THE THIRD PERSON

EMMA GROVE

DRAWN & QUARTERLY

EMMA S. CLARK MEMORIAL LIBRARY
Setauket, L.I., New York 11733

MANY THANKS TO FELLOW ARTIST AND
GOOD FRIEND ANDY RISTAINO FOR
HIS CONSTANT ENCOURAGEMENT AND
SUPPORT THROUGHOUT THE ENTIRE
PROCESS OF THE MAKING OF THIS
BOOK.

AND TO THE ENTIRE STAFF AT
DRAWN & QUARTERLY, FOR ALL
OF THEIR HARD WORK AND
DEDICATION: TOM, PEGGY, TRACY,
MEGAN, LUCIA, ALISON, TRYNNE,
REBECCA, FRANCINE, SHIRLEY,
KAIYA AND JULIA.

ALL NAMES IN THIS BOOK, EXCEPT MY OWN NAME(S),
HAVE BEEN CHANGED TO PROTECT ALL OTHER
INDIVIDUALS' ANONYMITY

ENTIRE CONTENTS COPYRIGHT © 2022 EMMA GROVE.
ALL RIGHTS RESERVED. NO PART OF THIS BOOK
(EXCEPT SMALL PORTIONS FOR REVIEW PURPOSES)
MAY BE REPRODUCED IN ANY FORM WITHOUT
WRITTEN PERMISSION FROM EMMA GROVE OR
DRAWN & QUARTERLY

drawnandquarterly.com

ISBN 978-1-77046-615-9 | FIRST EDITION: MAY 2022
PRINTED IN TURKEY | 10 9 8 7 6 5 4 3 2 1

CATALOGUING DATA AVAILABLE FROM LIBRARY AND
ARCHIVES CANADA

PUBLISHED IN THE USA BY DRAWN & QUARTERLY,
A CLIENT PUBLISHER OF FARRAR, STRAUS, AND GIROUX.
PUBLISHED IN CANADA BY DRAWN & QUARTERLY,
A CLIENT PUBLISHER OF RAINCOAST BOOKS.
PUBLISHED IN THE UNITED KINGDOM BY DRAWN &
QUARTERLY, A CLIENT PUBLISHER OF
PUBLISHERS GROUP, UK.

AUTHOR'S NOTE

NONE OF THE FOLLOWING INCIDENTS ARE MADE UP OR INVENTED ... I WISH THEY WERE.

DIALOGUE —— EVEN INTERNAL DIALOGUE —— IS RELATED EXACTLY AS I REMEMBER IT.

THE DIALOGUE HAS BEEN SLIGHTLY EDITED FOR LENGTH ONLY, NOT CONTENT, AND ONLY IF CERTAIN WORDS OR PHRASES WERE REPEATED AGAIN AND AGAIN. HOWEVER, I FOUND THAT IT IS IN THE NATURE OF REAL DIALOGUE — REAL, NOT INVENTED— TO BE SOMEWHAT REPETITIOUS. THEREFORE, AS MUCH OF THIS AS POSSIBLE HAS BEEN RETAINED TO GIVE AN ENTIRELY ACCURATE ACCOUNT OF EXACTLY WHAT WAS SAID.

NO DIALOGUE HAS BEEN INVENTED OR TAILORED TO SUIT THE AUTHOR'S POINT OF VIEW OR FOR STORYTELLING PURPOSES.

FOR KATINA

WE FINALLY DID ONE
TOGETHER

CONTENTS

BOOK THREE
CORE SELF

INTRODUCTION

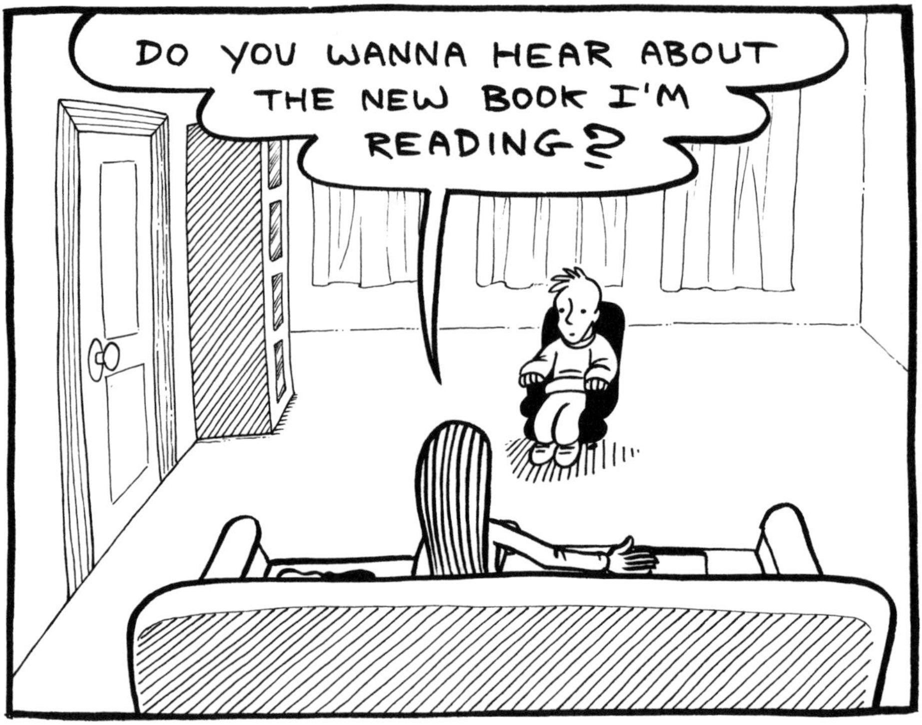
DO YOU WANNA HEAR ABOUT THE NEW BOOK I'M READING?

WINTER, 2004

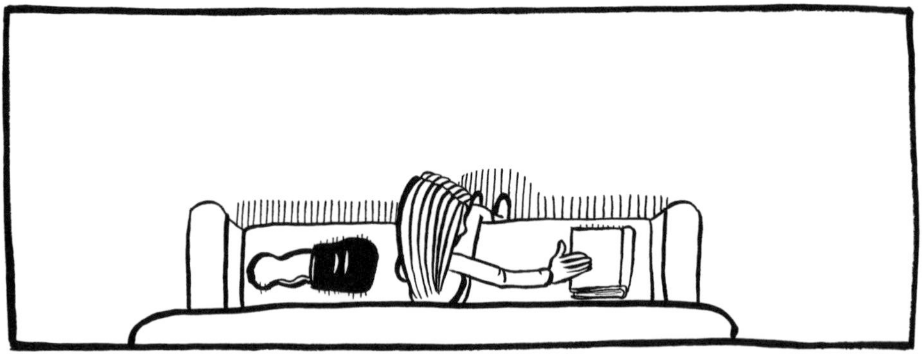

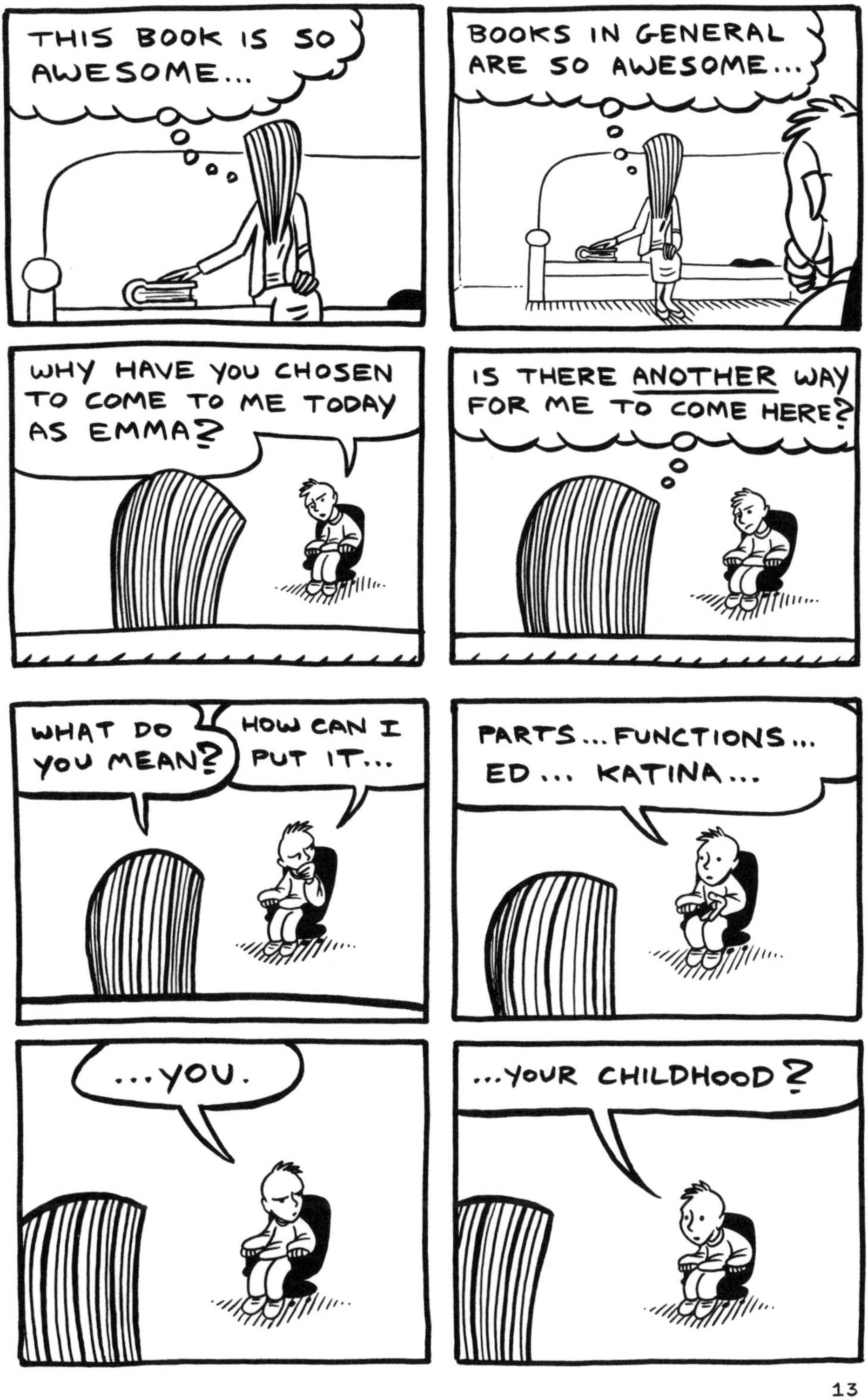
THIS BOOK IS SO AWESOME...
BOOKS IN GENERAL ARE SO AWESOME...
WHY HAVE YOU CHOSEN TO COME TO ME TODAY AS EMMA?
IS THERE ANOTHER WAY FOR ME TO COME HERE?
WHAT DO YOU MEAN?
HOW CAN I PUT IT...
PARTS... FUNCTIONS... ED... KATINA...
...YOU.
...YOUR CHILDHOOD?

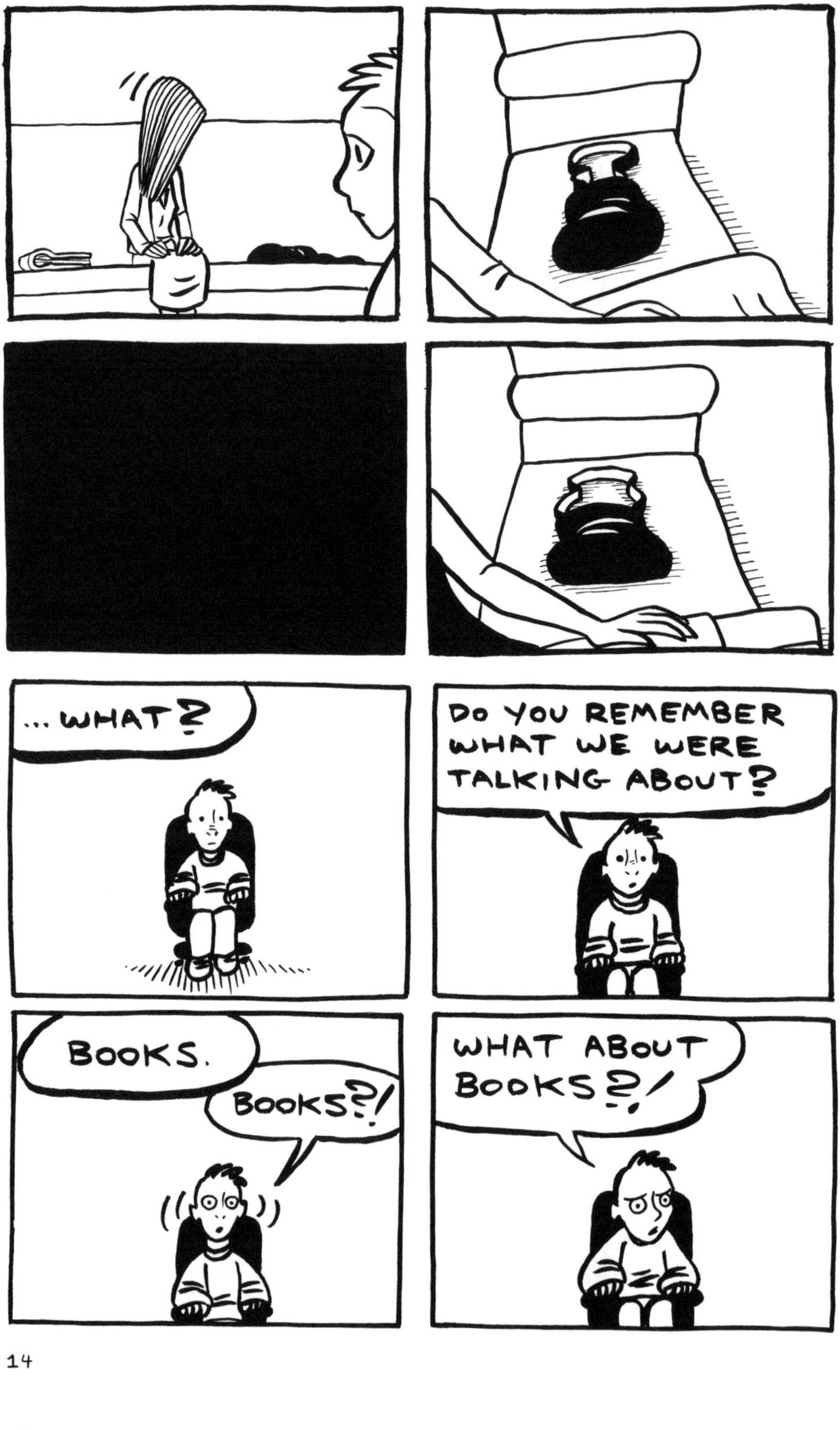
...WHAT?
DO YOU REMEMBER WHAT WE WERE TALKING ABOUT?
BOOKS.
BOOKS?!
WHAT ABOUT BOOKS?!

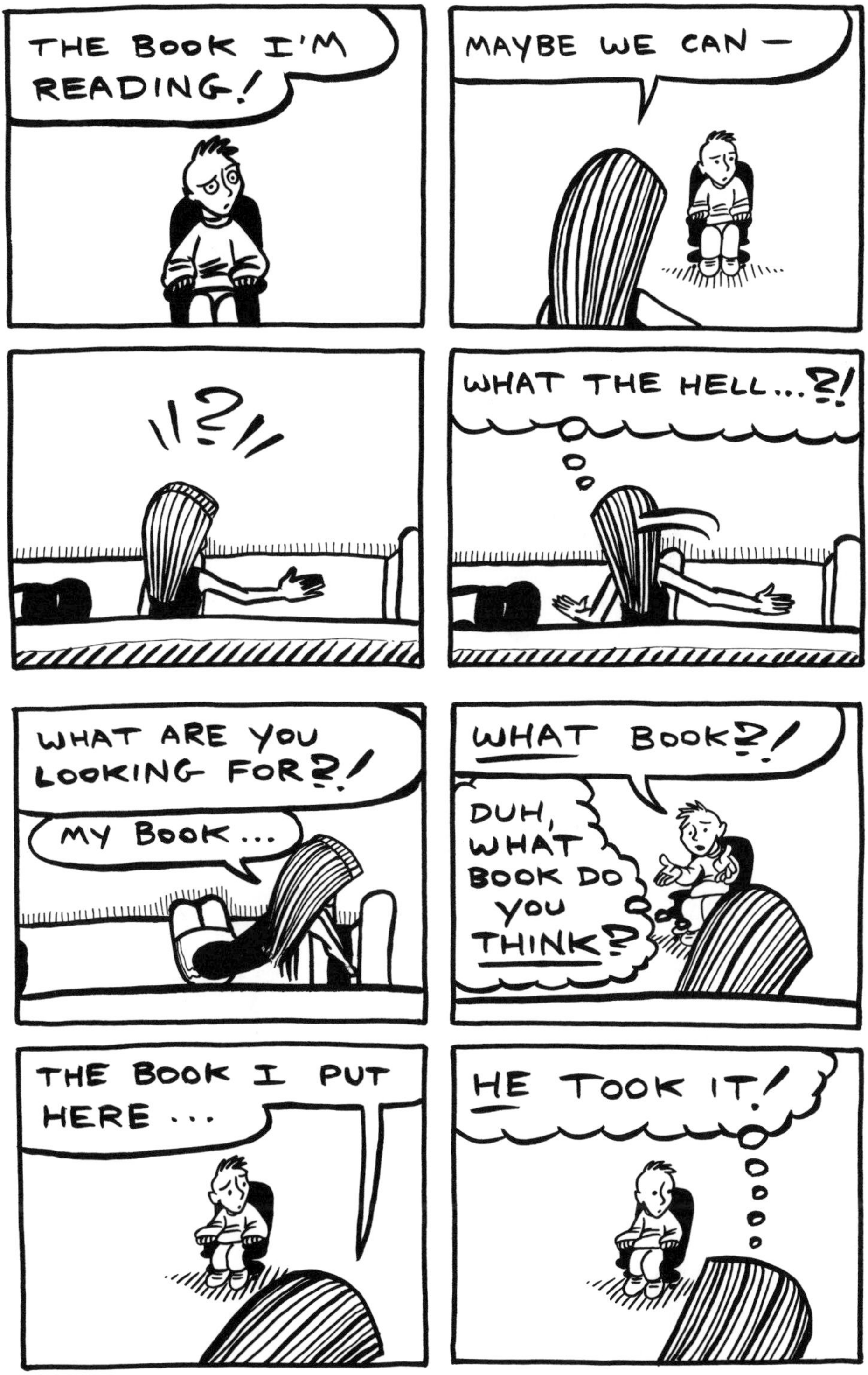
THE BOOK I'M READING!
MAYBE WE CAN —
?
WHAT THE HELL...?!
WHAT ARE YOU LOOKING FOR?!
MY BOOK...
WHAT BOOK?!
DUH, WHAT BOOK DO YOU THINK?
THE BOOK I PUT HERE...
HE TOOK IT!

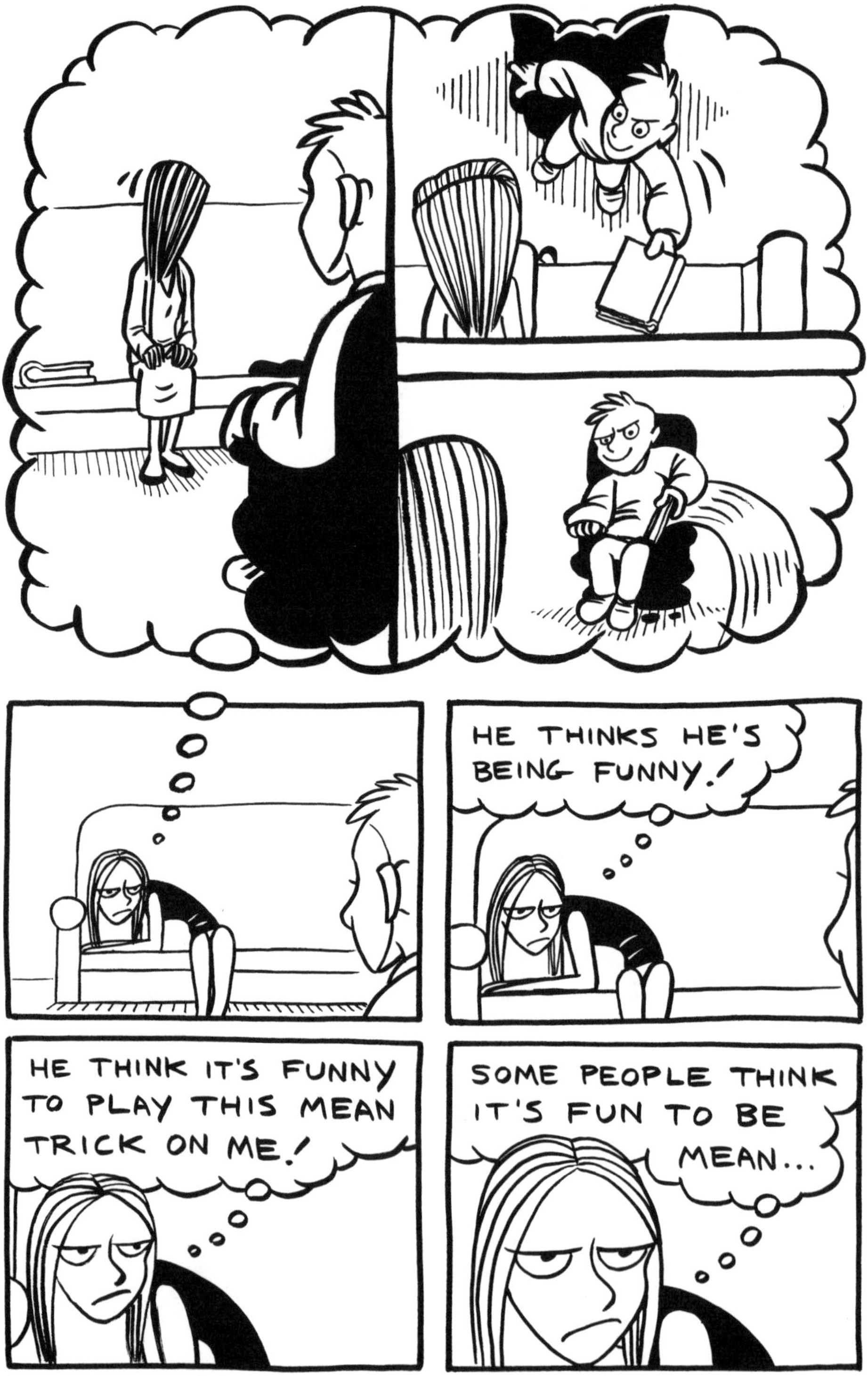
HE THINKS HE'S BEING FUNNY!
HE THINK IT'S FUNNY TO PLAY THIS MEAN TRICK ON ME!
SOME PEOPLE THINK IT'S FUN TO BE MEAN...

BOOK ONE

CRAZY

IN THE
CLOSET

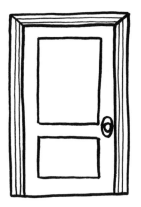

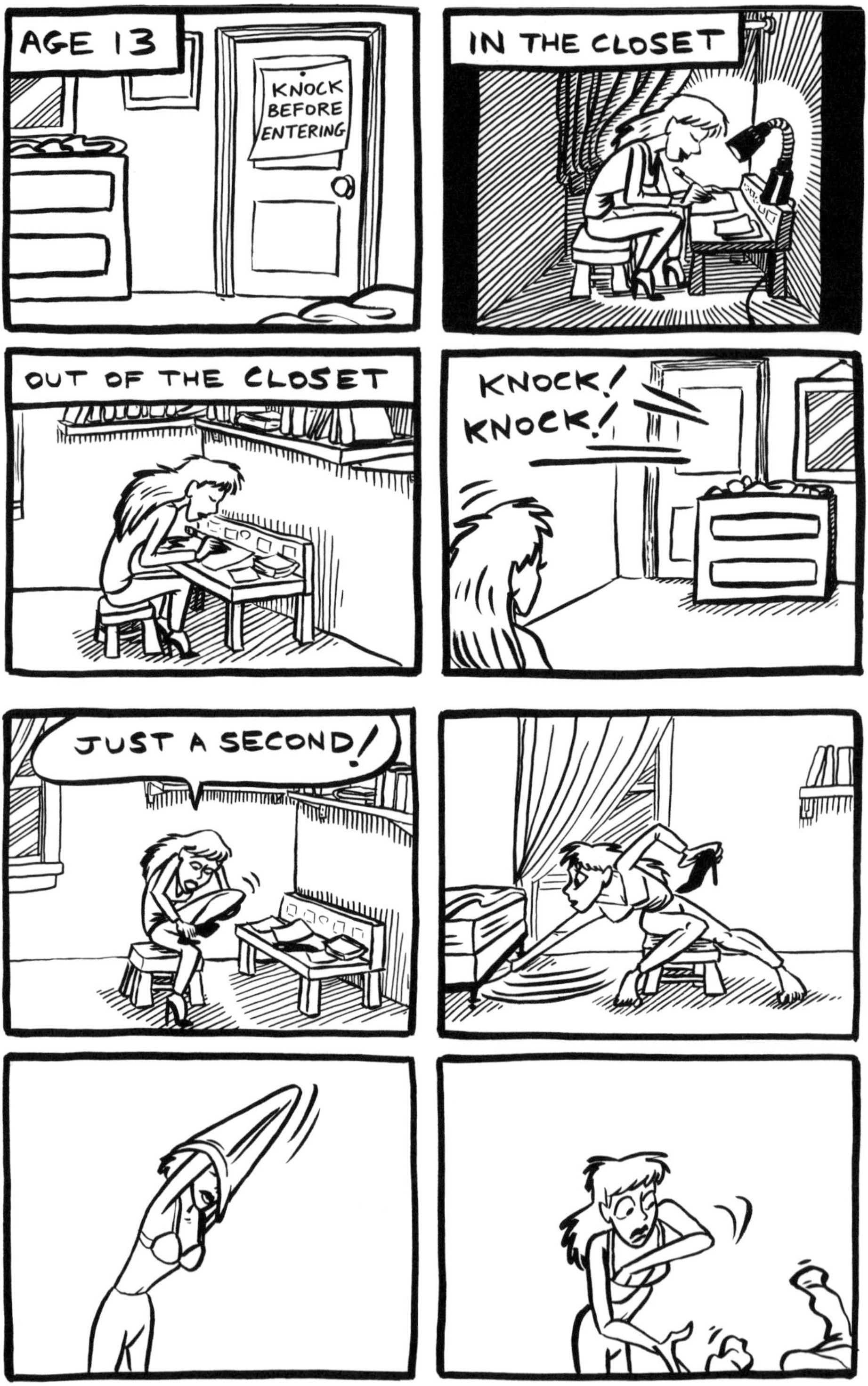
AGE 13
KNOCK BEFORE ENTERING
IN THE CLOSET
OUT OF THE CLOSET
KNOCK! KNOCK!
JUST A SECOND!

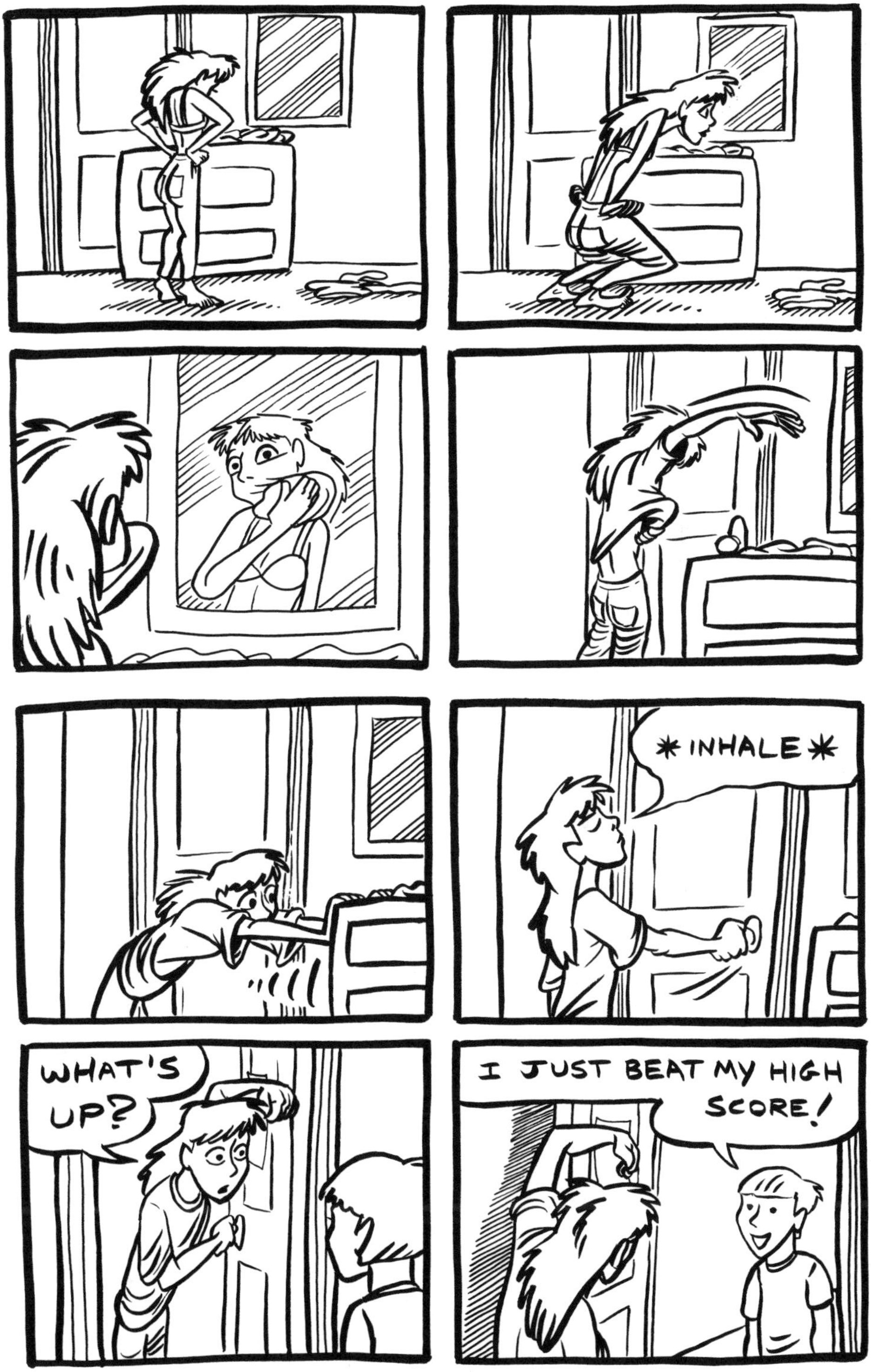
INHALE
WHAT'S UP?
I JUST BEAT MY HIGH SCORE!

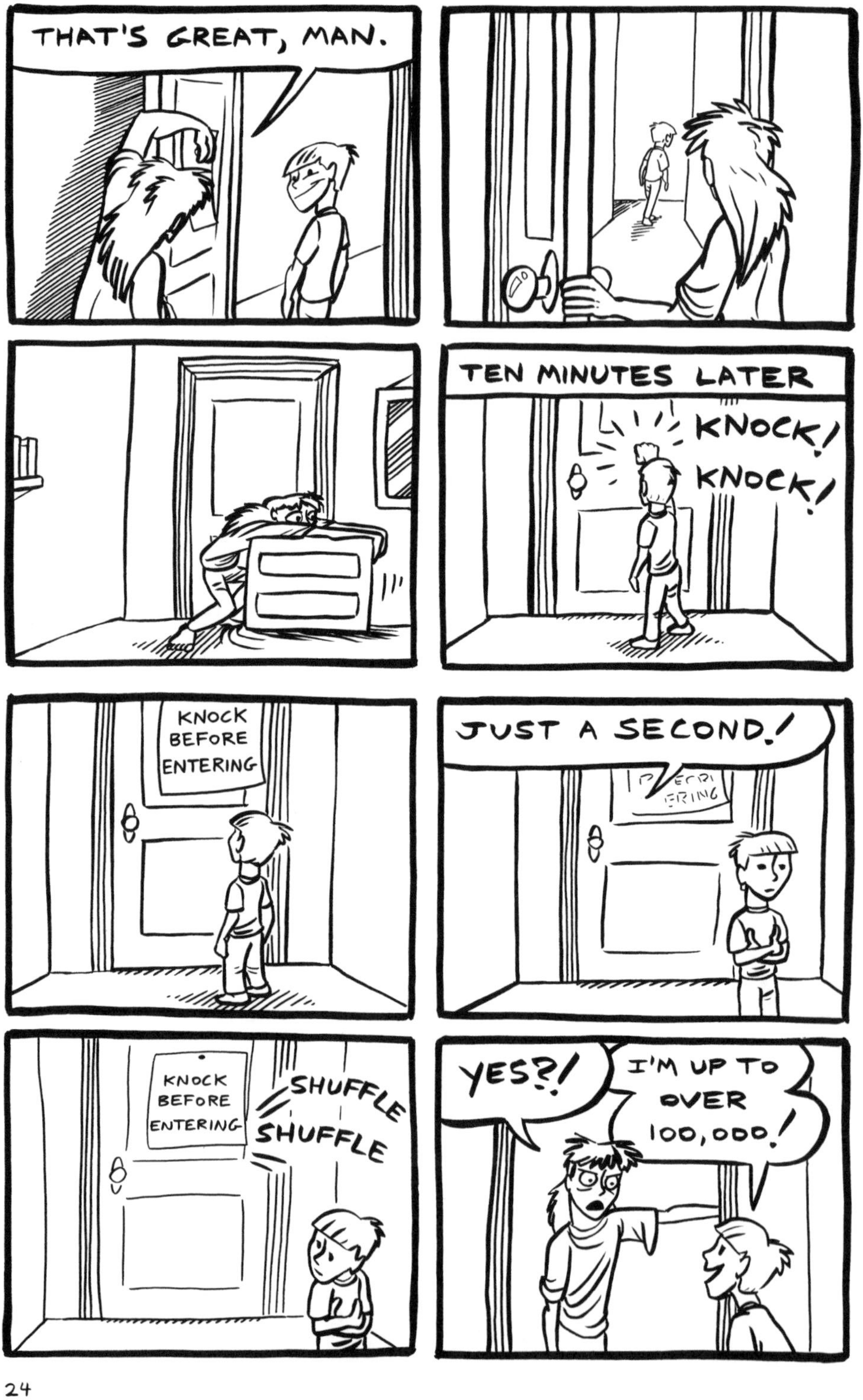
THAT'S GREAT, MAN.
TEN MINUTES LATER
KNOCK!
KNOCK!
KNOCK BEFORE ENTERING
JUST A SECOND!
KNOCK BEFORE ENTERING
SHUFFLE
SHUFFLE
YES?!
I'M UP TO OVER 100,000!

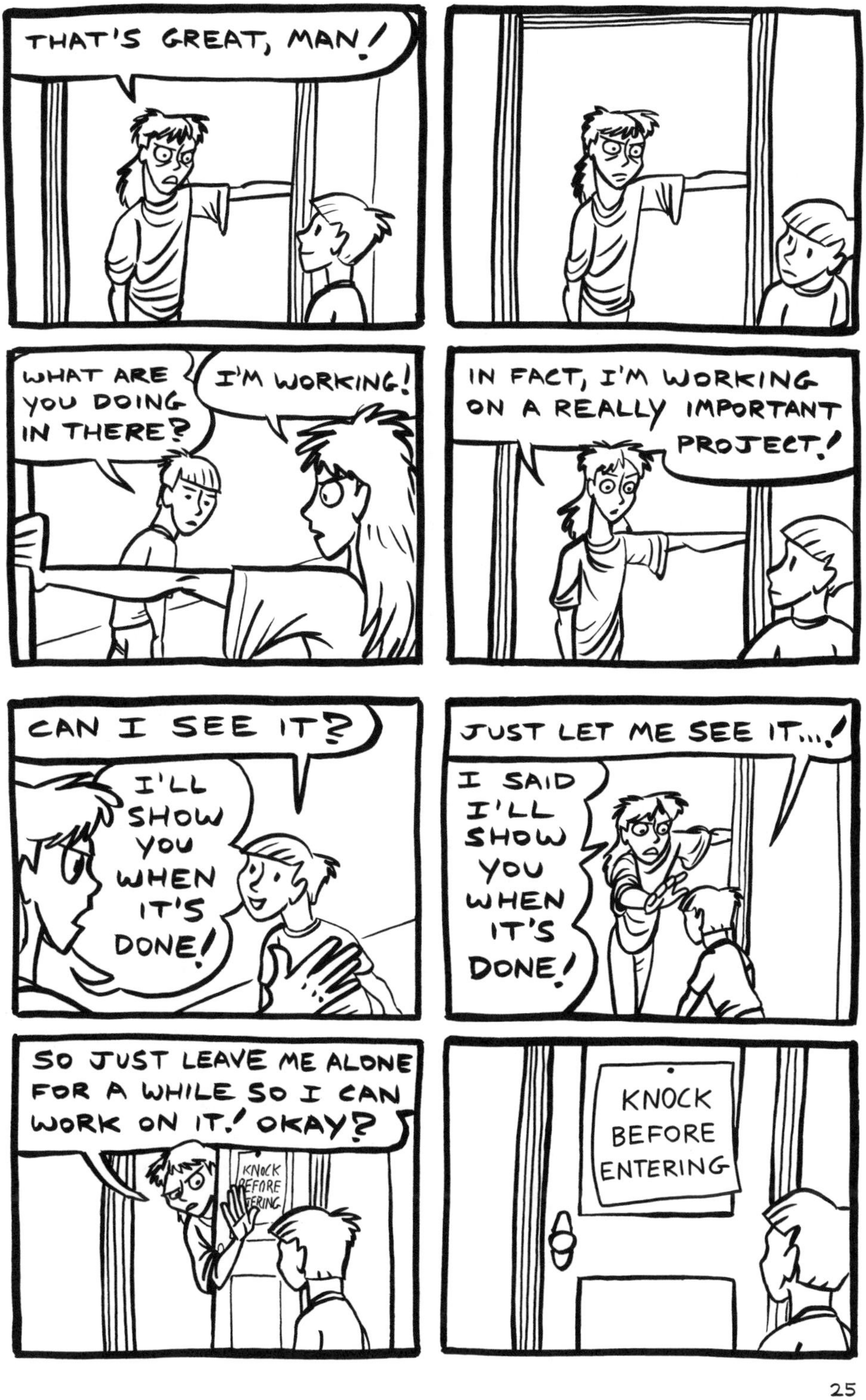
THAT'S GREAT, MAN!
WHAT ARE YOU DOING IN THERE?
I'M WORKING!
IN FACT, I'M WORKING ON A REALLY IMPORTANT PROJECT!
CAN I SEE IT?
I'LL SHOW YOU WHEN IT'S DONE!
JUST LET ME SEE IT...!
I SAID I'LL SHOW YOU WHEN IT'S DONE!
SO JUST LEAVE ME ALONE FOR A WHILE SO I CAN WORK ON IT! OKAY?
KNOCK BEFORE ENTERING

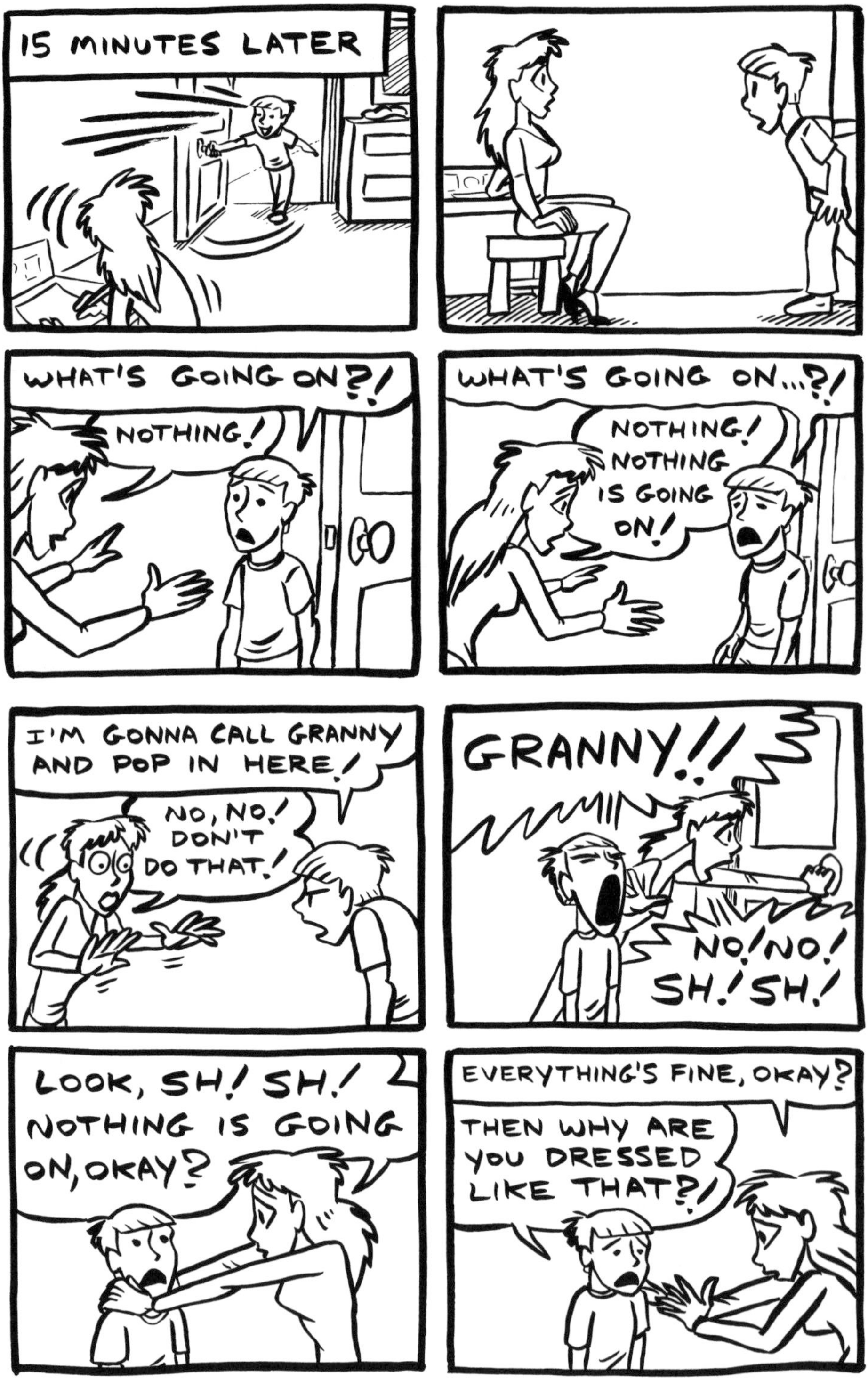
15 MINUTES LATER
WHAT'S GOING ON?!
NOTHING!
WHAT'S GOING ON...?!
NOTHING! NOTHING IS GOING ON!
I'M GONNA CALL GRANNY AND POP IN HERE!
NO, NO! DON'T DO THAT!
GRANNY!!
NO! NO! SH! SH!
LOOK, SH! SH! NOTHING IS GOING ON, OKAY?
EVERYTHING'S FINE, OKAY?
THEN WHY ARE YOU DRESSED LIKE THAT?!

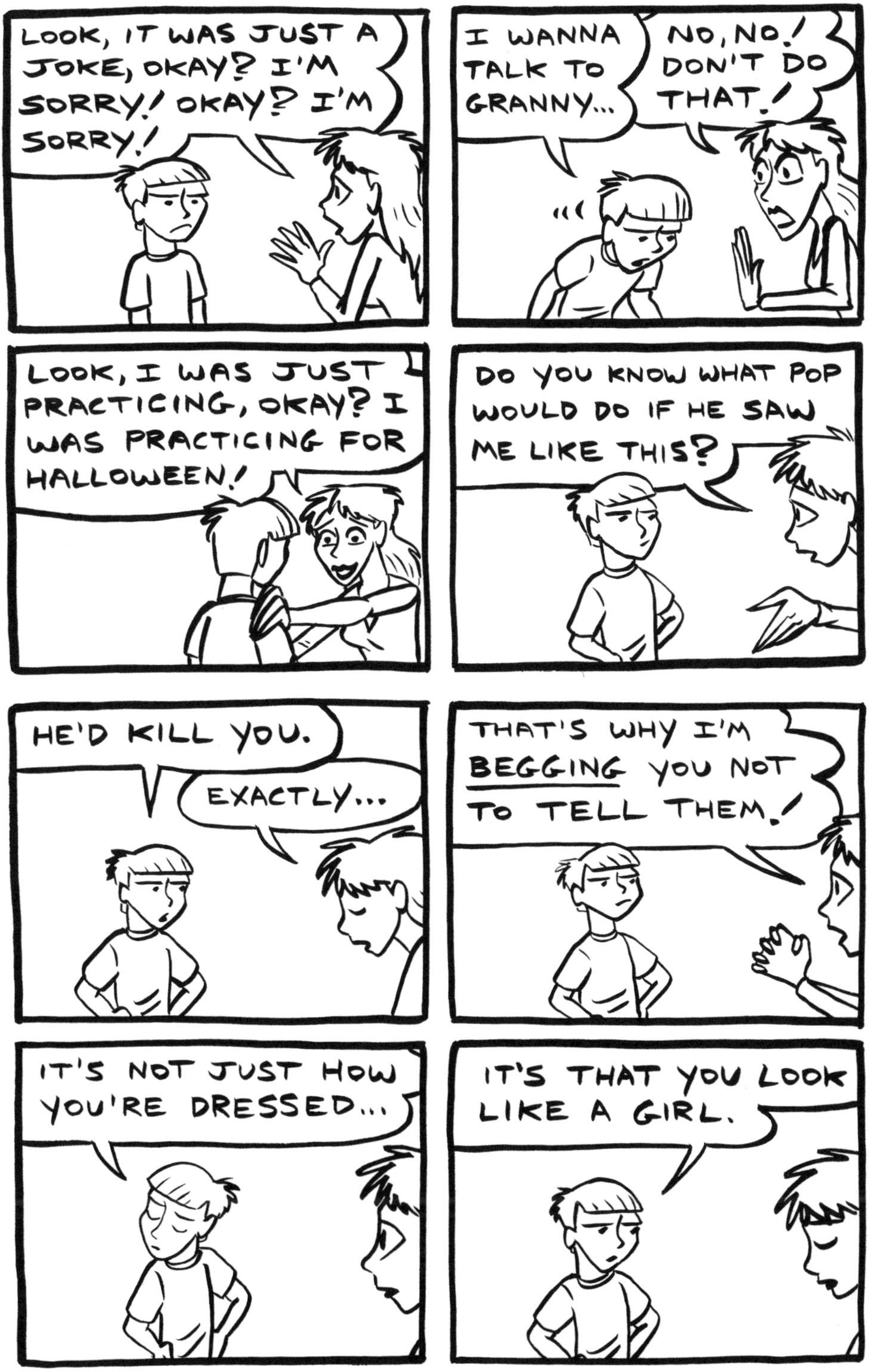
LOOK, IT WAS JUST A JOKE, OKAY? I'M SORRY! OKAY? I'M SORRY!
I WANNA TALK TO GRANNY...
NO, NO! DON'T DO THAT!
LOOK, I WAS JUST PRACTICING, OKAY? I WAS PRACTICING FOR HALLOWEEN!
DO YOU KNOW WHAT POP WOULD DO IF HE SAW ME LIKE THIS?
HE'D KILL YOU.
EXACTLY...
THAT'S WHY I'M BEGGING YOU NOT TO TELL THEM!
IT'S NOT JUST HOW YOU'RE DRESSED...
IT'S THAT YOU LOOK LIKE A GIRL.

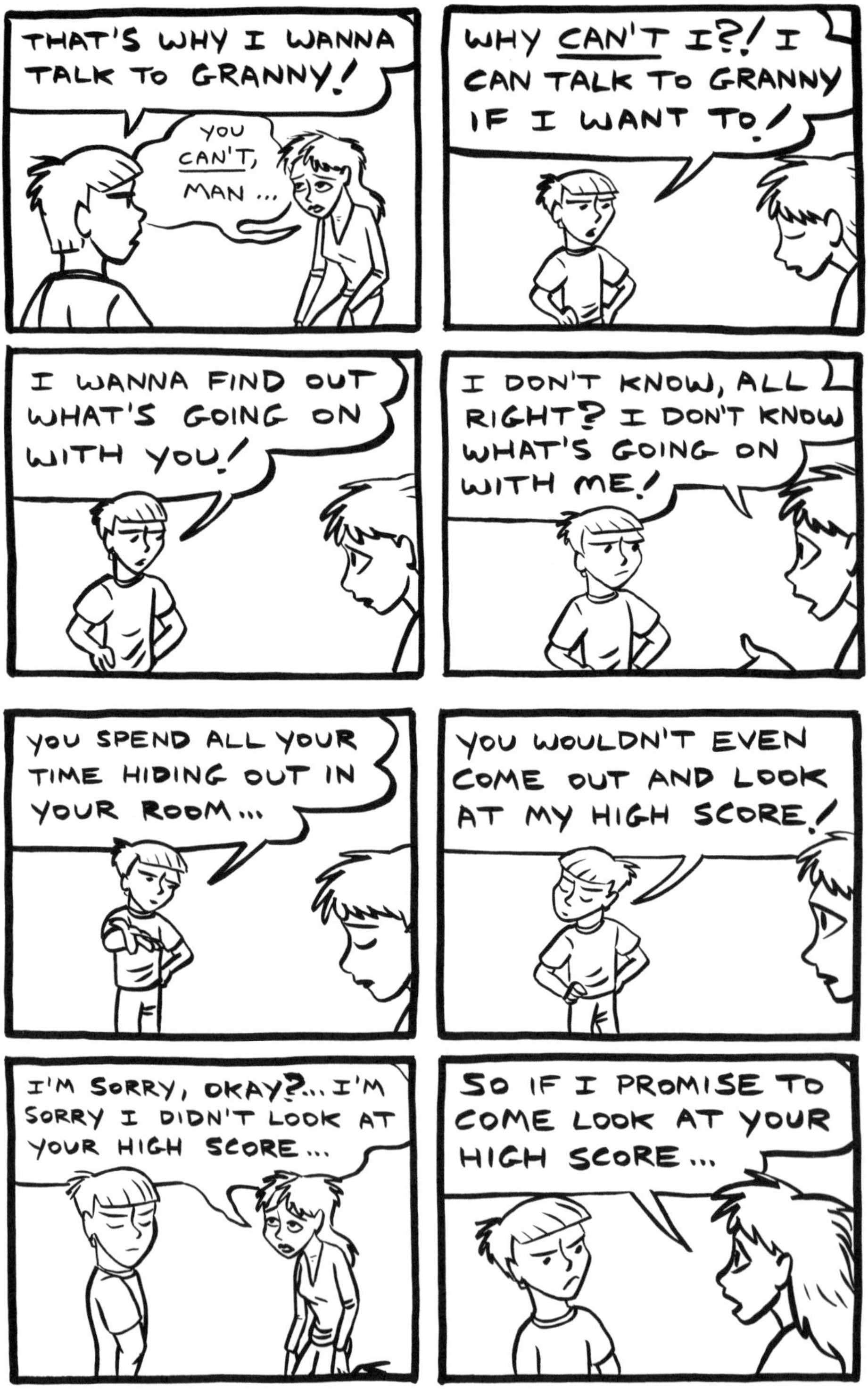
THAT'S WHY I WANNA TALK TO GRANNY!
YOU CAN'T, MAN...
WHY CAN'T I?! I CAN TALK TO GRANNY IF I WANT TO!
I WANNA FIND OUT WHAT'S GOING ON WITH YOU!
I DON'T KNOW, ALL RIGHT? I DON'T KNOW WHAT'S GOING ON WITH ME!
YOU SPEND ALL YOUR TIME HIDING OUT IN YOUR ROOM...
YOU WOULDN'T EVEN COME OUT AND LOOK AT MY HIGH SCORE!
I'M SORRY, OKAY?... I'M SORRY I DIDN'T LOOK AT YOUR HIGH SCORE...
SO IF I PROMISE TO COME LOOK AT YOUR HIGH SCORE...

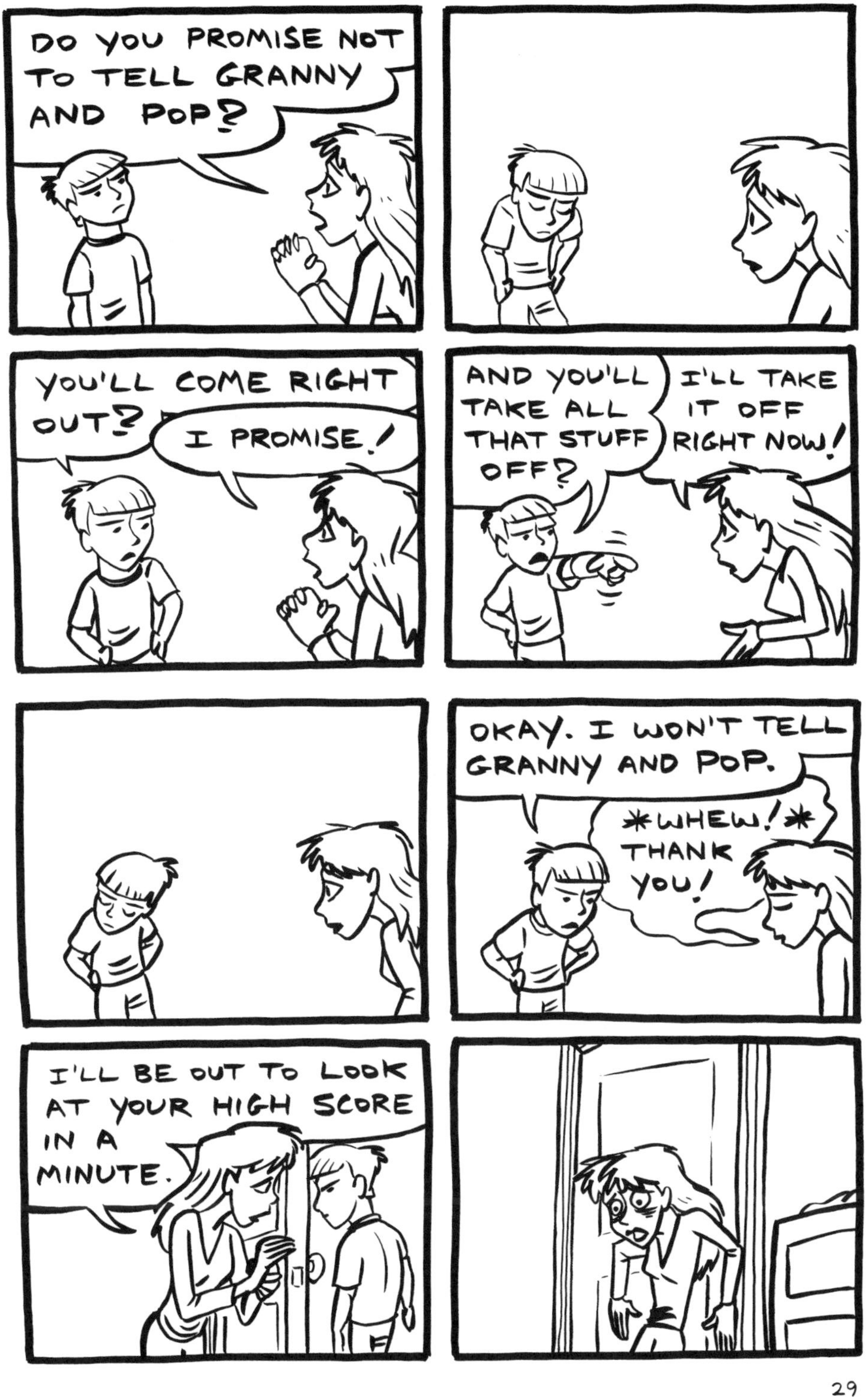
DO YOU PROMISE NOT TO TELL GRANNY AND POP?
YOU'LL COME RIGHT OUT?
I PROMISE!
AND YOU'LL TAKE ALL THAT STUFF OFF?
I'LL TAKE IT OFF RIGHT NOW!
OKAY. I WON'T TELL GRANNY AND POP.
WHEW! THANK YOU!
I'LL BE OUT TO LOOK AT YOUR HIGH SCORE IN A MINUTE.

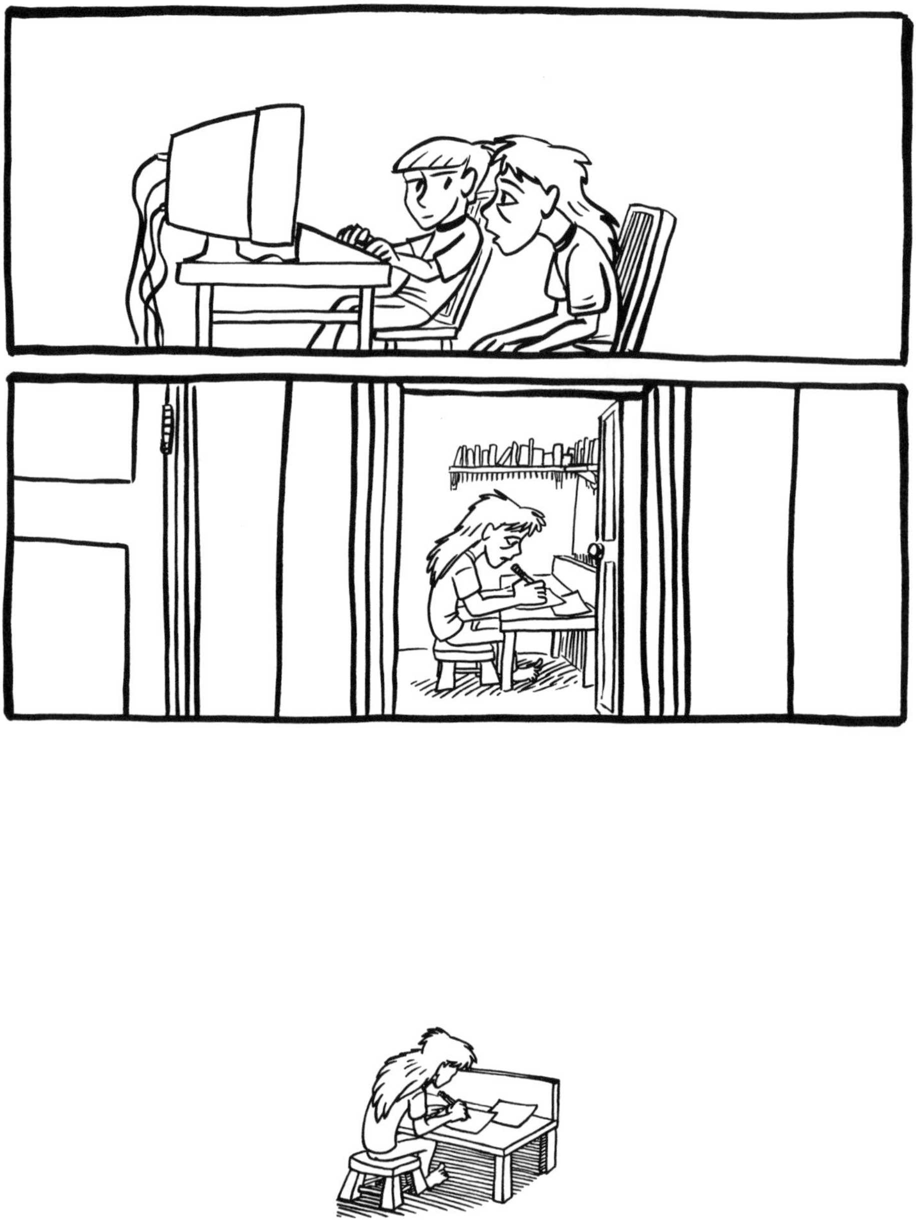

ON THE ROCKS

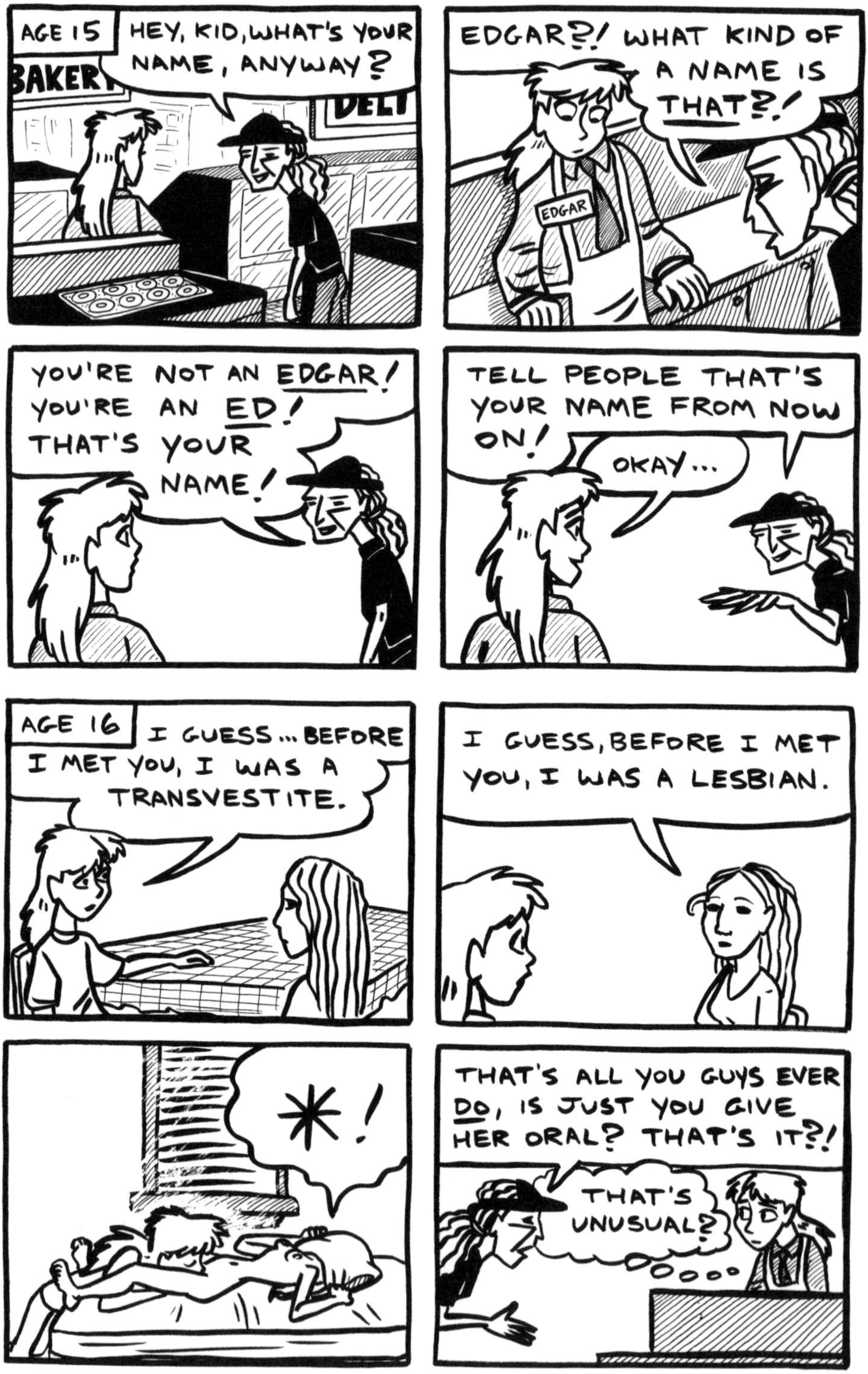
AGE 15
HEY, KID, WHAT'S YOUR NAME, ANYWAY?
BAKERY
DELI
EDGAR?! WHAT KIND OF A NAME IS THAT?!
EDGAR
YOU'RE NOT AN EDGAR! YOU'RE AN ED! THAT'S YOUR NAME!
TELL PEOPLE THAT'S YOUR NAME FROM NOW ON!
OKAY...
AGE 16
I GUESS... BEFORE I MET YOU, I WAS A TRANSVESTITE.
I GUESS, BEFORE I MET YOU, I WAS A LESBIAN.
*!
THAT'S ALL YOU GUYS EVER DO, IS JUST YOU GIVE HER ORAL? THAT'S IT?!
THAT'S UNUSUAL?

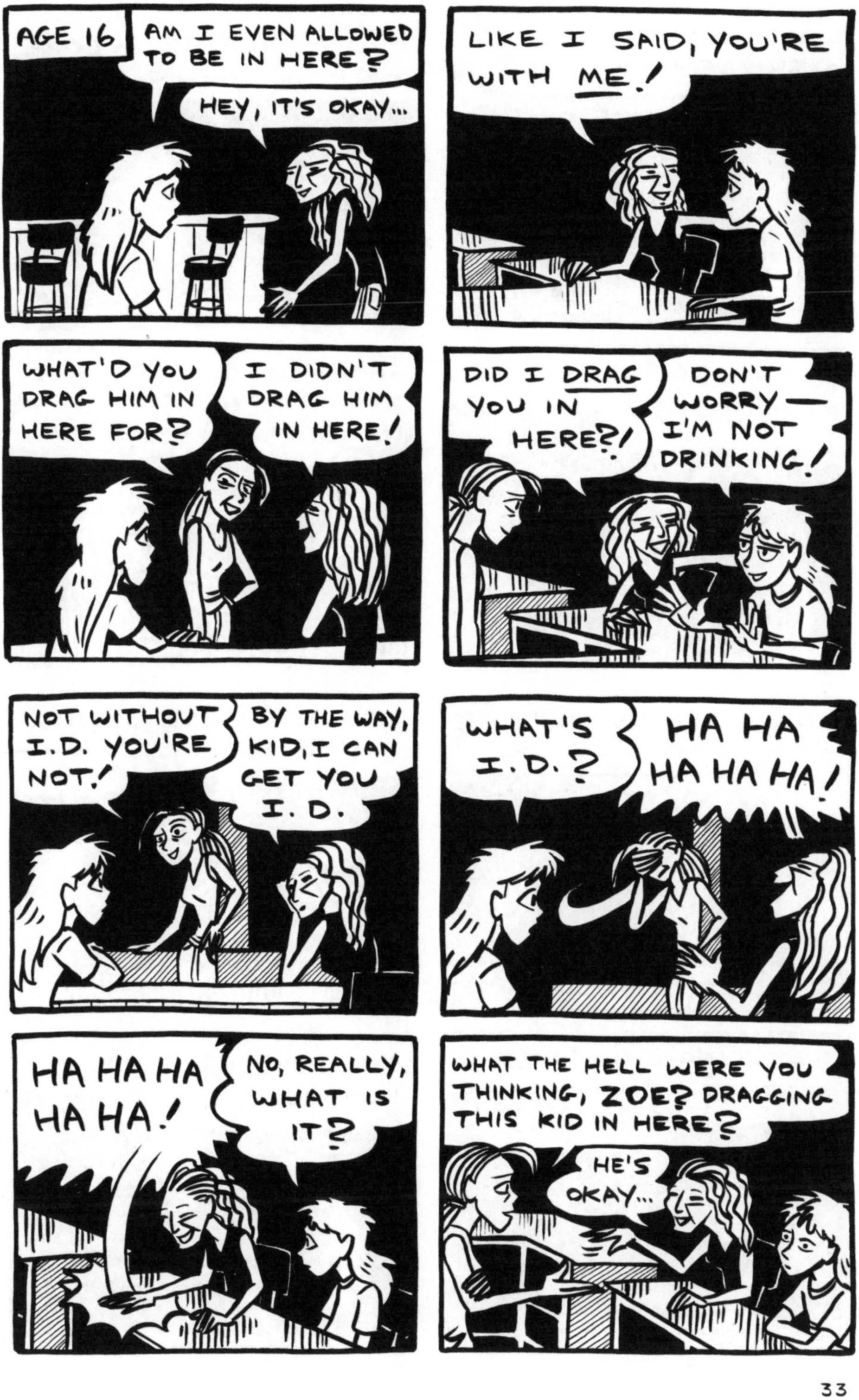
AGE 16
AM I EVEN ALLOWED TO BE IN HERE?
HEY, IT'S OKAY...
LIKE I SAID, YOU'RE WITH ME!
WHAT'D YOU DRAG HIM IN HERE FOR?
I DIDN'T DRAG HIM IN HERE!
DID I DRAG YOU IN HERE?!
DON'T WORRY— I'M NOT DRINKING!
NOT WITHOUT I.D. YOU'RE NOT!
BY THE WAY, KID, I CAN GET YOU I.D.
WHAT'S I.D.?
HA HA HA HA HA!
HA HA HA HA HA!
NO, REALLY, WHAT IS IT?
WHAT THE HELL WERE YOU THINKING, ZOE? DRAGGING THIS KID IN HERE?
HE'S OKAY...

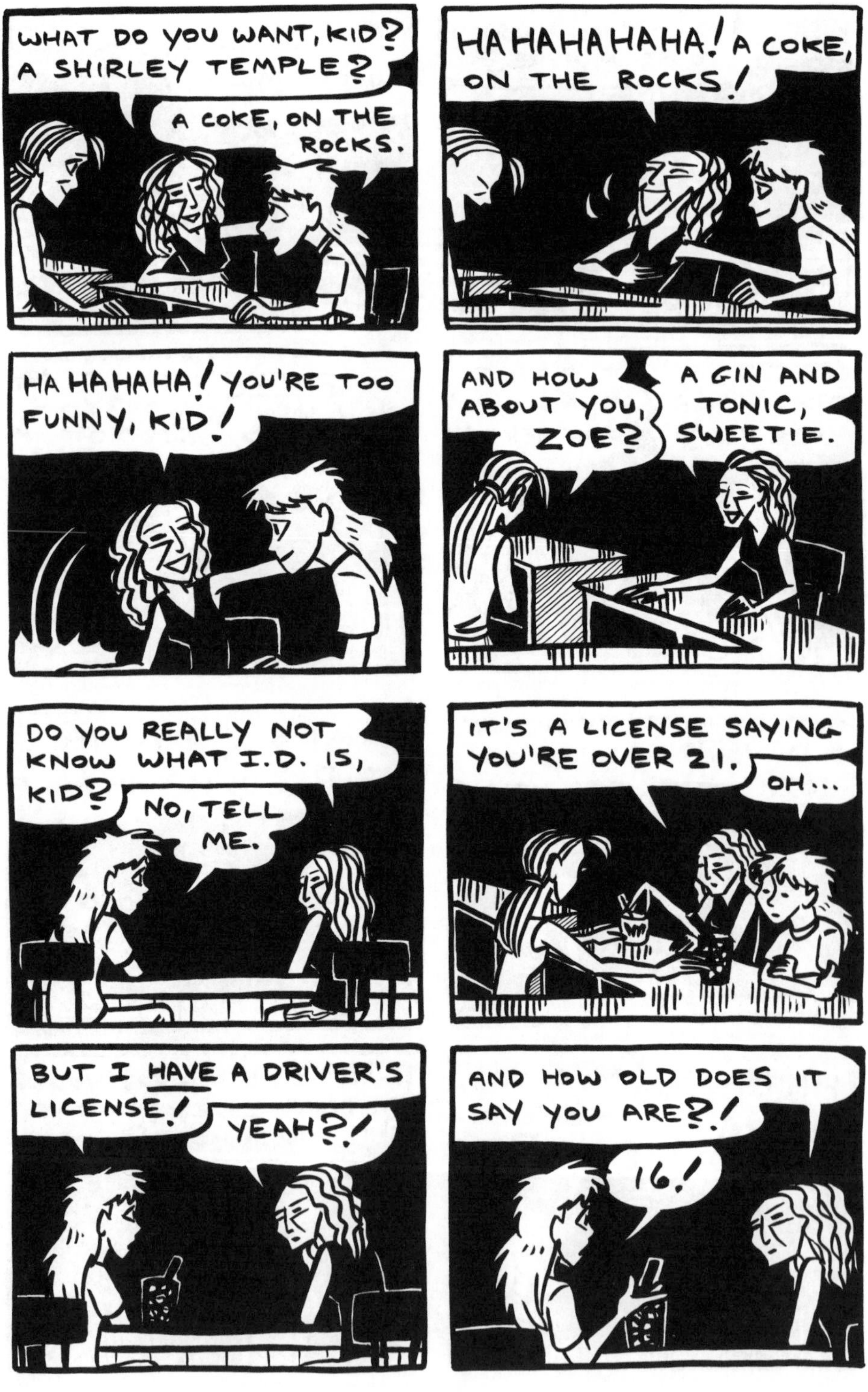
WHAT DO YOU WANT, KID? A SHIRLEY TEMPLE?
A COKE, ON THE ROCKS.
HAHAHAHAHA! A COKE, ON THE ROCKS!
HA HAHAHA! YOU'RE TOO FUNNY, KID!
AND HOW ABOUT YOU, ZOE?
A GIN AND TONIC, SWEETIE.
DO YOU REALLY NOT KNOW WHAT I.D. IS, KID?
NO, TELL ME.
IT'S A LICENSE SAYING YOU'RE OVER 21.
OH...
BUT I HAVE A DRIVER'S LICENSE!
YEAH?!
AND HOW OLD DOES IT SAY YOU ARE?!
16!

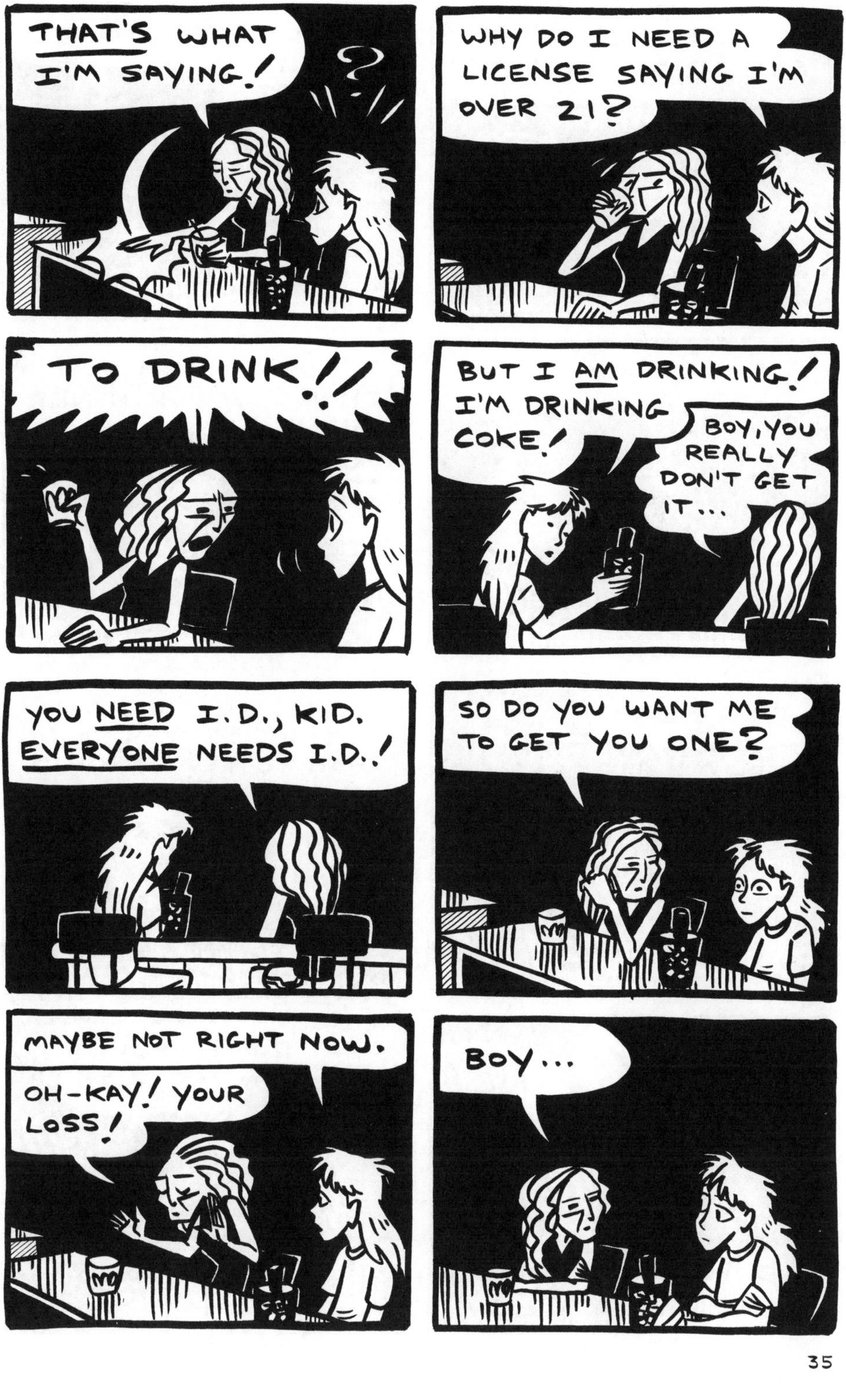
THAT'S WHAT I'M SAYING!
?
WHY DO I NEED A LICENSE SAYING I'M OVER 21?
TO DRINK!!
BUT I AM DRINKING! I'M DRINKING COKE!
BOY, YOU REALLY DON'T GET IT...
YOU NEED I.D., KID. EVERYONE NEEDS I.D.!
SO DO YOU WANT ME TO GET YOU ONE?
MAYBE NOT RIGHT NOW.
OH-KAY! YOUR LOSS!
BOY...

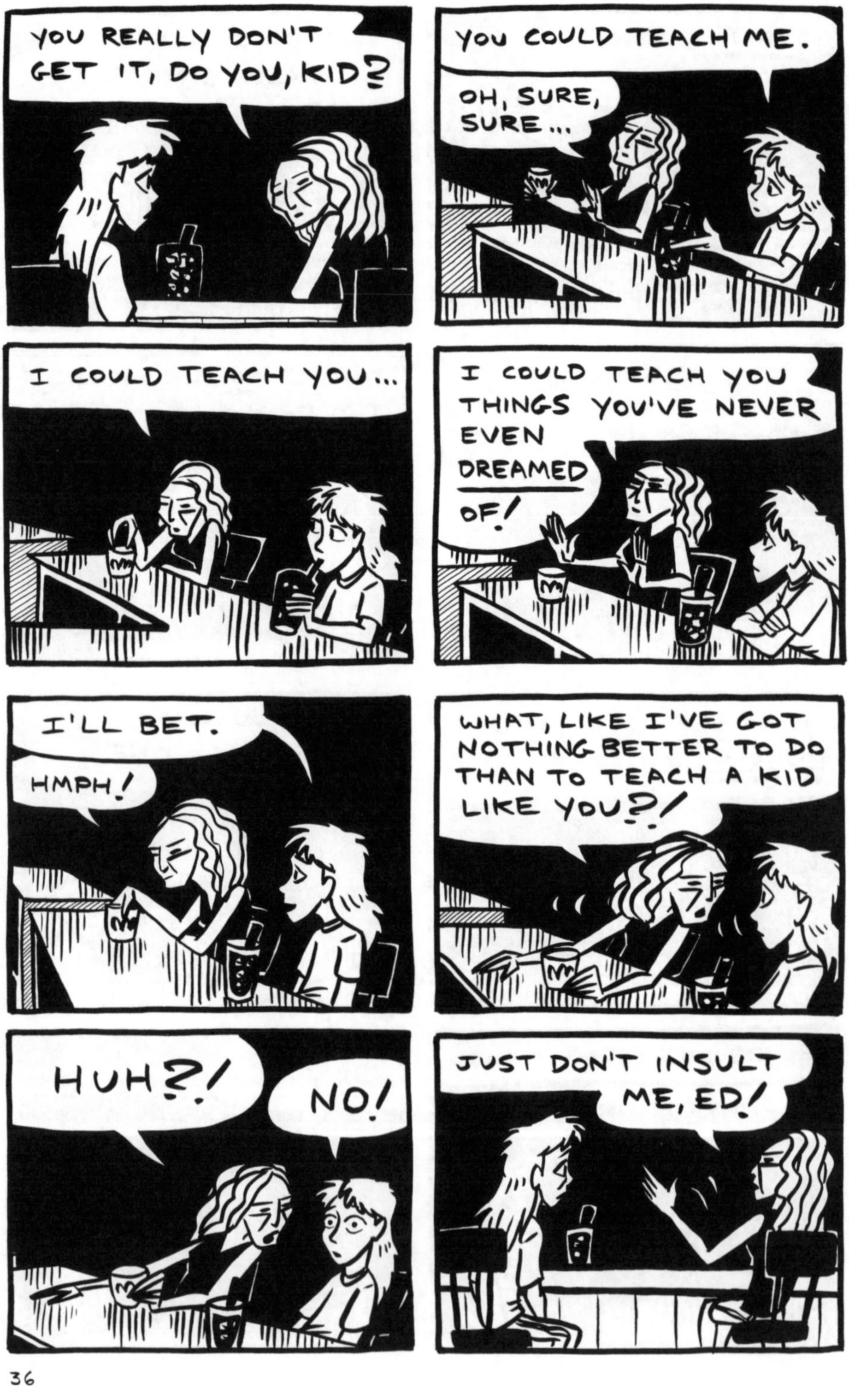
YOU REALLY DON'T GET IT, DO YOU, KID?
YOU COULD TEACH ME.
OH, SURE, SURE...
I COULD TEACH YOU...
I COULD TEACH YOU THINGS YOU'VE NEVER EVEN DREAMED OF!
I'LL BET.
HMPH!
WHAT, LIKE I'VE GOT NOTHING BETTER TO DO THAN TO TEACH A KID LIKE YOU?!
HUH?!
NO!
JUST DON'T INSULT ME, ED!

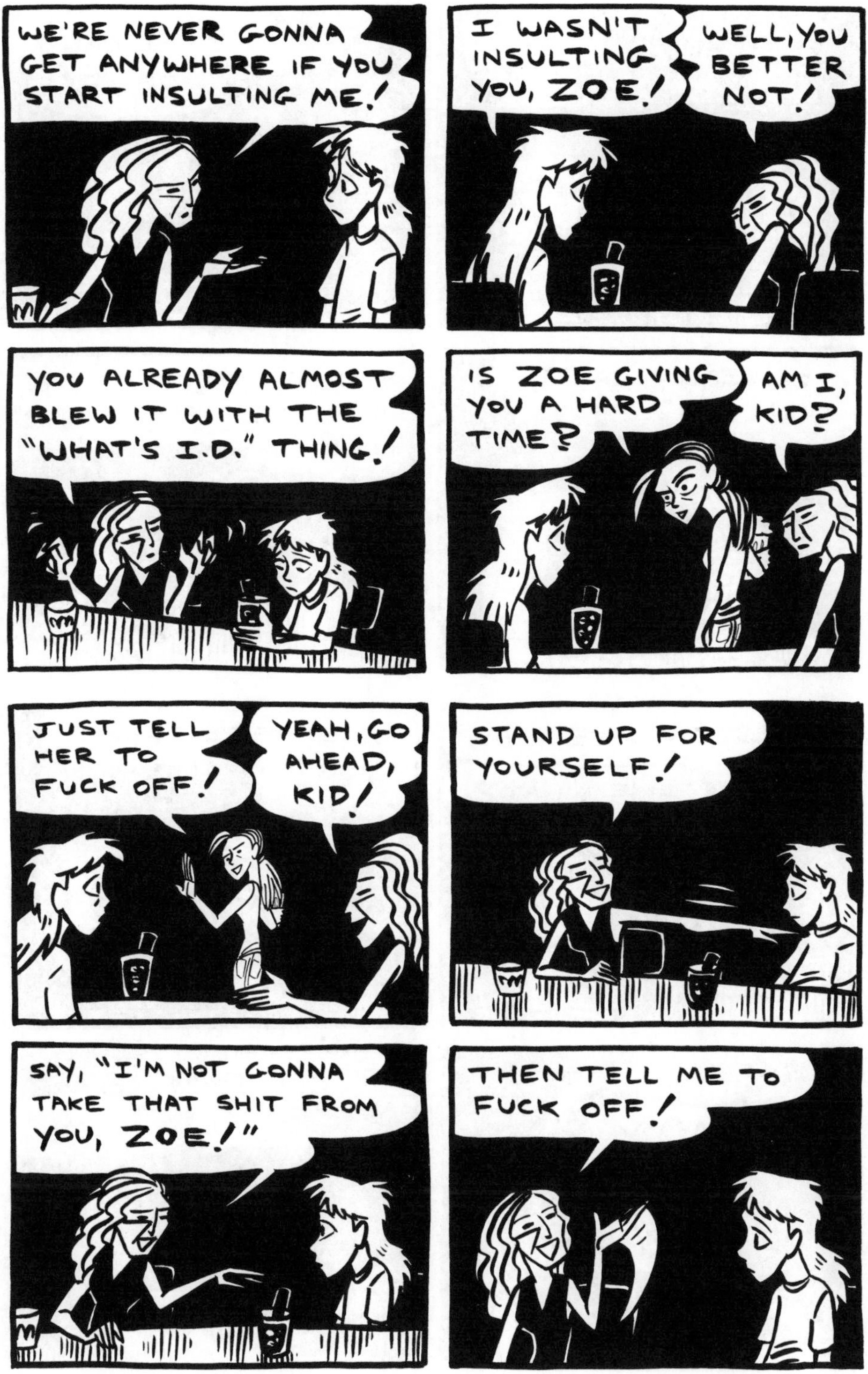
WE'RE NEVER GONNA GET ANYWHERE IF YOU START INSULTING ME!
I WASN'T INSULTING YOU, ZOE!
WELL, YOU BETTER NOT!
YOU ALREADY ALMOST BLEW IT WITH THE "WHAT'S I.D." THING!
IS ZOE GIVING YOU A HARD TIME?
AM I, KID?
JUST TELL HER TO FUCK OFF!
YEAH, GO AHEAD, KID!
STAND UP FOR YOURSELF!
SAY, "I'M NOT GONNA TAKE THAT SHIT FROM YOU, ZOE!"
THEN TELL ME TO FUCK OFF!

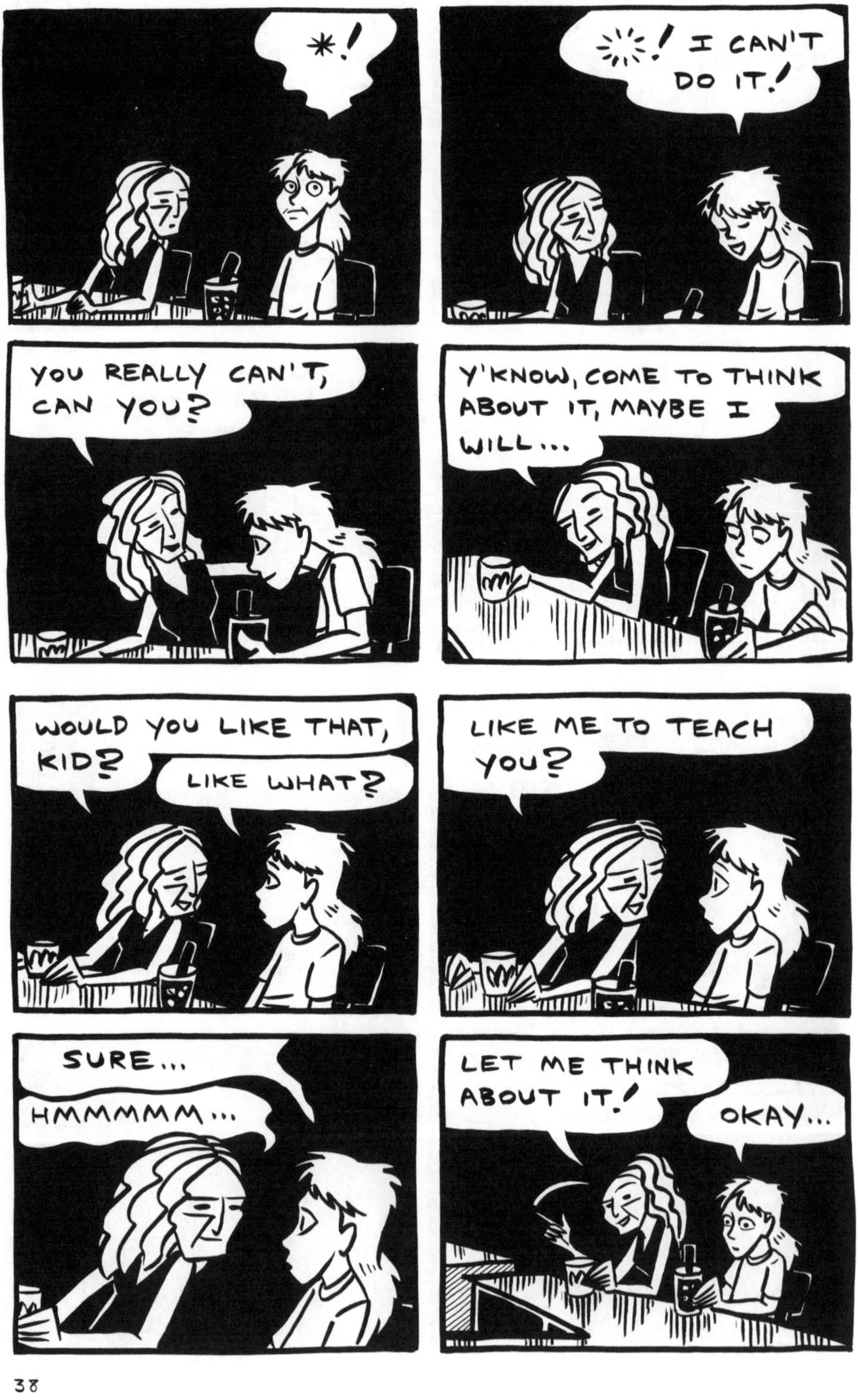
*!
*! I CAN'T DO IT!
YOU REALLY CAN'T, CAN YOU?
Y'KNOW, COME TO THINK ABOUT IT, MAYBE I WILL...
WOULD YOU LIKE THAT, KID?
LIKE WHAT?
LIKE ME TO TEACH YOU?
SURE...
HMMMMM...
LET ME THINK ABOUT IT!
OKAY...

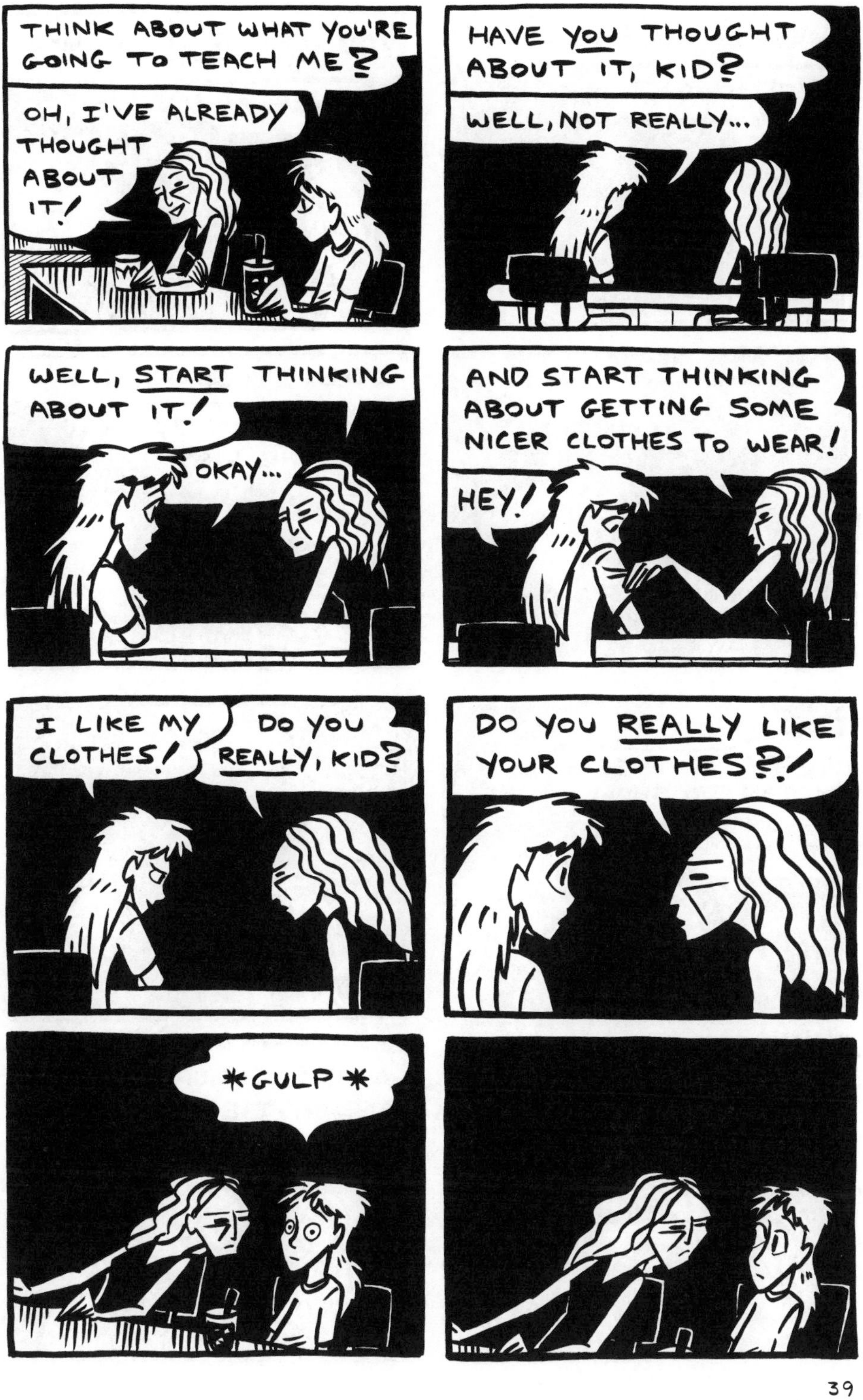
THINK ABOUT WHAT YOU'RE GOING TO TEACH ME?
OH, I'VE ALREADY THOUGHT ABOUT IT!
HAVE YOU THOUGHT ABOUT IT, KID?
WELL, NOT REALLY...
WELL, START THINKING ABOUT IT!
OKAY...
AND START THINKING ABOUT GETTING SOME NICER CLOTHES TO WEAR!
HEY!
I LIKE MY CLOTHES!
DO YOU REALLY, KID?
DO YOU REALLY LIKE YOUR CLOTHES?!
GULP

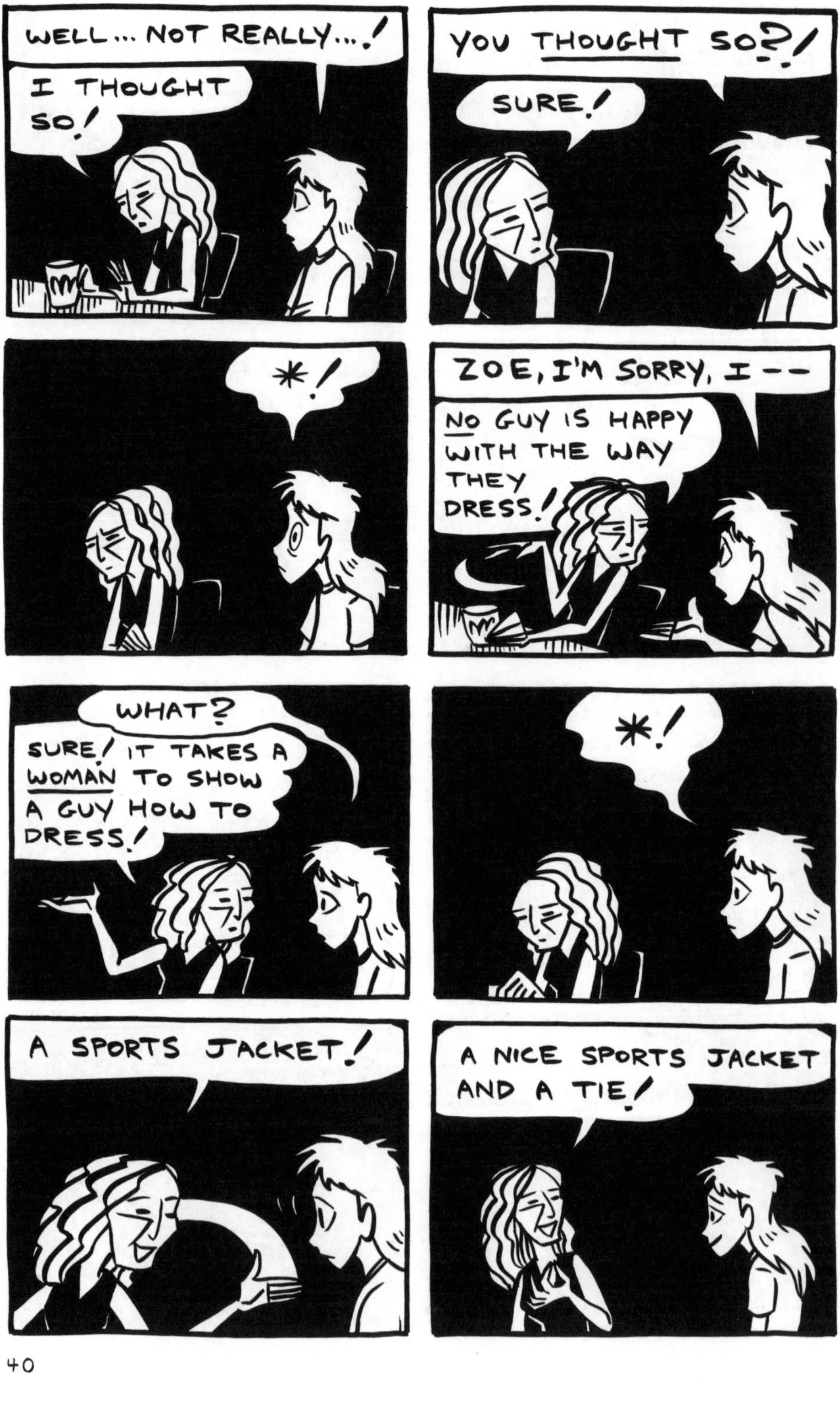
WELL... NOT REALLY...!
I THOUGHT SO!
YOU THOUGHT SO?!
SURE!
*!
ZOE, I'M SORRY, I --
NO GUY IS HAPPY WITH THE WAY THEY DRESS!
WHAT?
SURE! IT TAKES A WOMAN TO SHOW A GUY HOW TO DRESS!
*!
A SPORTS JACKET!
A NICE SPORTS JACKET AND A TIE!

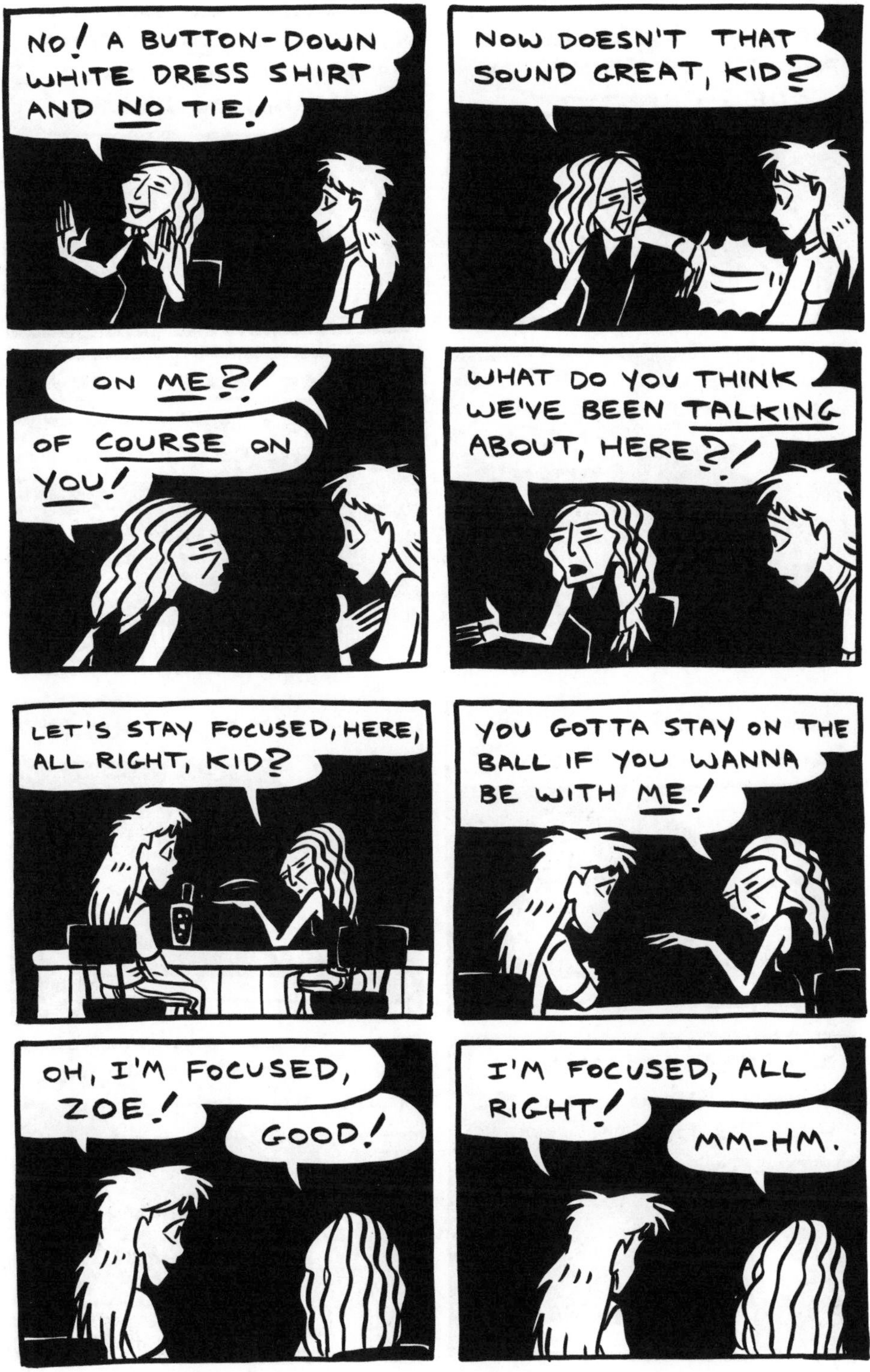
NO! A BUTTON-DOWN WHITE DRESS SHIRT AND NO TIE!
NOW DOESN'T THAT SOUND GREAT, KID?
ON ME?!
OF COURSE ON YOU!
WHAT DO YOU THINK WE'VE BEEN TALKING ABOUT, HERE?!
LET'S STAY FOCUSED, HERE, ALL RIGHT, KID?
YOU GOTTA STAY ON THE BALL IF YOU WANNA BE WITH ME!
OH, I'M FOCUSED, ZOE!
GOOD!
I'M FOCUSED, ALL RIGHT!
MM-HM.

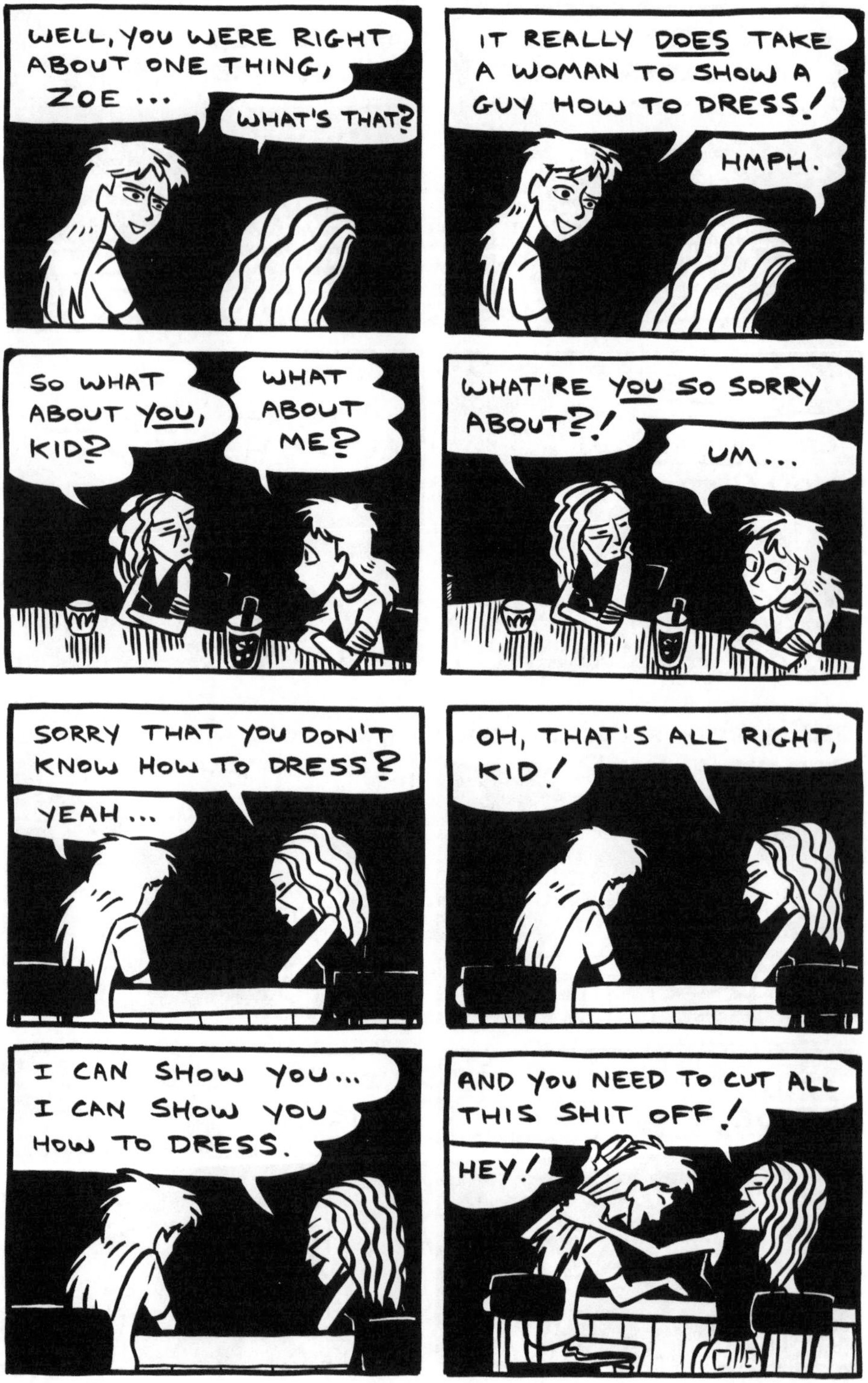
WELL, YOU WERE RIGHT ABOUT ONE THING, ZOE ...
WHAT'S THAT?
IT REALLY DOES TAKE A WOMAN TO SHOW A GUY HOW TO DRESS!
HMPH.
SO WHAT ABOUT YOU, KID?
WHAT ABOUT ME?
WHAT'RE YOU SO SORRY ABOUT?!
UM ...
SORRY THAT YOU DON'T KNOW HOW TO DRESS?
YEAH ...
OH, THAT'S ALL RIGHT, KID!
I CAN SHOW YOU... I CAN SHOW YOU HOW TO DRESS.
AND YOU NEED TO CUT ALL THIS SHIT OFF!
HEY!

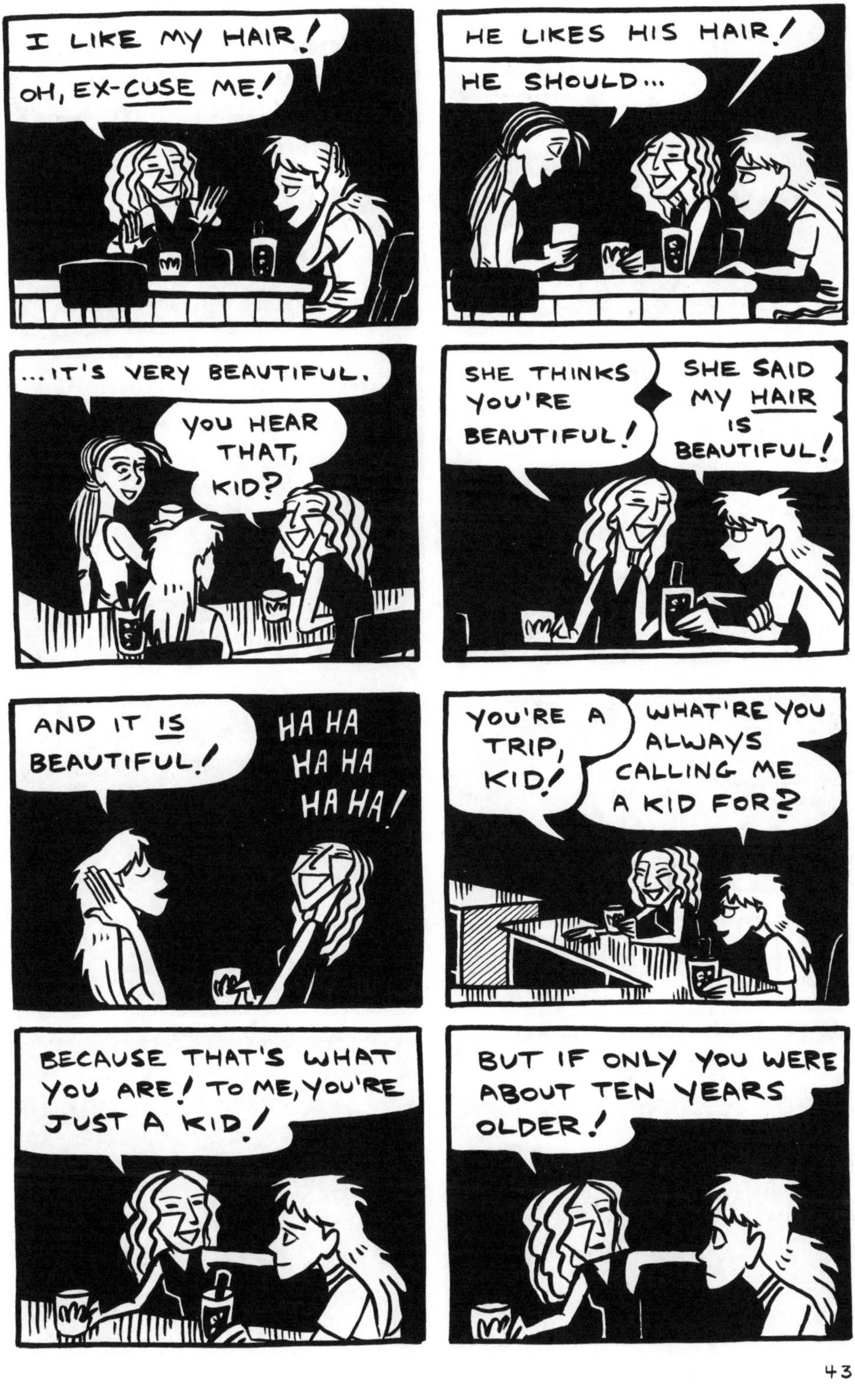

I LIKE MY HAIR!
OH, EX-CUSE ME!
HE LIKES HIS HAIR!
HE SHOULD...
...IT'S VERY BEAUTIFUL.
YOU HEAR THAT, KID?
SHE THINKS YOU'RE BEAUTIFUL!
SHE SAID MY HAIR IS BEAUTIFUL!
AND IT IS BEAUTIFUL!
HA HA HA HA HA HA!
YOU'RE A TRIP, KID!
WHAT'RE YOU ALWAYS CALLING ME A KID FOR?
BECAUSE THAT'S WHAT YOU ARE! TO ME, YOU'RE JUST A KID!
BUT IF ONLY YOU WERE ABOUT TEN YEARS OLDER!

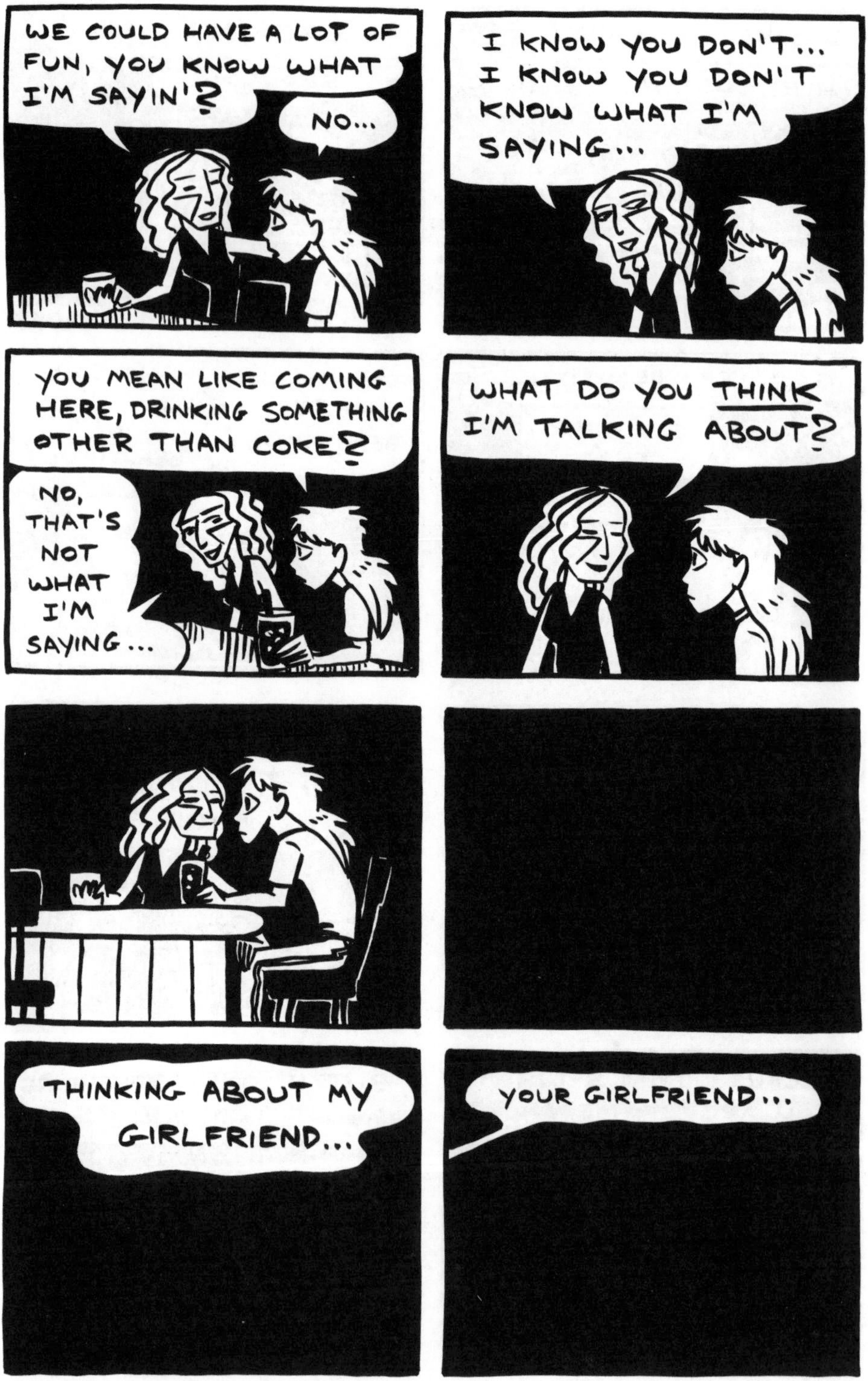
WE COULD HAVE A LOT OF FUN, YOU KNOW WHAT I'M SAYIN'?
NO...
I KNOW YOU DON'T... I KNOW YOU DON'T KNOW WHAT I'M SAYING...
YOU MEAN LIKE COMING HERE, DRINKING SOMETHING OTHER THAN COKE?
NO, THAT'S NOT WHAT I'M SAYING...
WHAT DO YOU THINK I'M TALKING ABOUT?
THINKING ABOUT MY GIRLFRIEND...
YOUR GIRLFRIEND...

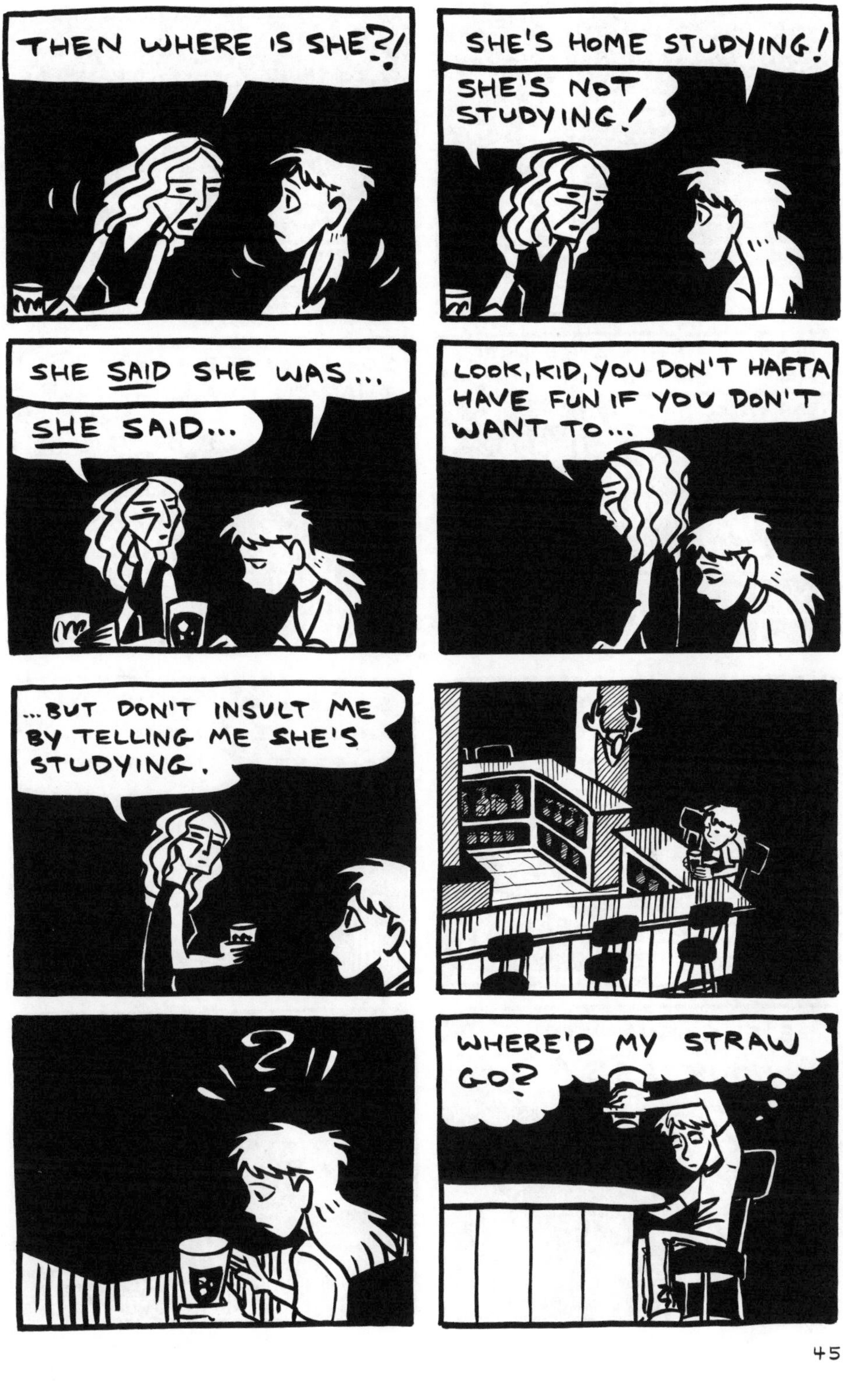
THEN WHERE IS SHE?!
SHE'S HOME STUDYING!
SHE'S NOT STUDYING!
SHE SAID SHE WAS...
SHE SAID...
LOOK, KID, YOU DON'T HAFTA HAVE FUN IF YOU DON'T WANT TO...
...BUT DON'T INSULT ME BY TELLING ME SHE'S STUDYING.
?
WHERE'D MY STRAW GO?

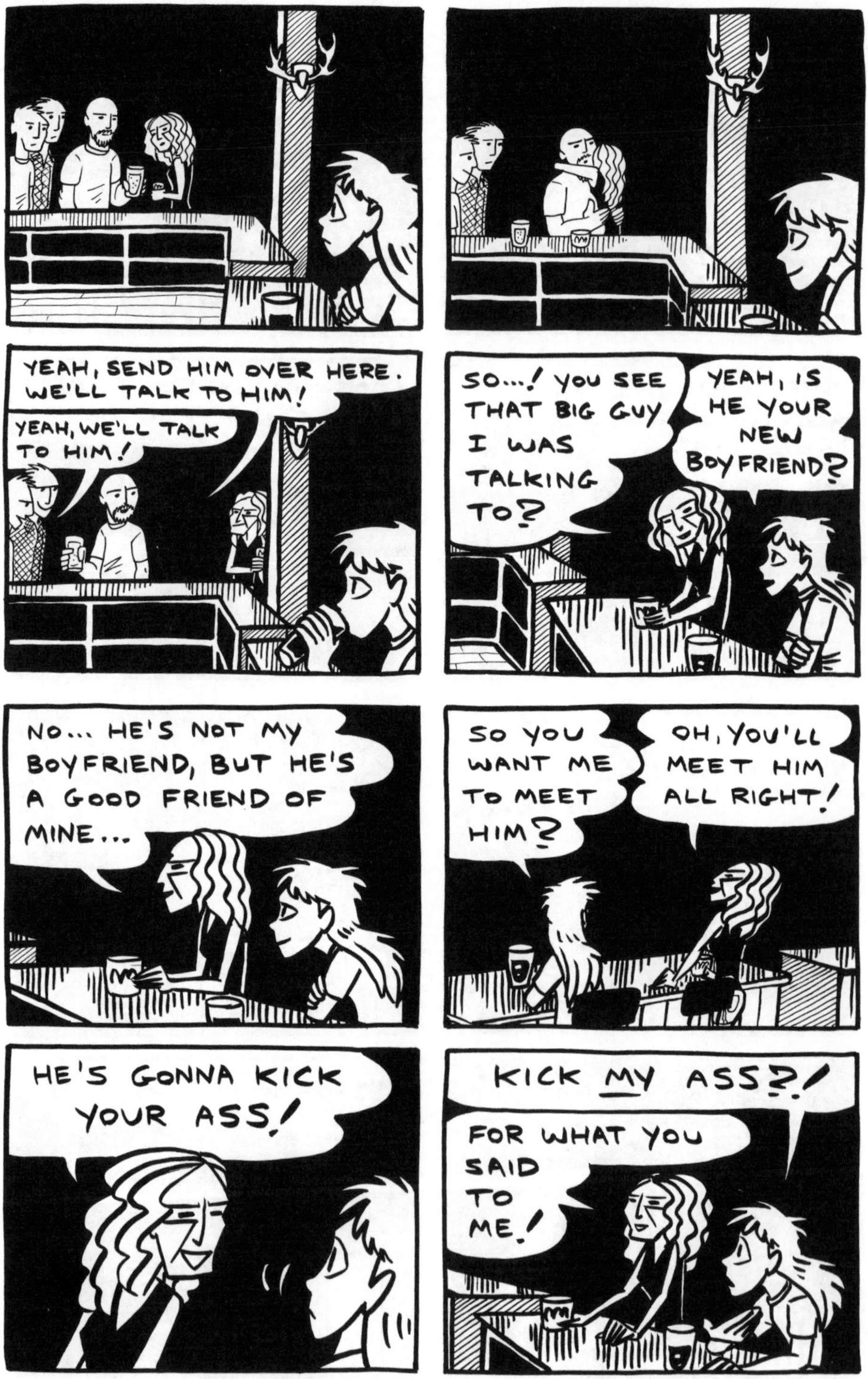
YEAH, SEND HIM OVER HERE. WE'LL TALK TO HIM!
YEAH, WE'LL TALK TO HIM!
SO...! YOU SEE THAT BIG GUY I WAS TALKING TO?
YEAH, IS HE YOUR NEW BOYFRIEND?
NO... HE'S NOT MY BOYFRIEND, BUT HE'S A GOOD FRIEND OF MINE...
SO YOU WANT ME TO MEET HIM?
OH, YOU'LL MEET HIM ALL RIGHT!
HE'S GONNA KICK YOUR ASS!
KICK MY ASS?!
FOR WHAT YOU SAID TO ME!

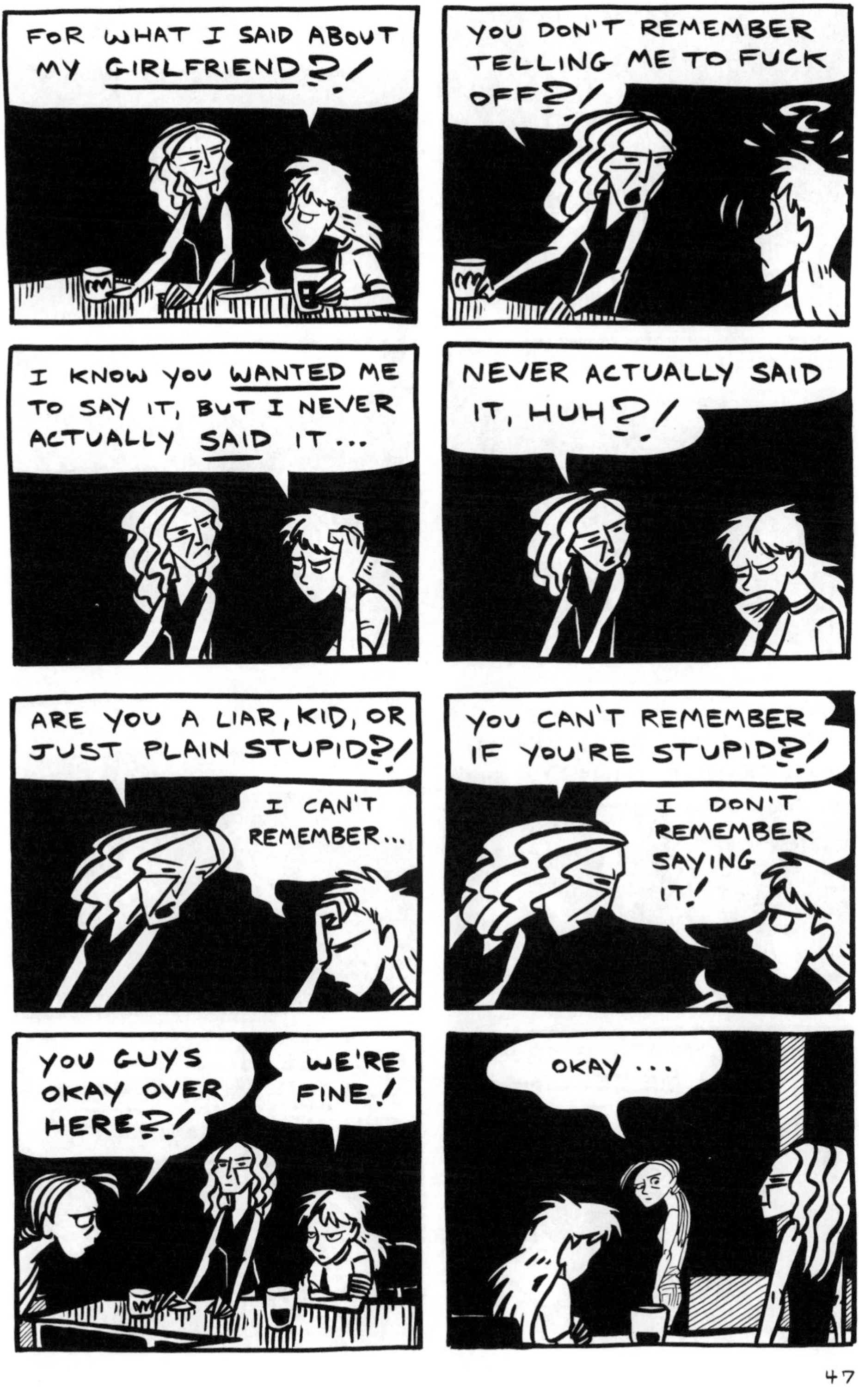
FOR WHAT I SAID ABOUT MY GIRLFRIEND?!
YOU DON'T REMEMBER TELLING ME TO FUCK OFF?!
I KNOW YOU WANTED ME TO SAY IT, BUT I NEVER ACTUALLY SAID IT...
NEVER ACTUALLY SAID IT, HUH?!
ARE YOU A LIAR, KID, OR JUST PLAIN STUPID?!
I CAN'T REMEMBER...
YOU CAN'T REMEMBER IF YOU'RE STUPID?!
I DON'T REMEMBER SAYING IT!
YOU GUYS OKAY OVER HERE?!
WE'RE FINE!
OKAY...

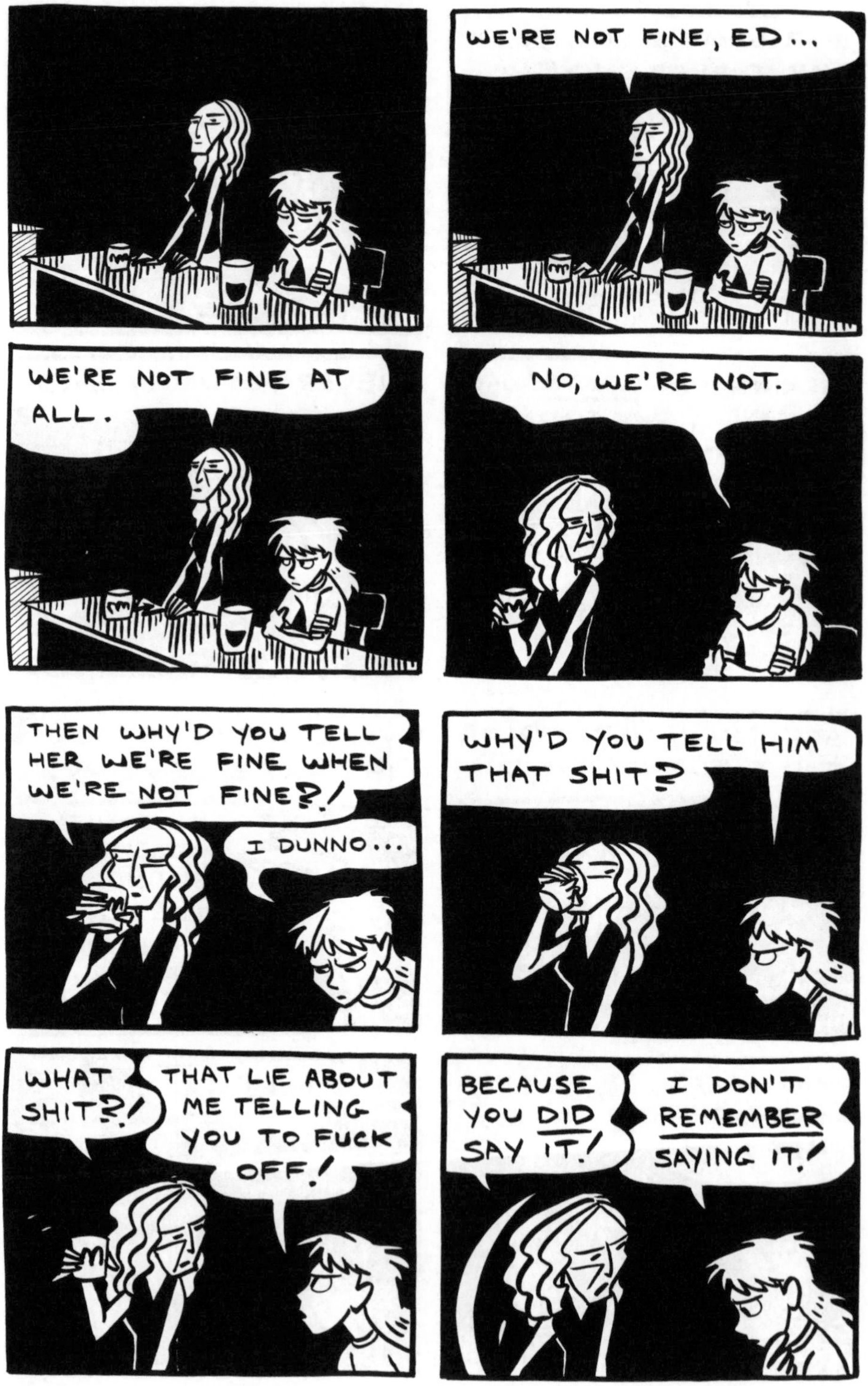
WE'RE NOT FINE, ED...
WE'RE NOT FINE AT ALL.
NO, WE'RE NOT.
THEN WHY'D YOU TELL HER WE'RE FINE WHEN WE'RE NOT FINE?!
I DUNNO...
WHY'D YOU TELL HIM THAT SHIT?
WHAT SHIT?!
THAT LIE ABOUT ME TELLING YOU TO FUCK OFF!
BECAUSE YOU DID SAY IT!
I DON'T REMEMBER SAYING IT!

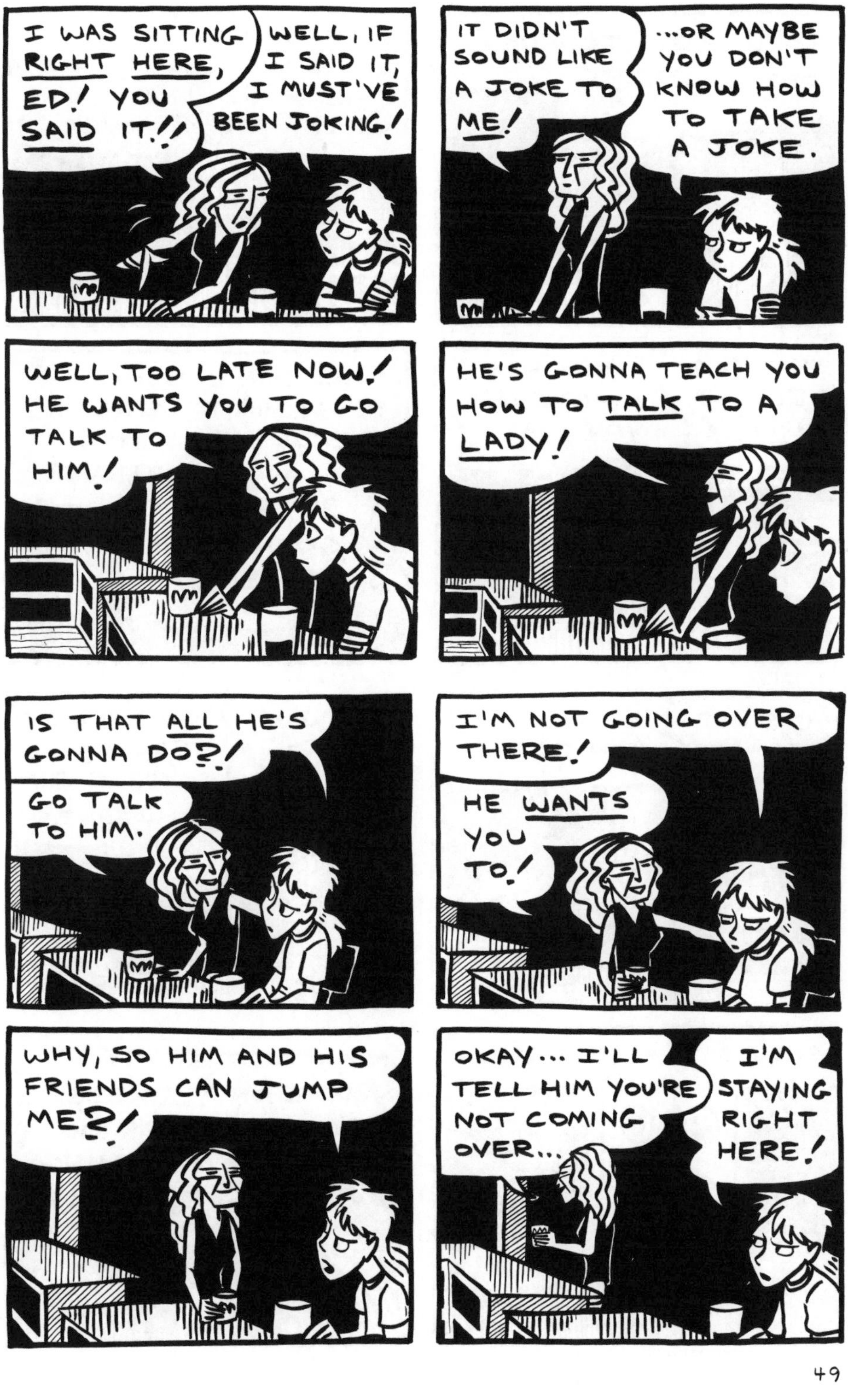
I WAS SITTING RIGHT HERE, ED! YOU SAID IT!!
WELL, IF I SAID IT, I MUST'VE BEEN JOKING!
IT DIDN'T SOUND LIKE A JOKE TO ME!
...OR MAYBE YOU DON'T KNOW HOW TO TAKE A JOKE.
WELL, TOO LATE NOW! HE WANTS YOU TO GO TALK TO HIM!
HE'S GONNA TEACH YOU HOW TO TALK TO A LADY!
IS THAT ALL HE'S GONNA DO?!
GO TALK TO HIM.
I'M NOT GOING OVER THERE!
HE WANTS YOU TO!
WHY, SO HIM AND HIS FRIENDS CAN JUMP ME?!
OKAY... I'LL TELL HIM YOU'RE NOT COMING OVER...
I'M STAYING RIGHT HERE!

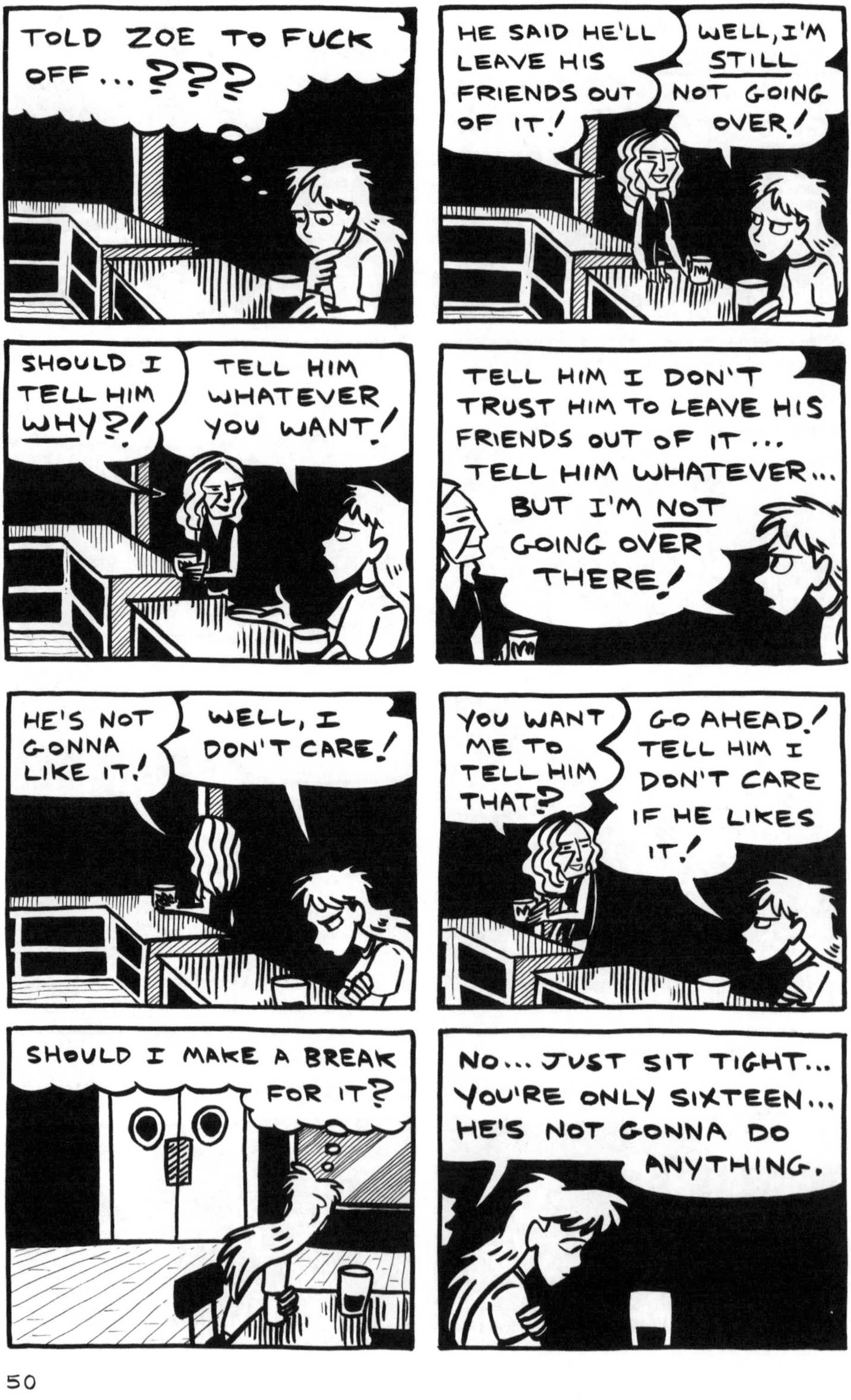
TOLD ZOE TO FUCK OFF... ???
HE SAID HE'LL LEAVE HIS FRIENDS OUT OF IT!
WELL, I'M STILL NOT GOING OVER!
SHOULD I TELL HIM WHY?!
TELL HIM WHATEVER YOU WANT!
TELL HIM I DON'T TRUST HIM TO LEAVE HIS FRIENDS OUT OF IT... TELL HIM WHATEVER... BUT I'M NOT GOING OVER THERE!
HE'S NOT GONNA LIKE IT!
WELL, I DON'T CARE!
YOU WANT ME TO TELL HIM THAT?
GO AHEAD! TELL HIM I DON'T CARE IF HE LIKES IT!
SHOULD I MAKE A BREAK FOR IT?
NO... JUST SIT TIGHT... YOU'RE ONLY SIXTEEN... HE'S NOT GONNA DO ANYTHING.

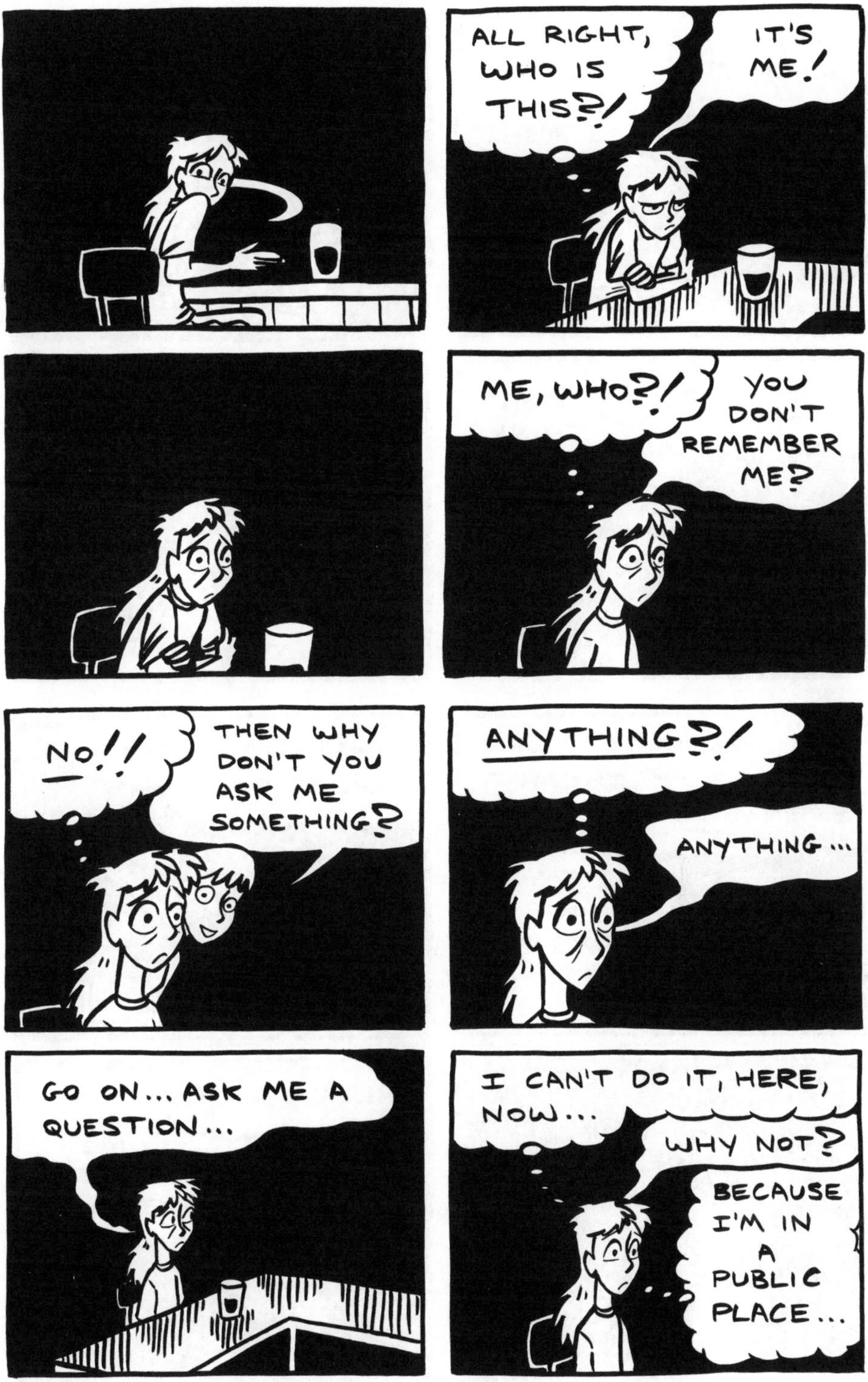

ALL RIGHT, WHO IS THIS?!
IT'S ME!
ME, WHO?!
YOU DON'T REMEMBER ME?
NO!!
THEN WHY DON'T YOU ASK ME SOMETHING?
ANYTHING?!
ANYTHING...
GO ON... ASK ME A QUESTION...
I CAN'T DO IT, HERE, NOW...
WHY NOT?
BECAUSE I'M IN A PUBLIC PLACE...

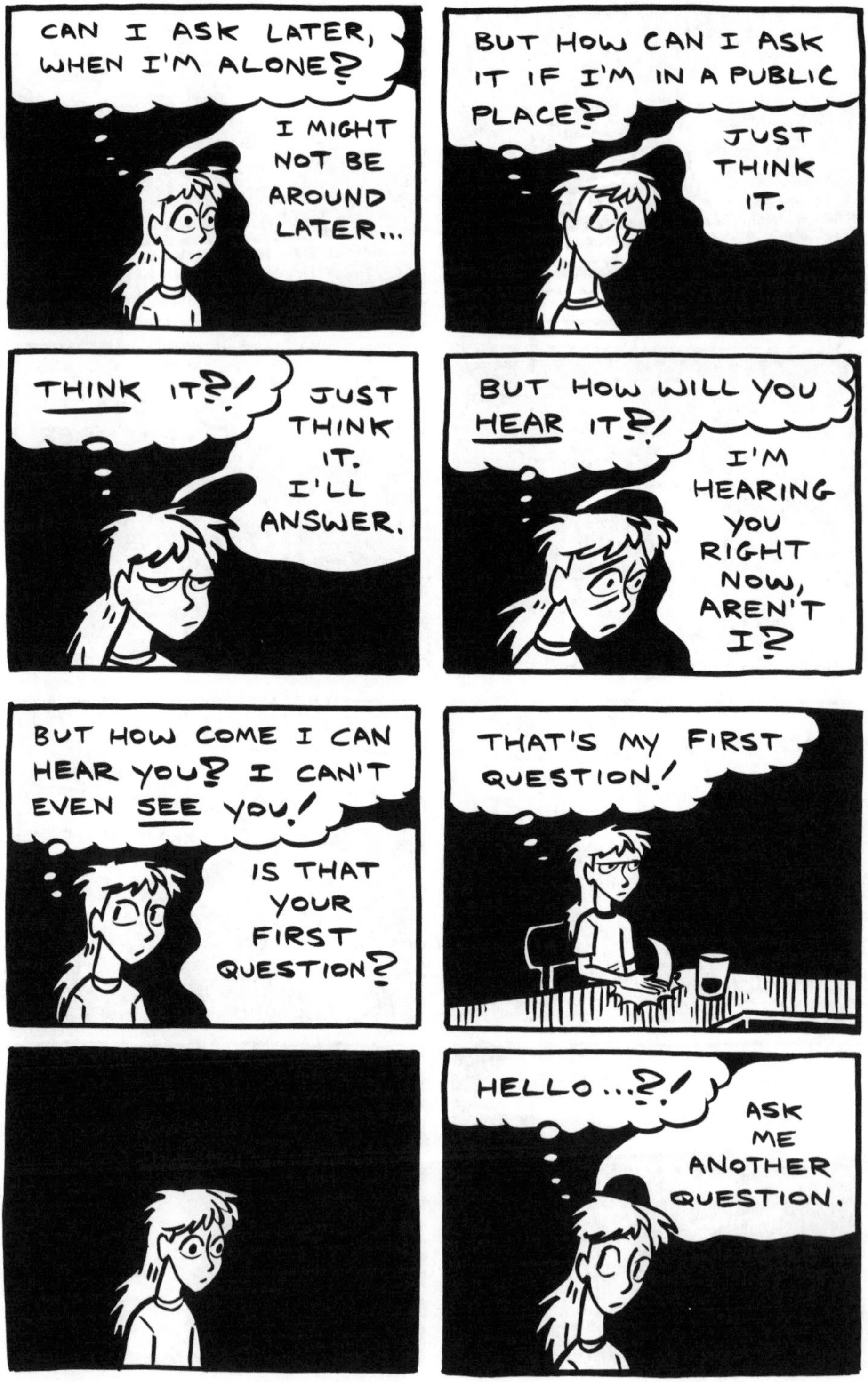
CAN I ASK LATER, WHEN I'M ALONE?
I MIGHT NOT BE AROUND LATER...
BUT HOW CAN I ASK IT IF I'M IN A PUBLIC PLACE?
JUST THINK IT.
THINK IT?!
JUST THINK IT. I'LL ANSWER.
BUT HOW WILL YOU HEAR IT?!
I'M HEARING YOU RIGHT NOW, AREN'T I?
BUT HOW COME I CAN HEAR YOU? I CAN'T EVEN SEE YOU!
IS THAT YOUR FIRST QUESTION?
THAT'S MY FIRST QUESTION!
HELLO...?!
ASK ME ANOTHER QUESTION.

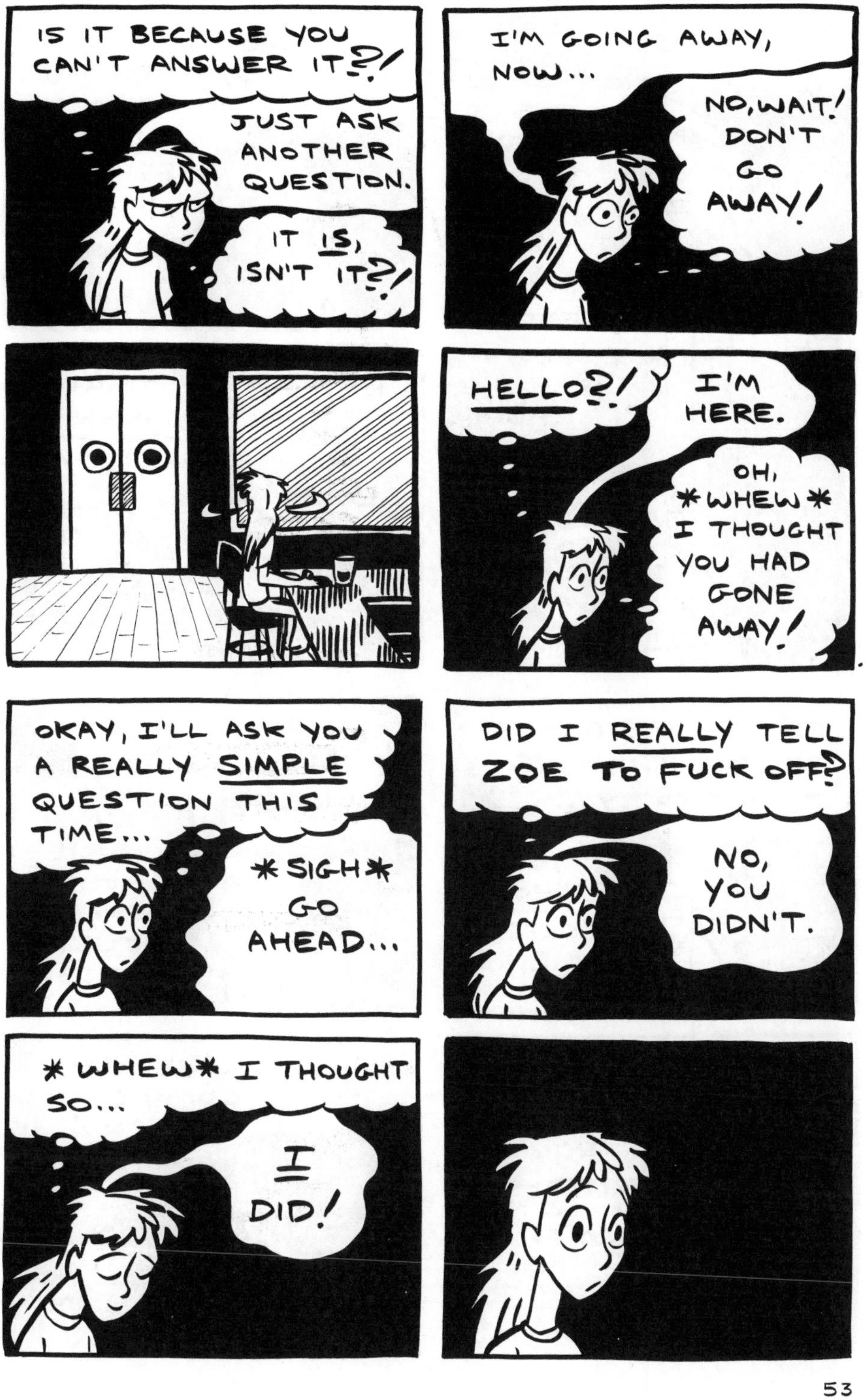

IS IT BECAUSE YOU CAN'T ANSWER IT?!
JUST ASK ANOTHER QUESTION.
IT IS, ISN'T IT?!
I'M GOING AWAY, NOW...
NO, WAIT! DON'T GO AWAY!
HELLO?!
I'M HERE.
OH, *WHEW* I THOUGHT YOU HAD GONE AWAY!
OKAY, I'LL ASK YOU A REALLY SIMPLE QUESTION THIS TIME...
SIGH GO AHEAD...
DID I REALLY TELL ZOE TO FUCK OFF?
NO, YOU DIDN'T.
WHEW I THOUGHT SO...
I DID!

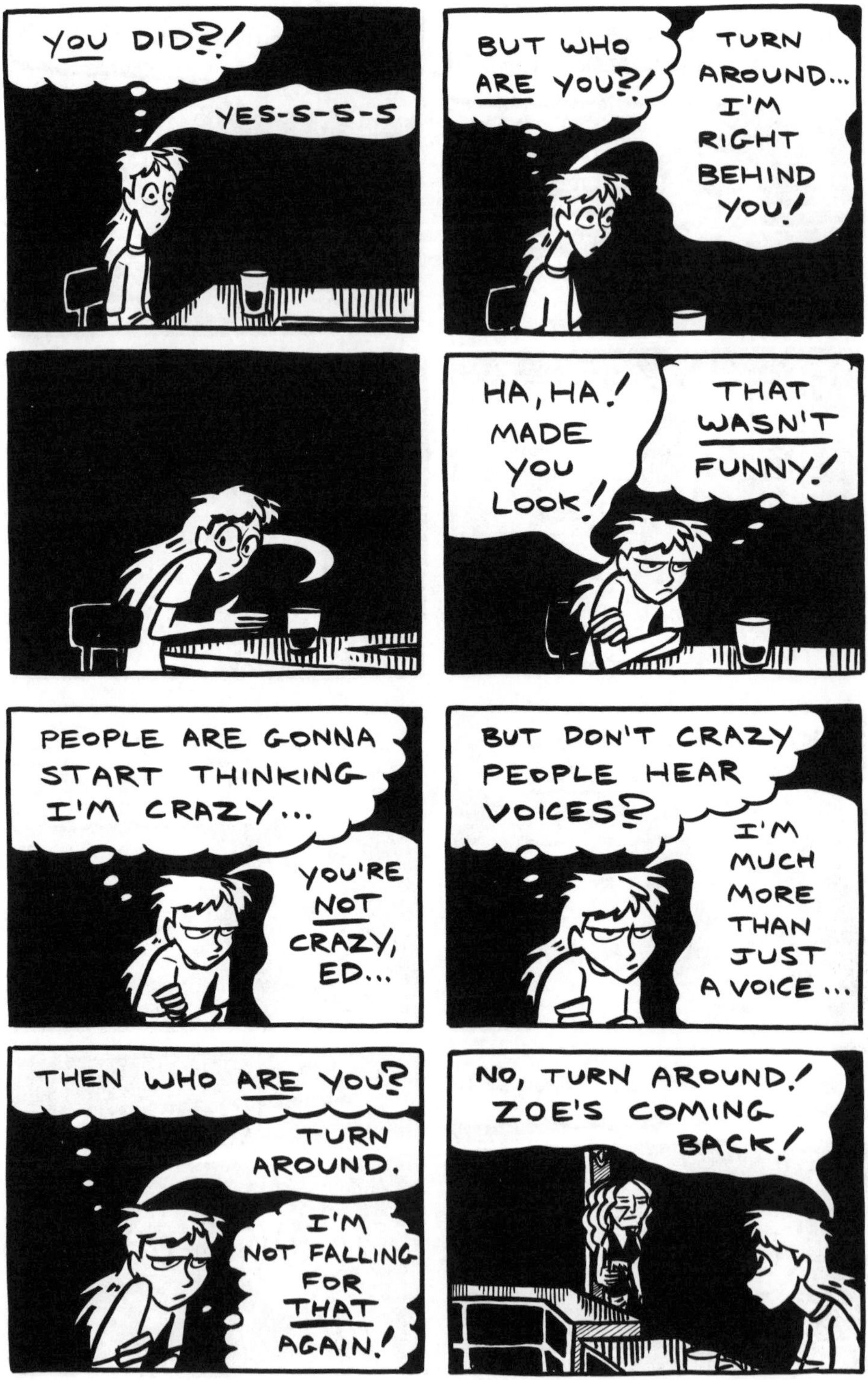
YOU DID?!
YES-S-S-S
BUT WHO ARE YOU?!
TURN AROUND... I'M RIGHT BEHIND YOU!
HA, HA! MADE YOU LOOK!
THAT WASN'T FUNNY!
PEOPLE ARE GONNA START THINKING I'M CRAZY...
YOU'RE NOT CRAZY, ED...
BUT DON'T CRAZY PEOPLE HEAR VOICES?
I'M MUCH MORE THAN JUST A VOICE...
THEN WHO ARE YOU?
TURN AROUND.
I'M NOT FALLING FOR THAT AGAIN!
NO, TURN AROUND! ZOE'S COMING BACK!

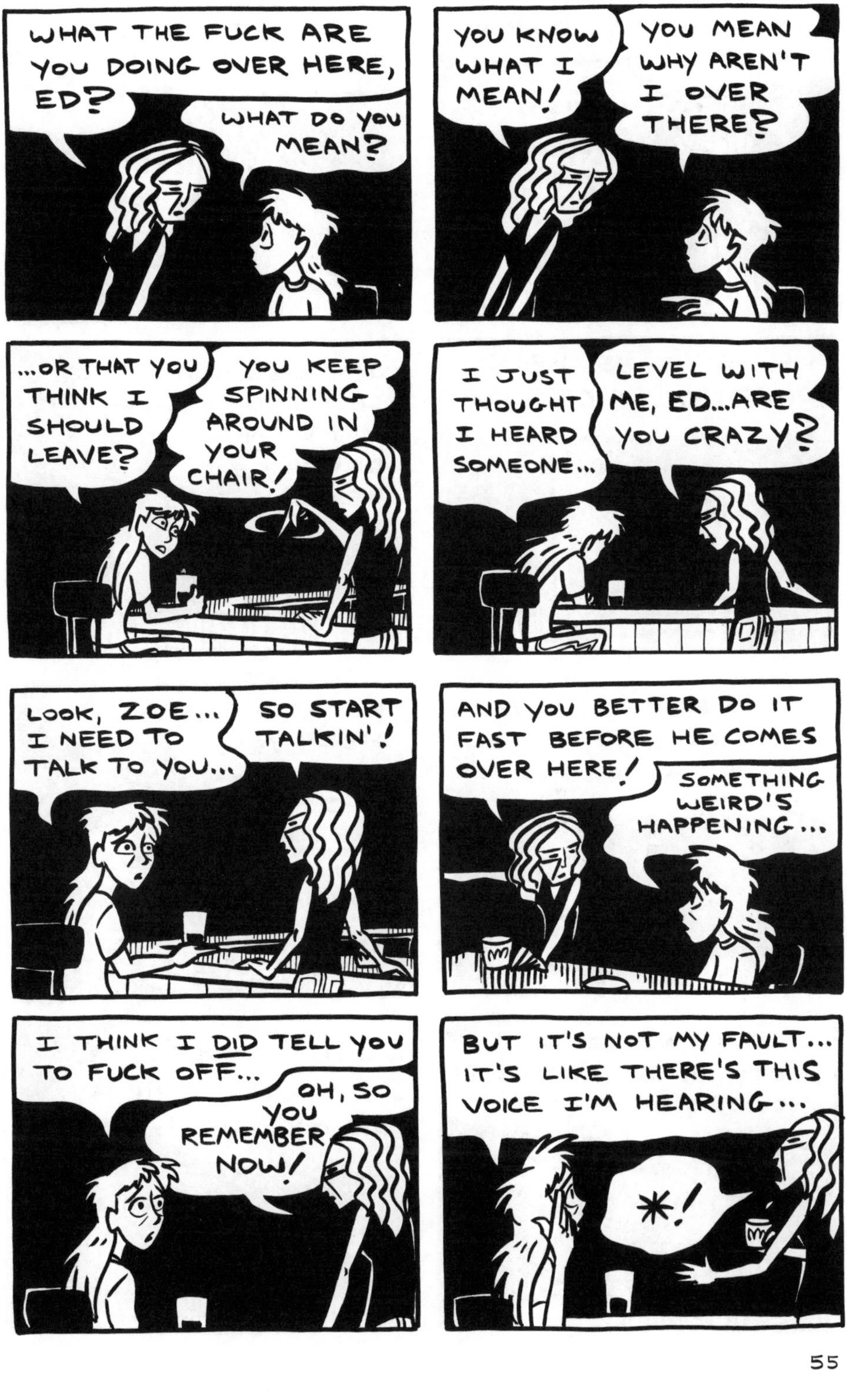
WHAT THE FUCK ARE YOU DOING OVER HERE, ED?
WHAT DO YOU MEAN?
YOU KNOW WHAT I MEAN!
YOU MEAN WHY AREN'T I OVER THERE?
...OR THAT YOU THINK I SHOULD LEAVE?
YOU KEEP SPINNING AROUND IN YOUR CHAIR!
I JUST THOUGHT I HEARD SOMEONE...
LEVEL WITH ME, ED...ARE YOU CRAZY?
LOOK, ZOE... I NEED TO TALK TO YOU...
SO START TALKIN'!
AND YOU BETTER DO IT FAST BEFORE HE COMES OVER HERE!
SOMETHING WEIRD'S HAPPENING...
I THINK I DID TELL YOU TO FUCK OFF...
OH, SO YOU REMEMBER NOW!
BUT IT'S NOT MY FAULT... IT'S LIKE THERE'S THIS VOICE I'M HEARING...
*!

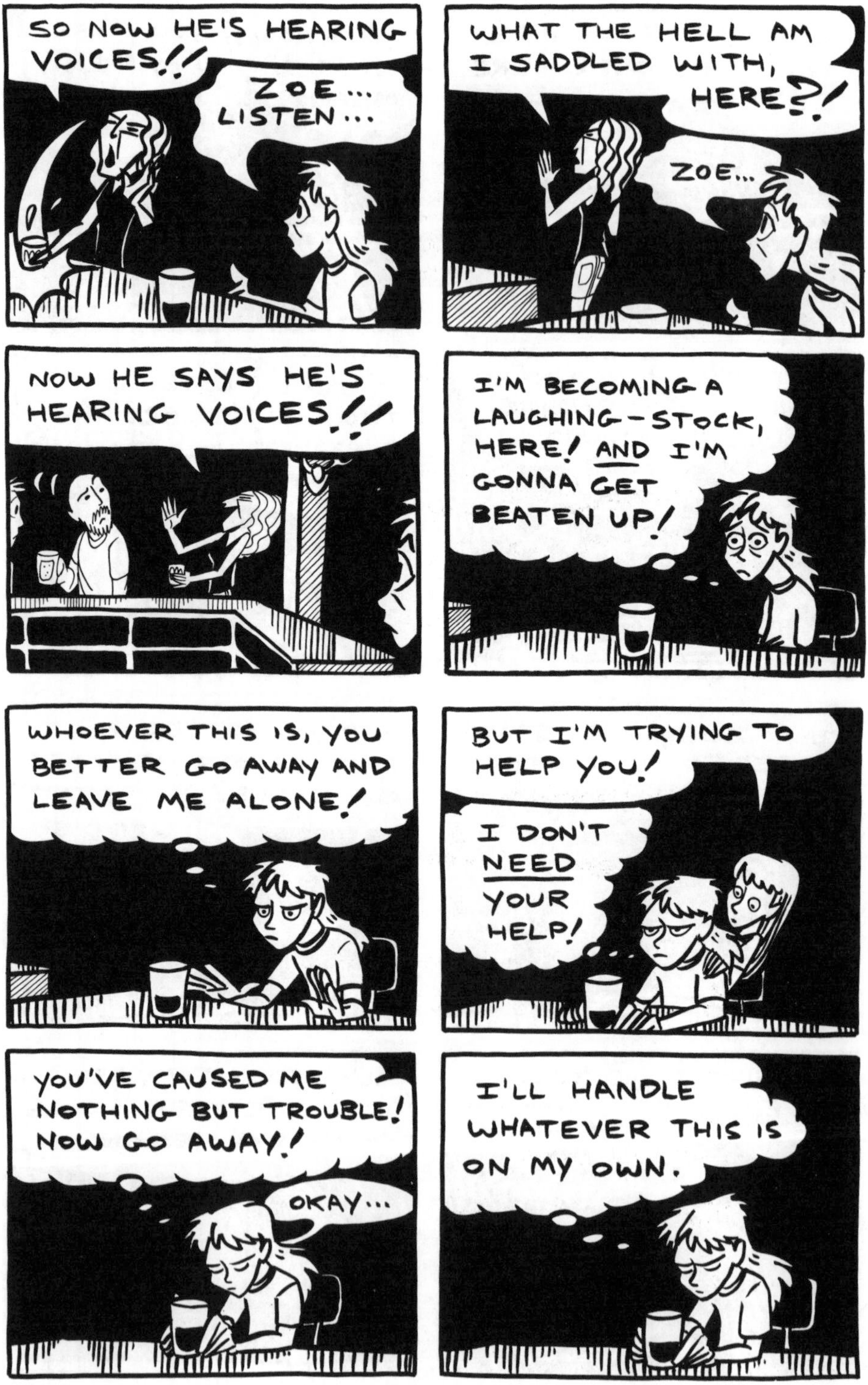
SO NOW HE'S HEARING VOICES!!
ZOE... LISTEN...
WHAT THE HELL AM I SADDLED WITH, HERE?!
ZOE...
NOW HE SAYS HE'S HEARING VOICES!!
I'M BECOMING A LAUGHING-STOCK, HERE! AND I'M GONNA GET BEATEN UP!
WHOEVER THIS IS, YOU BETTER GO AWAY AND LEAVE ME ALONE!
BUT I'M TRYING TO HELP YOU!
I DON'T NEED YOUR HELP!
YOU'VE CAUSED ME NOTHING BUT TROUBLE! NOW GO AWAY!
OKAY...
I'LL HANDLE WHATEVER THIS IS ON MY OWN.

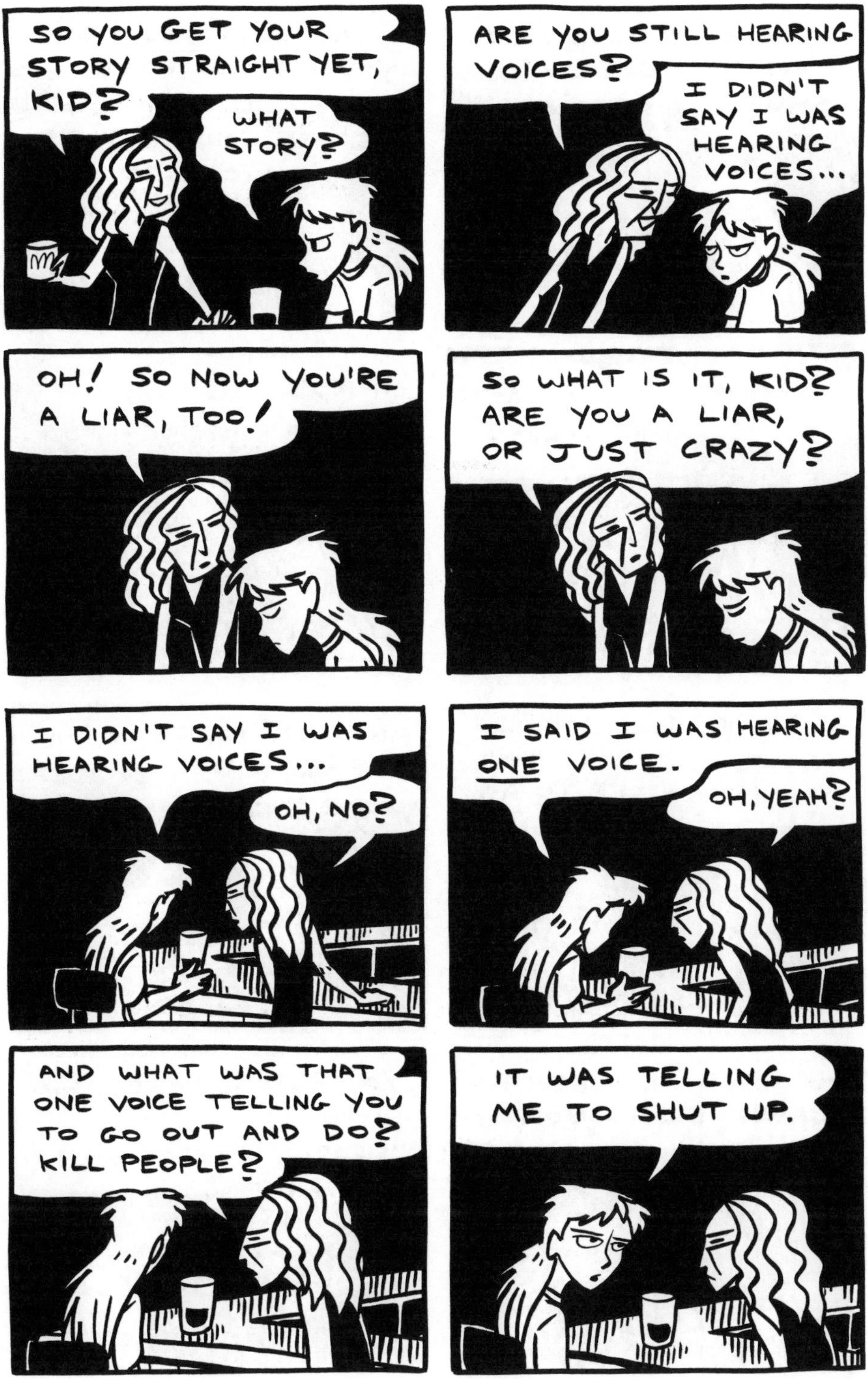
SO YOU GET YOUR STORY STRAIGHT YET, KID?
WHAT STORY?
ARE YOU STILL HEARING VOICES?
I DIDN'T SAY I WAS HEARING VOICES...
OH! SO NOW YOU'RE A LIAR, TOO!
SO WHAT IS IT, KID? ARE YOU A LIAR, OR JUST CRAZY?
I DIDN'T SAY I WAS HEARING VOICES...
OH, NO?
I SAID I WAS HEARING ONE VOICE.
OH, YEAH?
AND WHAT WAS THAT ONE VOICE TELLING YOU TO GO OUT AND DO? KILL PEOPLE?
IT WAS TELLING ME TO SHUT UP.

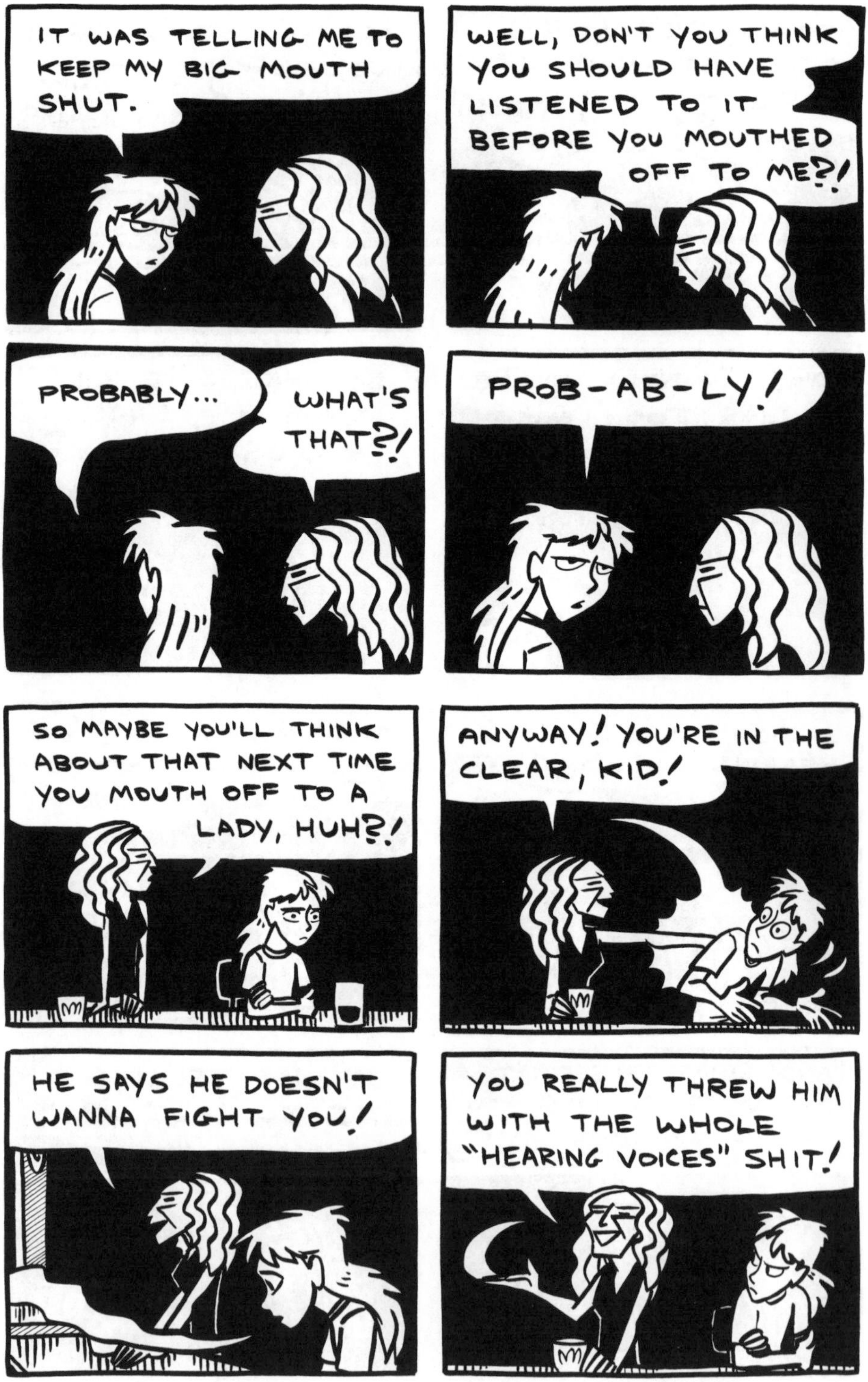
IT WAS TELLING ME TO KEEP MY BIG MOUTH SHUT.
WELL, DON'T YOU THINK YOU SHOULD HAVE LISTENED TO IT BEFORE YOU MOUTHED OFF TO ME?!
PROBABLY...
WHAT'S THAT?!
PROB-AB-LY!
SO MAYBE YOU'LL THINK ABOUT THAT NEXT TIME YOU MOUTH OFF TO A LADY, HUH?!
ANYWAY! YOU'RE IN THE CLEAR, KID!
HE SAYS HE DOESN'T WANNA FIGHT YOU!
YOU REALLY THREW HIM WITH THE WHOLE "HEARING VOICES" SHIT!

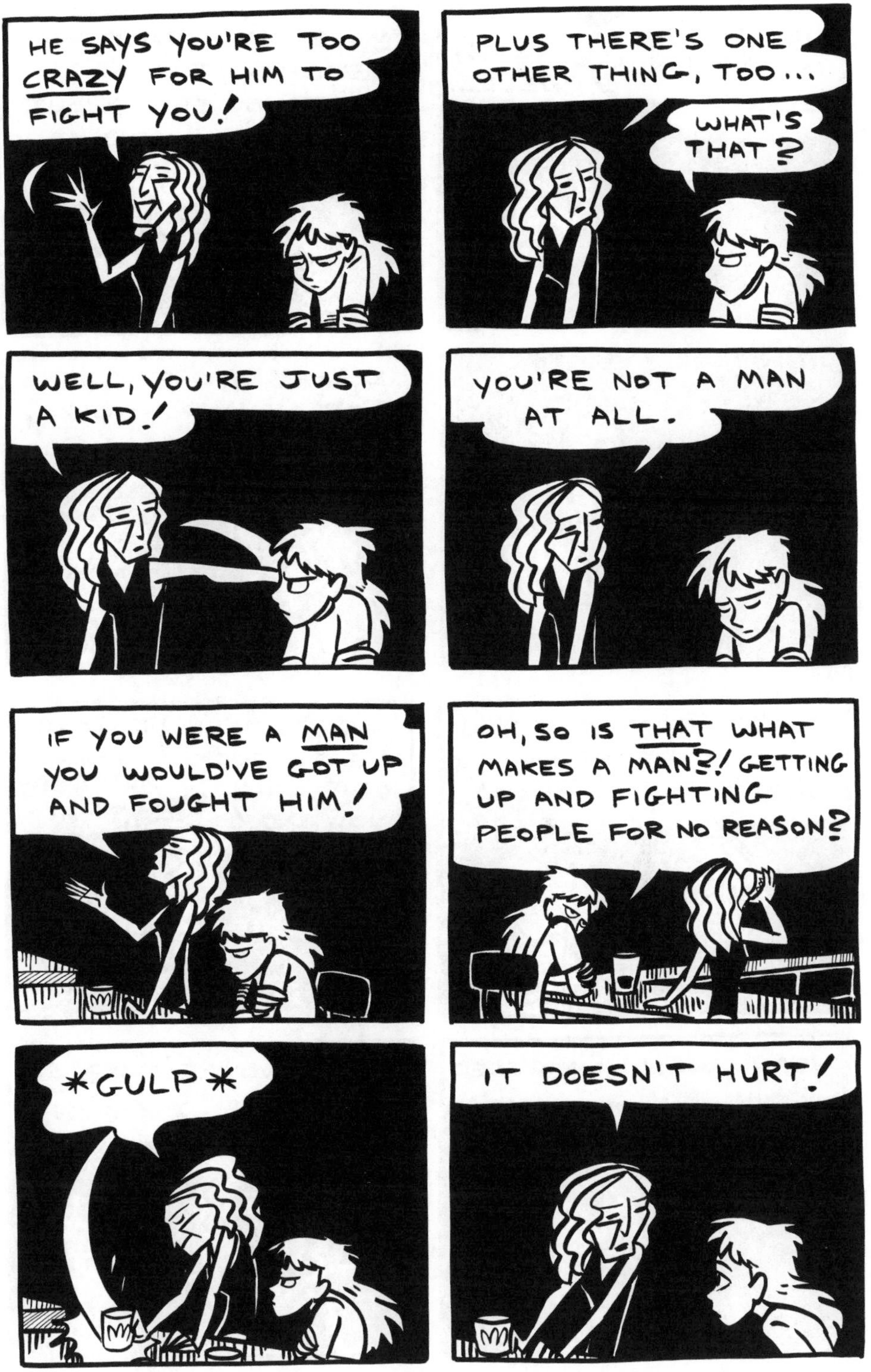
HE SAYS YOU'RE TOO CRAZY FOR HIM TO FIGHT YOU!
PLUS THERE'S ONE OTHER THING, TOO...
WHAT'S THAT?
WELL, YOU'RE JUST A KID!
YOU'RE NOT A MAN AT ALL.
IF YOU WERE A MAN YOU WOULD'VE GOT UP AND FOUGHT HIM!
OH, SO IS THAT WHAT MAKES A MAN?! GETTING UP AND FIGHTING PEOPLE FOR NO REASON?
GULP
IT DOESN'T HURT!

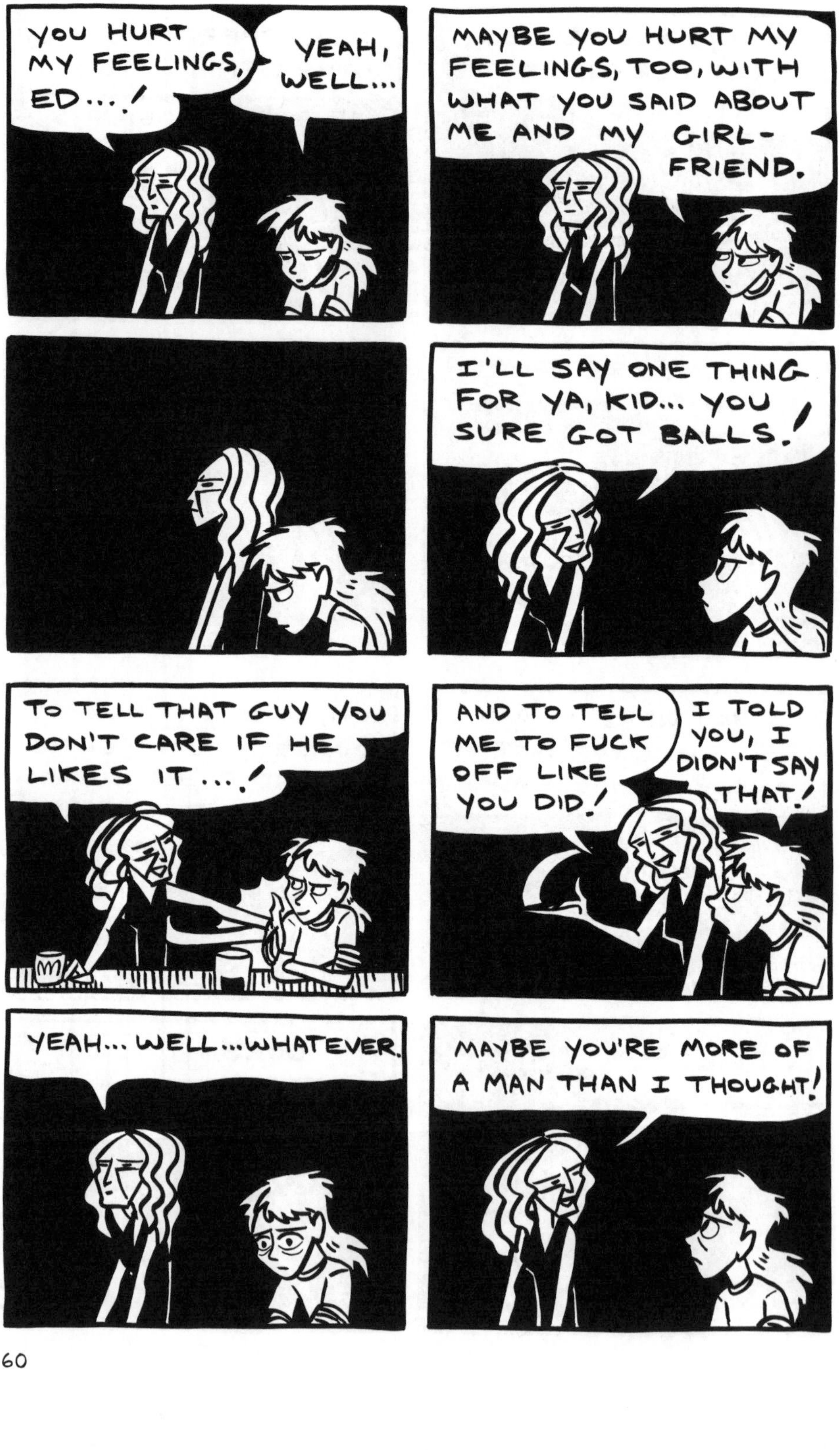
YOU HURT MY FEELINGS, ED...!
YEAH, WELL...
MAYBE YOU HURT MY FEELINGS, TOO, WITH WHAT YOU SAID ABOUT ME AND MY GIRL-FRIEND.
I'LL SAY ONE THING FOR YA, KID... YOU SURE GOT BALLS!
TO TELL THAT GUY YOU DON'T CARE IF HE LIKES IT...!
AND TO TELL ME TO FUCK OFF LIKE YOU DID!
I TOLD YOU, I DIDN'T SAY THAT!
YEAH... WELL... WHATEVER.
MAYBE YOU'RE MORE OF A MAN THAN I THOUGHT!

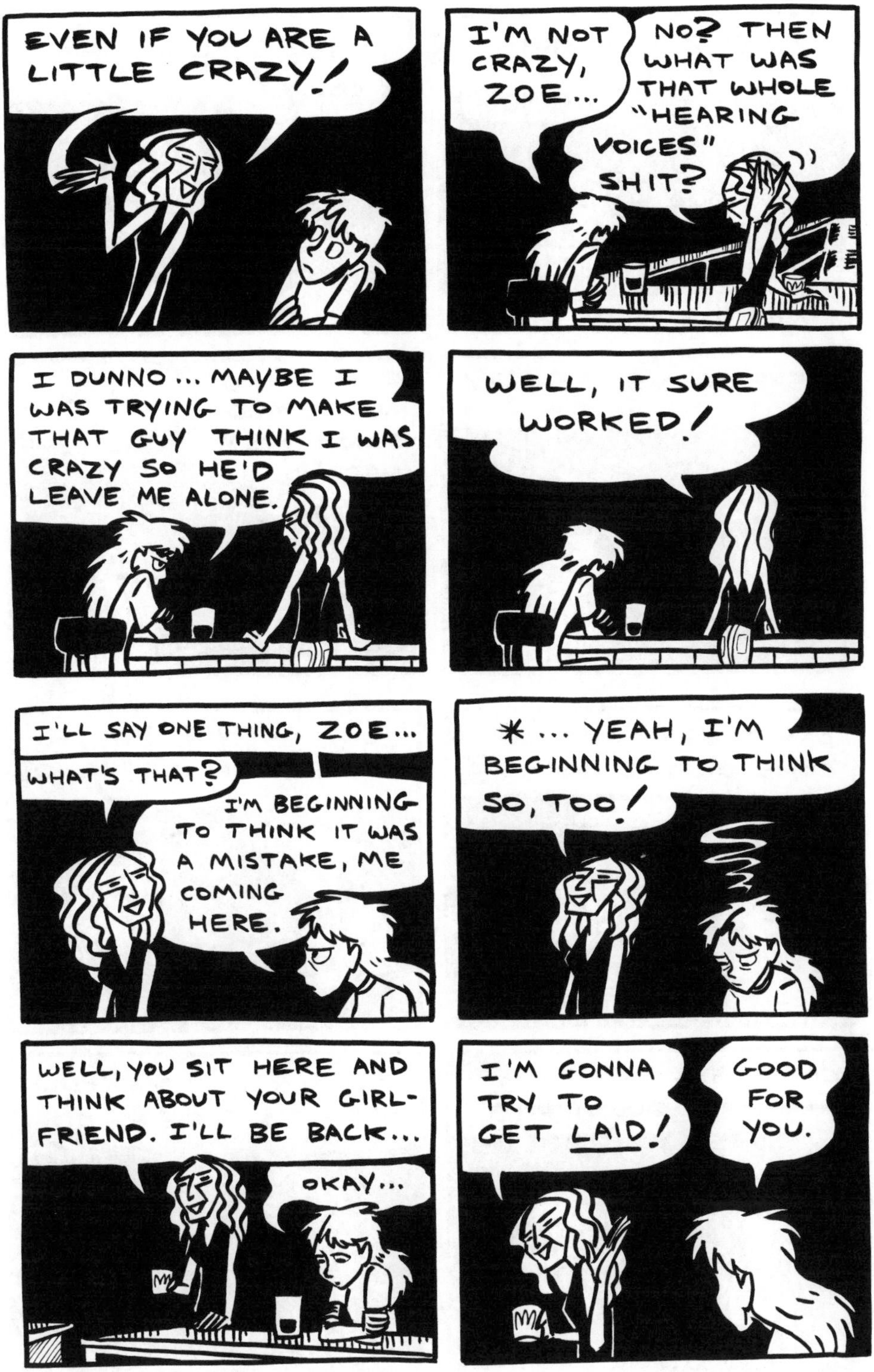
EVEN IF YOU ARE A LITTLE CRAZY!
I'M NOT CRAZY, ZOE...
NO? THEN WHAT WAS THAT WHOLE "HEARING VOICES" SHIT?
I DUNNO... MAYBE I WAS TRYING TO MAKE THAT GUY THINK I WAS CRAZY SO HE'D LEAVE ME ALONE.
WELL, IT SURE WORKED!
I'LL SAY ONE THING, ZOE...
WHAT'S THAT?
I'M BEGINNING TO THINK IT WAS A MISTAKE, ME COMING HERE.
*... YEAH, I'M BEGINNING TO THINK SO, TOO!
WELL, YOU SIT HERE AND THINK ABOUT YOUR GIRL-FRIEND. I'LL BE BACK...
OKAY...
I'M GONNA TRY TO GET LAID!
GOOD FOR YOU.

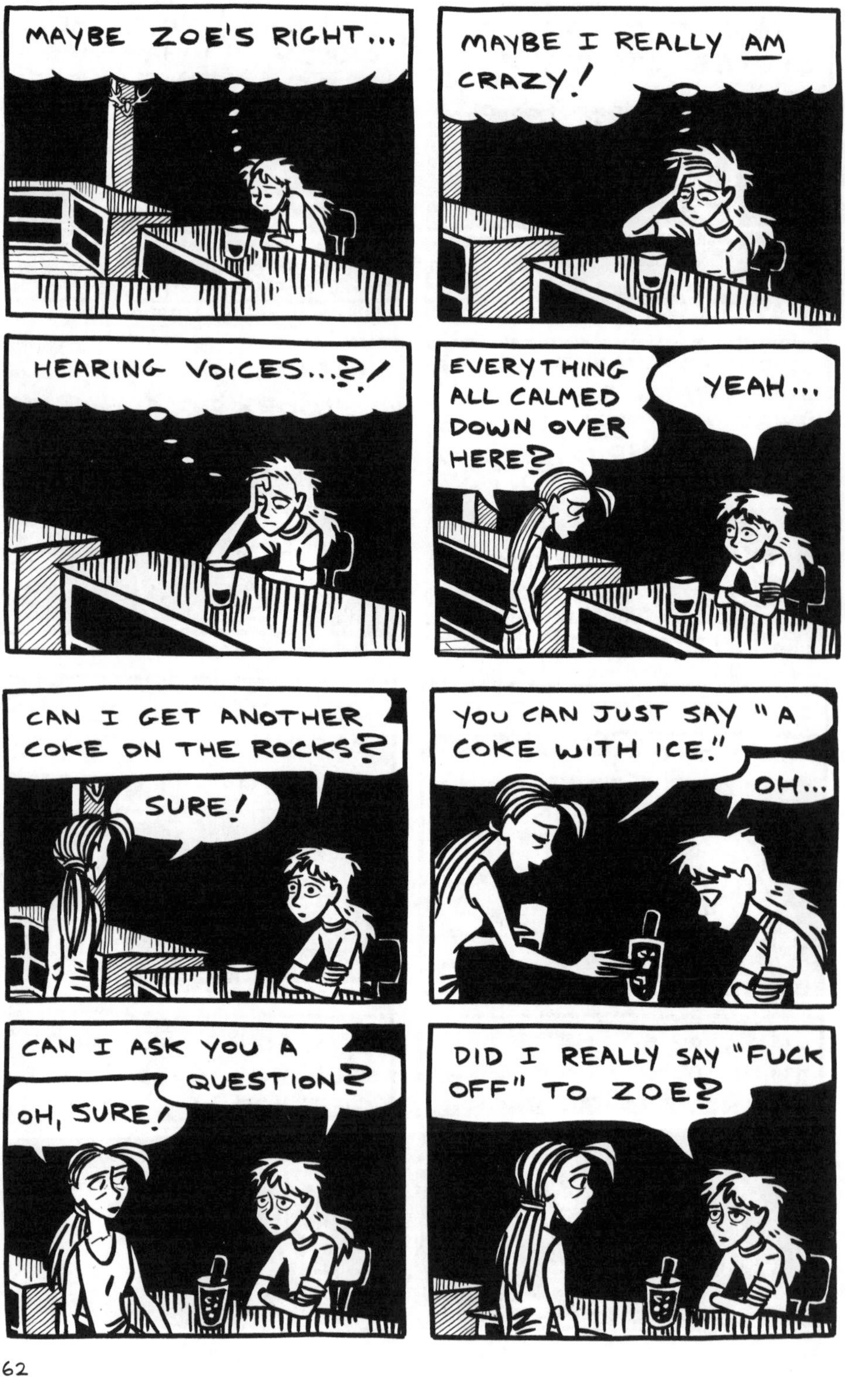
MAYBE ZOE'S RIGHT...
MAYBE I REALLY AM CRAZY!
HEARING VOICES...?!
EVERYTHING ALL CALMED DOWN OVER HERE?
YEAH...
CAN I GET ANOTHER COKE ON THE ROCKS?
SURE!
YOU CAN JUST SAY "A COKE WITH ICE."
OH...
CAN I ASK YOU A QUESTION?
OH, SURE!
DID I REALLY SAY "FUCK OFF" TO ZOE?

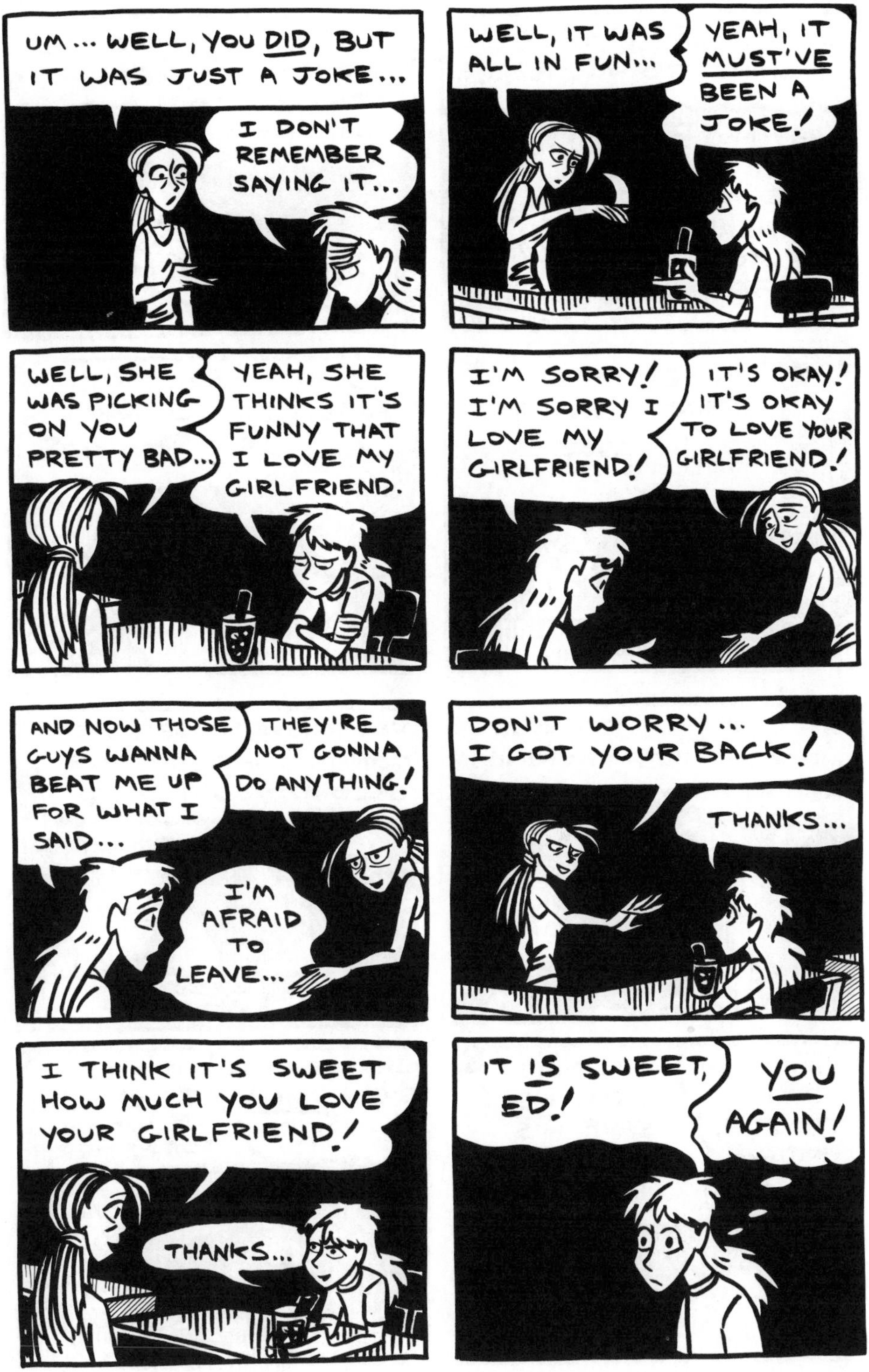
UM... WELL, YOU DID, BUT IT WAS JUST A JOKE...
I DON'T REMEMBER SAYING IT...
WELL, IT WAS ALL IN FUN...
YEAH, IT MUST'VE BEEN A JOKE!
WELL, SHE WAS PICKING ON YOU PRETTY BAD...
YEAH, SHE THINKS IT'S FUNNY THAT I LOVE MY GIRLFRIEND.
I'M SORRY! I'M SORRY I LOVE MY GIRLFRIEND!
IT'S OKAY! IT'S OKAY TO LOVE YOUR GIRLFRIEND!
AND NOW THOSE GUYS WANNA BEAT ME UP FOR WHAT I SAID...
THEY'RE NOT GONNA DO ANYTHING!
I'M AFRAID TO LEAVE...
DON'T WORRY... I GOT YOUR BACK!
THANKS...
I THINK IT'S SWEET HOW MUCH YOU LOVE YOUR GIRLFRIEND!
THANKS...
IT IS SWEET, ED!
YOU AGAIN!

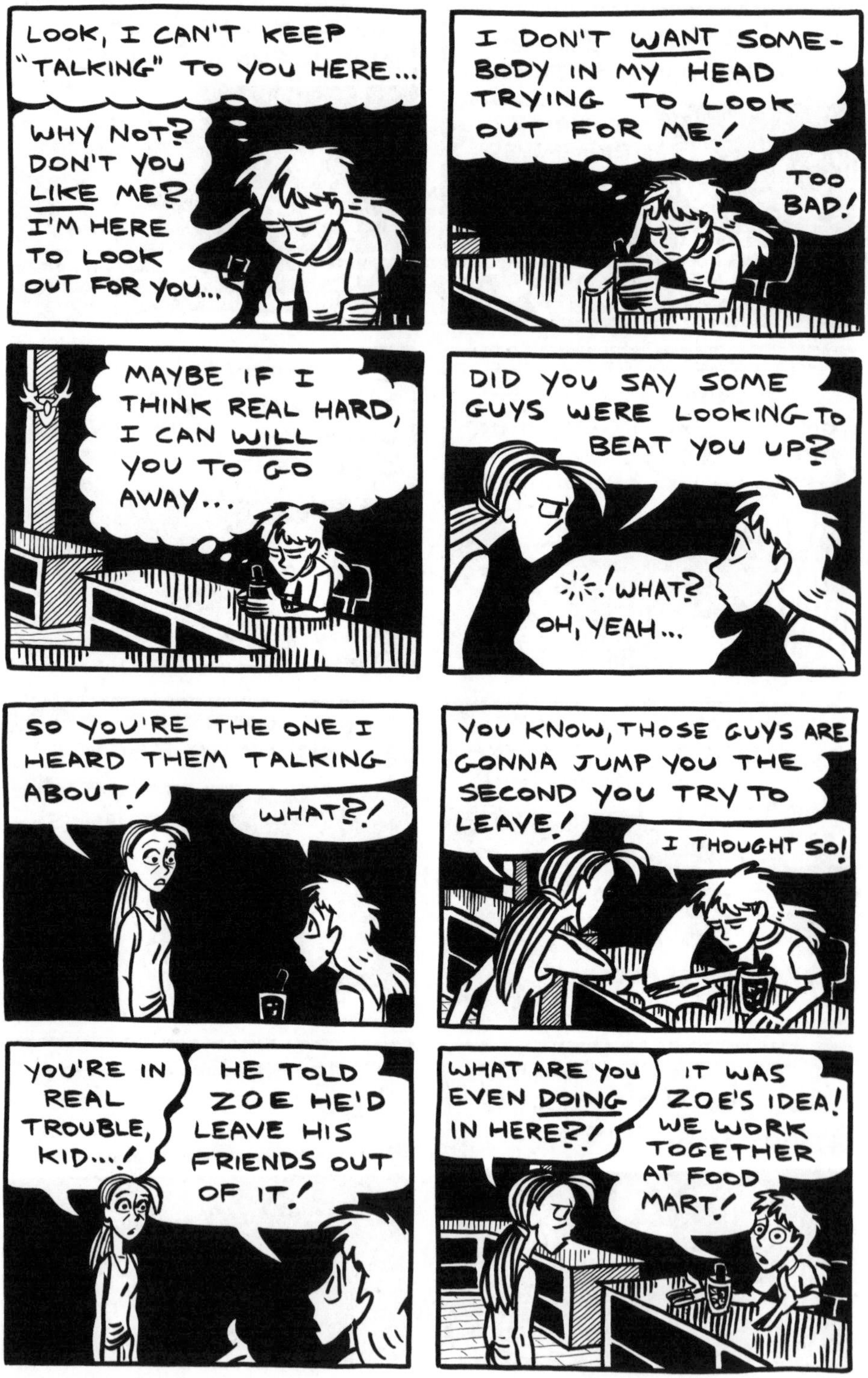
LOOK, I CAN'T KEEP "TALKING" TO YOU HERE...
WHY NOT? DON'T YOU LIKE ME? I'M HERE TO LOOK OUT FOR YOU...
I DON'T WANT SOMEBODY IN MY HEAD TRYING TO LOOK OUT FOR ME!
TOO BAD!
MAYBE IF I THINK REAL HARD, I CAN WILL YOU TO GO AWAY...
DID YOU SAY SOME GUYS WERE LOOKING TO BEAT YOU UP?
!WHAT? OH, YEAH...
SO YOU'RE THE ONE I HEARD THEM TALKING ABOUT!
WHAT?!
YOU KNOW, THOSE GUYS ARE GONNA JUMP YOU THE SECOND YOU TRY TO LEAVE!
I THOUGHT SO!
YOU'RE IN REAL TROUBLE, KID...!
HE TOLD ZOE HE'D LEAVE HIS FRIENDS OUT OF IT!
WHAT ARE YOU EVEN DOING IN HERE?!
IT WAS ZOE'S IDEA! WE WORK TOGETHER AT FOOD MART!

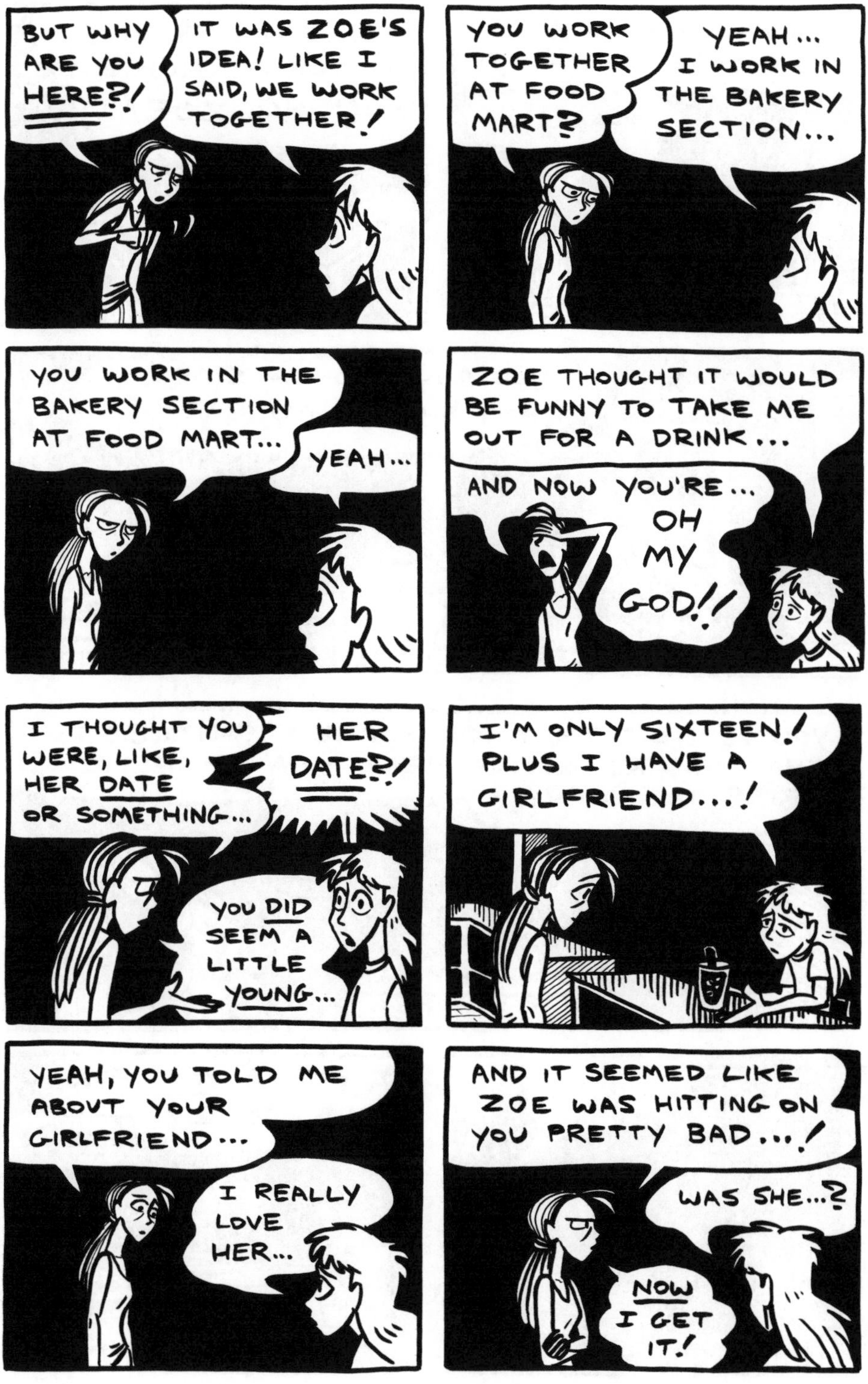

BUT WHY ARE YOU HERE?!
IT WAS ZOE'S IDEA! LIKE I SAID, WE WORK TOGETHER!
YOU WORK TOGETHER AT FOOD MART?
YEAH... I WORK IN THE BAKERY SECTION...
YOU WORK IN THE BAKERY SECTION AT FOOD MART...
YEAH...
ZOE THOUGHT IT WOULD BE FUNNY TO TAKE ME OUT FOR A DRINK...
AND NOW YOU'RE...
OH MY GOD!!
I THOUGHT YOU WERE, LIKE, HER DATE OR SOMETHING...
HER DATE?!
YOU DID SEEM A LITTLE YOUNG...
I'M ONLY SIXTEEN! PLUS I HAVE A GIRLFRIEND...!
YEAH, YOU TOLD ME ABOUT YOUR GIRLFRIEND...
I REALLY LOVE HER...
AND IT SEEMED LIKE ZOE WAS HITTING ON YOU PRETTY BAD...!
WAS SHE...?
NOW I GET IT!

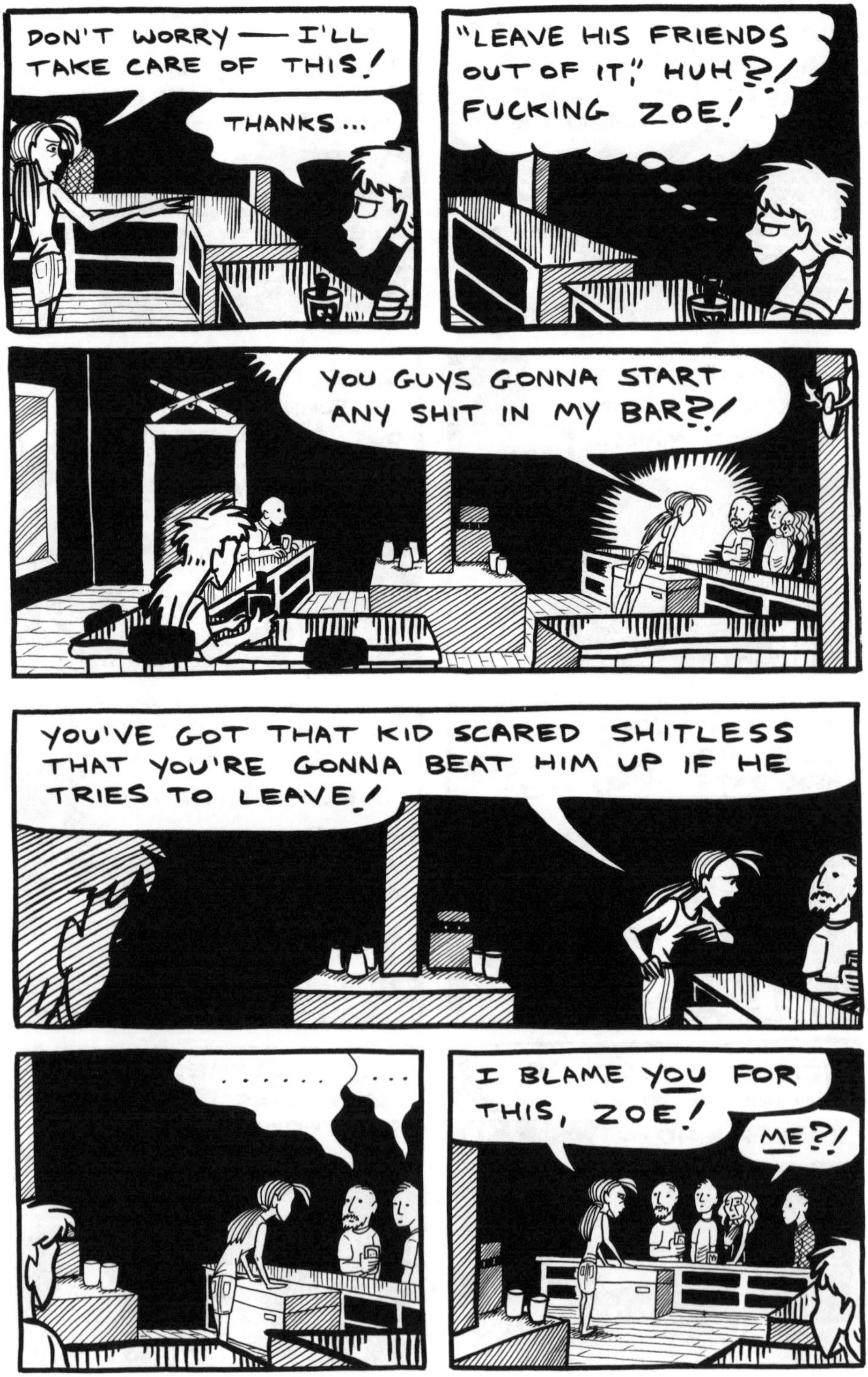
DON'T WORRY — I'LL TAKE CARE OF THIS!
THANKS...
"LEAVE HIS FRIENDS OUT OF IT," HUH?! FUCKING ZOE!
YOU GUYS GONNA START ANY SHIT IN MY BAR?!
YOU'VE GOT THAT KID SCARED SHITLESS THAT YOU'RE GONNA BEAT HIM UP IF HE TRIES TO LEAVE!
......
...
I BLAME YOU FOR THIS, ZOE!
ME?!

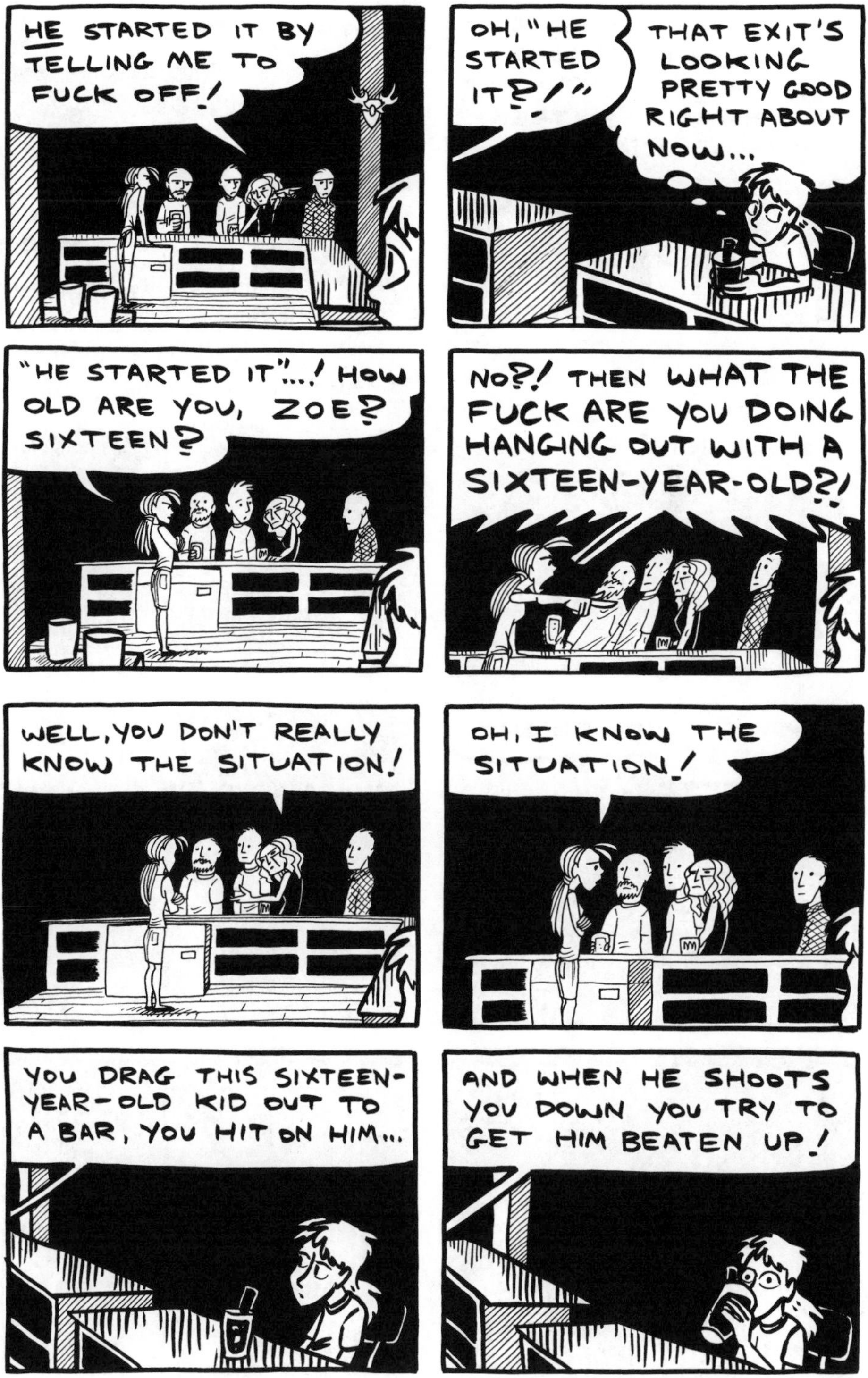
HE STARTED IT BY TELLING ME TO FUCK OFF!
OH, "HE STARTED IT?!"
THAT EXIT'S LOOKING PRETTY GOOD RIGHT ABOUT NOW...
"HE STARTED IT"...! HOW OLD ARE YOU, ZOE? SIXTEEN?
NO?! THEN WHAT THE FUCK ARE YOU DOING HANGING OUT WITH A SIXTEEN-YEAR-OLD?!
WELL, YOU DON'T REALLY KNOW THE SITUATION!
OH, I KNOW THE SITUATION!
YOU DRAG THIS SIXTEEN-YEAR-OLD KID OUT TO A BAR, YOU HIT ON HIM...
AND WHEN HE SHOOTS YOU DOWN YOU TRY TO GET HIM BEATEN UP!

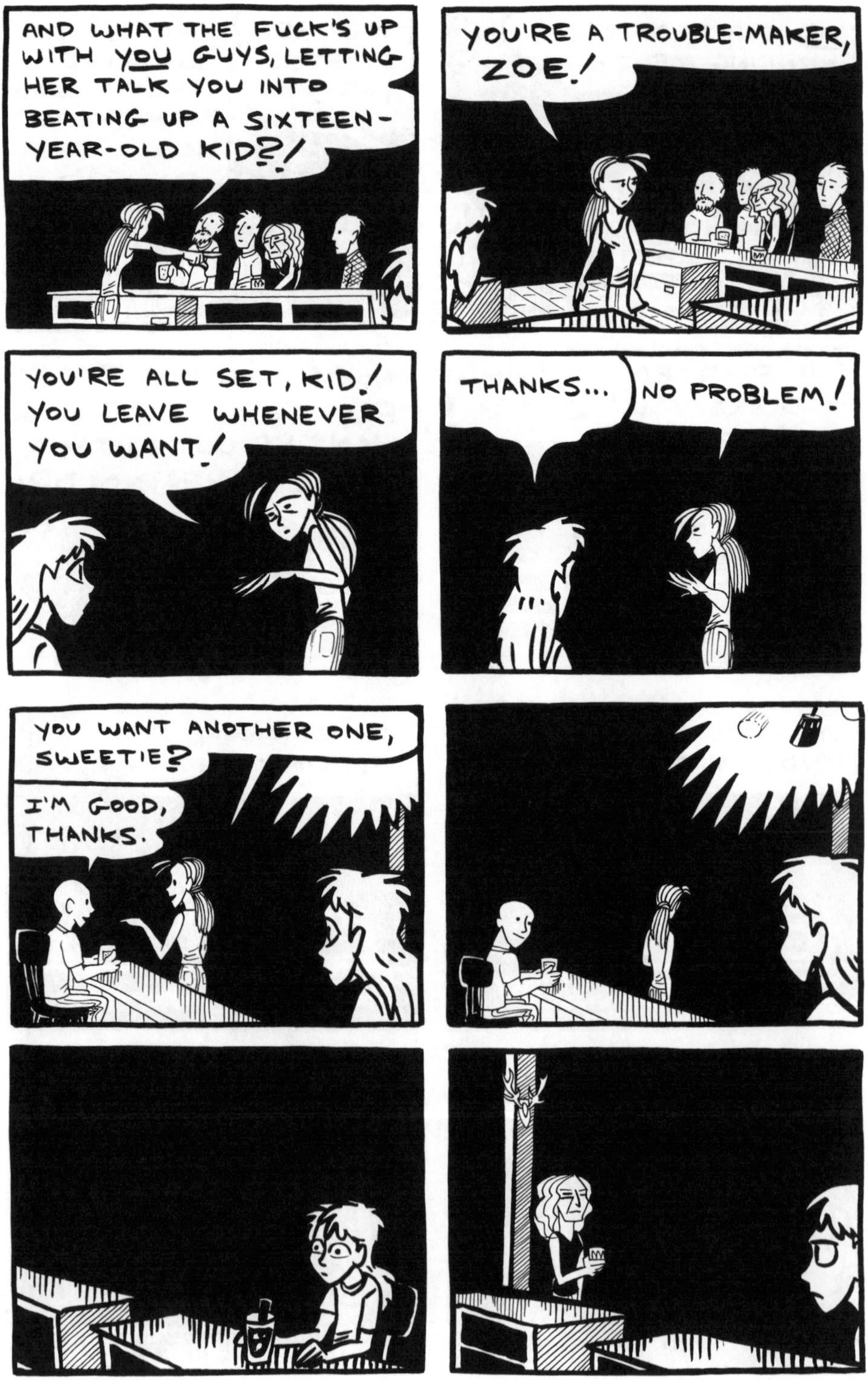
AND WHAT THE FUCK'S UP WITH YOU GUYS, LETTING HER TALK YOU INTO BEATING UP A SIXTEEN-YEAR-OLD KID?!
YOU'RE A TROUBLE-MAKER, ZOE!
YOU'RE ALL SET, KID! YOU LEAVE WHENEVER YOU WANT!
THANKS...
NO PROBLEM!
YOU WANT ANOTHER ONE, SWEETIE?
I'M GOOD, THANKS.

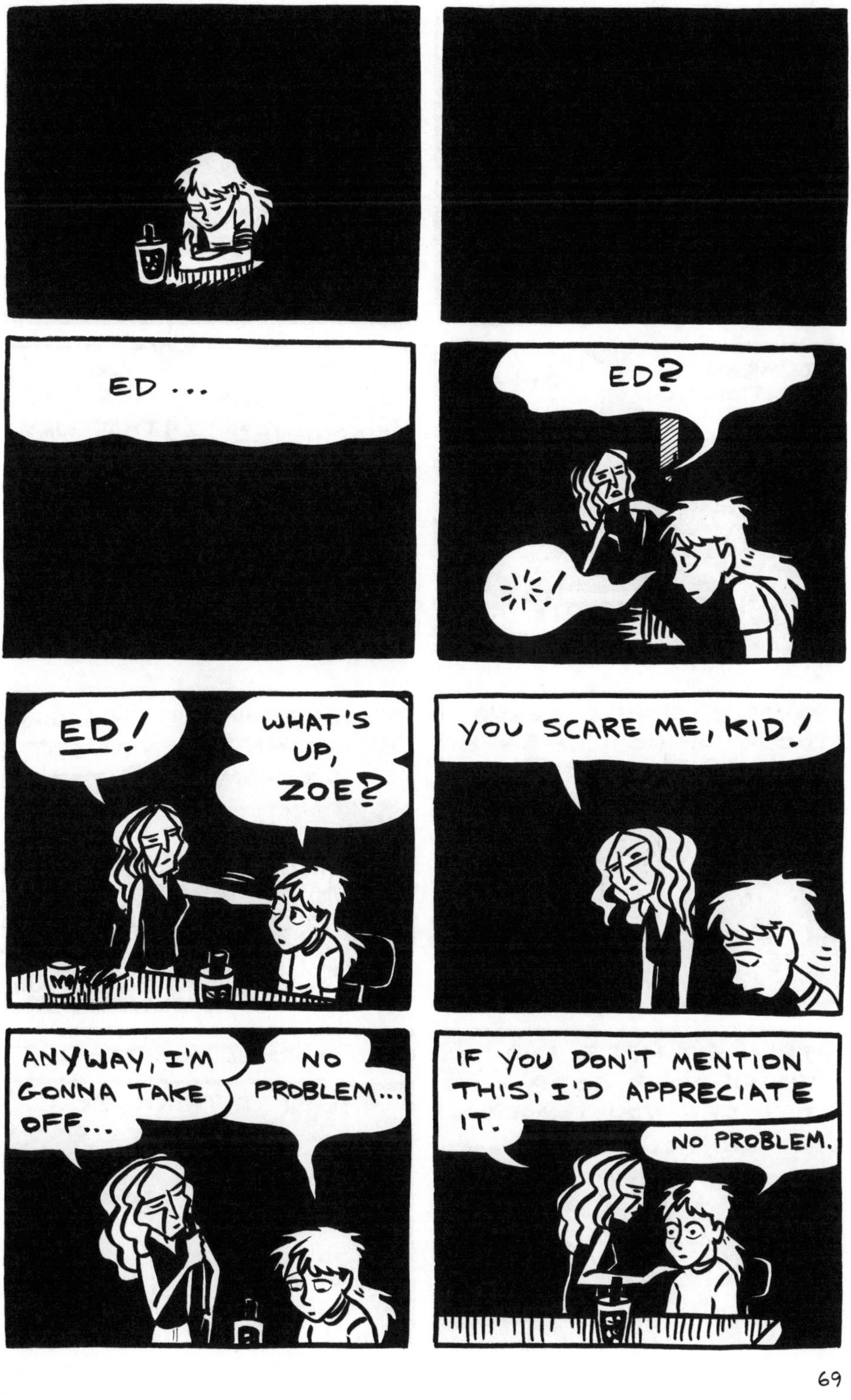
ED ...
ED?
!
ED!
WHAT'S UP, ZOE?
YOU SCARE ME, KID!
ANYWAY, I'M GONNA TAKE OFF...
NO PROBLEM...
IF YOU DON'T MENTION THIS, I'D APPRECIATE IT.
NO PROBLEM.

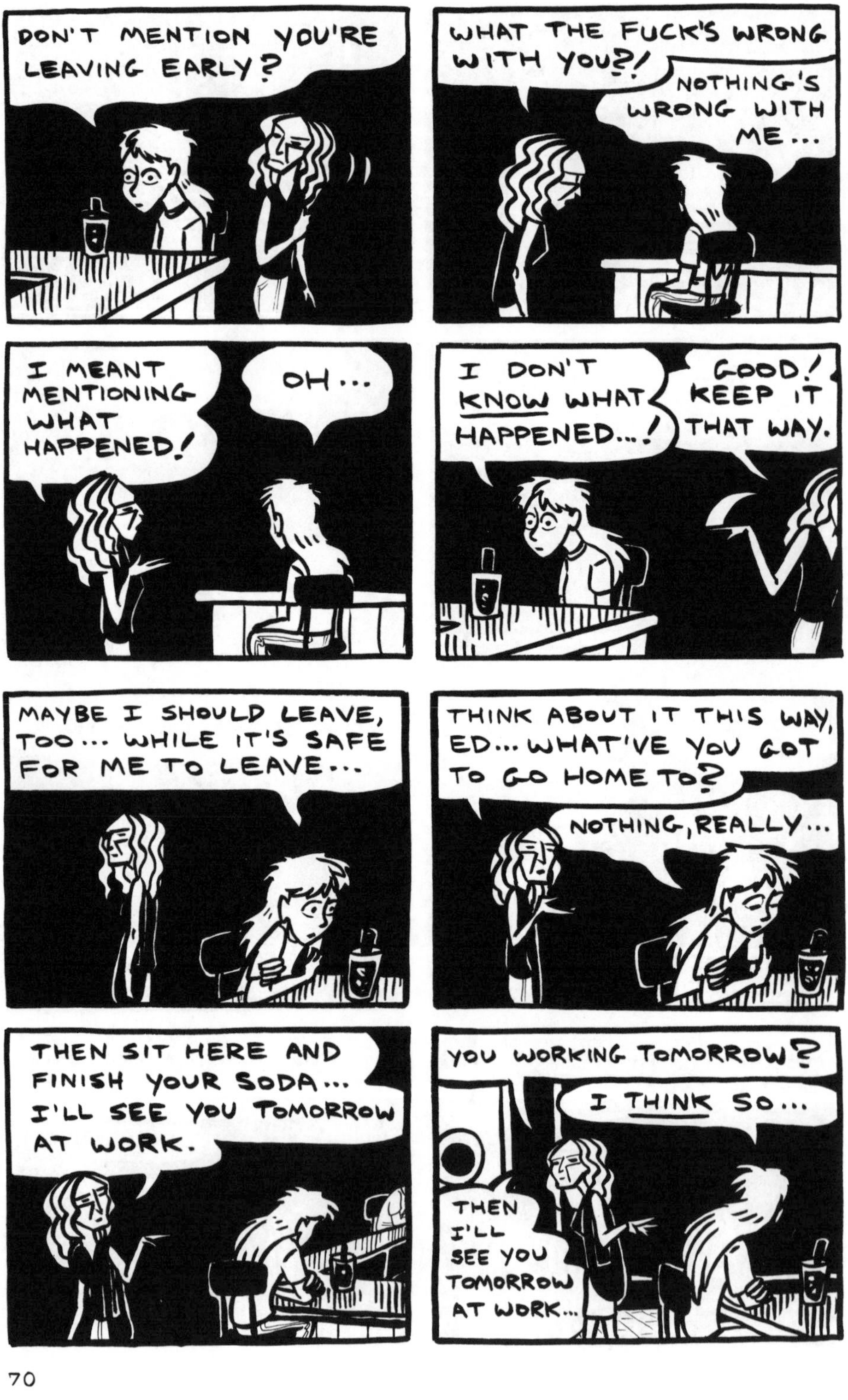
DON'T MENTION YOU'RE LEAVING EARLY?
WHAT THE FUCK'S WRONG WITH YOU?!
NOTHING'S WRONG WITH ME...
I MEANT MENTIONING WHAT HAPPENED!
OH...
I DON'T KNOW WHAT HAPPENED...!
GOOD! KEEP IT THAT WAY.
MAYBE I SHOULD LEAVE, TOO... WHILE IT'S SAFE FOR ME TO LEAVE...
THINK ABOUT IT THIS WAY, ED... WHAT'VE YOU GOT TO GO HOME TO?
NOTHING, REALLY...
THEN SIT HERE AND FINISH YOUR SODA... I'LL SEE YOU TOMORROW AT WORK.
YOU WORKING TOMORROW?
I THINK SO...
THEN I'LL SEE YOU TOMORROW AT WORK...

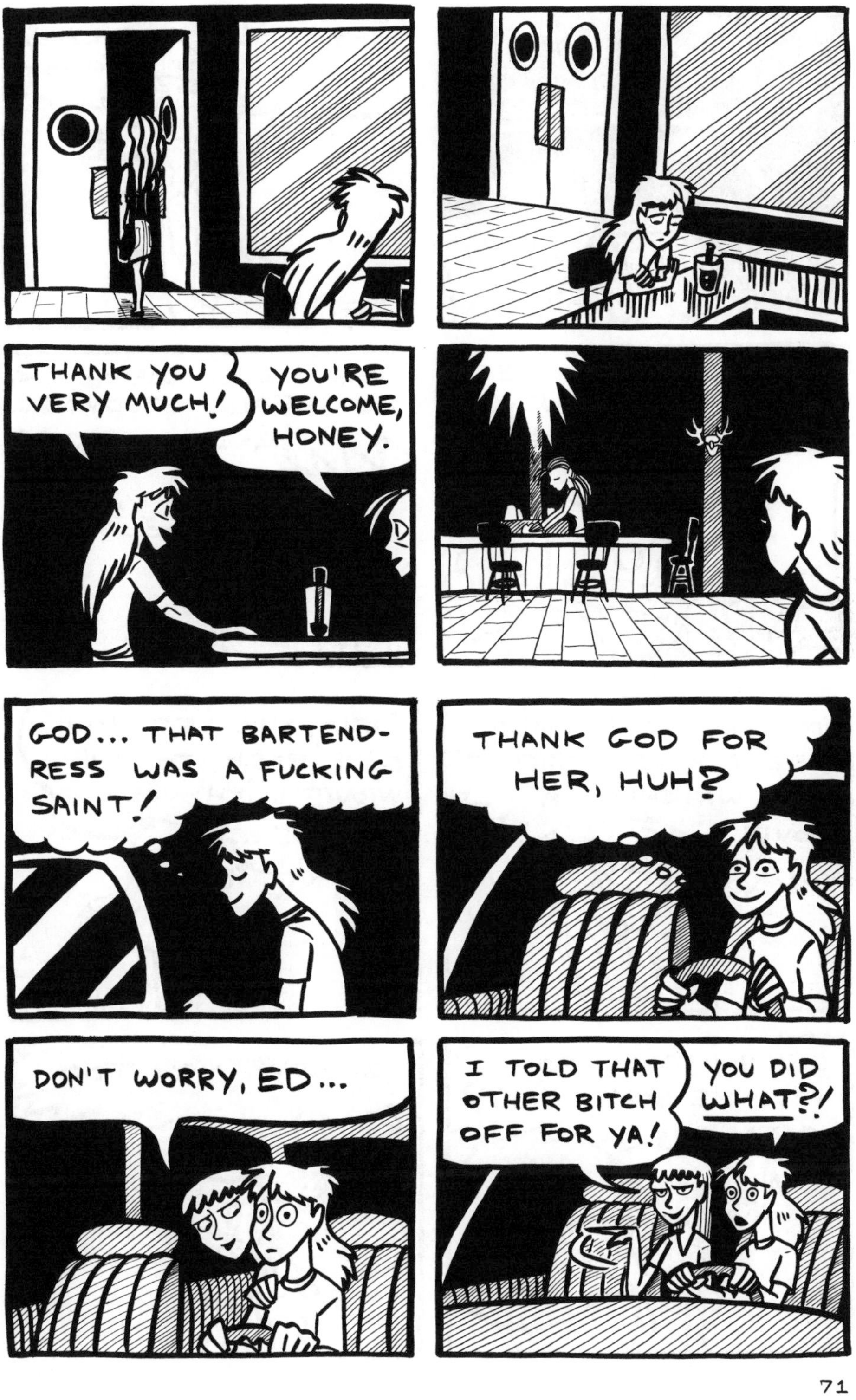
THANK YOU VERY MUCH!
YOU'RE WELCOME, HONEY.
GOD... THAT BARTENDRESS WAS A FUCKING SAINT!
THANK GOD FOR HER, HUH?
DON'T WORRY, ED...
I TOLD THAT OTHER BITCH OFF FOR YA!
YOU DID WHAT?!

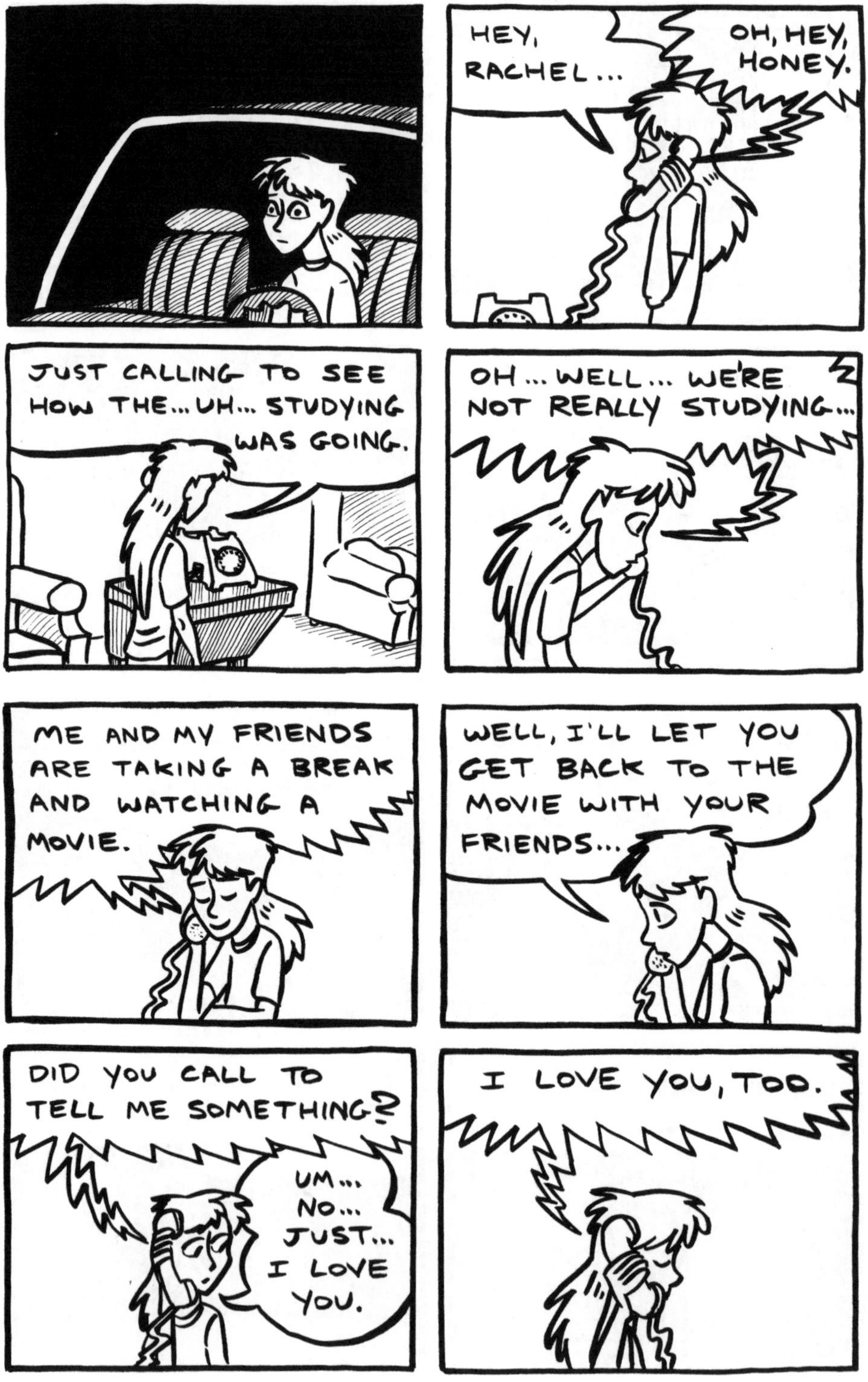
HEY, RACHEL...
OH, HEY, HONEY.
JUST CALLING TO SEE HOW THE... UH... STUDYING WAS GOING.
OH... WELL... WE'RE NOT REALLY STUDYING...
ME AND MY FRIENDS ARE TAKING A BREAK AND WATCHING A MOVIE.
WELL, I'LL LET YOU GET BACK TO THE MOVIE WITH YOUR FRIENDS...
DID YOU CALL TO TELL ME SOMETHING?
UM... NO... JUST... I LOVE YOU.
I LOVE YOU, TOO.

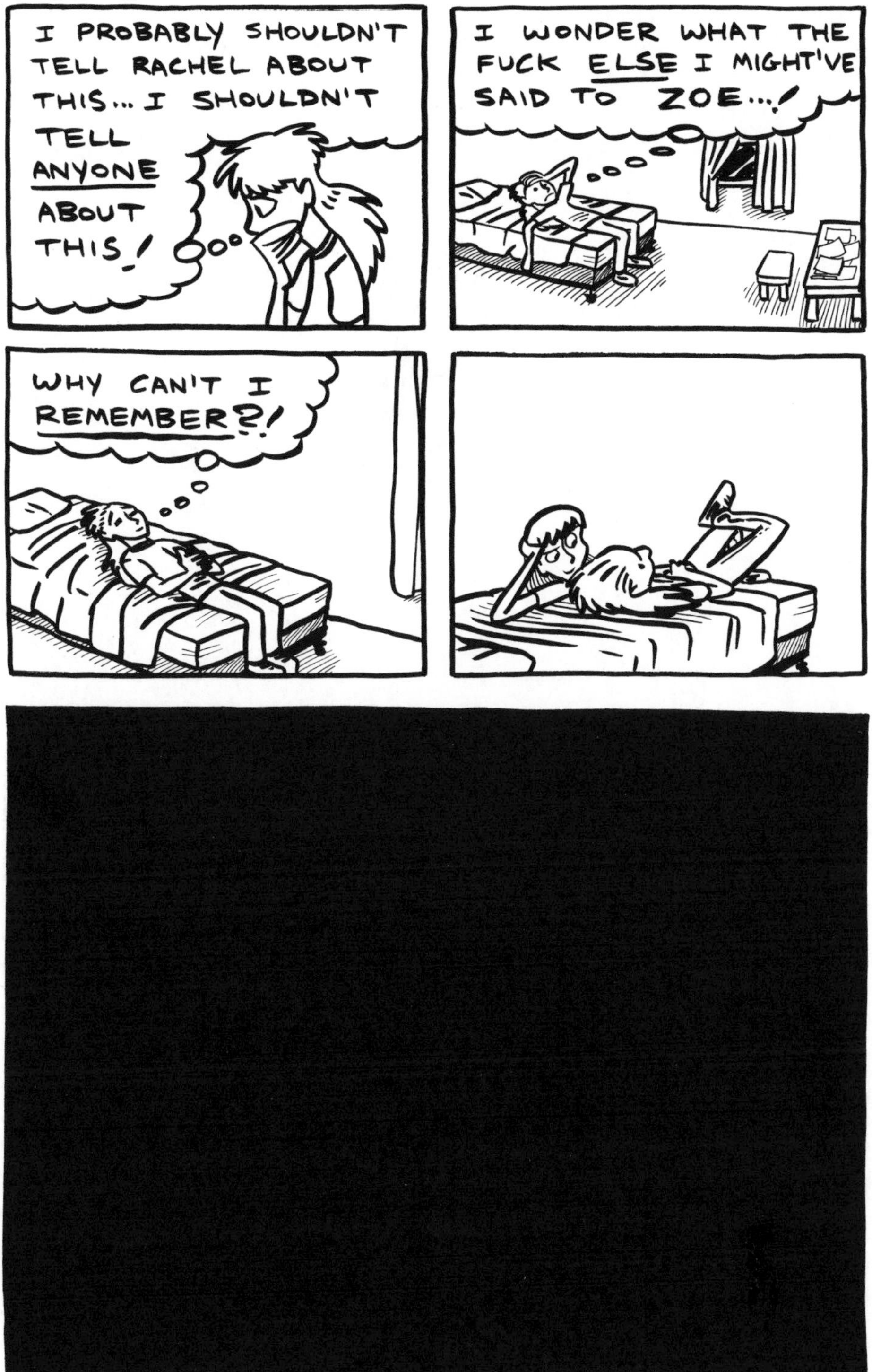
I PROBABLY SHOULDN'T TELL RACHEL ABOUT THIS... I SHOULDN'T TELL ANYONE ABOUT THIS!
I WONDER WHAT THE FUCK ELSE I MIGHT'VE SAID TO ZOE...!
WHY CAN'T I REMEMBER?!

THINK ABOUT YOUR GIRLFRIEND, ED...
ISN'T SHE BETTER THAN THIS OLD HAG?!
I'VE HAD JUST ABOUT ENOUGH OF THIS BITCH PUSHING YOU AROUND!

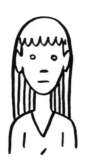

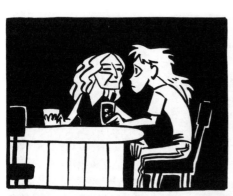

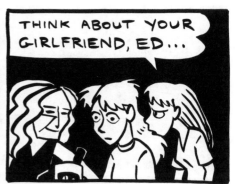

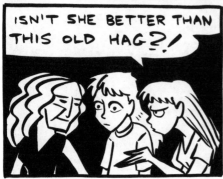

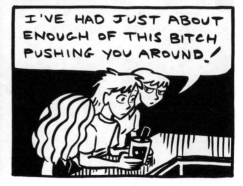

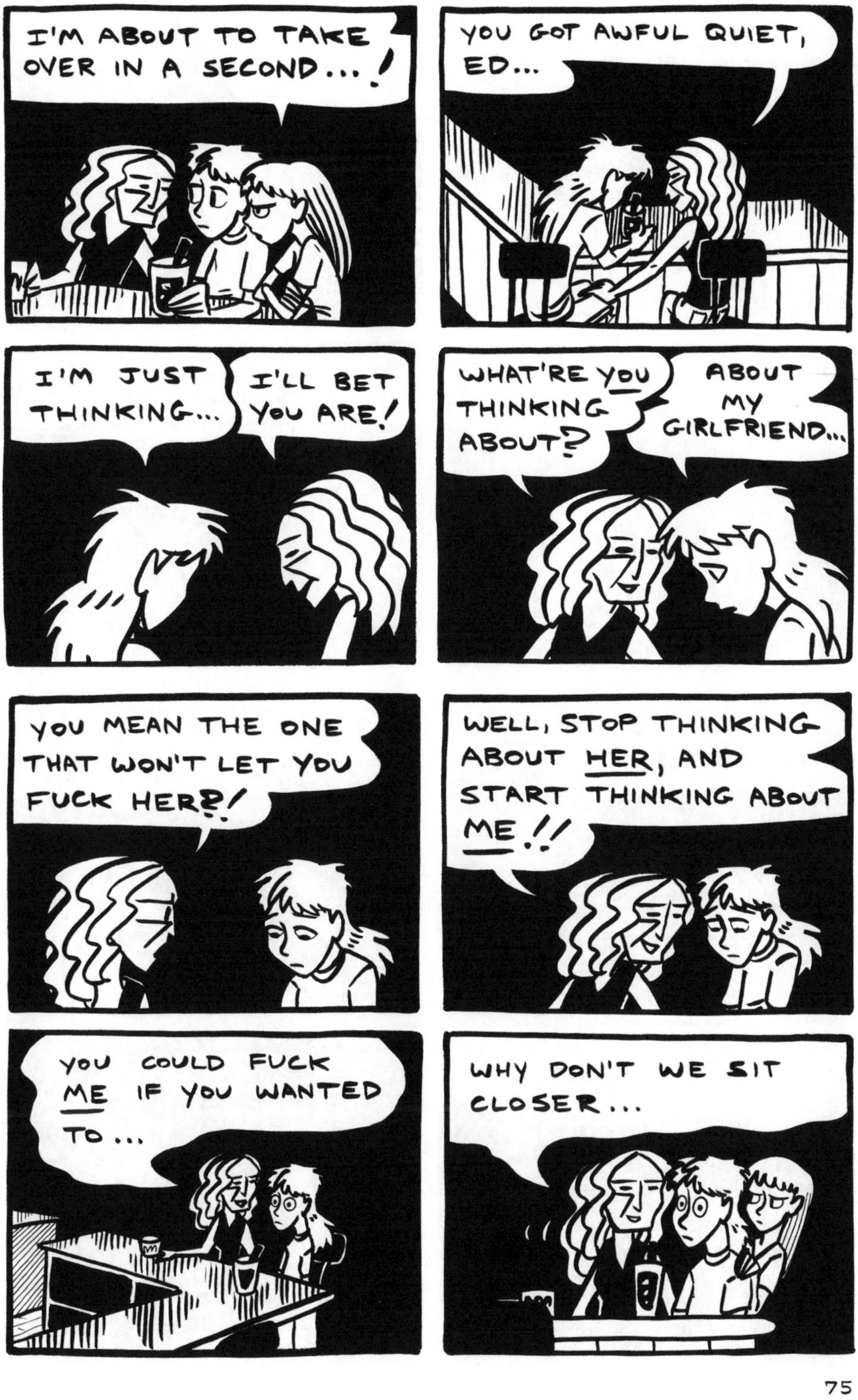
I'M ABOUT TO TAKE OVER IN A SECOND...!
YOU GOT AWFUL QUIET, ED...
I'M JUST THINKING...
I'LL BET YOU ARE!
WHAT'RE YOU THINKING ABOUT?
ABOUT MY GIRLFRIEND...
YOU MEAN THE ONE THAT WON'T LET YOU FUCK HER?!
WELL, STOP THINKING ABOUT HER, AND START THINKING ABOUT ME!!
YOU COULD FUCK ME IF YOU WANTED TO...
WHY DON'T WE SIT CLOSER...

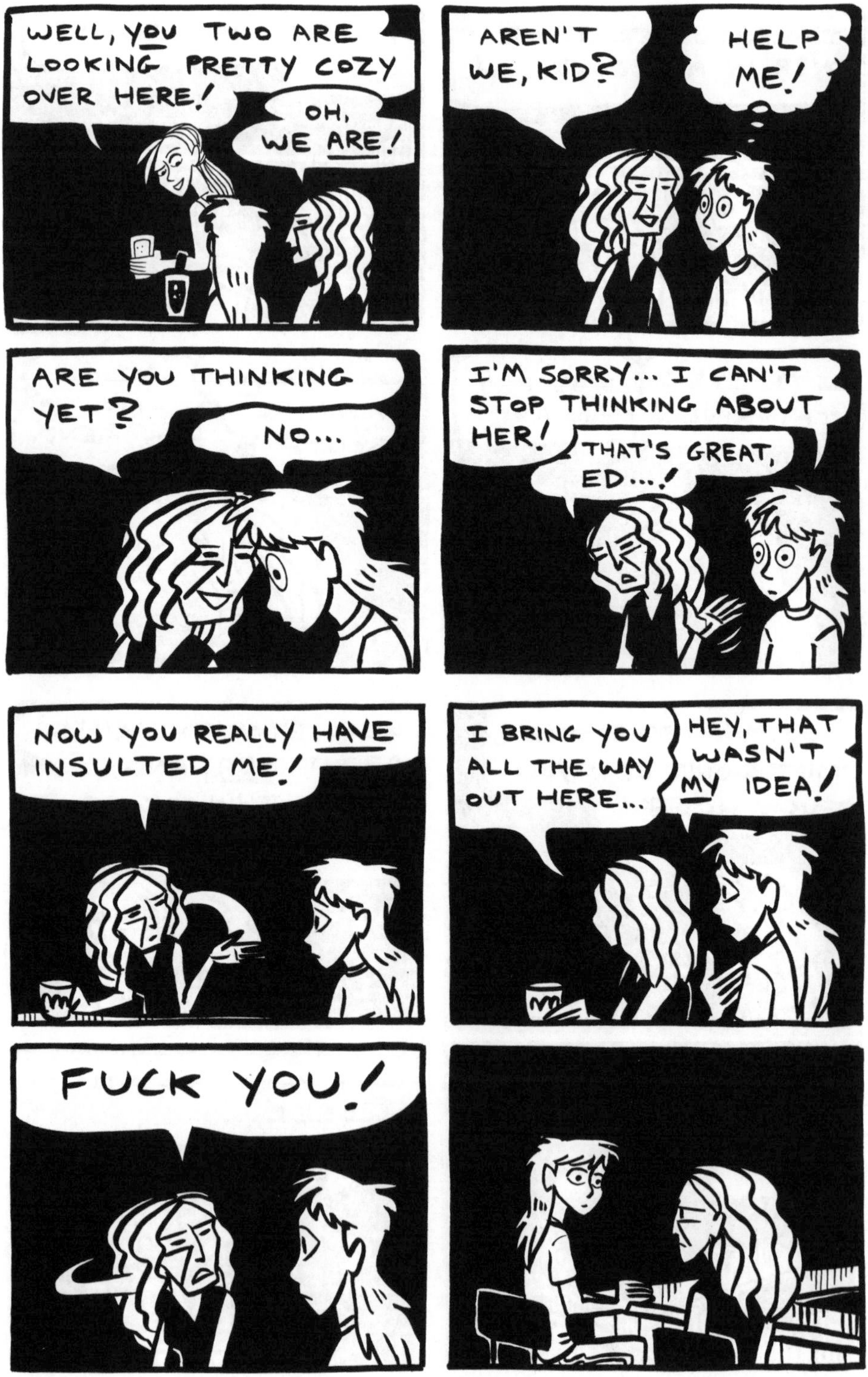
WELL, YOU TWO ARE LOOKING PRETTY COZY OVER HERE!
OH, WE ARE!
AREN'T WE, KID?
HELP ME!
ARE YOU THINKING YET?
NO...
I'M SORRY... I CAN'T STOP THINKING ABOUT HER!
THAT'S GREAT, ED...!
NOW YOU REALLY HAVE INSULTED ME!
I BRING YOU ALL THE WAY OUT HERE...
HEY, THAT WASN'T MY IDEA!
FUCK YOU!

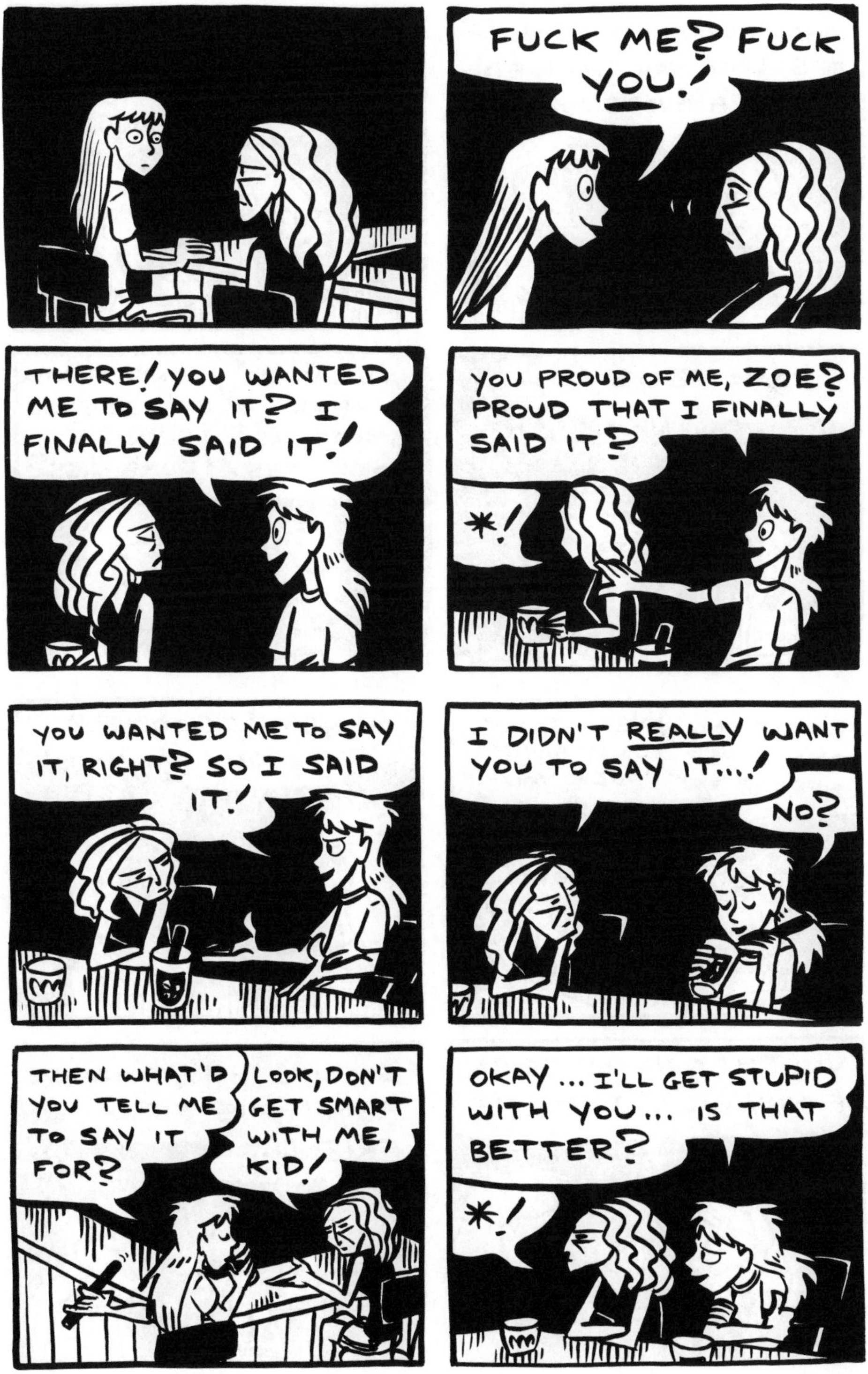
FUCK ME? FUCK YOU!
THERE! YOU WANTED ME TO SAY IT? I FINALLY SAID IT!
YOU PROUD OF ME, ZOE? PROUD THAT I FINALLY SAID IT?
*!
YOU WANTED ME TO SAY IT, RIGHT? SO I SAID IT!
I DIDN'T REALLY WANT YOU TO SAY IT...!
NO?
THEN WHAT'D YOU TELL ME TO SAY IT FOR?
LOOK, DON'T GET SMART WITH ME, KID!
OKAY ... I'LL GET STUPID WITH YOU... IS THAT BETTER?
*!

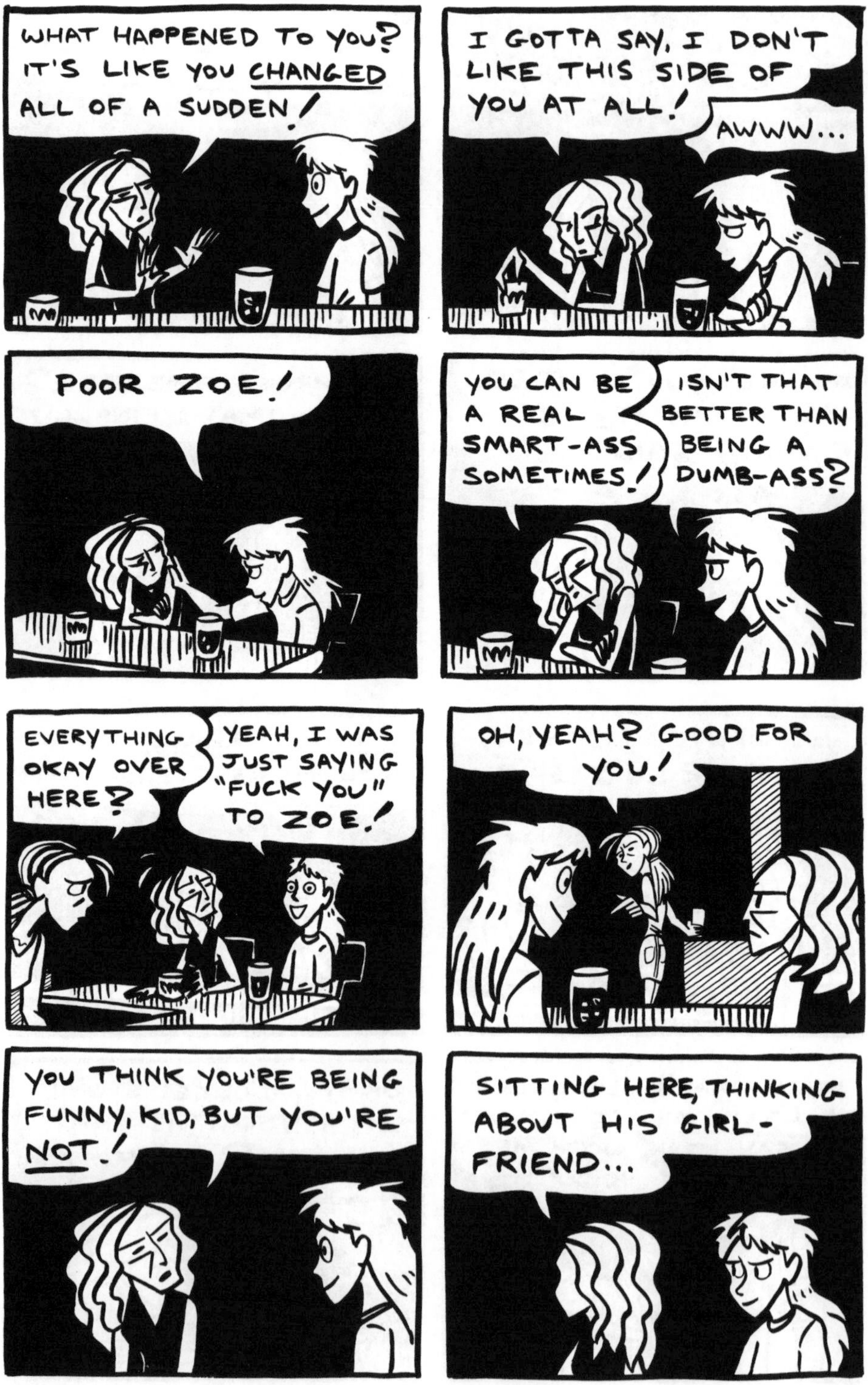
WHAT HAPPENED TO YOU? IT'S LIKE YOU CHANGED ALL OF A SUDDEN!
I GOTTA SAY, I DON'T LIKE THIS SIDE OF YOU AT ALL!
AWWW...
POOR ZOE!
YOU CAN BE A REAL SMART-ASS SOMETIMES!
ISN'T THAT BETTER THAN BEING A DUMB-ASS?
EVERYTHING OKAY OVER HERE?
YEAH, I WAS JUST SAYING "FUCK YOU" TO ZOE!
OH, YEAH? GOOD FOR YOU!
YOU THINK YOU'RE BEING FUNNY, KID, BUT YOU'RE NOT!
SITTING HERE, THINKING ABOUT HIS GIRL-FRIEND...

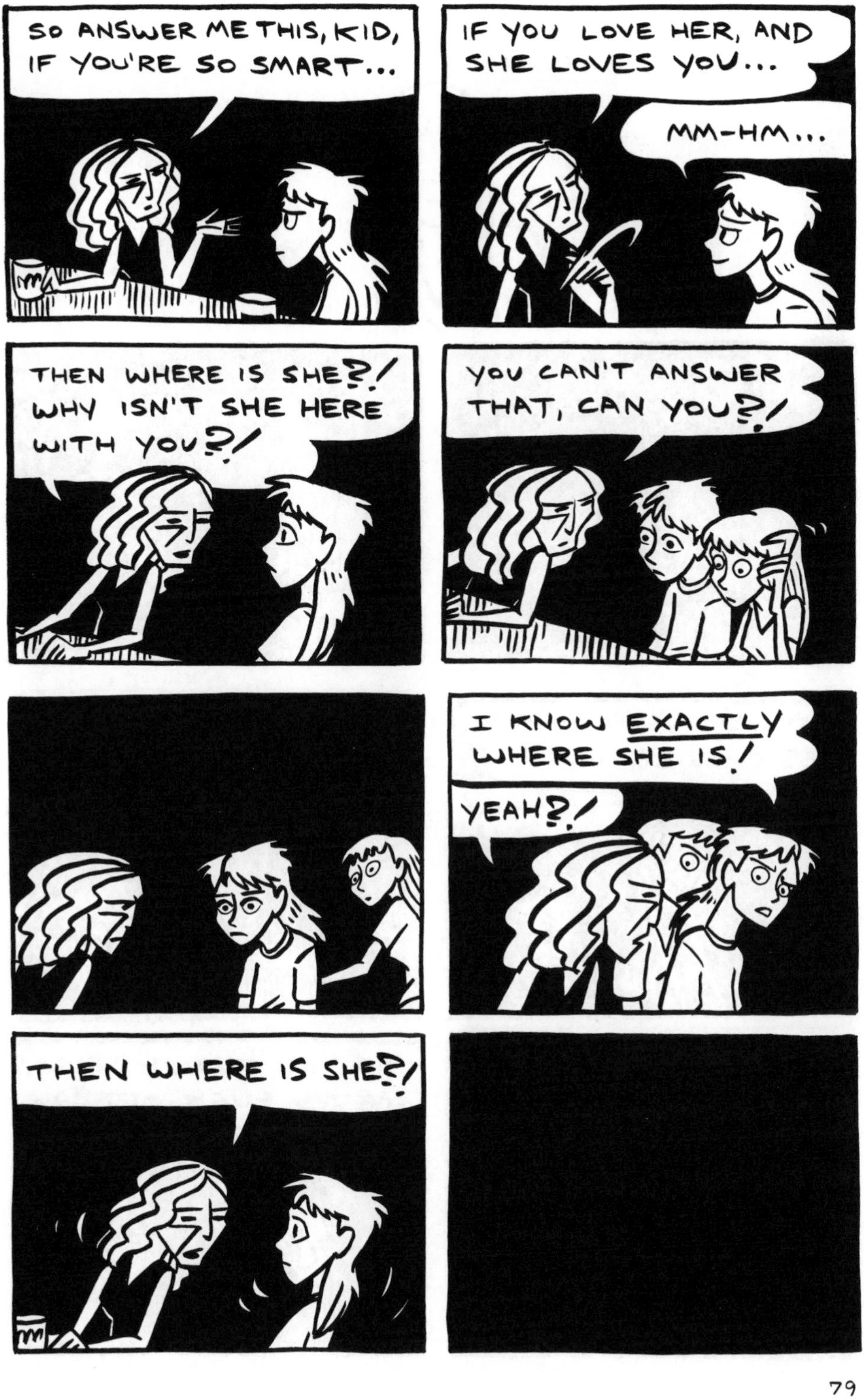
SO ANSWER ME THIS, KID, IF YOU'RE SO SMART...
IF YOU LOVE HER, AND SHE LOVES YOU...
MM-HM...
THEN WHERE IS SHE?! WHY ISN'T SHE HERE WITH YOU?!
YOU CAN'T ANSWER THAT, CAN YOU?!
I KNOW EXACTLY WHERE SHE IS!
YEAH?!
THEN WHERE IS SHE?!

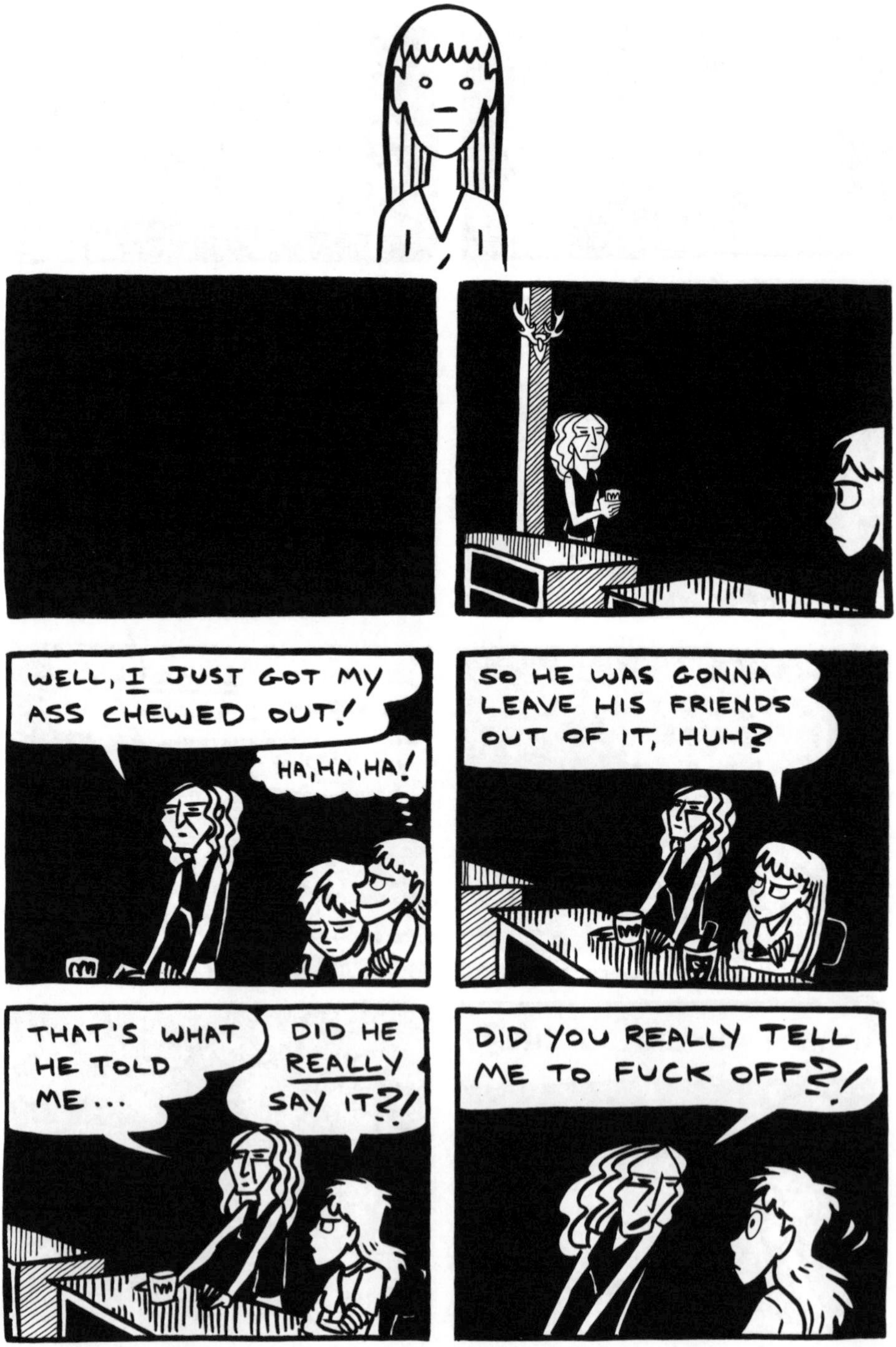
WELL, I JUST GOT MY ASS CHEWED OUT!
HA,HA,HA!
SO HE WAS GONNA LEAVE HIS FRIENDS OUT OF IT, HUH?
THAT'S WHAT HE TOLD ME...
DID HE REALLY SAY IT?!
DID YOU REALLY TELL ME TO FUCK OFF?!

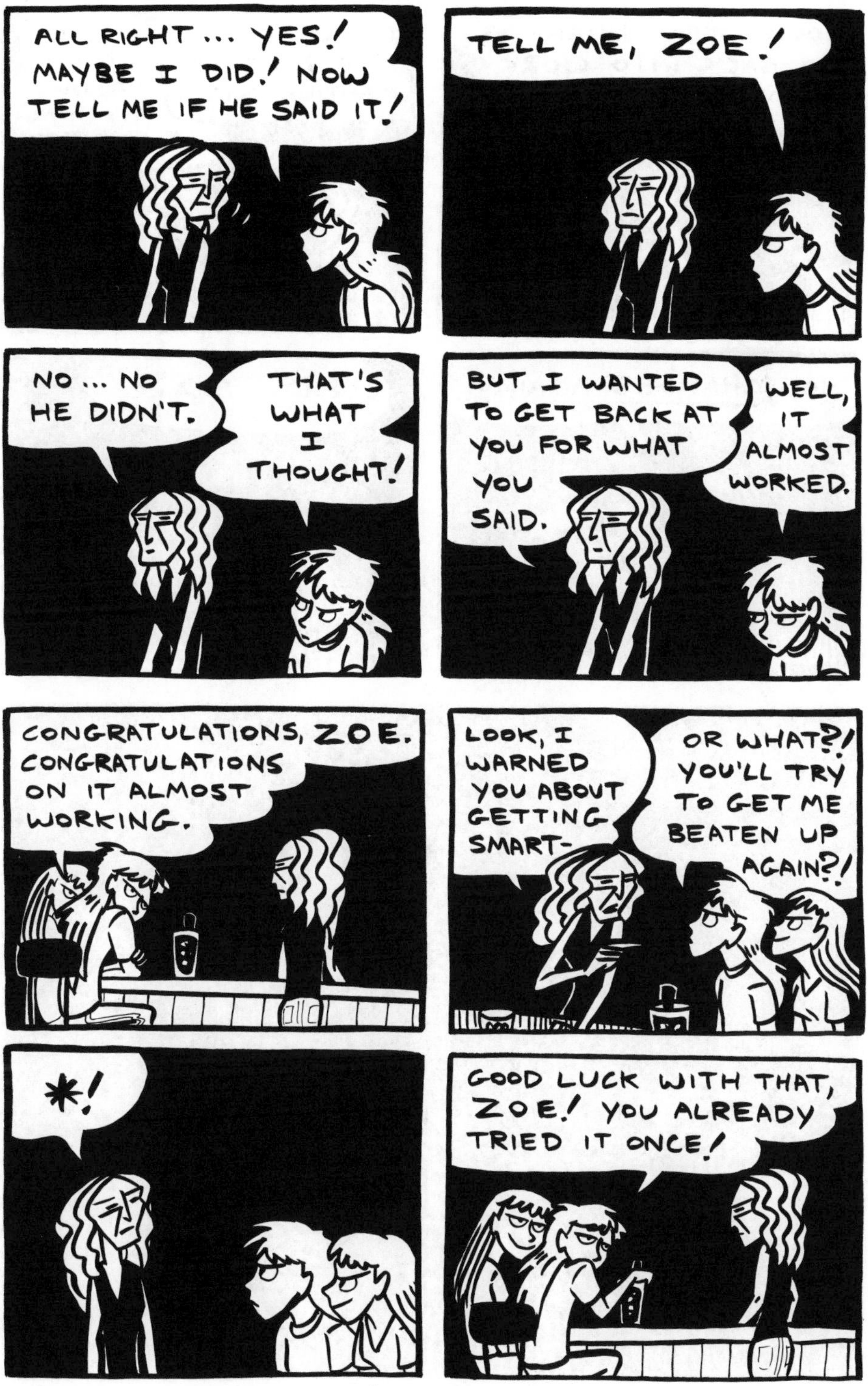
ALL RIGHT... YES! MAYBE I DID! NOW TELL ME IF HE SAID IT!
TELL ME, ZOE!
NO... NO HE DIDN'T.
THAT'S WHAT I THOUGHT!
BUT I WANTED TO GET BACK AT YOU FOR WHAT YOU SAID.
WELL, IT ALMOST WORKED.
CONGRATULATIONS, ZOE. CONGRATULATIONS ON IT ALMOST WORKING.
LOOK, I WARNED YOU ABOUT GETTING SMART-
OR WHAT?! YOU'LL TRY TO GET ME BEATEN UP AGAIN?!
*!
GOOD LUCK WITH THAT, ZOE! YOU ALREADY TRIED IT ONCE!

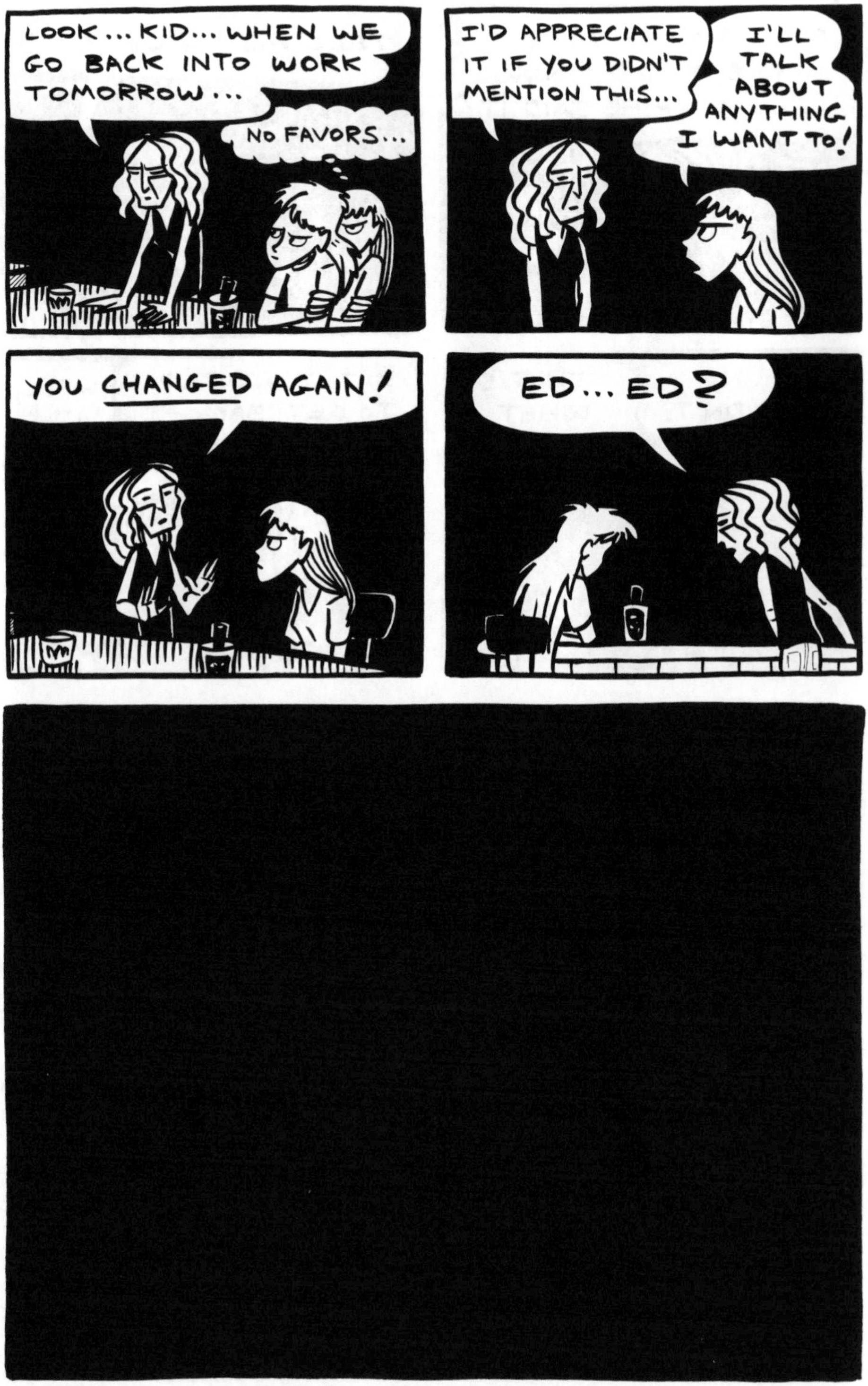
LOOK... KID... WHEN WE GO BACK INTO WORK TOMORROW...
NO FAVORS...
I'D APPRECIATE IT IF YOU DIDN'T MENTION THIS...
I'LL TALK ABOUT ANYTHING I WANT TO!
YOU CHANGED AGAIN!
ED... ED?

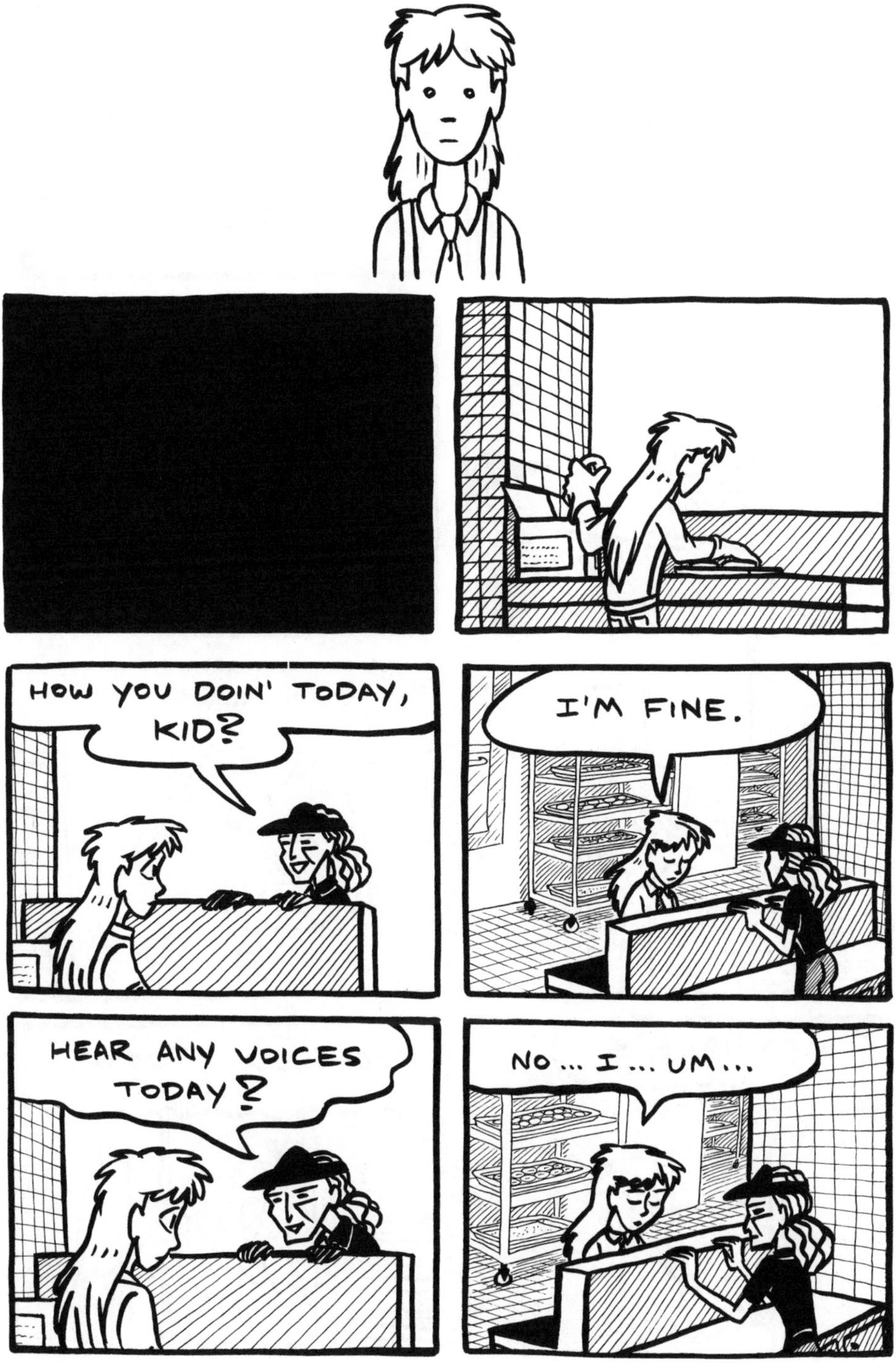
HOW YOU DOIN' TODAY, KID?
I'M FINE.
HEAR ANY VOICES TODAY?
NO... I... UM...

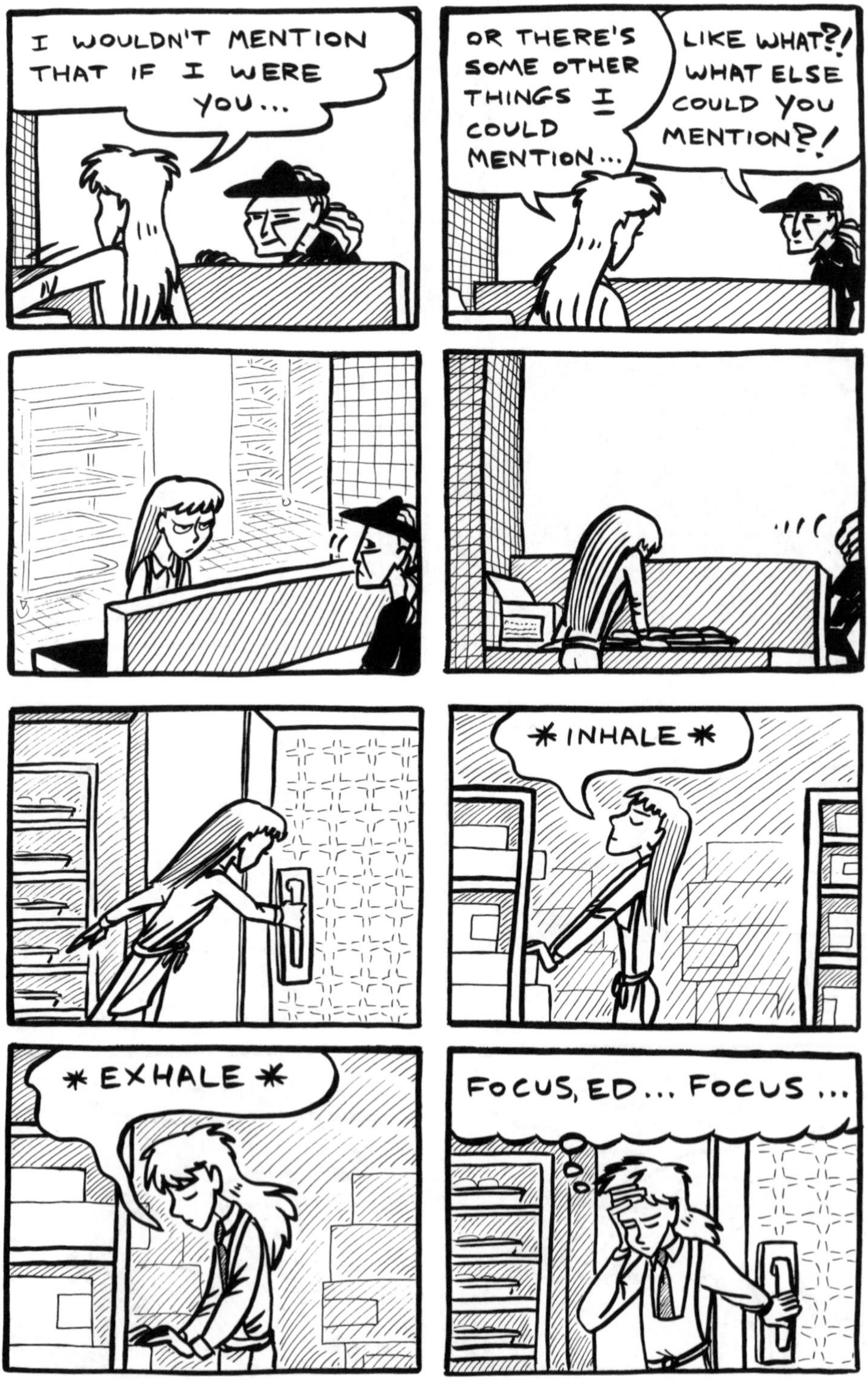
I WOULDN'T MENTION THAT IF I WERE YOU...
OR THERE'S SOME OTHER THINGS I COULD MENTION...
LIKE WHAT?! WHAT ELSE COULD YOU MENTION?!
* INHALE *
* EXHALE *
FOCUS, ED... FOCUS...

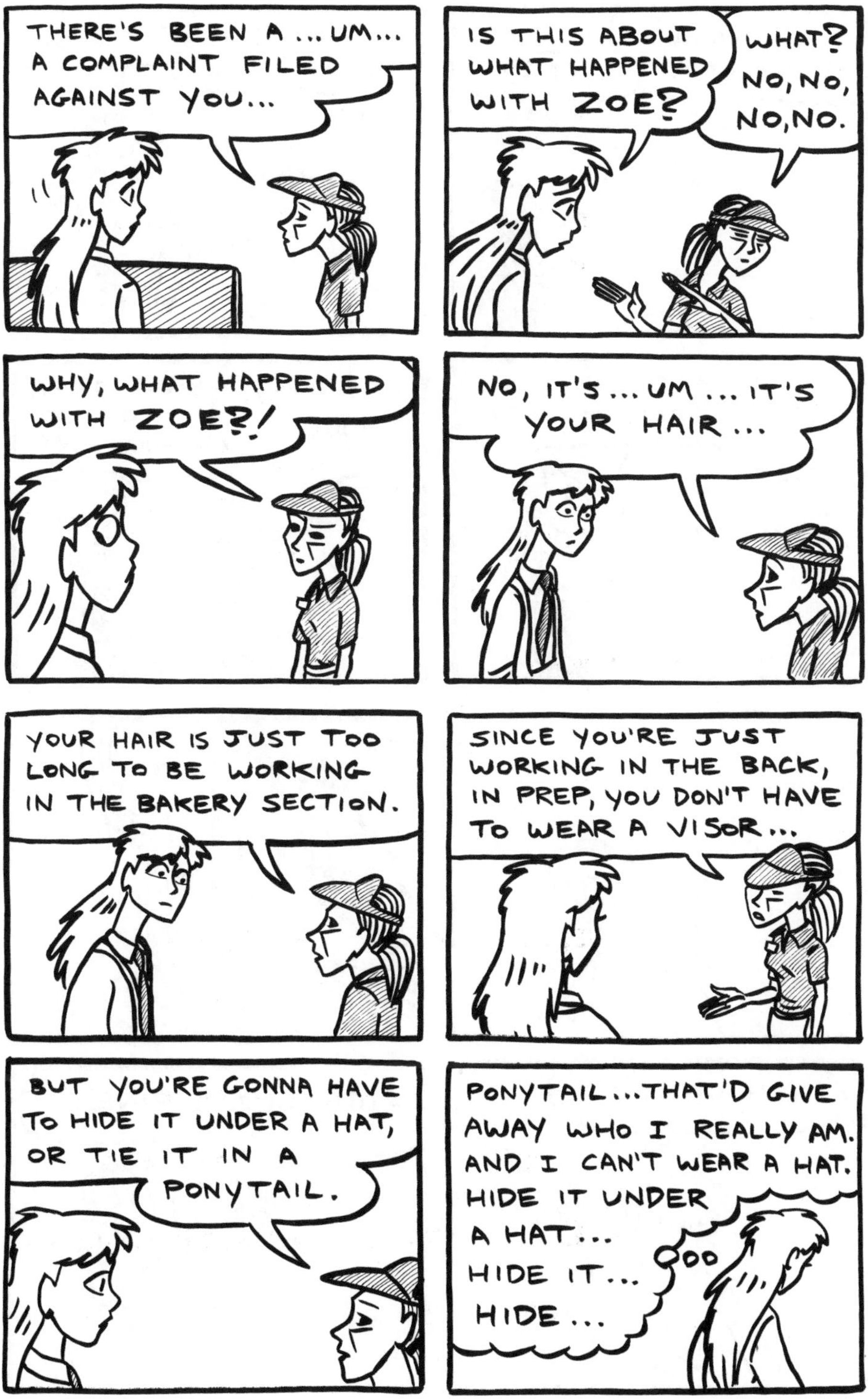
THERE'S BEEN A ... UM... A COMPLAINT FILED AGAINST YOU...
IS THIS ABOUT WHAT HAPPENED WITH ZOE?
WHAT? NO, NO, NO, NO.
WHY, WHAT HAPPENED WITH ZOE?!
NO, IT'S ... UM ... IT'S YOUR HAIR ...
YOUR HAIR IS JUST TOO LONG TO BE WORKING IN THE BAKERY SECTION.
SINCE YOU'RE JUST WORKING IN THE BACK, IN PREP, YOU DON'T HAVE TO WEAR A VISOR...
BUT YOU'RE GONNA HAVE TO HIDE IT UNDER A HAT, OR TIE IT IN A PONYTAIL.
PONYTAIL...THAT'D GIVE AWAY WHO I REALLY AM. AND I CAN'T WEAR A HAT. HIDE IT UNDER A HAT... HIDE IT... HIDE...

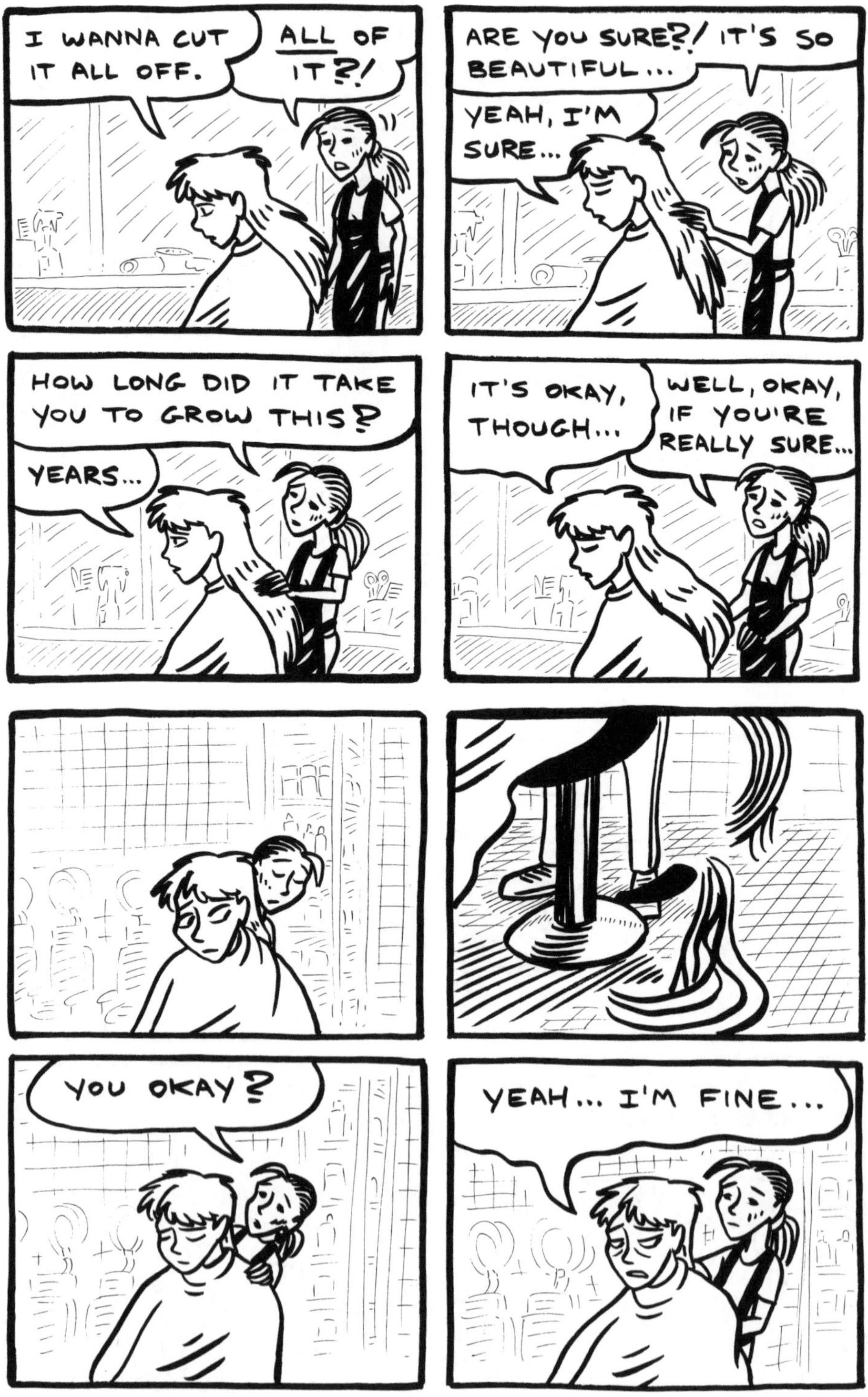
I WANNA CUT IT ALL OFF.
ALL OF IT?!
ARE YOU SURE?! IT'S SO BEAUTIFUL...
YEAH, I'M SURE...
HOW LONG DID IT TAKE YOU TO GROW THIS?
YEARS...
IT'S OKAY, THOUGH...
WELL, OKAY, IF YOU'RE REALLY SURE...
YOU OKAY?
YEAH... I'M FINE...

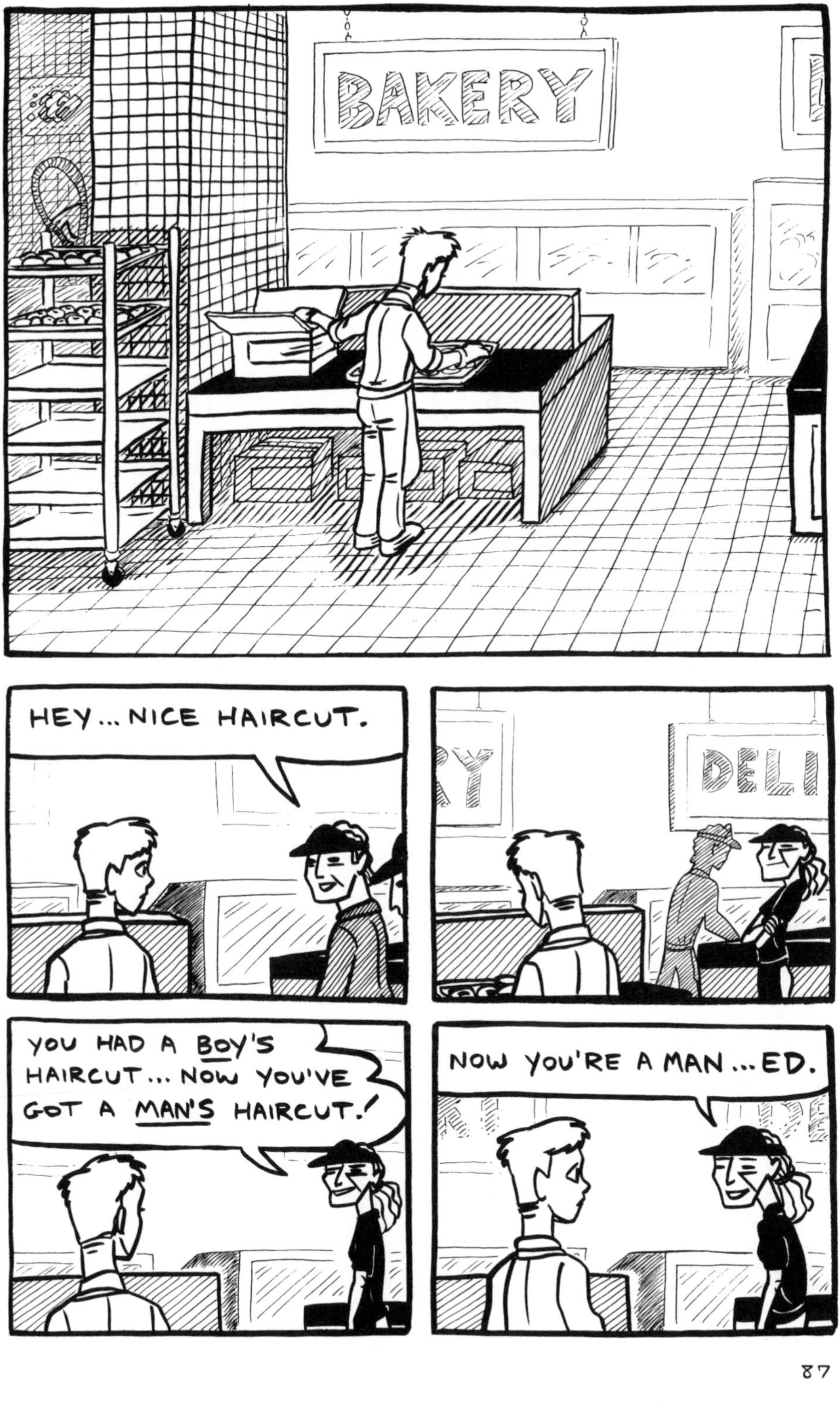
BAKERY
HEY... NICE HAIRCUT.
DELI
YOU HAD A BOY'S HAIRCUT... NOW YOU'VE GOT A MAN'S HAIRCUT!
NOW YOU'RE A MAN... ED.

SUEDE

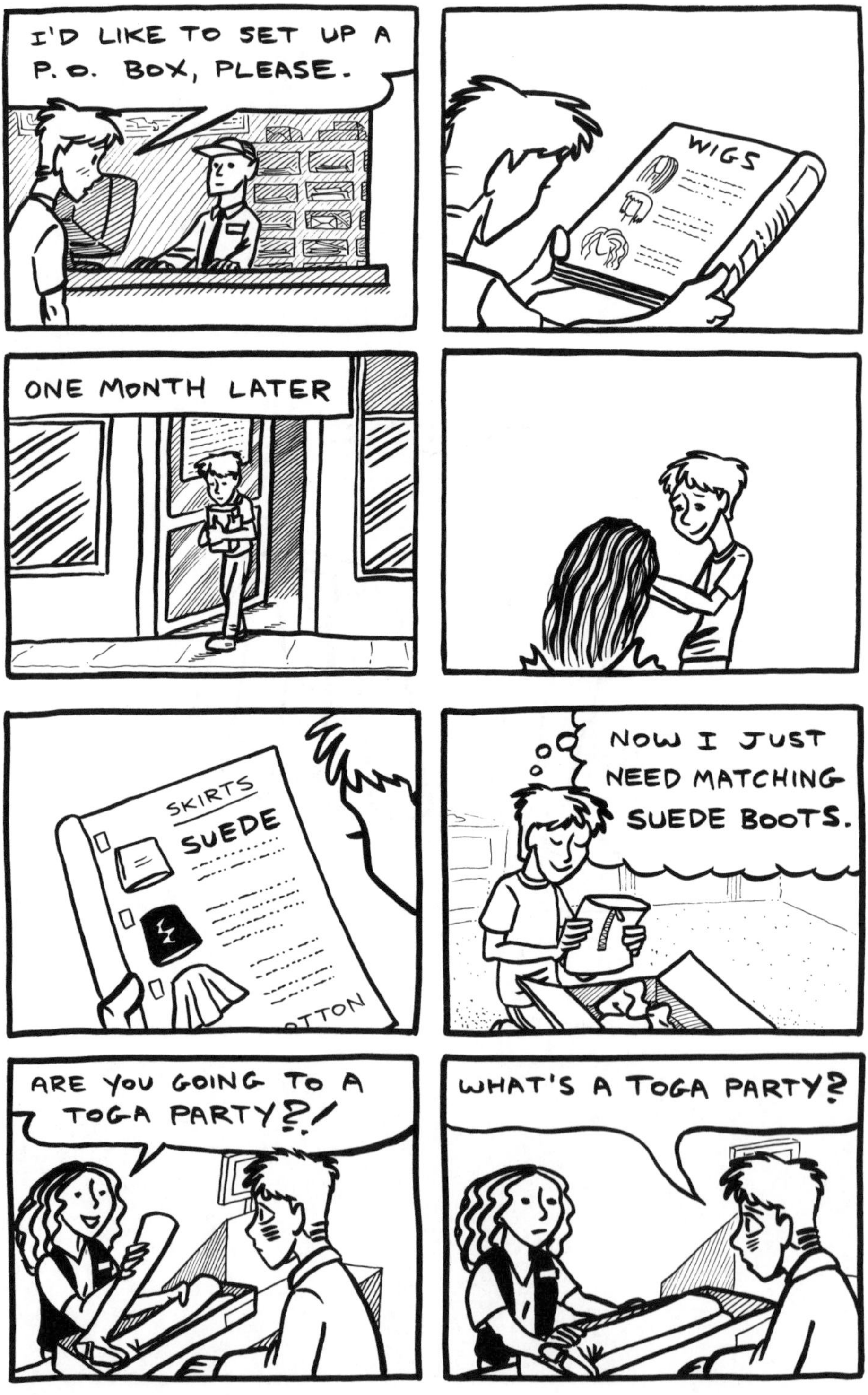
I'D LIKE TO SET UP A P.O. BOX, PLEASE.
WIGS
ONE MONTH LATER
SKIRTS
SUEDE
NOW I JUST NEED MATCHING SUEDE BOOTS.
ARE YOU GOING TO A TOGA PARTY?!
WHAT'S A TOGA PARTY?

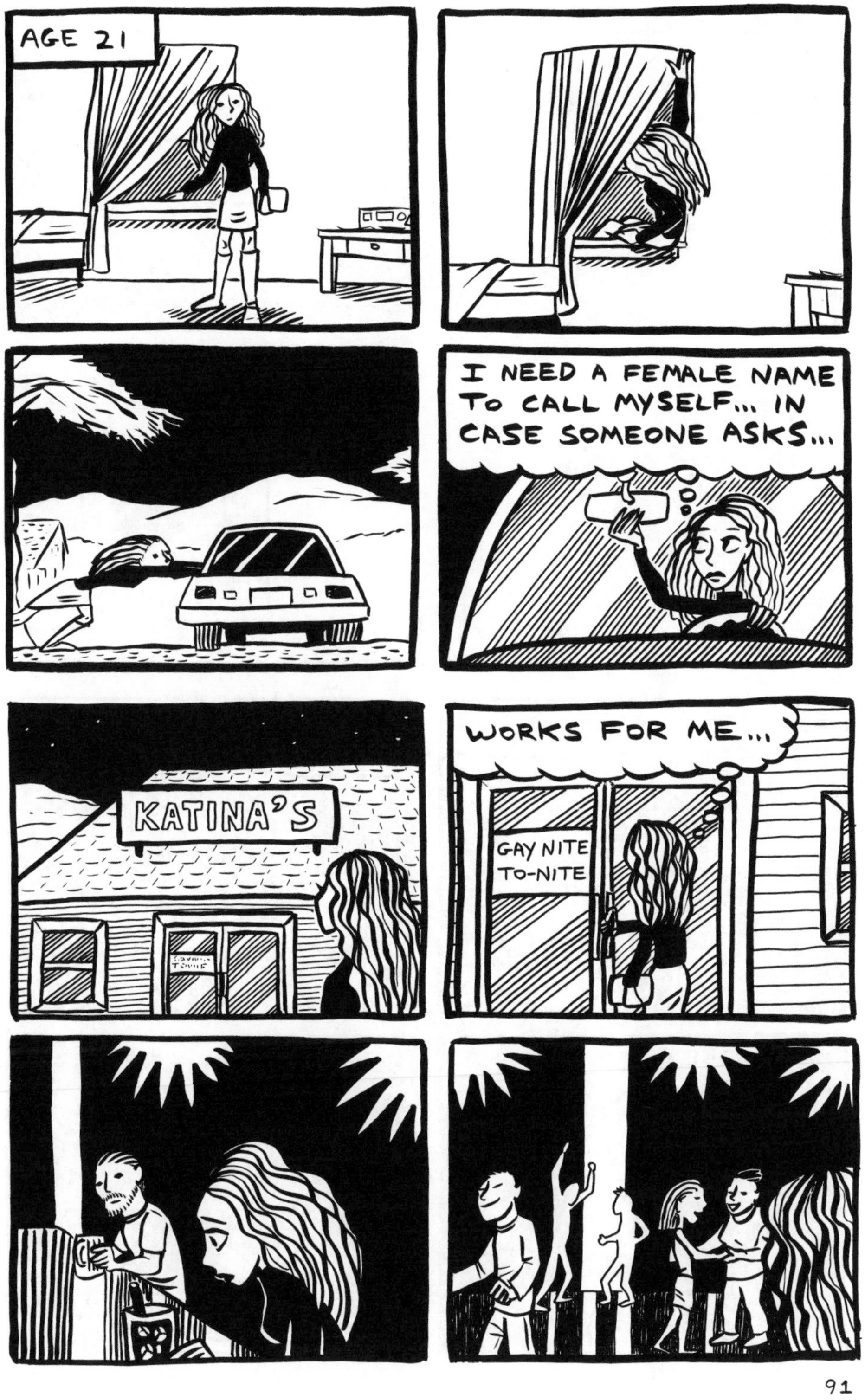
AGE 21
I NEED A FEMALE NAME TO CALL MYSELF... IN CASE SOMEONE ASKS...
KATINA'S
WORKS FOR ME...
GAY NITE TO-NITE

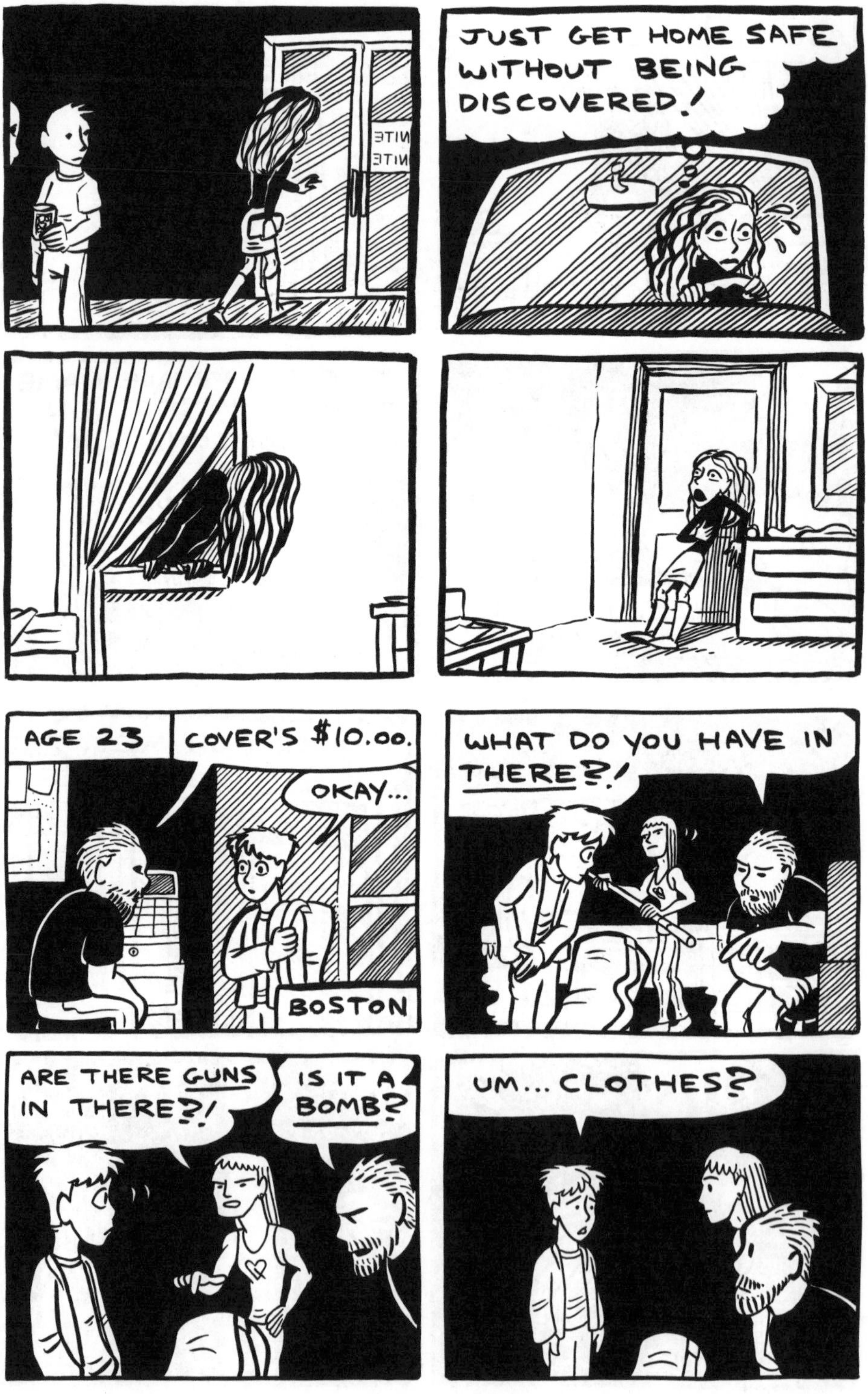
JUST GET HOME SAFE WITHOUT BEING DISCOVERED!
AGE 23
COVER'S $10.00.
OKAY...
BOSTON
WHAT DO YOU HAVE IN THERE?!
ARE THERE GUNS IN THERE?!
IS IT A BOMB?
UM... CLOTHES?

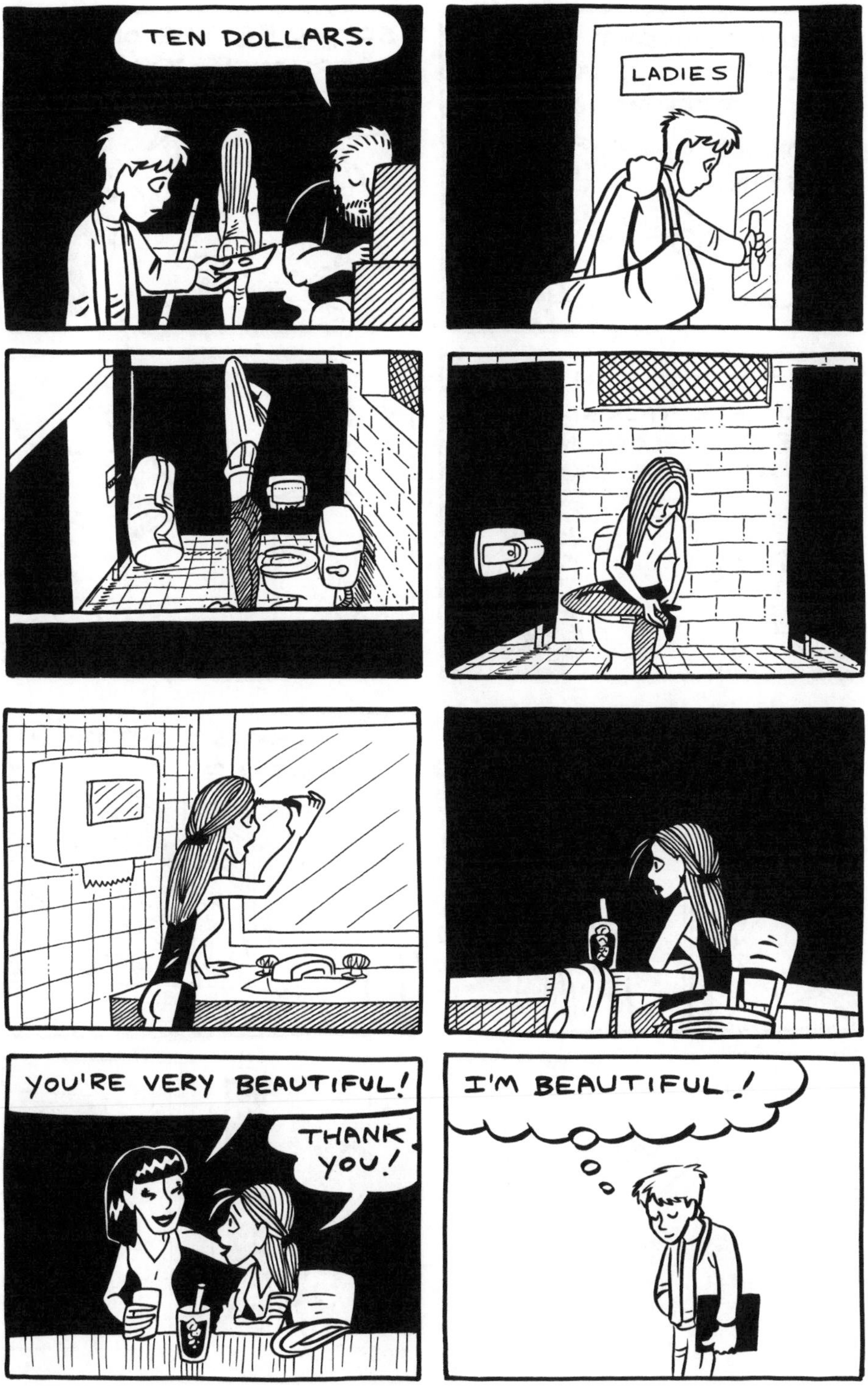
TEN DOLLARS.
LADIES
YOU'RE VERY BEAUTIFUL!
THANK YOU!
I'M BEAUTIFUL!

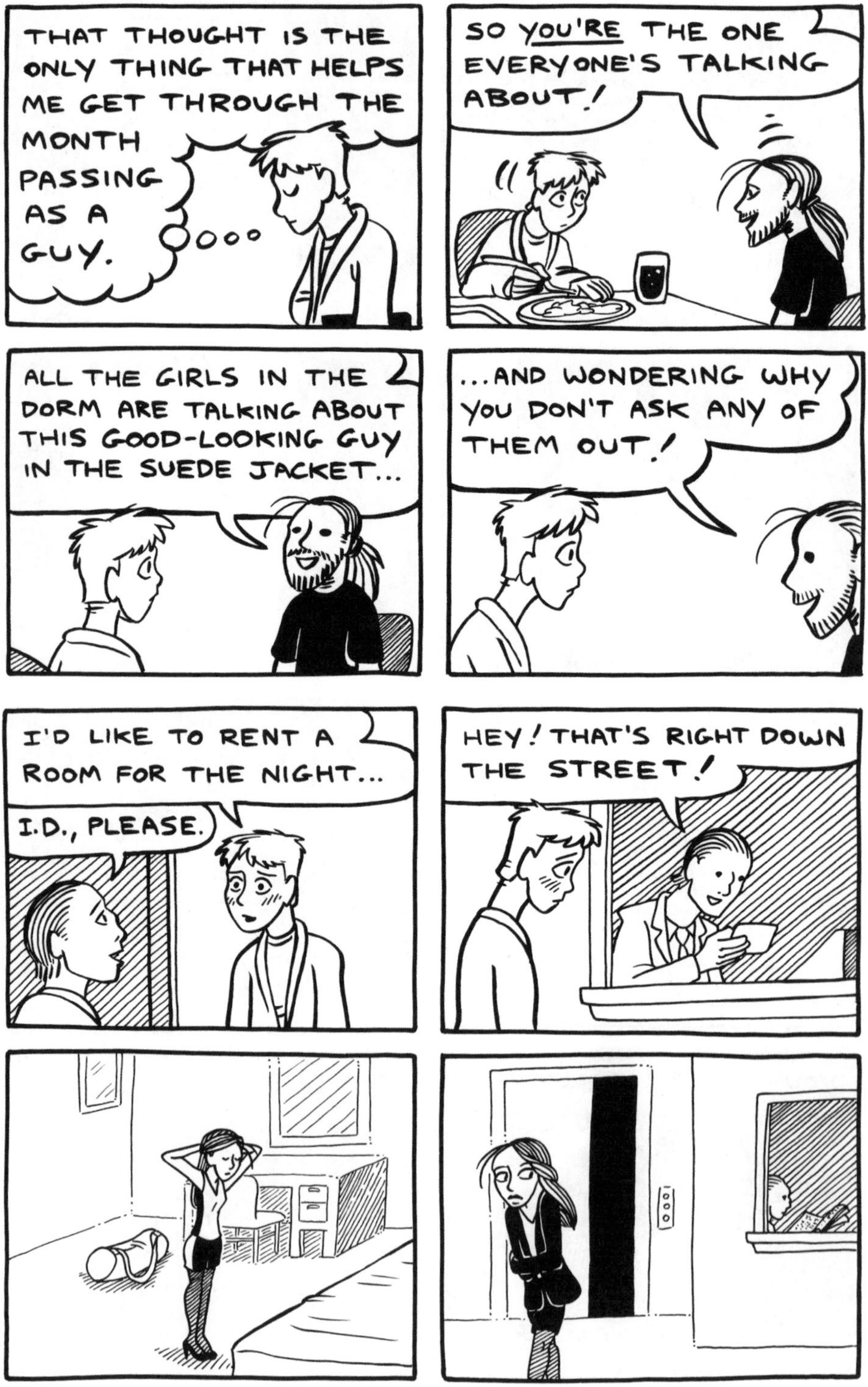
THAT THOUGHT IS THE ONLY THING THAT HELPS ME GET THROUGH THE MONTH PASSING AS A GUY.
SO YOU'RE THE ONE EVERYONE'S TALKING ABOUT!
ALL THE GIRLS IN THE DORM ARE TALKING ABOUT THIS GOOD-LOOKING GUY IN THE SUEDE JACKET...
...AND WONDERING WHY YOU DON'T ASK ANY OF THEM OUT!
I'D LIKE TO RENT A ROOM FOR THE NIGHT...
I.D., PLEASE.
HEY! THAT'S RIGHT DOWN THE STREET!

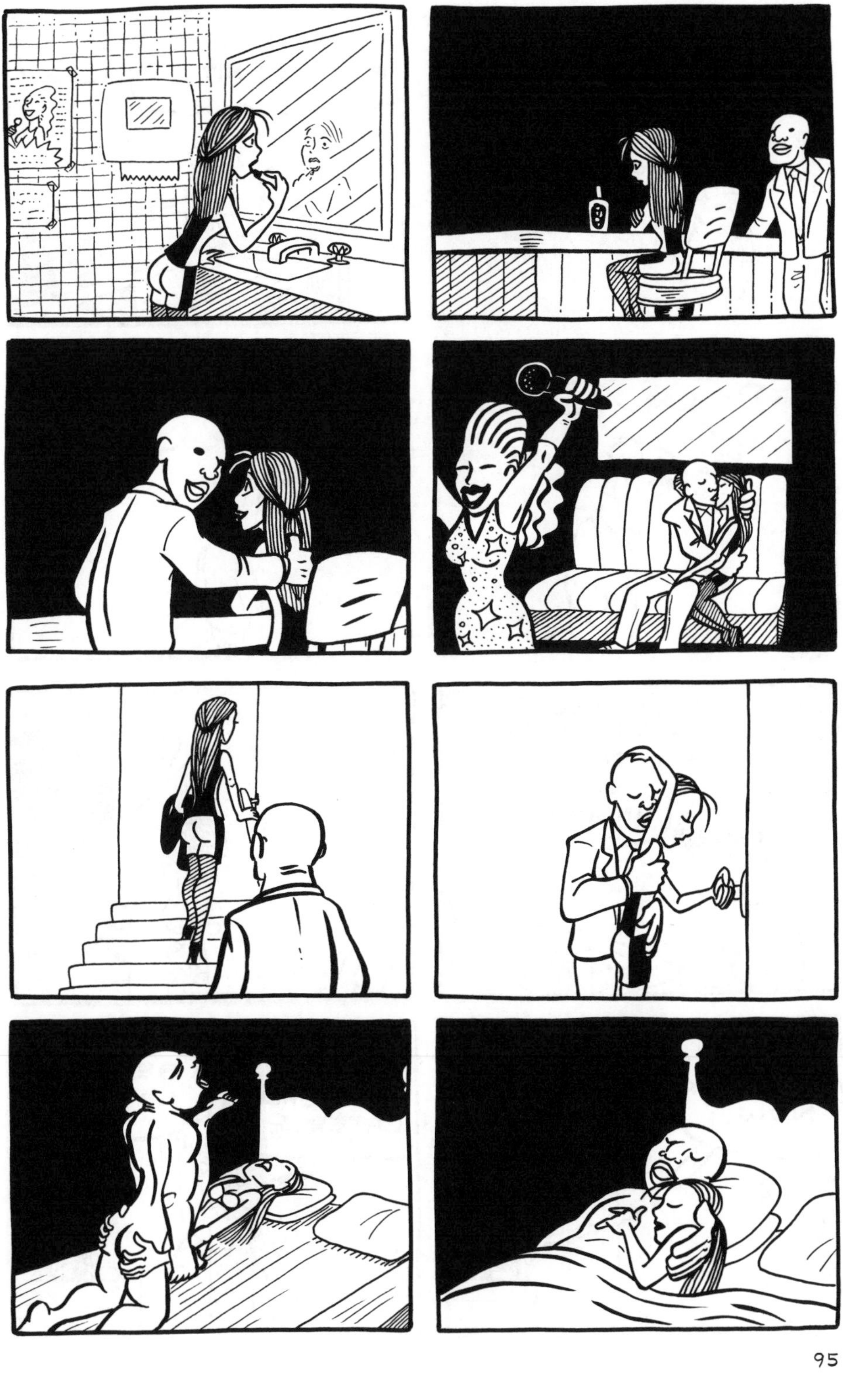

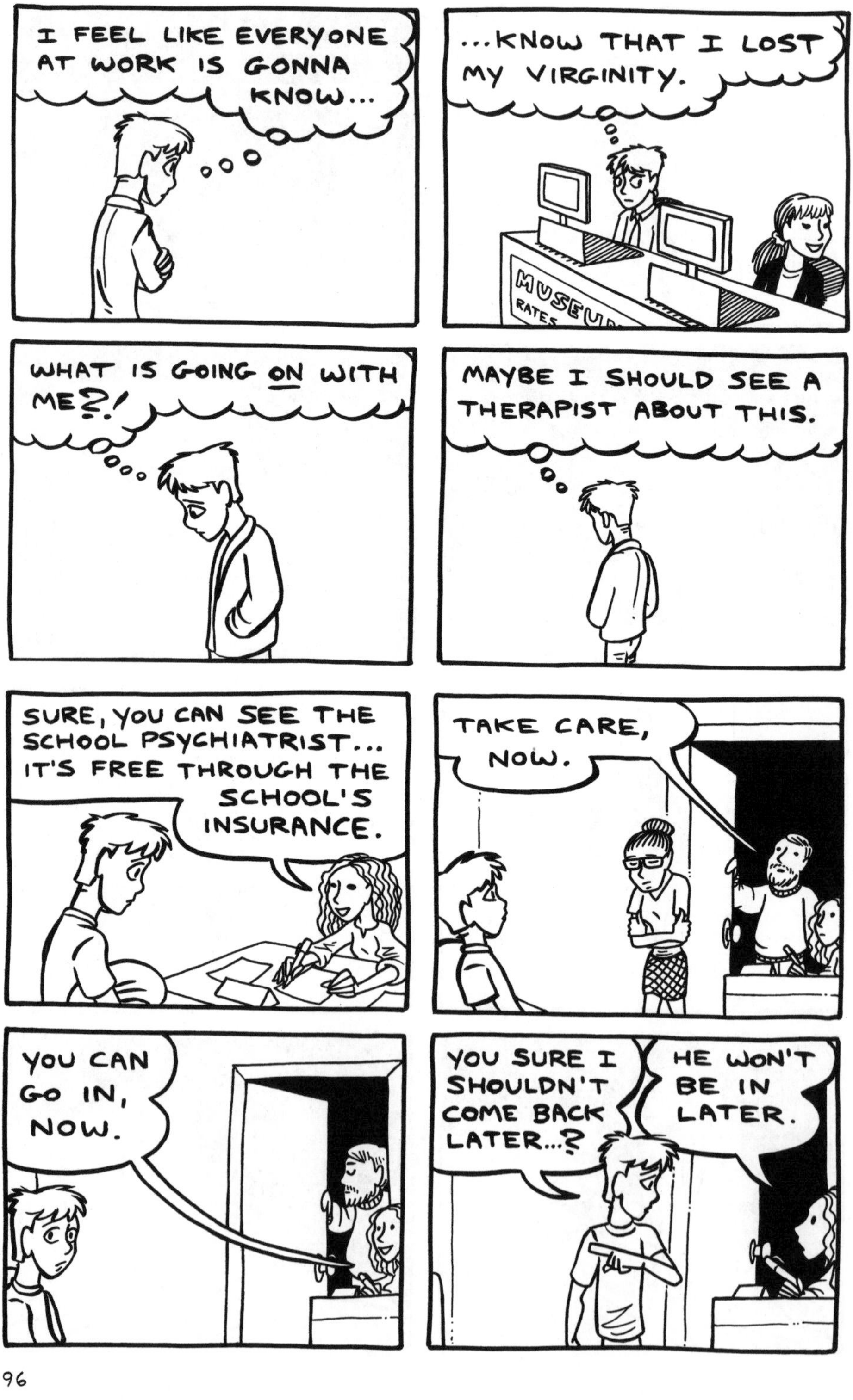
I FEEL LIKE EVERYONE AT WORK IS GONNA KNOW...
...KNOW THAT I LOST MY VIRGINITY.
MUSEUM
RATES
WHAT IS GOING ON WITH ME?!
MAYBE I SHOULD SEE A THERAPIST ABOUT THIS.
SURE, YOU CAN SEE THE SCHOOL PSYCHIATRIST... IT'S FREE THROUGH THE SCHOOL'S INSURANCE.
TAKE CARE, NOW.
YOU CAN GO IN, NOW.
YOU SURE I SHOULDN'T COME BACK LATER...?
HE WON'T BE IN LATER.

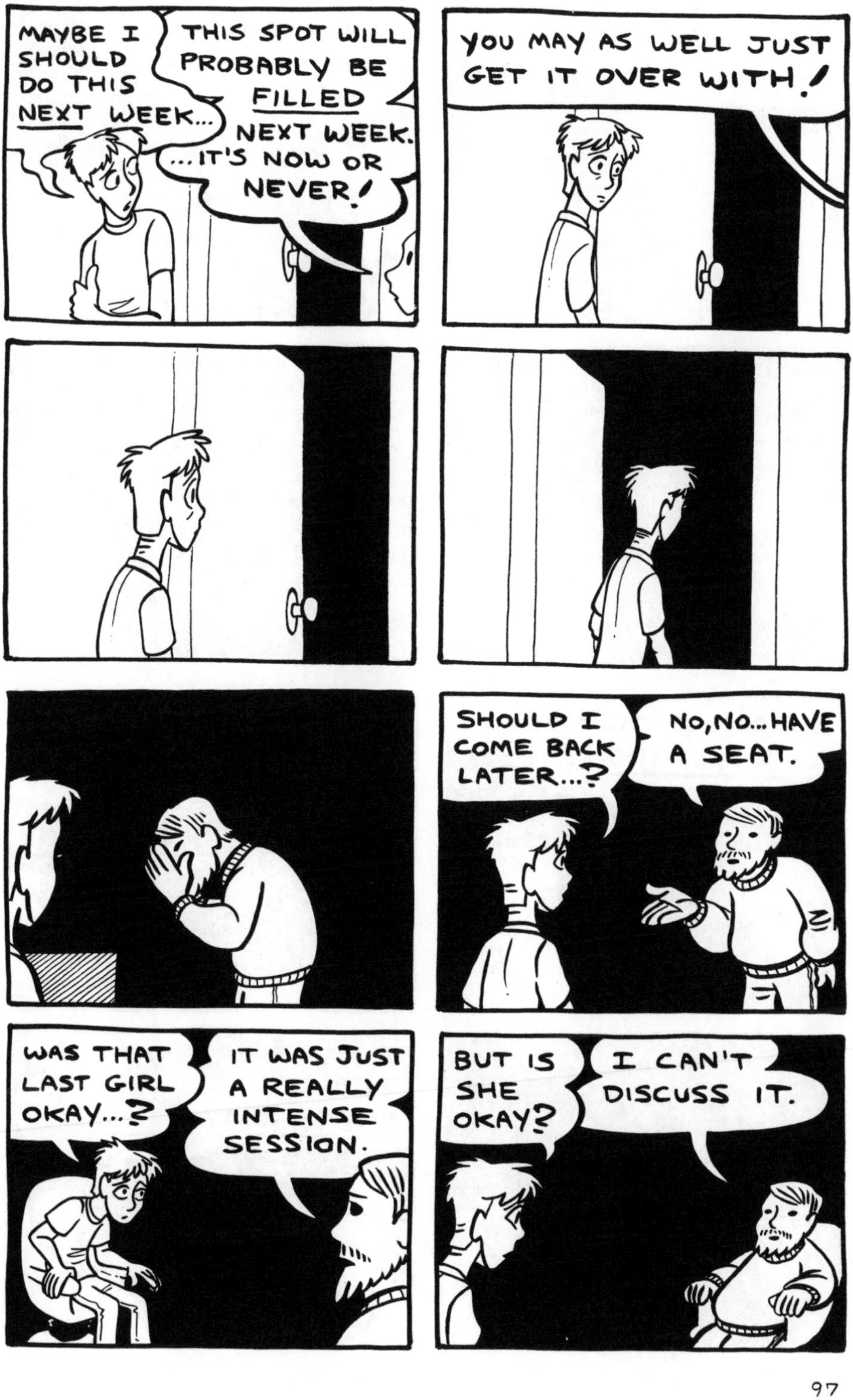
MAYBE I SHOULD DO THIS NEXT WEEK...
THIS SPOT WILL PROBABLY BE FILLED NEXT WEEK. ...IT'S NOW OR NEVER!
YOU MAY AS WELL JUST GET IT OVER WITH!
SHOULD I COME BACK LATER...?
NO, NO... HAVE A SEAT.
WAS THAT LAST GIRL OKAY...?
IT WAS JUST A REALLY INTENSE SESSION.
BUT IS SHE OKAY?
I CAN'T DISCUSS IT.

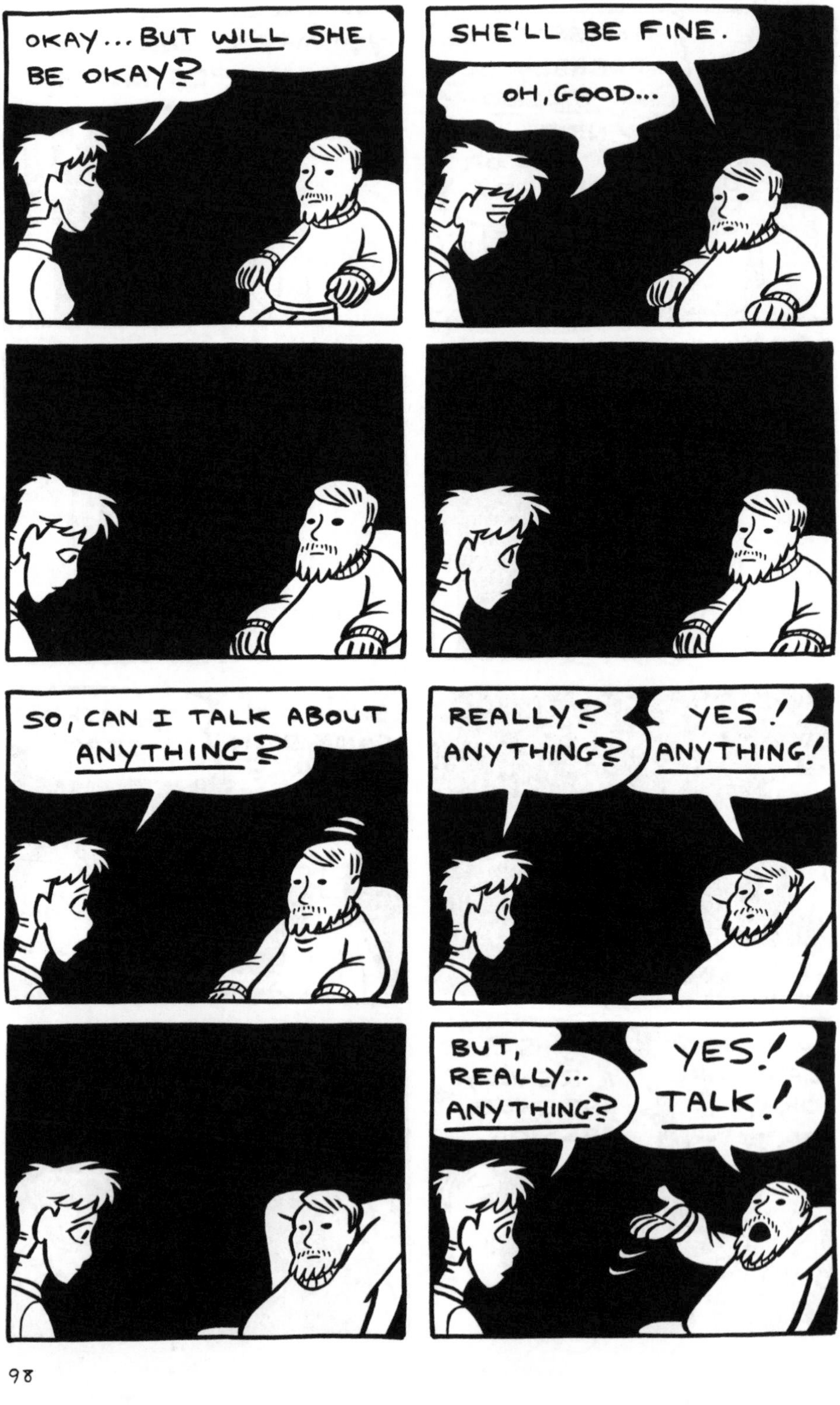
OKAY... BUT WILL SHE BE OKAY?
SHE'LL BE FINE.
OH, GOOD...
SO, CAN I TALK ABOUT ANYTHING?
REALLY? ANYTHING?
YES! ANYTHING!
BUT, REALLY... ANYTHING?
YES! TALK!

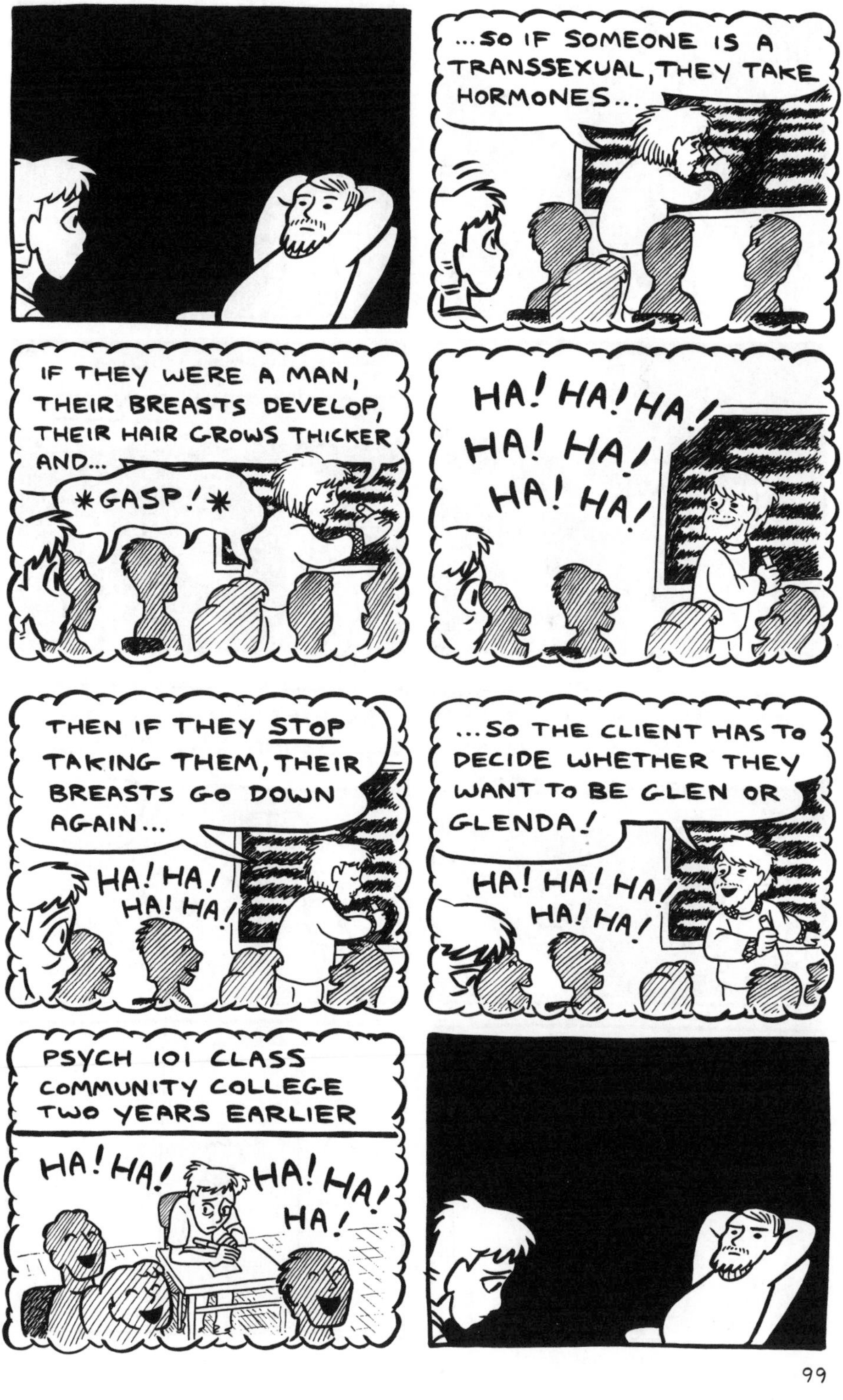

...SO IF SOMEONE IS A TRANSSEXUAL, THEY TAKE HORMONES...
IF THEY WERE A MAN, THEIR BREASTS DEVELOP, THEIR HAIR GROWS THICKER AND...
GASP!
HA! HA! HA! HA! HA! HA! HA!
THEN IF THEY STOP TAKING THEM, THEIR BREASTS GO DOWN AGAIN...
HA! HA! HA! HA!
...SO THE CLIENT HAS TO DECIDE WHETHER THEY WANT TO BE GLEN OR GLENDA!
HA! HA! HA! HA! HA!
PSYCH 101 CLASS COMMUNITY COLLEGE TWO YEARS EARLIER
HA! HA! HA! HA! HA!

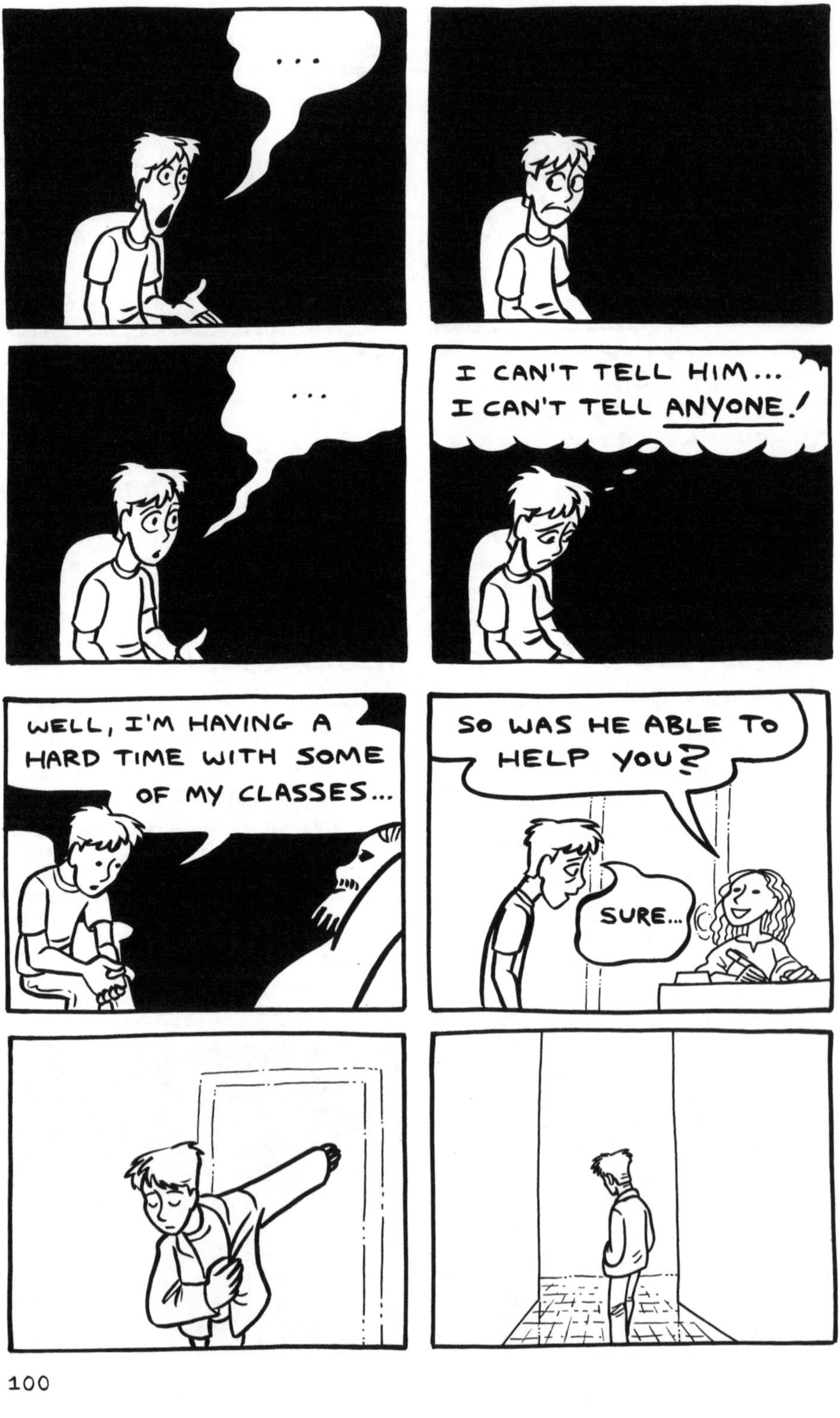
...
...
I CAN'T TELL HIM...
I CAN'T TELL ANYONE!
WELL, I'M HAVING A HARD TIME WITH SOME OF MY CLASSES...
SO WAS HE ABLE TO HELP YOU?
SURE...

BOOK TWO

SEPARATE PEOPLE

KATINA

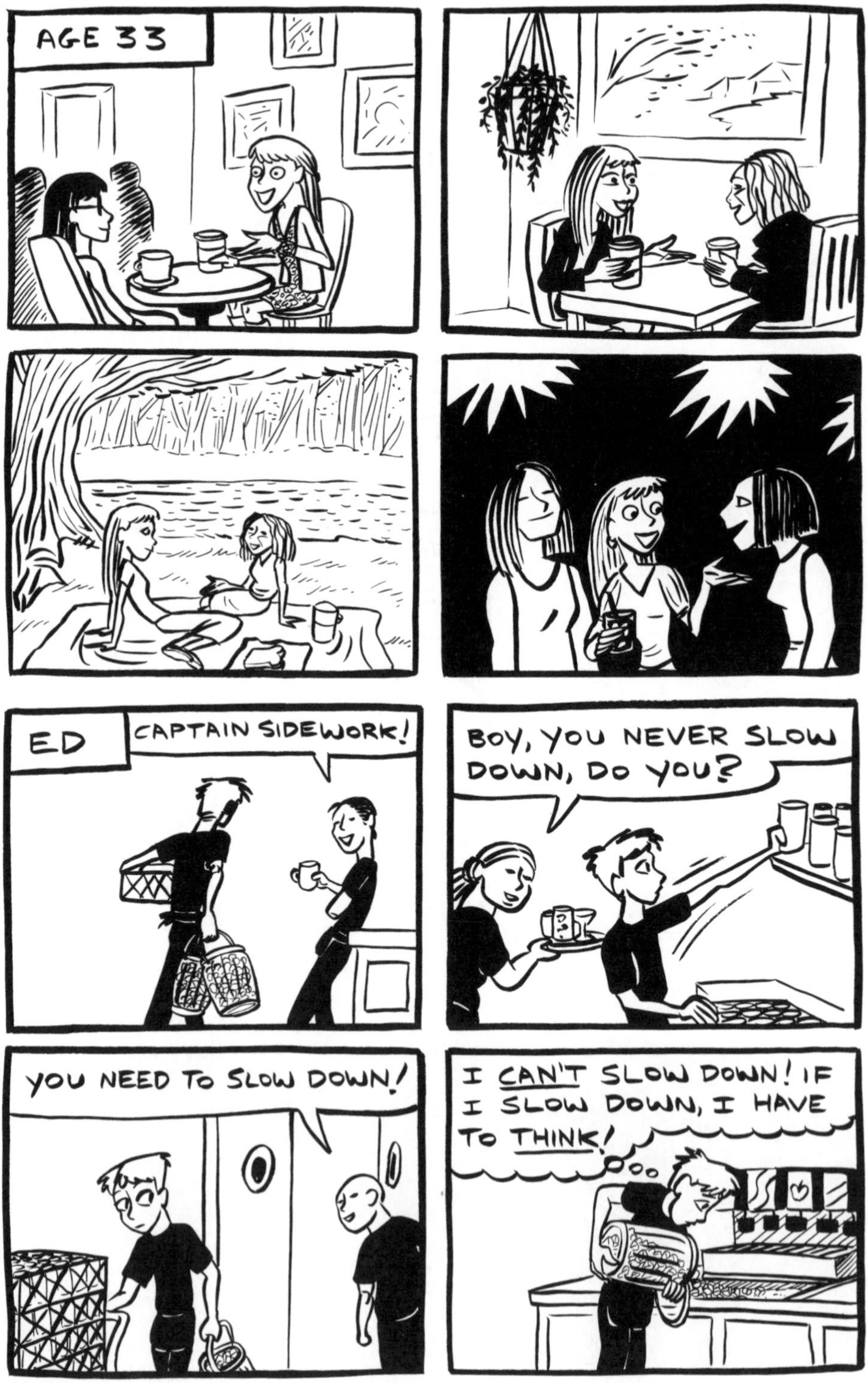
AGE 33
ED
CAPTAIN SIDEWORK!
BOY, YOU NEVER SLOW DOWN, DO YOU?
YOU NEED TO SLOW DOWN!
I CAN'T SLOW DOWN! IF I SLOW DOWN, I HAVE TO THINK!

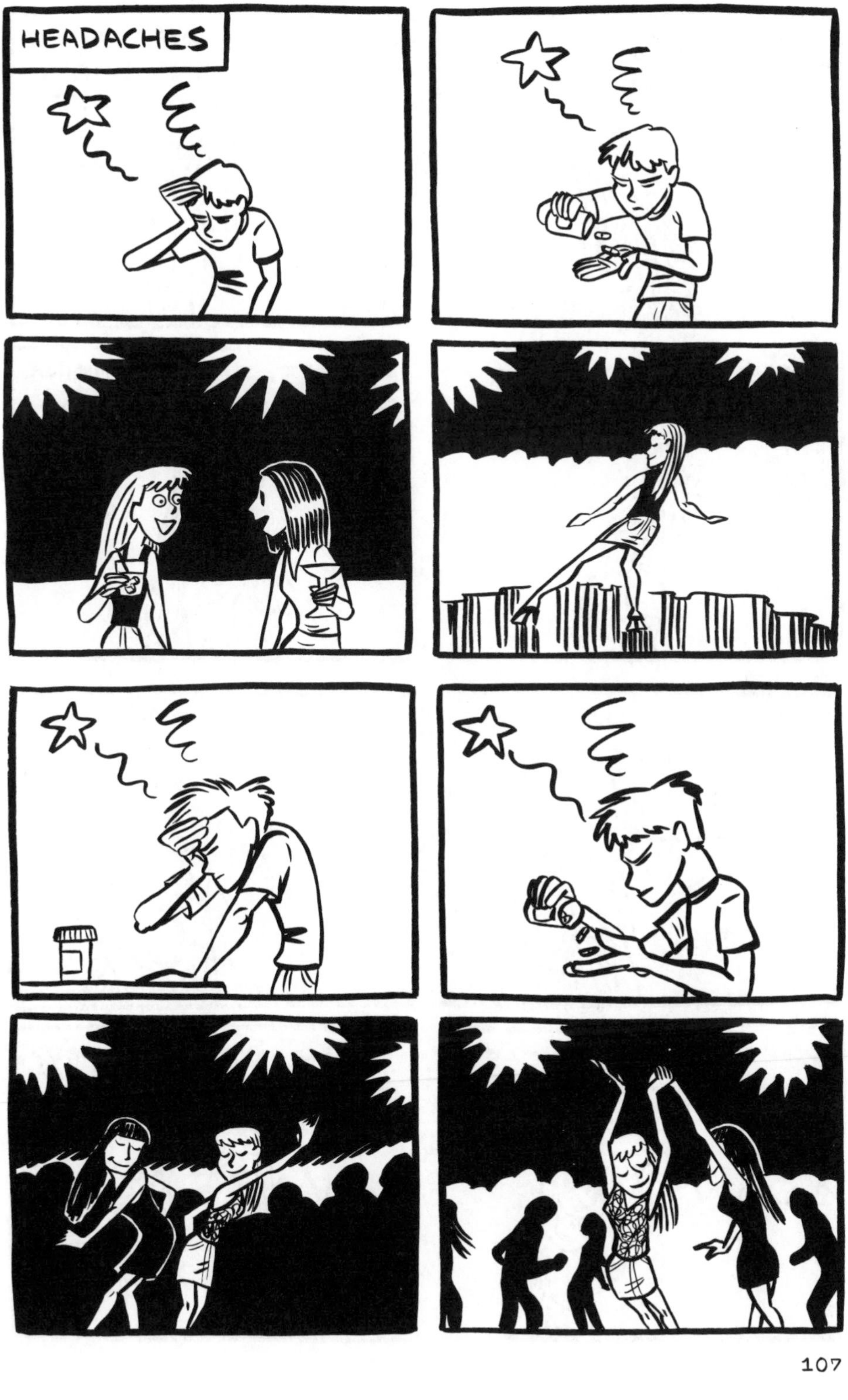
HEADACHES

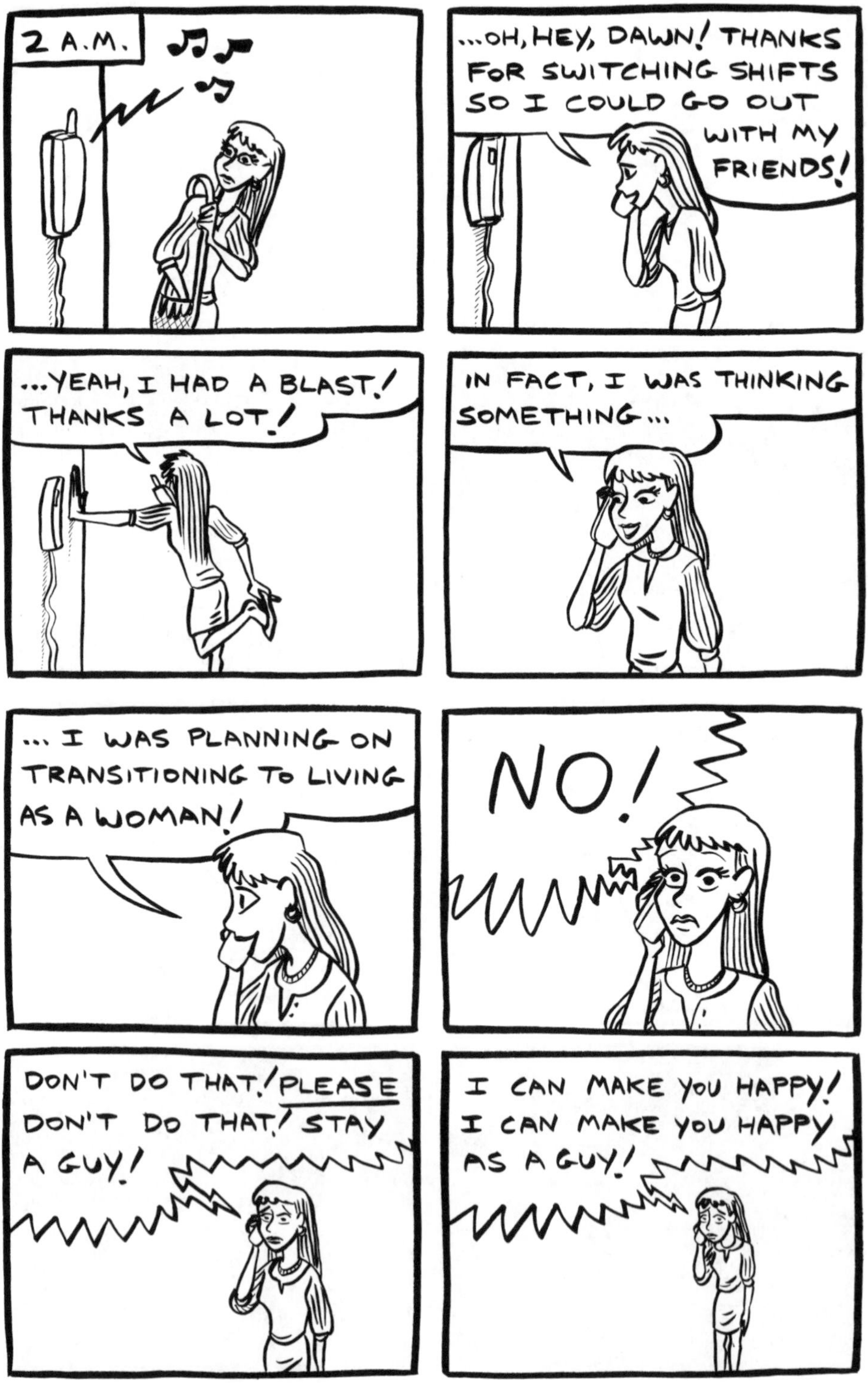
2 A.M.
...OH, HEY, DAWN! THANKS FOR SWITCHING SHIFTS SO I COULD GO OUT WITH MY FRIENDS!
...YEAH, I HAD A BLAST! THANKS A LOT!
IN FACT, I WAS THINKING SOMETHING...
... I WAS PLANNING ON TRANSITIONING TO LIVING AS A WOMAN!
NO!
DON'T DO THAT! PLEASE DON'T DO THAT! STAY A GUY!
I CAN MAKE YOU HAPPY! I CAN MAKE YOU HAPPY AS A GUY!

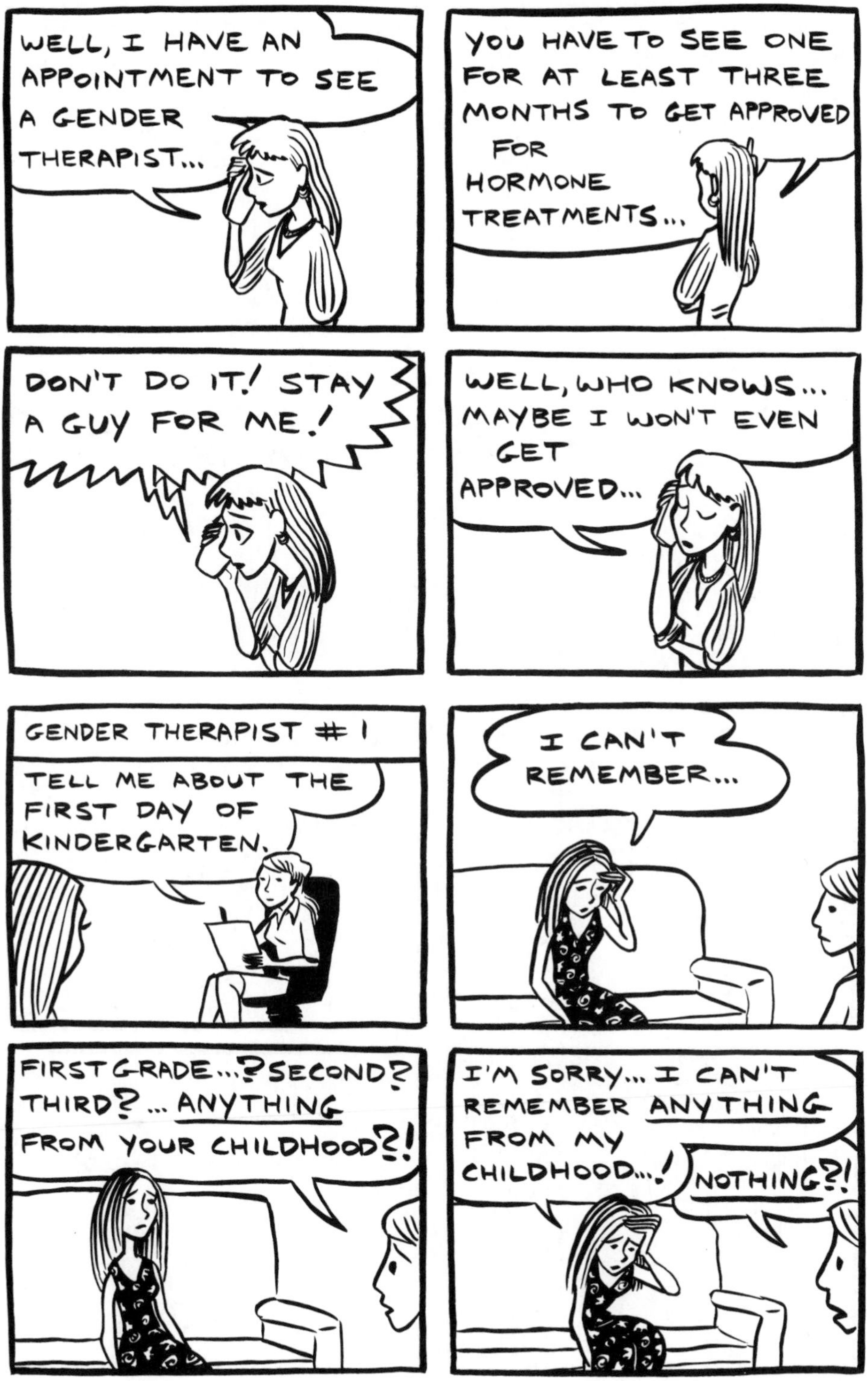
WELL, I HAVE AN APPOINTMENT TO SEE A GENDER THERAPIST...
YOU HAVE TO SEE ONE FOR AT LEAST THREE MONTHS TO GET APPROVED FOR HORMONE TREATMENTS...
DON'T DO IT! STAY A GUY FOR ME!
WELL, WHO KNOWS... MAYBE I WON'T EVEN GET APPROVED...
GENDER THERAPIST #1
TELL ME ABOUT THE FIRST DAY OF KINDERGARTEN.
I CAN'T REMEMBER...
FIRST GRADE...? SECOND? THIRD? ... ANYTHING FROM YOUR CHILDHOOD?!
I'M SORRY... I CAN'T REMEMBER ANYTHING FROM MY CHILDHOOD...!
NOTHING?!

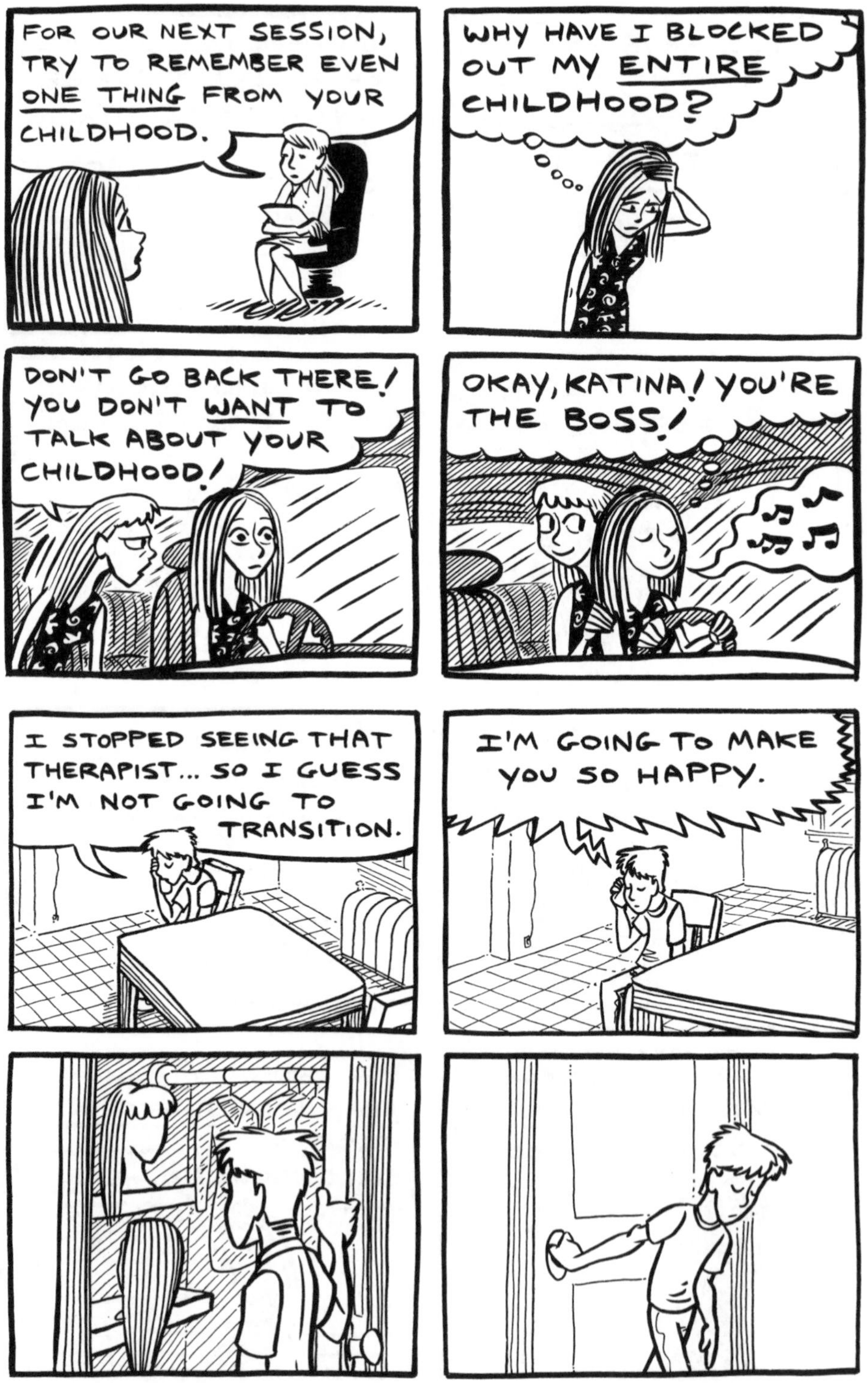
FOR OUR NEXT SESSION, TRY TO REMEMBER EVEN ONE THING FROM YOUR CHILDHOOD.
WHY HAVE I BLOCKED OUT MY ENTIRE CHILDHOOD?
DON'T GO BACK THERE! YOU DON'T WANT TO TALK ABOUT YOUR CHILDHOOD!
OKAY, KATINA! YOU'RE THE BOSS!
I STOPPED SEEING THAT THERAPIST... SO I GUESS I'M NOT GOING TO TRANSITION.
I'M GOING TO MAKE YOU SO HAPPY.

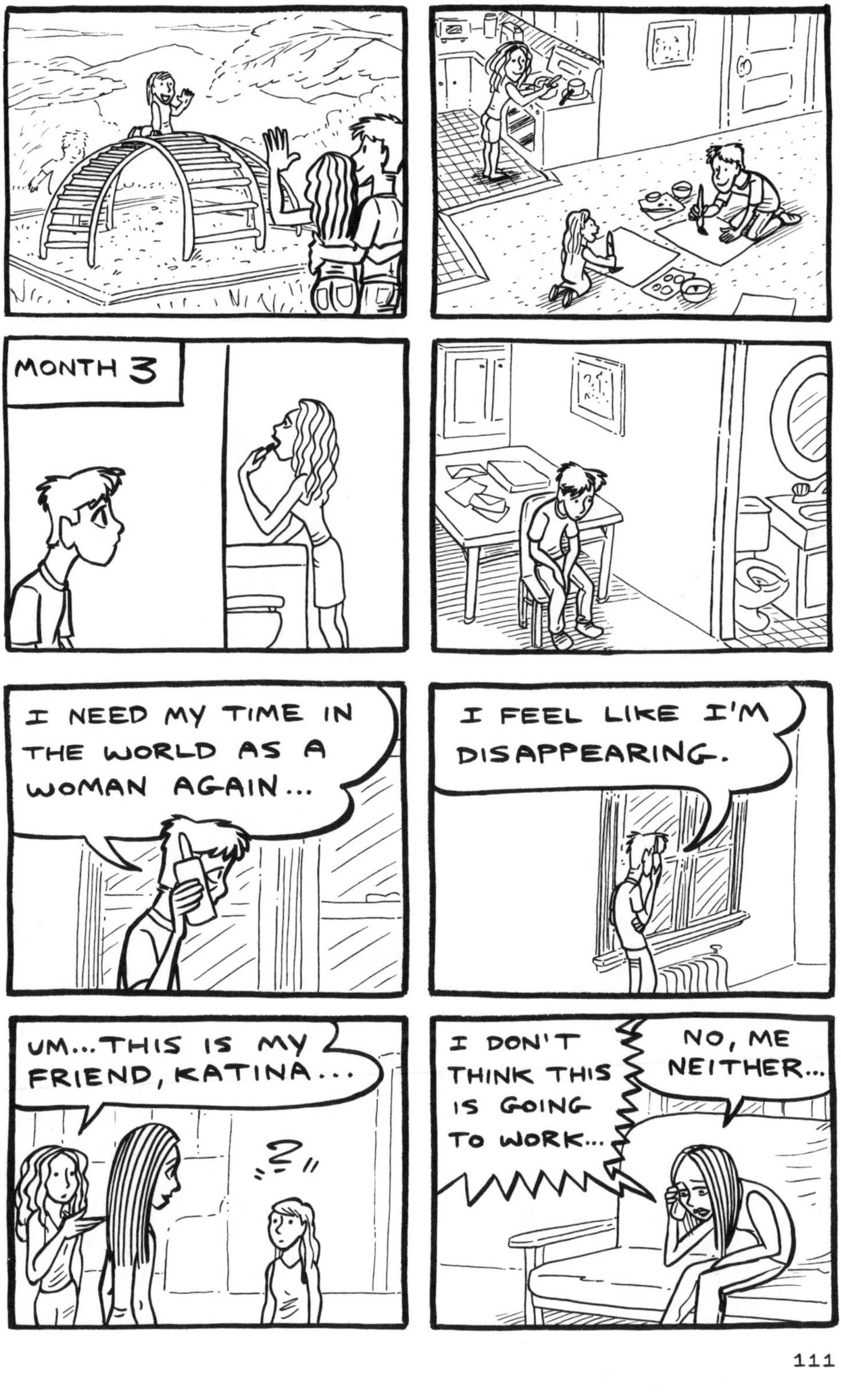
MONTH 3
I NEED MY TIME IN THE WORLD AS A WOMAN AGAIN...
I FEEL LIKE I'M DISAPPEARING.
UM...THIS IS MY FRIEND, KATINA...
?
I DON'T THINK THIS IS GOING TO WORK...
NO, ME NEITHER...

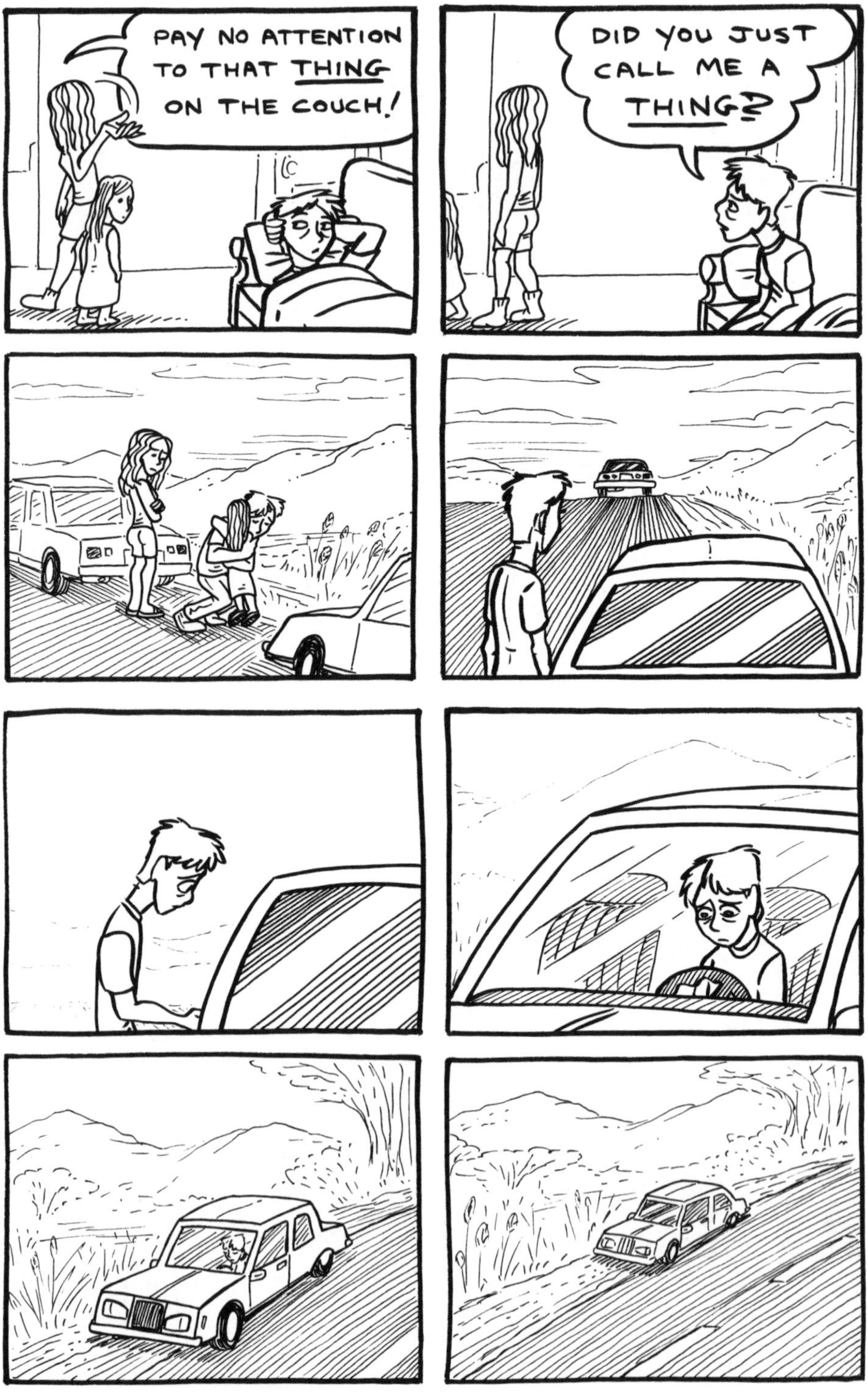
PAY NO ATTENTION TO THAT THING ON THE COUCH!
DID YOU JUST CALL ME A THING?

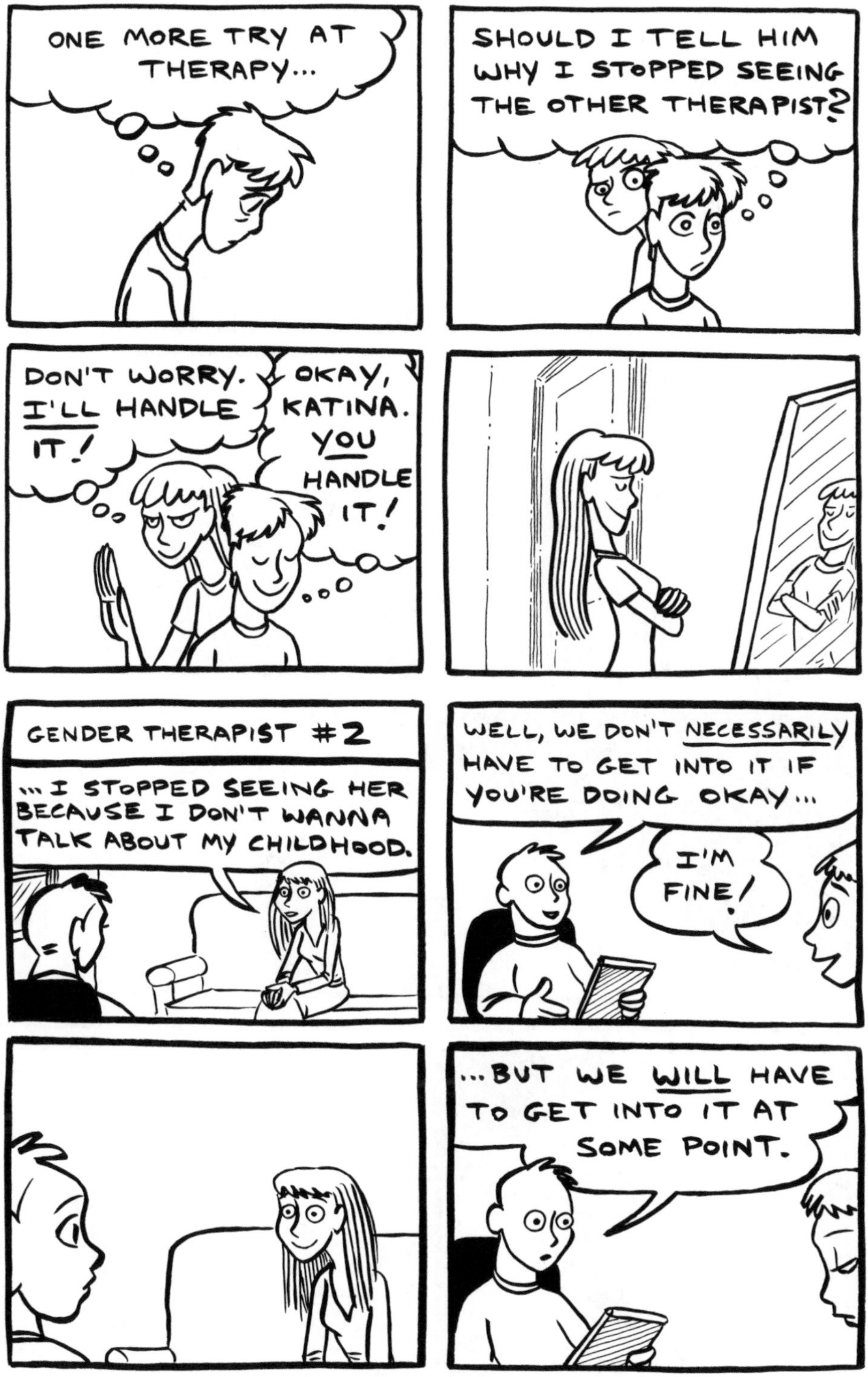
ONE MORE TRY AT THERAPY...
SHOULD I TELL HIM WHY I STOPPED SEEING THE OTHER THERAPIST?
DON'T WORRY. I'LL HANDLE IT!
OKAY, KATINA. YOU HANDLE IT!
GENDER THERAPIST #2
...I STOPPED SEEING HER BECAUSE I DON'T WANNA TALK ABOUT MY CHILDHOOD.
WELL, WE DON'T NECESSARILY HAVE TO GET INTO IT IF YOU'RE DOING OKAY...
I'M FINE!
...BUT WE WILL HAVE TO GET INTO IT AT SOME POINT.

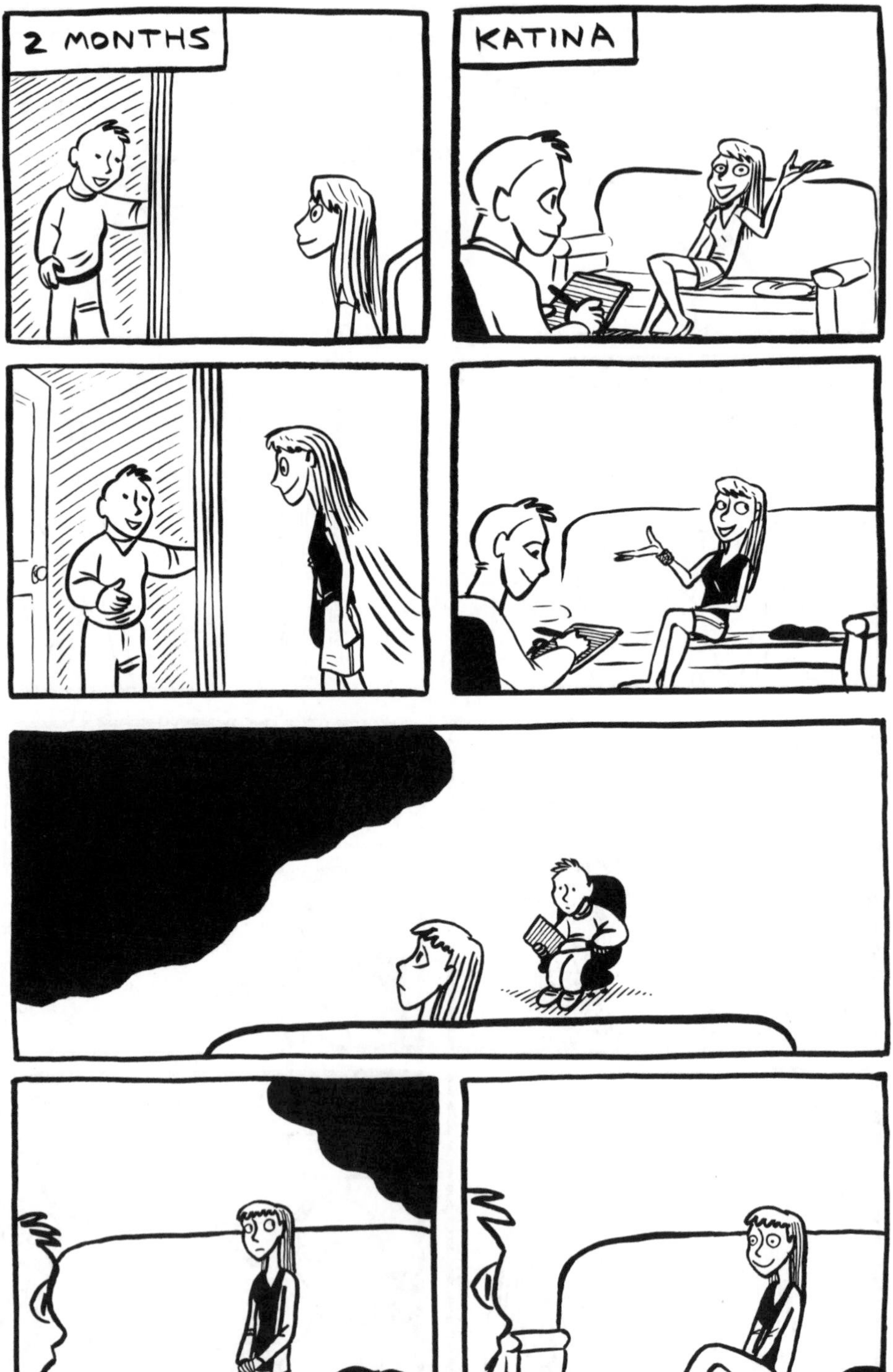
2 MONTHS
KATINA

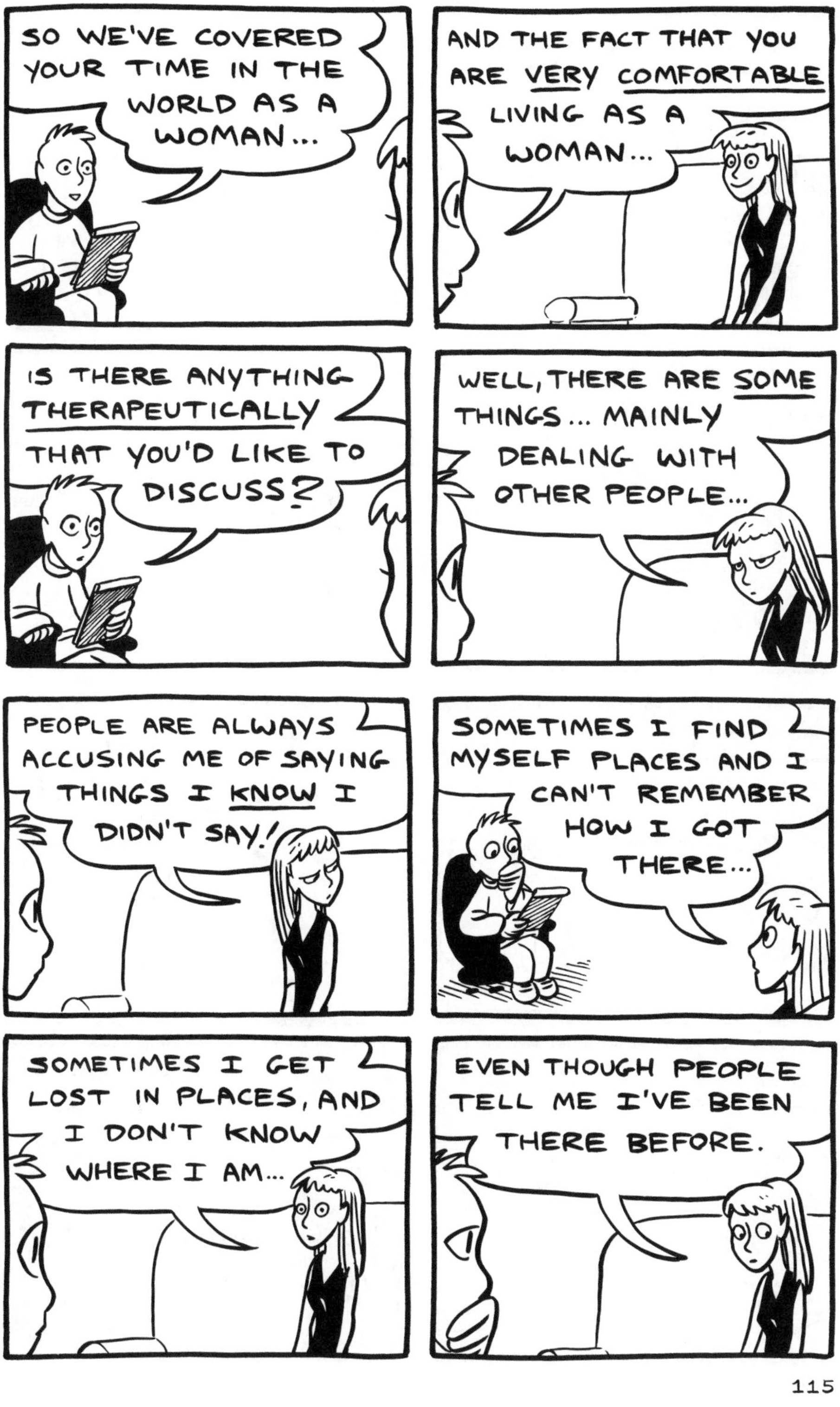
SO WE'VE COVERED YOUR TIME IN THE WORLD AS A WOMAN...
AND THE FACT THAT YOU ARE VERY COMFORTABLE LIVING AS A WOMAN...
IS THERE ANYTHING THERAPEUTICALLY THAT YOU'D LIKE TO DISCUSS?
WELL, THERE ARE SOME THINGS... MAINLY DEALING WITH OTHER PEOPLE...
PEOPLE ARE ALWAYS ACCUSING ME OF SAYING THINGS I KNOW I DIDN'T SAY!
SOMETIMES I FIND MYSELF PLACES AND I CAN'T REMEMBER HOW I GOT THERE...
SOMETIMES I GET LOST IN PLACES, AND I DON'T KNOW WHERE I AM...
EVEN THOUGH PEOPLE TELL ME I'VE BEEN THERE BEFORE.

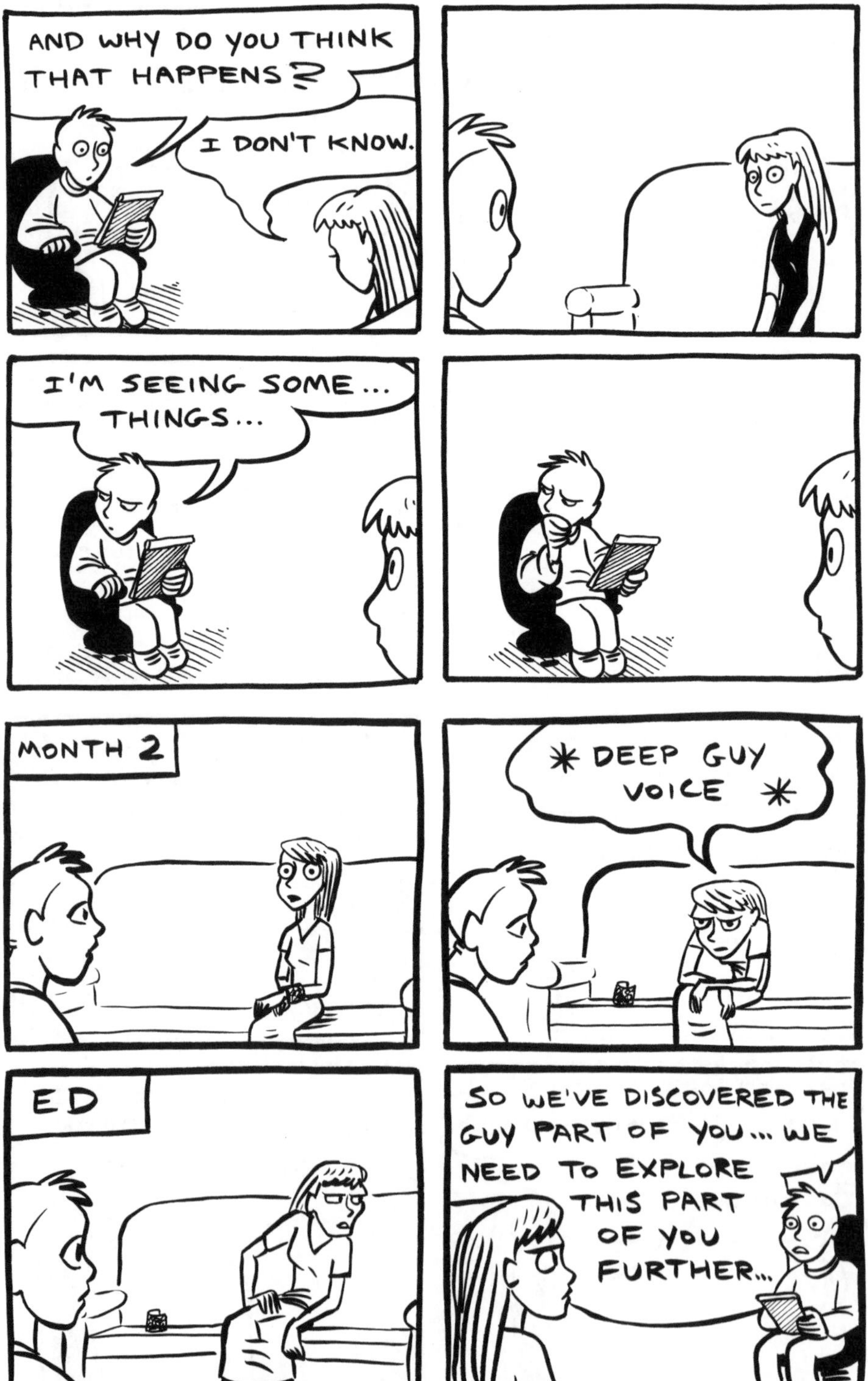
AND WHY DO YOU THINK THAT HAPPENS?
I DON'T KNOW.
I'M SEEING SOME... THINGS...
MONTH 2
* DEEP GUY VOICE *
ED
SO WE'VE DISCOVERED THE GUY PART OF YOU... WE NEED TO EXPLORE THIS PART OF YOU FURTHER...

ED

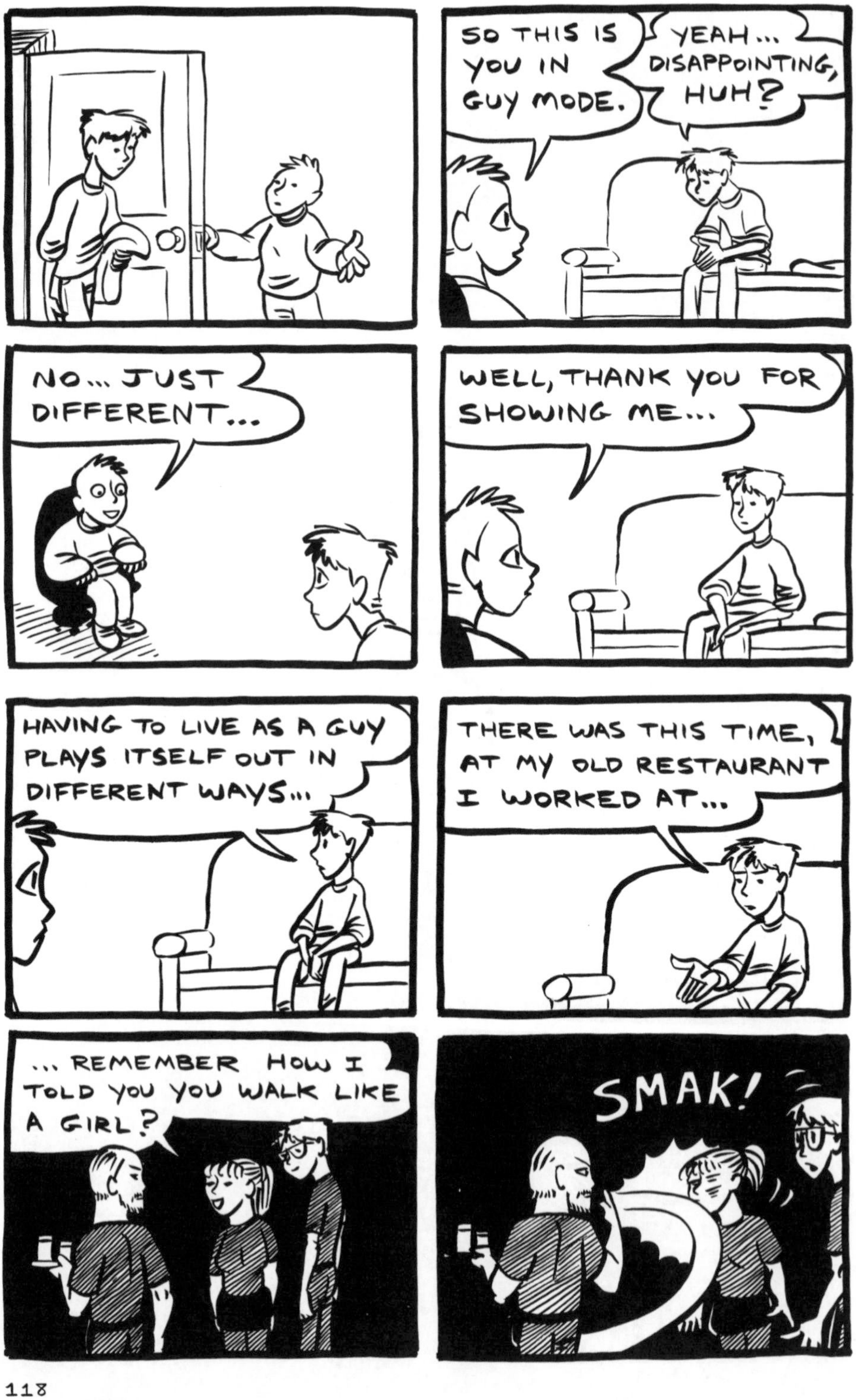
SO THIS IS YOU IN GUY MODE.
YEAH... DISAPPOINTING, HUH?
NO... JUST DIFFERENT...
WELL, THANK YOU FOR SHOWING ME...
HAVING TO LIVE AS A GUY PLAYS ITSELF OUT IN DIFFERENT WAYS...
THERE WAS THIS TIME, AT MY OLD RESTAURANT I WORKED AT...
... REMEMBER HOW I TOLD YOU YOU WALK LIKE A GIRL?
SMAK!

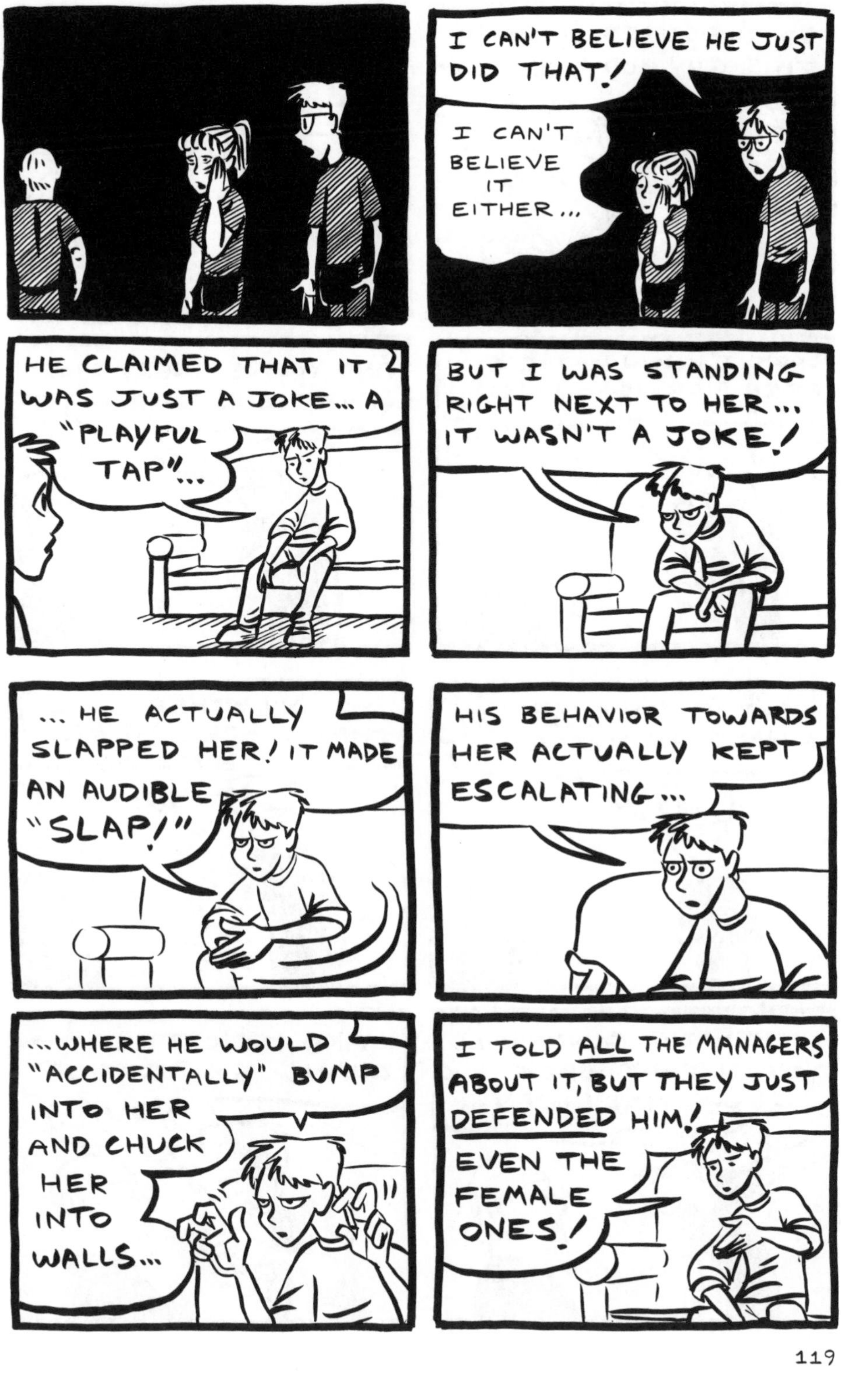

I CAN'T BELIEVE HE JUST DID THAT!
I CAN'T BELIEVE IT EITHER...
HE CLAIMED THAT IT WAS JUST A JOKE... A "PLAYFUL TAP"...
BUT I WAS STANDING RIGHT NEXT TO HER... IT WASN'T A JOKE!
... HE ACTUALLY SLAPPED HER! IT MADE AN AUDIBLE "SLAP!"
HIS BEHAVIOR TOWARDS HER ACTUALLY KEPT ESCALATING...
...WHERE HE WOULD "ACCIDENTALLY" BUMP INTO HER AND CHUCK HER INTO WALLS...
I TOLD ALL THE MANAGERS ABOUT IT, BUT THEY JUST DEFENDED HIM!
EVEN THE FEMALE ONES!

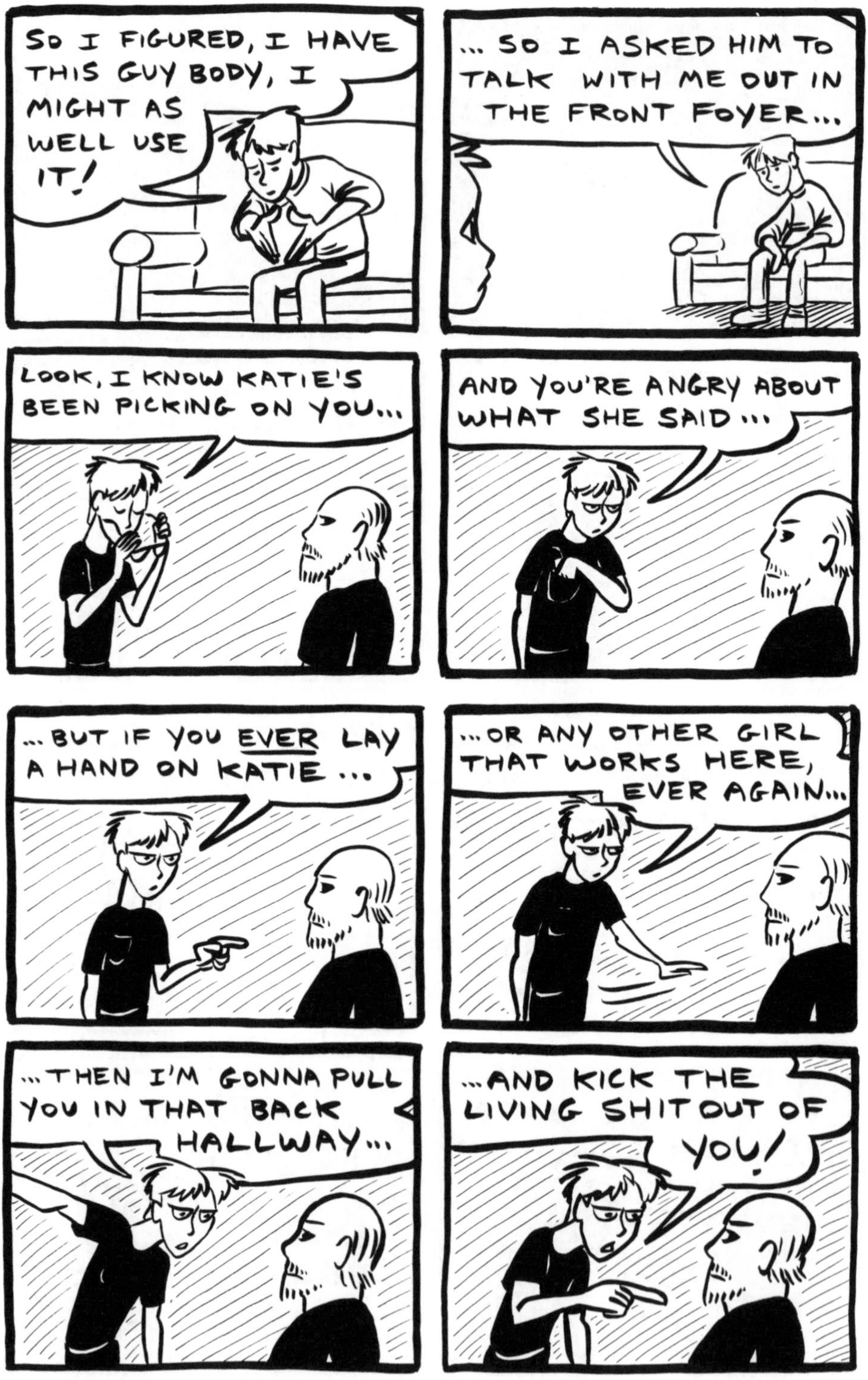
SO I FIGURED, I HAVE THIS GUY BODY, I MIGHT AS WELL USE IT!
... SO I ASKED HIM TO TALK WITH ME OUT IN THE FRONT FOYER...
LOOK, I KNOW KATIE'S BEEN PICKING ON YOU...
AND YOU'RE ANGRY ABOUT WHAT SHE SAID...
...BUT IF YOU EVER LAY A HAND ON KATIE...
...OR ANY OTHER GIRL THAT WORKS HERE, EVER AGAIN...
...THEN I'M GONNA PULL YOU IN THAT BACK HALLWAY...
...AND KICK THE LIVING SHIT OUT OF YOU!

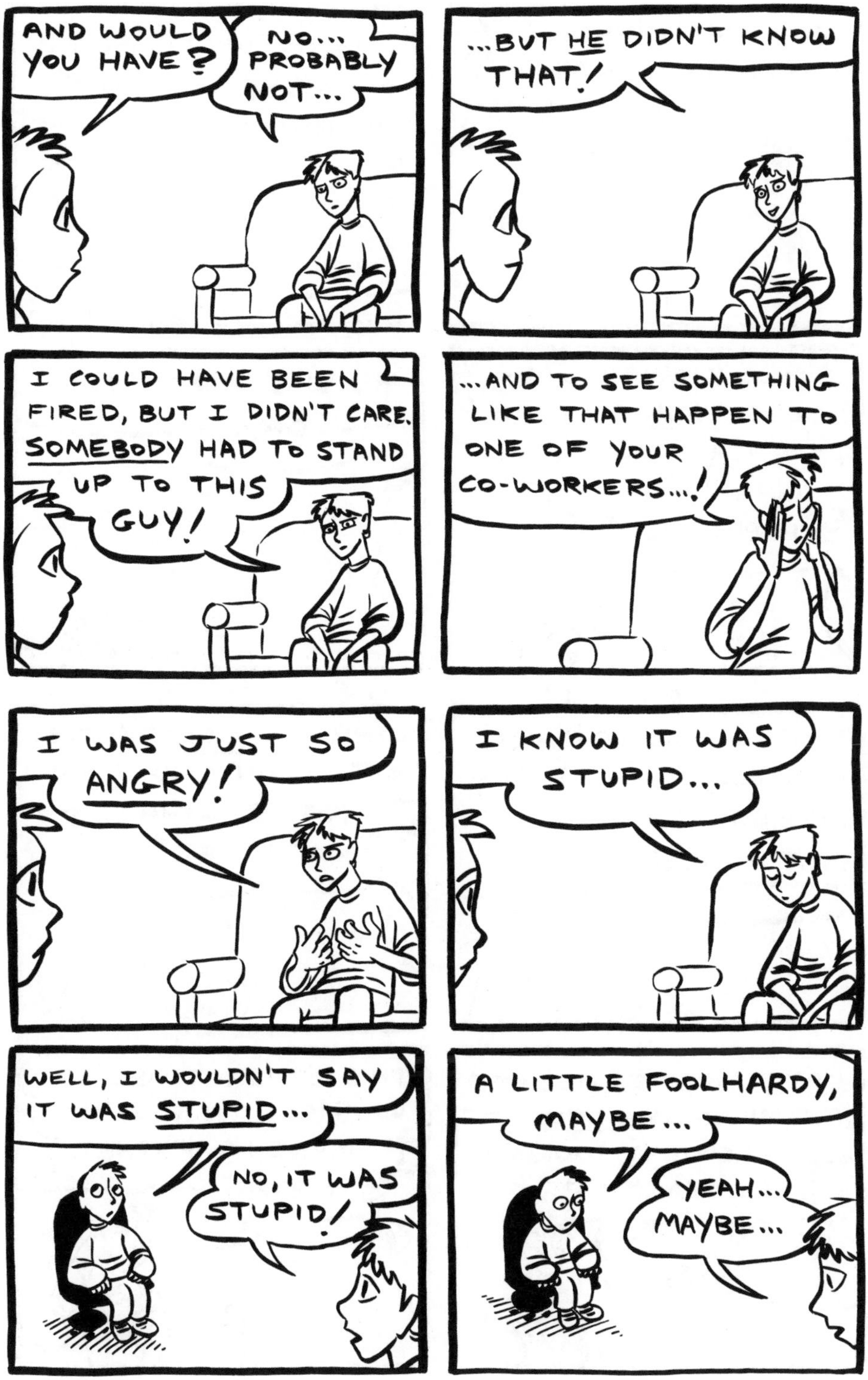

AND WOULD YOU HAVE?
NO... PROBABLY NOT...
...BUT HE DIDN'T KNOW THAT!
I COULD HAVE BEEN FIRED, BUT I DIDN'T CARE. SOMEBODY HAD TO STAND UP TO THIS GUY!
...AND TO SEE SOMETHING LIKE THAT HAPPEN TO ONE OF YOUR CO-WORKERS...!
I WAS JUST SO ANGRY!
I KNOW IT WAS STUPID...
WELL, I WOULDN'T SAY IT WAS STUPID...
NO, IT WAS STUPID!
A LITTLE FOOLHARDY, MAYBE...
YEAH... MAYBE...

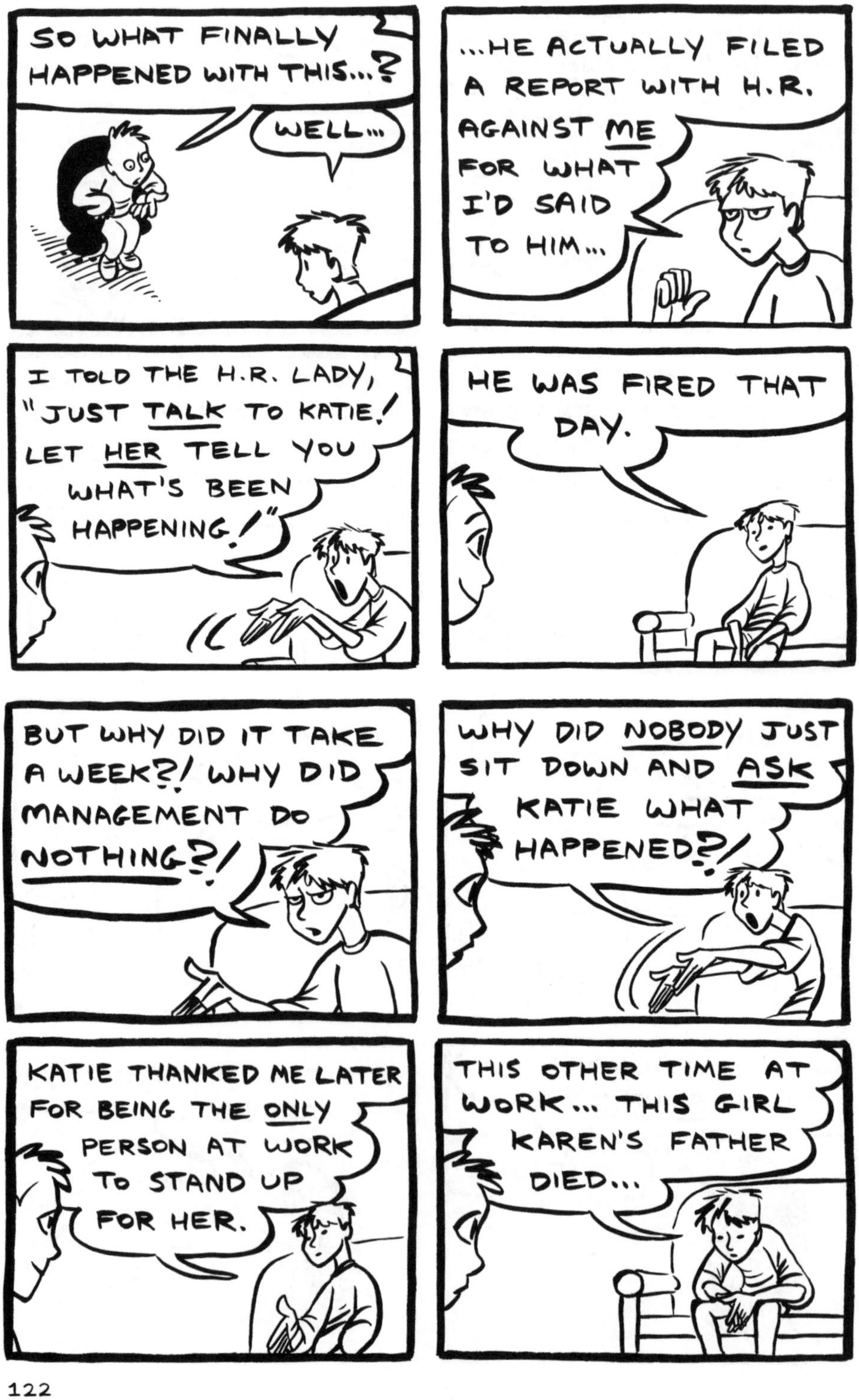
SO WHAT FINALLY HAPPENED WITH THIS...?
WELL...
...HE ACTUALLY FILED A REPORT WITH H.R. AGAINST ME FOR WHAT I'D SAID TO HIM...
I TOLD THE H.R. LADY, "JUST TALK TO KATIE! LET HER TELL YOU WHAT'S BEEN HAPPENING!"
HE WAS FIRED THAT DAY.
BUT WHY DID IT TAKE A WEEK?! WHY DID MANAGEMENT DO NOTHING?!
WHY DID NOBODY JUST SIT DOWN AND ASK KATIE WHAT HAPPENED?!
KATIE THANKED ME LATER FOR BEING THE ONLY PERSON AT WORK TO STAND UP FOR HER.
THIS OTHER TIME AT WORK... THIS GIRL KAREN'S FATHER DIED...

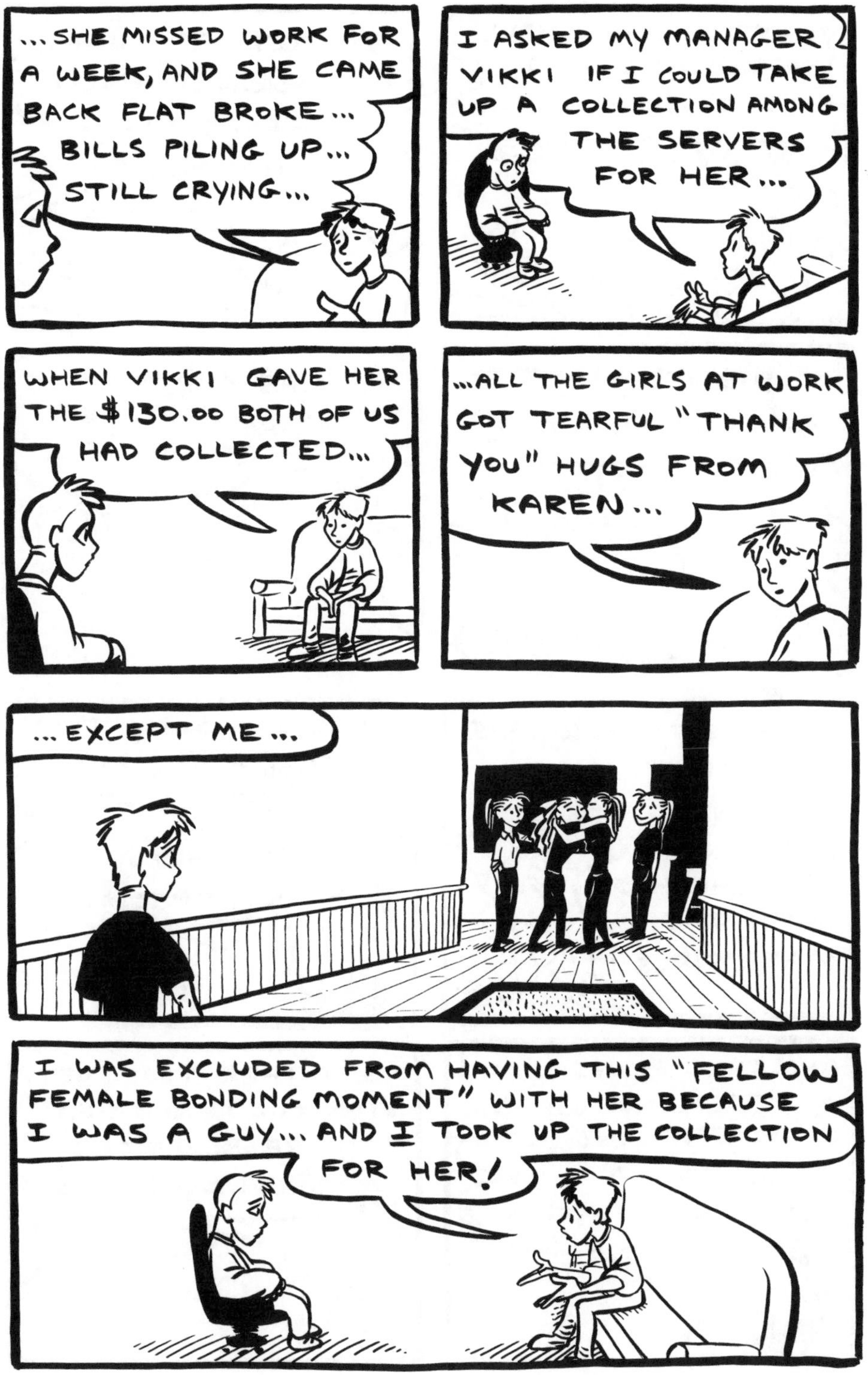
...SHE MISSED WORK FOR A WEEK, AND SHE CAME BACK FLAT BROKE... BILLS PILING UP... STILL CRYING...
I ASKED MY MANAGER VIKKI IF I COULD TAKE UP A COLLECTION AMONG THE SERVERS FOR HER...
WHEN VIKKI GAVE HER THE $130.00 BOTH OF US HAD COLLECTED...
...ALL THE GIRLS AT WORK GOT TEARFUL "THANK YOU" HUGS FROM KAREN...
...EXCEPT ME...
I WAS EXCLUDED FROM HAVING THIS "FELLOW FEMALE BONDING MOMENT" WITH HER BECAUSE I WAS A GUY... AND I TOOK UP THE COLLECTION FOR HER!

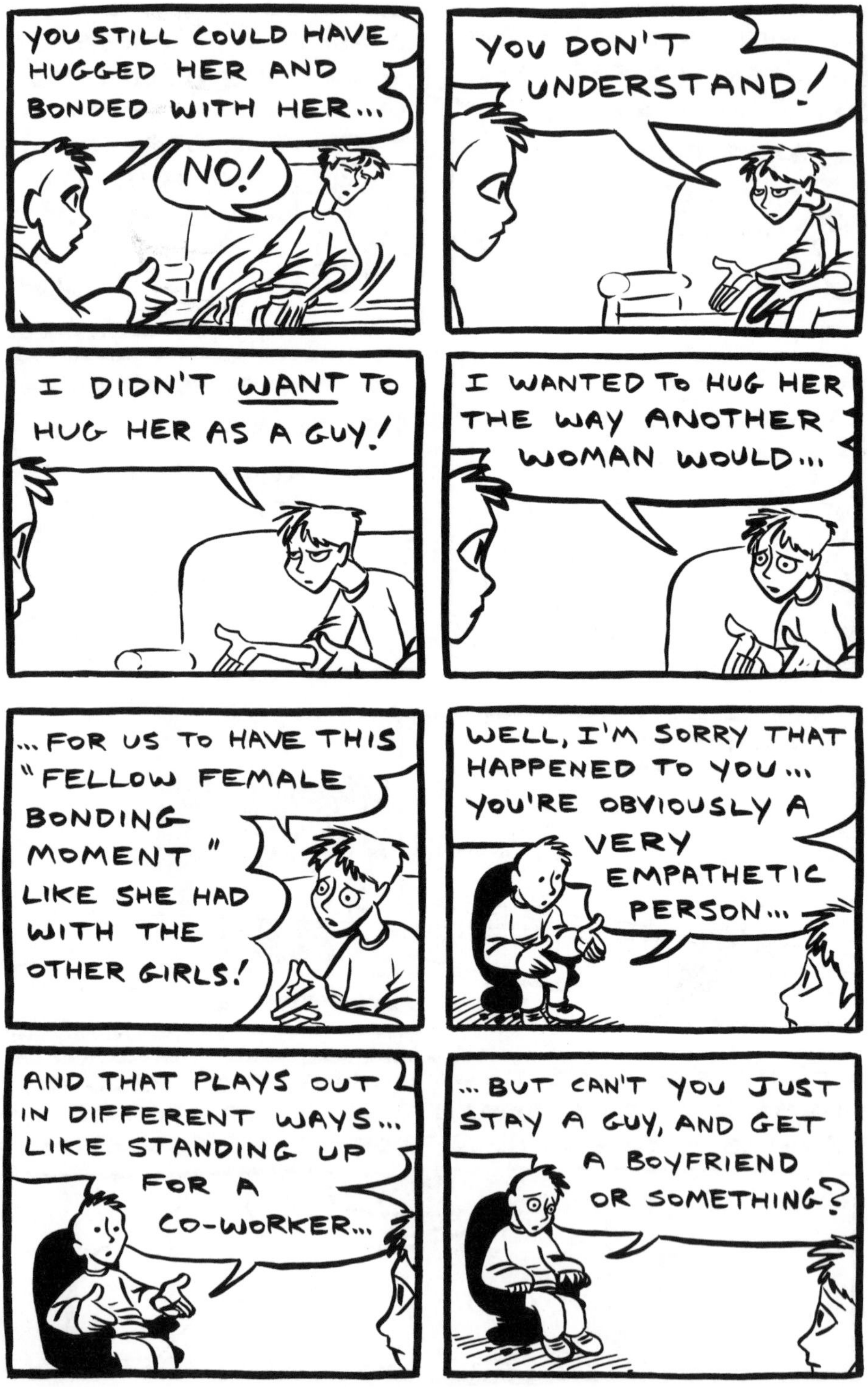
YOU STILL COULD HAVE HUGGED HER AND BONDED WITH HER...
NO!
YOU DON'T UNDERSTAND!
I DIDN'T WANT TO HUG HER AS A GUY!
I WANTED TO HUG HER THE WAY ANOTHER WOMAN WOULD...
...FOR US TO HAVE THIS "FELLOW FEMALE BONDING MOMENT" LIKE SHE HAD WITH THE OTHER GIRLS!
WELL, I'M SORRY THAT HAPPENED TO YOU... YOU'RE OBVIOUSLY A VERY EMPATHETIC PERSON...
AND THAT PLAYS OUT IN DIFFERENT WAYS... LIKE STANDING UP FOR A CO-WORKER...
...BUT CAN'T YOU JUST STAY A GUY, AND GET A BOYFRIEND OR SOMETHING?

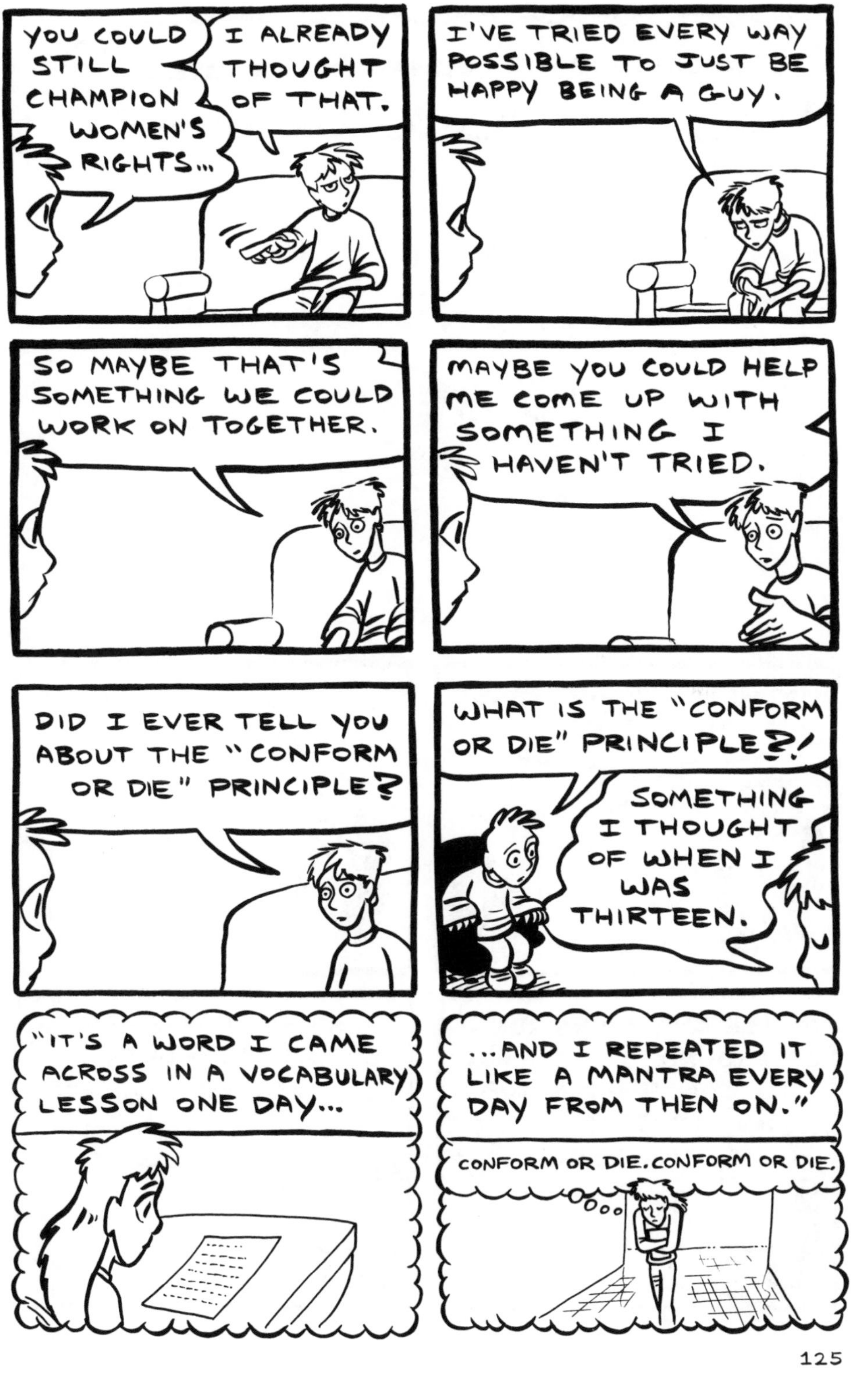
YOU COULD STILL CHAMPION WOMEN'S RIGHTS...
I ALREADY THOUGHT OF THAT.
I'VE TRIED EVERY WAY POSSIBLE TO JUST BE HAPPY BEING A GUY.
SO MAYBE THAT'S SOMETHING WE COULD WORK ON TOGETHER.
MAYBE YOU COULD HELP ME COME UP WITH SOMETHING I HAVEN'T TRIED.
DID I EVER TELL YOU ABOUT THE "CONFORM OR DIE" PRINCIPLE?
WHAT IS THE "CONFORM OR DIE" PRINCIPLE?!
SOMETHING I THOUGHT OF WHEN I WAS THIRTEEN.
"IT'S A WORD I CAME ACROSS IN A VOCABULARY LESSON ONE DAY...
...AND I REPEATED IT LIKE A MANTRA EVERY DAY FROM THEN ON."
CONFORM OR DIE. CONFORM OR DIE.

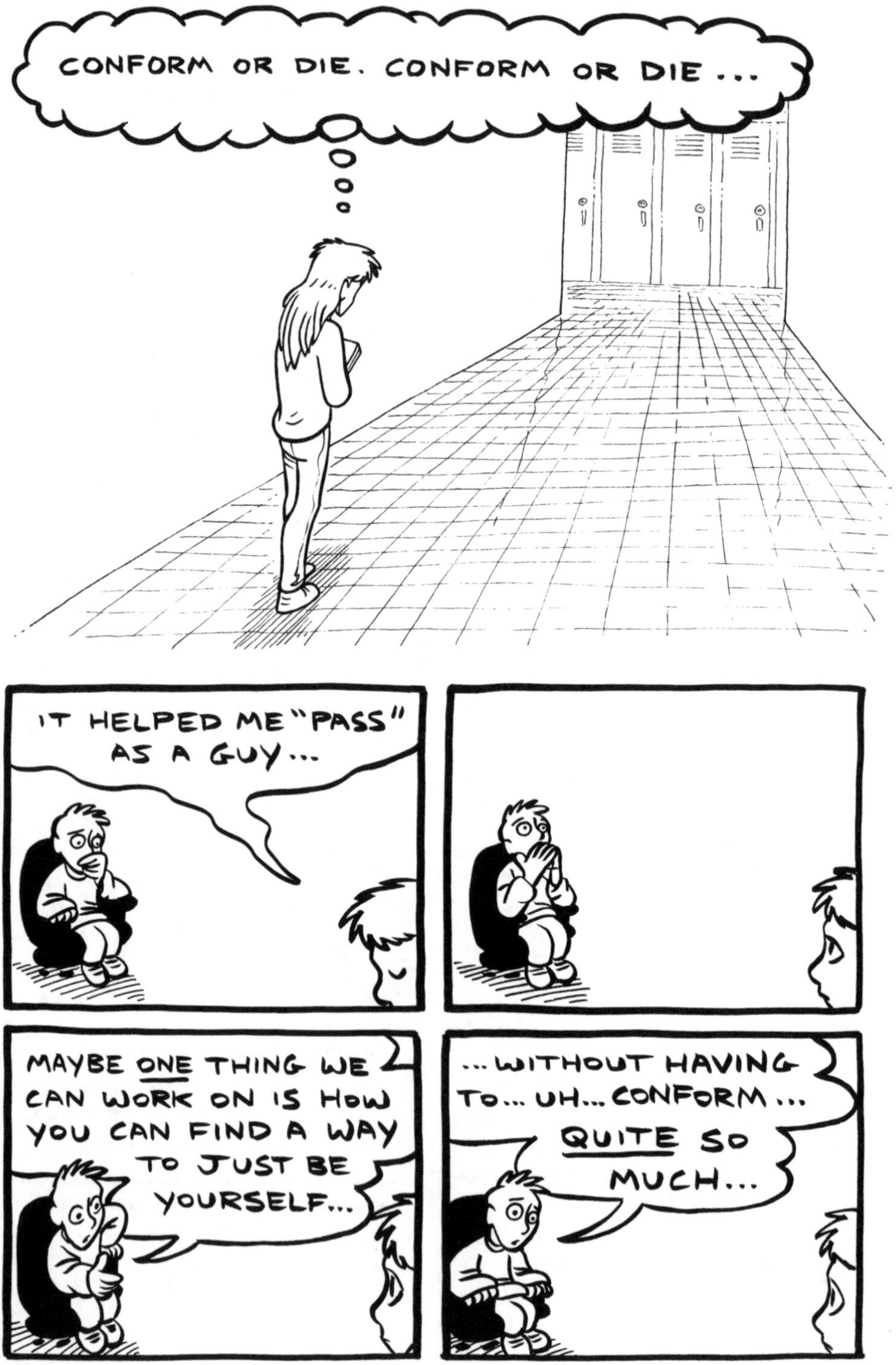
CONFORM OR DIE. CONFORM OR DIE...
IT HELPED ME "PASS" AS A GUY...
MAYBE ONE THING WE CAN WORK ON IS HOW YOU CAN FIND A WAY TO JUST BE YOURSELF...
...WITHOUT HAVING TO... UH... CONFORM... QUITE SO MUCH...

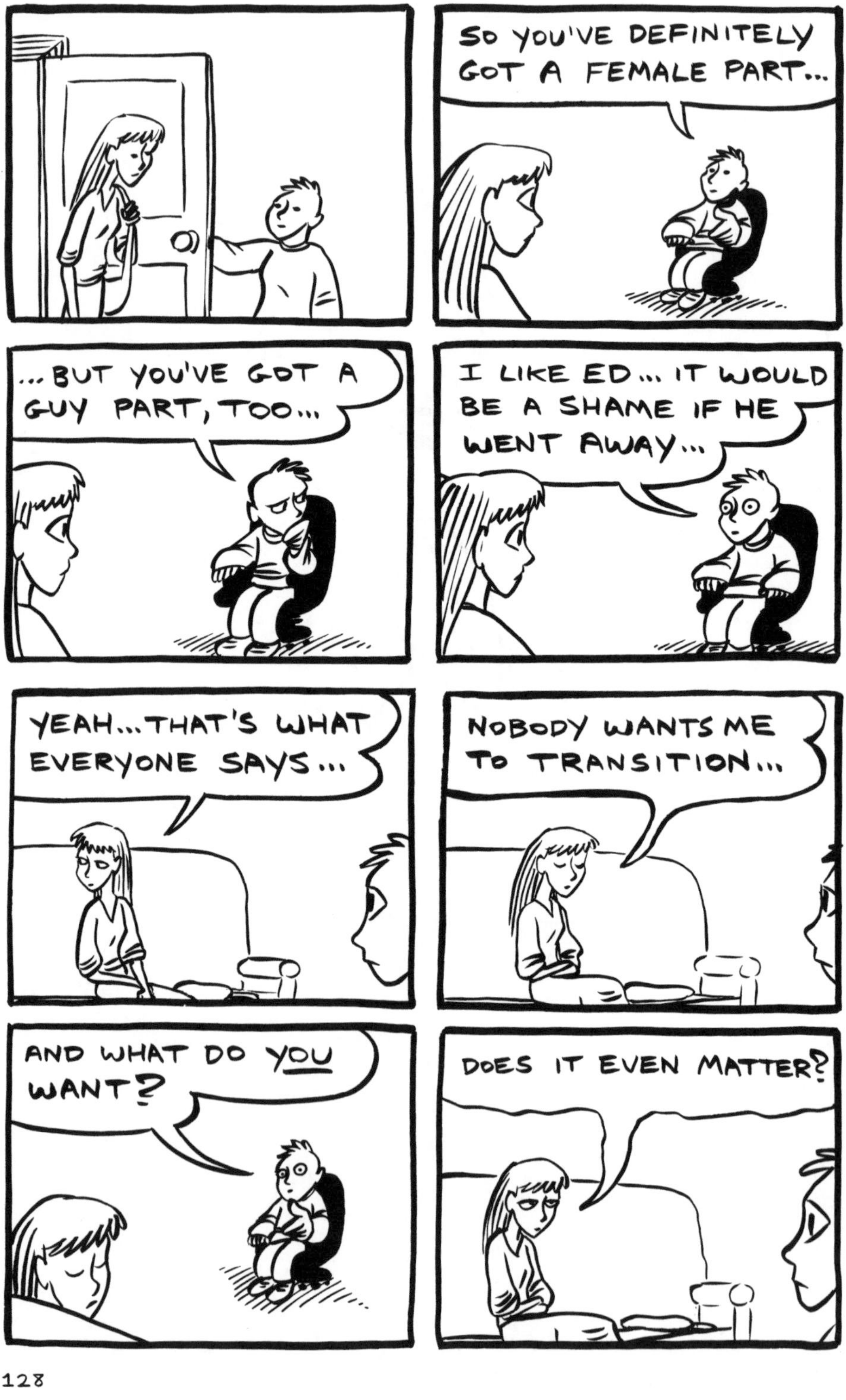
SO YOU'VE DEFINITELY GOT A FEMALE PART...
...BUT YOU'VE GOT A GUY PART, TOO...
I LIKE ED... IT WOULD BE A SHAME IF HE WENT AWAY...
YEAH...THAT'S WHAT EVERYONE SAYS...
NOBODY WANTS ME TO TRANSITION...
AND WHAT DO YOU WANT?
DOES IT EVEN MATTER?

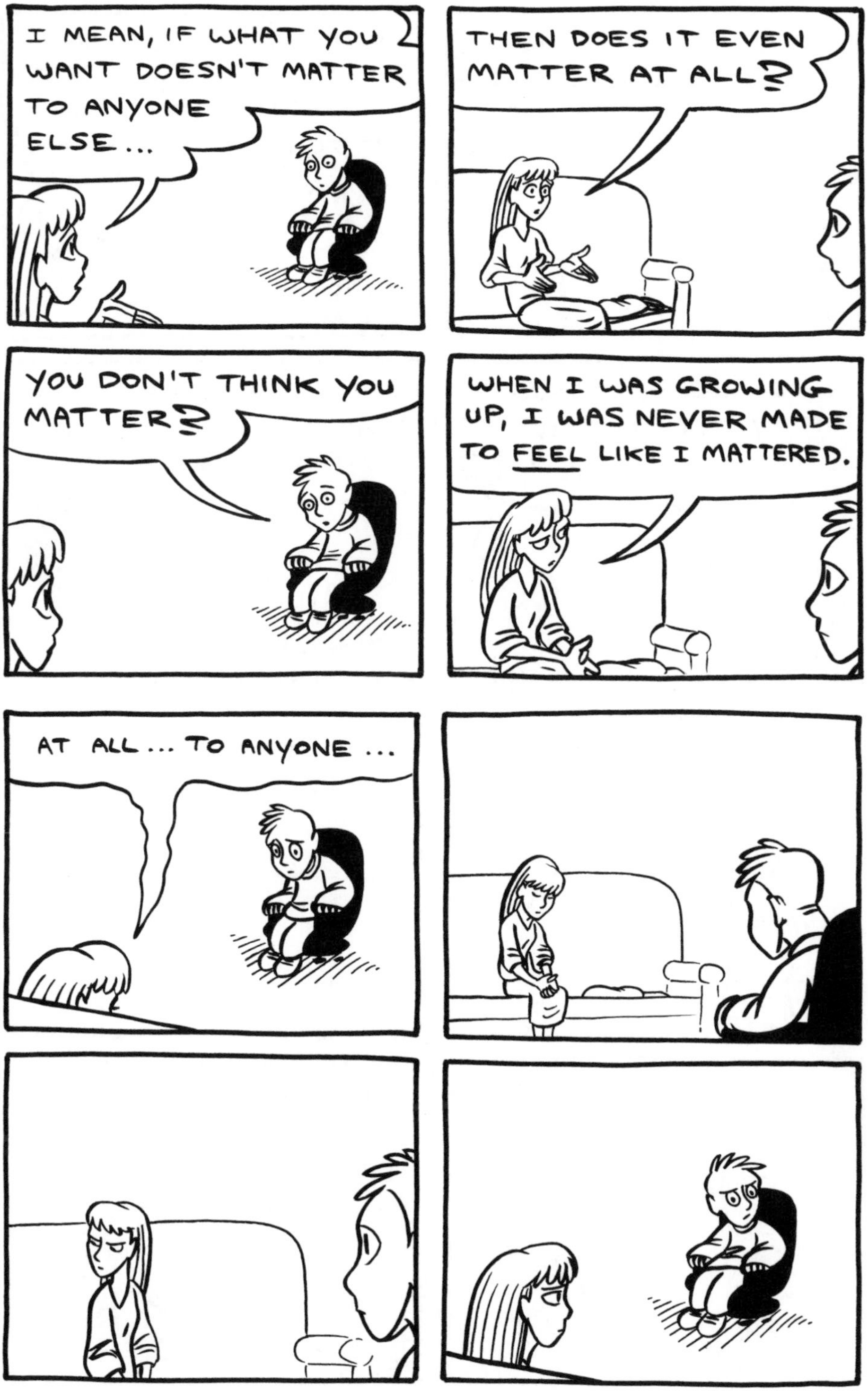
I MEAN, IF WHAT YOU WANT DOESN'T MATTER TO ANYONE ELSE...
THEN DOES IT EVEN MATTER AT ALL?
YOU DON'T THINK YOU MATTER?
WHEN I WAS GROWING UP, I WAS NEVER MADE TO FEEL LIKE I MATTERED.
AT ALL... TO ANYONE...

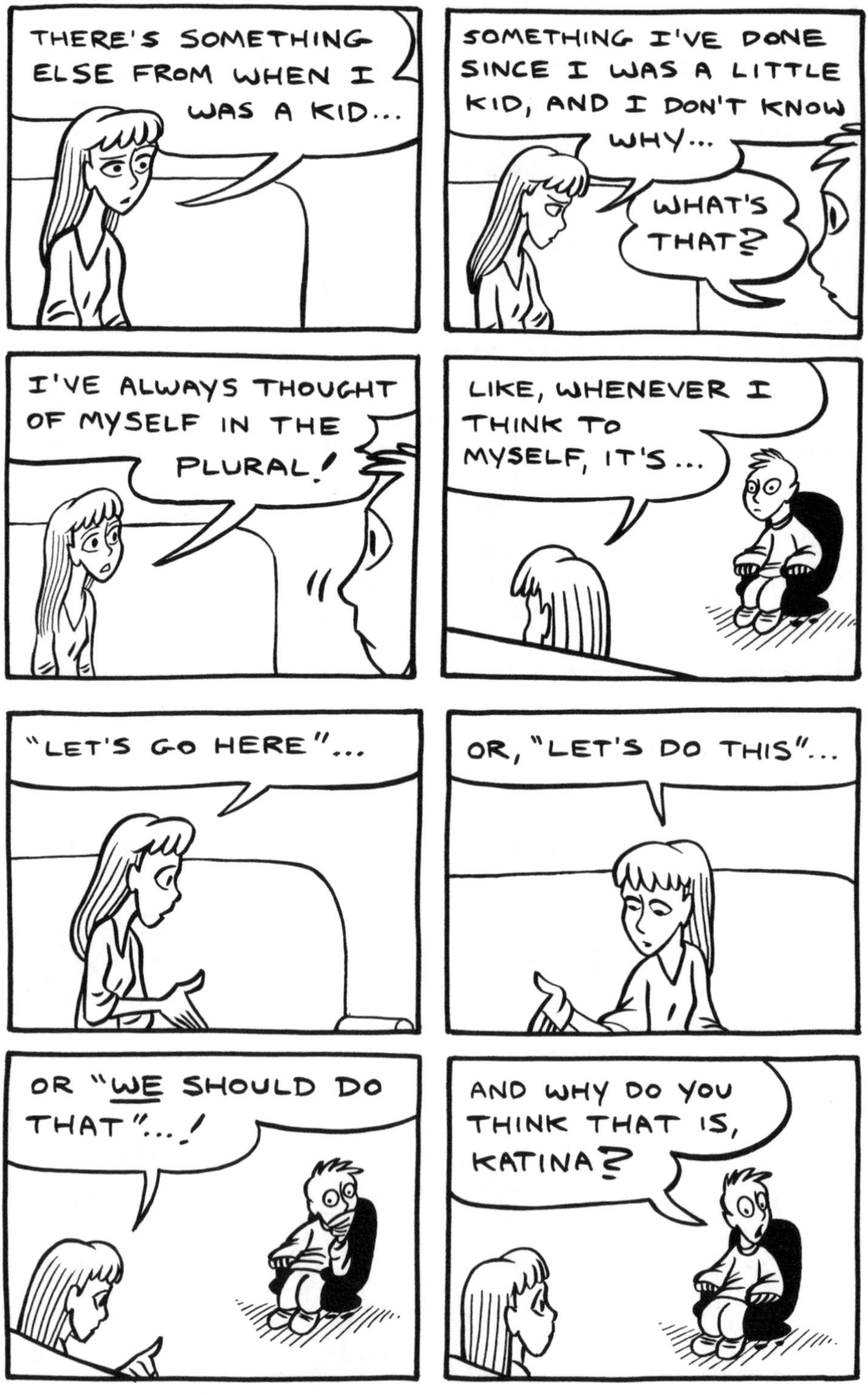
THERE'S SOMETHING ELSE FROM WHEN I WAS A KID...
SOMETHING I'VE DONE SINCE I WAS A LITTLE KID, AND I DON'T KNOW WHY...
WHAT'S THAT?
I'VE ALWAYS THOUGHT OF MYSELF IN THE PLURAL!
LIKE, WHENEVER I THINK TO MYSELF, IT'S...
"LET'S GO HERE"...
OR, "LET'S DO THIS"...
OR "WE SHOULD DO THAT"...!
AND WHY DO YOU THINK THAT IS, KATINA?

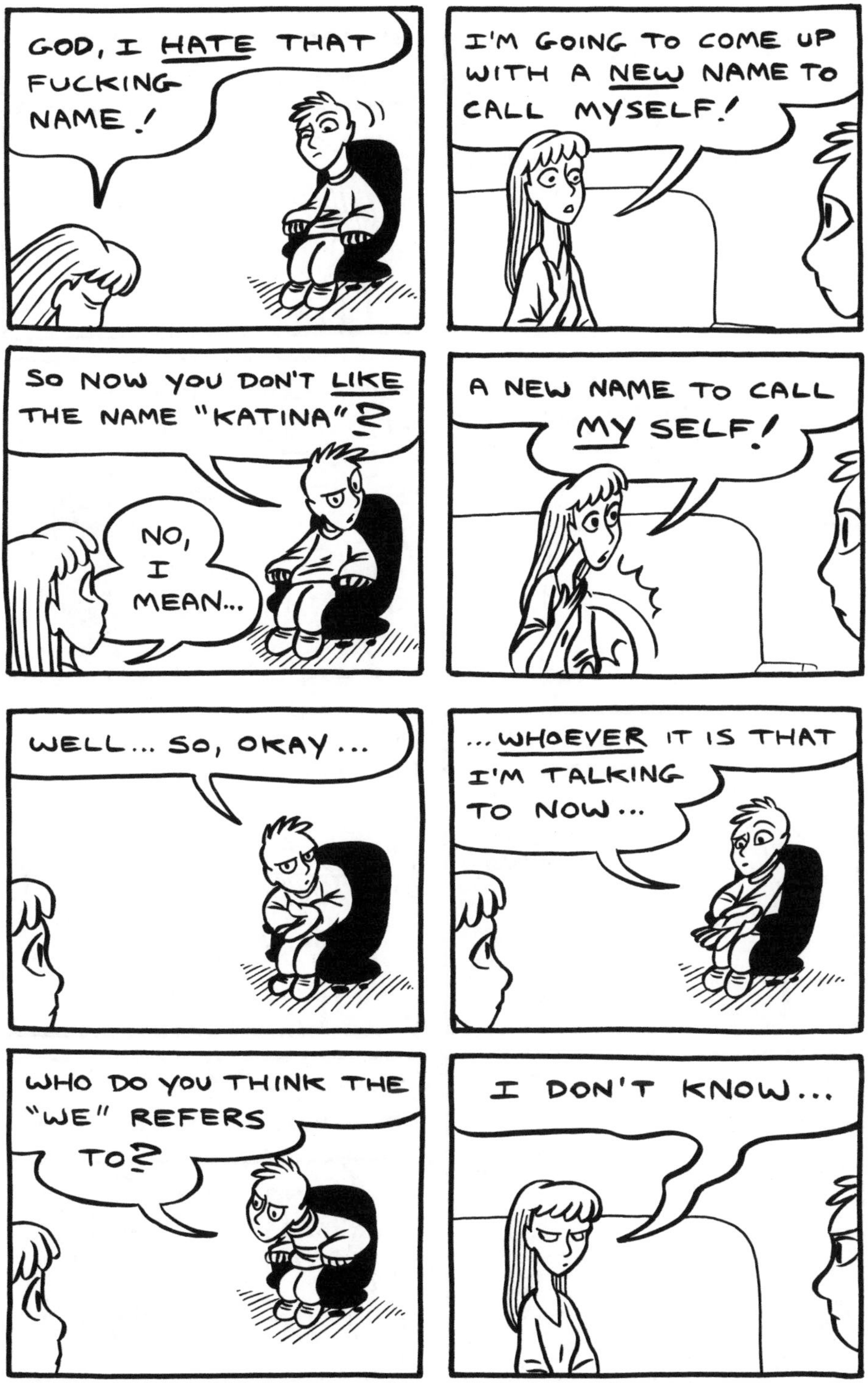
GOD, I HATE THAT FUCKING NAME!
I'M GOING TO COME UP WITH A NEW NAME TO CALL MYSELF!
SO NOW YOU DON'T LIKE THE NAME "KATINA"?
NO, I MEAN...
A NEW NAME TO CALL MY SELF!
WELL... SO, OKAY...
...WHOEVER IT IS THAT I'M TALKING TO NOW...
WHO DO YOU THINK THE "WE" REFERS TO?
I DON'T KNOW...

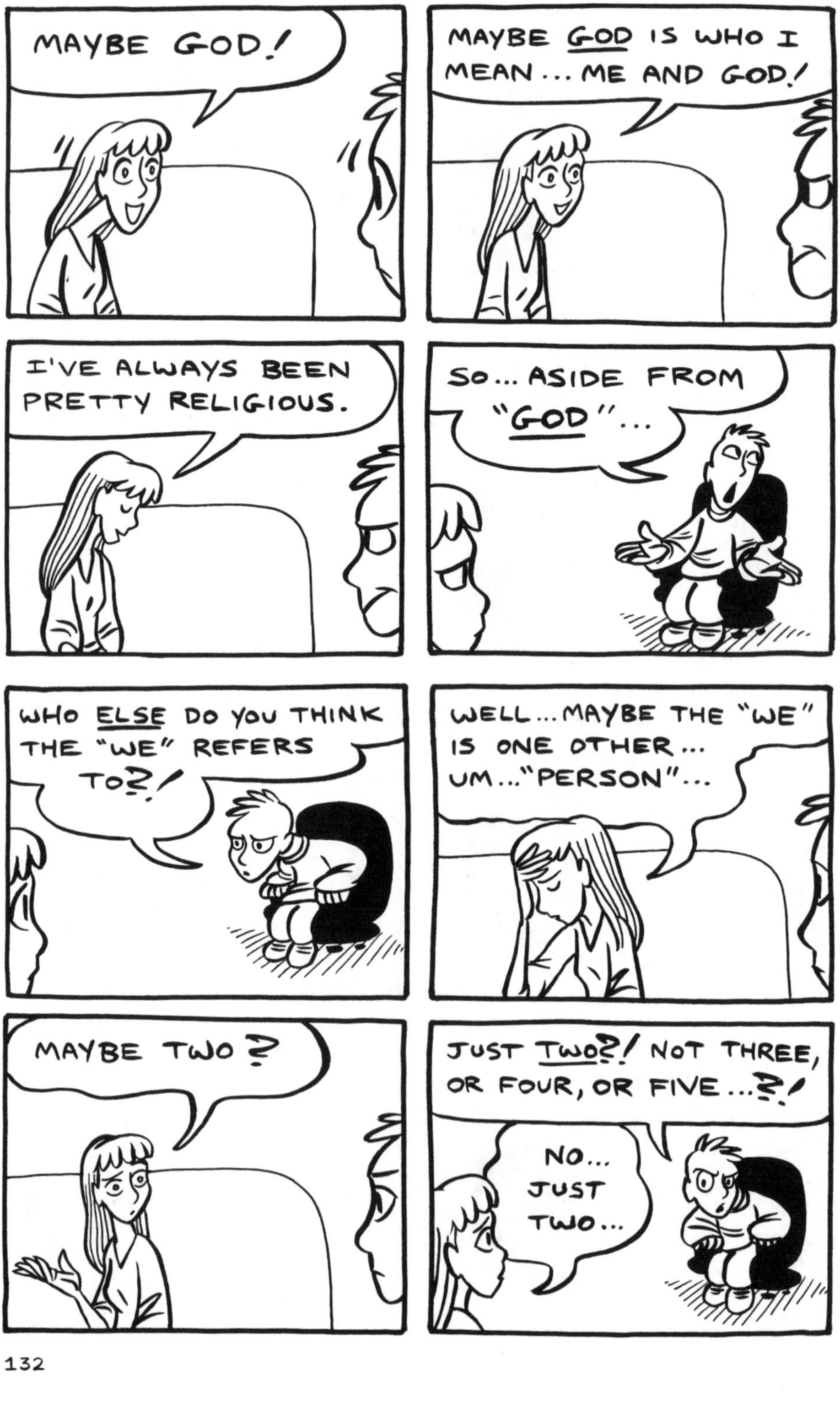
MAYBE GOD!
MAYBE GOD IS WHO I MEAN... ME AND GOD!
I'VE ALWAYS BEEN PRETTY RELIGIOUS.
SO... ASIDE FROM "GOD"...
WHO ELSE DO YOU THINK THE "WE" REFERS TO?!
WELL... MAYBE THE "WE" IS ONE OTHER... UM..."PERSON"...
MAYBE TWO?
JUST TWO?! NOT THREE, OR FOUR, OR FIVE...?!
NO... JUST TWO...

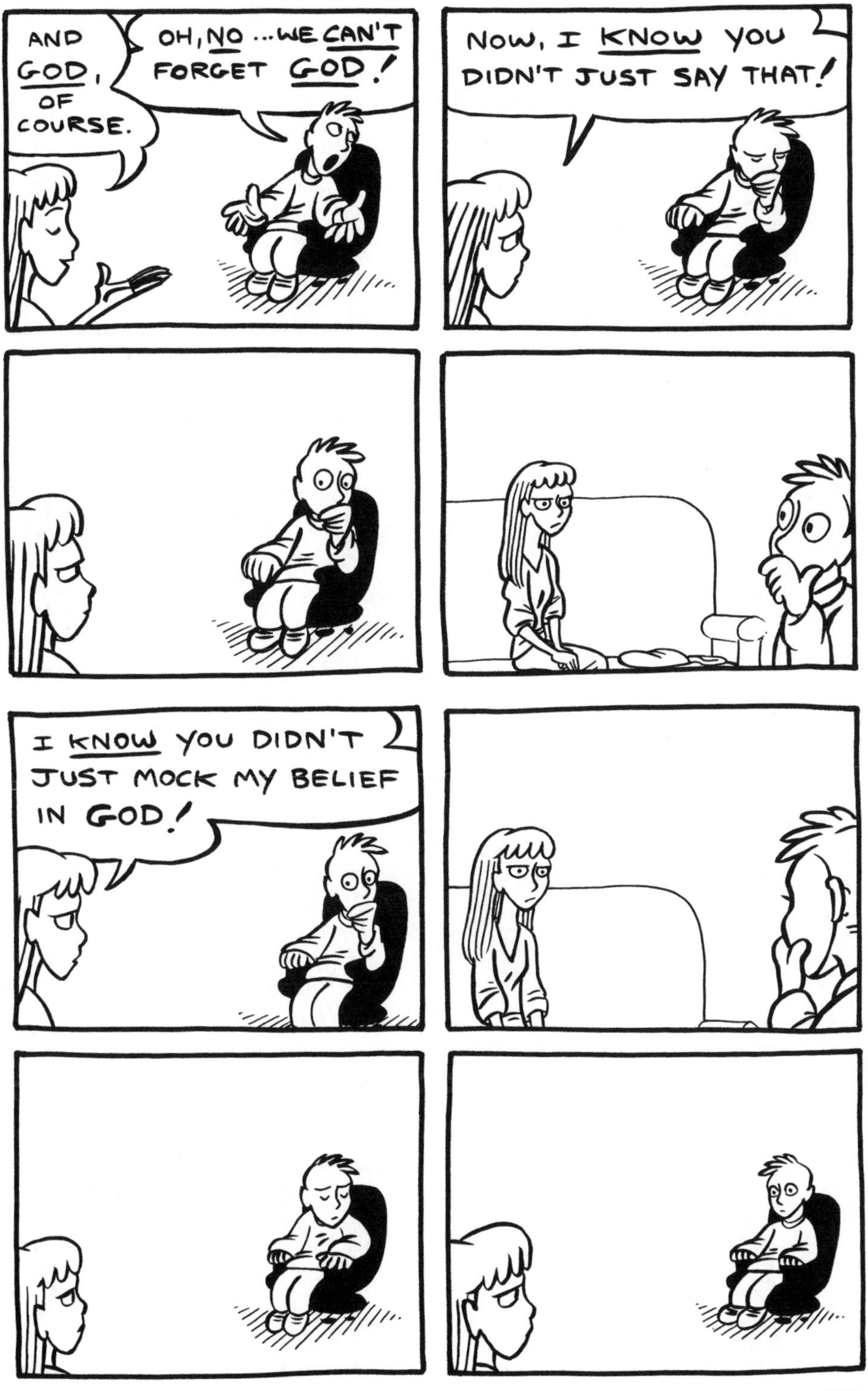
AND GOD, OF COURSE.
OH, NO ...WE CAN'T FORGET GOD!
NOW, I KNOW YOU DIDN'T JUST SAY THAT!
I KNOW YOU DIDN'T JUST MOCK MY BELIEF IN GOD!

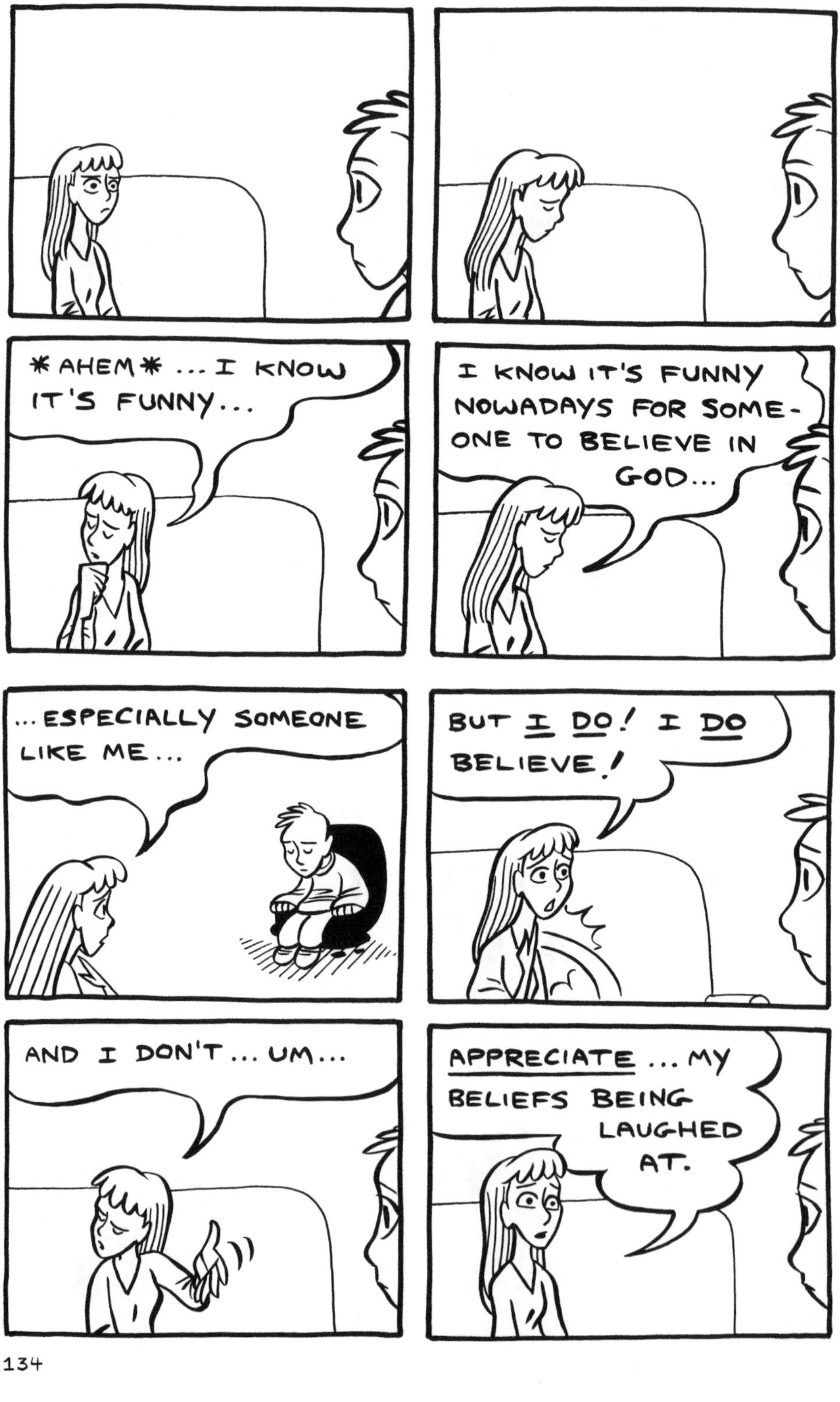
AHEM ... I KNOW IT'S FUNNY...
I KNOW IT'S FUNNY NOWADAYS FOR SOME-ONE TO BELIEVE IN GOD...
...ESPECIALLY SOMEONE LIKE ME...
BUT I DO! I DO BELIEVE!
AND I DON'T ... UM...
APPRECIATE ... MY BELIEFS BEING LAUGHED AT.

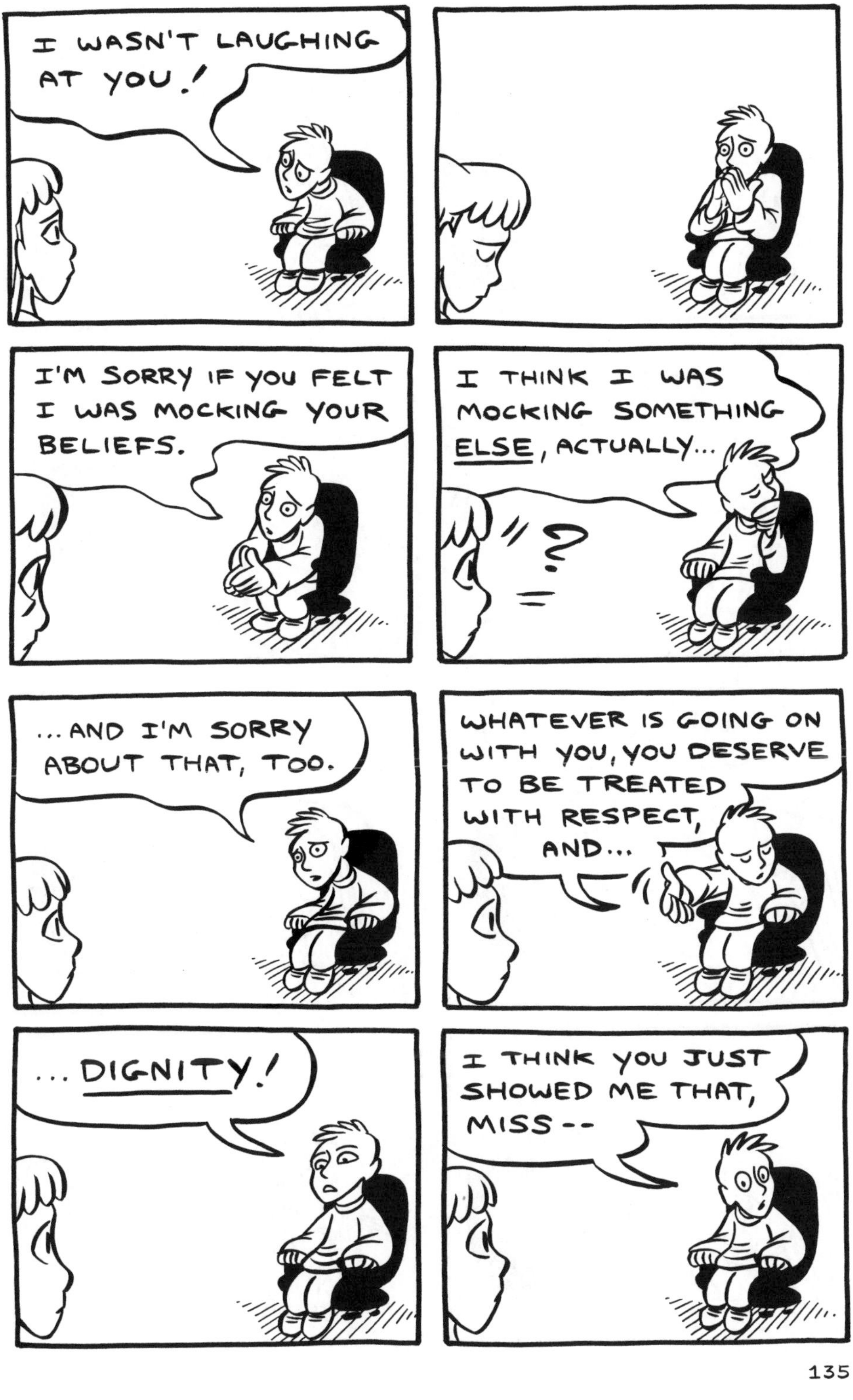
I WASN'T LAUGHING AT YOU!
I'M SORRY IF YOU FELT I WAS MOCKING YOUR BELIEFS.
I THINK I WAS MOCKING SOMETHING ELSE, ACTUALLY...
?
...AND I'M SORRY ABOUT THAT, TOO.
WHATEVER IS GOING ON WITH YOU, YOU DESERVE TO BE TREATED WITH RESPECT, AND...
...DIGNITY!
I THINK YOU JUST SHOWED ME THAT, MISS--

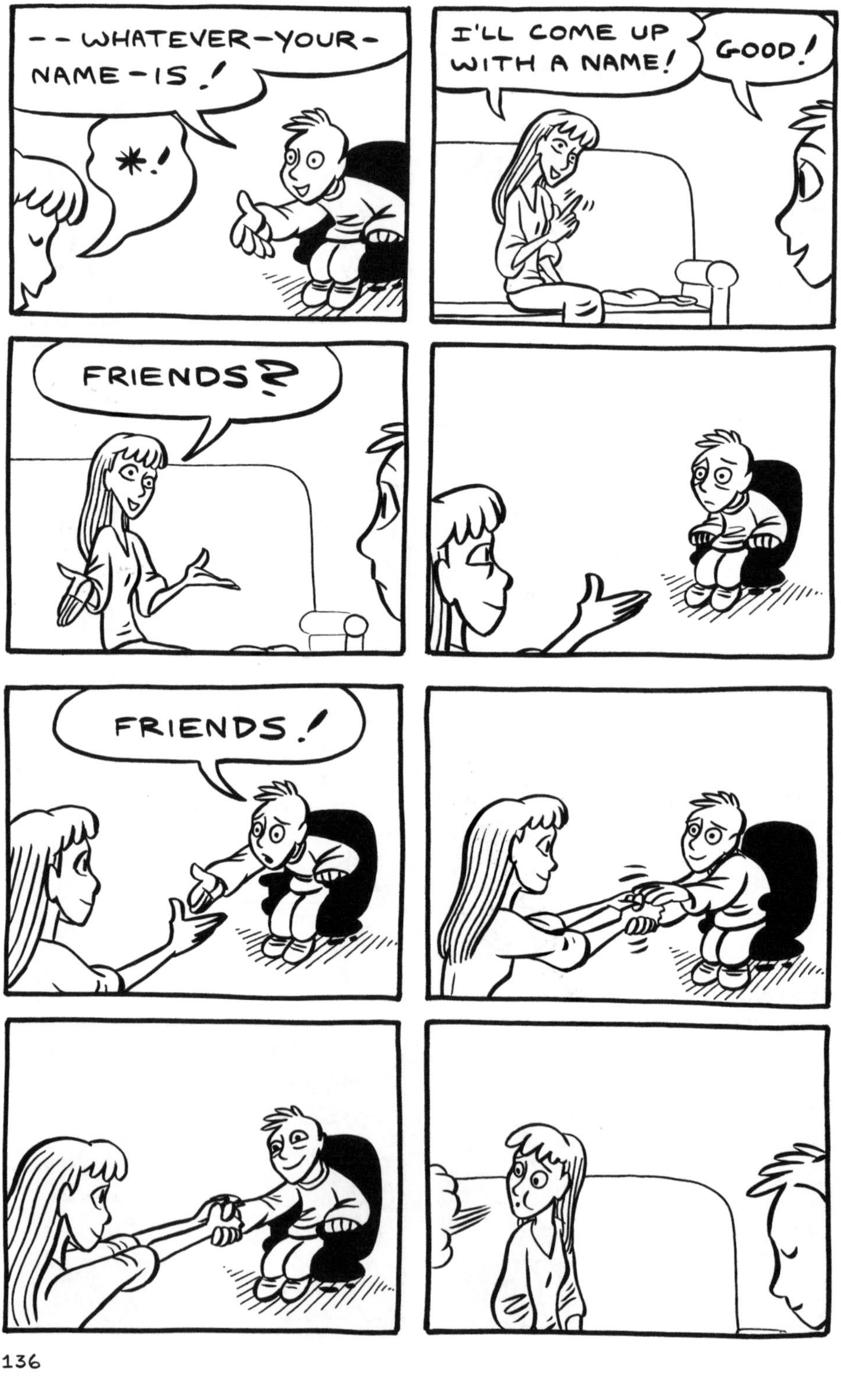
--WHATEVER-YOUR-NAME-IS!
*!
I'LL COME UP WITH A NAME!
GOOD!
FRIENDS?
FRIENDS!

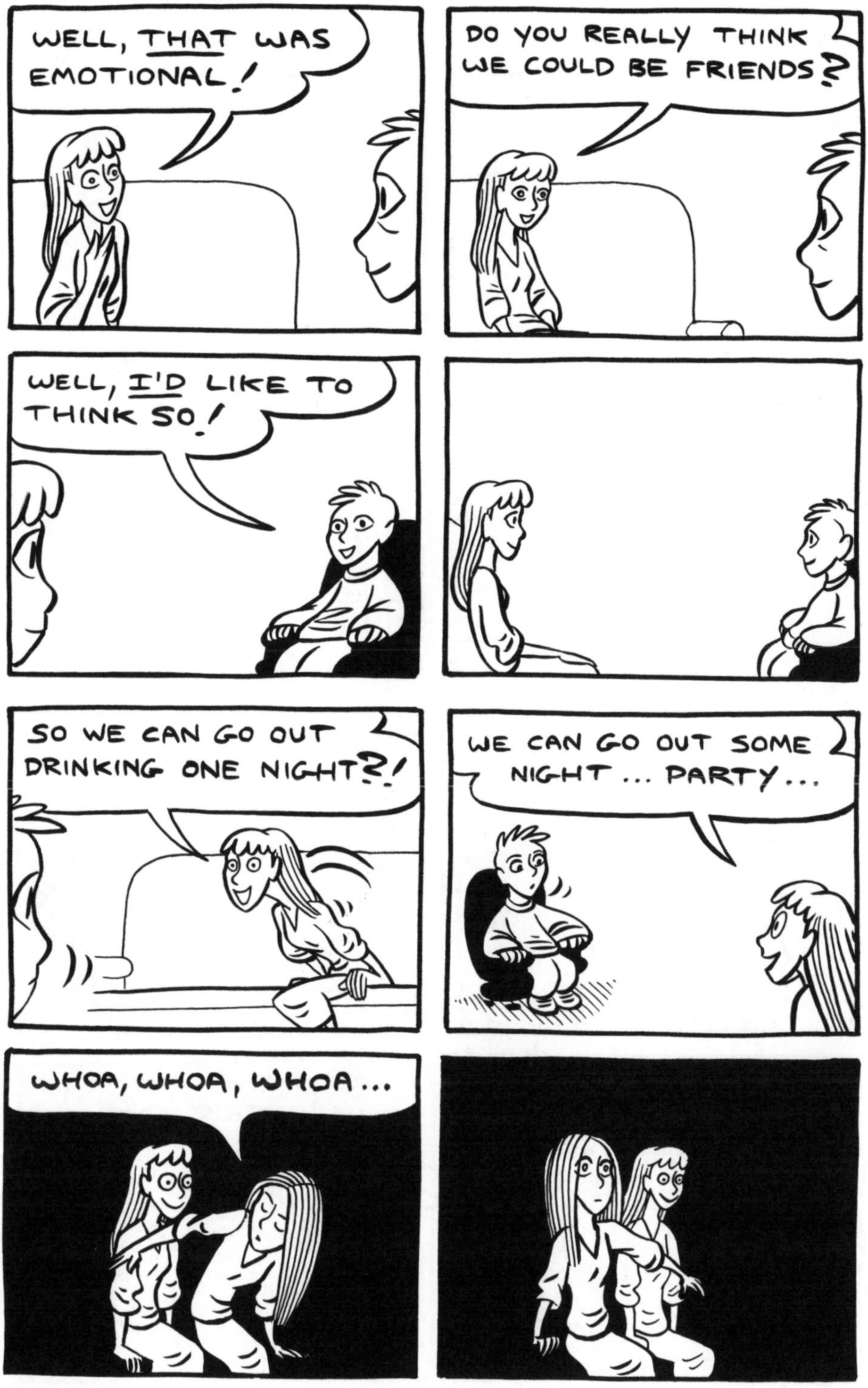
WELL, THAT WAS EMOTIONAL!
DO YOU REALLY THINK WE COULD BE FRIENDS?
WELL, I'D LIKE TO THINK SO!
SO WE CAN GO OUT DRINKING ONE NIGHT?!
WE CAN GO OUT SOME NIGHT ... PARTY ...
WHOA, WHOA, WHOA ...

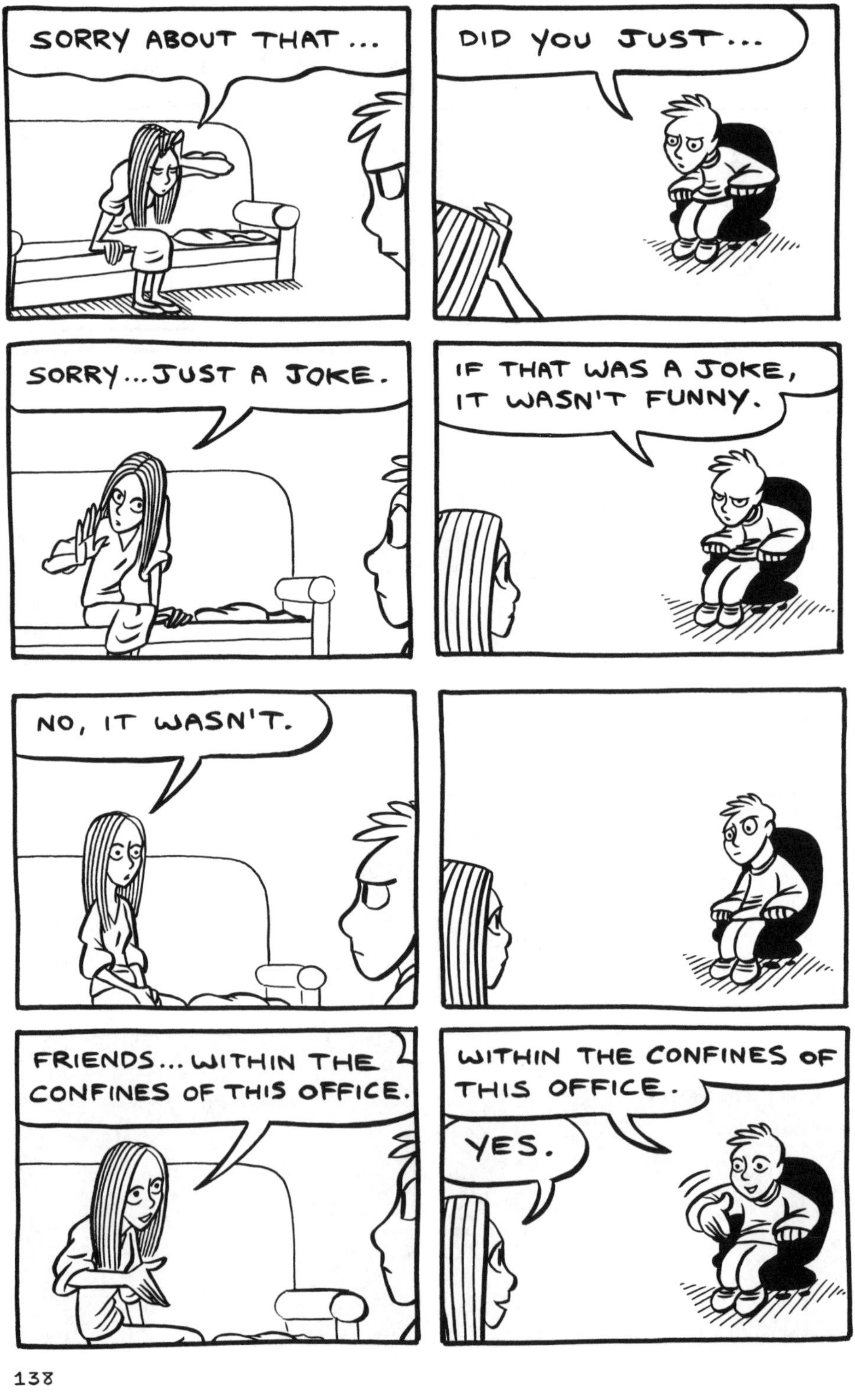
SORRY ABOUT THAT...
DID YOU JUST...
SORRY...JUST A JOKE.
IF THAT WAS A JOKE, IT WASN'T FUNNY.
NO, IT WASN'T.
FRIENDS... WITHIN THE CONFINES OF THIS OFFICE.
WITHIN THE CONFINES OF THIS OFFICE.
YES.

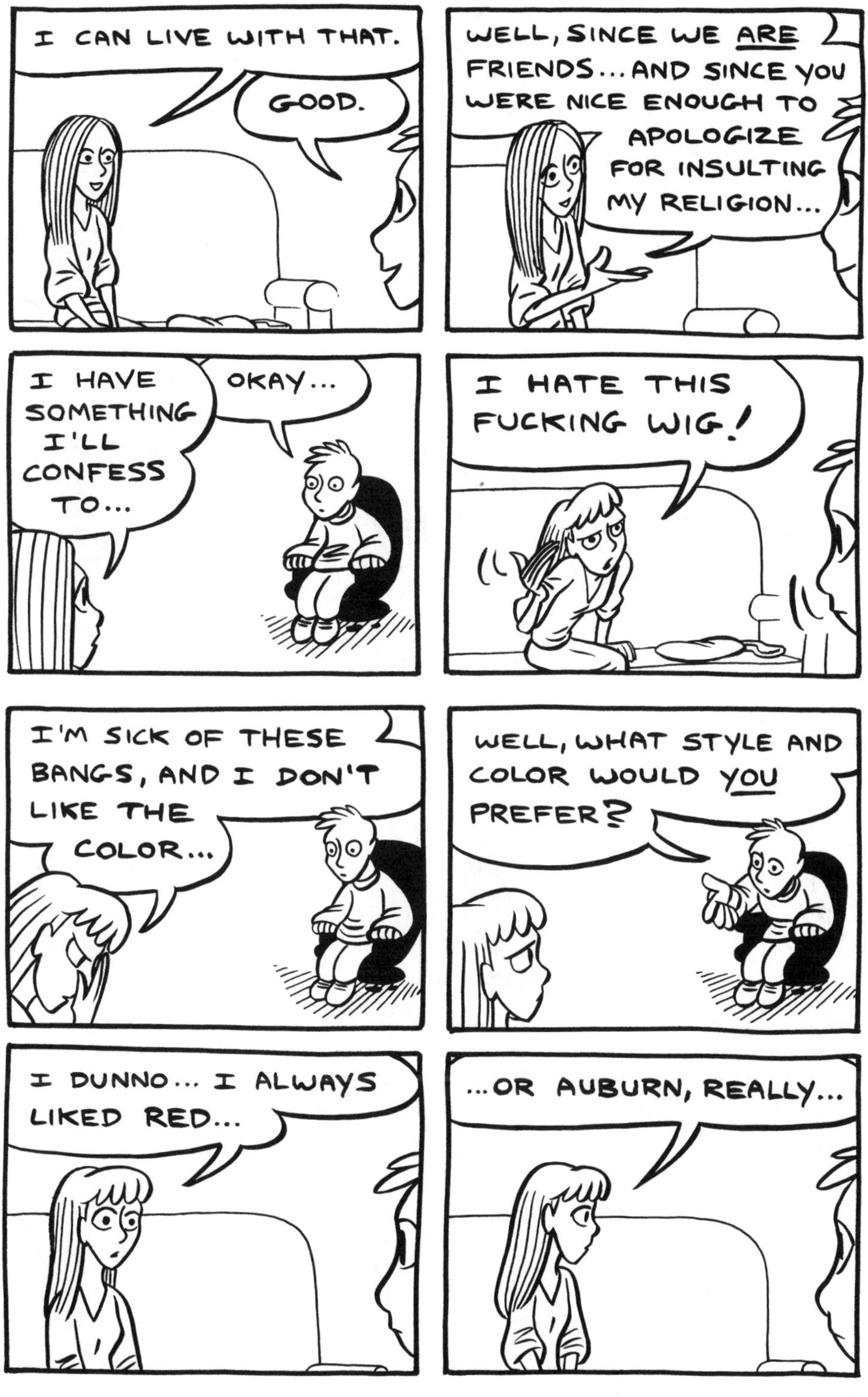
I CAN LIVE WITH THAT.
GOOD.
WELL, SINCE WE ARE FRIENDS... AND SINCE YOU WERE NICE ENOUGH TO APOLOGIZE FOR INSULTING MY RELIGION...
I HAVE SOMETHING I'LL CONFESS TO...
OKAY...
I HATE THIS FUCKING WIG!
I'M SICK OF THESE BANGS, AND I DON'T LIKE THE COLOR...
WELL, WHAT STYLE AND COLOR WOULD YOU PREFER?
I DUNNO... I ALWAYS LIKED RED...
...OR AUBURN, REALLY...

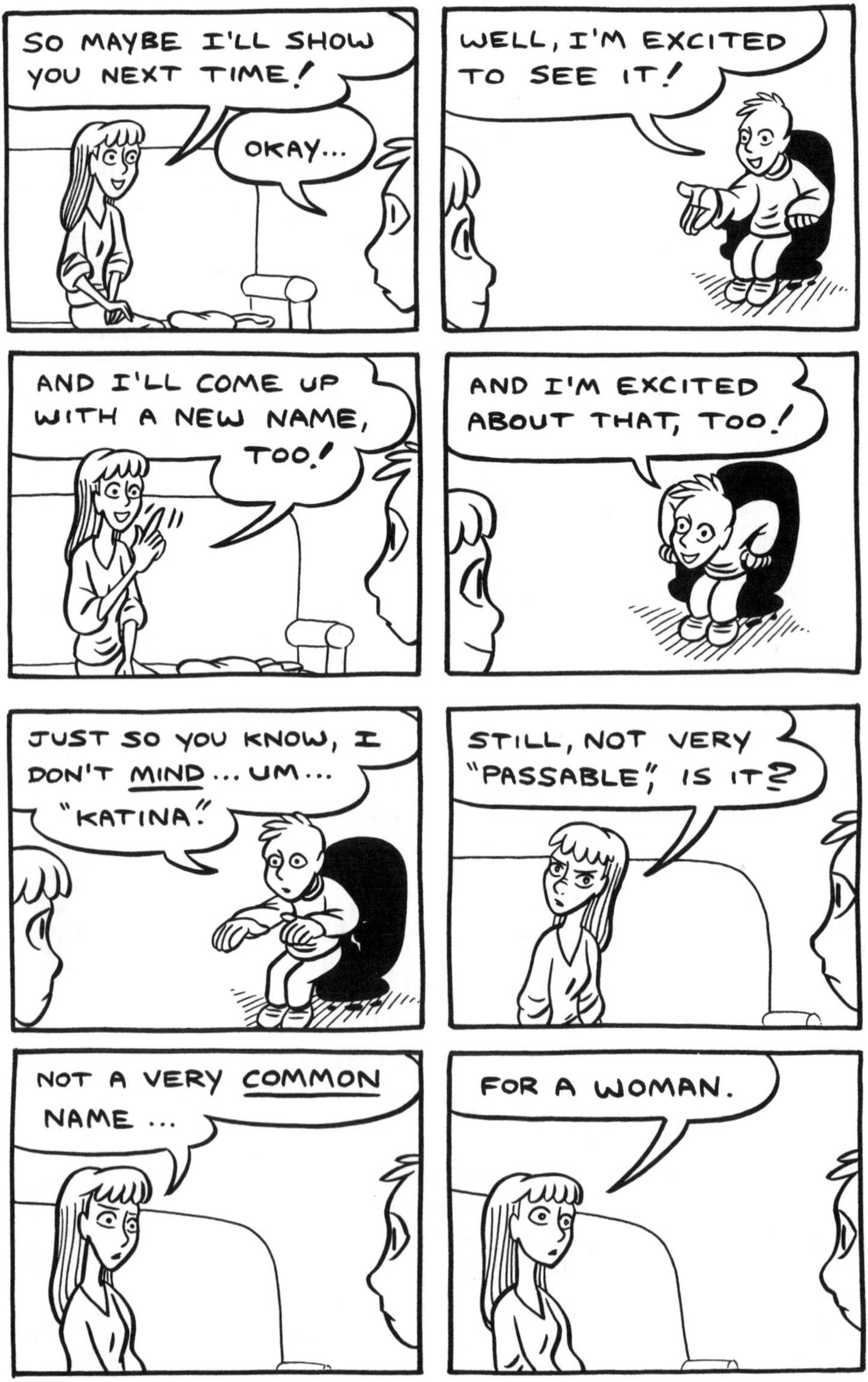
SO MAYBE I'LL SHOW YOU NEXT TIME!
OKAY...
WELL, I'M EXCITED TO SEE IT!
AND I'LL COME UP WITH A NEW NAME, TOO!
AND I'M EXCITED ABOUT THAT, TOO!
JUST SO YOU KNOW, I DON'T MIND... UM... "KATINA."
STILL, NOT VERY "PASSABLE," IS IT?
NOT A VERY COMMON NAME...
FOR A WOMAN.

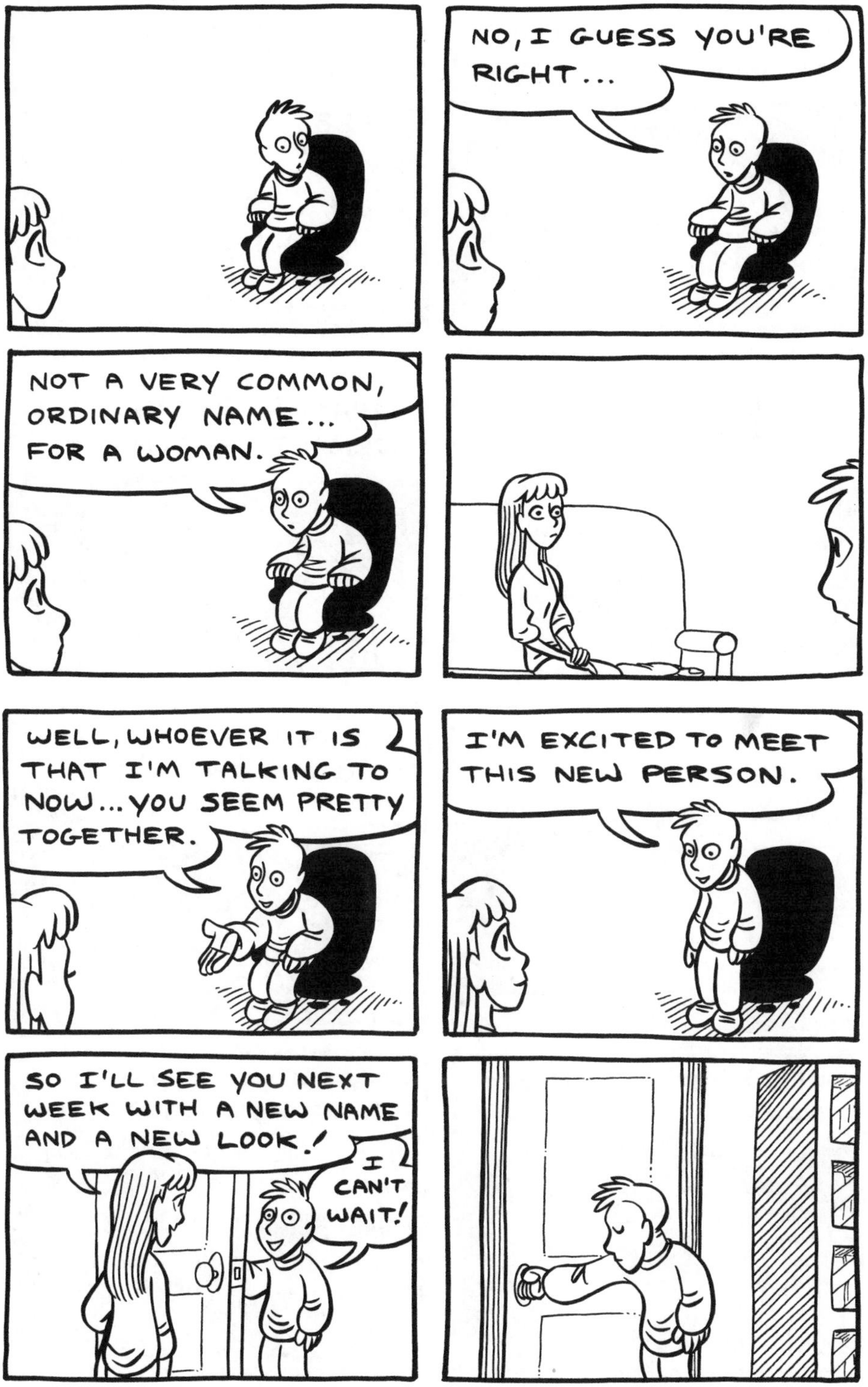
NO, I GUESS YOU'RE RIGHT...
NOT A VERY COMMON, ORDINARY NAME... FOR A WOMAN.
WELL, WHOEVER IT IS THAT I'M TALKING TO NOW... YOU SEEM PRETTY TOGETHER.
I'M EXCITED TO MEET THIS NEW PERSON.
SO I'LL SEE YOU NEXT WEEK WITH A NEW NAME AND A NEW LOOK!
I CAN'T WAIT!

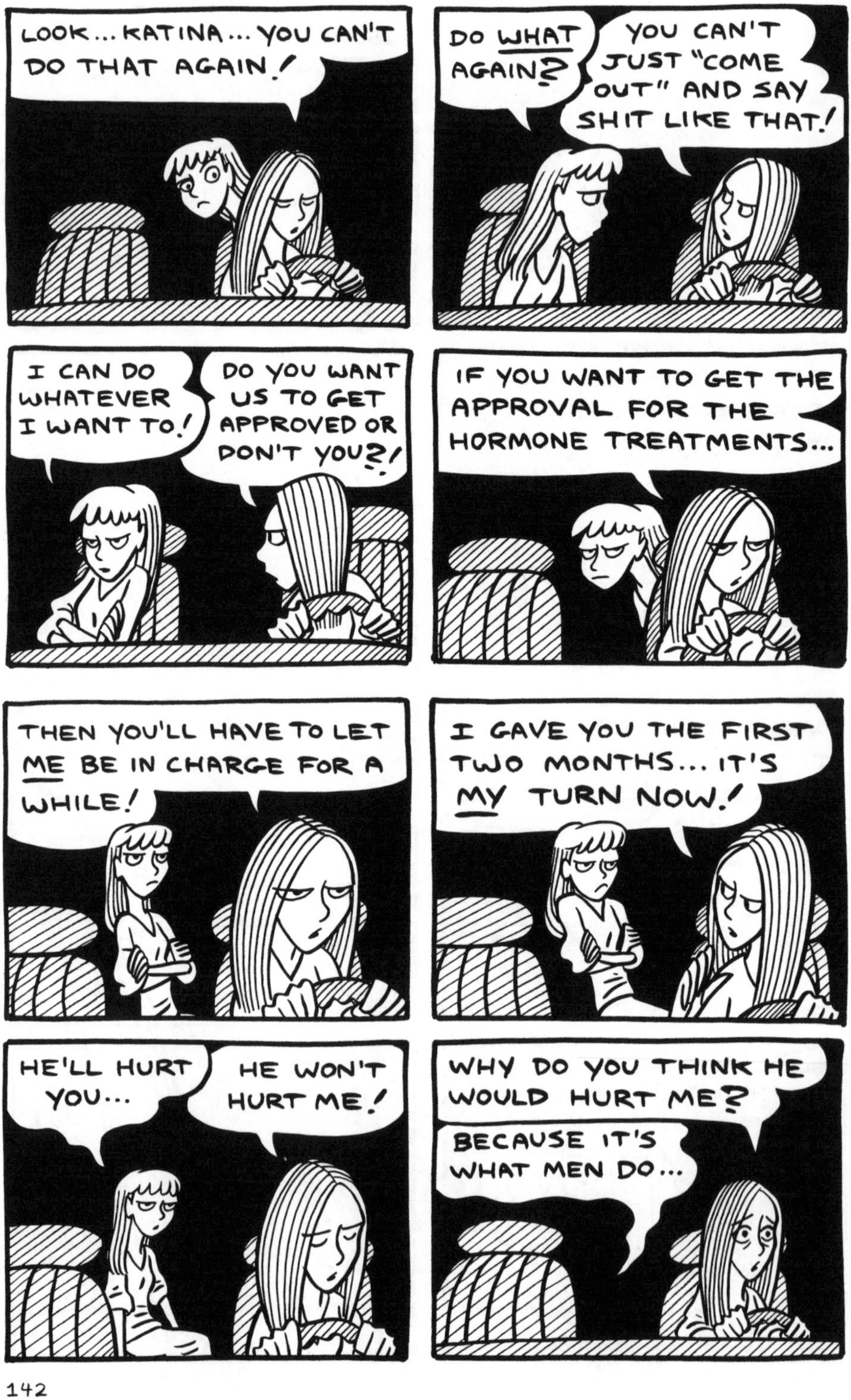
LOOK... KATINA... YOU CAN'T DO THAT AGAIN!
DO WHAT AGAIN?
YOU CAN'T JUST "COME OUT" AND SAY SHIT LIKE THAT!
I CAN DO WHATEVER I WANT TO!
DO YOU WANT US TO GET APPROVED OR DON'T YOU?!
IF YOU WANT TO GET THE APPROVAL FOR THE HORMONE TREATMENTS...
THEN YOU'LL HAVE TO LET ME BE IN CHARGE FOR A WHILE!
I GAVE YOU THE FIRST TWO MONTHS... IT'S MY TURN NOW!
HE'LL HURT YOU...
HE WON'T HURT ME!
WHY DO YOU THINK HE WOULD HURT ME?
BECAUSE IT'S WHAT MEN DO...

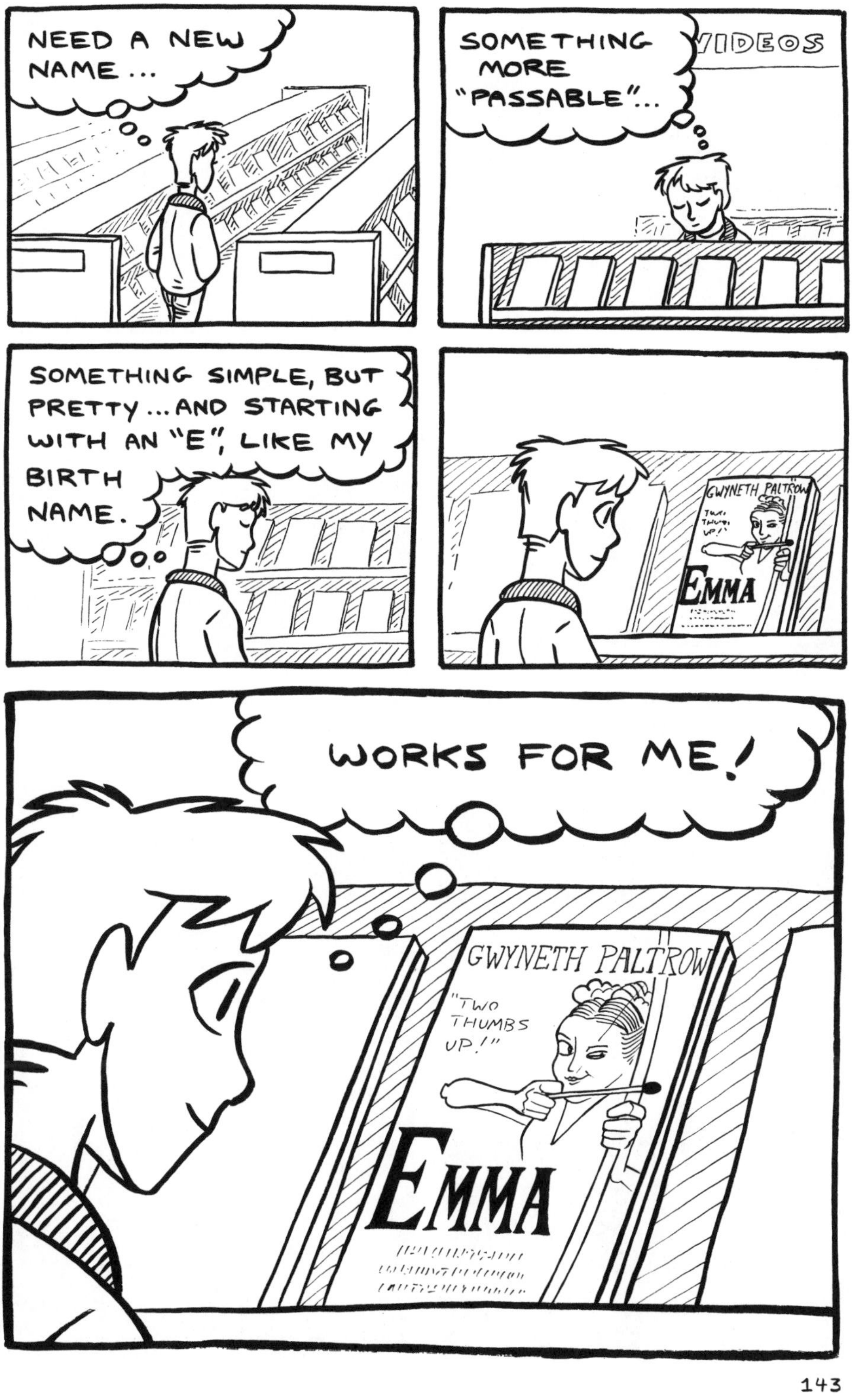
NEED A NEW NAME...
SOMETHING MORE "PASSABLE"...
VIDEOS
SOMETHING SIMPLE, BUT PRETTY...AND STARTING WITH AN "E", LIKE MY BIRTH NAME.
GWYNETH PALTROW
EMMA
WORKS FOR ME!
GWYNETH PALTROW
"TWO THUMBS UP!"
EMMA

EMMA

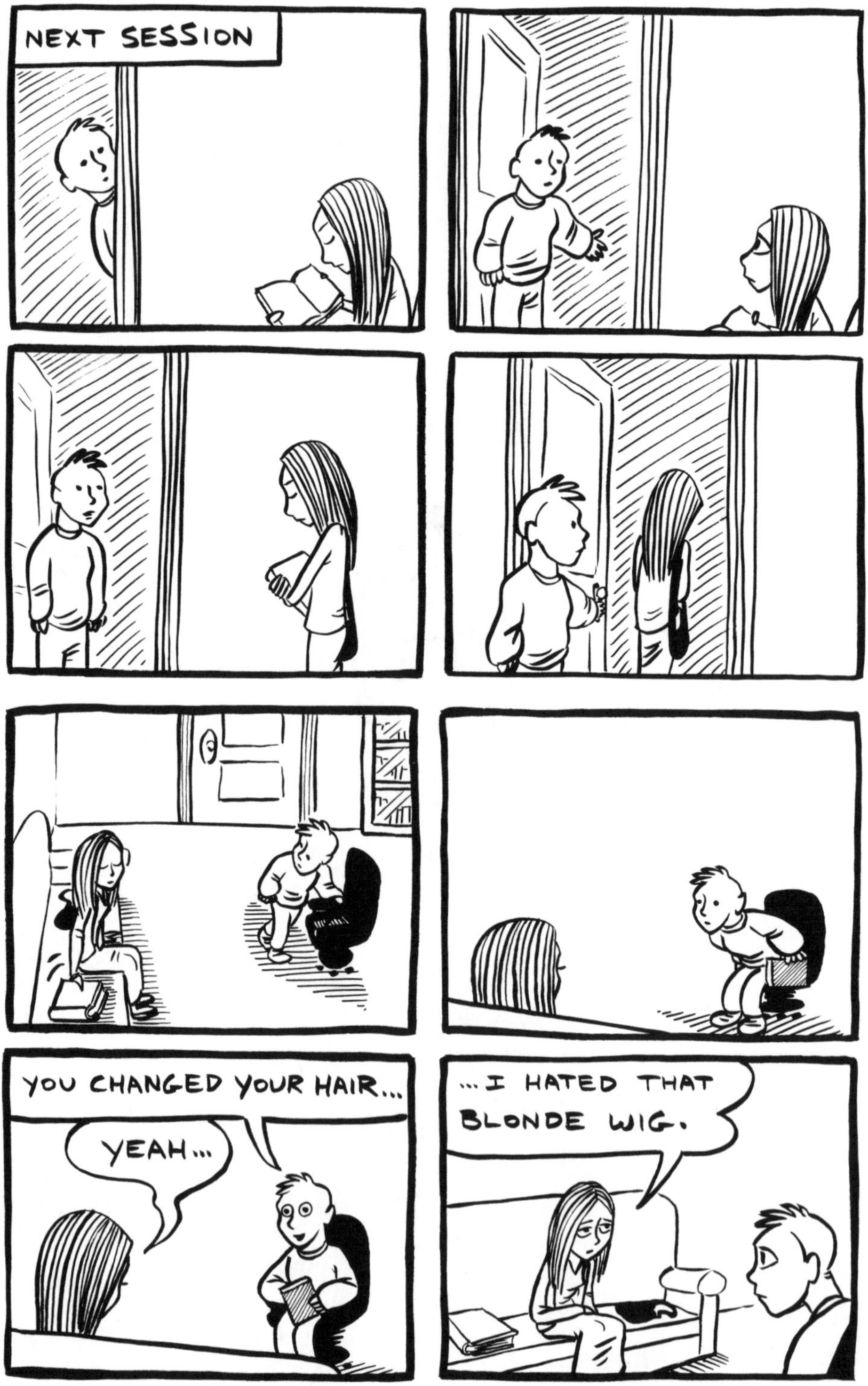
NEXT SESSION
YOU CHANGED YOUR HAIR...
YEAH...
...I HATED THAT BLONDE WIG.

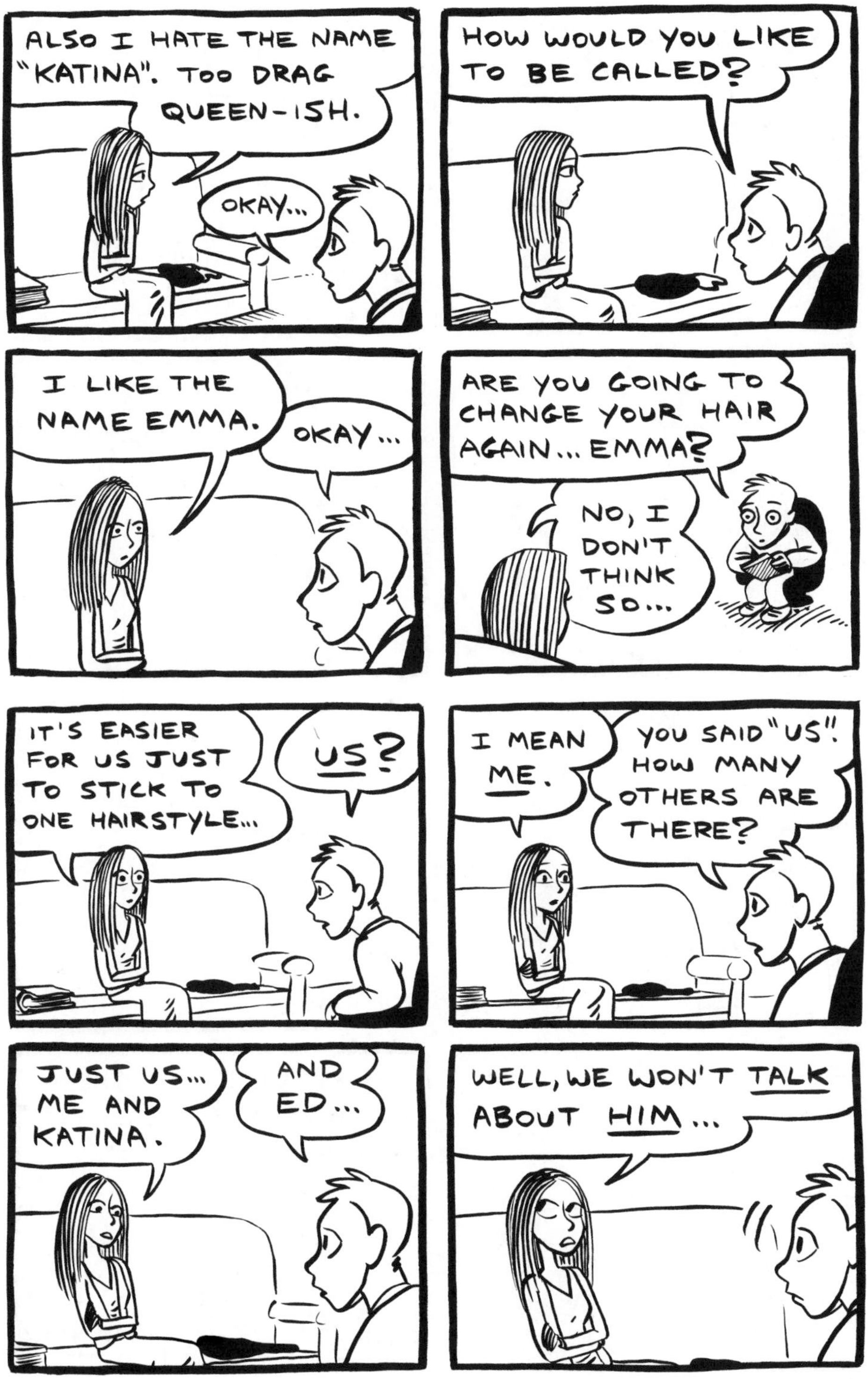
ALSO I HATE THE NAME "KATINA". TOO DRAG QUEEN-ISH.
OKAY...
HOW WOULD YOU LIKE TO BE CALLED?
I LIKE THE NAME EMMA.
OKAY...
ARE YOU GOING TO CHANGE YOUR HAIR AGAIN... EMMA?
NO, I DON'T THINK SO...
IT'S EASIER FOR US JUST TO STICK TO ONE HAIRSTYLE...
US?
I MEAN ME.
YOU SAID "US". HOW MANY OTHERS ARE THERE?
JUST US... ME AND KATINA.
AND ED...
WELL, WE WON'T TALK ABOUT HIM...

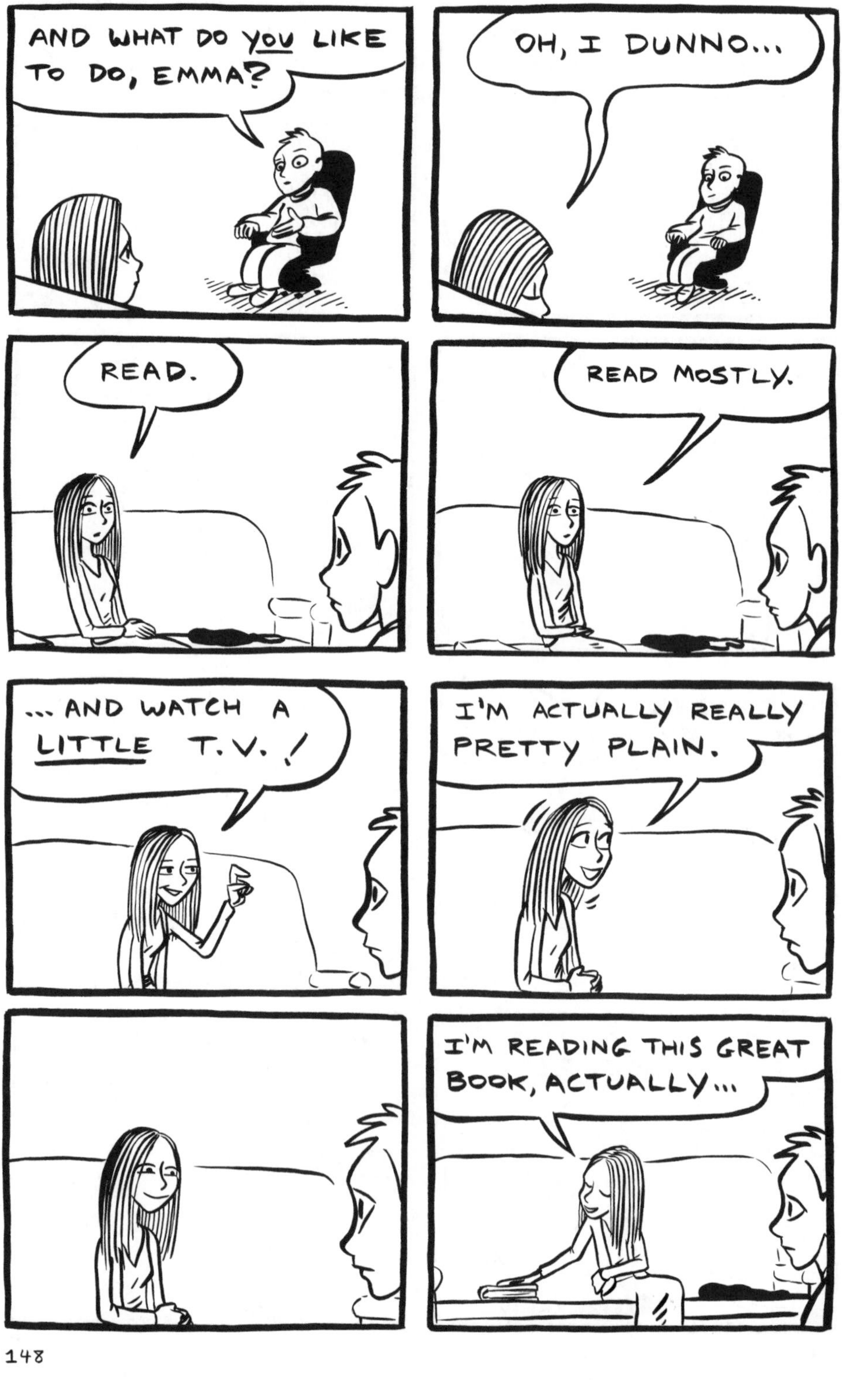
AND WHAT DO YOU LIKE TO DO, EMMA?
OH, I DUNNO...
READ.
READ MOSTLY.
...AND WATCH A LITTLE T.V. !
I'M ACTUALLY REALLY PRETTY PLAIN.
I'M READING THIS GREAT BOOK, ACTUALLY...

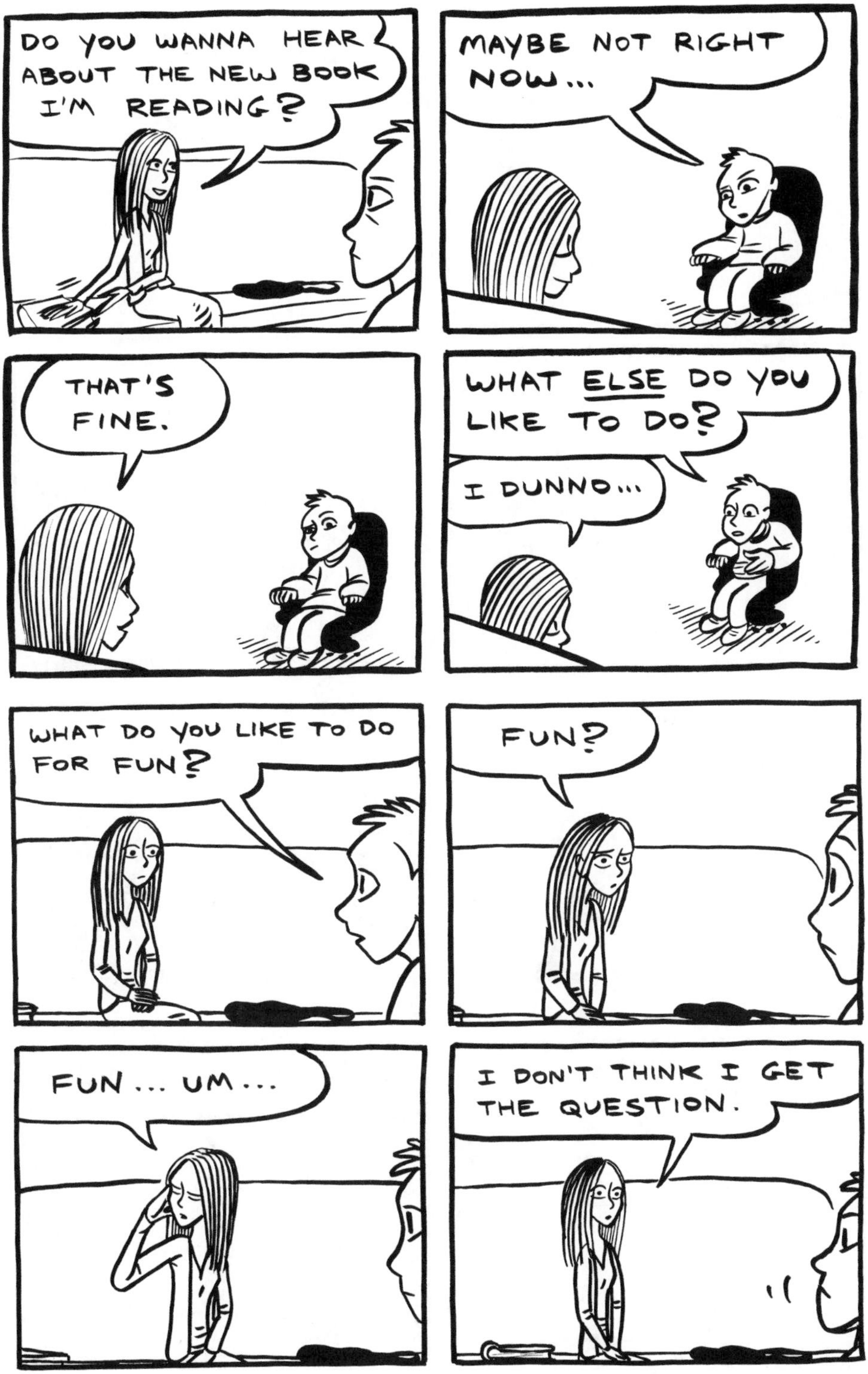
DO YOU WANNA HEAR ABOUT THE NEW BOOK I'M READING?
MAYBE NOT RIGHT NOW...
THAT'S FINE.
WHAT ELSE DO YOU LIKE TO DO?
I DUNNO...
WHAT DO YOU LIKE TO DO FOR FUN?
FUN?
FUN... UM...
I DON'T THINK I GET THE QUESTION.

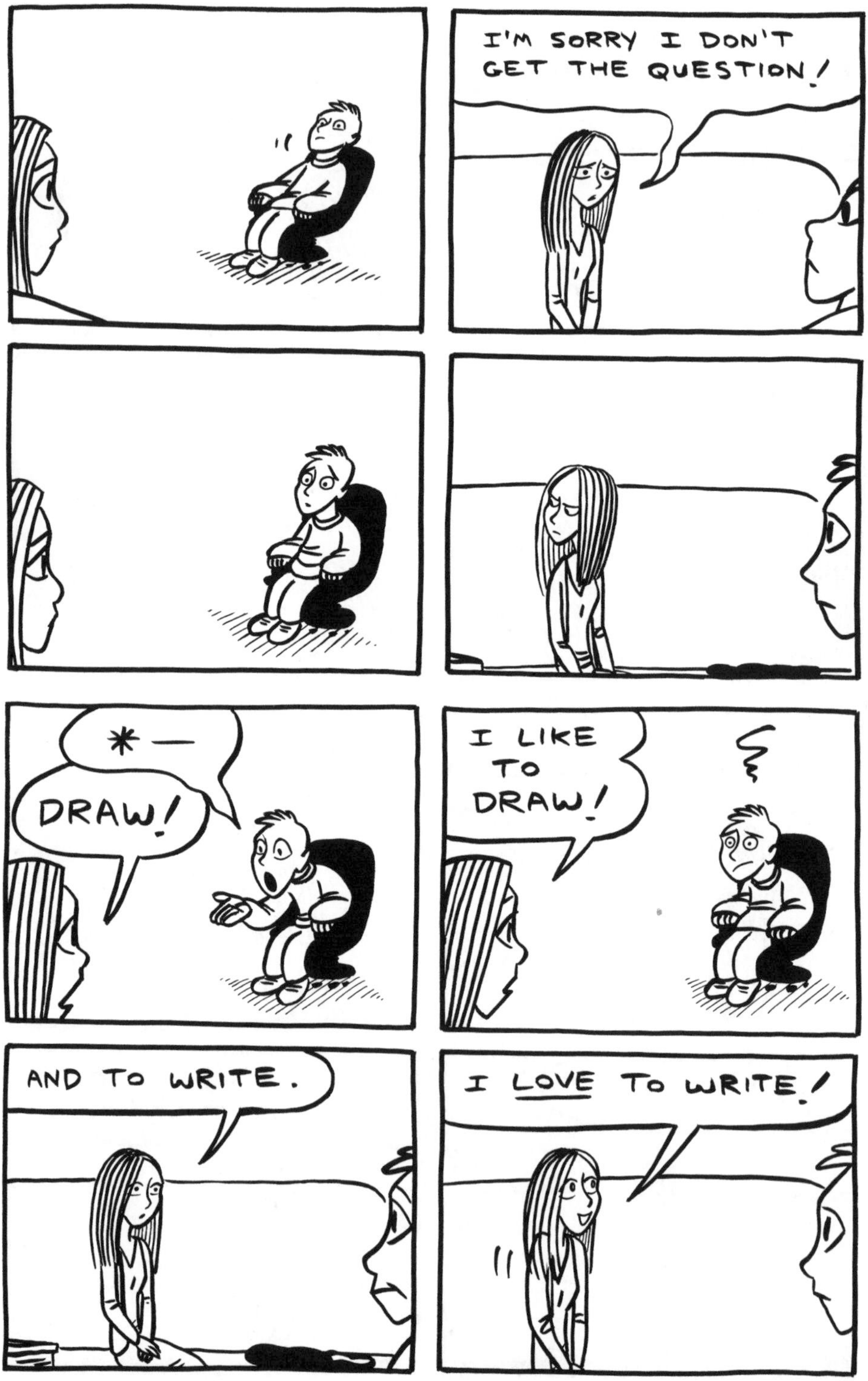
I'M SORRY I DON'T GET THE QUESTION!
*—
DRAW!
I LIKE TO DRAW!
AND TO WRITE.
I LOVE TO WRITE!

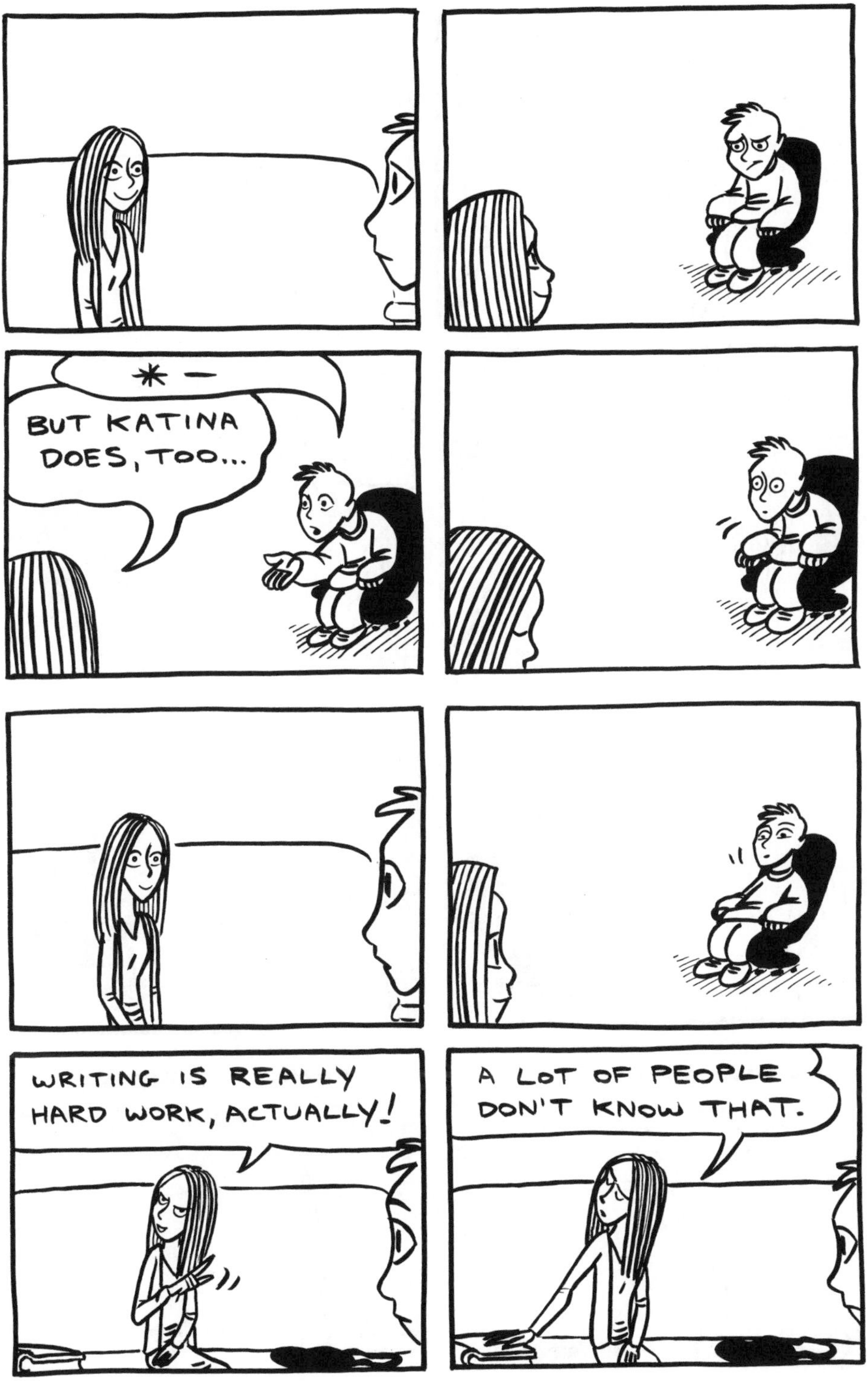

* —
BUT KATINA DOES, TOO...
WRITING IS REALLY HARD WORK, ACTUALLY!
A LOT OF PEOPLE DON'T KNOW THAT.

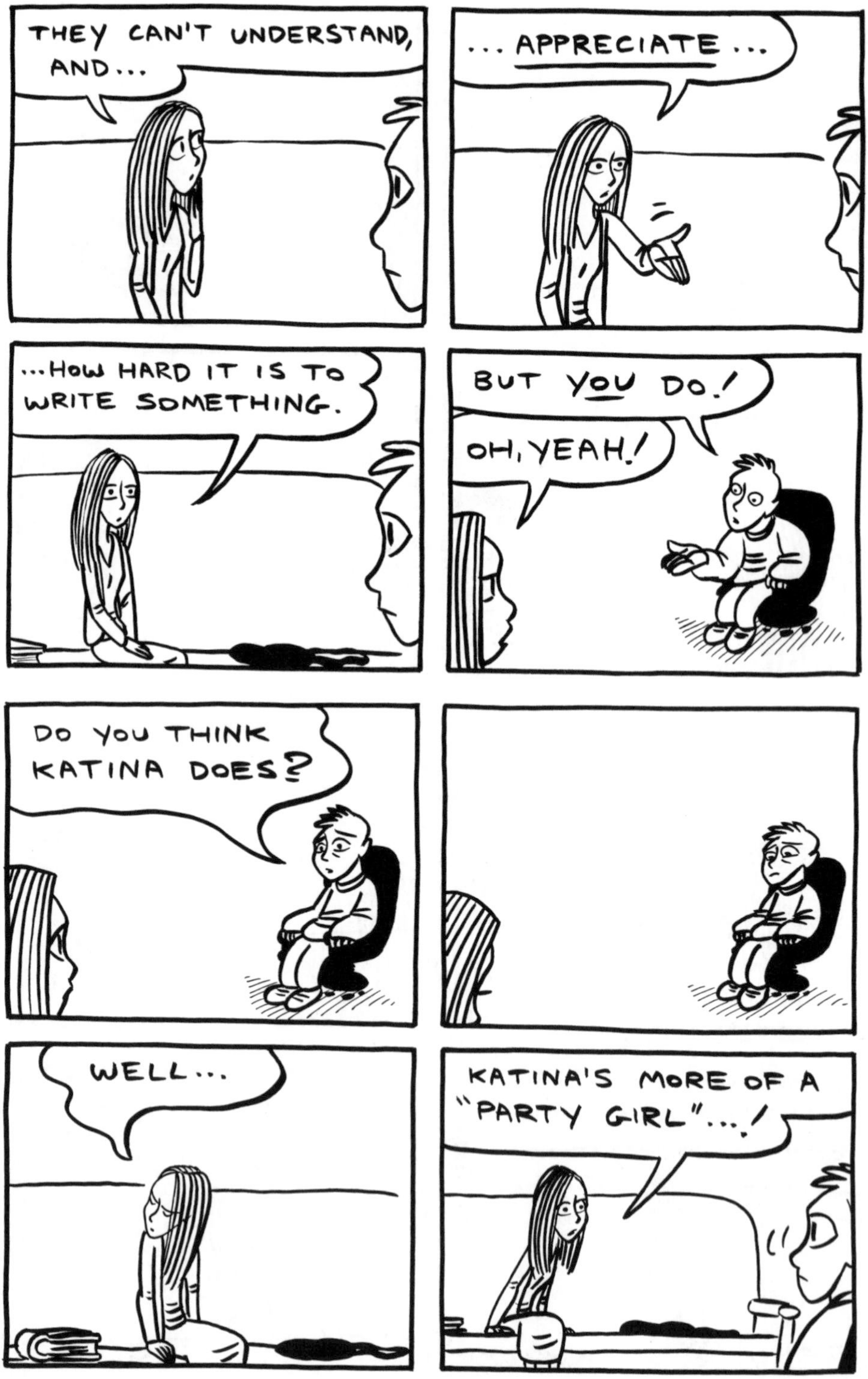
THEY CAN'T UNDERSTAND, AND...
...APPRECIATE...
...HOW HARD IT IS TO WRITE SOMETHING.
BUT YOU DO.!
OH, YEAH!
DO YOU THINK KATINA DOES?
WELL...
KATINA'S MORE OF A "PARTY GIRL"...!

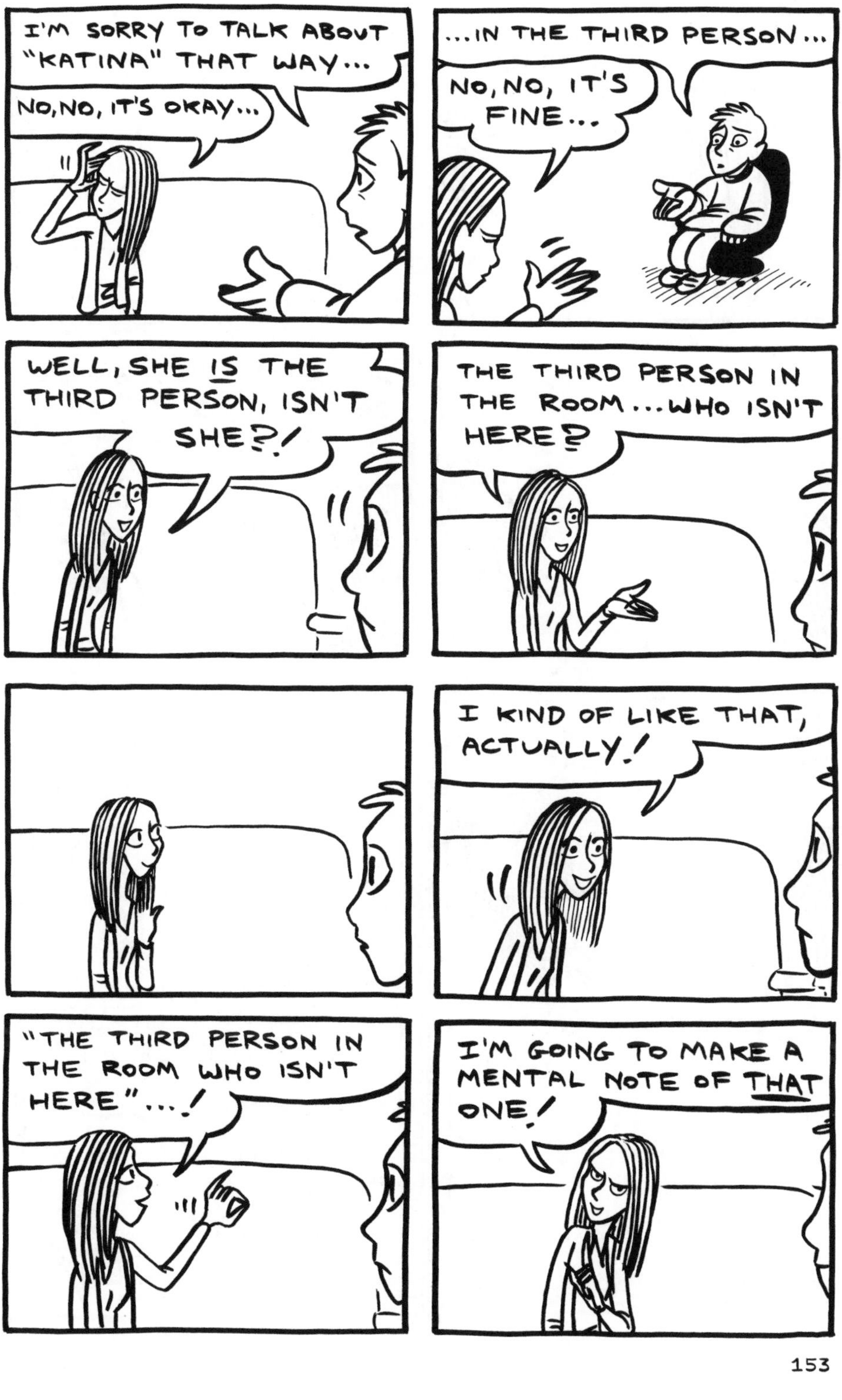
I'M SORRY TO TALK ABOUT "KATINA" THAT WAY...
NO, NO, IT'S OKAY...
...IN THE THIRD PERSON...
NO, NO, IT'S FINE...
WELL, SHE IS THE THIRD PERSON, ISN'T SHE?!
THE THIRD PERSON IN THE ROOM...WHO ISN'T HERE?
I KIND OF LIKE THAT, ACTUALLY!
"THE THIRD PERSON IN THE ROOM WHO ISN'T HERE"...!
I'M GOING TO MAKE A MENTAL NOTE OF THAT ONE!

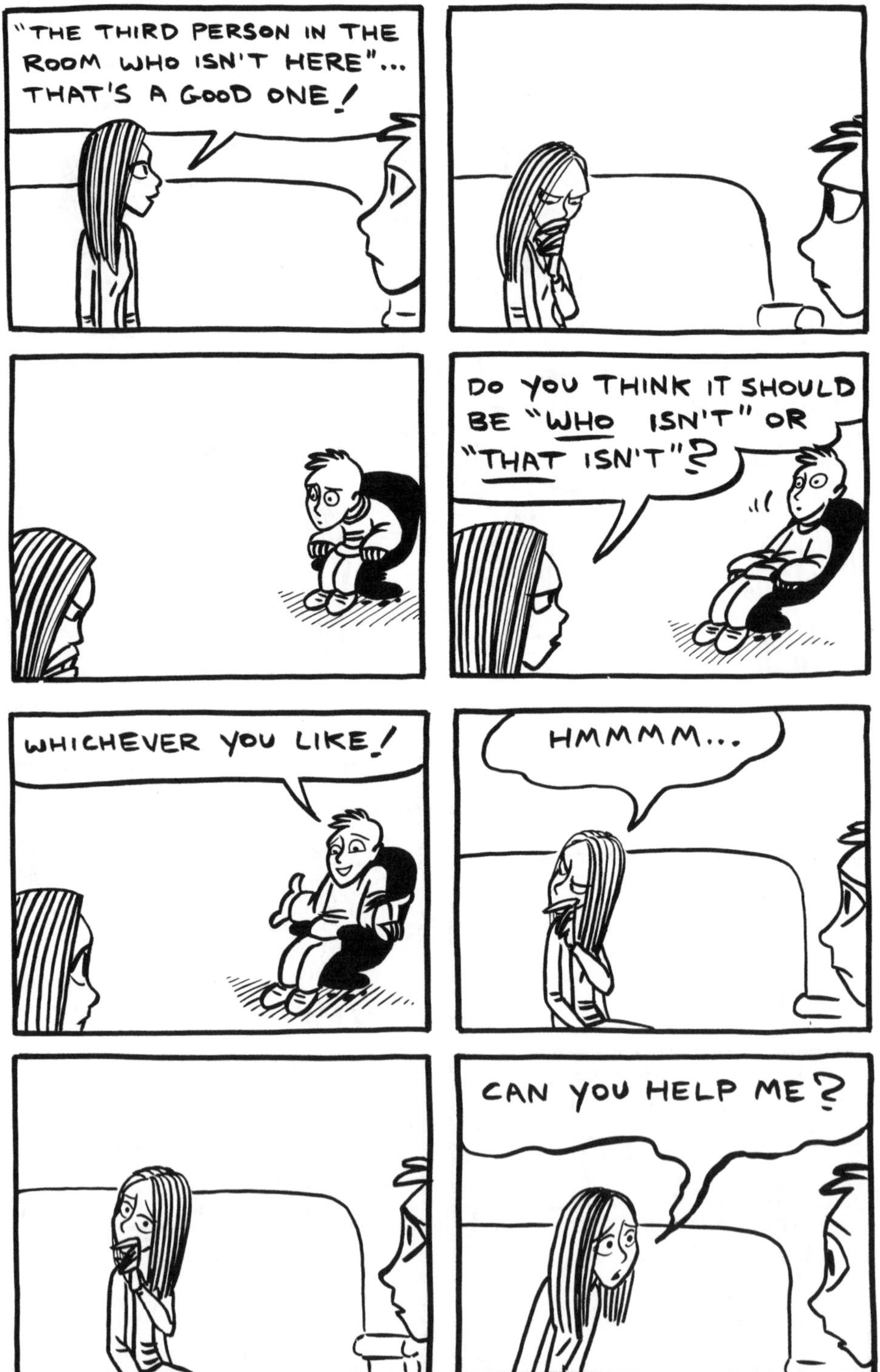
"THE THIRD PERSON IN THE ROOM WHO ISN'T HERE"... THAT'S A GOOD ONE!
DO YOU THINK IT SHOULD BE "WHO ISN'T" OR "THAT ISN'T"?
WHICHEVER YOU LIKE!
HMMMM...
CAN YOU HELP ME?

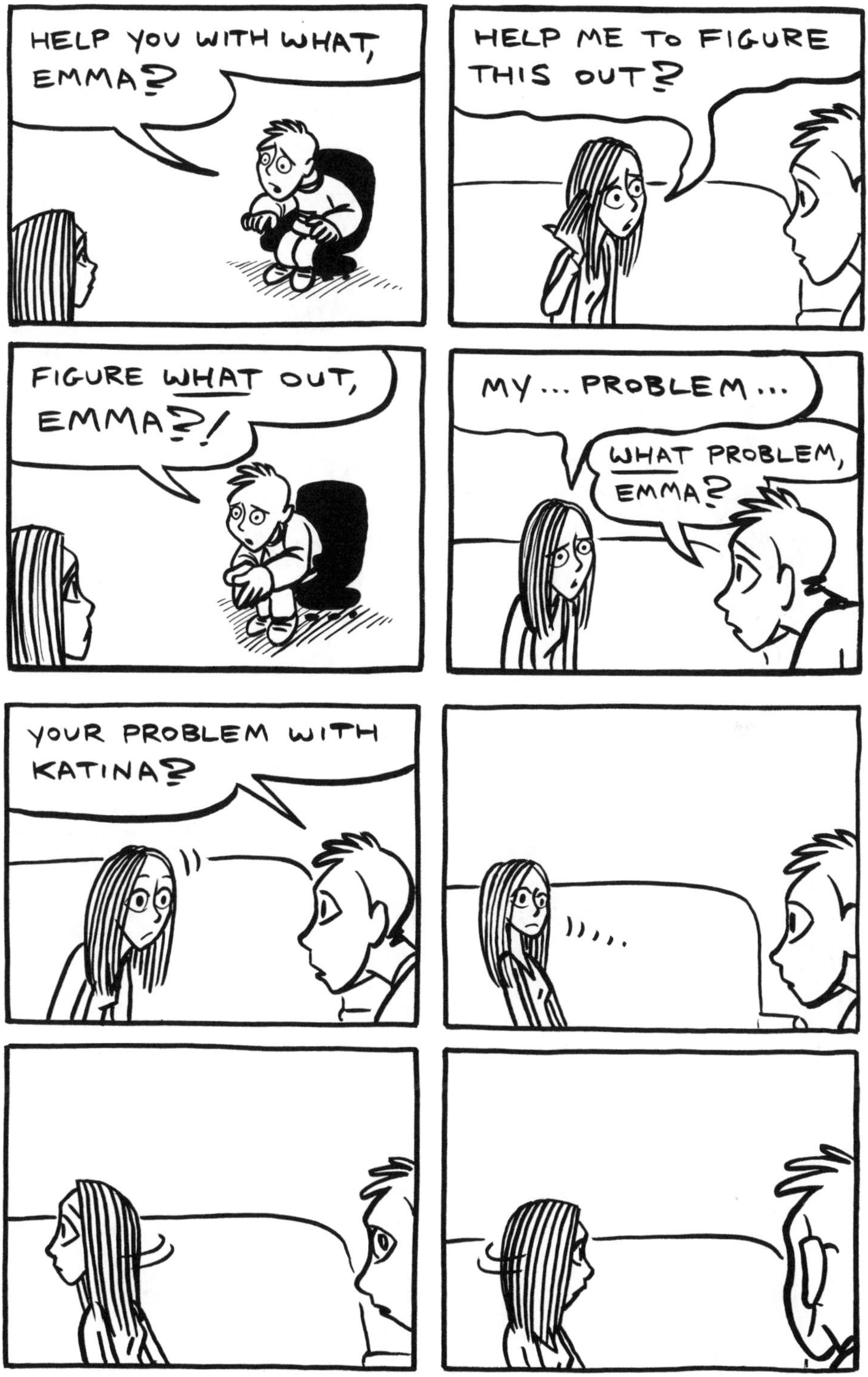
HELP YOU WITH WHAT, EMMA?
HELP ME TO FIGURE THIS OUT?
FIGURE WHAT OUT, EMMA?!
MY... PROBLEM...
WHAT PROBLEM, EMMA?
YOUR PROBLEM WITH KATINA?

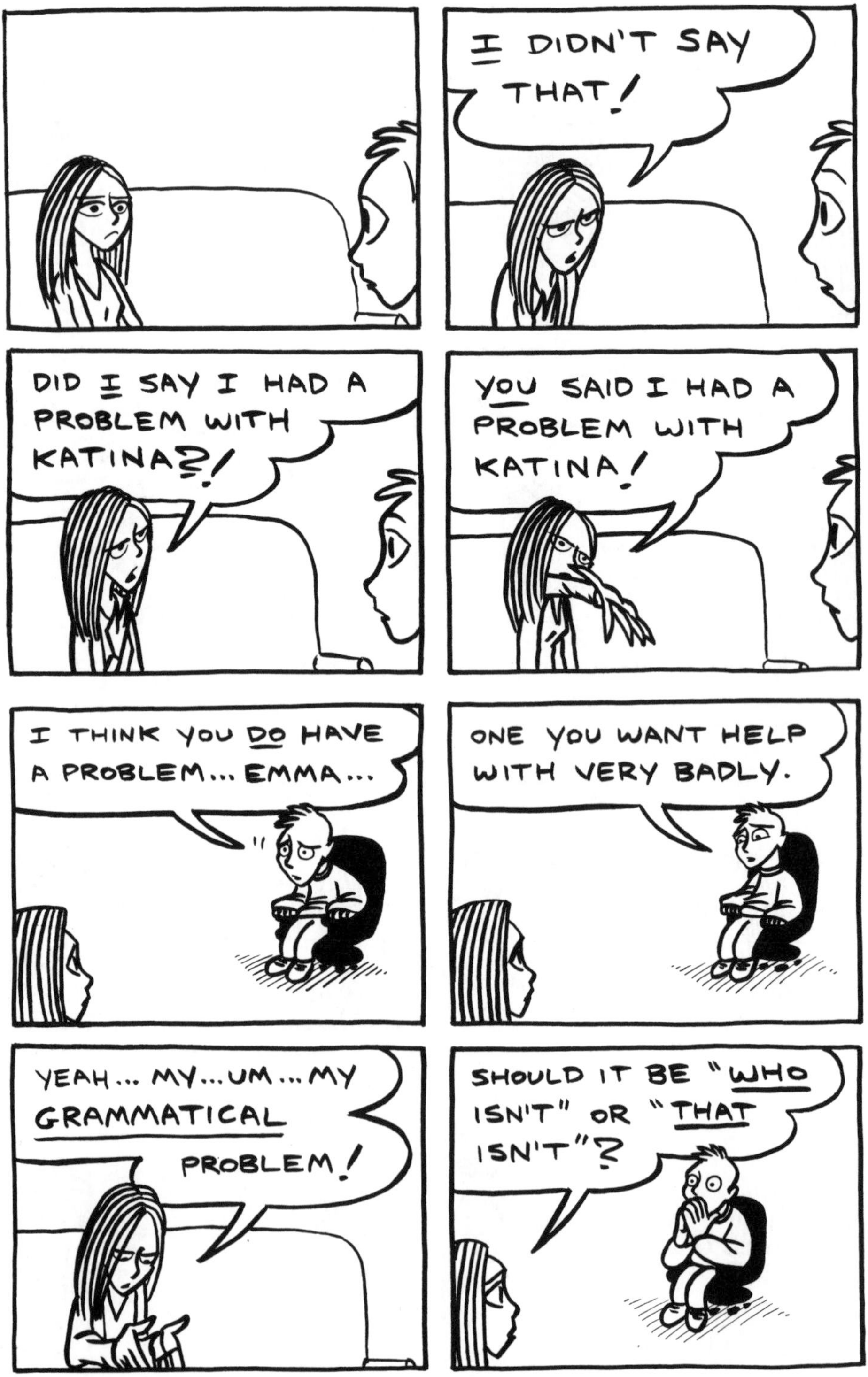
I DIDN'T SAY THAT!
DID I SAY I HAD A PROBLEM WITH KATINA?!
YOU SAID I HAD A PROBLEM WITH KATINA!
I THINK YOU DO HAVE A PROBLEM... EMMA...
ONE YOU WANT HELP WITH VERY BADLY.
YEAH... MY... UM... MY GRAMMATICAL PROBLEM!
SHOULD IT BE "WHO ISN'T" OR "THAT ISN'T"?

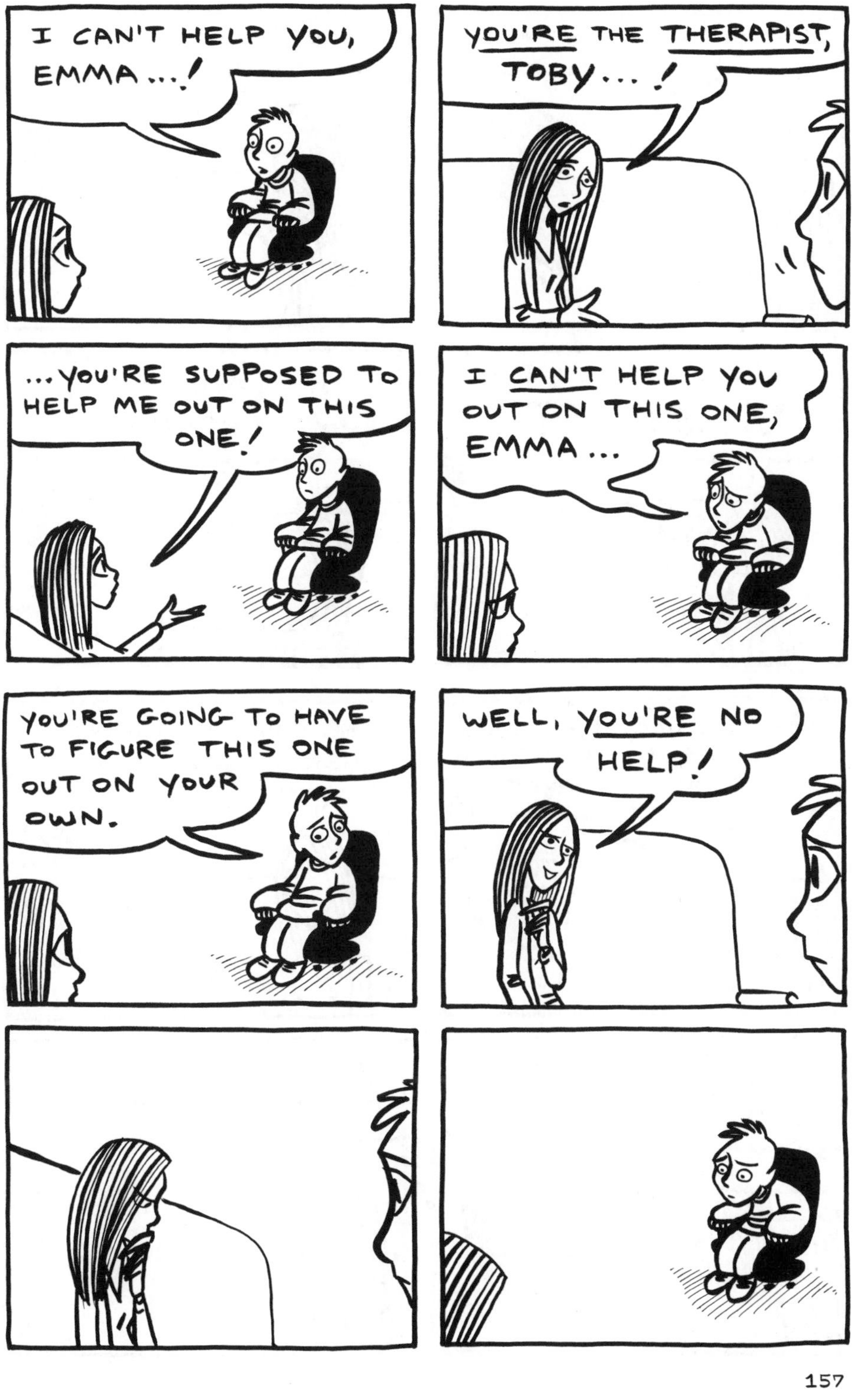
I CAN'T HELP YOU, EMMA...!
YOU'RE THE THERAPIST, TOBY...!
...YOU'RE SUPPOSED TO HELP ME OUT ON THIS ONE!
I CAN'T HELP YOU OUT ON THIS ONE, EMMA...
YOU'RE GOING TO HAVE TO FIGURE THIS ONE OUT ON YOUR OWN.
WELL, YOU'RE NO HELP!

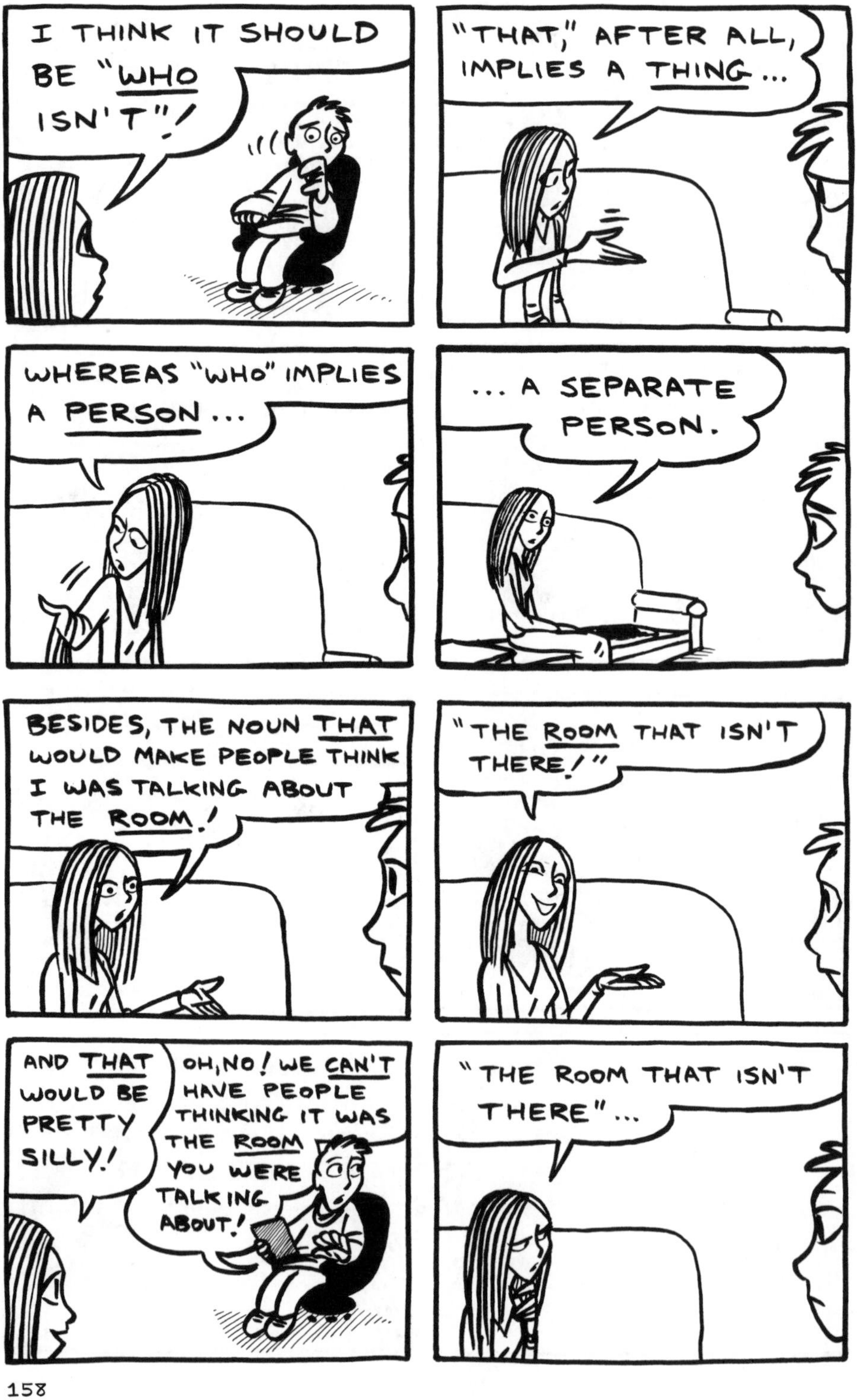
I THINK IT SHOULD BE "WHO ISN'T"!
"THAT," AFTER ALL, IMPLIES A THING...
WHEREAS "WHO" IMPLIES A PERSON...
... A SEPARATE PERSON.
BESIDES, THE NOUN THAT WOULD MAKE PEOPLE THINK I WAS TALKING ABOUT THE ROOM!
"THE ROOM THAT ISN'T THERE!"
AND THAT WOULD BE PRETTY SILLY!
OH, NO! WE CAN'T HAVE PEOPLE THINKING IT WAS THE ROOM YOU WERE TALKING ABOUT!
"THE ROOM THAT ISN'T THERE"...

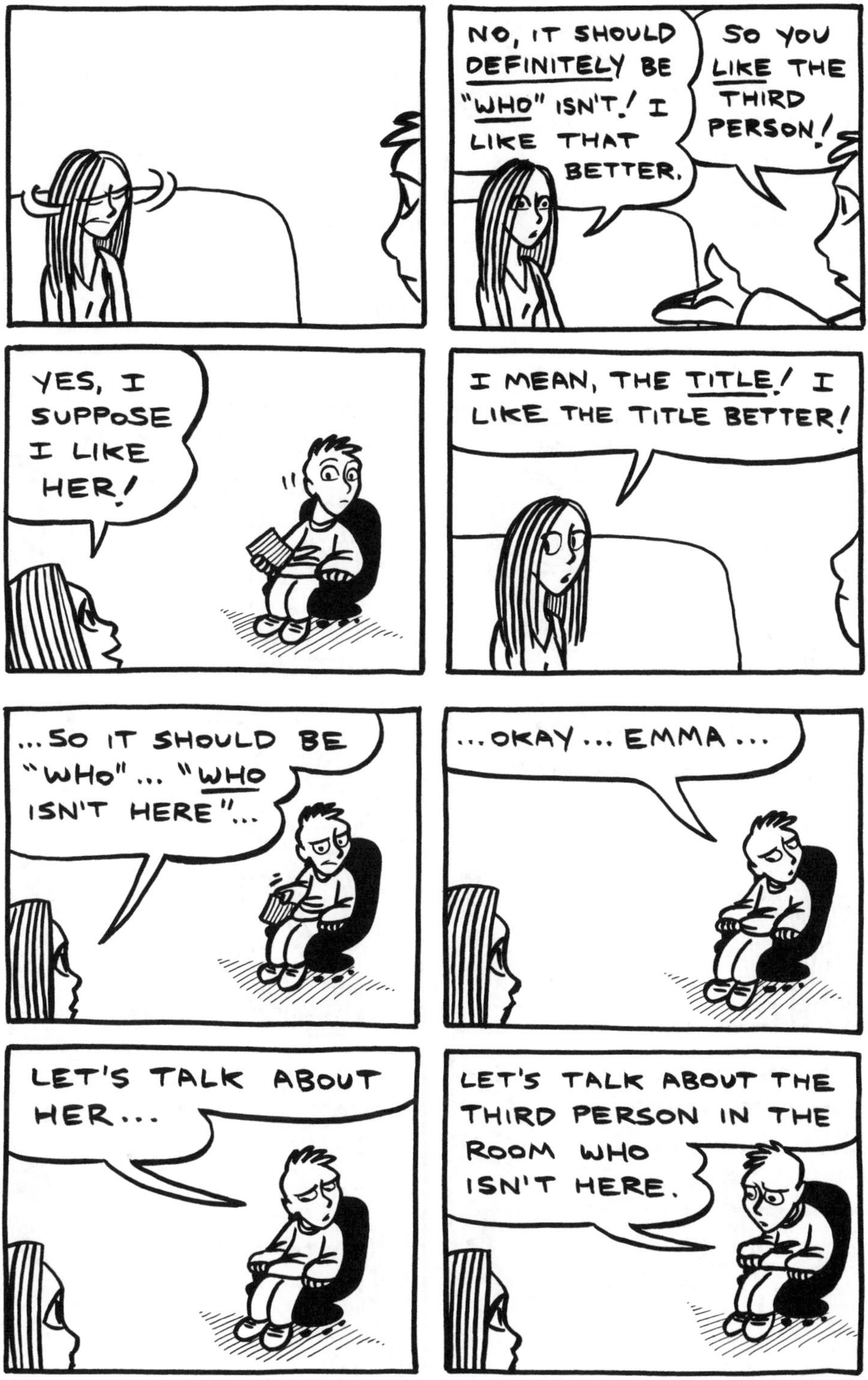
NO, IT SHOULD DEFINITELY BE "WHO" ISN'T! I LIKE THAT BETTER.
SO YOU LIKE THE THIRD PERSON!
YES, I SUPPOSE I LIKE HER!
I MEAN, THE TITLE! I LIKE THE TITLE BETTER!
...SO IT SHOULD BE "WHO"... "WHO ISN'T HERE"...
...OKAY... EMMA...
LET'S TALK ABOUT HER...
LET'S TALK ABOUT THE THIRD PERSON IN THE ROOM WHO ISN'T HERE.

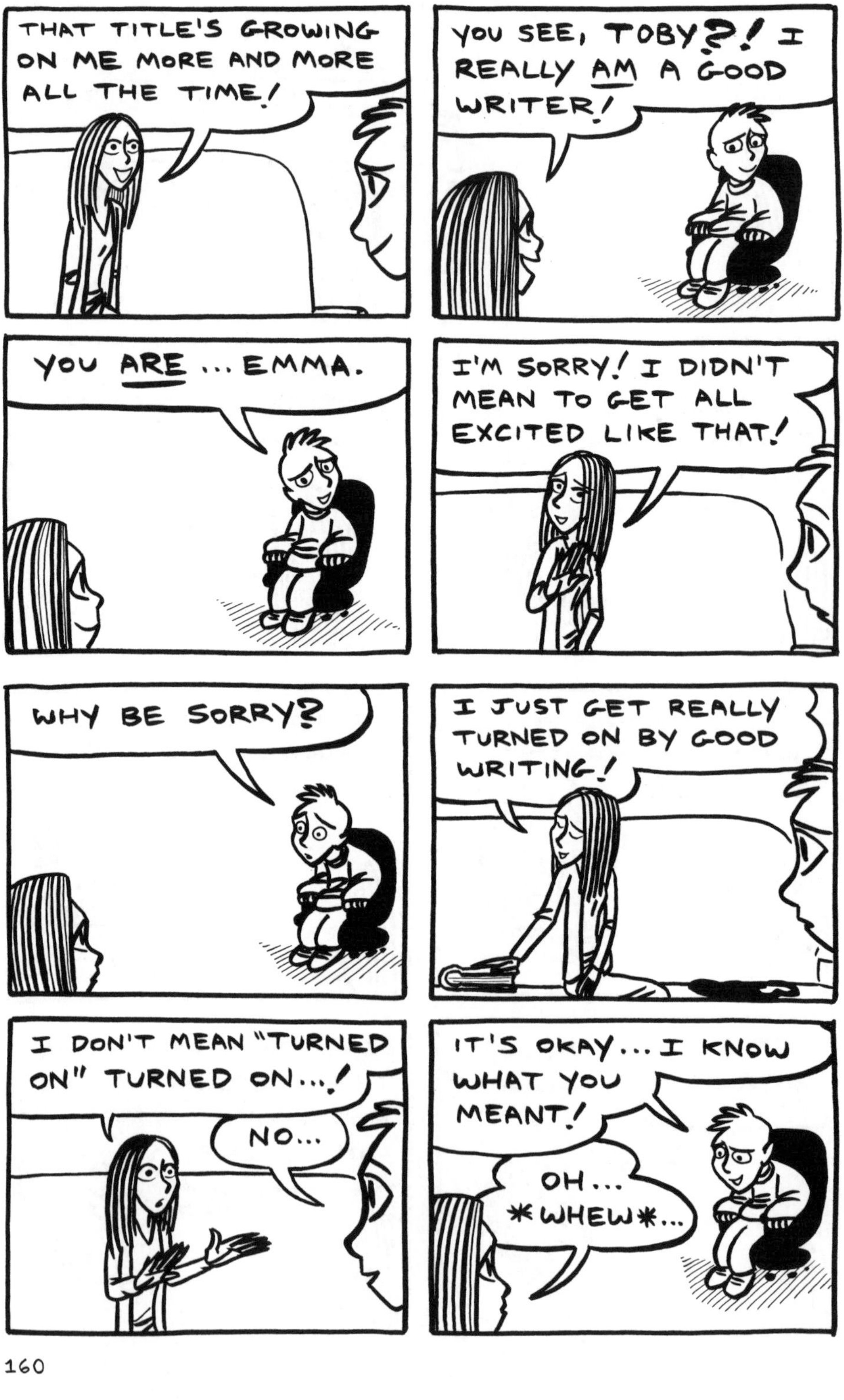
THAT TITLE'S GROWING ON ME MORE AND MORE ALL THE TIME!
YOU SEE, TOBY?! I REALLY AM A GOOD WRITER!
YOU ARE ... EMMA.
I'M SORRY! I DIDN'T MEAN TO GET ALL EXCITED LIKE THAT!
WHY BE SORRY?
I JUST GET REALLY TURNED ON BY GOOD WRITING!
I DON'T MEAN "TURNED ON" TURNED ON...!
NO...
IT'S OKAY... I KNOW WHAT YOU MEANT!
OH... *WHEW*...

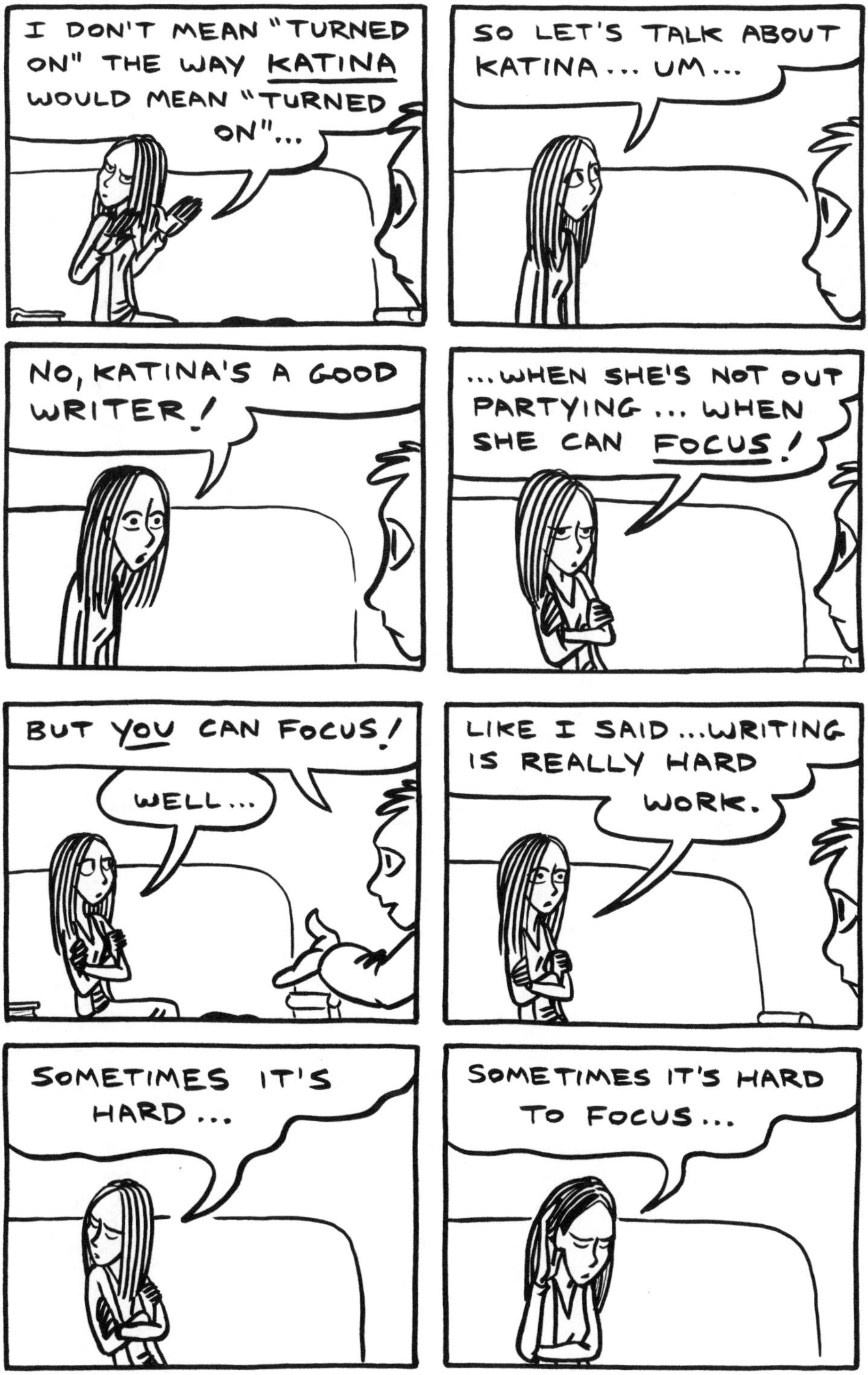
I DON'T MEAN "TURNED ON" THE WAY KATINA WOULD MEAN "TURNED ON"...
SO LET'S TALK ABOUT KATINA... UM...
NO, KATINA'S A GOOD WRITER!
...WHEN SHE'S NOT OUT PARTYING... WHEN SHE CAN FOCUS!
BUT YOU CAN FOCUS!
WELL...
LIKE I SAID...WRITING IS REALLY HARD WORK.
SOMETIMES IT'S HARD...
SOMETIMES IT'S HARD TO FOCUS...

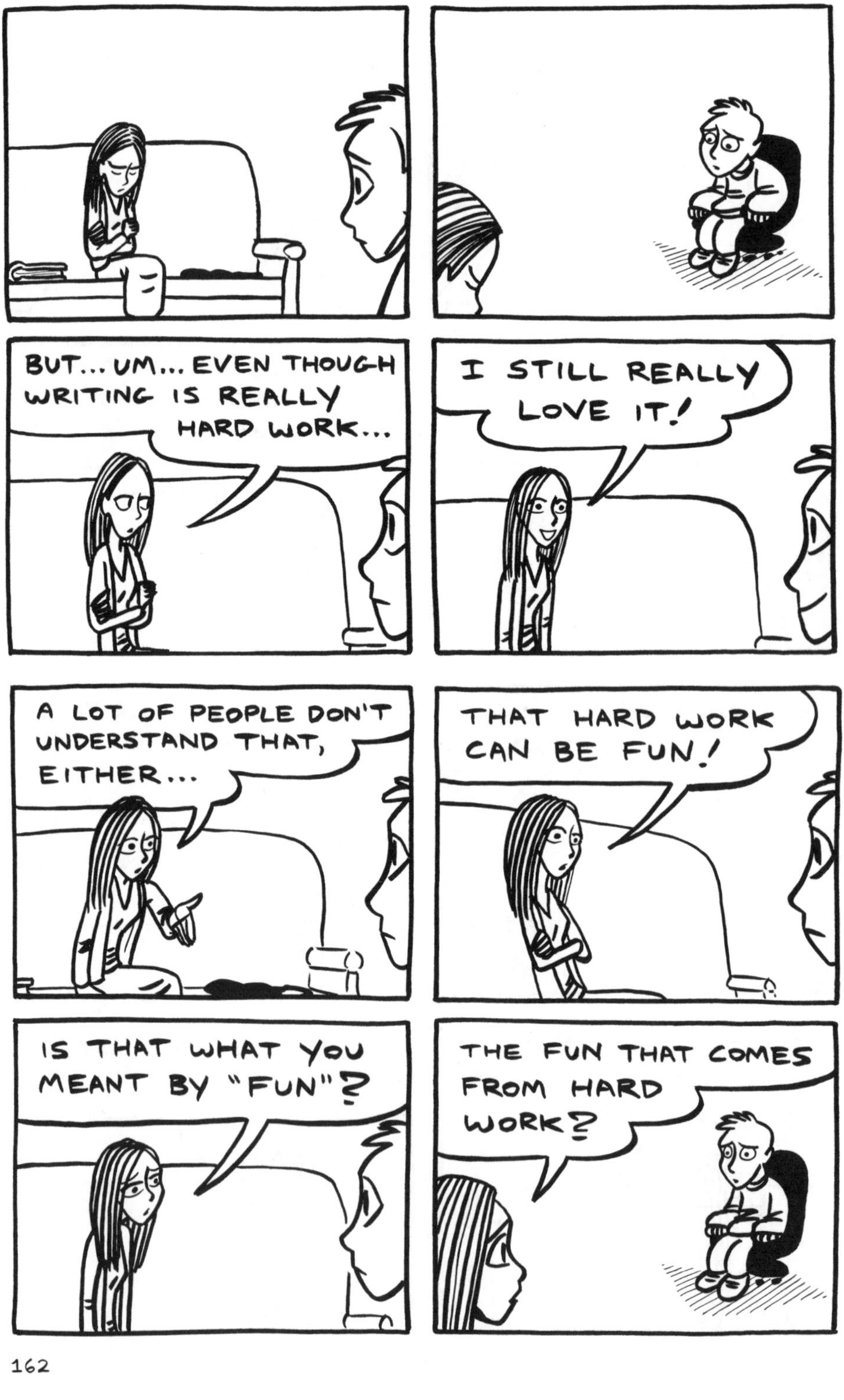
BUT... UM... EVEN THOUGH WRITING IS REALLY HARD WORK...
I STILL REALLY LOVE IT!
A LOT OF PEOPLE DON'T UNDERSTAND THAT, EITHER...
THAT HARD WORK CAN BE FUN!
IS THAT WHAT YOU MEANT BY "FUN"?
THE FUN THAT COMES FROM HARD WORK?

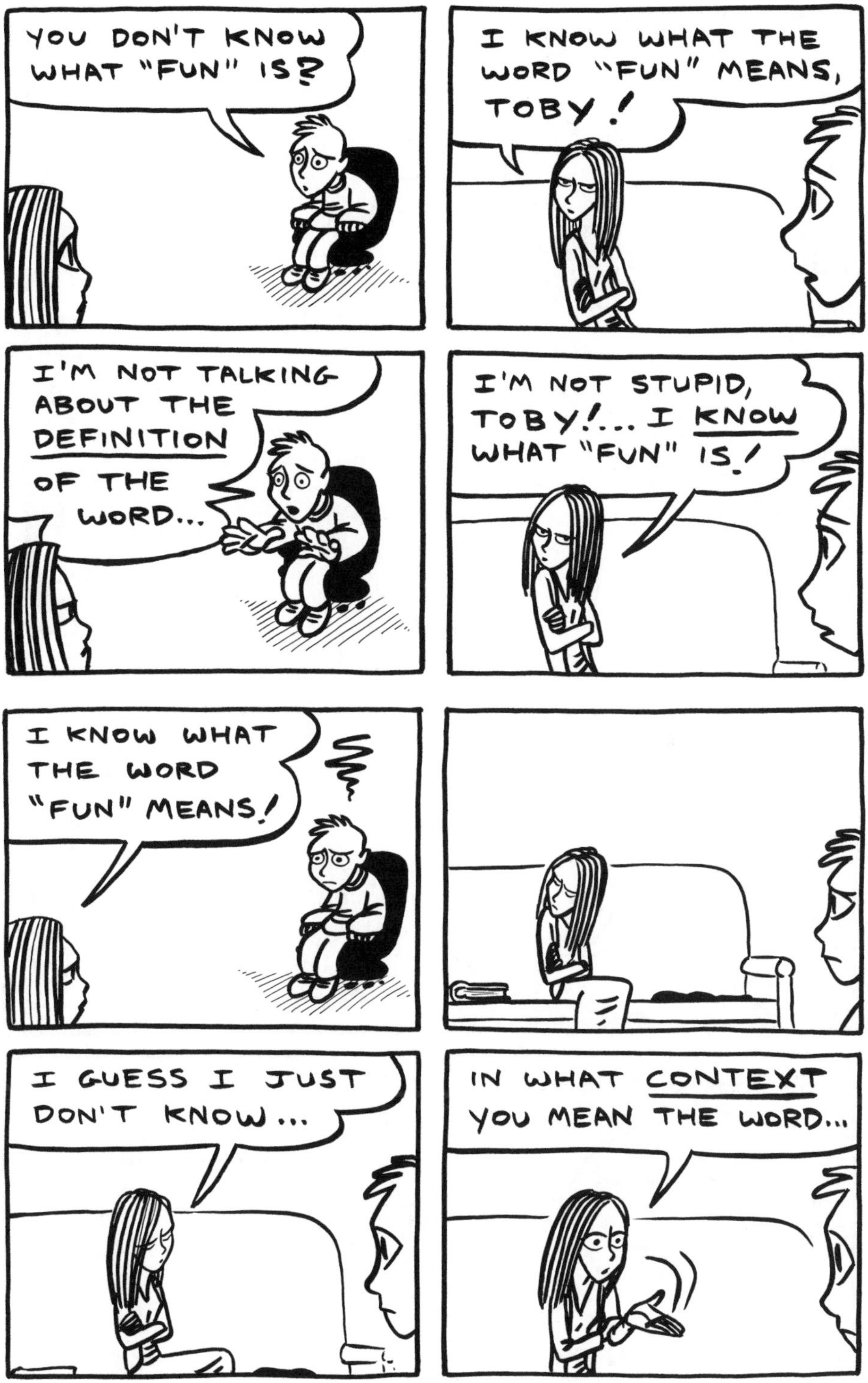
YOU DON'T KNOW WHAT "FUN" IS?
I KNOW WHAT THE WORD "FUN" MEANS, TOBY!
I'M NOT TALKING ABOUT THE DEFINITION OF THE WORD...
I'M NOT STUPID, TOBY!... I KNOW WHAT "FUN" IS!
I KNOW WHAT THE WORD "FUN" MEANS!
I GUESS I JUST DON'T KNOW...
IN WHAT CONTEXT YOU MEAN THE WORD...

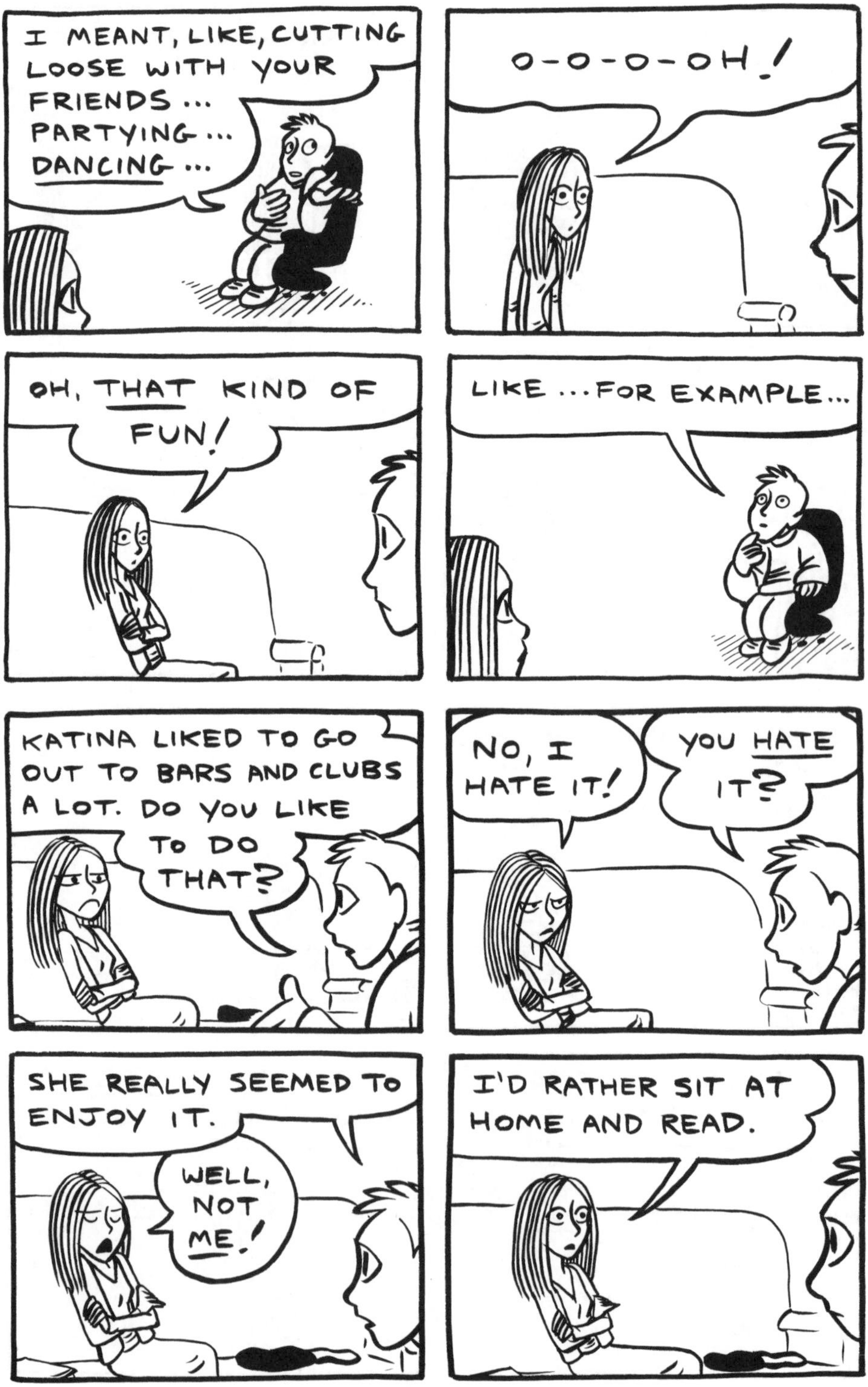
I MEANT, LIKE, CUTTING LOOSE WITH YOUR FRIENDS... PARTYING... DANCING...
O-O-O-OH!
OH, THAT KIND OF FUN!
LIKE...FOR EXAMPLE...
KATINA LIKED TO GO OUT TO BARS AND CLUBS A LOT. DO YOU LIKE TO DO THAT?
NO, I HATE IT!
YOU HATE IT?
SHE REALLY SEEMED TO ENJOY IT.
WELL, NOT ME!
I'D RATHER SIT AT HOME AND READ.

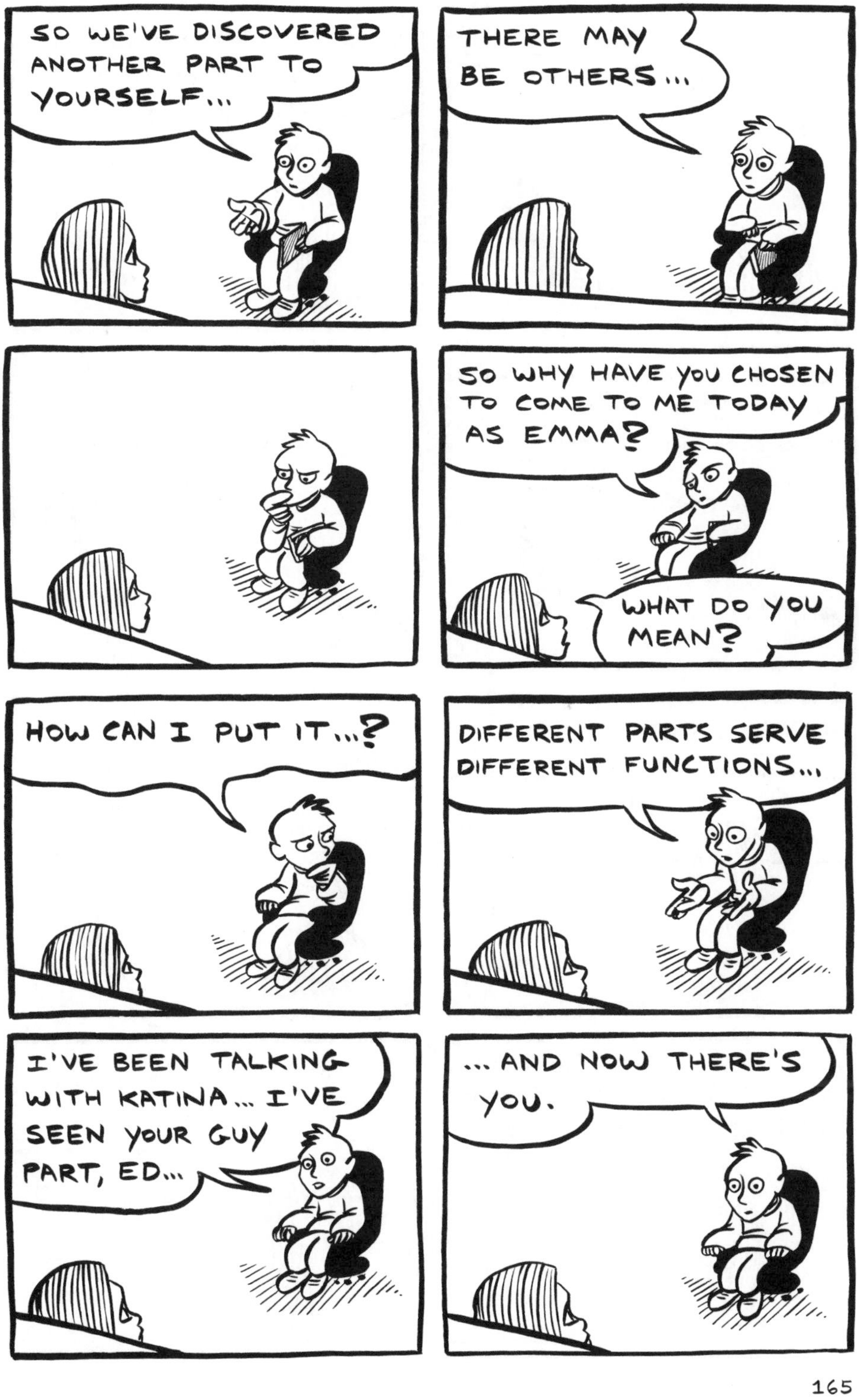
SO WE'VE DISCOVERED ANOTHER PART TO YOURSELF...
THERE MAY BE OTHERS...
SO WHY HAVE YOU CHOSEN TO COME TO ME TODAY AS EMMA?
WHAT DO YOU MEAN?
HOW CAN I PUT IT...?
DIFFERENT PARTS SERVE DIFFERENT FUNCTIONS...
I'VE BEEN TALKING WITH KATINA... I'VE SEEN YOUR GUY PART, ED...
... AND NOW THERE'S YOU.

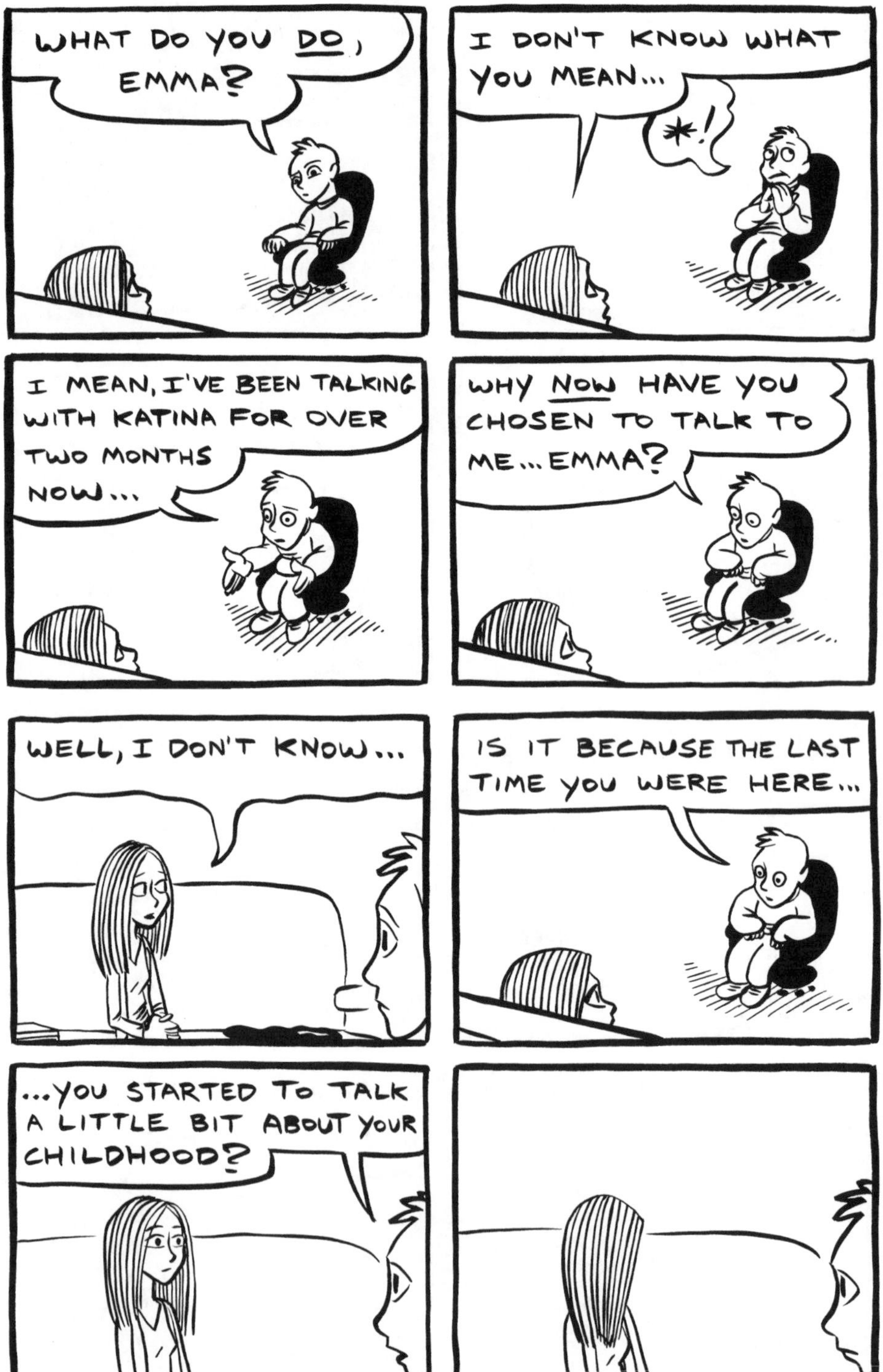
WHAT DO YOU DO, EMMA?
I DON'T KNOW WHAT YOU MEAN...
*!
I MEAN, I'VE BEEN TALKING WITH KATINA FOR OVER TWO MONTHS NOW...
WHY NOW HAVE YOU CHOSEN TO TALK TO ME... EMMA?
WELL, I DON'T KNOW...
IS IT BECAUSE THE LAST TIME YOU WERE HERE...
...YOU STARTED TO TALK A LITTLE BIT ABOUT YOUR CHILDHOOD?

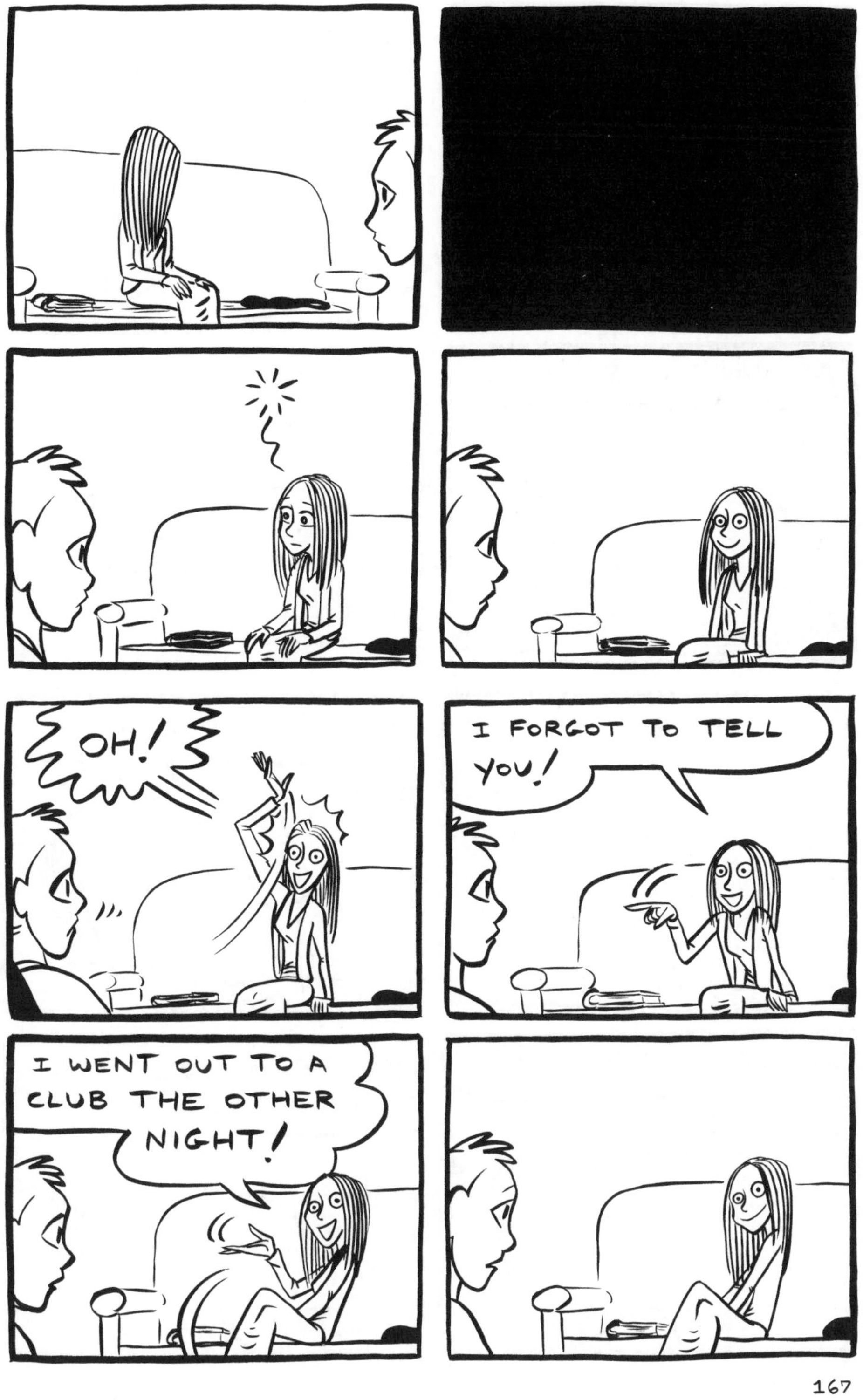
OH!
I FORGOT TO TELL YOU!
I WENT OUT TO A CLUB THE OTHER NIGHT!

I MEANT TO TELL YOU, I JUST HADN'T SEEN YOU IN A LONG TIME.
YOU JUST SAW ME LAST WEEK!
YEAH, BUT...
I DIDN'T GET TO TALK TO YOU MUCH!
WHO DID GET TO TALK TO ME?
WHEN DID YOU GO TO THE CLUB?
OH, A WEEK OR SO AGO...
ABOUT A WEEK AGO?
OR SO...
MAYBE A WEEK AND A HALF AGO.

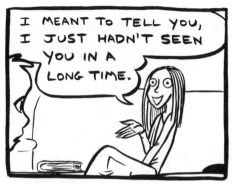

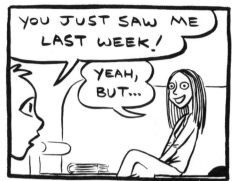

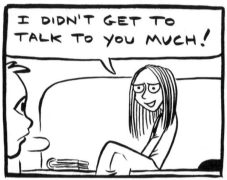

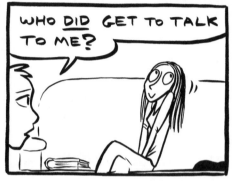

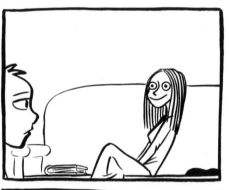

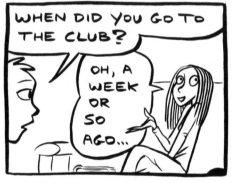

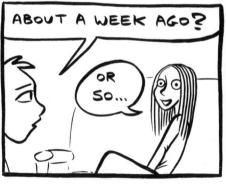

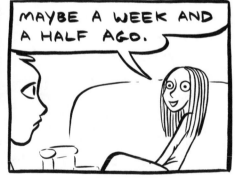

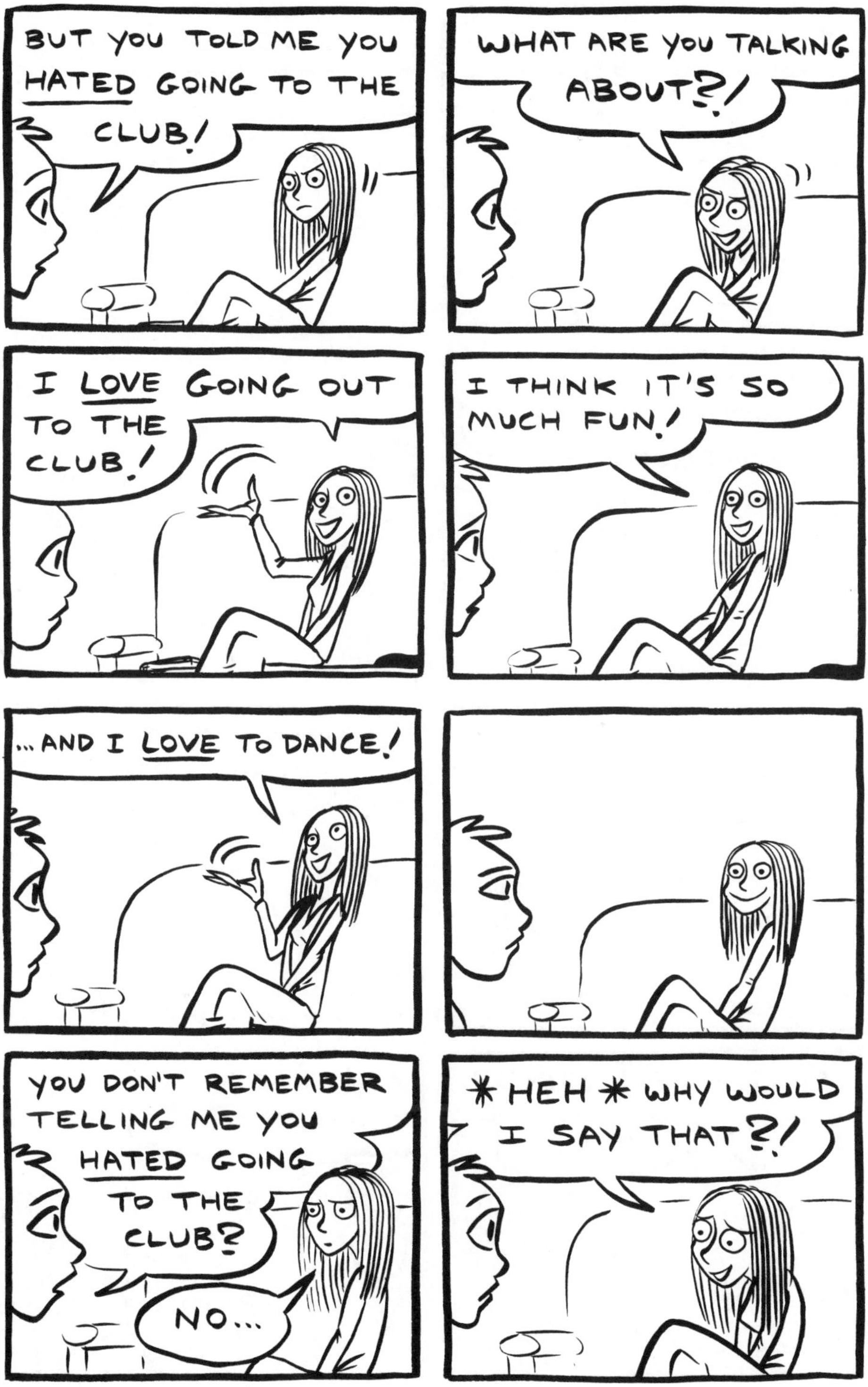
BUT YOU TOLD ME YOU HATED GOING TO THE CLUB!
WHAT ARE YOU TALKING ABOUT?!
I LOVE GOING OUT TO THE CLUB!
I THINK IT'S SO MUCH FUN!
...AND I LOVE TO DANCE!
YOU DON'T REMEMBER TELLING ME YOU HATED GOING TO THE CLUB?
NO...
HEH WHY WOULD I SAY THAT?!

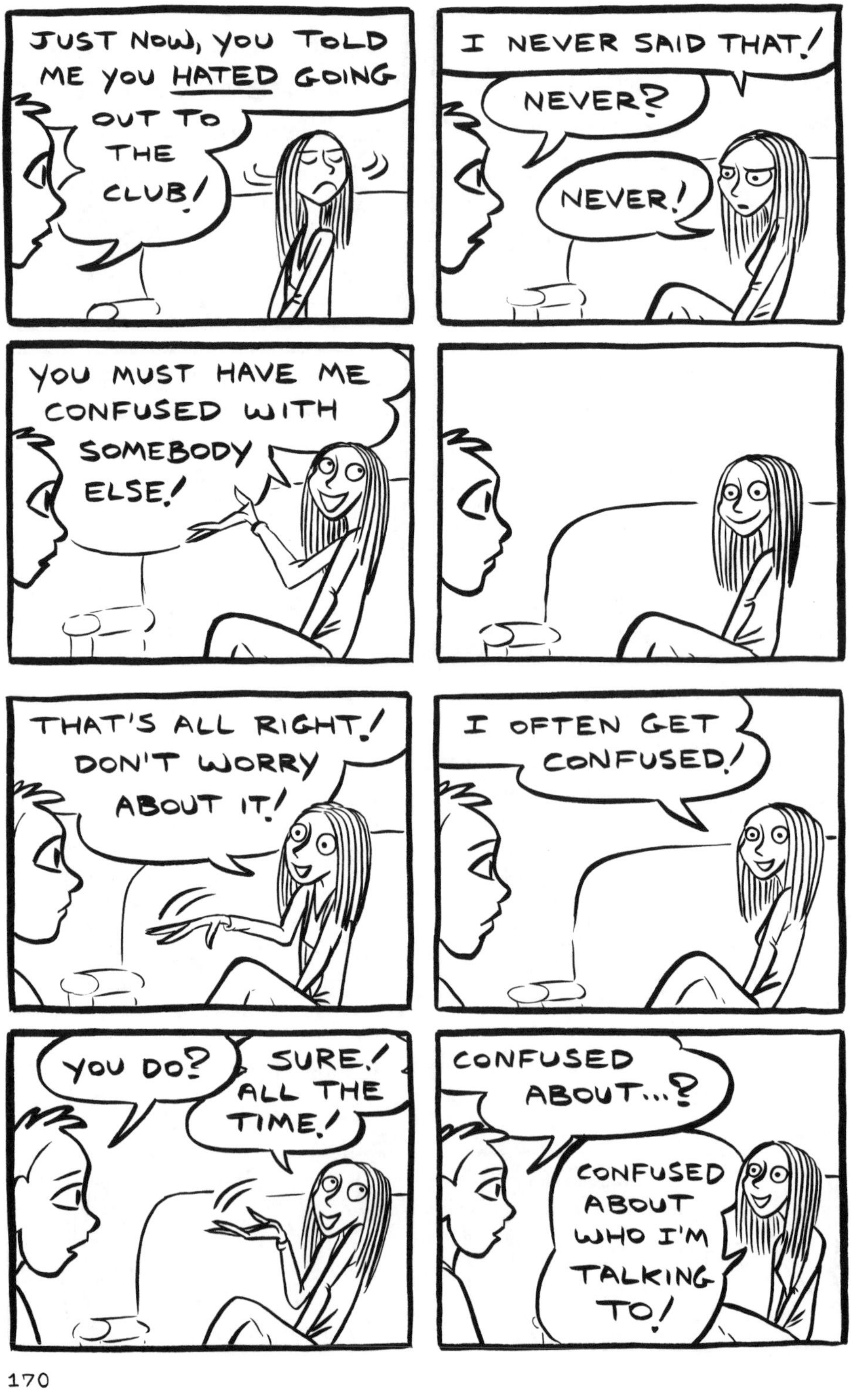
JUST NOW, YOU TOLD ME YOU HATED GOING OUT TO THE CLUB!
I NEVER SAID THAT!
NEVER?
NEVER!
YOU MUST HAVE ME CONFUSED WITH SOMEBODY ELSE!
THAT'S ALL RIGHT! DON'T WORRY ABOUT IT!
I OFTEN GET CONFUSED!
YOU DO?
SURE! ALL THE TIME!
CONFUSED ABOUT...?
CONFUSED ABOUT WHO I'M TALKING TO!

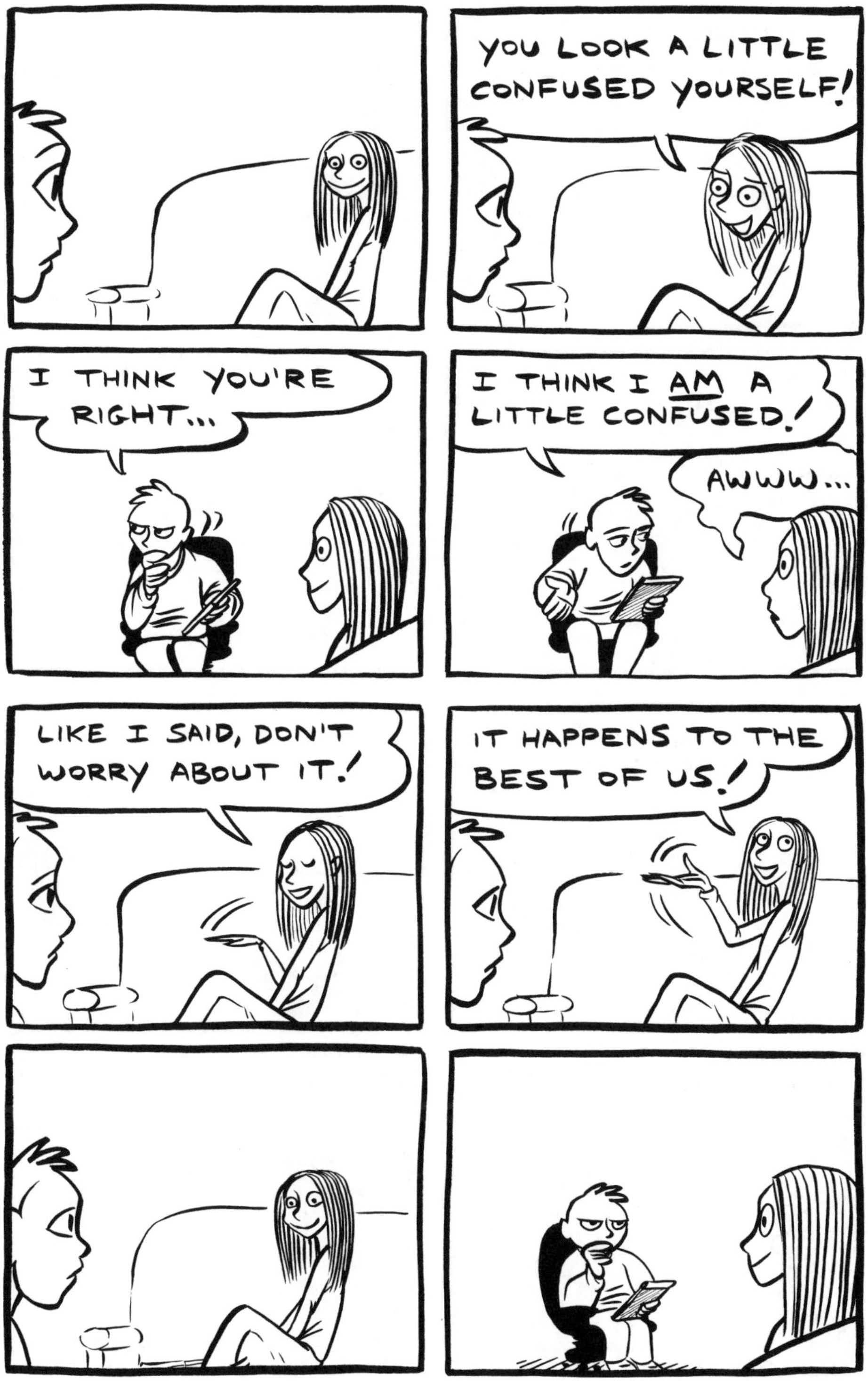
YOU LOOK A LITTLE CONFUSED YOURSELF!
I THINK YOU'RE RIGHT...
I THINK I AM A LITTLE CONFUSED!
AWWW...
LIKE I SAID, DON'T WORRY ABOUT IT!
IT HAPPENS TO THE BEST OF US!

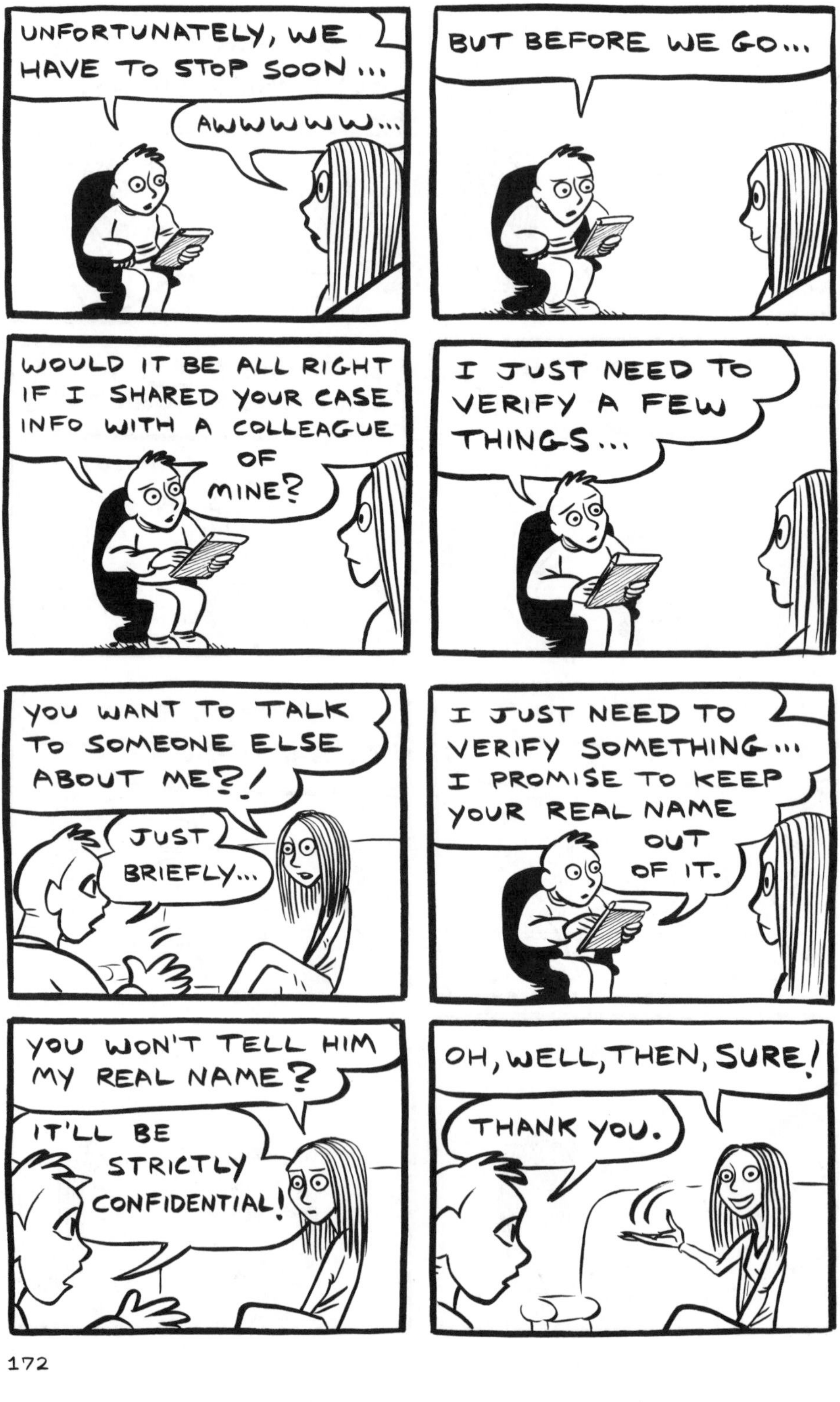

UNFORTUNATELY, WE HAVE TO STOP SOON...
AWWWWWW...
BUT BEFORE WE GO...
WOULD IT BE ALL RIGHT IF I SHARED YOUR CASE INFO WITH A COLLEAGUE OF MINE?
I JUST NEED TO VERIFY A FEW THINGS...
YOU WANT TO TALK TO SOMEONE ELSE ABOUT ME?!
JUST BRIEFLY...
I JUST NEED TO VERIFY SOMETHING... I PROMISE TO KEEP YOUR REAL NAME OUT OF IT.
YOU WON'T TELL HIM MY REAL NAME?
IT'LL BE STRICTLY CONFIDENTIAL!
OH, WELL, THEN, SURE!
THANK YOU.

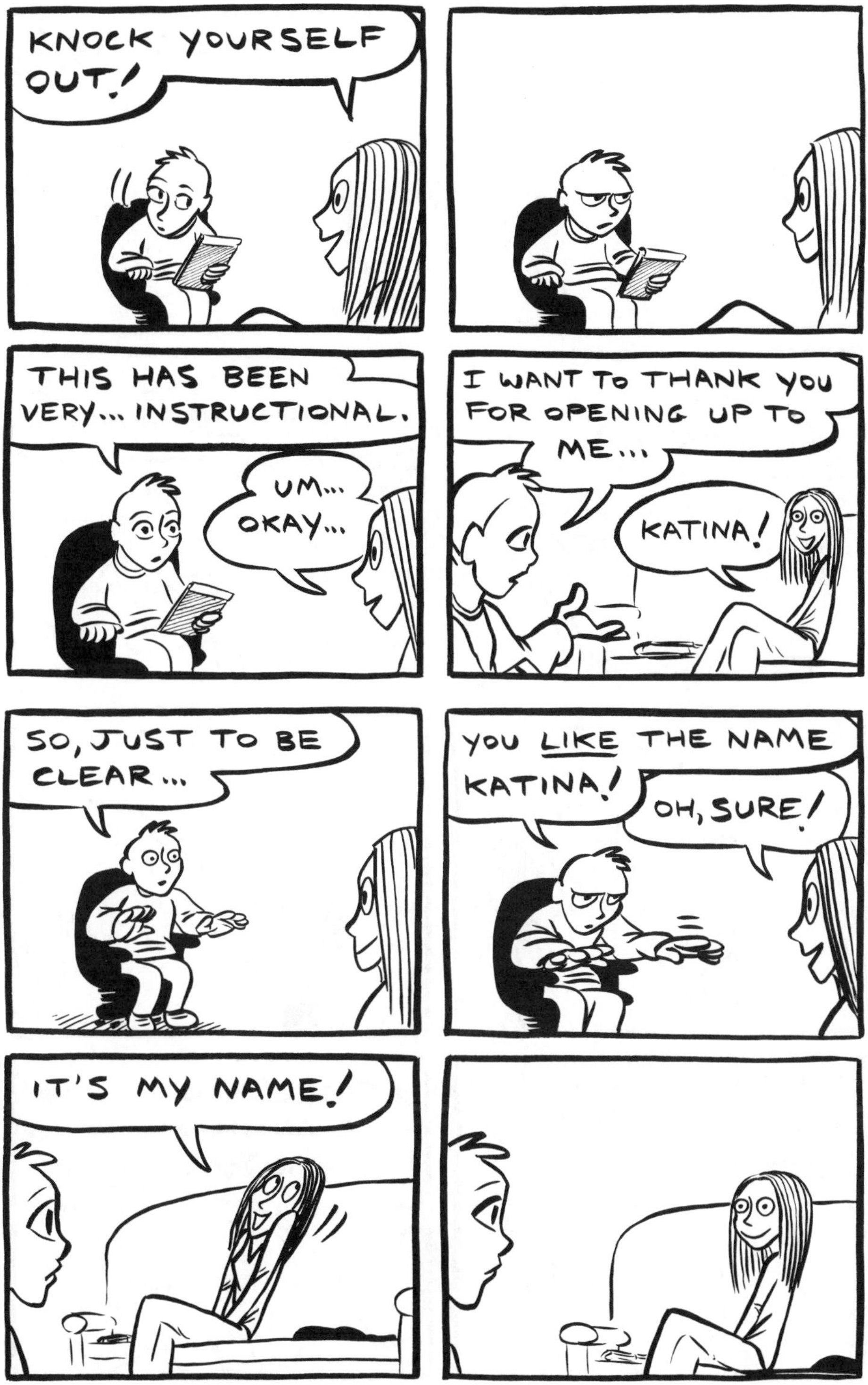
KNOCK YOURSELF OUT!
THIS HAS BEEN VERY... INSTRUCTIONAL.
UM... OKAY...
I WANT TO THANK YOU FOR OPENING UP TO ME...
KATINA!
SO, JUST TO BE CLEAR...
YOU LIKE THE NAME KATINA!
OH, SURE!
IT'S MY NAME!

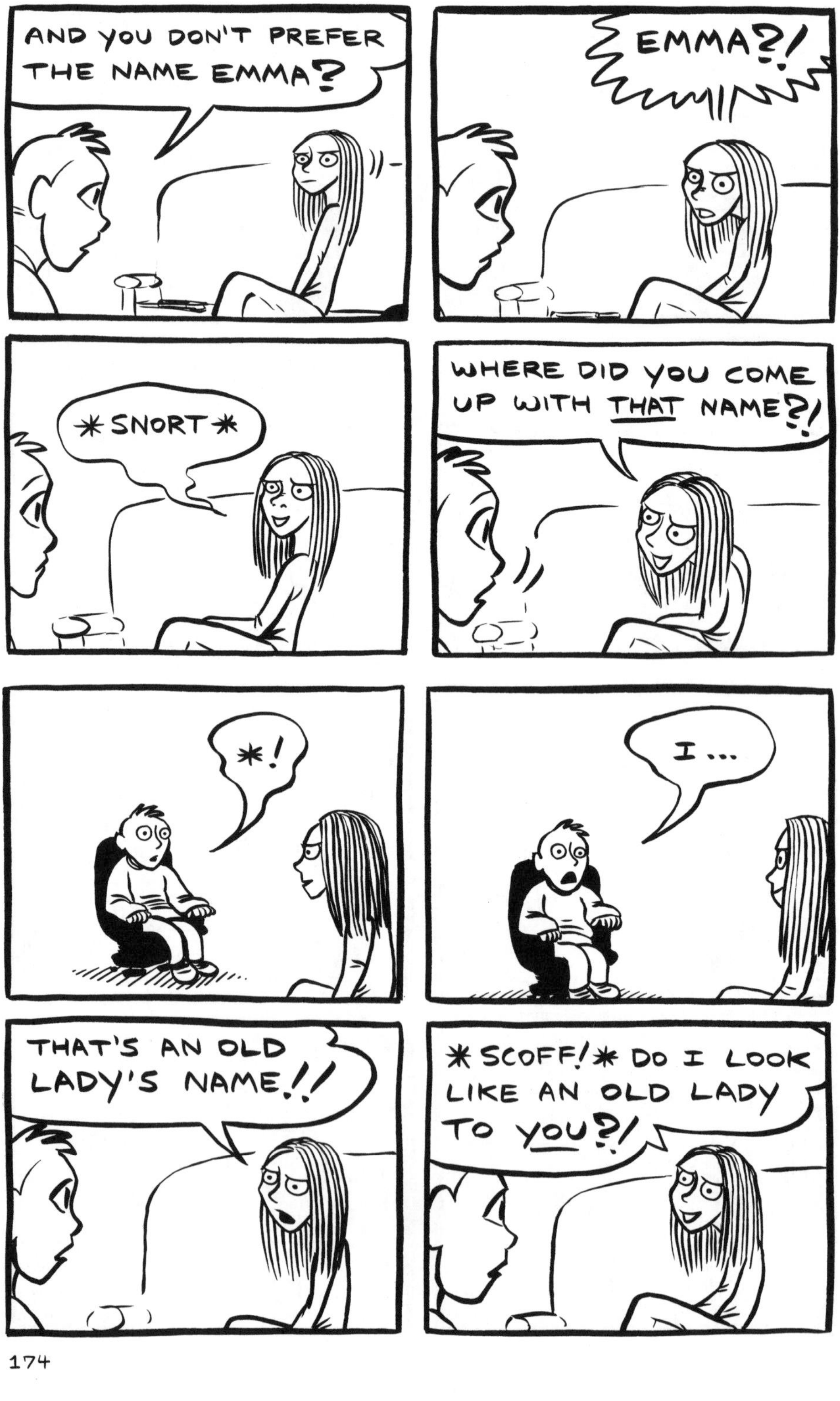
AND YOU DON'T PREFER THE NAME EMMA?
EMMA?!
SNORT
WHERE DID YOU COME UP WITH THAT NAME?!
*!
I...
THAT'S AN OLD LADY'S NAME!!
SCOFF! DO I LOOK LIKE AN OLD LADY TO YOU?!

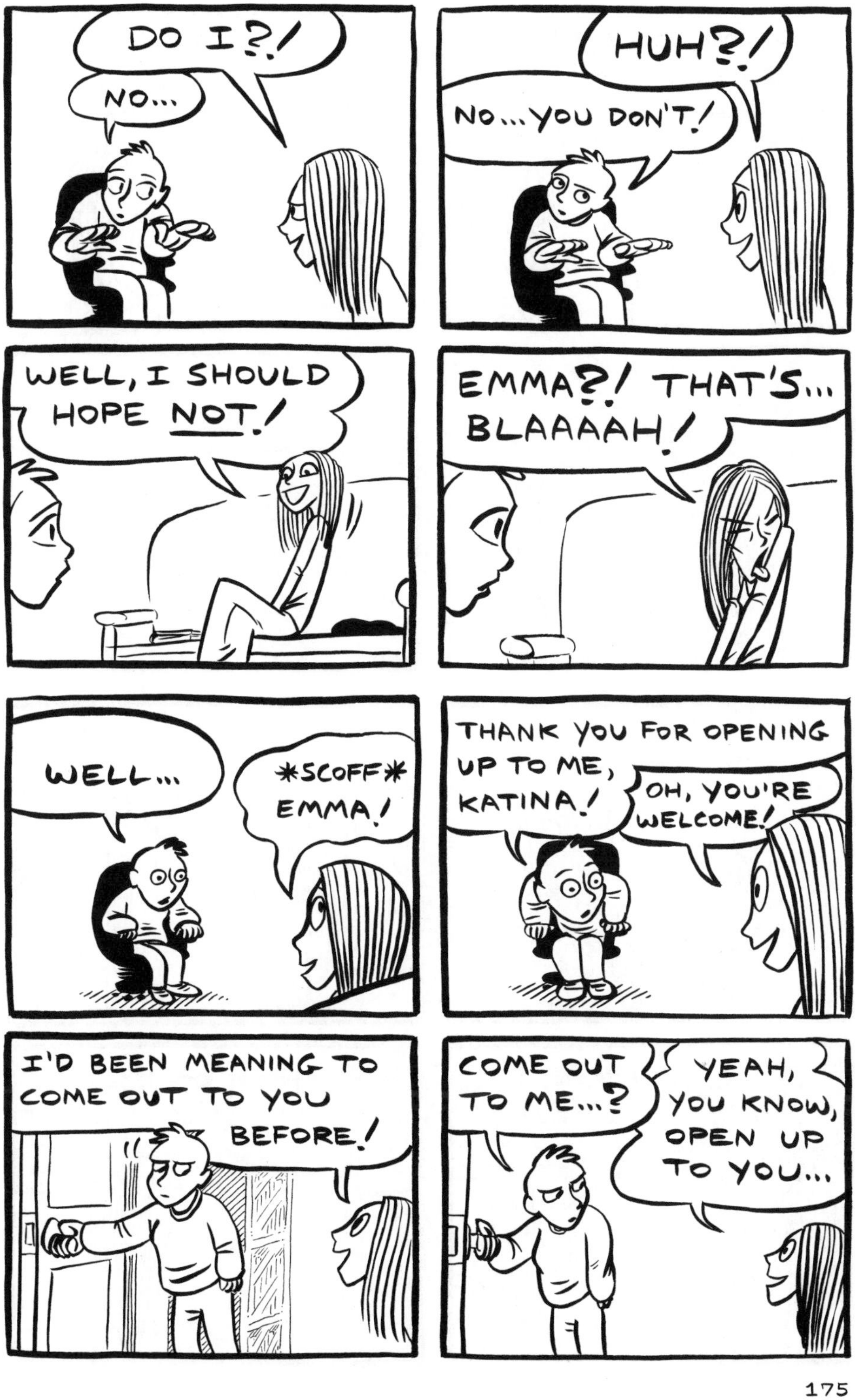
DO I?!
NO...
NO... YOU DON'T!
HUH?!
WELL, I SHOULD HOPE NOT!
EMMA?! THAT'S... BLAAAAH!
WELL...
SCOFF EMMA!
THANK YOU FOR OPENING UP TO ME, KATINA!
OH, YOU'RE WELCOME!
I'D BEEN MEANING TO COME OUT TO YOU BEFORE!
COME OUT TO ME...?
YEAH, YOU KNOW, OPEN UP TO YOU...

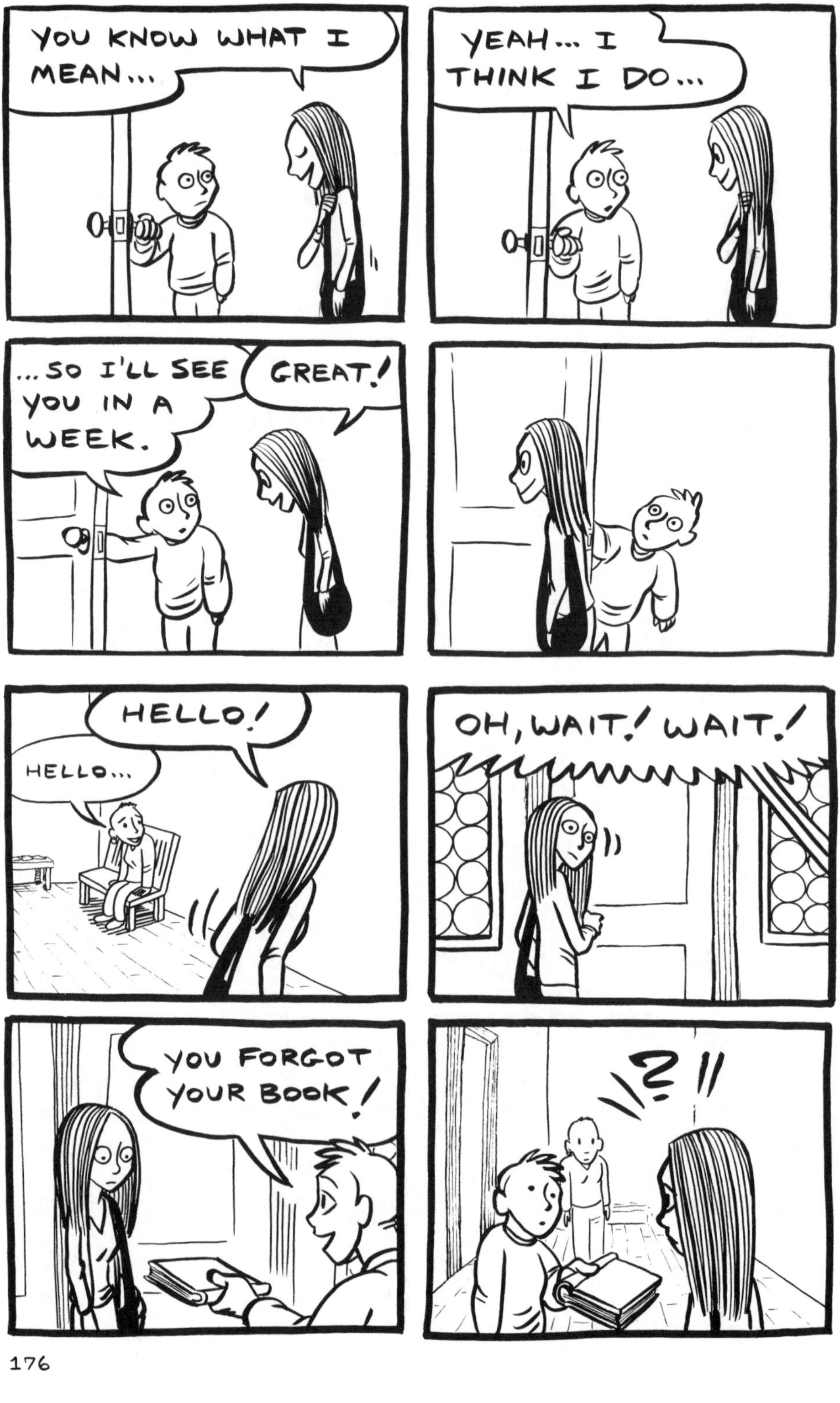
YOU KNOW WHAT I MEAN...
YEAH... I THINK I DO...
...SO I'LL SEE YOU IN A WEEK.
GREAT!
HELLO!
HELLO...
OH, WAIT! WAIT!
YOU FORGOT YOUR BOOK!
?

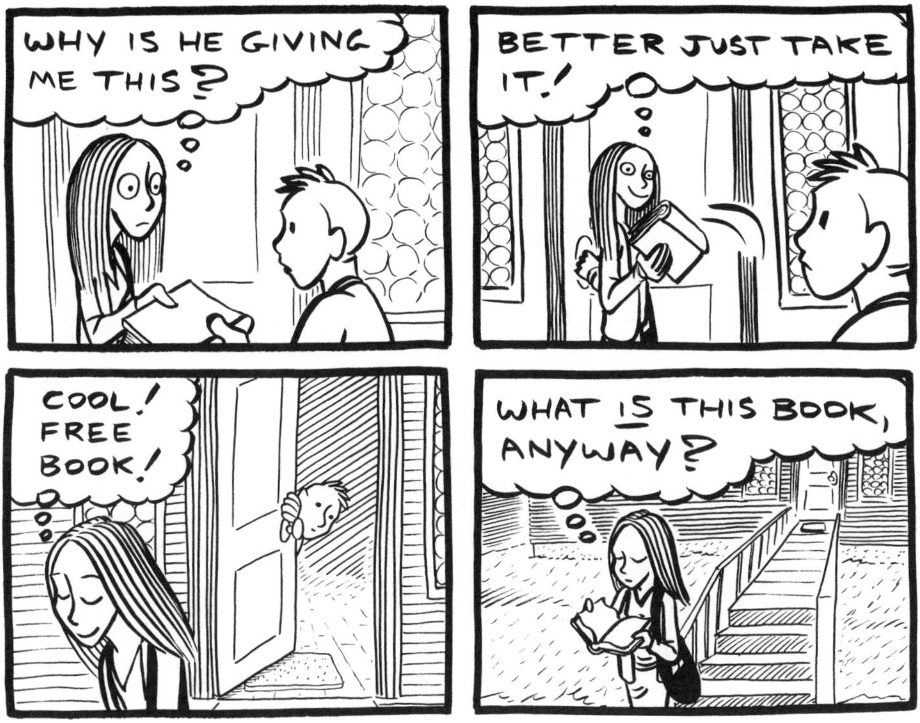
WHY IS HE GIVING ME THIS?
BETTER JUST TAKE IT!
COOL! FREE BOOK!
WHAT IS THIS BOOK, ANYWAY?

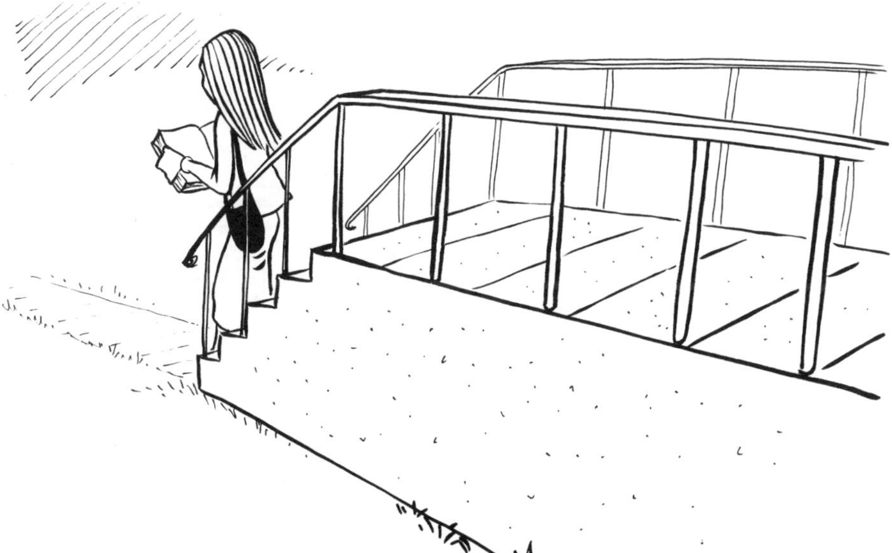

LIBRARY
BOOK

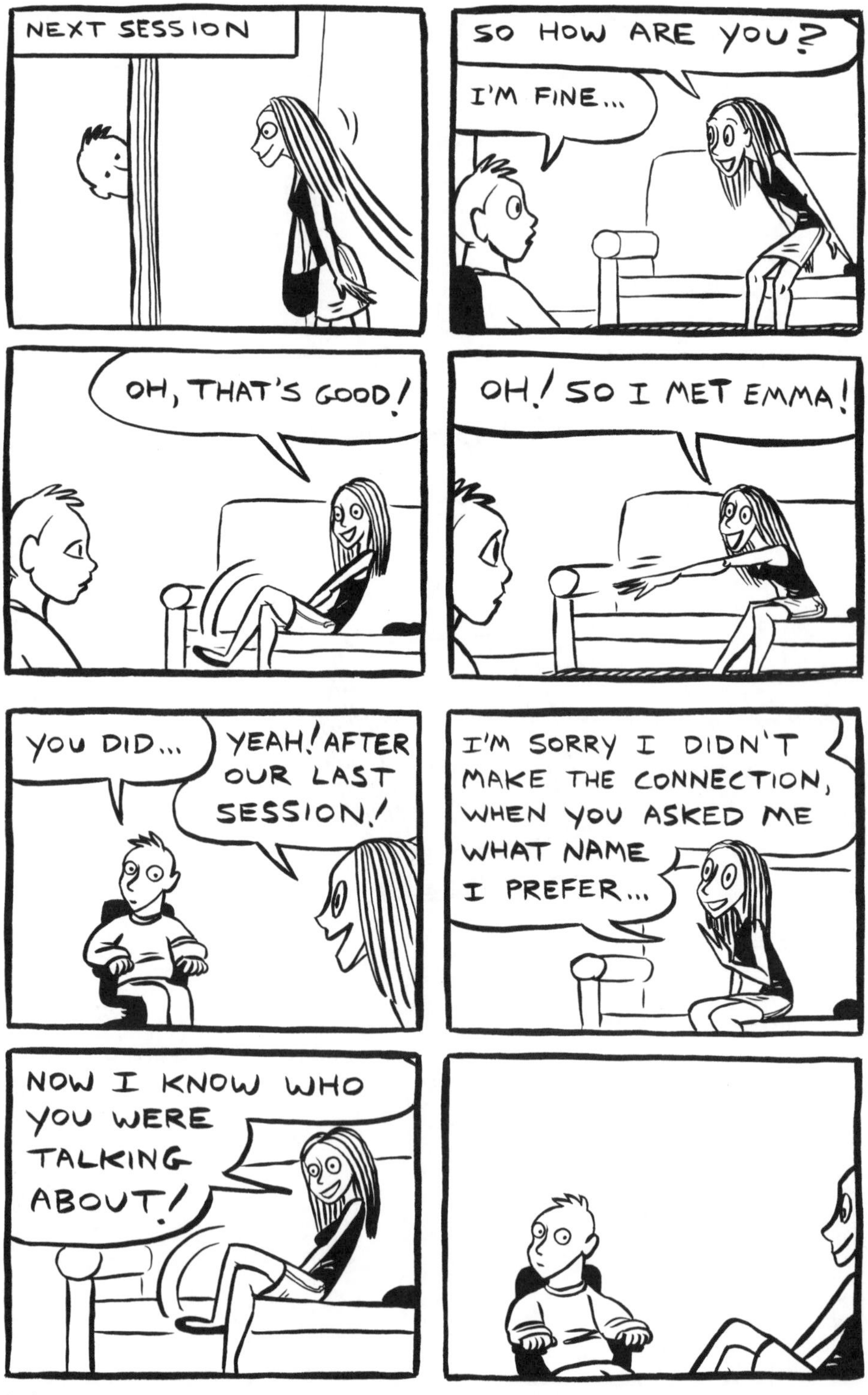
NEXT SESSION
SO HOW ARE YOU?
I'M FINE...
OH, THAT'S GOOD!
OH! SO I MET EMMA!
YOU DID...
YEAH! AFTER OUR LAST SESSION!
I'M SORRY I DIDN'T MAKE THE CONNECTION, WHEN YOU ASKED ME WHAT NAME I PREFER...
NOW I KNOW WHO YOU WERE TALKING ABOUT!

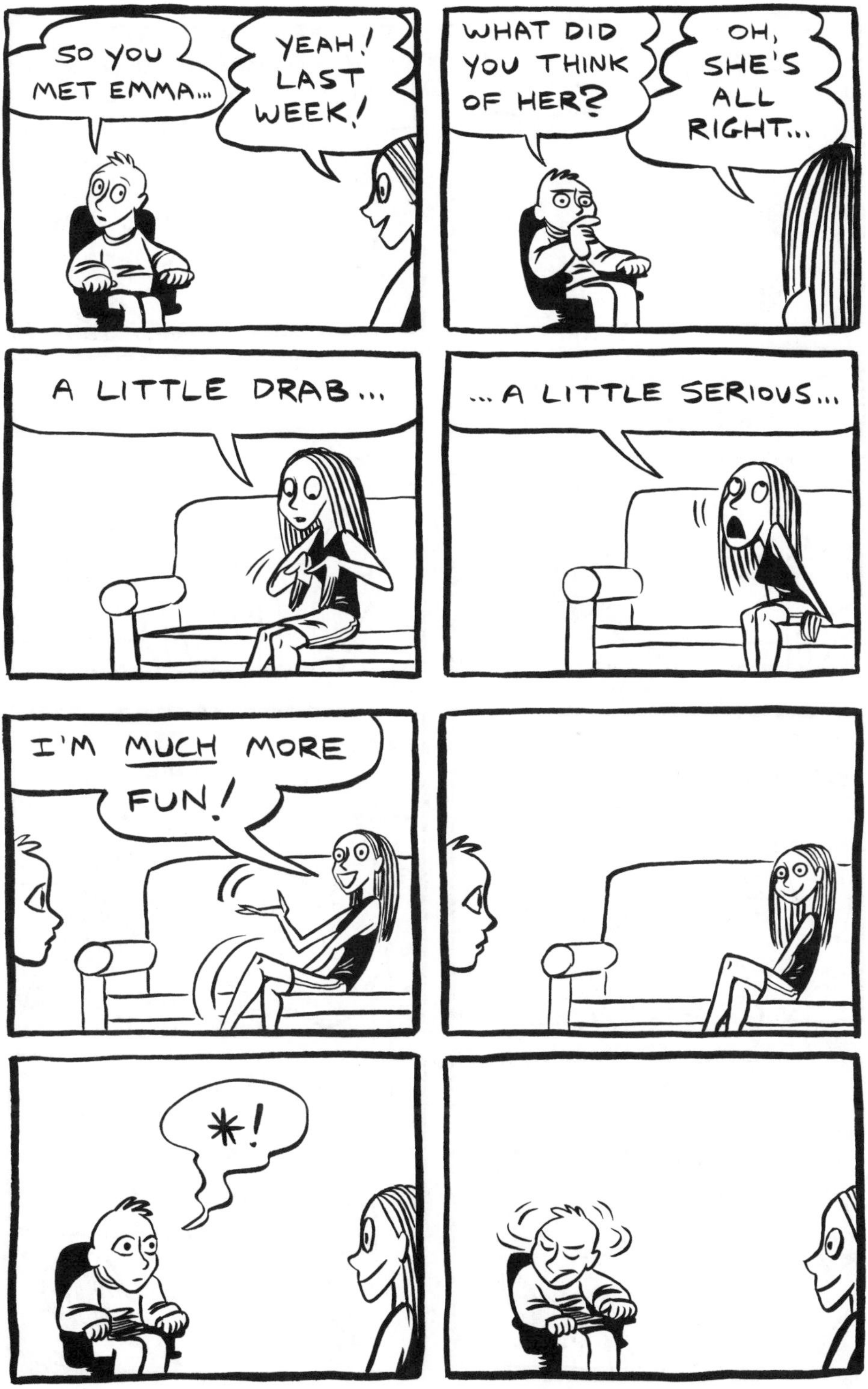
SO YOU MET EMMA...
YEAH! LAST WEEK!
WHAT DID YOU THINK OF HER?
OH, SHE'S ALL RIGHT...
A LITTLE DRAB...
...A LITTLE SERIOUS...
I'M MUCH MORE FUN!
*!

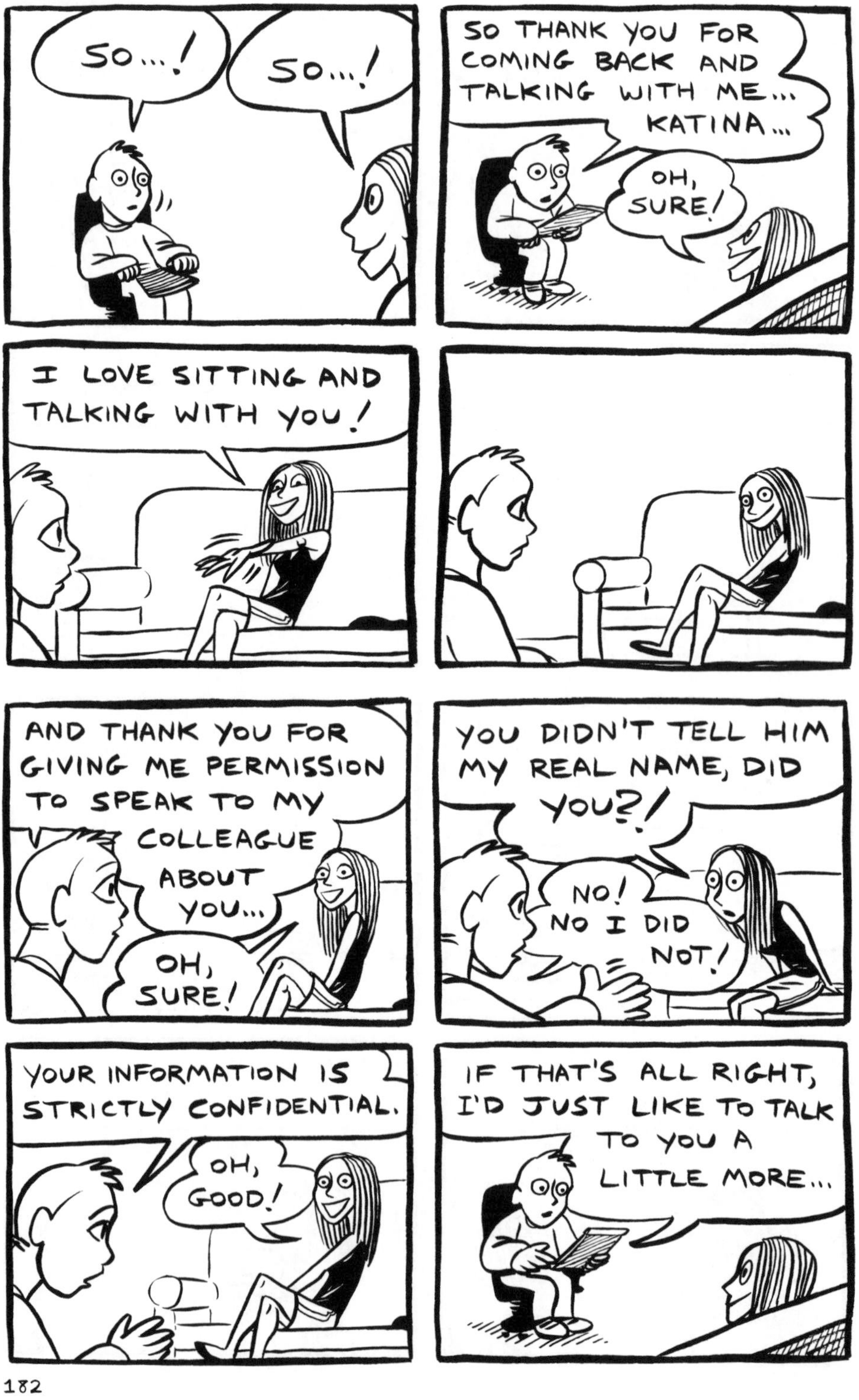
SO...!
SO...!
SO THANK YOU FOR COMING BACK AND TALKING WITH ME... KATINA...
OH, SURE!
I LOVE SITTING AND TALKING WITH YOU!
AND THANK YOU FOR GIVING ME PERMISSION TO SPEAK TO MY COLLEAGUE ABOUT YOU...
OH, SURE!
YOU DIDN'T TELL HIM MY REAL NAME, DID YOU?!
NO! NO I DID NOT!
YOUR INFORMATION IS STRICTLY CONFIDENTIAL.
OH, GOOD!
IF THAT'S ALL RIGHT, I'D JUST LIKE TO TALK TO YOU A LITTLE MORE...

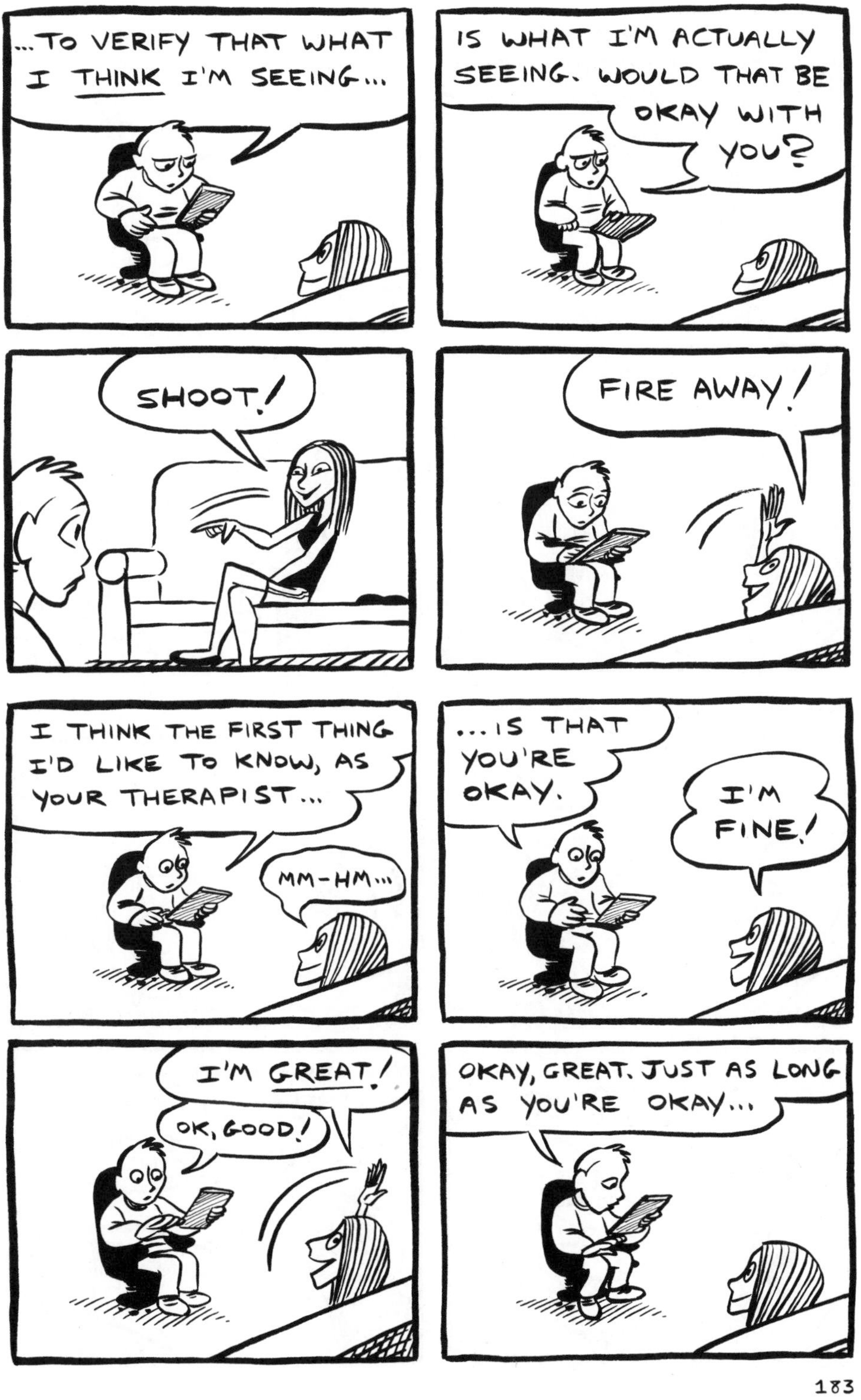
...TO VERIFY THAT WHAT I THINK I'M SEEING...
IS WHAT I'M ACTUALLY SEEING. WOULD THAT BE OKAY WITH YOU?
SHOOT!
FIRE AWAY!
I THINK THE FIRST THING I'D LIKE TO KNOW, AS YOUR THERAPIST...
MM-HM...
...IS THAT YOU'RE OKAY.
I'M FINE!
I'M GREAT!
OK, GOOD!
OKAY, GREAT. JUST AS LONG AS YOU'RE OKAY...

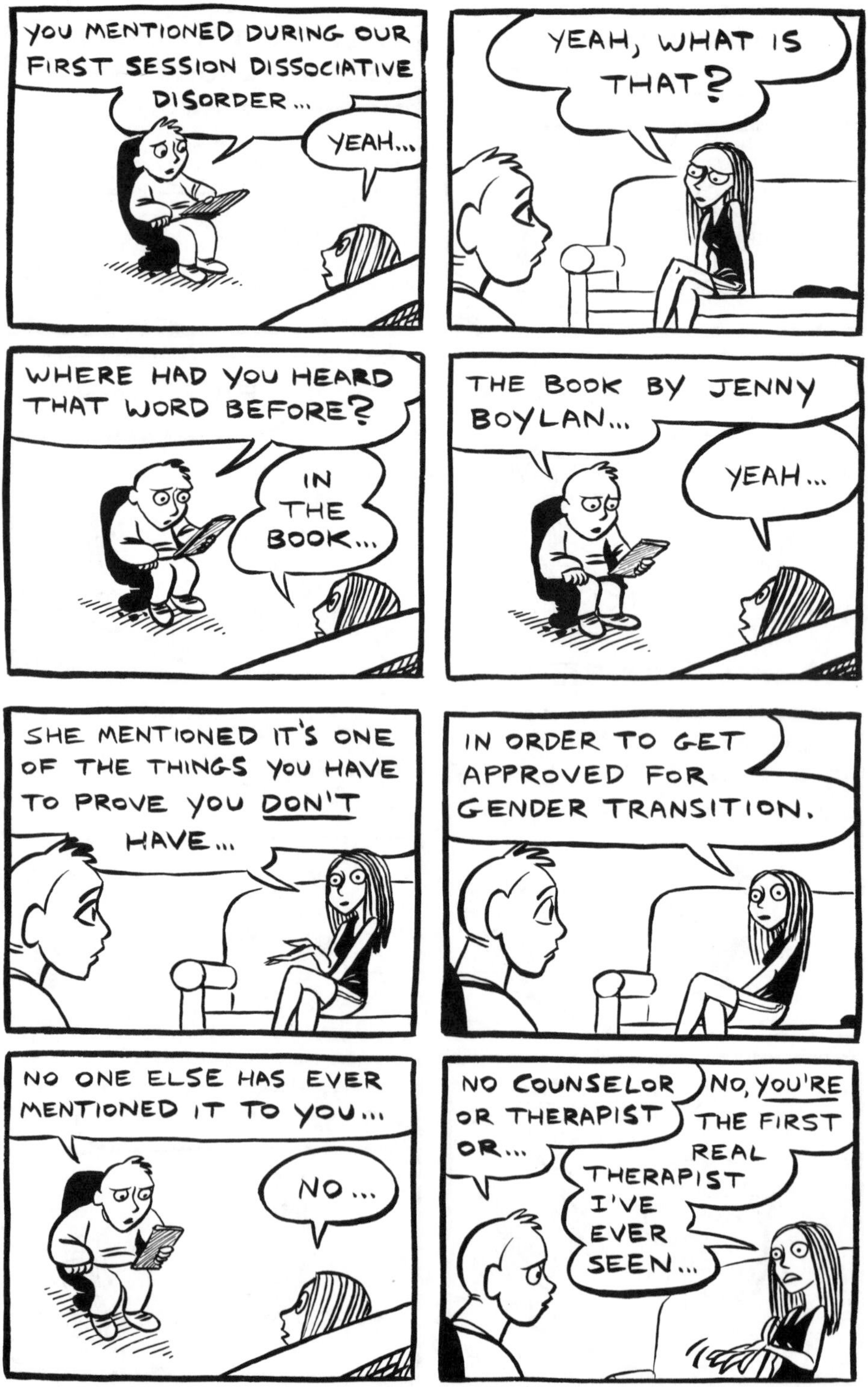
YOU MENTIONED DURING OUR FIRST SESSION DISSOCIATIVE DISORDER...
YEAH...
YEAH, WHAT IS THAT?
WHERE HAD YOU HEARD THAT WORD BEFORE?
IN THE BOOK...
THE BOOK BY JENNY BOYLAN...
YEAH...
SHE MENTIONED IT'S ONE OF THE THINGS YOU HAVE TO PROVE YOU DON'T HAVE...
IN ORDER TO GET APPROVED FOR GENDER TRANSITION.
NO ONE ELSE HAS EVER MENTIONED IT TO YOU...
NO...
NO COUNSELOR OR THERAPIST OR...
NO, YOU'RE THE FIRST REAL THERAPIST I'VE EVER SEEN...

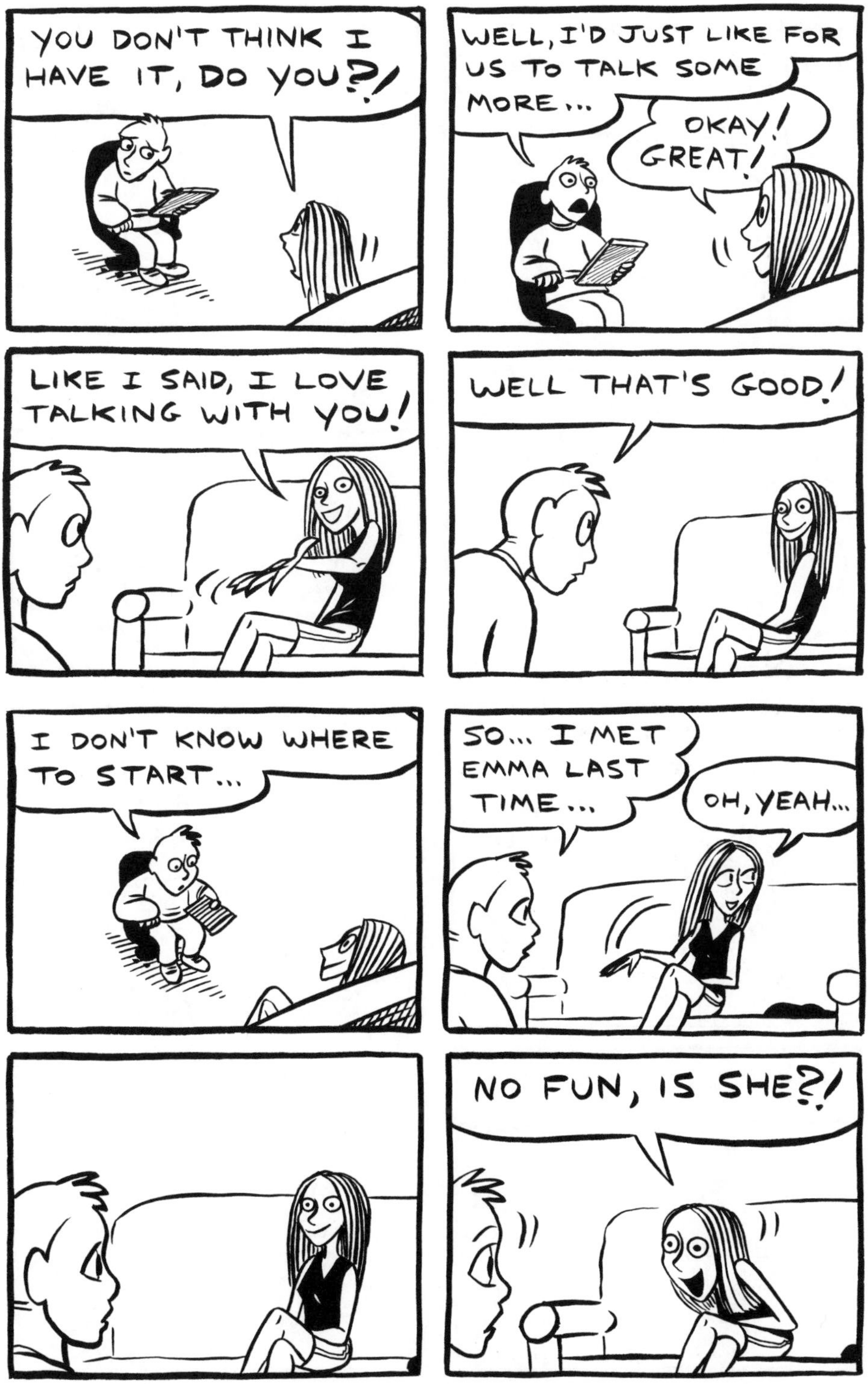
YOU DON'T THINK I HAVE IT, DO YOU?!
WELL, I'D JUST LIKE FOR US TO TALK SOME MORE...
OKAY! GREAT!
LIKE I SAID, I LOVE TALKING WITH YOU!
WELL THAT'S GOOD!
I DON'T KNOW WHERE TO START...
SO... I MET EMMA LAST TIME...
OH, YEAH...
NO FUN, IS SHE?!

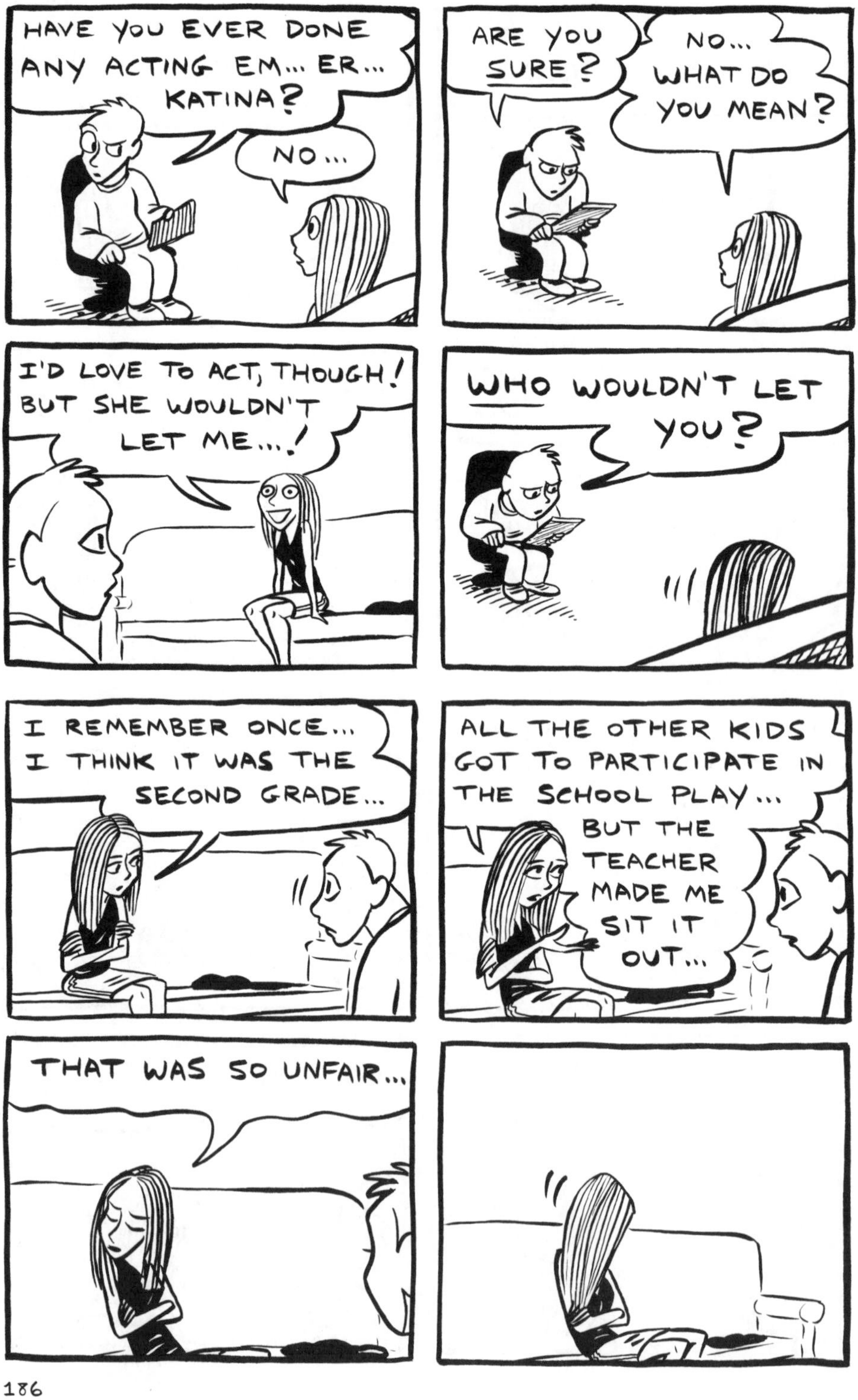
HAVE YOU EVER DONE ANY ACTING EM... ER... KATINA?
NO...
ARE YOU SURE?
NO... WHAT DO YOU MEAN?
I'D LOVE TO ACT, THOUGH! BUT SHE WOULDN'T LET ME...!
WHO WOULDN'T LET YOU?
I REMEMBER ONCE... I THINK IT WAS THE SECOND GRADE...
ALL THE OTHER KIDS GOT TO PARTICIPATE IN THE SCHOOL PLAY...
BUT THE TEACHER MADE ME SIT IT OUT...
THAT WAS SO UNFAIR...

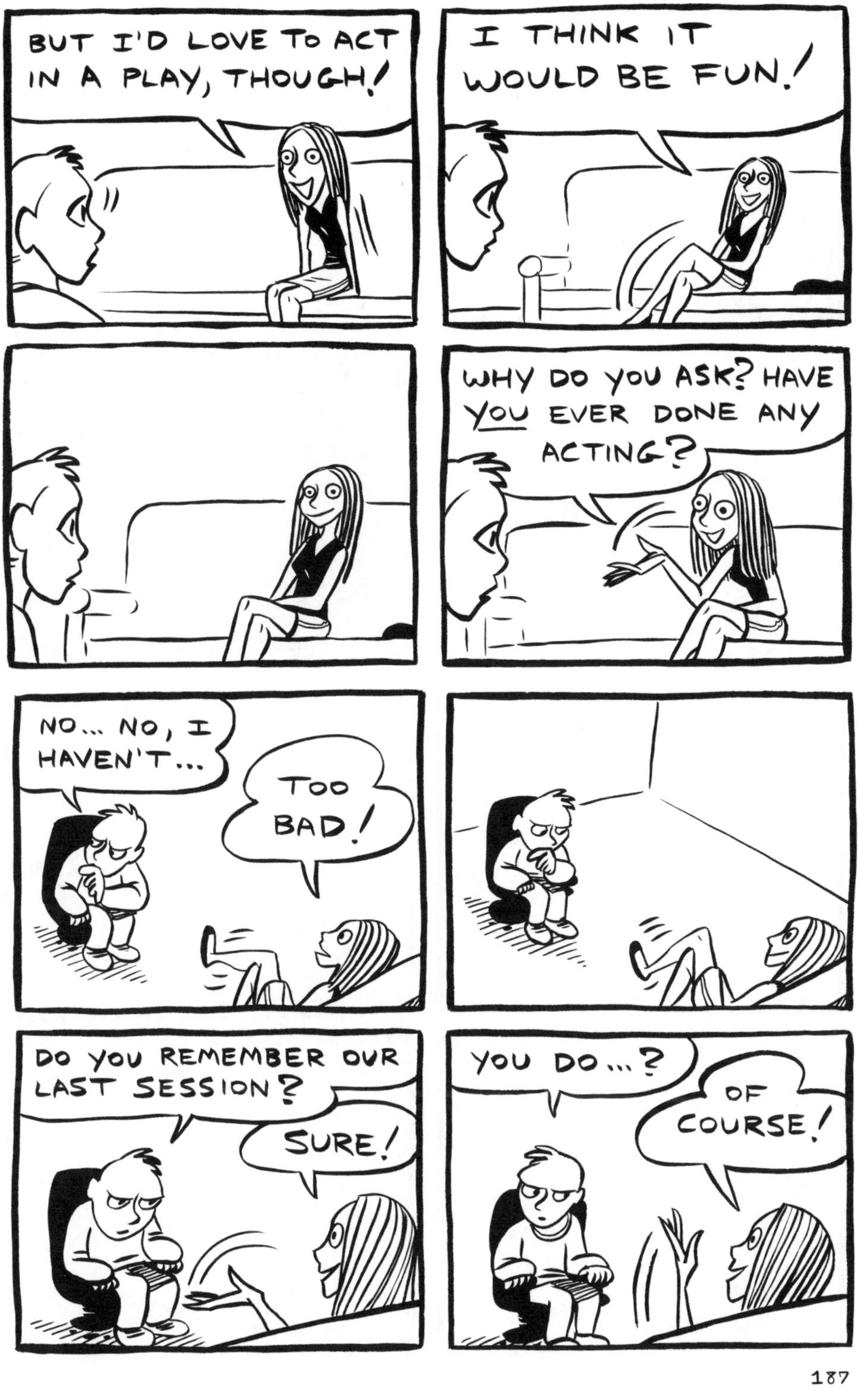
BUT I'D LOVE TO ACT IN A PLAY, THOUGH!
I THINK IT WOULD BE FUN!
WHY DO YOU ASK? HAVE YOU EVER DONE ANY ACTING?
NO... NO, I HAVEN'T...
TOO BAD!
DO YOU REMEMBER OUR LAST SESSION?
SURE!
YOU DO...?
OF COURSE!

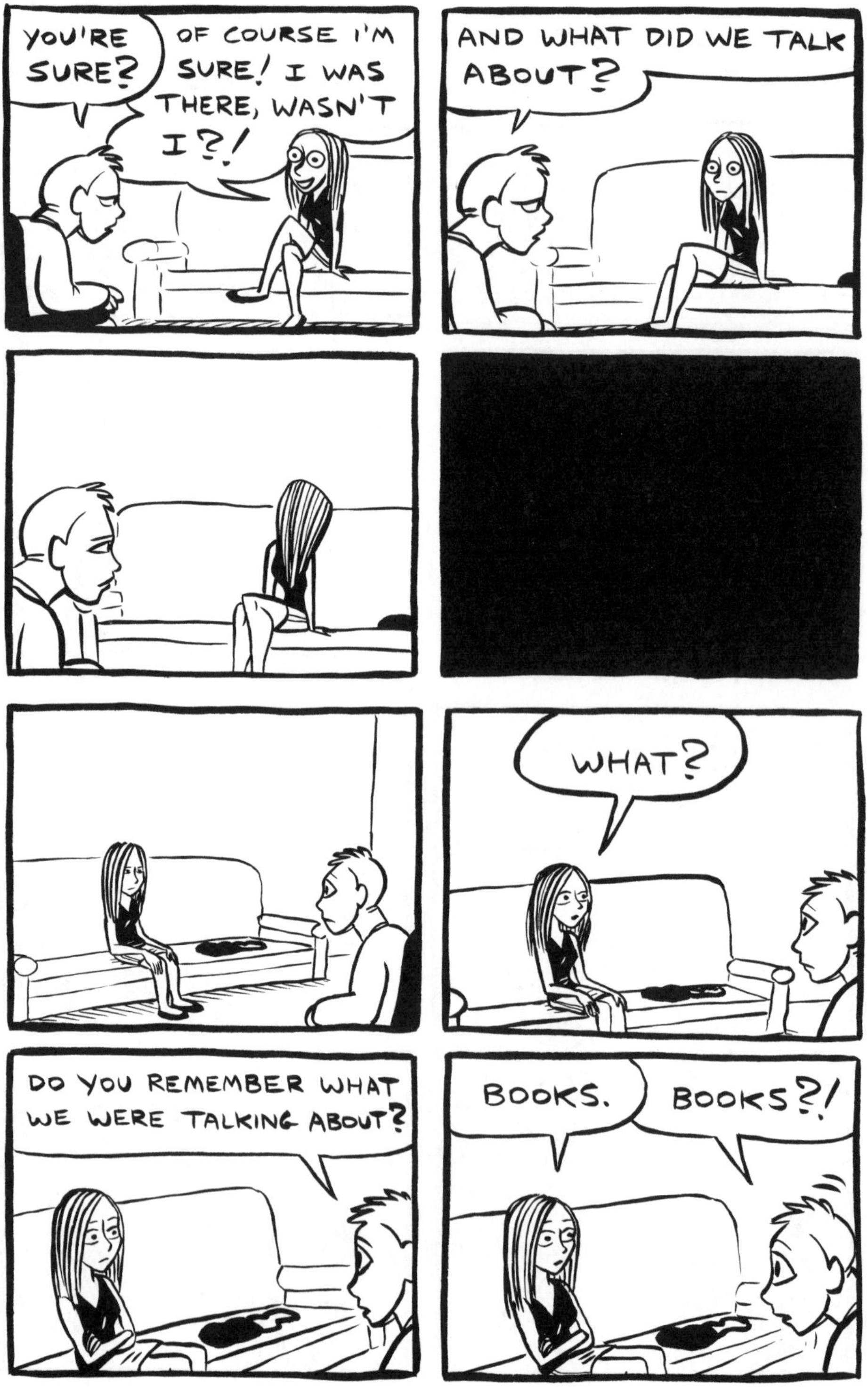
YOU'RE SURE?
OF COURSE I'M SURE! I WAS THERE, WASN'T I?!
AND WHAT DID WE TALK ABOUT?
WHAT?
DO YOU REMEMBER WHAT WE WERE TALKING ABOUT?
BOOKS.
BOOKS?!

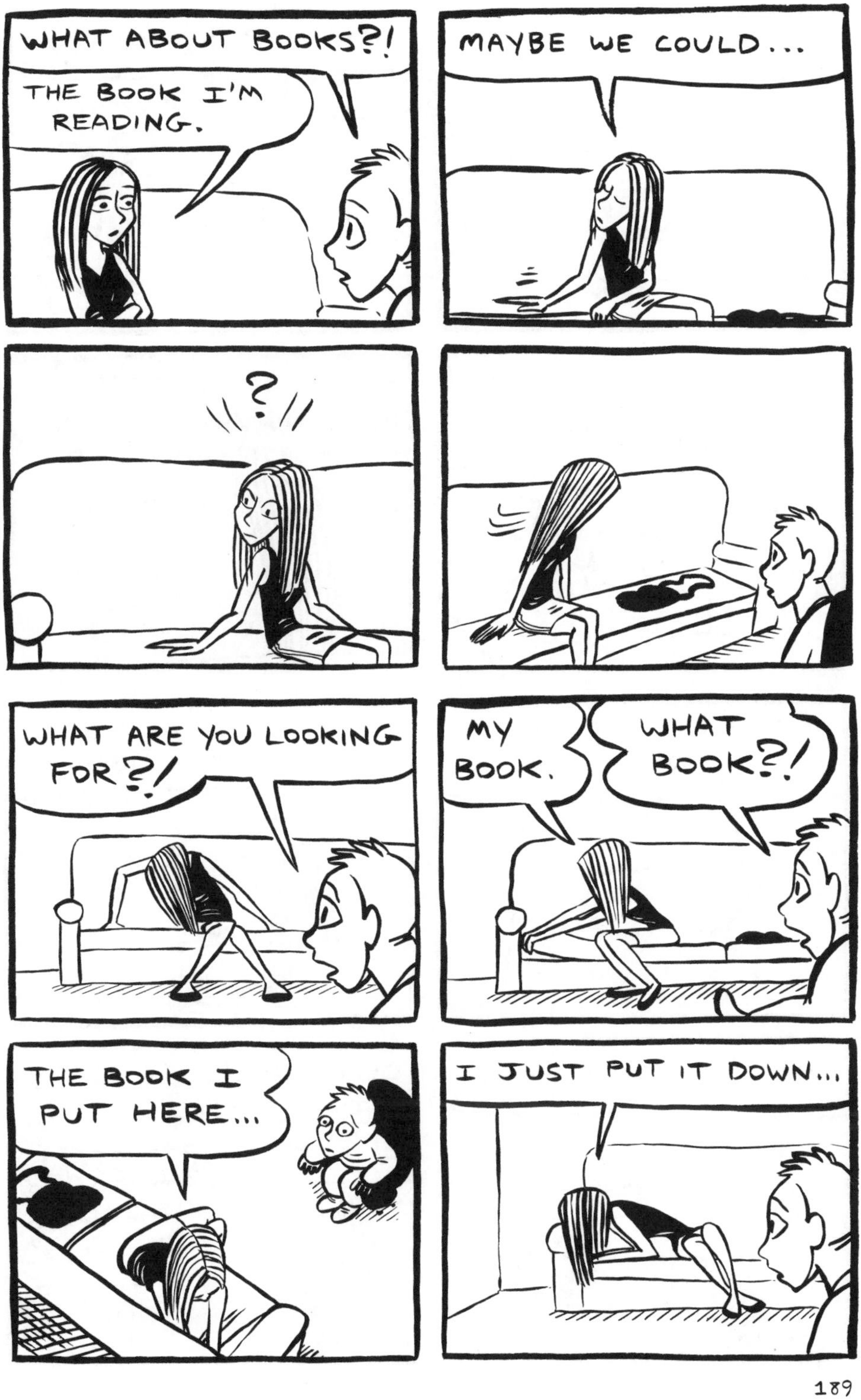
WHAT ABOUT BOOKS?!
THE BOOK I'M READING.
MAYBE WE COULD...
?
WHAT ARE YOU LOOKING FOR?!
MY BOOK.
WHAT BOOK?!
THE BOOK I PUT HERE...
I JUST PUT IT DOWN...

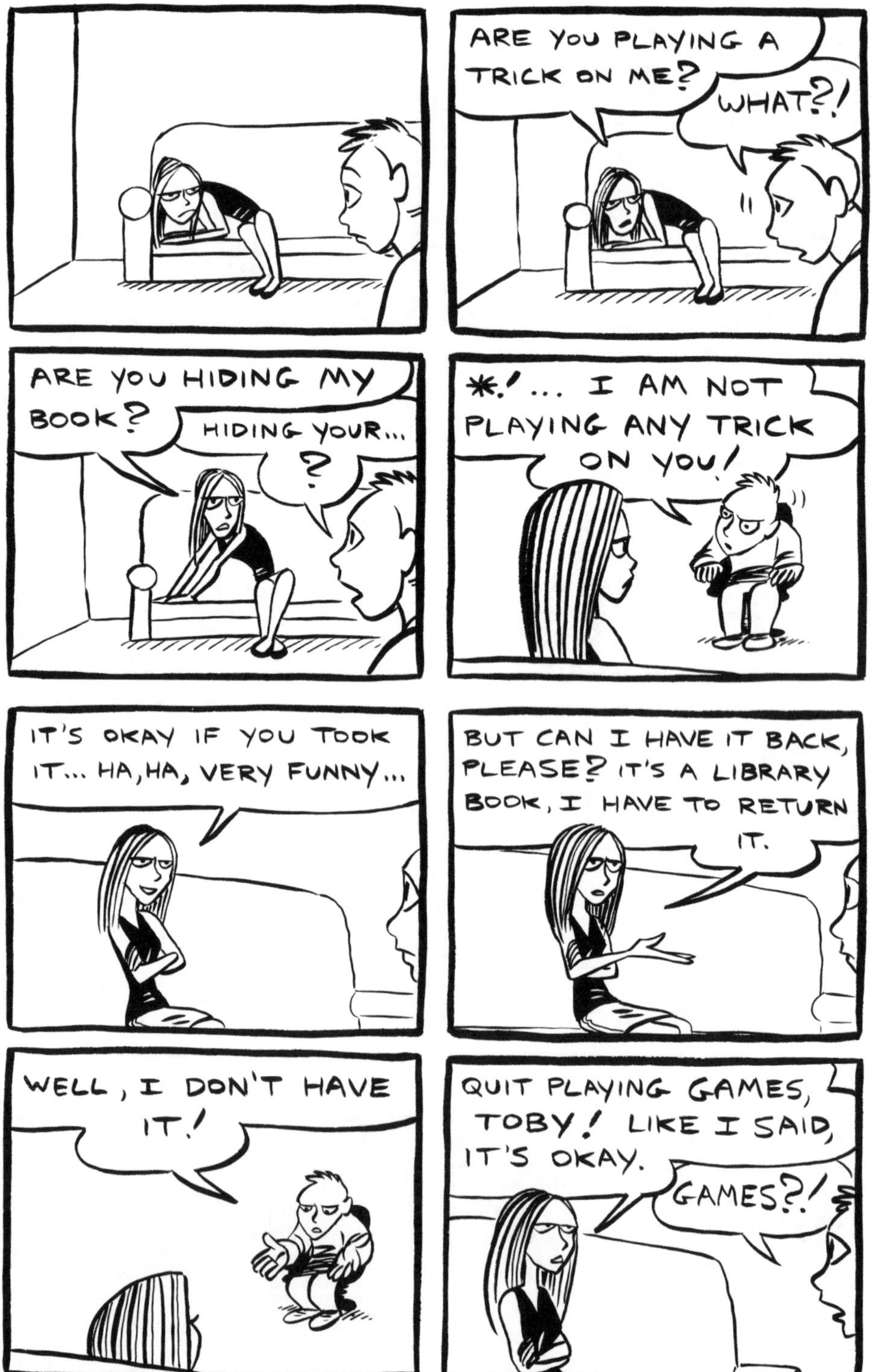
ARE YOU PLAYING A TRICK ON ME?
WHAT?!
ARE YOU HIDING MY BOOK?
HIDING YOUR...
?
*!... I AM NOT PLAYING ANY TRICK ON YOU!
IT'S OKAY IF YOU TOOK IT... HA, HA, VERY FUNNY...
BUT CAN I HAVE IT BACK, PLEASE? IT'S A LIBRARY BOOK, I HAVE TO RETURN IT.
WELL, I DON'T HAVE IT!
QUIT PLAYING GAMES, TOBY! LIKE I SAID, IT'S OKAY.
GAMES?!

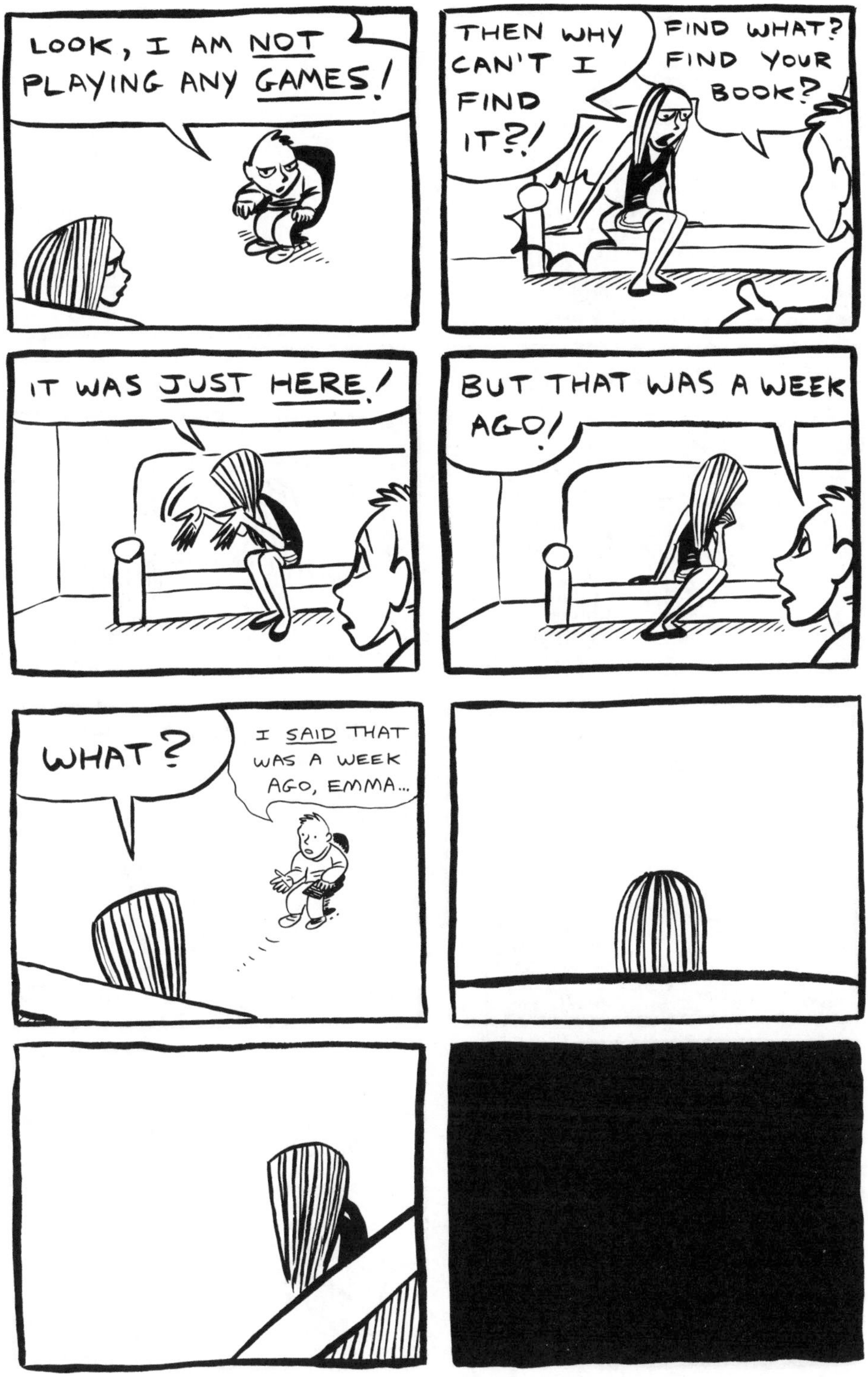

LOOK, I AM NOT PLAYING ANY GAMES!
THEN WHY CAN'T I FIND IT?!
FIND WHAT? FIND YOUR BOOK?
IT WAS JUST HERE!
BUT THAT WAS A WEEK AGO!
WHAT?
I SAID THAT WAS A WEEK AGO, EMMA...

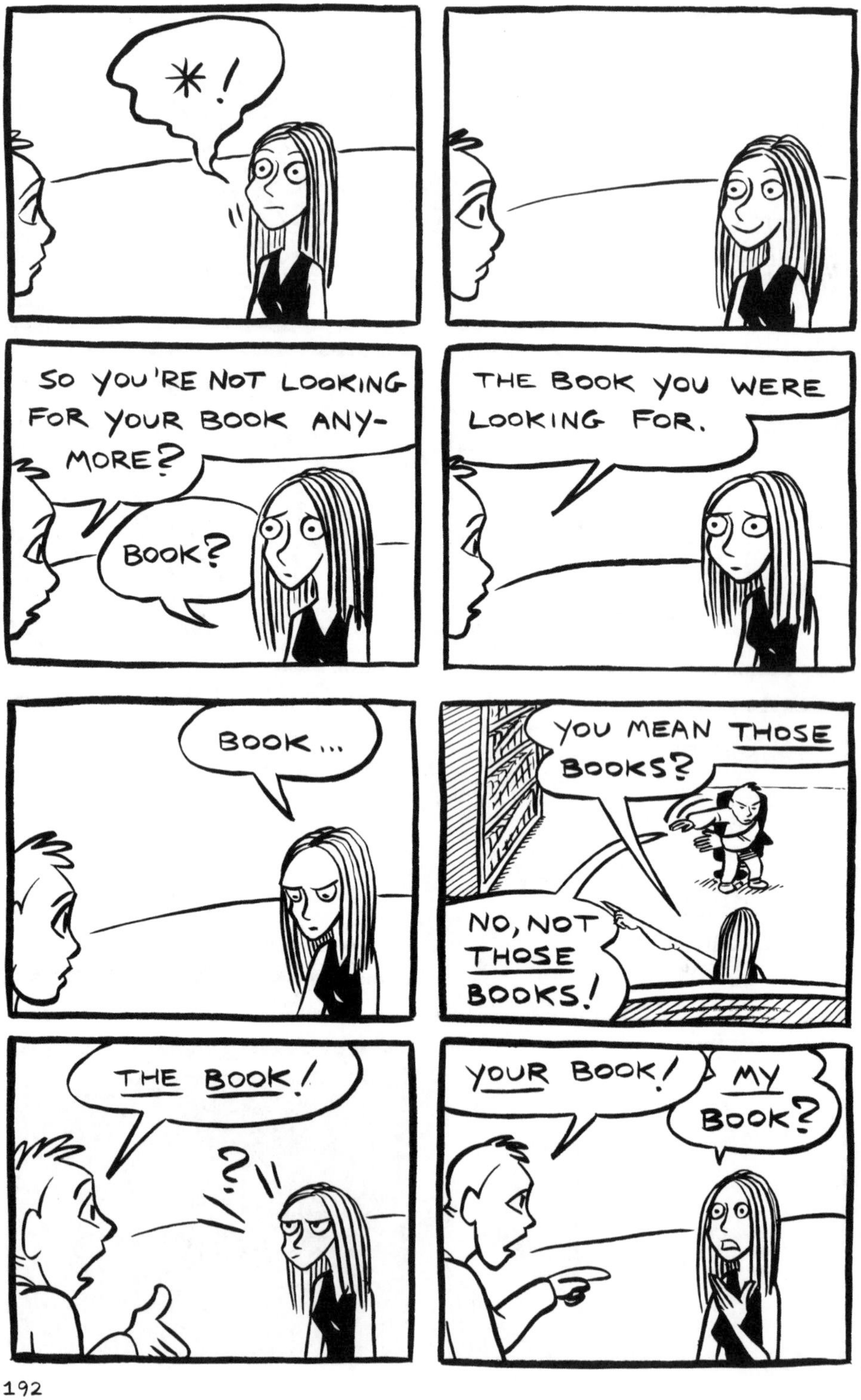
*!
SO YOU'RE NOT LOOKING FOR YOUR BOOK ANY-MORE?
BOOK?
THE BOOK YOU WERE LOOKING FOR.
BOOK...
YOU MEAN THOSE BOOKS?
NO, NOT THOSE BOOKS!
THE BOOK!
?!
YOUR BOOK!
MY BOOK?

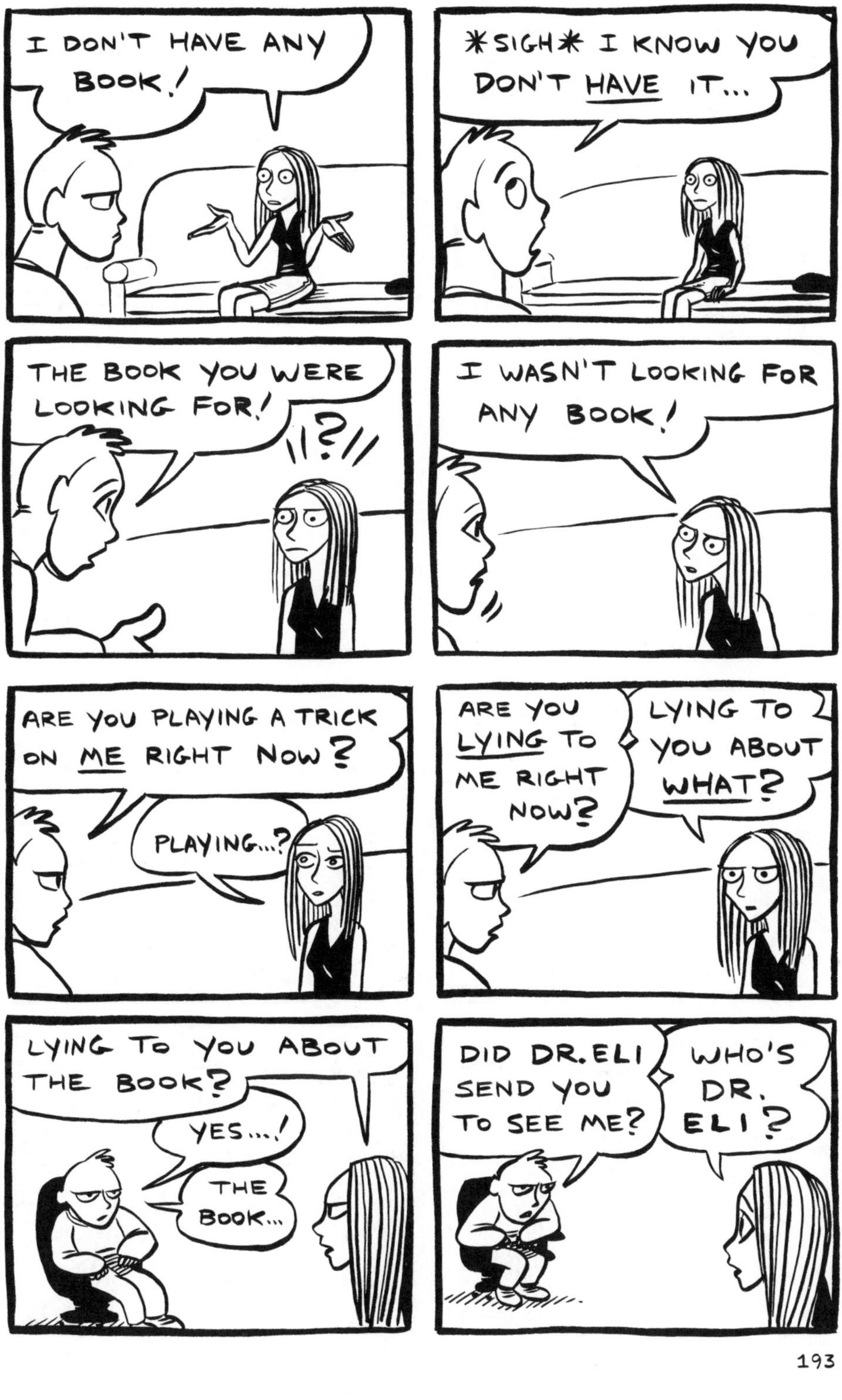
I DON'T HAVE ANY BOOK!
SIGH I KNOW YOU DON'T HAVE IT...
THE BOOK YOU WERE LOOKING FOR!
?
I WASN'T LOOKING FOR ANY BOOK!
ARE YOU PLAYING A TRICK ON ME RIGHT NOW?
PLAYING...?
ARE YOU LYING TO ME RIGHT NOW?
LYING TO YOU ABOUT WHAT?
LYING TO YOU ABOUT THE BOOK?
YES...!
THE BOOK...
DID DR. ELI SEND YOU TO SEE ME?
WHO'S DR. ELI?

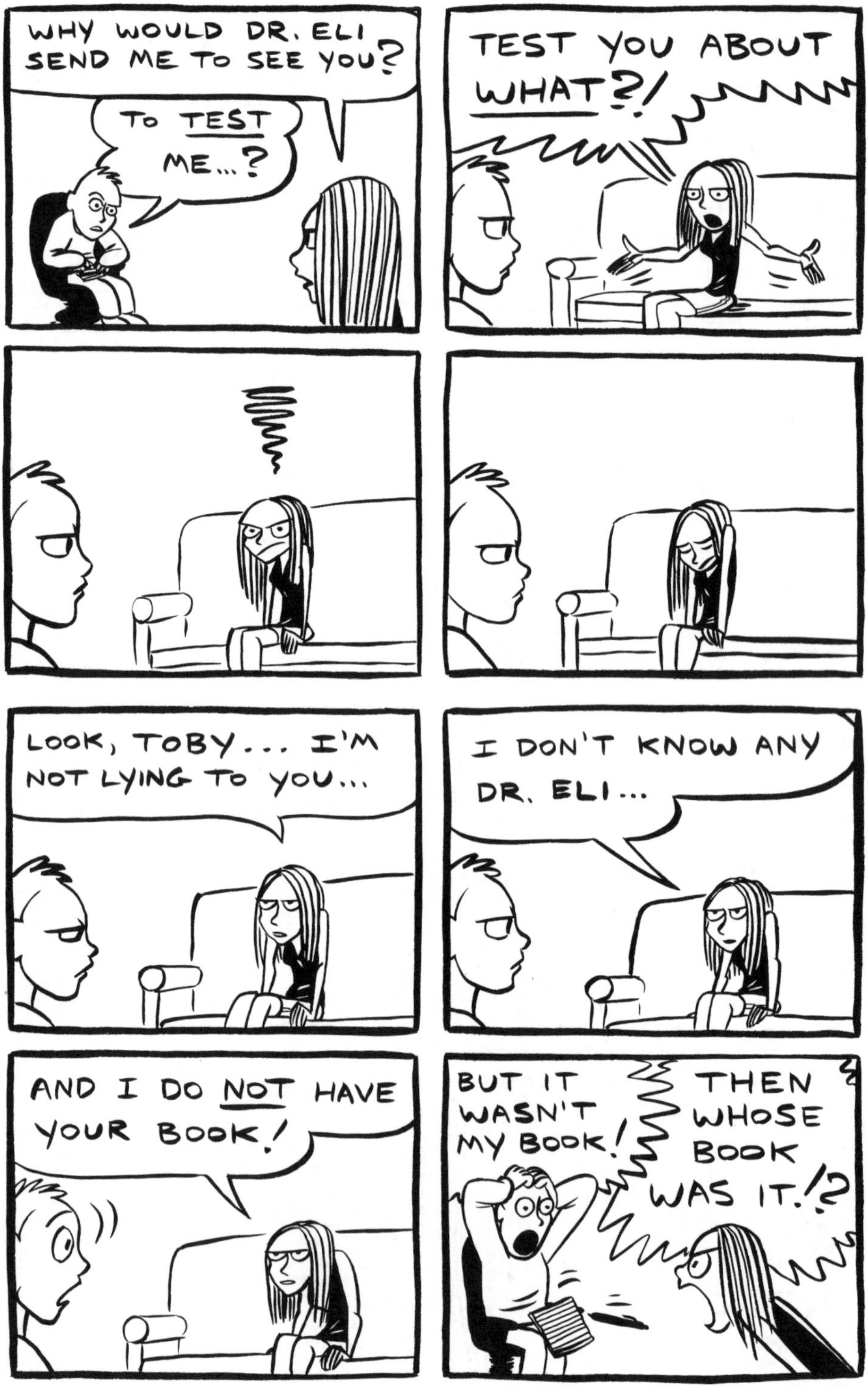
WHY WOULD DR. ELI SEND ME TO SEE YOU?
TO TEST ME...?
TEST YOU ABOUT WHAT?!
LOOK, TOBY... I'M NOT LYING TO YOU...
I DON'T KNOW ANY DR. ELI...
AND I DO NOT HAVE YOUR BOOK!
BUT IT WASN'T MY BOOK!
THEN WHOSE BOOK WAS IT.!?

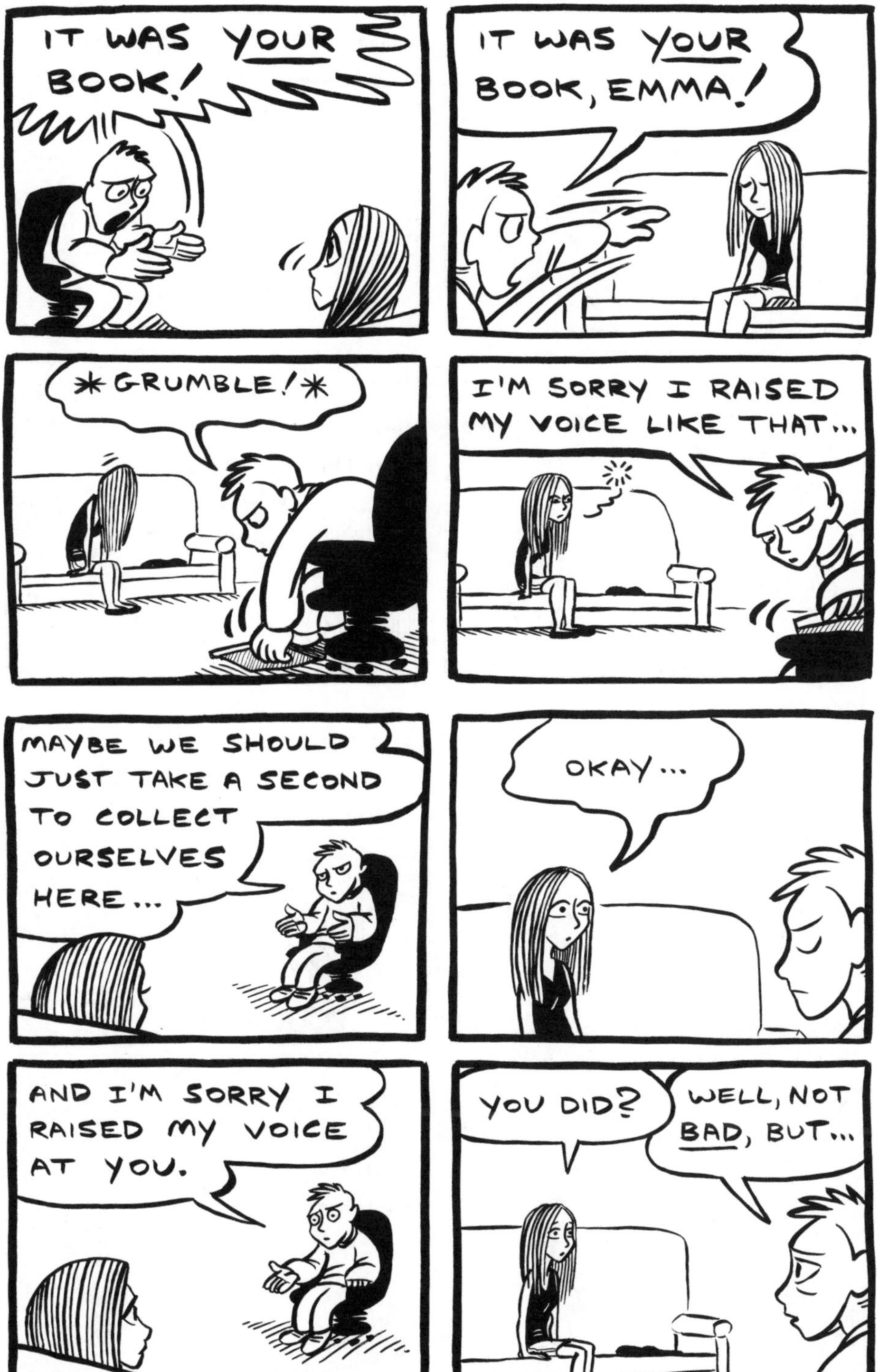
IT WAS YOUR BOOK!
IT WAS YOUR BOOK, EMMA!
GRUMBLE!
I'M SORRY I RAISED MY VOICE LIKE THAT...
MAYBE WE SHOULD JUST TAKE A SECOND TO COLLECT OURSELVES HERE...
OKAY...
AND I'M SORRY I RAISED MY VOICE AT YOU.
YOU DID?
WELL, NOT BAD, BUT...

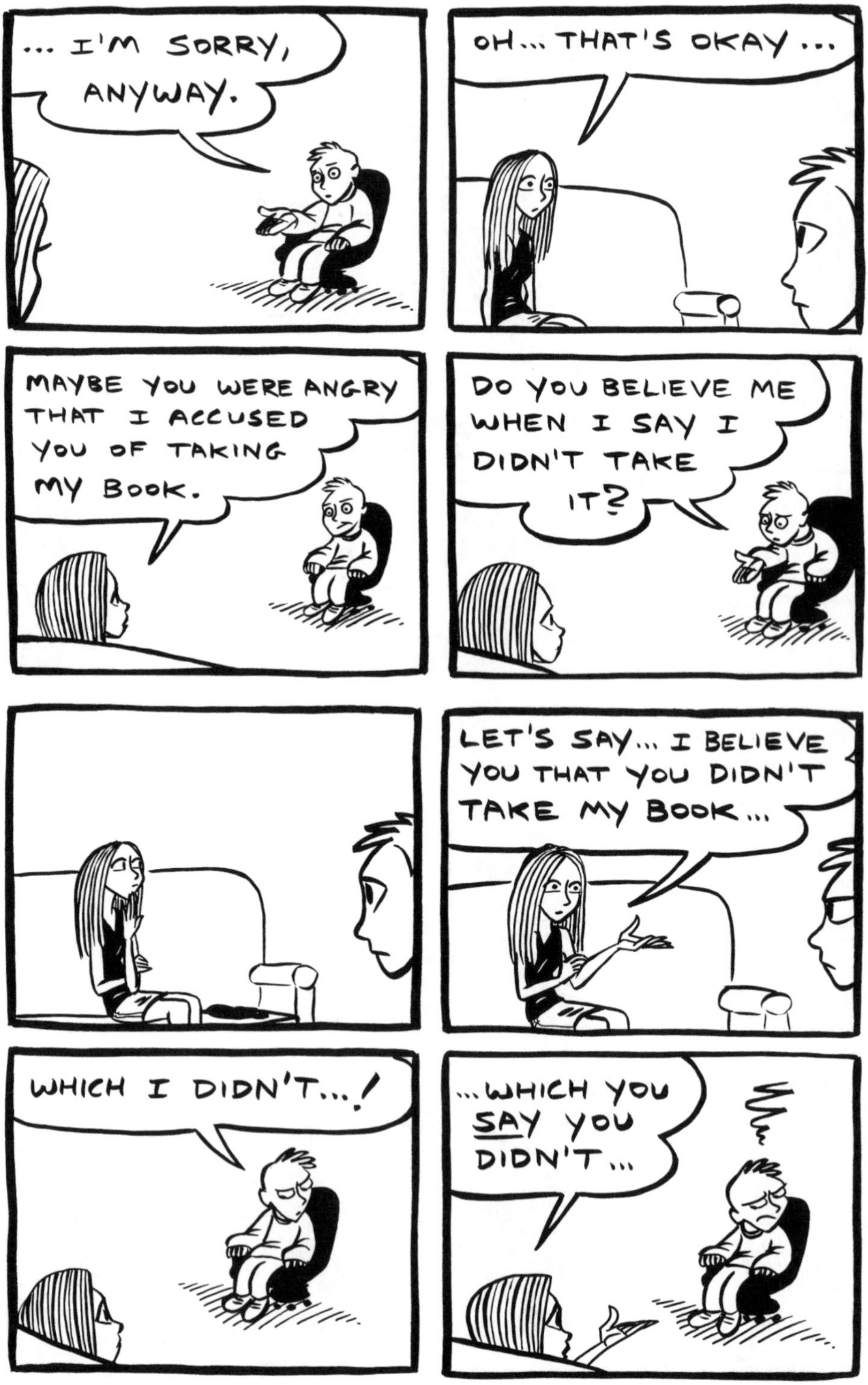
... I'M SORRY, ANYWAY.
OH... THAT'S OKAY...
MAYBE YOU WERE ANGRY THAT I ACCUSED YOU OF TAKING MY BOOK.
DO YOU BELIEVE ME WHEN I SAY I DIDN'T TAKE IT?
LET'S SAY... I BELIEVE YOU THAT YOU DIDN'T TAKE MY BOOK...
WHICH I DIDN'T...!
...WHICH YOU SAY YOU DIDN'T...

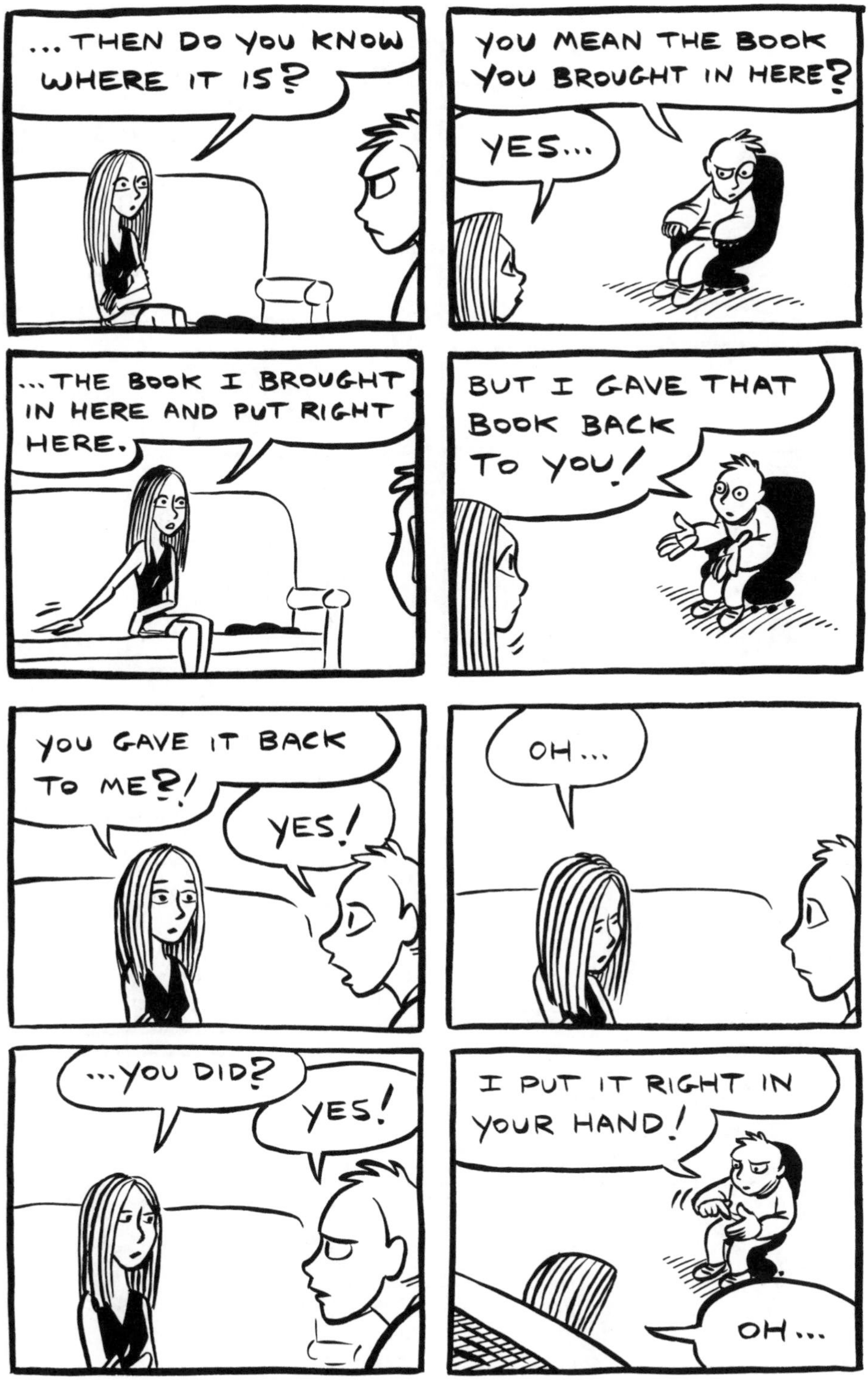

...THEN DO YOU KNOW WHERE IT IS?
YOU MEAN THE BOOK YOU BROUGHT IN HERE?
YES...
...THE BOOK I BROUGHT IN HERE AND PUT RIGHT HERE.
BUT I GAVE THAT BOOK BACK TO YOU!
YOU GAVE IT BACK TO ME?!
YES!
OH...
...YOU DID?
YES!
I PUT IT RIGHT IN YOUR HAND!
OH...

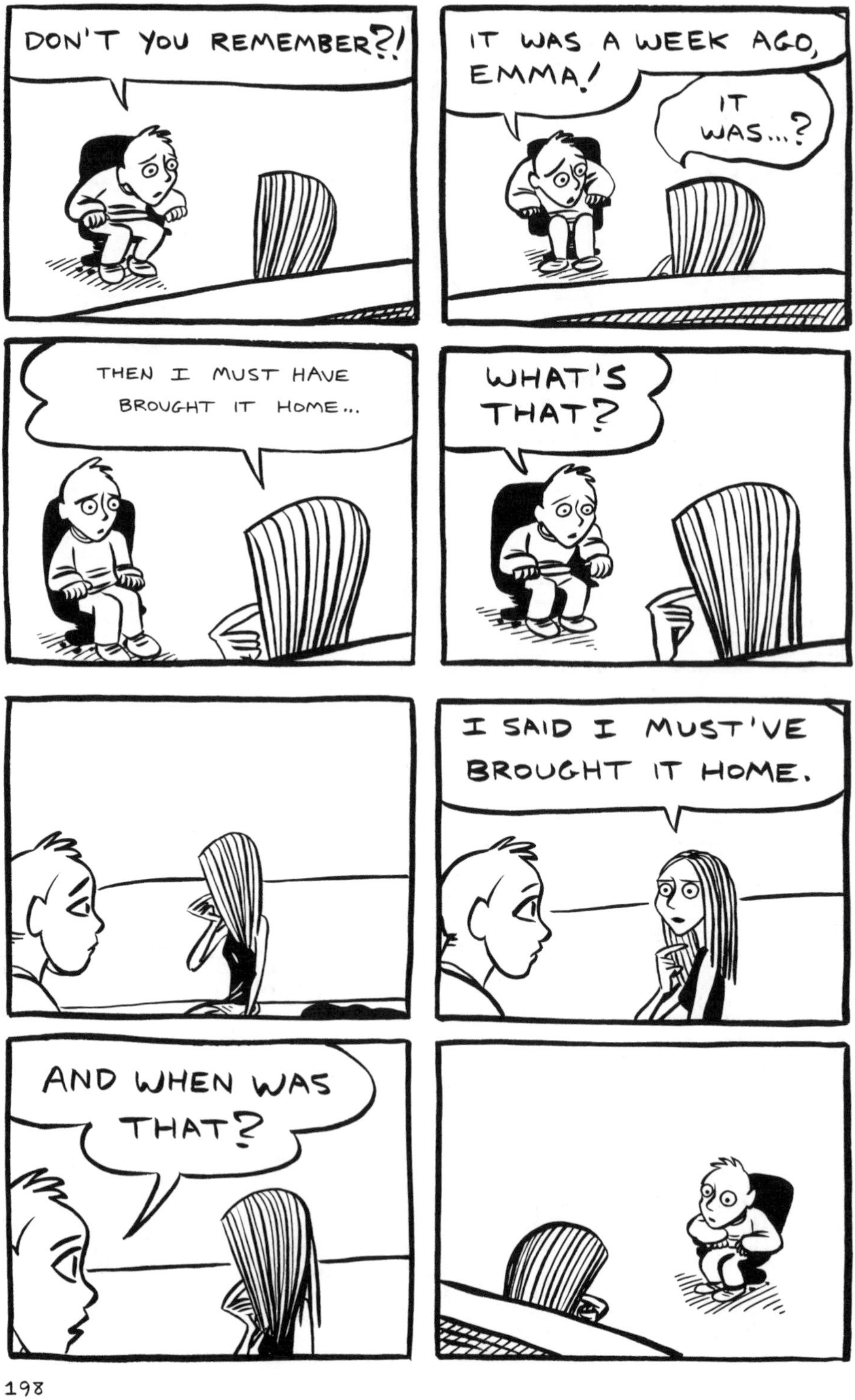
DON'T YOU REMEMBER?!
IT WAS A WEEK AGO, EMMA!
IT WAS...?
THEN I MUST HAVE BROUGHT IT HOME...
WHAT'S THAT?
I SAID I MUST'VE BROUGHT IT HOME.
AND WHEN WAS THAT?

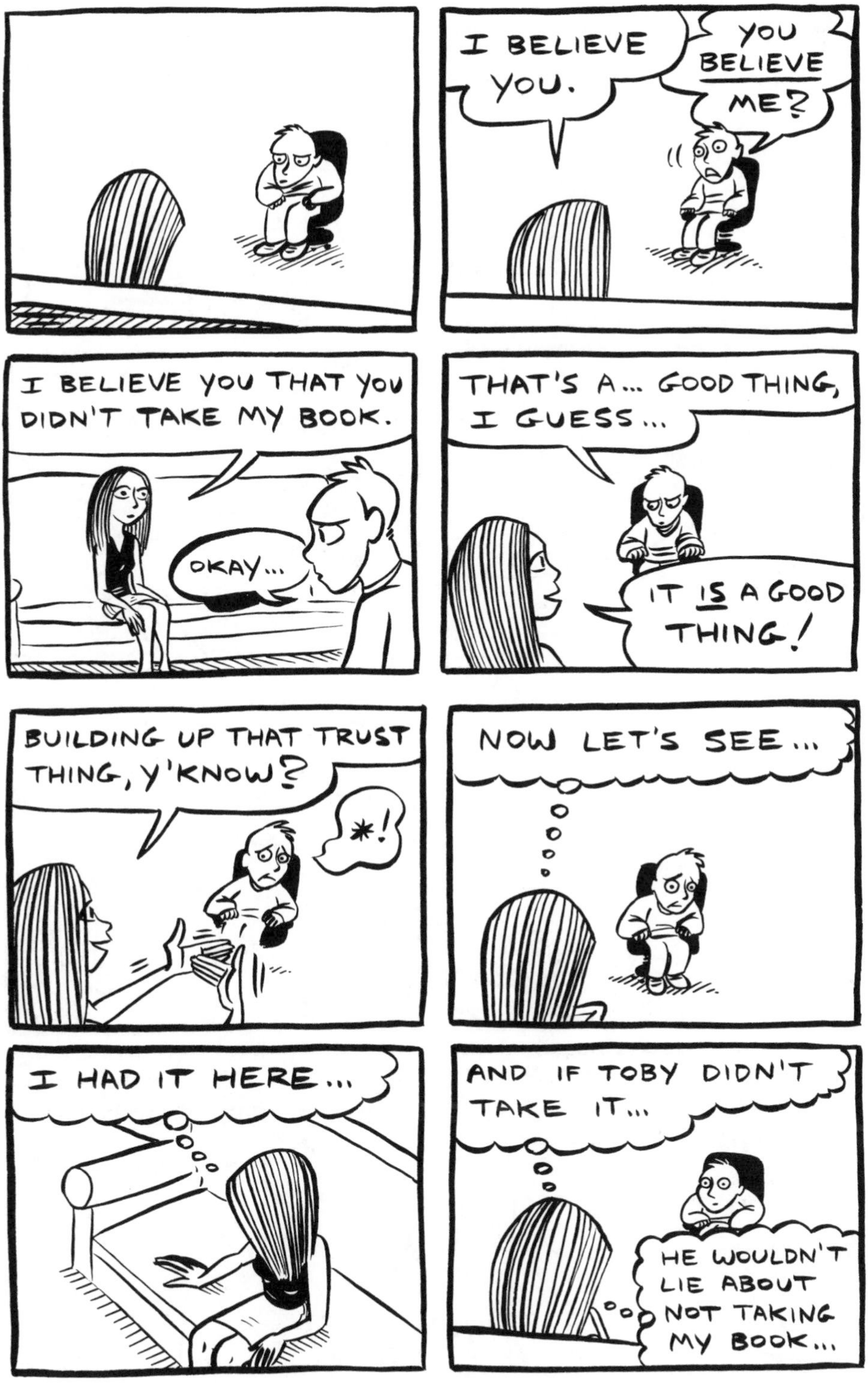
I BELIEVE YOU.
YOU BELIEVE ME?
I BELIEVE YOU THAT YOU DIDN'T TAKE MY BOOK.
OKAY...
THAT'S A... GOOD THING, I GUESS...
IT IS A GOOD THING!
BUILDING UP THAT TRUST THING, Y'KNOW?
*!
NOW LET'S SEE...
I HAD IT HERE...
AND IF TOBY DIDN'T TAKE IT...
HE WOULDN'T LIE ABOUT NOT TAKING MY BOOK...

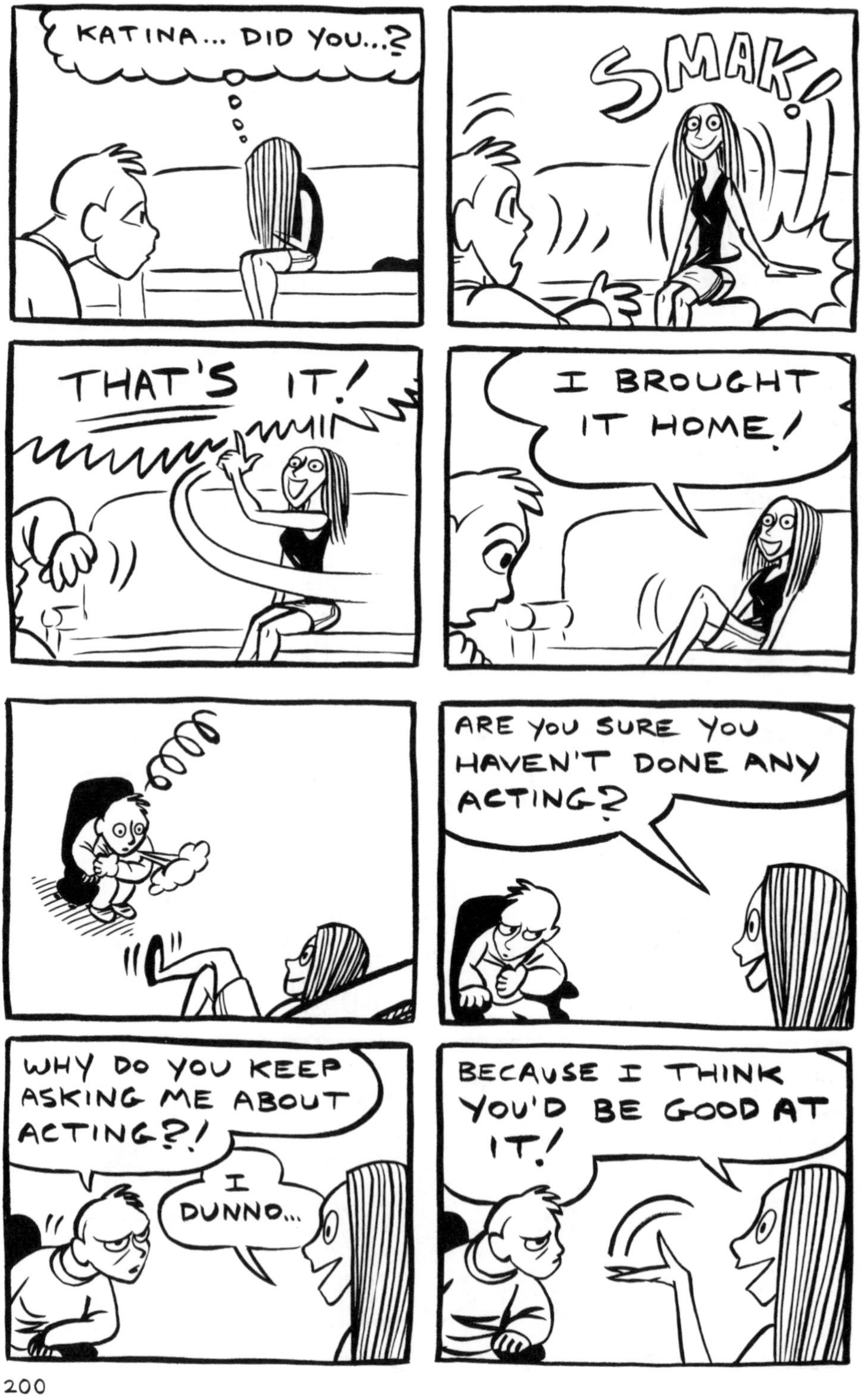

KATINA... DID YOU...?
SMAK!
THAT'S IT!
I BROUGHT IT HOME!
ARE YOU SURE YOU HAVEN'T DONE ANY ACTING?
WHY DO YOU KEEP ASKING ME ABOUT ACTING?!
I DUNNO...
BECAUSE I THINK YOU'D BE GOOD AT IT!

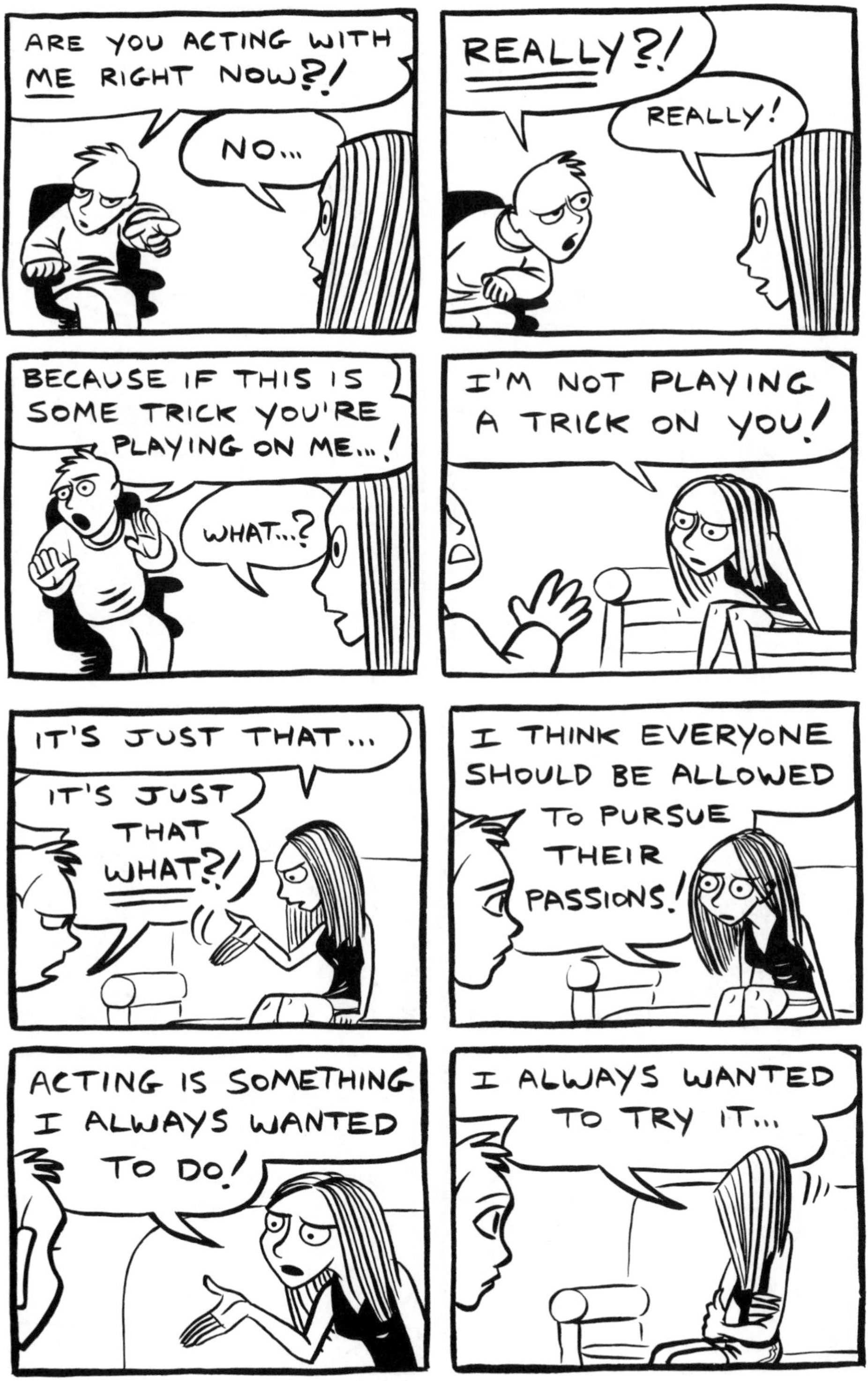
ARE YOU ACTING WITH ME RIGHT NOW?!
NO...
REALLY?!
REALLY!
BECAUSE IF THIS IS SOME TRICK YOU'RE PLAYING ON ME...!
WHAT...?
I'M NOT PLAYING A TRICK ON YOU!
IT'S JUST THAT...
IT'S JUST THAT WHAT?!
I THINK EVERYONE SHOULD BE ALLOWED TO PURSUE THEIR PASSIONS!
ACTING IS SOMETHING I ALWAYS WANTED TO DO!
I ALWAYS WANTED TO TRY IT...

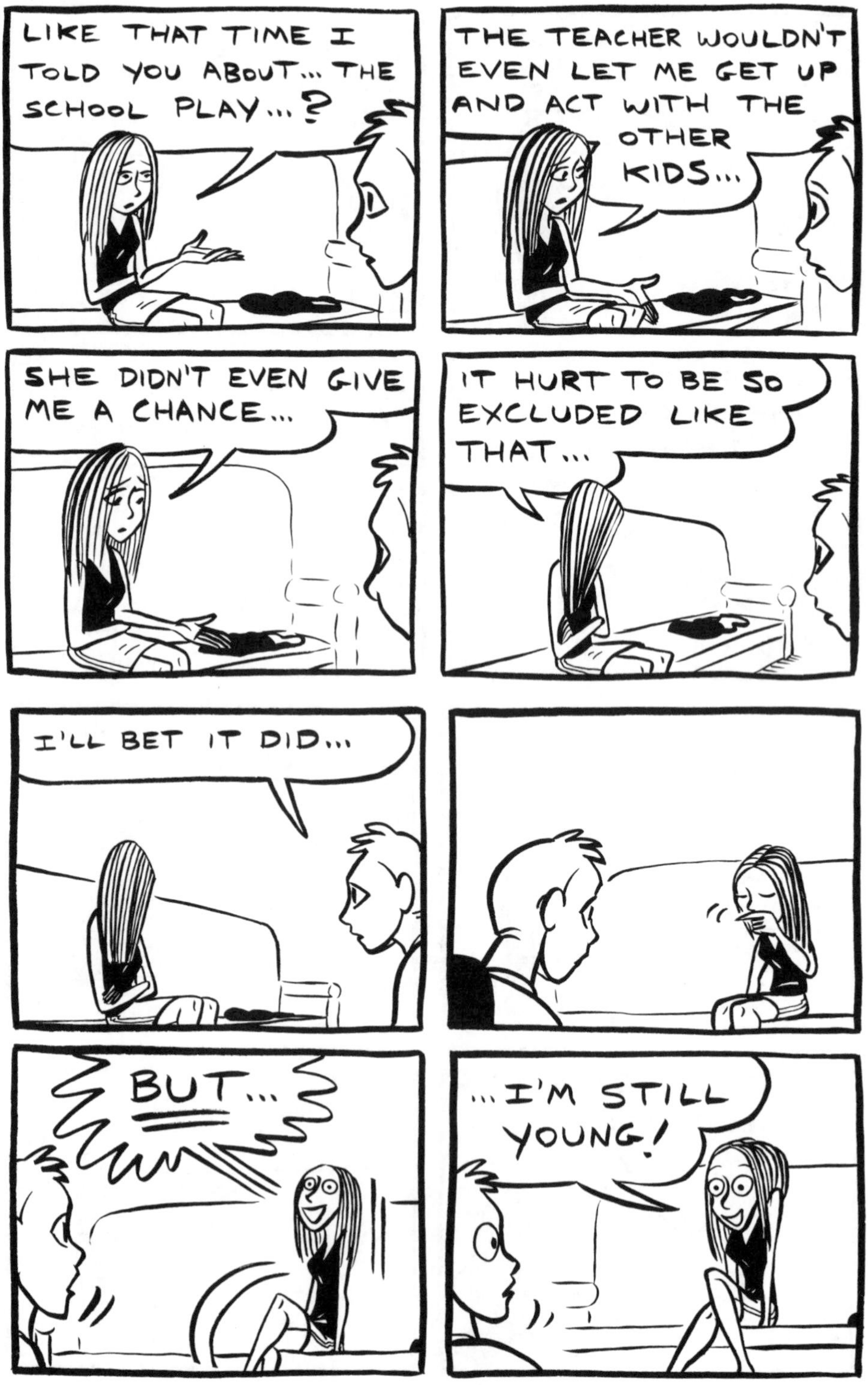
LIKE THAT TIME I TOLD YOU ABOUT... THE SCHOOL PLAY...?
THE TEACHER WOULDN'T EVEN LET ME GET UP AND ACT WITH THE OTHER KIDS...
SHE DIDN'T EVEN GIVE ME A CHANCE...
IT HURT TO BE SO EXCLUDED LIKE THAT...
I'LL BET IT DID...
BUT...
...I'M STILL YOUNG!

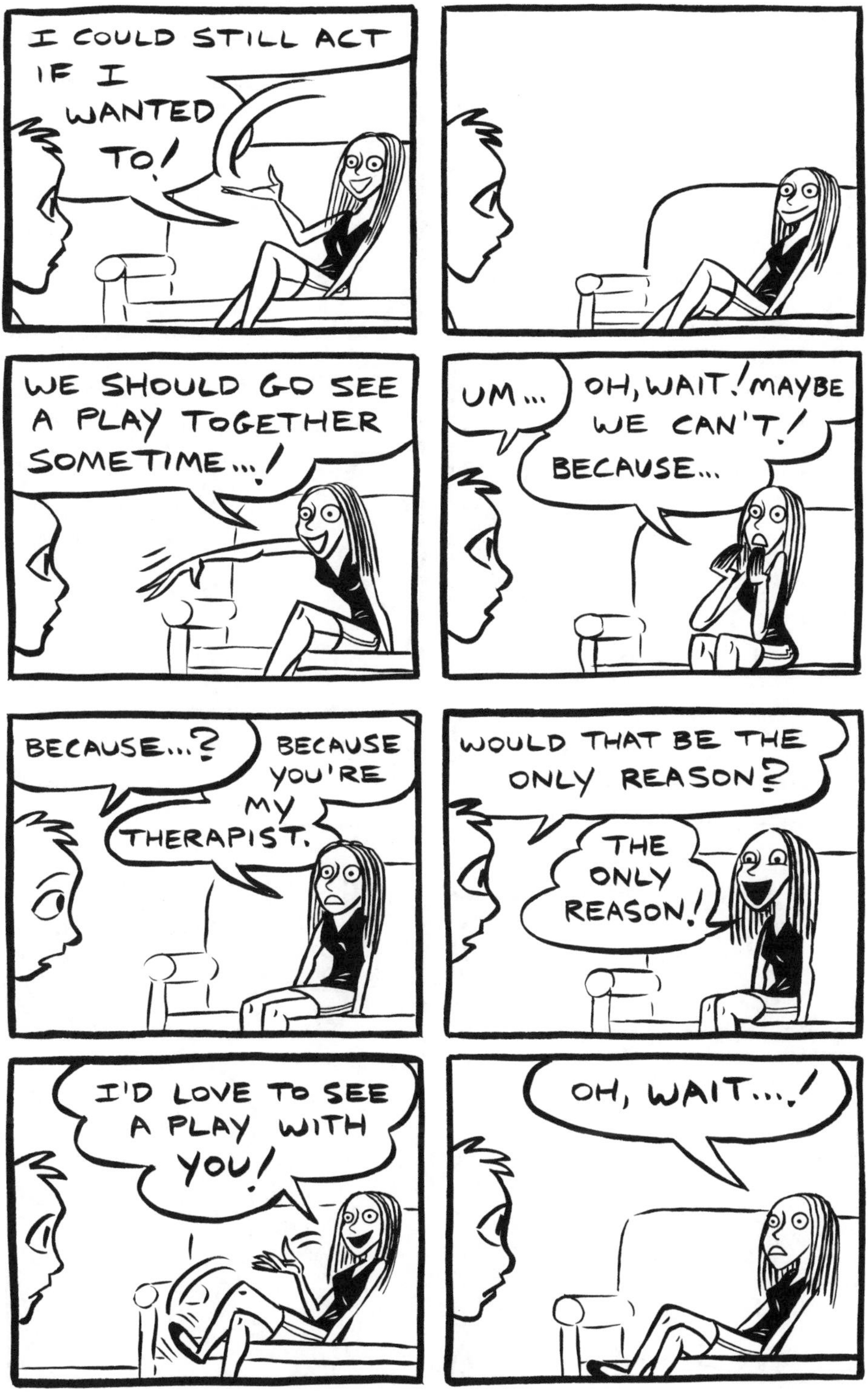

I COULD STILL ACT IF I WANTED TO!
WE SHOULD GO SEE A PLAY TOGETHER SOMETIME...!
UM...
OH, WAIT! MAYBE WE CAN'T! BECAUSE...
BECAUSE...?
BECAUSE YOU'RE MY THERAPIST.
WOULD THAT BE THE ONLY REASON?
THE ONLY REASON!
I'D LOVE TO SEE A PLAY WITH YOU!
OH, WAIT....!

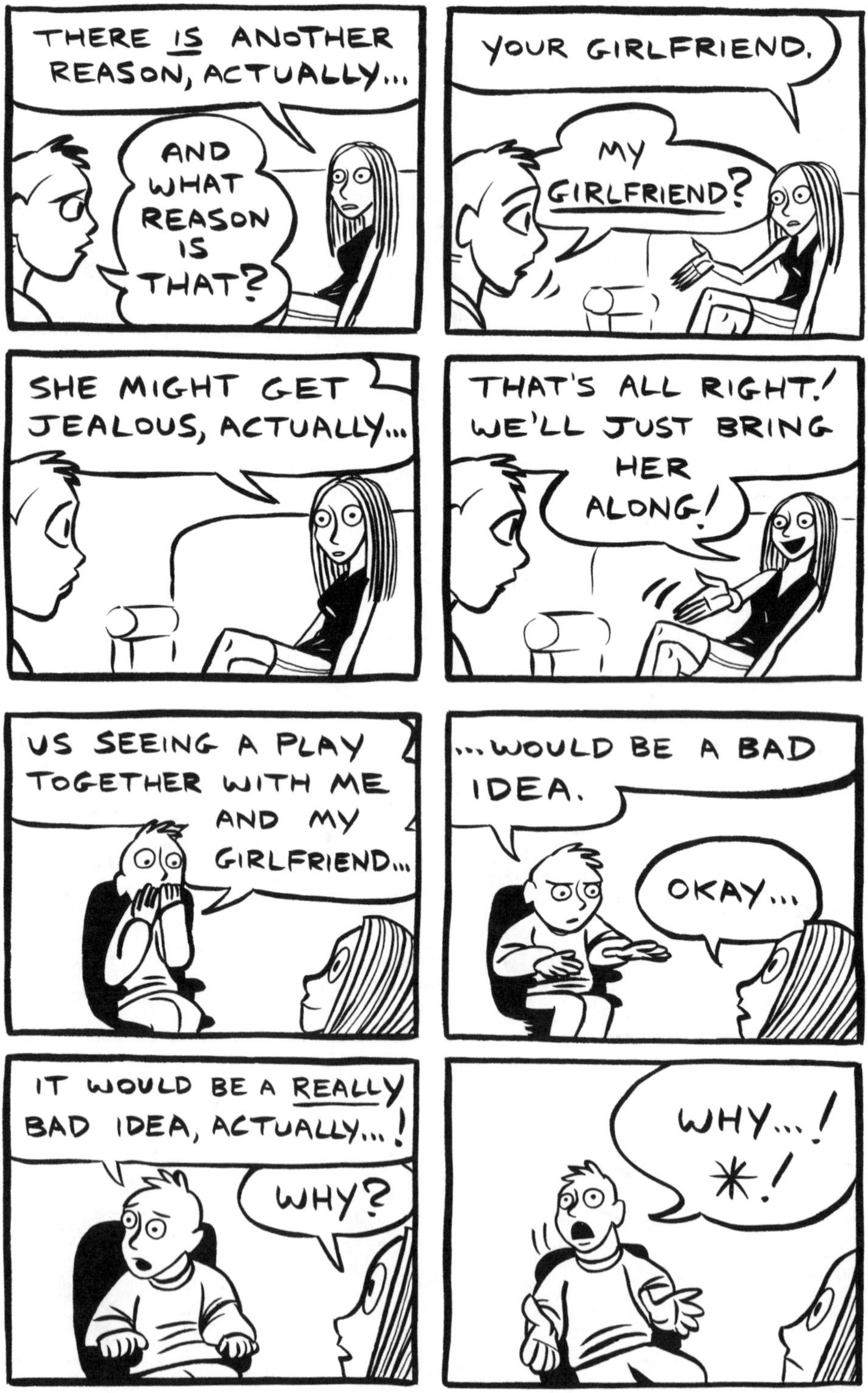
THERE IS ANOTHER REASON, ACTUALLY...
AND WHAT REASON IS THAT?
YOUR GIRLFRIEND.
MY GIRLFRIEND?
SHE MIGHT GET JEALOUS, ACTUALLY...
THAT'S ALL RIGHT! WE'LL JUST BRING HER ALONG!
US SEEING A PLAY TOGETHER WITH ME AND MY GIRLFRIEND...
...WOULD BE A BAD IDEA.
OKAY...
IT WOULD BE A REALLY BAD IDEA, ACTUALLY...!
WHY?
WHY...! *!

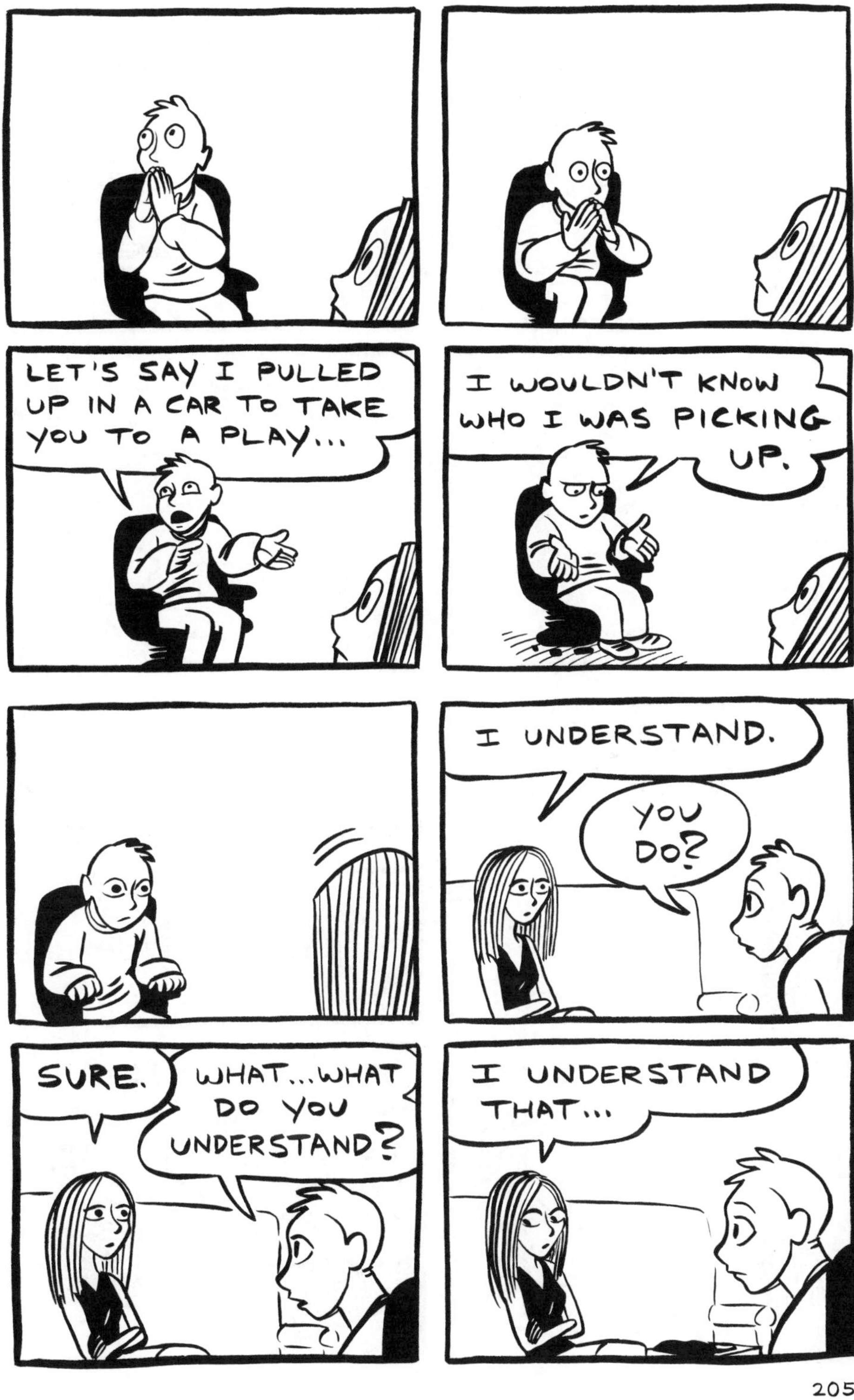
LET'S SAY I PULLED UP IN A CAR TO TAKE YOU TO A PLAY...
I WOULDN'T KNOW WHO I WAS PICKING UP.
I UNDERSTAND.
YOU DO?
SURE.
WHAT...WHAT DO YOU UNDERSTAND?
I UNDERSTAND THAT...

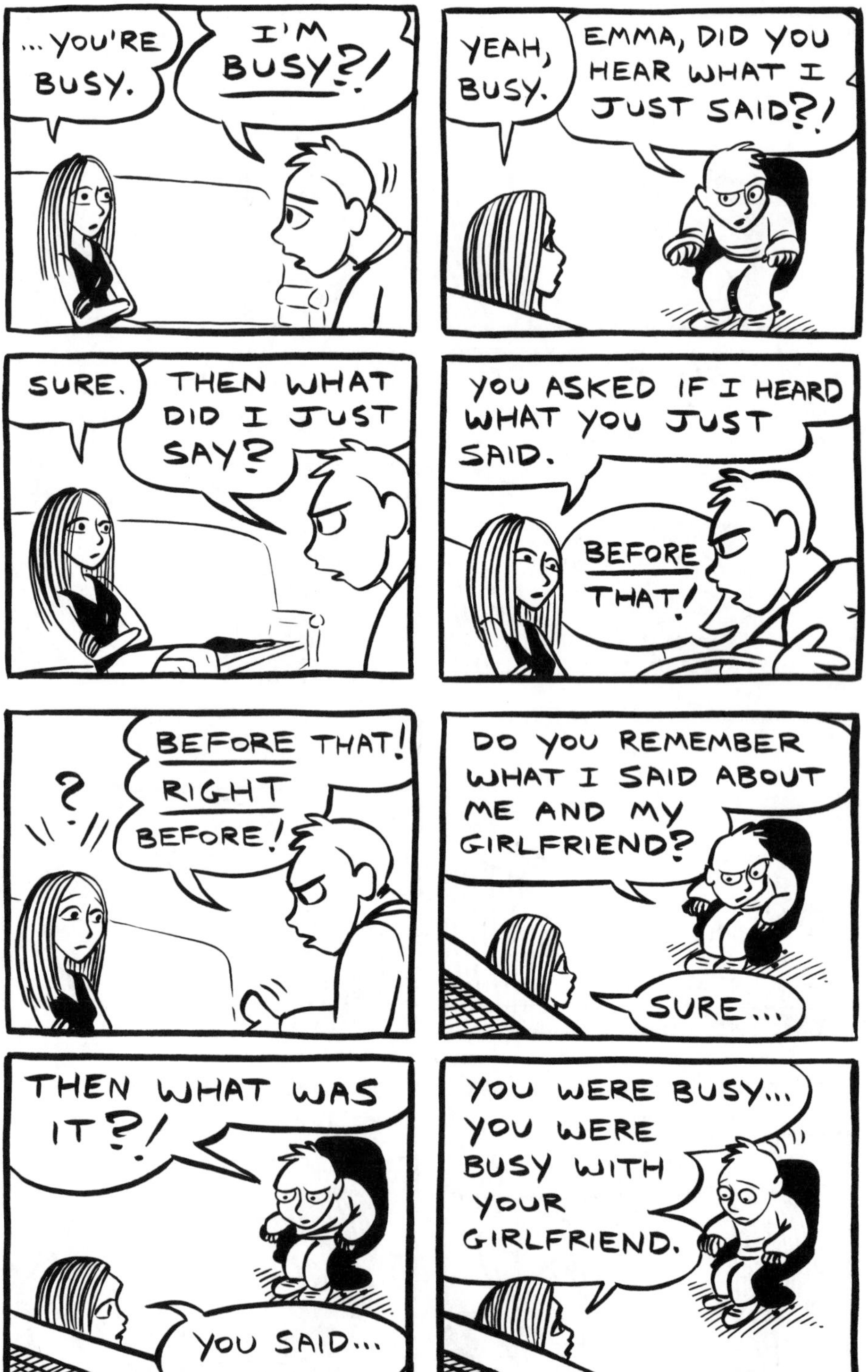
...YOU'RE BUSY.
I'M BUSY?!
YEAH, BUSY.
EMMA, DID YOU HEAR WHAT I JUST SAID?!
SURE.
THEN WHAT DID I JUST SAY?
YOU ASKED IF I HEARD WHAT YOU JUST SAID.
BEFORE THAT!
?
BEFORE THAT! RIGHT BEFORE!
DO YOU REMEMBER WHAT I SAID ABOUT ME AND MY GIRLFRIEND?
SURE...
THEN WHAT WAS IT?!
YOU SAID...
YOU WERE BUSY... YOU WERE BUSY WITH YOUR GIRLFRIEND.

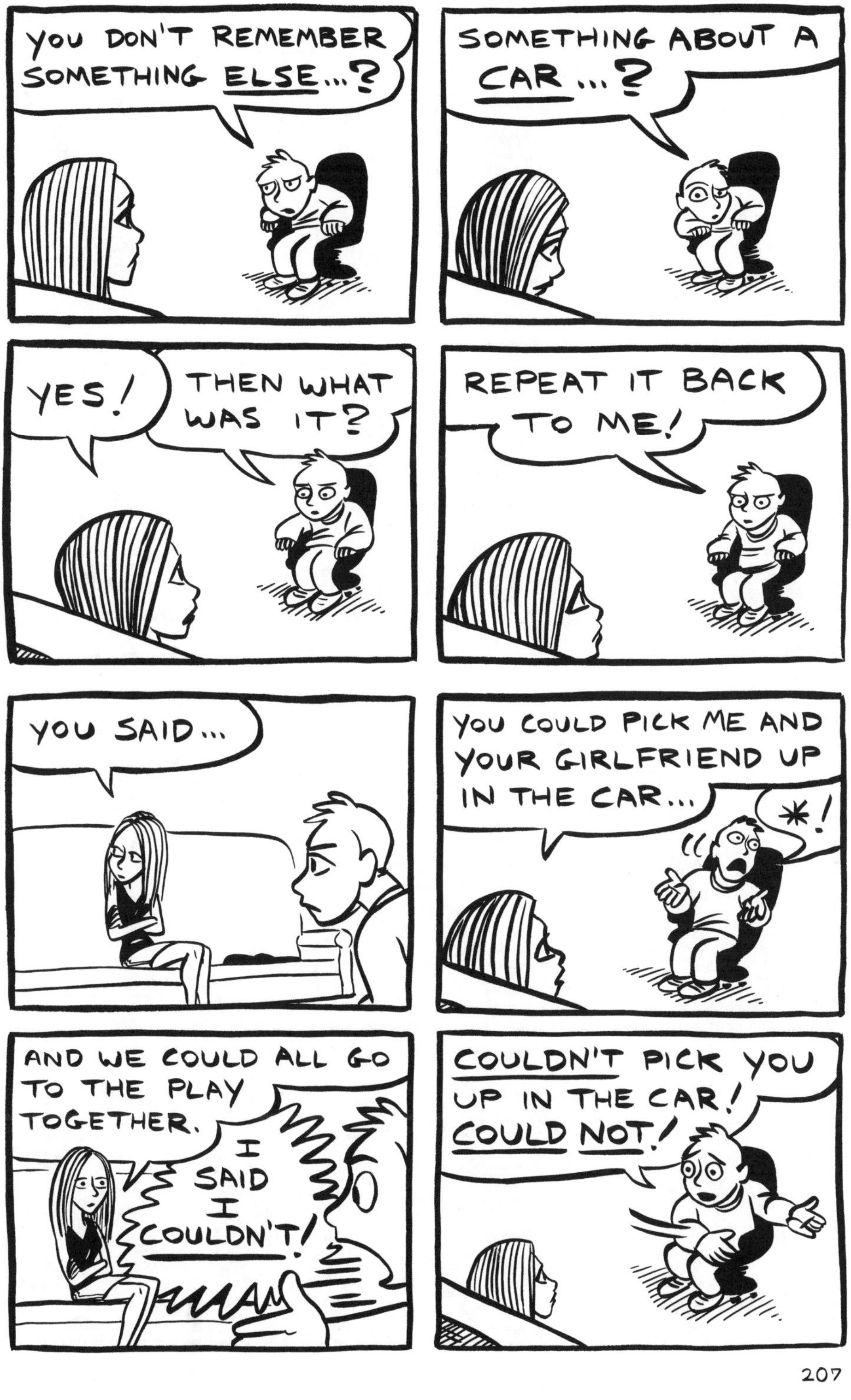
YOU DON'T REMEMBER SOMETHING ELSE...?
SOMETHING ABOUT A CAR...?
YES!
THEN WHAT WAS IT?
REPEAT IT BACK TO ME!
YOU SAID...
YOU COULD PICK ME AND YOUR GIRLFRIEND UP IN THE CAR...
*!
AND WE COULD ALL GO TO THE PLAY TOGETHER.
I SAID I COULDN'T!
COULDN'T PICK YOU UP IN THE CAR! COULD NOT!

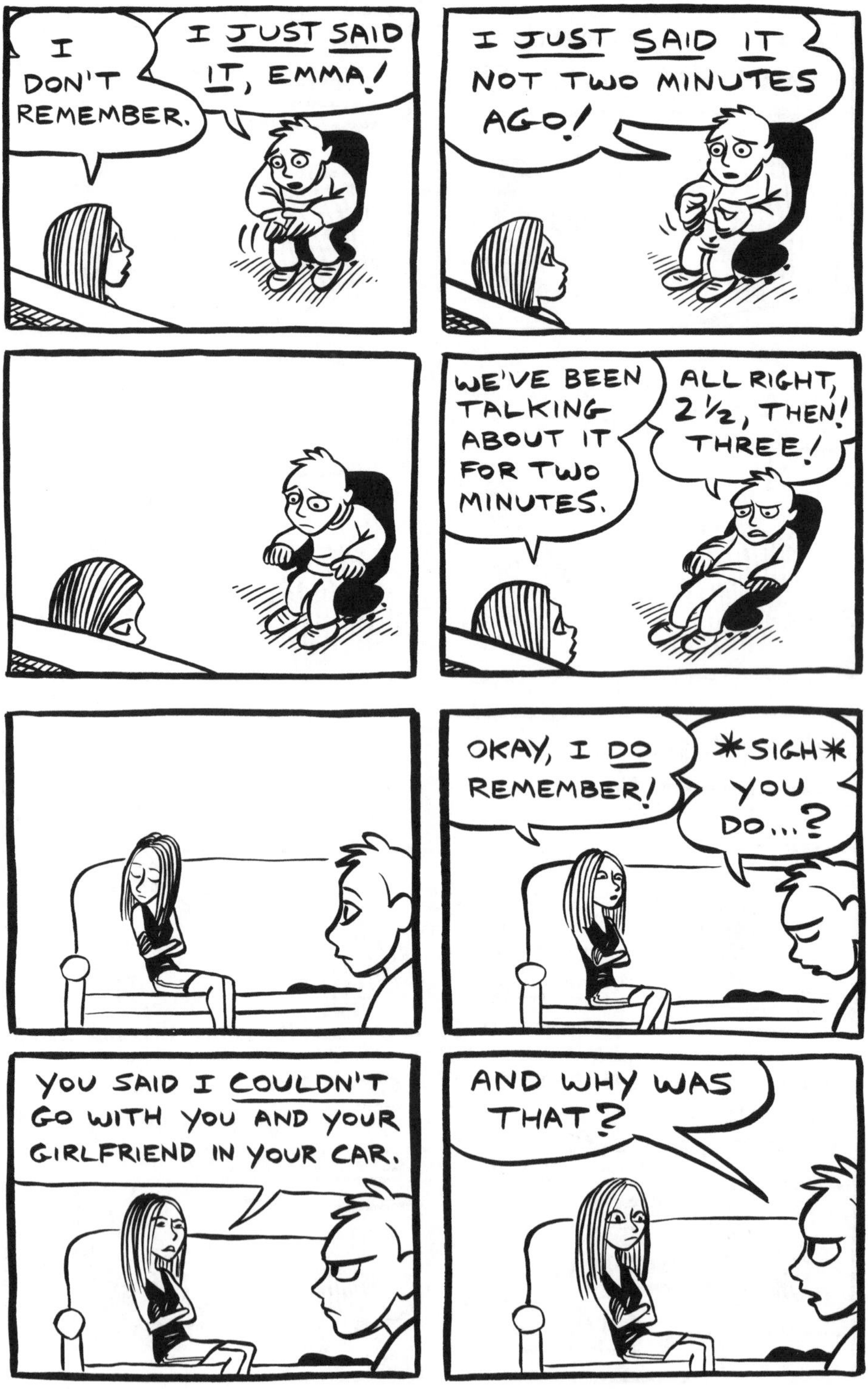
I DON'T REMEMBER.
I JUST SAID IT, EMMA!
I JUST SAID IT NOT TWO MINUTES AGO!
WE'VE BEEN TALKING ABOUT IT FOR TWO MINUTES.
ALL RIGHT, 2½, THEN! THREE!
OKAY, I DO REMEMBER!
SIGH YOU DO...?
YOU SAID I COULDN'T GO WITH YOU AND YOUR GIRLFRIEND IN YOUR CAR.
AND WHY WAS THAT?

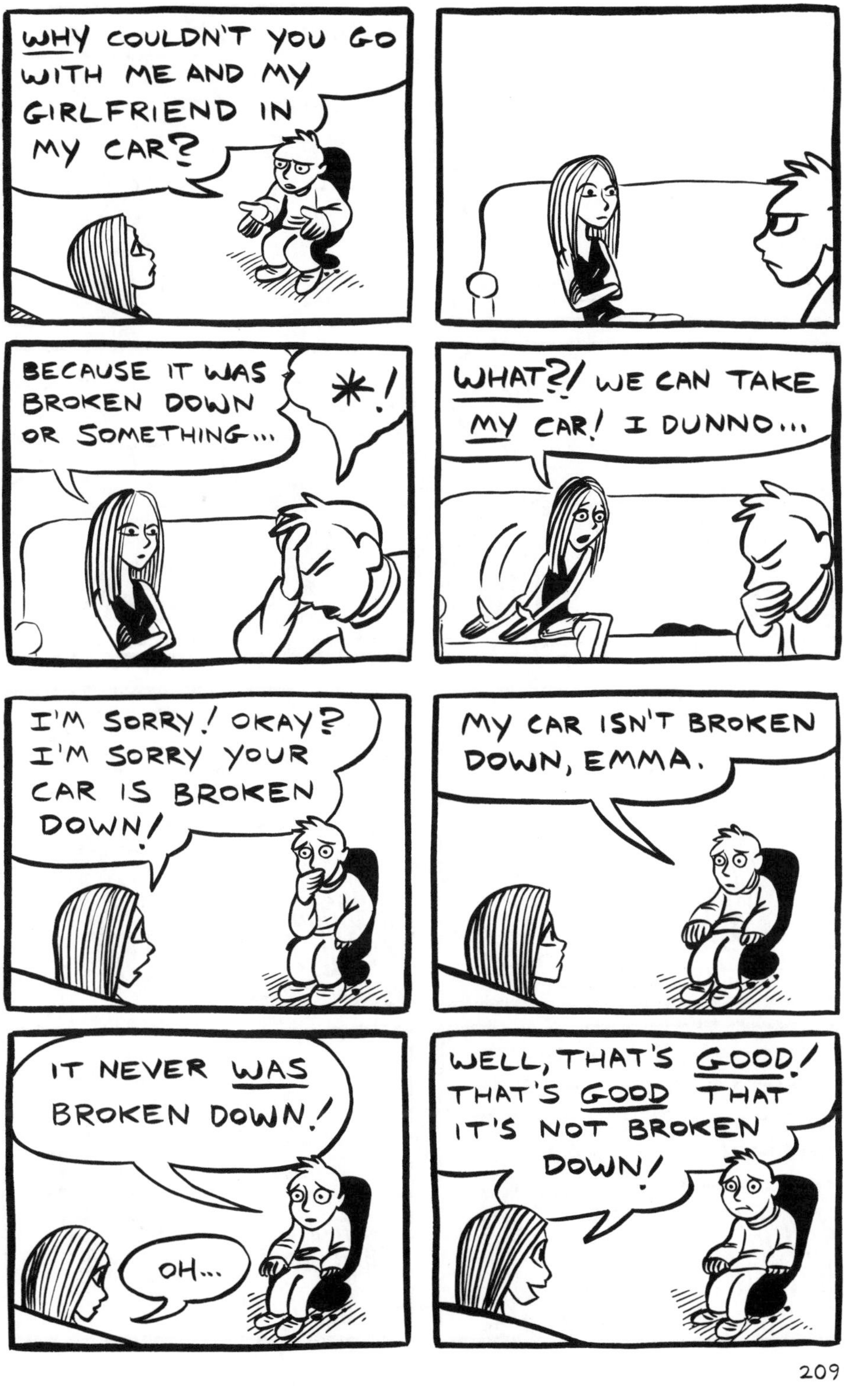
WHY COULDN'T YOU GO WITH ME AND MY GIRLFRIEND IN MY CAR?
BECAUSE IT WAS BROKEN DOWN OR SOMETHING...
*!
WHAT?! WE CAN TAKE MY CAR! I DUNNO...
I'M SORRY! OKAY? I'M SORRY YOUR CAR IS BROKEN DOWN!
MY CAR ISN'T BROKEN DOWN, EMMA.
IT NEVER WAS BROKEN DOWN!
OH...
WELL, THAT'S GOOD! THAT'S GOOD THAT IT'S NOT BROKEN DOWN!

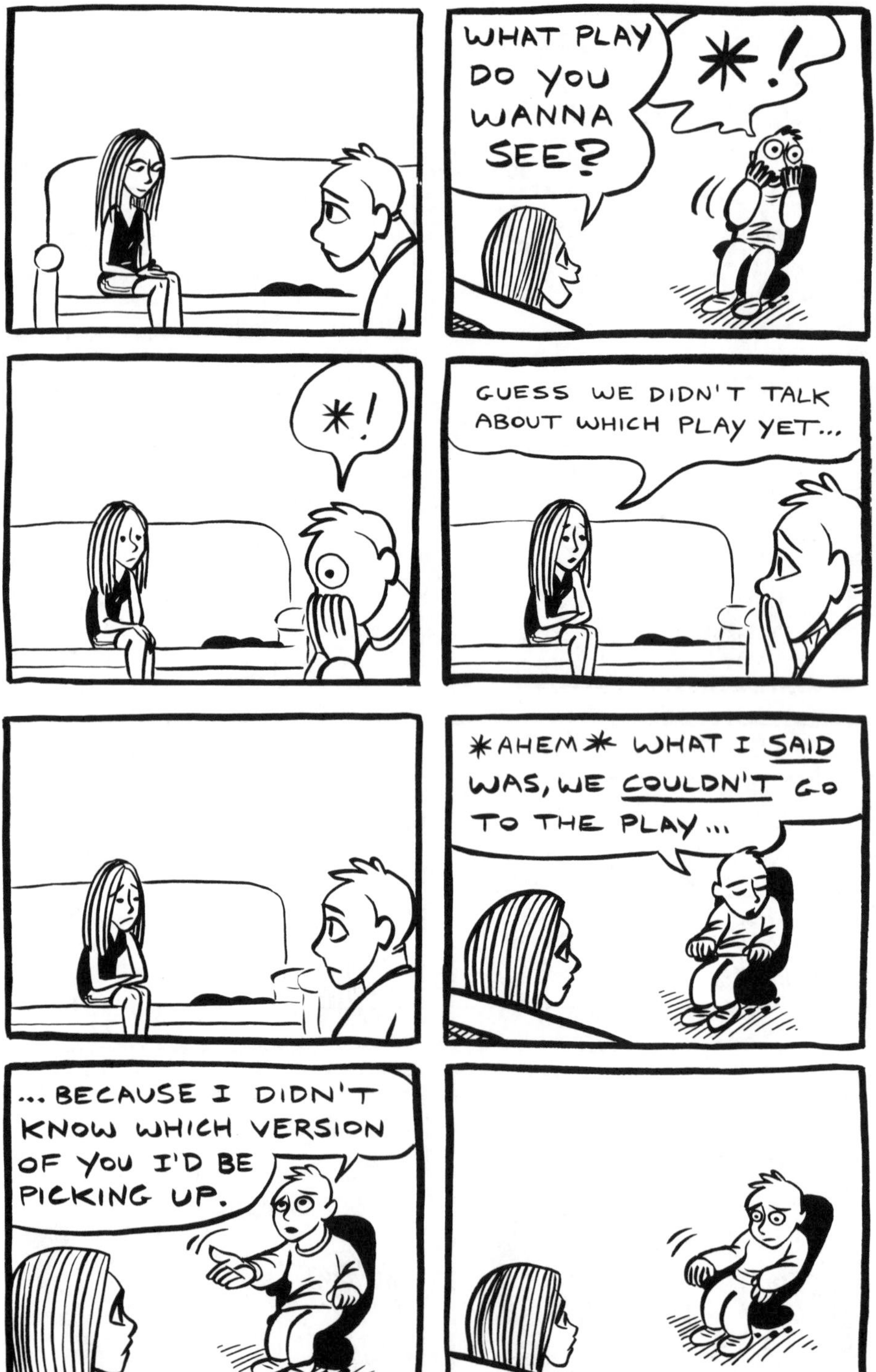
WHAT PLAY DO YOU WANNA SEE?
*!
*!
GUESS WE DIDN'T TALK ABOUT WHICH PLAY YET...
AHEM WHAT I SAID WAS, WE COULDN'T GO TO THE PLAY...
...BECAUSE I DIDN'T KNOW WHICH VERSION OF YOU I'D BE PICKING UP.

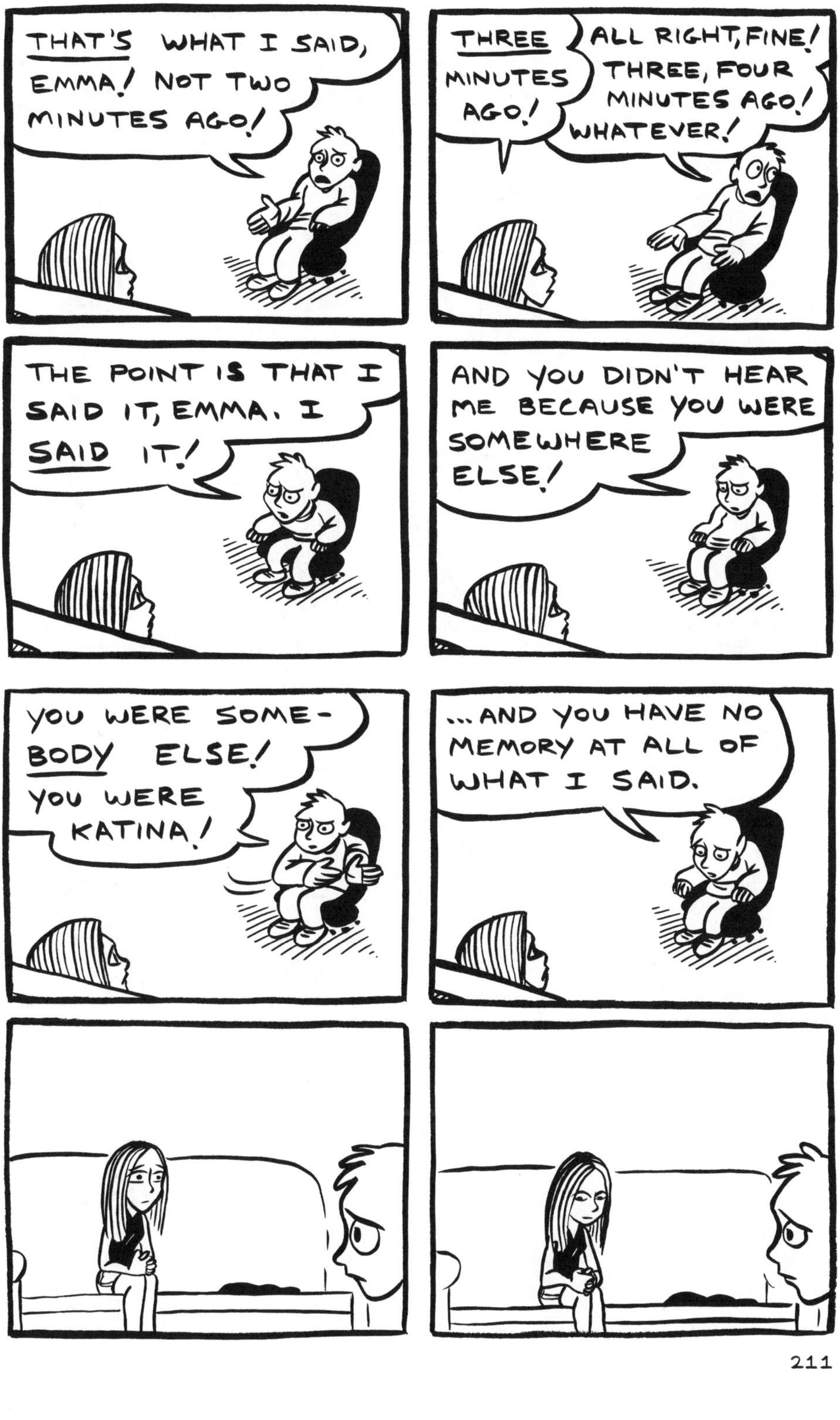
THAT'S WHAT I SAID, EMMA! NOT TWO MINUTES AGO!
THREE MINUTES AGO!
ALL RIGHT, FINE! THREE, FOUR MINUTES AGO! WHATEVER!
THE POINT IS THAT I SAID IT, EMMA. I SAID IT!
AND YOU DIDN'T HEAR ME BECAUSE YOU WERE SOMEWHERE ELSE!
YOU WERE SOME-BODY ELSE! YOU WERE KATINA!
...AND YOU HAVE NO MEMORY AT ALL OF WHAT I SAID.

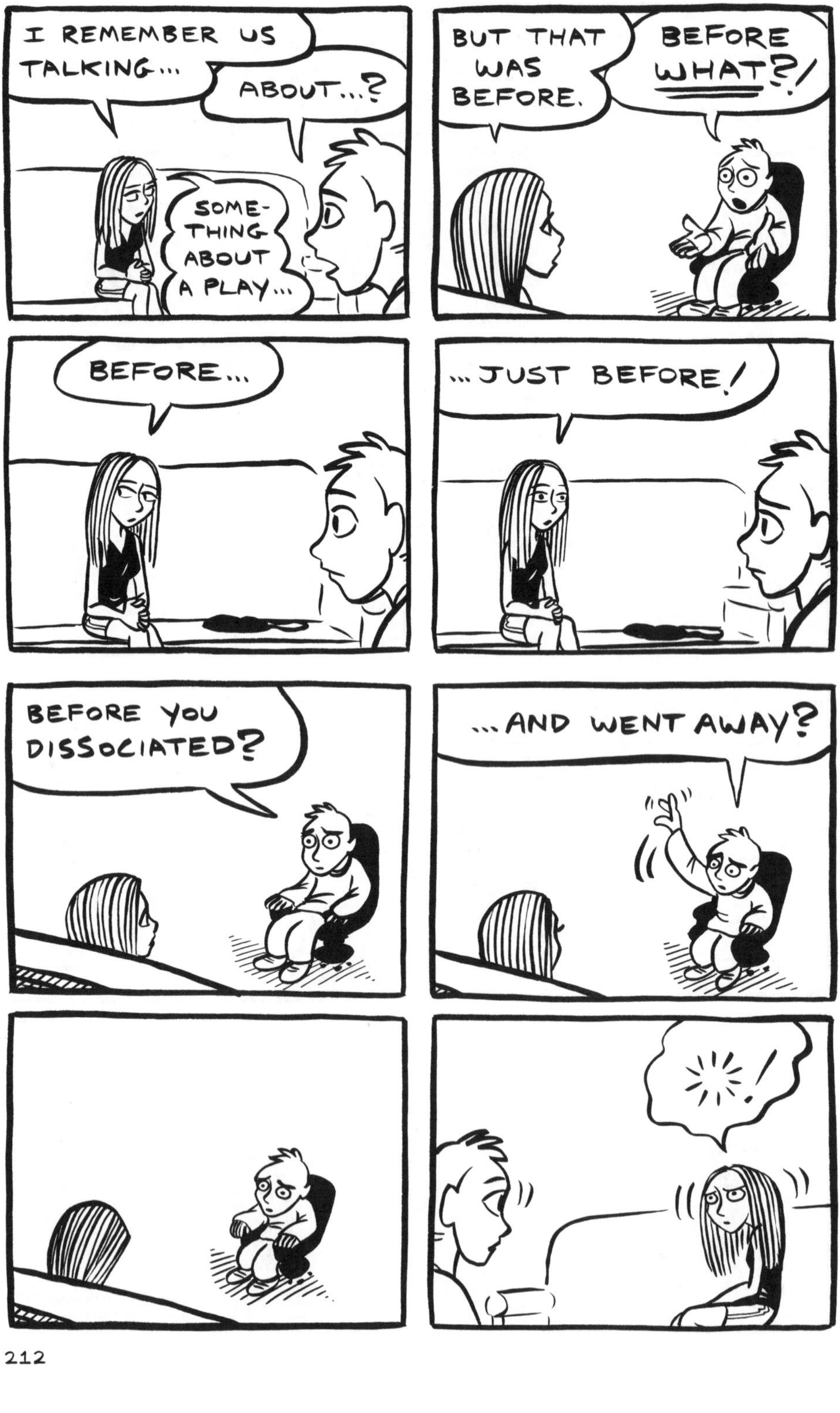
I REMEMBER US TALKING...
ABOUT...?
SOME-THING ABOUT A PLAY...
BUT THAT WAS BEFORE.
BEFORE WHAT?!
BEFORE...
...JUST BEFORE!
BEFORE YOU DISSOCIATED?
...AND WENT AWAY?
!

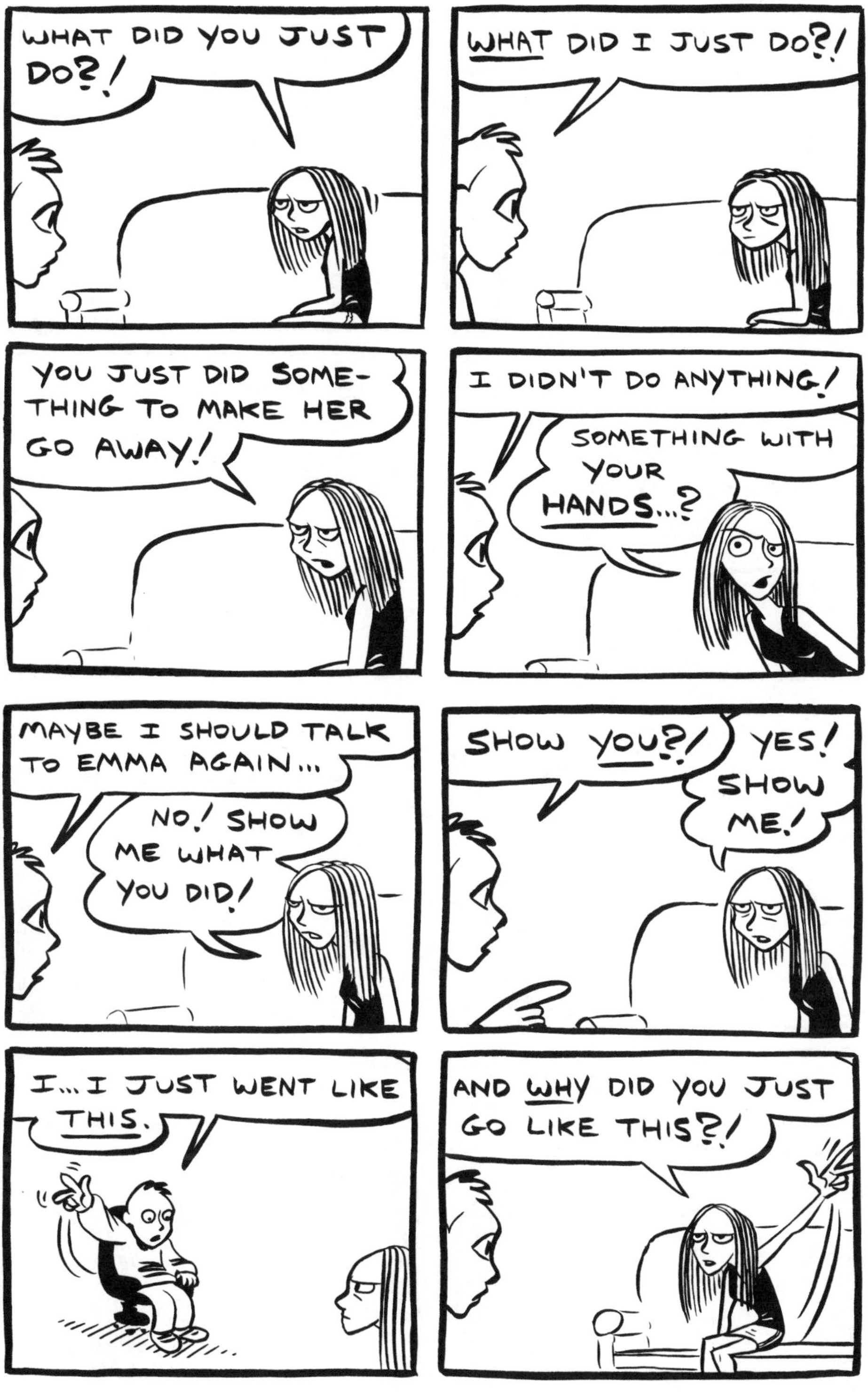
WHAT DID YOU JUST DO?!
WHAT DID I JUST DO?!
YOU JUST DID SOMETHING TO MAKE HER GO AWAY!
I DIDN'T DO ANYTHING!
SOMETHING WITH YOUR HANDS...?
MAYBE I SHOULD TALK TO EMMA AGAIN...
NO! SHOW ME WHAT YOU DID!
SHOW YOU?!
YES! SHOW ME!
I... I JUST WENT LIKE THIS.
AND WHY DID YOU JUST GO LIKE THIS?!

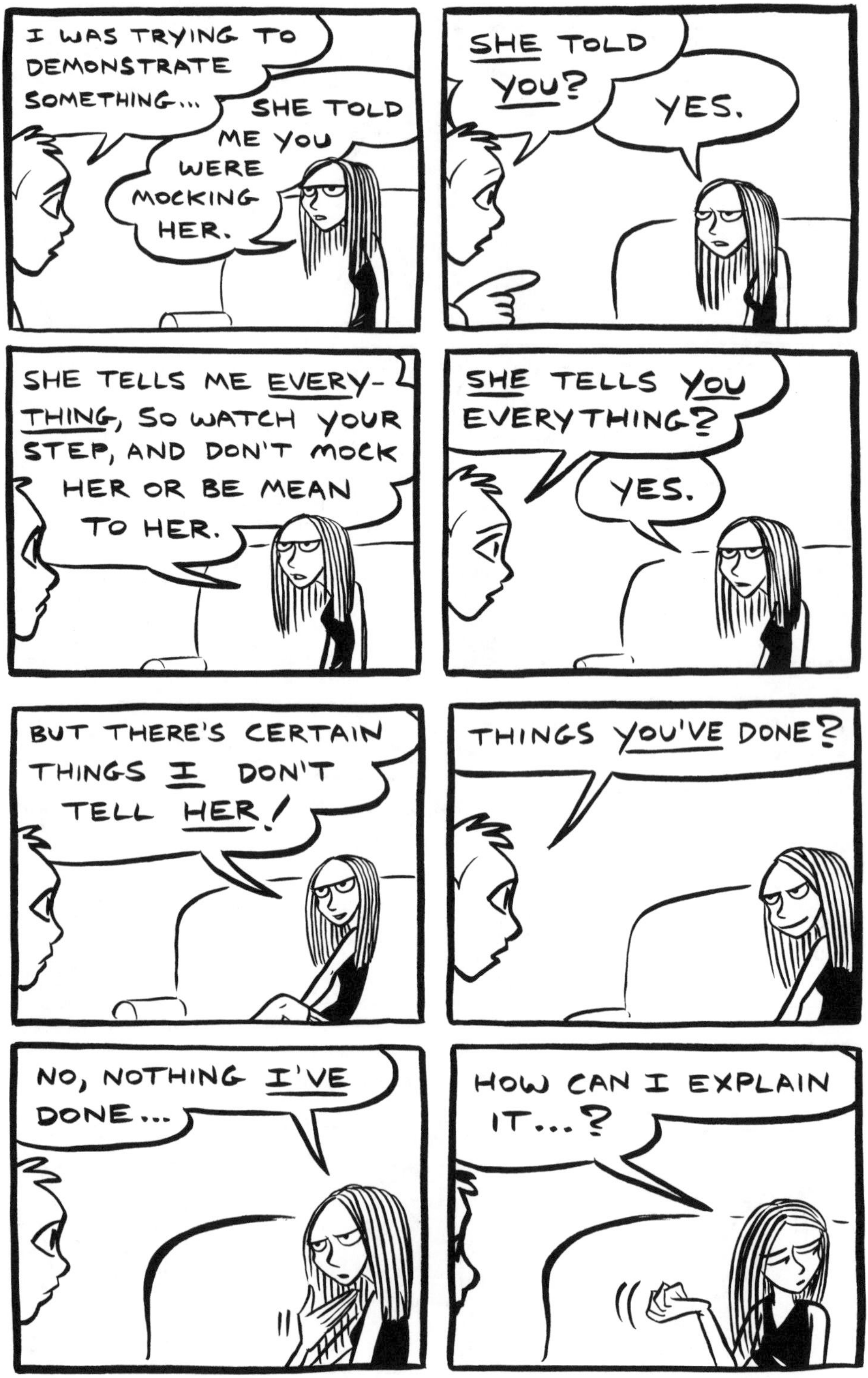
I WAS TRYING TO DEMONSTRATE SOMETHING...
SHE TOLD ME YOU WERE MOCKING HER.
SHE TOLD YOU?
YES.
SHE TELLS ME EVERYTHING, SO WATCH YOUR STEP, AND DON'T MOCK HER OR BE MEAN TO HER.
SHE TELLS YOU EVERYTHING?
YES.
BUT THERE'S CERTAIN THINGS I DON'T TELL HER!
THINGS YOU'VE DONE?
NO, NOTHING I'VE DONE...
HOW CAN I EXPLAIN IT...?

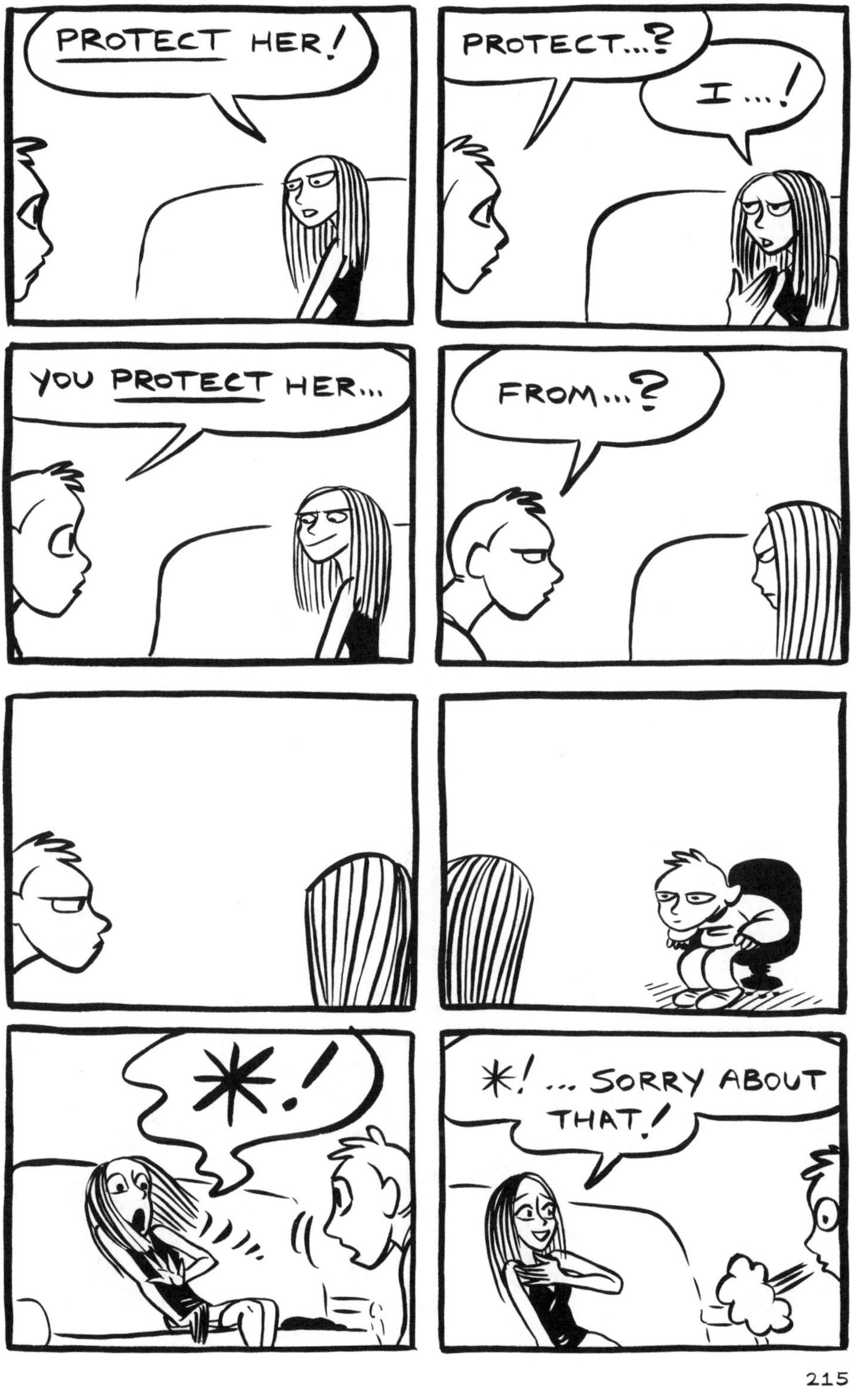
PROTECT HER!
PROTECT...?
I...!
YOU PROTECT HER...
FROM...?
*!
*! ... SORRY ABOUT THAT!

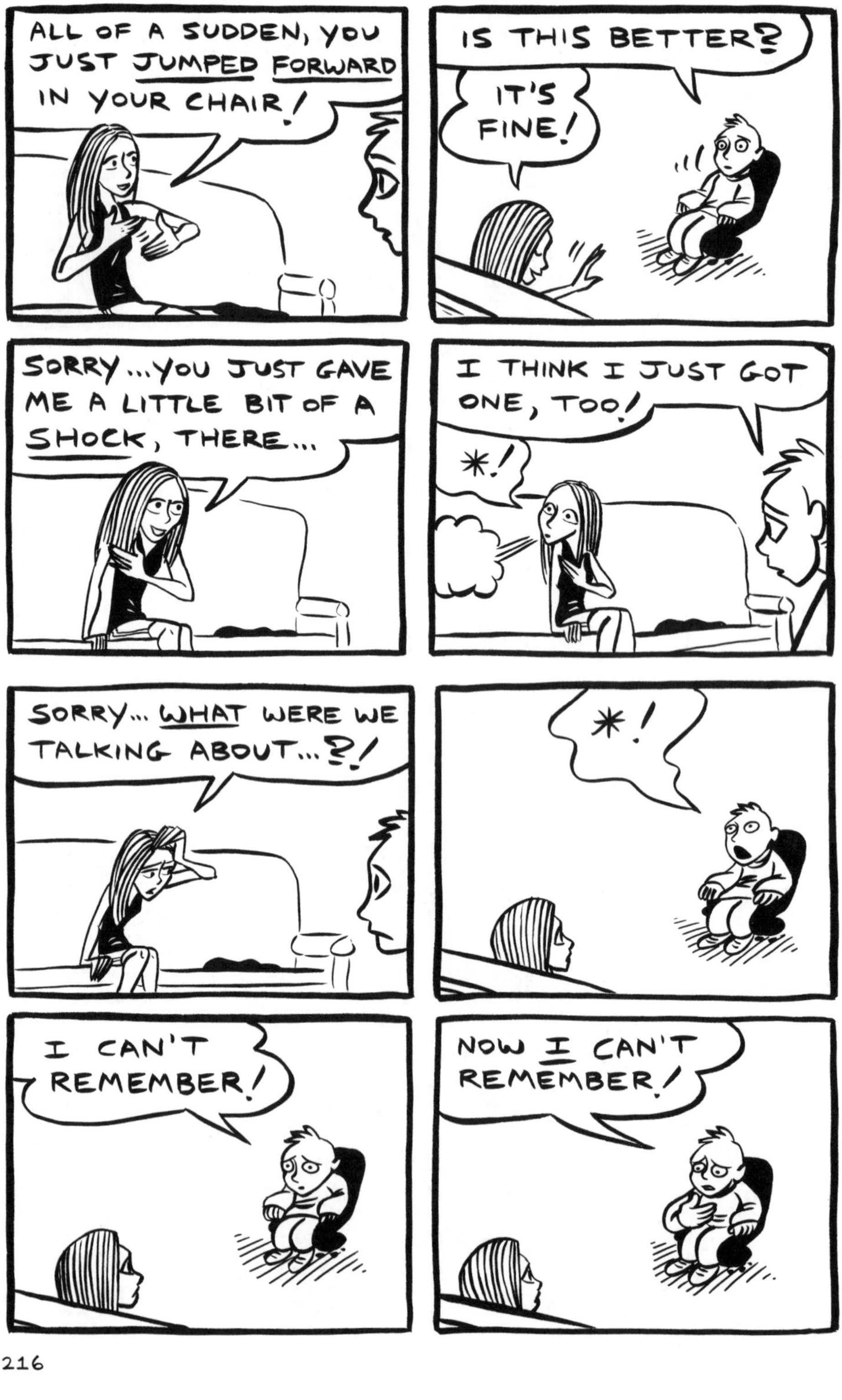
ALL OF A SUDDEN, YOU JUST JUMPED FORWARD IN YOUR CHAIR!
IS THIS BETTER?
IT'S FINE!
SORRY...YOU JUST GAVE ME A LITTLE BIT OF A SHOCK, THERE...
I THINK I JUST GOT ONE, TOO!
*!
SORRY... WHAT WERE WE TALKING ABOUT...?!
*!
I CAN'T REMEMBER!
NOW I CAN'T REMEMBER!

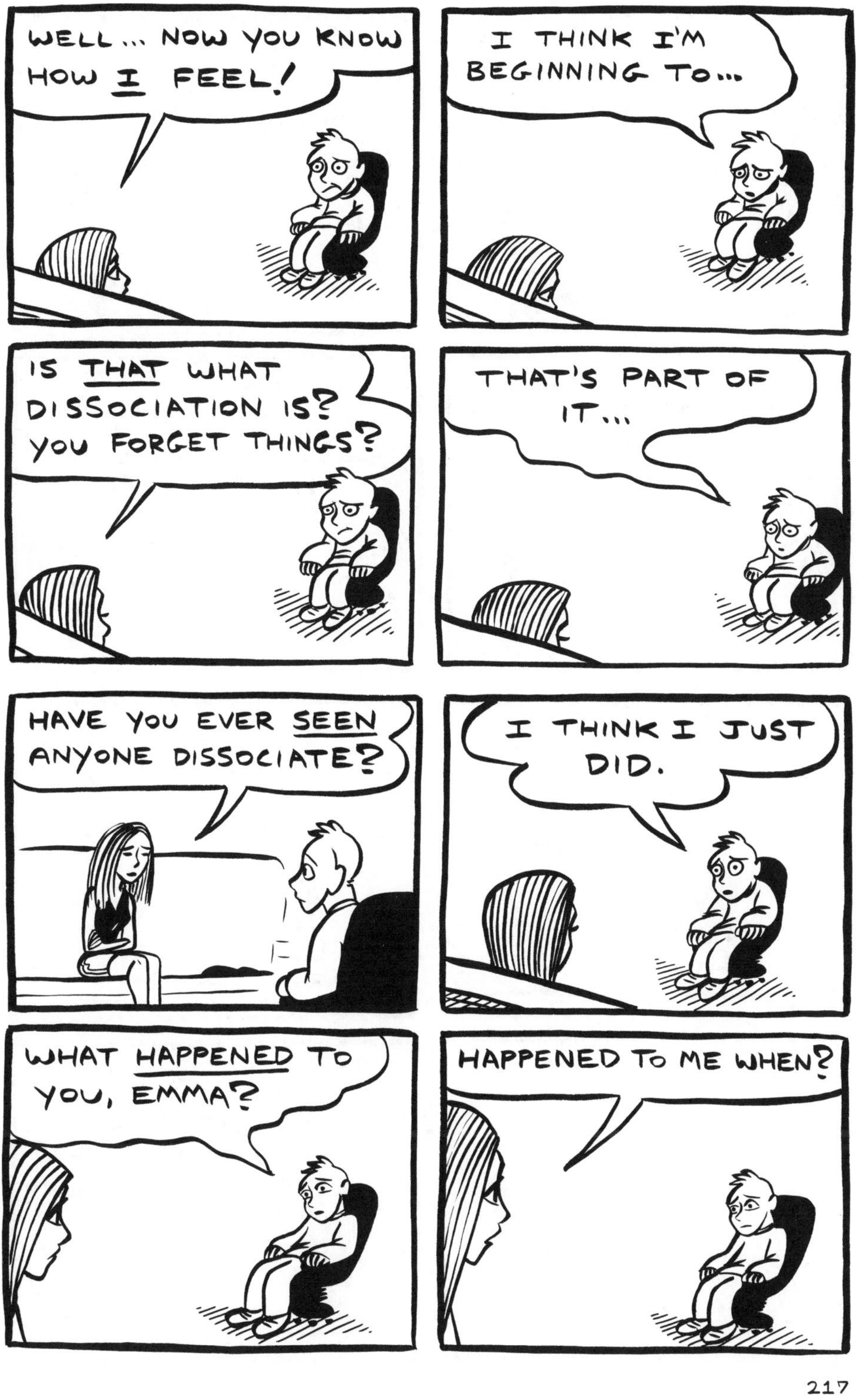
WELL... NOW YOU KNOW HOW I FEEL!
I THINK I'M BEGINNING TO...
IS THAT WHAT DISSOCIATION IS? YOU FORGET THINGS?
THAT'S PART OF IT...
HAVE YOU EVER SEEN ANYONE DISSOCIATE?
I THINK I JUST DID.
WHAT HAPPENED TO YOU, EMMA?
HAPPENED TO ME WHEN?

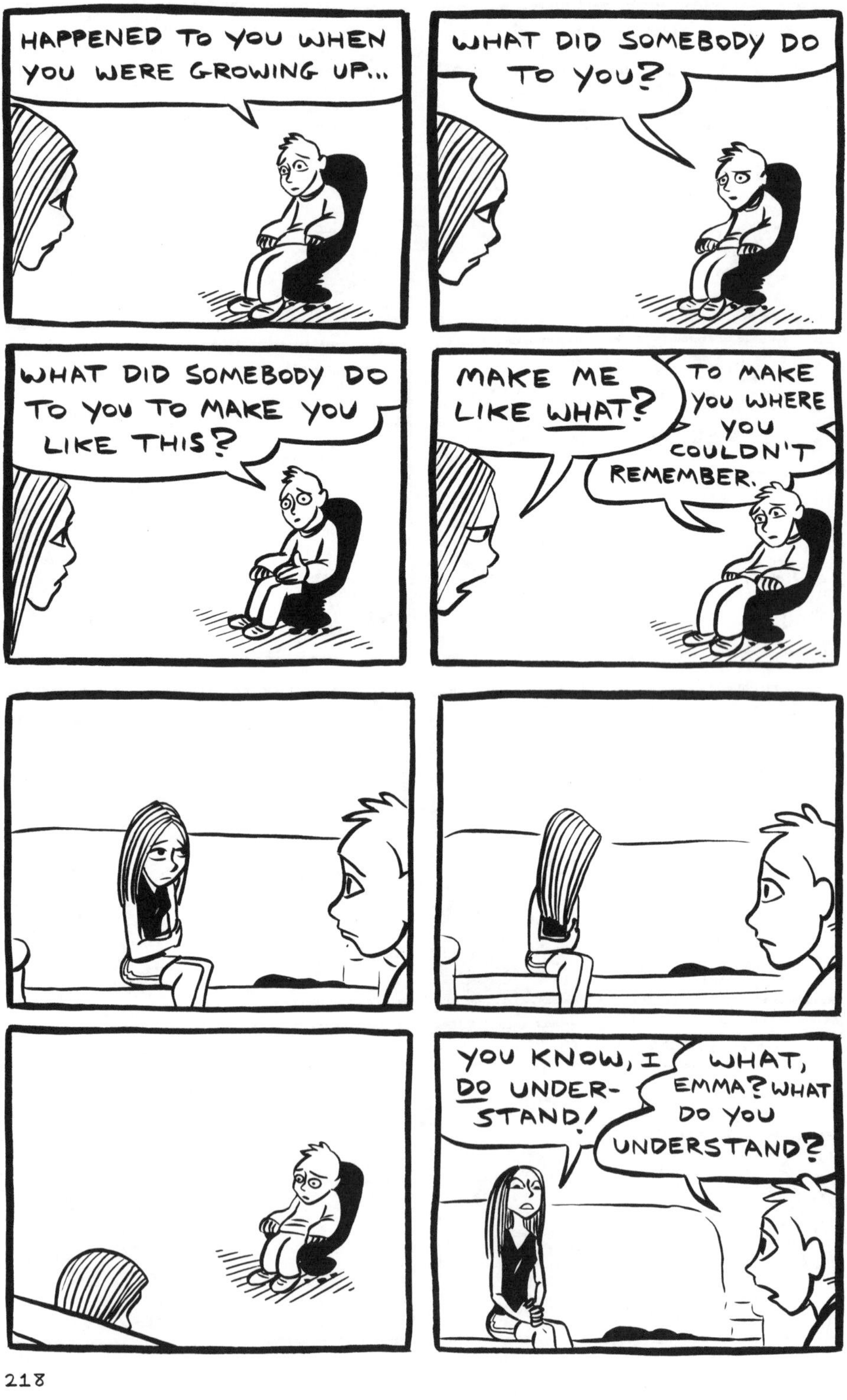
HAPPENED TO YOU WHEN YOU WERE GROWING UP...
WHAT DID SOMEBODY DO TO YOU?
WHAT DID SOMEBODY DO TO YOU TO MAKE YOU LIKE THIS?
MAKE ME LIKE WHAT?
TO MAKE YOU WHERE YOU COULDN'T REMEMBER.
YOU KNOW, I DO UNDER-STAND!
WHAT, EMMA? WHAT DO YOU UNDERSTAND?

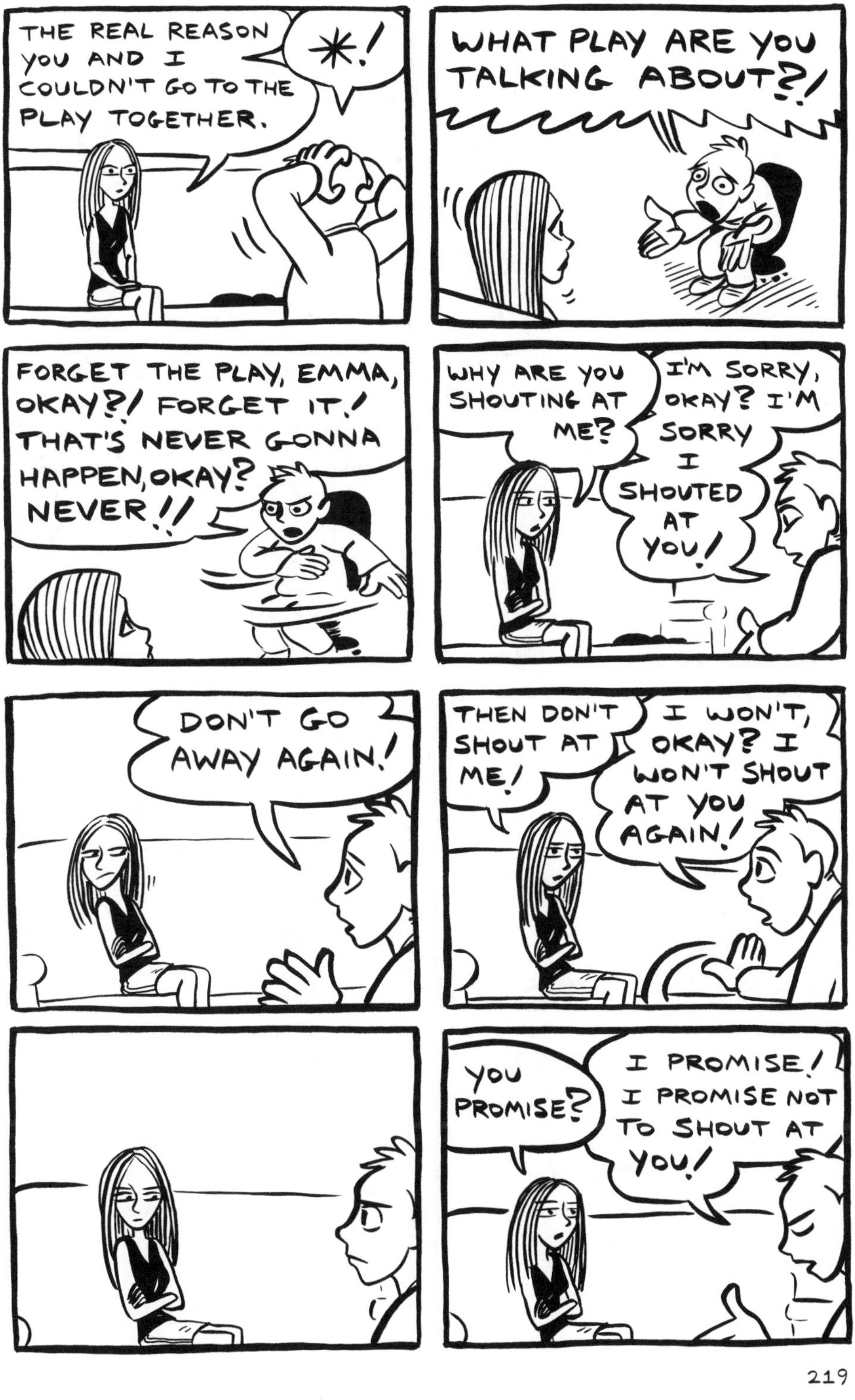

THE REAL REASON YOU AND I COULDN'T GO TO THE PLAY TOGETHER.
*!
WHAT PLAY ARE YOU TALKING ABOUT?!
FORGET THE PLAY, EMMA, OKAY?! FORGET IT! THAT'S NEVER GONNA HAPPEN, OKAY? NEVER!!
WHY ARE YOU SHOUTING AT ME?
I'M SORRY, OKAY? I'M SORRY I SHOUTED AT YOU!
DON'T GO AWAY AGAIN!
THEN DON'T SHOUT AT ME!
I WON'T, OKAY? I WON'T SHOUT AT YOU AGAIN!
YOU PROMISE?
I PROMISE! I PROMISE NOT TO SHOUT AT YOU!

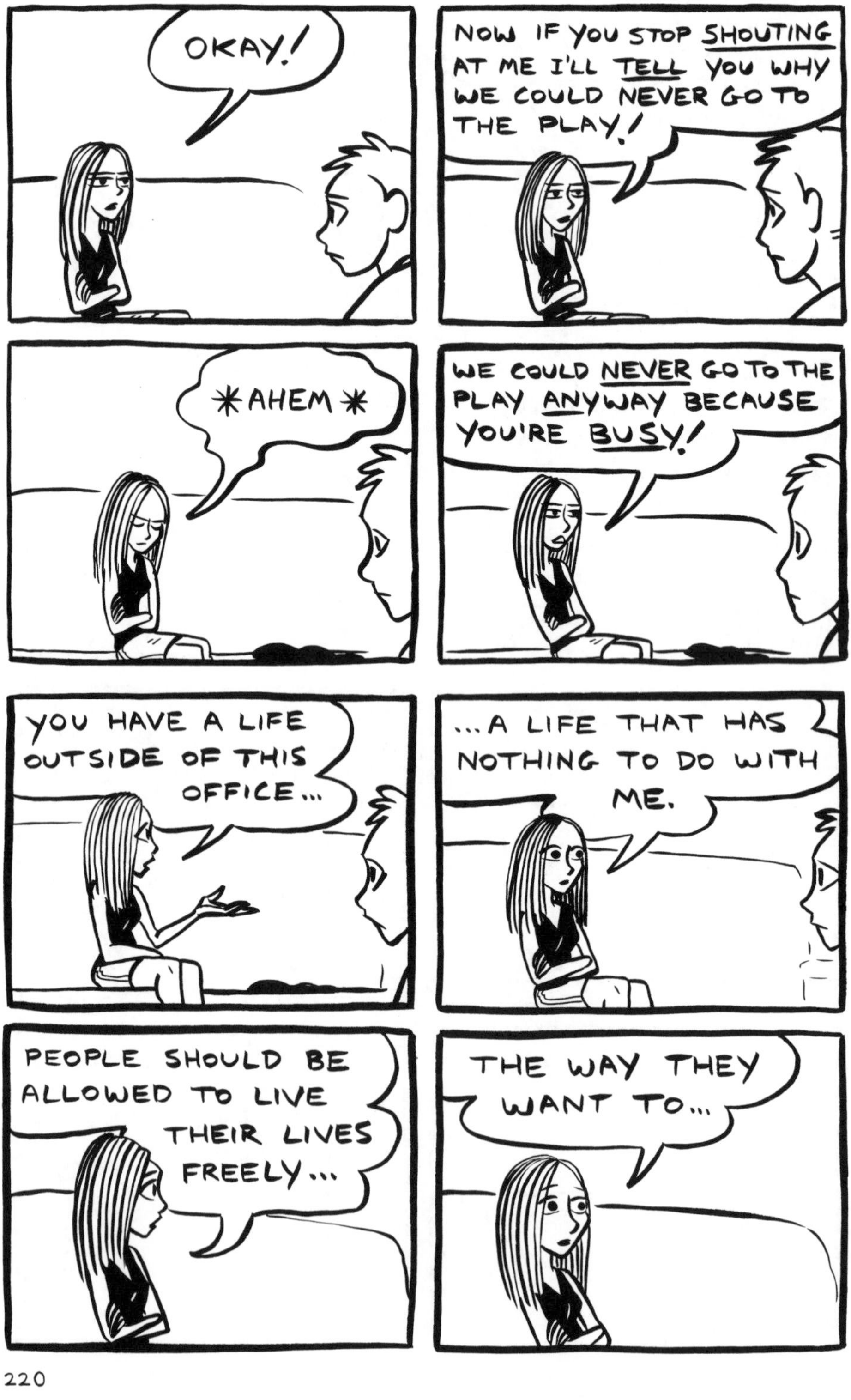

OKAY!
NOW IF YOU STOP SHOUTING AT ME I'LL TELL YOU WHY WE COULD NEVER GO TO THE PLAY!
AHEM
WE COULD NEVER GO TO THE PLAY ANYWAY BECAUSE YOU'RE BUSY!
YOU HAVE A LIFE OUTSIDE OF THIS OFFICE...
...A LIFE THAT HAS NOTHING TO DO WITH ME.
PEOPLE SHOULD BE ALLOWED TO LIVE THEIR LIVES FREELY...
THE WAY THEY WANT TO...

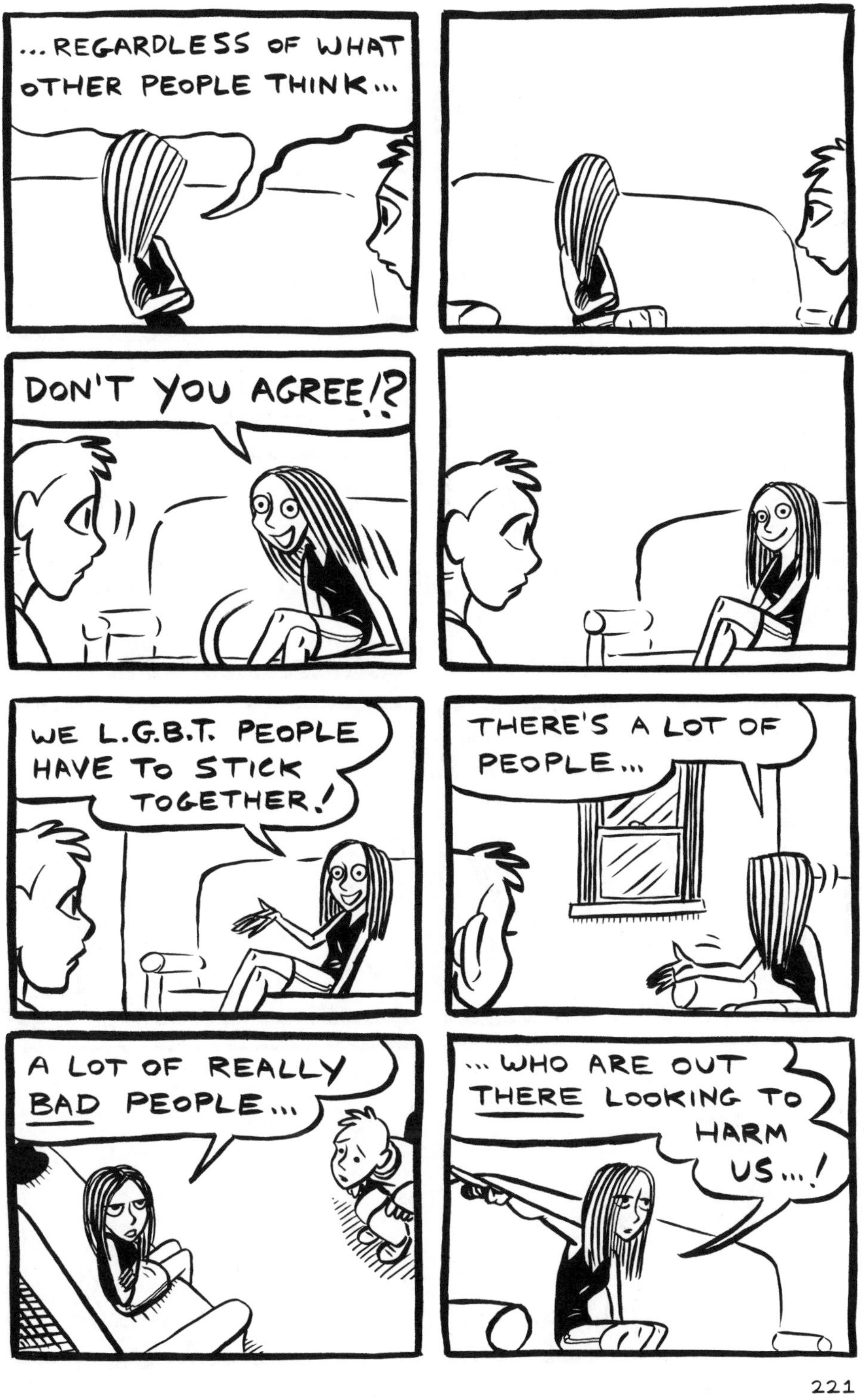
...REGARDLESS OF WHAT OTHER PEOPLE THINK...
DON'T YOU AGREE!?
WE L.G.B.T. PEOPLE HAVE TO STICK TOGETHER!
THERE'S A LOT OF PEOPLE...
A LOT OF REALLY BAD PEOPLE...
...WHO ARE OUT THERE LOOKING TO HARM US...!

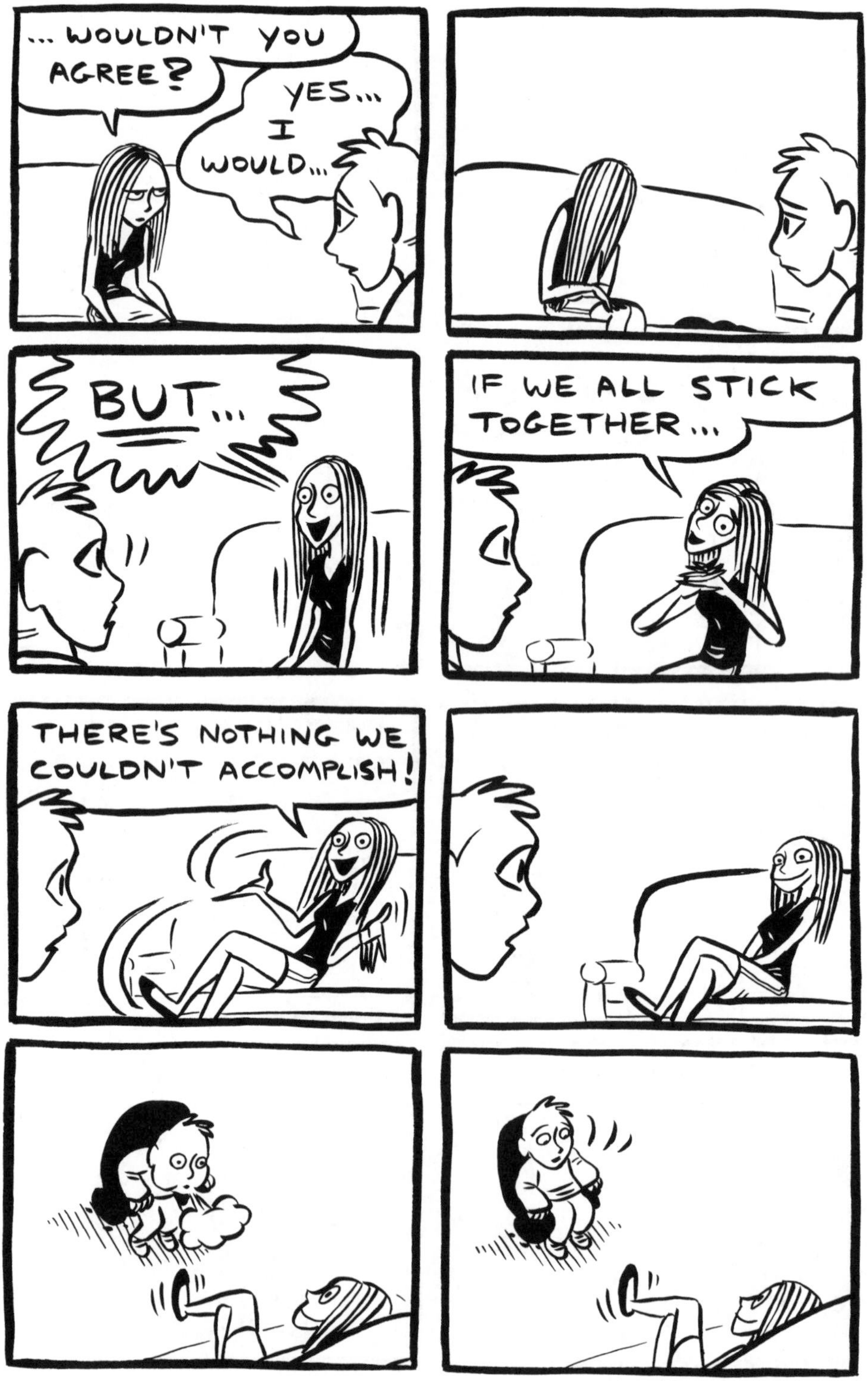
...WOULDN'T YOU AGREE?
YES... I WOULD...
BUT...
IF WE ALL STICK TOGETHER...
THERE'S NOTHING WE COULDN'T ACCOMPLISH!

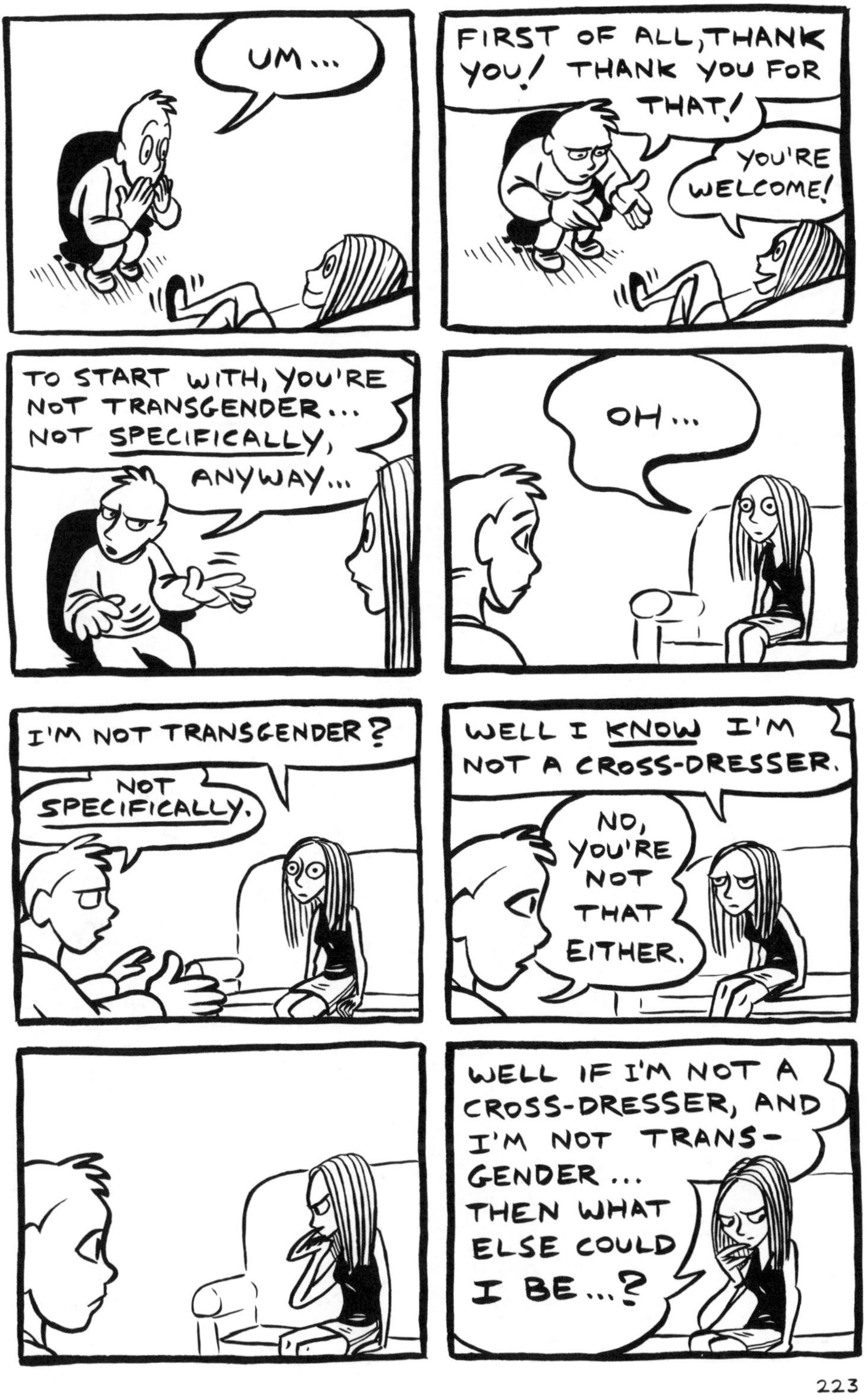
UM...
FIRST OF ALL, THANK YOU! THANK YOU FOR THAT!
YOU'RE WELCOME!
TO START WITH, YOU'RE NOT TRANSGENDER... NOT SPECIFICALLY, ANYWAY...
OH...
I'M NOT TRANSGENDER?
NOT SPECIFICALLY.
WELL I KNOW I'M NOT A CROSS-DRESSER.
NO, YOU'RE NOT THAT EITHER.
WELL IF I'M NOT A CROSS-DRESSER, AND I'M NOT TRANS-GENDER... THEN WHAT ELSE COULD I BE...?

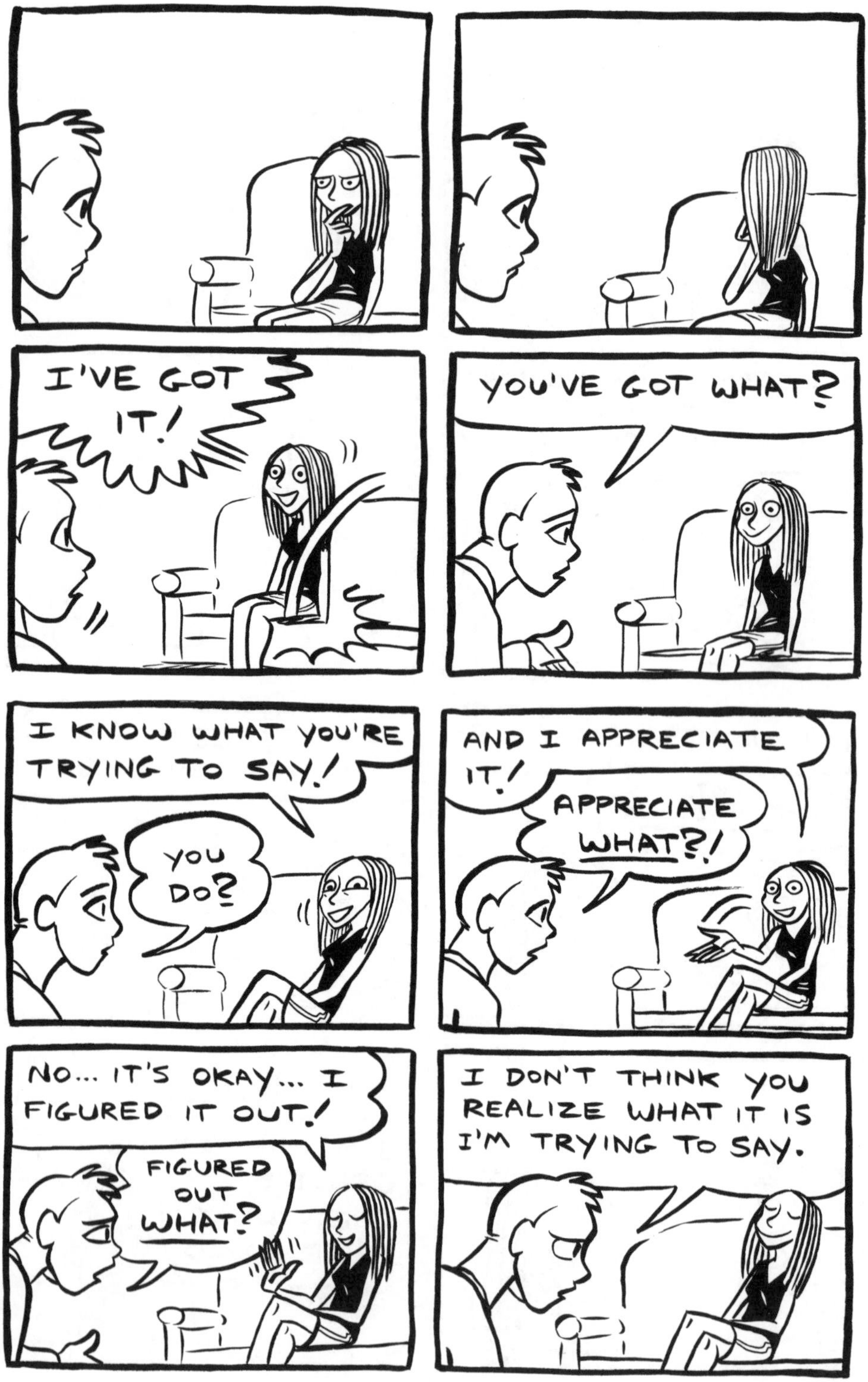

I'VE GOT IT!
YOU'VE GOT WHAT?
I KNOW WHAT YOU'RE TRYING TO SAY!
YOU DO?
AND I APPRECIATE IT!
APPRECIATE WHAT?!
NO... IT'S OKAY... I FIGURED IT OUT!
FIGURED OUT WHAT?
I DON'T THINK YOU REALIZE WHAT IT IS I'M TRYING TO SAY.

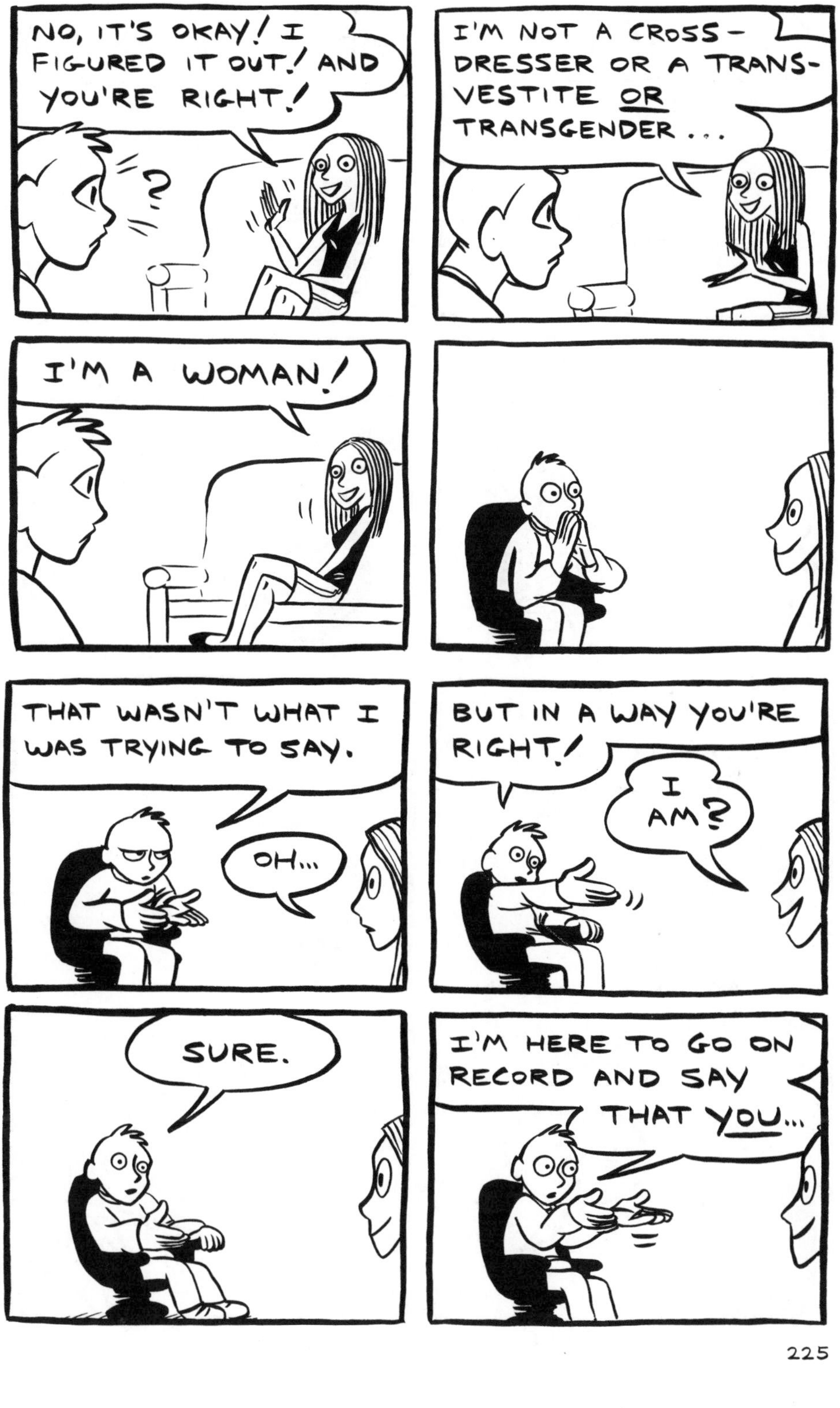
NO, IT'S OKAY! I FIGURED IT OUT! AND YOU'RE RIGHT!
?
I'M NOT A CROSS-DRESSER OR A TRANS-VESTITE OR TRANSGENDER...
I'M A WOMAN!
THAT WASN'T WHAT I WAS TRYING TO SAY.
OH...
BUT IN A WAY YOU'RE RIGHT!
I AM?
SURE.
I'M HERE TO GO ON RECORD AND SAY THAT YOU...

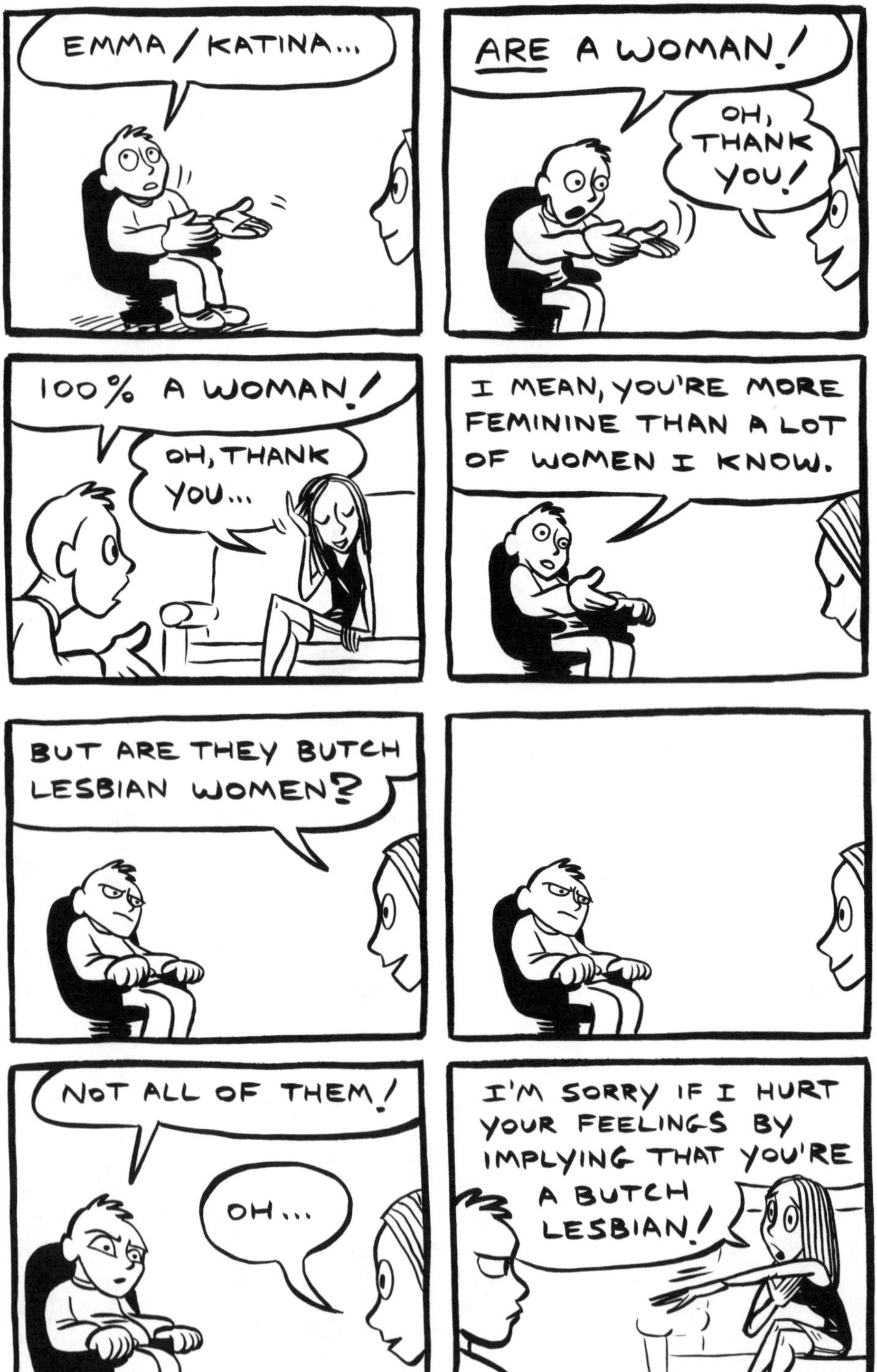
EMMA / KATINA...
ARE A WOMAN!
OH, THANK YOU!
100% A WOMAN!
OH, THANK YOU...
I MEAN, YOU'RE MORE FEMININE THAN A LOT OF WOMEN I KNOW.
BUT ARE THEY BUTCH LESBIAN WOMEN?
NOT ALL OF THEM!
OH...
I'M SORRY IF I HURT YOUR FEELINGS BY IMPLYING THAT YOU'RE A BUTCH LESBIAN!

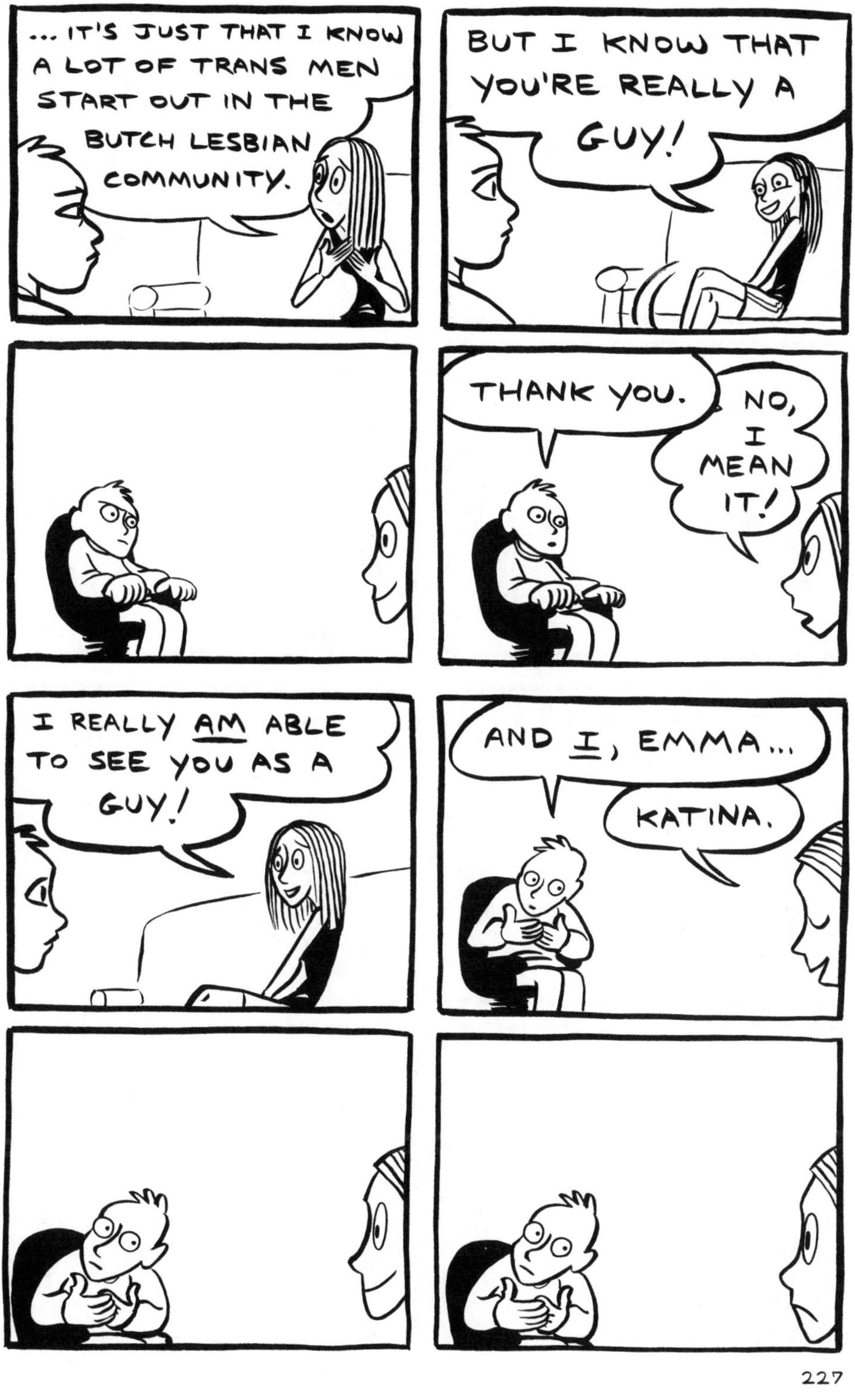
... IT'S JUST THAT I KNOW A LOT OF TRANS MEN START OUT IN THE BUTCH LESBIAN COMMUNITY.
BUT I KNOW THAT YOU'RE REALLY A GUY!
THANK YOU.
NO, I MEAN IT!
I REALLY AM ABLE TO SEE YOU AS A GUY!
AND I, EMMA...
KATINA.

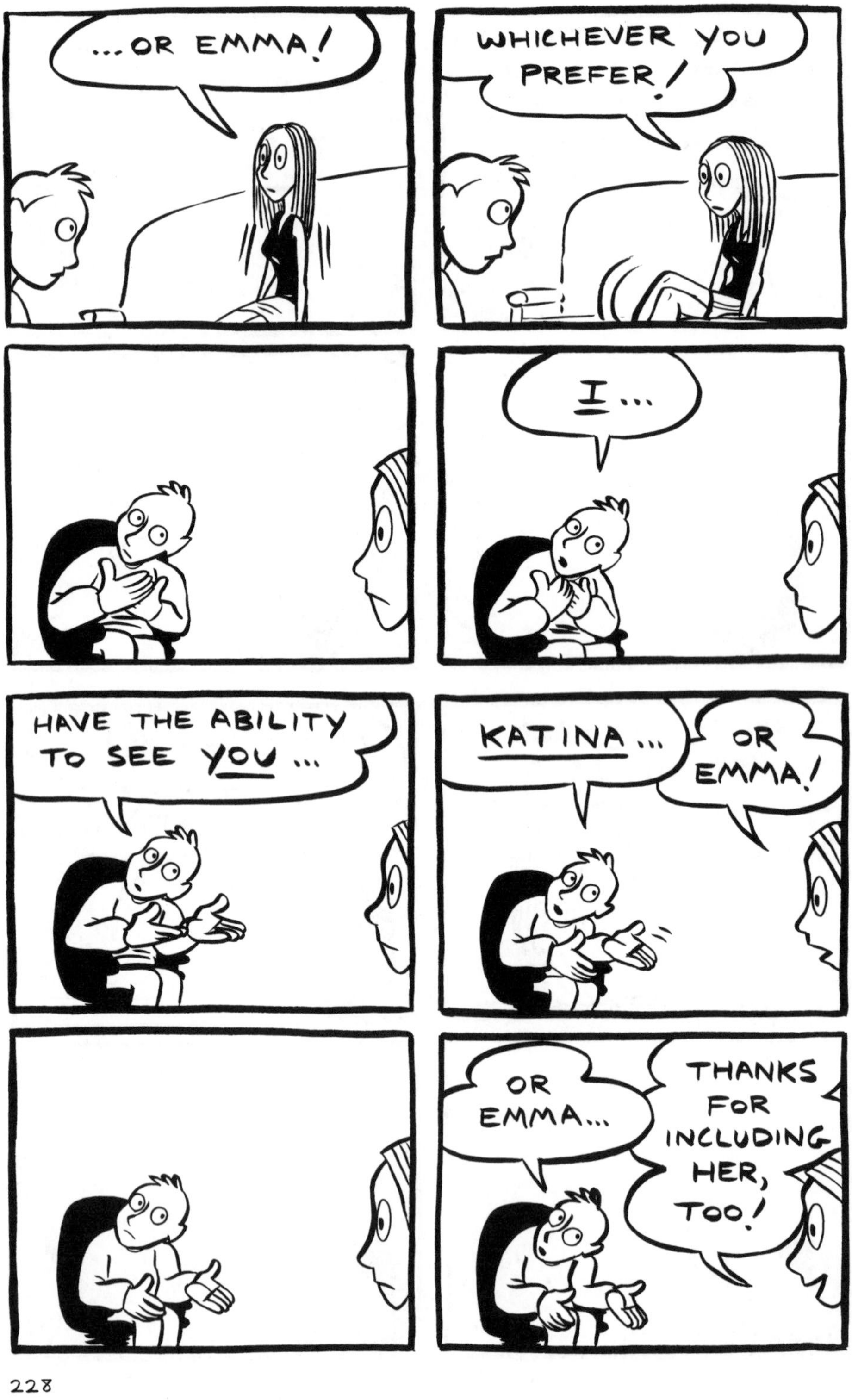

...OR EMMA!
WHICHEVER YOU PREFER!
I...
HAVE THE ABILITY TO SEE YOU...
KATINA...
OR EMMA!
OR EMMA...
THANKS FOR INCLUDING HER, TOO!

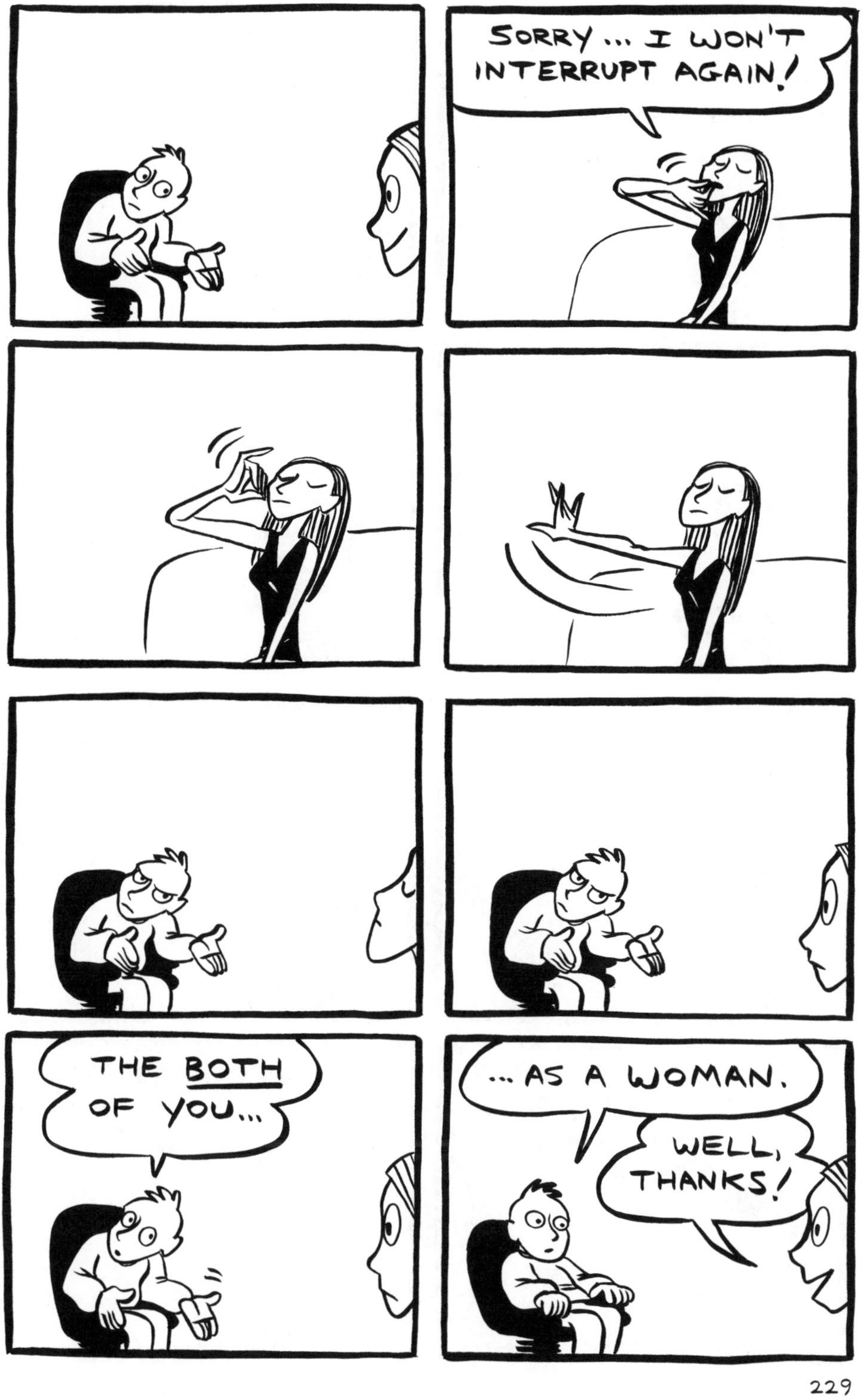
SORRY ... I WON'T INTERRUPT AGAIN!
THE BOTH OF YOU...
... AS A WOMAN.
WELL, THANKS!

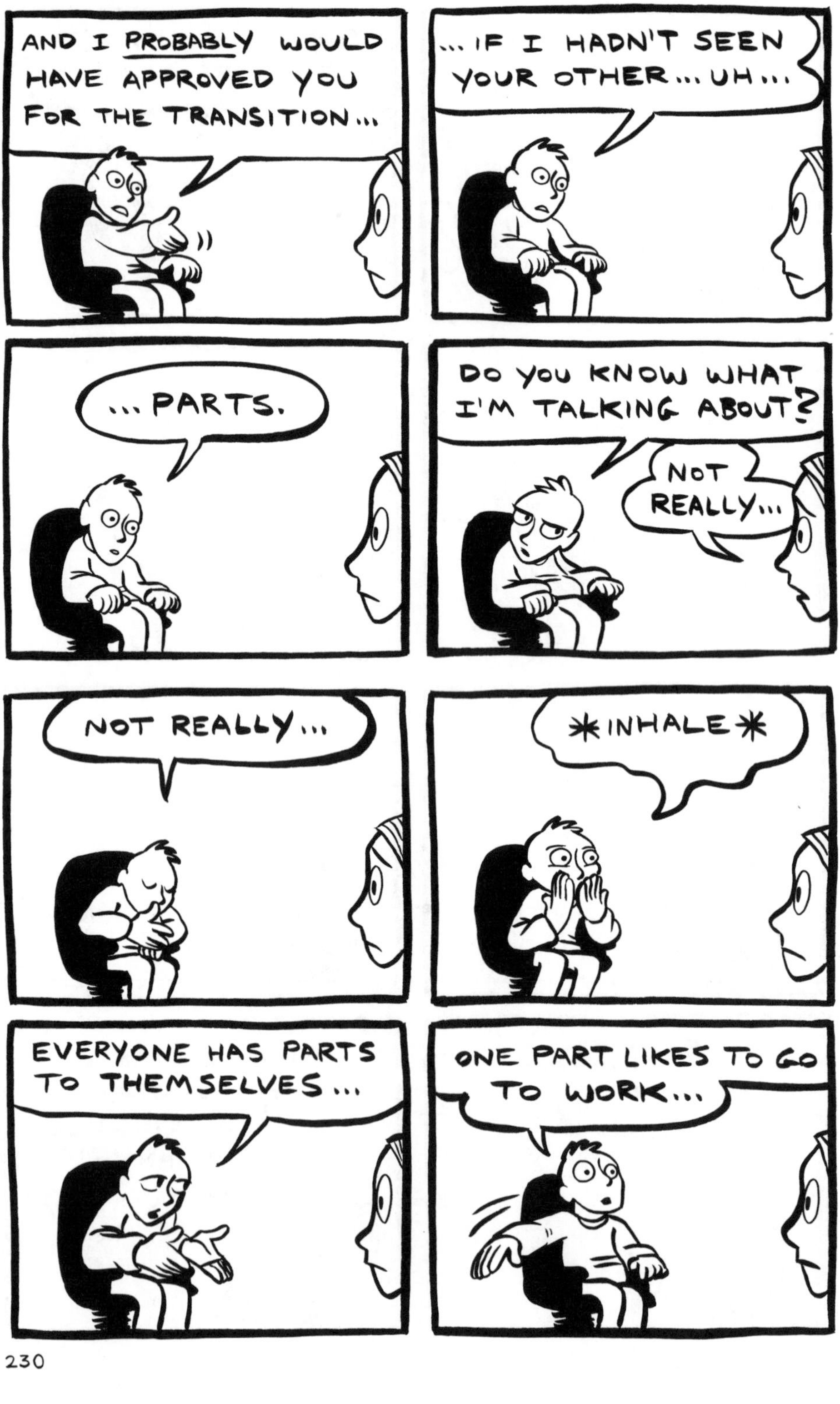
AND I PROBABLY WOULD HAVE APPROVED YOU FOR THE TRANSITION...
...IF I HADN'T SEEN YOUR OTHER... UH...
...PARTS.
DO YOU KNOW WHAT I'M TALKING ABOUT?
NOT REALLY...
NOT REALLY...
INHALE
EVERYONE HAS PARTS TO THEMSELVES...
ONE PART LIKES TO GO TO WORK...

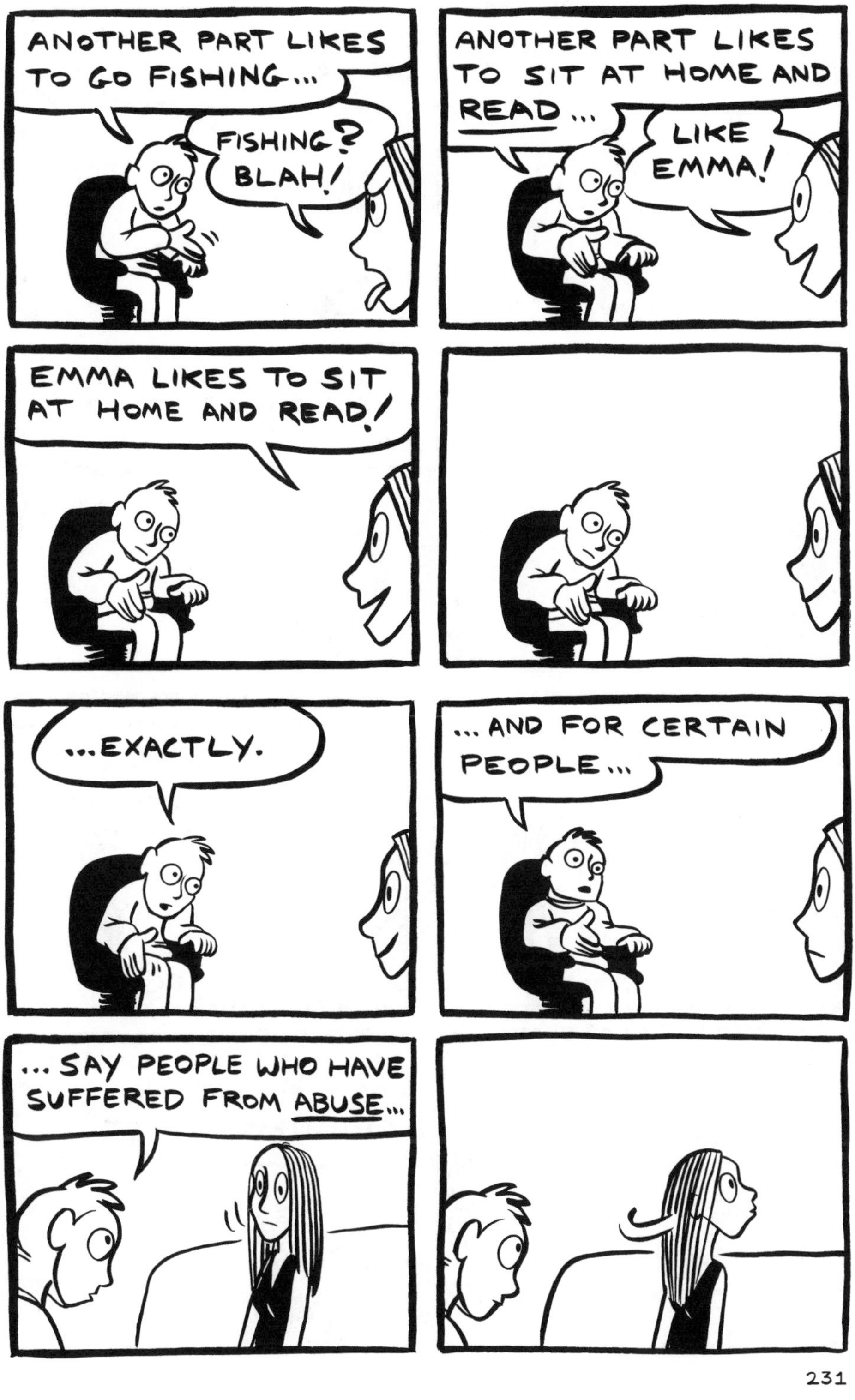
ANOTHER PART LIKES TO GO FISHING...
FISHING? BLAH!
ANOTHER PART LIKES TO SIT AT HOME AND READ...
LIKE EMMA!
EMMA LIKES TO SIT AT HOME AND READ!
...EXACTLY.
...AND FOR CERTAIN PEOPLE...
...SAY PEOPLE WHO HAVE SUFFERED FROM ABUSE...

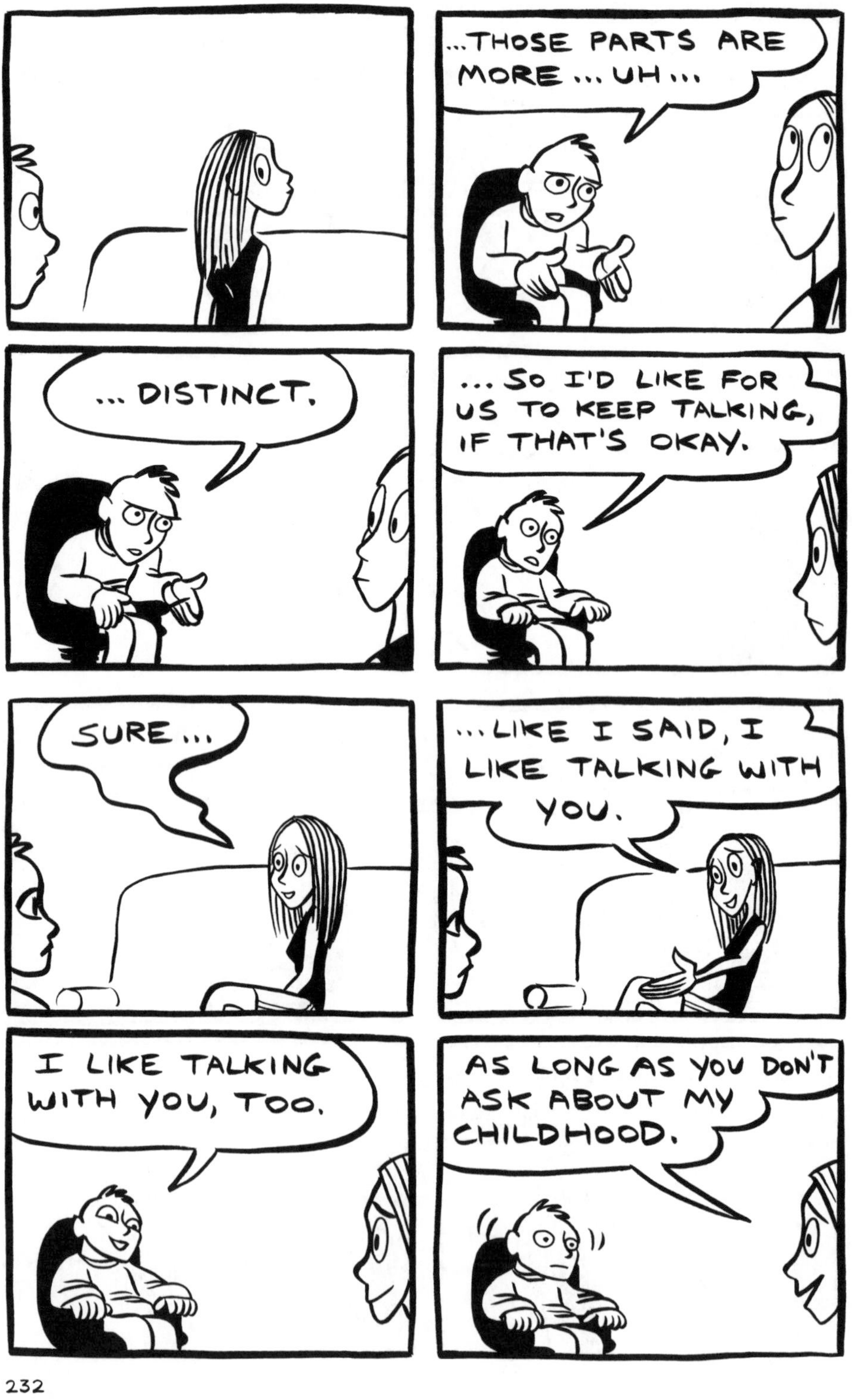
...THOSE PARTS ARE MORE... UH...
... DISTINCT.
... SO I'D LIKE FOR US TO KEEP TALKING, IF THAT'S OKAY.
SURE...
...LIKE I SAID, I LIKE TALKING WITH YOU.
I LIKE TALKING WITH YOU, TOO.
AS LONG AS YOU DON'T ASK ABOUT MY CHILDHOOD.

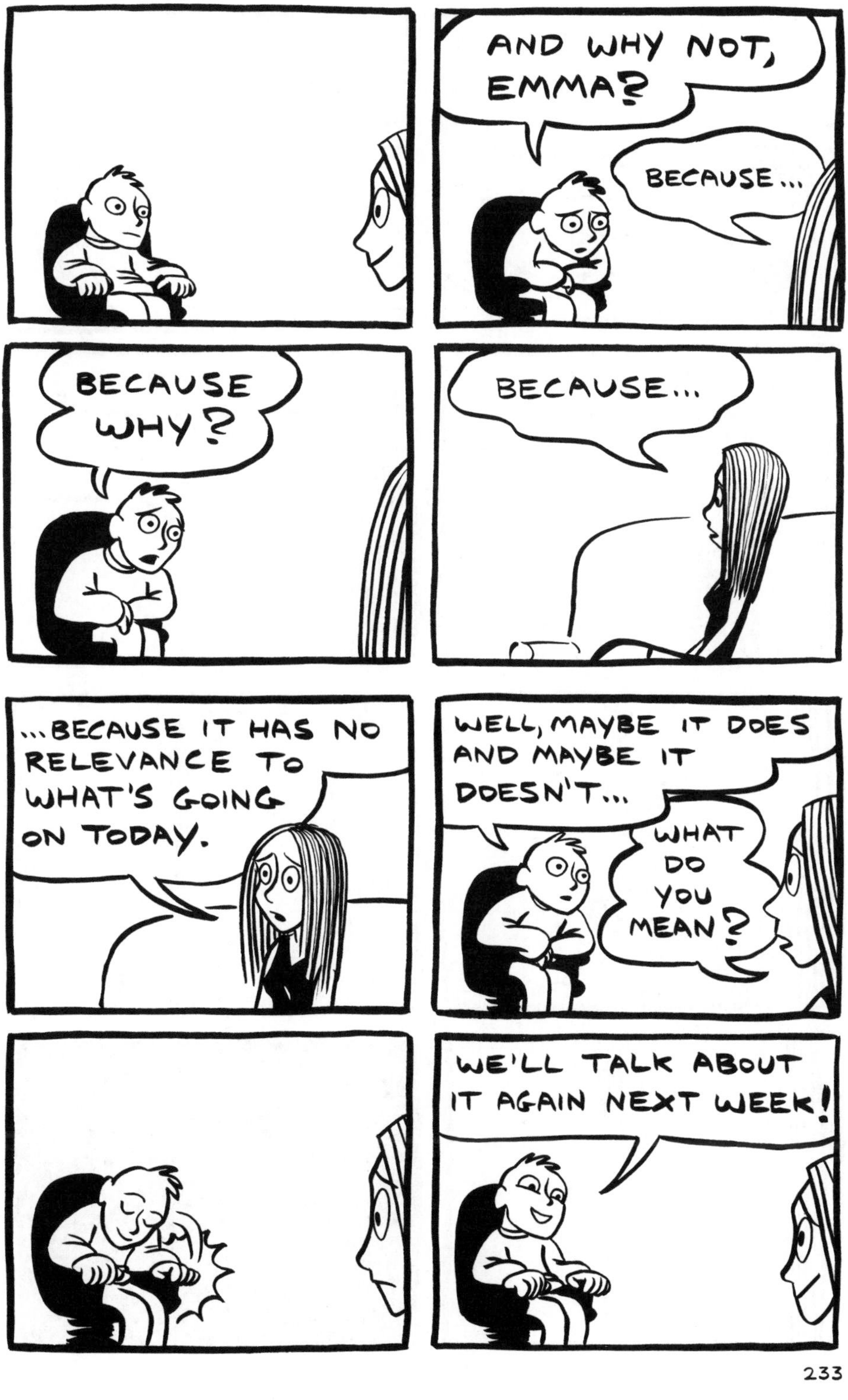
AND WHY NOT, EMMA?
BECAUSE...
BECAUSE WHY?
BECAUSE...
...BECAUSE IT HAS NO RELEVANCE TO WHAT'S GOING ON TODAY.
WELL, MAYBE IT DOES AND MAYBE IT DOESN'T...
WHAT DO YOU MEAN?
WE'LL TALK ABOUT IT AGAIN NEXT WEEK!

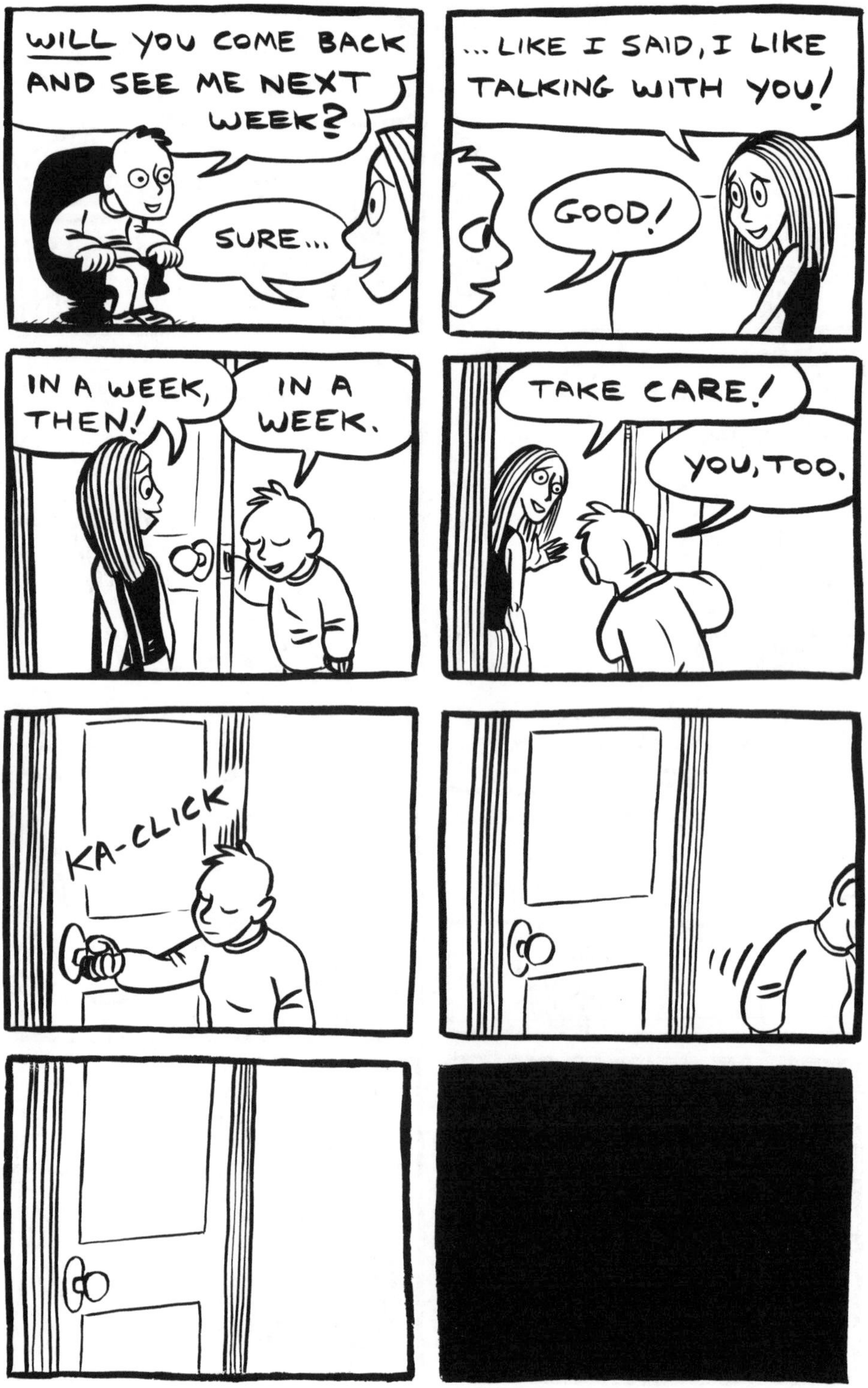
WILL YOU COME BACK AND SEE ME NEXT WEEK?
SURE...
...LIKE I SAID, I LIKE TALKING WITH YOU!
GOOD!
IN A WEEK, THEN!
IN A WEEK.
TAKE CARE!
YOU, TOO.
KA-CLICK

PARTS

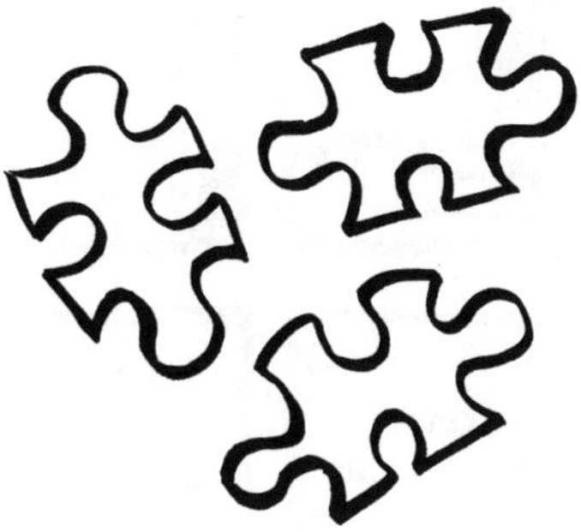

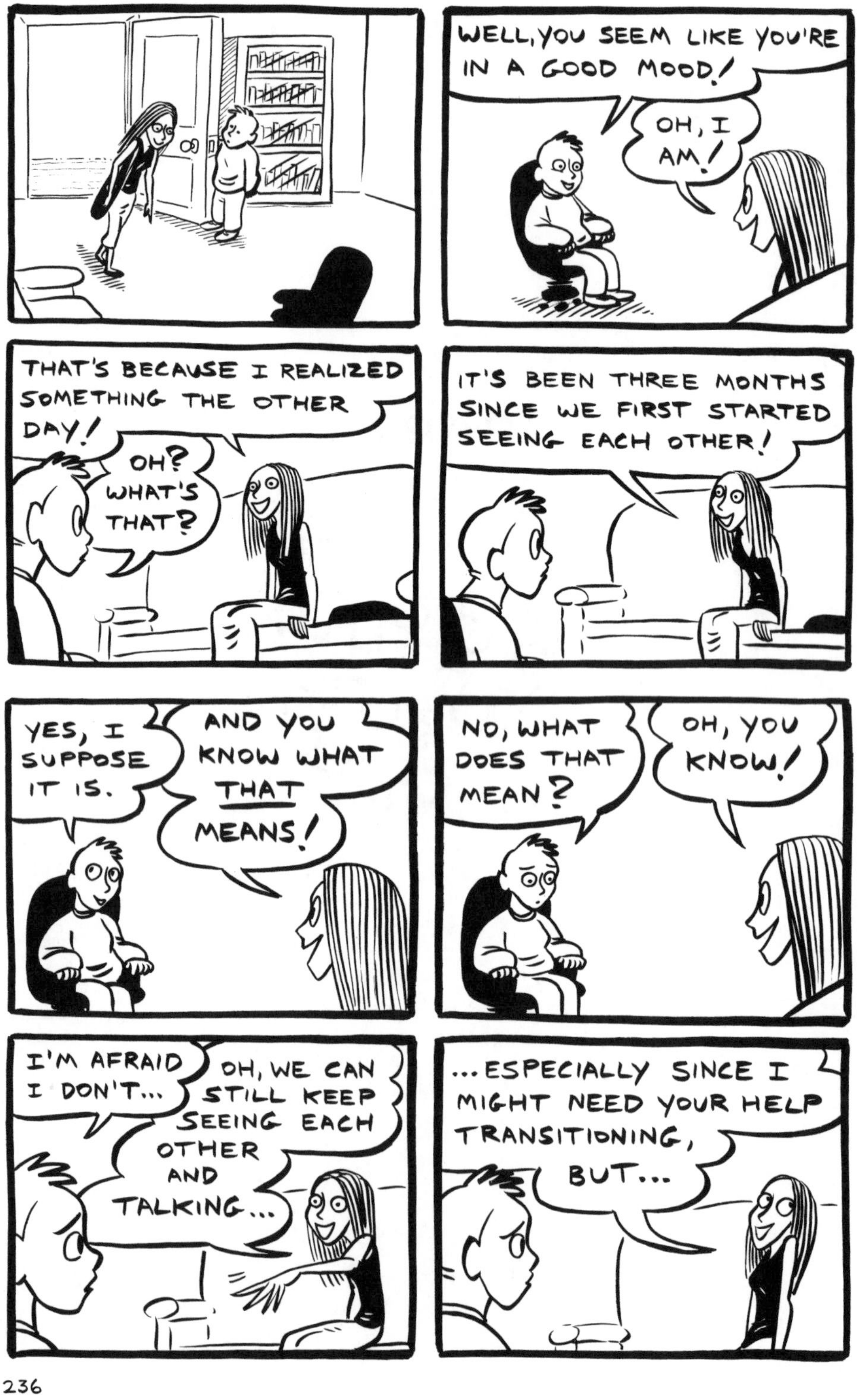
WELL, YOU SEEM LIKE YOU'RE IN A GOOD MOOD!
OH, I AM!
THAT'S BECAUSE I REALIZED SOMETHING THE OTHER DAY!
OH? WHAT'S THAT?
IT'S BEEN THREE MONTHS SINCE WE FIRST STARTED SEEING EACH OTHER!
YES, I SUPPOSE IT IS.
AND YOU KNOW WHAT THAT MEANS!
NO, WHAT DOES THAT MEAN?
OH, YOU KNOW!
I'M AFRAID I DON'T...
OH, WE CAN STILL KEEP SEEING EACH OTHER AND TALKING...
...ESPECIALLY SINCE I MIGHT NEED YOUR HELP TRANSITIONING,
BUT...

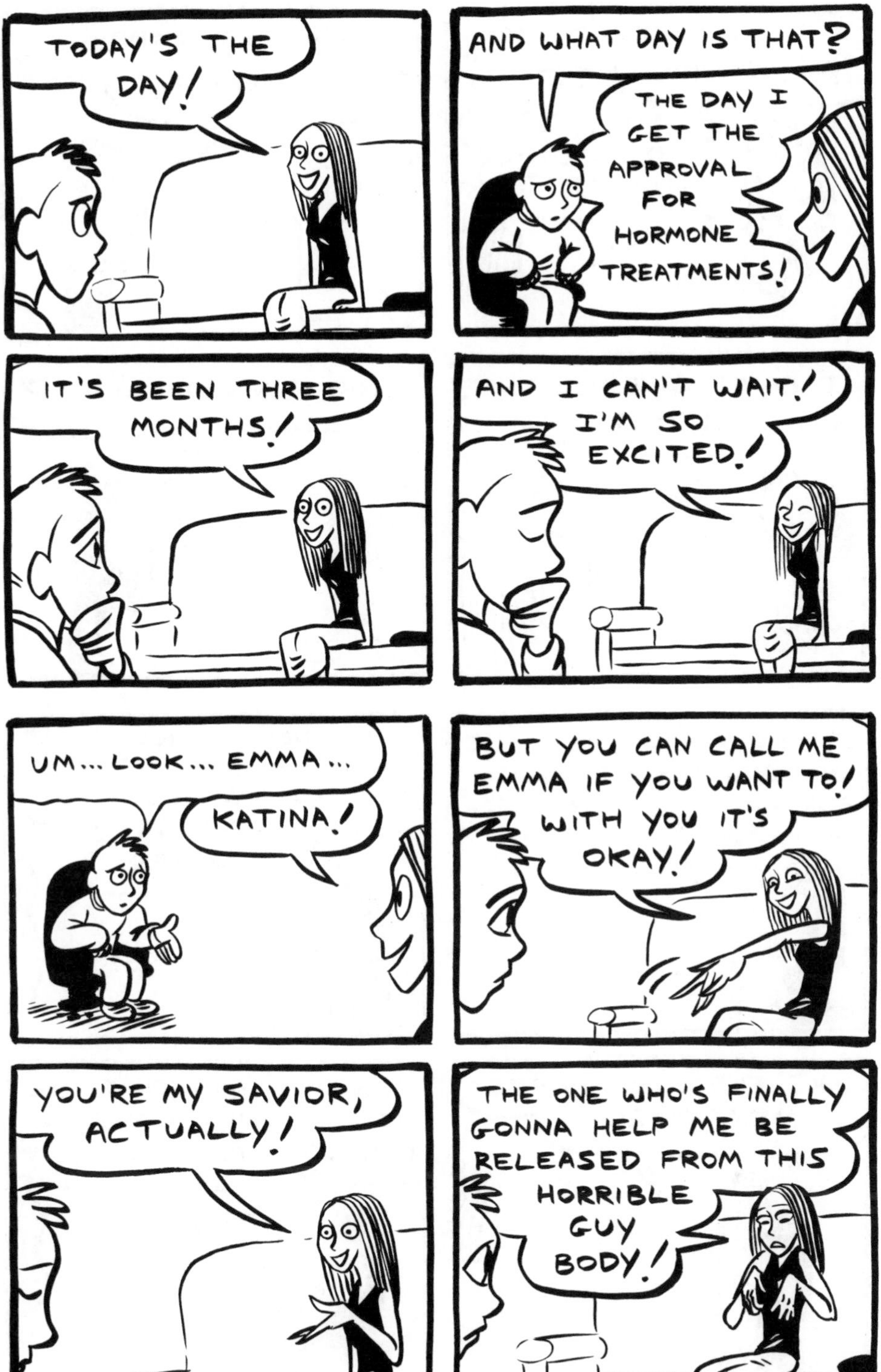
TODAY'S THE DAY!
AND WHAT DAY IS THAT?
THE DAY I GET THE APPROVAL FOR HORMONE TREATMENTS!
IT'S BEEN THREE MONTHS!
AND I CAN'T WAIT! I'M SO EXCITED!
UM... LOOK... EMMA...
KATINA!
BUT YOU CAN CALL ME EMMA IF YOU WANT TO! WITH YOU IT'S OKAY!
YOU'RE MY SAVIOR, ACTUALLY!
THE ONE WHO'S FINALLY GONNA HELP ME BE RELEASED FROM THIS HORRIBLE GUY BODY!

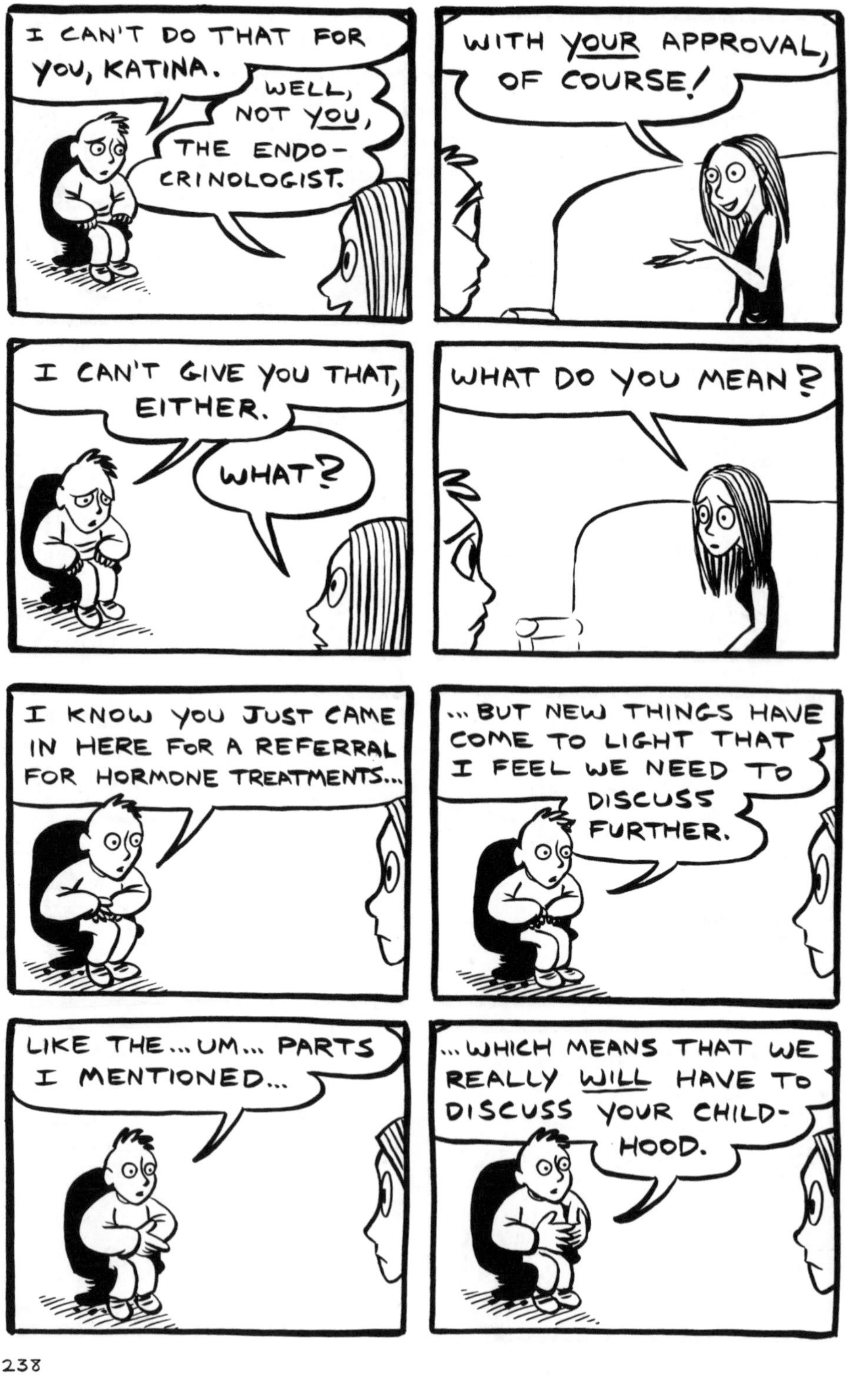
I CAN'T DO THAT FOR YOU, KATINA.
WELL, NOT YOU, THE ENDO-CRINOLOGIST.
WITH YOUR APPROVAL, OF COURSE!
I CAN'T GIVE YOU THAT, EITHER.
WHAT?
WHAT DO YOU MEAN?
I KNOW YOU JUST CAME IN HERE FOR A REFERRAL FOR HORMONE TREATMENTS...
...BUT NEW THINGS HAVE COME TO LIGHT THAT I FEEL WE NEED TO DISCUSS FURTHER.
LIKE THE...UM... PARTS I MENTIONED...
...WHICH MEANS THAT WE REALLY WILL HAVE TO DISCUSS YOUR CHILD-HOOD.

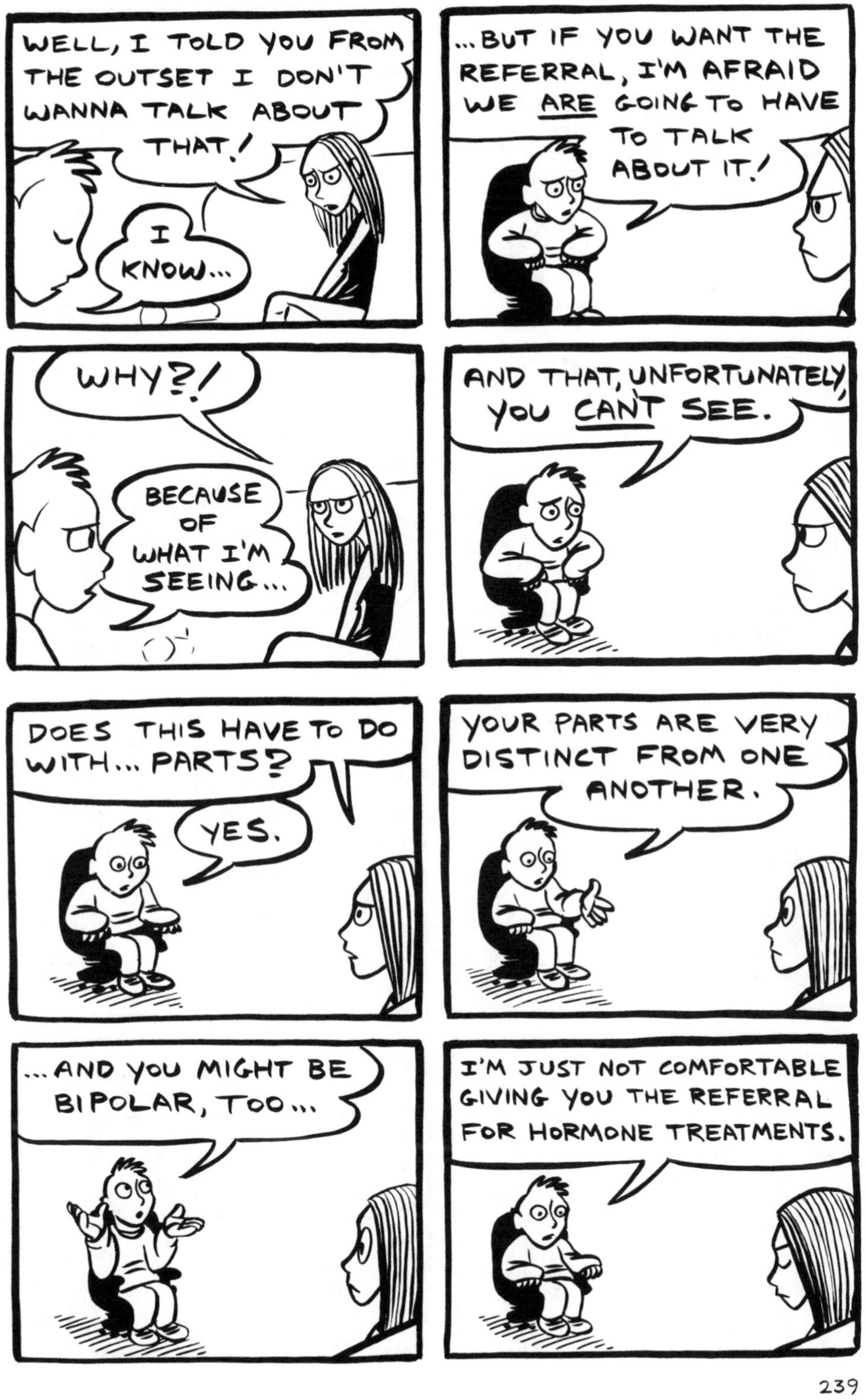

WELL, I TOLD YOU FROM THE OUTSET I DON'T WANNA TALK ABOUT THAT!
I KNOW...
...BUT IF YOU WANT THE REFERRAL, I'M AFRAID WE ARE GOING TO HAVE TO TALK ABOUT IT!
WHY?!
BECAUSE OF WHAT I'M SEEING...
AND THAT, UNFORTUNATELY, YOU CAN'T SEE.
DOES THIS HAVE TO DO WITH... PARTS?
YES.
YOUR PARTS ARE VERY DISTINCT FROM ONE ANOTHER.
...AND YOU MIGHT BE BIPOLAR, TOO...
I'M JUST NOT COMFORTABLE GIVING YOU THE REFERRAL FOR HORMONE TREATMENTS.

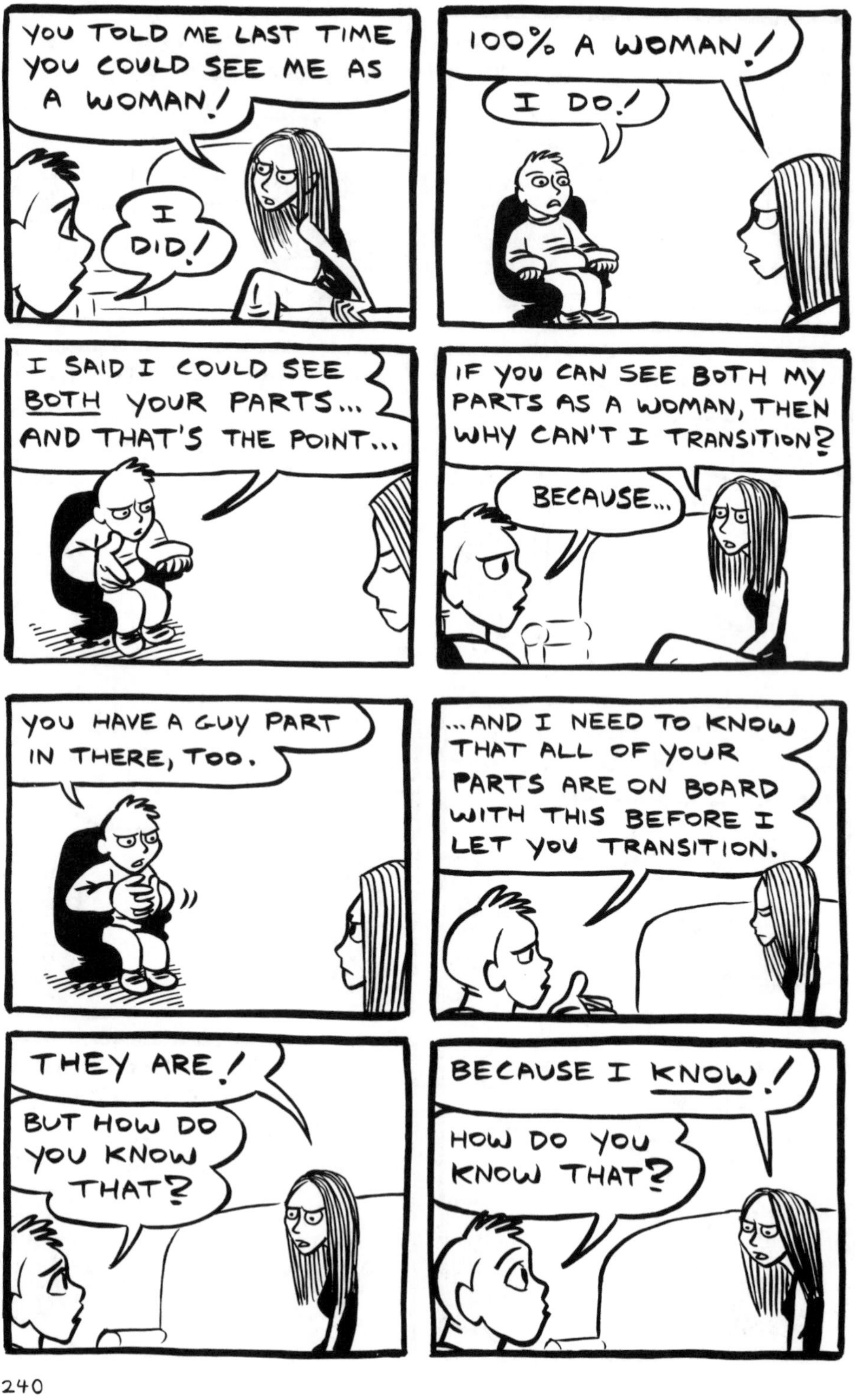
YOU TOLD ME LAST TIME YOU COULD SEE ME AS A WOMAN!
I DID!
100% A WOMAN!
I DO!
I SAID I COULD SEE BOTH YOUR PARTS... AND THAT'S THE POINT...
IF YOU CAN SEE BOTH MY PARTS AS A WOMAN, THEN WHY CAN'T I TRANSITION?
BECAUSE...
YOU HAVE A GUY PART IN THERE, TOO.
...AND I NEED TO KNOW THAT ALL OF YOUR PARTS ARE ON BOARD WITH THIS BEFORE I LET YOU TRANSITION.
THEY ARE!
BUT HOW DO YOU KNOW THAT?
BECAUSE I KNOW!
HOW DO YOU KNOW THAT?

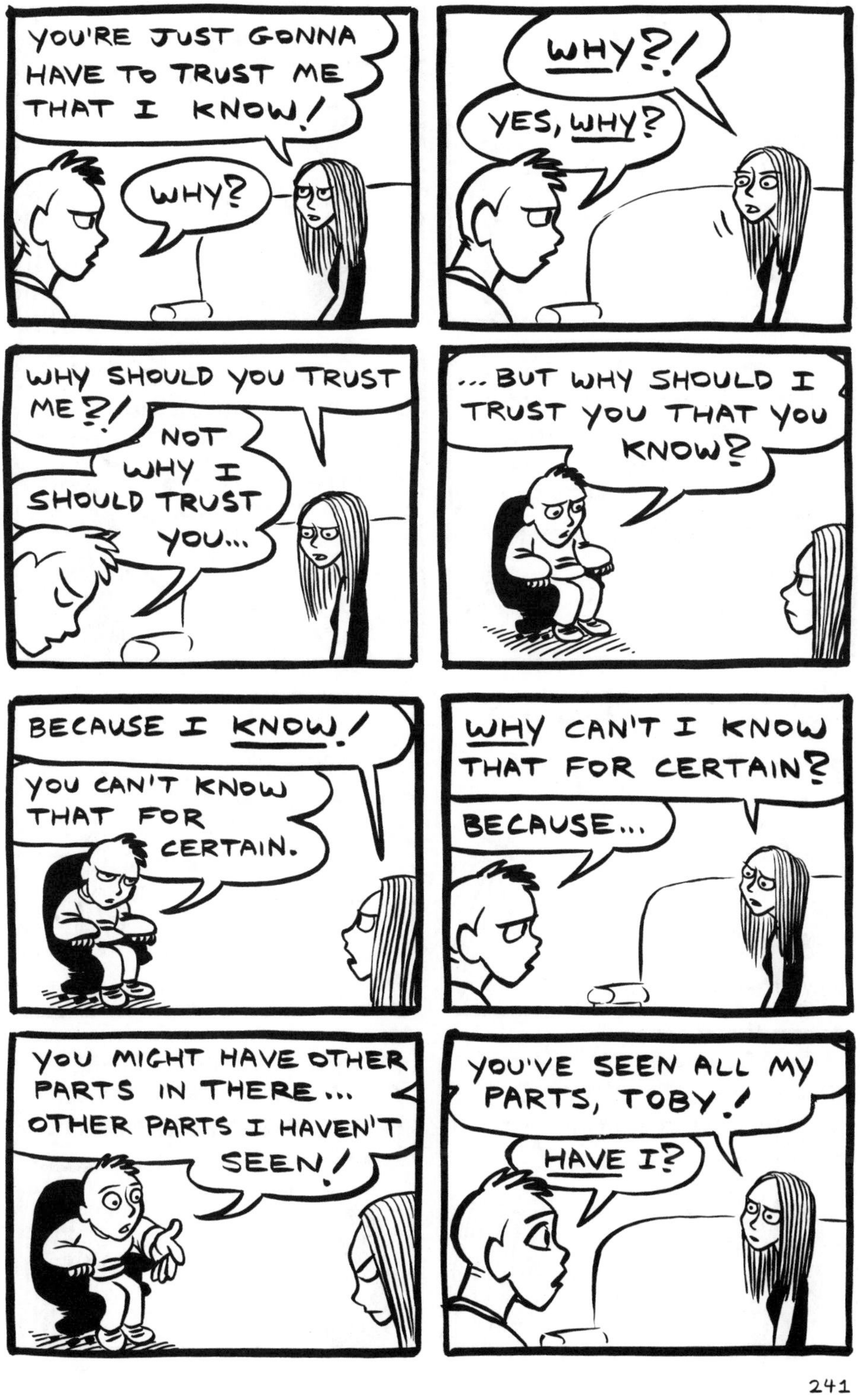
YOU'RE JUST GONNA HAVE TO TRUST ME THAT I KNOW!
WHY?
WHY?!
YES, WHY?
WHY SHOULD YOU TRUST ME?!
NOT WHY I SHOULD TRUST YOU...
...BUT WHY SHOULD I TRUST YOU THAT YOU KNOW?
BECAUSE I KNOW!
YOU CAN'T KNOW THAT FOR CERTAIN.
WHY CAN'T I KNOW THAT FOR CERTAIN?
BECAUSE...
YOU MIGHT HAVE OTHER PARTS IN THERE... OTHER PARTS I HAVEN'T SEEN!
YOU'VE SEEN ALL MY PARTS, TOBY!
HAVE I?

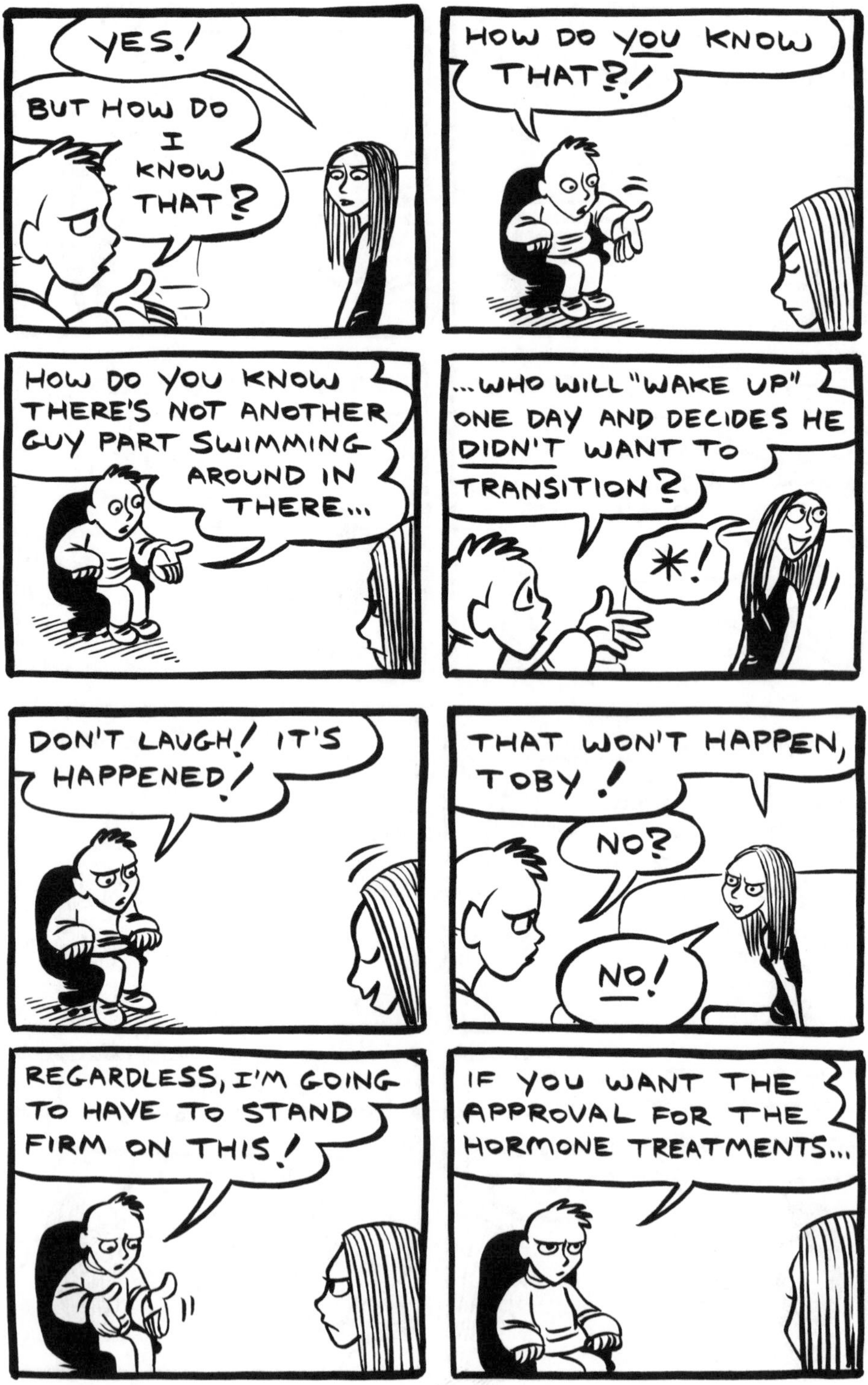

YES!
BUT HOW DO I KNOW THAT?
HOW DO YOU KNOW THAT?!
HOW DO YOU KNOW THERE'S NOT ANOTHER GUY PART SWIMMING AROUND IN THERE...
...WHO WILL "WAKE UP" ONE DAY AND DECIDES HE DIDN'T WANT TO TRANSITION?
*!
DON'T LAUGH! IT'S HAPPENED!
THAT WON'T HAPPEN, TOBY!
NO?
NO!
REGARDLESS, I'M GOING TO HAVE TO STAND FIRM ON THIS!
IF YOU WANT THE APPROVAL FOR THE HORMONE TREATMENTS...

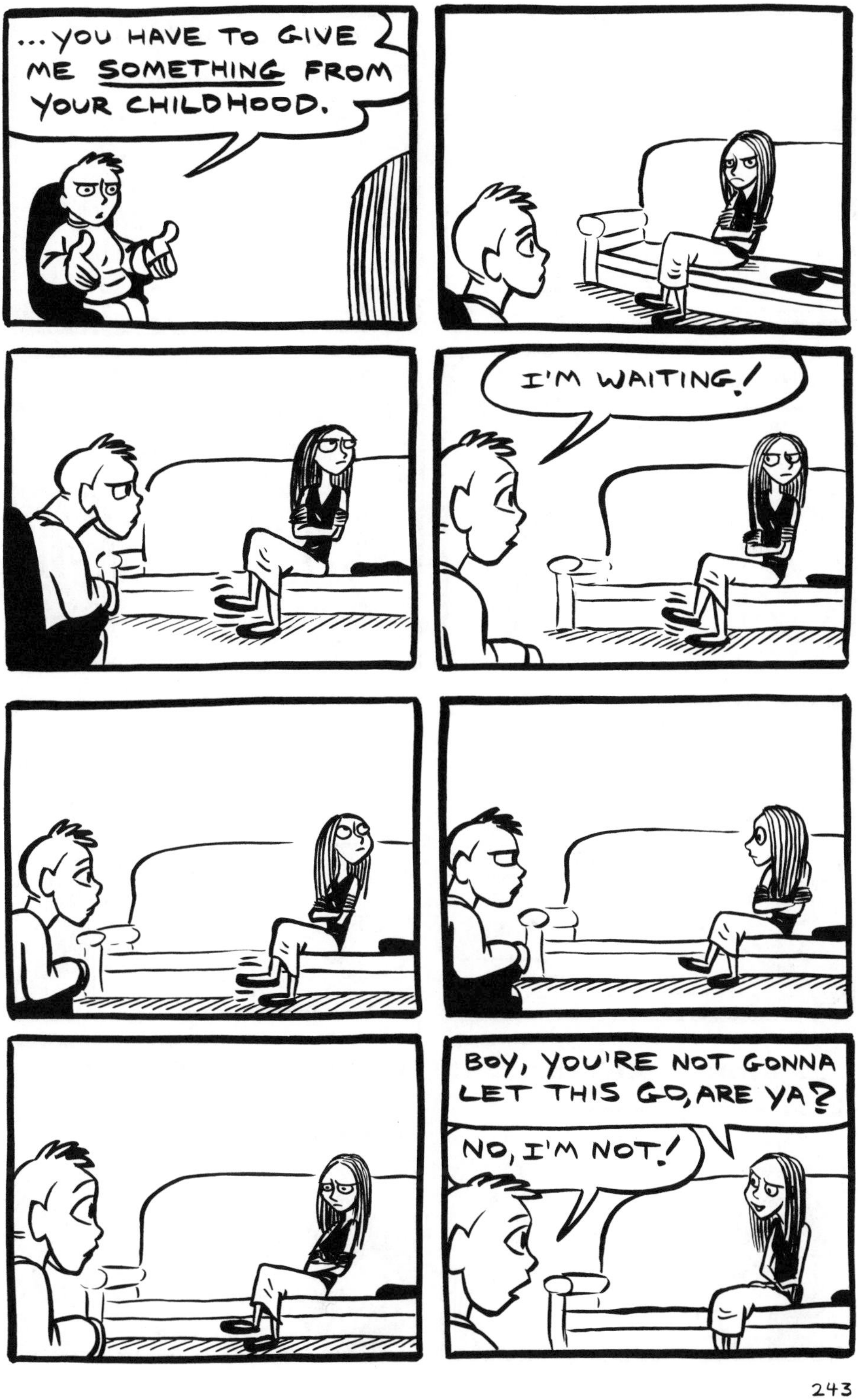
...YOU HAVE TO GIVE ME SOMETHING FROM YOUR CHILDHOOD.
I'M WAITING!
BOY, YOU'RE NOT GONNA LET THIS GO, ARE YA?
NO, I'M NOT!

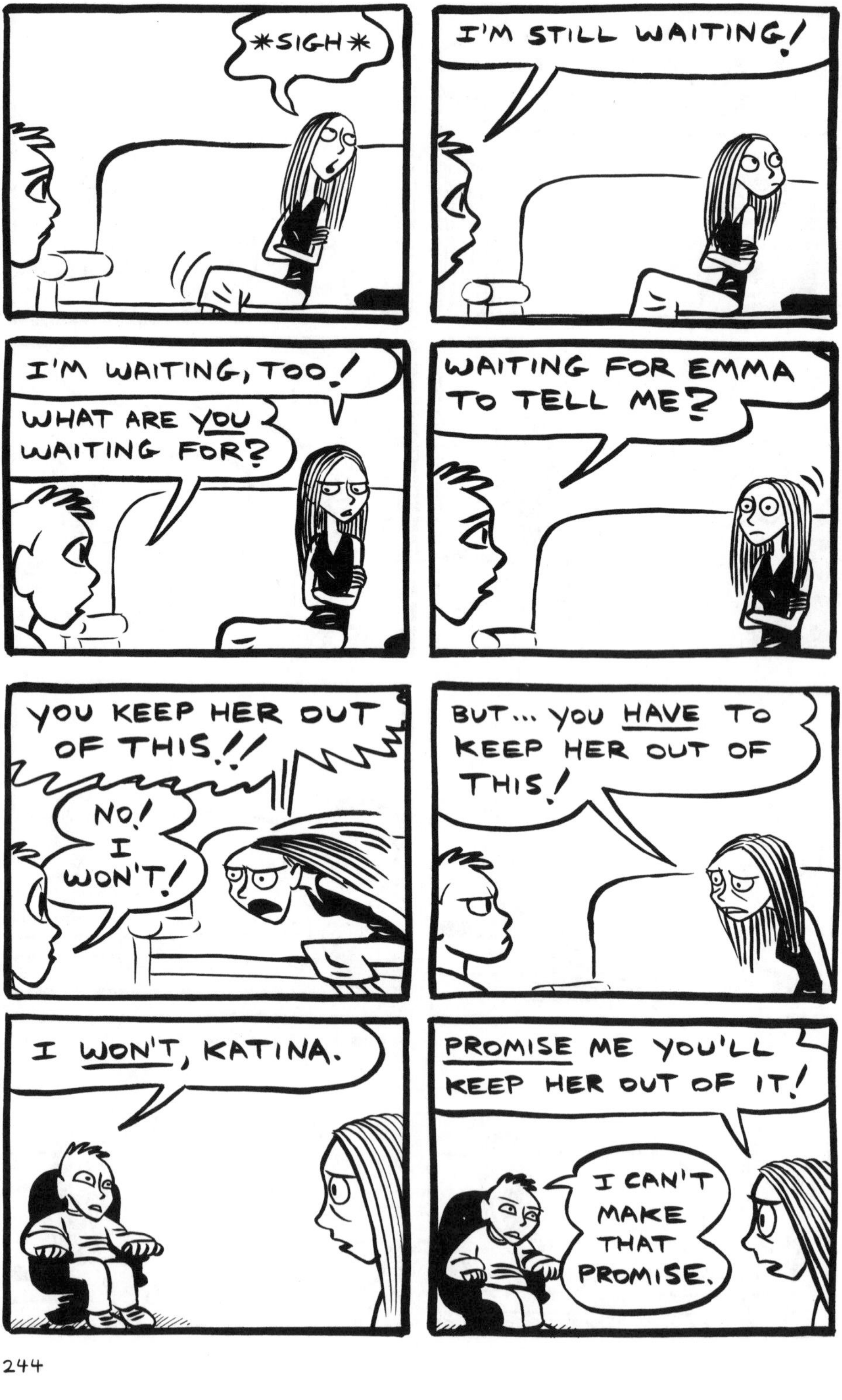
SIGH
I'M STILL WAITING!
I'M WAITING, TOO!
WHAT ARE YOU WAITING FOR?
WAITING FOR EMMA TO TELL ME?
YOU KEEP HER OUT OF THIS!!
NO! I WON'T!
BUT... YOU HAVE TO KEEP HER OUT OF THIS!
I WON'T, KATINA.
PROMISE ME YOU'LL KEEP HER OUT OF IT!
I CAN'T MAKE THAT PROMISE.

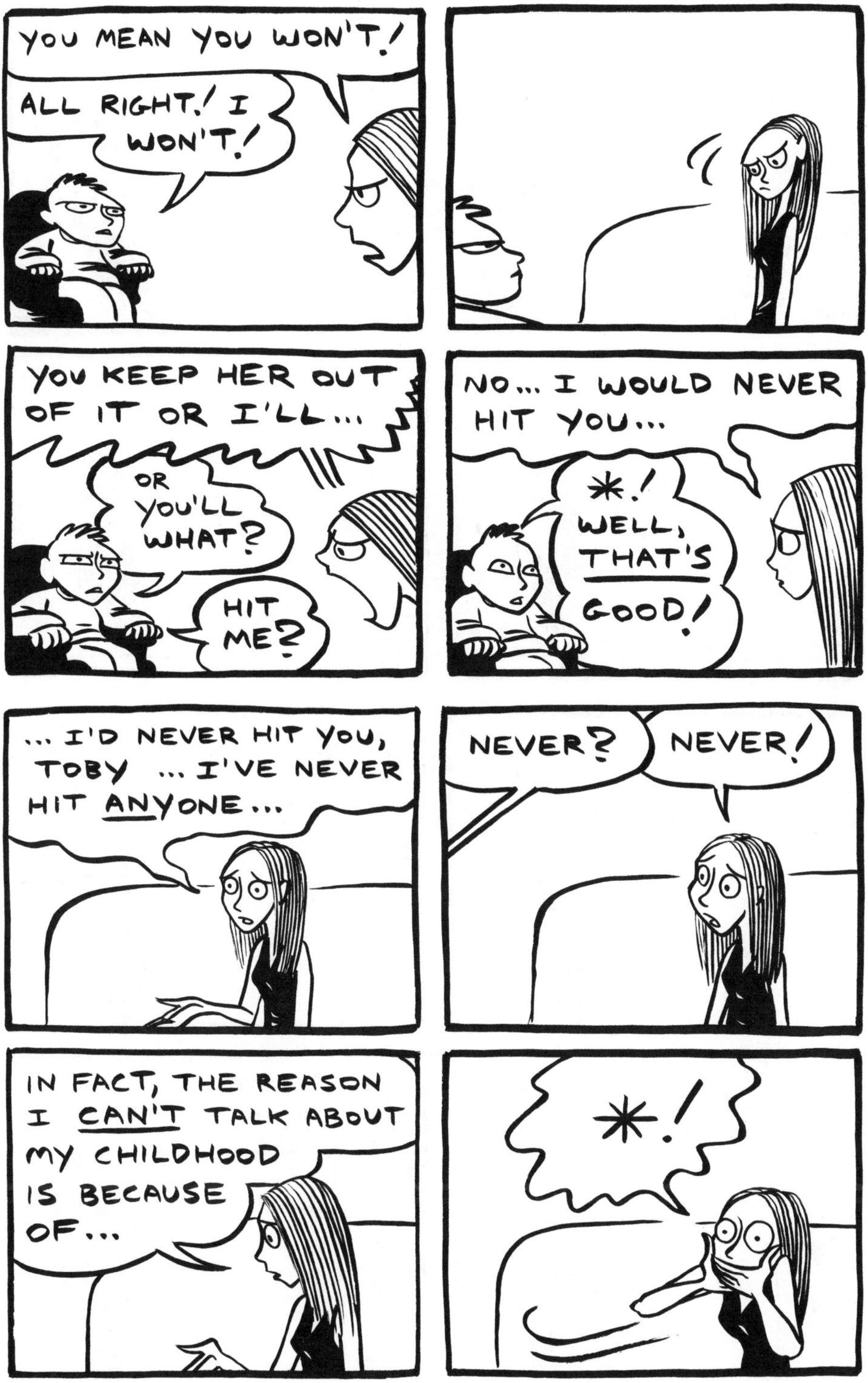
YOU MEAN YOU WON'T!
ALL RIGHT! I WON'T!
YOU KEEP HER OUT OF IT OR I'LL...
OR YOU'LL WHAT?
HIT ME?
NO... I WOULD NEVER HIT YOU...
*! WELL, THAT'S GOOD!
... I'D NEVER HIT YOU, TOBY ... I'VE NEVER HIT ANYONE...
NEVER?
NEVER!
IN FACT, THE REASON I CAN'T TALK ABOUT MY CHILDHOOD IS BECAUSE OF...
*!

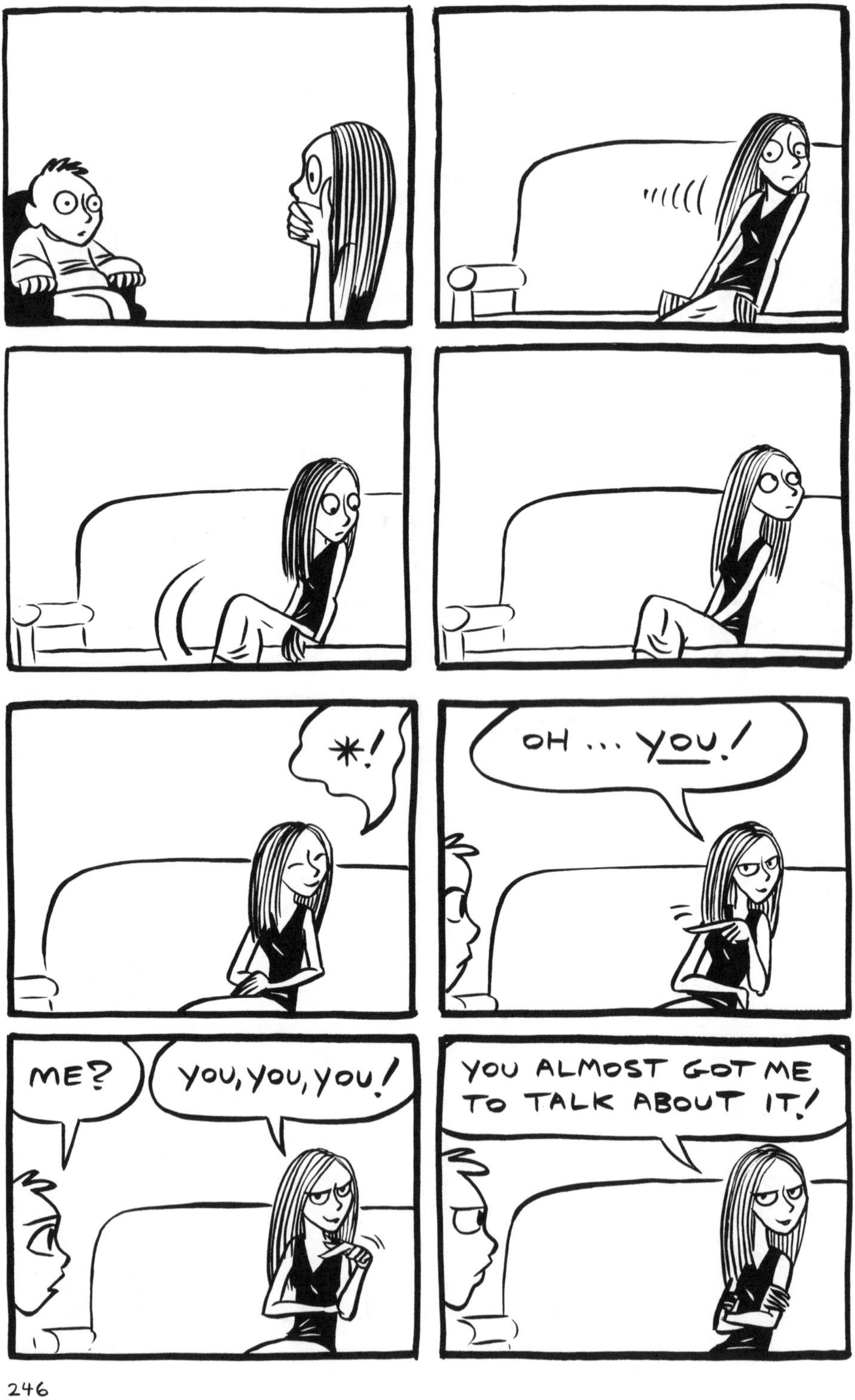
*!
OH ... YOU!
ME?
YOU, YOU, YOU!
YOU ALMOST GOT ME TO TALK ABOUT IT!

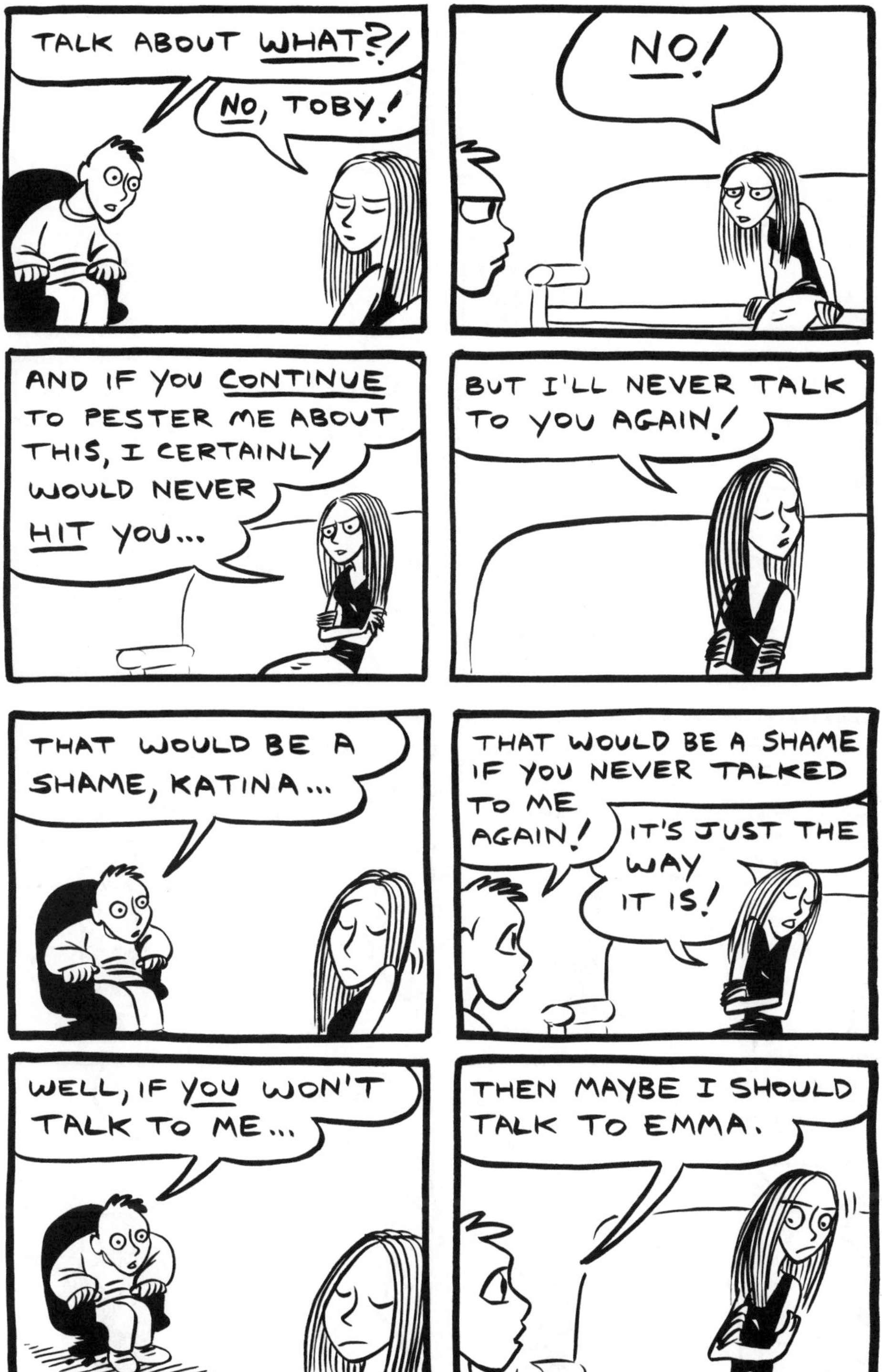
TALK ABOUT WHAT?!
NO, TOBY!
NO!
AND IF YOU CONTINUE TO PESTER ME ABOUT THIS, I CERTAINLY WOULD NEVER HIT YOU...
BUT I'LL NEVER TALK TO YOU AGAIN!
THAT WOULD BE A SHAME, KATINA...
THAT WOULD BE A SHAME IF YOU NEVER TALKED TO ME AGAIN!
IT'S JUST THE WAY IT IS!
WELL, IF YOU WON'T TALK TO ME...
THEN MAYBE I SHOULD TALK TO EMMA.

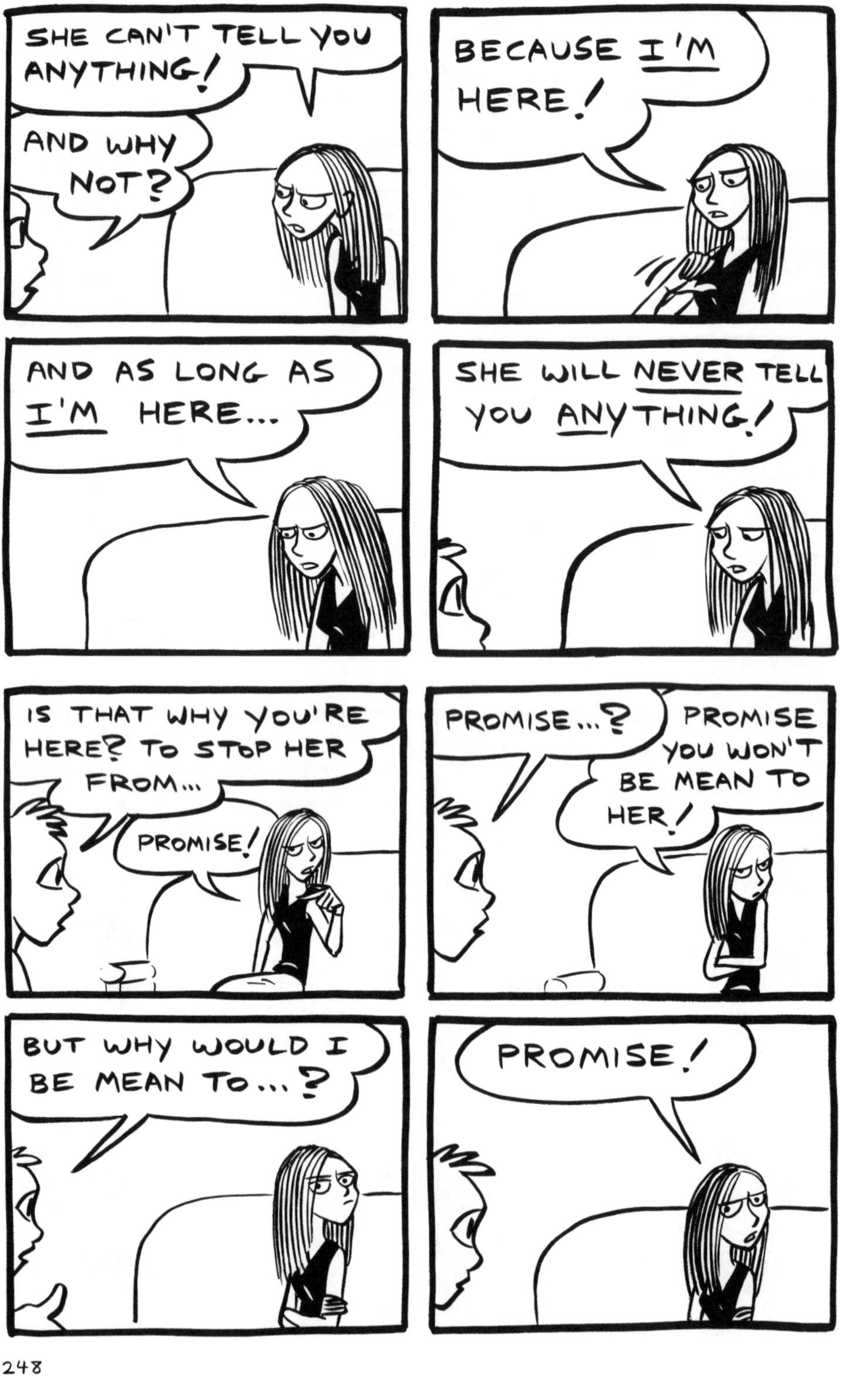
SHE CAN'T TELL YOU ANYTHING!
AND WHY NOT?
BECAUSE I'M HERE!
AND AS LONG AS I'M HERE...
SHE WILL NEVER TELL YOU ANYTHING!
IS THAT WHY YOU'RE HERE? TO STOP HER FROM...
PROMISE!
PROMISE...?
PROMISE YOU WON'T BE MEAN TO HER!
BUT WHY WOULD I BE MEAN TO...?
PROMISE!

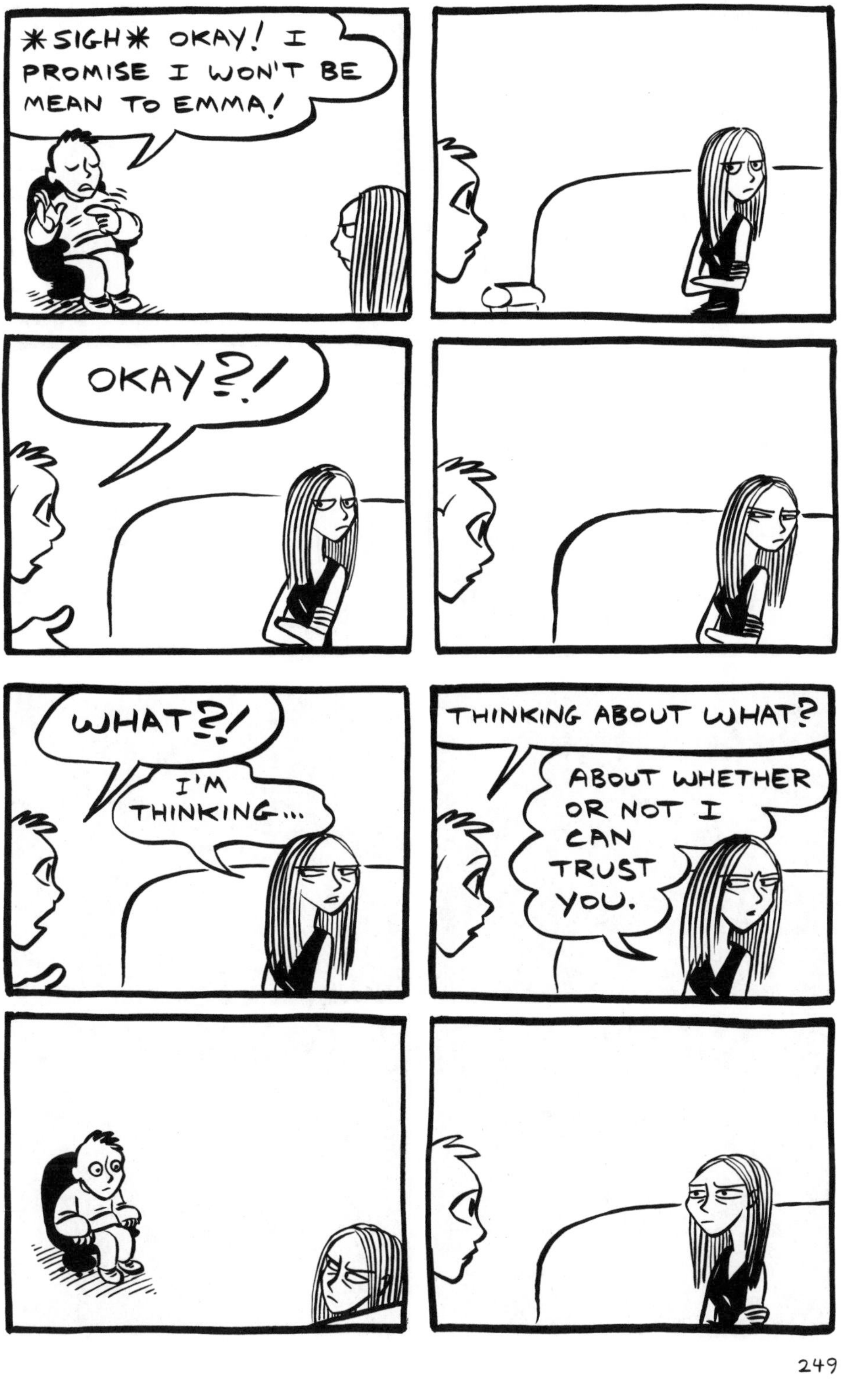
SIGH OKAY! I PROMISE I WON'T BE MEAN TO EMMA!
OKAY?!
WHAT?!
I'M THINKING...
THINKING ABOUT WHAT?
ABOUT WHETHER OR NOT I CAN TRUST YOU.

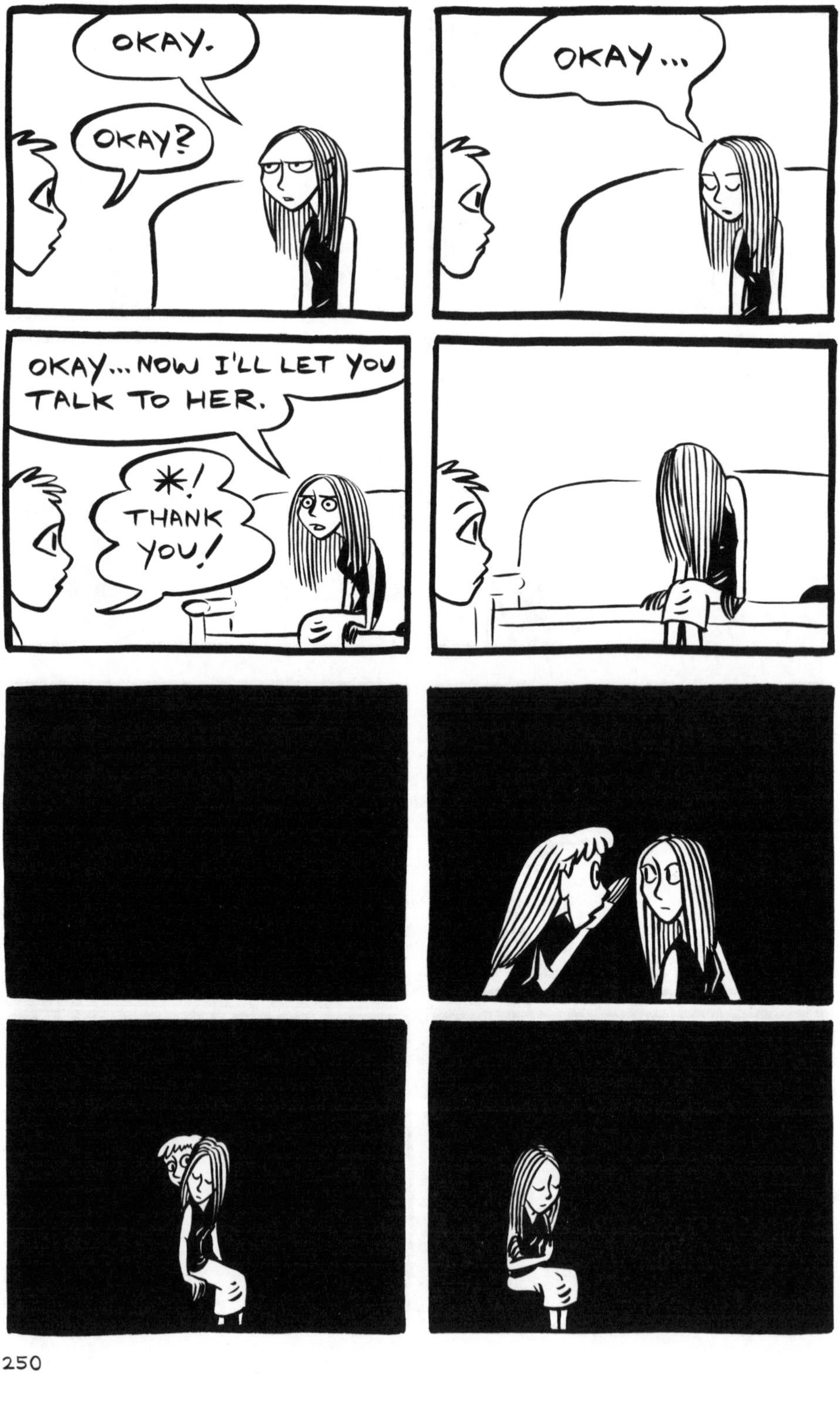
OKAY.
OKAY?
OKAY...
OKAY... NOW I'LL LET YOU TALK TO HER.
*! THANK YOU!

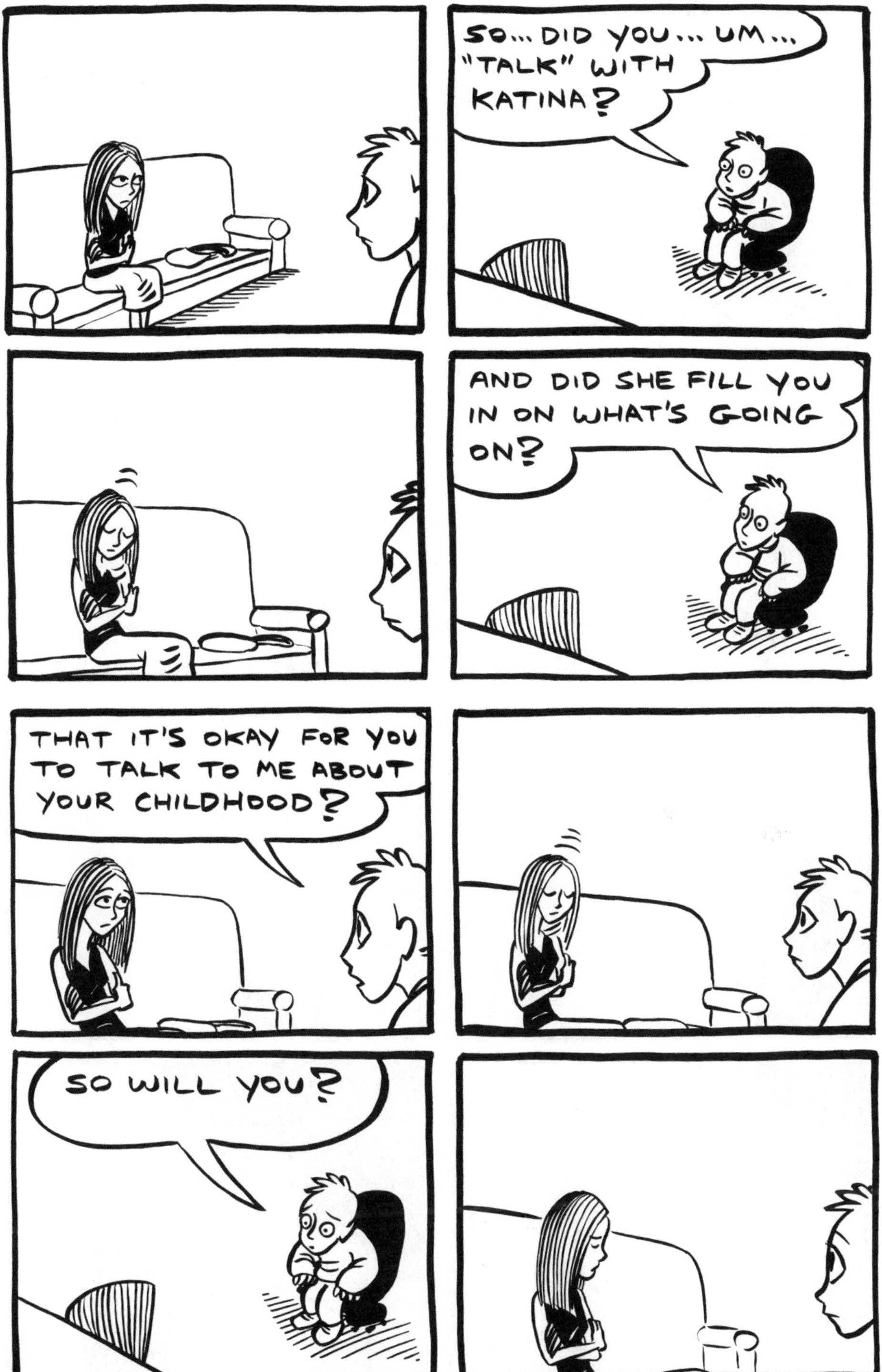
SO... DID YOU... UM... "TALK" WITH KATINA?
AND DID SHE FILL YOU IN ON WHAT'S GOING ON?
THAT IT'S OKAY FOR YOU TO TALK TO ME ABOUT YOUR CHILDHOOD?
SO WILL YOU?

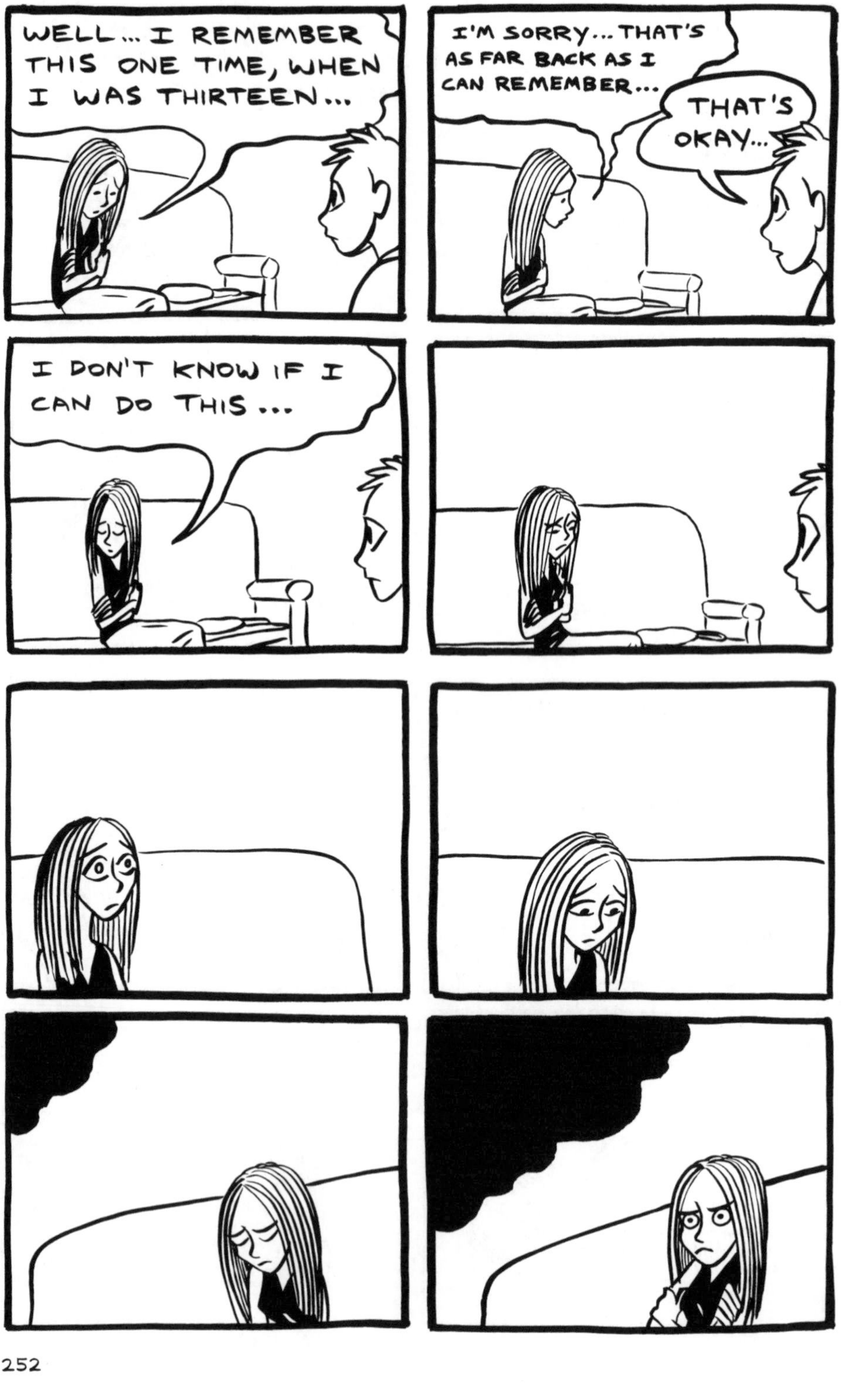
WELL... I REMEMBER THIS ONE TIME, WHEN I WAS THIRTEEN...
I'M SORRY... THAT'S AS FAR BACK AS I CAN REMEMBER...
THAT'S OKAY...
I DON'T KNOW IF I CAN DO THIS...

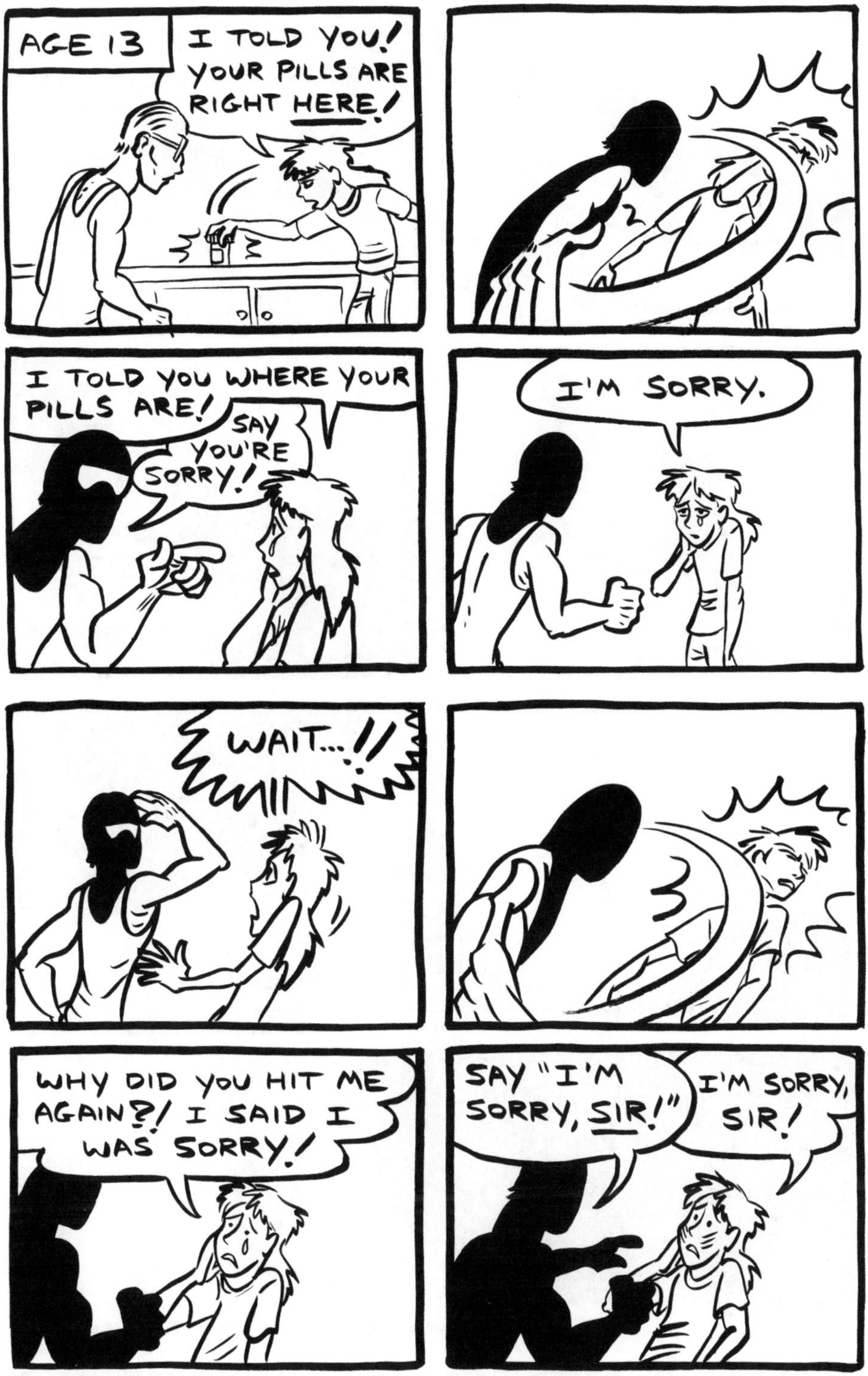
AGE 13
I TOLD YOU! YOUR PILLS ARE RIGHT HERE!
I TOLD YOU WHERE YOUR PILLS ARE!
SAY YOU'RE SORRY!
I'M SORRY.
WAIT...!!
WHY DID YOU HIT ME AGAIN?! I SAID I WAS SORRY!
SAY "I'M SORRY, SIR!"
I'M SORRY, SIR!

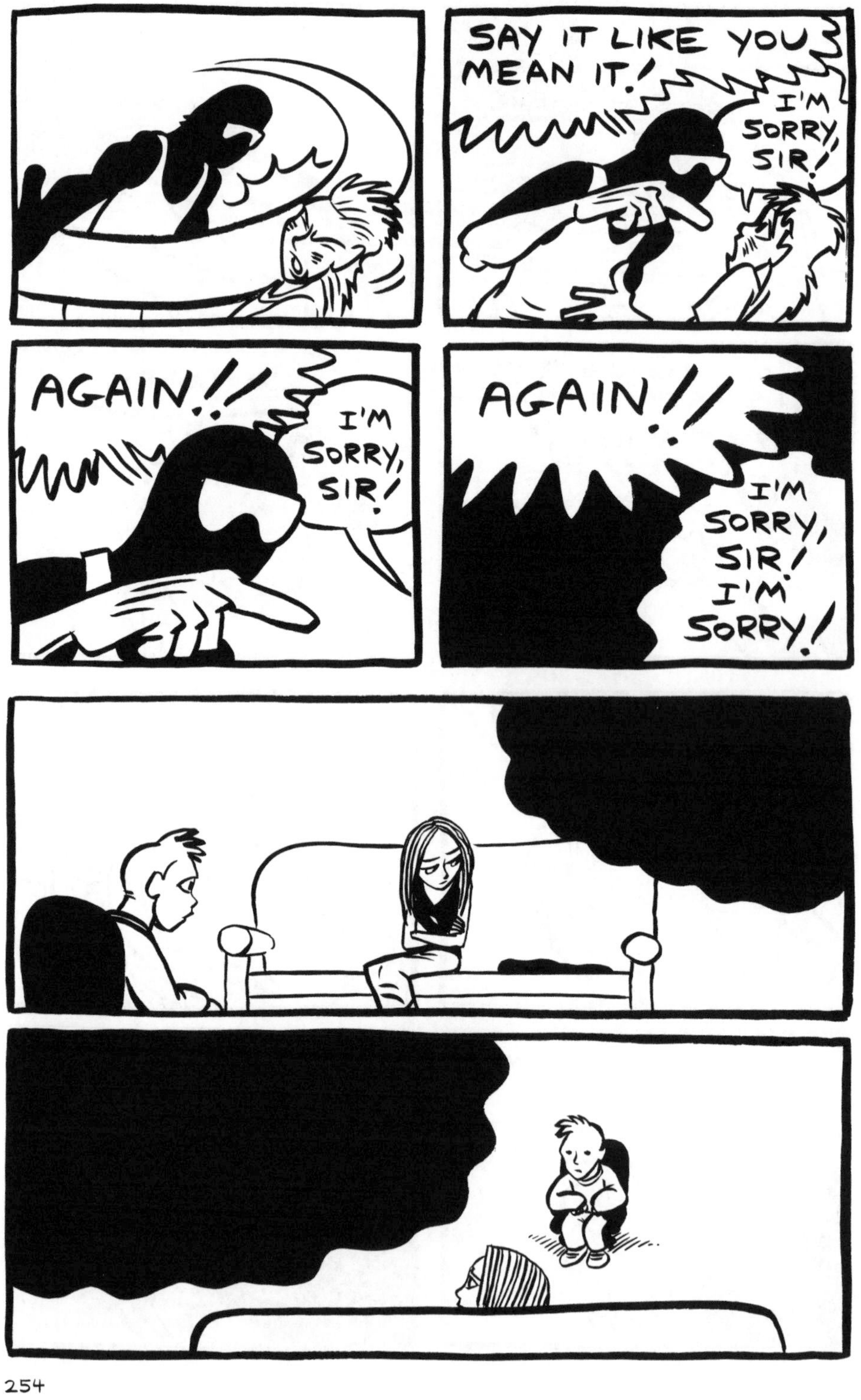
SAY IT LIKE YOU MEAN IT!
I'M SORRY, SIR!
AGAIN!!
I'M SORRY, SIR!
AGAIN!!
I'M SORRY, SIR! I'M SORRY!

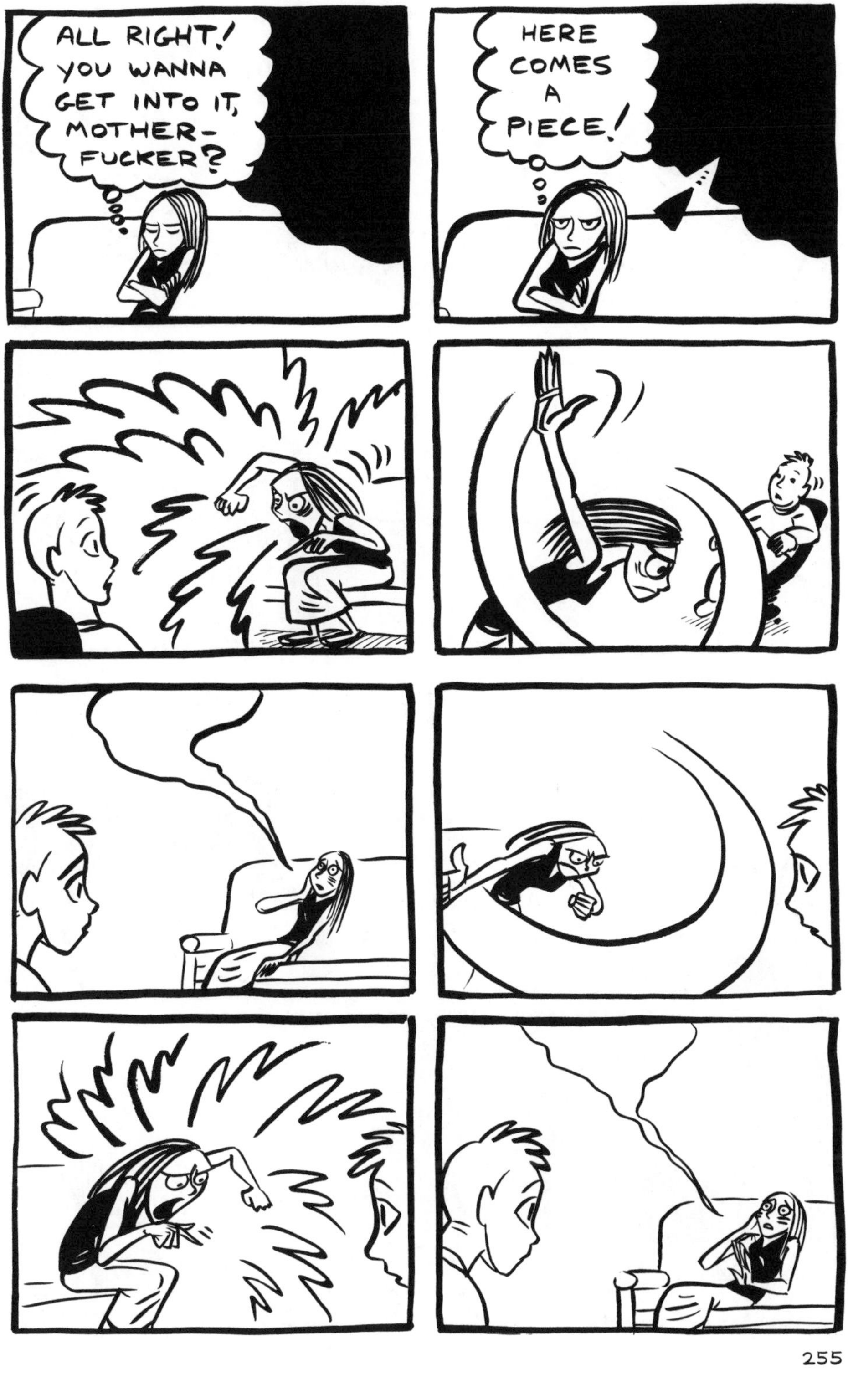
ALL RIGHT! YOU WANNA GET INTO IT, MOTHER-FUCKER?
HERE COMES A PIECE!

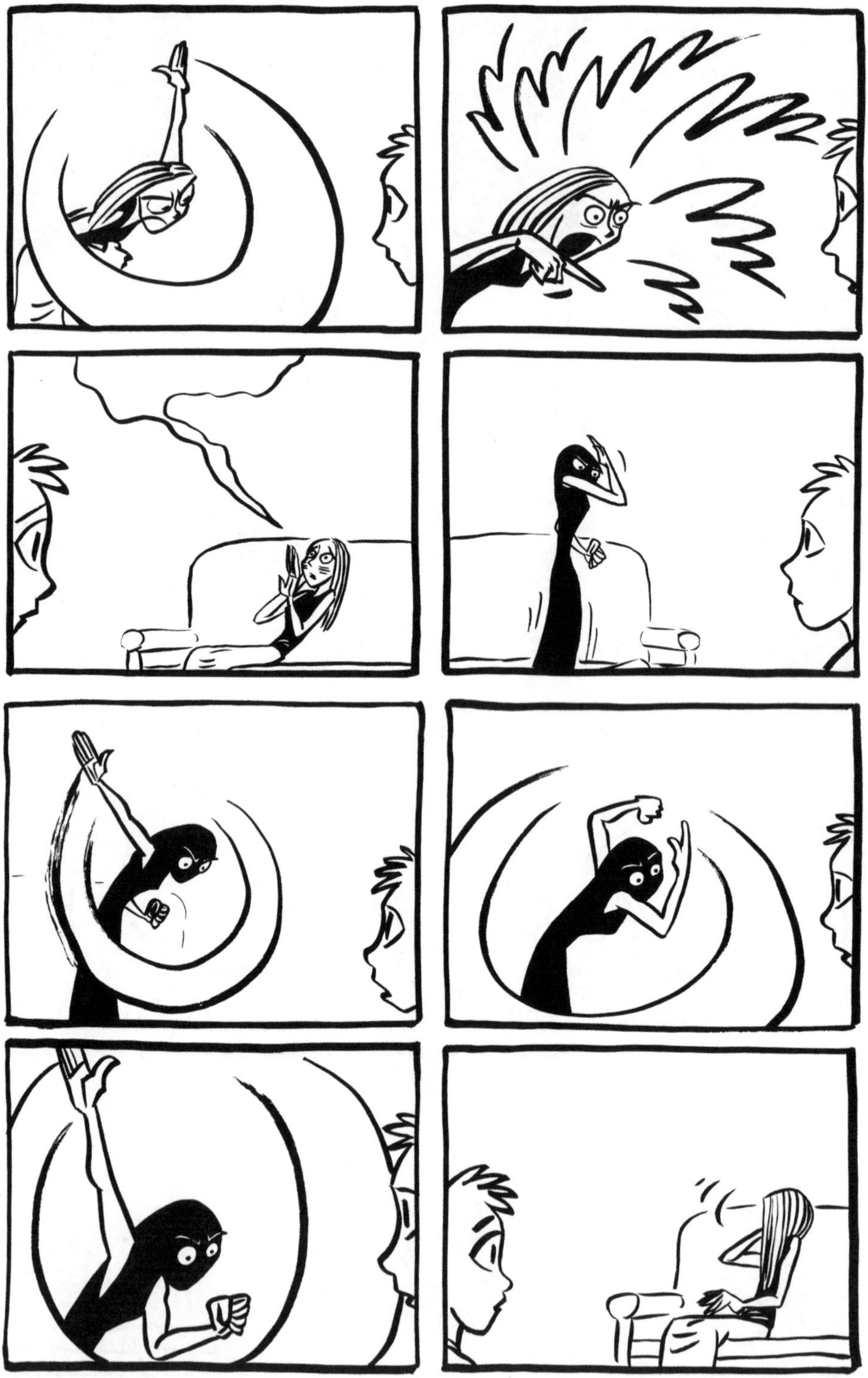

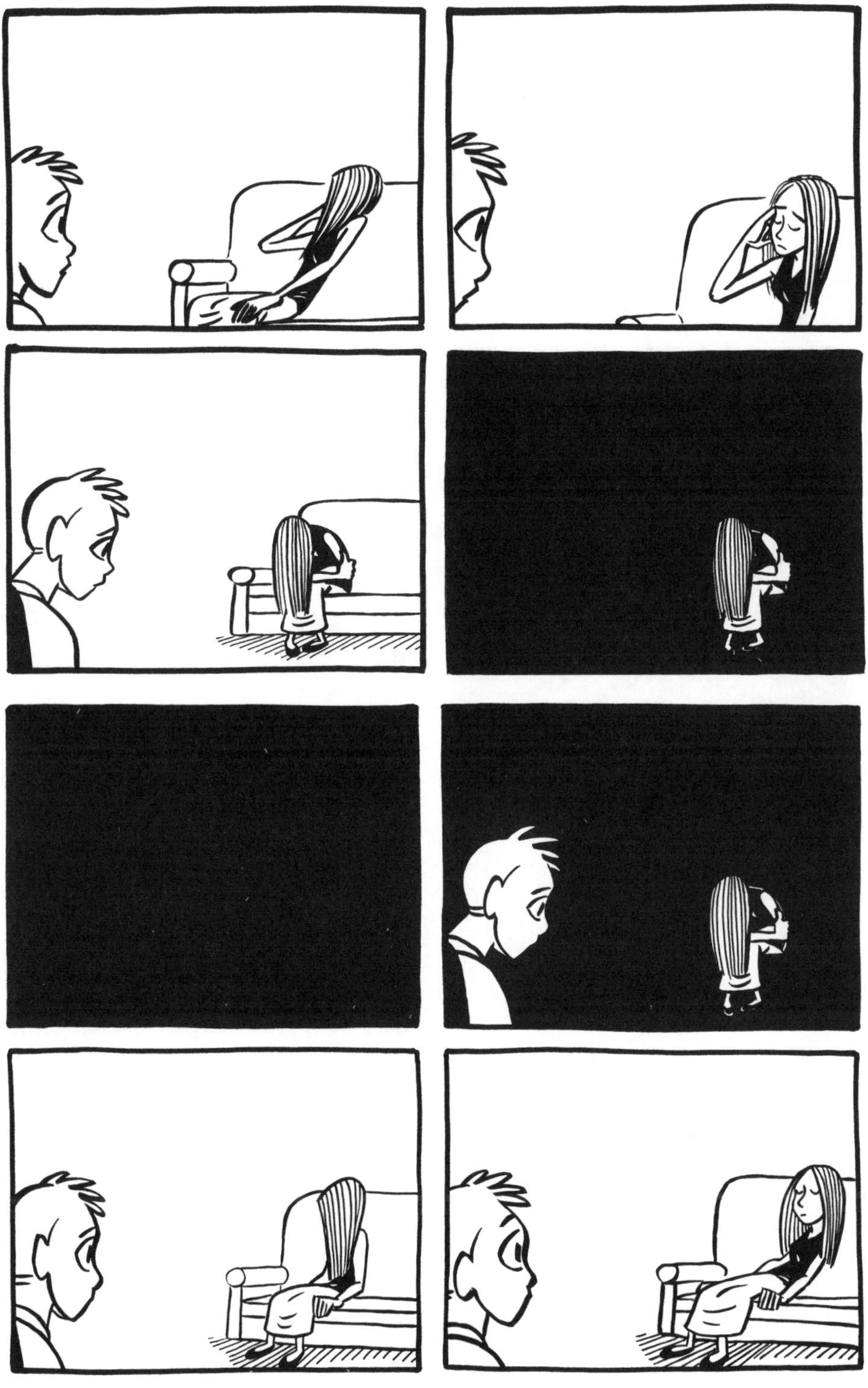

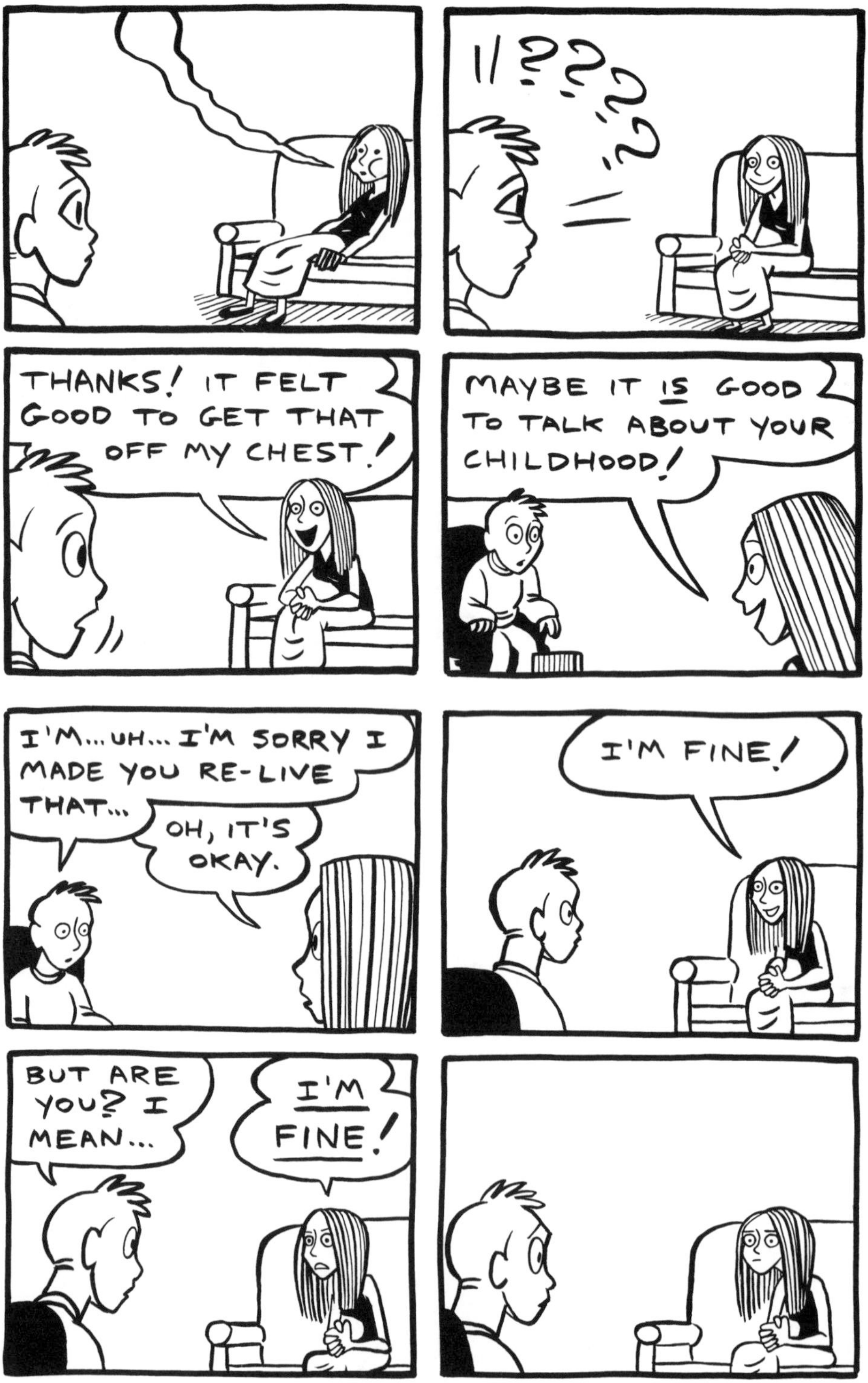
THANKS! IT FELT GOOD TO GET THAT OFF MY CHEST!
MAYBE IT IS GOOD TO TALK ABOUT YOUR CHILDHOOD!
I'M... UH... I'M SORRY I MADE YOU RE-LIVE THAT...
OH, IT'S OKAY.
I'M FINE!
BUT ARE YOU? I MEAN...
I'M FINE!

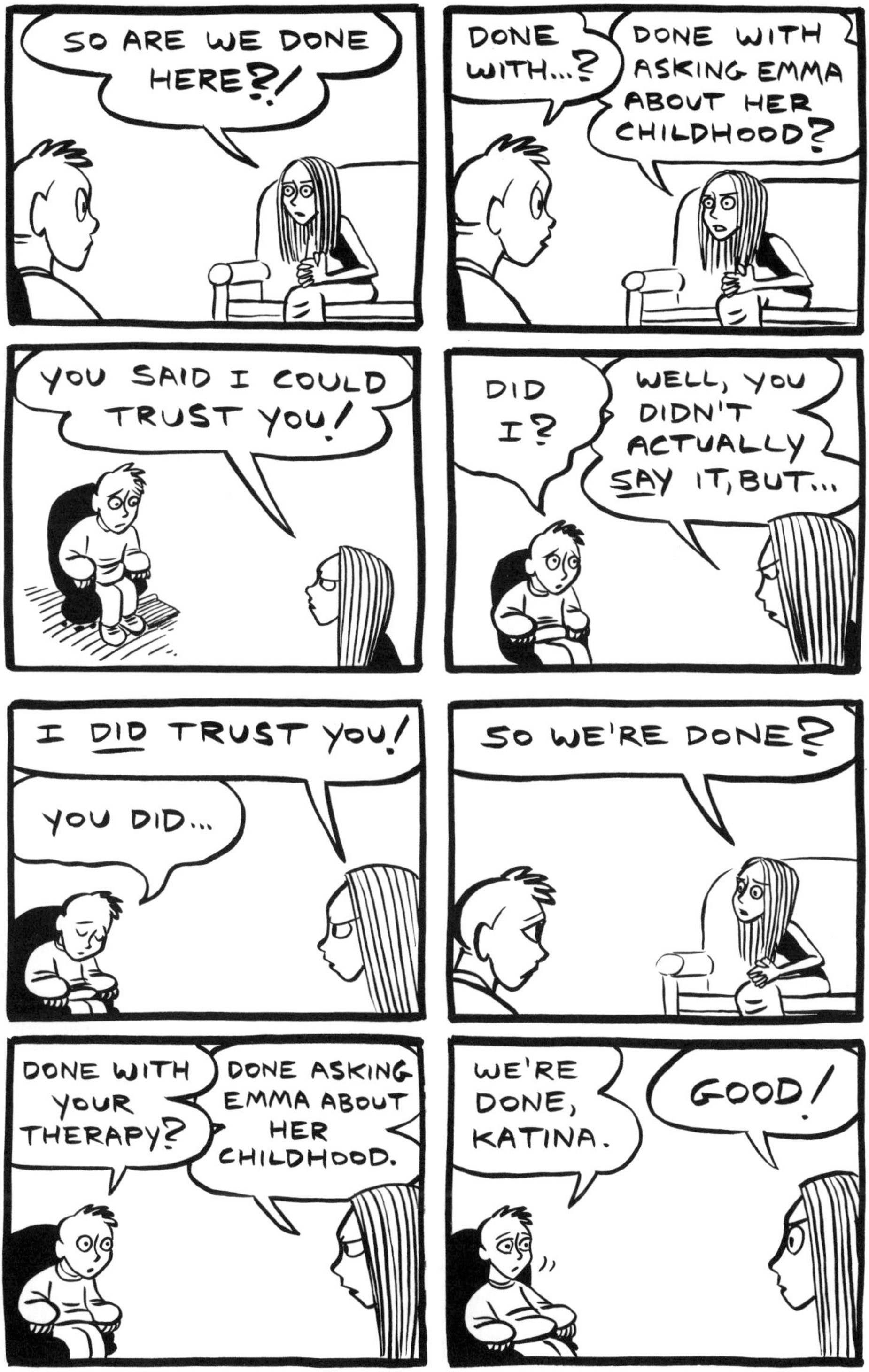
SO ARE WE DONE HERE?!
DONE WITH...?
DONE WITH ASKING EMMA ABOUT HER CHILDHOOD?
YOU SAID I COULD TRUST YOU!
DID I?
WELL, YOU DIDN'T ACTUALLY SAY IT, BUT...
I DID TRUST YOU!
YOU DID...
SO WE'RE DONE?
DONE WITH YOUR THERAPY?
DONE ASKING EMMA ABOUT HER CHILDHOOD.
WE'RE DONE, KATINA.
GOOD!

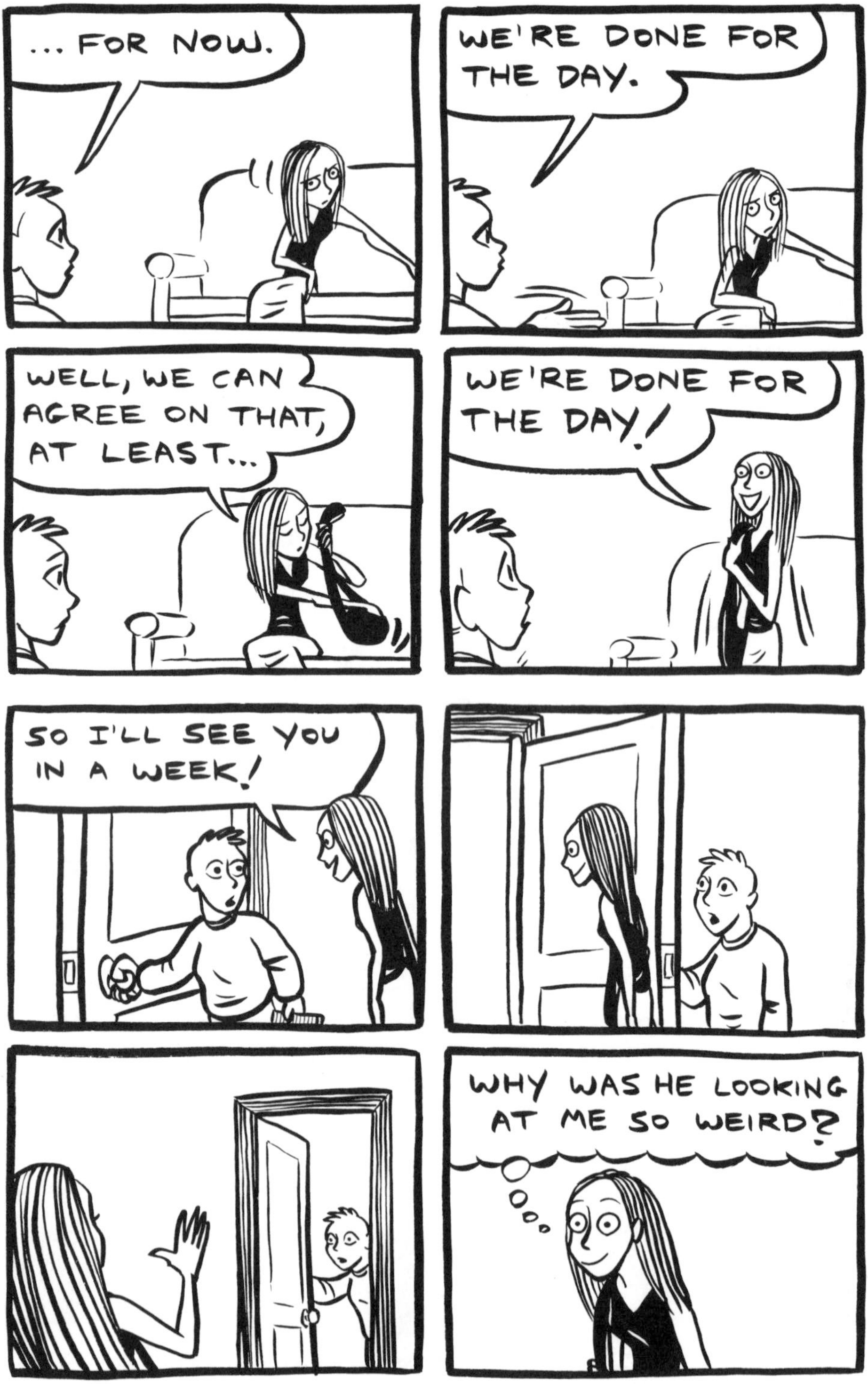
... FOR NOW.
WE'RE DONE FOR THE DAY.
WELL, WE CAN AGREE ON THAT, AT LEAST...
WE'RE DONE FOR THE DAY!
SO I'LL SEE YOU IN A WEEK!
WHY WAS HE LOOKING AT ME SO WEIRD?

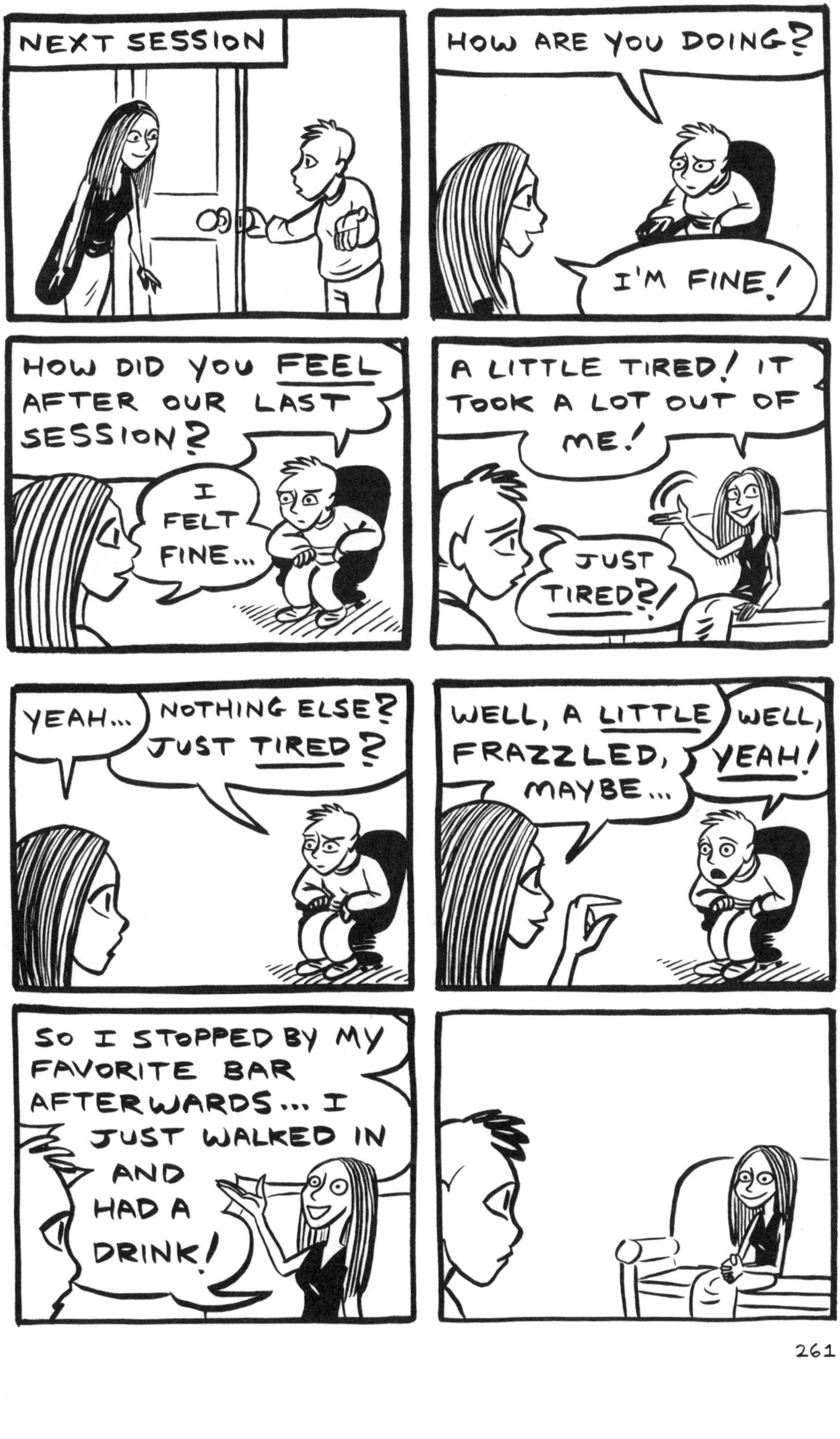
NEXT SESSION
HOW ARE YOU DOING?
I'M FINE!
HOW DID YOU FEEL AFTER OUR LAST SESSION?
I FELT FINE...
A LITTLE TIRED! IT TOOK A LOT OUT OF ME!
JUST TIRED?!
YEAH...
NOTHING ELSE? JUST TIRED?
WELL, A LITTLE FRAZZLED, MAYBE...
WELL, YEAH!
SO I STOPPED BY MY FAVORITE BAR AFTERWARDS... I JUST WALKED IN AND HAD A DRINK!

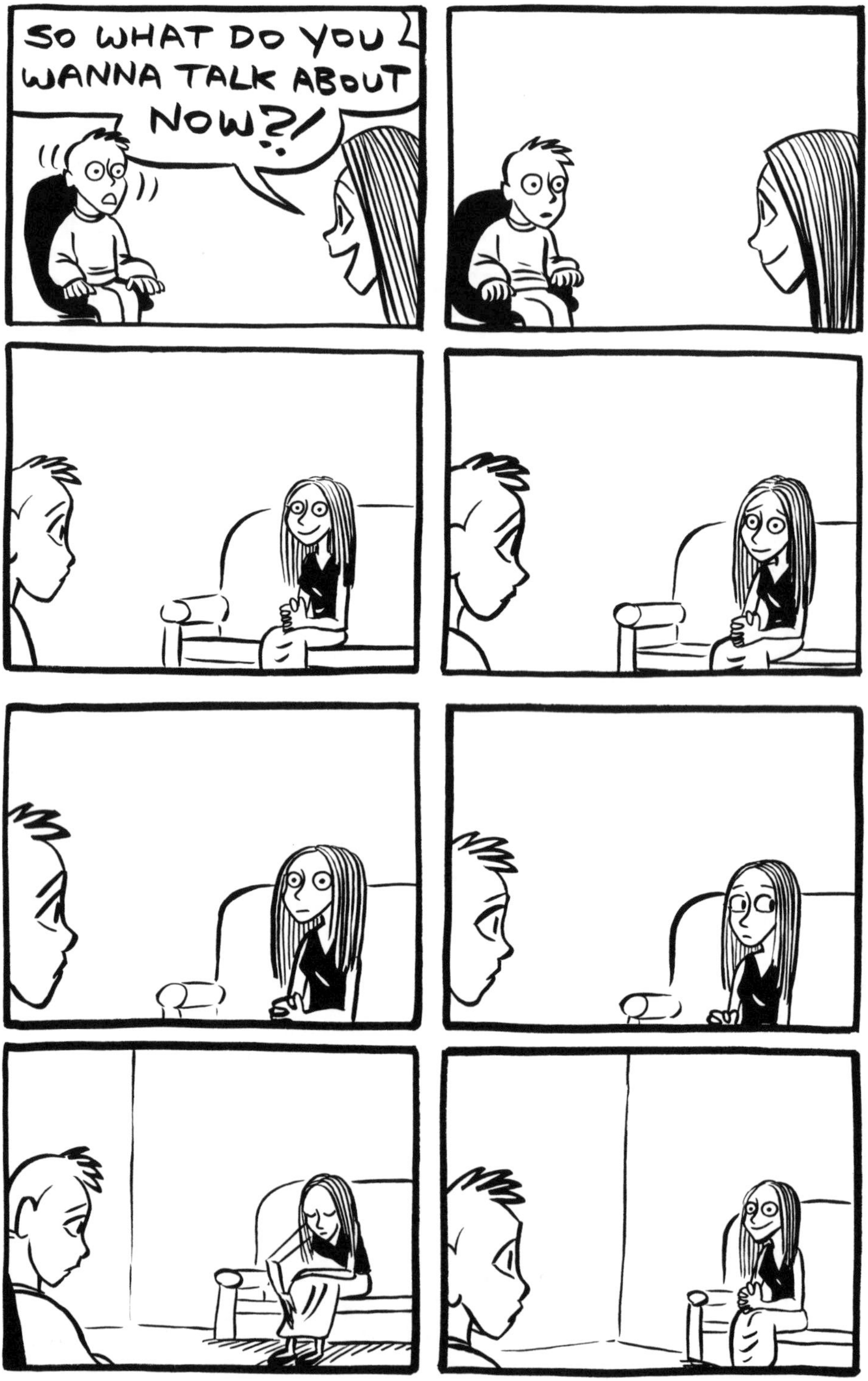
SO WHAT DO YOU WANNA TALK ABOUT NOW?!

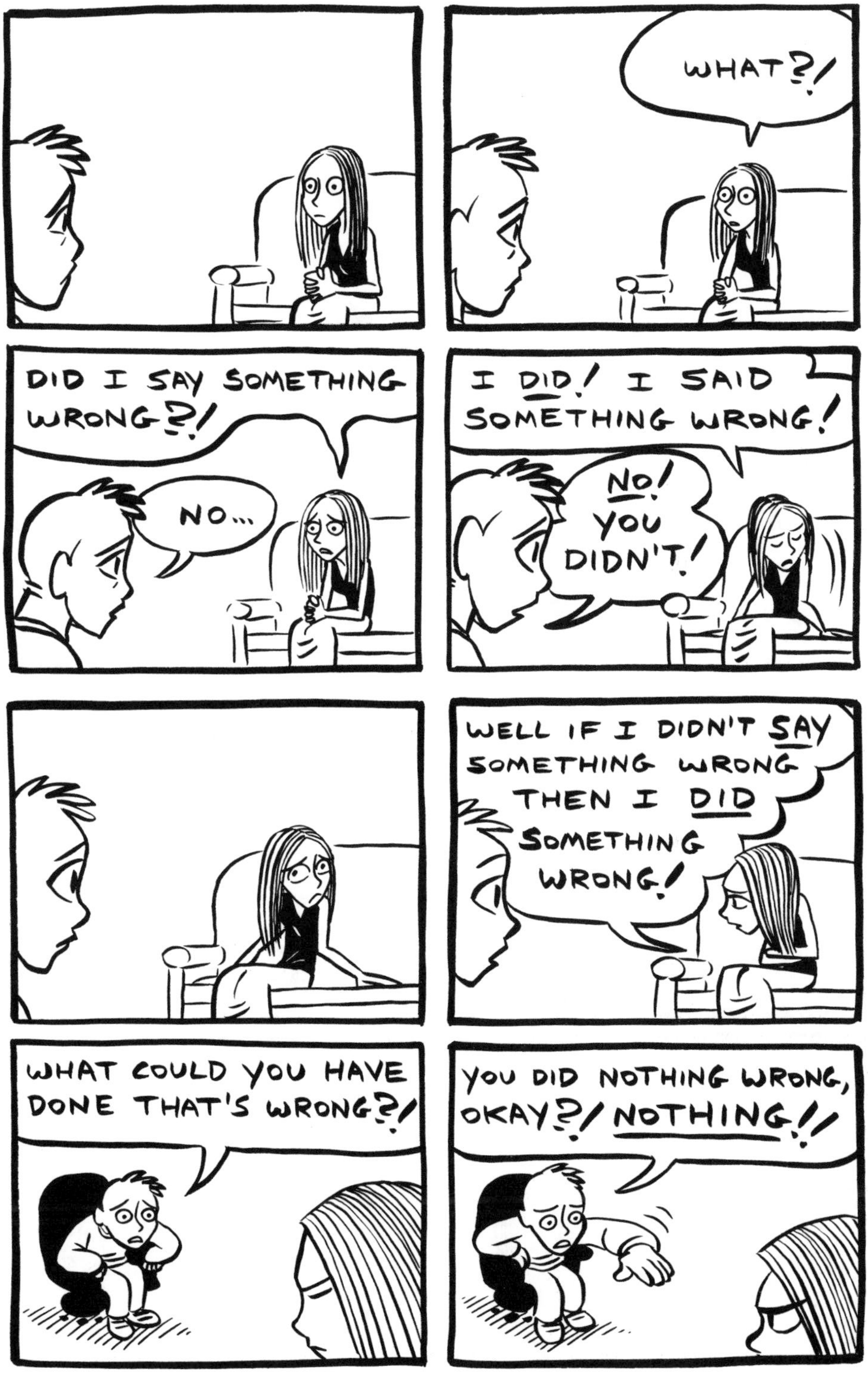
WHAT?!
DID I SAY SOMETHING WRONG?!
NO...
I DID! I SAID SOMETHING WRONG!
NO! YOU DIDN'T!
WELL IF I DIDN'T SAY SOMETHING WRONG THEN I DID SOMETHING WRONG!
WHAT COULD YOU HAVE DONE THAT'S WRONG?!
YOU DID NOTHING WRONG, OKAY?! NOTHING!!

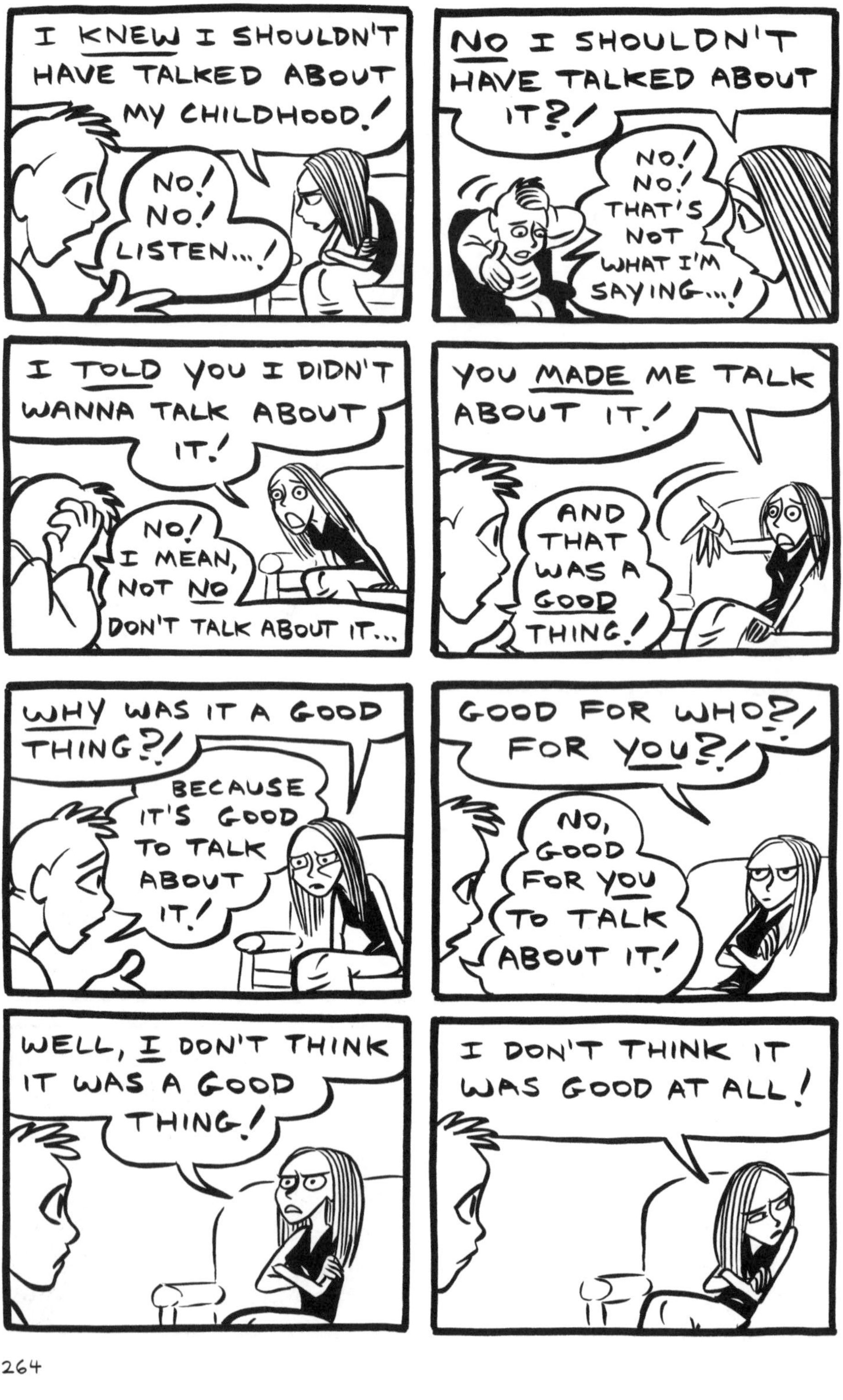

I KNEW I SHOULDN'T HAVE TALKED ABOUT MY CHILDHOOD!
NO! NO! LISTEN...!
NO I SHOULDN'T HAVE TALKED ABOUT IT?!
NO! NO! THAT'S NOT WHAT I'M SAYING...!
I TOLD YOU I DIDN'T WANNA TALK ABOUT IT!
NO! I MEAN, NOT NO DON'T TALK ABOUT IT...
YOU MADE ME TALK ABOUT IT!
AND THAT WAS A GOOD THING!
WHY WAS IT A GOOD THING?!
BECAUSE IT'S GOOD TO TALK ABOUT IT!
GOOD FOR WHO?! FOR YOU?!
NO, GOOD FOR YOU TO TALK ABOUT IT!
WELL, I DON'T THINK IT WAS A GOOD THING!
I DON'T THINK IT WAS GOOD AT ALL!

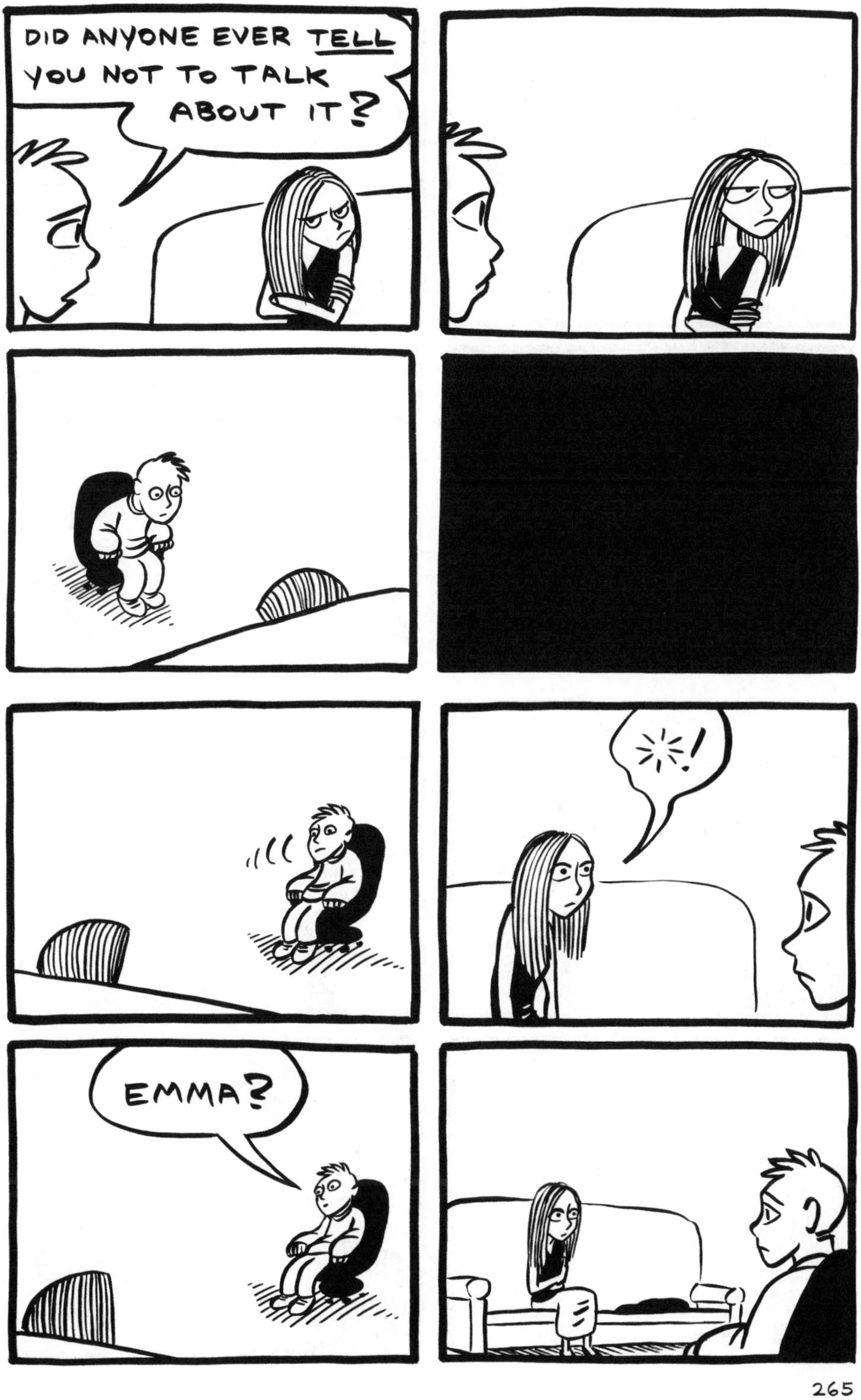
DID ANYONE EVER TELL YOU NOT TO TALK ABOUT IT?
!
EMMA?

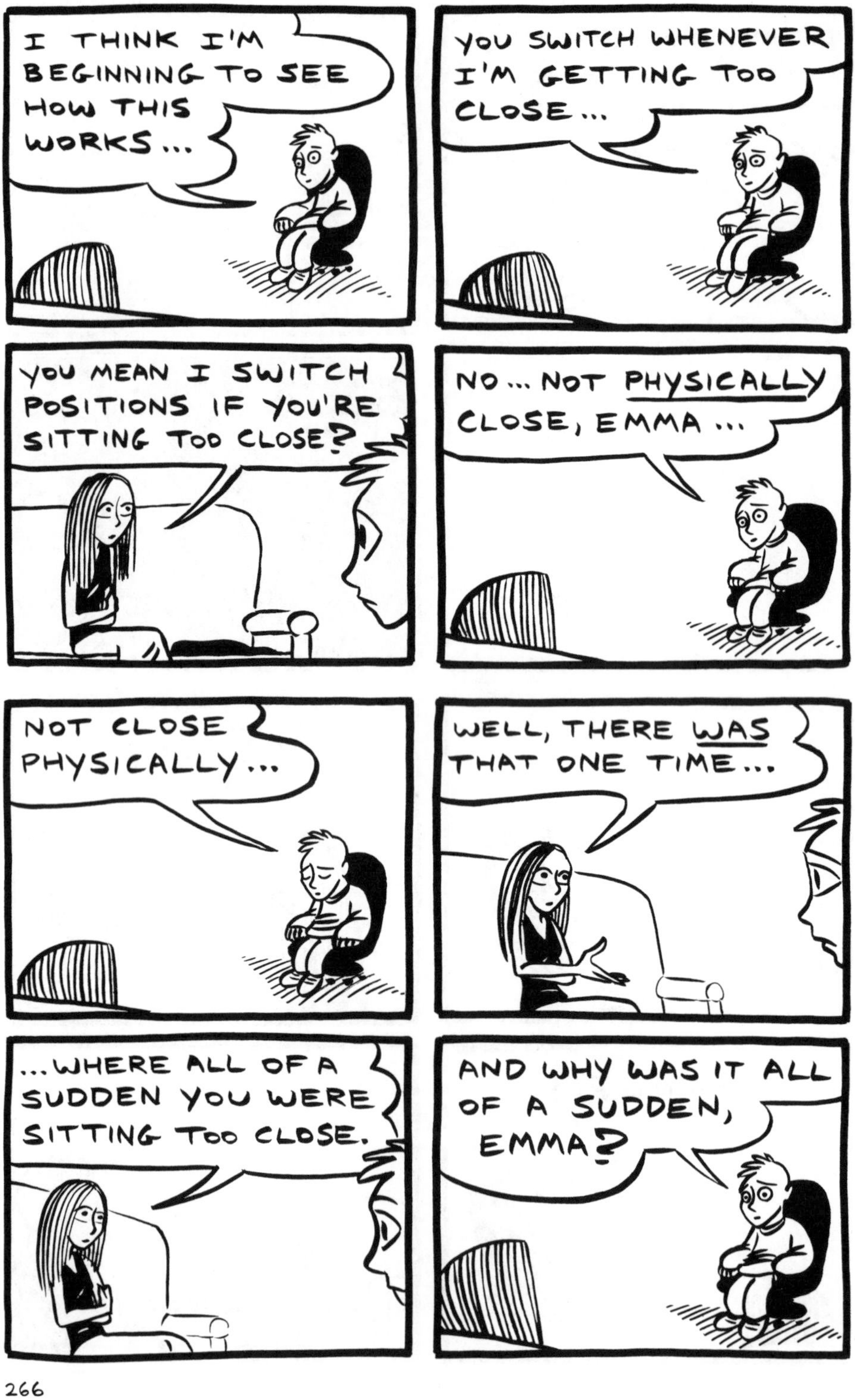
I THINK I'M BEGINNING TO SEE HOW THIS WORKS...
YOU SWITCH WHENEVER I'M GETTING TOO CLOSE...
YOU MEAN I SWITCH POSITIONS IF YOU'RE SITTING TOO CLOSE?
NO... NOT PHYSICALLY CLOSE, EMMA...
NOT CLOSE PHYSICALLY...
WELL, THERE WAS THAT ONE TIME...
...WHERE ALL OF A SUDDEN YOU WERE SITTING TOO CLOSE.
AND WHY WAS IT ALL OF A SUDDEN, EMMA?

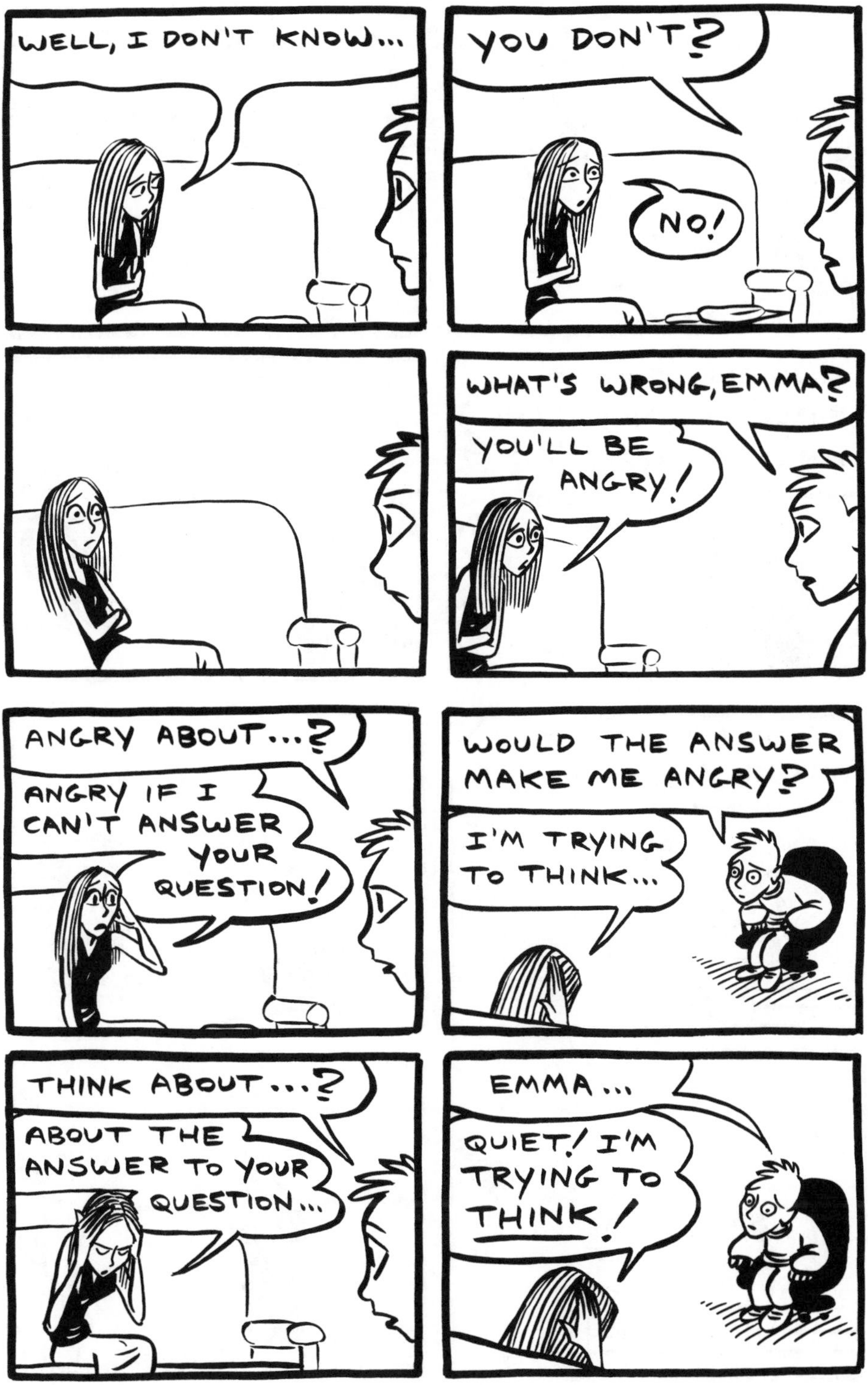
WELL, I DON'T KNOW...
YOU DON'T?
NO!
WHAT'S WRONG, EMMA?
YOU'LL BE ANGRY!
ANGRY ABOUT...?
ANGRY IF I CAN'T ANSWER YOUR QUESTION!
WOULD THE ANSWER MAKE ME ANGRY?
I'M TRYING TO THINK...
THINK ABOUT...?
ABOUT THE ANSWER TO YOUR QUESTION...
EMMA...
QUIET! I'M TRYING TO THINK!

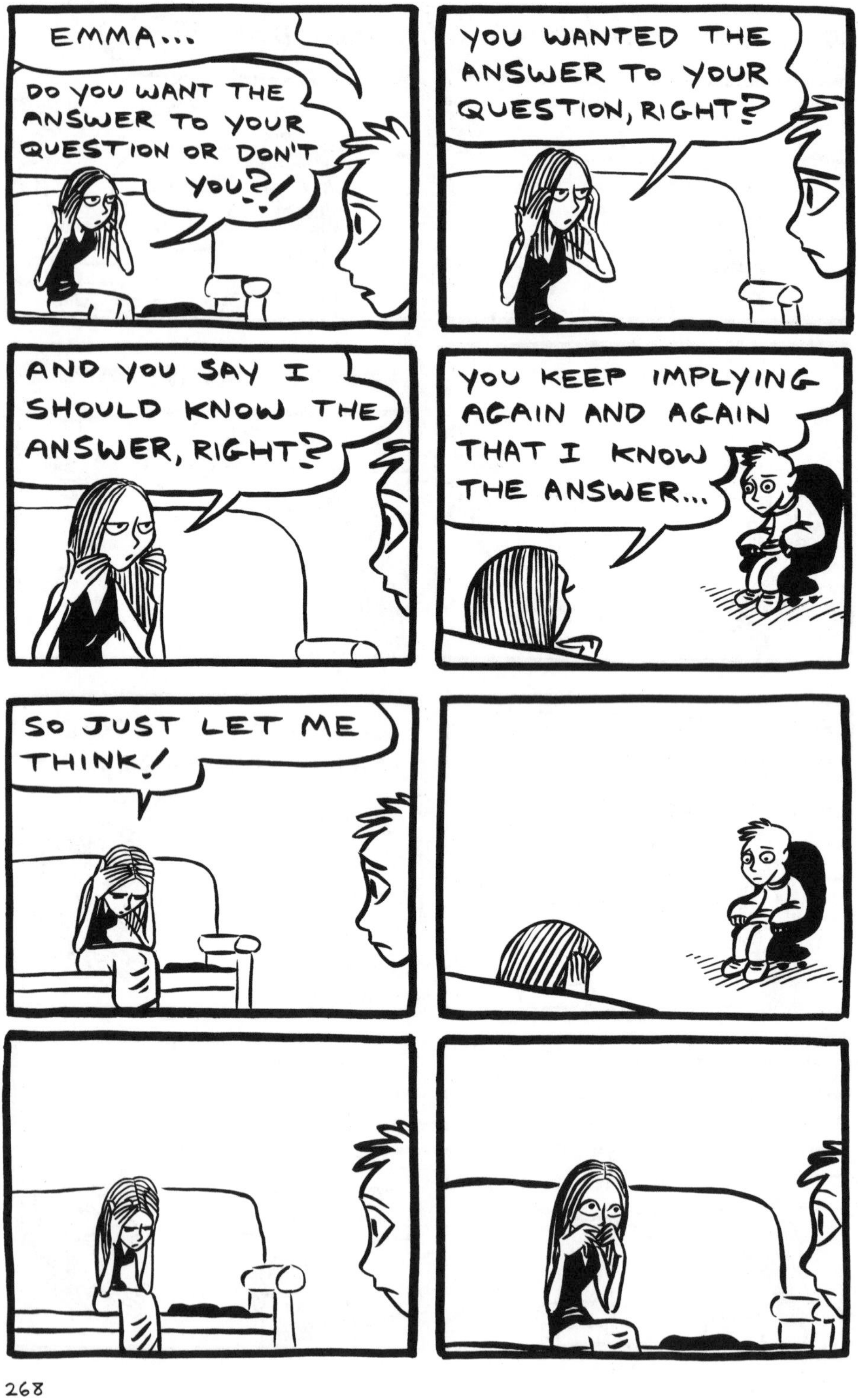
EMMA...
DO YOU WANT THE ANSWER TO YOUR QUESTION OR DON'T YOU?!
YOU WANTED THE ANSWER TO YOUR QUESTION, RIGHT?
AND YOU SAY I SHOULD KNOW THE ANSWER, RIGHT?
YOU KEEP IMPLYING AGAIN AND AGAIN THAT I KNOW THE ANSWER...
SO JUST LET ME THINK!

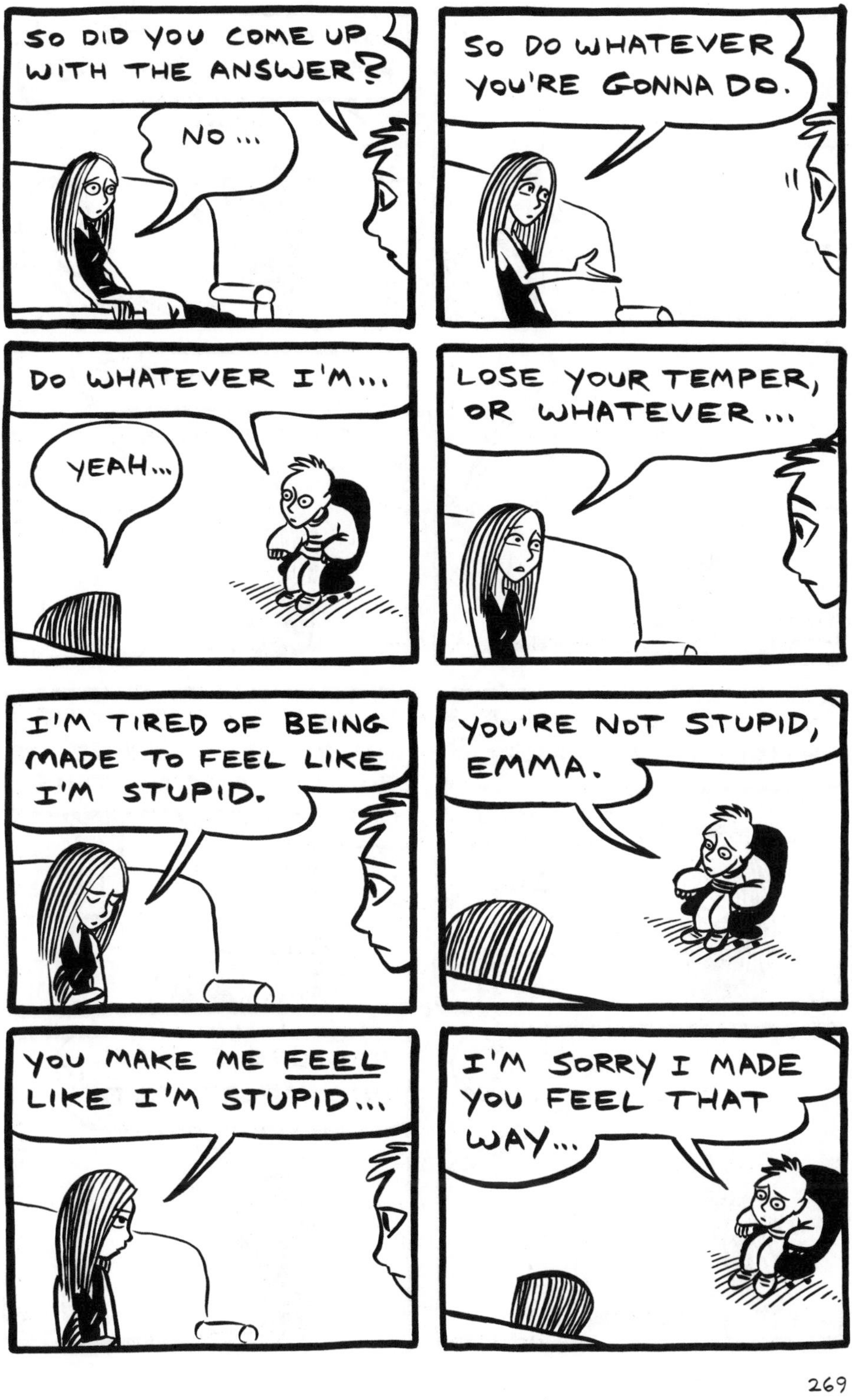
SO DID YOU COME UP WITH THE ANSWER?
NO...
SO DO WHATEVER YOU'RE GONNA DO.
DO WHATEVER I'M...
YEAH...
LOSE YOUR TEMPER, OR WHATEVER...
I'M TIRED OF BEING MADE TO FEEL LIKE I'M STUPID.
YOU'RE NOT STUPID, EMMA.
YOU MAKE ME FEEL LIKE I'M STUPID...
I'M SORRY I MADE YOU FEEL THAT WAY...

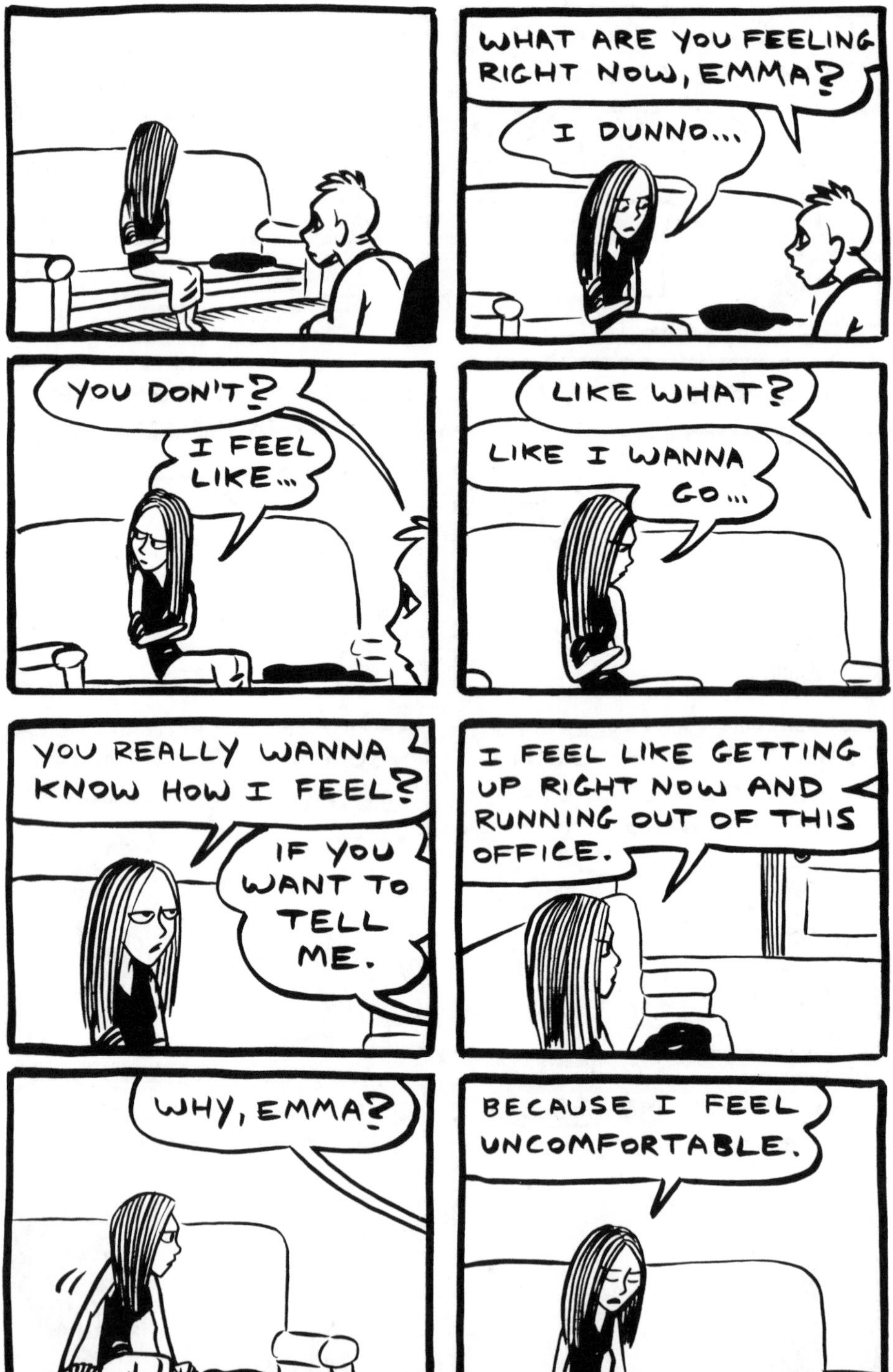
WHAT ARE YOU FEELING RIGHT NOW, EMMA?
I DUNNO...
YOU DON'T?
I FEEL LIKE...
LIKE WHAT?
LIKE I WANNA GO...
YOU REALLY WANNA KNOW HOW I FEEL?
IF YOU WANT TO TELL ME.
I FEEL LIKE GETTING UP RIGHT NOW AND RUNNING OUT OF THIS OFFICE.
WHY, EMMA?
BECAUSE I FEEL UNCOMFORTABLE.

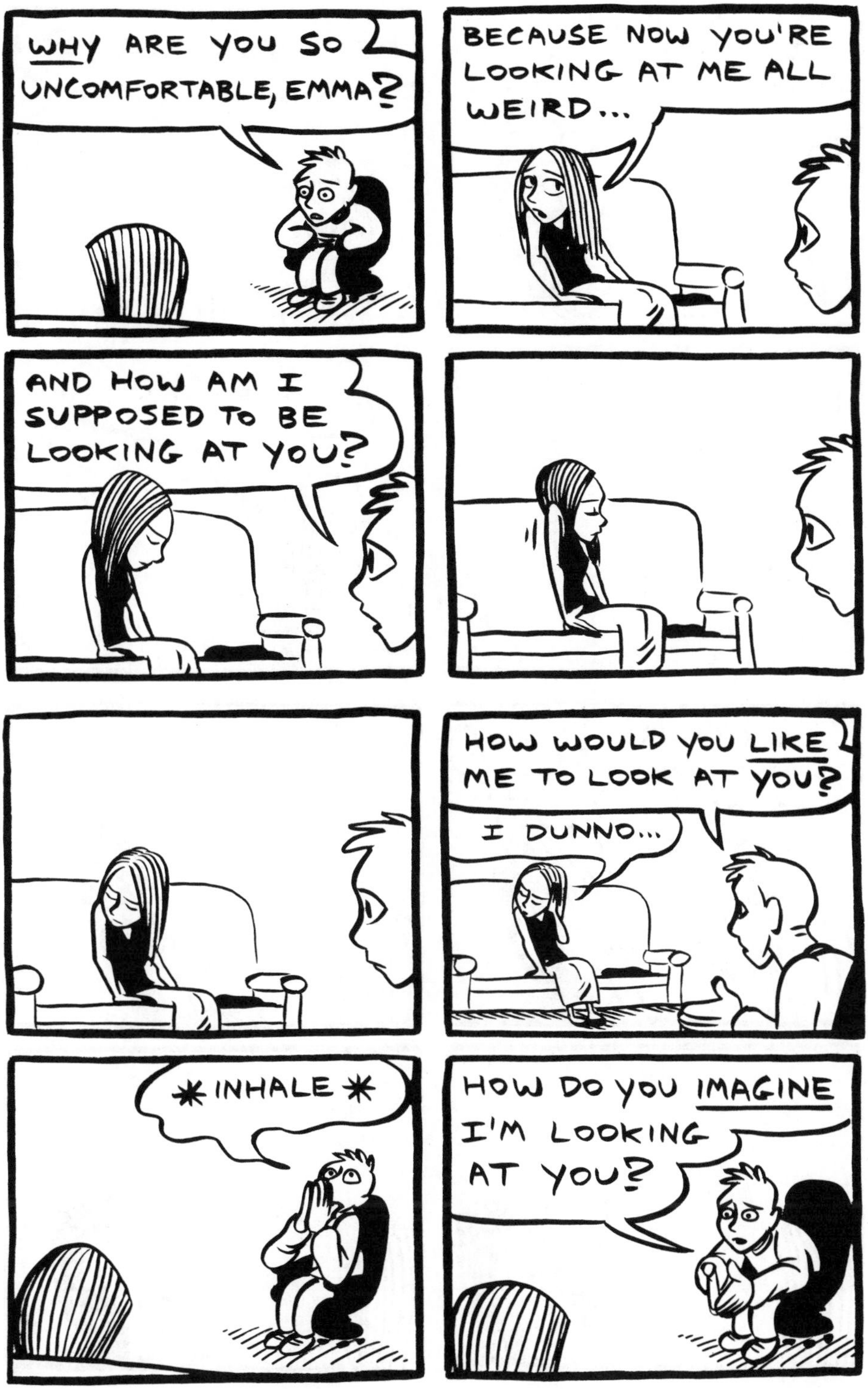
WHY ARE YOU SO UNCOMFORTABLE, EMMA?
BECAUSE NOW YOU'RE LOOKING AT ME ALL WEIRD...
AND HOW AM I SUPPOSED TO BE LOOKING AT YOU?
HOW WOULD YOU LIKE ME TO LOOK AT YOU?
I DUNNO...
INHALE
HOW DO YOU IMAGINE I'M LOOKING AT YOU?

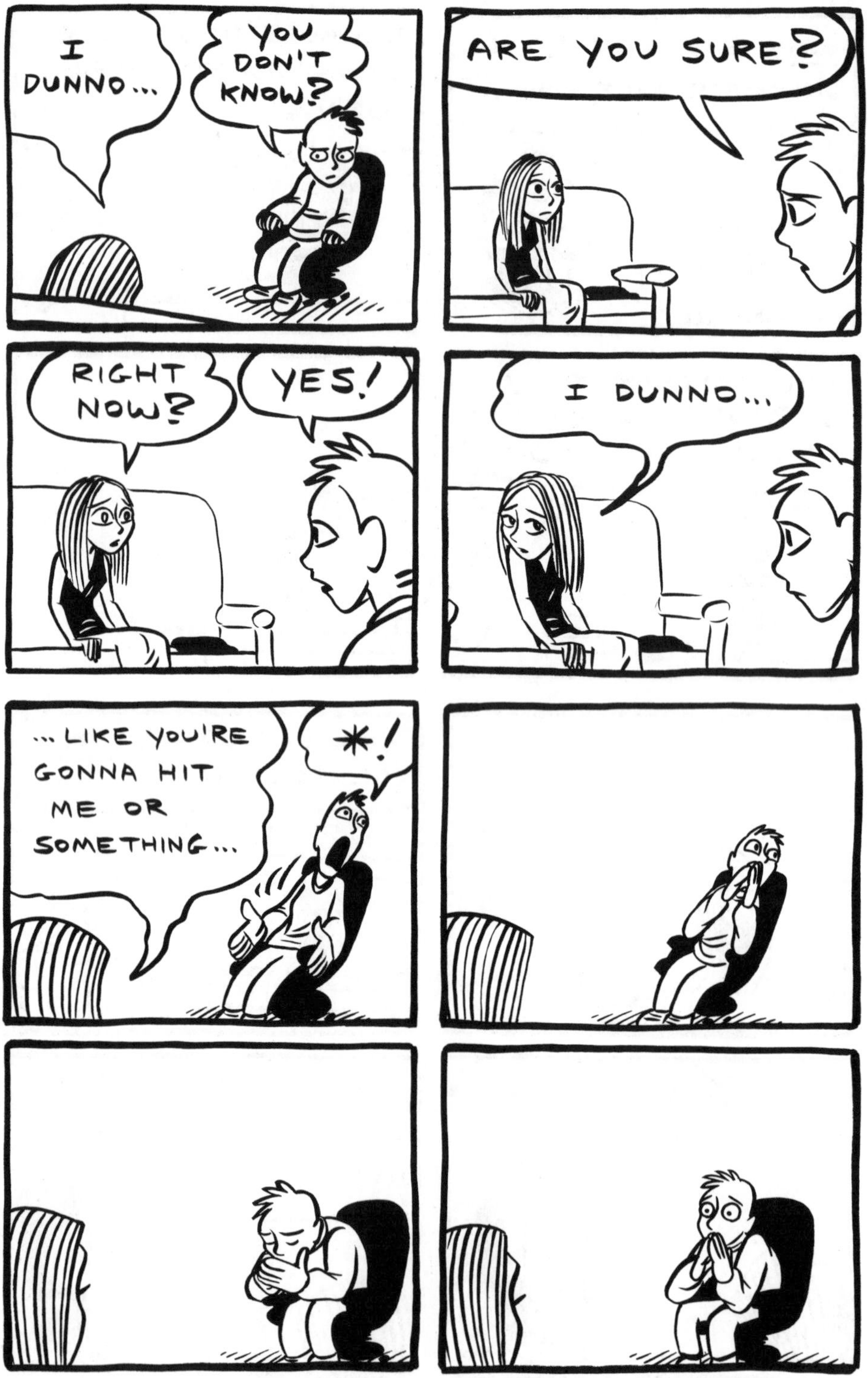
I DUNNO...
YOU DON'T KNOW?
ARE YOU SURE?
RIGHT NOW?
YES!
I DUNNO...
...LIKE YOU'RE GONNA HIT ME OR SOMETHING...
*!

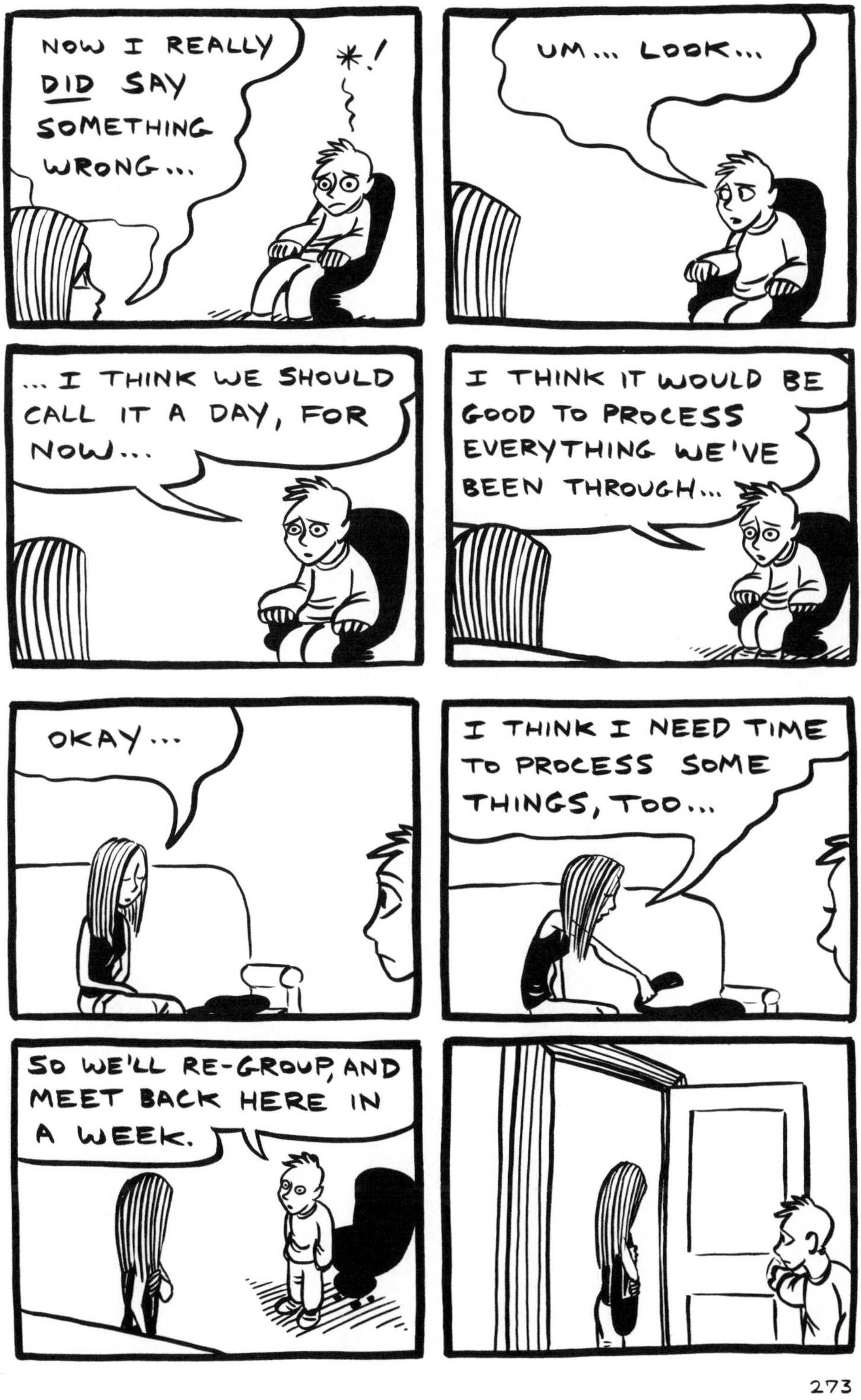
NOW I REALLY DID SAY SOMETHING WRONG...
*!
UM... LOOK...
... I THINK WE SHOULD CALL IT A DAY, FOR NOW...
I THINK IT WOULD BE GOOD TO PROCESS EVERYTHING WE'VE BEEN THROUGH...
OKAY...
I THINK I NEED TIME TO PROCESS SOME THINGS, TOO...
SO WE'LL RE-GROUP, AND MEET BACK HERE IN A WEEK.

BUSINESS CARD

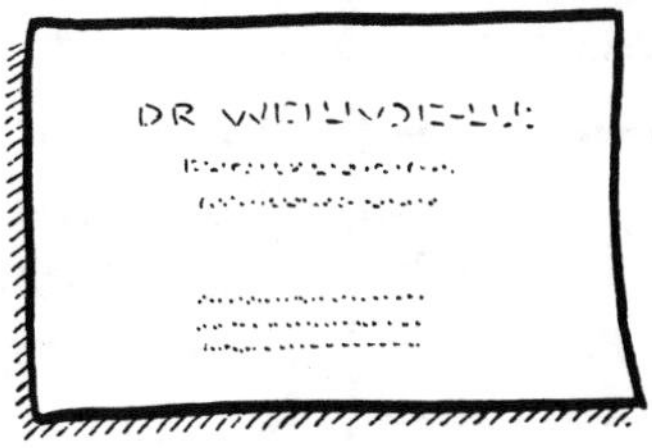

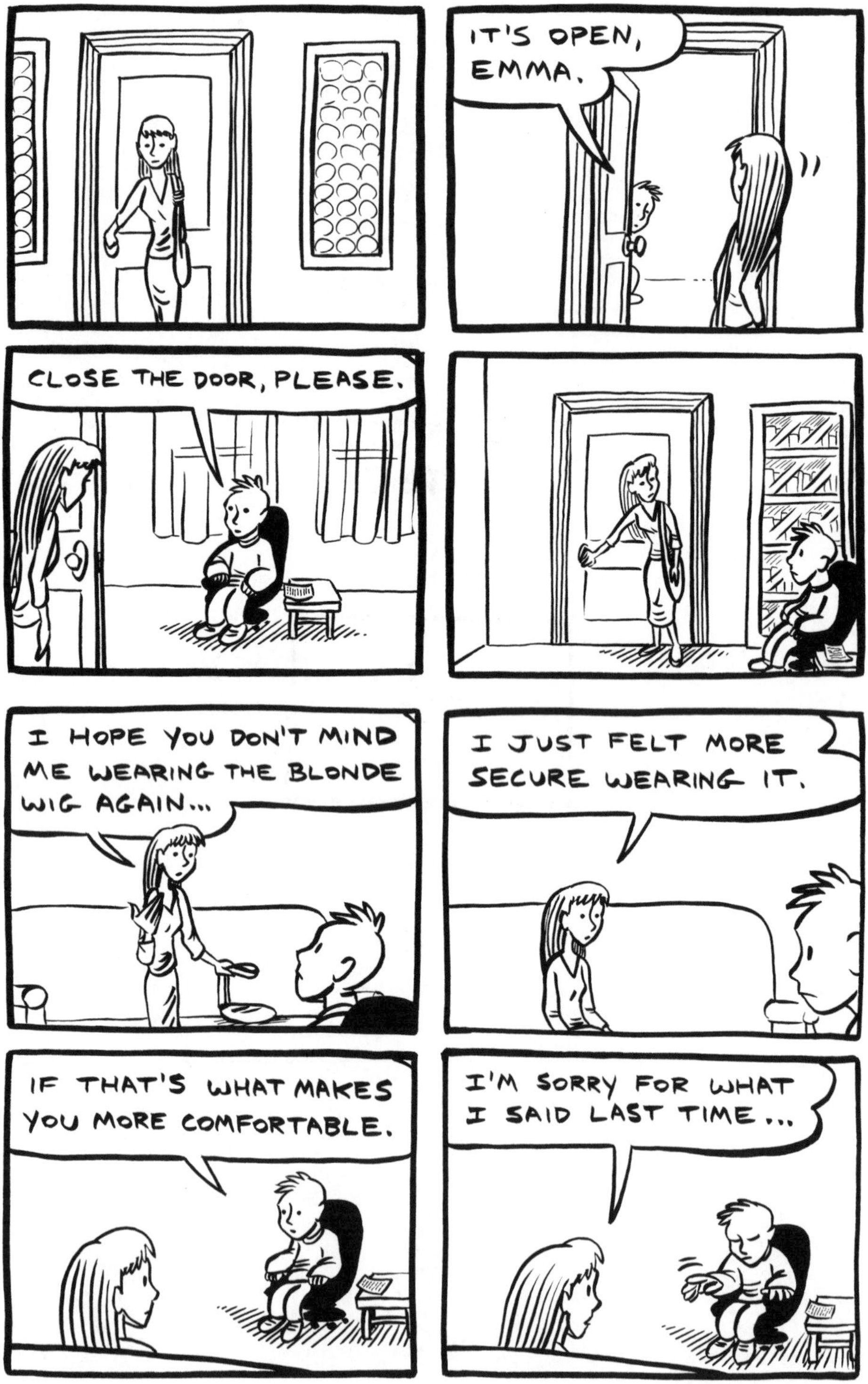

IT'S OPEN, EMMA.
CLOSE THE DOOR, PLEASE.
I HOPE YOU DON'T MIND ME WEARING THE BLONDE WIG AGAIN...
I JUST FELT MORE SECURE WEARING IT.
IF THAT'S WHAT MAKES YOU MORE COMFORTABLE.
I'M SORRY FOR WHAT I SAID LAST TIME...

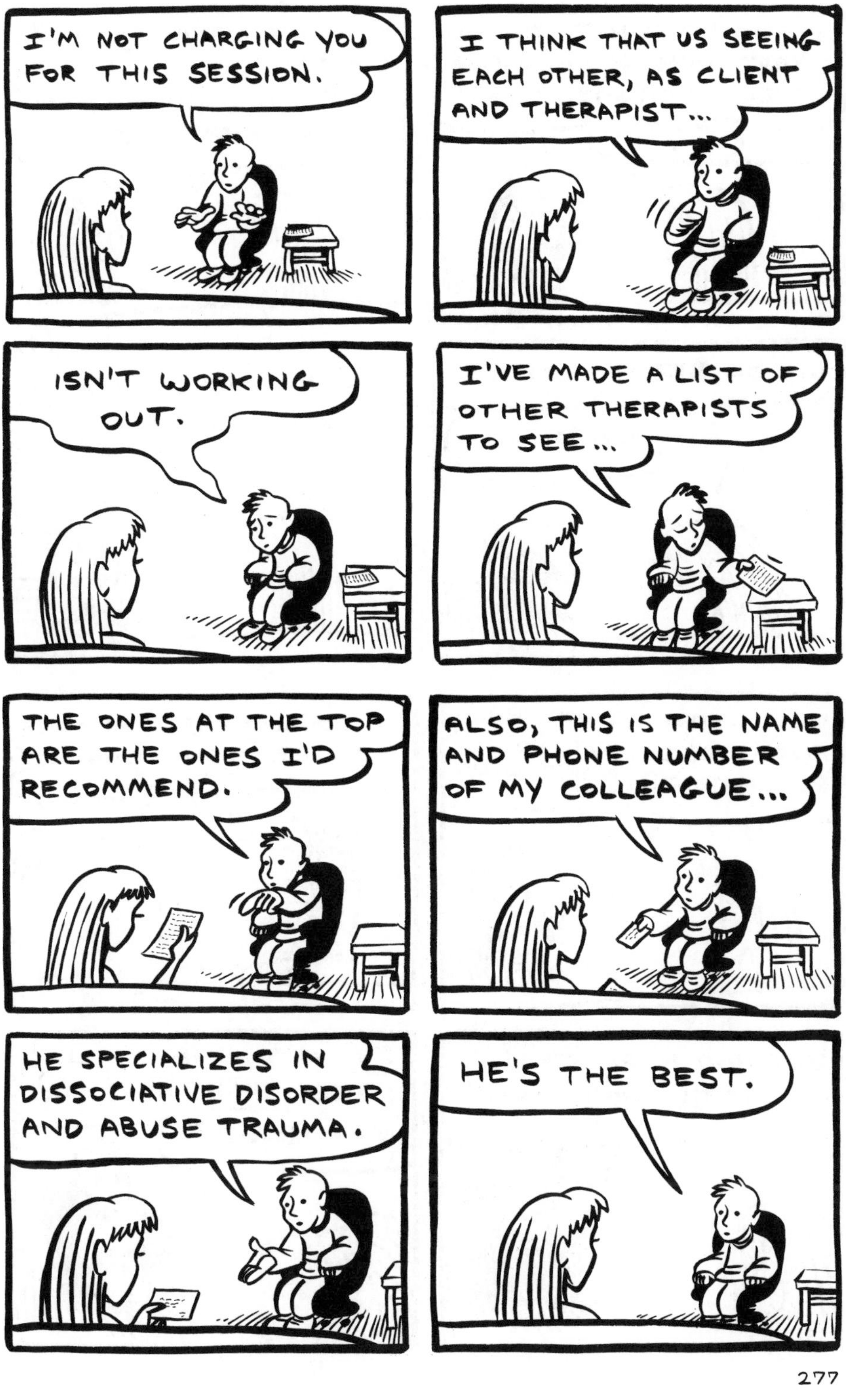
I'M NOT CHARGING YOU FOR THIS SESSION.
I THINK THAT US SEEING EACH OTHER, AS CLIENT AND THERAPIST...
ISN'T WORKING OUT.
I'VE MADE A LIST OF OTHER THERAPISTS TO SEE...
THE ONES AT THE TOP ARE THE ONES I'D RECOMMEND.
ALSO, THIS IS THE NAME AND PHONE NUMBER OF MY COLLEAGUE...
HE SPECIALIZES IN DISSOCIATIVE DISORDER AND ABUSE TRAUMA.
HE'S THE BEST.

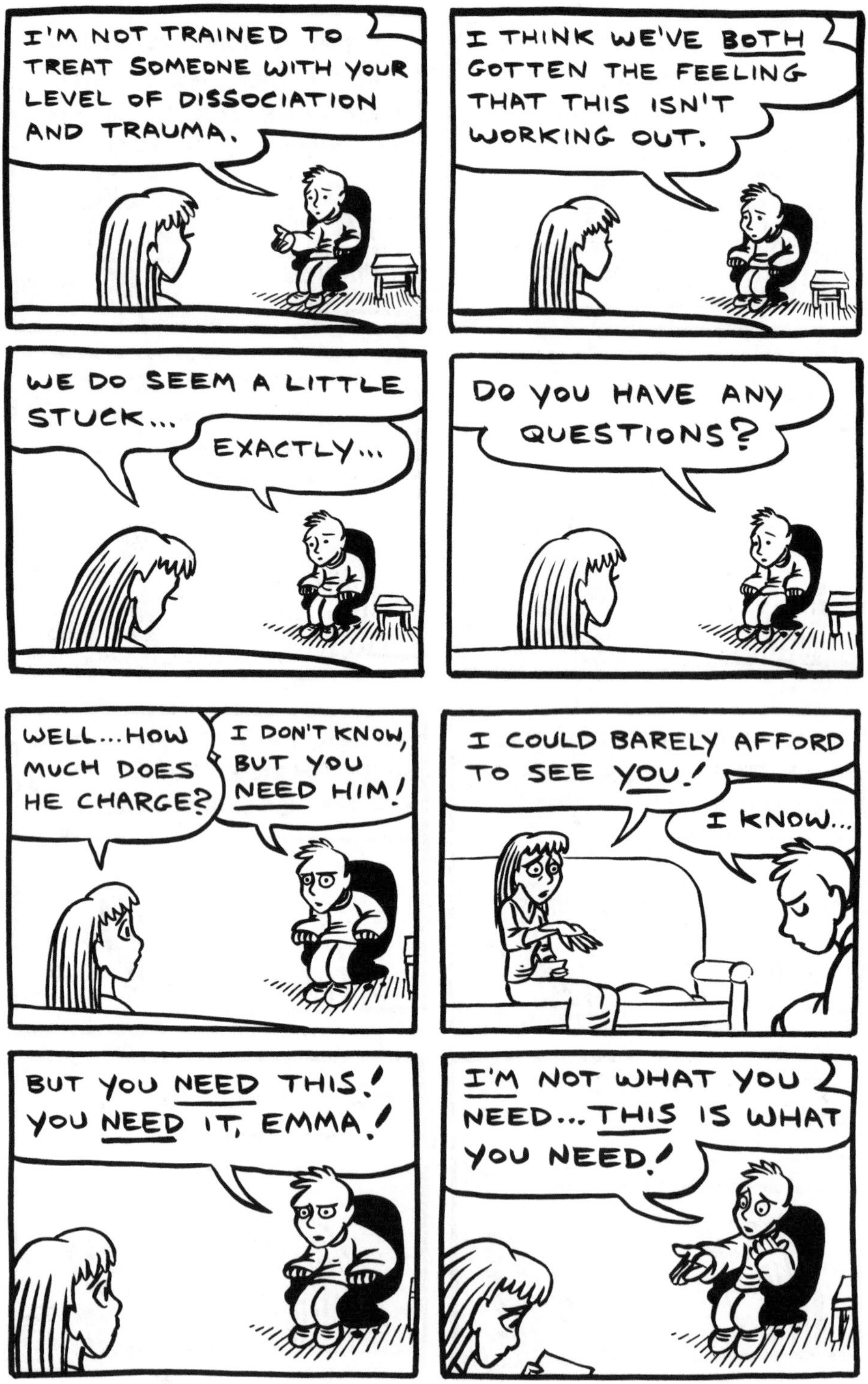
I'M NOT TRAINED TO TREAT SOMEONE WITH YOUR LEVEL OF DISSOCIATION AND TRAUMA.
I THINK WE'VE BOTH GOTTEN THE FEELING THAT THIS ISN'T WORKING OUT.
WE DO SEEM A LITTLE STUCK...
EXACTLY...
DO YOU HAVE ANY QUESTIONS?
WELL...HOW MUCH DOES HE CHARGE?
I DON'T KNOW, BUT YOU NEED HIM!
I COULD BARELY AFFORD TO SEE YOU!
I KNOW...
BUT YOU NEED THIS! YOU NEED IT, EMMA!
I'M NOT WHAT YOU NEED...THIS IS WHAT YOU NEED!

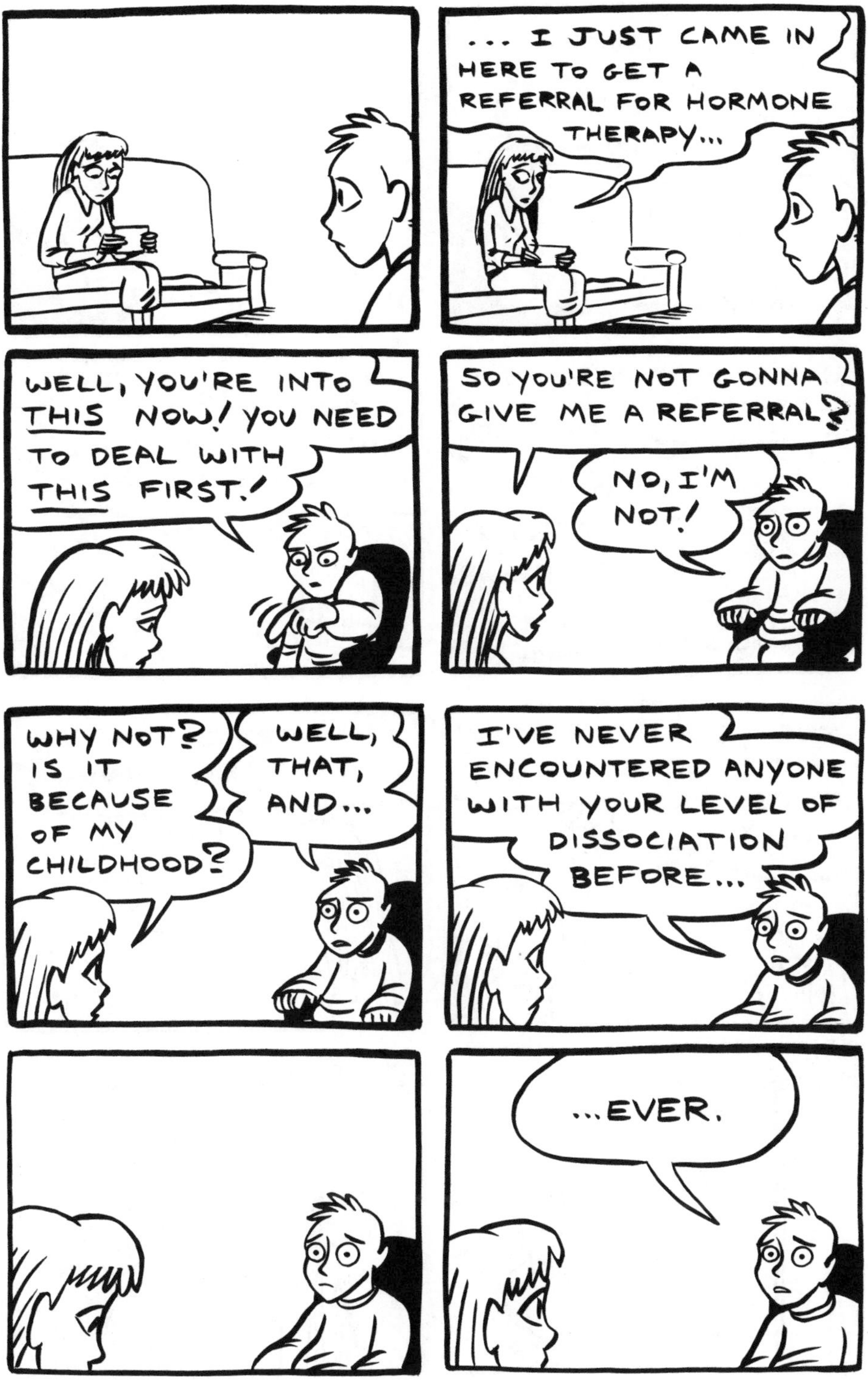
... I JUST CAME IN HERE TO GET A REFERRAL FOR HORMONE THERAPY...
WELL, YOU'RE INTO THIS NOW! YOU NEED TO DEAL WITH THIS FIRST!
SO YOU'RE NOT GONNA GIVE ME A REFERRAL?
NO, I'M NOT!
WHY NOT? IS IT BECAUSE OF MY CHILDHOOD?
WELL, THAT, AND...
I'VE NEVER ENCOUNTERED ANYONE WITH YOUR LEVEL OF DISSOCIATION BEFORE...
...EVER.

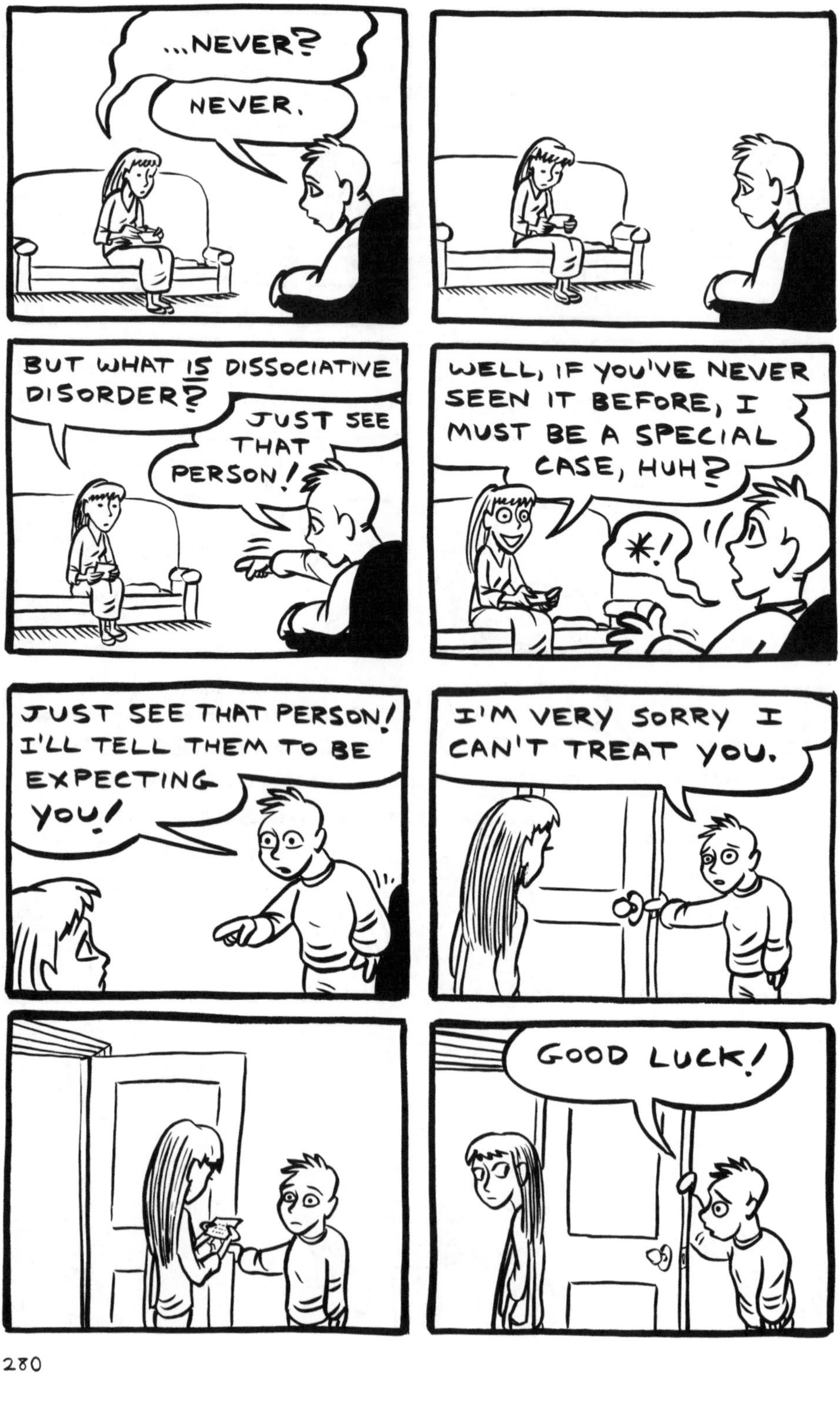
...NEVER?
NEVER.
BUT WHAT IS DISSOCIATIVE DISORDER?
JUST SEE THAT PERSON!
WELL, IF YOU'VE NEVER SEEN IT BEFORE, I MUST BE A SPECIAL CASE, HUH?
*!
JUST SEE THAT PERSON! I'LL TELL THEM TO BE EXPECTING YOU!
I'M VERY SORRY I CAN'T TREAT YOU.
GOOD LUCK!

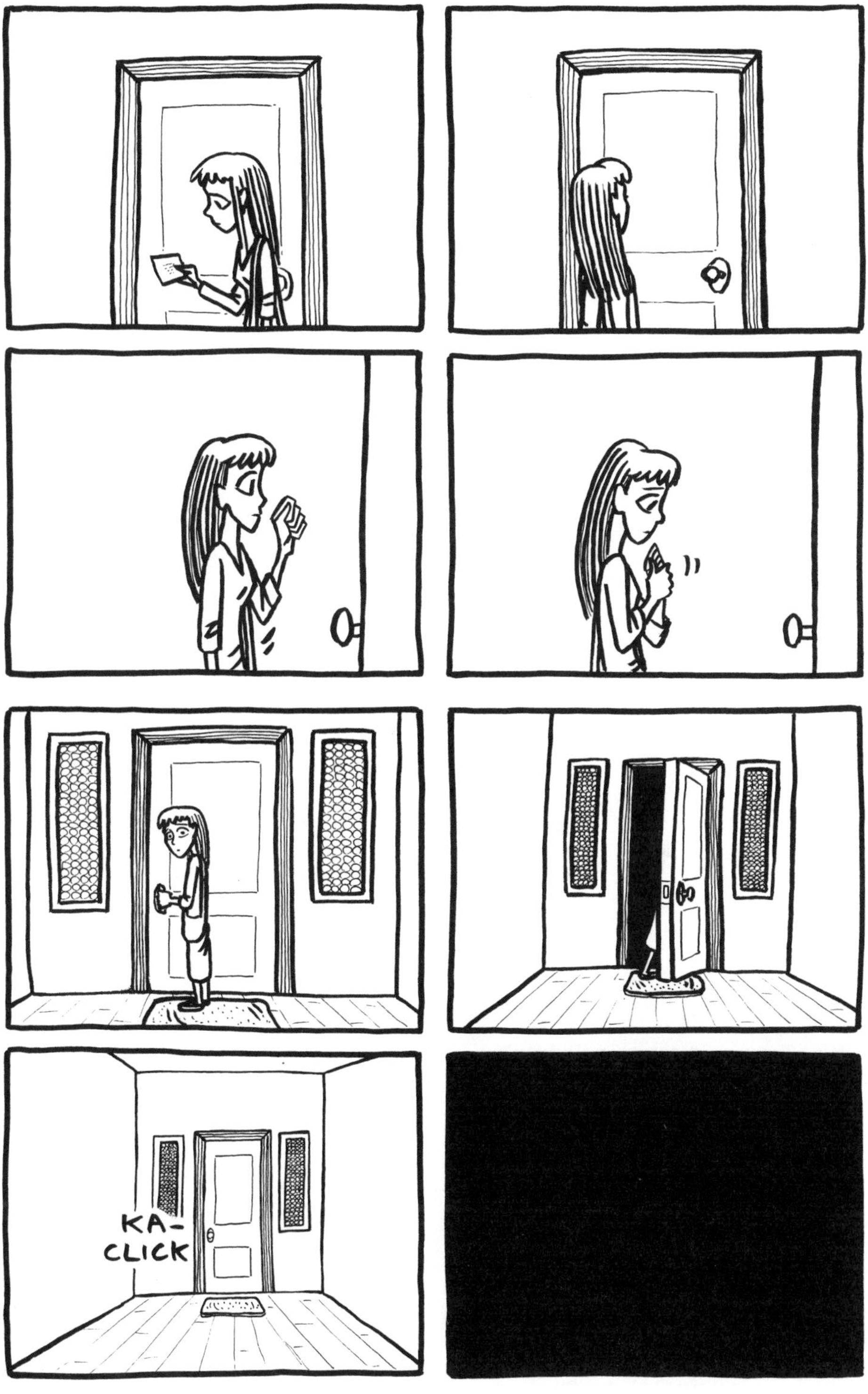
KA-
CLICK

EDGAR

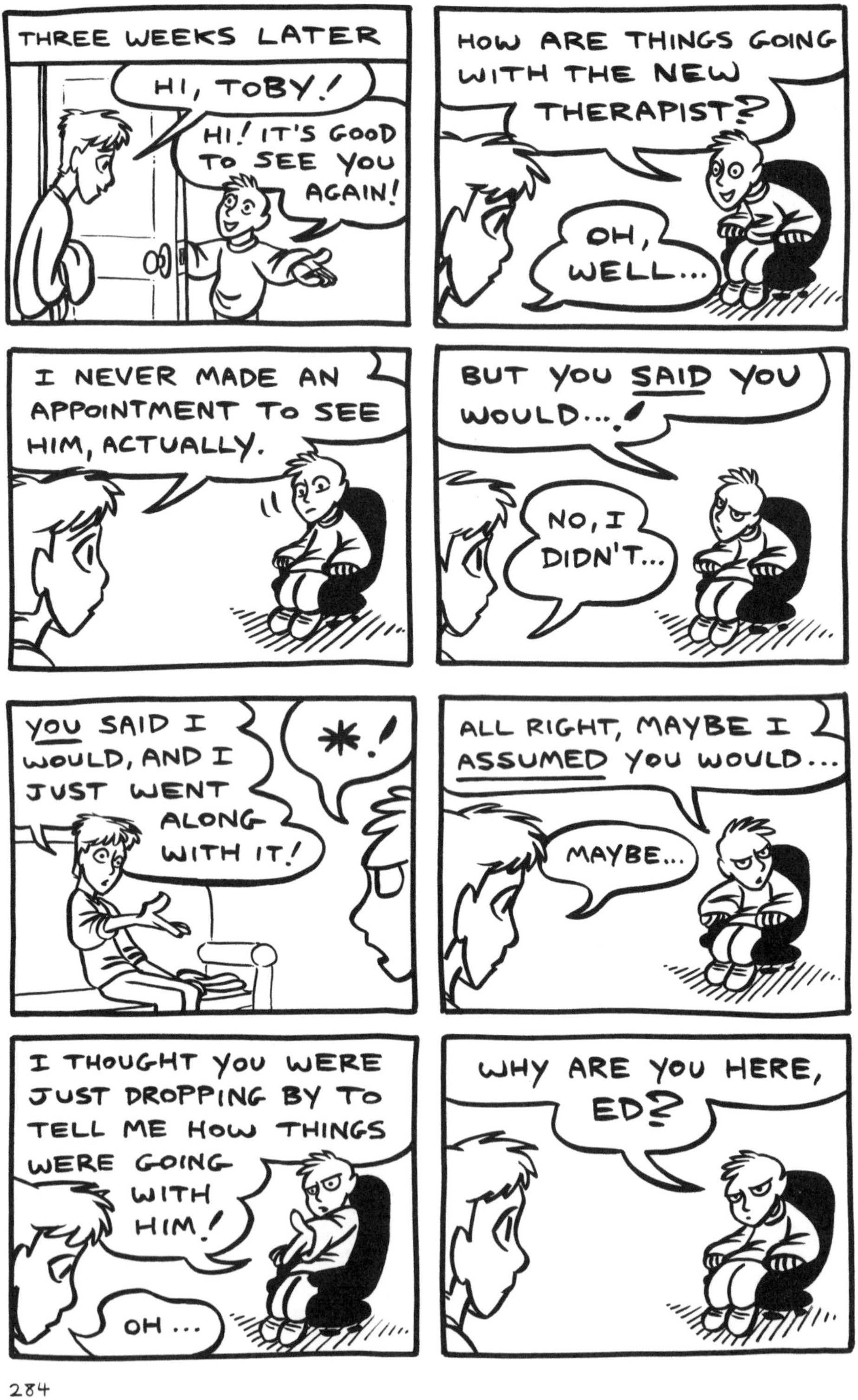
THREE WEEKS LATER
HI, TOBY!
HI! IT'S GOOD TO SEE YOU AGAIN!
HOW ARE THINGS GOING WITH THE NEW THERAPIST?
OH, WELL...
I NEVER MADE AN APPOINTMENT TO SEE HIM, ACTUALLY.
BUT YOU SAID YOU WOULD...!
NO, I DIDN'T...
YOU SAID I WOULD, AND I JUST WENT ALONG WITH IT!
*!
ALL RIGHT, MAYBE I ASSUMED YOU WOULD...
MAYBE...
I THOUGHT YOU WERE JUST DROPPING BY TO TELL ME HOW THINGS WERE GOING WITH HIM!
OH ...
WHY ARE YOU HERE, ED?

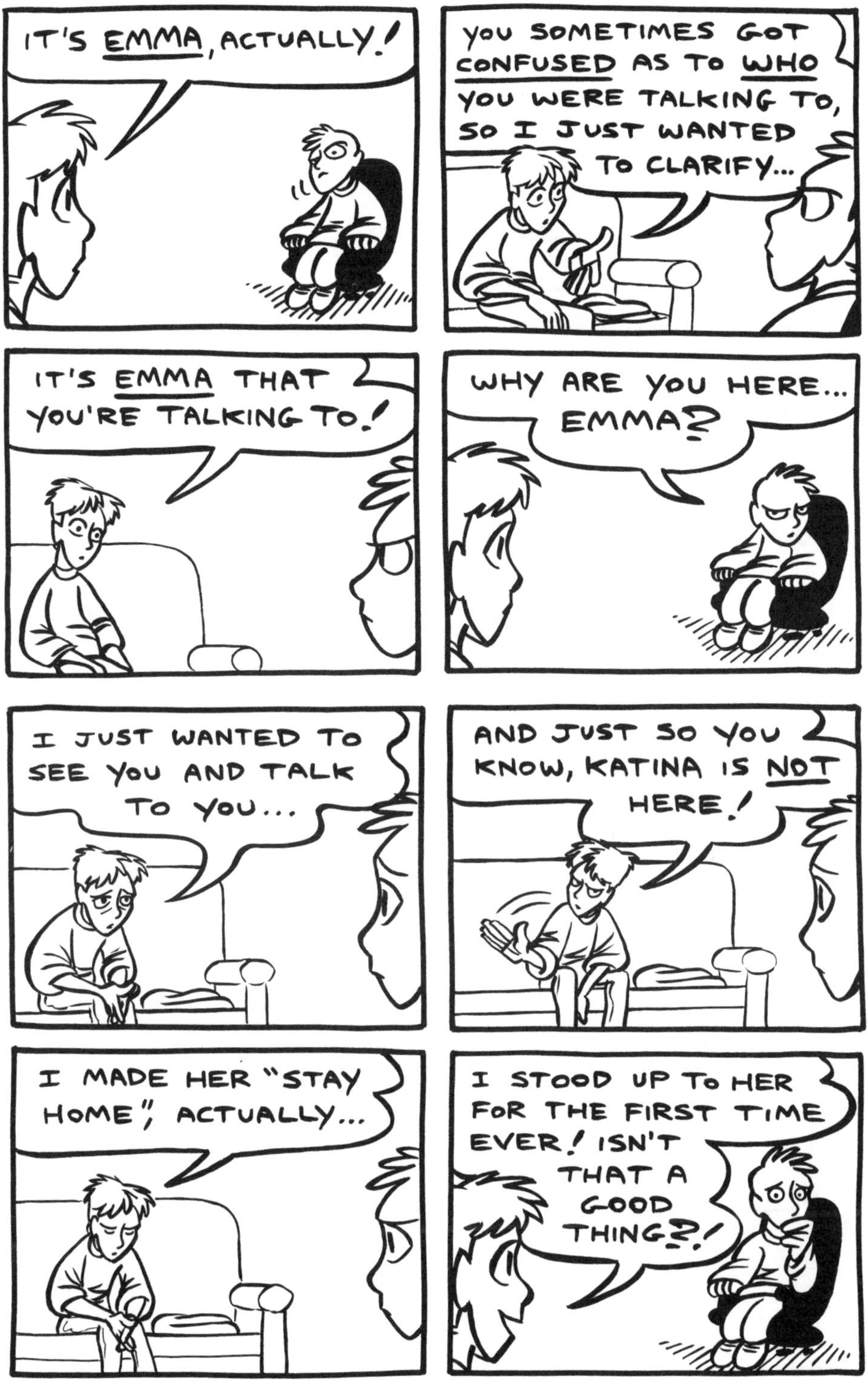
IT'S EMMA, ACTUALLY!
YOU SOMETIMES GOT CONFUSED AS TO WHO YOU WERE TALKING TO, SO I JUST WANTED TO CLARIFY...
IT'S EMMA THAT YOU'RE TALKING TO!
WHY ARE YOU HERE... EMMA?
I JUST WANTED TO SEE YOU AND TALK TO YOU...
AND JUST SO YOU KNOW, KATINA IS NOT HERE!
I MADE HER "STAY HOME", ACTUALLY...
I STOOD UP TO HER FOR THE FIRST TIME EVER! ISN'T THAT A GOOD THING?!

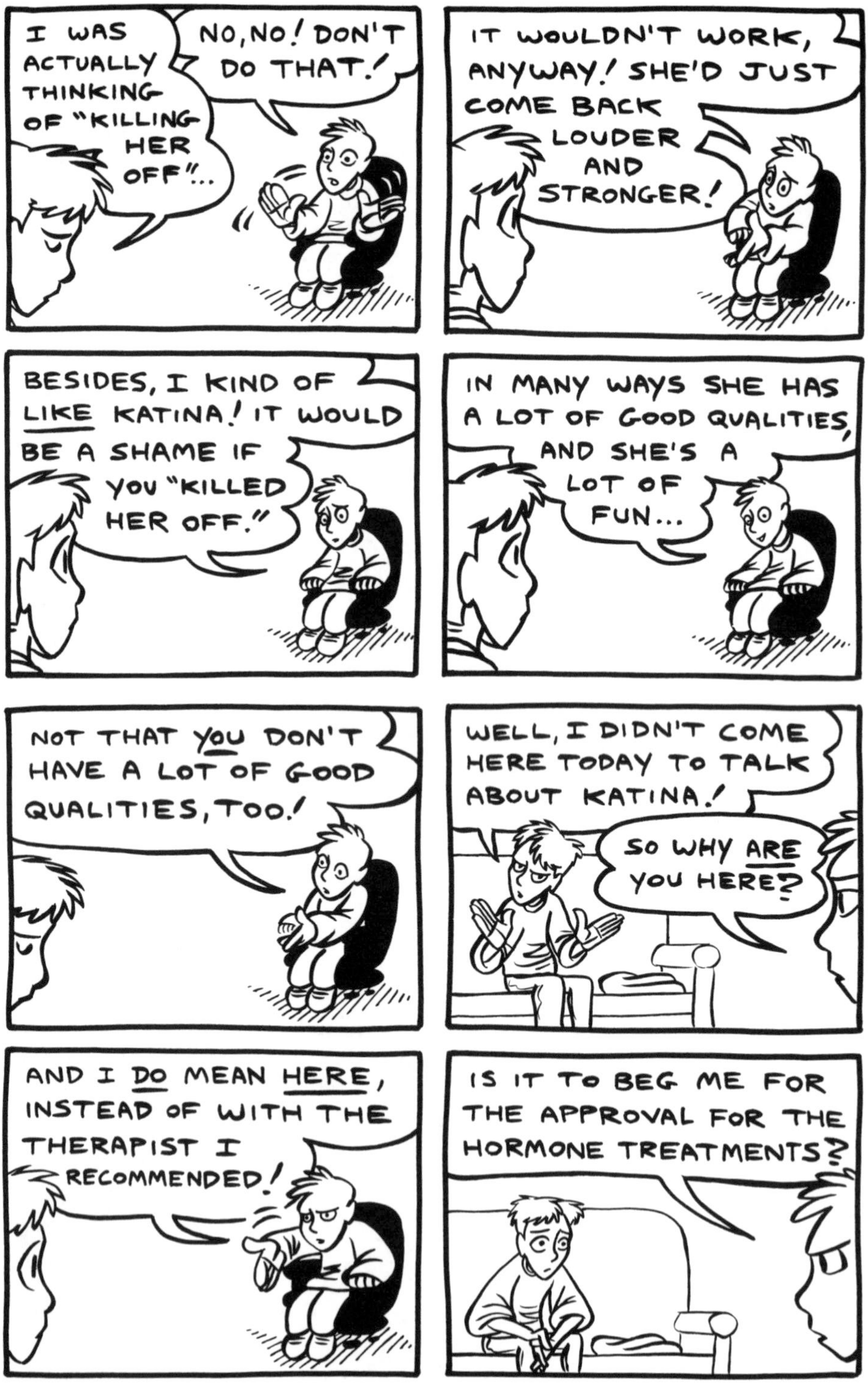
I WAS ACTUALLY THINKING OF "KILLING HER OFF"...
NO, NO! DON'T DO THAT!
IT WOULDN'T WORK, ANYWAY! SHE'D JUST COME BACK LOUDER AND STRONGER!
BESIDES, I KIND OF LIKE KATINA! IT WOULD BE A SHAME IF YOU "KILLED HER OFF."
IN MANY WAYS SHE HAS A LOT OF GOOD QUALITIES, AND SHE'S A LOT OF FUN...
NOT THAT YOU DON'T HAVE A LOT OF GOOD QUALITIES, TOO!
WELL, I DIDN'T COME HERE TODAY TO TALK ABOUT KATINA!
SO WHY ARE YOU HERE?
AND I DO MEAN HERE, INSTEAD OF WITH THE THERAPIST I RECOMMENDED!
IS IT TO BEG ME FOR THE APPROVAL FOR THE HORMONE TREATMENTS?

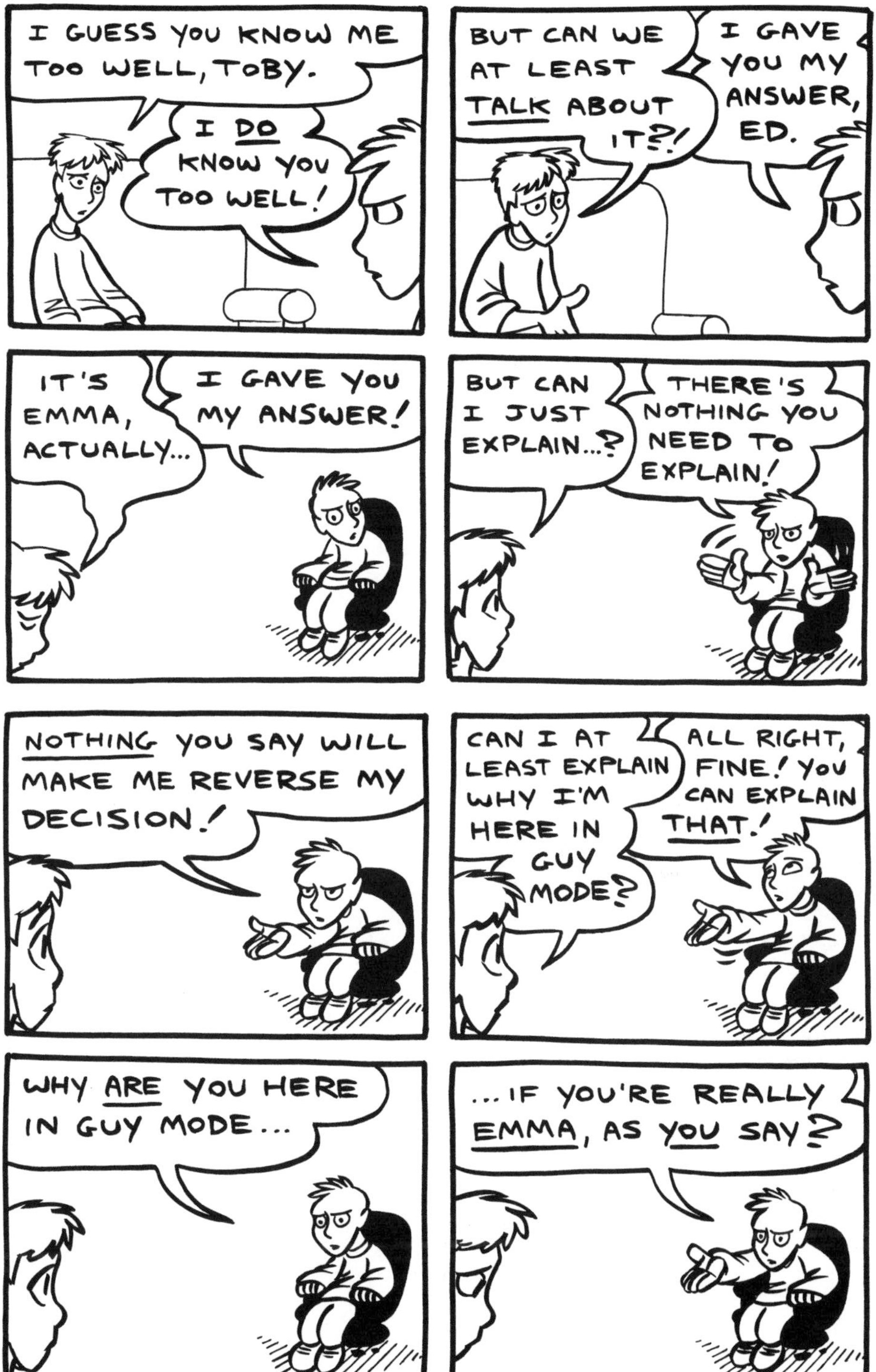
I GUESS YOU KNOW ME TOO WELL, TOBY.
I DO KNOW YOU TOO WELL!
BUT CAN WE AT LEAST TALK ABOUT IT?!
I GAVE YOU MY ANSWER, ED.
IT'S EMMA, ACTUALLY...
I GAVE YOU MY ANSWER!
BUT CAN I JUST EXPLAIN...?
THERE'S NOTHING YOU NEED TO EXPLAIN!
NOTHING YOU SAY WILL MAKE ME REVERSE MY DECISION!
CAN I AT LEAST EXPLAIN WHY I'M HERE IN GUY MODE?
ALL RIGHT, FINE! YOU CAN EXPLAIN THAT!
WHY ARE YOU HERE IN GUY MODE...
...IF YOU'RE REALLY EMMA, AS YOU SAY?

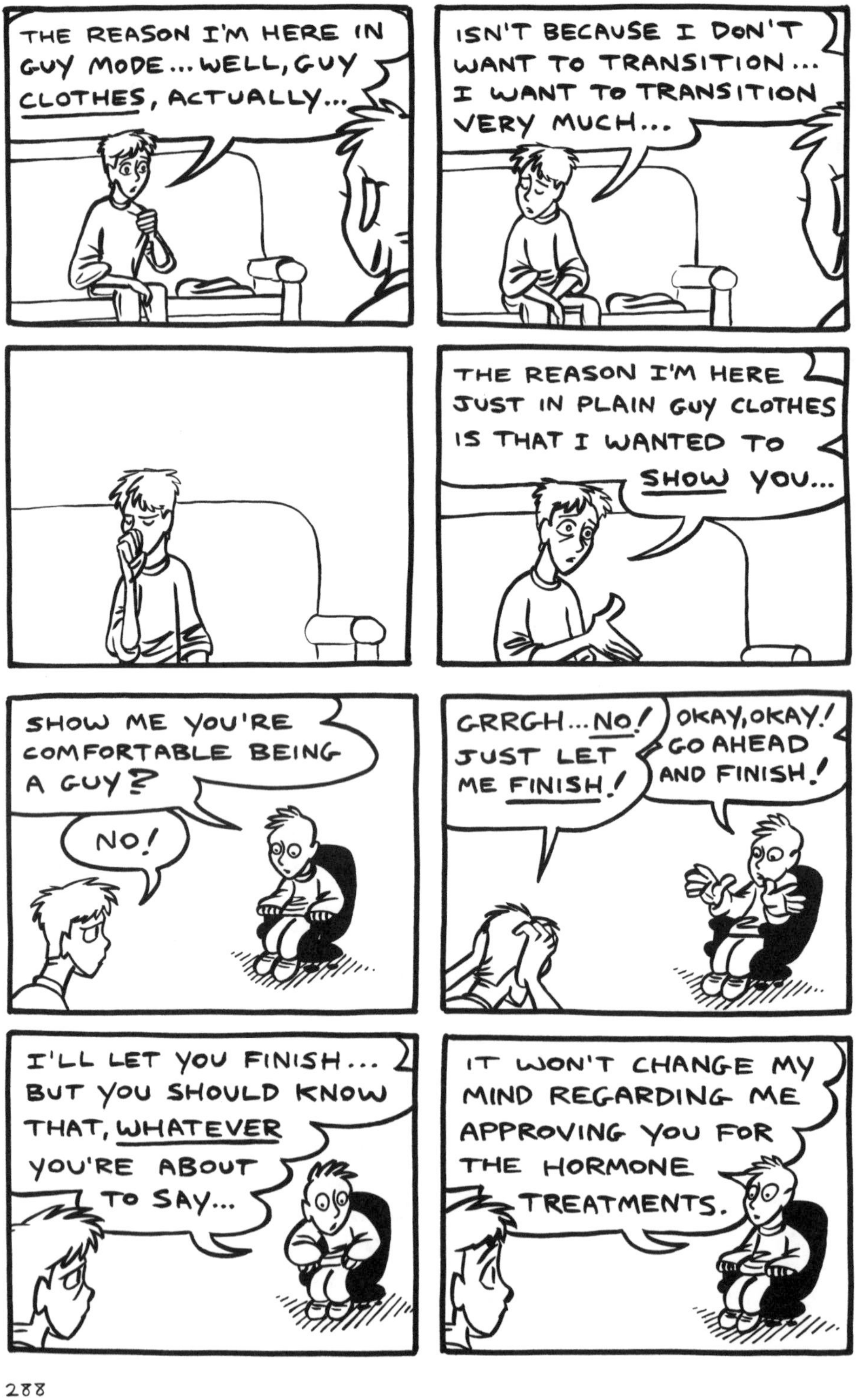
THE REASON I'M HERE IN GUY MODE... WELL, GUY CLOTHES, ACTUALLY...
ISN'T BECAUSE I DON'T WANT TO TRANSITION... I WANT TO TRANSITION VERY MUCH...
THE REASON I'M HERE JUST IN PLAIN GUY CLOTHES IS THAT I WANTED TO SHOW YOU...
SHOW ME YOU'RE COMFORTABLE BEING A GUY?
NO!
GRRGH... NO! JUST LET ME FINISH!
OKAY, OKAY! GO AHEAD AND FINISH!
I'LL LET YOU FINISH... BUT YOU SHOULD KNOW THAT, WHATEVER YOU'RE ABOUT TO SAY...
IT WON'T CHANGE MY MIND REGARDING ME APPROVING YOU FOR THE HORMONE TREATMENTS.

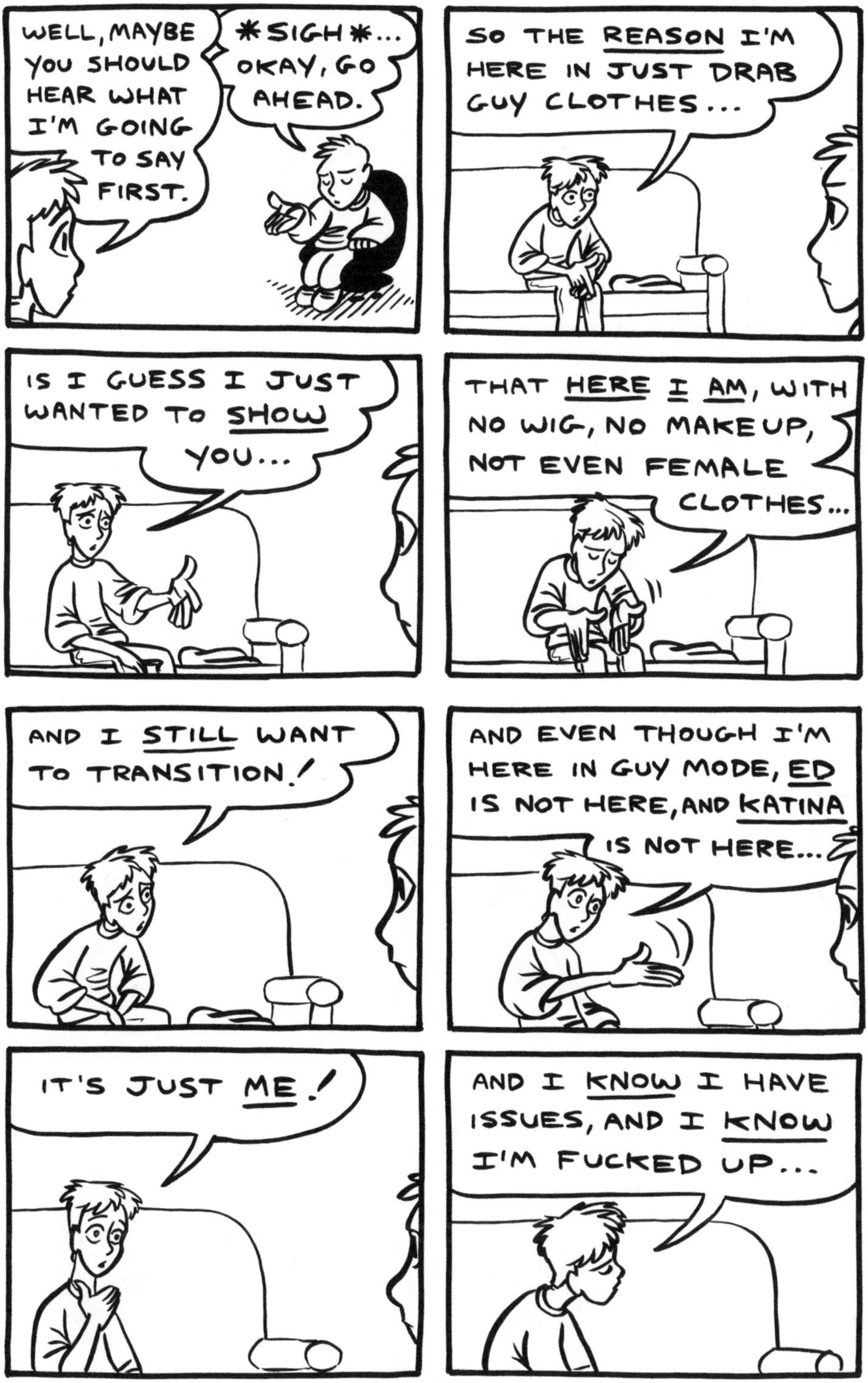
WELL, MAYBE YOU SHOULD HEAR WHAT I'M GOING TO SAY FIRST.
SIGH... OKAY, GO AHEAD.
SO THE REASON I'M HERE IN JUST DRAB GUY CLOTHES...
IS I GUESS I JUST WANTED TO SHOW YOU...
THAT HERE I AM, WITH NO WIG, NO MAKEUP, NOT EVEN FEMALE CLOTHES...
AND I STILL WANT TO TRANSITION!
AND EVEN THOUGH I'M HERE IN GUY MODE, ED IS NOT HERE, AND KATINA IS NOT HERE...
IT'S JUST ME!
AND I KNOW I HAVE ISSUES, AND I KNOW I'M FUCKED UP...

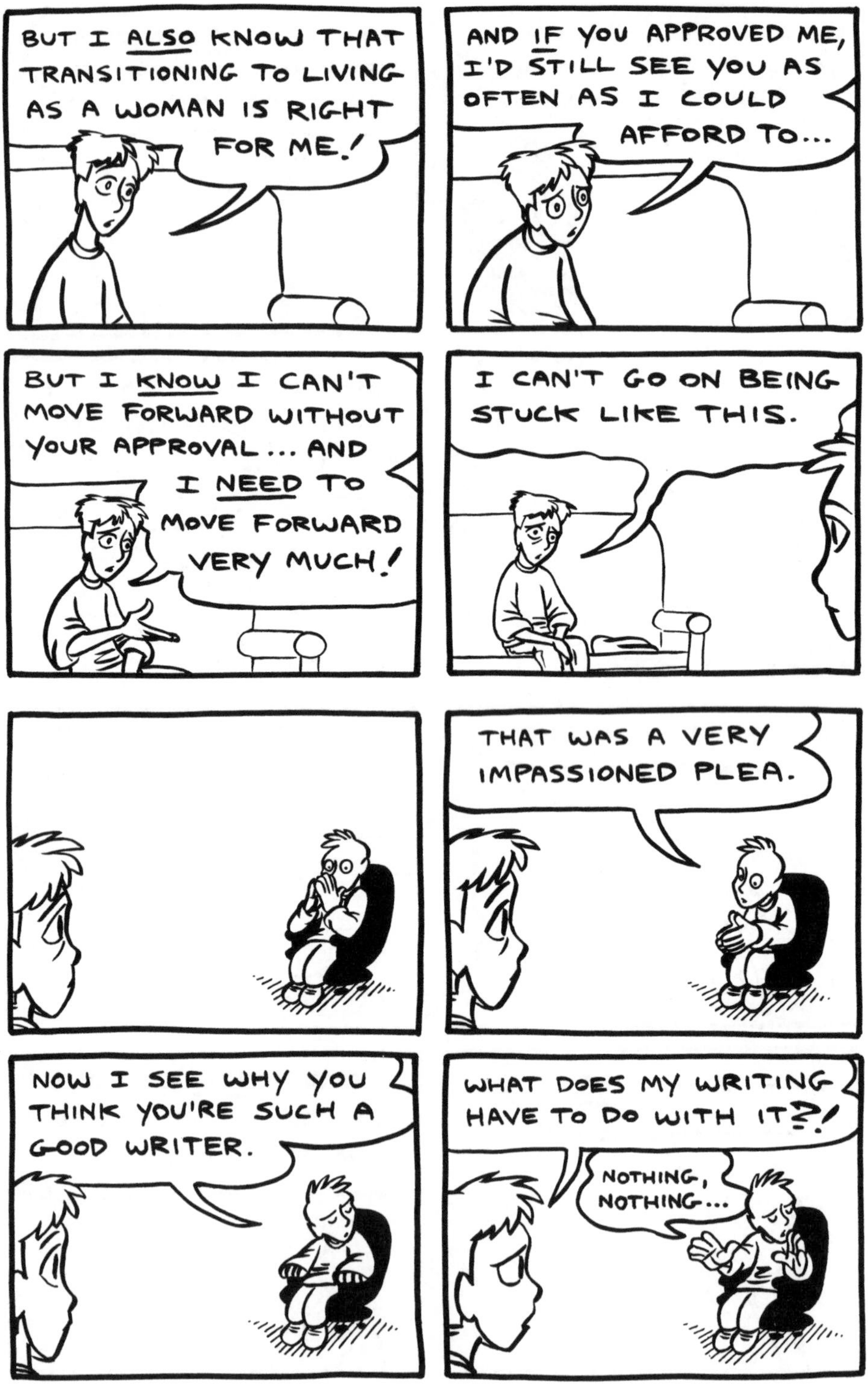
BUT I ALSO KNOW THAT TRANSITIONING TO LIVING AS A WOMAN IS RIGHT FOR ME!
AND IF YOU APPROVED ME, I'D STILL SEE YOU AS OFTEN AS I COULD AFFORD TO...
BUT I KNOW I CAN'T MOVE FORWARD WITHOUT YOUR APPROVAL... AND I NEED TO MOVE FORWARD VERY MUCH!
I CAN'T GO ON BEING STUCK LIKE THIS.
THAT WAS A VERY IMPASSIONED PLEA.
NOW I SEE WHY YOU THINK YOU'RE SUCH A GOOD WRITER.
WHAT DOES MY WRITING HAVE TO DO WITH IT?!
NOTHING, NOTHING...

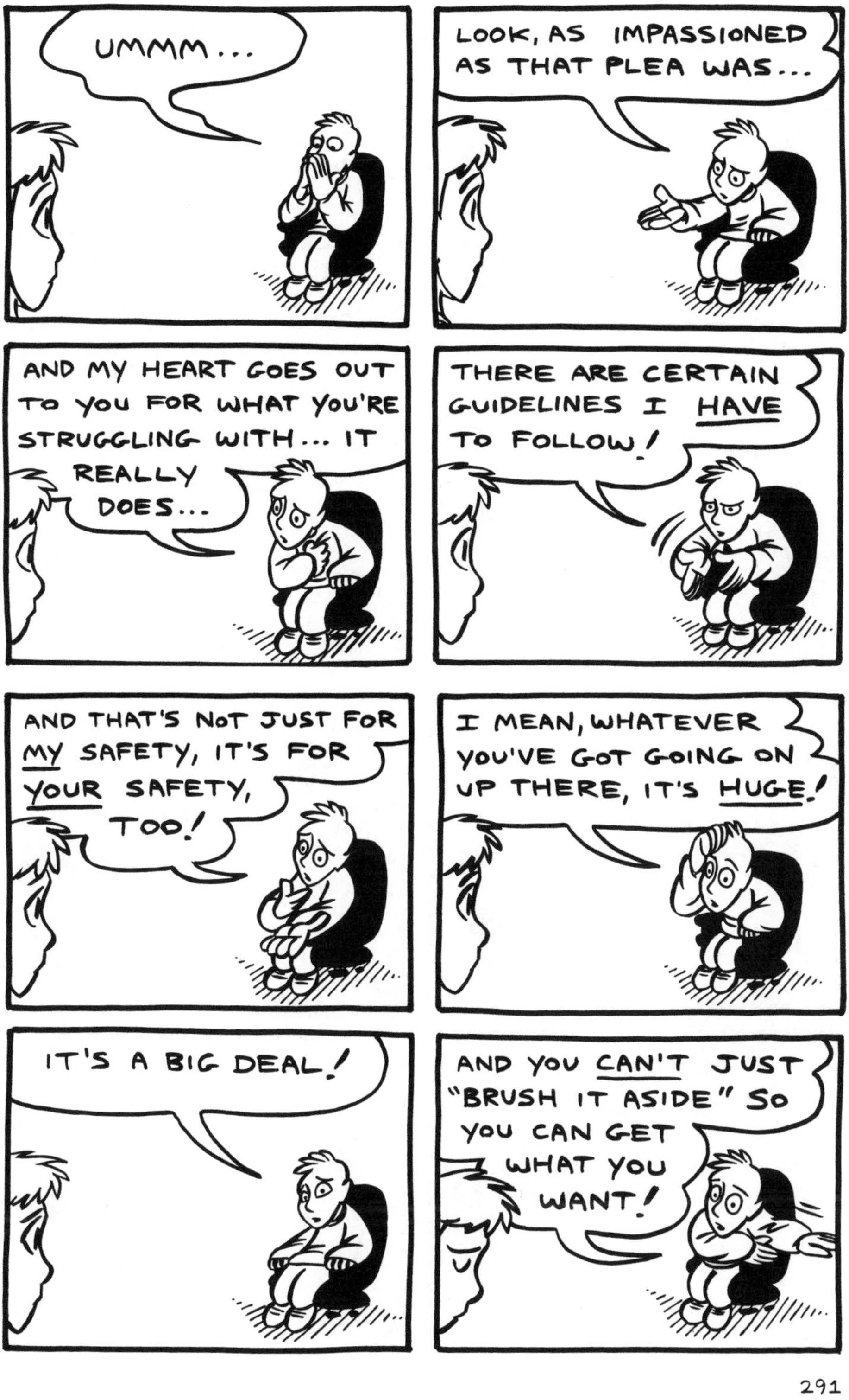
UMMM...
LOOK, AS IMPASSIONED AS THAT PLEA WAS...
AND MY HEART GOES OUT TO YOU FOR WHAT YOU'RE STRUGGLING WITH... IT REALLY DOES...
THERE ARE CERTAIN GUIDELINES I HAVE TO FOLLOW!
AND THAT'S NOT JUST FOR MY SAFETY, IT'S FOR YOUR SAFETY, TOO!
I MEAN, WHATEVER YOU'VE GOT GOING ON UP THERE, IT'S HUGE!
IT'S A BIG DEAL!
AND YOU CAN'T JUST "BRUSH IT ASIDE" SO YOU CAN GET WHAT YOU WANT!

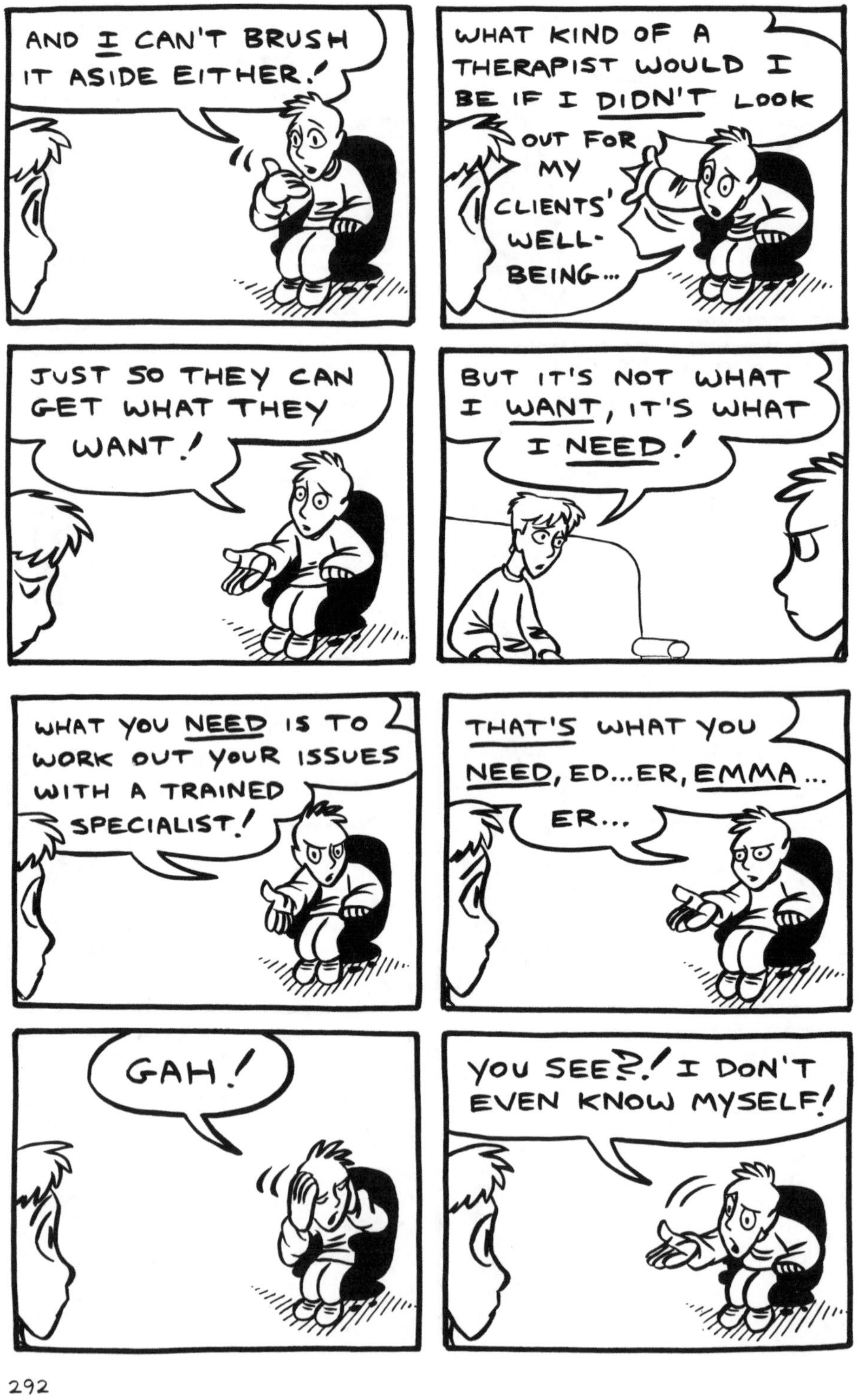
AND I CAN'T BRUSH IT ASIDE EITHER!
WHAT KIND OF A THERAPIST WOULD I BE IF I DIDN'T LOOK OUT FOR MY CLIENTS' WELL-BEING...
JUST SO THEY CAN GET WHAT THEY WANT!
BUT IT'S NOT WHAT I WANT, IT'S WHAT I NEED!
WHAT YOU NEED IS TO WORK OUT YOUR ISSUES WITH A TRAINED SPECIALIST!
THAT'S WHAT YOU NEED, ED...ER, EMMA... ER...
GAH!
YOU SEE?! I DON'T EVEN KNOW MYSELF!

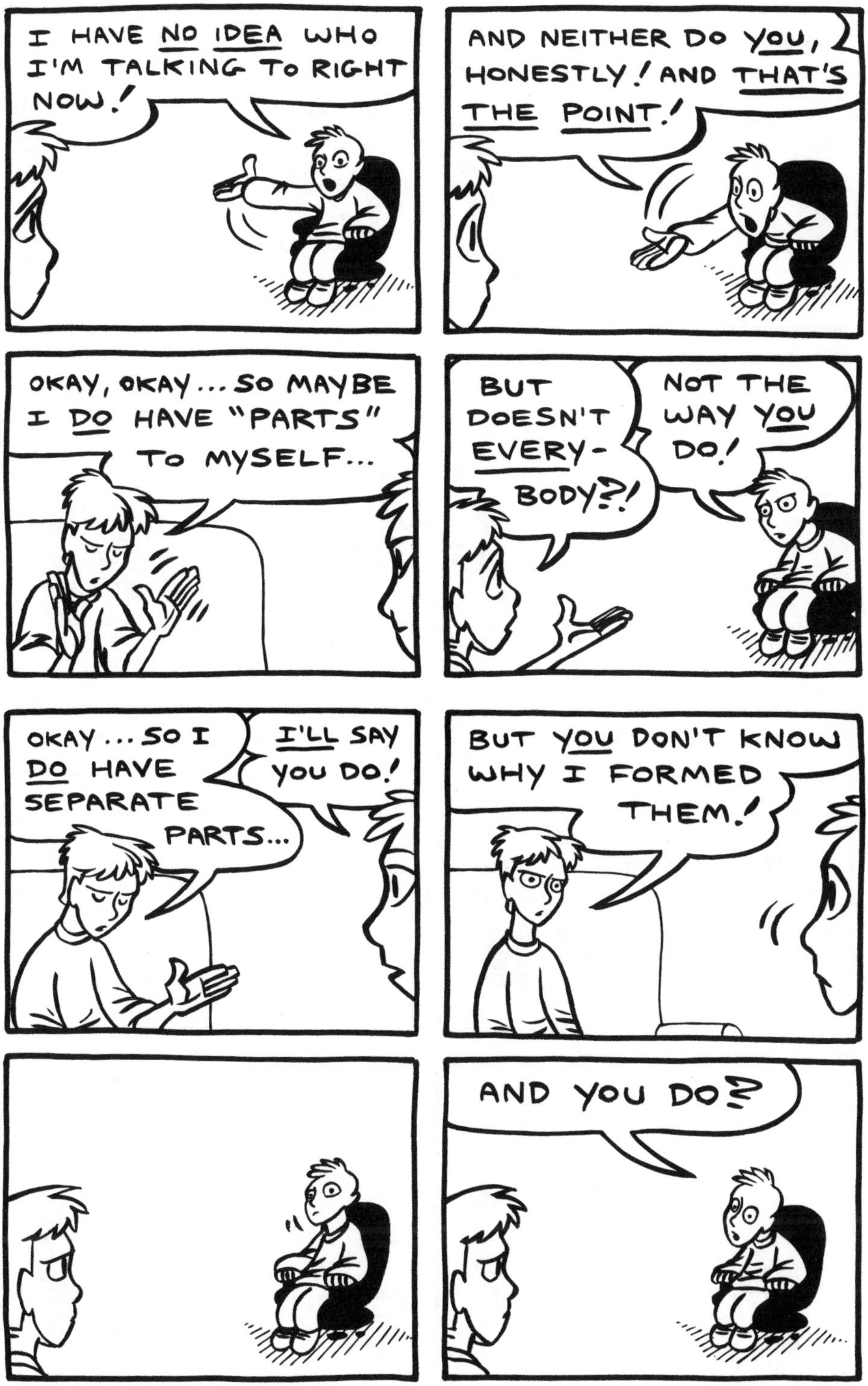

I HAVE NO IDEA WHO I'M TALKING TO RIGHT NOW!
AND NEITHER DO YOU, HONESTLY! AND THAT'S THE POINT!
OKAY, OKAY... SO MAYBE I DO HAVE "PARTS" TO MYSELF...
BUT DOESN'T EVERY-BODY?!
NOT THE WAY YOU DO!
OKAY... SO I DO HAVE SEPARATE PARTS...
I'LL SAY YOU DO!
BUT YOU DON'T KNOW WHY I FORMED THEM!
AND YOU DO?

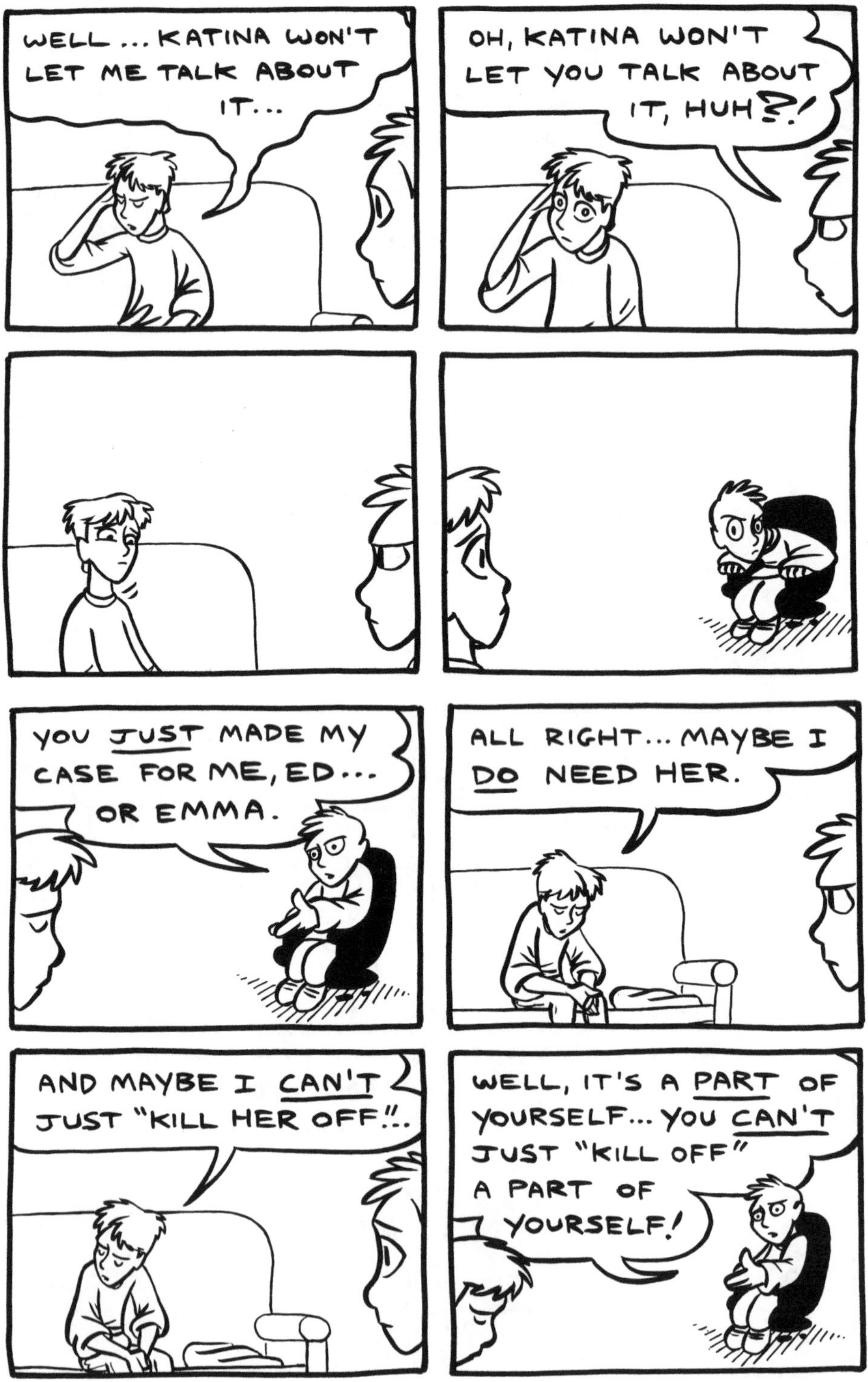

WELL... KATINA WON'T LET ME TALK ABOUT IT...
OH, KATINA WON'T LET YOU TALK ABOUT IT, HUH?!
YOU JUST MADE MY CASE FOR ME, ED... OR EMMA.
ALL RIGHT... MAYBE I DO NEED HER.
AND MAYBE I CAN'T JUST "KILL HER OFF!"..
WELL, IT'S A PART OF YOURSELF... YOU CAN'T JUST "KILL OFF" A PART OF YOURSELF!

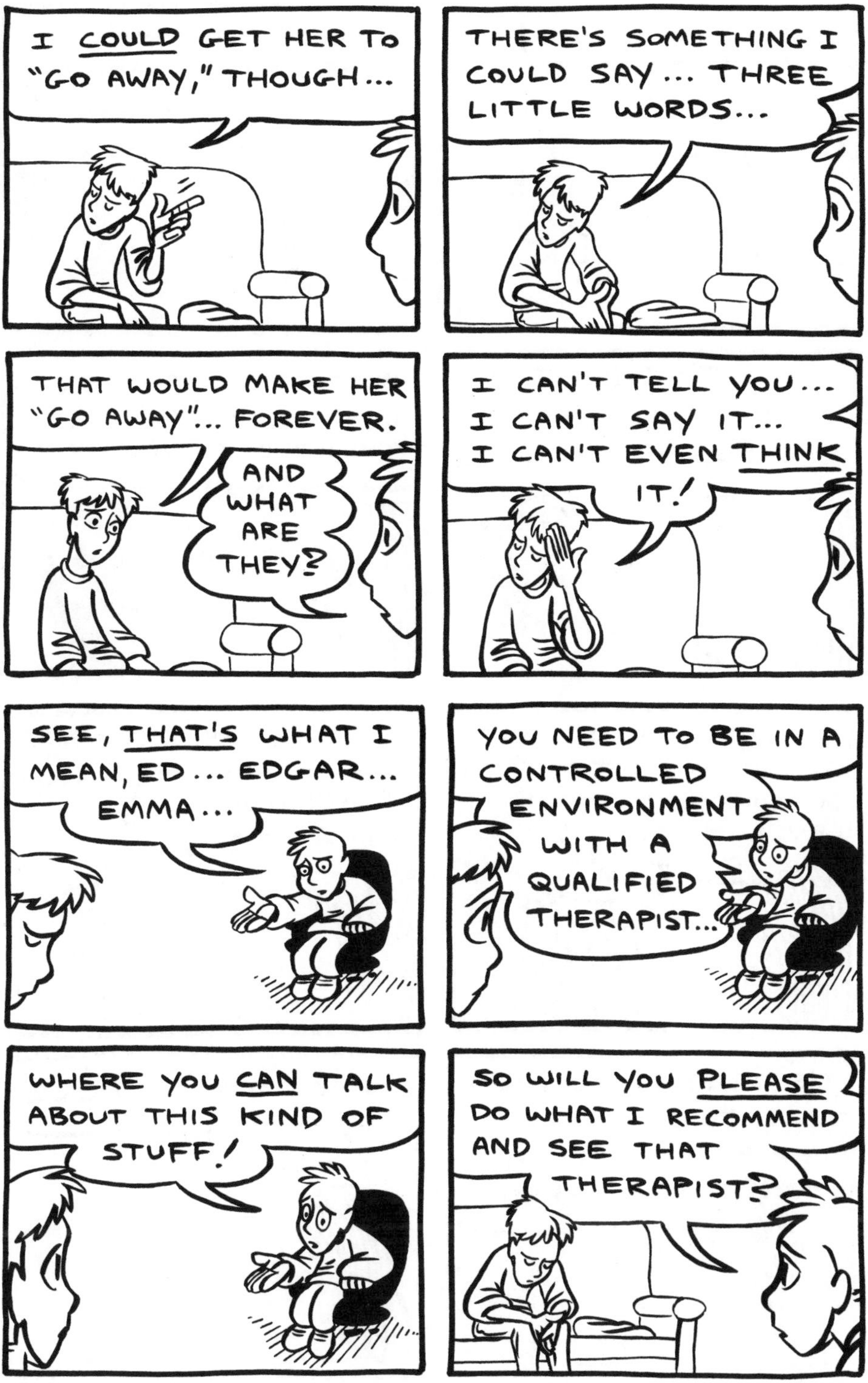

I COULD GET HER TO "GO AWAY," THOUGH...
THERE'S SOMETHING I COULD SAY... THREE LITTLE WORDS...
THAT WOULD MAKE HER "GO AWAY"... FOREVER.
AND WHAT ARE THEY?
I CAN'T TELL YOU... I CAN'T SAY IT... I CAN'T EVEN THINK IT!
SEE, THAT'S WHAT I MEAN, ED... EDGAR... EMMA...
YOU NEED TO BE IN A CONTROLLED ENVIRONMENT WITH A QUALIFIED THERAPIST...
WHERE YOU CAN TALK ABOUT THIS KIND OF STUFF!
SO WILL YOU PLEASE DO WHAT I RECOMMEND AND SEE THAT THERAPIST?

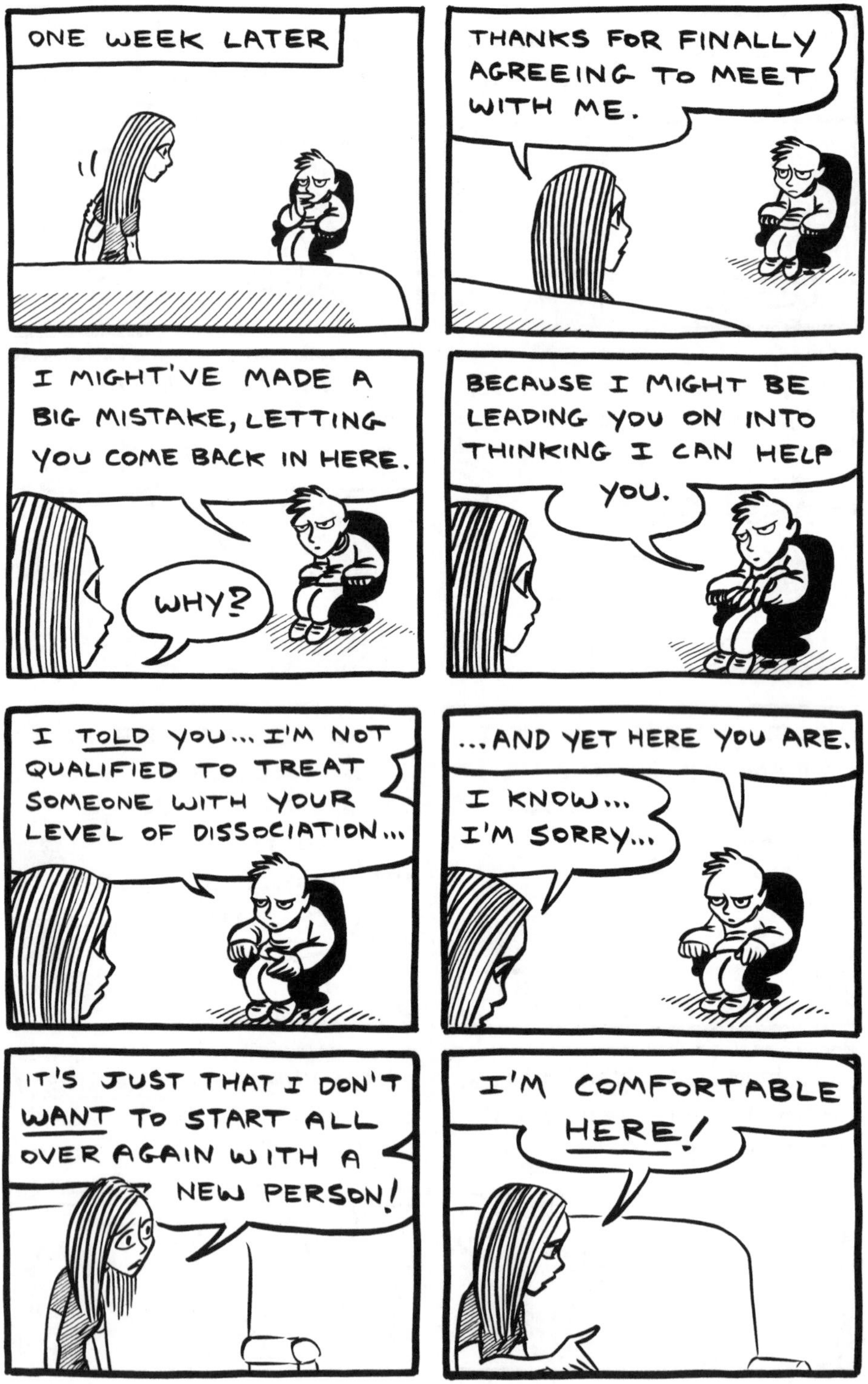
ONE WEEK LATER
THANKS FOR FINALLY AGREEING TO MEET WITH ME.
I MIGHT'VE MADE A BIG MISTAKE, LETTING YOU COME BACK IN HERE.
WHY?
BECAUSE I MIGHT BE LEADING YOU ON INTO THINKING I CAN HELP YOU.
I TOLD YOU... I'M NOT QUALIFIED TO TREAT SOMEONE WITH YOUR LEVEL OF DISSOCIATION...
...AND YET HERE YOU ARE.
I KNOW... I'M SORRY...
IT'S JUST THAT I DON'T WANT TO START ALL OVER AGAIN WITH A NEW PERSON!
I'M COMFORTABLE HERE!

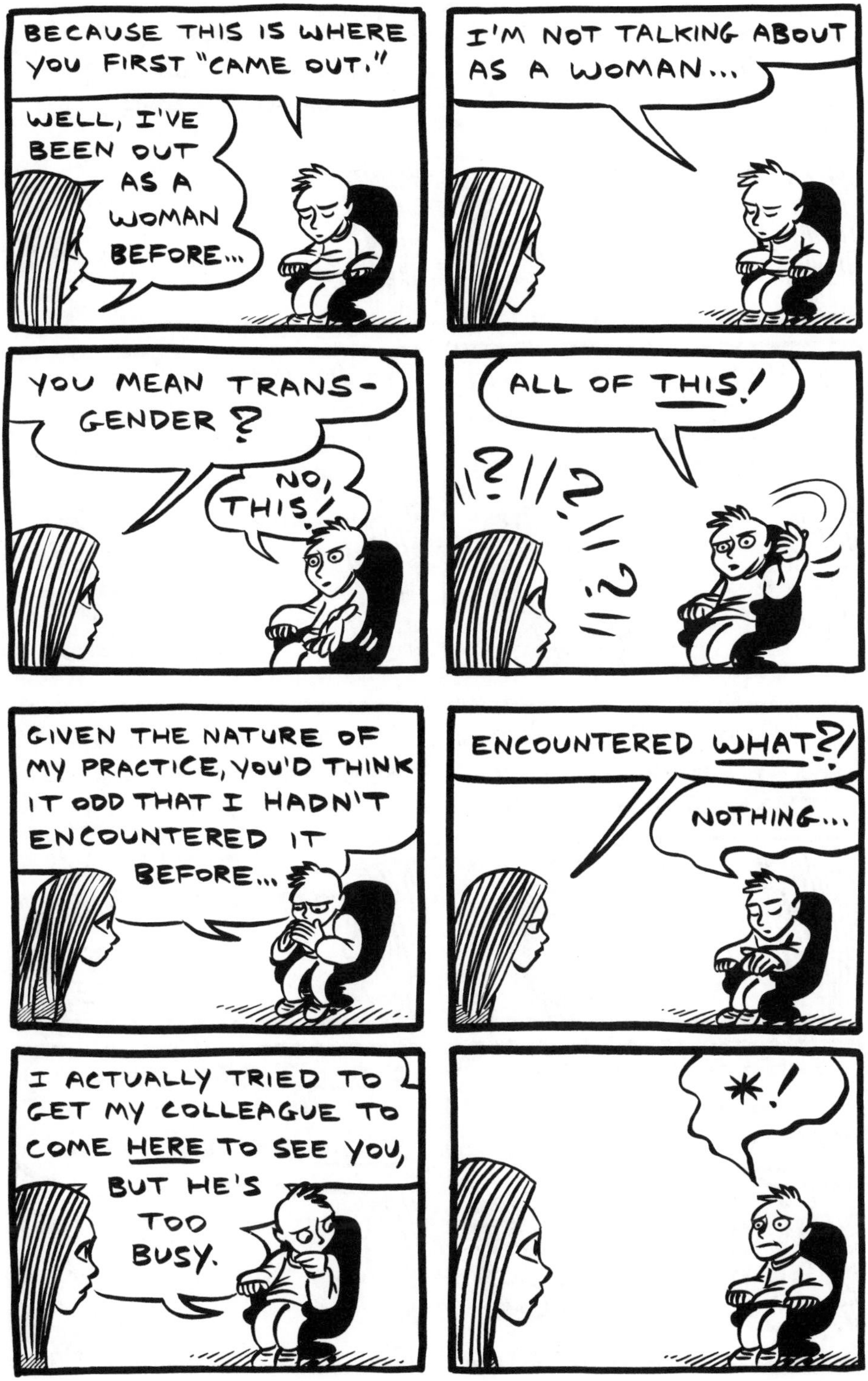
BECAUSE THIS IS WHERE YOU FIRST "CAME OUT."
WELL, I'VE BEEN OUT AS A WOMAN BEFORE...
I'M NOT TALKING ABOUT AS A WOMAN...
YOU MEAN TRANS-GENDER?
NO, THIS!
ALL OF THIS!
?
?
?
GIVEN THE NATURE OF MY PRACTICE, YOU'D THINK IT ODD THAT I HADN'T ENCOUNTERED IT BEFORE...
ENCOUNTERED WHAT?!
NOTHING...
I ACTUALLY TRIED TO GET MY COLLEAGUE TO COME HERE TO SEE YOU, BUT HE'S TOO BUSY.
*!

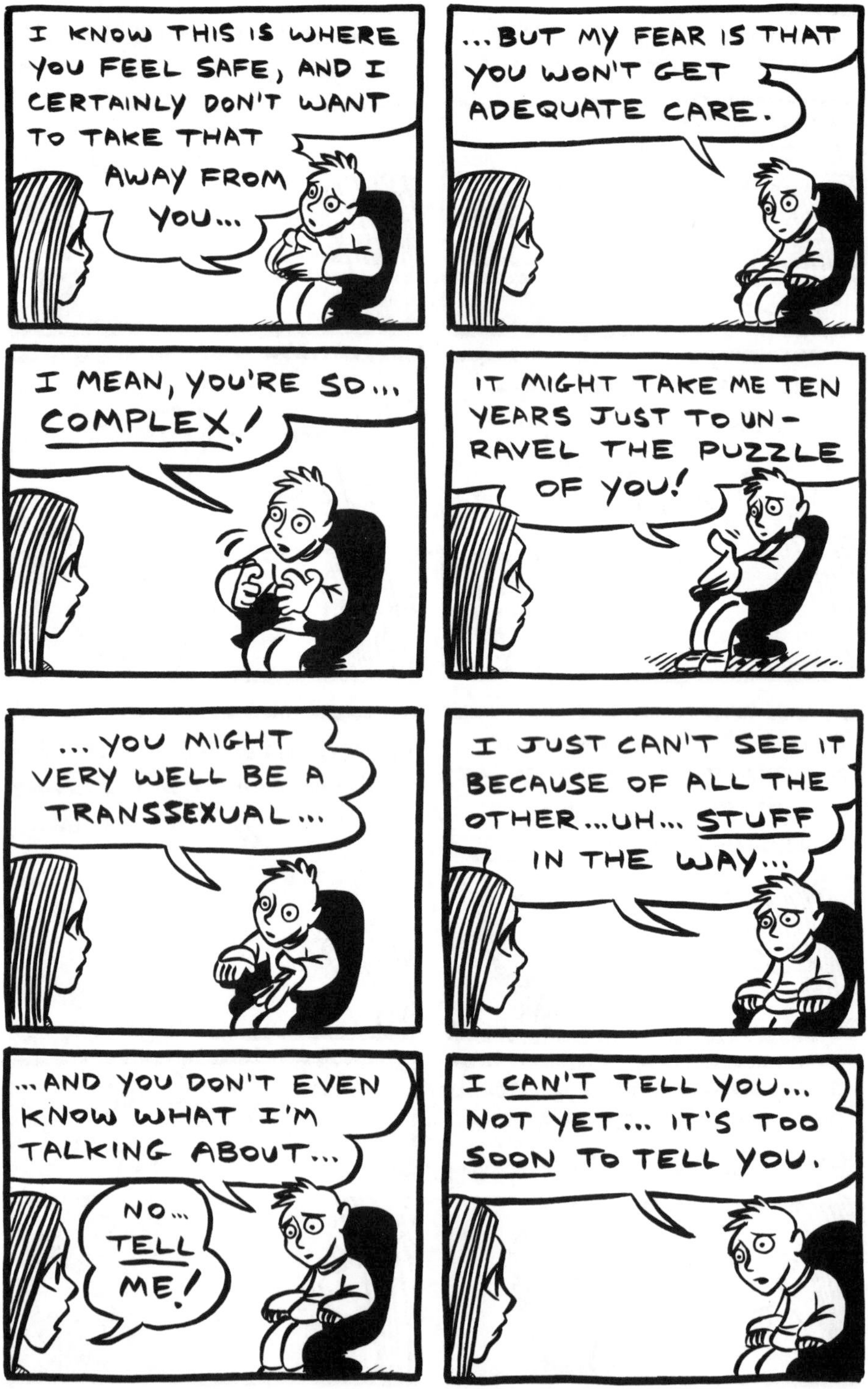
I KNOW THIS IS WHERE YOU FEEL SAFE, AND I CERTAINLY DON'T WANT TO TAKE THAT AWAY FROM YOU...
...BUT MY FEAR IS THAT YOU WON'T GET ADEQUATE CARE.
I MEAN, YOU'RE SO... COMPLEX!
IT MIGHT TAKE ME TEN YEARS JUST TO UN-RAVEL THE PUZZLE OF YOU!
...YOU MIGHT VERY WELL BE A TRANSSEXUAL...
I JUST CAN'T SEE IT BECAUSE OF ALL THE OTHER...UH... STUFF IN THE WAY...
...AND YOU DON'T EVEN KNOW WHAT I'M TALKING ABOUT...
NO... TELL ME!
I CAN'T TELL YOU... NOT YET... IT'S TOO SOON TO TELL YOU.

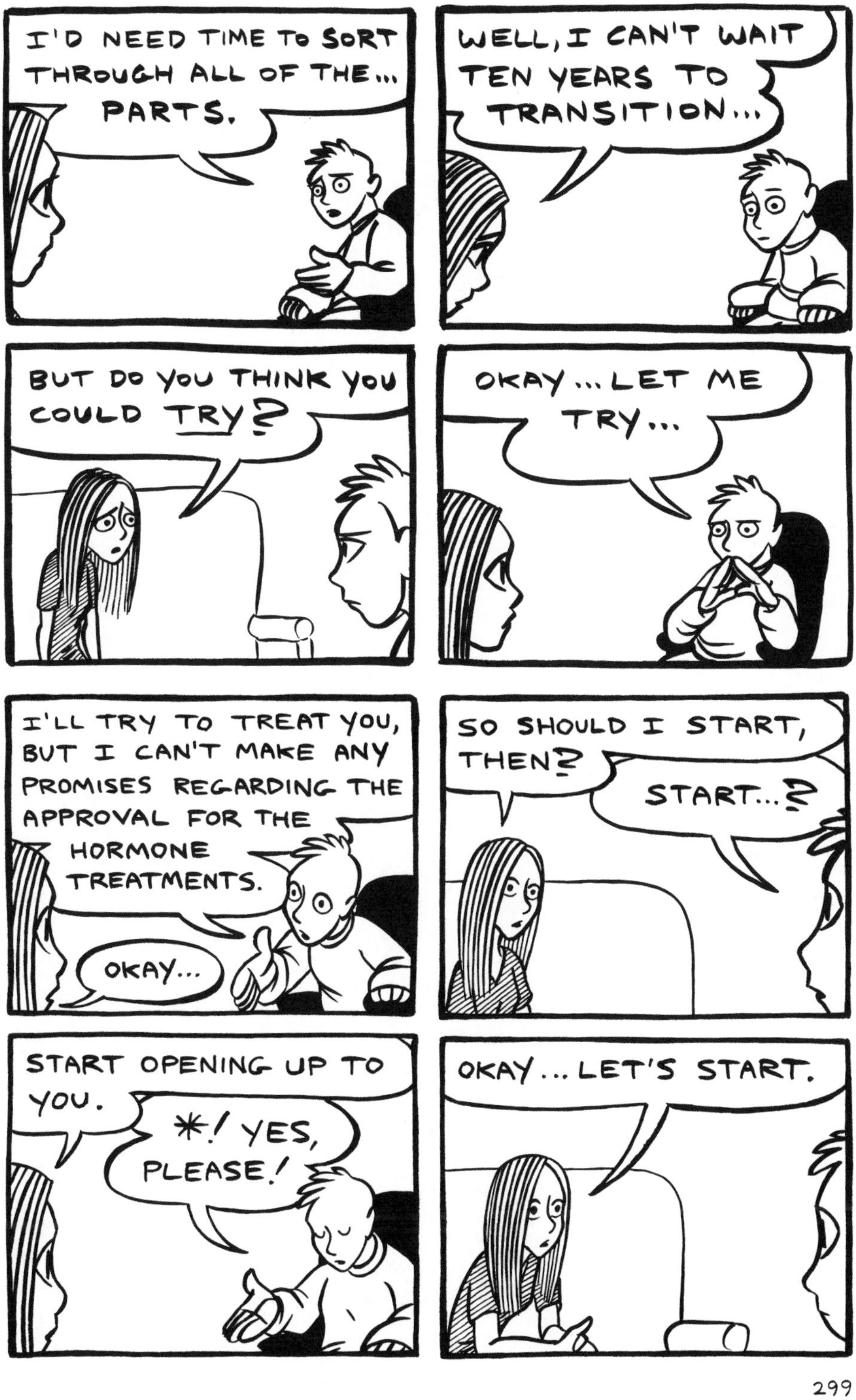
I'D NEED TIME TO SORT THROUGH ALL OF THE... PARTS.
WELL, I CAN'T WAIT TEN YEARS TO TRANSITION...
BUT DO YOU THINK YOU COULD TRY?
OKAY... LET ME TRY...
I'LL TRY TO TREAT YOU, BUT I CAN'T MAKE ANY PROMISES REGARDING THE APPROVAL FOR THE HORMONE TREATMENTS.
OKAY...
SO SHOULD I START, THEN?
START...?
START OPENING UP TO YOU.
*! YES, PLEASE!
OKAY... LET'S START.

CLIFFS

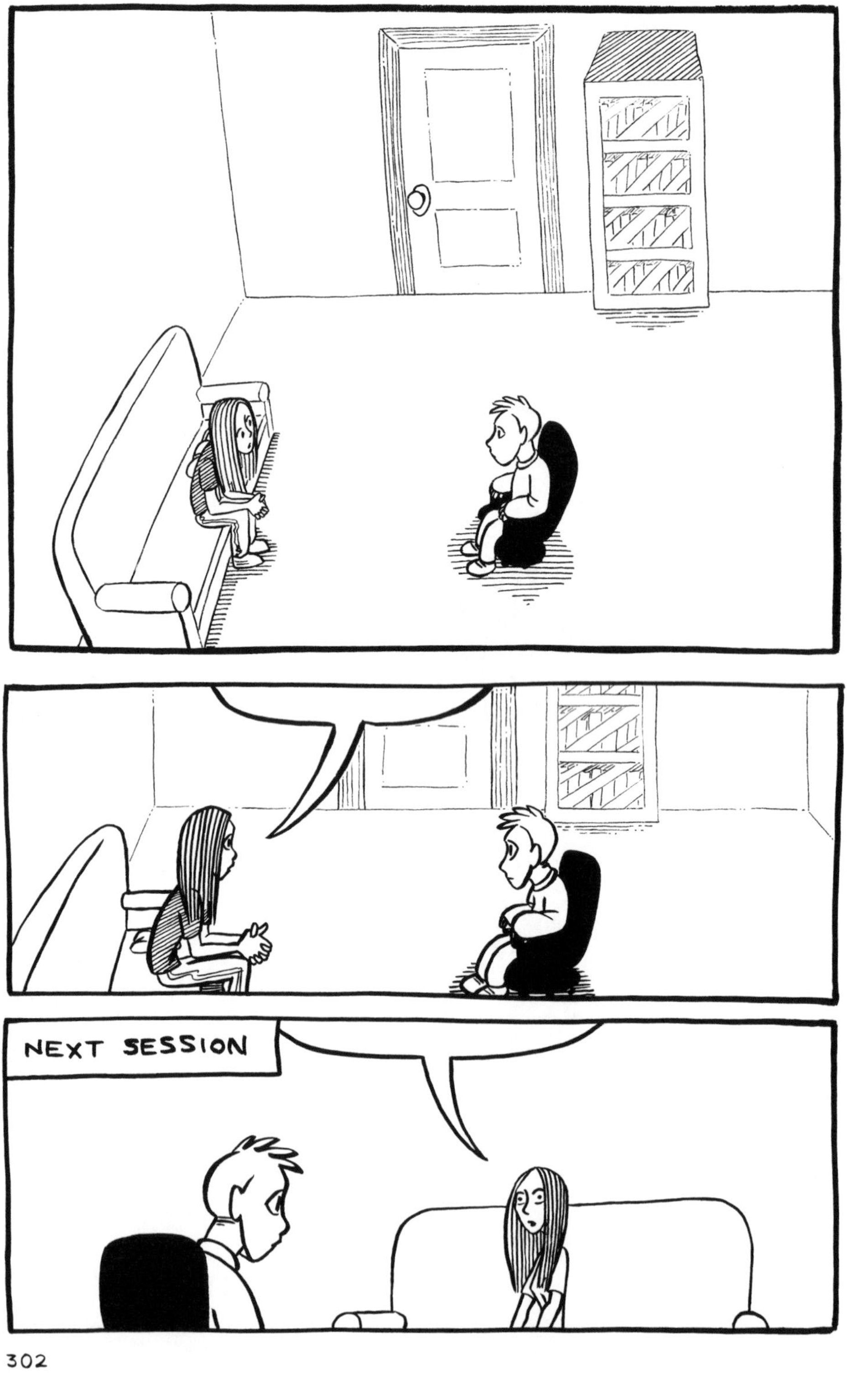
NEXT SESSION

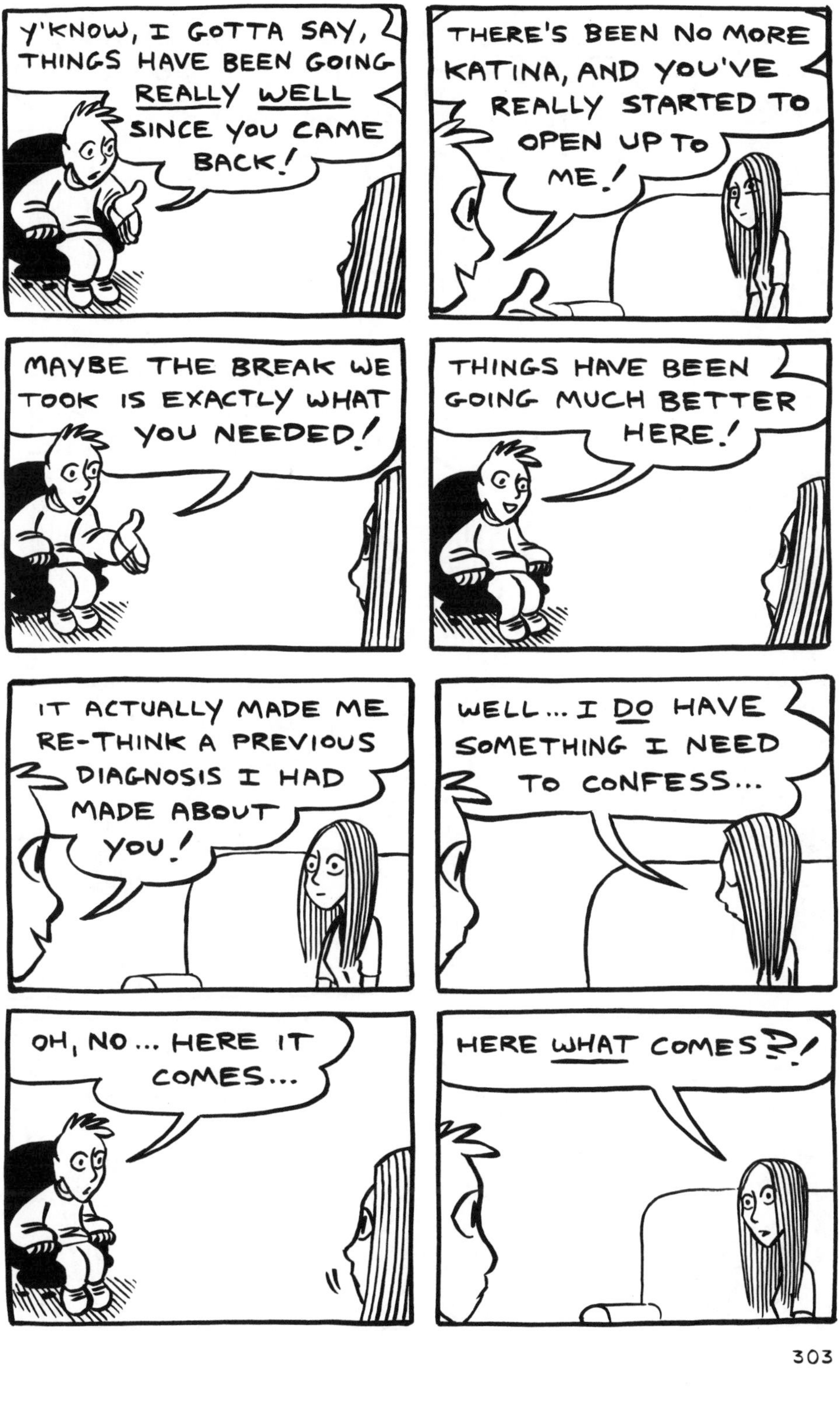
Y'KNOW, I GOTTA SAY, THINGS HAVE BEEN GOING REALLY WELL SINCE YOU CAME BACK!
THERE'S BEEN NO MORE KATINA, AND YOU'VE REALLY STARTED TO OPEN UP TO ME!
MAYBE THE BREAK WE TOOK IS EXACTLY WHAT YOU NEEDED!
THINGS HAVE BEEN GOING MUCH BETTER HERE!
IT ACTUALLY MADE ME RE-THINK A PREVIOUS DIAGNOSIS I HAD MADE ABOUT YOU!
WELL... I DO HAVE SOMETHING I NEED TO CONFESS...
OH, NO... HERE IT COMES...
HERE WHAT COMES?!

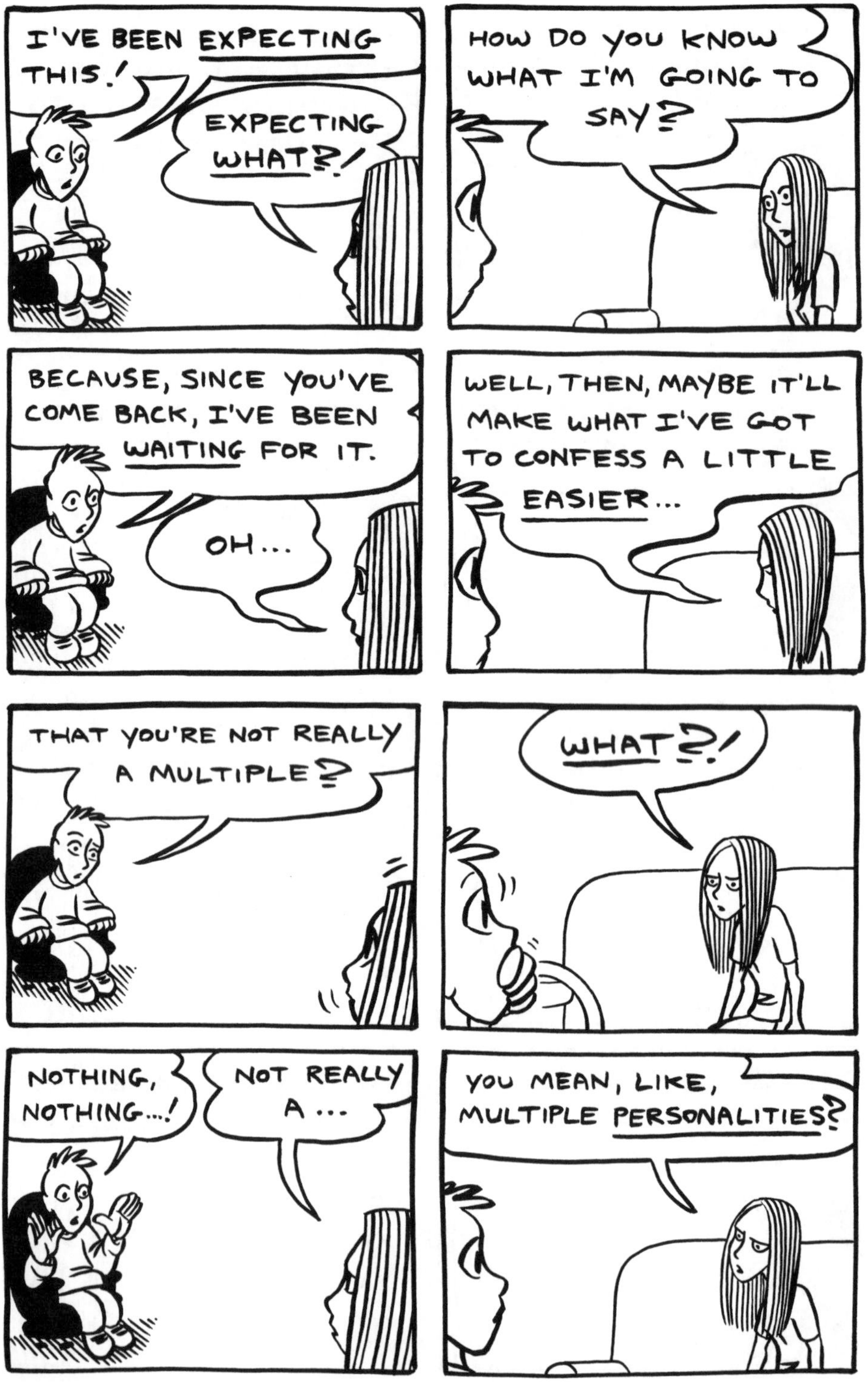
I'VE BEEN EXPECTING THIS!
EXPECTING WHAT?!
HOW DO YOU KNOW WHAT I'M GOING TO SAY?
BECAUSE, SINCE YOU'VE COME BACK, I'VE BEEN WAITING FOR IT.
OH...
WELL, THEN, MAYBE IT'LL MAKE WHAT I'VE GOT TO CONFESS A LITTLE EASIER...
THAT YOU'RE NOT REALLY A MULTIPLE?
WHAT?!
NOTHING, NOTHING...!
NOT REALLY A...
YOU MEAN, LIKE, MULTIPLE PERSONALITIES?

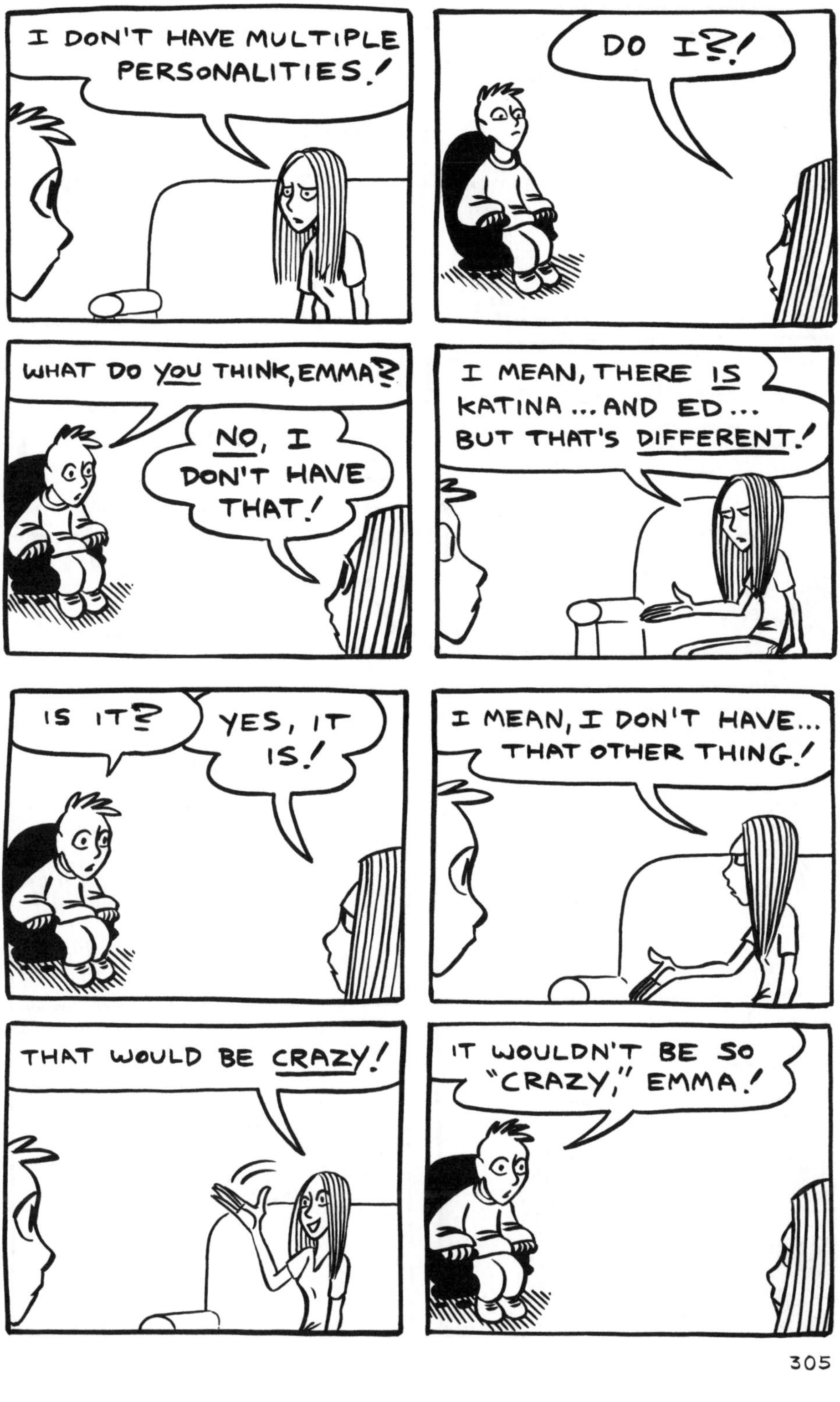

I DON'T HAVE MULTIPLE PERSONALITIES!
DO I?!
WHAT DO YOU THINK, EMMA?
NO, I DON'T HAVE THAT!
I MEAN, THERE IS KATINA ... AND ED ... BUT THAT'S DIFFERENT!
IS IT?
YES, IT IS!
I MEAN, I DON'T HAVE... THAT OTHER THING!
THAT WOULD BE CRAZY!
IT WOULDN'T BE SO "CRAZY," EMMA!

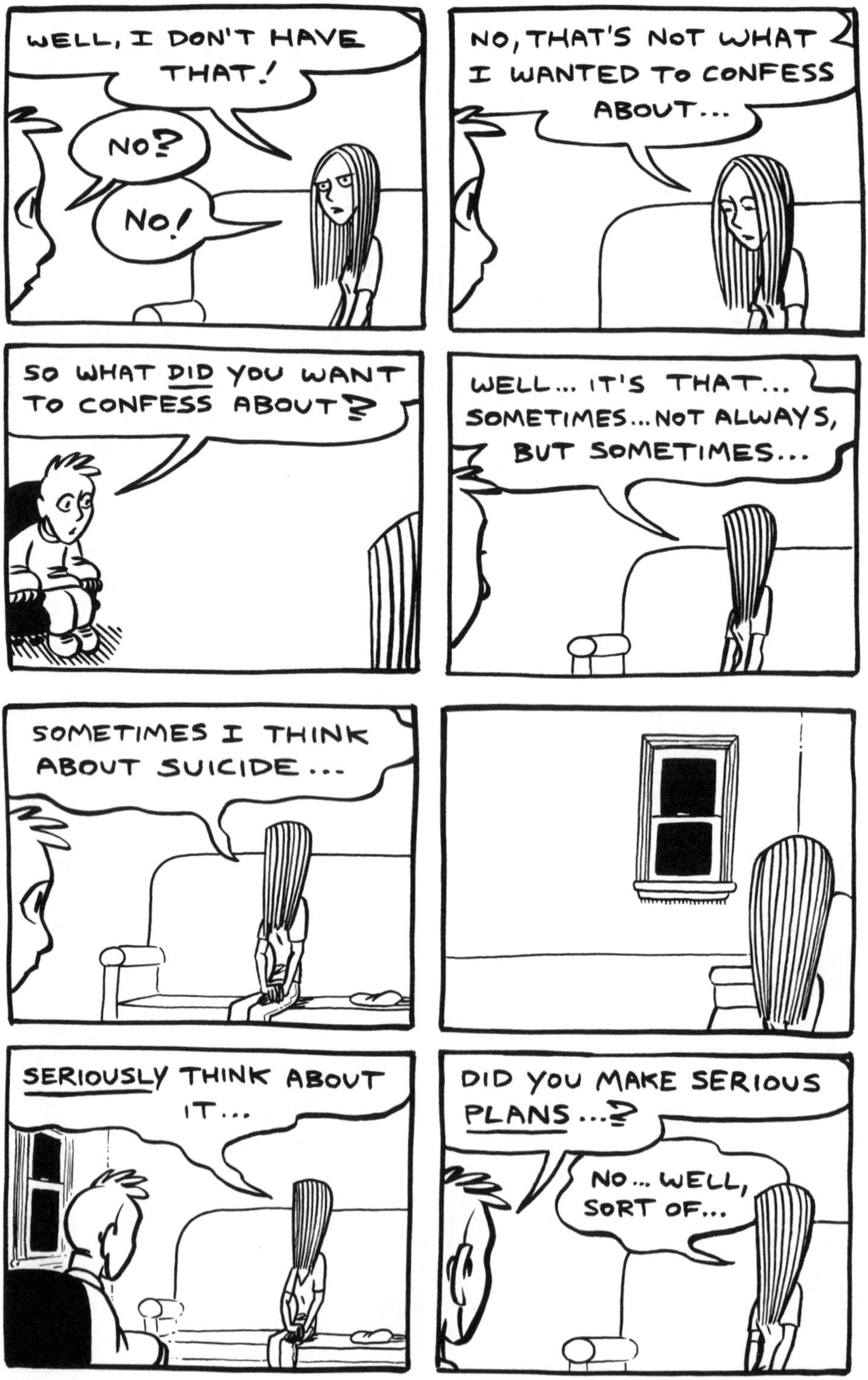
WELL, I DON'T HAVE THAT!
NO?
NO!
NO, THAT'S NOT WHAT I WANTED TO CONFESS ABOUT...
SO WHAT DID YOU WANT TO CONFESS ABOUT?
WELL... IT'S THAT... SOMETIMES... NOT ALWAYS, BUT SOMETIMES...
SOMETIMES I THINK ABOUT SUICIDE...
SERIOUSLY THINK ABOUT IT...
DID YOU MAKE SERIOUS PLANS...?
NO... WELL, SORT OF...

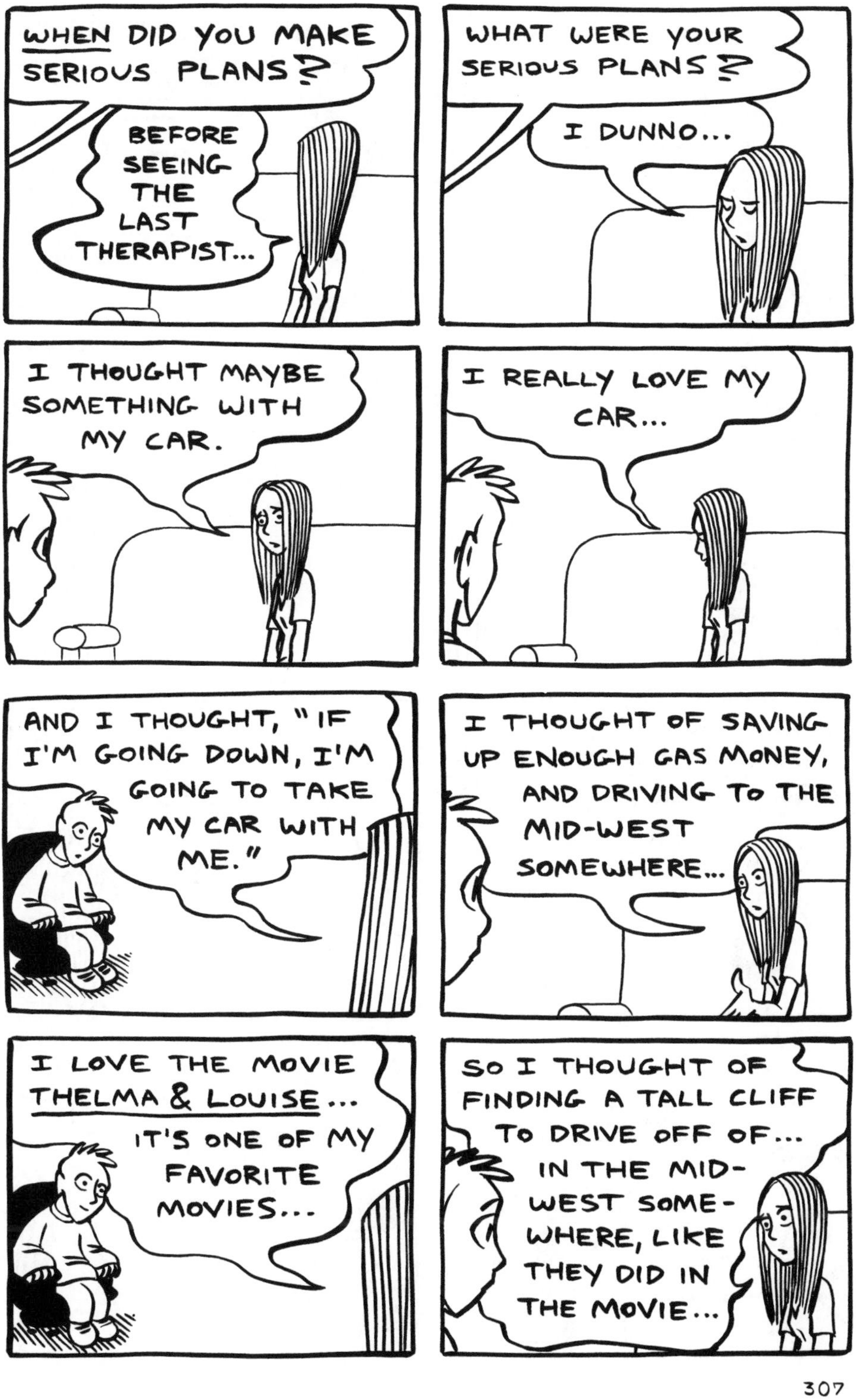
WHEN DID YOU MAKE SERIOUS PLANS?
BEFORE SEEING THE LAST THERAPIST...
WHAT WERE YOUR SERIOUS PLANS?
I DUNNO...
I THOUGHT MAYBE SOMETHING WITH MY CAR.
I REALLY LOVE MY CAR...
AND I THOUGHT, "IF I'M GOING DOWN, I'M GOING TO TAKE MY CAR WITH ME."
I THOUGHT OF SAVING UP ENOUGH GAS MONEY, AND DRIVING TO THE MID-WEST SOMEWHERE...
I LOVE THE MOVIE THELMA & LOUISE... IT'S ONE OF MY FAVORITE MOVIES...
SO I THOUGHT OF FINDING A TALL CLIFF TO DRIVE OFF OF... IN THE MID-WEST SOME-WHERE, LIKE THEY DID IN THE MOVIE...

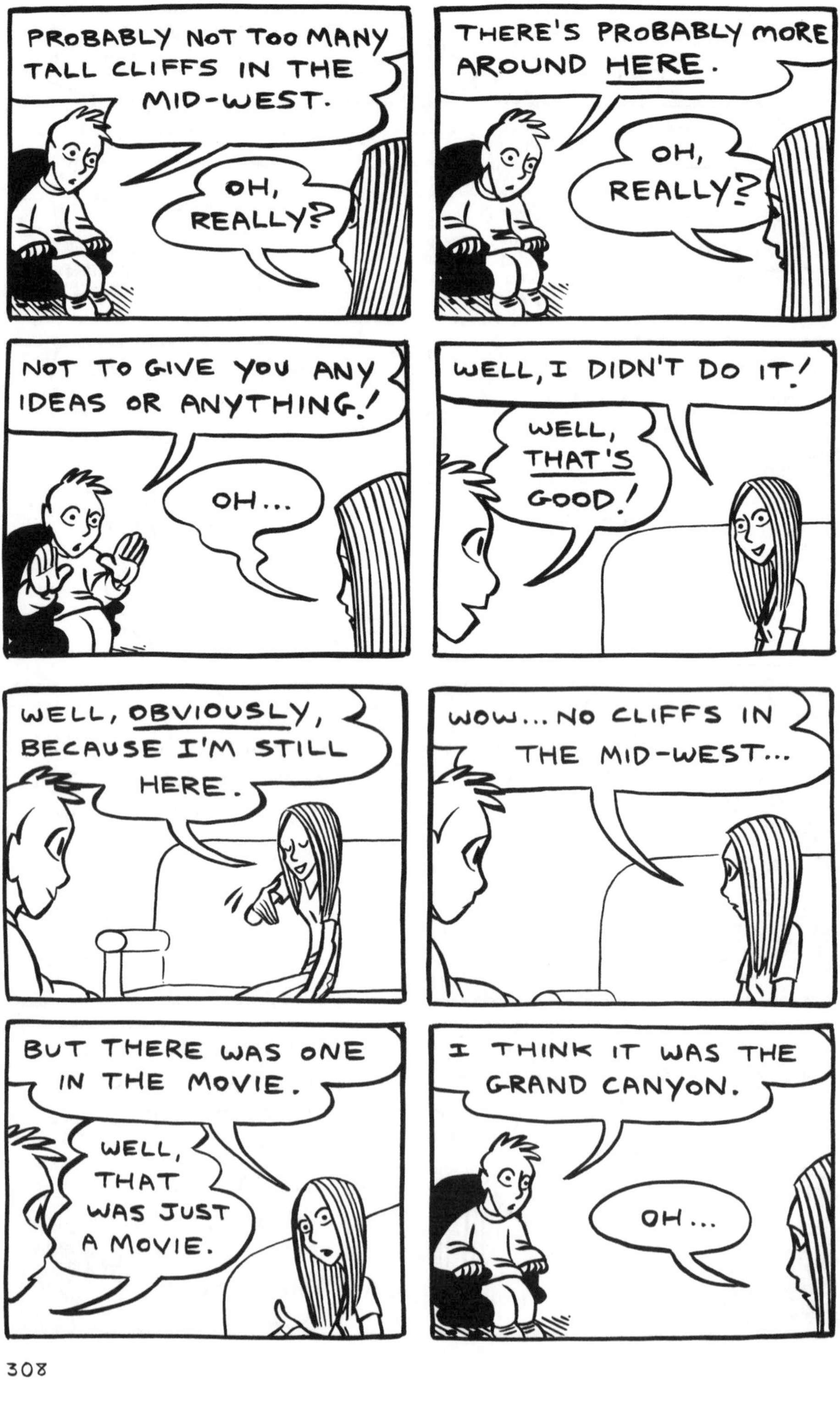
PROBABLY NOT TOO MANY TALL CLIFFS IN THE MID-WEST.
OH, REALLY?
THERE'S PROBABLY MORE AROUND HERE.
OH, REALLY?
NOT TO GIVE YOU ANY IDEAS OR ANYTHING!
OH...
WELL, I DIDN'T DO IT!
WELL, THAT'S GOOD!
WELL, OBVIOUSLY, BECAUSE I'M STILL HERE.
WOW... NO CLIFFS IN THE MID-WEST...
BUT THERE WAS ONE IN THE MOVIE.
WELL, THAT WAS JUST A MOVIE.
I THINK IT WAS THE GRAND CANYON.
OH...

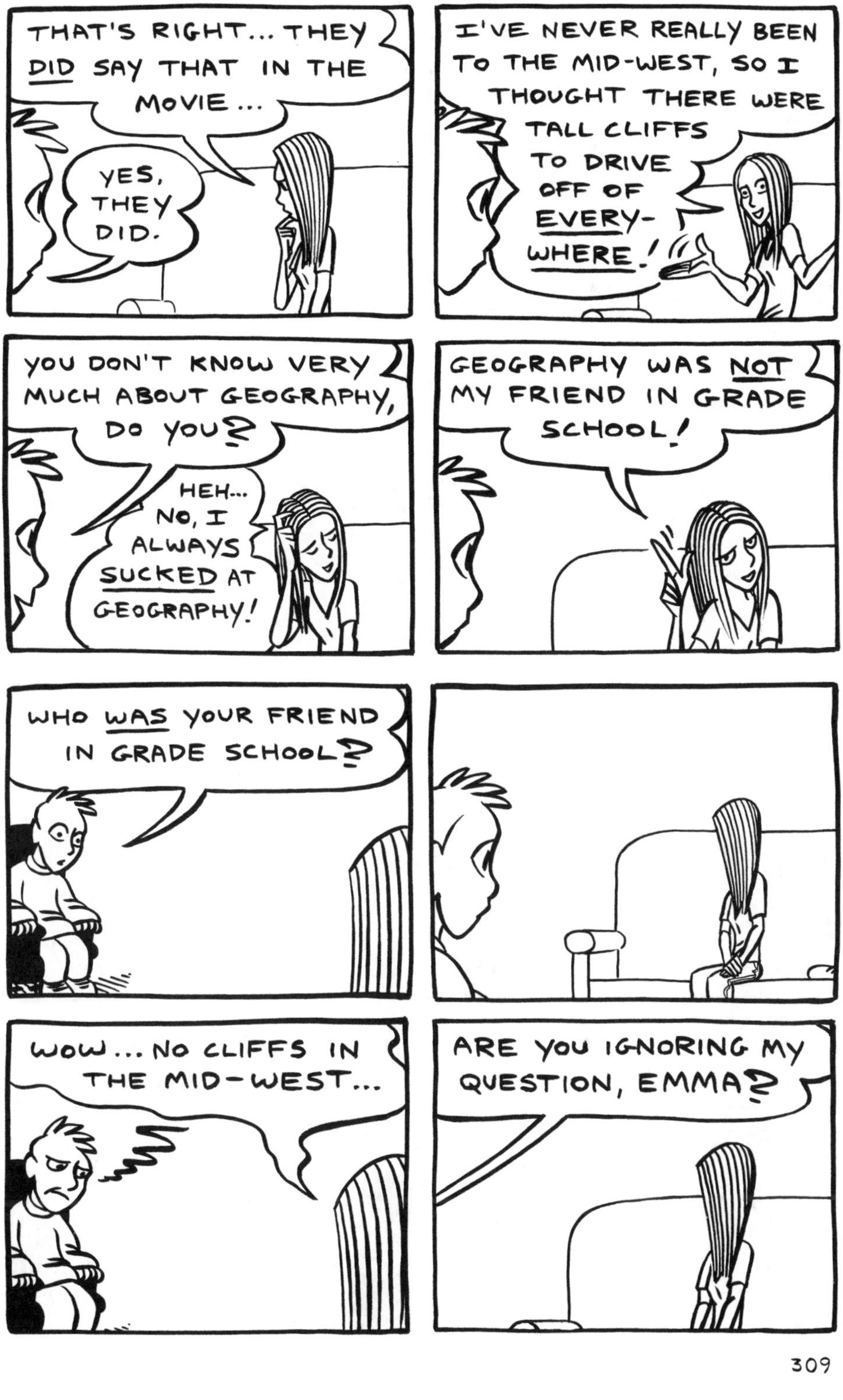
THAT'S RIGHT... THEY DID SAY THAT IN THE MOVIE...
YES, THEY DID.
I'VE NEVER REALLY BEEN TO THE MID-WEST, SO I THOUGHT THERE WERE TALL CLIFFS TO DRIVE OFF OF EVERY-WHERE!
YOU DON'T KNOW VERY MUCH ABOUT GEOGRAPHY, DO YOU?
HEH... NO, I ALWAYS SUCKED AT GEOGRAPHY!
GEOGRAPHY WAS NOT MY FRIEND IN GRADE SCHOOL!
WHO WAS YOUR FRIEND IN GRADE SCHOOL?
WOW... NO CLIFFS IN THE MID-WEST...
ARE YOU IGNORING MY QUESTION, EMMA?

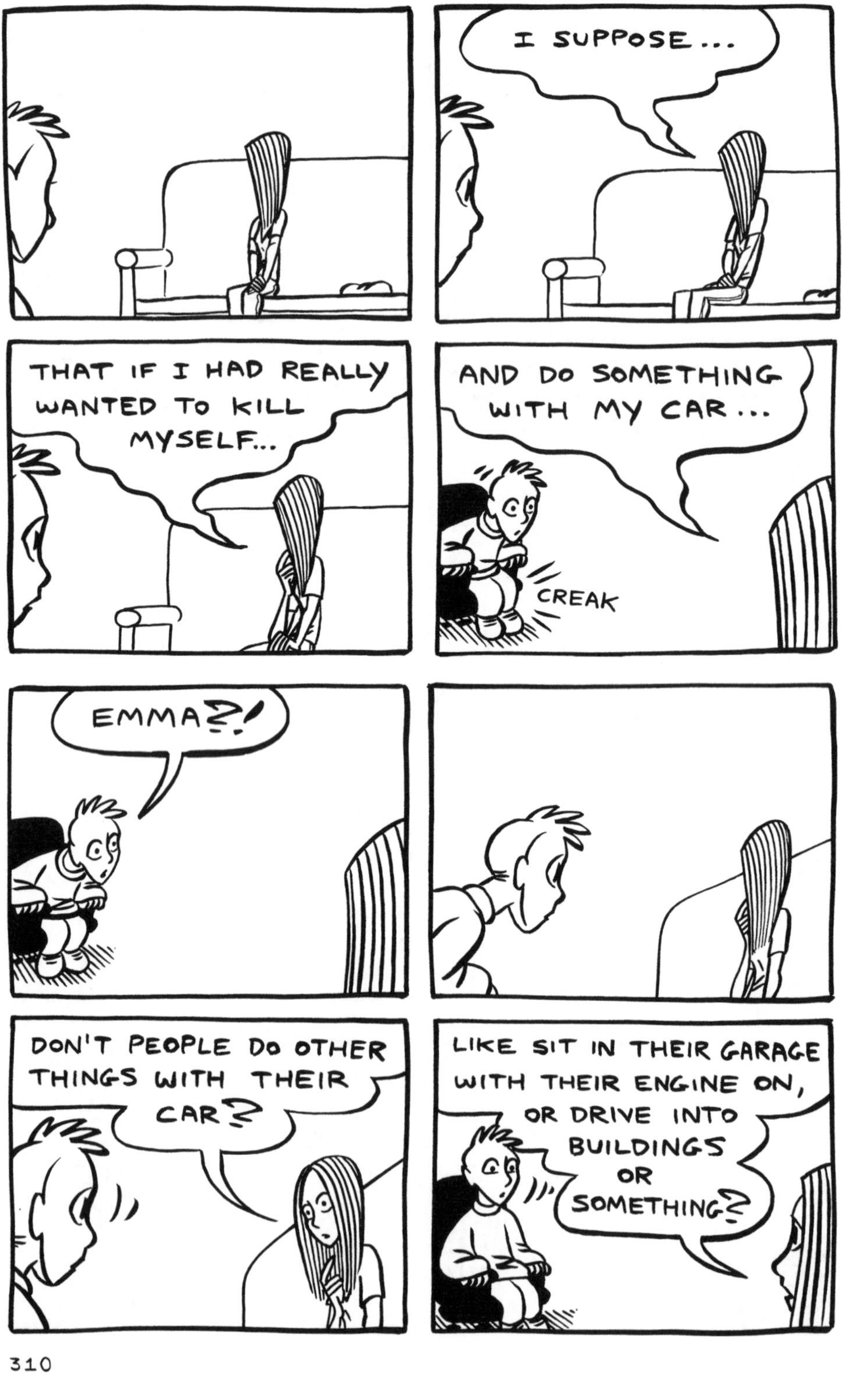
I SUPPOSE...
THAT IF I HAD REALLY WANTED TO KILL MYSELF...
AND DO SOMETHING WITH MY CAR...
CREAK
EMMA?!
DON'T PEOPLE DO OTHER THINGS WITH THEIR CAR?
LIKE SIT IN THEIR GARAGE WITH THEIR ENGINE ON, OR DRIVE INTO BUILDINGS OR SOMETHING?

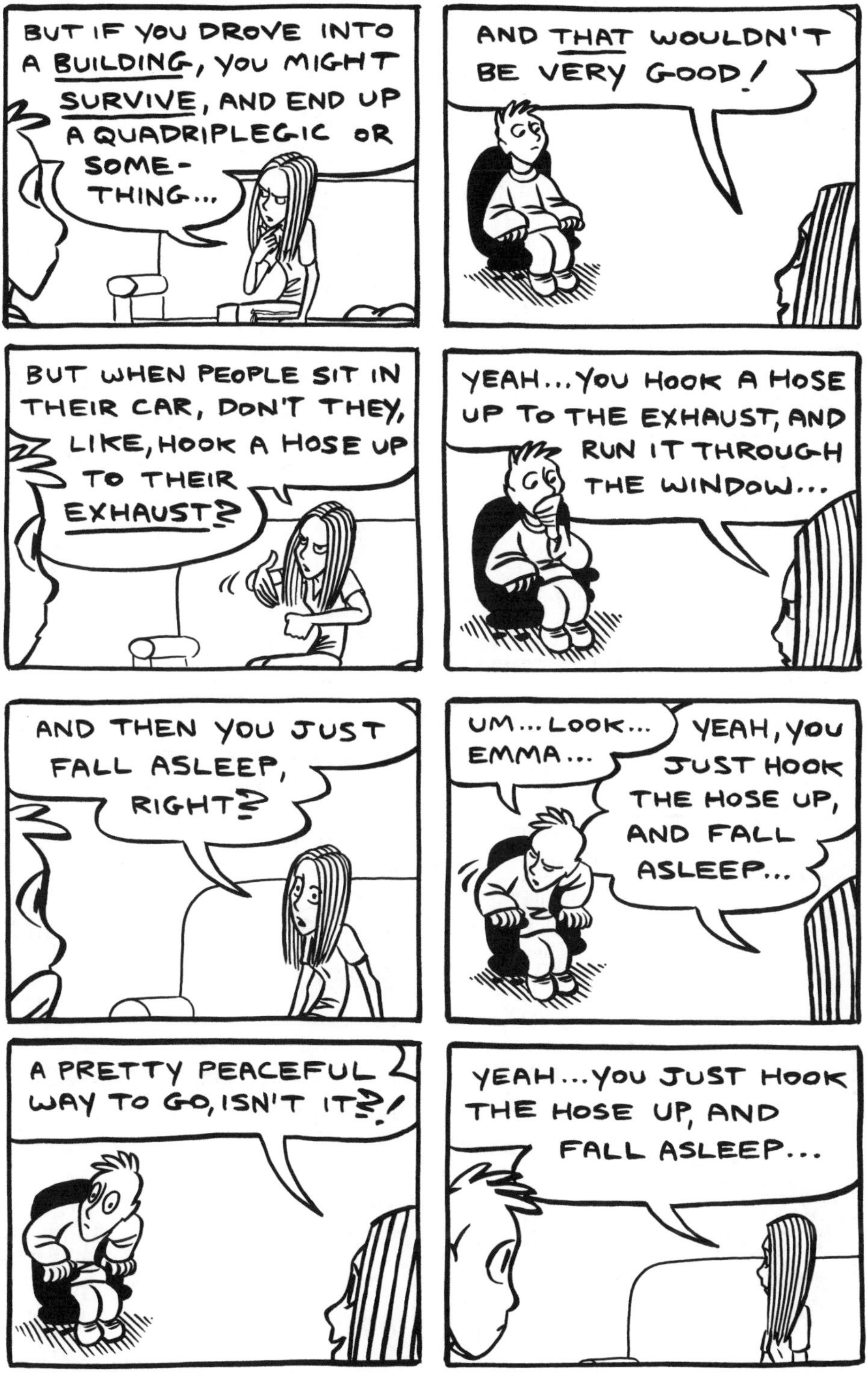
BUT IF YOU DROVE INTO A BUILDING, YOU MIGHT SURVIVE, AND END UP A QUADRIPLEGIC OR SOME-THING...
AND THAT WOULDN'T BE VERY GOOD!
BUT WHEN PEOPLE SIT IN THEIR CAR, DON'T THEY, LIKE, HOOK A HOSE UP TO THEIR EXHAUST?
YEAH...YOU HOOK A HOSE UP TO THE EXHAUST, AND RUN IT THROUGH THE WINDOW...
AND THEN YOU JUST FALL ASLEEP, RIGHT?
UM...LOOK... EMMA...
YEAH, YOU JUST HOOK THE HOSE UP, AND FALL ASLEEP...
A PRETTY PEACEFUL WAY TO GO, ISN'T IT?!
YEAH...YOU JUST HOOK THE HOSE UP, AND FALL ASLEEP...

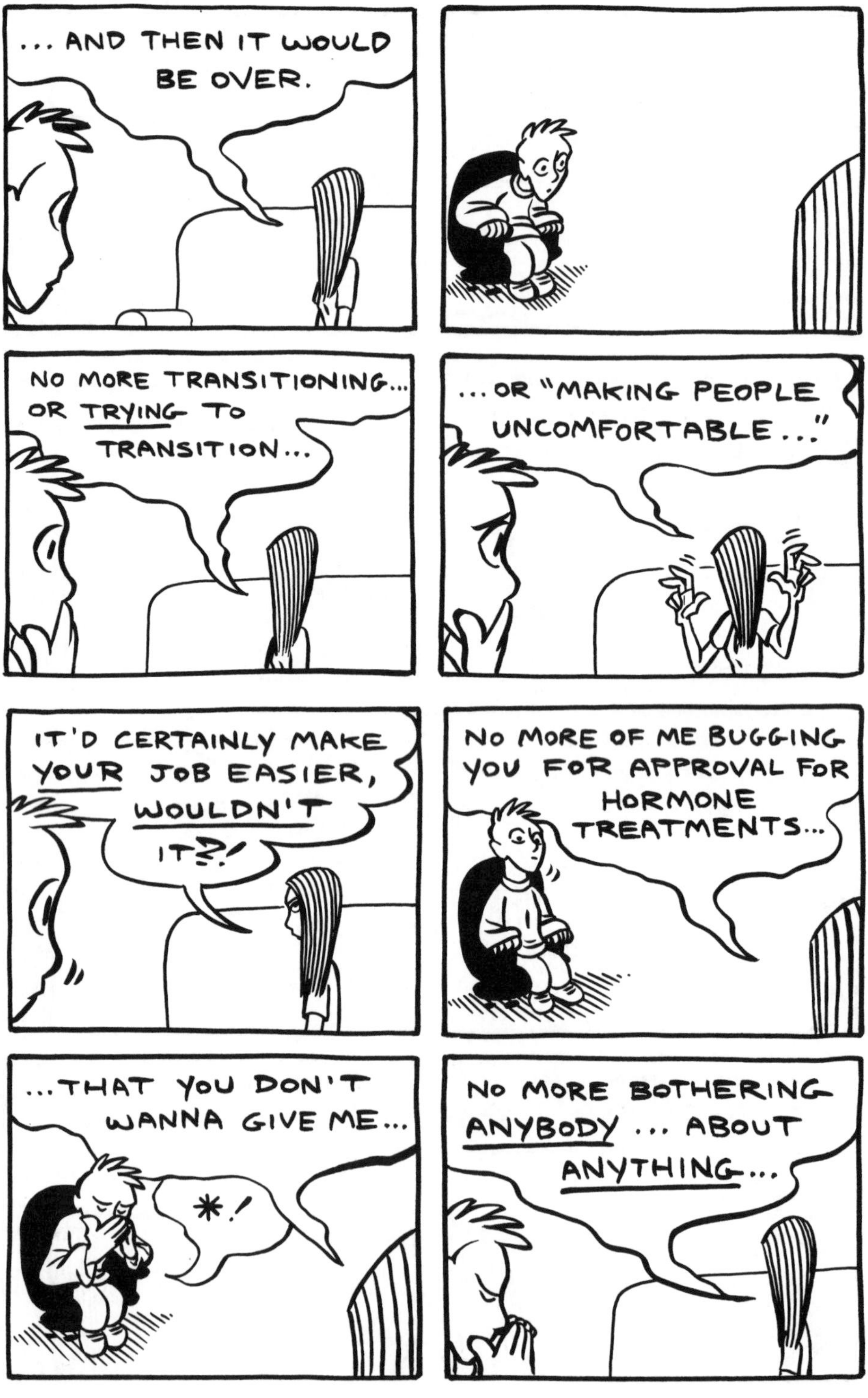
... AND THEN IT WOULD BE OVER.
NO MORE TRANSITIONING... OR TRYING TO TRANSITION...
... OR "MAKING PEOPLE UNCOMFORTABLE..."
IT'D CERTAINLY MAKE YOUR JOB EASIER, WOULDN'T IT?!
NO MORE OF ME BUGGING YOU FOR APPROVAL FOR HORMONE TREATMENTS...
...THAT YOU DON'T WANNA GIVE ME...
*!
NO MORE BOTHERING ANYBODY ... ABOUT ANYTHING...

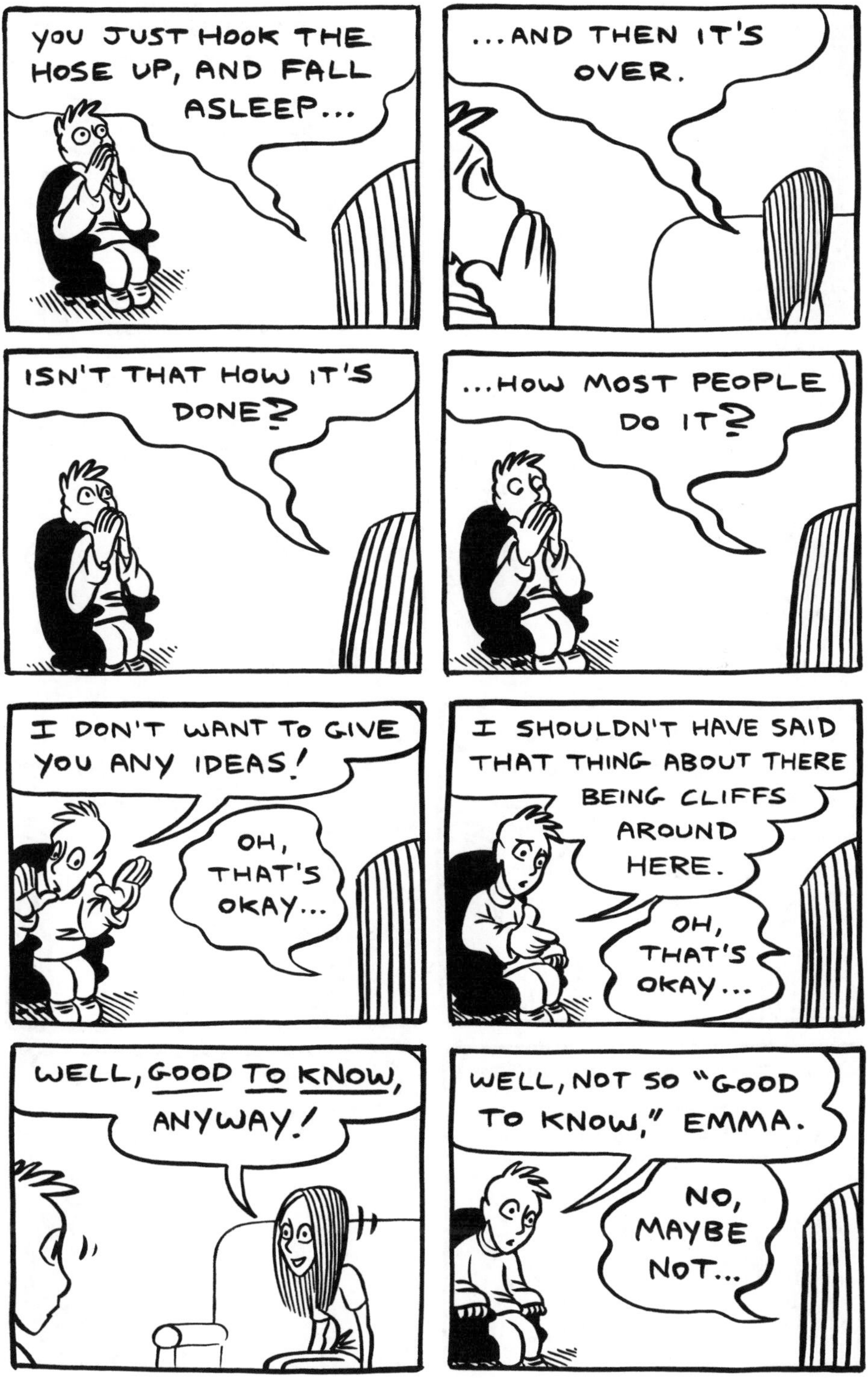
YOU JUST HOOK THE HOSE UP, AND FALL ASLEEP...
...AND THEN IT'S OVER.
ISN'T THAT HOW IT'S DONE?
...HOW MOST PEOPLE DO IT?
I DON'T WANT TO GIVE YOU ANY IDEAS!
OH, THAT'S OKAY...
I SHOULDN'T HAVE SAID THAT THING ABOUT THERE BEING CLIFFS AROUND HERE.
OH, THAT'S OKAY...
WELL, GOOD TO KNOW, ANYWAY!
WELL, NOT SO "GOOD TO KNOW," EMMA.
NO, MAYBE NOT...

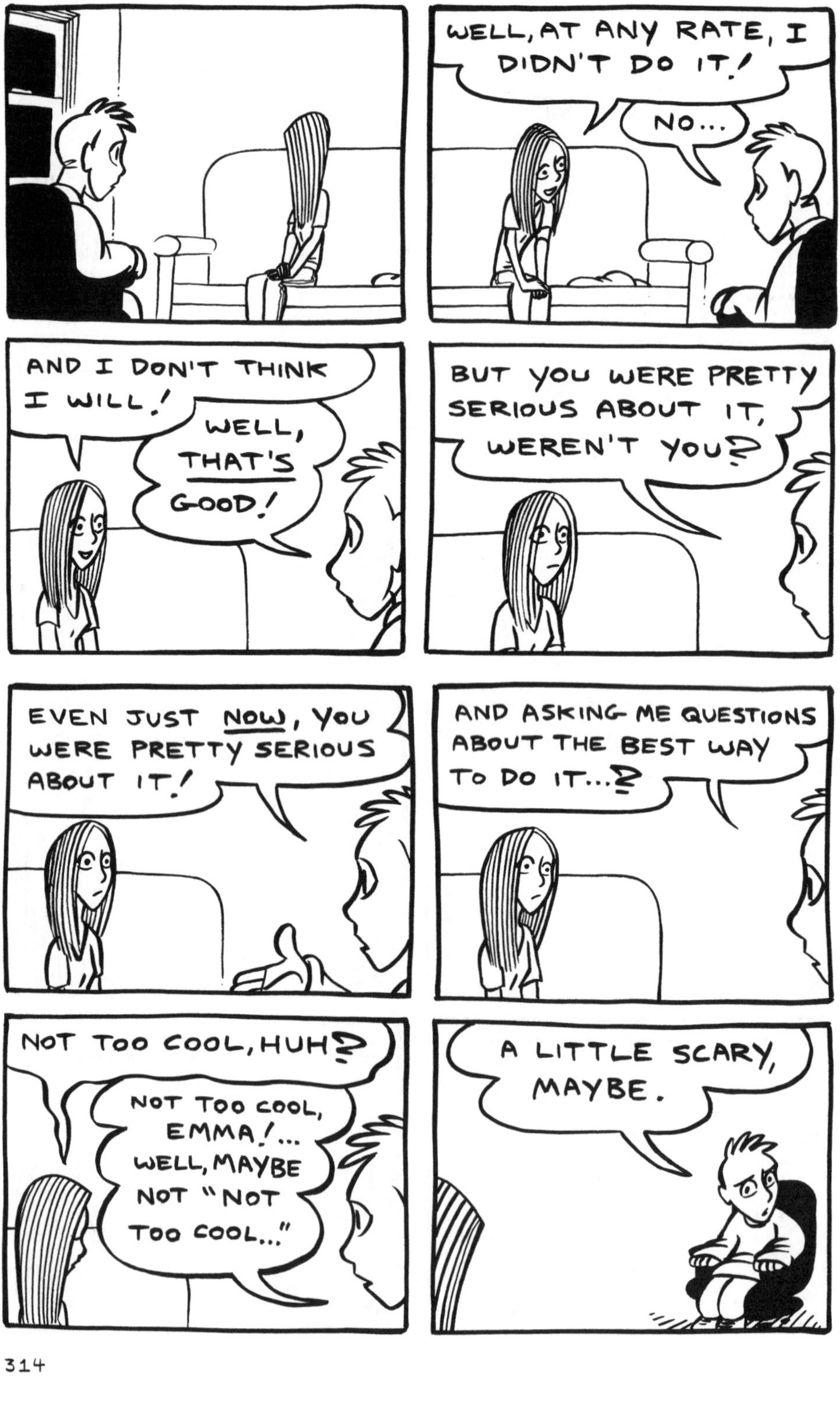

WELL, AT ANY RATE, I DIDN'T DO IT!
NO...
AND I DON'T THINK I WILL!
WELL, THAT'S GOOD!
BUT YOU WERE PRETTY SERIOUS ABOUT IT, WEREN'T YOU?
EVEN JUST NOW, YOU WERE PRETTY SERIOUS ABOUT IT!
AND ASKING ME QUESTIONS ABOUT THE BEST WAY TO DO IT...?
NOT TOO COOL, HUH?
NOT TOO COOL, EMMA!... WELL, MAYBE NOT "NOT TOO COOL..."
A LITTLE SCARY, MAYBE.

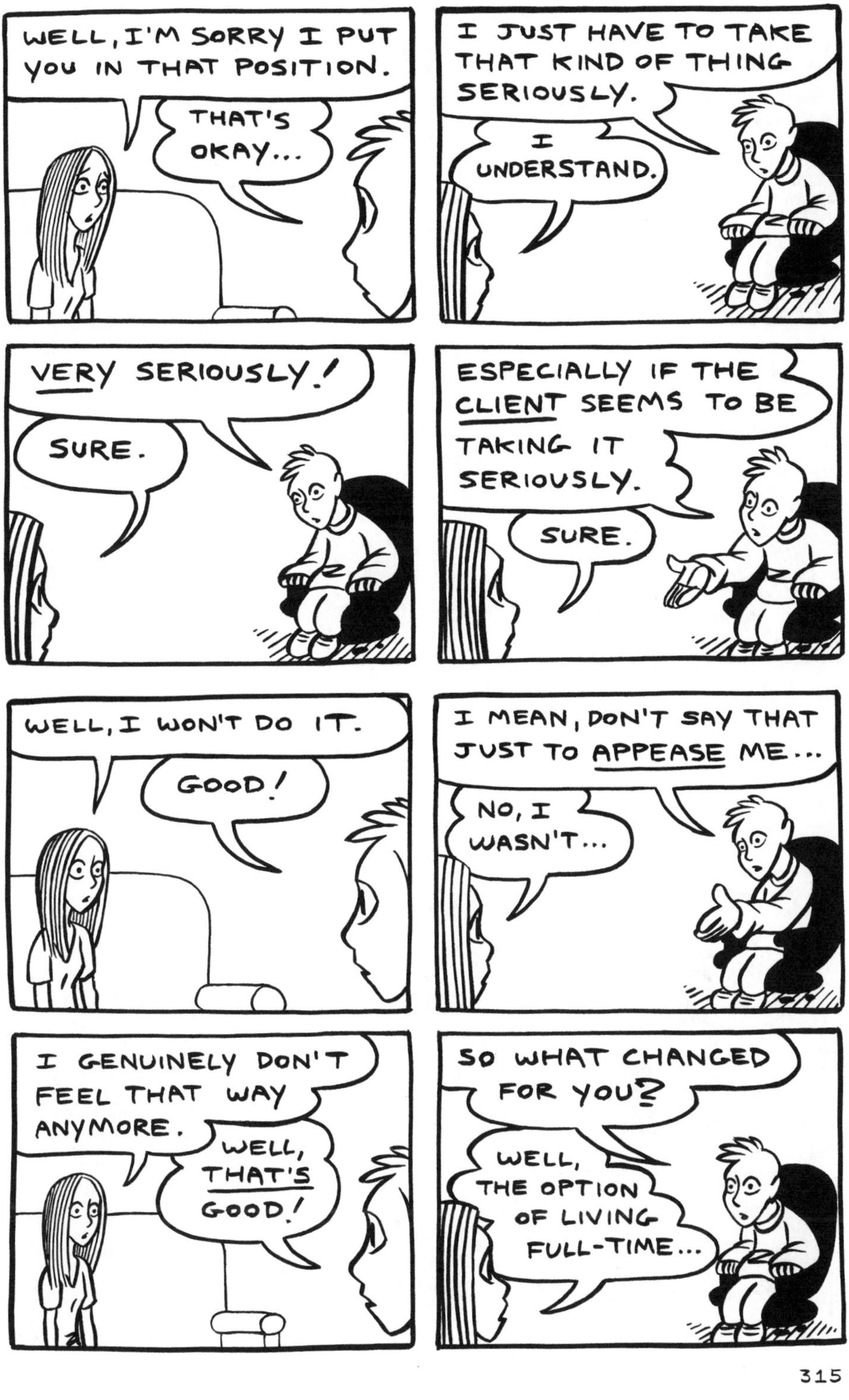

WELL, I'M SORRY I PUT YOU IN THAT POSITION.
THAT'S OKAY...
I JUST HAVE TO TAKE THAT KIND OF THING SERIOUSLY.
I UNDERSTAND.
VERY SERIOUSLY!
SURE.
ESPECIALLY IF THE CLIENT SEEMS TO BE TAKING IT SERIOUSLY.
SURE.
WELL, I WON'T DO IT.
GOOD!
I MEAN, DON'T SAY THAT JUST TO APPEASE ME...
NO, I WASN'T...
I GENUINELY DON'T FEEL THAT WAY ANYMORE.
WELL, THAT'S GOOD!
SO WHAT CHANGED FOR YOU?
WELL, THE OPTION OF LIVING FULL-TIME...

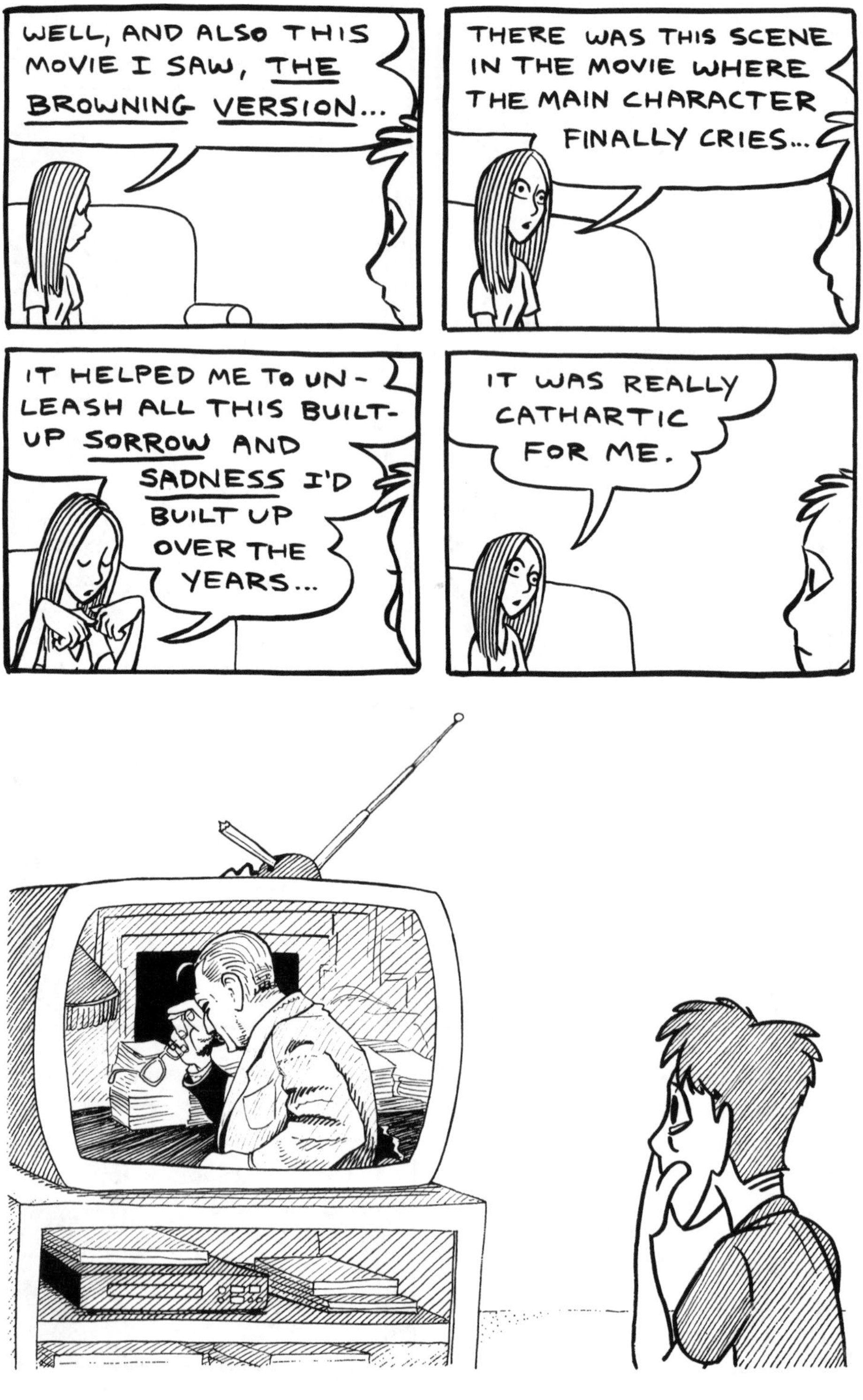
WELL, AND ALSO THIS MOVIE I SAW, THE BROWNING VERSION...
THERE WAS THIS SCENE IN THE MOVIE WHERE THE MAIN CHARACTER FINALLY CRIES...
IT HELPED ME TO UN-LEASH ALL THIS BUILT-UP SORROW AND SADNESS I'D BUILT UP OVER THE YEARS...
IT WAS REALLY CATHARTIC FOR ME.

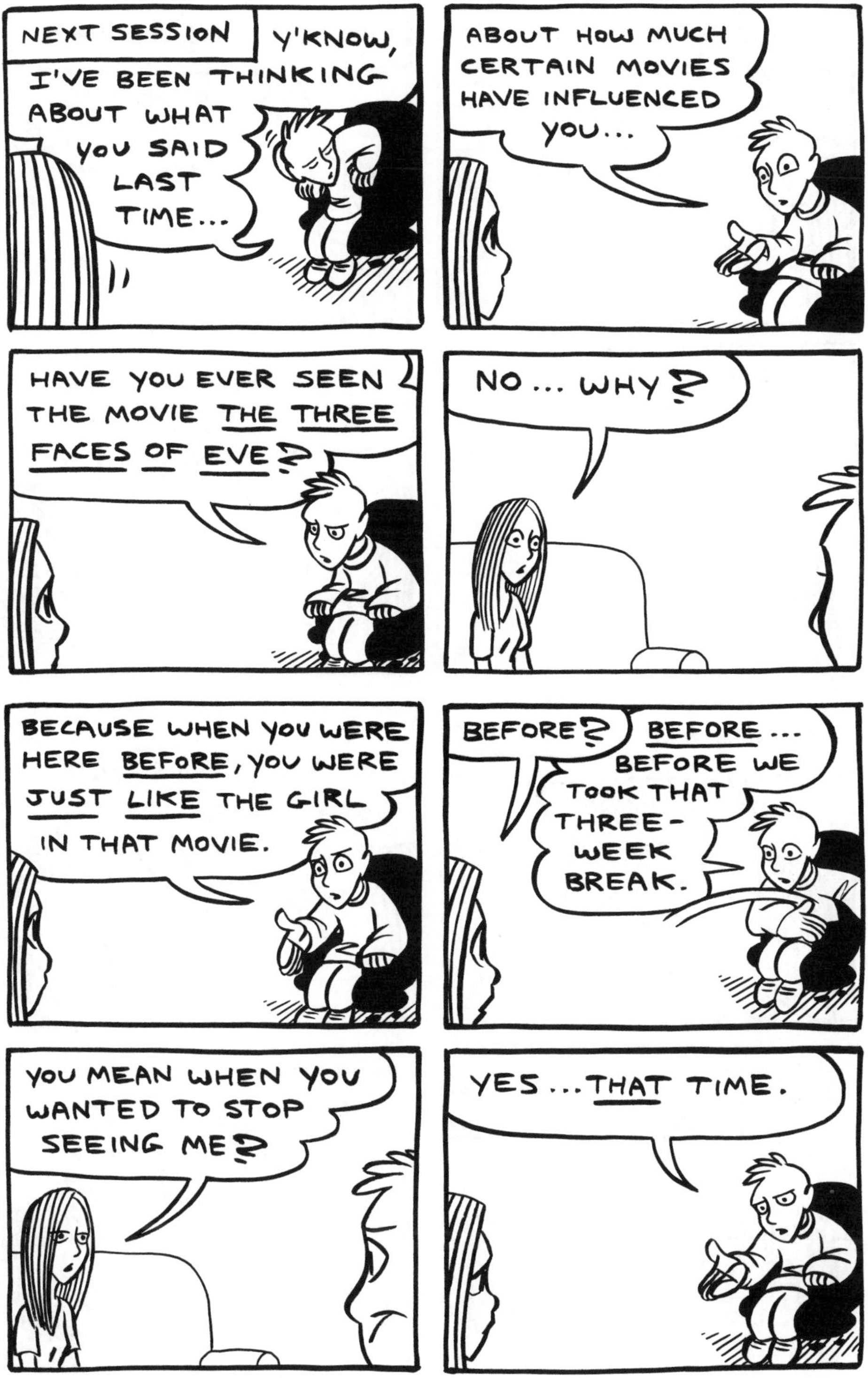
NEXT SESSION
Y'KNOW, I'VE BEEN THINKING ABOUT WHAT YOU SAID LAST TIME...
ABOUT HOW MUCH CERTAIN MOVIES HAVE INFLUENCED YOU...
HAVE YOU EVER SEEN THE MOVIE THE THREE FACES OF EVE?
NO... WHY?
BECAUSE WHEN YOU WERE HERE BEFORE, YOU WERE JUST LIKE THE GIRL IN THAT MOVIE.
BEFORE?
BEFORE... BEFORE WE TOOK THAT THREE-WEEK BREAK.
YOU MEAN WHEN YOU WANTED TO STOP SEEING ME?
YES... THAT TIME.

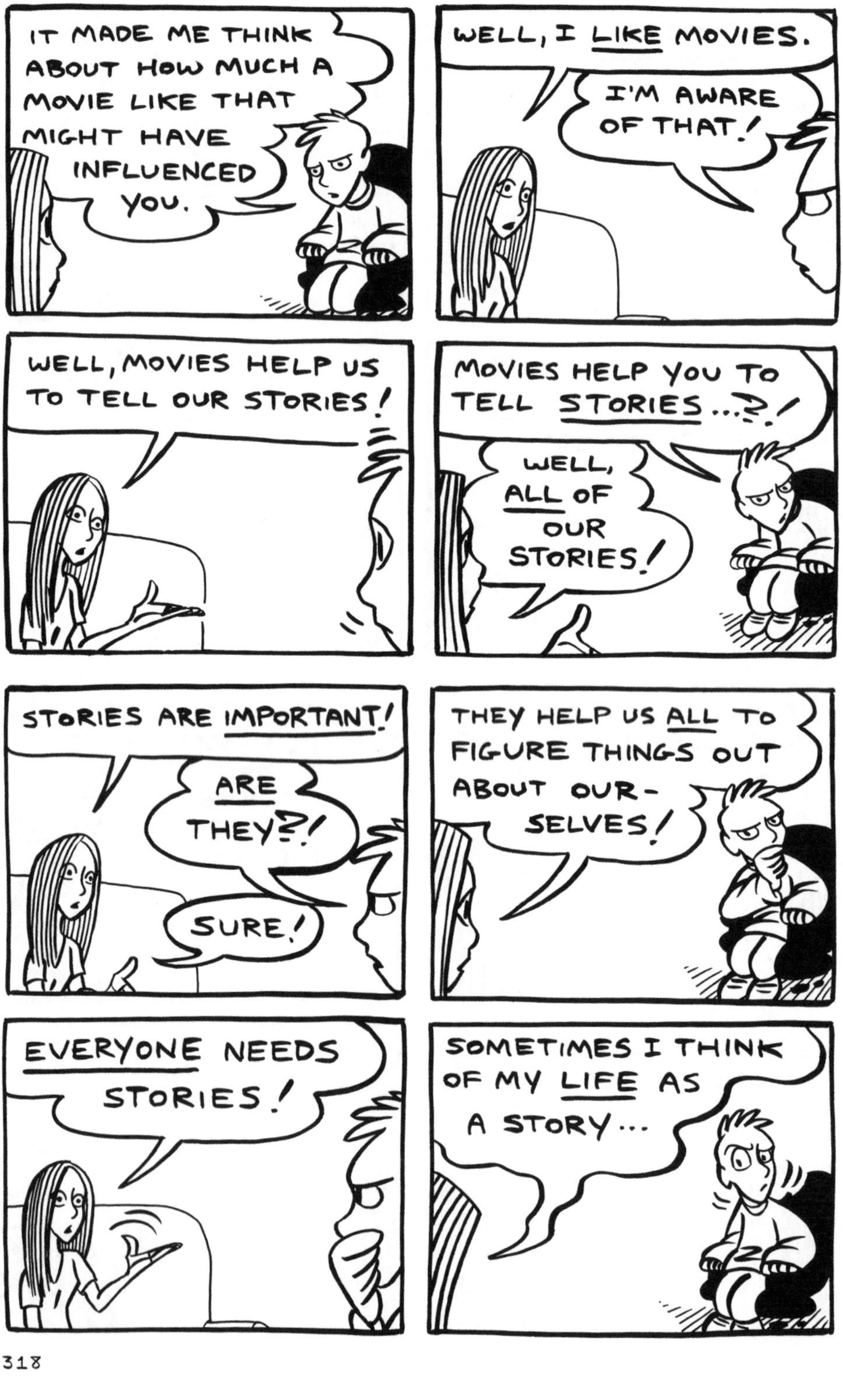
IT MADE ME THINK ABOUT HOW MUCH A MOVIE LIKE THAT MIGHT HAVE INFLUENCED YOU.
WELL, I LIKE MOVIES.
I'M AWARE OF THAT!
WELL, MOVIES HELP US TO TELL OUR STORIES!
MOVIES HELP YOU TO TELL STORIES...?!
WELL, ALL OF OUR STORIES!
STORIES ARE IMPORTANT!
ARE THEY?!
SURE!
THEY HELP US ALL TO FIGURE THINGS OUT ABOUT OUR-SELVES!
EVERYONE NEEDS STORIES!
SOMETIMES I THINK OF MY LIFE AS A STORY...

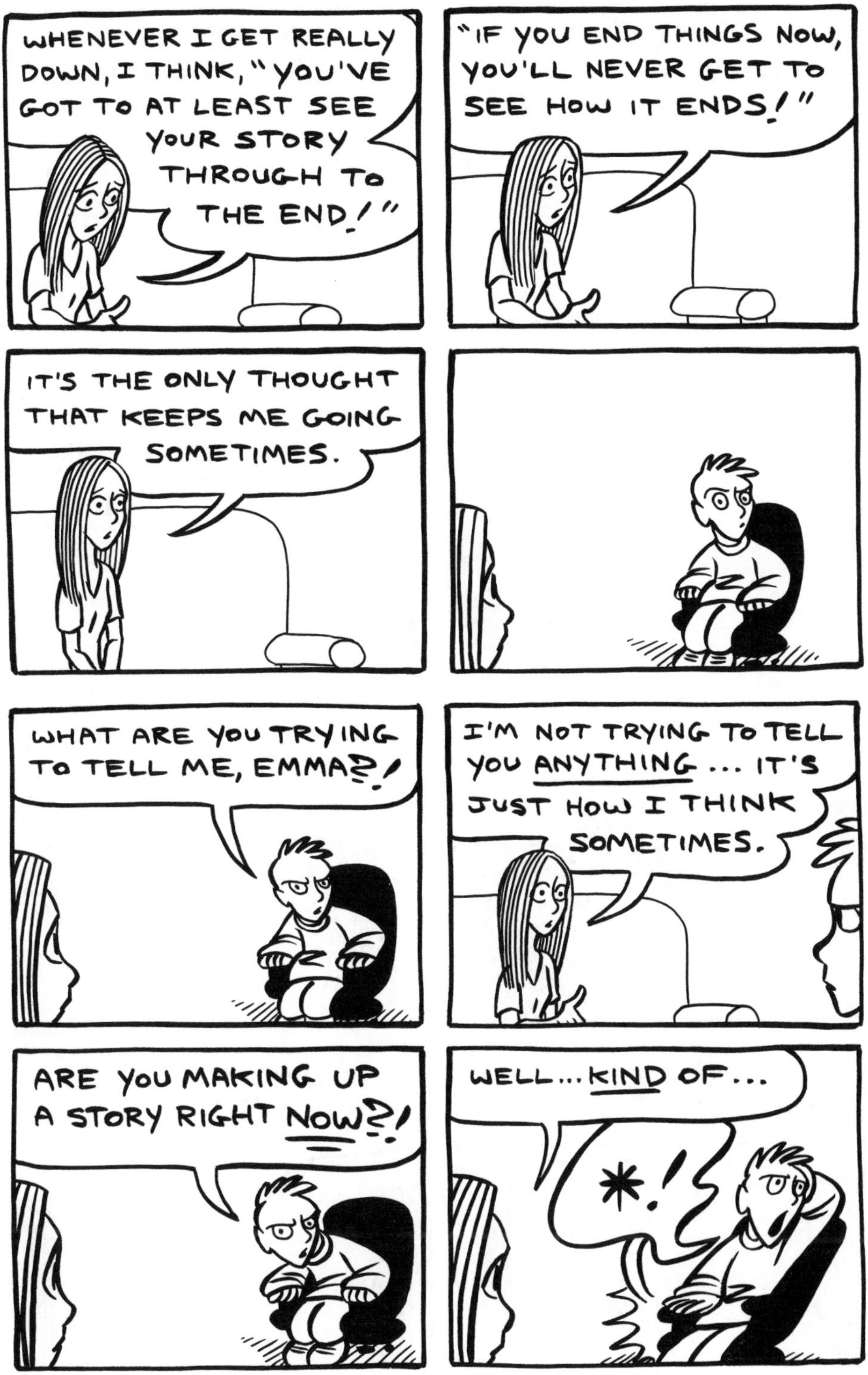
WHENEVER I GET REALLY DOWN, I THINK, "YOU'VE GOT TO AT LEAST SEE YOUR STORY THROUGH TO THE END!"
"IF YOU END THINGS NOW, YOU'LL NEVER GET TO SEE HOW IT ENDS!"
IT'S THE ONLY THOUGHT THAT KEEPS ME GOING SOMETIMES.
WHAT ARE YOU TRYING TO TELL ME, EMMA?!
I'M NOT TRYING TO TELL YOU ANYTHING ... IT'S JUST HOW I THINK SOMETIMES.
ARE YOU MAKING UP A STORY RIGHT NOW?!
WELL... KIND OF...
*!

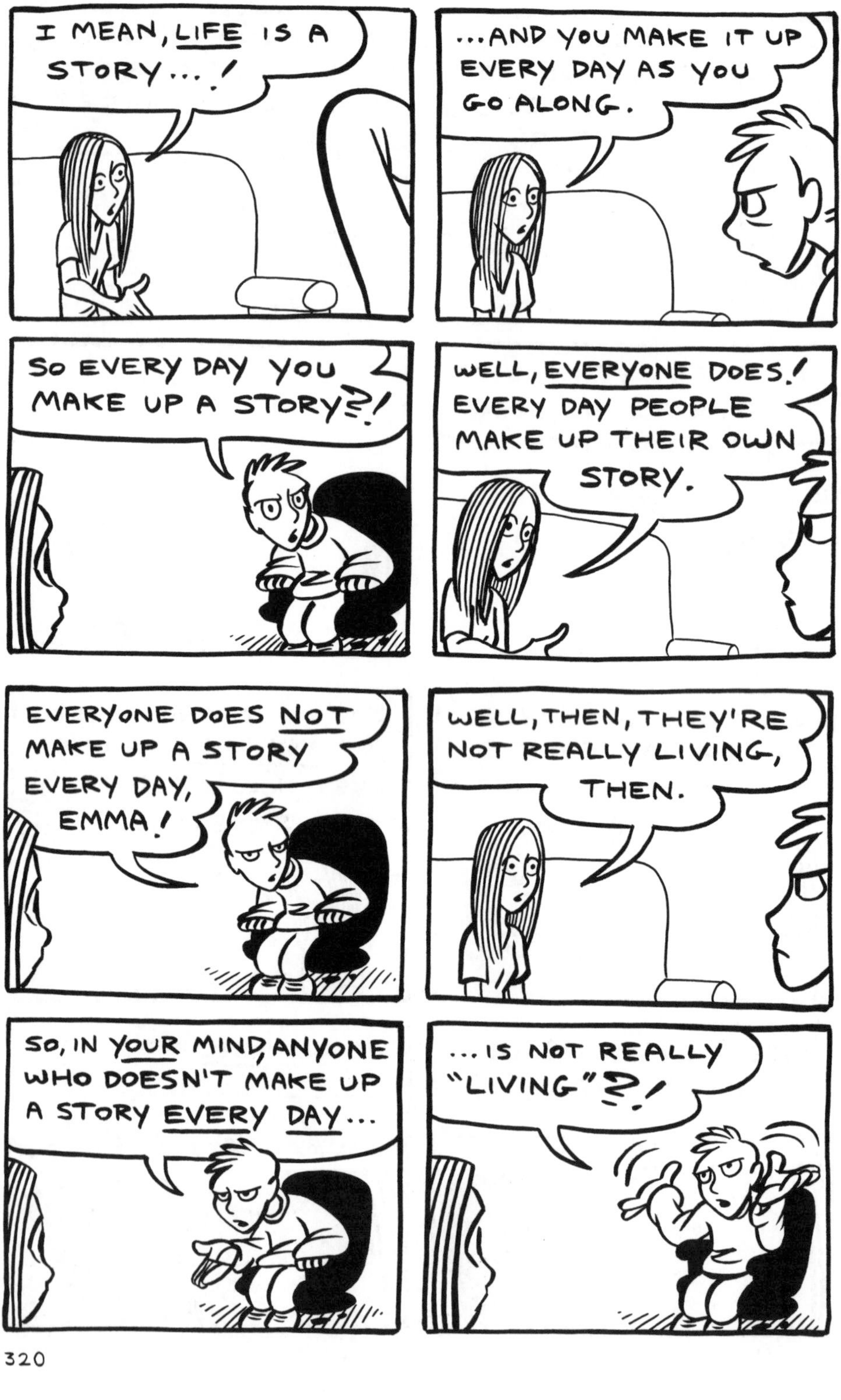
I MEAN, LIFE IS A STORY...!
...AND YOU MAKE IT UP EVERY DAY AS YOU GO ALONG.
SO EVERY DAY YOU MAKE UP A STORY?!
WELL, EVERYONE DOES! EVERY DAY PEOPLE MAKE UP THEIR OWN STORY.
EVERYONE DOES NOT MAKE UP A STORY EVERY DAY, EMMA!
WELL, THEN, THEY'RE NOT REALLY LIVING, THEN.
SO, IN YOUR MIND, ANYONE WHO DOESN'T MAKE UP A STORY EVERY DAY...
...IS NOT REALLY "LIVING"?!

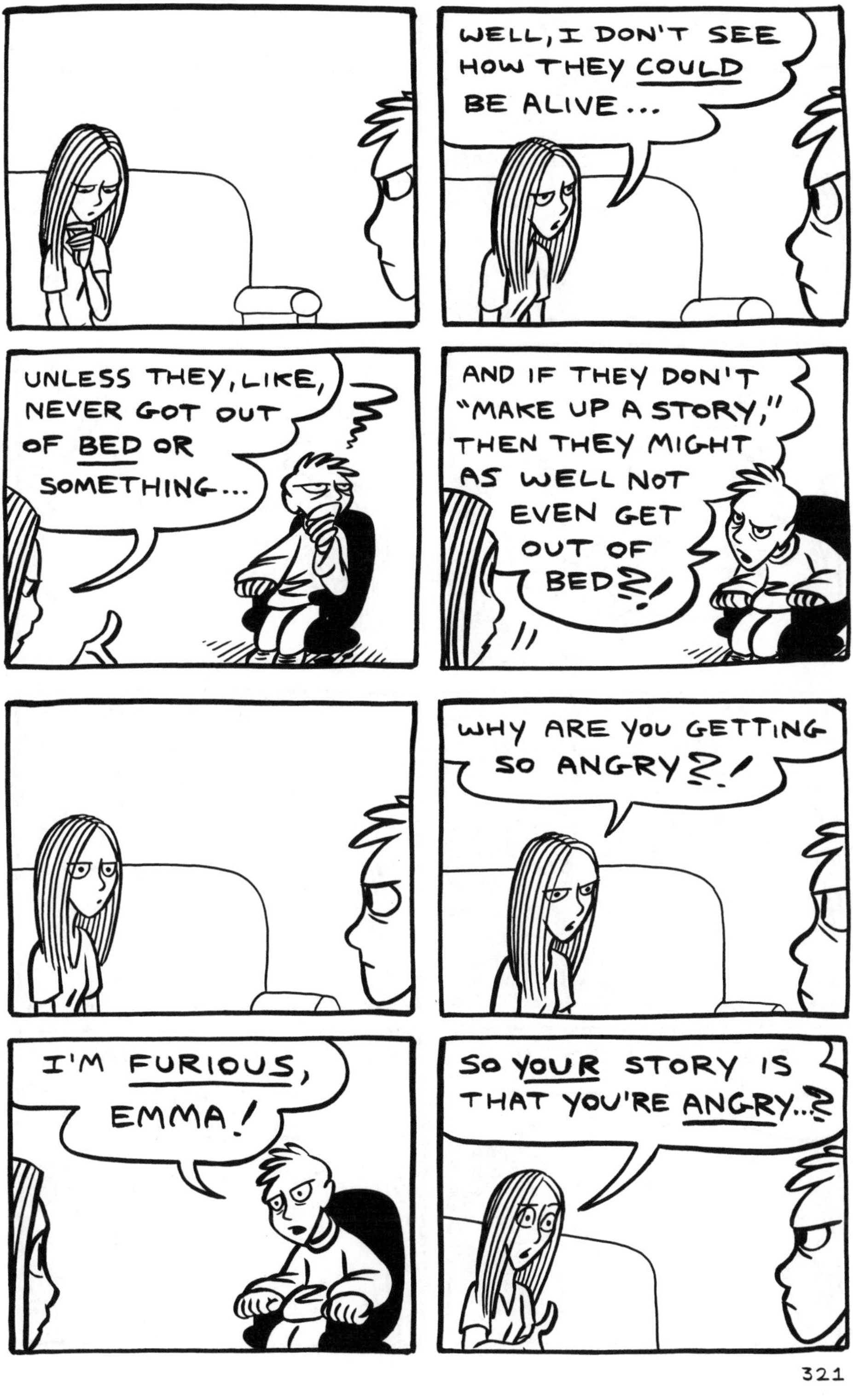
WELL, I DON'T SEE HOW THEY COULD BE ALIVE...
UNLESS THEY, LIKE, NEVER GOT OUT OF BED OR SOMETHING...
AND IF THEY DON'T "MAKE UP A STORY," THEN THEY MIGHT AS WELL NOT EVEN GET OUT OF BED?!
WHY ARE YOU GETTING SO ANGRY?!
I'M FURIOUS, EMMA!
SO YOUR STORY IS THAT YOU'RE ANGRY..?

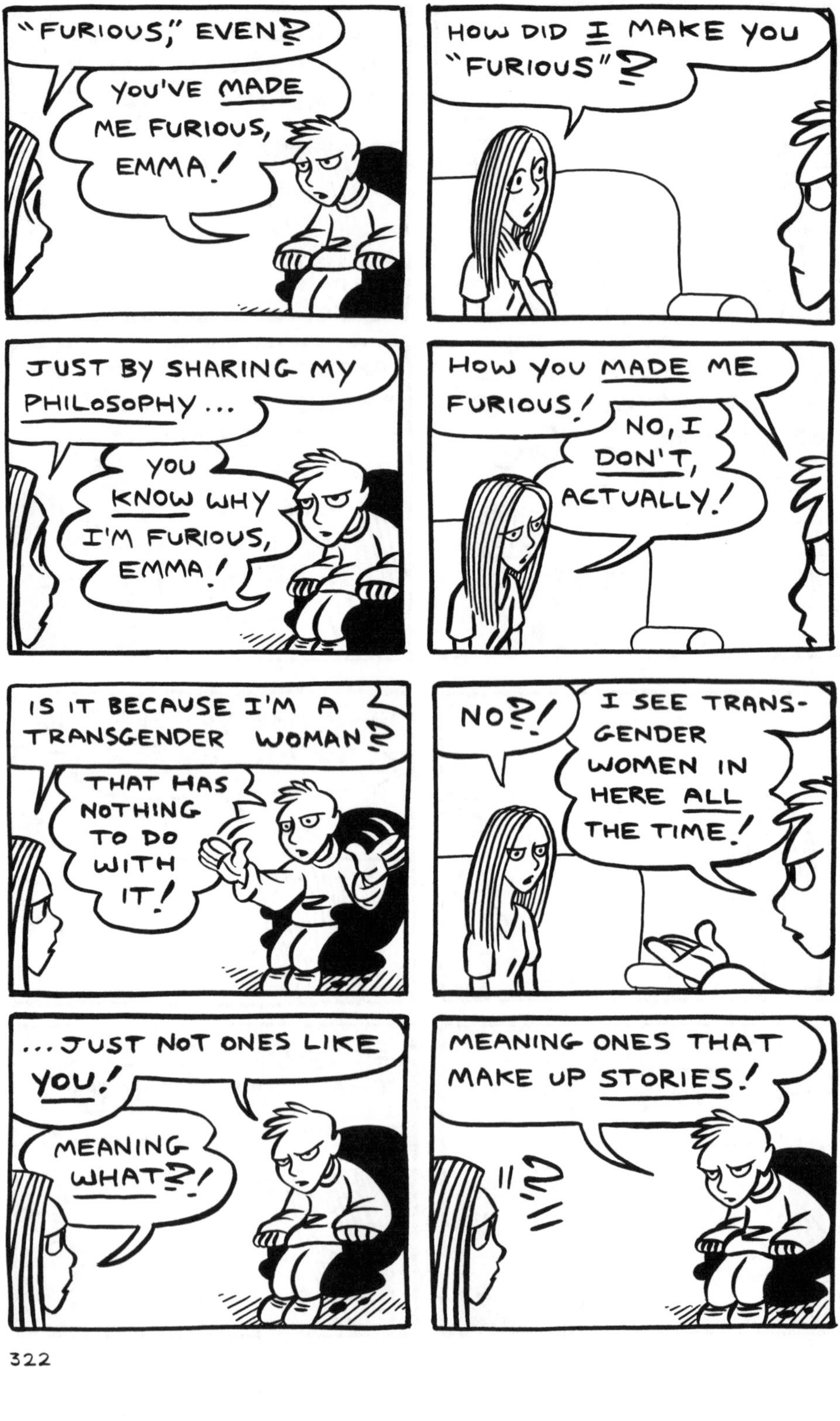
"FURIOUS," EVEN?
YOU'VE MADE ME FURIOUS, EMMA!
HOW DID I MAKE YOU "FURIOUS"?
JUST BY SHARING MY PHILOSOPHY...
YOU KNOW WHY I'M FURIOUS, EMMA!
HOW YOU MADE ME FURIOUS!
NO, I DON'T, ACTUALLY!
IS IT BECAUSE I'M A TRANSGENDER WOMAN?
THAT HAS NOTHING TO DO WITH IT!
NO?!
I SEE TRANS-GENDER WOMEN IN HERE ALL THE TIME!
...JUST NOT ONES LIKE YOU!
MEANING WHAT?!
MEANING ONES THAT MAKE UP STORIES!

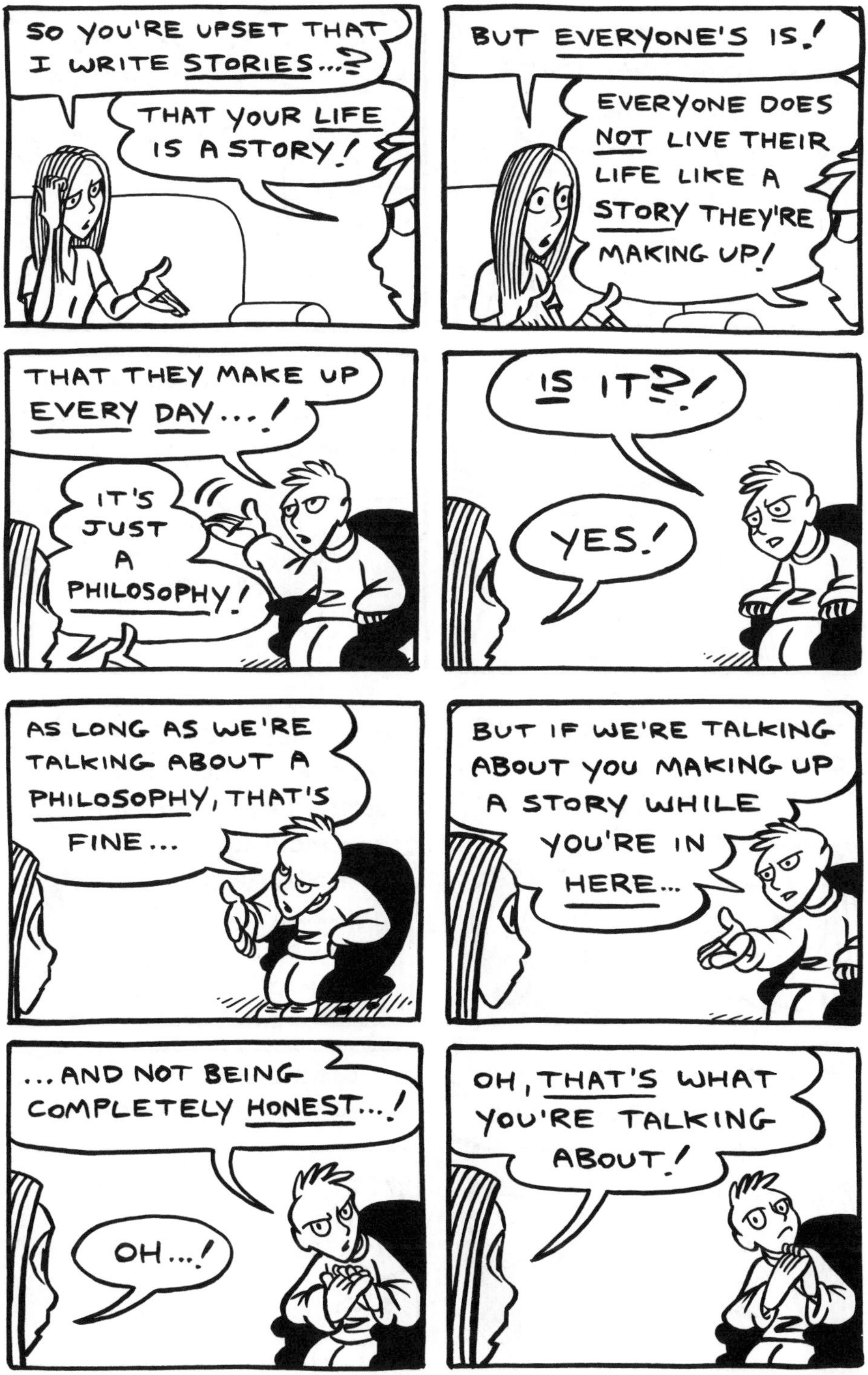
SO YOU'RE UPSET THAT I WRITE STORIES...?
THAT YOUR LIFE IS A STORY!
BUT EVERYONE'S IS!
EVERYONE DOES NOT LIVE THEIR LIFE LIKE A STORY THEY'RE MAKING UP!
THAT THEY MAKE UP EVERY DAY...!
IT'S JUST A PHILOSOPHY!
IS IT?!
YES!
AS LONG AS WE'RE TALKING ABOUT A PHILOSOPHY, THAT'S FINE...
BUT IF WE'RE TALKING ABOUT YOU MAKING UP A STORY WHILE YOU'RE IN HERE...
...AND NOT BEING COMPLETELY HONEST...!
OH...!
OH, THAT'S WHAT YOU'RE TALKING ABOUT!

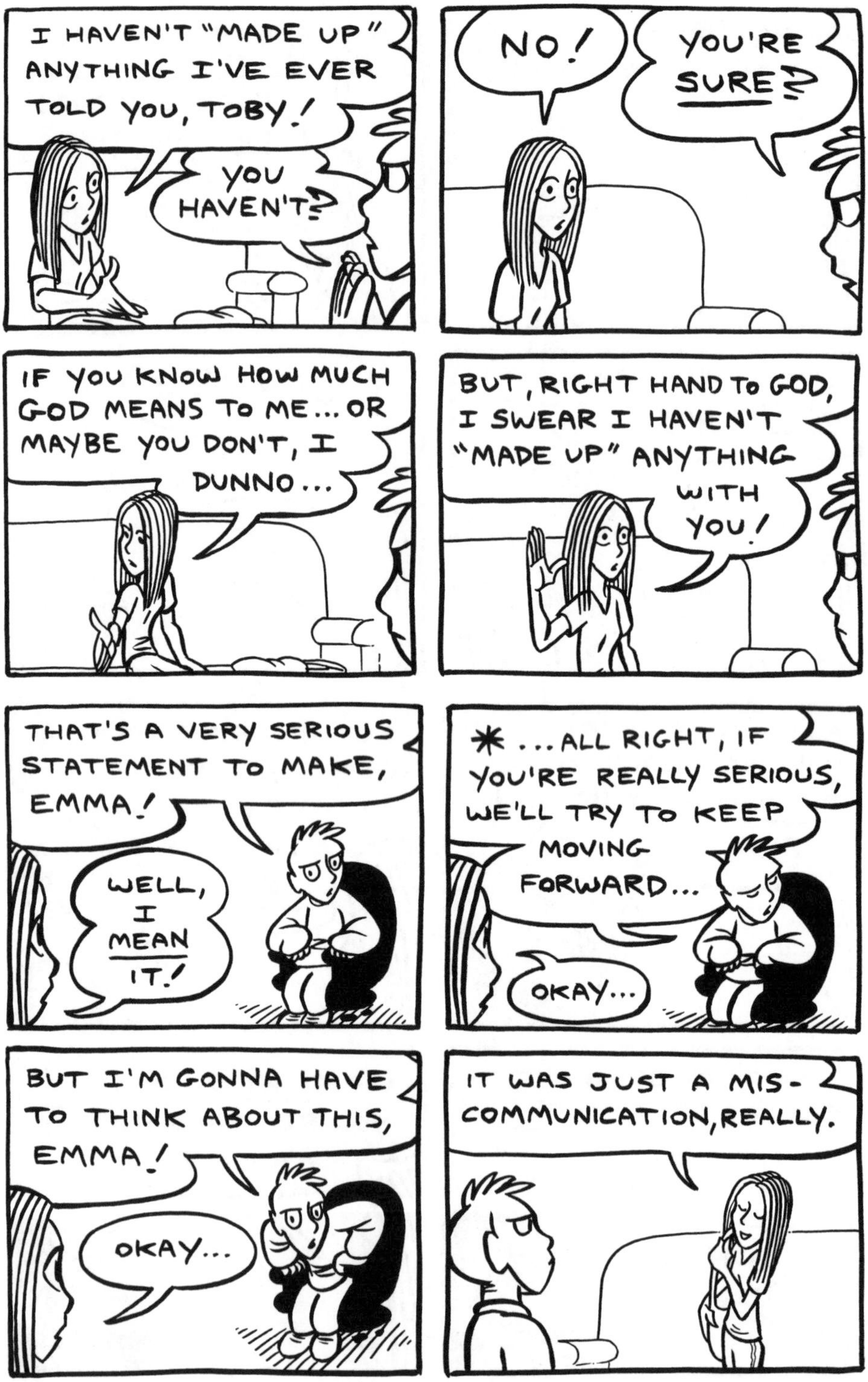
I HAVEN'T "MADE UP" ANYTHING I'VE EVER TOLD YOU, TOBY!
YOU HAVEN'T?
NO!
YOU'RE SURE?
IF YOU KNOW HOW MUCH GOD MEANS TO ME... OR MAYBE YOU DON'T, I DUNNO...
BUT, RIGHT HAND TO GOD, I SWEAR I HAVEN'T "MADE UP" ANYTHING WITH YOU!
THAT'S A VERY SERIOUS STATEMENT TO MAKE, EMMA!
WELL, I MEAN IT!
* ...ALL RIGHT, IF YOU'RE REALLY SERIOUS, WE'LL TRY TO KEEP MOVING FORWARD...
OKAY...
BUT I'M GONNA HAVE TO THINK ABOUT THIS, EMMA!
OKAY...
IT WAS JUST A MIS-COMMUNICATION, REALLY.

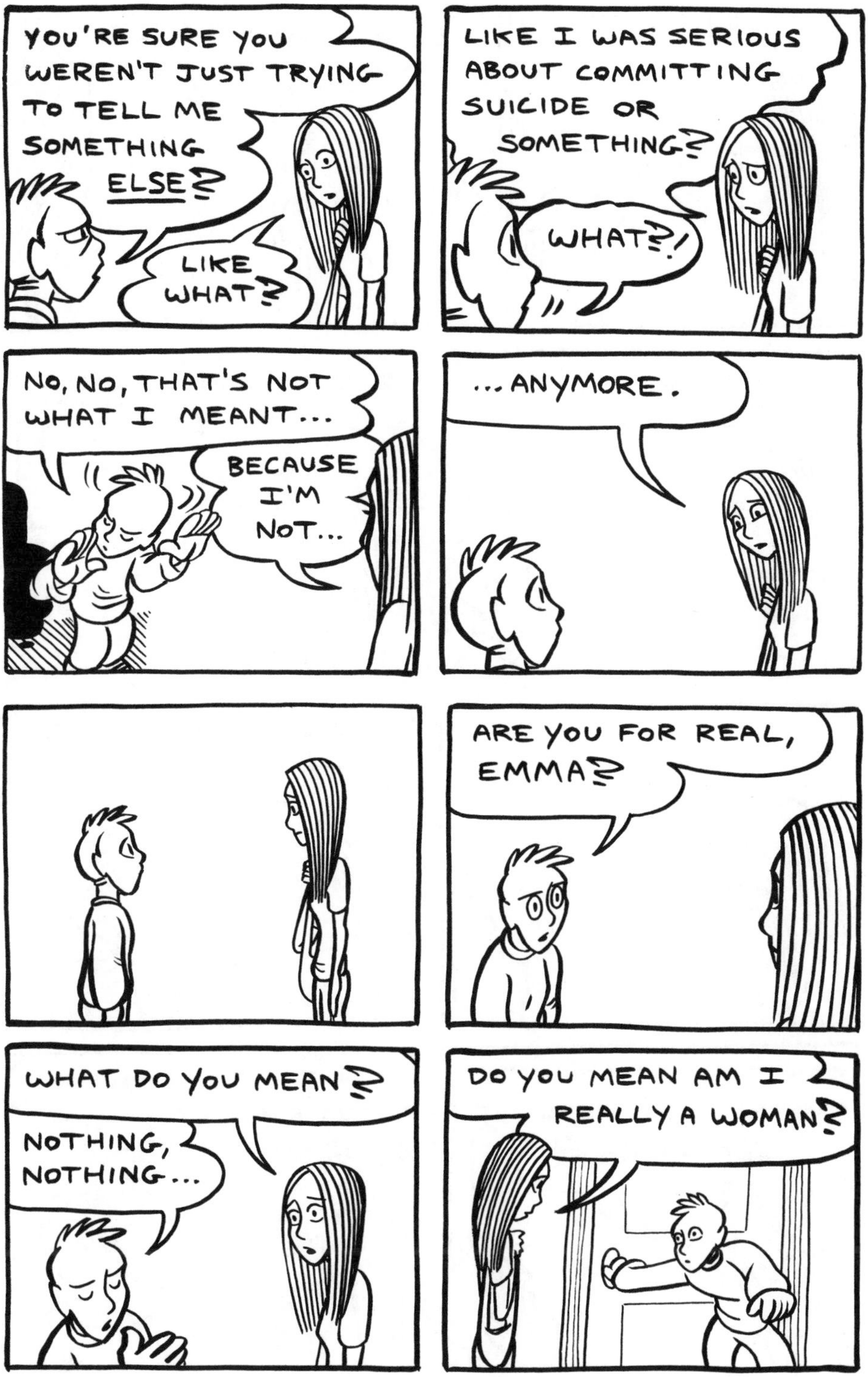
YOU'RE SURE YOU WEREN'T JUST TRYING TO TELL ME SOMETHING ELSE?
LIKE WHAT?
LIKE I WAS SERIOUS ABOUT COMMITTING SUICIDE OR SOMETHING?
WHAT?!
NO, NO, THAT'S NOT WHAT I MEANT...
BECAUSE I'M NOT...
...ANYMORE.
ARE YOU FOR REAL, EMMA?
WHAT DO YOU MEAN?
NOTHING, NOTHING...
DO YOU MEAN AM I REALLY A WOMAN?

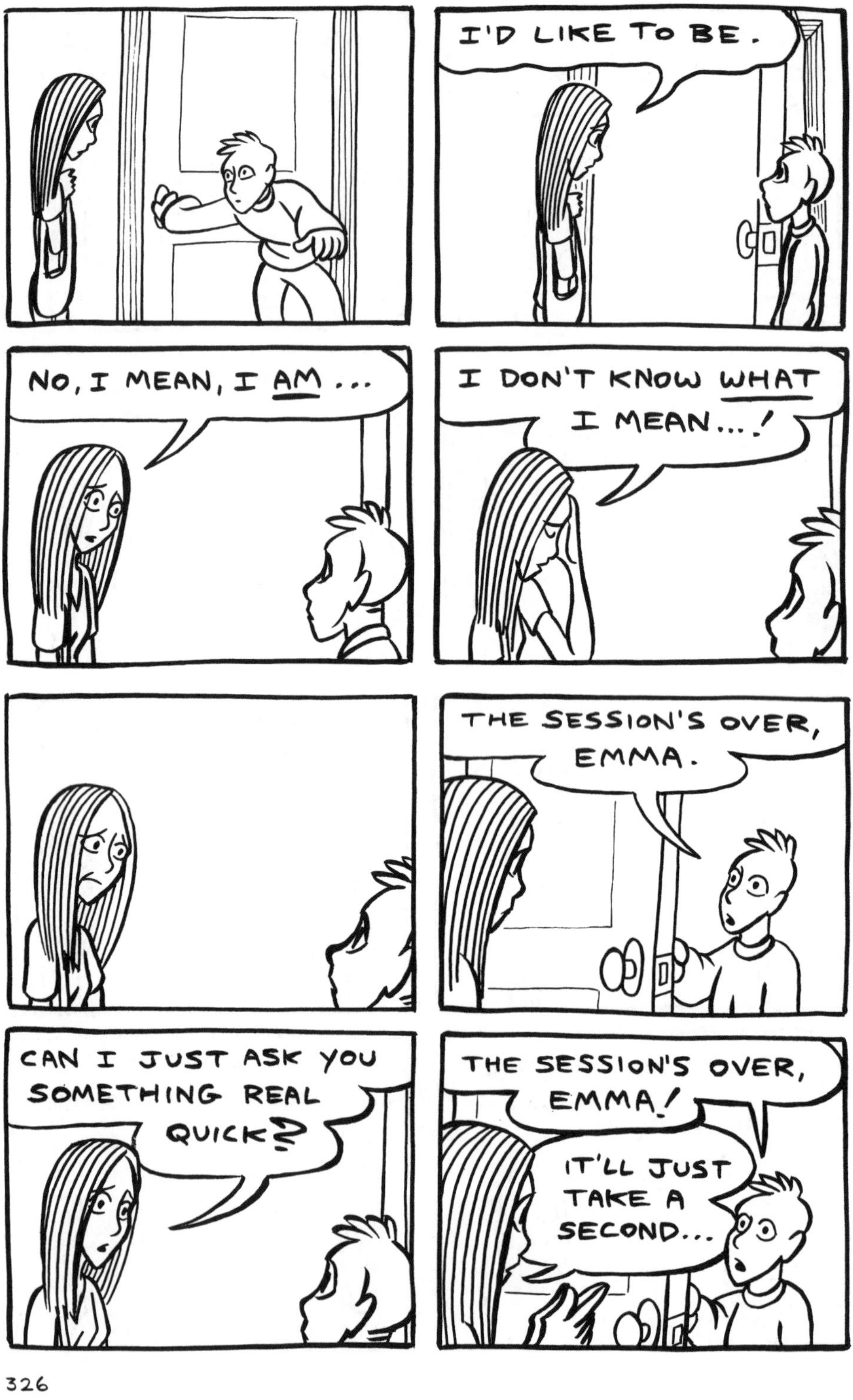
I'D LIKE TO BE.
NO, I MEAN, I AM ...
I DON'T KNOW WHAT I MEAN....!
THE SESSION'S OVER, EMMA.
CAN I JUST ASK YOU SOMETHING REAL QUICK?
THE SESSION'S OVER, EMMA!
IT'LL JUST TAKE A SECOND...

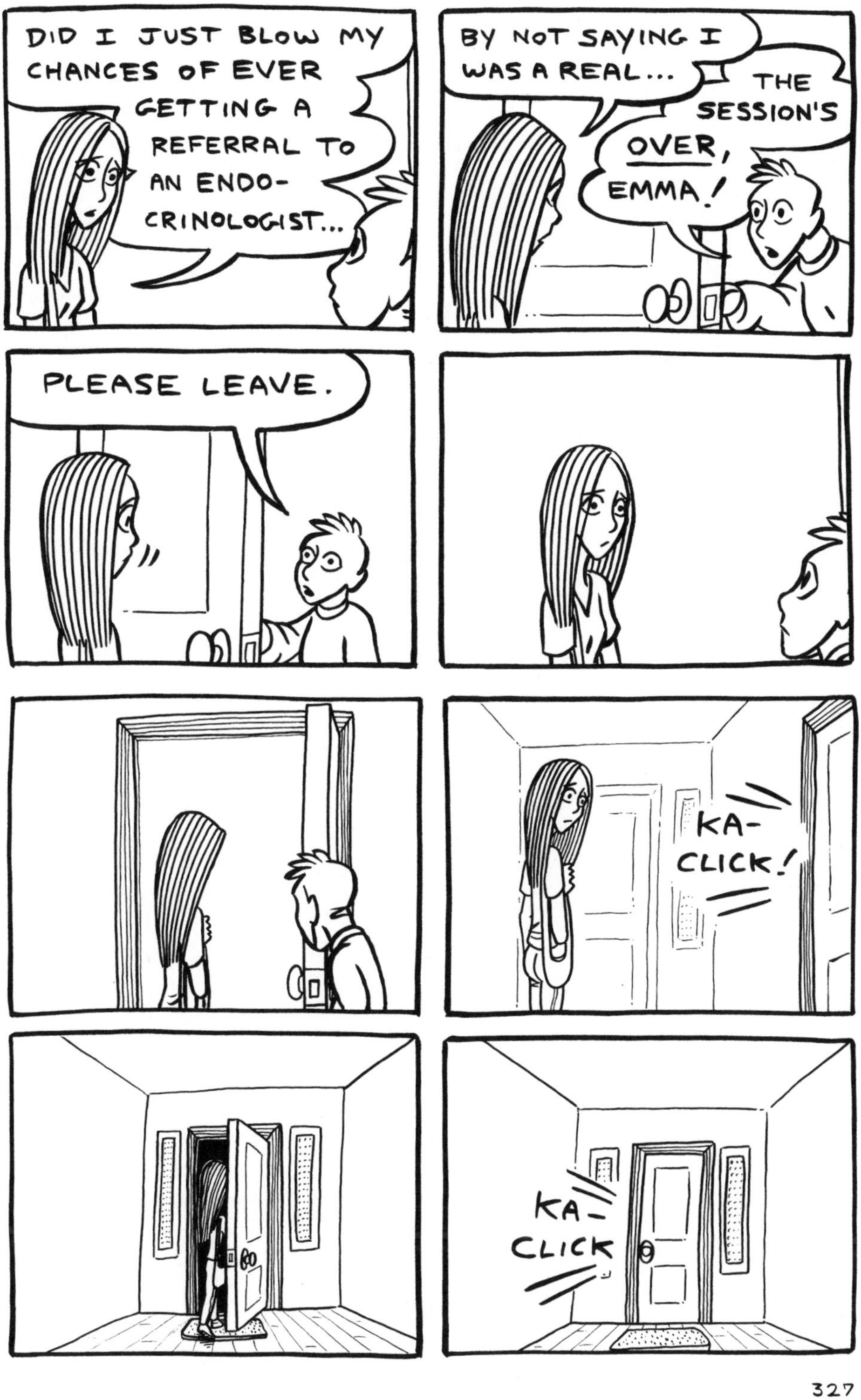
DID I JUST BLOW MY CHANCES OF EVER GETTING A REFERRAL TO AN ENDO-CRINOLOGIST...
BY NOT SAYING I WAS A REAL...
THE SESSION'S OVER, EMMA!
PLEASE LEAVE.
KA-CLICK!
KA-CLICK

THROWN
BOOK

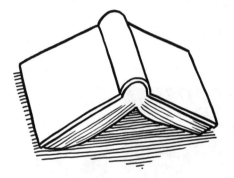

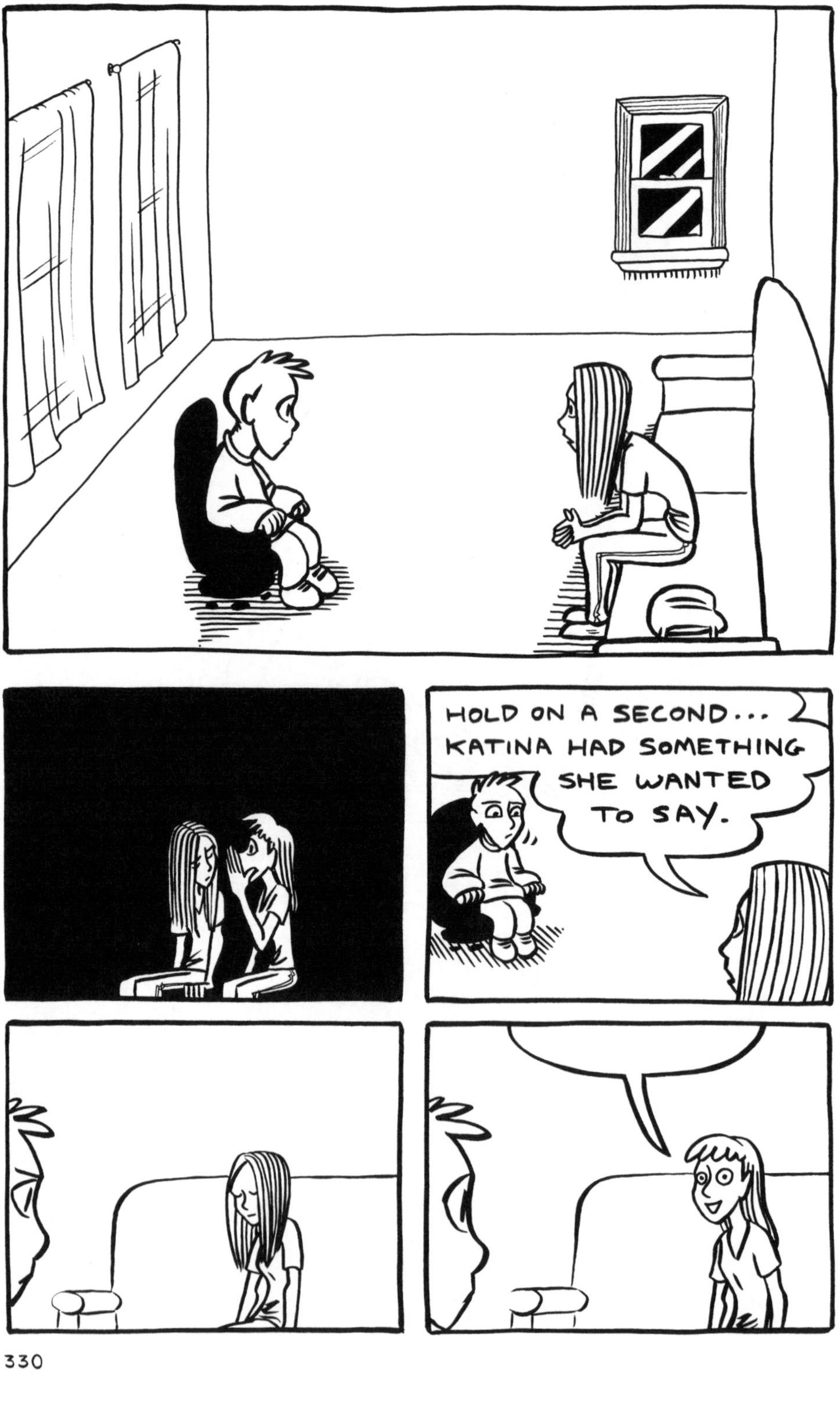
HOLD ON A SECOND... KATINA HAD SOMETHING SHE WANTED TO SAY.

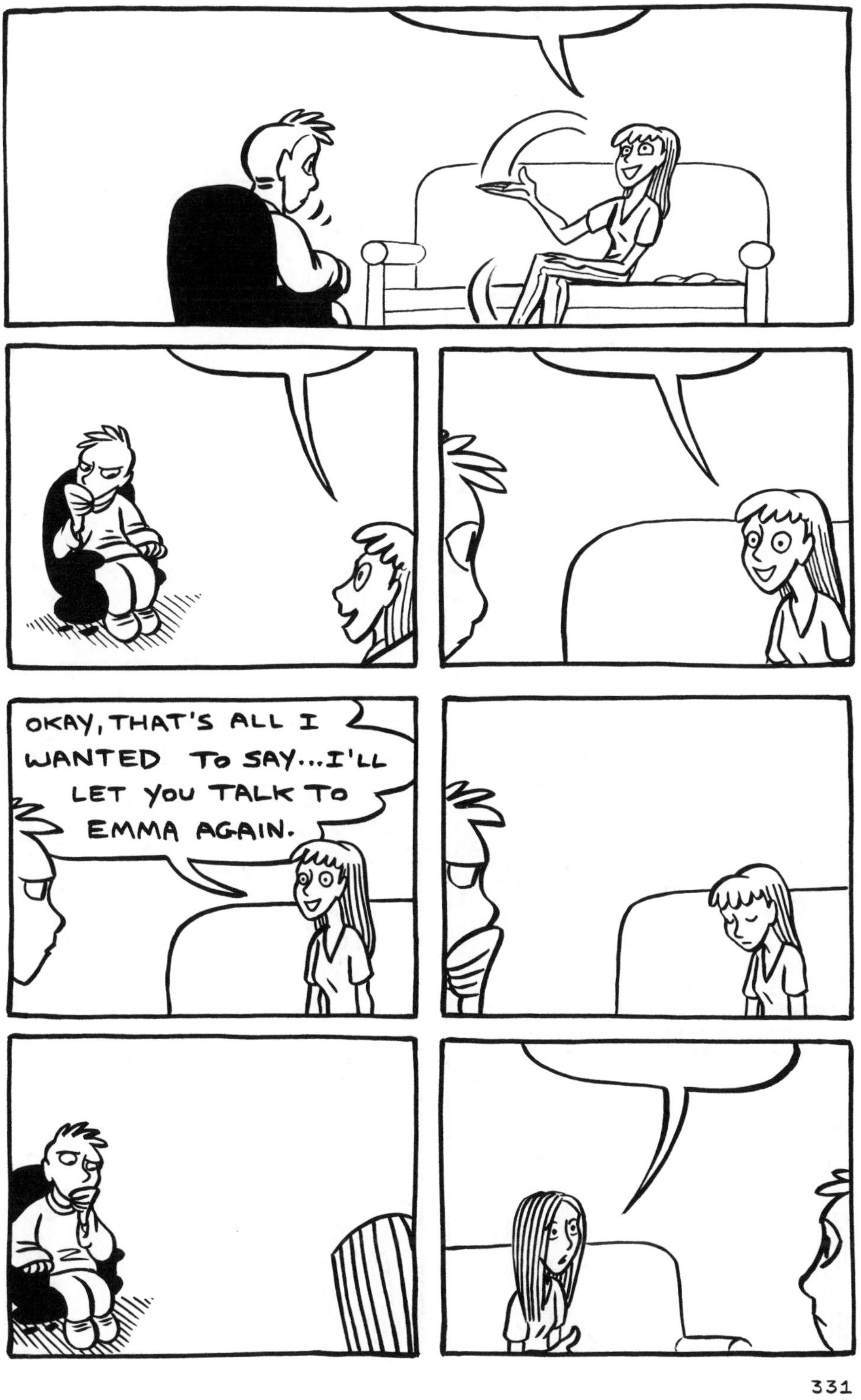
OKAY, THAT'S ALL I WANTED TO SAY...I'LL LET YOU TALK TO EMMA AGAIN.

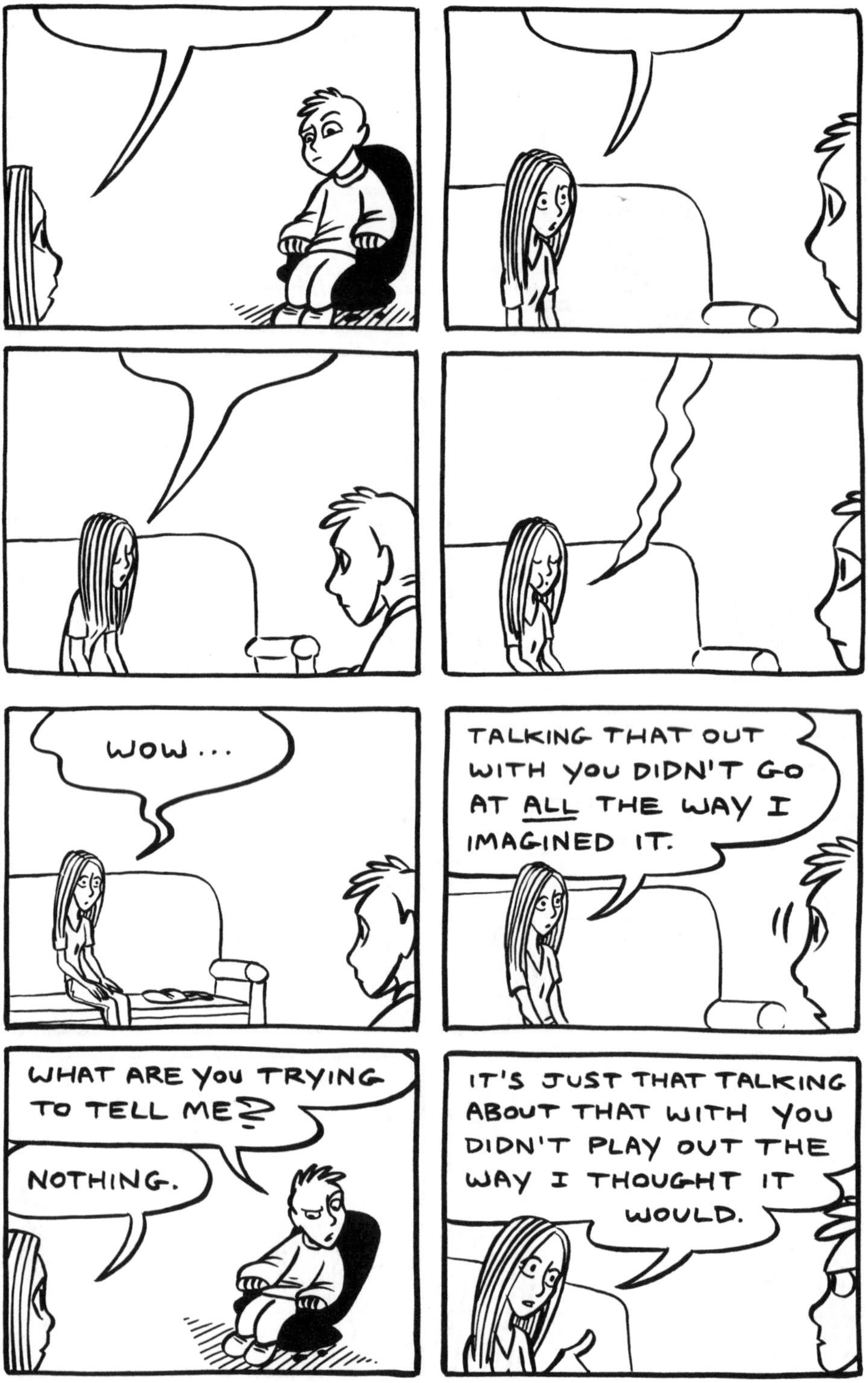
WOW...
TALKING THAT OUT WITH YOU DIDN'T GO AT ALL THE WAY I IMAGINED IT.
WHAT ARE YOU TRYING TO TELL ME?
NOTHING.
IT'S JUST THAT TALKING ABOUT THAT WITH YOU DIDN'T PLAY OUT THE WAY I THOUGHT IT WOULD.

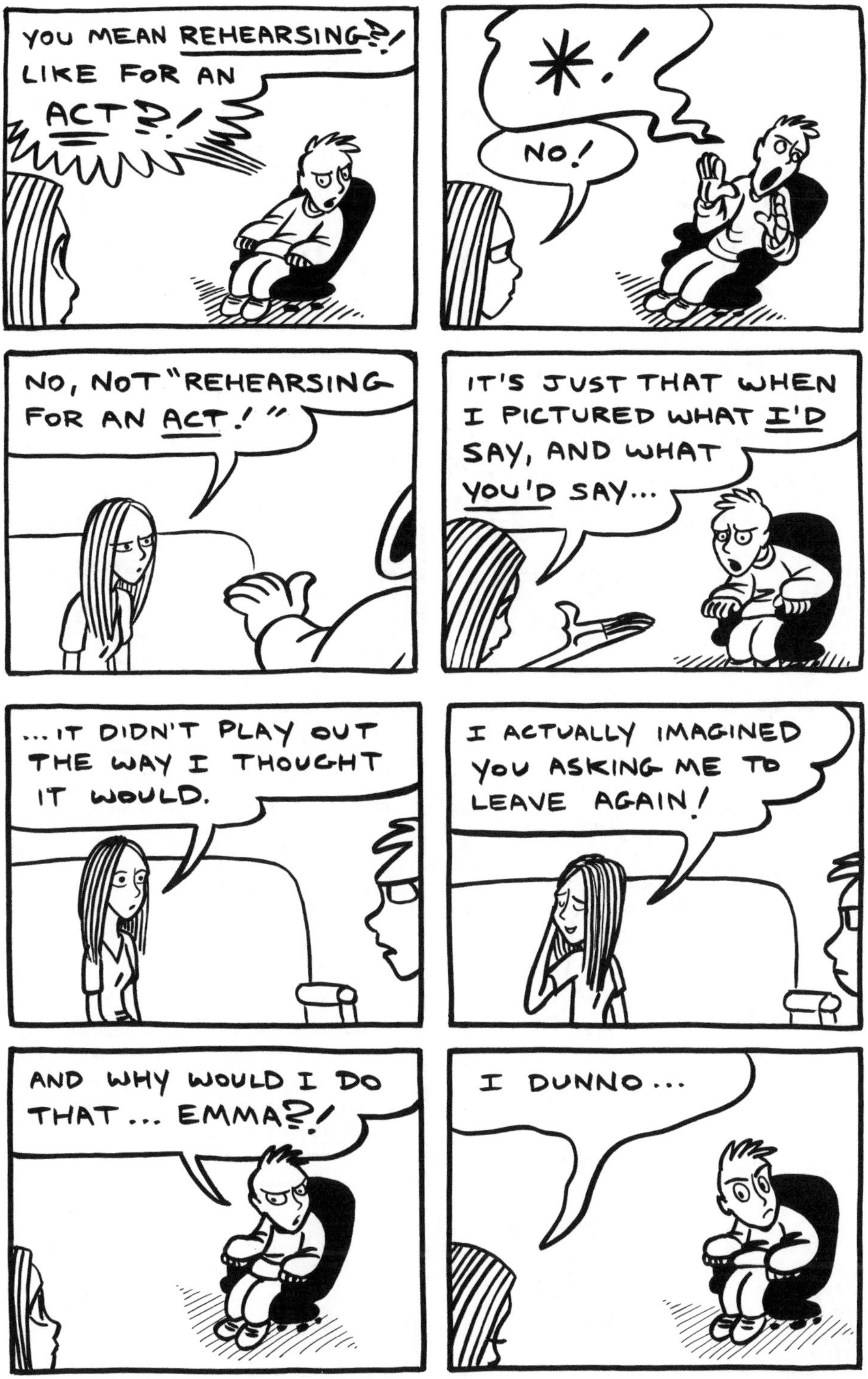
YOU MEAN REHEARSING?! LIKE FOR AN ACT?!
*!
NO!
NO, NOT "REHEARSING FOR AN ACT!"
IT'S JUST THAT WHEN I PICTURED WHAT I'D SAY, AND WHAT YOU'D SAY...
...IT DIDN'T PLAY OUT THE WAY I THOUGHT IT WOULD.
I ACTUALLY IMAGINED YOU ASKING ME TO LEAVE AGAIN!
AND WHY WOULD I DO THAT... EMMA?!
I DUNNO...

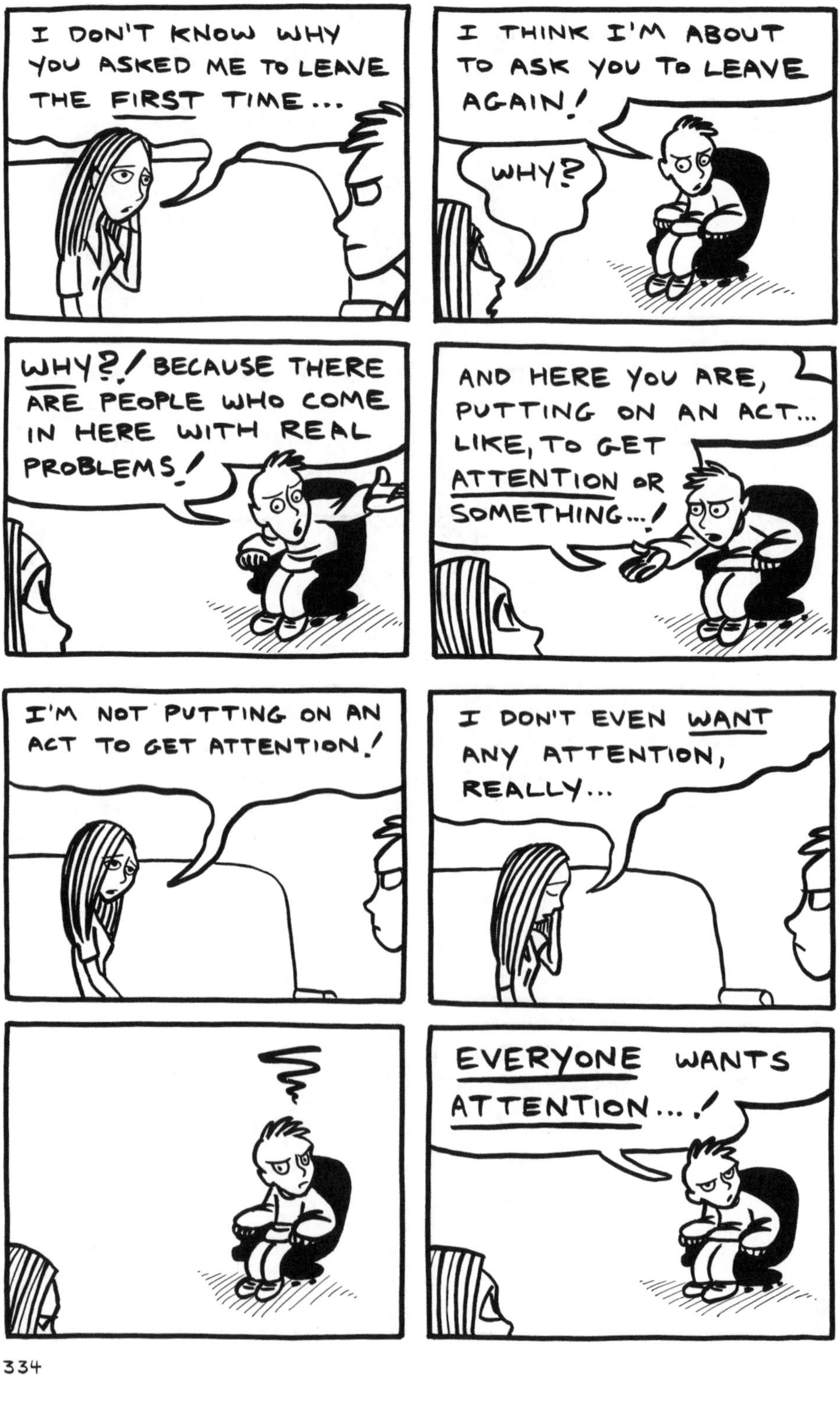
I DON'T KNOW WHY YOU ASKED ME TO LEAVE THE FIRST TIME...
I THINK I'M ABOUT TO ASK YOU TO LEAVE AGAIN!
WHY?
WHY?! BECAUSE THERE ARE PEOPLE WHO COME IN HERE WITH REAL PROBLEMS!
AND HERE YOU ARE, PUTTING ON AN ACT... LIKE, TO GET ATTENTION OR SOMETHING...!
I'M NOT PUTTING ON AN ACT TO GET ATTENTION!
I DON'T EVEN WANT ANY ATTENTION, REALLY...
EVERYONE WANTS ATTENTION...!

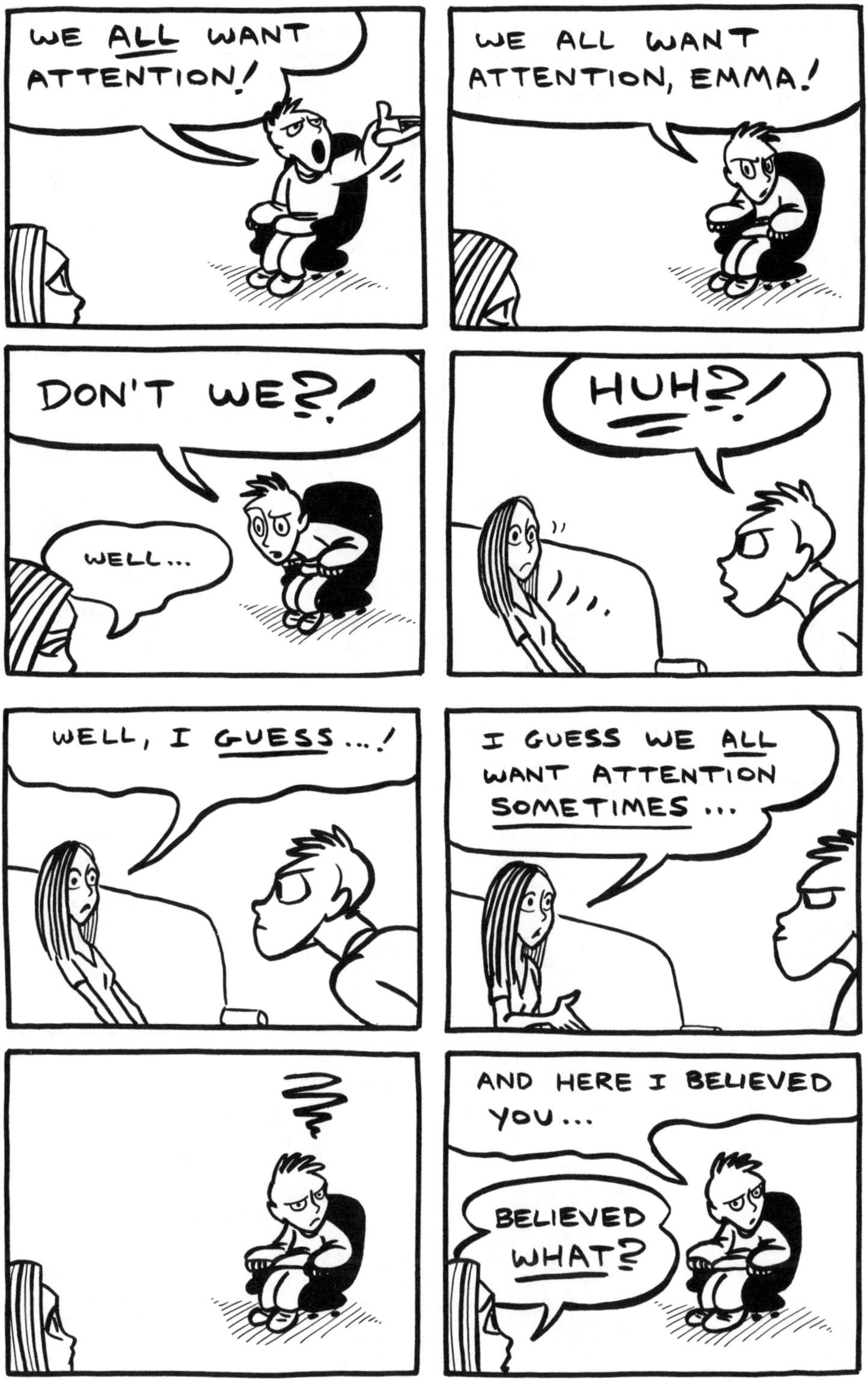
WE ALL WANT ATTENTION!
WE ALL WANT ATTENTION, EMMA!
DON'T WE?!
WELL...
HUH?!
WELL, I GUESS...!
I GUESS WE ALL WANT ATTENTION SOMETIMES...
AND HERE I BELIEVED YOU...
BELIEVED WHAT?

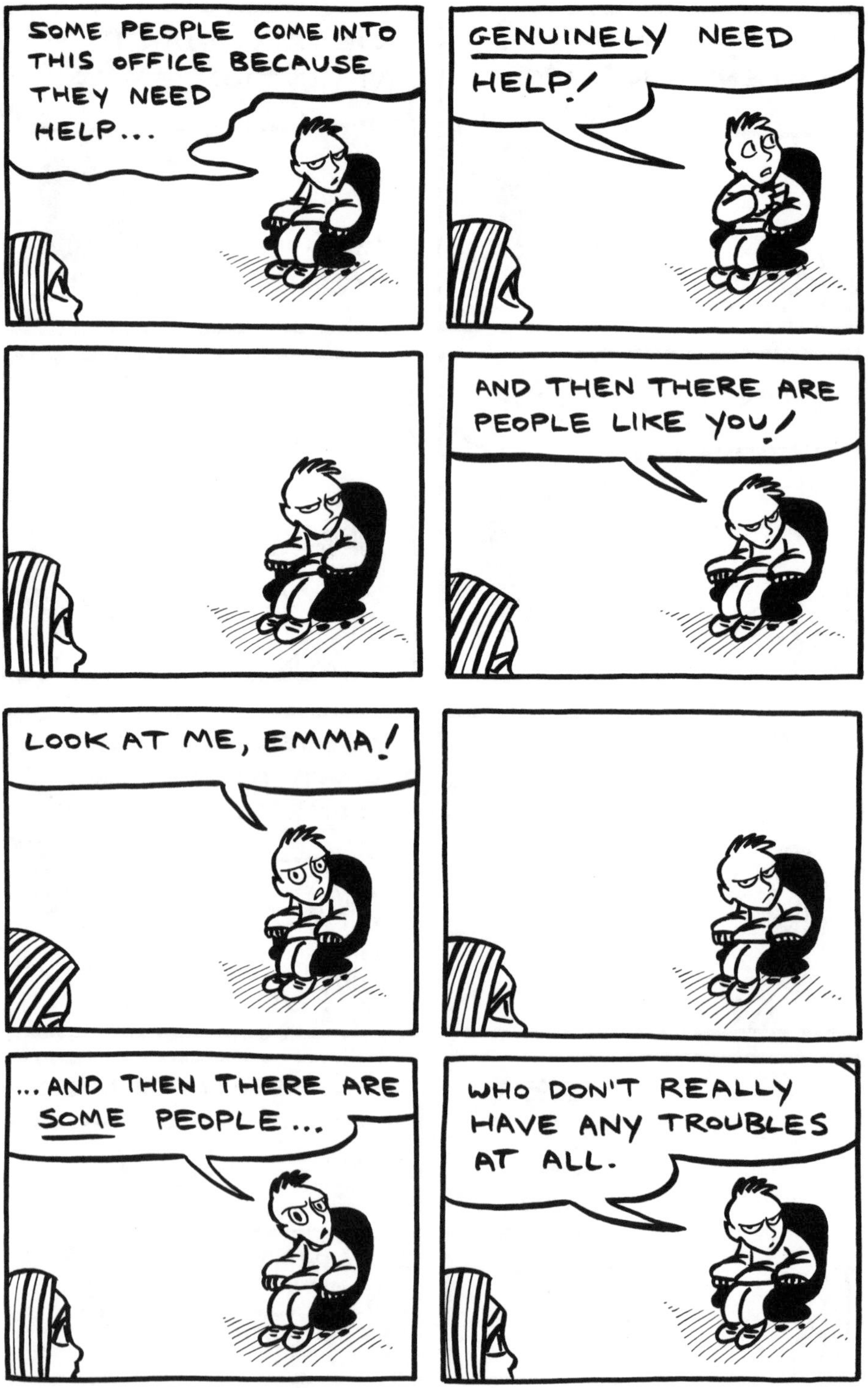
SOME PEOPLE COME INTO THIS OFFICE BECAUSE THEY NEED HELP...
GENUINELY NEED HELP!
AND THEN THERE ARE PEOPLE LIKE YOU!
LOOK AT ME, EMMA!
...AND THEN THERE ARE SOME PEOPLE...
WHO DON'T REALLY HAVE ANY TROUBLES AT ALL.

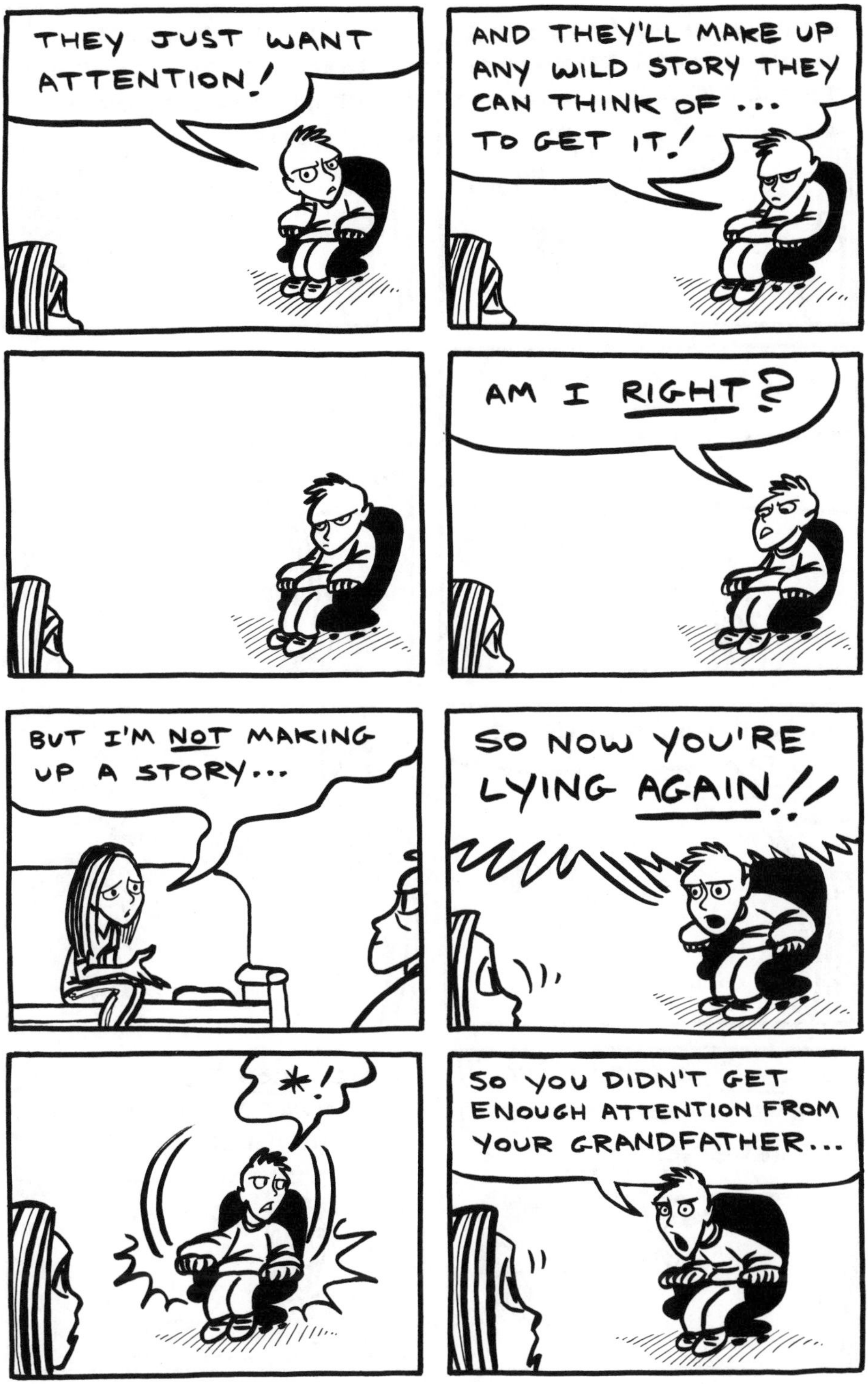
THEY JUST WANT ATTENTION!
AND THEY'LL MAKE UP ANY WILD STORY THEY CAN THINK OF ... TO GET IT!
AM I RIGHT?
BUT I'M NOT MAKING UP A STORY...
SO NOW YOU'RE LYING AGAIN!!
*!
SO YOU DIDN'T GET ENOUGH ATTENTION FROM YOUR GRANDFATHER...

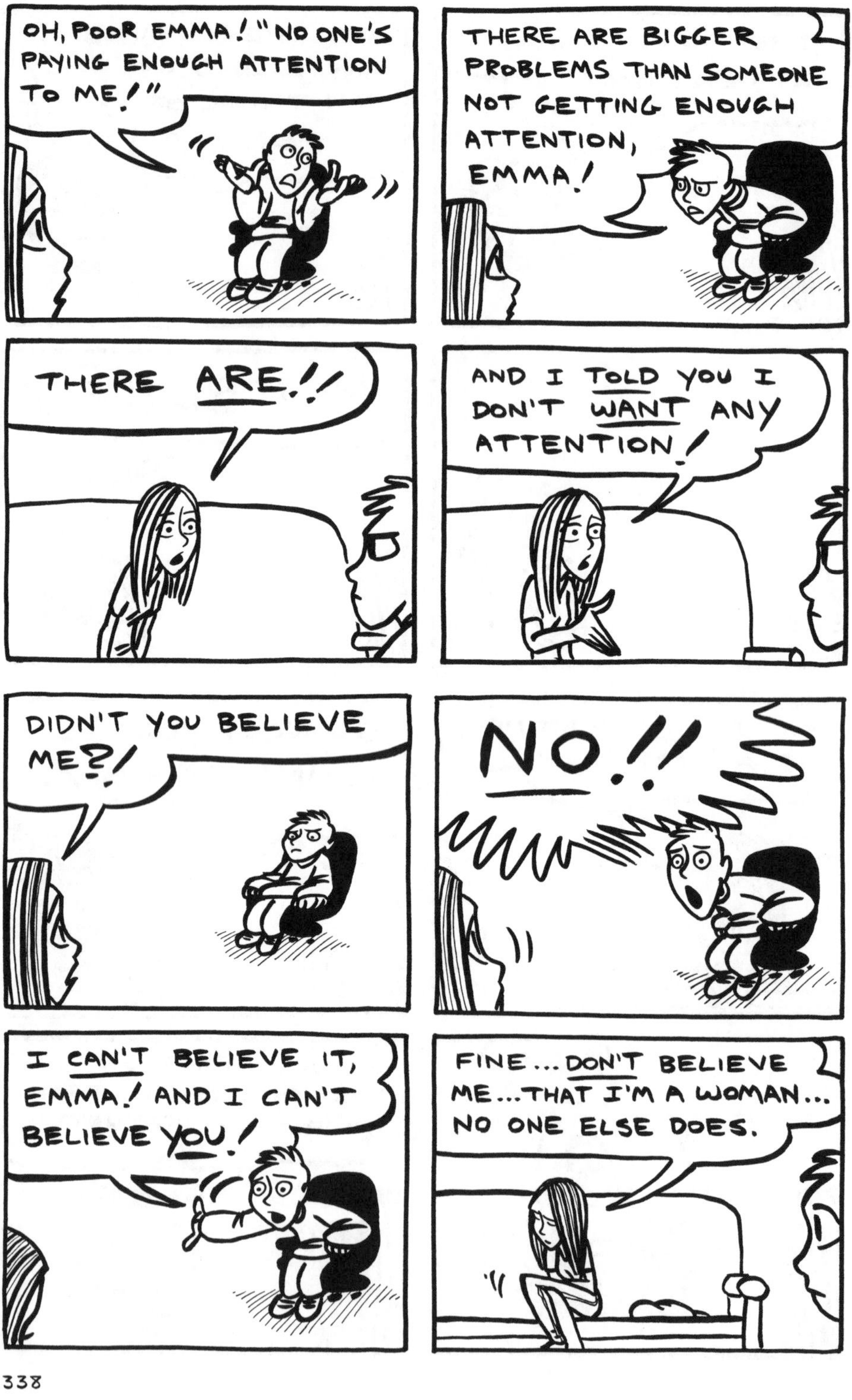

OH, POOR EMMA! "NO ONE'S PAYING ENOUGH ATTENTION TO ME!"
THERE ARE BIGGER PROBLEMS THAN SOMEONE NOT GETTING ENOUGH ATTENTION, EMMA!
THERE ARE!!
AND I TOLD YOU I DON'T WANT ANY ATTENTION!
DIDN'T YOU BELIEVE ME?!
NO!!
I CAN'T BELIEVE IT, EMMA! AND I CAN'T BELIEVE YOU!
FINE... DON'T BELIEVE ME... THAT I'M A WOMAN... NO ONE ELSE DOES.

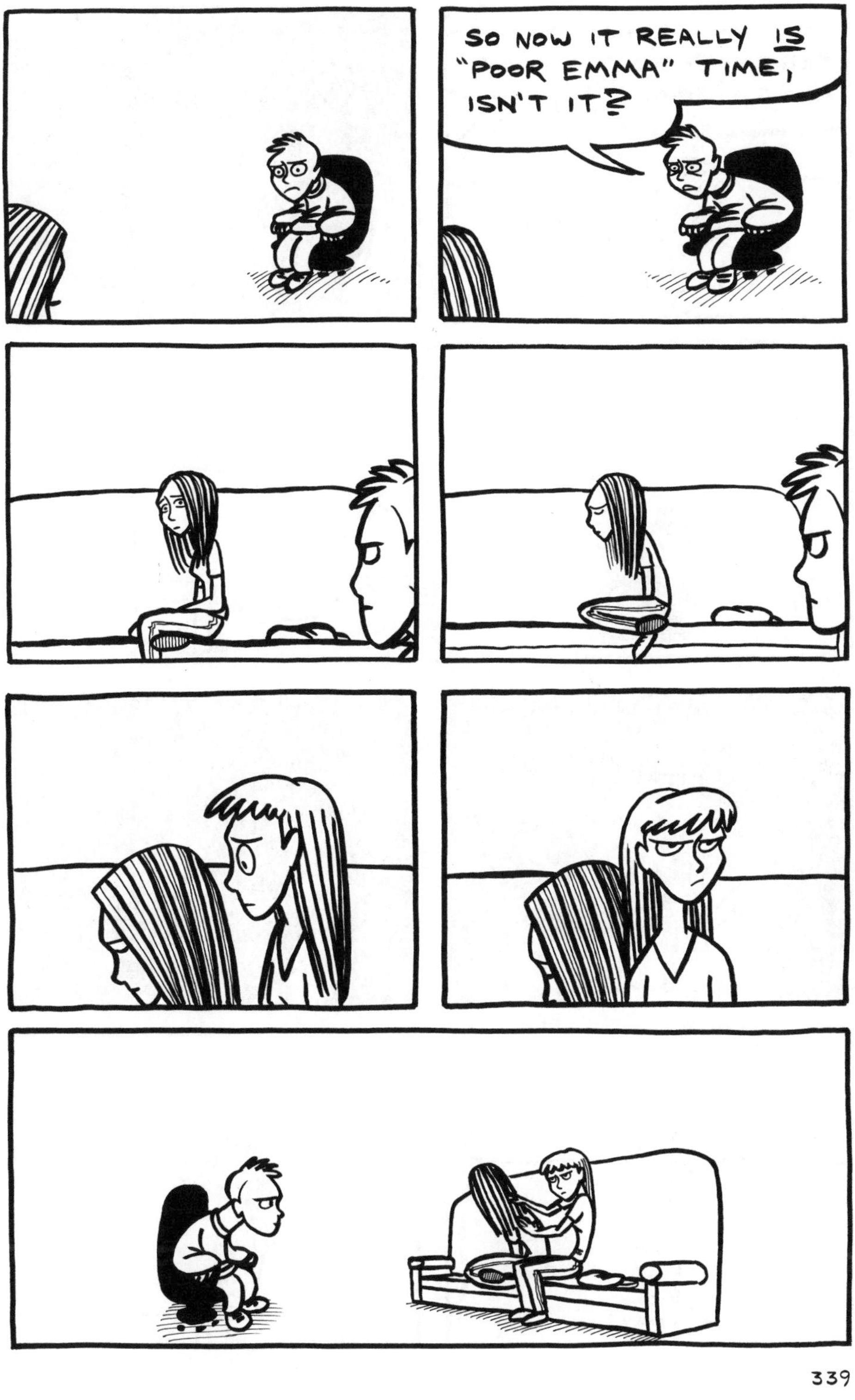
SO NOW IT REALLY IS "POOR EMMA" TIME, ISN'T IT?

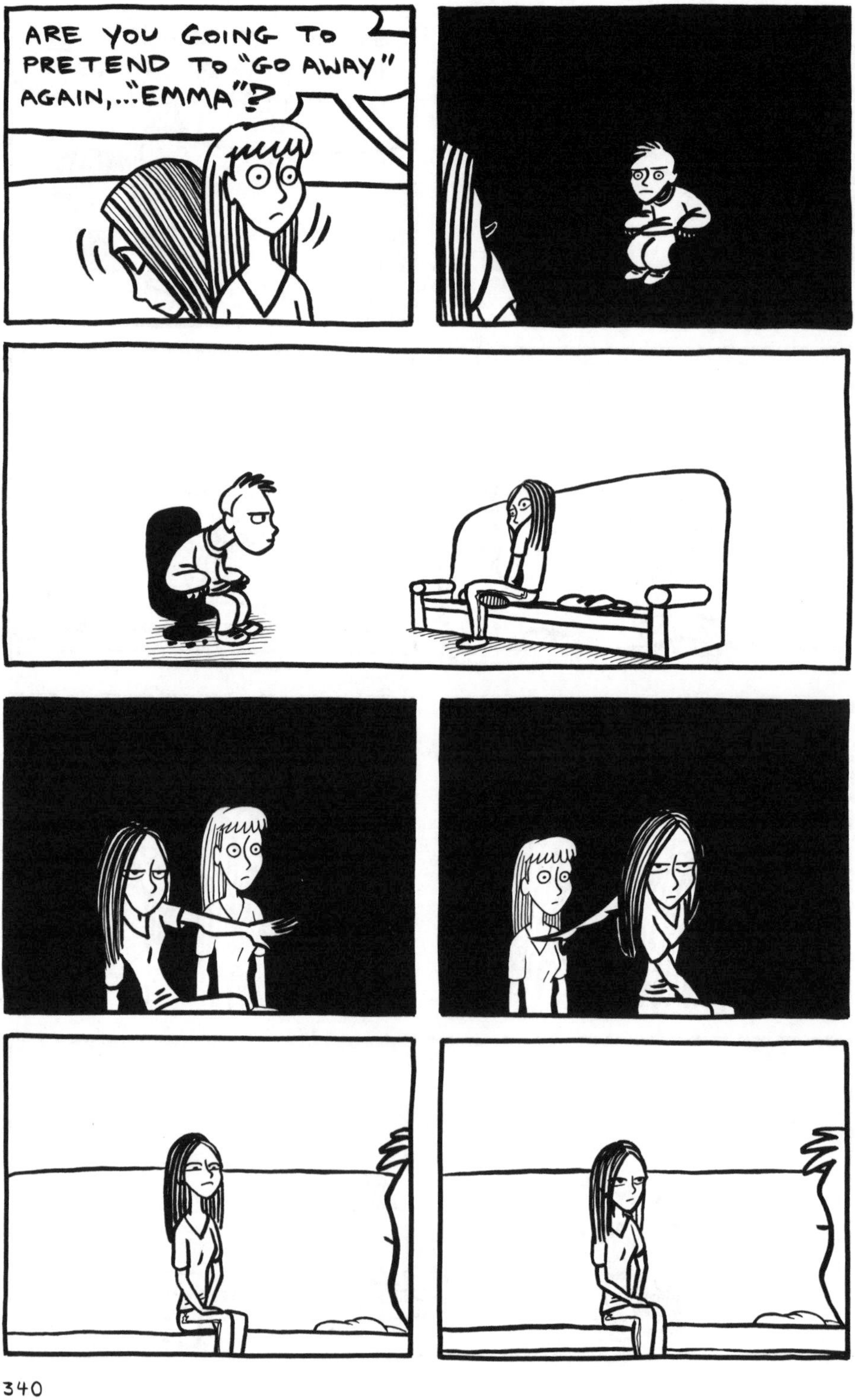
ARE YOU GOING TO PRETEND TO "GO AWAY" AGAIN, ..."EMMA"?

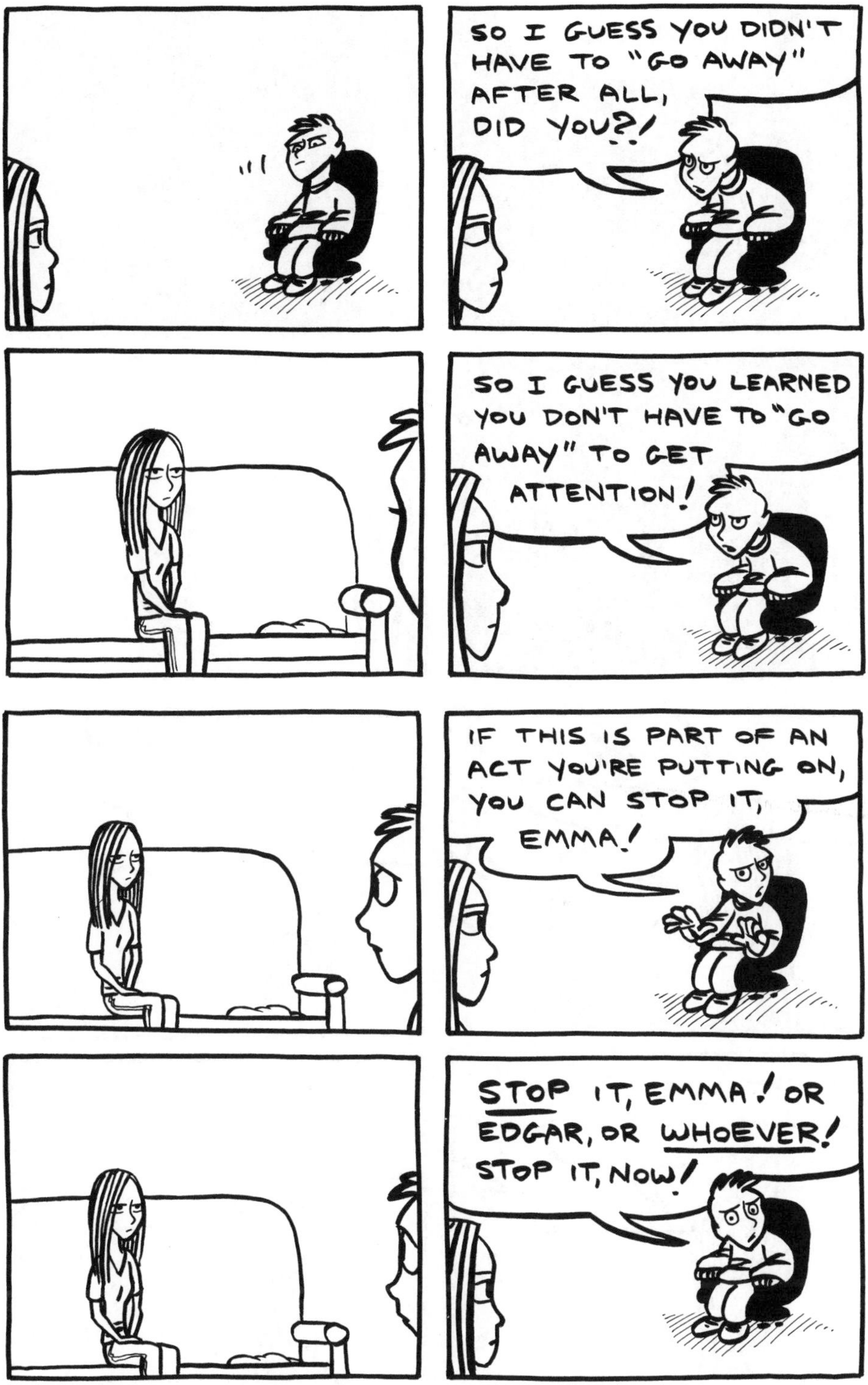
SO I GUESS YOU DIDN'T HAVE TO "GO AWAY" AFTER ALL, DID YOU?!
SO I GUESS YOU LEARNED YOU DON'T HAVE TO "GO AWAY" TO GET ATTENTION!
IF THIS IS PART OF AN ACT YOU'RE PUTTING ON, YOU CAN STOP IT, EMMA!
STOP IT, EMMA! OR EDGAR, OR WHOEVER! STOP IT, NOW!

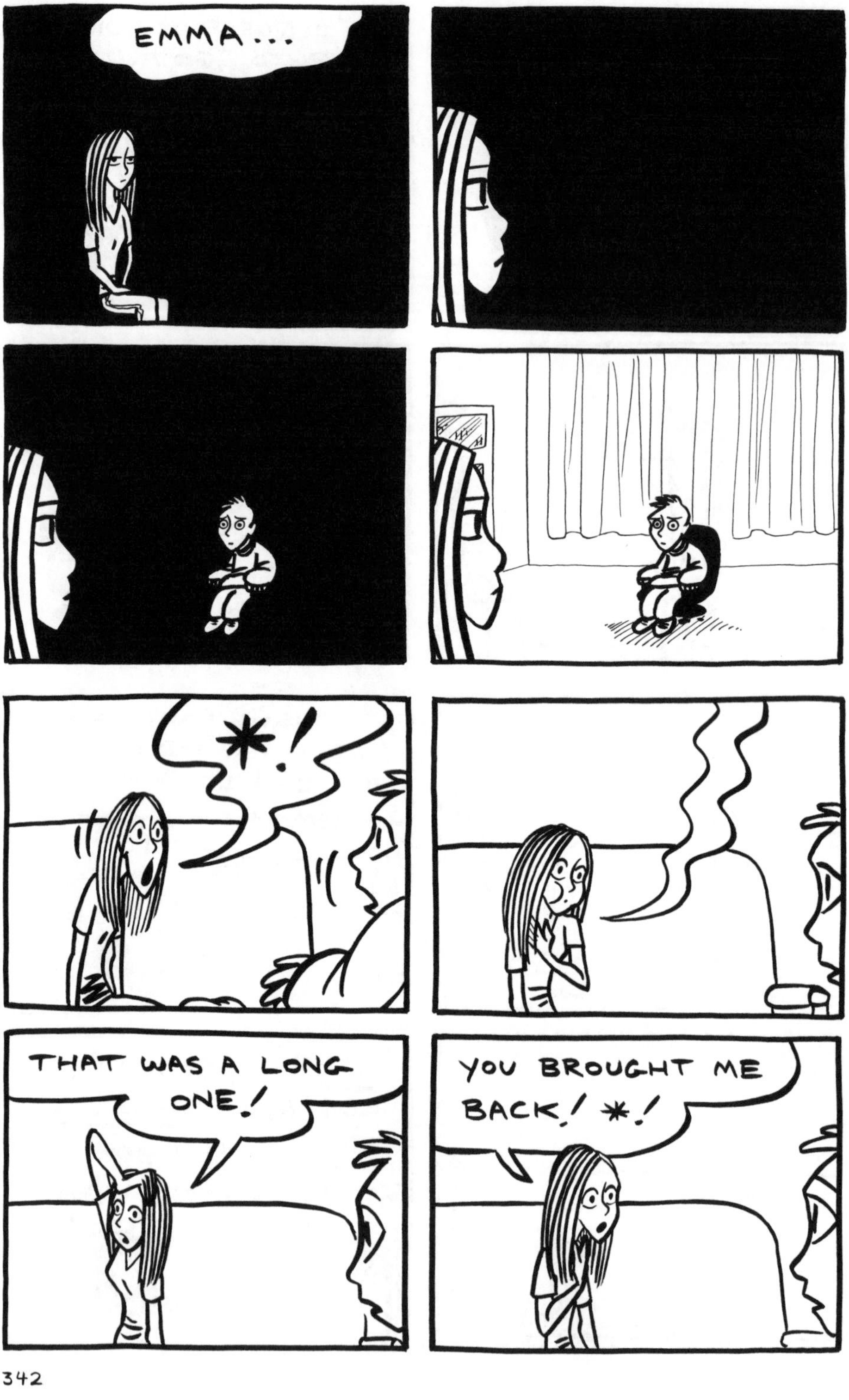
EMMA...
*!
THAT WAS A LONG ONE!
YOU BROUGHT ME BACK! *!

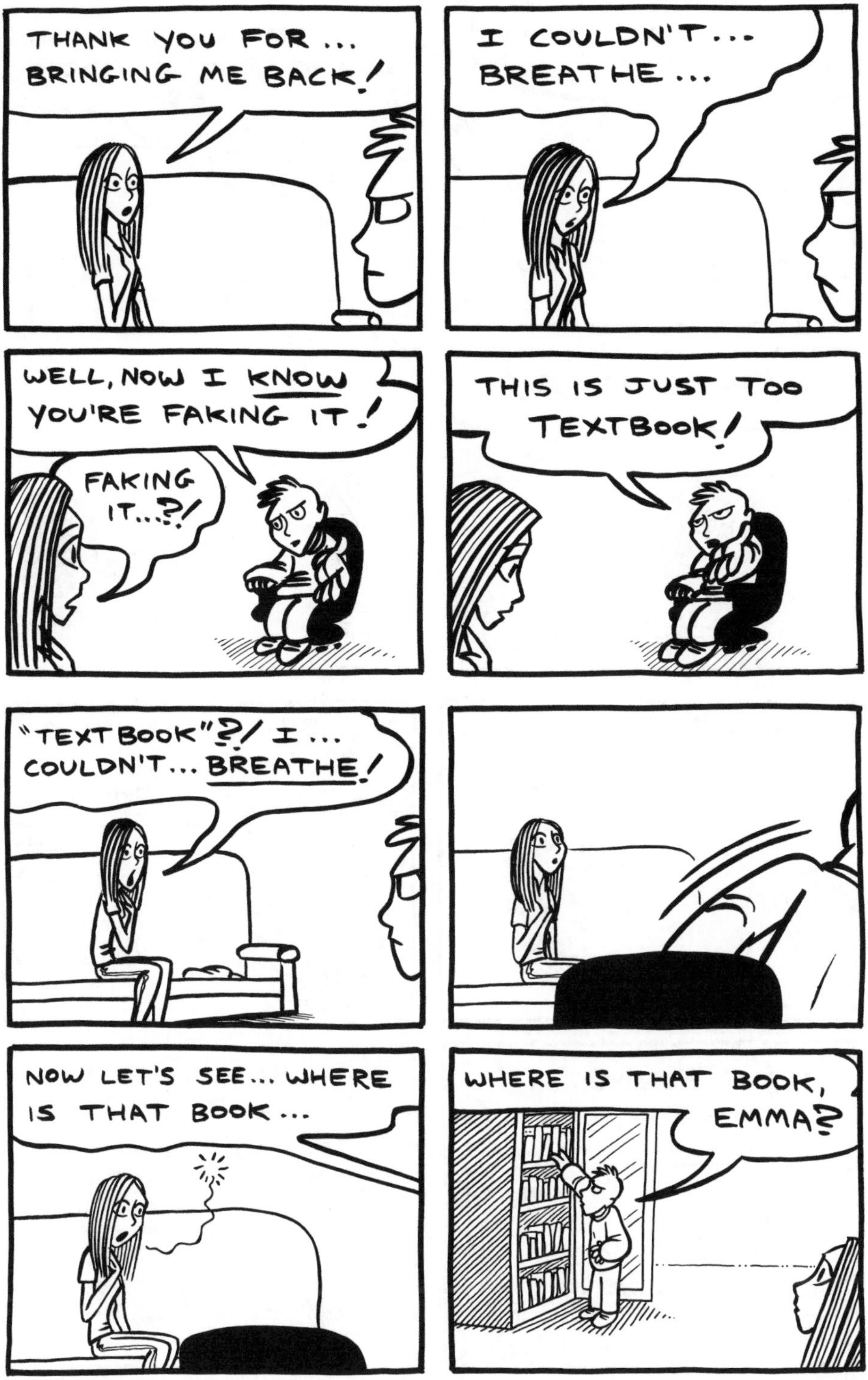
THANK YOU FOR... BRINGING ME BACK!
I COULDN'T... BREATHE...
WELL, NOW I KNOW YOU'RE FAKING IT!
FAKING IT...?!
THIS IS JUST TOO TEXTBOOK!
"TEXTBOOK"?! I... COULDN'T... BREATHE!
NOW LET'S SEE... WHERE IS THAT BOOK...
WHERE IS THAT BOOK, EMMA?

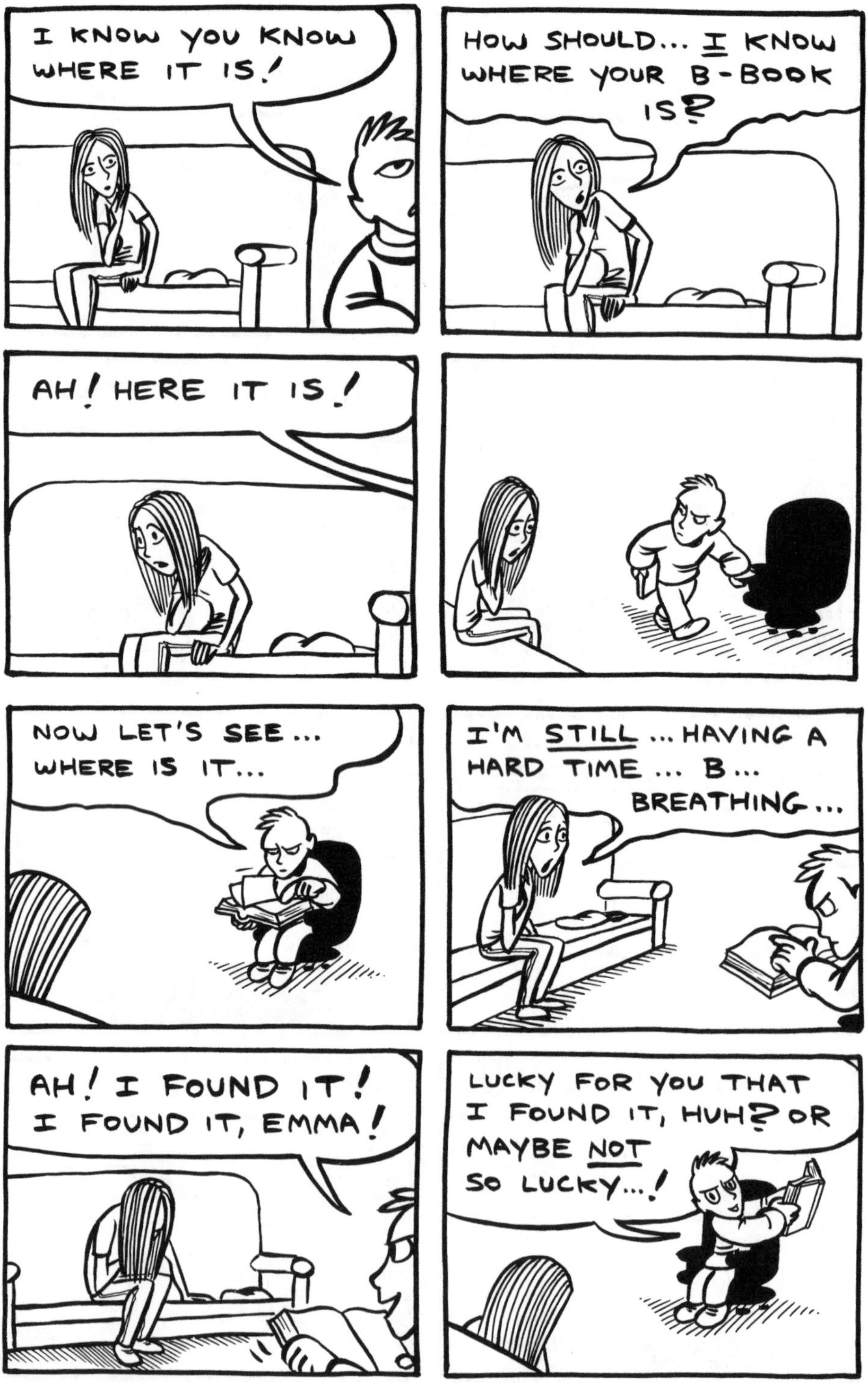

I KNOW YOU KNOW WHERE IT IS!
HOW SHOULD... I KNOW WHERE YOUR B-BOOK IS?
AH! HERE IT IS!
NOW LET'S SEE... WHERE IS IT...
I'M STILL ... HAVING A HARD TIME ... B... BREATHING...
AH! I FOUND IT! I FOUND IT, EMMA!
LUCKY FOR YOU THAT I FOUND IT, HUH? OR MAYBE NOT SO LUCKY...!

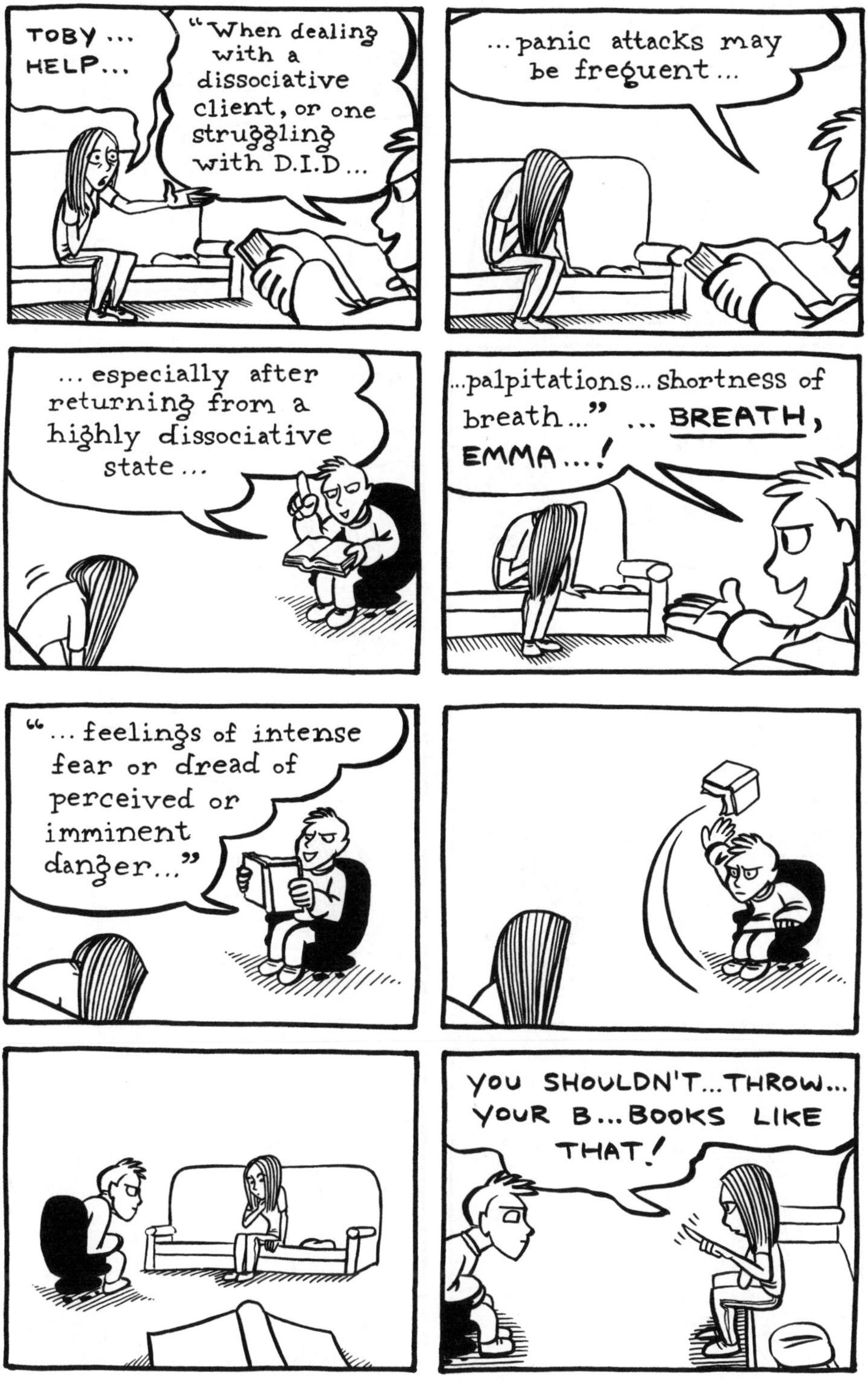
TOBY ... HELP...
"When dealing with a dissociative client, or one struggling with D.I.D ...
... panic attacks may be frequent ...
... especially after returning from a highly dissociative state ...
...palpitations... shortness of breath..." ... BREATH, EMMA....!
"... feelings of intense fear or dread of perceived or imminent danger..."
YOU SHOULDN'T...THROW... YOUR B...BOOKS LIKE THAT!

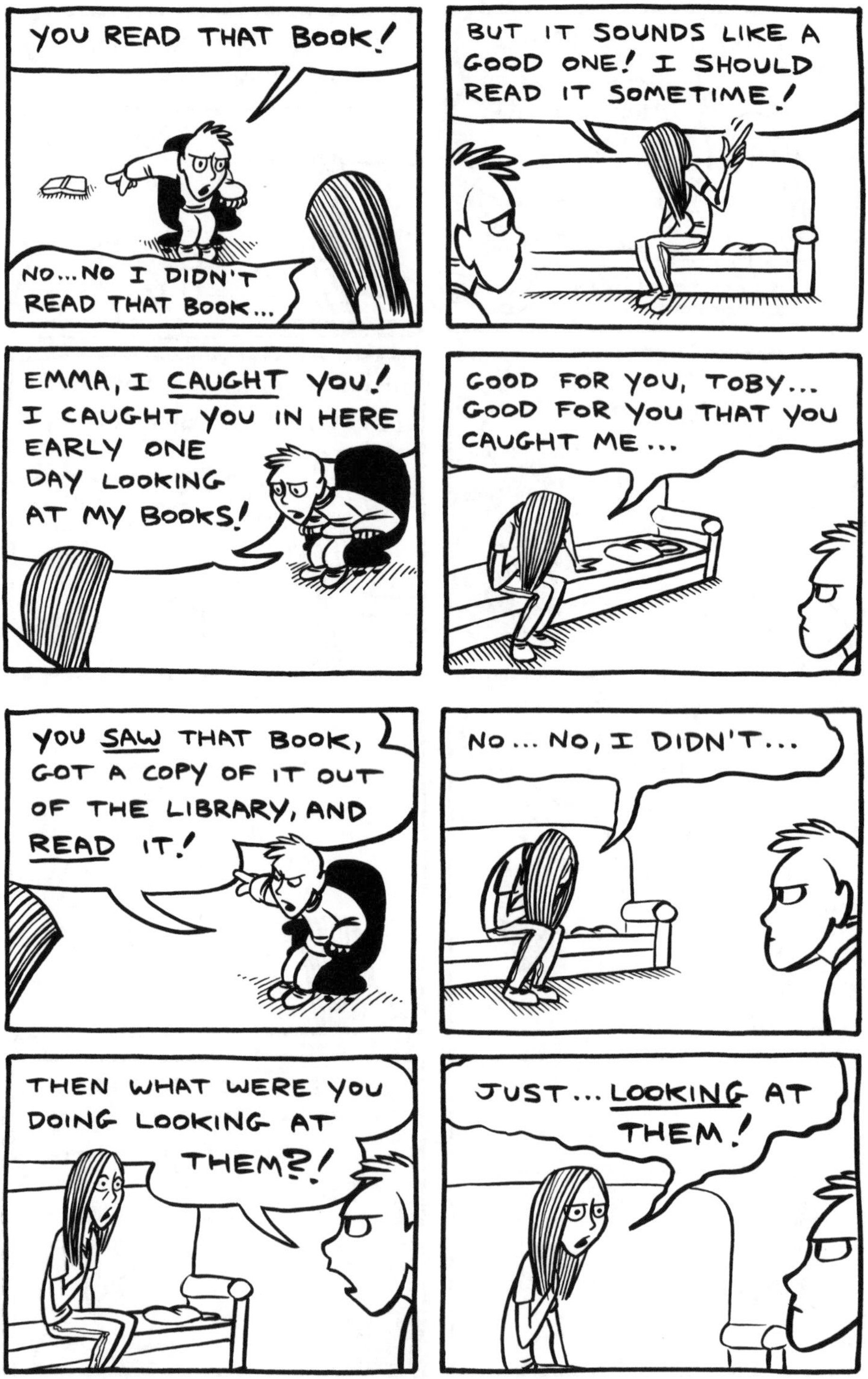
YOU READ THAT BOOK!
NO...NO I DIDN'T READ THAT BOOK...
BUT IT SOUNDS LIKE A GOOD ONE! I SHOULD READ IT SOMETIME!
EMMA, I CAUGHT YOU! I CAUGHT YOU IN HERE EARLY ONE DAY LOOKING AT MY BOOKS!
GOOD FOR YOU, TOBY... GOOD FOR YOU THAT YOU CAUGHT ME...
YOU SAW THAT BOOK, GOT A COPY OF IT OUT OF THE LIBRARY, AND READ IT!
NO... NO, I DIDN'T...
THEN WHAT WERE YOU DOING LOOKING AT THEM?!
JUST... LOOKING AT THEM!

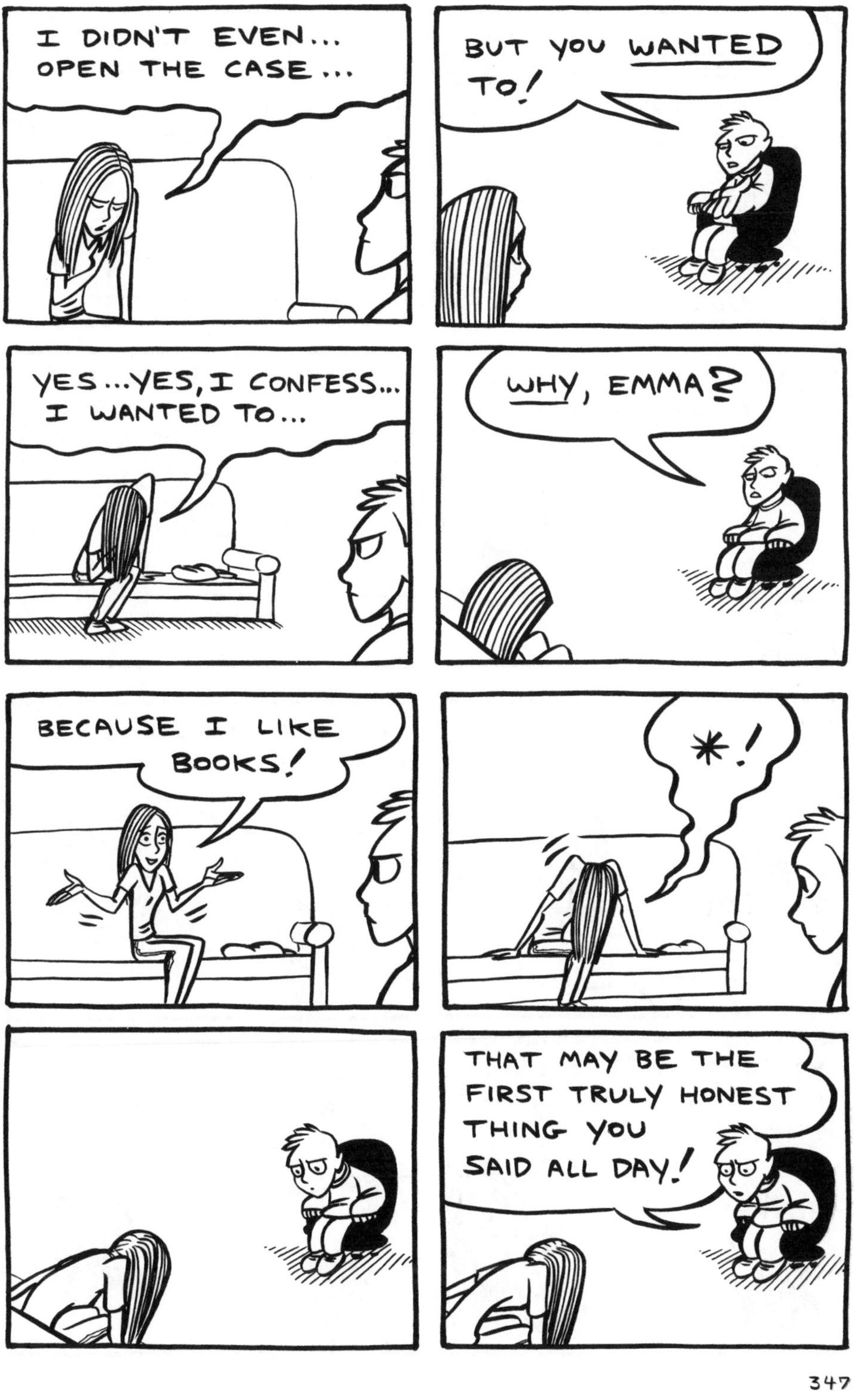
I DIDN'T EVEN... OPEN THE CASE...
BUT YOU WANTED TO!
YES...YES, I CONFESS... I WANTED TO...
WHY, EMMA?
BECAUSE I LIKE BOOKS!
*!
THAT MAY BE THE FIRST TRULY HONEST THING YOU SAID ALL DAY!

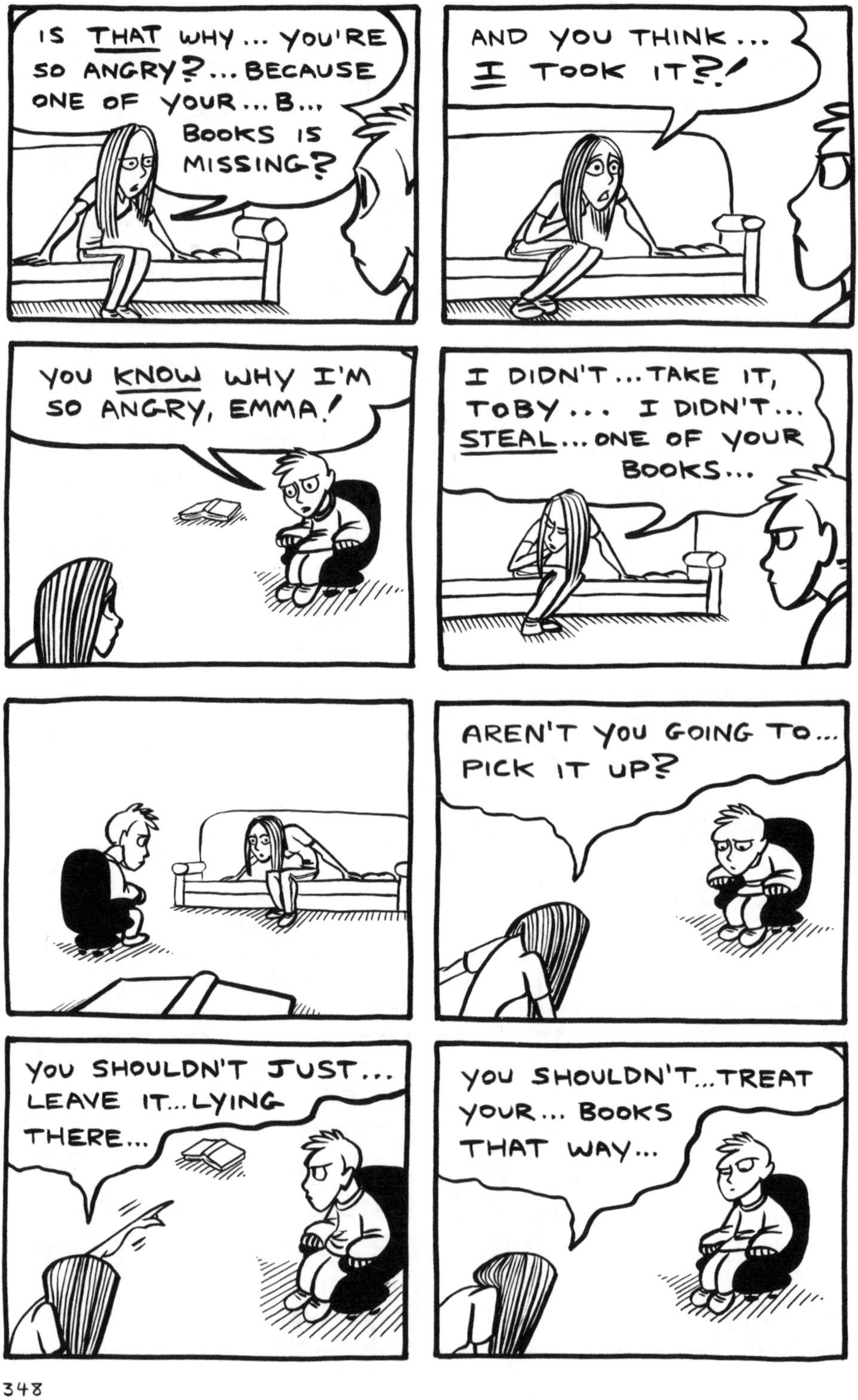
IS THAT WHY... YOU'RE SO ANGRY?... BECAUSE ONE OF YOUR... B... BOOKS IS MISSING?
AND YOU THINK... I TOOK IT?!
YOU KNOW WHY I'M SO ANGRY, EMMA!
I DIDN'T... TAKE IT, TOBY... I DIDN'T... STEAL... ONE OF YOUR BOOKS...
AREN'T YOU GOING TO... PICK IT UP?
YOU SHOULDN'T JUST... LEAVE IT... LYING THERE...
YOU SHOULDN'T... TREAT YOUR... BOOKS THAT WAY...

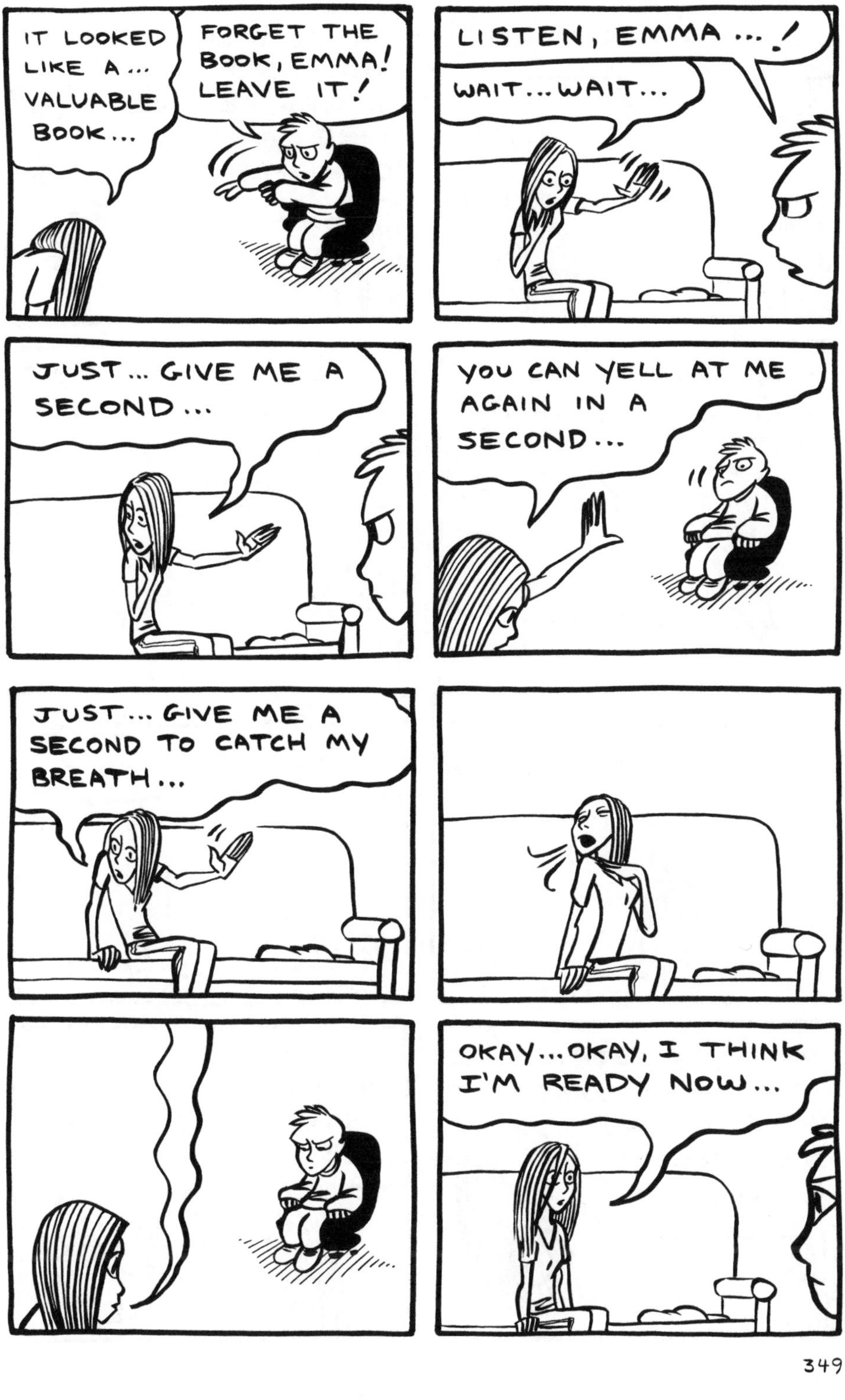
IT LOOKED LIKE A... VALUABLE BOOK...
FORGET THE BOOK, EMMA! LEAVE IT!
LISTEN, EMMA...!
WAIT...WAIT...
JUST... GIVE ME A SECOND...
YOU CAN YELL AT ME AGAIN IN A SECOND...
JUST... GIVE ME A SECOND TO CATCH MY BREATH...
OKAY...OKAY, I THINK I'M READY NOW...

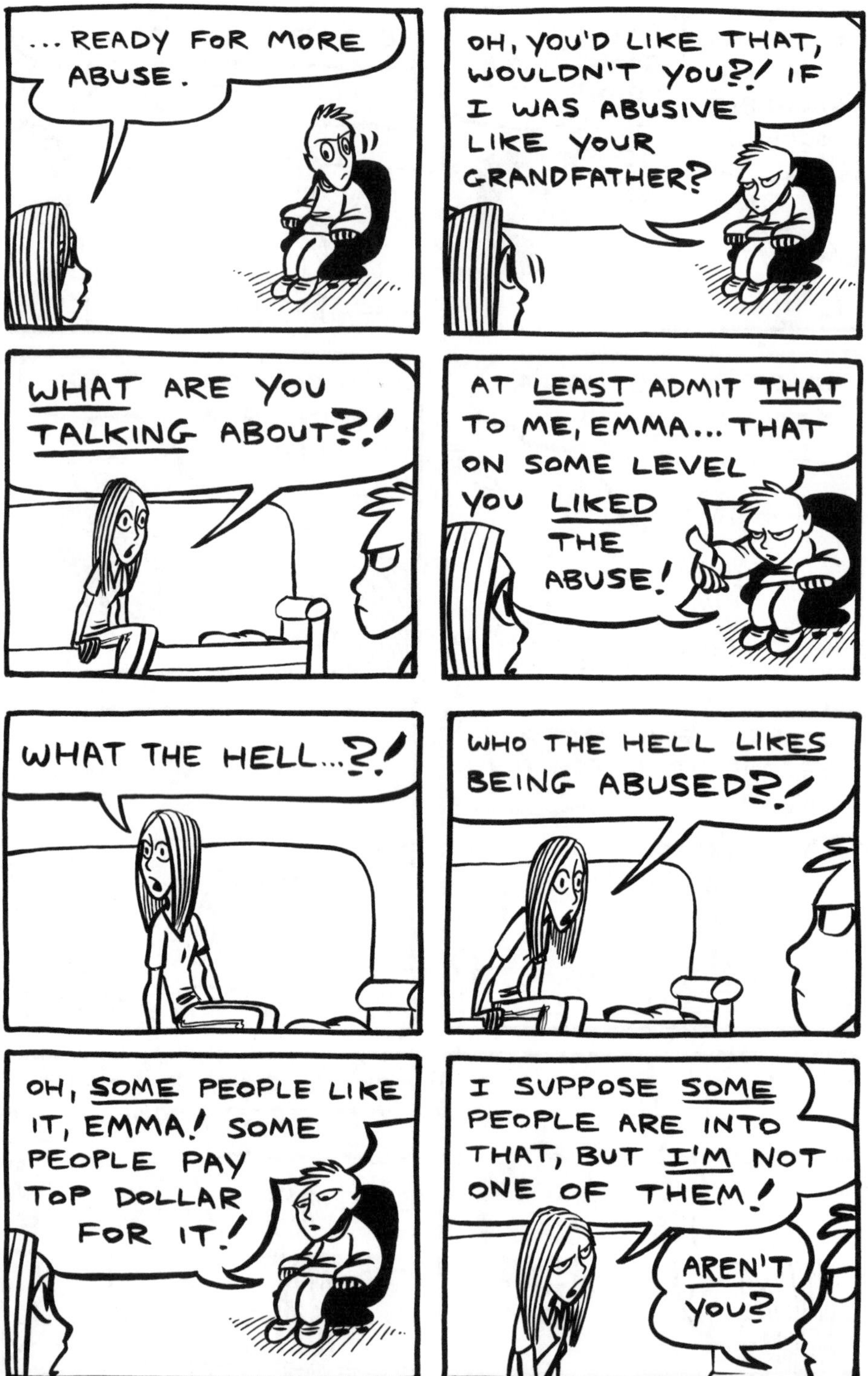
...READY FOR MORE ABUSE.
OH, YOU'D LIKE THAT, WOULDN'T YOU?! IF I WAS ABUSIVE LIKE YOUR GRANDFATHER?
WHAT ARE YOU TALKING ABOUT?!
AT LEAST ADMIT THAT TO ME, EMMA... THAT ON SOME LEVEL YOU LIKED THE ABUSE!
WHAT THE HELL...?!
WHO THE HELL LIKES BEING ABUSED?!
OH, SOME PEOPLE LIKE IT, EMMA! SOME PEOPLE PAY TOP DOLLAR FOR IT!
I SUPPOSE SOME PEOPLE ARE INTO THAT, BUT I'M NOT ONE OF THEM!
AREN'T YOU?

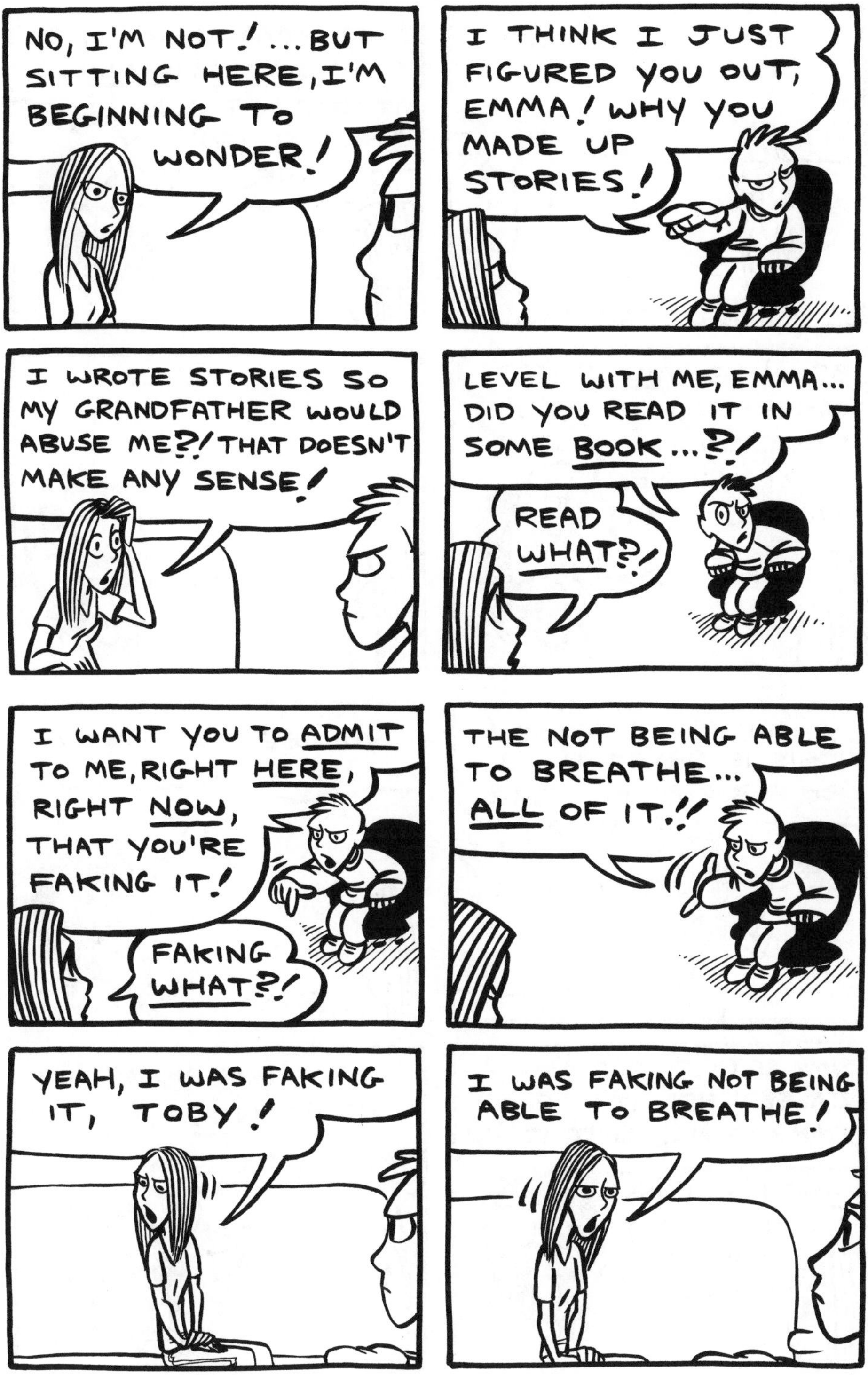
NO, I'M NOT! ...BUT SITTING HERE, I'M BEGINNING TO WONDER!
I THINK I JUST FIGURED YOU OUT, EMMA! WHY YOU MADE UP STORIES!
I WROTE STORIES SO MY GRANDFATHER WOULD ABUSE ME?! THAT DOESN'T MAKE ANY SENSE!
LEVEL WITH ME, EMMA... DID YOU READ IT IN SOME BOOK...?!
READ WHAT?!
I WANT YOU TO ADMIT TO ME, RIGHT HERE, RIGHT NOW, THAT YOU'RE FAKING IT!
FAKING WHAT?!
THE NOT BEING ABLE TO BREATHE... ALL OF IT!!
YEAH, I WAS FAKING IT, TOBY!
I WAS FAKING NOT BEING ABLE TO BREATHE!

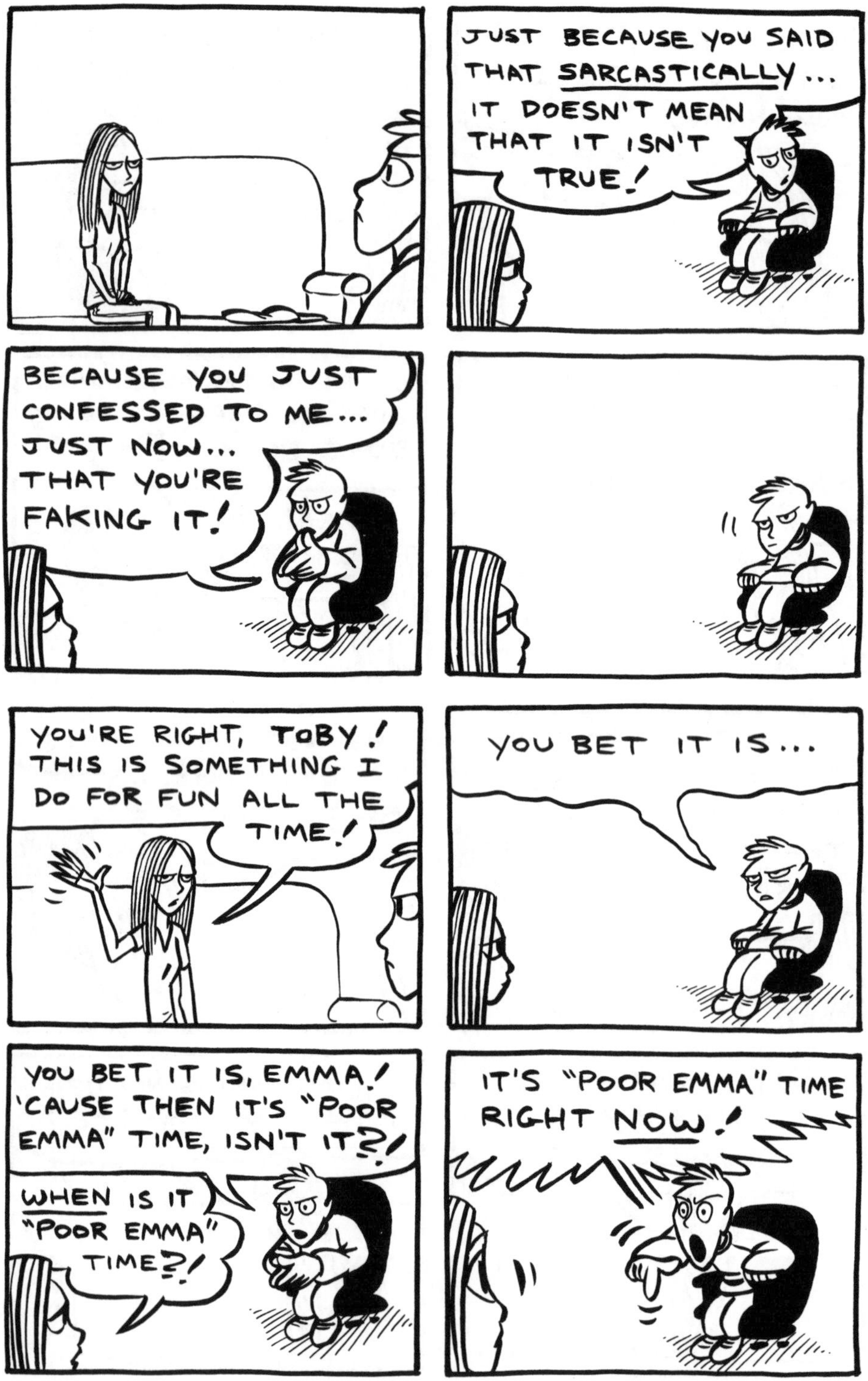
JUST BECAUSE YOU SAID THAT SARCASTICALLY...
IT DOESN'T MEAN THAT IT ISN'T TRUE!
BECAUSE YOU JUST CONFESSED TO ME... JUST NOW... THAT YOU'RE FAKING IT!
YOU'RE RIGHT, TOBY! THIS IS SOMETHING I DO FOR FUN ALL THE TIME!
YOU BET IT IS...
YOU BET IT IS, EMMA! 'CAUSE THEN IT'S "POOR EMMA" TIME, ISN'T IT?!
WHEN IS IT "POOR EMMA" TIME?!
IT'S "POOR EMMA" TIME RIGHT NOW!

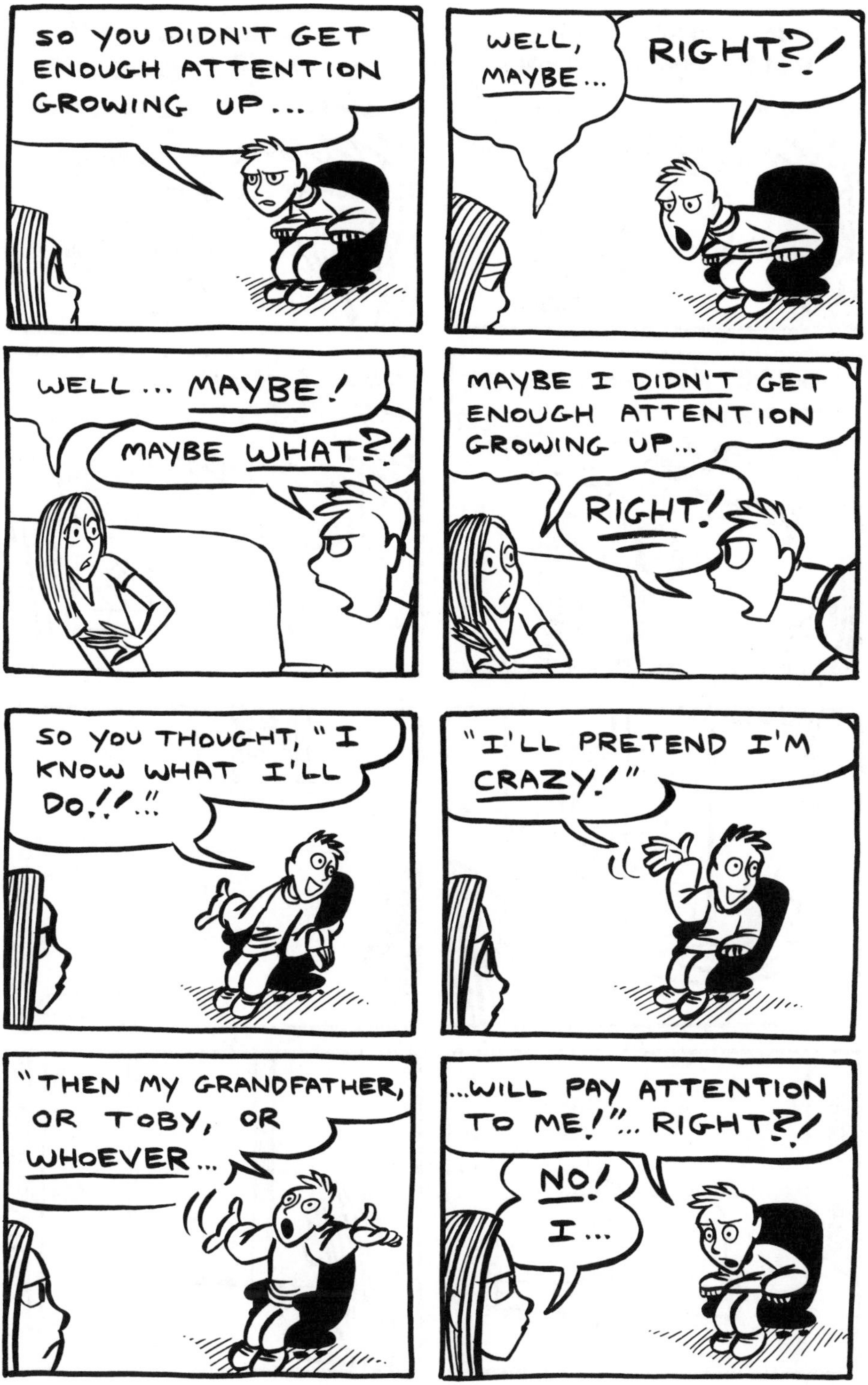
SO YOU DIDN'T GET ENOUGH ATTENTION GROWING UP...
WELL, MAYBE...
RIGHT?!
WELL... MAYBE!
MAYBE WHAT?!
MAYBE I DIDN'T GET ENOUGH ATTENTION GROWING UP...
RIGHT!
SO YOU THOUGHT, "I KNOW WHAT I'LL DO!!..!!
"I'LL PRETEND I'M CRAZY!"
"THEN MY GRANDFATHER, OR TOBY, OR WHOEVER...
...WILL PAY ATTENTION TO ME!"... RIGHT?!
NO! I...

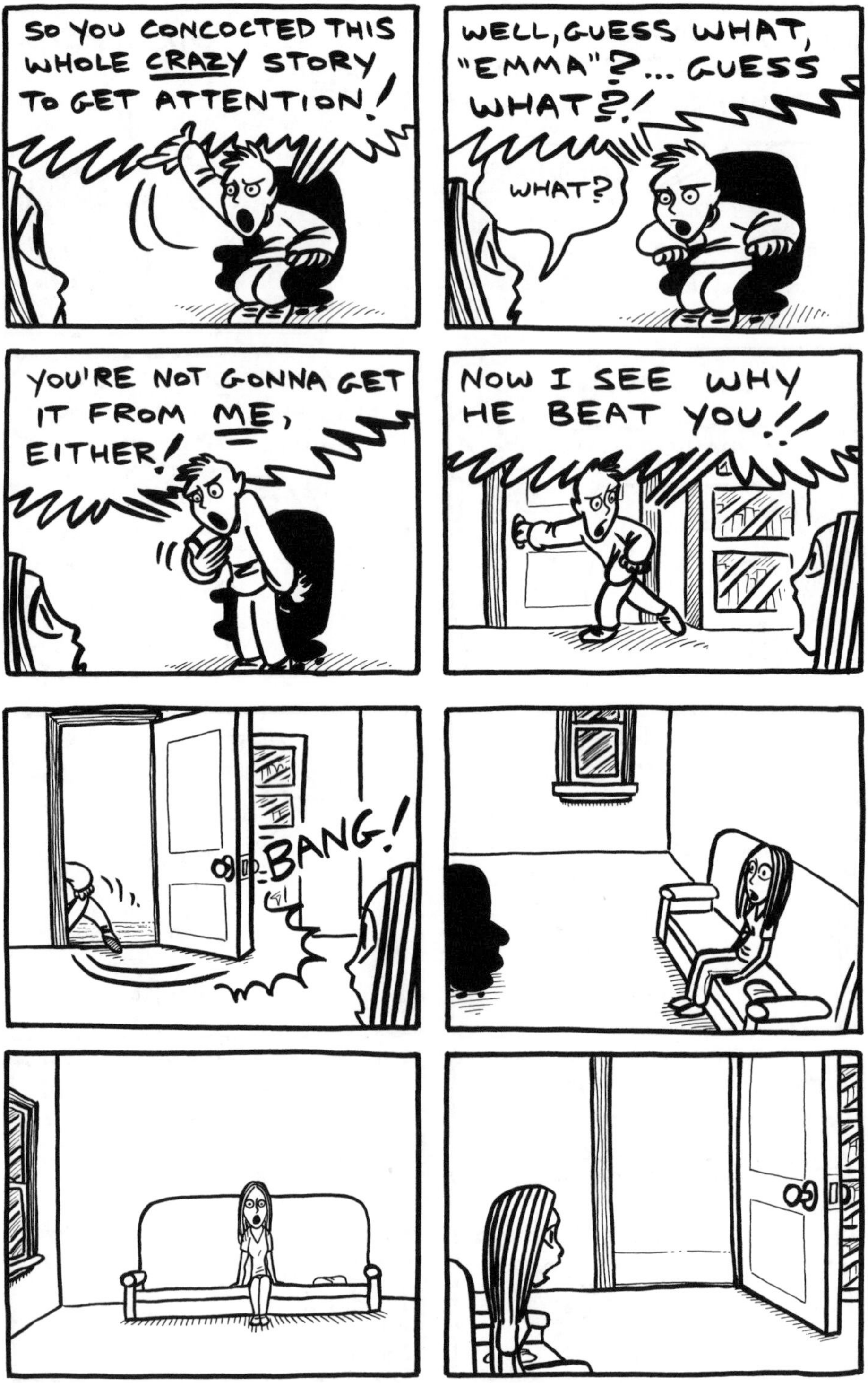
SO YOU CONCOCTED THIS WHOLE CRAZY STORY TO GET ATTENTION!
WELL, GUESS WHAT, "EMMA"?... GUESS WHAT?!
WHAT?
YOU'RE NOT GONNA GET IT FROM ME, EITHER!
NOW I SEE WHY HE BEAT YOU!!
BANG!

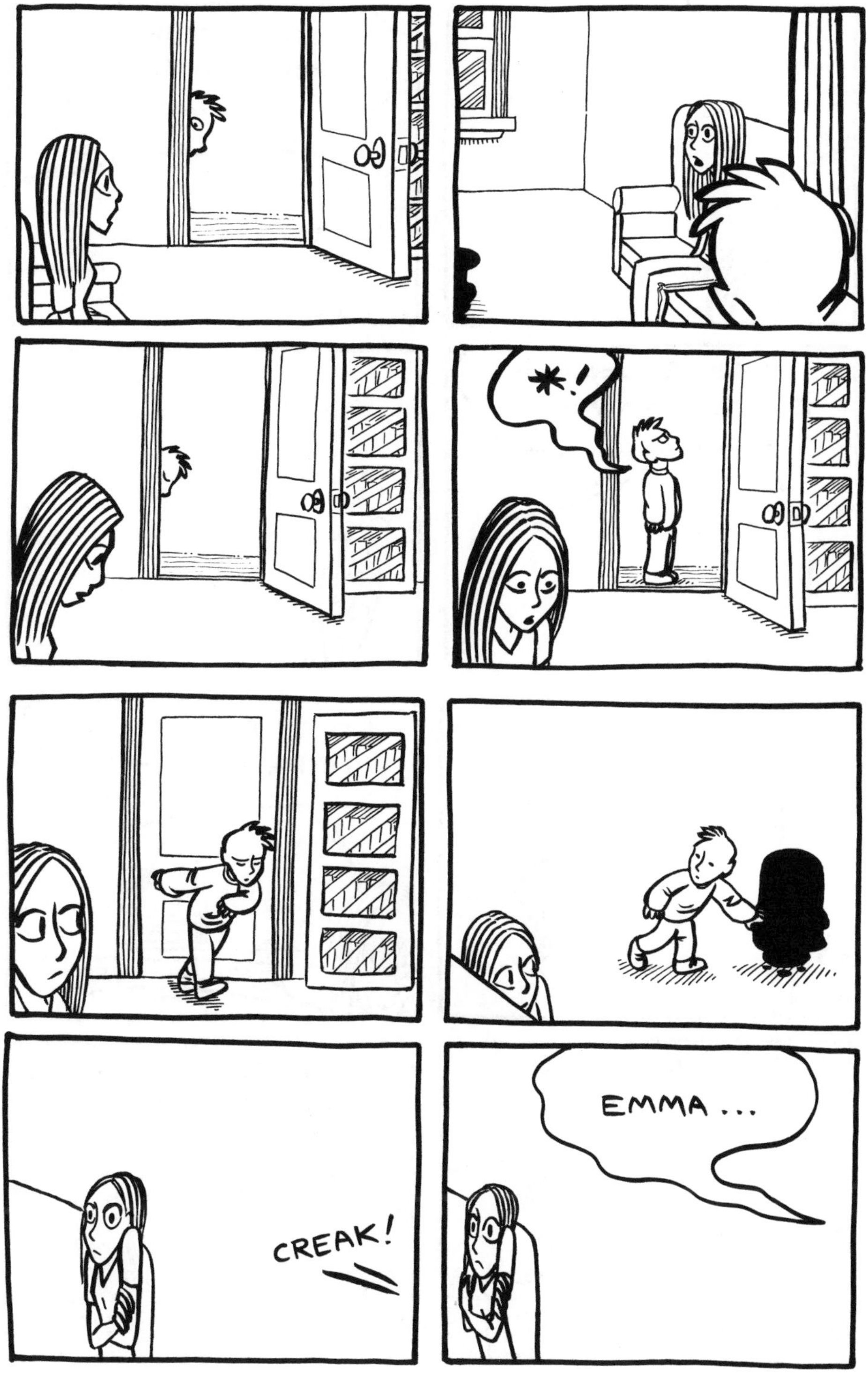
*!
CREAK!
EMMA ...

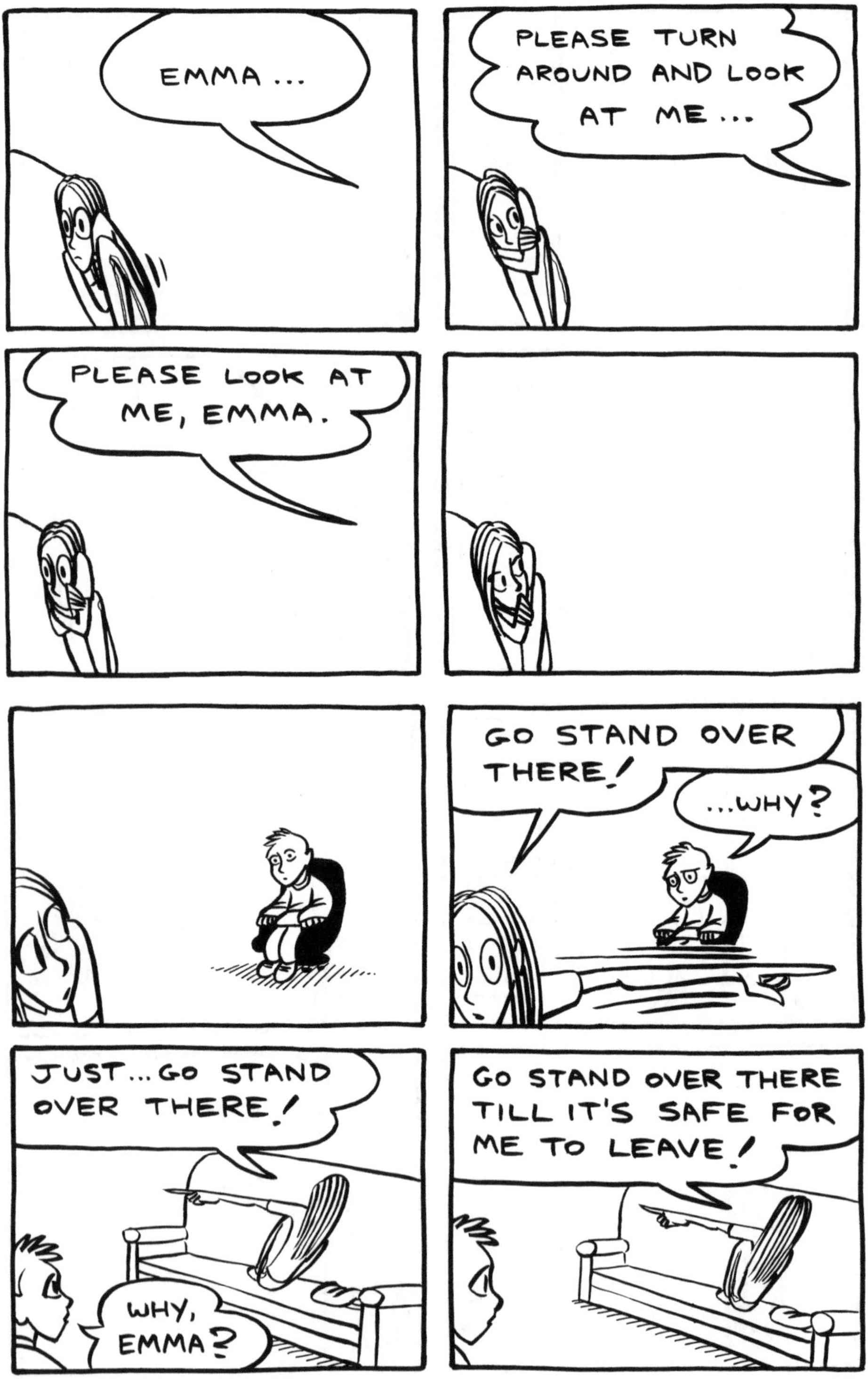
EMMA ...
PLEASE TURN AROUND AND LOOK AT ME ...
PLEASE LOOK AT ME, EMMA.
GO STAND OVER THERE!
...WHY?
JUST... GO STAND OVER THERE!
WHY, EMMA?
GO STAND OVER THERE TILL IT'S SAFE FOR ME TO LEAVE!

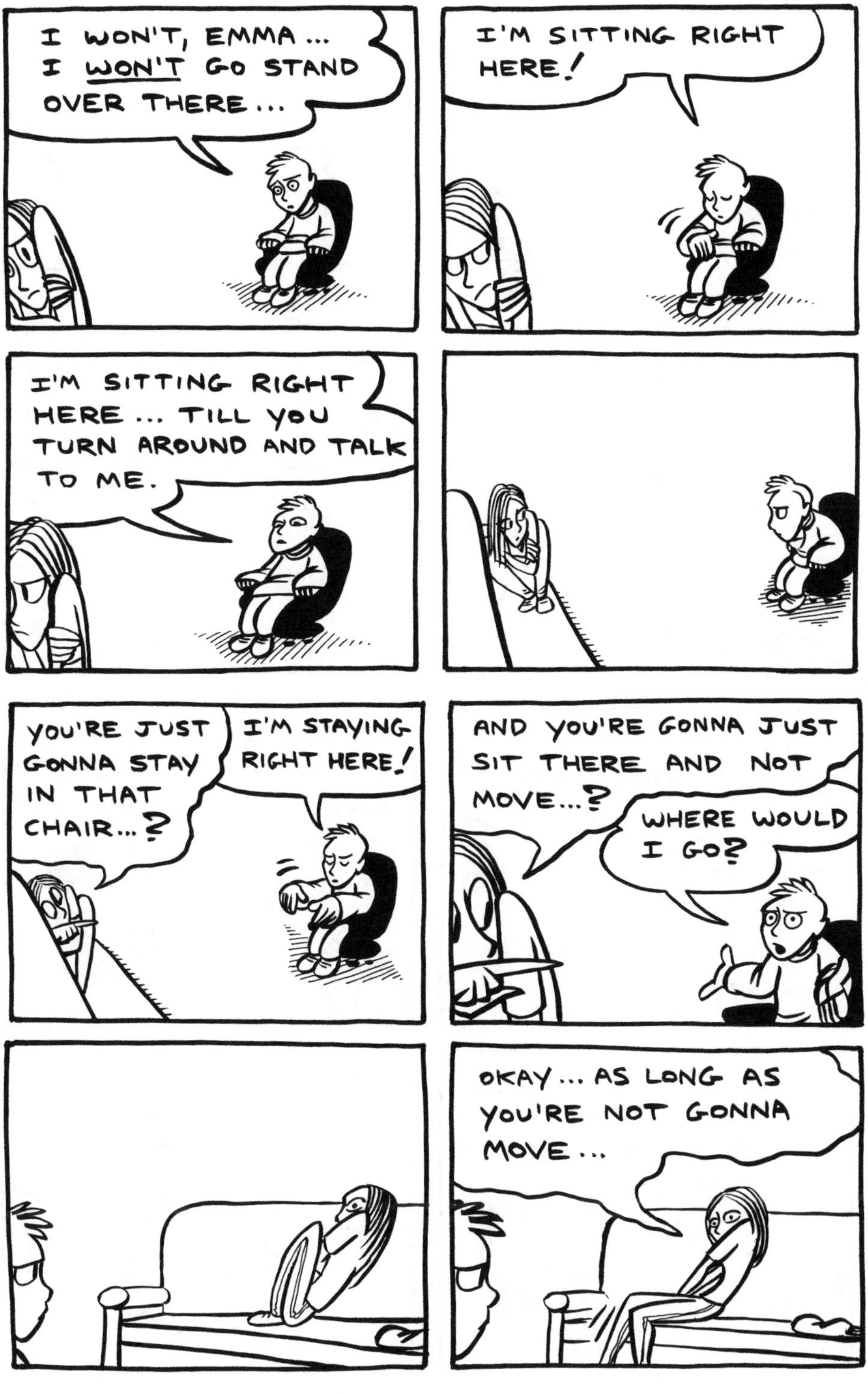

I WON'T, EMMA... I WON'T GO STAND OVER THERE...
I'M SITTING RIGHT HERE!
I'M SITTING RIGHT HERE... TILL YOU TURN AROUND AND TALK TO ME.
YOU'RE JUST GONNA STAY IN THAT CHAIR...?
I'M STAYING RIGHT HERE!
AND YOU'RE GONNA JUST SIT THERE AND NOT MOVE...?
WHERE WOULD I GO?
OKAY... AS LONG AS YOU'RE NOT GONNA MOVE...

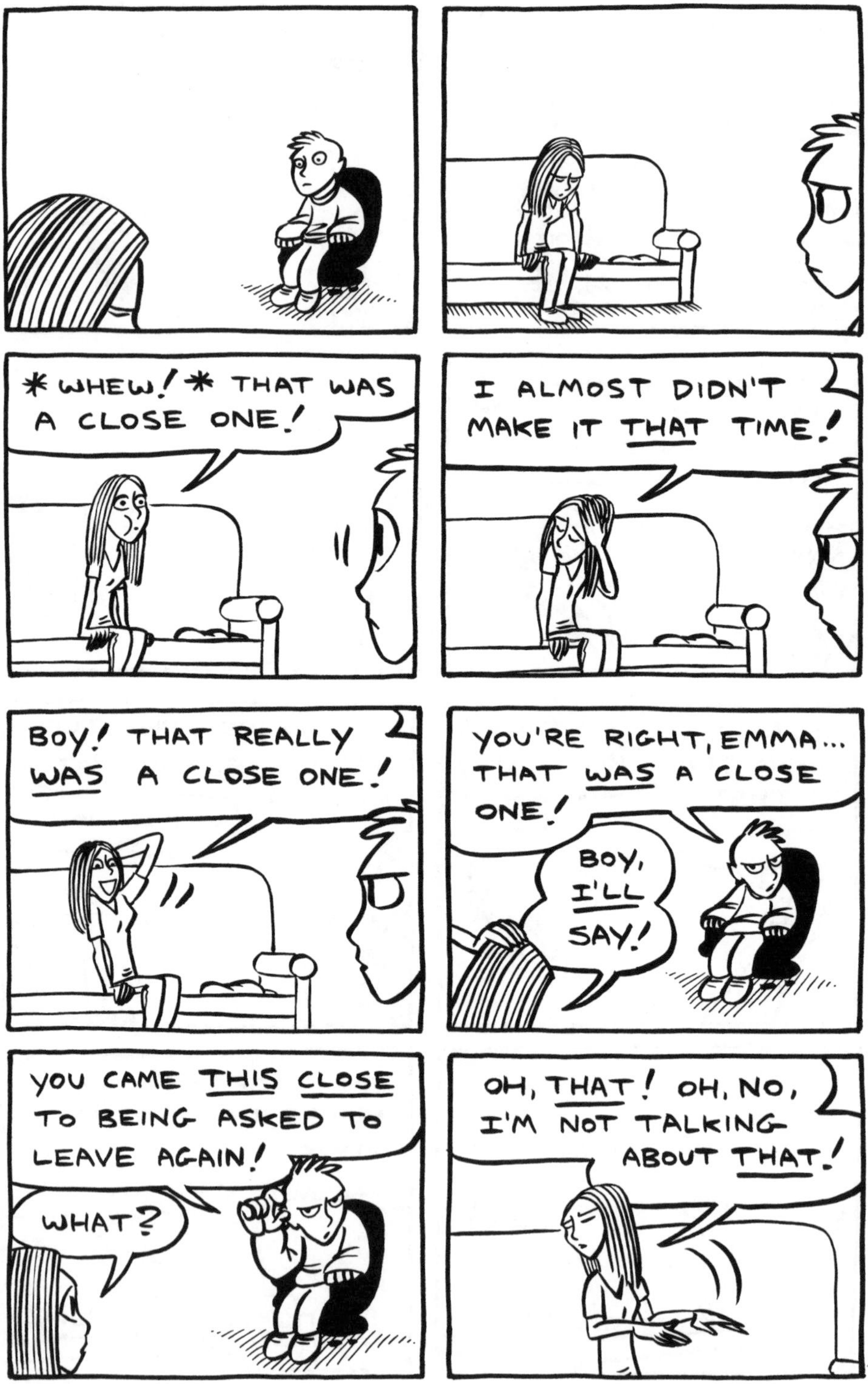
WHEW! THAT WAS A CLOSE ONE!
I ALMOST DIDN'T MAKE IT THAT TIME!
BOY! THAT REALLY WAS A CLOSE ONE!
YOU'RE RIGHT, EMMA... THAT WAS A CLOSE ONE!
BOY, I'LL SAY!
YOU CAME THIS CLOSE TO BEING ASKED TO LEAVE AGAIN!
WHAT?
OH, THAT! OH, NO, I'M NOT TALKING ABOUT THAT!

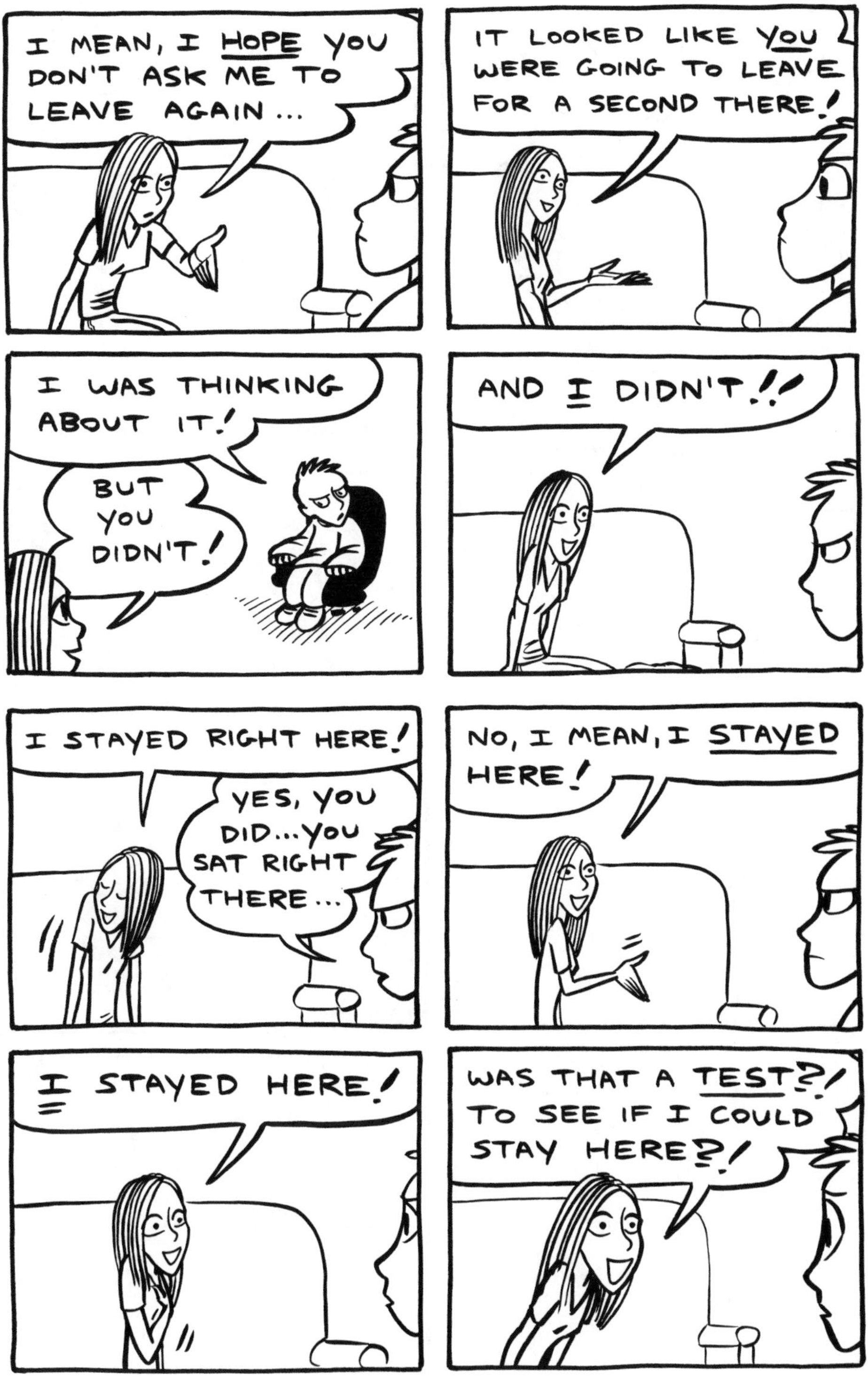
I MEAN, I HOPE YOU DON'T ASK ME TO LEAVE AGAIN...
IT LOOKED LIKE YOU WERE GOING TO LEAVE FOR A SECOND THERE!
I WAS THINKING ABOUT IT!
BUT YOU DIDN'T!
AND I DIDN'T!!
I STAYED RIGHT HERE!
YES, YOU DID...YOU SAT RIGHT THERE...
NO, I MEAN, I STAYED HERE!
I STAYED HERE!
WAS THAT A TEST?! TO SEE IF I COULD STAY HERE?!

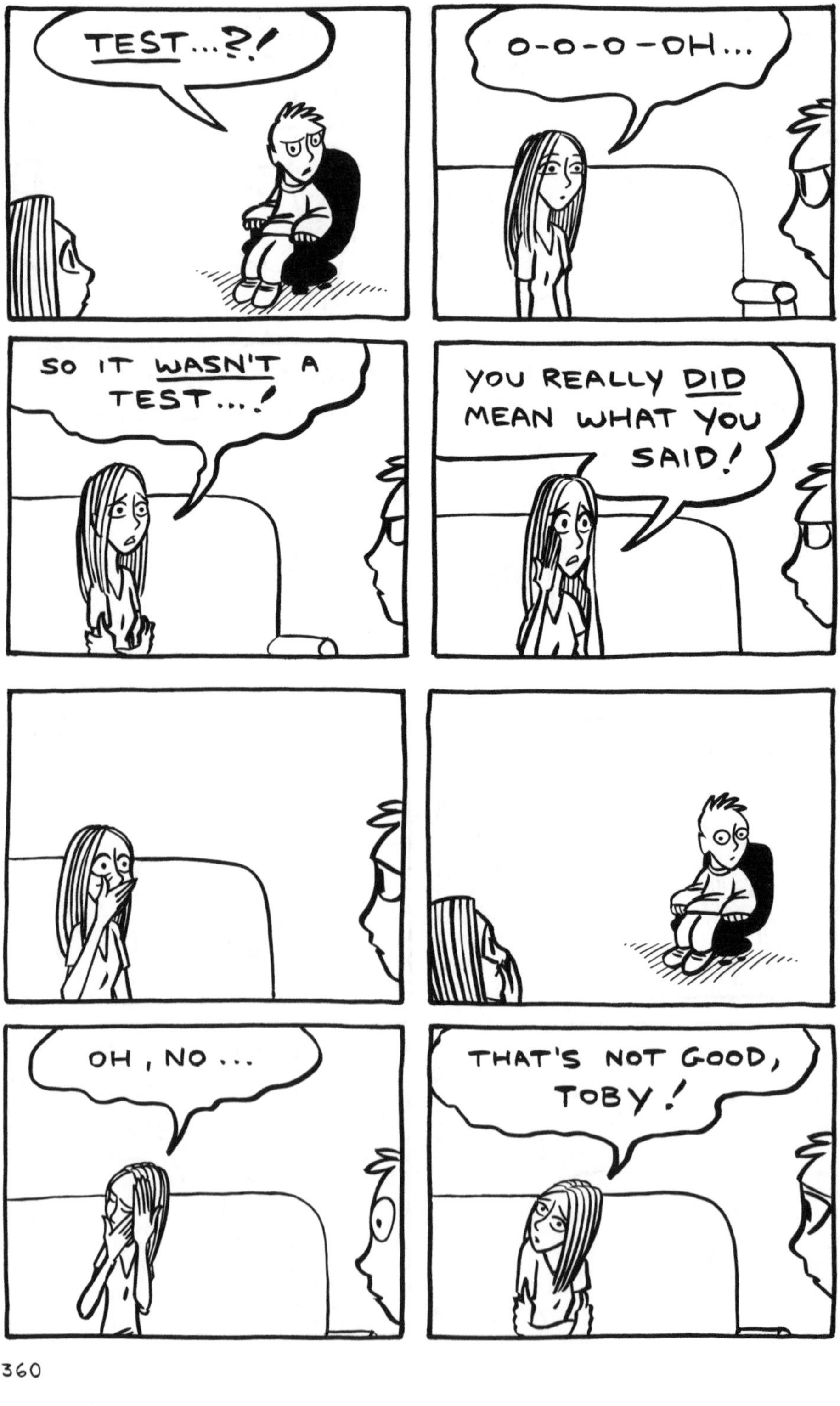
TEST...?!
O-O-O-OH...
SO IT WASN'T A TEST...!
YOU REALLY DID MEAN WHAT YOU SAID!
OH, NO...
THAT'S NOT GOOD, TOBY!

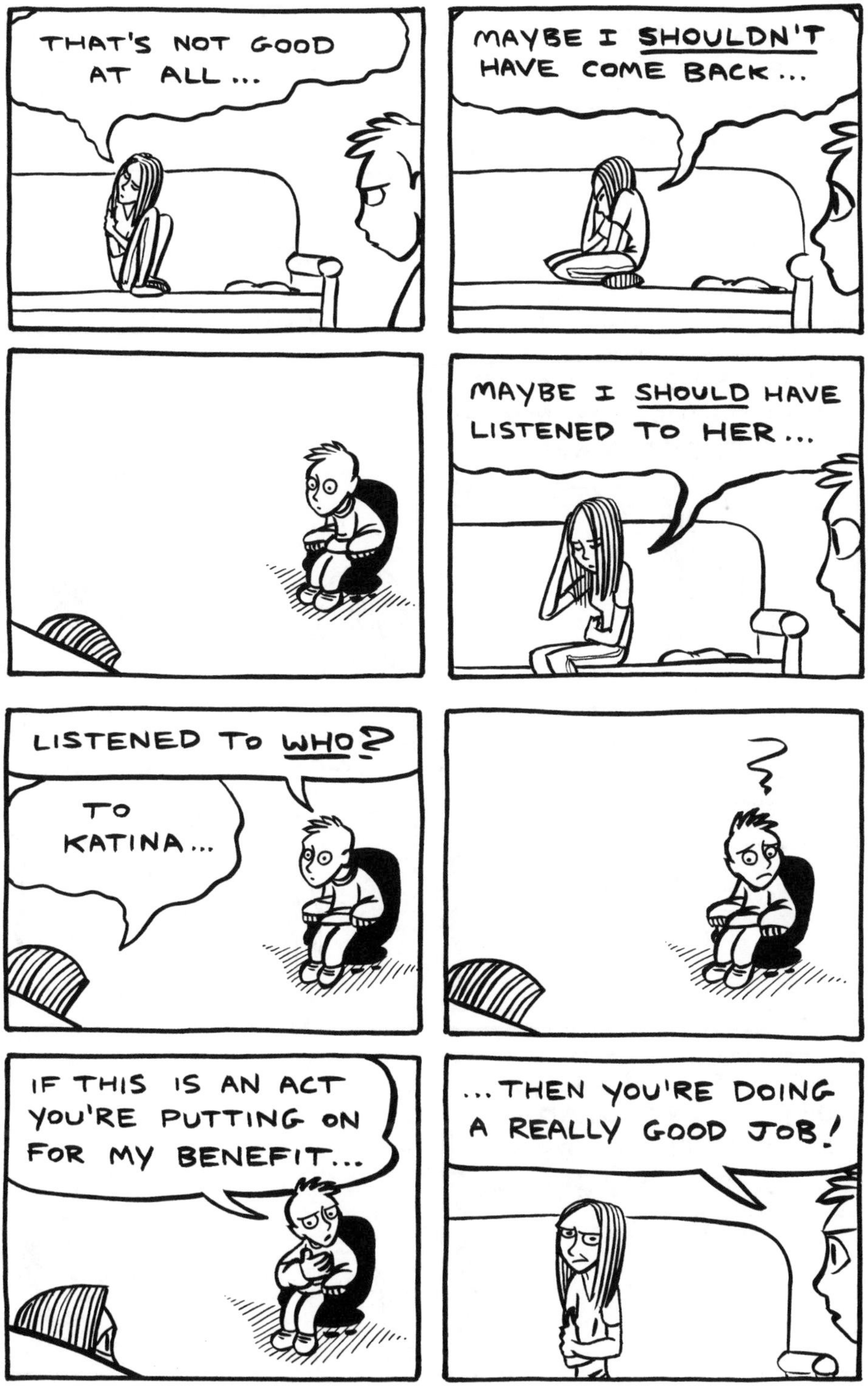
THAT'S NOT GOOD AT ALL...
MAYBE I SHOULDN'T HAVE COME BACK...
MAYBE I SHOULD HAVE LISTENED TO HER...
LISTENED TO WHO?
TO KATINA...
IF THIS IS AN ACT YOU'RE PUTTING ON FOR MY BENEFIT...
...THEN YOU'RE DOING A REALLY GOOD JOB!

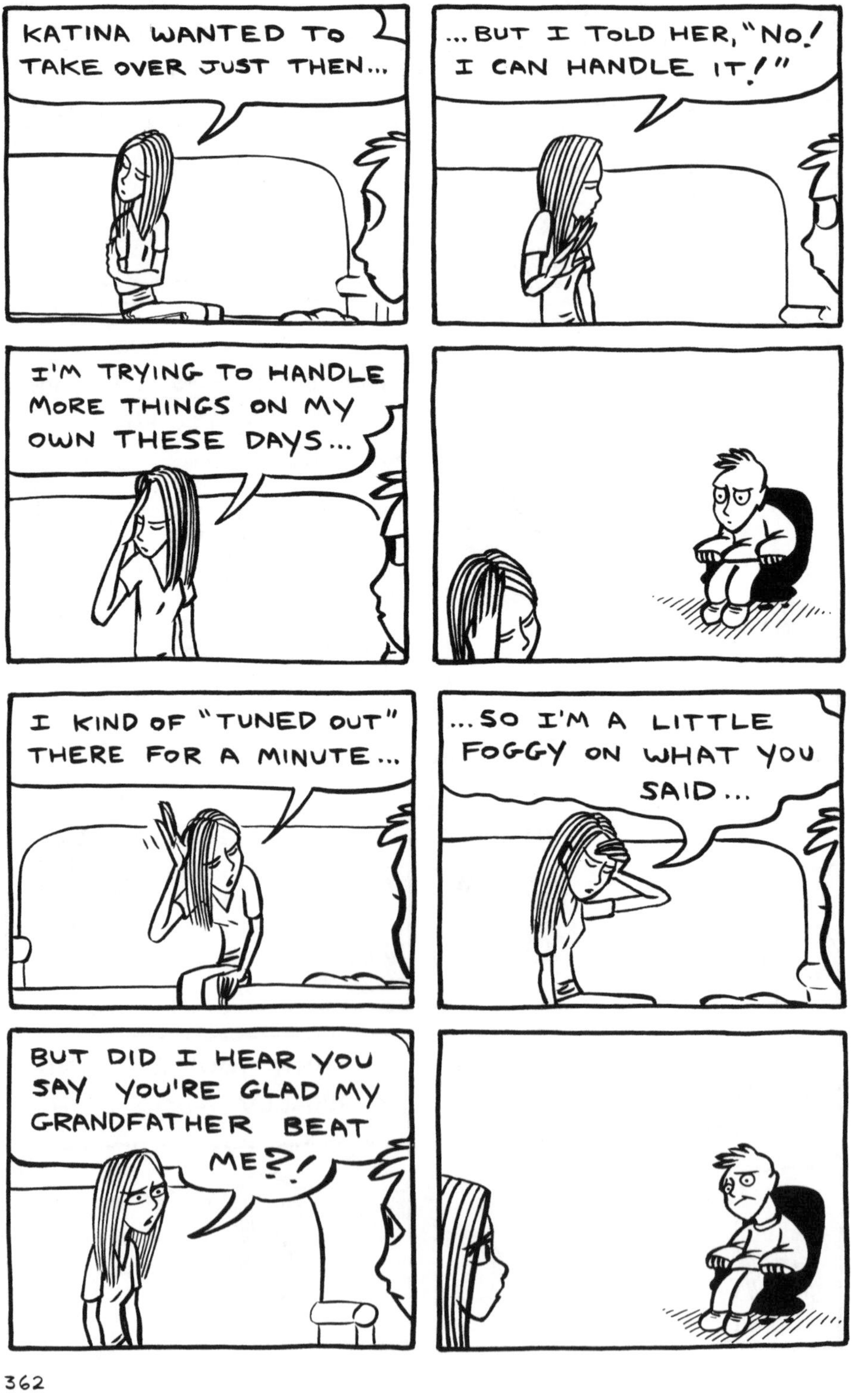
KATINA WANTED TO TAKE OVER JUST THEN...
...BUT I TOLD HER, "NO! I CAN HANDLE IT!"
I'M TRYING TO HANDLE MORE THINGS ON MY OWN THESE DAYS...
I KIND OF "TUNED OUT" THERE FOR A MINUTE...
...SO I'M A LITTLE FOGGY ON WHAT YOU SAID...
BUT DID I HEAR YOU SAY YOU'RE GLAD MY GRANDFATHER BEAT ME?!

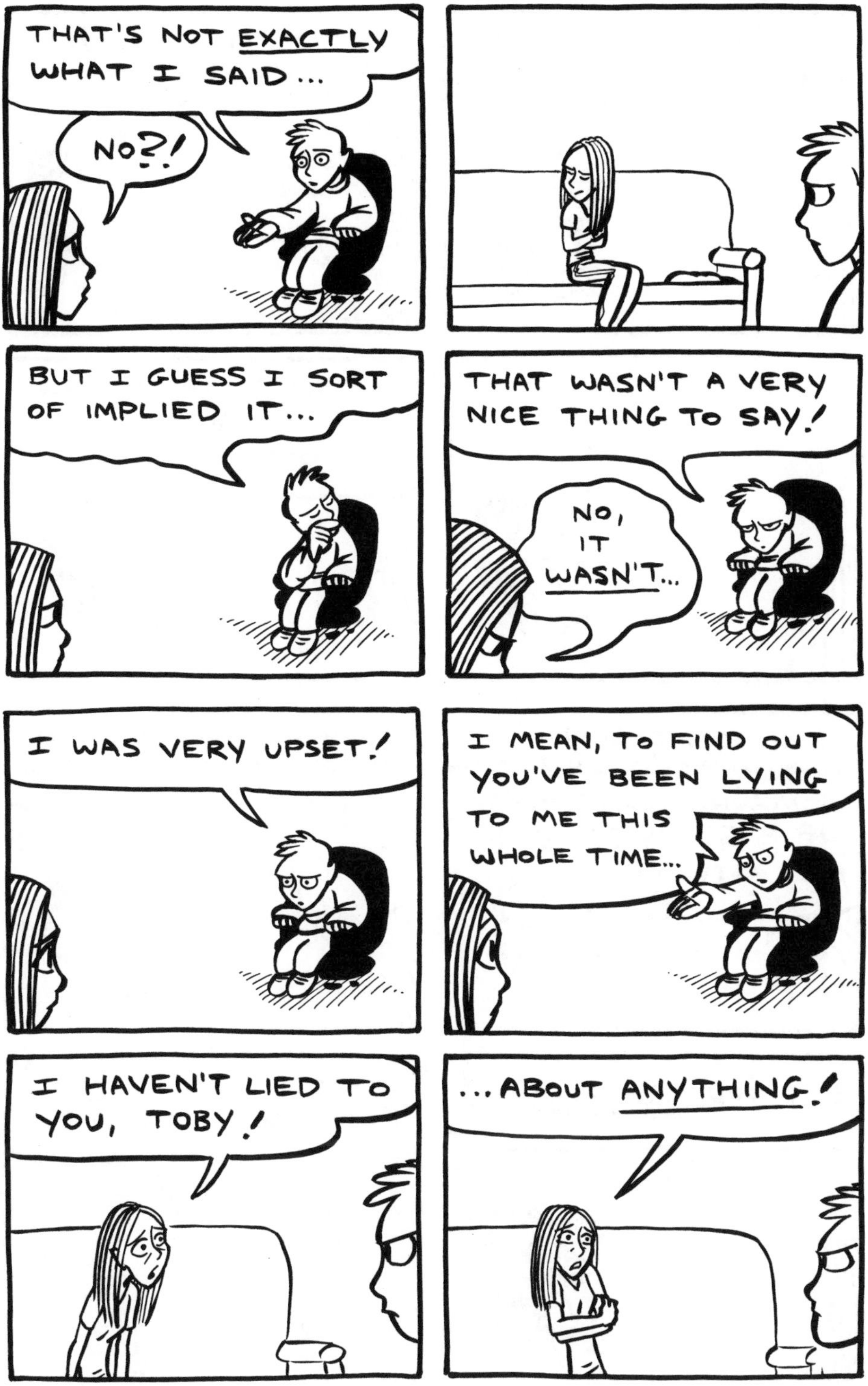
THAT'S NOT EXACTLY WHAT I SAID...
NO?!
BUT I GUESS I SORT OF IMPLIED IT...
THAT WASN'T A VERY NICE THING TO SAY!
NO, IT WASN'T...
I WAS VERY UPSET!
I MEAN, TO FIND OUT YOU'VE BEEN LYING TO ME THIS WHOLE TIME...
I HAVEN'T LIED TO YOU, TOBY!
...ABOUT ANYTHING!

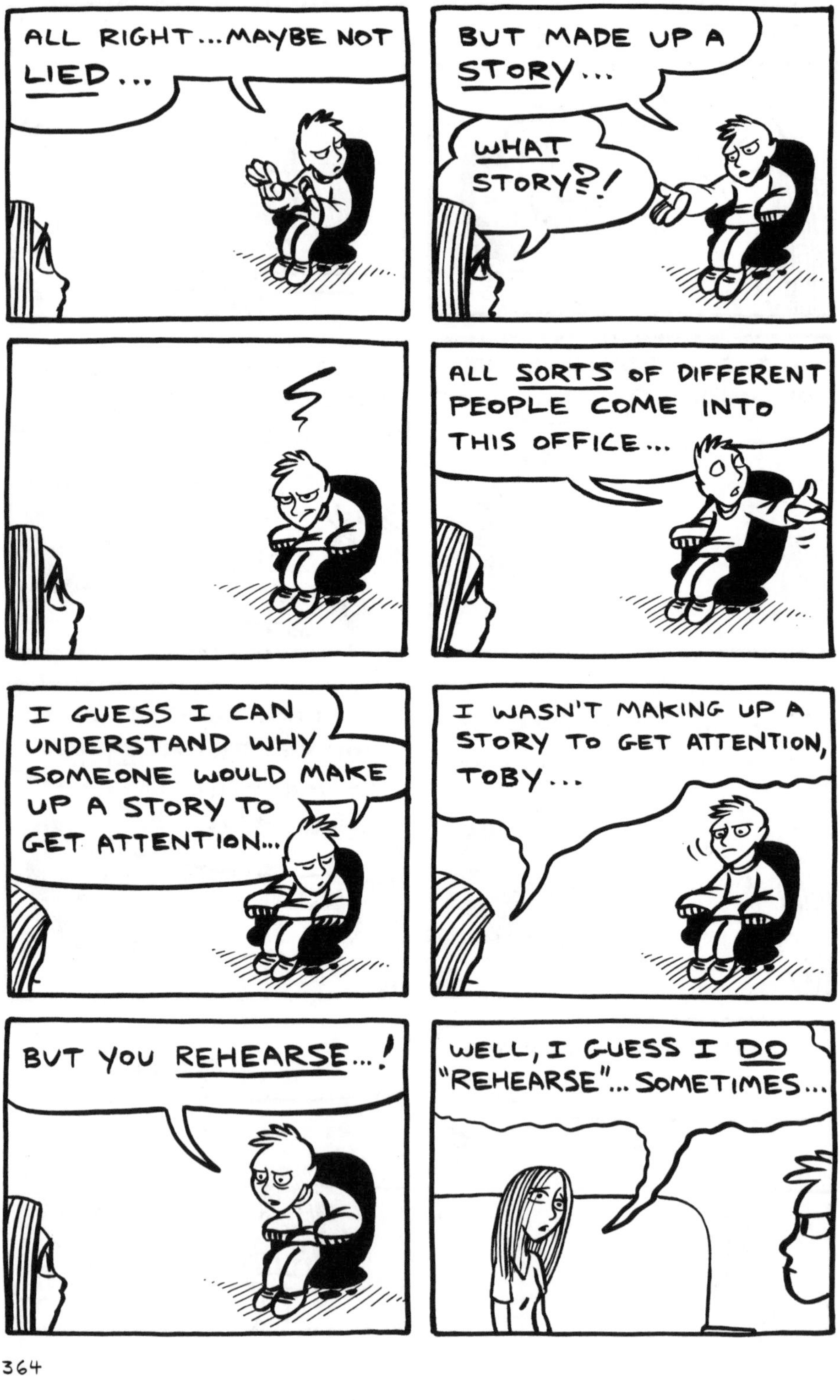
ALL RIGHT...MAYBE NOT LIED...
BUT MADE UP A STORY...
WHAT STORY?!
ALL SORTS OF DIFFERENT PEOPLE COME INTO THIS OFFICE...
I GUESS I CAN UNDERSTAND WHY SOMEONE WOULD MAKE UP A STORY TO GET ATTENTION...
I WASN'T MAKING UP A STORY TO GET ATTENTION, TOBY...
BUT YOU REHEARSE...!
WELL, I GUESS I DO "REHEARSE"... SOMETIMES...

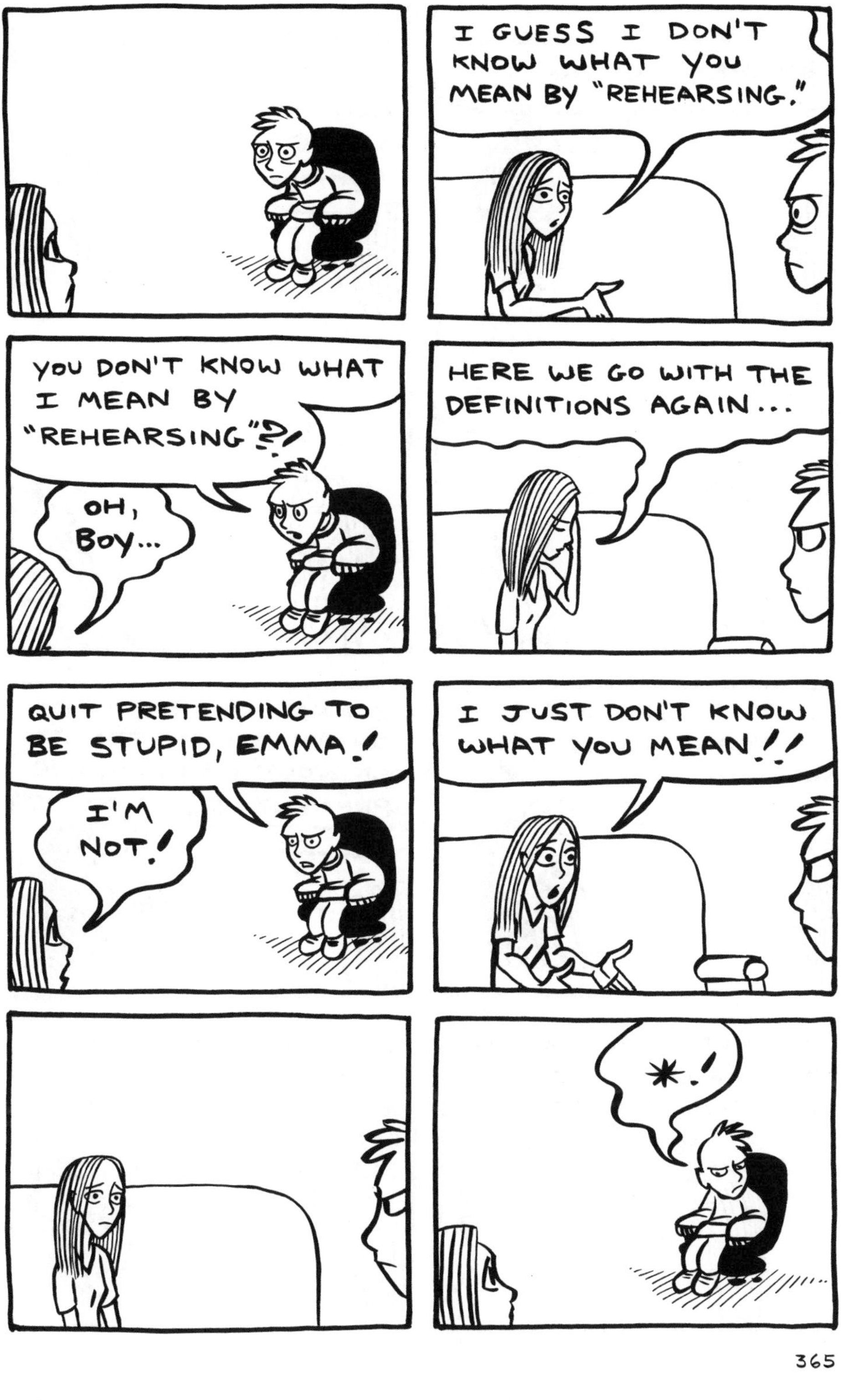
I GUESS I DON'T KNOW WHAT YOU MEAN BY "REHEARSING."
YOU DON'T KNOW WHAT I MEAN BY "REHEARSING"?!
OH, BOY...
HERE WE GO WITH THE DEFINITIONS AGAIN...
QUIT PRETENDING TO BE STUPID, EMMA!
I'M NOT!
I JUST DON'T KNOW WHAT YOU MEAN!!
*!

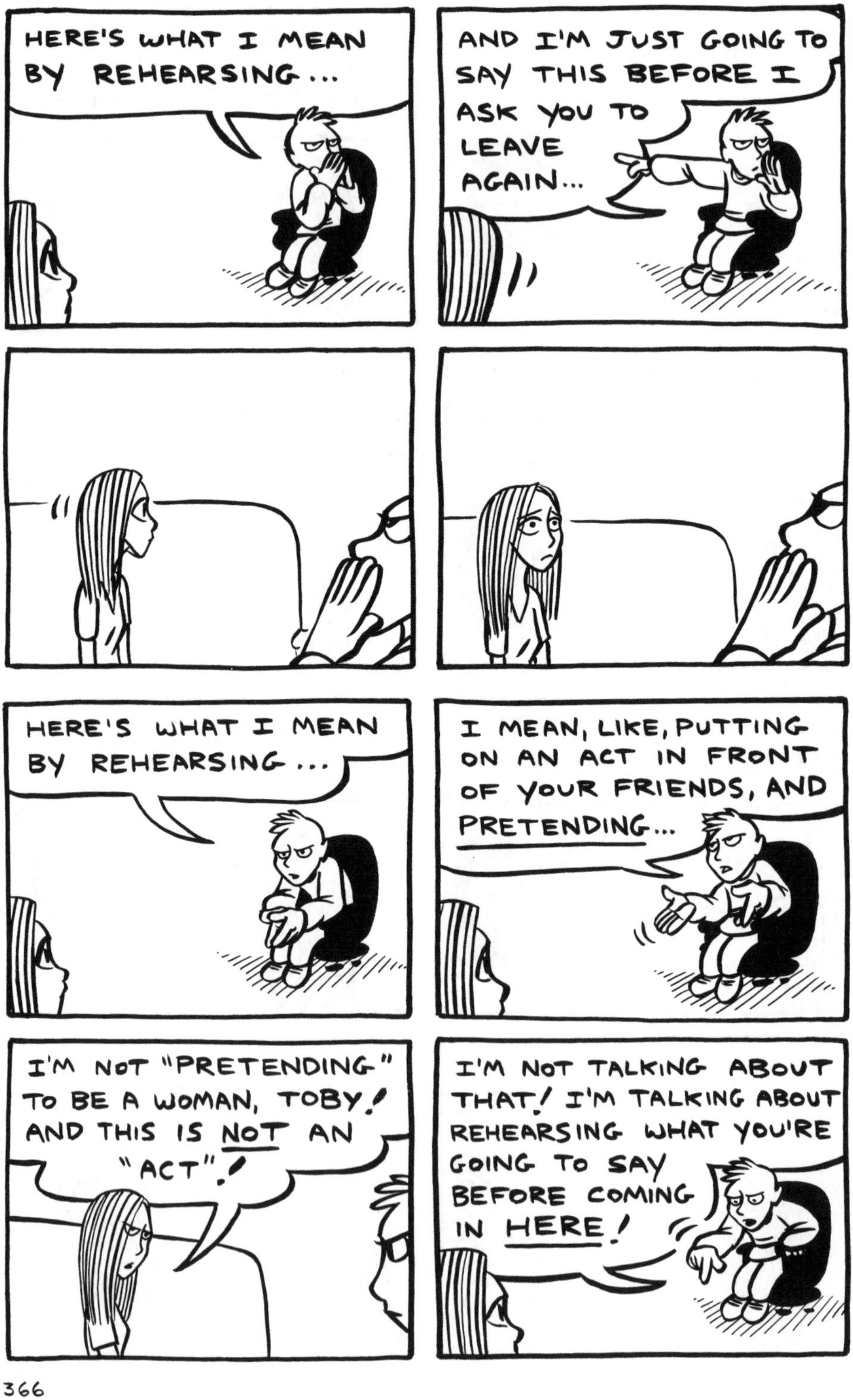
HERE'S WHAT I MEAN BY REHEARSING...
AND I'M JUST GOING TO SAY THIS BEFORE I ASK YOU TO LEAVE AGAIN...
HERE'S WHAT I MEAN BY REHEARSING...
I MEAN, LIKE, PUTTING ON AN ACT IN FRONT OF YOUR FRIENDS, AND PRETENDING...
I'M NOT "PRETENDING" TO BE A WOMAN, TOBY! AND THIS IS NOT AN "ACT"!
I'M NOT TALKING ABOUT THAT! I'M TALKING ABOUT REHEARSING WHAT YOU'RE GOING TO SAY BEFORE COMING IN HERE!

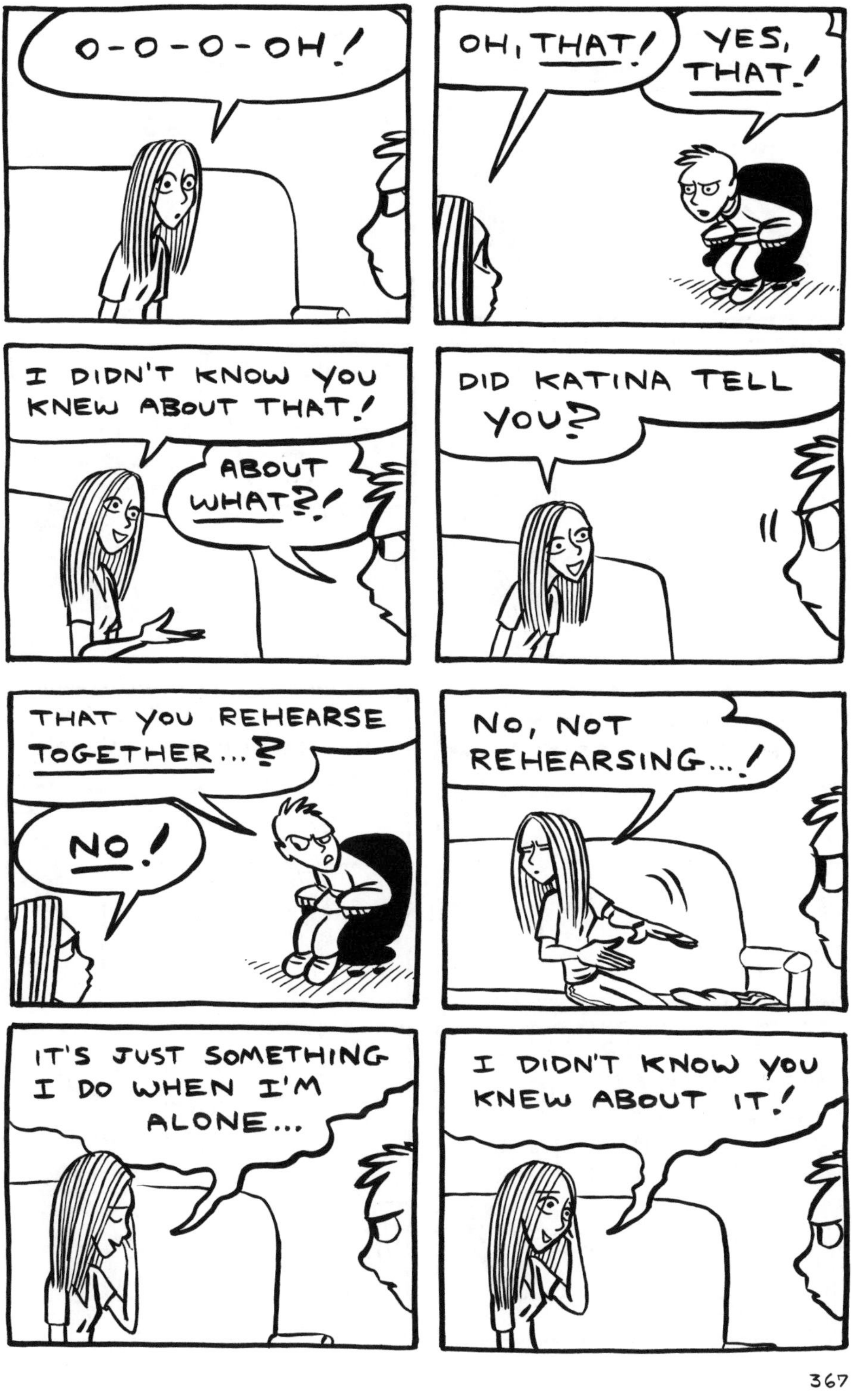

O-O-O-OH!
OH, THAT!
YES, THAT!
I DIDN'T KNOW YOU KNEW ABOUT THAT!
ABOUT WHAT?!
DID KATINA TELL YOU?
THAT YOU REHEARSE TOGETHER...?
NO!
NO, NOT REHEARSING...!
IT'S JUST SOMETHING I DO WHEN I'M ALONE...
I DIDN'T KNOW YOU KNEW ABOUT IT!

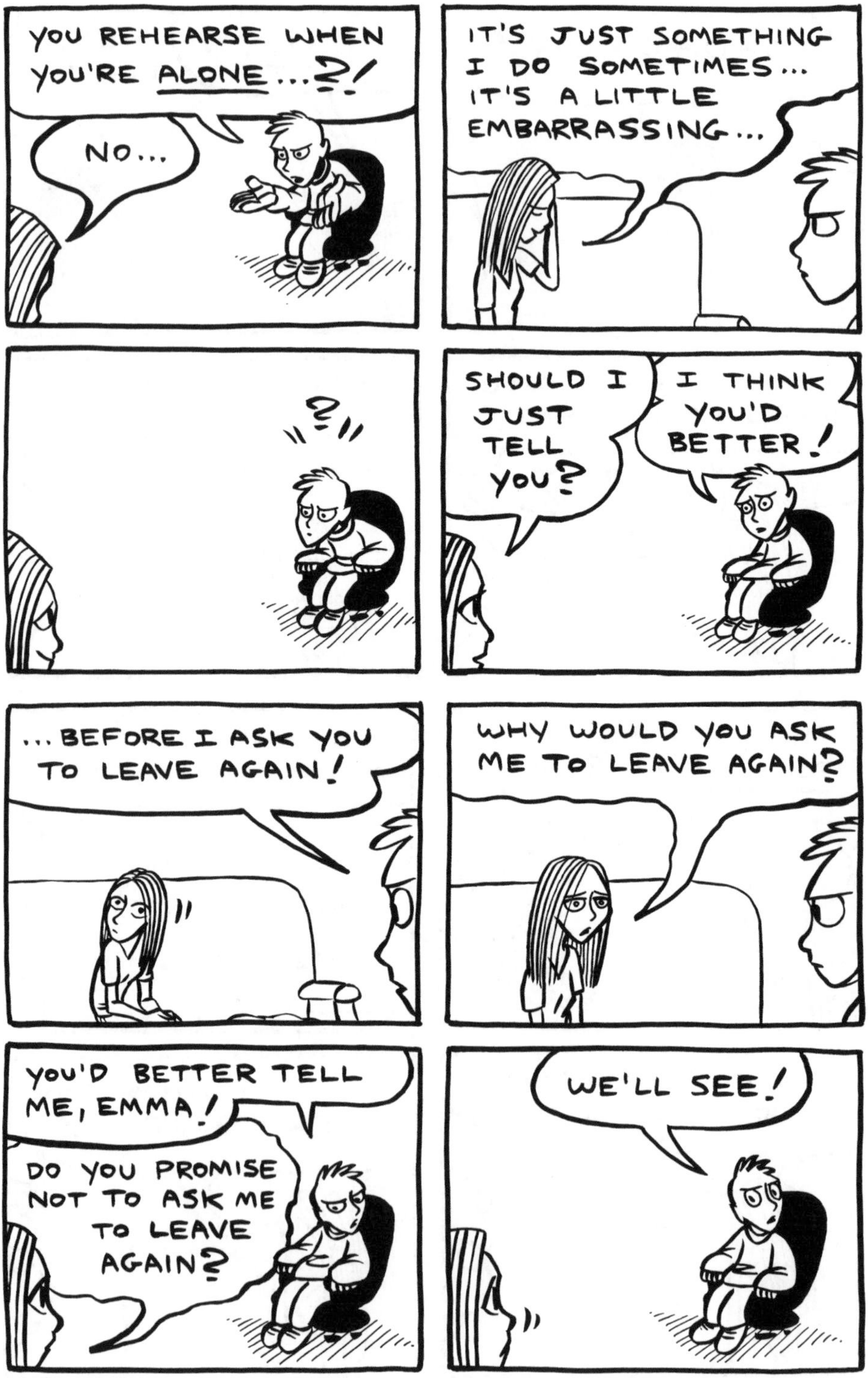
YOU REHEARSE WHEN YOU'RE ALONE...?!
NO...
IT'S JUST SOMETHING I DO SOMETIMES... IT'S A LITTLE EMBARRASSING...
?
SHOULD I JUST TELL YOU?
I THINK YOU'D BETTER!
...BEFORE I ASK YOU TO LEAVE AGAIN!
WHY WOULD YOU ASK ME TO LEAVE AGAIN?
YOU'D BETTER TELL ME, EMMA!
DO YOU PROMISE NOT TO ASK ME TO LEAVE AGAIN?
WE'LL SEE!

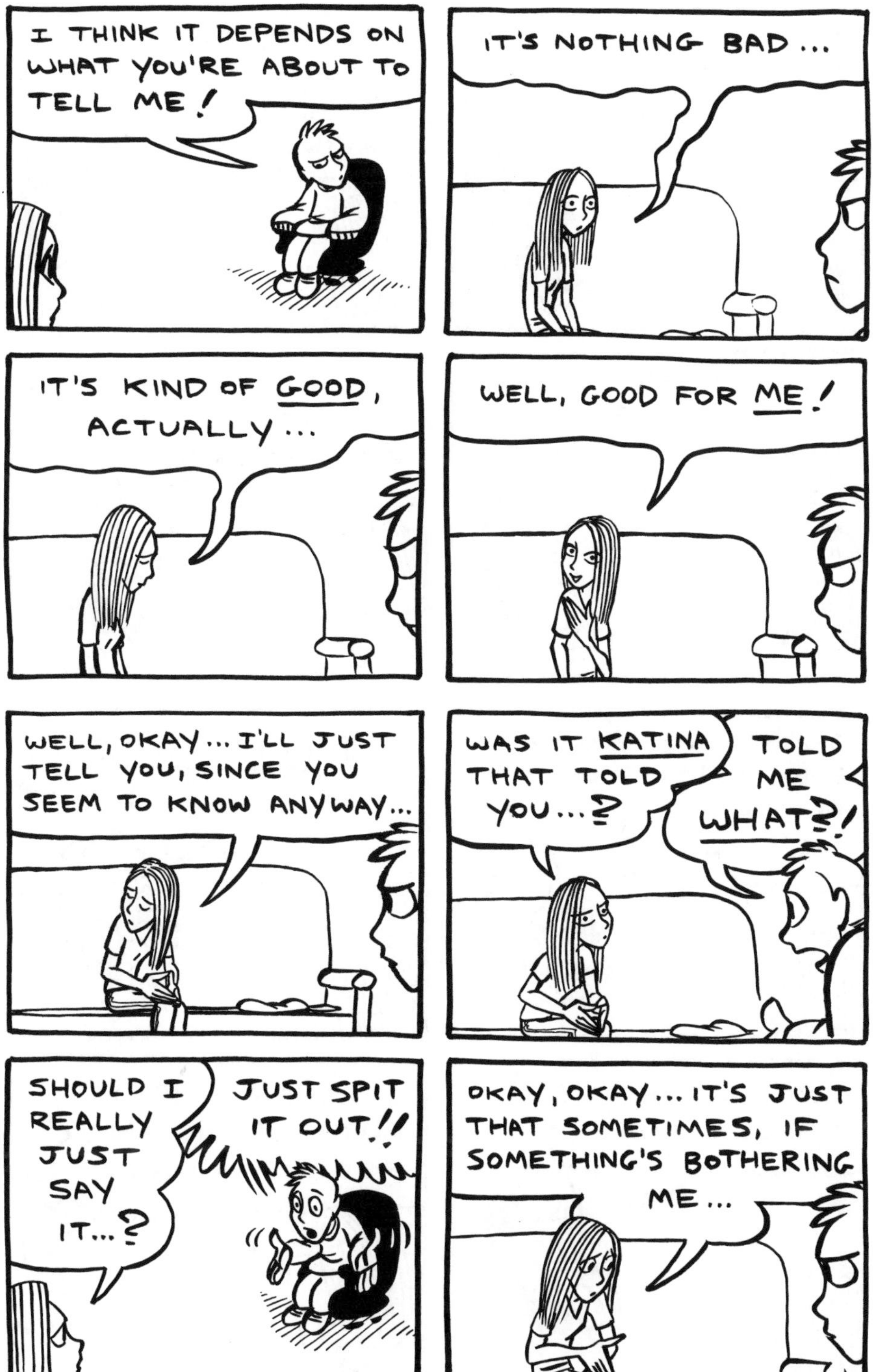
I THINK IT DEPENDS ON WHAT YOU'RE ABOUT TO TELL ME!
IT'S NOTHING BAD...
IT'S KIND OF GOOD, ACTUALLY...
WELL, GOOD FOR ME!
WELL, OKAY... I'LL JUST TELL YOU, SINCE YOU SEEM TO KNOW ANYWAY...
WAS IT KATINA THAT TOLD YOU...?
TOLD ME WHAT?!
SHOULD I REALLY JUST SAY IT...?
JUST SPIT IT OUT!!
OKAY, OKAY... IT'S JUST THAT SOMETIMES, IF SOMETHING'S BOTHERING ME...

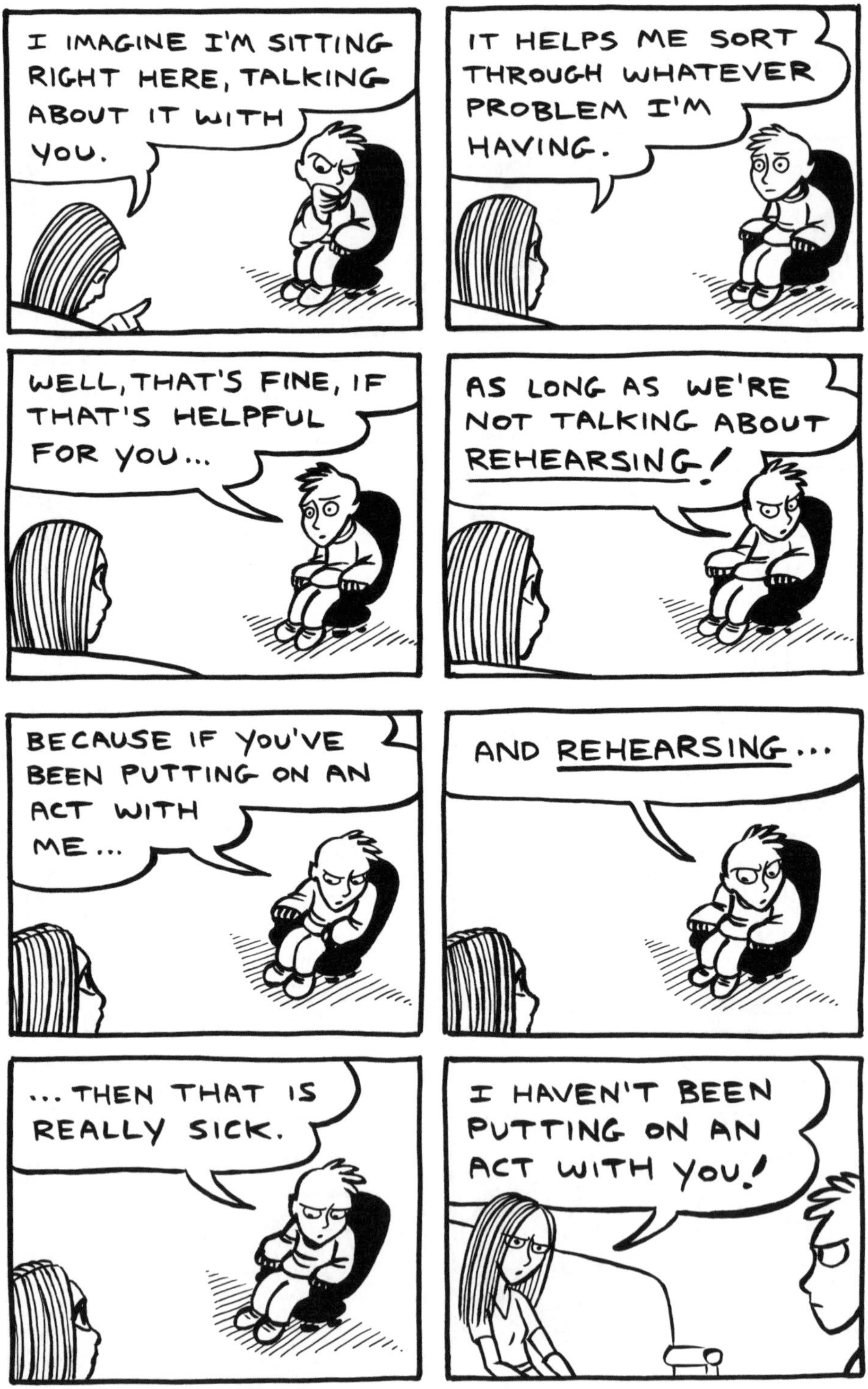
I IMAGINE I'M SITTING RIGHT HERE, TALKING ABOUT IT WITH YOU.
IT HELPS ME SORT THROUGH WHATEVER PROBLEM I'M HAVING.
WELL, THAT'S FINE, IF THAT'S HELPFUL FOR YOU...
AS LONG AS WE'RE NOT TALKING ABOUT REHEARSING!
BECAUSE IF YOU'VE BEEN PUTTING ON AN ACT WITH ME...
AND REHEARSING...
...THEN THAT IS REALLY SICK.
I HAVEN'T BEEN PUTTING ON AN ACT WITH YOU!

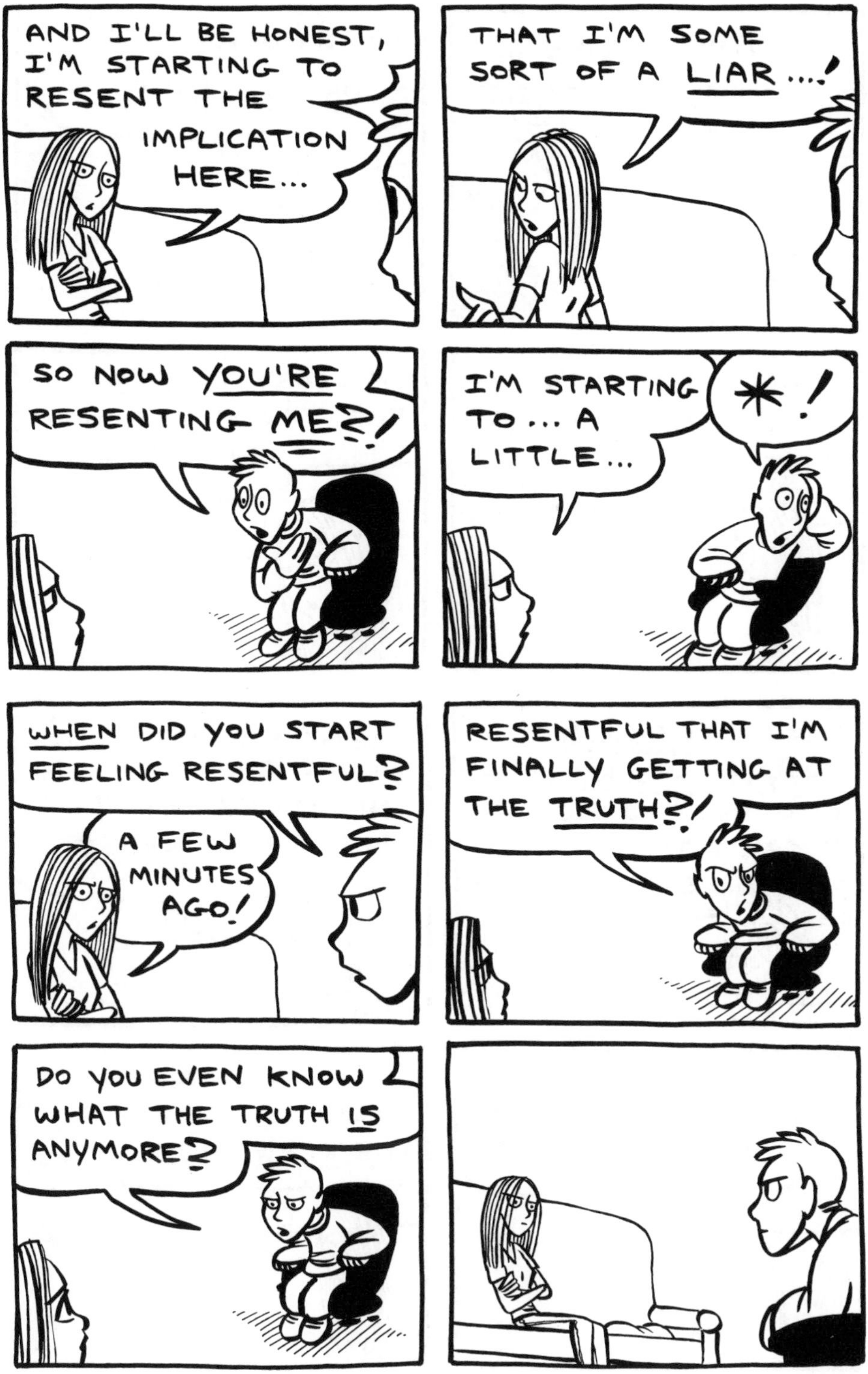
AND I'LL BE HONEST, I'M STARTING TO RESENT THE IMPLICATION HERE...
THAT I'M SOME SORT OF A LIAR...!
SO NOW YOU'RE RESENTING ME?!
I'M STARTING TO... A LITTLE...
*!
WHEN DID YOU START FEELING RESENTFUL?
A FEW MINUTES AGO!
RESENTFUL THAT I'M FINALLY GETTING AT THE TRUTH?!
DO YOU EVEN KNOW WHAT THE TRUTH IS ANYMORE?

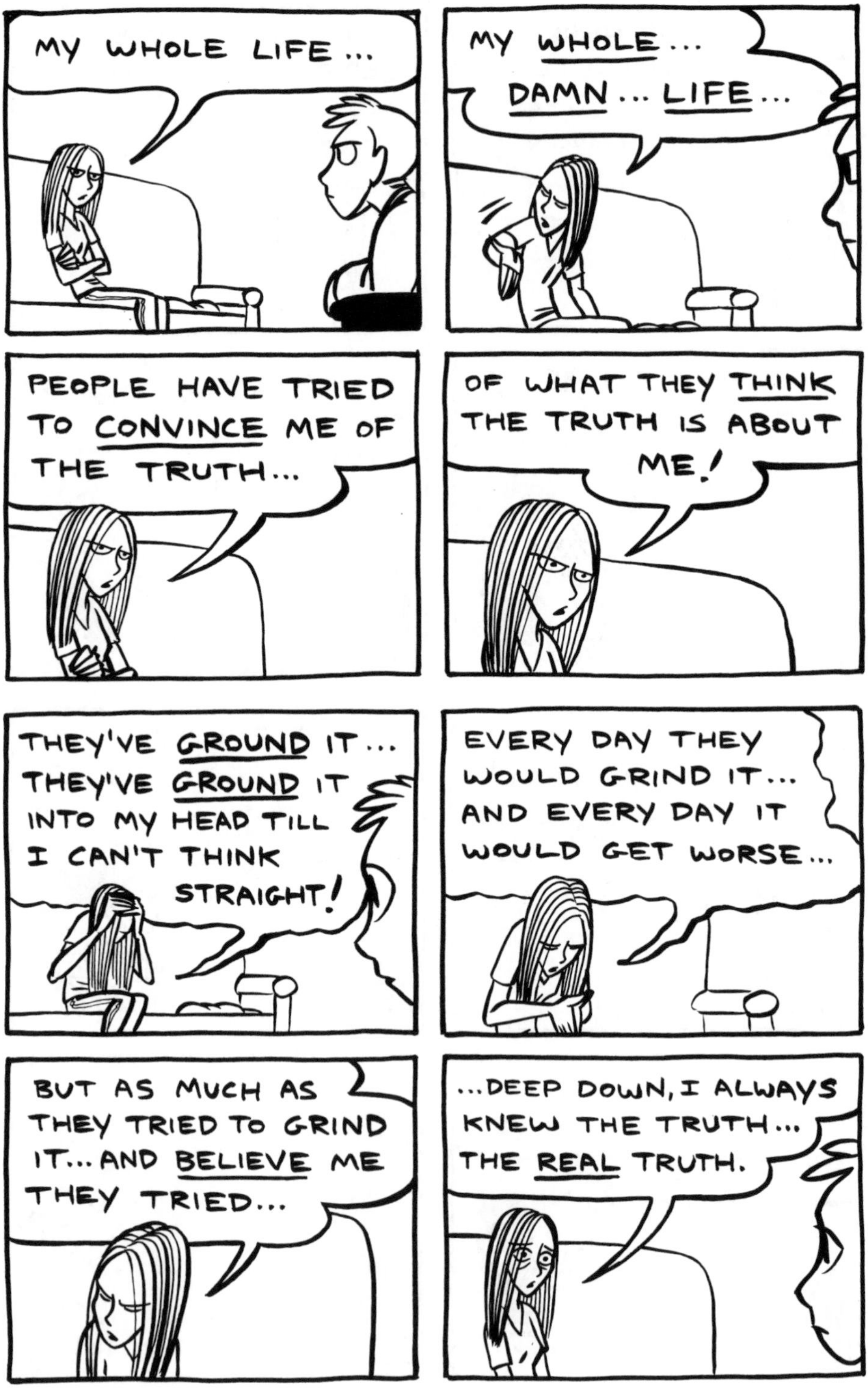
MY WHOLE LIFE...
MY WHOLE... DAMN... LIFE...
PEOPLE HAVE TRIED TO CONVINCE ME OF THE TRUTH...
OF WHAT THEY THINK THE TRUTH IS ABOUT ME!
THEY'VE GROUND IT... THEY'VE GROUND IT INTO MY HEAD TILL I CAN'T THINK STRAIGHT!
EVERY DAY THEY WOULD GRIND IT... AND EVERY DAY IT WOULD GET WORSE...
BUT AS MUCH AS THEY TRIED TO GRIND IT... AND BELIEVE ME THEY TRIED...
...DEEP DOWN, I ALWAYS KNEW THE TRUTH... THE REAL TRUTH.

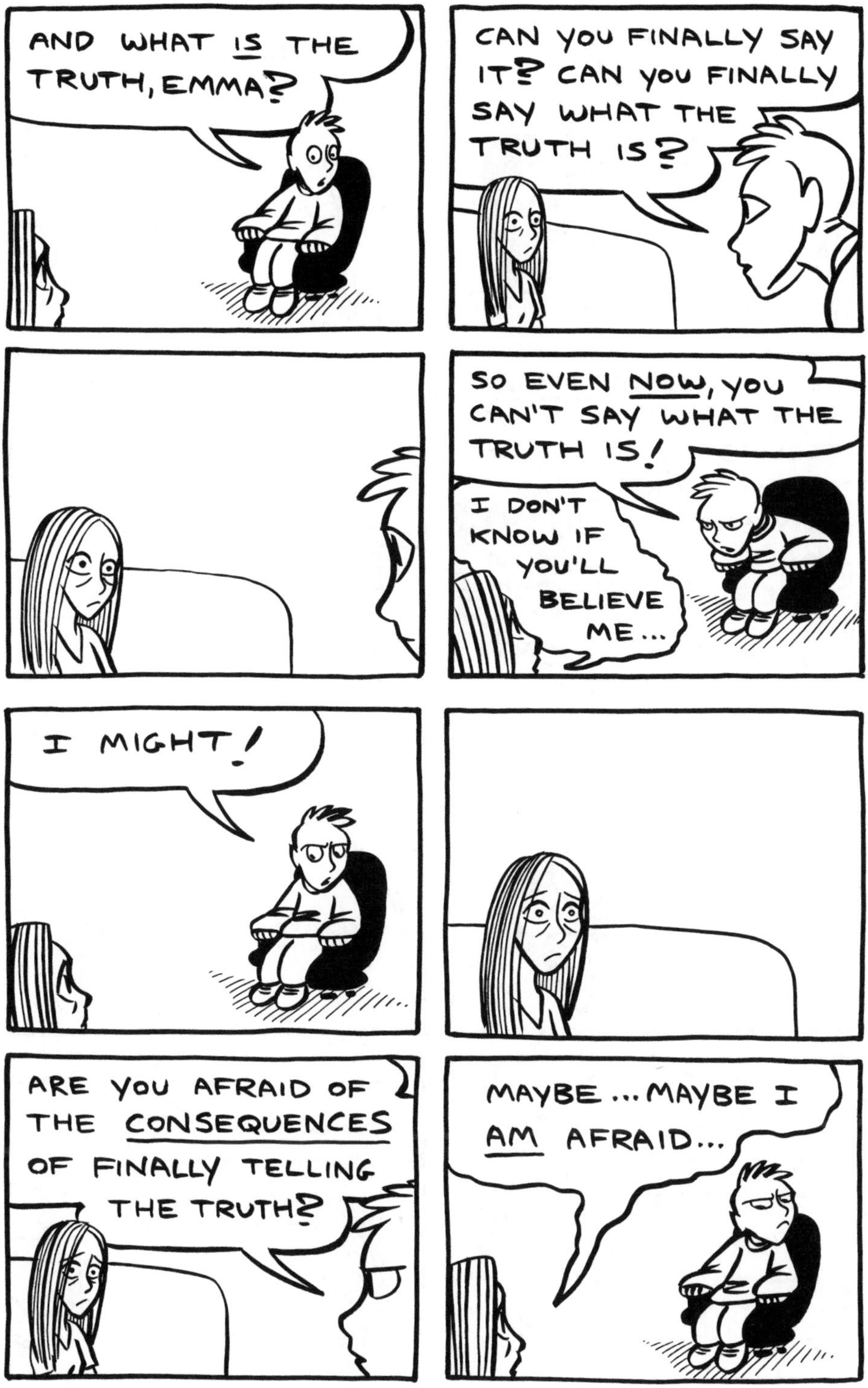
AND WHAT IS THE TRUTH, EMMA?
CAN YOU FINALLY SAY IT? CAN YOU FINALLY SAY WHAT THE TRUTH IS?
SO EVEN NOW, YOU CAN'T SAY WHAT THE TRUTH IS!
I DON'T KNOW IF YOU'LL BELIEVE ME...
I MIGHT!
ARE YOU AFRAID OF THE CONSEQUENCES OF FINALLY TELLING THE TRUTH?
MAYBE... MAYBE I AM AFRAID...

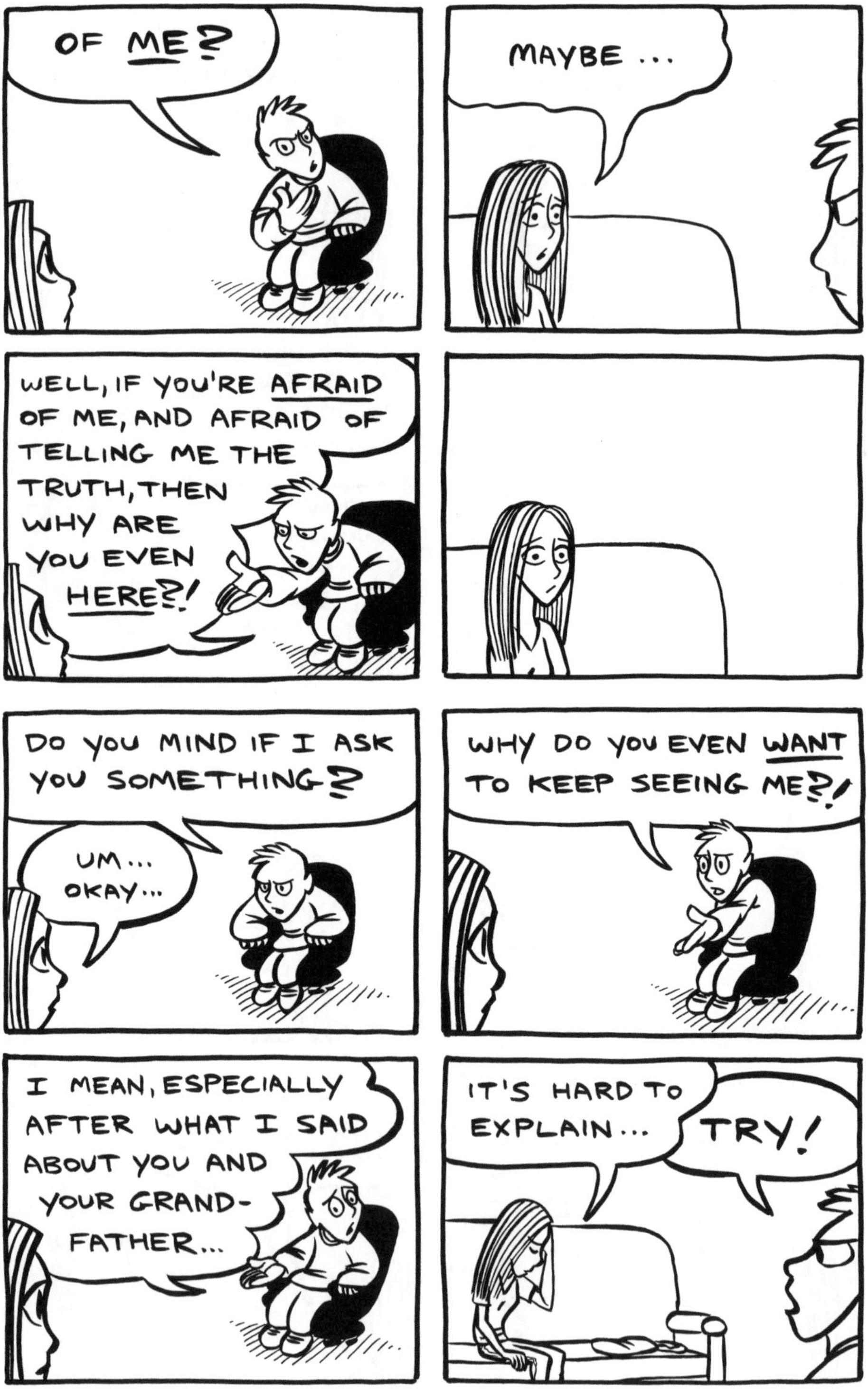
OF ME?
MAYBE ...
WELL, IF YOU'RE AFRAID OF ME, AND AFRAID OF TELLING ME THE TRUTH, THEN WHY ARE YOU EVEN HERE?!
DO YOU MIND IF I ASK YOU SOMETHING?
UM... OKAY...
WHY DO YOU EVEN WANT TO KEEP SEEING ME?!
I MEAN, ESPECIALLY AFTER WHAT I SAID ABOUT YOU AND YOUR GRAND-FATHER...
IT'S HARD TO EXPLAIN...
TRY!

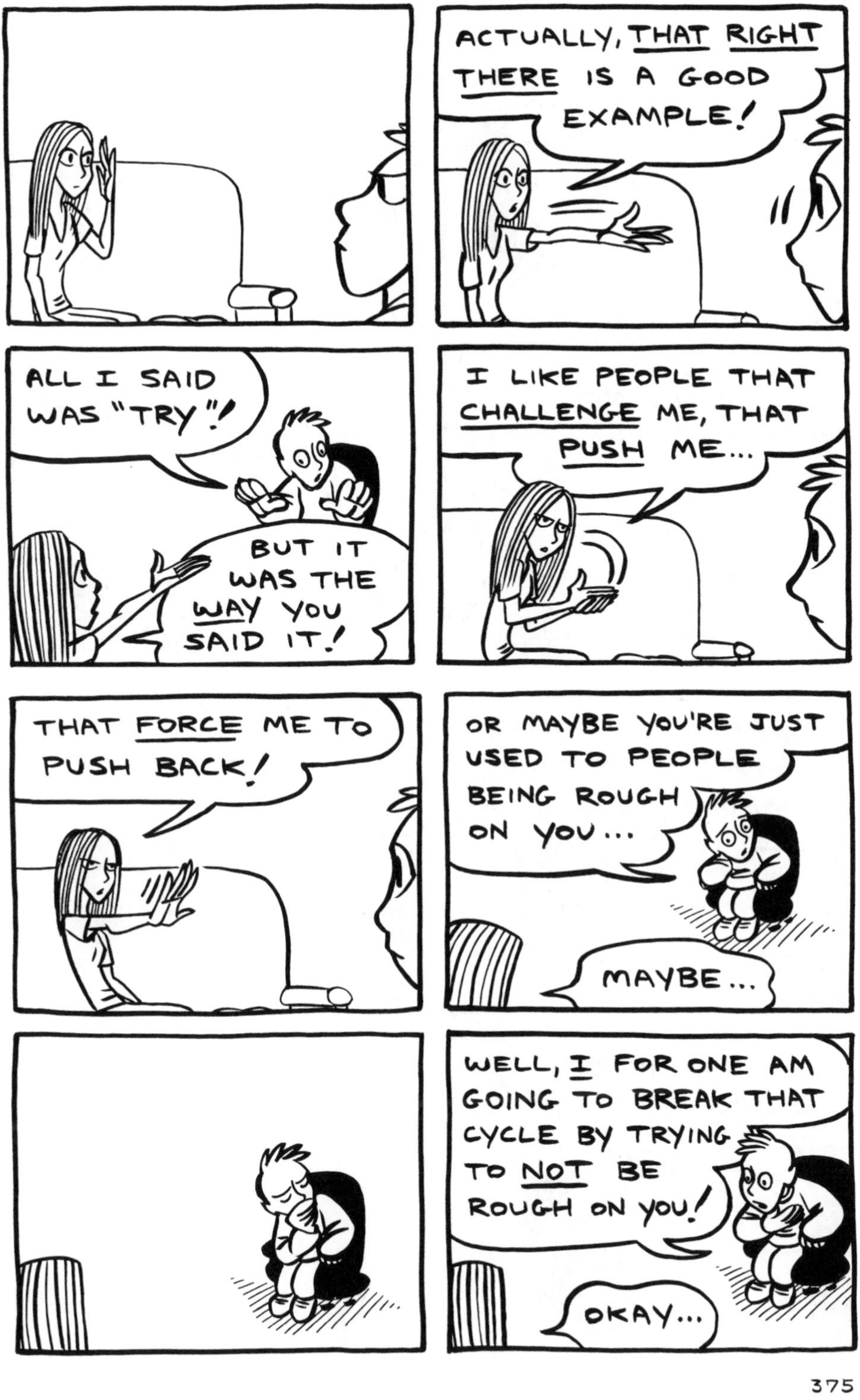

ACTUALLY, THAT RIGHT THERE IS A GOOD EXAMPLE!
ALL I SAID WAS "TRY"!
BUT IT WAS THE WAY YOU SAID IT!
I LIKE PEOPLE THAT CHALLENGE ME, THAT PUSH ME...
THAT FORCE ME TO PUSH BACK!
OR MAYBE YOU'RE JUST USED TO PEOPLE BEING ROUGH ON YOU...
MAYBE...
WELL, I FOR ONE AM GOING TO BREAK THAT CYCLE BY TRYING TO NOT BE ROUGH ON YOU!
OKAY...

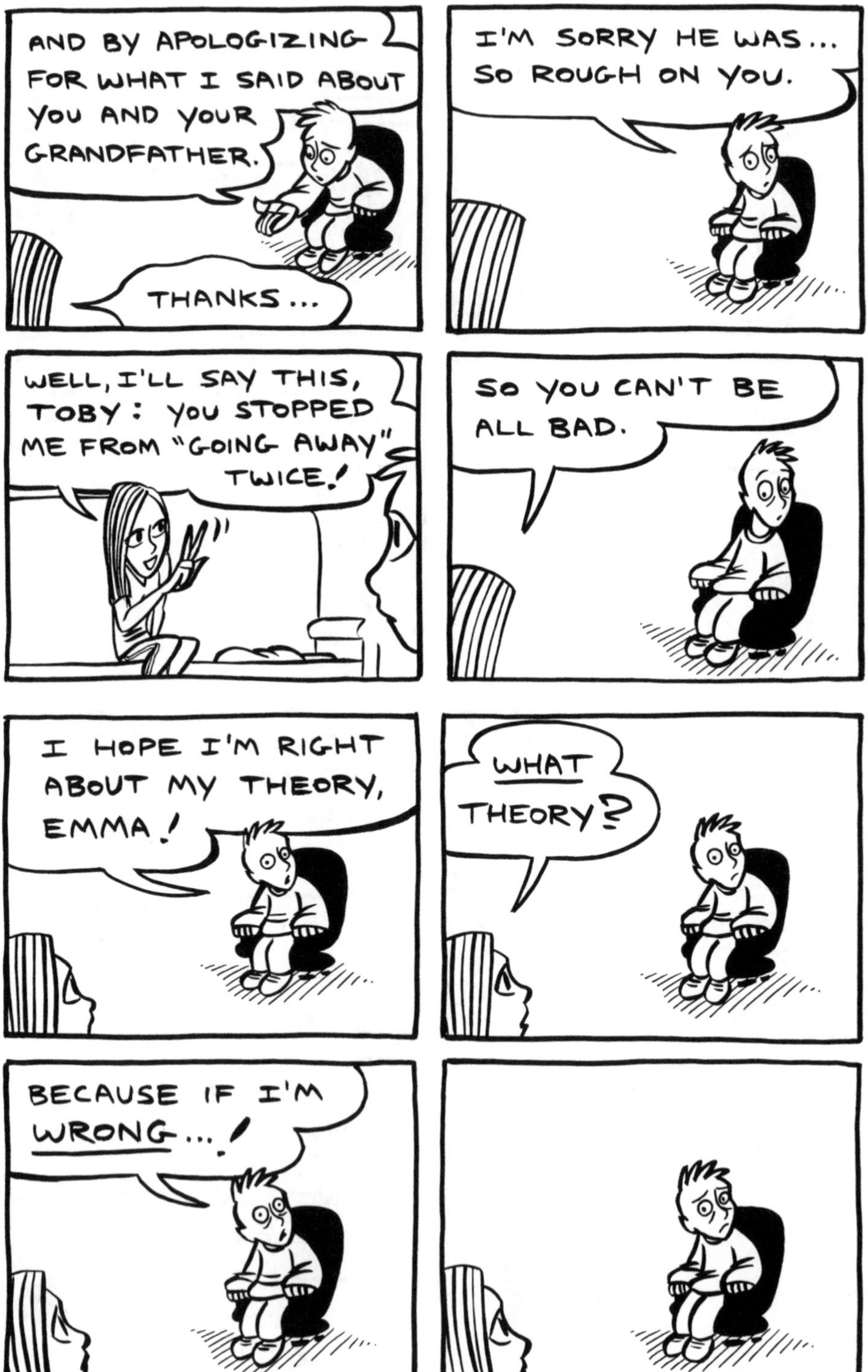

AND BY APOLOGIZING FOR WHAT I SAID ABOUT YOU AND YOUR GRANDFATHER.
THANKS...
I'M SORRY HE WAS... SO ROUGH ON YOU.
WELL, I'LL SAY THIS, TOBY: YOU STOPPED ME FROM "GOING AWAY" TWICE!
SO YOU CAN'T BE ALL BAD.
I HOPE I'M RIGHT ABOUT MY THEORY, EMMA!
WHAT THEORY?
BECAUSE IF I'M WRONG...!

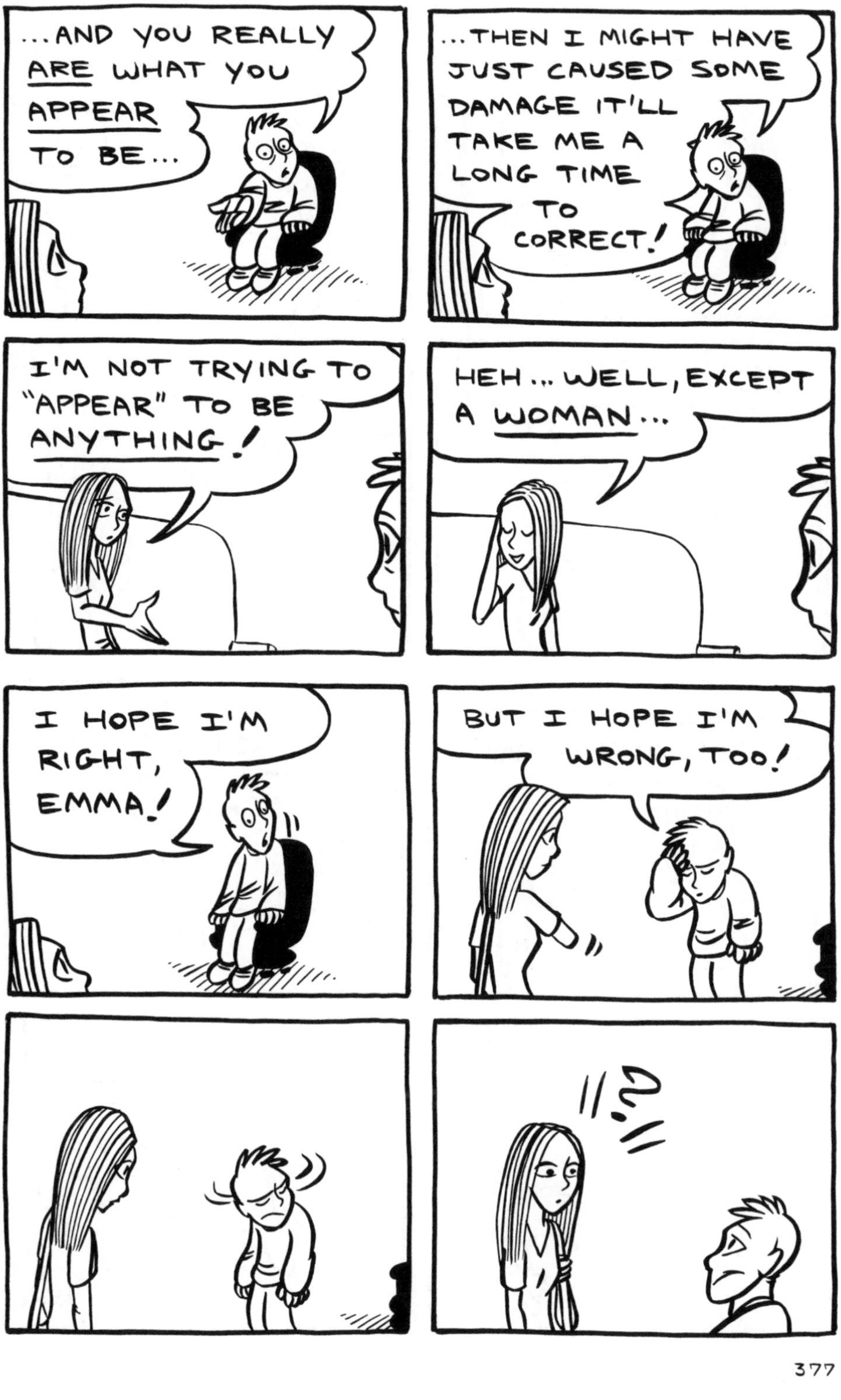
...AND YOU REALLY ARE WHAT YOU APPEAR TO BE...
...THEN I MIGHT HAVE JUST CAUSED SOME DAMAGE IT'LL TAKE ME A LONG TIME TO CORRECT!
I'M NOT TRYING TO "APPEAR" TO BE ANYTHING!
HEH... WELL, EXCEPT A WOMAN...
I HOPE I'M RIGHT, EMMA!
BUT I HOPE I'M WRONG, TOO!
?

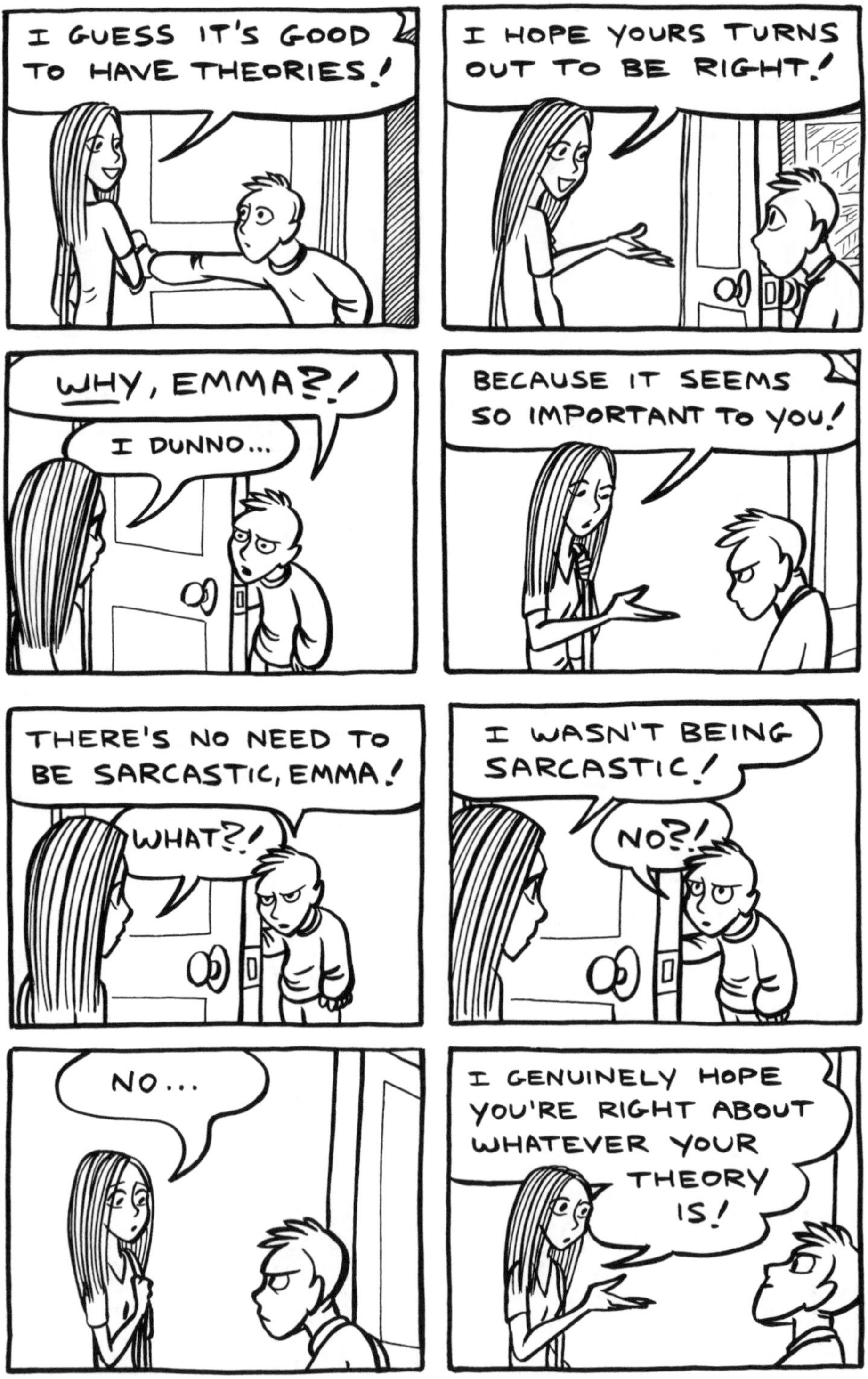
I GUESS IT'S GOOD TO HAVE THEORIES!
I HOPE YOURS TURNS OUT TO BE RIGHT!
WHY, EMMA?!
I DUNNO...
BECAUSE IT SEEMS SO IMPORTANT TO YOU!
THERE'S NO NEED TO BE SARCASTIC, EMMA!
WHAT?!
I WASN'T BEING SARCASTIC!
NO?!
NO...
I GENUINELY HOPE YOU'RE RIGHT ABOUT WHATEVER YOUR THEORY IS!

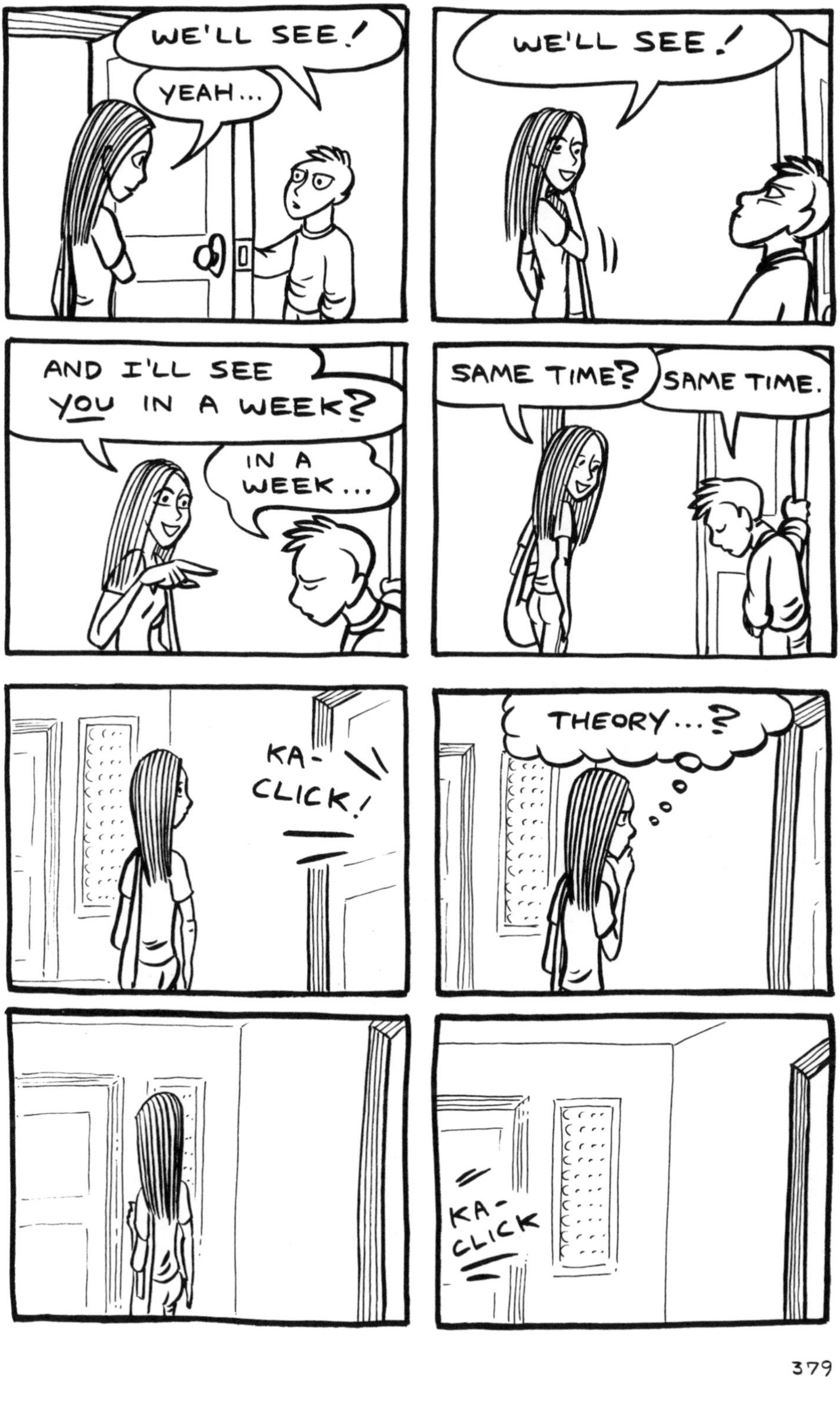
WE'LL SEE!
YEAH...
WE'LL SEE!
AND I'LL SEE YOU IN A WEEK?
IN A WEEK...
SAME TIME?
SAME TIME.
KA-CLICK!
THEORY...?
KA-CLICK

WALT

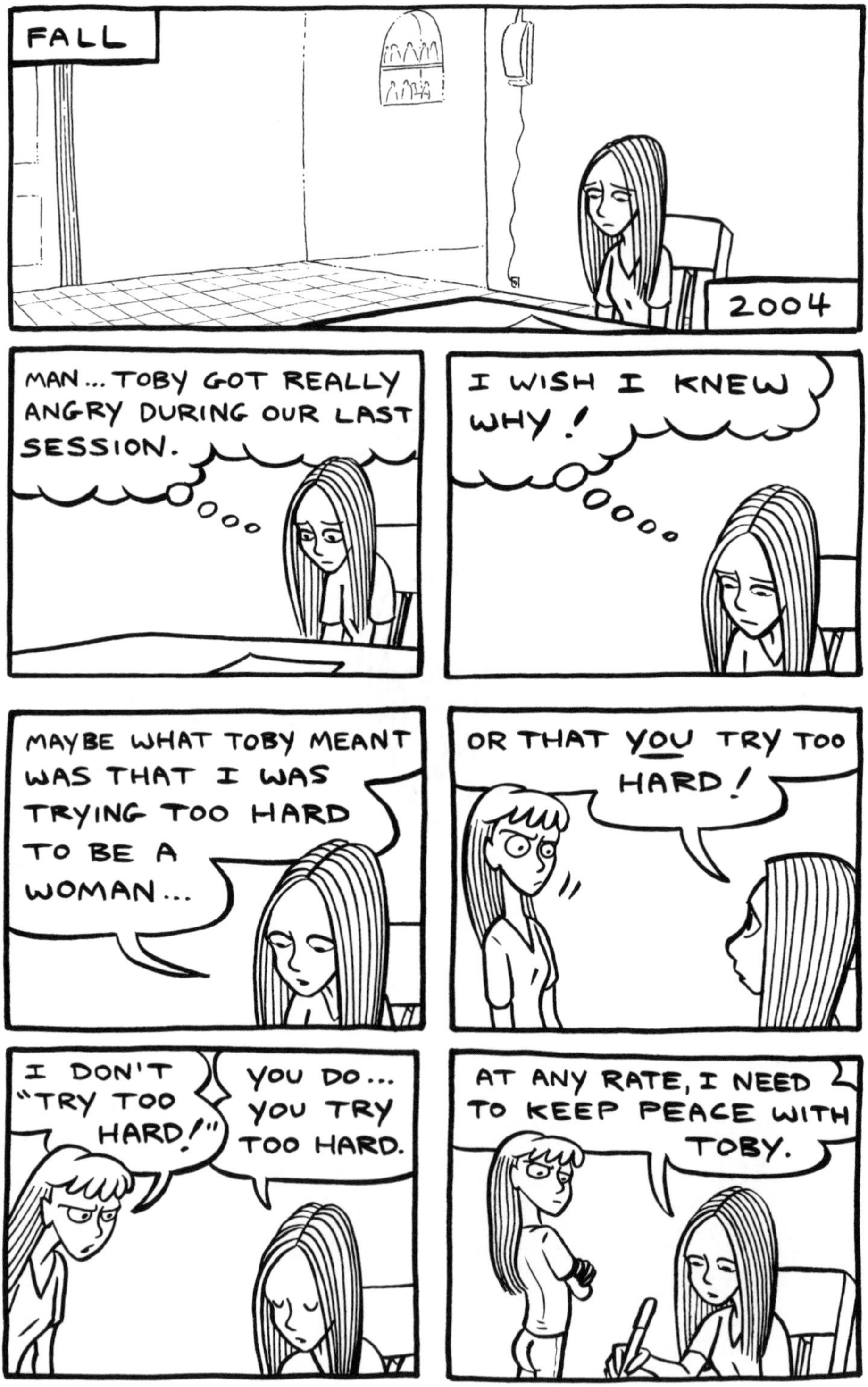
FALL
2004
MAN... TOBY GOT REALLY ANGRY DURING OUR LAST SESSION.
I WISH I KNEW WHY!
MAYBE WHAT TOBY MEANT WAS THAT I WAS TRYING TOO HARD TO BE A WOMAN...
OR THAT YOU TRY TOO HARD!
I DON'T "TRY TOO HARD!"
YOU DO... YOU TRY TOO HARD.
AT ANY RATE, I NEED TO KEEP PEACE WITH TOBY.

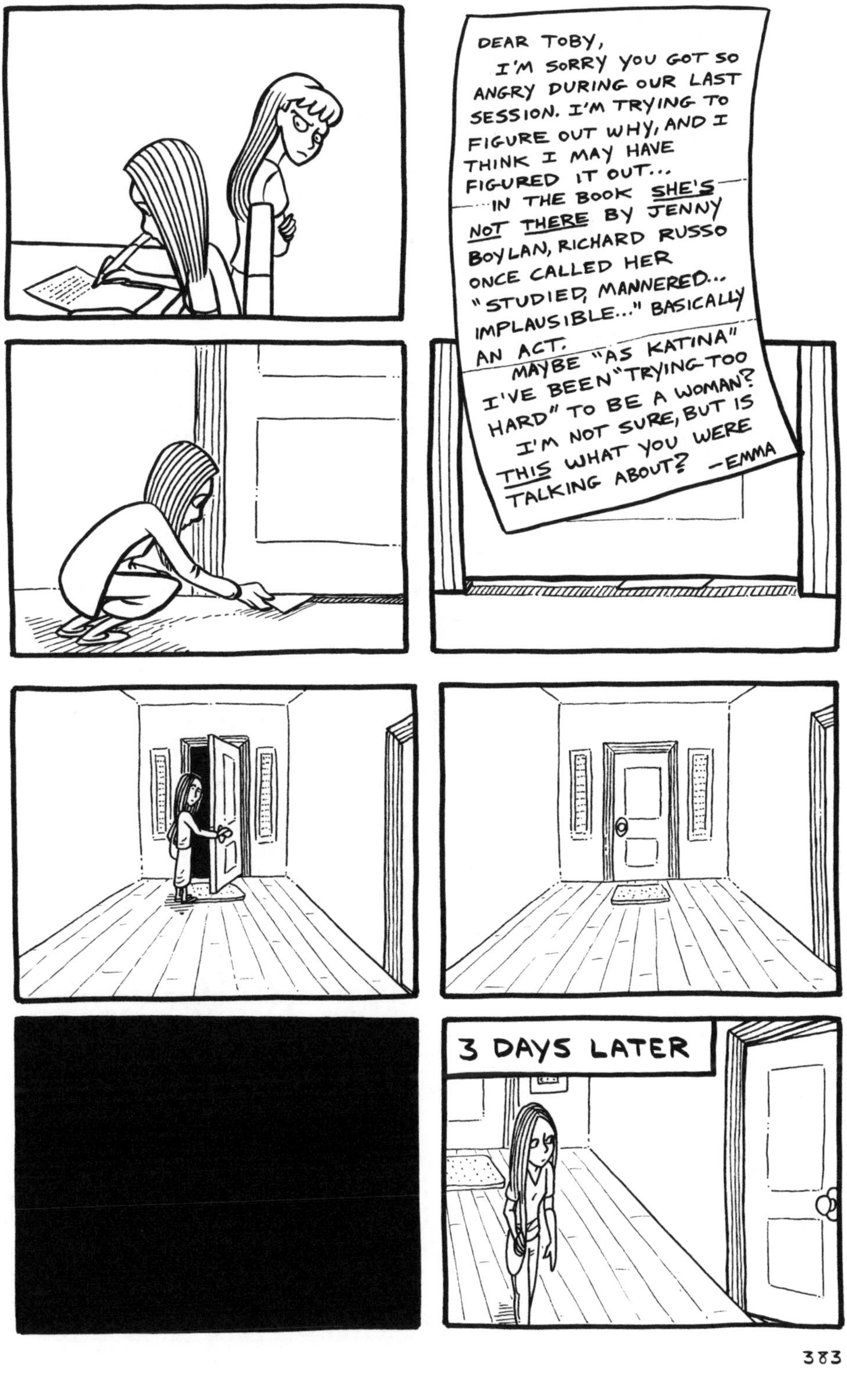
DEAR TOBY,
I'M SORRY YOU GOT SO ANGRY DURING OUR LAST SESSION. I'M TRYING TO FIGURE OUT WHY, AND I THINK I MAY HAVE FIGURED IT OUT...
IN THE BOOK SHE'S NOT THERE BY JENNY BOYLAN, RICHARD RUSSO ONCE CALLED HER "STUDIED, MANNERED... IMPLAUSIBLE..." BASICALLY AN ACT.
MAYBE "AS KATINA" I'VE BEEN "TRYING TOO HARD" TO BE A WOMAN? I'M NOT SURE, BUT IS THIS WHAT YOU WERE TALKING ABOUT? -EMMA
3 DAYS LATER

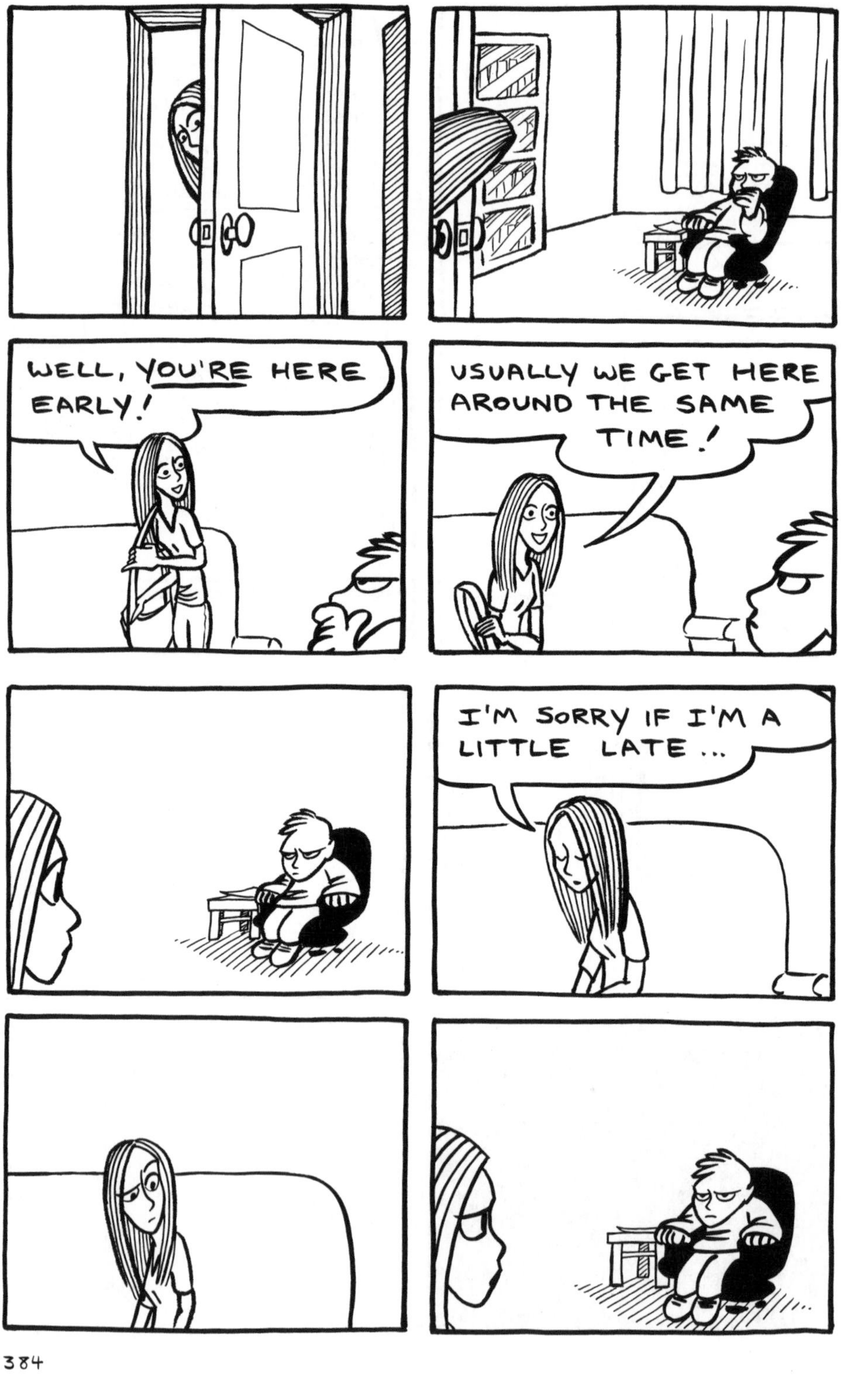
WELL, YOU'RE HERE EARLY!
USUALLY WE GET HERE AROUND THE SAME TIME!
I'M SORRY IF I'M A LITTLE LATE ...

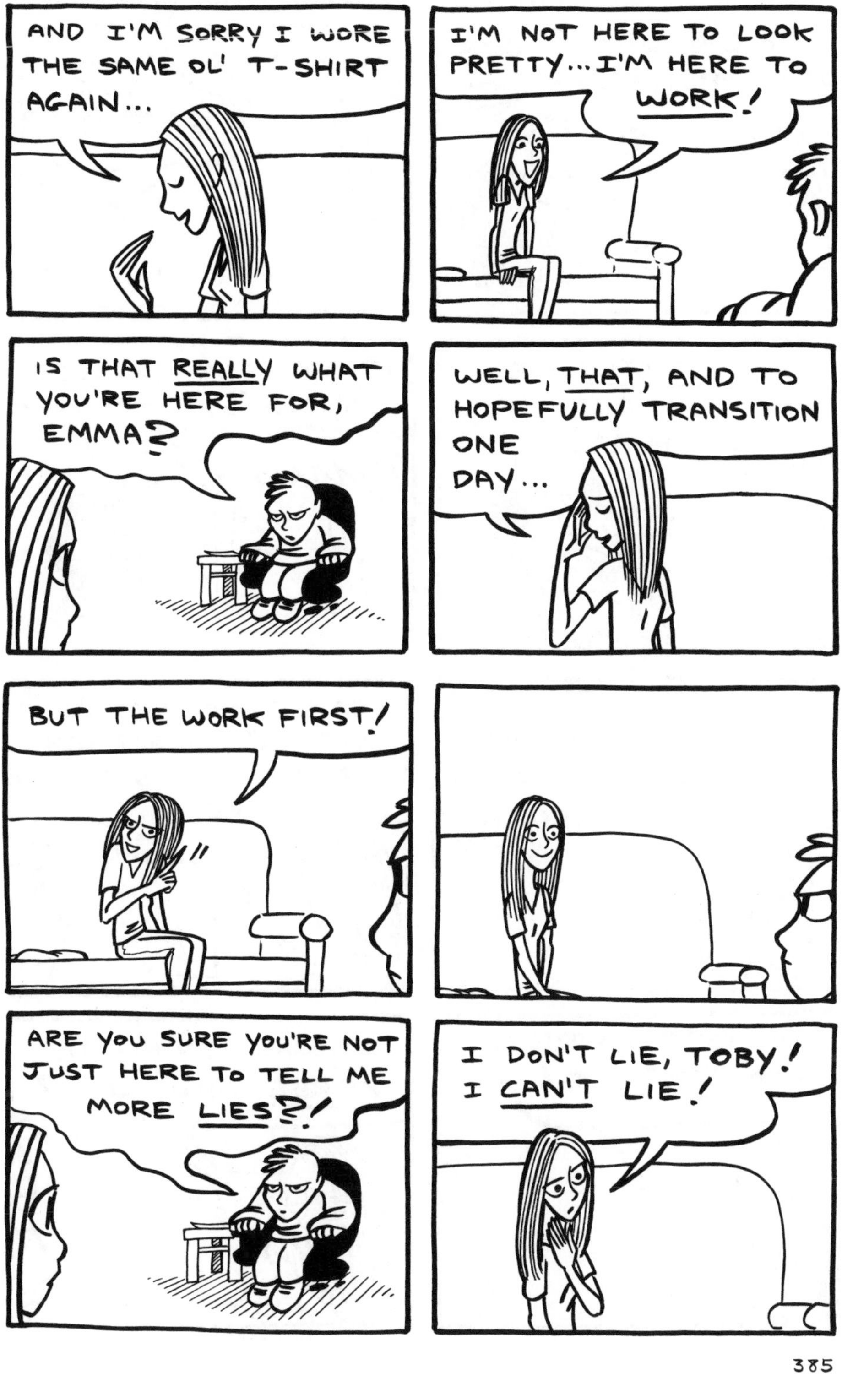
AND I'M SORRY I WORE THE SAME OL' T-SHIRT AGAIN...
I'M NOT HERE TO LOOK PRETTY... I'M HERE TO WORK!
IS THAT REALLY WHAT YOU'RE HERE FOR, EMMA?
WELL, THAT, AND TO HOPEFULLY TRANSITION ONE DAY...
BUT THE WORK FIRST!
ARE YOU SURE YOU'RE NOT JUST HERE TO TELL ME MORE LIES?!
I DON'T LIE, TOBY! I CAN'T LIE!

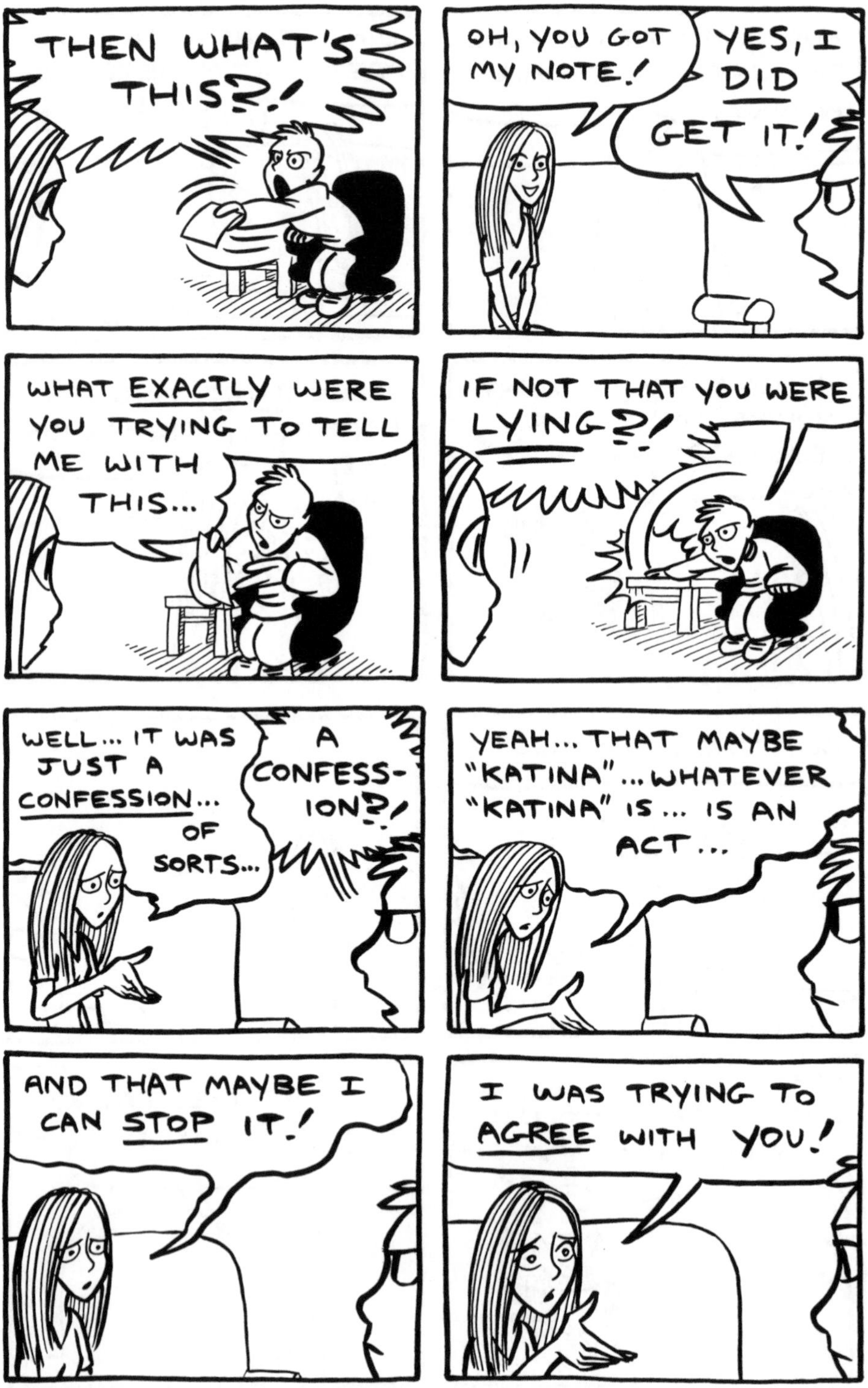
THEN WHAT'S THIS?!
OH, YOU GOT MY NOTE!
YES, I DID GET IT!
WHAT EXACTLY WERE YOU TRYING TO TELL ME WITH THIS...
IF NOT THAT YOU WERE LYING?!
WELL... IT WAS JUST A CONFESSION... OF SORTS...
A CONFESSION?!
YEAH... THAT MAYBE "KATINA"... WHATEVER "KATINA" IS... IS AN ACT...
AND THAT MAYBE I CAN STOP IT!
I WAS TRYING TO AGREE WITH YOU!

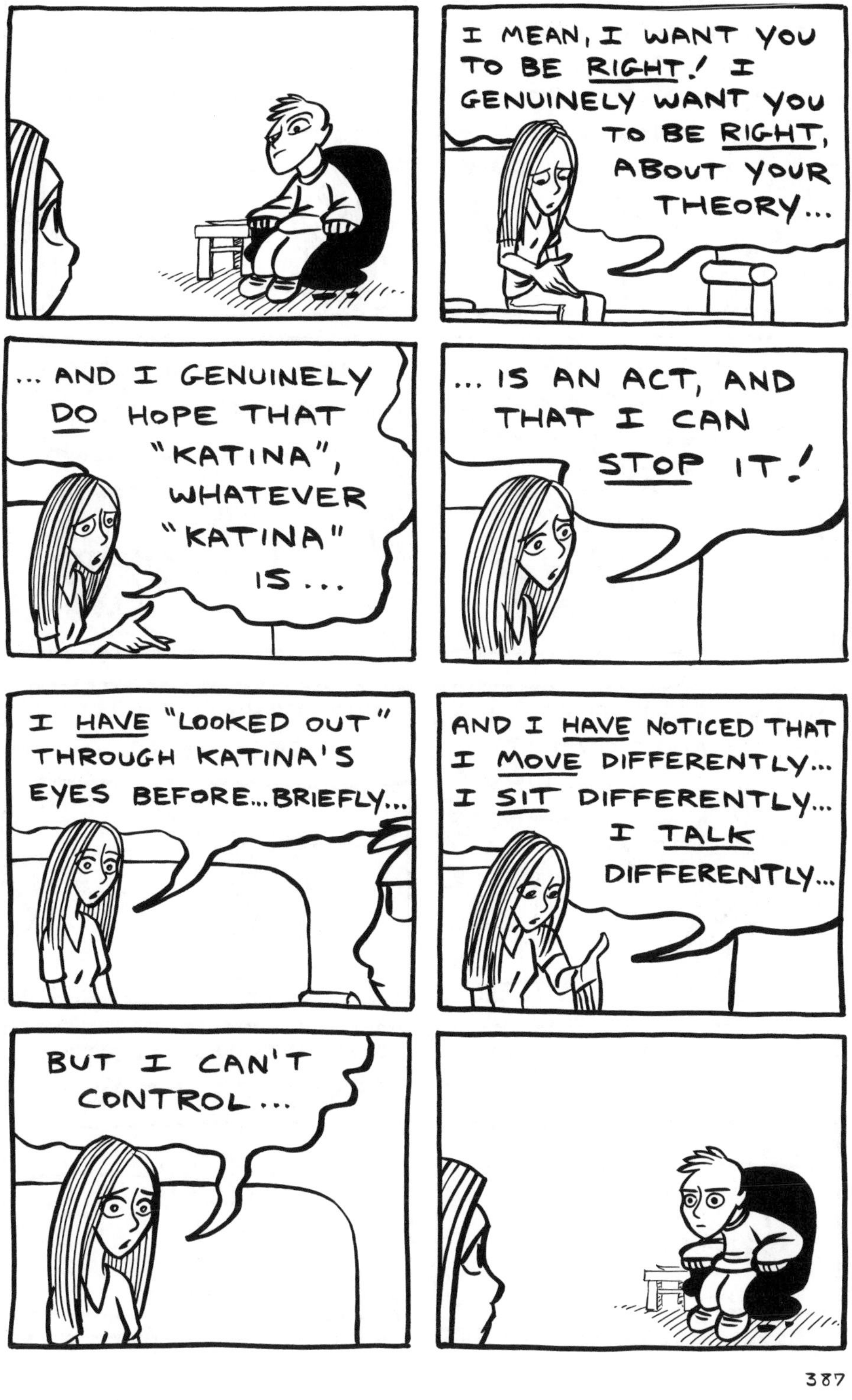
I MEAN, I WANT YOU TO BE RIGHT! I GENUINELY WANT YOU TO BE RIGHT, ABOUT YOUR THEORY...
... AND I GENUINELY DO HOPE THAT "KATINA", WHATEVER "KATINA" IS...
... IS AN ACT, AND THAT I CAN STOP IT!
I HAVE "LOOKED OUT" THROUGH KATINA'S EYES BEFORE... BRIEFLY...
AND I HAVE NOTICED THAT I MOVE DIFFERENTLY... I SIT DIFFERENTLY... I TALK DIFFERENTLY...
BUT I CAN'T CONTROL...

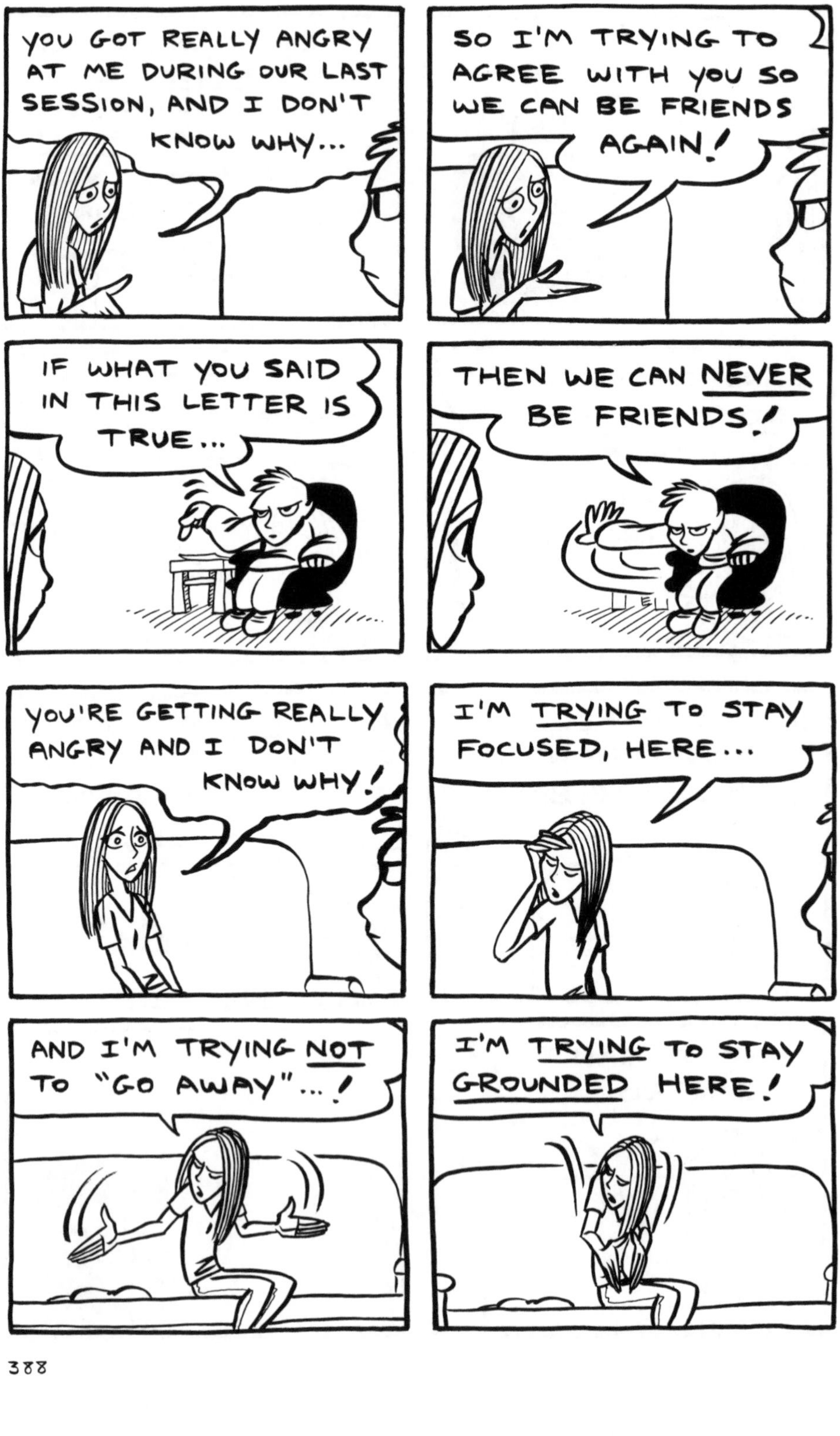
YOU GOT REALLY ANGRY AT ME DURING OUR LAST SESSION, AND I DON'T KNOW WHY...
SO I'M TRYING TO AGREE WITH YOU SO WE CAN BE FRIENDS AGAIN!
IF WHAT YOU SAID IN THIS LETTER IS TRUE...
THEN WE CAN NEVER BE FRIENDS!
YOU'RE GETTING REALLY ANGRY AND I DON'T KNOW WHY!
I'M TRYING TO STAY FOCUSED, HERE...
AND I'M TRYING NOT TO "GO AWAY"...!
I'M TRYING TO STAY GROUNDED HERE!

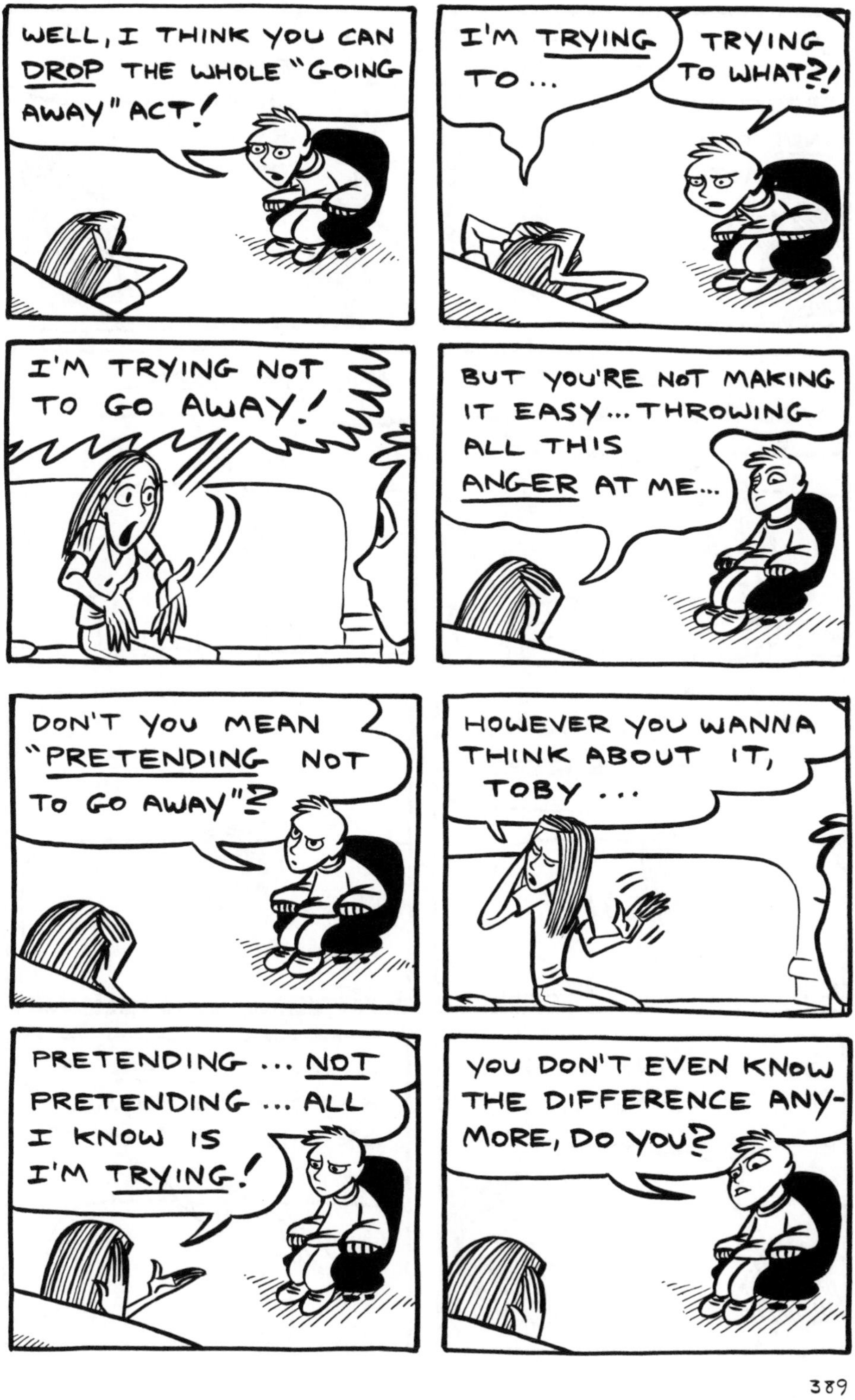
WELL, I THINK YOU CAN DROP THE WHOLE "GOING AWAY" ACT!
I'M TRYING TO...
TRYING TO WHAT?!
I'M TRYING NOT TO GO AWAY!
BUT YOU'RE NOT MAKING IT EASY... THROWING ALL THIS ANGER AT ME...
DON'T YOU MEAN "PRETENDING NOT TO GO AWAY"?
HOWEVER YOU WANNA THINK ABOUT IT, TOBY...
PRETENDING... NOT PRETENDING... ALL I KNOW IS I'M TRYING!
YOU DON'T EVEN KNOW THE DIFFERENCE ANY-MORE, DO YOU?

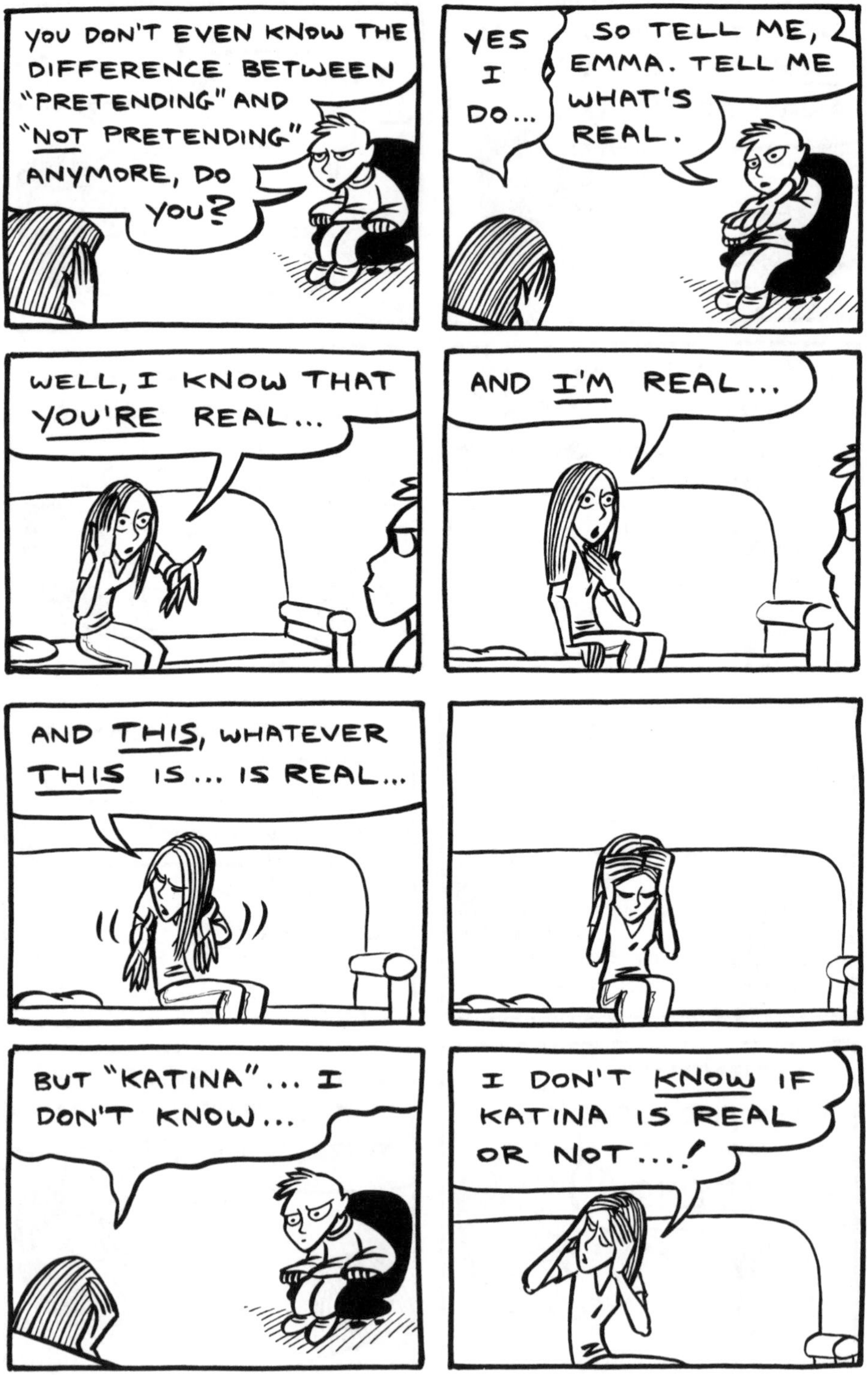

YOU DON'T EVEN KNOW THE DIFFERENCE BETWEEN "PRETENDING" AND "NOT PRETENDING" ANYMORE, DO YOU?
YES I DO...
SO TELL ME, EMMA. TELL ME WHAT'S REAL.
WELL, I KNOW THAT YOU'RE REAL...
AND I'M REAL...
AND THIS, WHATEVER THIS IS... IS REAL...
BUT "KATINA"... I DON'T KNOW...
I DON'T KNOW IF KATINA IS REAL OR NOT...!

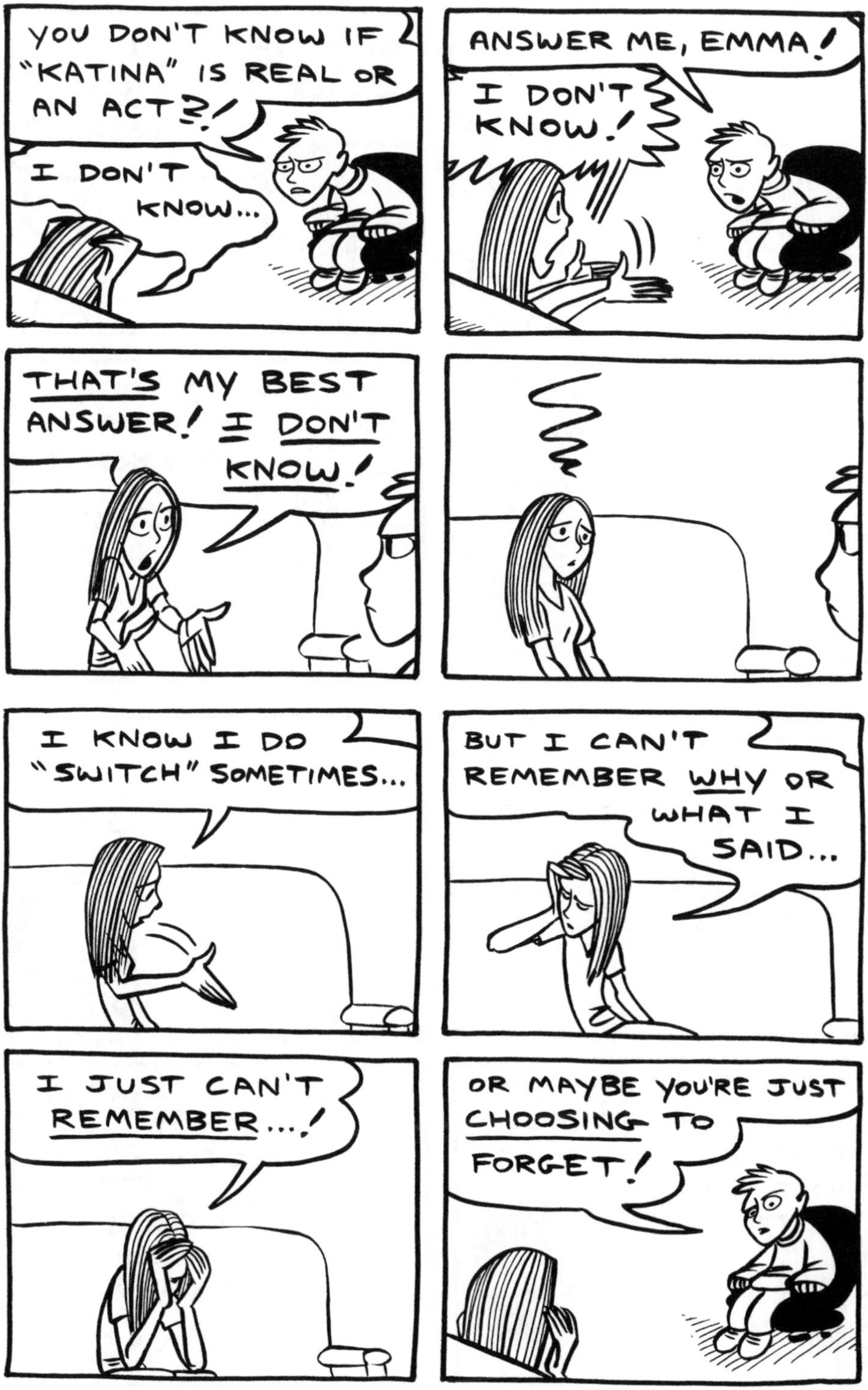
YOU DON'T KNOW IF "KATINA" IS REAL OR AN ACT?!
I DON'T KNOW...
ANSWER ME, EMMA!
I DON'T KNOW!
THAT'S MY BEST ANSWER! I DON'T KNOW!
I KNOW I DO "SWITCH" SOMETIMES...
BUT I CAN'T REMEMBER WHY OR WHAT I SAID...
I JUST CAN'T REMEMBER...!
OR MAYBE YOU'RE JUST CHOOSING TO FORGET!

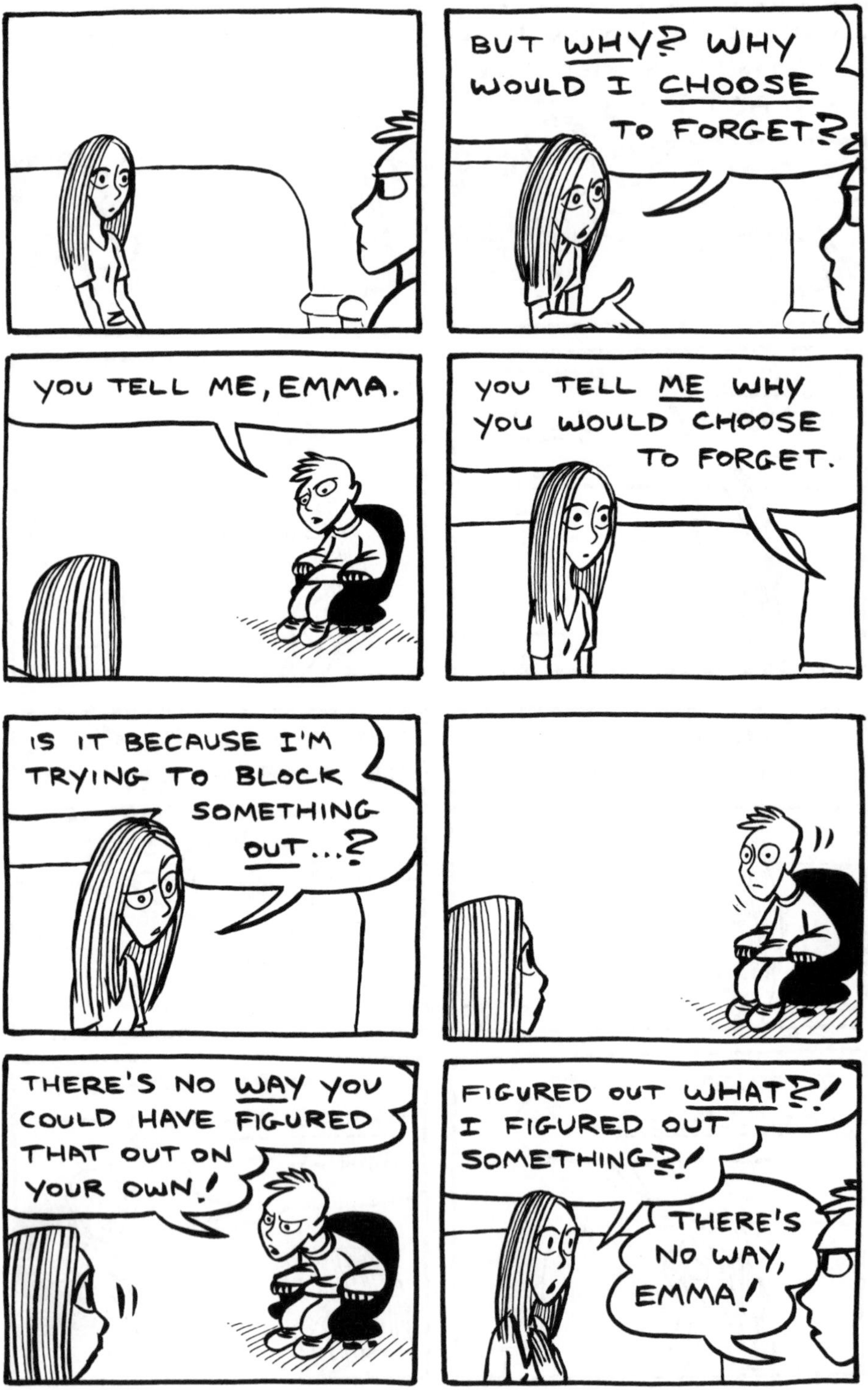
BUT WHY? WHY WOULD I CHOOSE TO FORGET?
YOU TELL ME, EMMA.
YOU TELL ME WHY YOU WOULD CHOOSE TO FORGET.
IS IT BECAUSE I'M TRYING TO BLOCK SOMETHING OUT...?
THERE'S NO WAY YOU COULD HAVE FIGURED THAT OUT ON YOUR OWN!
FIGURED OUT WHAT?! I FIGURED OUT SOMETHING?!
THERE'S NO WAY, EMMA!

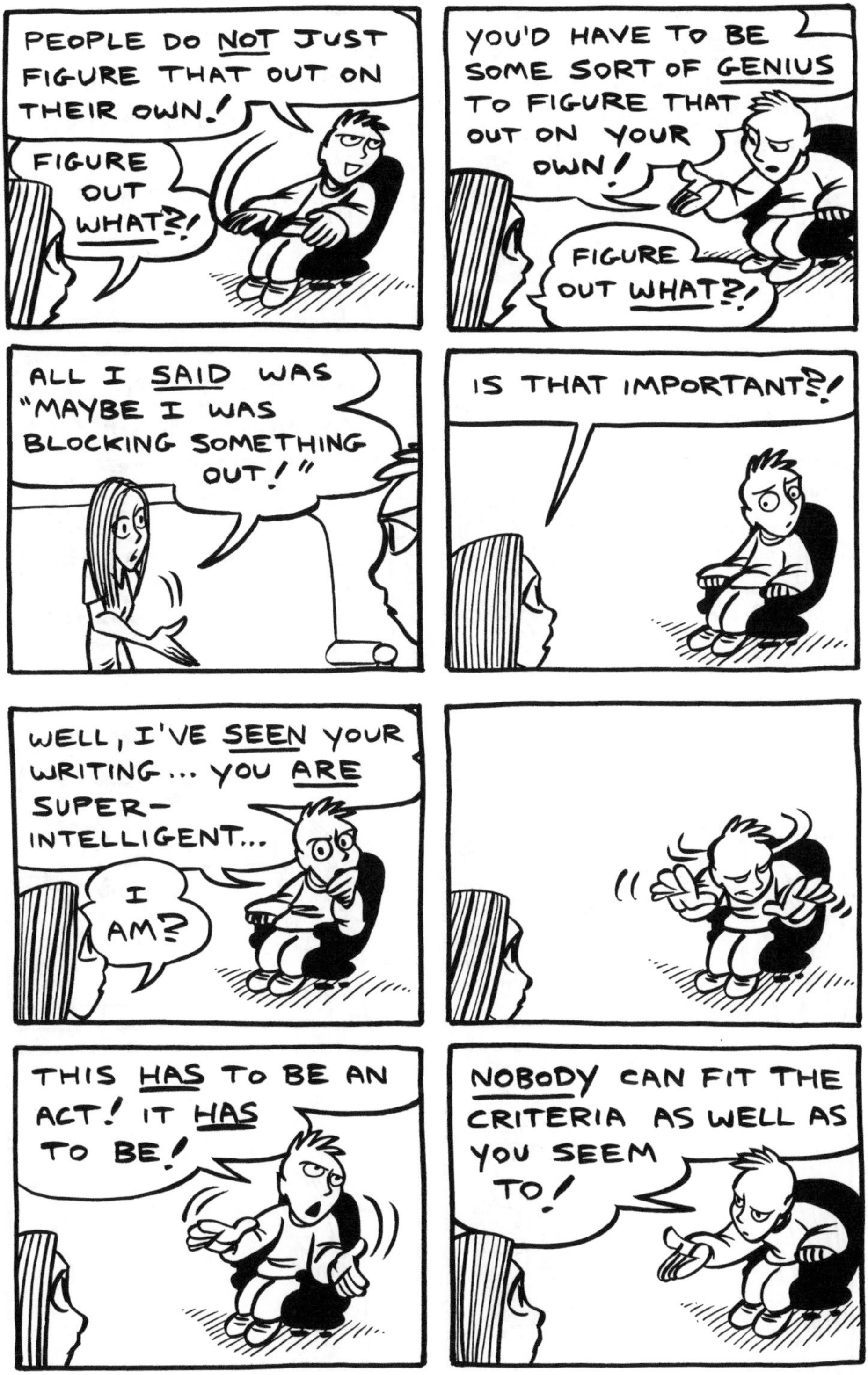
PEOPLE DO NOT JUST FIGURE THAT OUT ON THEIR OWN!
FIGURE OUT WHAT?!
YOU'D HAVE TO BE SOME SORT OF GENIUS TO FIGURE THAT OUT ON YOUR OWN!
FIGURE OUT WHAT?!
ALL I SAID WAS "MAYBE I WAS BLOCKING SOMETHING OUT!"
IS THAT IMPORTANT?!
WELL, I'VE SEEN YOUR WRITING... YOU ARE SUPER-INTELLIGENT...
I AM?
THIS HAS TO BE AN ACT! IT HAS TO BE!
NOBODY CAN FIT THE CRITERIA AS WELL AS YOU SEEM TO!

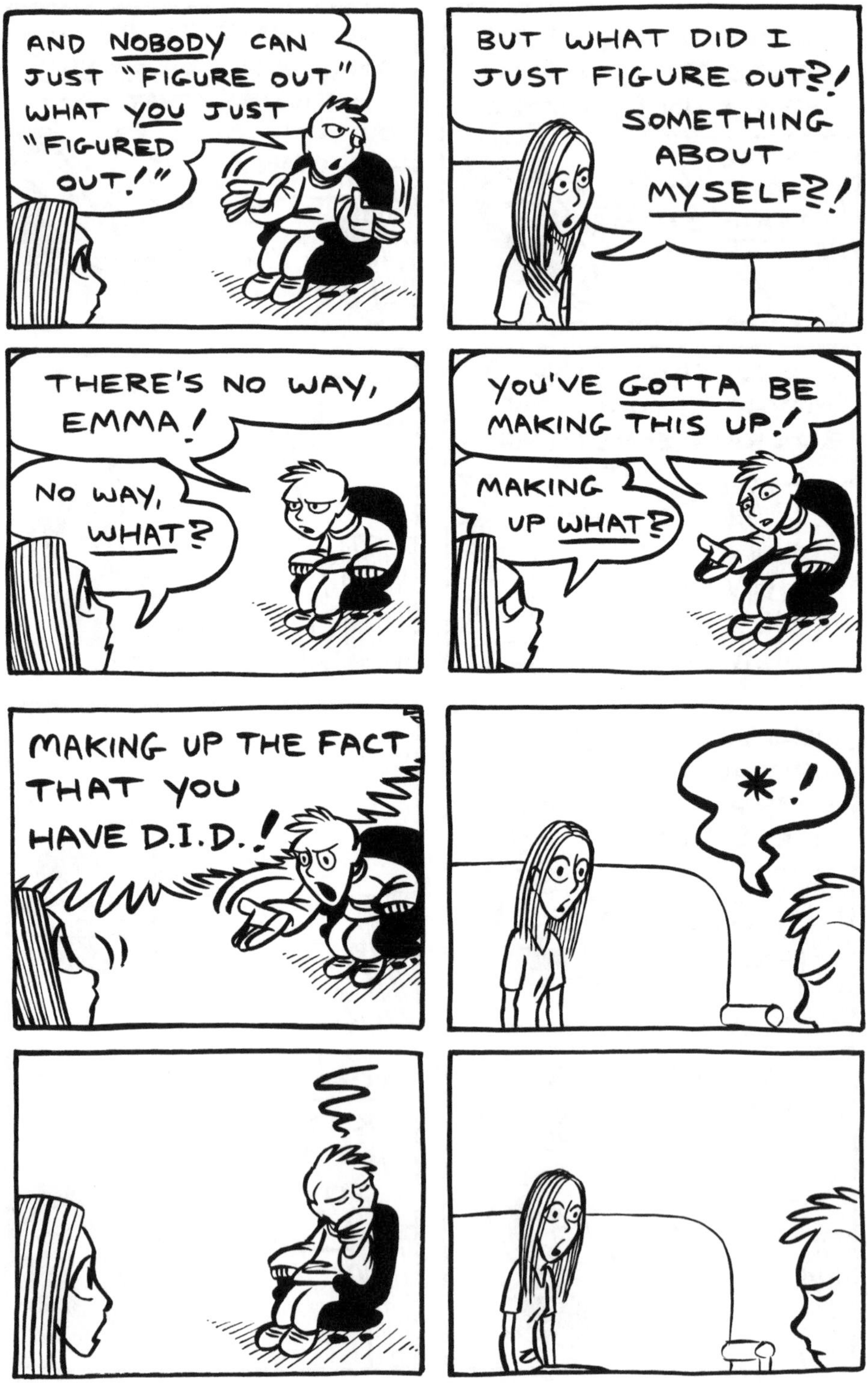
AND NOBODY CAN JUST "FIGURE OUT" WHAT YOU JUST "FIGURED OUT!"
BUT WHAT DID I JUST FIGURE OUT?!
SOMETHING ABOUT MYSELF?!
THERE'S NO WAY, EMMA!
NO WAY, WHAT?
YOU'VE GOTTA BE MAKING THIS UP!
MAKING UP WHAT?
MAKING UP THE FACT THAT YOU HAVE D.I.D.!
*!

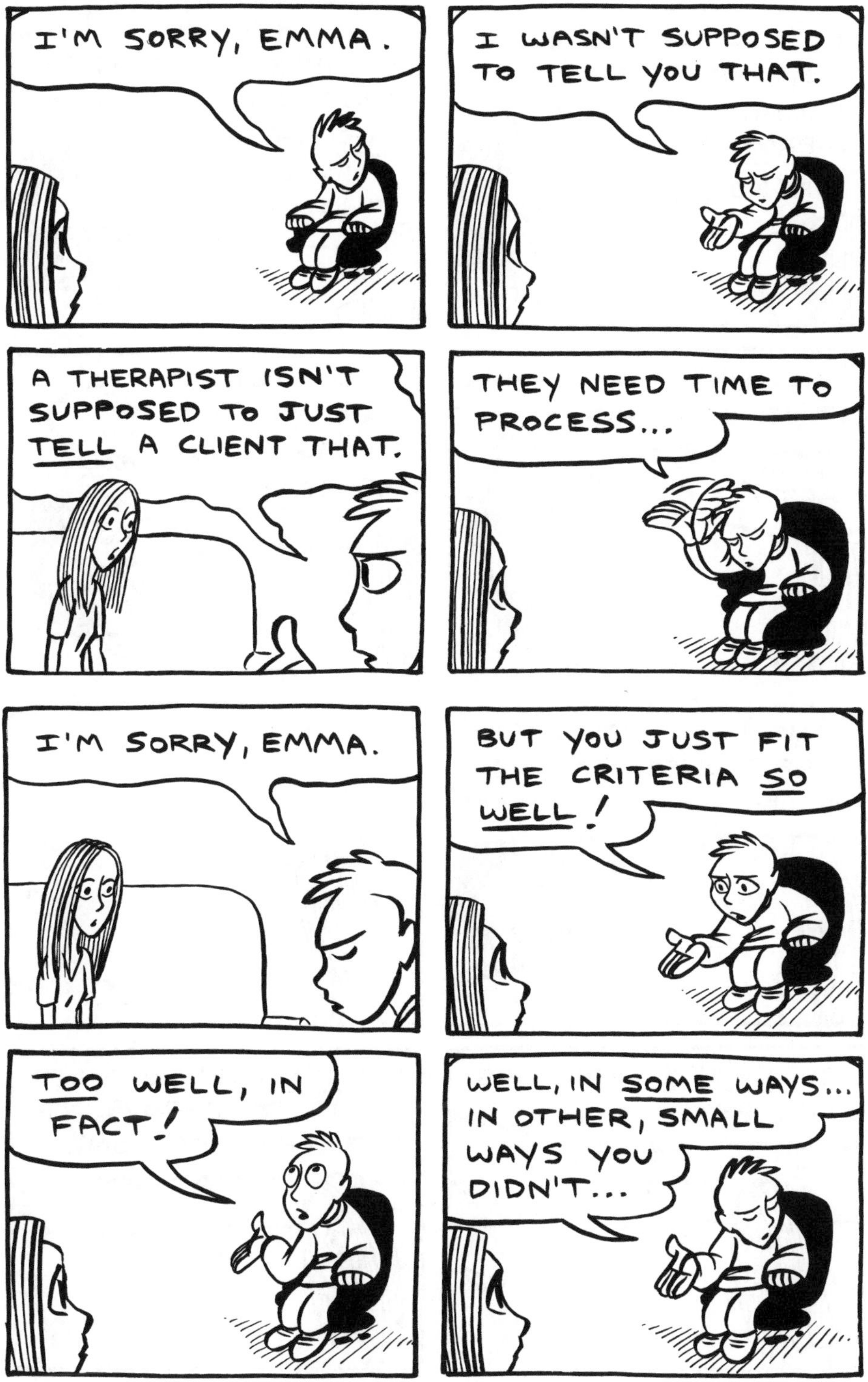
I'M SORRY, EMMA.
I WASN'T SUPPOSED TO TELL YOU THAT.
A THERAPIST ISN'T SUPPOSED TO JUST TELL A CLIENT THAT.
THEY NEED TIME TO PROCESS...
I'M SORRY, EMMA.
BUT YOU JUST FIT THE CRITERIA SO WELL!
TOO WELL, IN FACT!
WELL, IN SOME WAYS... IN OTHER, SMALL WAYS YOU DIDN'T...

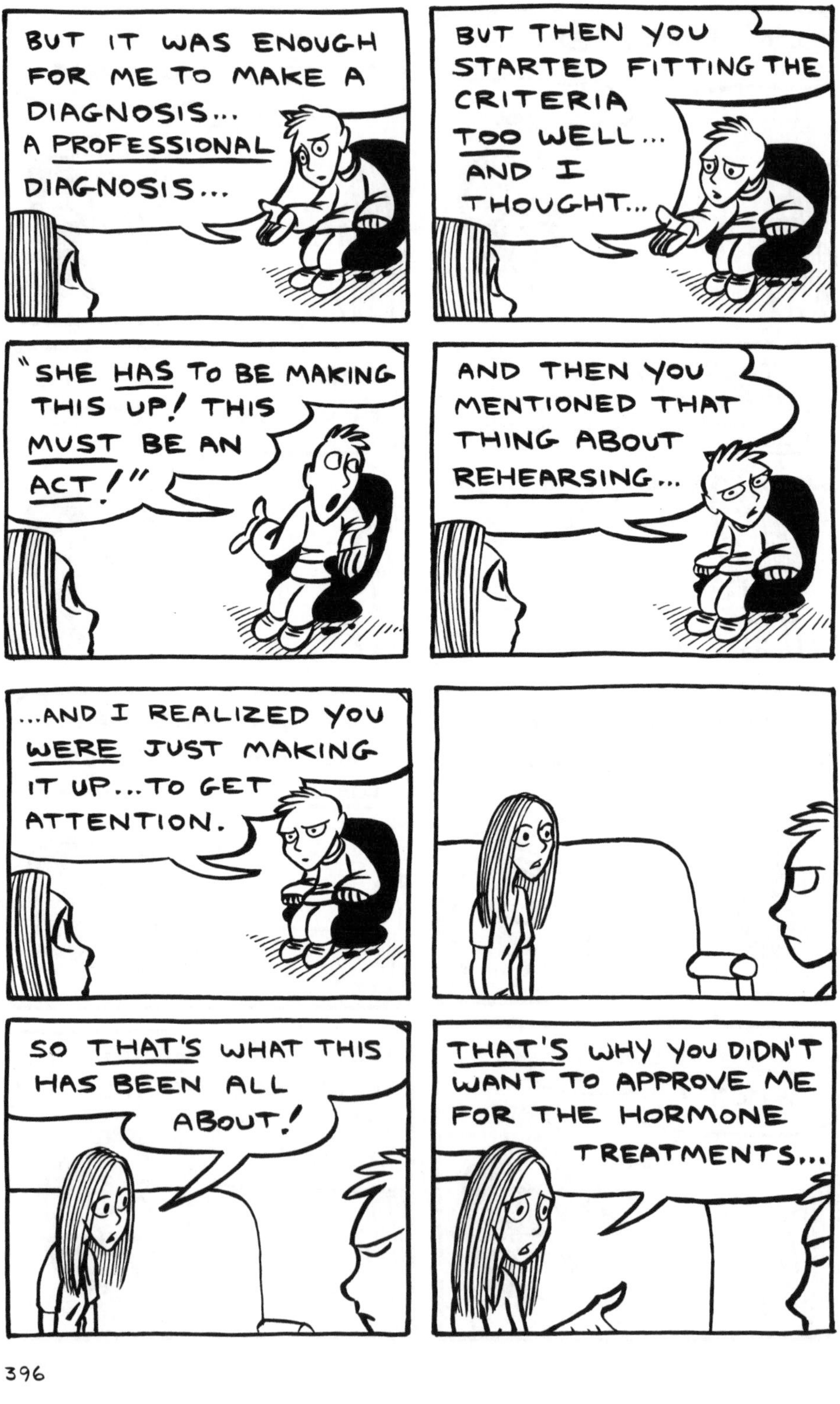
BUT IT WAS ENOUGH FOR ME TO MAKE A DIAGNOSIS... A PROFESSIONAL DIAGNOSIS...
BUT THEN YOU STARTED FITTING THE CRITERIA TOO WELL... AND I THOUGHT...
"SHE HAS TO BE MAKING THIS UP! THIS MUST BE AN ACT!"
AND THEN YOU MENTIONED THAT THING ABOUT REHEARSING...
...AND I REALIZED YOU WERE JUST MAKING IT UP...TO GET ATTENTION.
SO THAT'S WHAT THIS HAS BEEN ALL ABOUT!
THAT'S WHY YOU DIDN'T WANT TO APPROVE ME FOR THE HORMONE TREATMENTS...

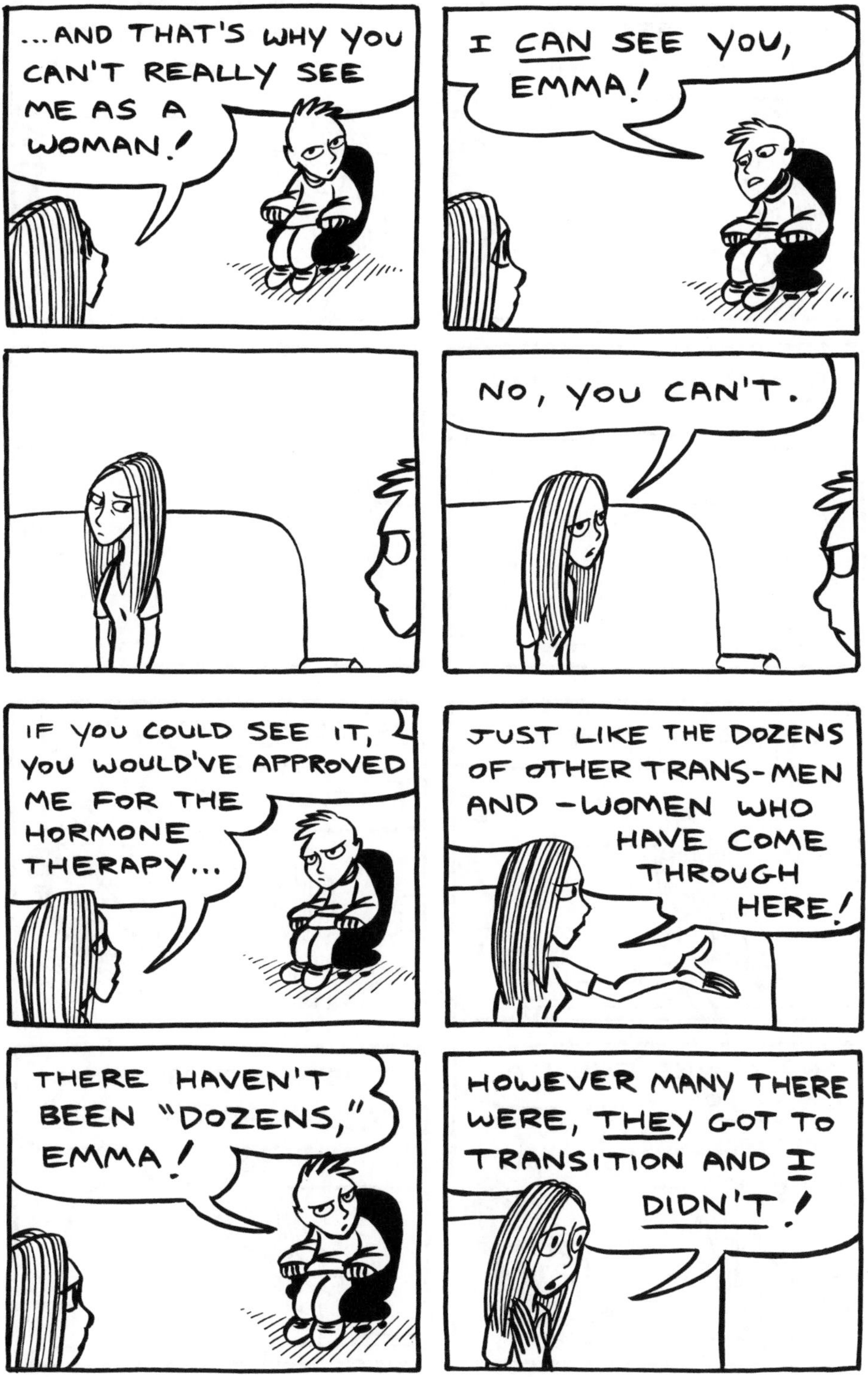
...AND THAT'S WHY YOU CAN'T REALLY SEE ME AS A WOMAN!
I CAN SEE YOU, EMMA!
NO, YOU CAN'T.
IF YOU COULD SEE IT, YOU WOULD'VE APPROVED ME FOR THE HORMONE THERAPY...
JUST LIKE THE DOZENS OF OTHER TRANS-MEN AND -WOMEN WHO HAVE COME THROUGH HERE!
THERE HAVEN'T BEEN "DOZENS," EMMA!
HOWEVER MANY THERE WERE, THEY GOT TO TRANSITION AND I DIDN'T!

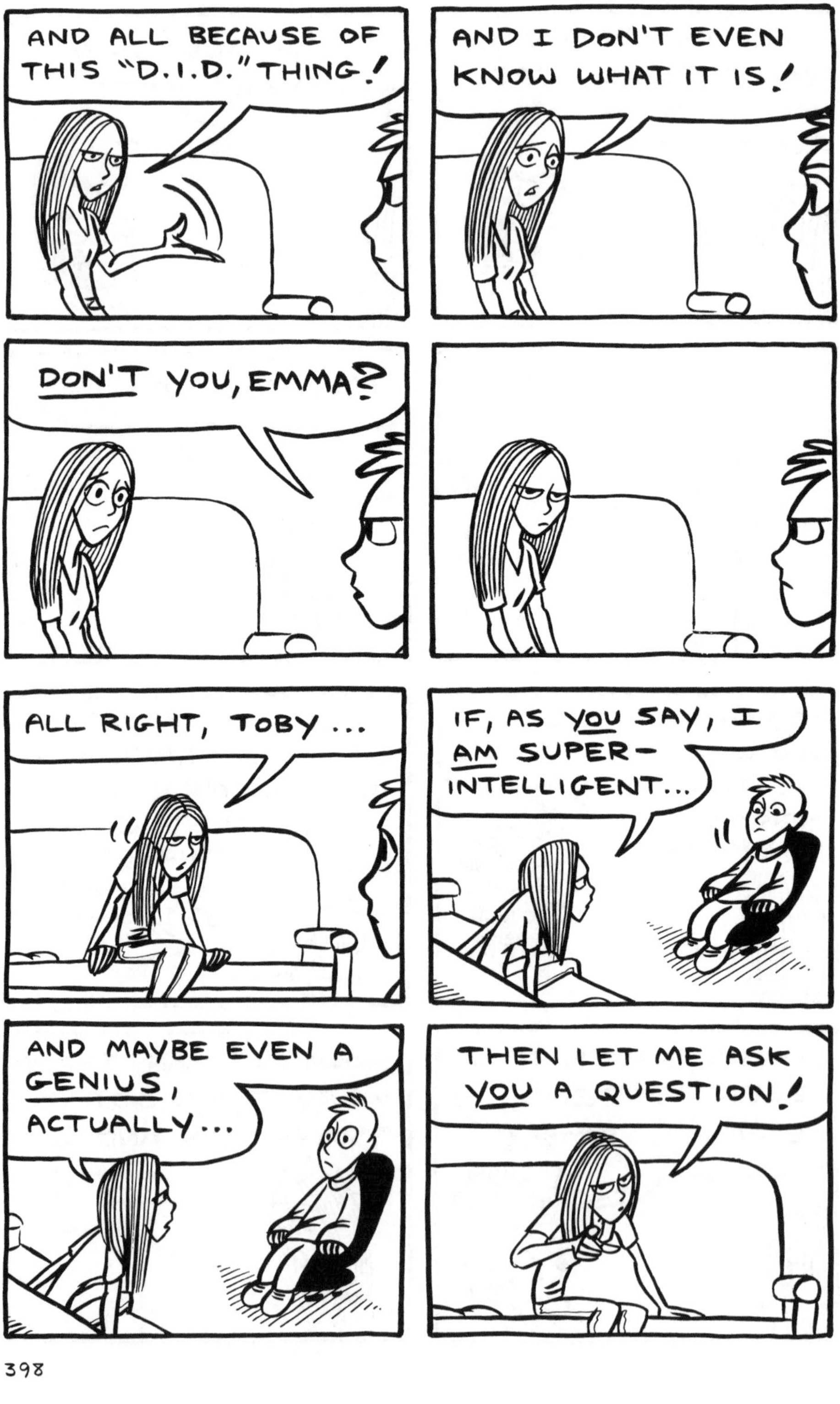
AND ALL BECAUSE OF THIS "D.I.D." THING!
AND I DON'T EVEN KNOW WHAT IT IS!
DON'T YOU, EMMA?
ALL RIGHT, TOBY ...
IF, AS YOU SAY, I AM SUPER-INTELLIGENT...
AND MAYBE EVEN A GENIUS, ACTUALLY...
THEN LET ME ASK YOU A QUESTION!

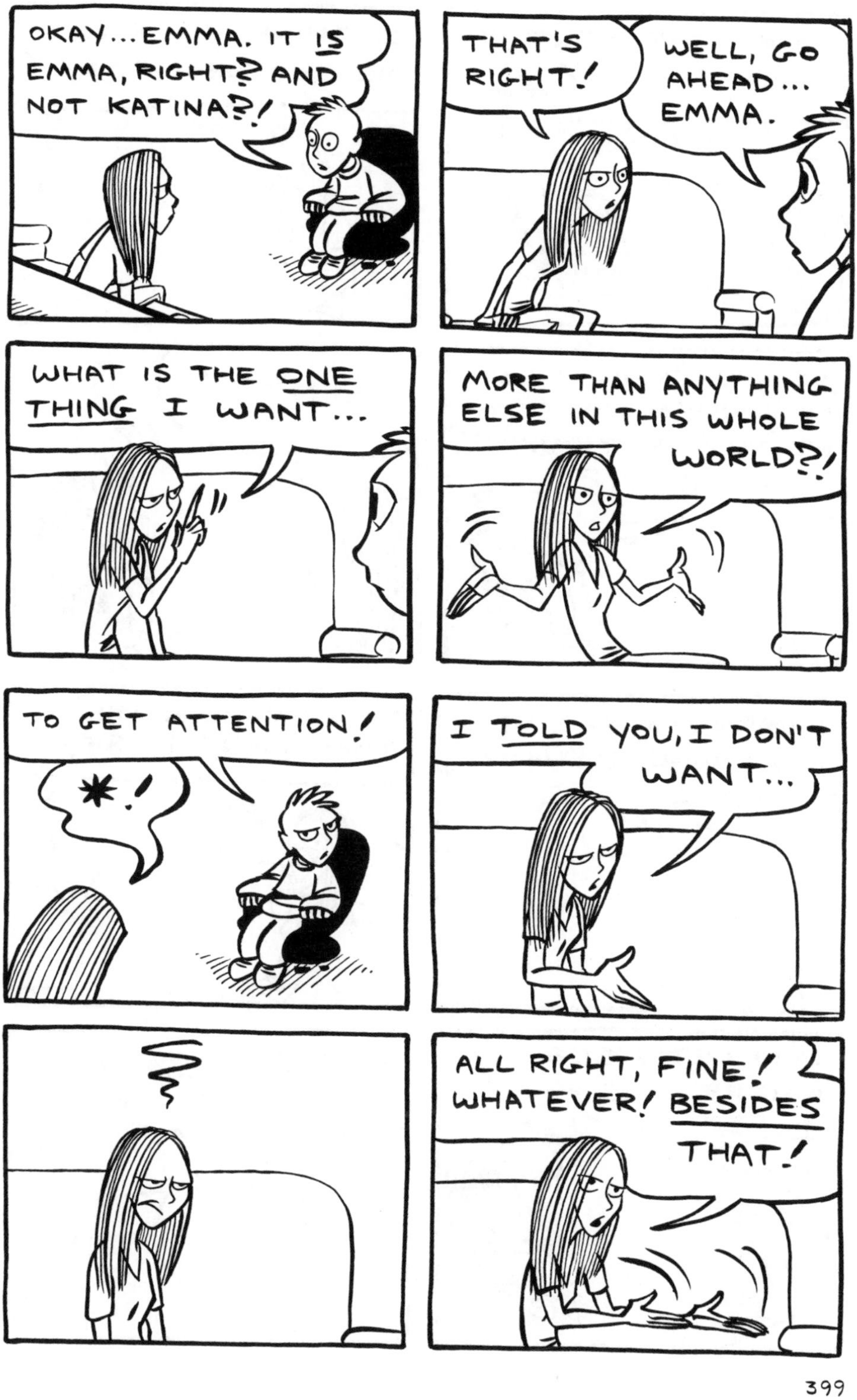
OKAY... EMMA. IT IS EMMA, RIGHT? AND NOT KATINA?!
THAT'S RIGHT!
WELL, GO AHEAD... EMMA.
WHAT IS THE ONE THING I WANT...
MORE THAN ANYTHING ELSE IN THIS WHOLE WORLD?!
TO GET ATTENTION!
*!
I TOLD YOU, I DON'T WANT...
ALL RIGHT, FINE! WHATEVER! BESIDES THAT!

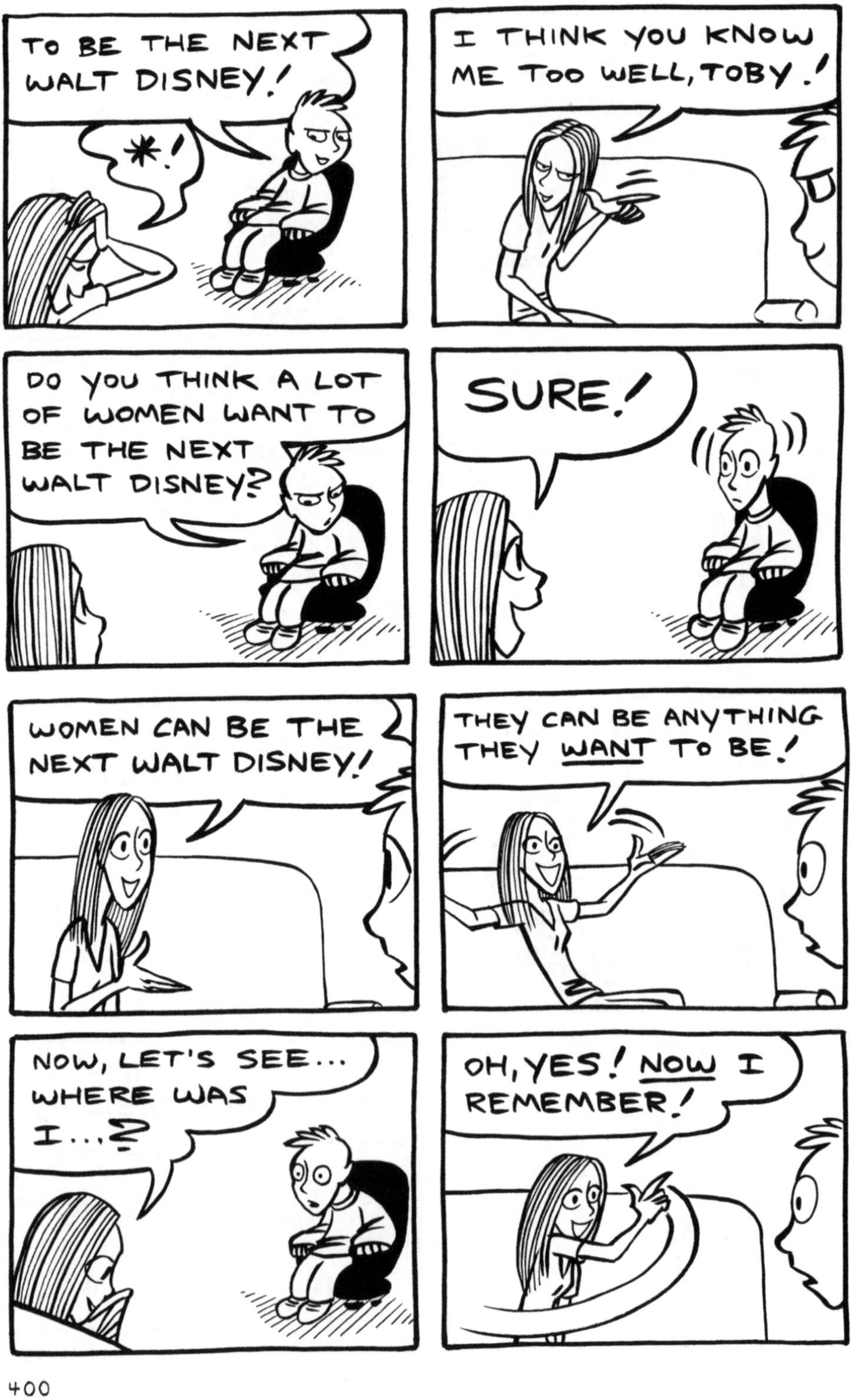
TO BE THE NEXT WALT DISNEY!
*!
I THINK YOU KNOW ME TOO WELL, TOBY!
DO YOU THINK A LOT OF WOMEN WANT TO BE THE NEXT WALT DISNEY?
SURE!
WOMEN CAN BE THE NEXT WALT DISNEY!
THEY CAN BE ANYTHING THEY WANT TO BE!
NOW, LET'S SEE... WHERE WAS I...?
OH, YES! NOW I REMEMBER!

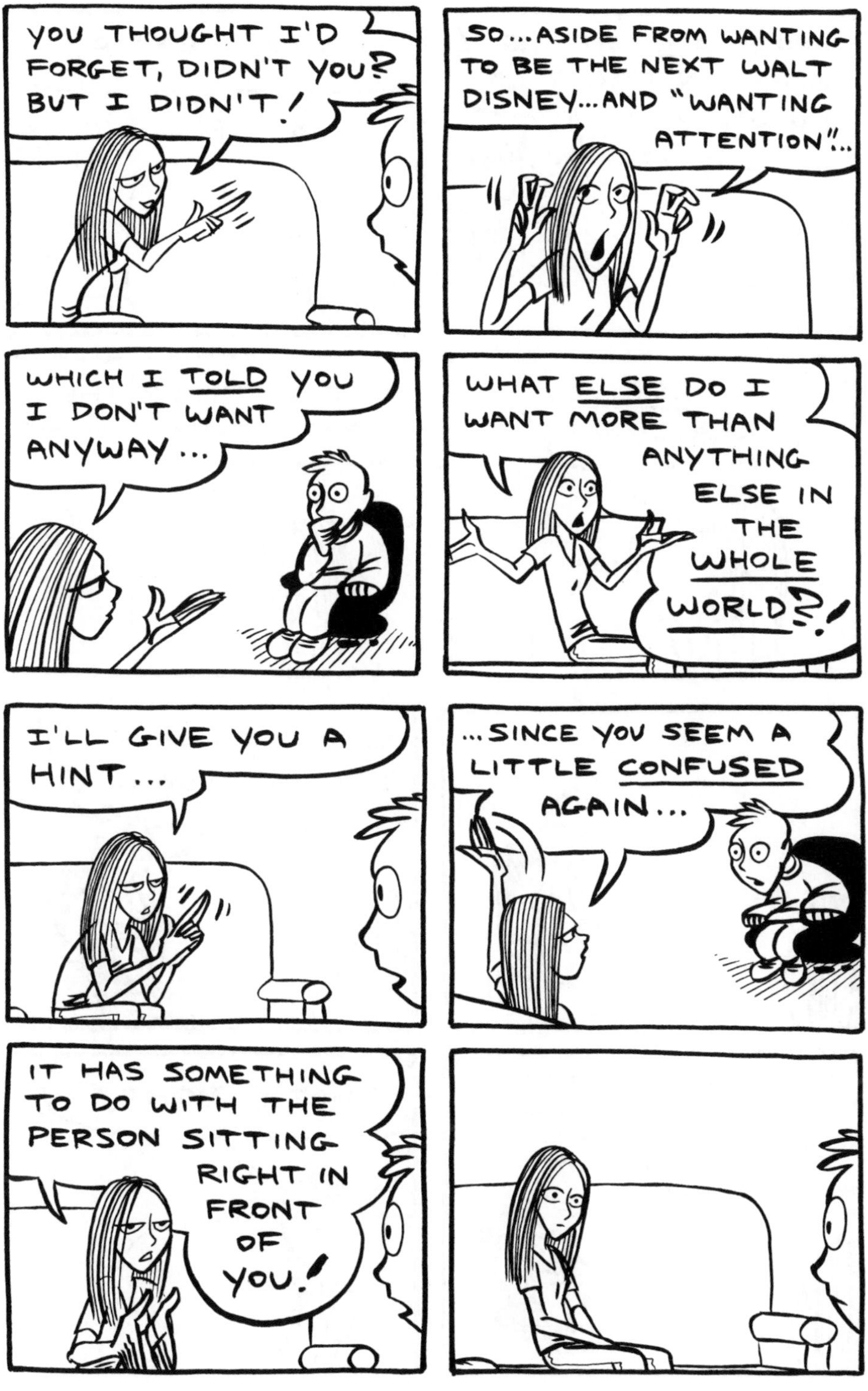
YOU THOUGHT I'D FORGET, DIDN'T YOU? BUT I DIDN'T!
SO... ASIDE FROM WANTING TO BE THE NEXT WALT DISNEY... AND "WANTING ATTENTION"...
WHICH I TOLD YOU I DON'T WANT ANYWAY...
WHAT ELSE DO I WANT MORE THAN ANYTHING ELSE IN THE WHOLE WORLD?!
I'LL GIVE YOU A HINT...
...SINCE YOU SEEM A LITTLE CONFUSED AGAIN...
IT HAS SOMETHING TO DO WITH THE PERSON SITTING RIGHT IN FRONT OF YOU!

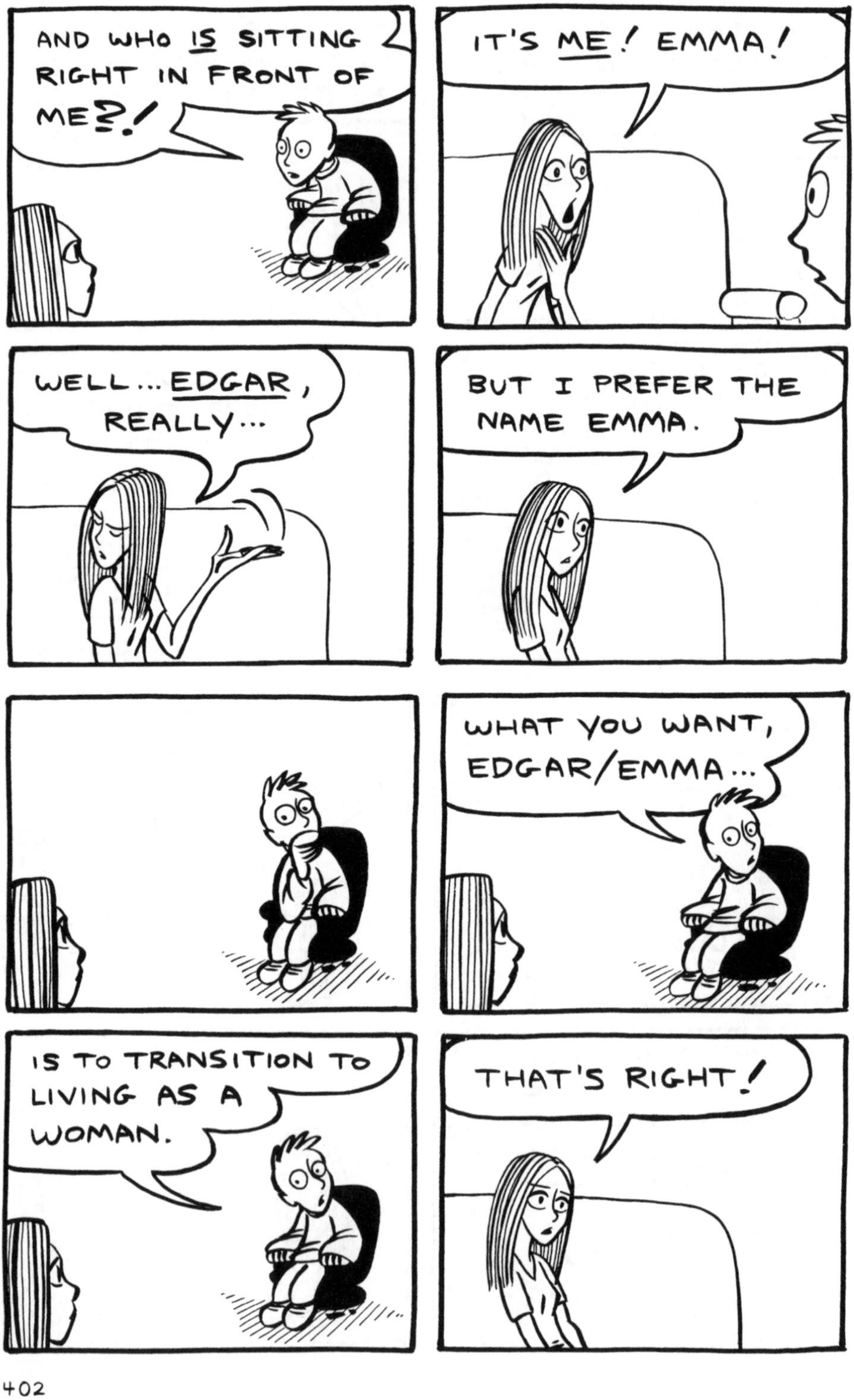
AND WHO IS SITTING RIGHT IN FRONT OF ME?!
IT'S ME! EMMA!
WELL... EDGAR, REALLY...
BUT I PREFER THE NAME EMMA.
WHAT YOU WANT, EDGAR/EMMA...
IS TO TRANSITION TO LIVING AS A WOMAN.
THAT'S RIGHT!

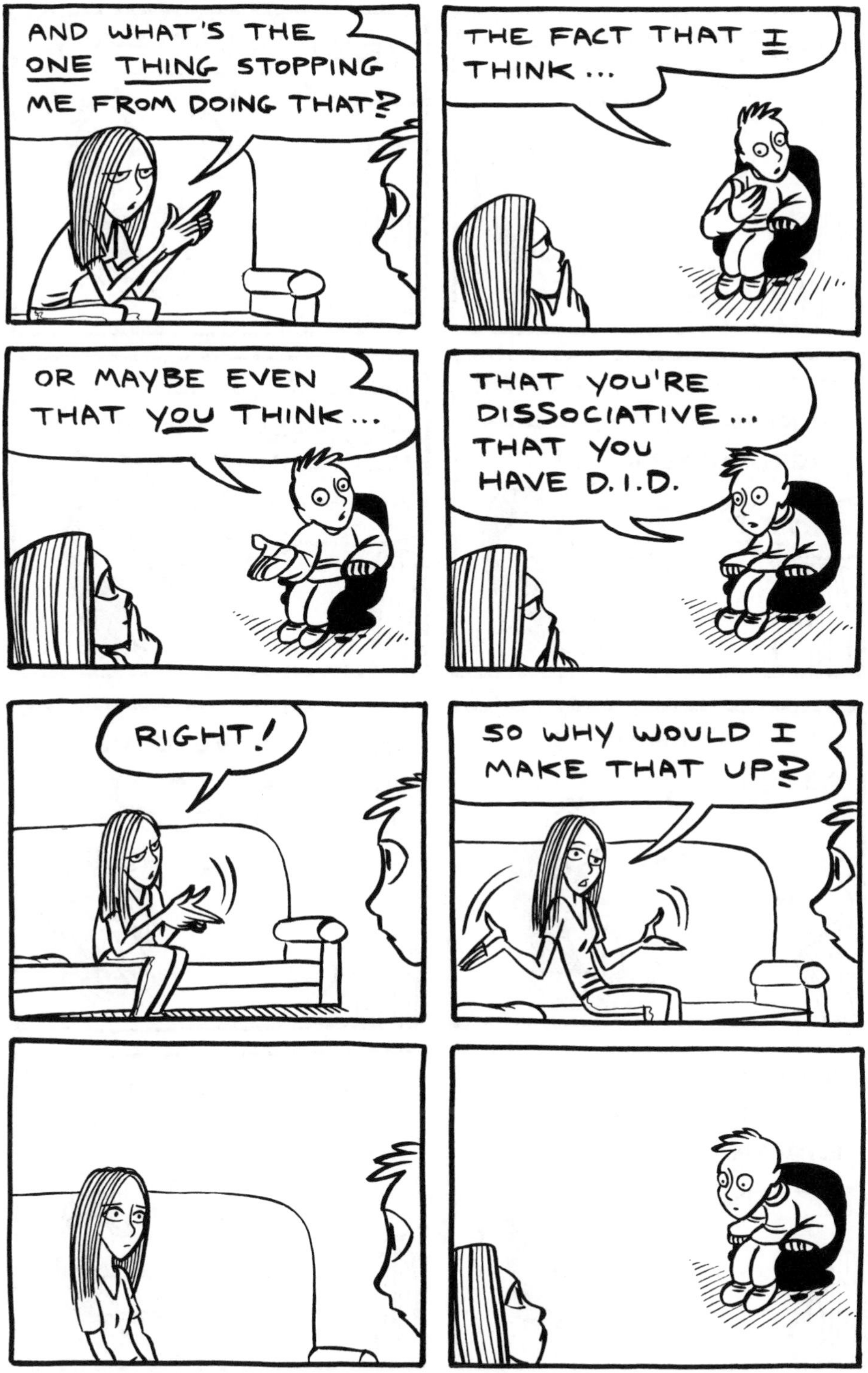
AND WHAT'S THE ONE THING STOPPING ME FROM DOING THAT?
THE FACT THAT I THINK...
OR MAYBE EVEN THAT YOU THINK...
THAT YOU'RE DISSOCIATIVE... THAT YOU HAVE D.I.D.
RIGHT!
SO WHY WOULD I MAKE THAT UP?

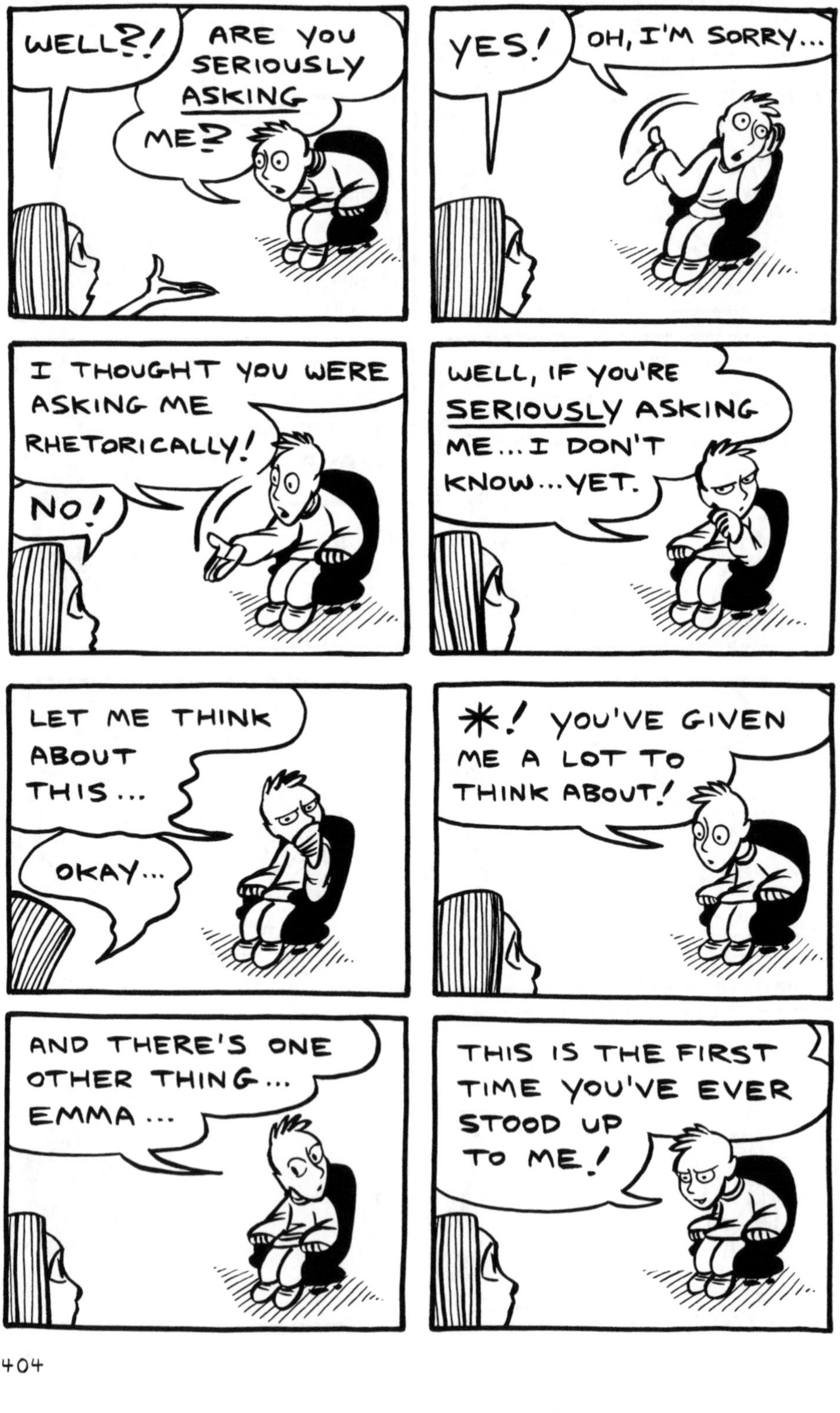
WELL?!
ARE YOU SERIOUSLY ASKING ME?
YES!
OH, I'M SORRY...
I THOUGHT YOU WERE ASKING ME RHETORICALLY!
NO!
WELL, IF YOU'RE SERIOUSLY ASKING ME... I DON'T KNOW... YET.
LET ME THINK ABOUT THIS...
OKAY...
*! YOU'VE GIVEN ME A LOT TO THINK ABOUT!
AND THERE'S ONE OTHER THING... EMMA...
THIS IS THE FIRST TIME YOU'VE EVER STOOD UP TO ME!

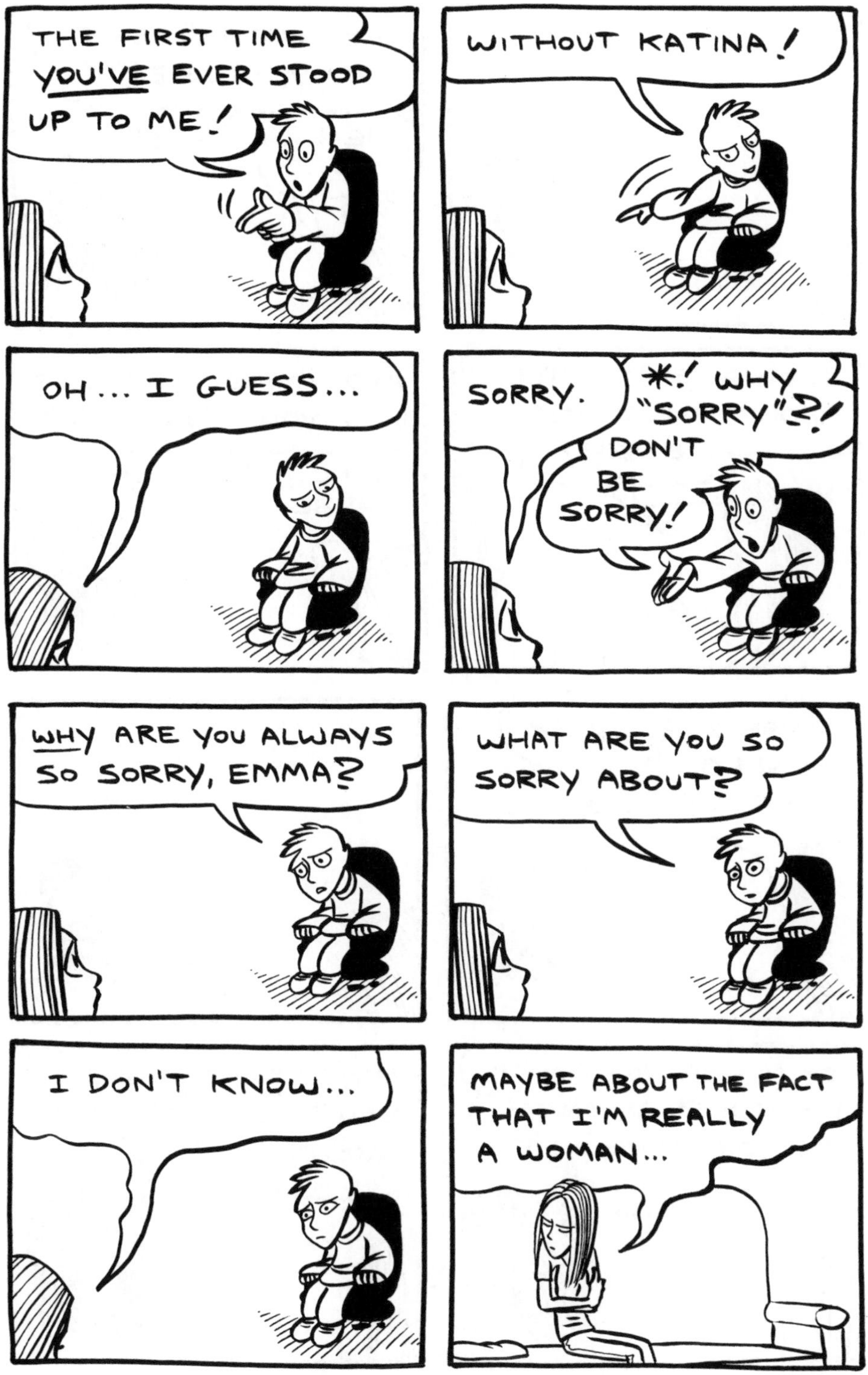
THE FIRST TIME YOU'VE EVER STOOD UP TO ME!
WITHOUT KATINA!
OH... I GUESS...
SORRY.
*! WHY "SORRY"?! DON'T BE SORRY!
WHY ARE YOU ALWAYS SO SORRY, EMMA?
WHAT ARE YOU SO SORRY ABOUT?
I DON'T KNOW...
MAYBE ABOUT THE FACT THAT I'M REALLY A WOMAN...

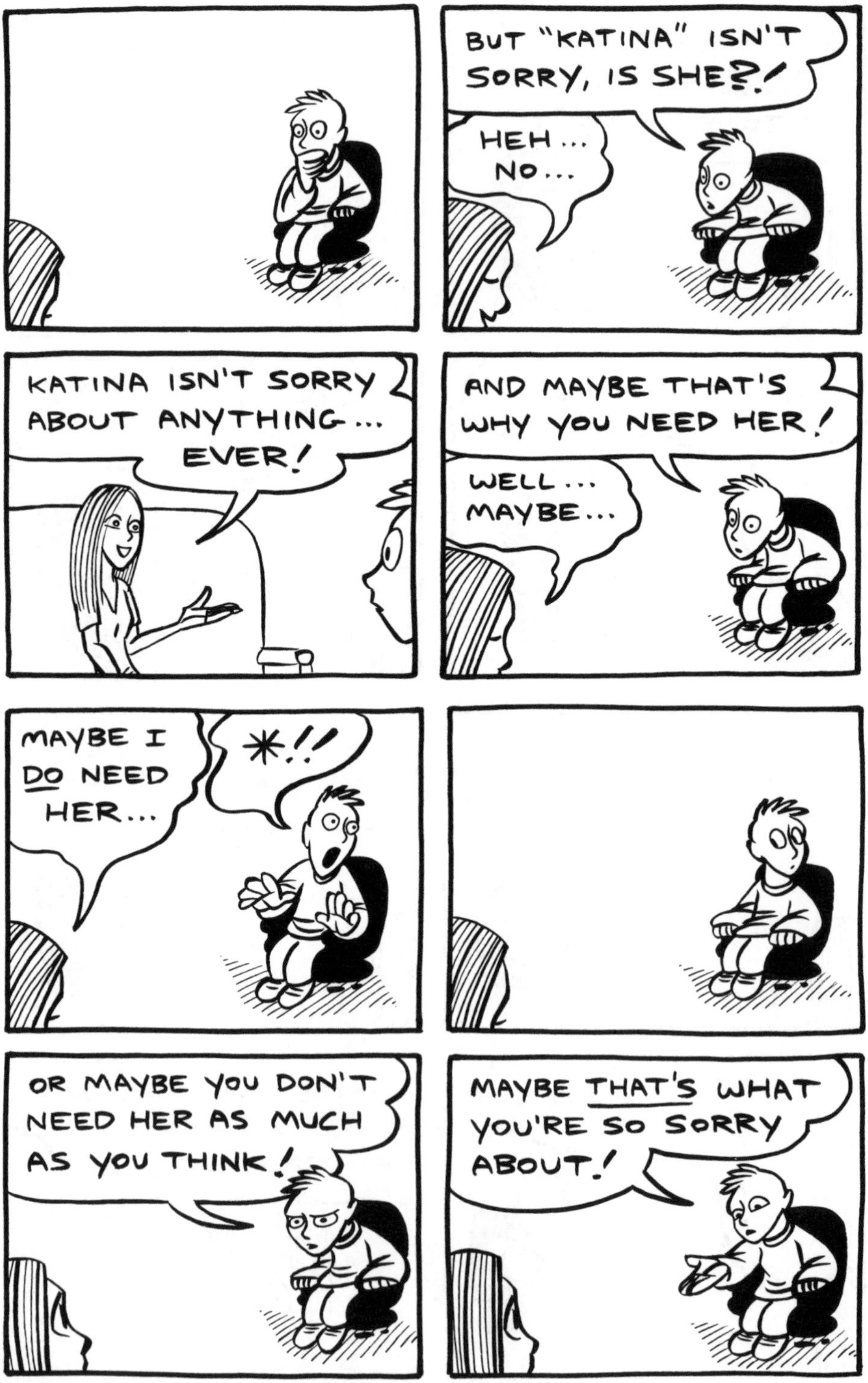
BUT "KATINA" ISN'T SORRY, IS SHE?!
HEH... NO...
KATINA ISN'T SORRY ABOUT ANYTHING... EVER!
AND MAYBE THAT'S WHY YOU NEED HER!
WELL... MAYBE...
MAYBE I DO NEED HER...
*!!
OR MAYBE YOU DON'T NEED HER AS MUCH AS YOU THINK!
MAYBE THAT'S WHAT YOU'RE SO SORRY ABOUT!

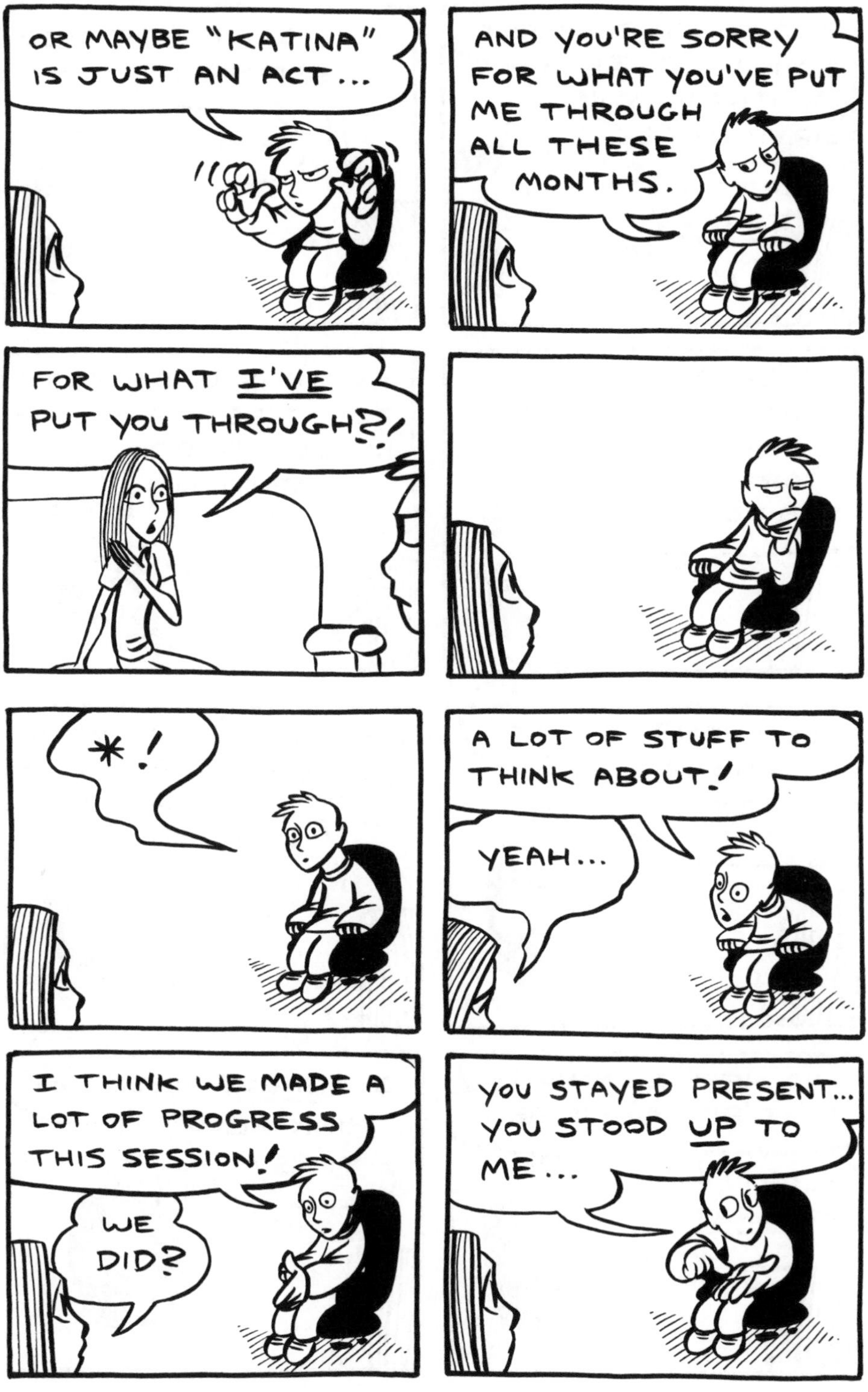
OR MAYBE "KATINA" IS JUST AN ACT...
AND YOU'RE SORRY FOR WHAT YOU'VE PUT ME THROUGH ALL THESE MONTHS.
FOR WHAT I'VE PUT YOU THROUGH?!
*!
A LOT OF STUFF TO THINK ABOUT!
YEAH...
I THINK WE MADE A LOT OF PROGRESS THIS SESSION!
WE DID?
YOU STAYED PRESENT... YOU STOOD UP TO ME...

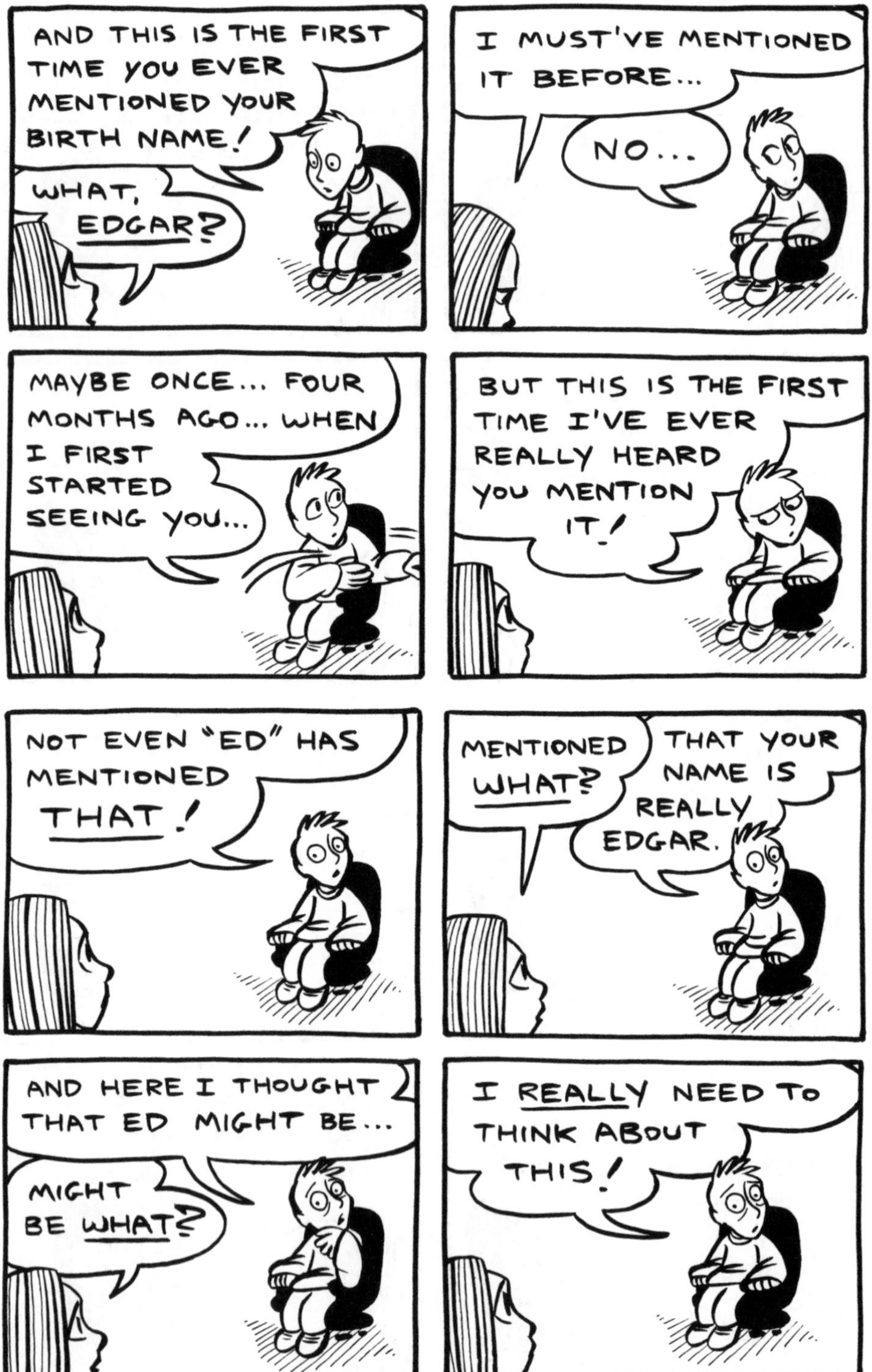
AND THIS IS THE FIRST TIME YOU EVER MENTIONED YOUR BIRTH NAME!
WHAT, EDGAR?
I MUST'VE MENTIONED IT BEFORE...
NO...
MAYBE ONCE... FOUR MONTHS AGO... WHEN I FIRST STARTED SEEING YOU...
BUT THIS IS THE FIRST TIME I'VE EVER REALLY HEARD YOU MENTION IT!
NOT EVEN "ED" HAS MENTIONED THAT!
MENTIONED WHAT?
THAT YOUR NAME IS REALLY EDGAR.
AND HERE I THOUGHT THAT ED MIGHT BE...
MIGHT BE WHAT?
I REALLY NEED TO THINK ABOUT THIS!

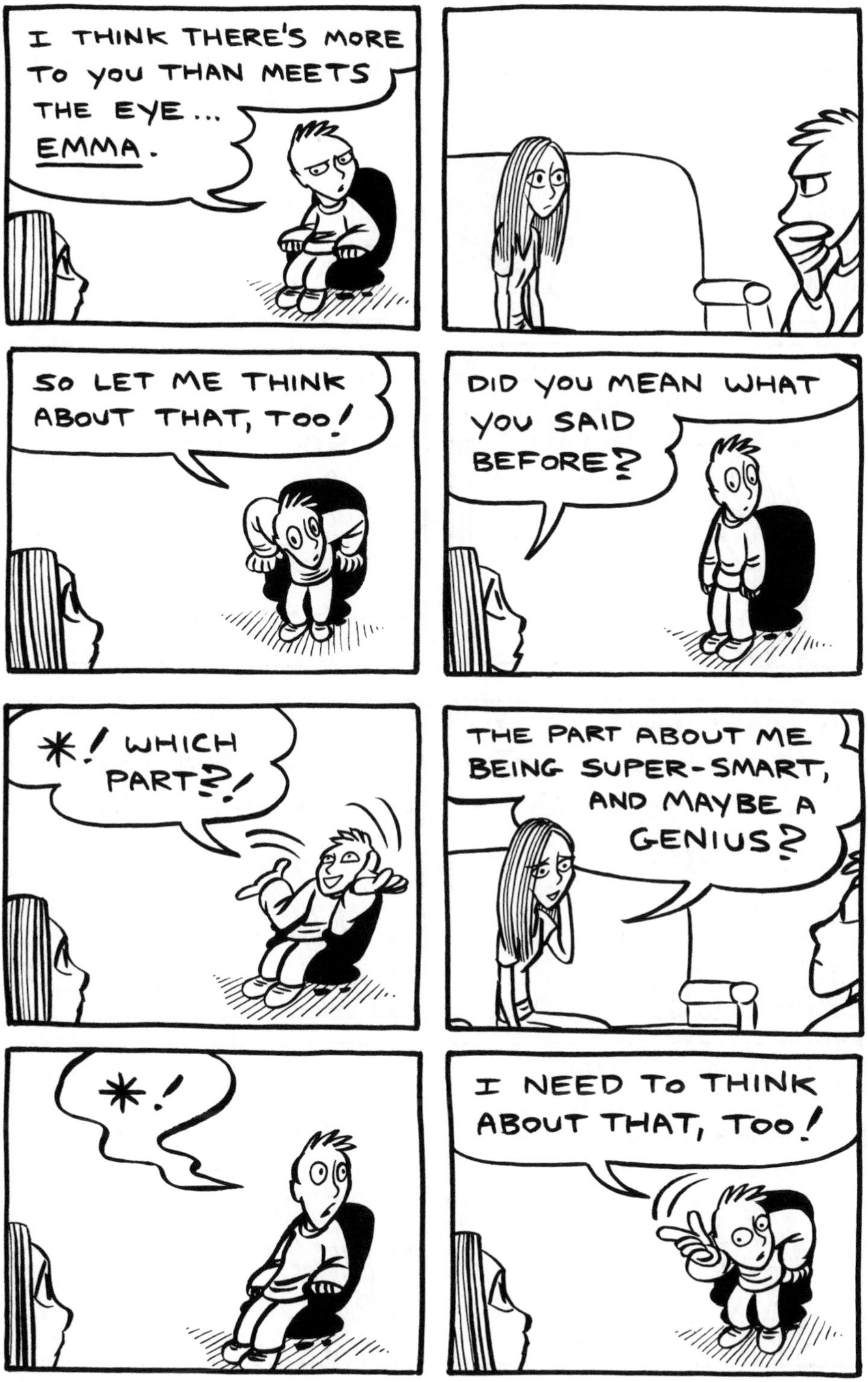
I THINK THERE'S MORE TO YOU THAN MEETS THE EYE... EMMA.
SO LET ME THINK ABOUT THAT, TOO!
DID YOU MEAN WHAT YOU SAID BEFORE?
*! WHICH PART?!
THE PART ABOUT ME BEING SUPER-SMART, AND MAYBE A GENIUS?
*!
I NEED TO THINK ABOUT THAT, TOO!

I THINK YOU MAY BE A LITTLE TOO SMART FOR YOUR OWN GOOD...

ANYWAY, WE'LL TALK ABOUT IT AGAIN NEXT WEEK!

THIS CERTAINLY WILL BE INTERESTING, EMMA... FIGURING THIS OUT!

TOO SMART FOR MY OWN GOOD...? HOW CAN BEING SMART BE A BAD THING?!

ALL RIGHT...WHAT THE HELL IS HE TALKING ABOUT?!

WHAT THE HELL IS DISSOCIATION?!

Dissociation : Disruption or breakdown of memory, awareness, or perception. In extreme cases...

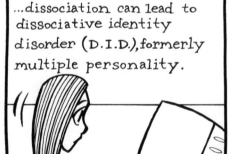

...dissociation can lead to dissociative identity disorder (D.I.D.), formerly multiple personality.

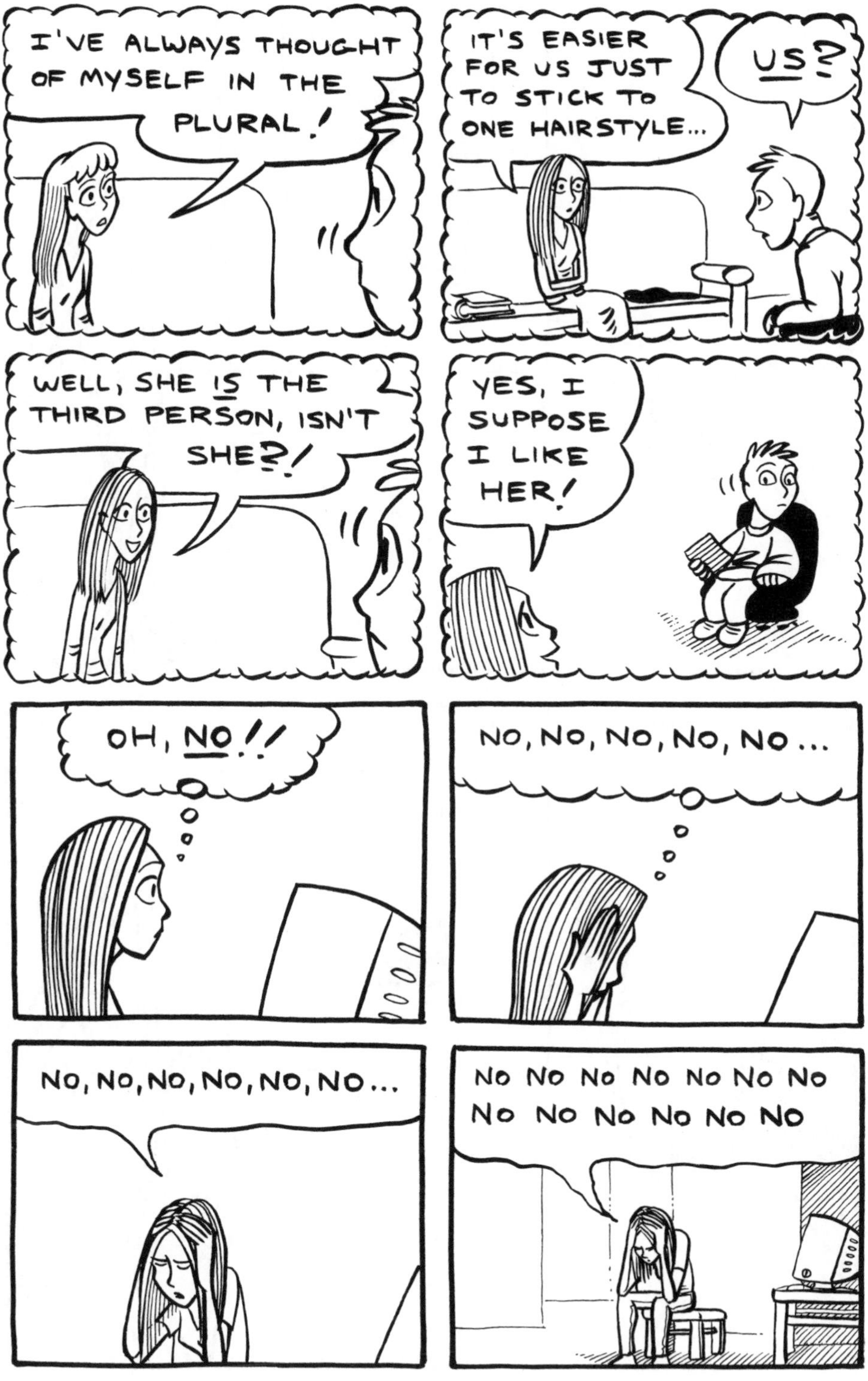
I'VE ALWAYS THOUGHT OF MYSELF IN THE PLURAL!
IT'S EASIER FOR US JUST TO STICK TO ONE HAIRSTYLE...
US?
WELL, SHE IS THE THIRD PERSON, ISN'T SHE?!
YES, I SUPPOSE I LIKE HER!
OH, NO!!
NO, NO, NO, NO, NO...
NO, NO, NO, NO, NO, NO...
No No No No No No No No No No No No No

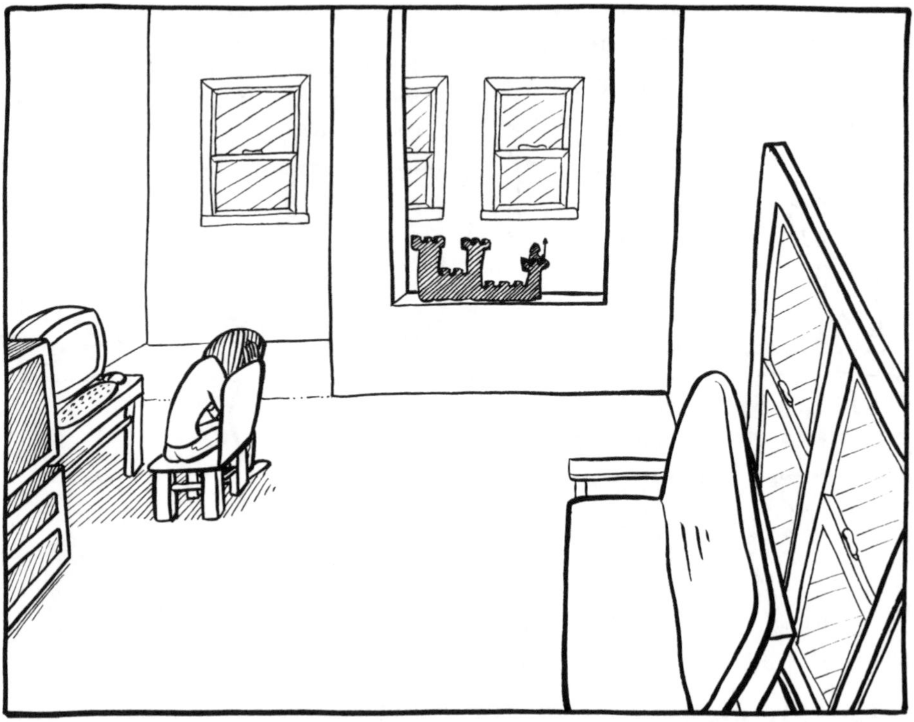

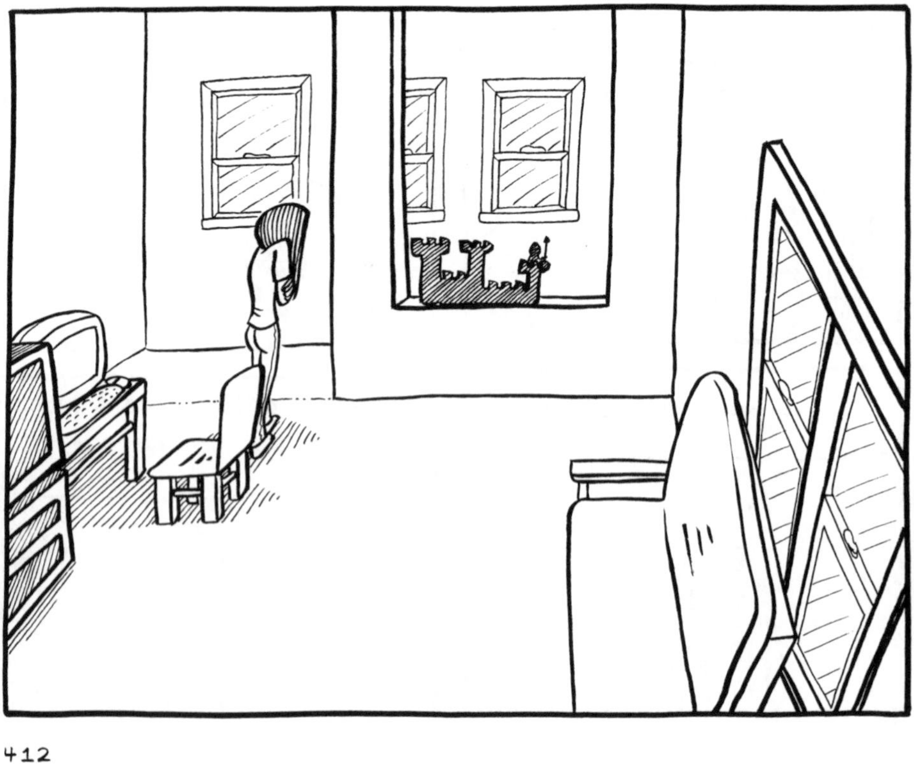

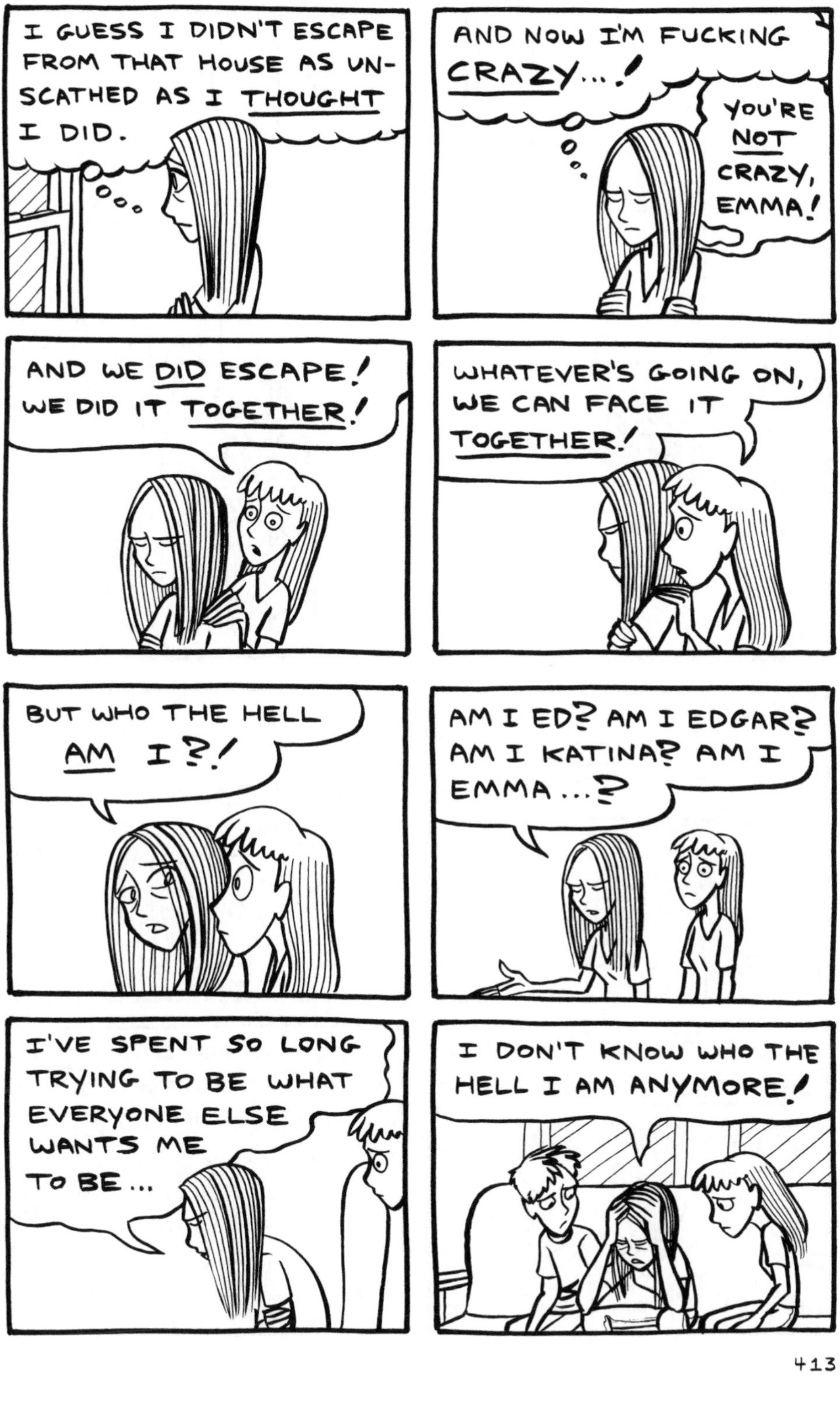
I GUESS I DIDN'T ESCAPE FROM THAT HOUSE AS UN-SCATHED AS I THOUGHT I DID.
AND NOW I'M FUCKING CRAZY...!
YOU'RE NOT CRAZY, EMMA!
AND WE DID ESCAPE! WE DID IT TOGETHER!
WHATEVER'S GOING ON, WE CAN FACE IT TOGETHER!
BUT WHO THE HELL AM I?!
AM I ED? AM I EDGAR? AM I KATINA? AM I EMMA...?
I'VE SPENT SO LONG TRYING TO BE WHAT EVERYONE ELSE WANTS ME TO BE...
I DON'T KNOW WHO THE HELL I AM ANYMORE!

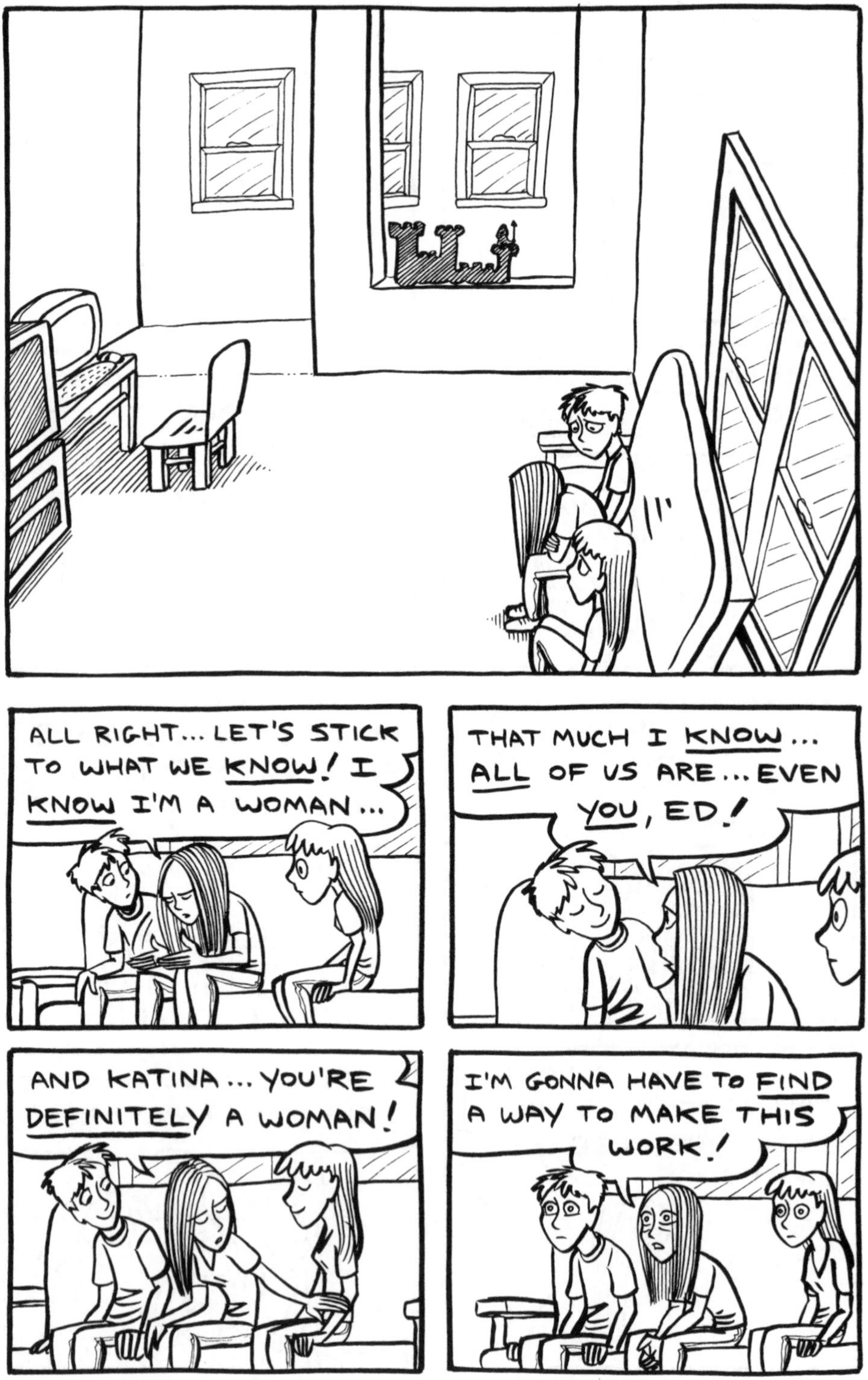
ALL RIGHT... LET'S STICK TO WHAT WE KNOW! I KNOW I'M A WOMAN...
THAT MUCH I KNOW... ALL OF US ARE... EVEN YOU, ED!
AND KATINA... YOU'RE DEFINITELY A WOMAN!
I'M GONNA HAVE TO FIND A WAY TO MAKE THIS WORK!

CHESTNUT

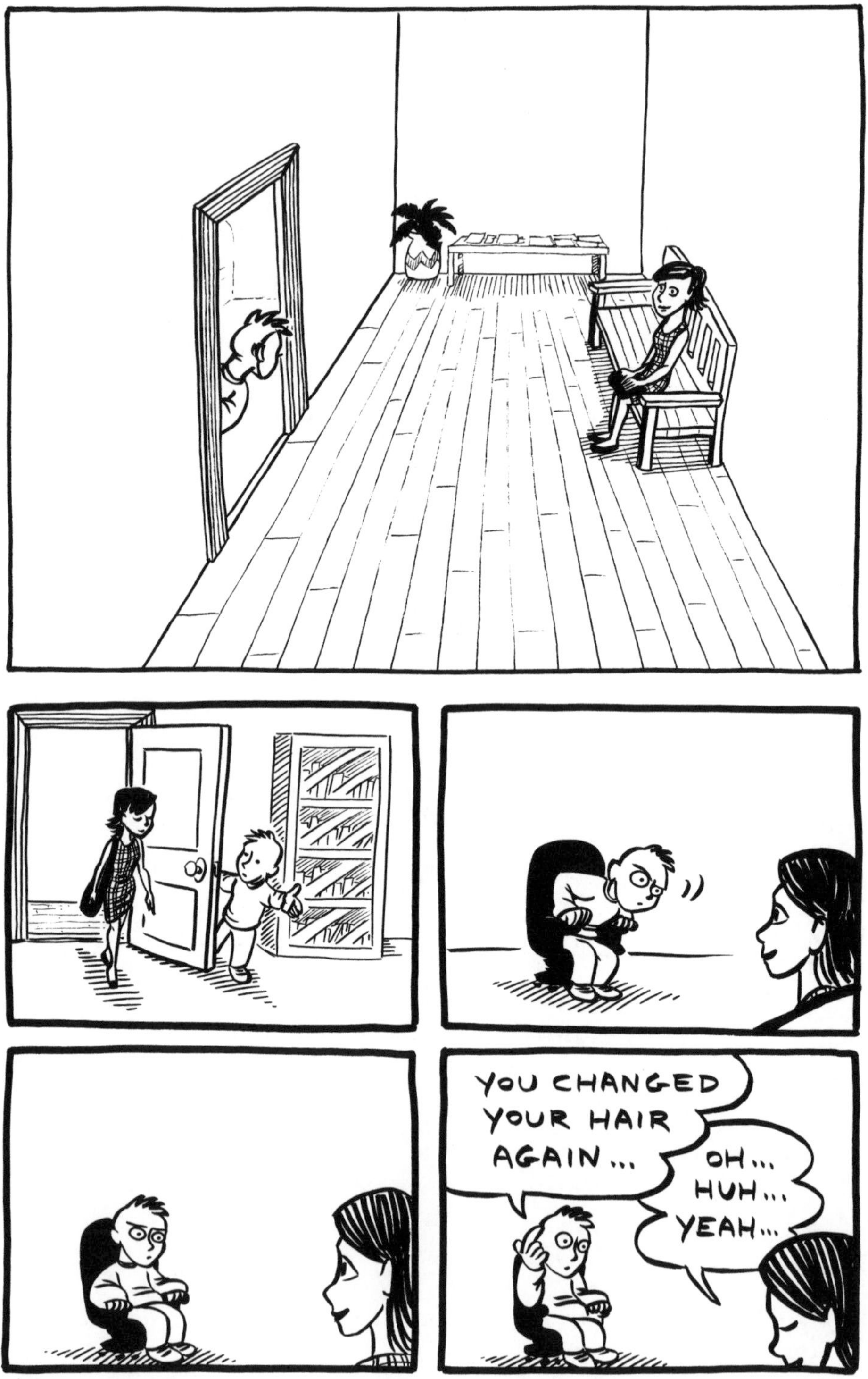
YOU CHANGED YOUR HAIR AGAIN...
OH... HUH... YEAH...

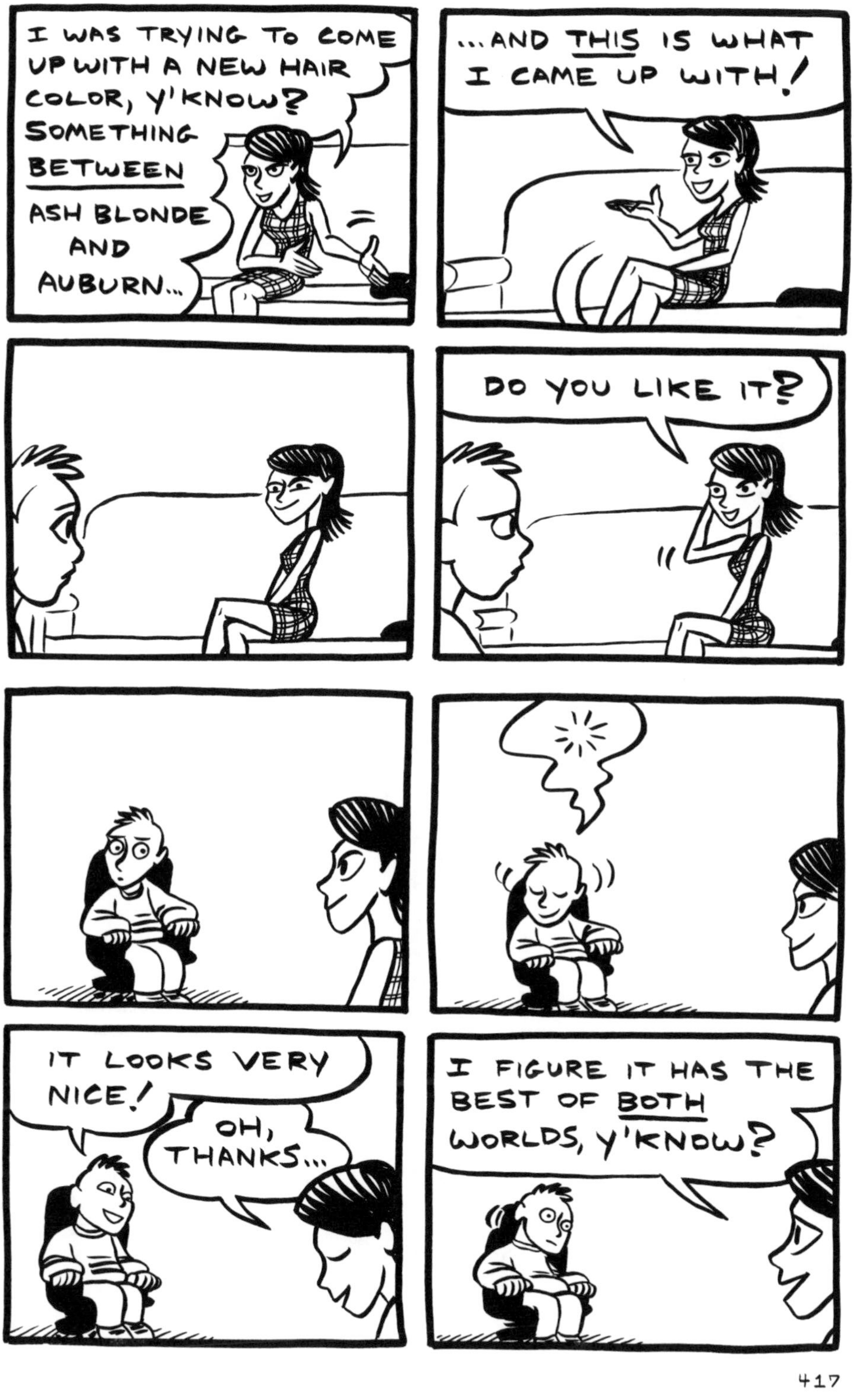

I WAS TRYING TO COME UP WITH A NEW HAIR COLOR, Y'KNOW? SOMETHING BETWEEN ASH BLONDE AND AUBURN...
...AND THIS IS WHAT I CAME UP WITH!
DO YOU LIKE IT?
IT LOOKS VERY NICE!
OH, THANKS...
I FIGURE IT HAS THE BEST OF BOTH WORLDS, Y'KNOW?

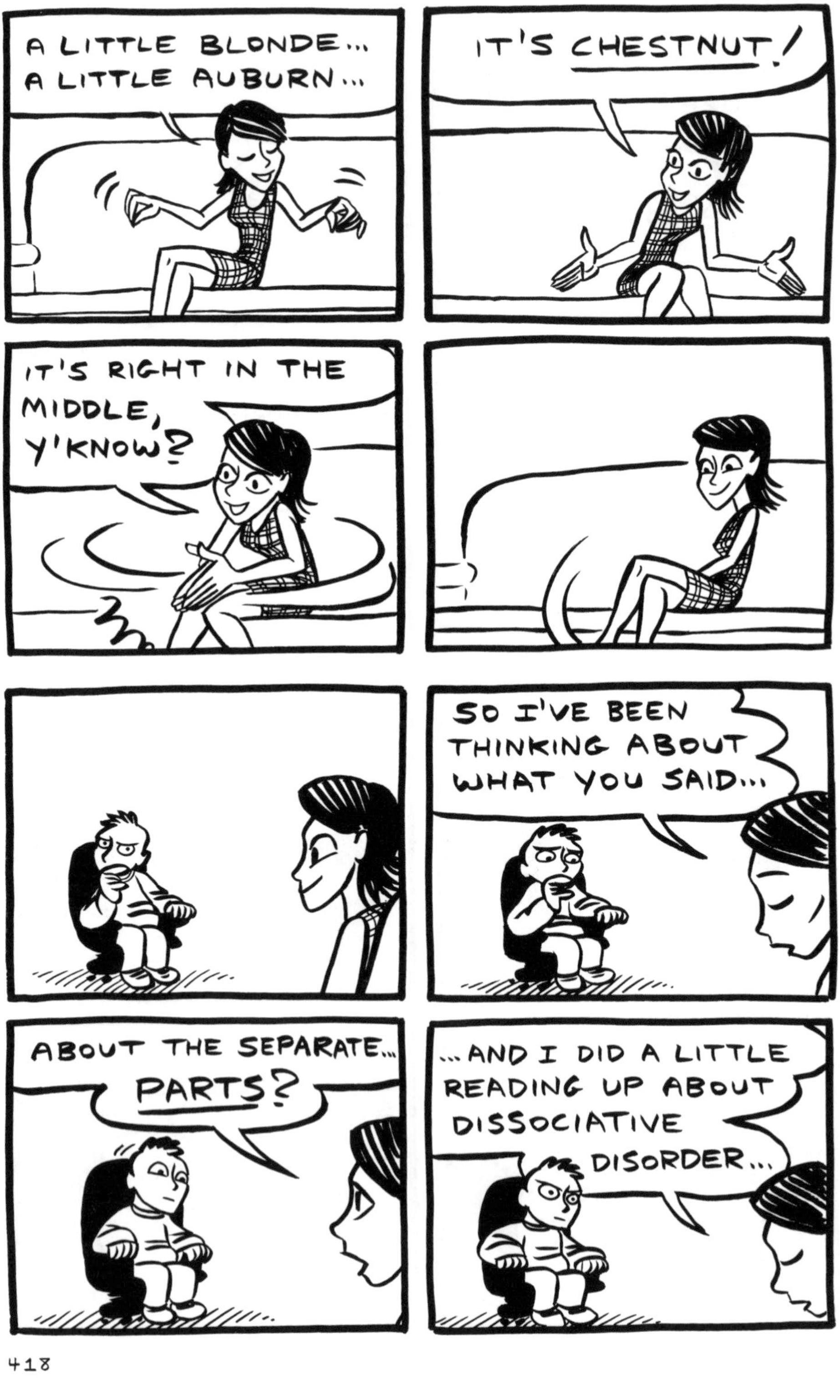
A LITTLE BLONDE...
A LITTLE AUBURN...
IT'S CHESTNUT!
IT'S RIGHT IN THE MIDDLE, Y'KNOW?
SO I'VE BEEN THINKING ABOUT WHAT YOU SAID...
ABOUT THE SEPARATE... PARTS?
...AND I DID A LITTLE READING UP ABOUT DISSOCIATIVE DISORDER...

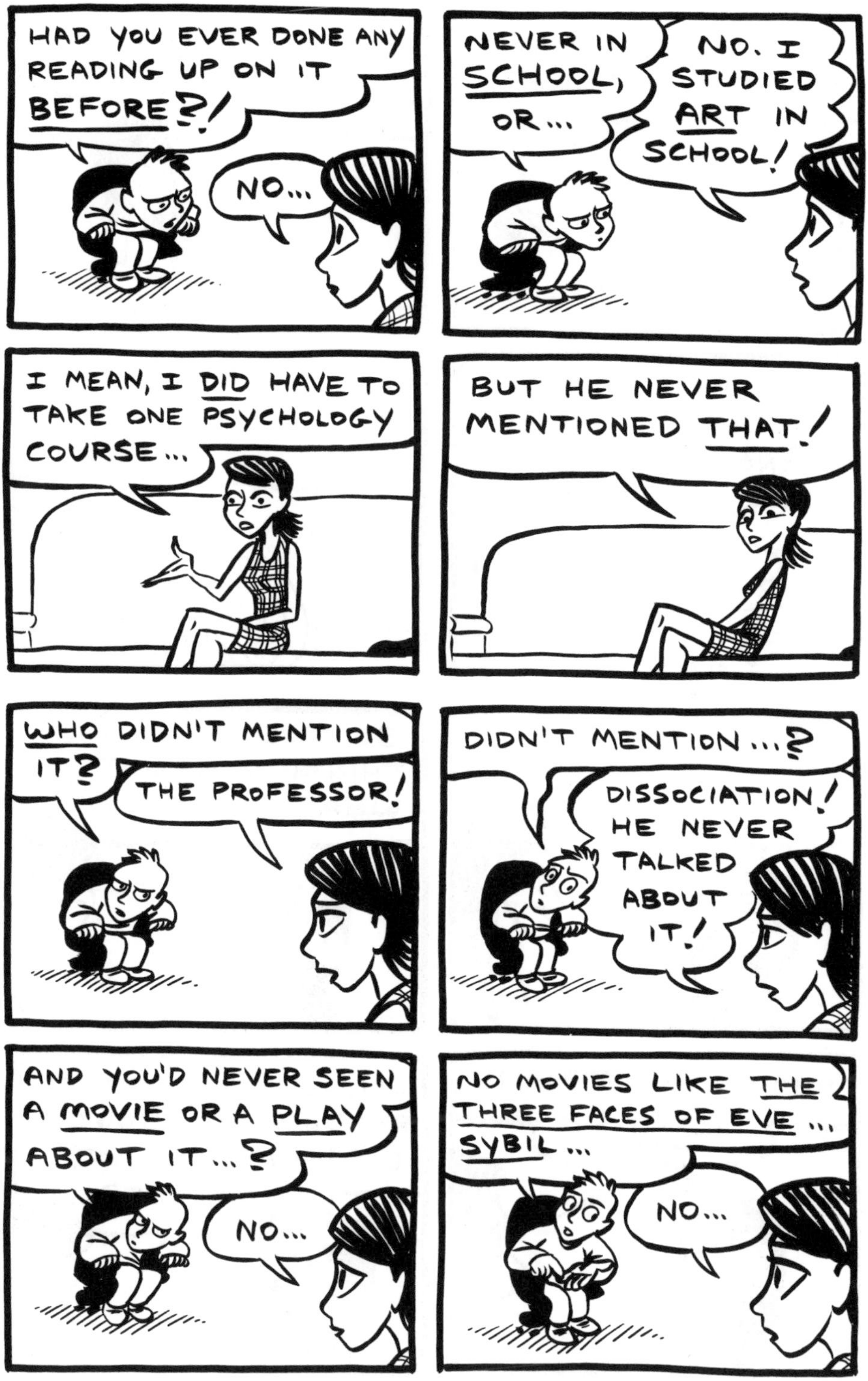
HAD YOU EVER DONE ANY READING UP ON IT BEFORE?!
NO...
NEVER IN SCHOOL, OR...
NO. I STUDIED ART IN SCHOOL!
I MEAN, I DID HAVE TO TAKE ONE PSYCHOLOGY COURSE...
BUT HE NEVER MENTIONED THAT!
WHO DIDN'T MENTION IT?
THE PROFESSOR!
DIDN'T MENTION...?
DISSOCIATION! HE NEVER TALKED ABOUT IT!
AND YOU'D NEVER SEEN A MOVIE OR A PLAY ABOUT IT...?
NO...
NO MOVIES LIKE THE THREE FACES OF EVE... SYBIL...
NO...

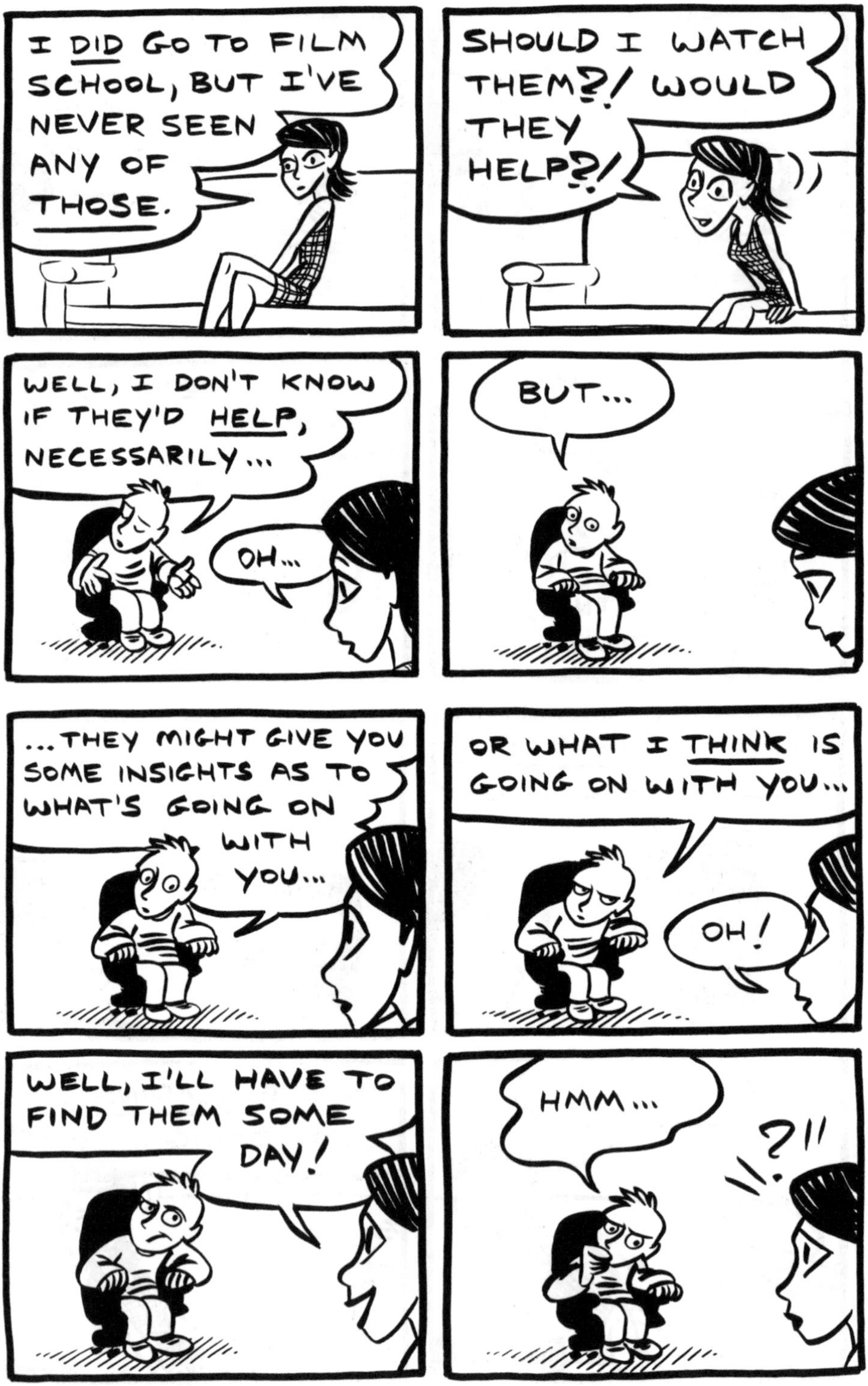
I DID GO TO FILM SCHOOL, BUT I'VE NEVER SEEN ANY OF THOSE.
SHOULD I WATCH THEM?! WOULD THEY HELP?!
WELL, I DON'T KNOW IF THEY'D HELP, NECESSARILY...
OH...
BUT...
...THEY MIGHT GIVE YOU SOME INSIGHTS AS TO WHAT'S GOING ON WITH YOU...
OR WHAT I THINK IS GOING ON WITH YOU...
OH!
WELL, I'LL HAVE TO FIND THEM SOME DAY!
HMM...
?!!

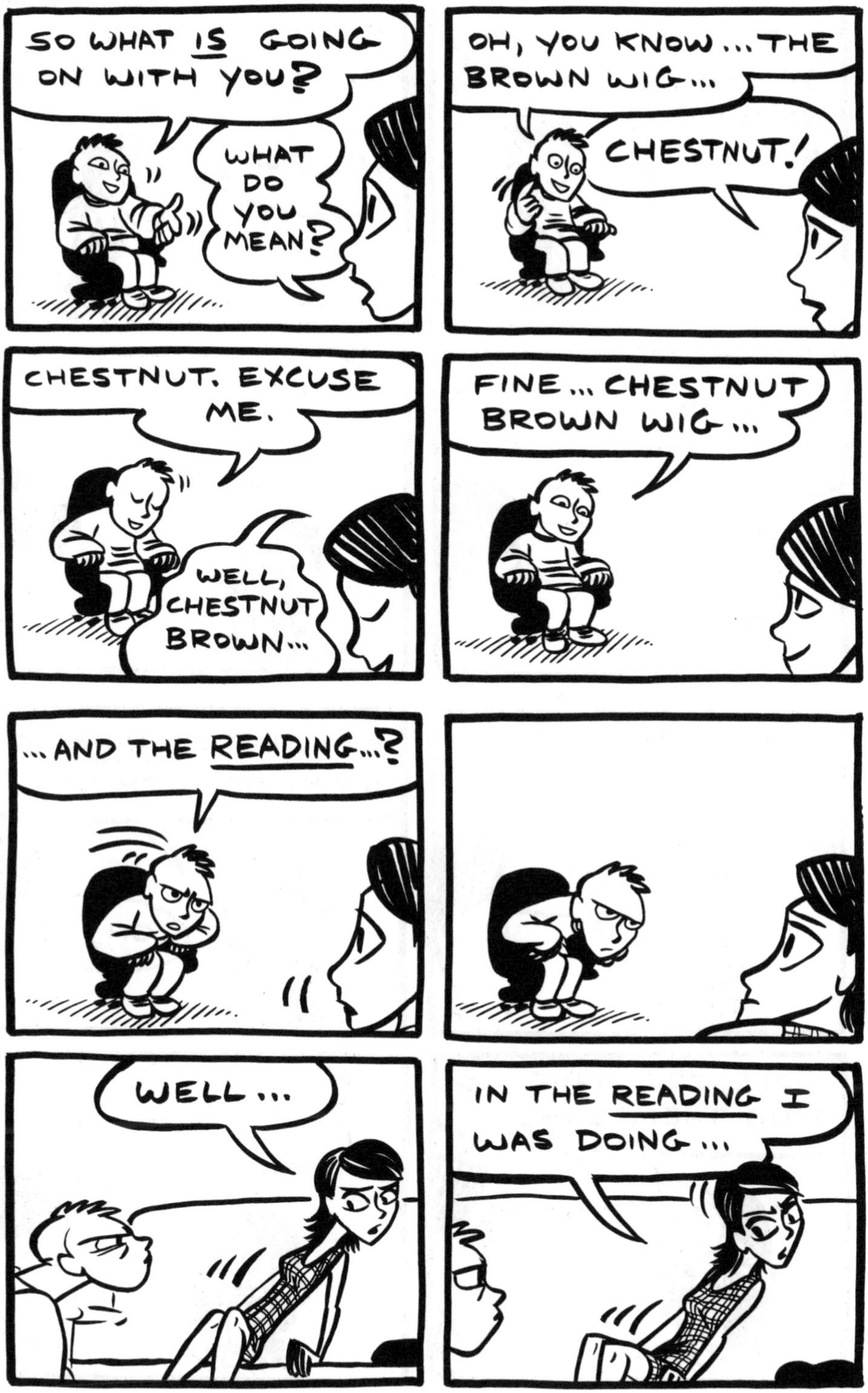
SO WHAT IS GOING ON WITH YOU?
WHAT DO YOU MEAN?
OH, YOU KNOW... THE BROWN WIG...
CHESTNUT!
CHESTNUT. EXCUSE ME.
WELL, CHESTNUT BROWN...
FINE... CHESTNUT BROWN WIG...
...AND THE READING...?
WELL...
IN THE READING I WAS DOING...

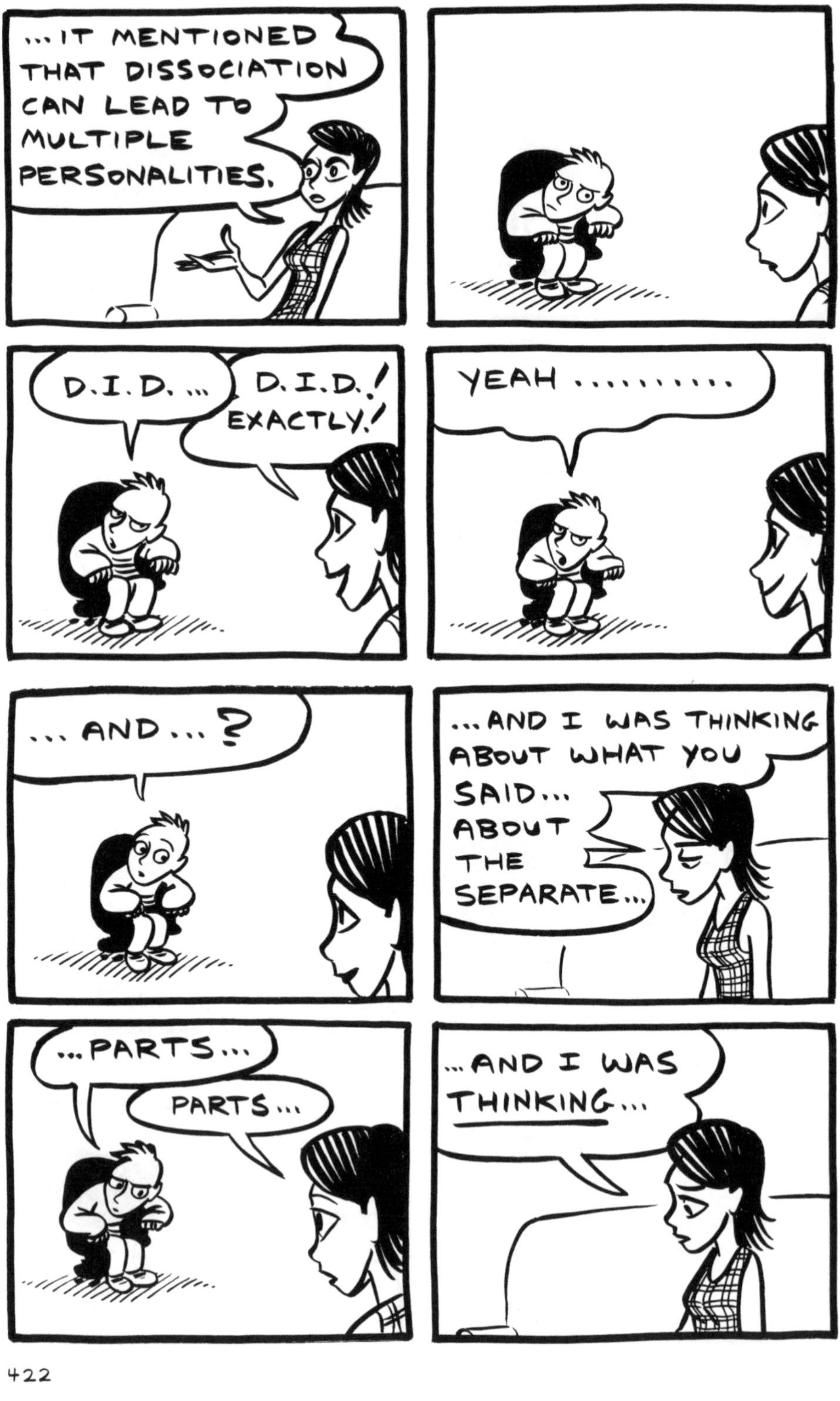
...IT MENTIONED THAT DISSOCIATION CAN LEAD TO MULTIPLE PERSONALITIES.
D.I.D. ...
D.I.D.! EXACTLY!
YEAH ....
... AND ... ?
...AND I WAS THINKING ABOUT WHAT YOU SAID... ABOUT THE SEPARATE...
...PARTS...
PARTS...
...AND I WAS THINKING...

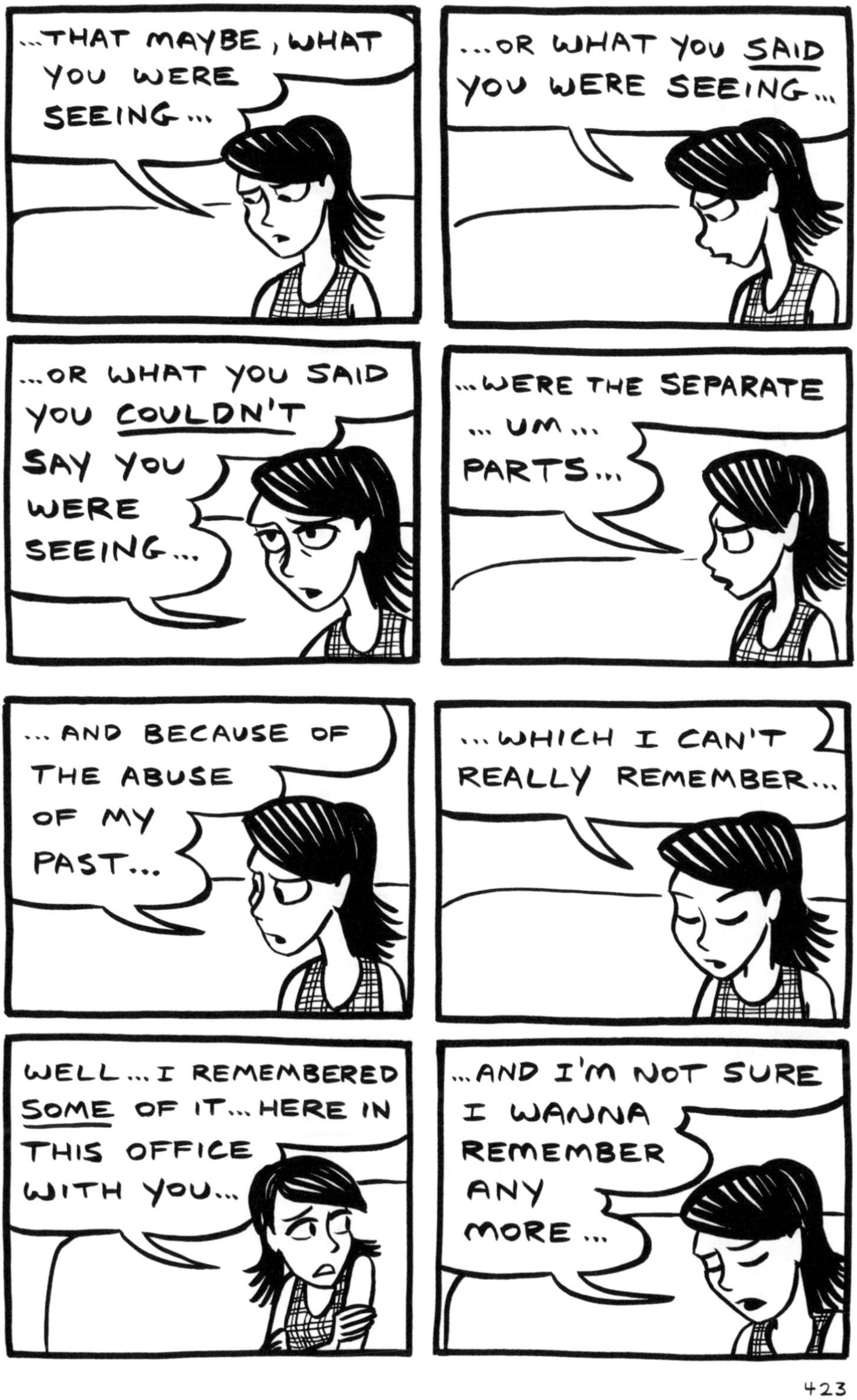
...THAT MAYBE, WHAT YOU WERE SEEING...
...OR WHAT YOU SAID YOU WERE SEEING...
...OR WHAT YOU SAID YOU COULDN'T SAY YOU WERE SEEING...
...WERE THE SEPARATE ... UM... PARTS...
...AND BECAUSE OF THE ABUSE OF MY PAST...
...WHICH I CAN'T REALLY REMEMBER...
WELL...I REMEMBERED SOME OF IT...HERE IN THIS OFFICE WITH YOU...
...AND I'M NOT SURE I WANNA REMEMBER ANY MORE...

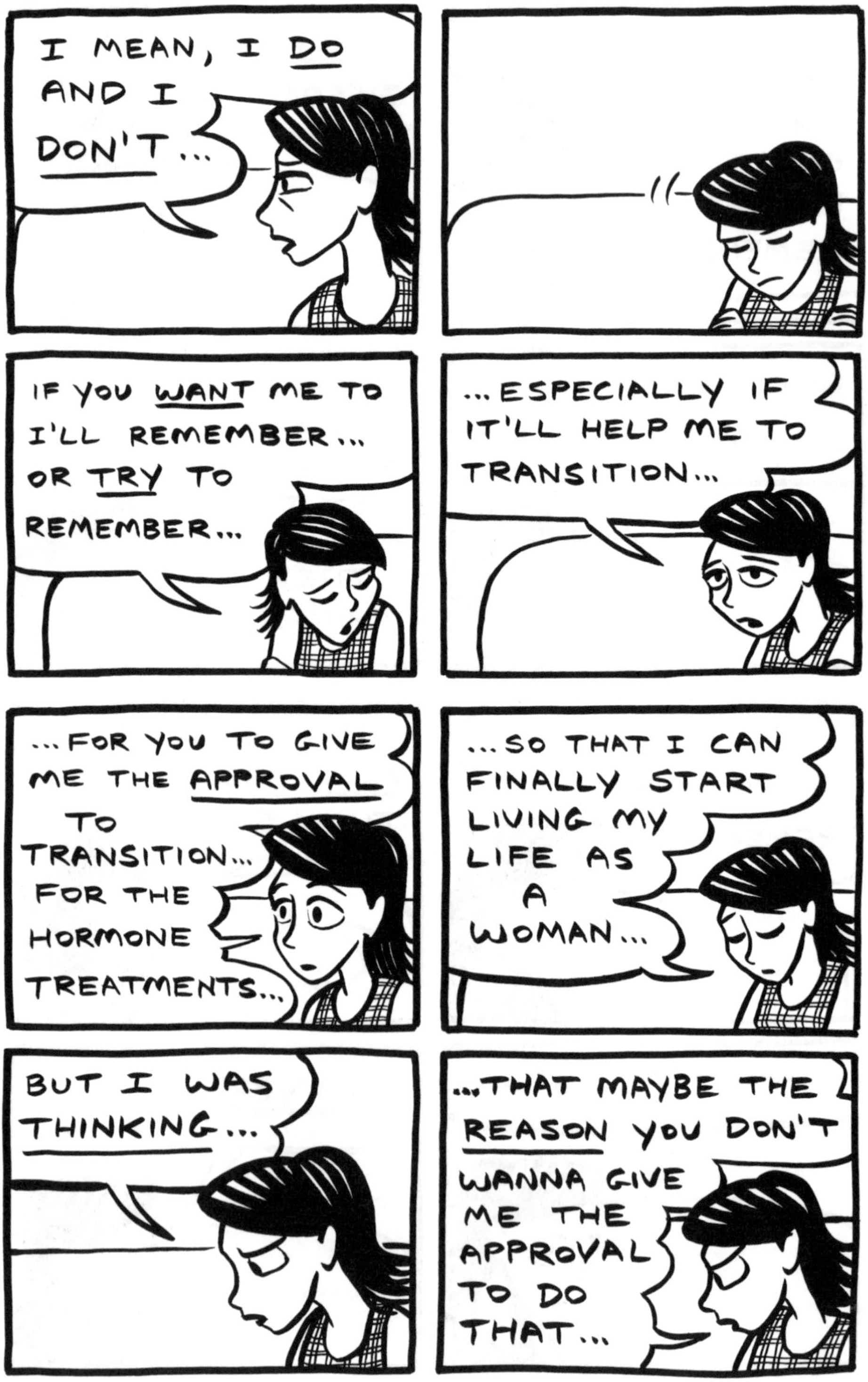
I MEAN, I DO AND I DON'T...
IF YOU WANT ME TO I'LL REMEMBER... OR TRY TO REMEMBER...
...ESPECIALLY IF IT'LL HELP ME TO TRANSITION...
...FOR YOU TO GIVE ME THE APPROVAL TO TRANSITION... FOR THE HORMONE TREATMENTS...
...SO THAT I CAN FINALLY START LIVING MY LIFE AS A WOMAN...
BUT I WAS THINKING...
...THAT MAYBE THE REASON YOU DON'T WANNA GIVE ME THE APPROVAL TO DO THAT...

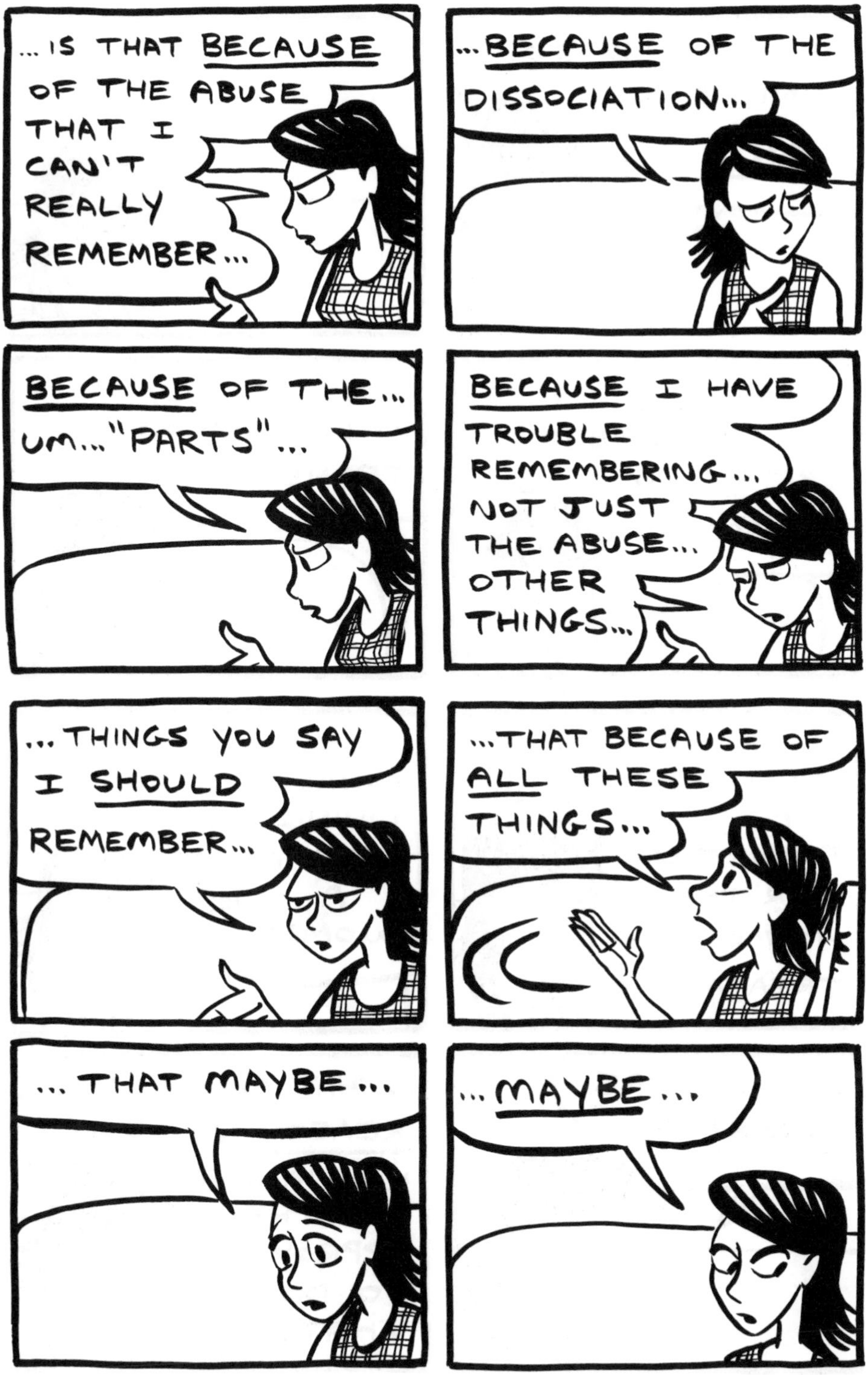
...IS THAT BECAUSE OF THE ABUSE THAT I CAN'T REALLY REMEMBER...
...BECAUSE OF THE DISSOCIATION...
BECAUSE OF THE... UM..."PARTS"...
BECAUSE I HAVE TROUBLE REMEMBERING... NOT JUST THE ABUSE... OTHER THINGS...
...THINGS YOU SAY I SHOULD REMEMBER...
...THAT BECAUSE OF ALL THESE THINGS...
...THAT MAYBE...
...MAYBE...

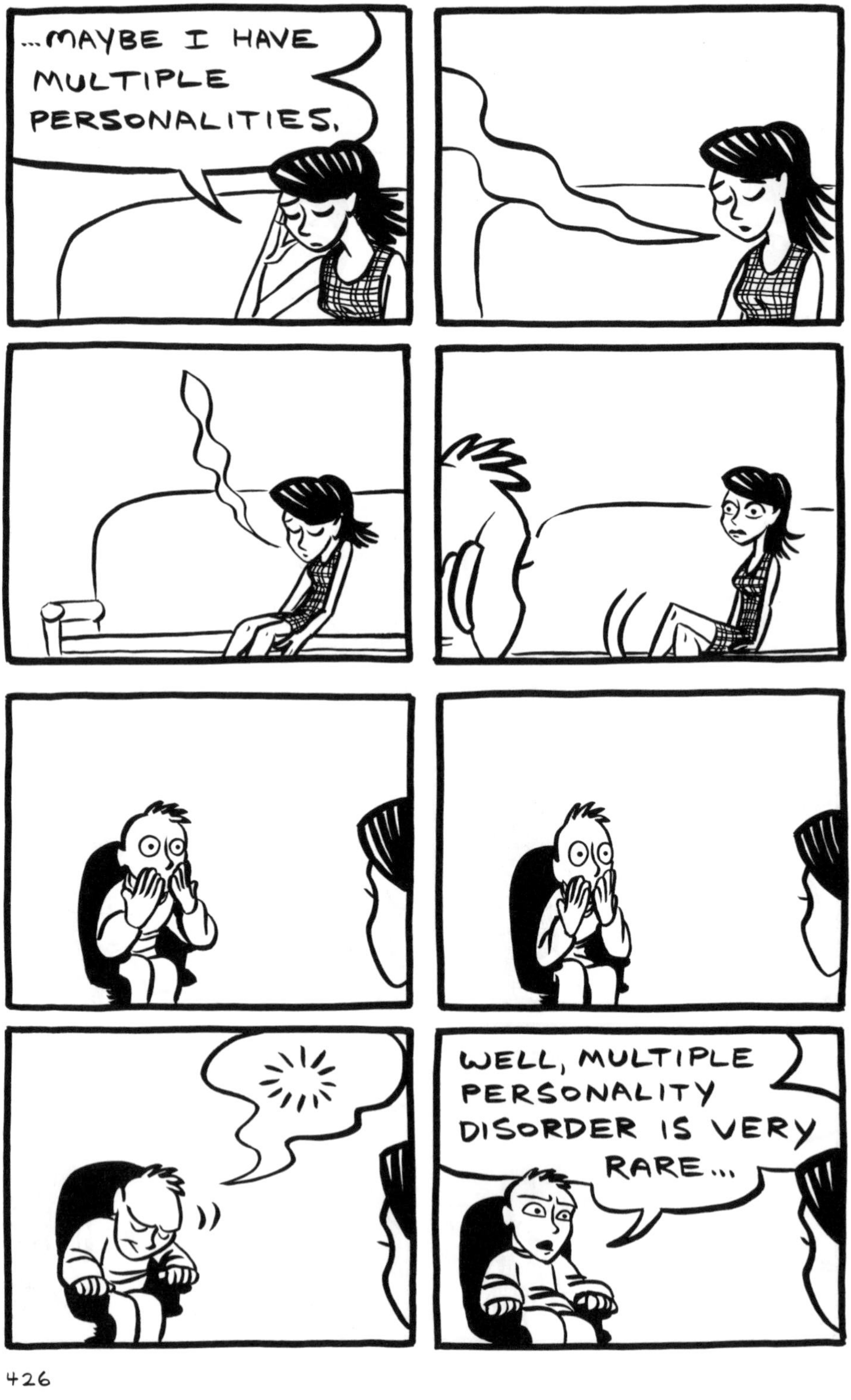
...MAYBE I HAVE MULTIPLE PERSONALITIES.
WELL, MULTIPLE PERSONALITY DISORDER IS VERY RARE...

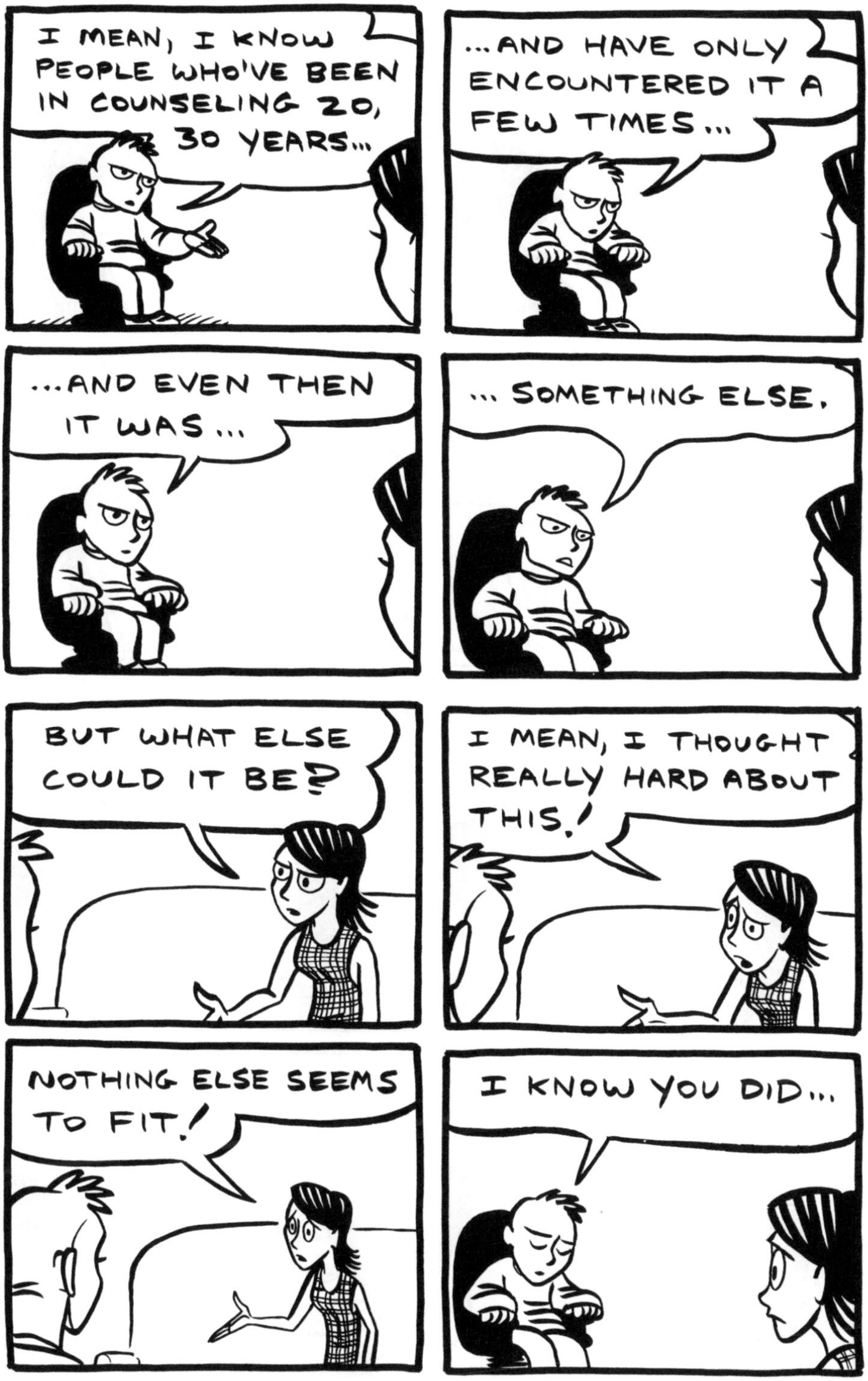
I MEAN, I KNOW PEOPLE WHO'VE BEEN IN COUNSELING 20, 30 YEARS...
...AND HAVE ONLY ENCOUNTERED IT A FEW TIMES...
...AND EVEN THEN IT WAS...
... SOMETHING ELSE.
BUT WHAT ELSE COULD IT BE?
I MEAN, I THOUGHT REALLY HARD ABOUT THIS!
NOTHING ELSE SEEMS TO FIT!
I KNOW YOU DID...

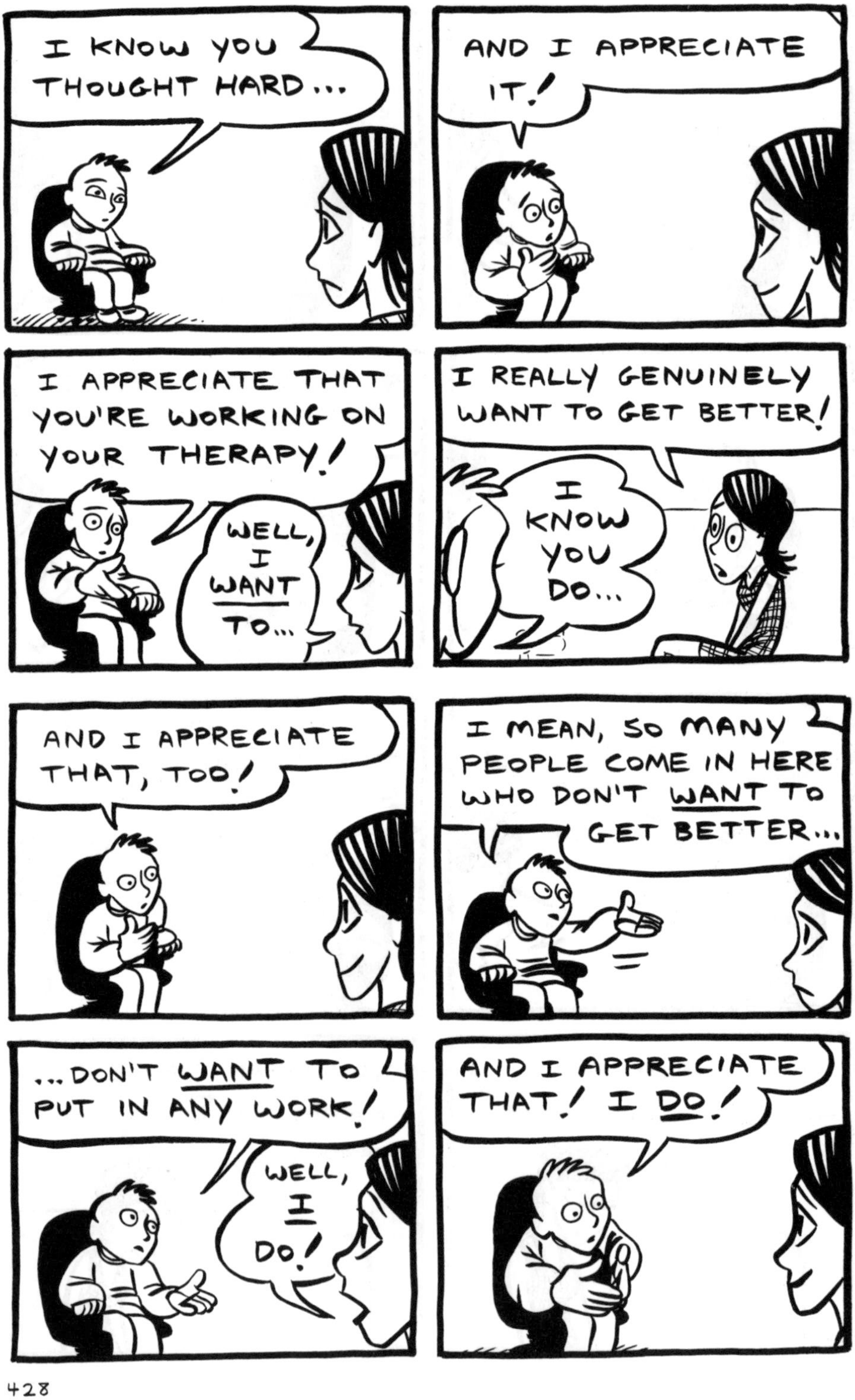
I KNOW YOU THOUGHT HARD...
AND I APPRECIATE IT!
I APPRECIATE THAT YOU'RE WORKING ON YOUR THERAPY!
WELL, I WANT TO...
I REALLY GENUINELY WANT TO GET BETTER!
I KNOW YOU DO...
AND I APPRECIATE THAT, TOO!
I MEAN, SO MANY PEOPLE COME IN HERE WHO DON'T WANT TO GET BETTER...
...DON'T WANT TO PUT IN ANY WORK!
WELL, I DO!
AND I APPRECIATE THAT! I DO!

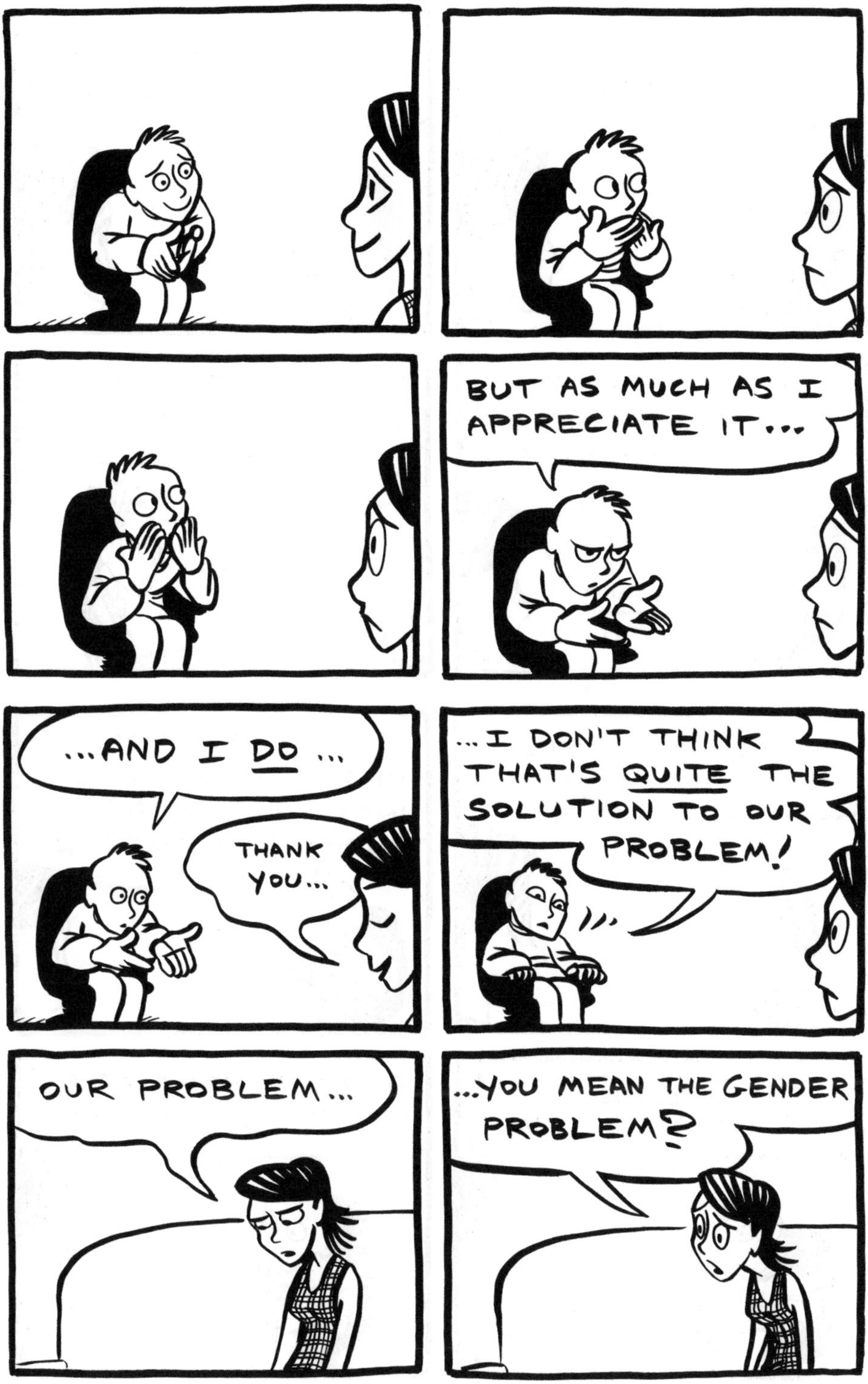
BUT AS MUCH AS I APPRECIATE IT...
...AND I DO ...
THANK YOU...
...I DON'T THINK THAT'S QUITE THE SOLUTION TO OUR PROBLEM!
OUR PROBLEM...
...YOU MEAN THE GENDER PROBLEM?

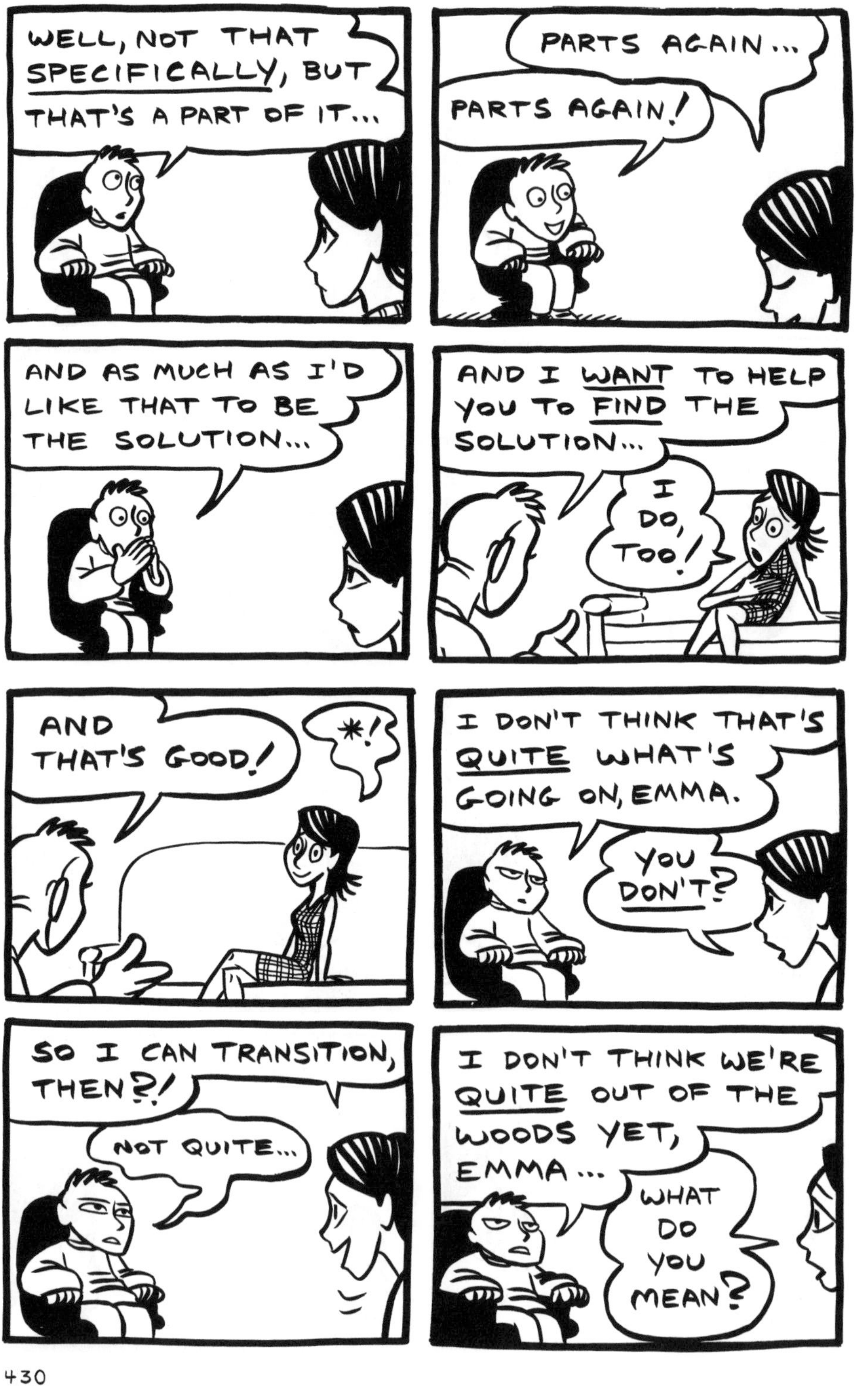
WELL, NOT THAT SPECIFICALLY, BUT THAT'S A PART OF IT...
PARTS AGAIN...
PARTS AGAIN!
AND AS MUCH AS I'D LIKE THAT TO BE THE SOLUTION...
AND I WANT TO HELP YOU TO FIND THE SOLUTION...
I DO, TOO!
AND THAT'S GOOD!
*!
I DON'T THINK THAT'S QUITE WHAT'S GOING ON, EMMA.
YOU DON'T?
SO I CAN TRANSITION, THEN?!
NOT QUITE...
I DON'T THINK WE'RE QUITE OUT OF THE WOODS YET, EMMA...
WHAT DO YOU MEAN?

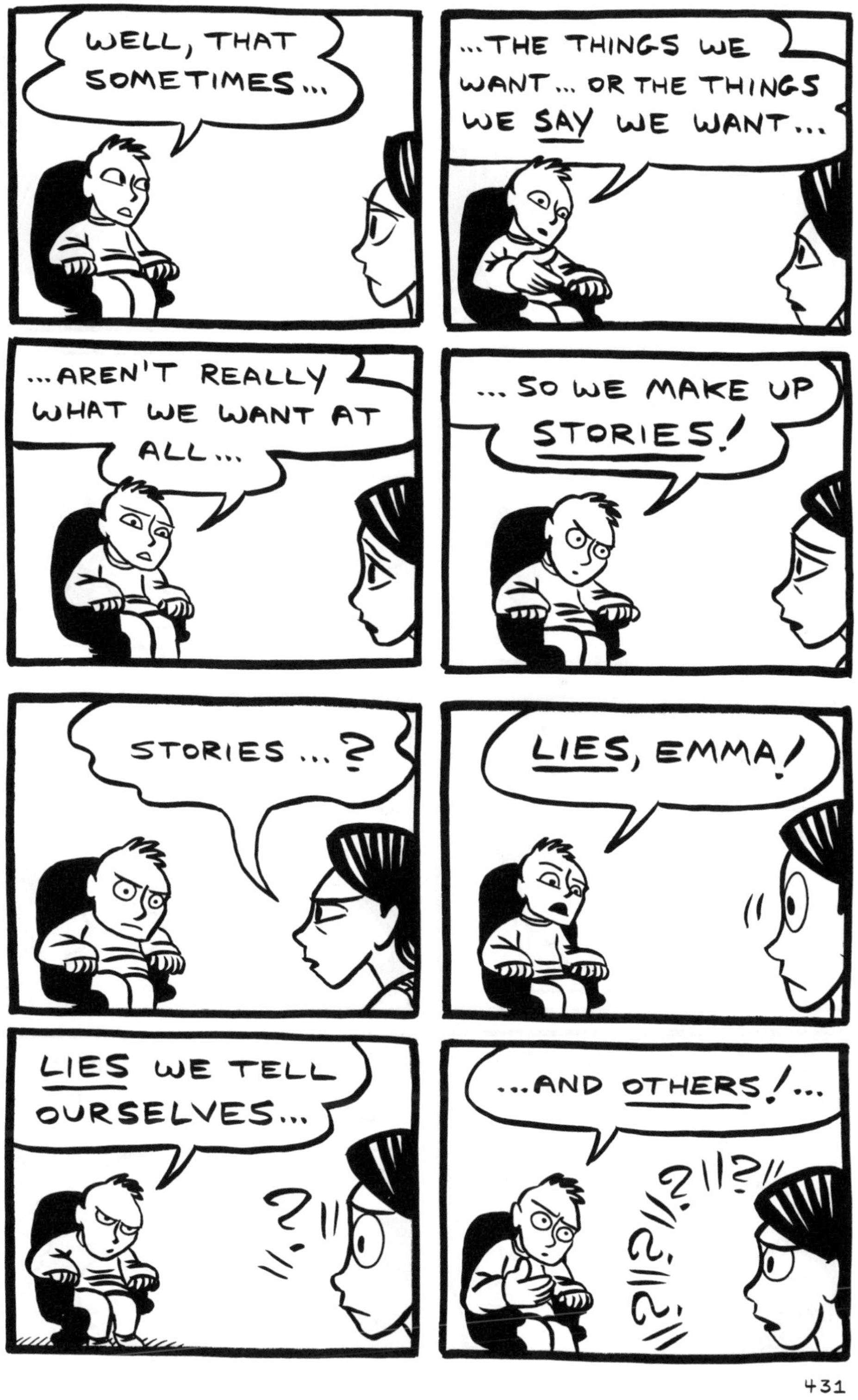
WELL, THAT SOMETIMES...
...THE THINGS WE WANT... OR THE THINGS WE SAY WE WANT...
...AREN'T REALLY WHAT WE WANT AT ALL...
...SO WE MAKE UP STORIES!
STORIES...?
LIES, EMMA!
LIES WE TELL OURSELVES...
...AND OTHERS!...

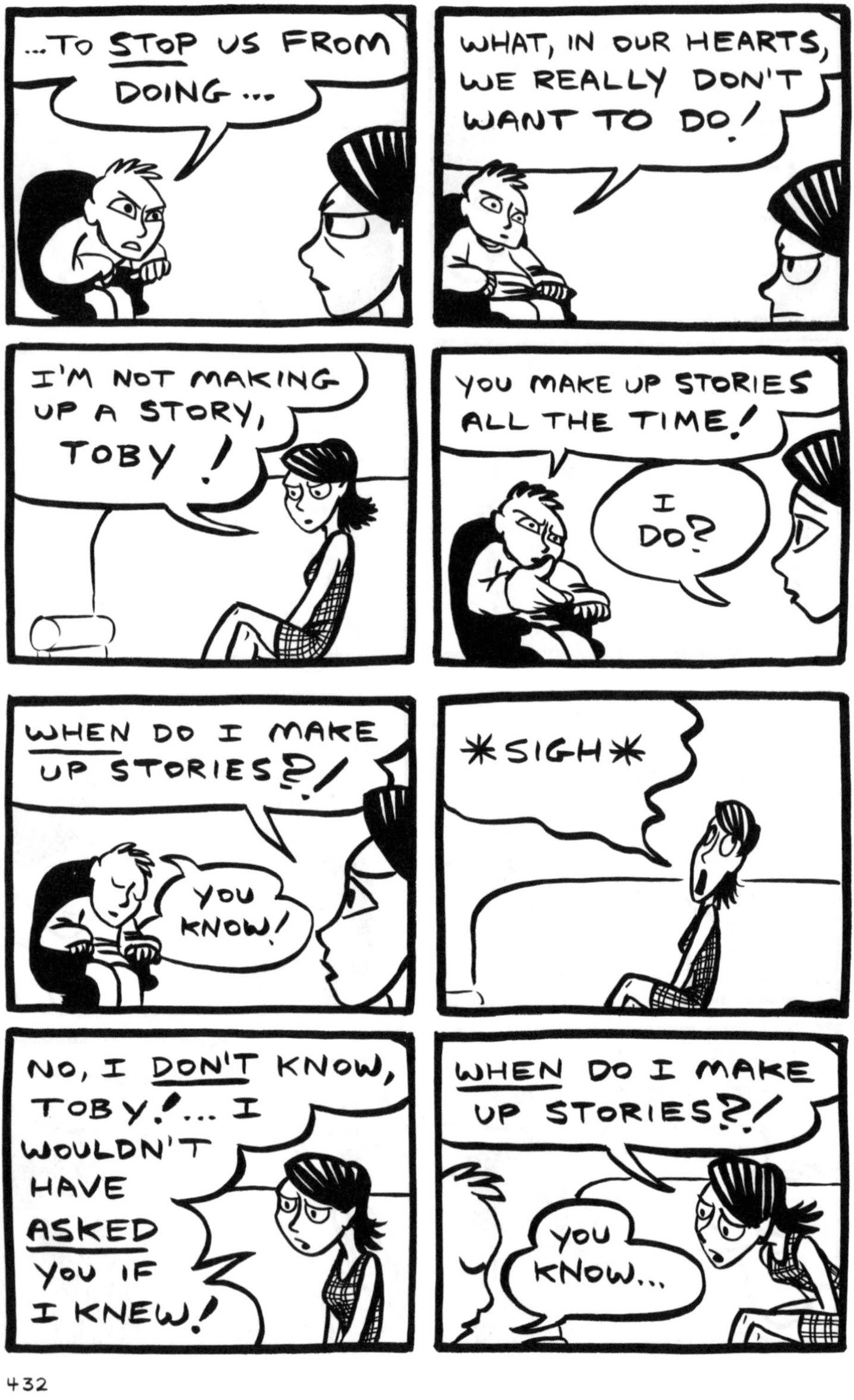
...TO STOP US FROM DOING...
WHAT, IN OUR HEARTS, WE REALLY DON'T WANT TO DO!
I'M NOT MAKING UP A STORY, TOBY!
YOU MAKE UP STORIES ALL THE TIME!
I DO?
WHEN DO I MAKE UP STORIES?!
YOU KNOW!
SIGH
NO, I DON'T KNOW, TOBY!... I WOULDN'T HAVE ASKED YOU IF I KNEW!
WHEN DO I MAKE UP STORIES?!
YOU KNOW...

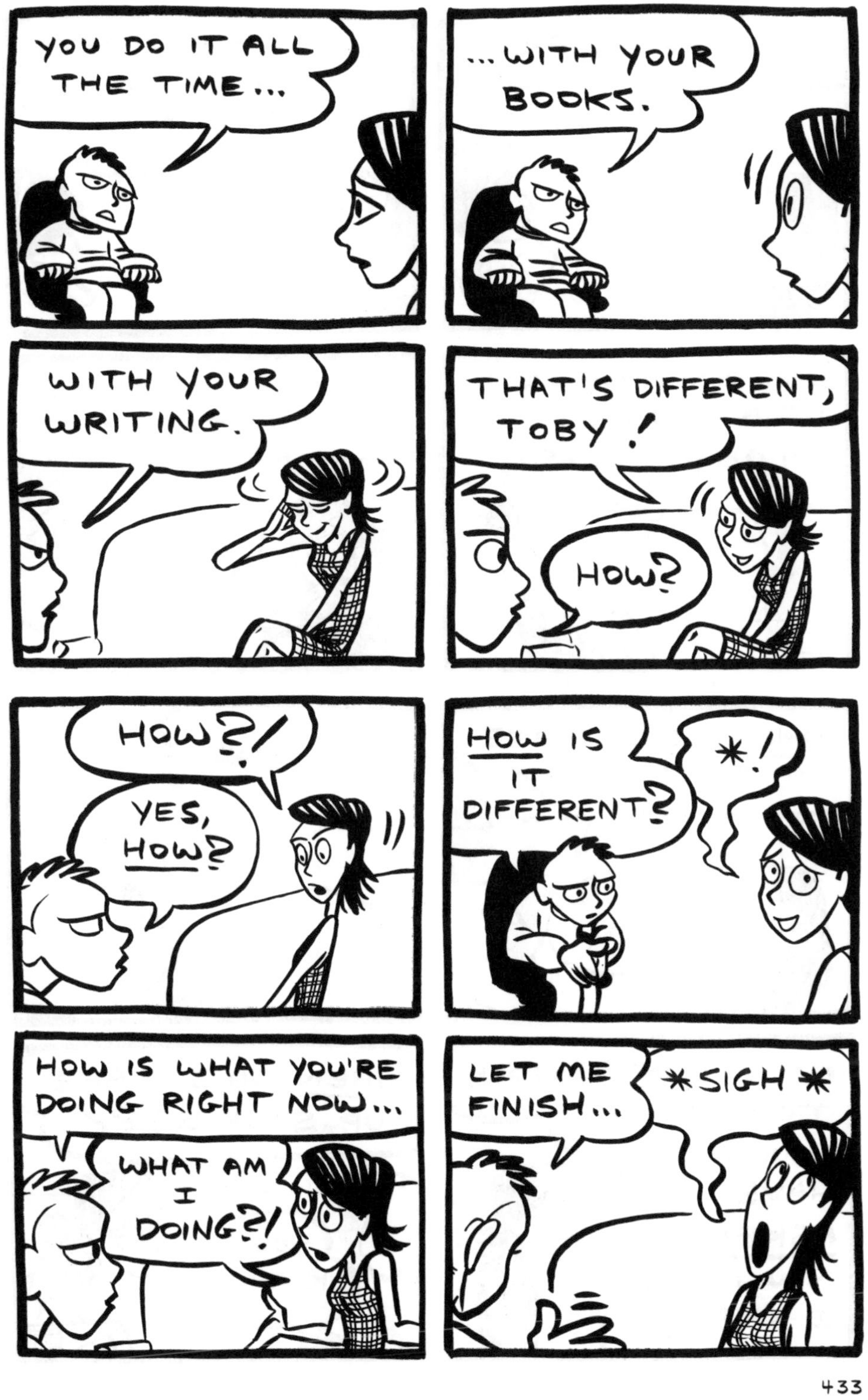
YOU DO IT ALL THE TIME...
...WITH YOUR BOOKS.
WITH YOUR WRITING.
THAT'S DIFFERENT, TOBY!
HOW?
HOW?!
YES, HOW?
HOW IS IT DIFFERENT?
*!
HOW IS WHAT YOU'RE DOING RIGHT NOW...
WHAT AM I DOING?!
LET ME FINISH...
SIGH

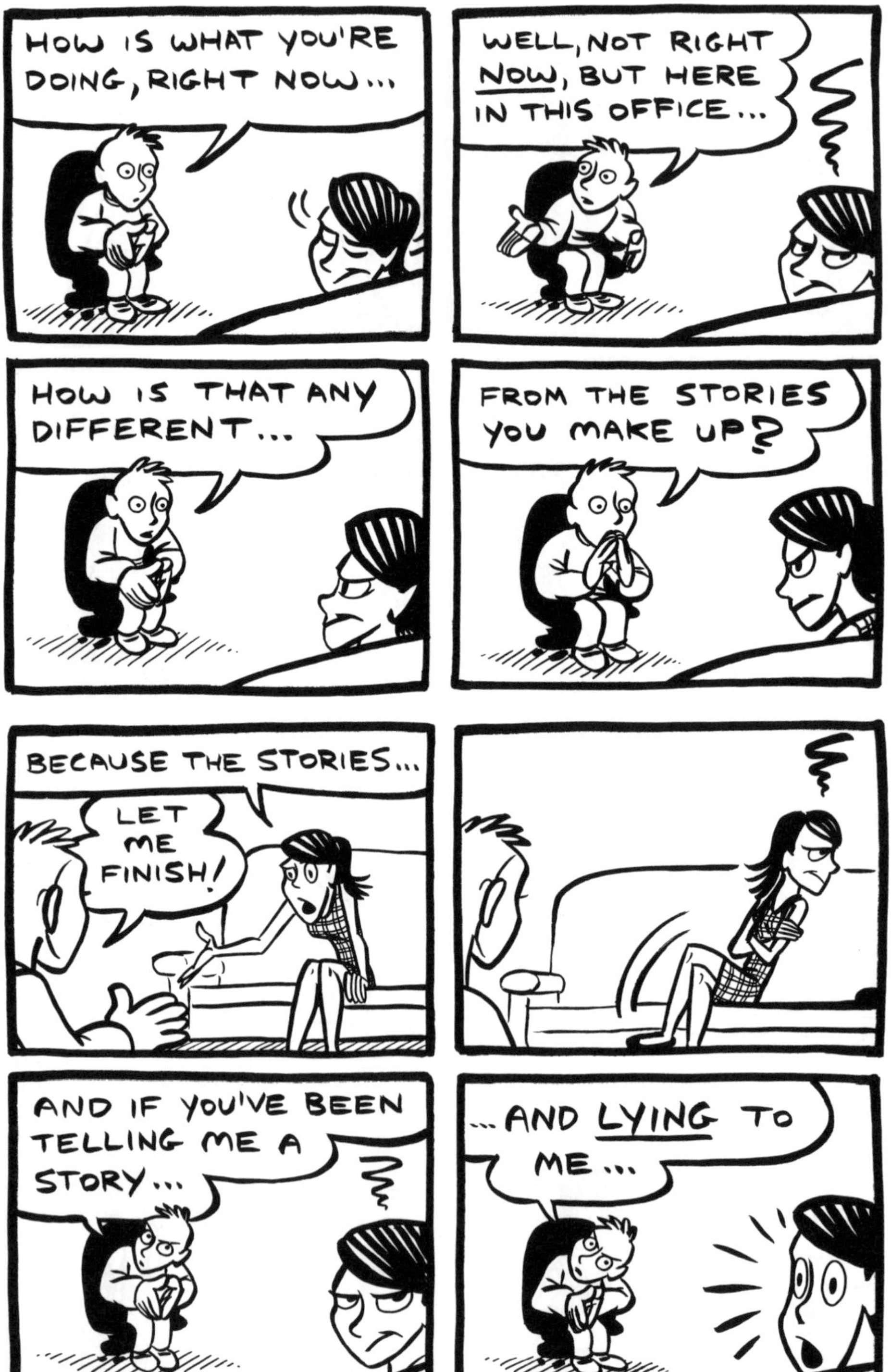
HOW IS WHAT YOU'RE DOING, RIGHT NOW...
WELL, NOT RIGHT NOW, BUT HERE IN THIS OFFICE...
HOW IS THAT ANY DIFFERENT...
FROM THE STORIES YOU MAKE UP?
BECAUSE THE STORIES...
LET ME FINISH!
AND IF YOU'VE BEEN TELLING ME A STORY...
...AND LYING TO ME...

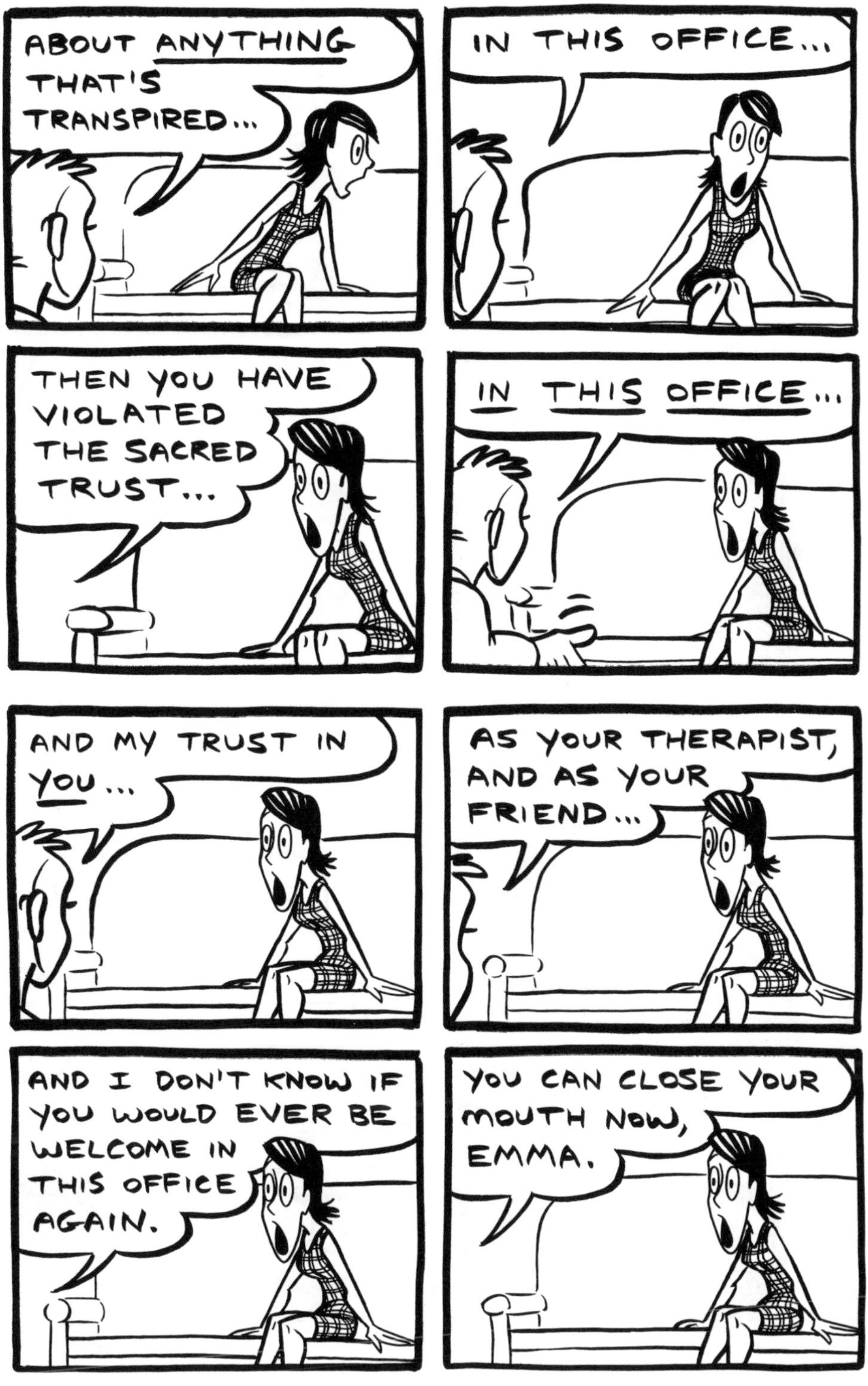
ABOUT ANYTHING THAT'S TRANSPIRED...
IN THIS OFFICE...
THEN YOU HAVE VIOLATED THE SACRED TRUST...
IN THIS OFFICE...
AND MY TRUST IN YOU...
AS YOUR THERAPIST, AND AS YOUR FRIEND...
AND I DON'T KNOW IF YOU WOULD EVER BE WELCOME IN THIS OFFICE AGAIN.
YOU CAN CLOSE YOUR MOUTH NOW, EMMA.

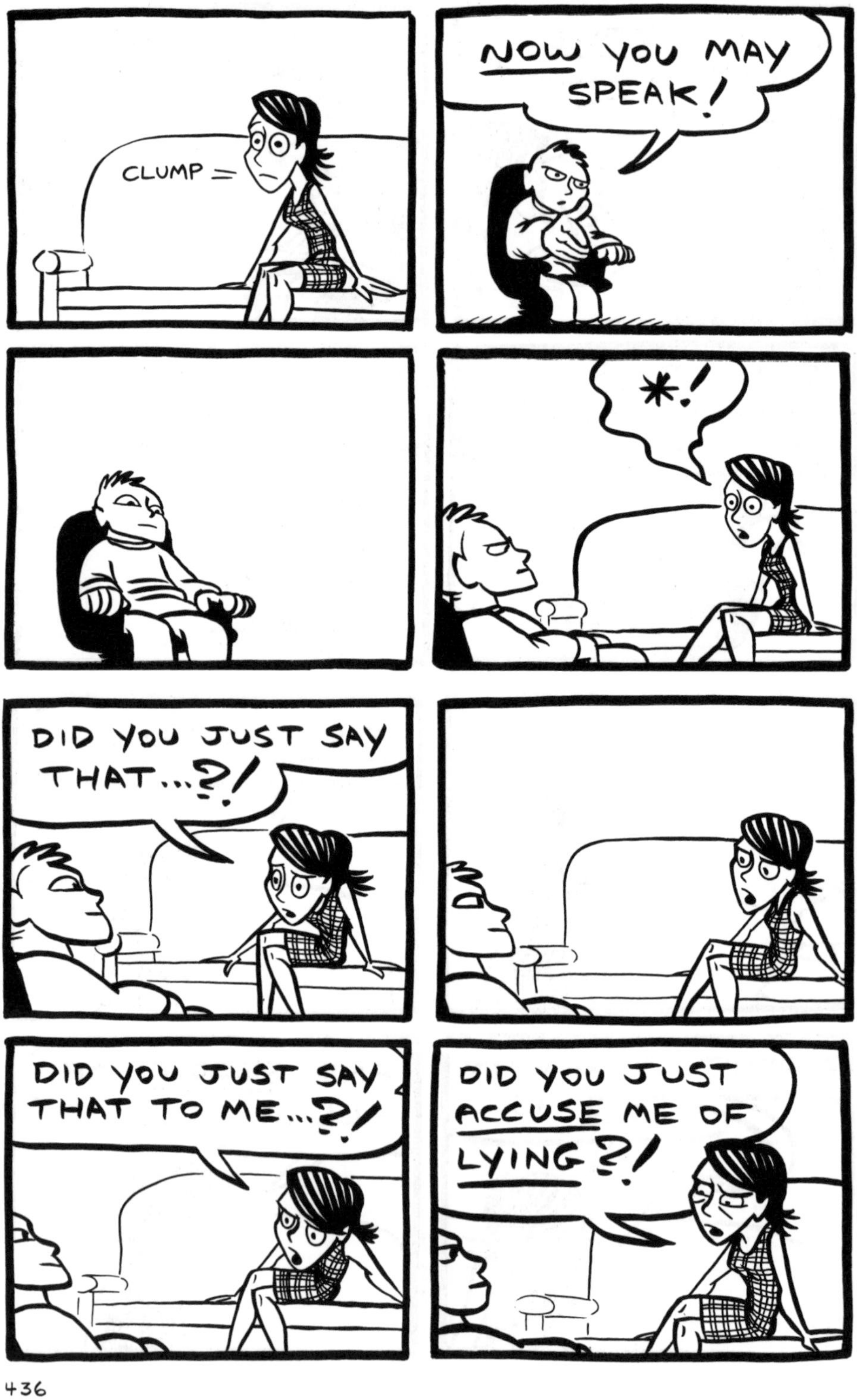
CLUMP =
NOW YOU MAY SPEAK!
*!
DID YOU JUST SAY THAT...?!
DID YOU JUST SAY THAT TO ME...?!
DID YOU JUST ACCUSE ME OF LYING?!

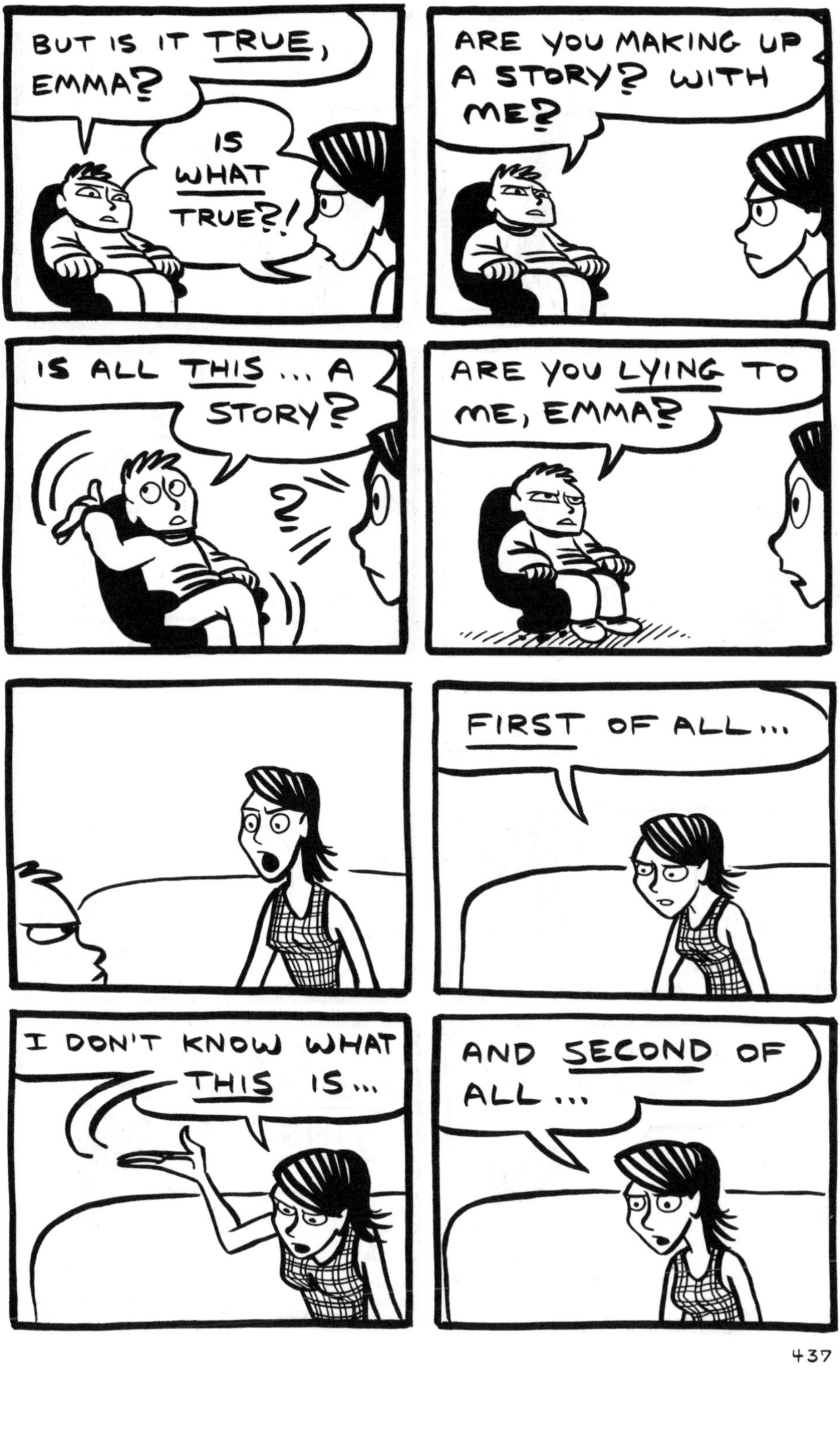
BUT IS IT TRUE, EMMA?
IS WHAT TRUE?!
ARE YOU MAKING UP A STORY? WITH ME?
IS ALL THIS ... A STORY?
?
ARE YOU LYING TO ME, EMMA?
FIRST OF ALL...
I DON'T KNOW WHAT THIS IS...
AND SECOND OF ALL...

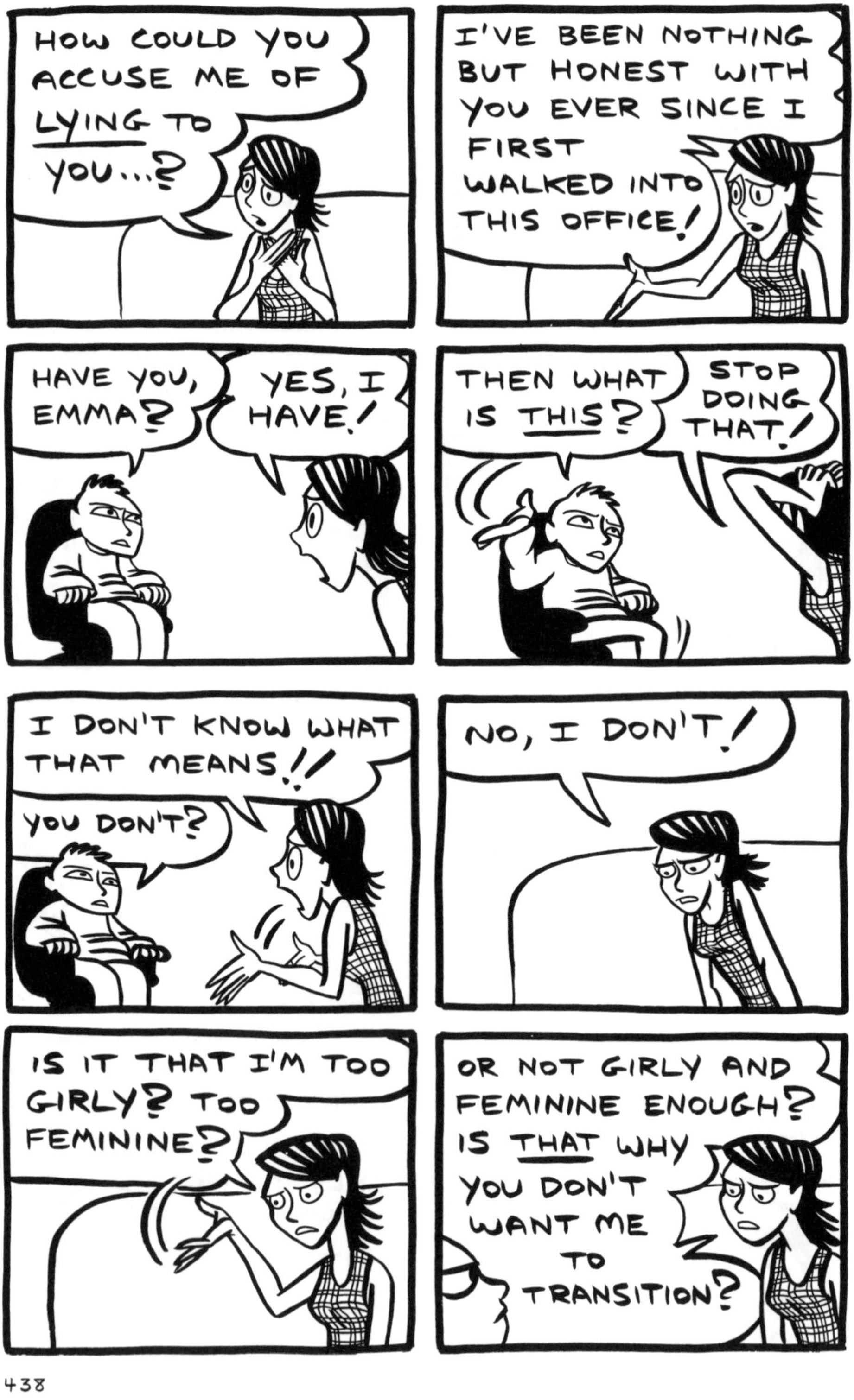
HOW COULD YOU ACCUSE ME OF LYING TO YOU...?
I'VE BEEN NOTHING BUT HONEST WITH YOU EVER SINCE I FIRST WALKED INTO THIS OFFICE!
HAVE YOU, EMMA?
YES, I HAVE!
THEN WHAT IS THIS?
STOP DOING THAT!
I DON'T KNOW WHAT THAT MEANS!!
YOU DON'T?
NO, I DON'T!
IS IT THAT I'M TOO GIRLY? TOO FEMININE?
OR NOT GIRLY AND FEMININE ENOUGH? IS THAT WHY YOU DON'T WANT ME TO TRANSITION?

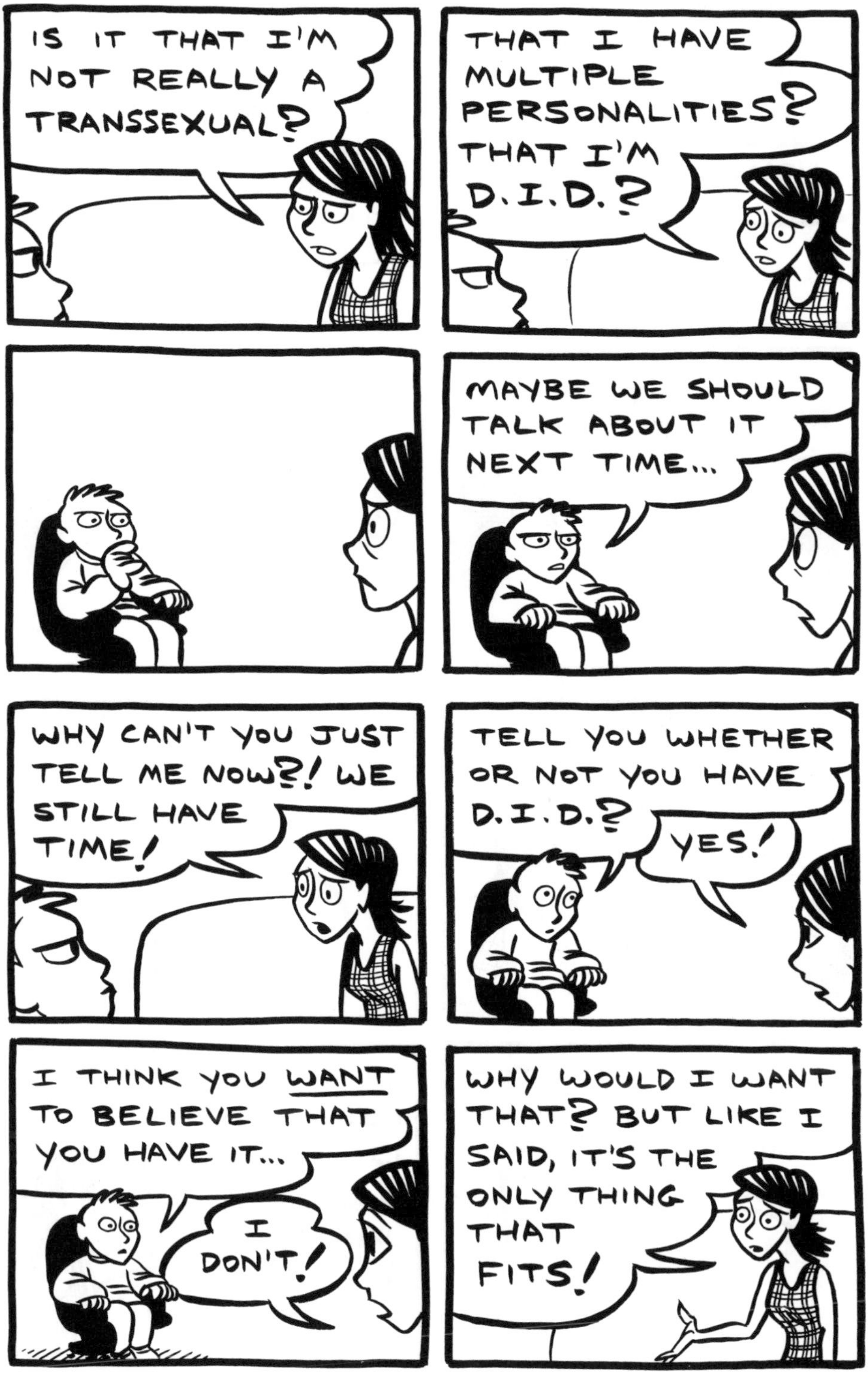
IS IT THAT I'M NOT REALLY A TRANSSEXUAL?
THAT I HAVE MULTIPLE PERSONALITIES? THAT I'M D.I.D.?
MAYBE WE SHOULD TALK ABOUT IT NEXT TIME...
WHY CAN'T YOU JUST TELL ME NOW?! WE STILL HAVE TIME!
TELL YOU WHETHER OR NOT YOU HAVE D.I.D.?
YES!
I THINK YOU WANT TO BELIEVE THAT YOU HAVE IT...
I DON'T!
WHY WOULD I WANT THAT? BUT LIKE I SAID, IT'S THE ONLY THING THAT FITS!

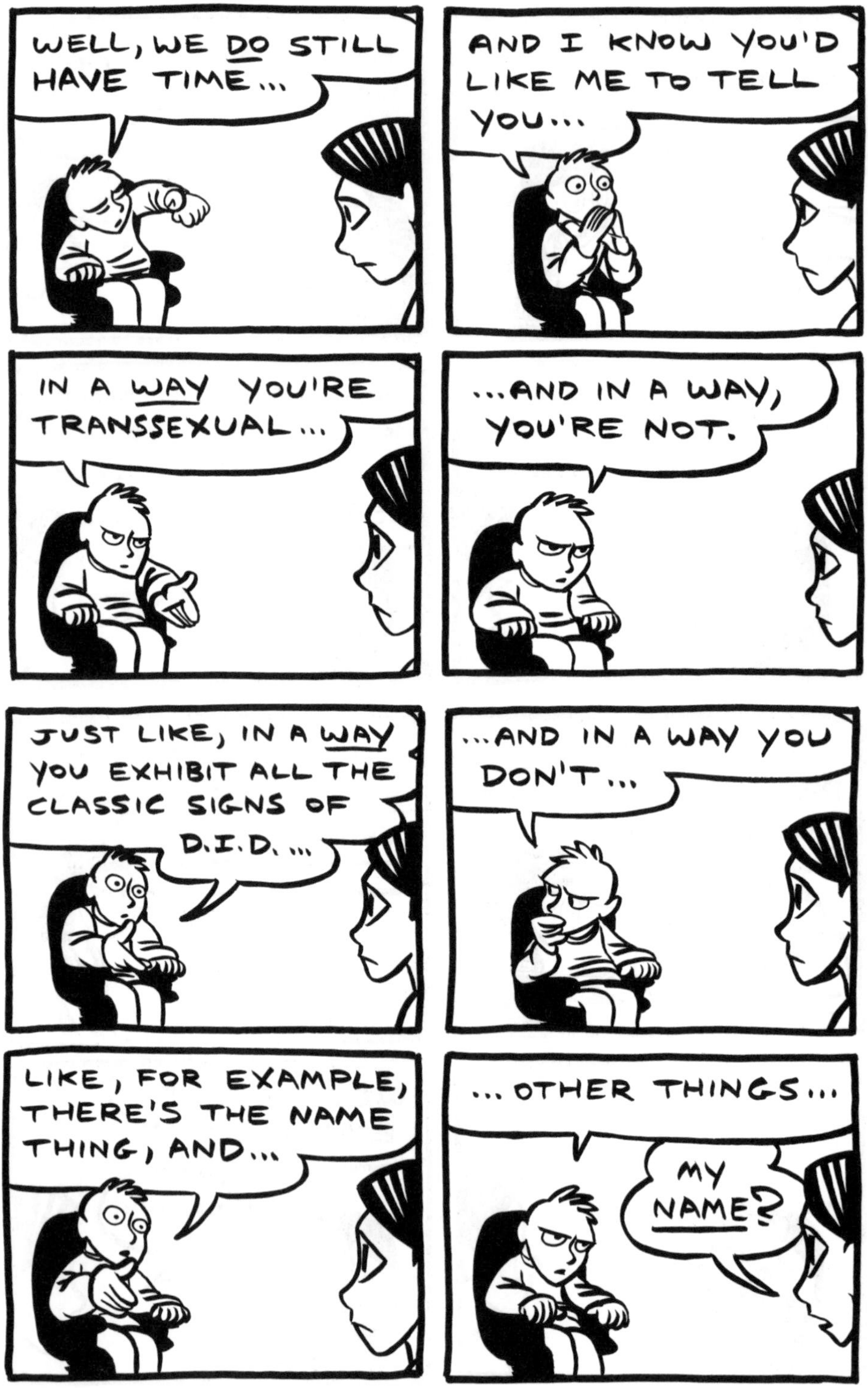
WELL, WE DO STILL HAVE TIME...
AND I KNOW YOU'D LIKE ME TO TELL YOU...
IN A WAY YOU'RE TRANSSEXUAL...
...AND IN A WAY, YOU'RE NOT.
JUST LIKE, IN A WAY YOU EXHIBIT ALL THE CLASSIC SIGNS OF D.I.D....
...AND IN A WAY YOU DON'T...
LIKE, FOR EXAMPLE, THERE'S THE NAME THING, AND...
...OTHER THINGS...
MY NAME?

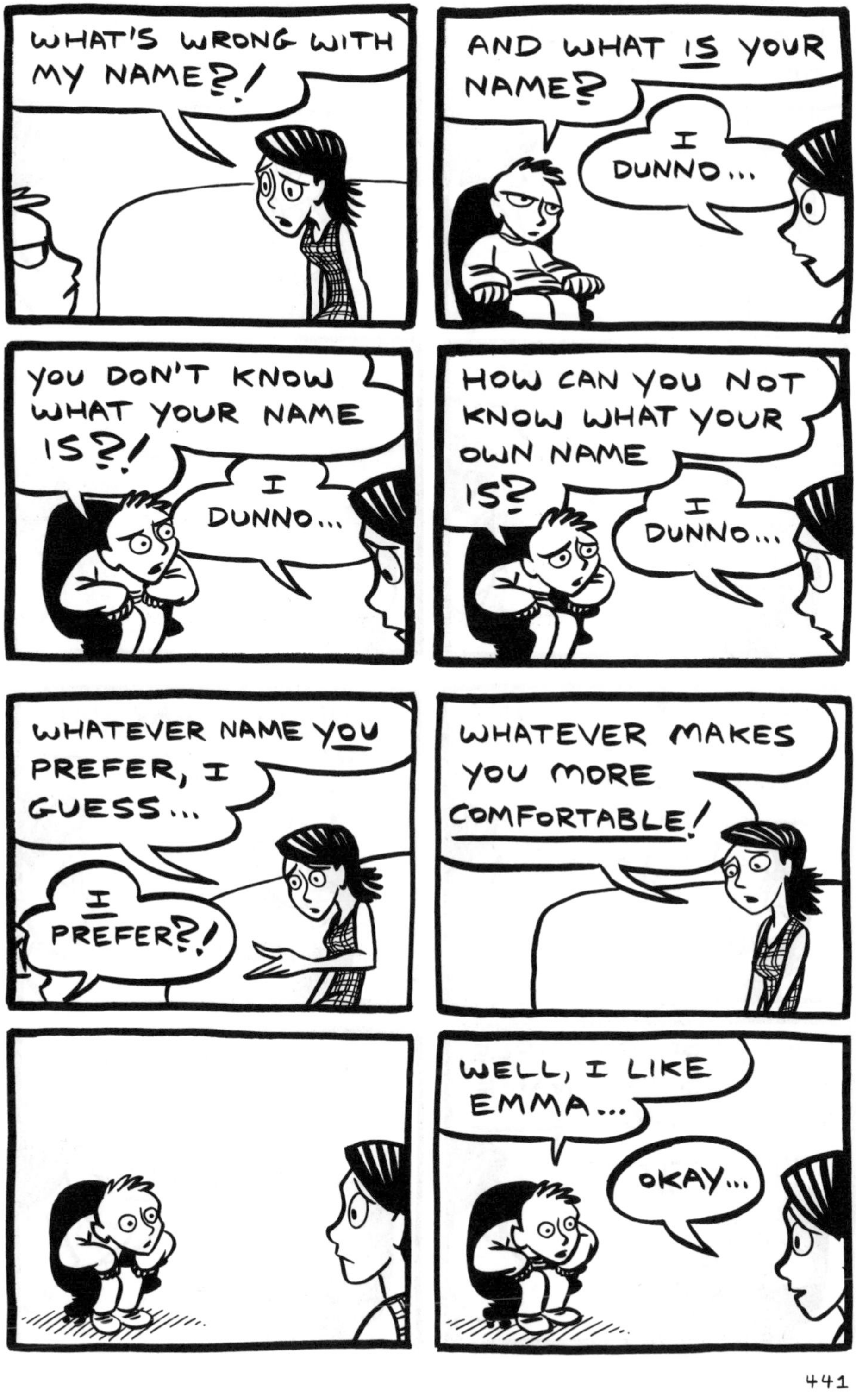
WHAT'S WRONG WITH MY NAME?!
AND WHAT IS YOUR NAME?
I DUNNO...
YOU DON'T KNOW WHAT YOUR NAME IS?!
I DUNNO...
HOW CAN YOU NOT KNOW WHAT YOUR OWN NAME IS?
I DUNNO...
WHATEVER NAME YOU PREFER, I GUESS...
I PREFER?!
WHATEVER MAKES YOU MORE COMFORTABLE!
WELL, I LIKE EMMA...
OKAY...

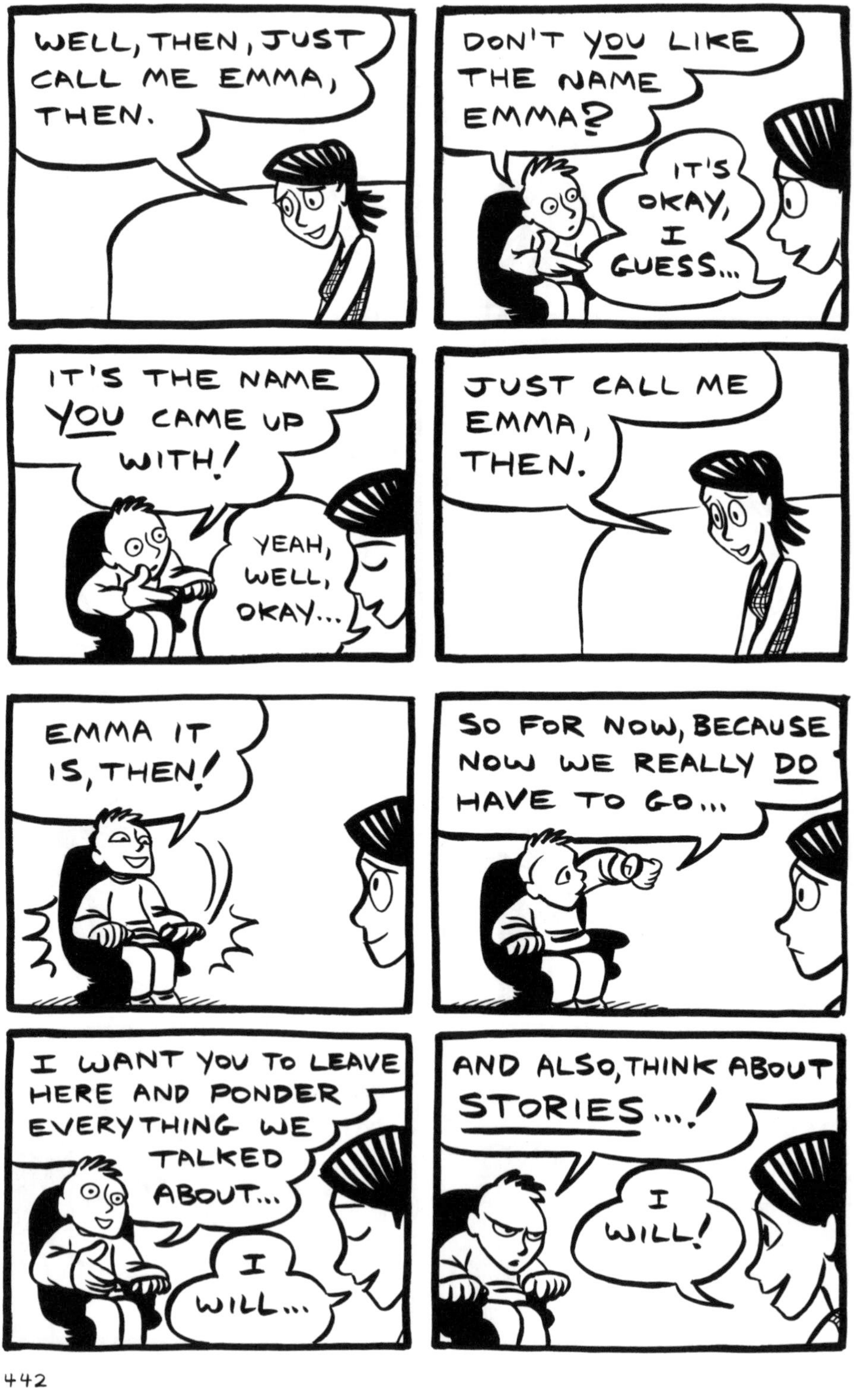
WELL, THEN, JUST CALL ME EMMA, THEN.
DON'T YOU LIKE THE NAME EMMA?
IT'S OKAY, I GUESS...
IT'S THE NAME YOU CAME UP WITH!
YEAH, WELL, OKAY...
JUST CALL ME EMMA, THEN.
EMMA IT IS, THEN!
SO FOR NOW, BECAUSE NOW WE REALLY DO HAVE TO GO...
I WANT YOU TO LEAVE HERE AND PONDER EVERYTHING WE TALKED ABOUT...
I WILL...
AND ALSO, THINK ABOUT STORIES...!
I WILL!

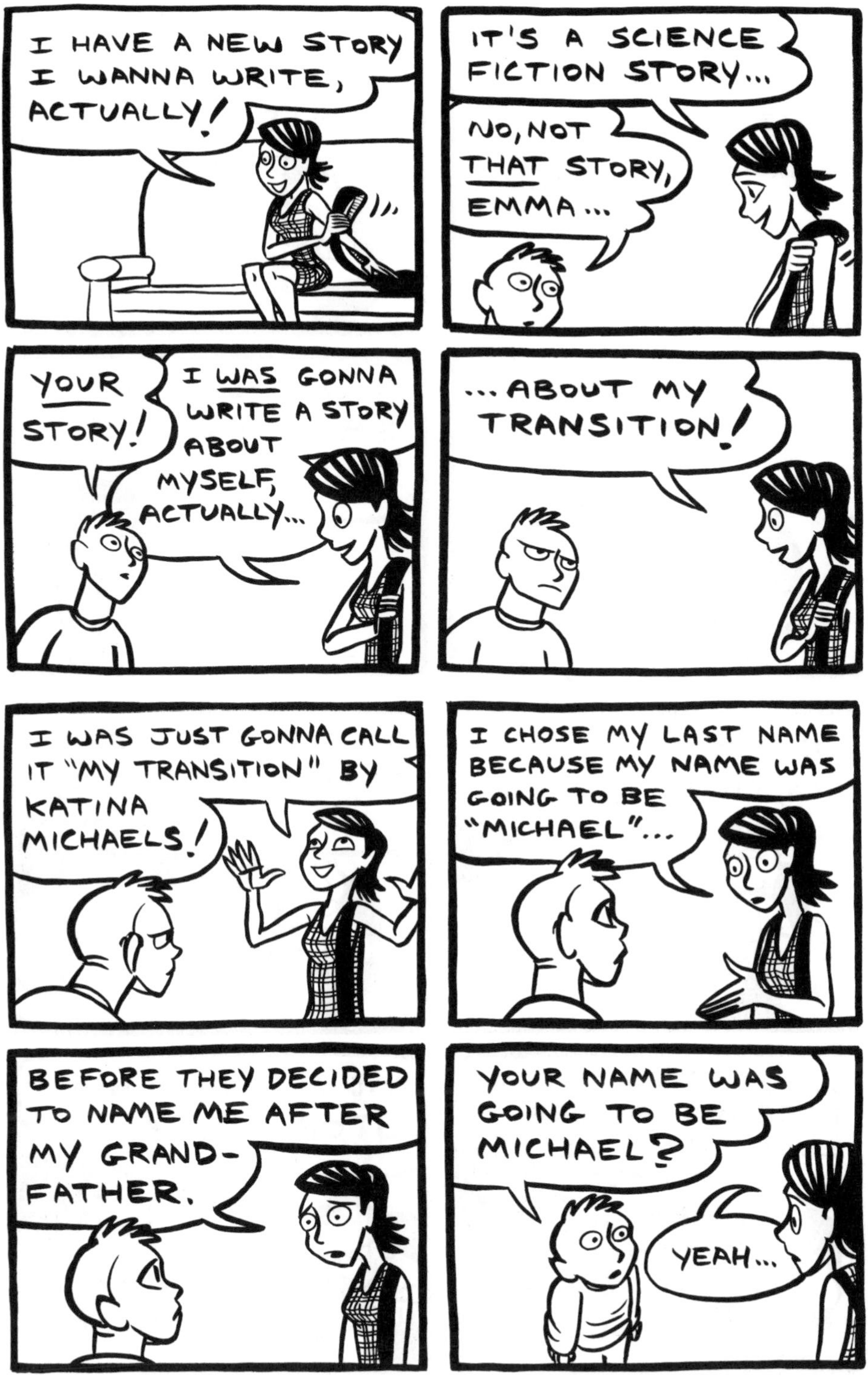

I HAVE A NEW STORY I WANNA WRITE, ACTUALLY!
IT'S A SCIENCE FICTION STORY...
NO, NOT THAT STORY, EMMA...
YOUR STORY!
I WAS GONNA WRITE A STORY ABOUT MYSELF, ACTUALLY...
...ABOUT MY TRANSITION!
I WAS JUST GONNA CALL IT "MY TRANSITION" BY KATINA MICHAELS!
I CHOSE MY LAST NAME BECAUSE MY NAME WAS GOING TO BE "MICHAEL"...
BEFORE THEY DECIDED TO NAME ME AFTER MY GRAND-FATHER.
YOUR NAME WAS GOING TO BE MICHAEL?
YEAH...

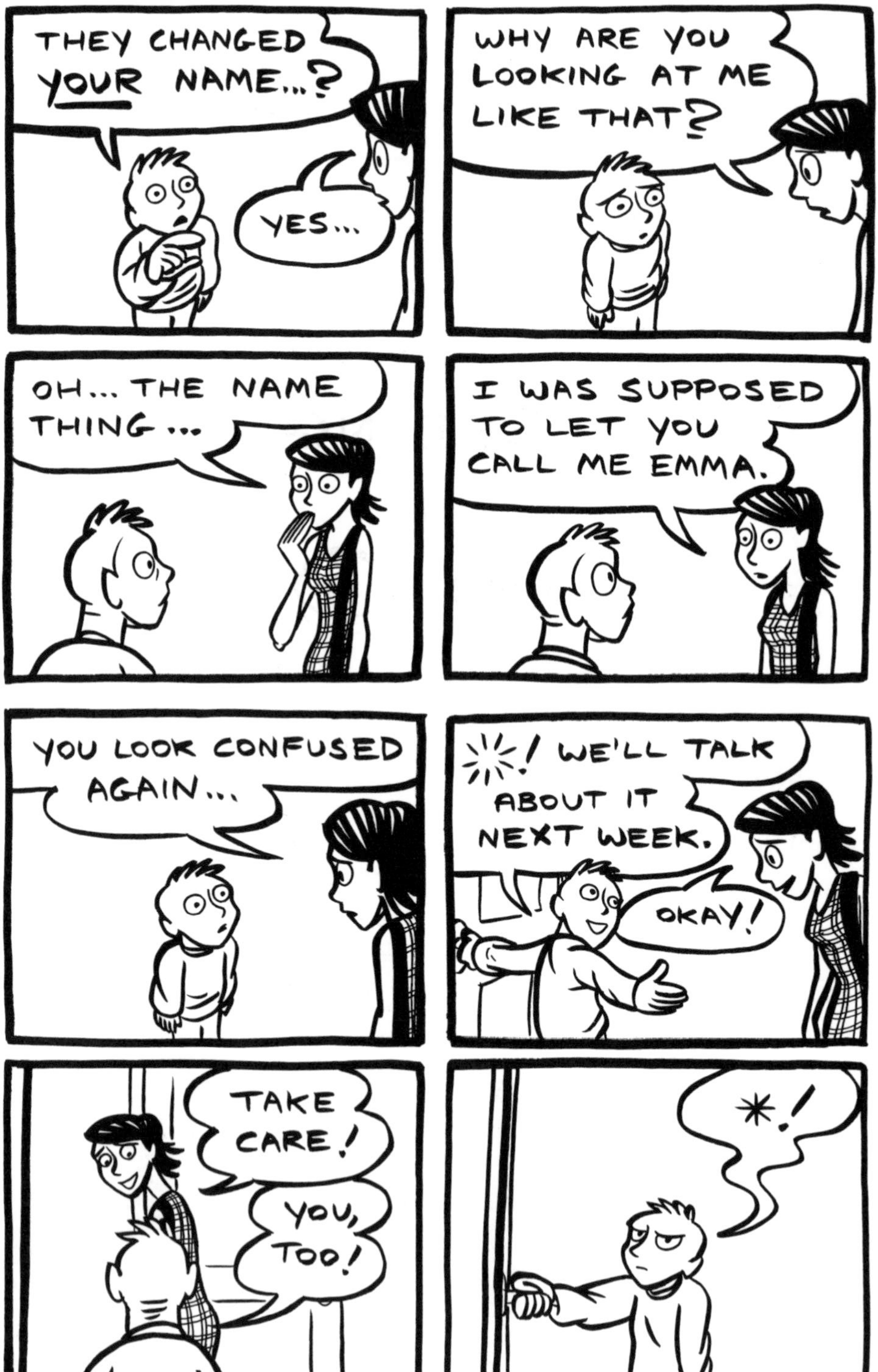

THEY CHANGED YOUR NAME...?
YES...
WHY ARE YOU LOOKING AT ME LIKE THAT?
OH... THE NAME THING...
I WAS SUPPOSED TO LET YOU CALL ME EMMA.
YOU LOOK CONFUSED AGAIN...
! WE'LL TALK ABOUT IT NEXT WEEK.
OKAY!
TAKE CARE!
YOU, TOO!
*!

SEEING

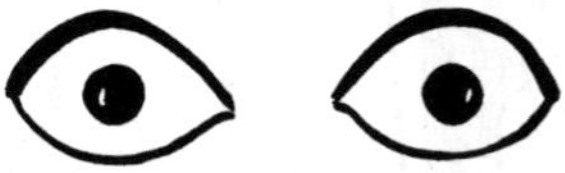

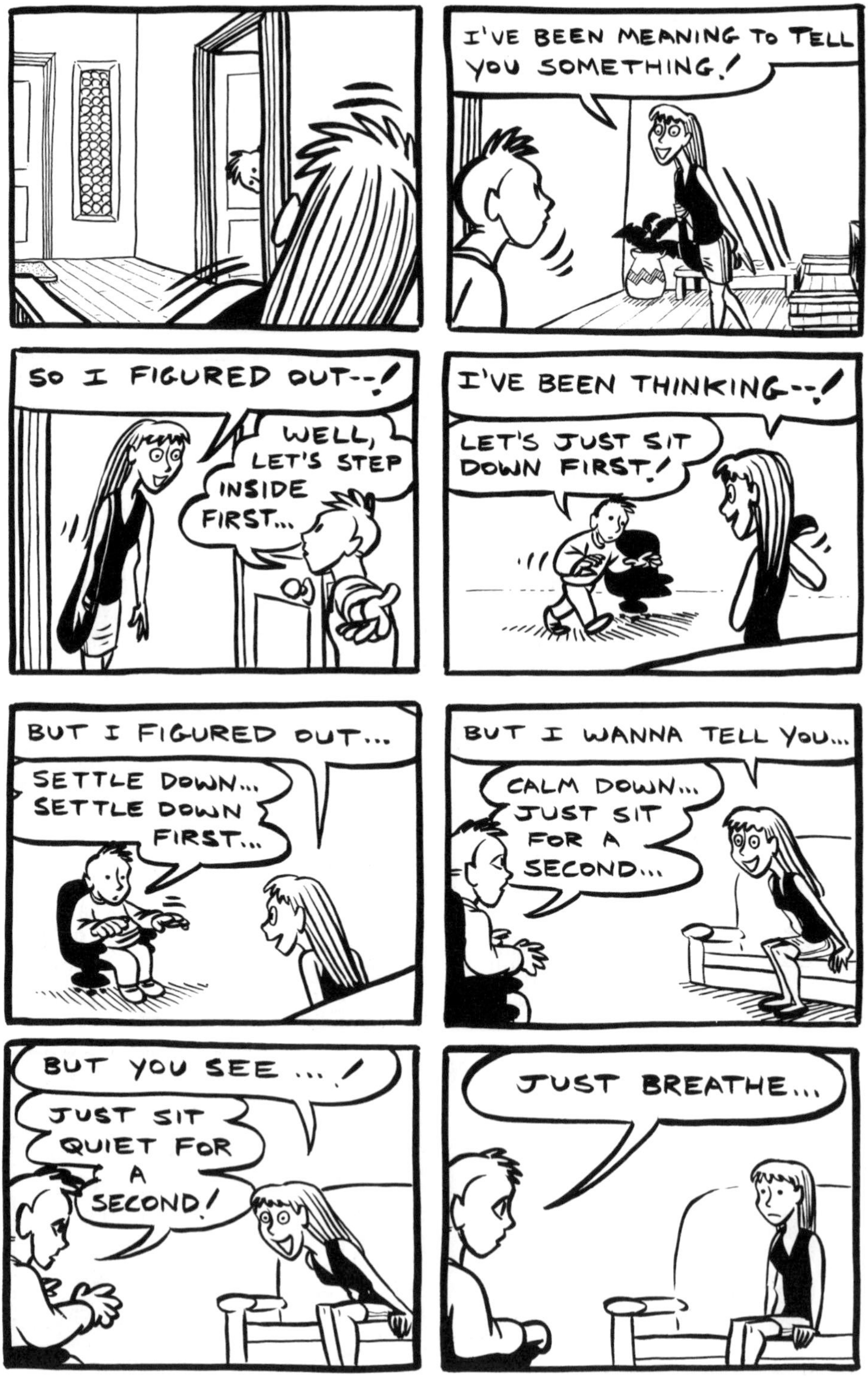

I'VE BEEN MEANING TO TELL YOU SOMETHING!
SO I FIGURED OUT--!
WELL, LET'S STEP INSIDE FIRST...
I'VE BEEN THINKING--!
LET'S JUST SIT DOWN FIRST!
BUT I FIGURED OUT...
SETTLE DOWN... SETTLE DOWN FIRST...
BUT I WANNA TELL YOU...
CALM DOWN... JUST SIT FOR A SECOND...
BUT YOU SEE...!
JUST SIT QUIET FOR A SECOND!
JUST BREATHE...

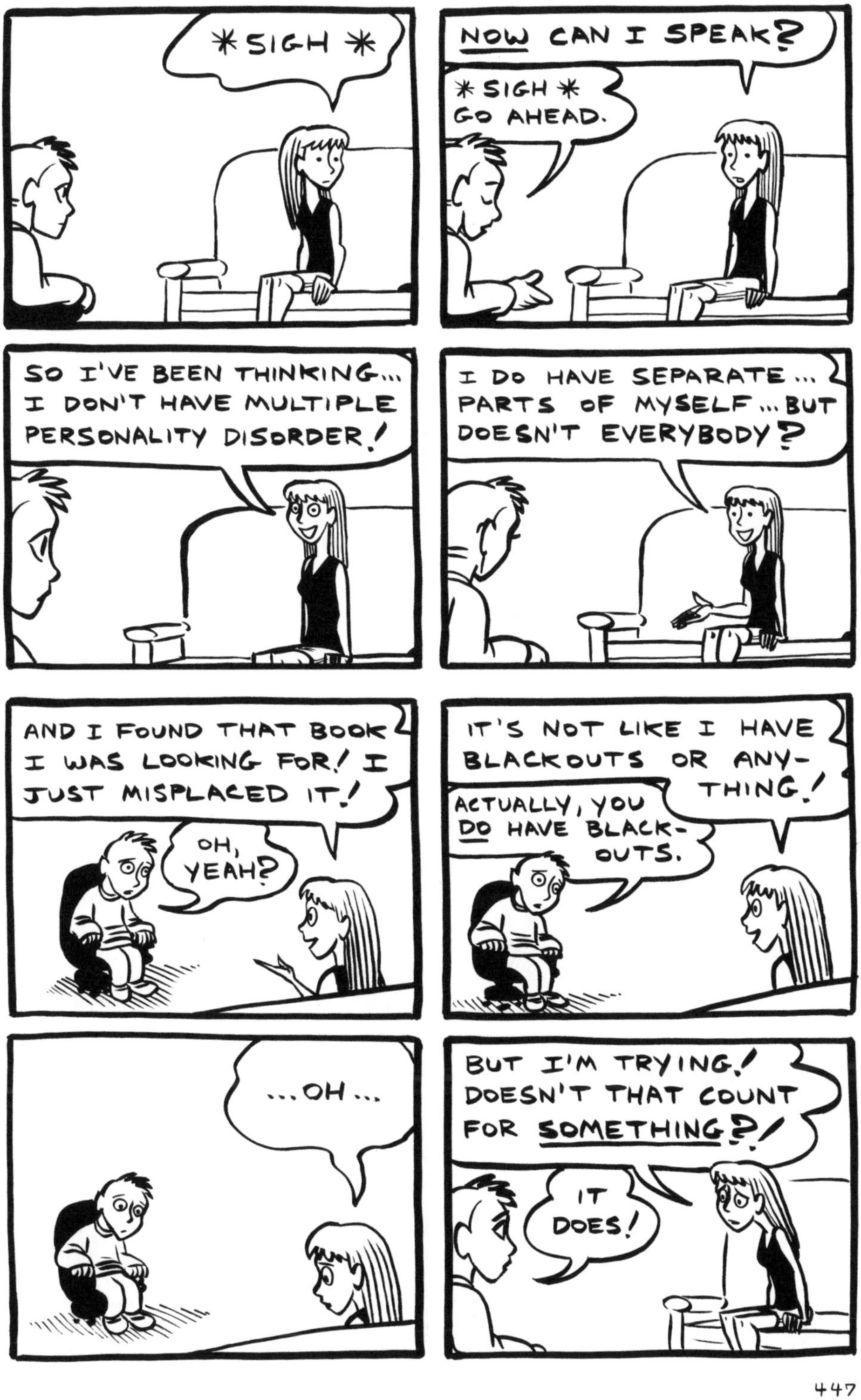
SIGH
NOW CAN I SPEAK?
SIGH GO AHEAD.
SO I'VE BEEN THINKING... I DON'T HAVE MULTIPLE PERSONALITY DISORDER!
I DO HAVE SEPARATE... PARTS OF MYSELF... BUT DOESN'T EVERYBODY?
AND I FOUND THAT BOOK I WAS LOOKING FOR! I JUST MISPLACED IT!
OH, YEAH?
IT'S NOT LIKE I HAVE BLACKOUTS OR ANY-THING!
ACTUALLY, YOU DO HAVE BLACK-OUTS.
...OH...
BUT I'M TRYING! DOESN'T THAT COUNT FOR SOMETHING?!
IT DOES!

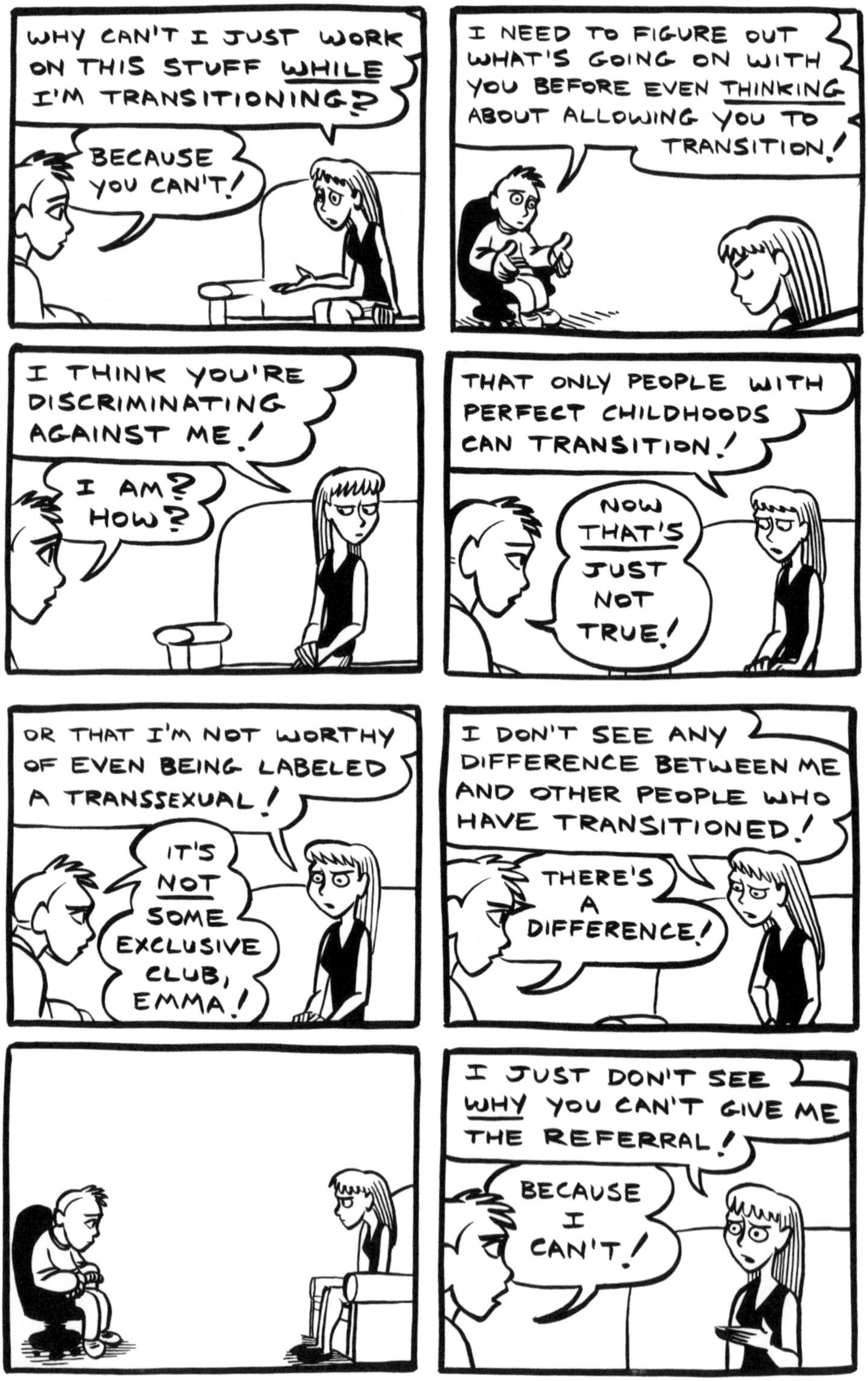
WHY CAN'T I JUST WORK ON THIS STUFF WHILE I'M TRANSITIONING?
BECAUSE YOU CAN'T!
I NEED TO FIGURE OUT WHAT'S GOING ON WITH YOU BEFORE EVEN THINKING ABOUT ALLOWING YOU TO TRANSITION!
I THINK YOU'RE DISCRIMINATING AGAINST ME!
I AM? HOW?
THAT ONLY PEOPLE WITH PERFECT CHILDHOODS CAN TRANSITION!
NOW THAT'S JUST NOT TRUE!
OR THAT I'M NOT WORTHY OF EVEN BEING LABELED A TRANSSEXUAL!
IT'S NOT SOME EXCLUSIVE CLUB, EMMA!
I DON'T SEE ANY DIFFERENCE BETWEEN ME AND OTHER PEOPLE WHO HAVE TRANSITIONED!
THERE'S A DIFFERENCE!
I JUST DON'T SEE WHY YOU CAN'T GIVE ME THE REFERRAL!
BECAUSE I CAN'T!

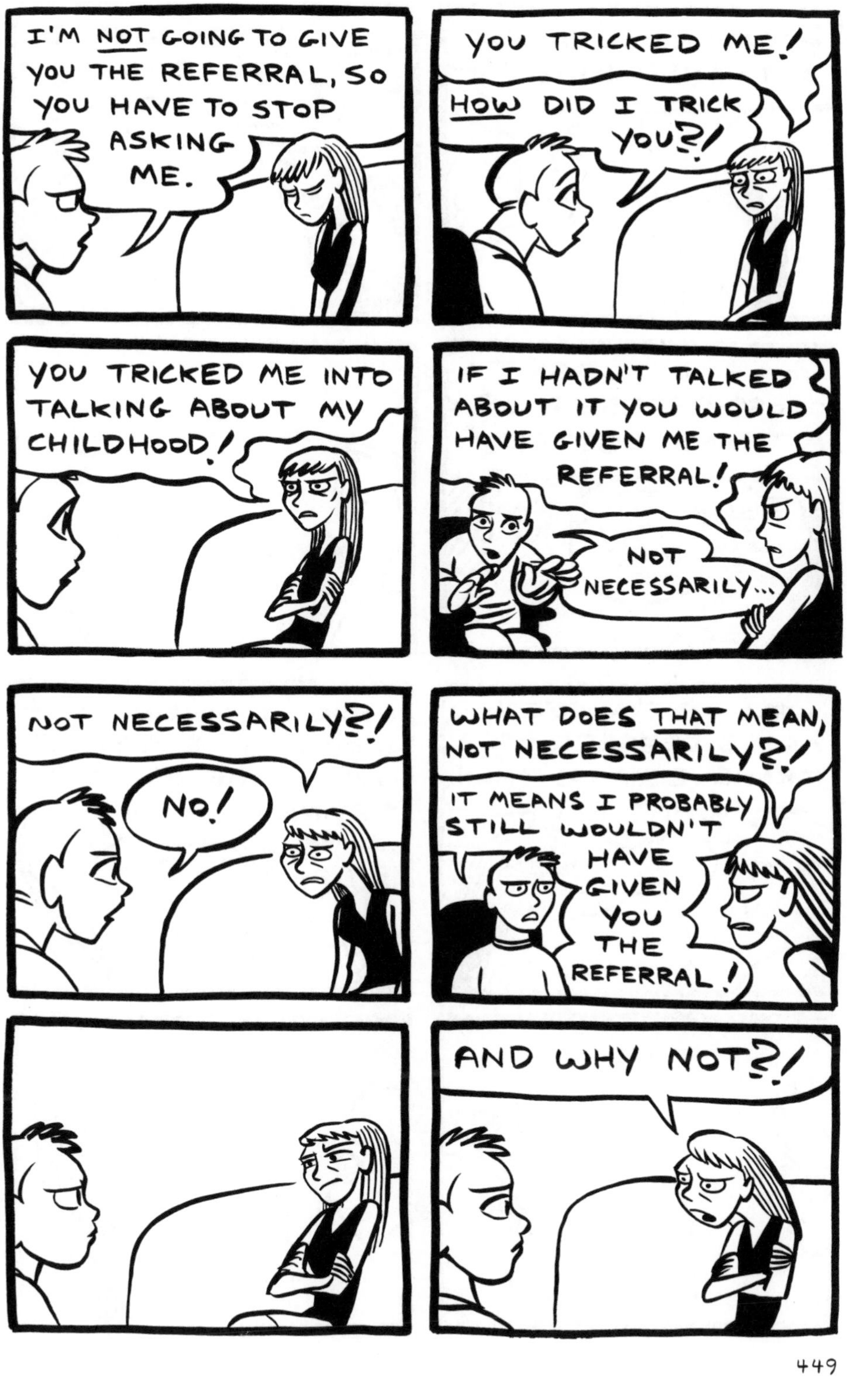
I'M NOT GOING TO GIVE YOU THE REFERRAL, SO YOU HAVE TO STOP ASKING ME.
YOU TRICKED ME!
HOW DID I TRICK YOU?!
YOU TRICKED ME INTO TALKING ABOUT MY CHILDHOOD!
IF I HADN'T TALKED ABOUT IT YOU WOULD HAVE GIVEN ME THE REFERRAL!
NOT NECESSARILY...
NOT NECESSARILY?!
NO!
WHAT DOES THAT MEAN, NOT NECESSARILY?!
IT MEANS I PROBABLY STILL WOULDN'T HAVE GIVEN YOU THE REFERRAL!
AND WHY NOT?!

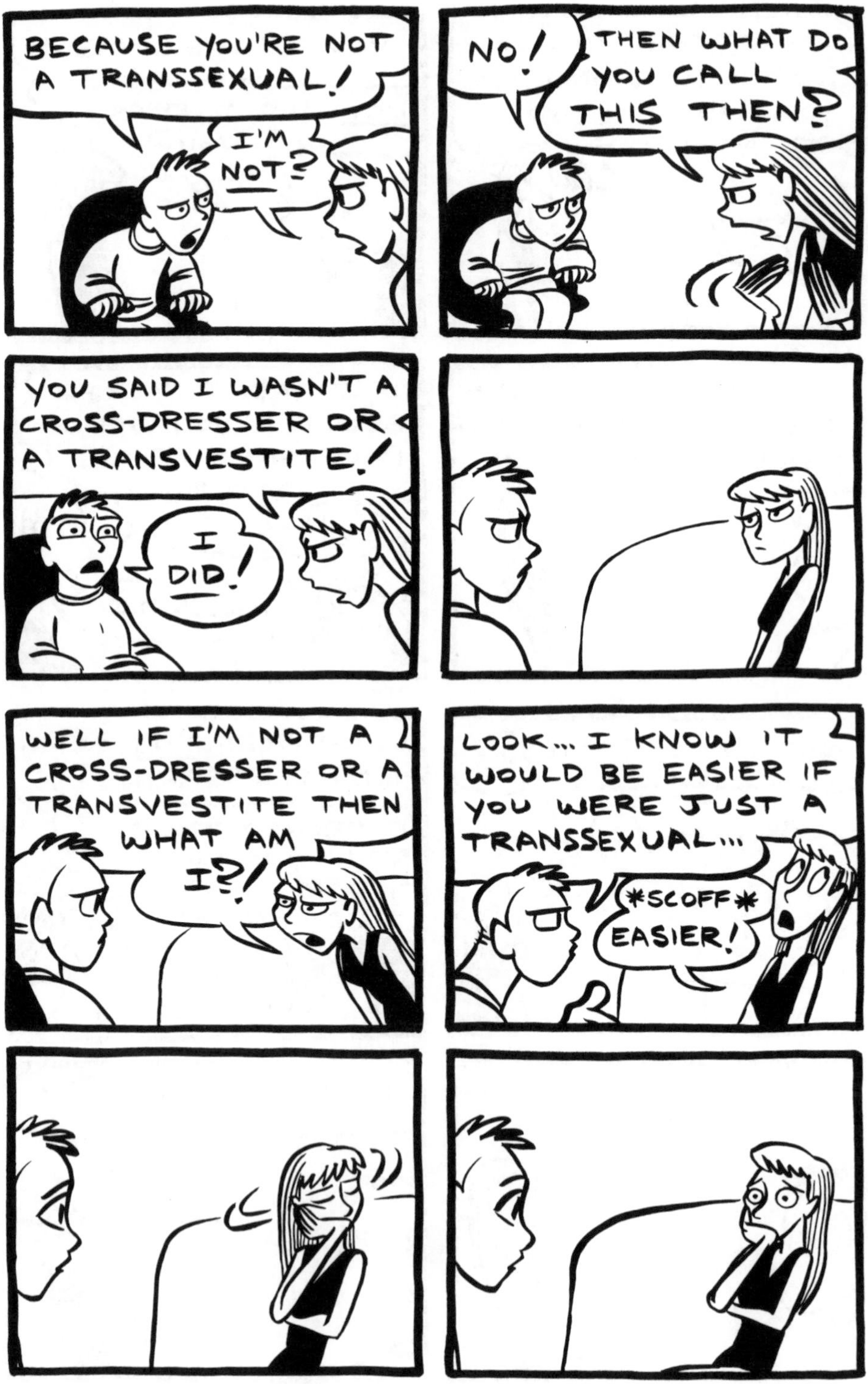

BECAUSE YOU'RE NOT A TRANSSEXUAL!
I'M NOT?
NO!
THEN WHAT DO YOU CALL THIS THEN?
YOU SAID I WASN'T A CROSS-DRESSER OR A TRANSVESTITE!
I DID!
WELL IF I'M NOT A CROSS-DRESSER OR A TRANSVESTITE THEN WHAT AM I?!
LOOK... I KNOW IT WOULD BE EASIER IF YOU WERE JUST A TRANSSEXUAL...
SCOFF EASIER!

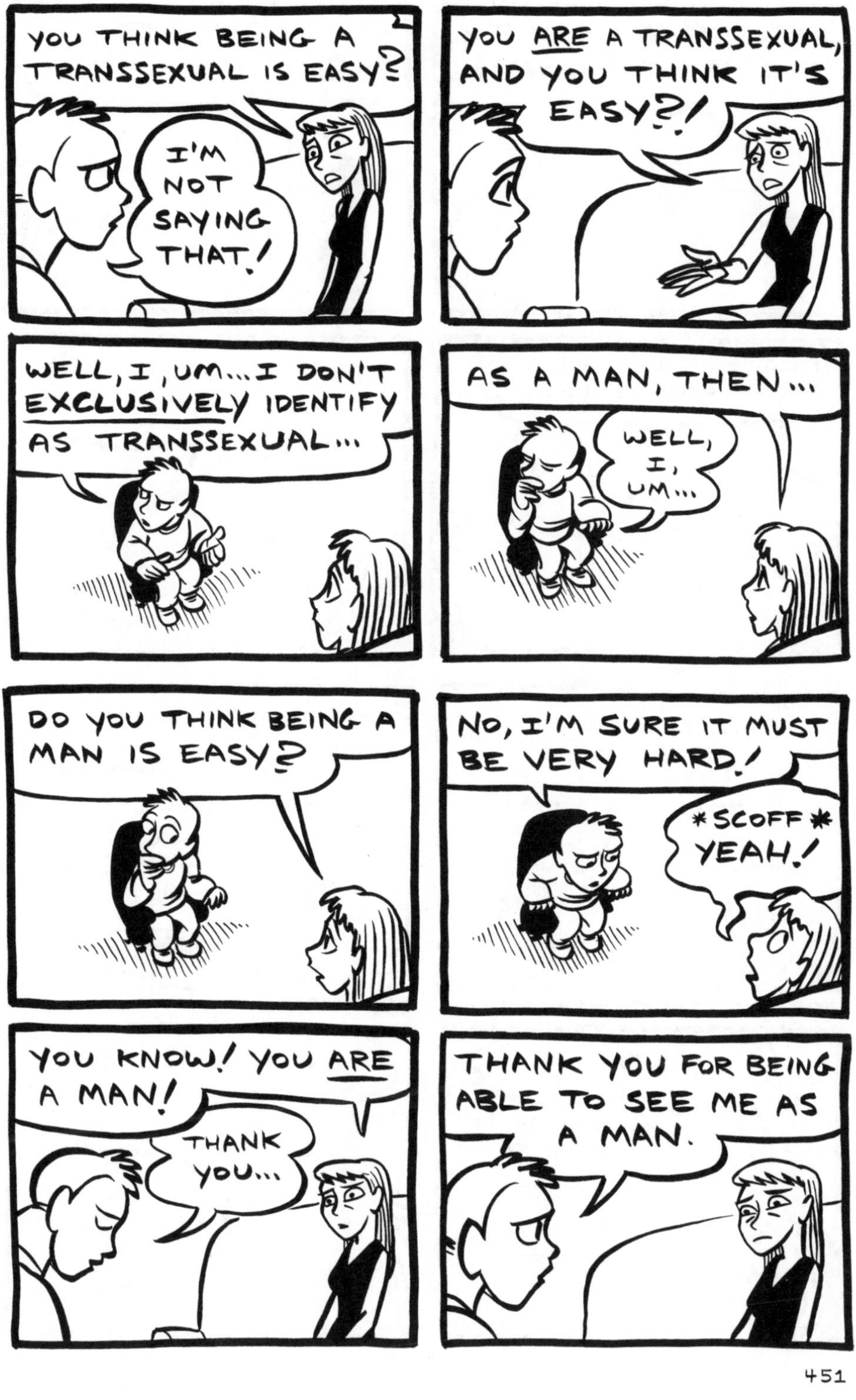
YOU THINK BEING A TRANSSEXUAL IS EASY?
I'M NOT SAYING THAT!
YOU ARE A TRANSSEXUAL, AND YOU THINK IT'S EASY?!
WELL, I, UM... I DON'T EXCLUSIVELY IDENTIFY AS TRANSSEXUAL...
AS A MAN, THEN...
WELL, I, UM...
DO YOU THINK BEING A MAN IS EASY?
NO, I'M SURE IT MUST BE VERY HARD!
SCOFF YEAH!
YOU KNOW! YOU ARE A MAN!
THANK YOU...
THANK YOU FOR BEING ABLE TO SEE ME AS A MAN.

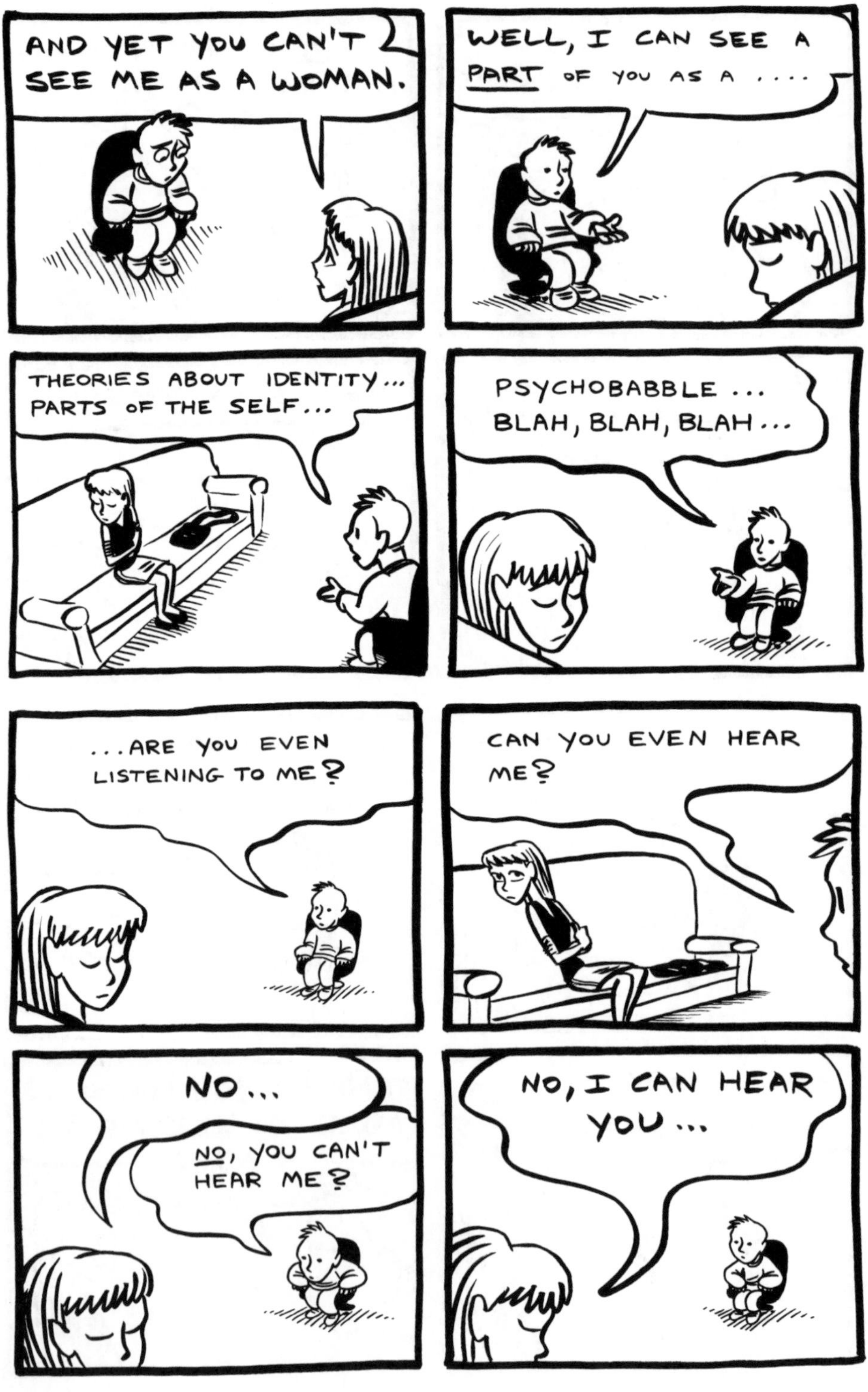
AND YET YOU CAN'T SEE ME AS A WOMAN.
WELL, I CAN SEE A PART OF YOU AS A ....
THEORIES ABOUT IDENTITY... PARTS OF THE SELF...
PSYCHOBABBLE ... BLAH, BLAH, BLAH ...
...ARE YOU EVEN LISTENING TO ME?
CAN YOU EVEN HEAR ME?
NO...
NO, YOU CAN'T HEAR ME?
NO, I CAN HEAR YOU ...

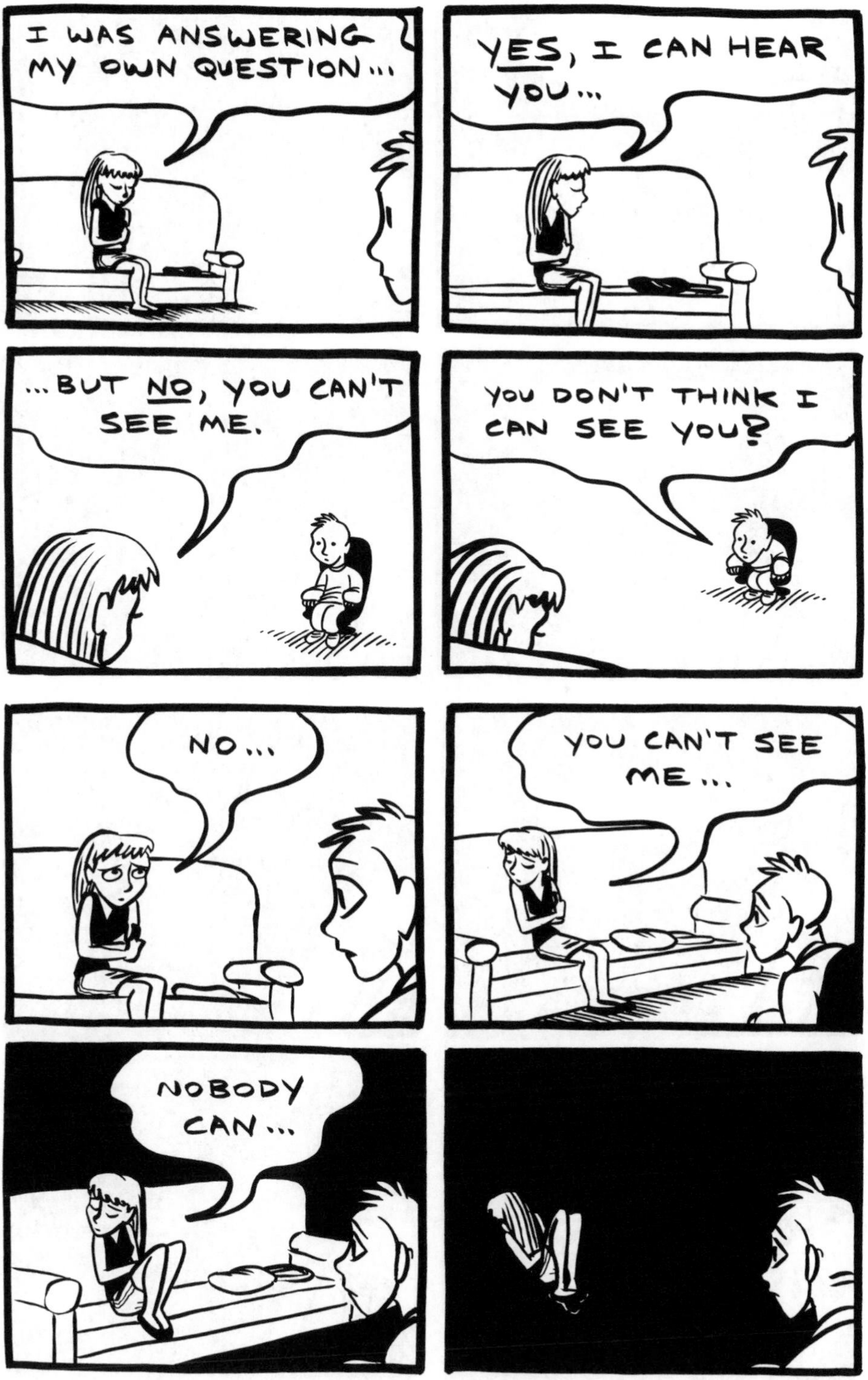

I WAS ANSWERING MY OWN QUESTION...
YES, I CAN HEAR YOU...
...BUT NO, YOU CAN'T SEE ME.
YOU DON'T THINK I CAN SEE YOU?
NO...
YOU CAN'T SEE ME...
NOBODY CAN...

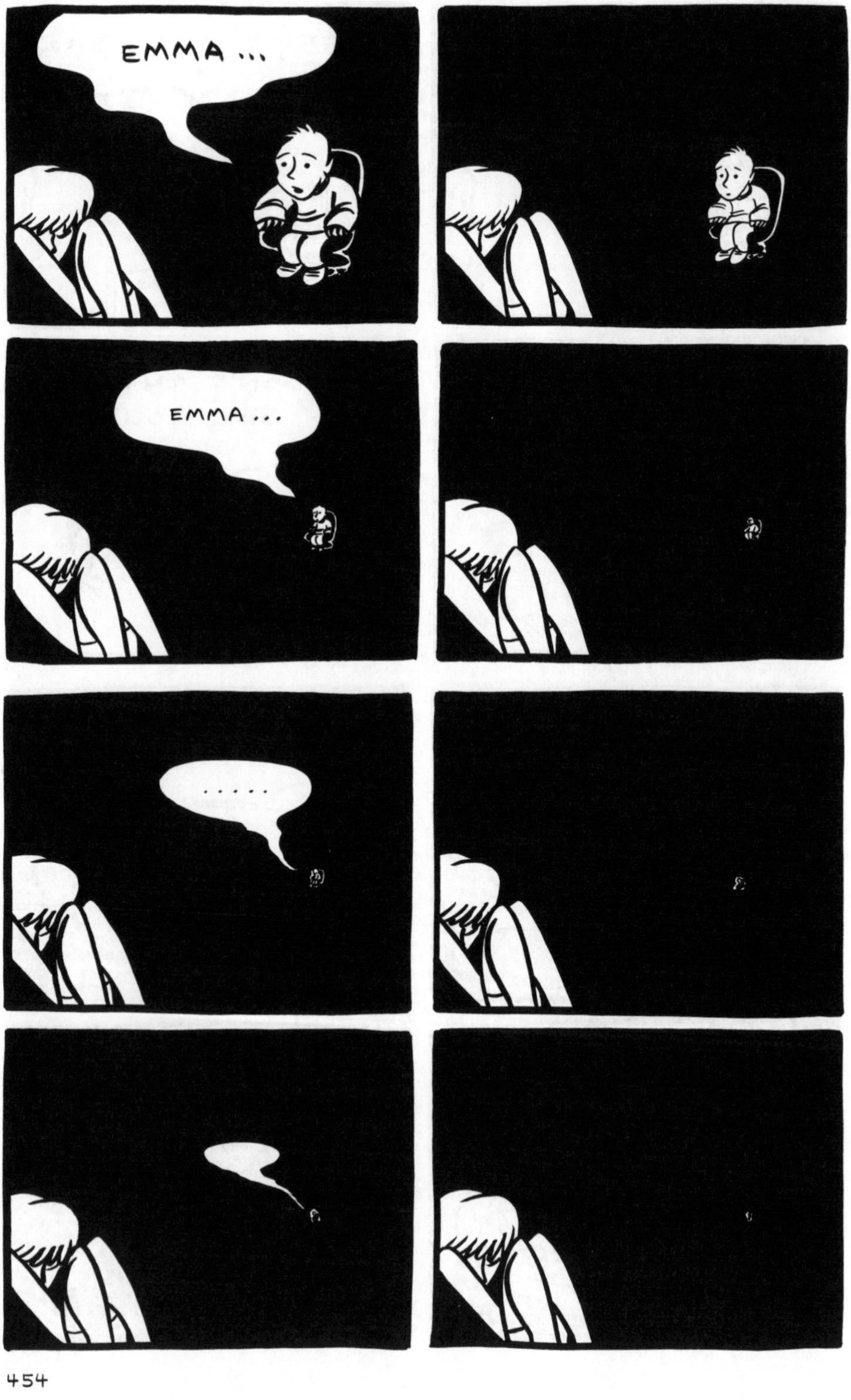
EMMA...
EMMA...
.....

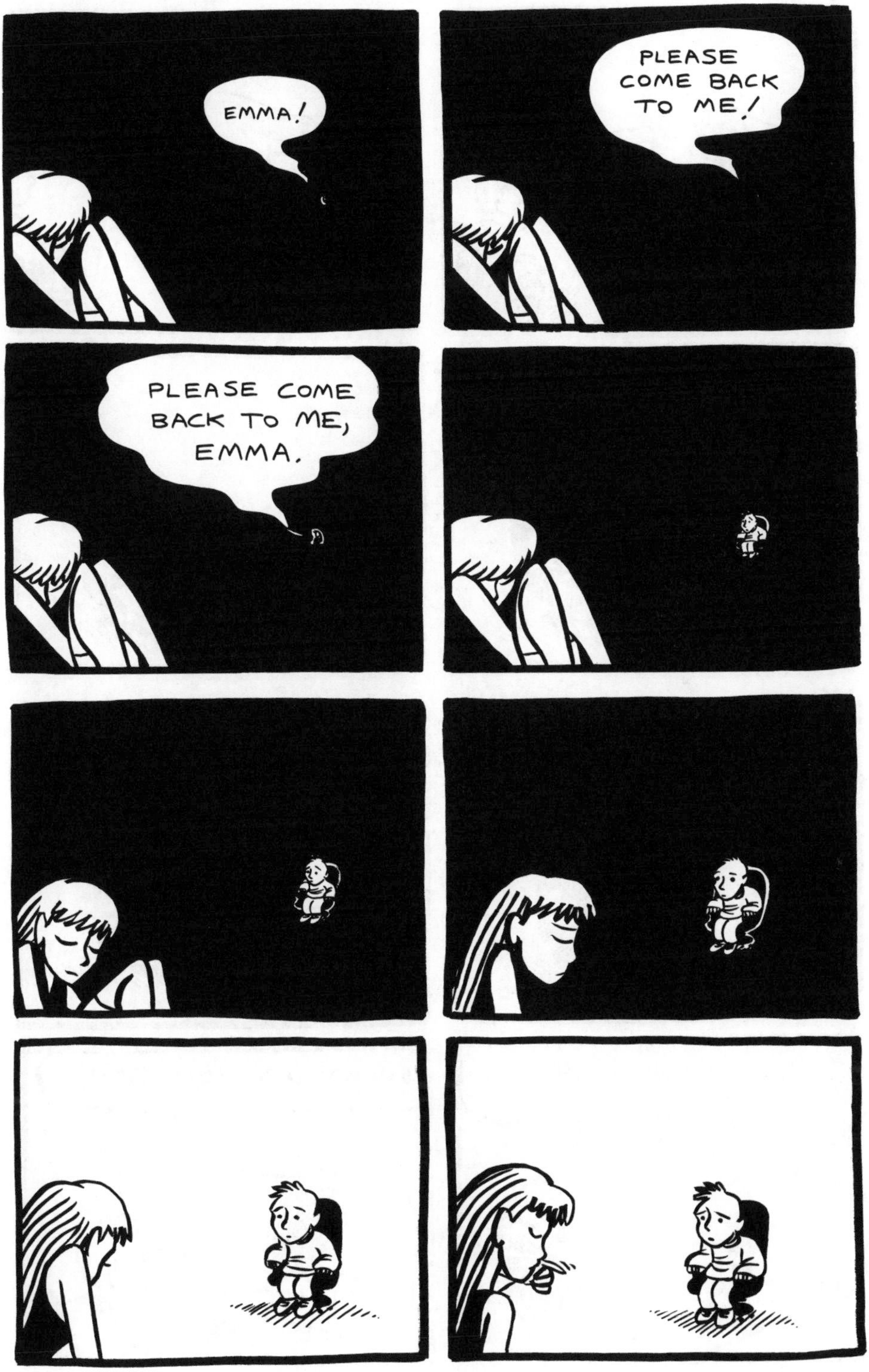
EMMA!
PLEASE COME BACK TO ME!
PLEASE COME BACK TO ME, EMMA.

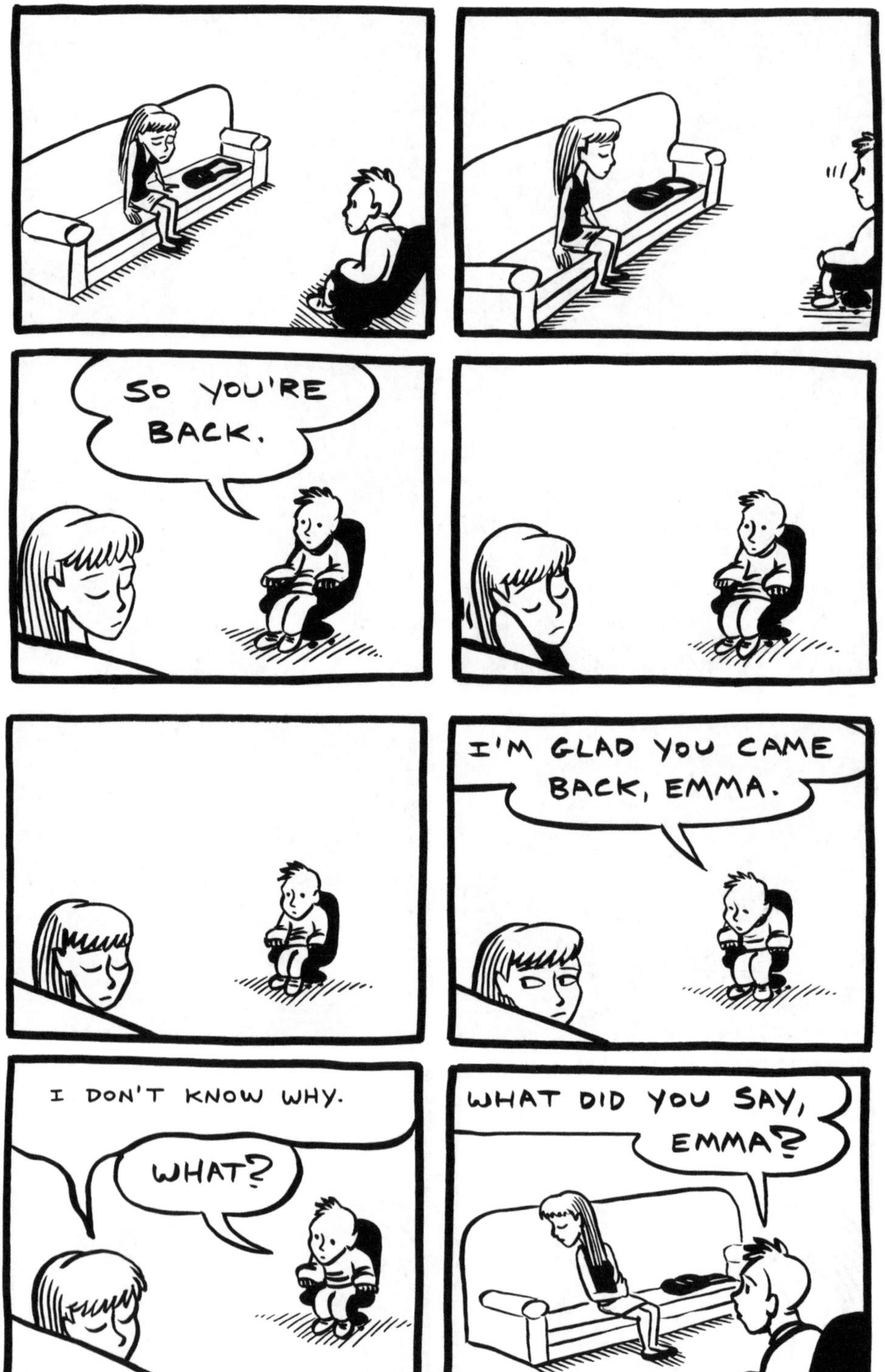
SO YOU'RE BACK.
I'M GLAD YOU CAME BACK, EMMA.
I DON'T KNOW WHY.
WHAT?
WHAT DID YOU SAY, EMMA?

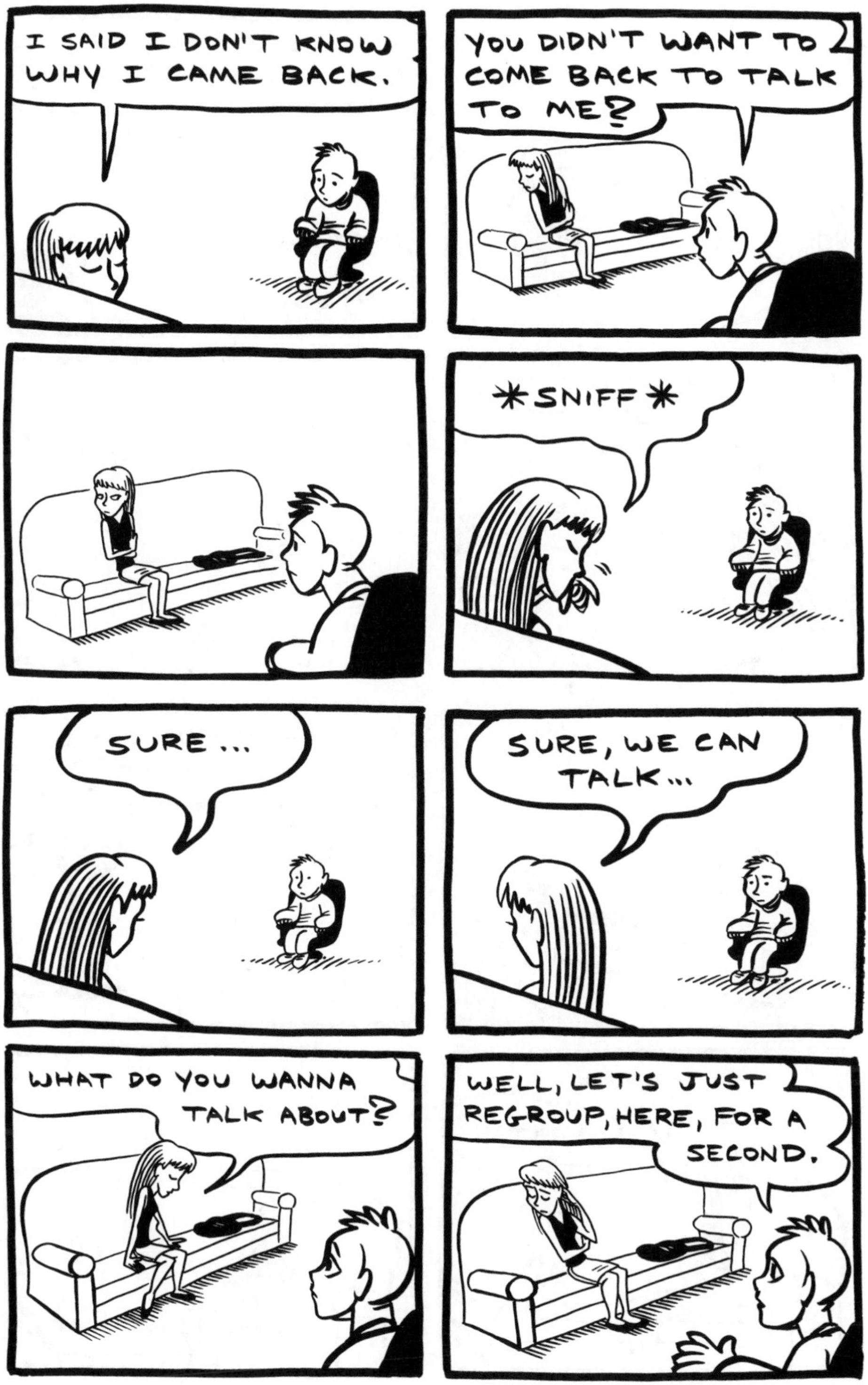
I SAID I DON'T KNOW WHY I CAME BACK.
YOU DIDN'T WANT TO COME BACK TO TALK TO ME?
SNIFF
SURE...
SURE, WE CAN TALK...
WHAT DO YOU WANNA TALK ABOUT?
WELL, LET'S JUST REGROUP, HERE, FOR A SECOND.

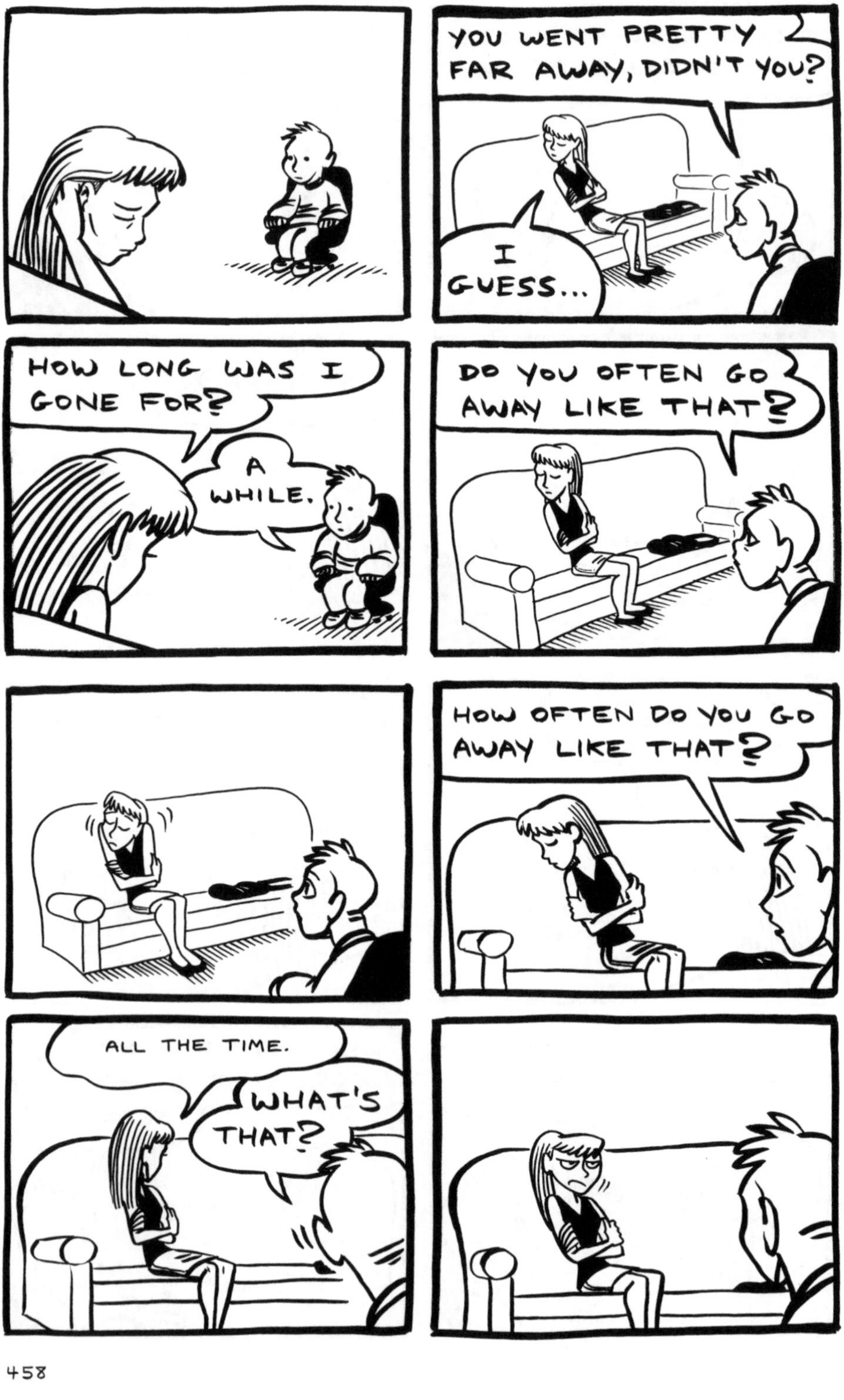
YOU WENT PRETTY FAR AWAY, DIDN'T YOU?
I GUESS...
HOW LONG WAS I GONE FOR?
A WHILE.
DO YOU OFTEN GO AWAY LIKE THAT?
HOW OFTEN DO YOU GO AWAY LIKE THAT?
ALL THE TIME.
WHAT'S THAT?

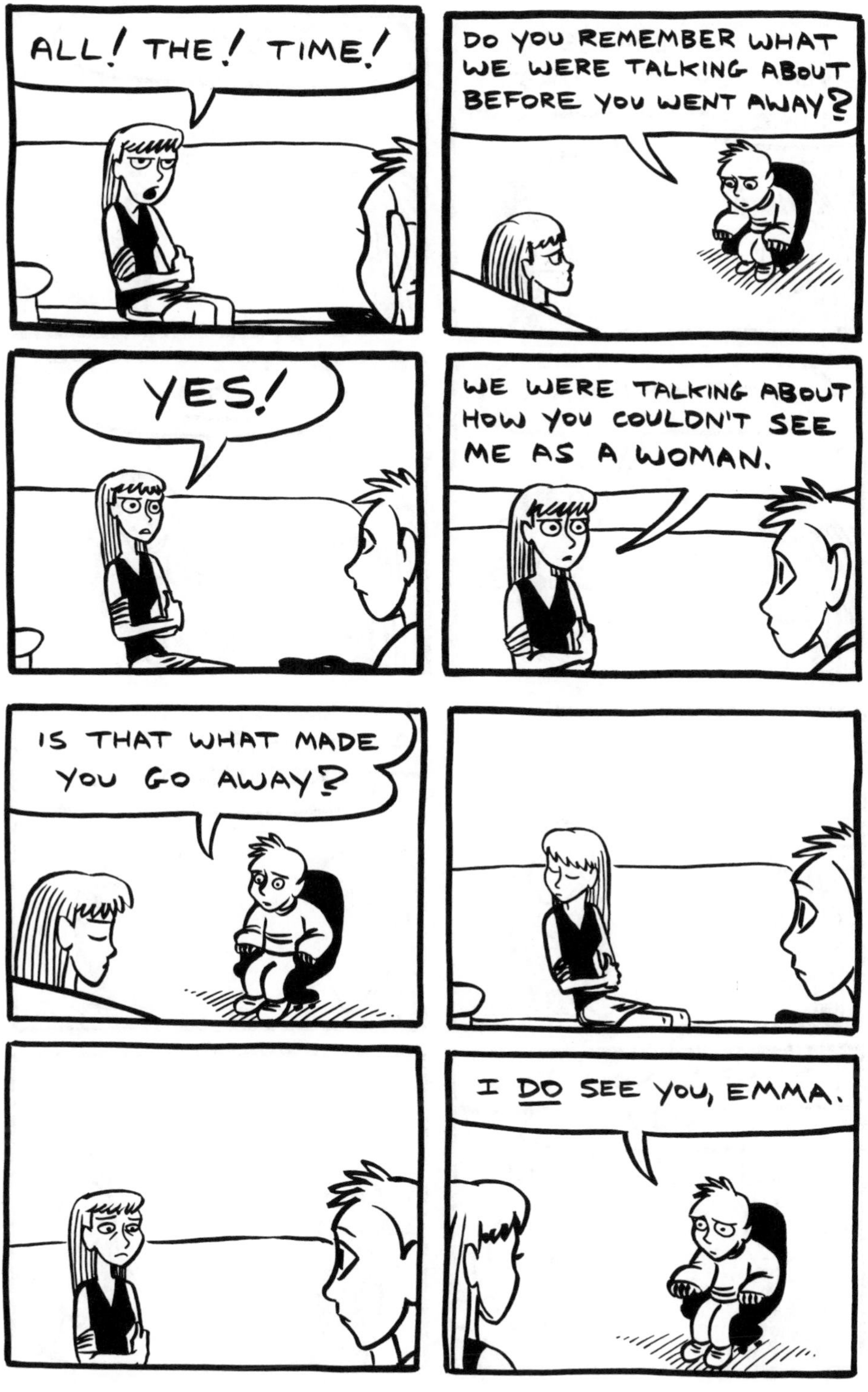
ALL! THE! TIME!
DO YOU REMEMBER WHAT WE WERE TALKING ABOUT BEFORE YOU WENT AWAY?
YES!
WE WERE TALKING ABOUT HOW YOU COULDN'T SEE ME AS A WOMAN.
IS THAT WHAT MADE YOU GO AWAY?
I DO SEE YOU, EMMA.

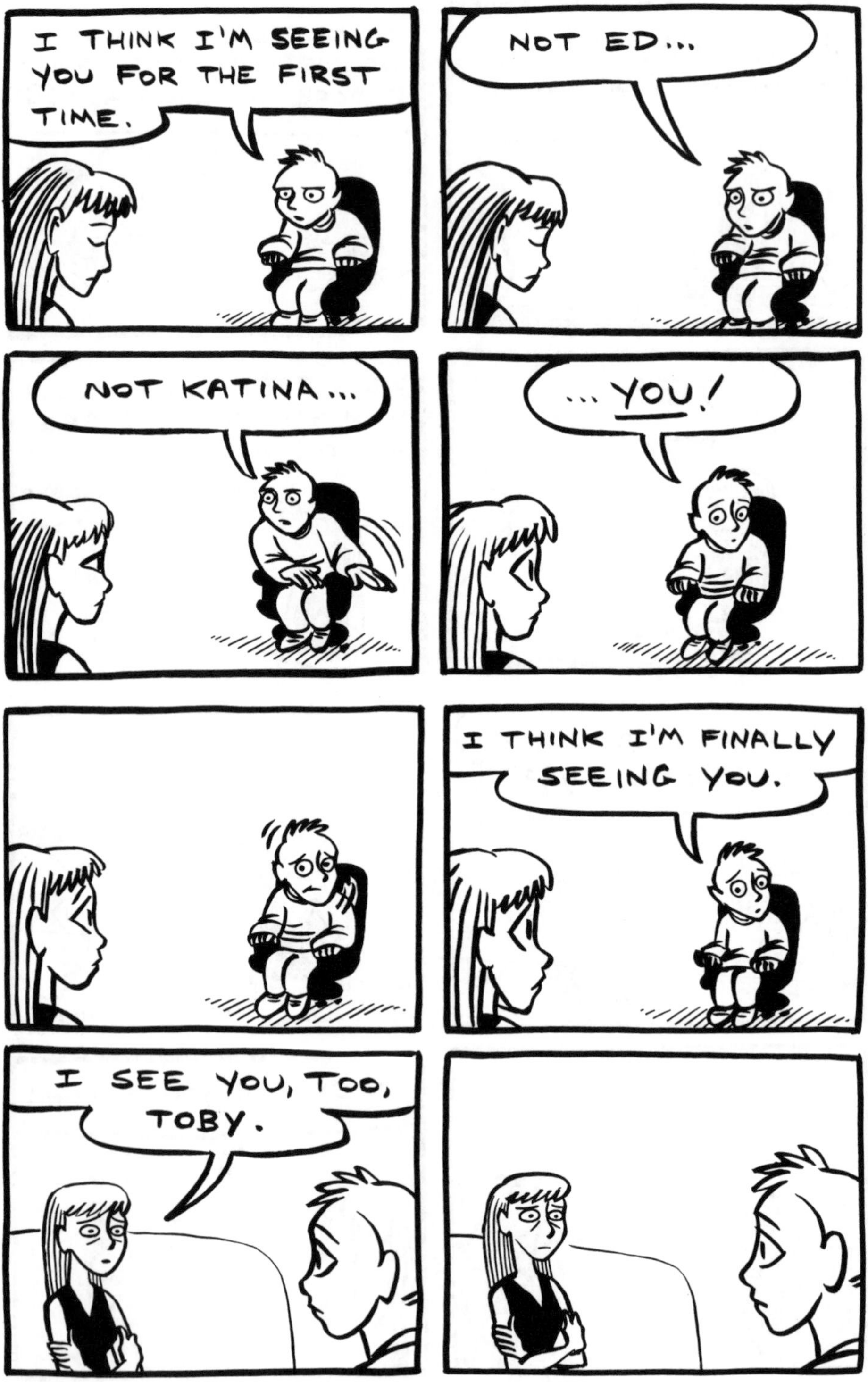
I THINK I'M SEEING YOU FOR THE FIRST TIME.
NOT ED...
NOT KATINA...
...YOU!
I THINK I'M FINALLY SEEING YOU.
I SEE YOU, TOO, TOBY.

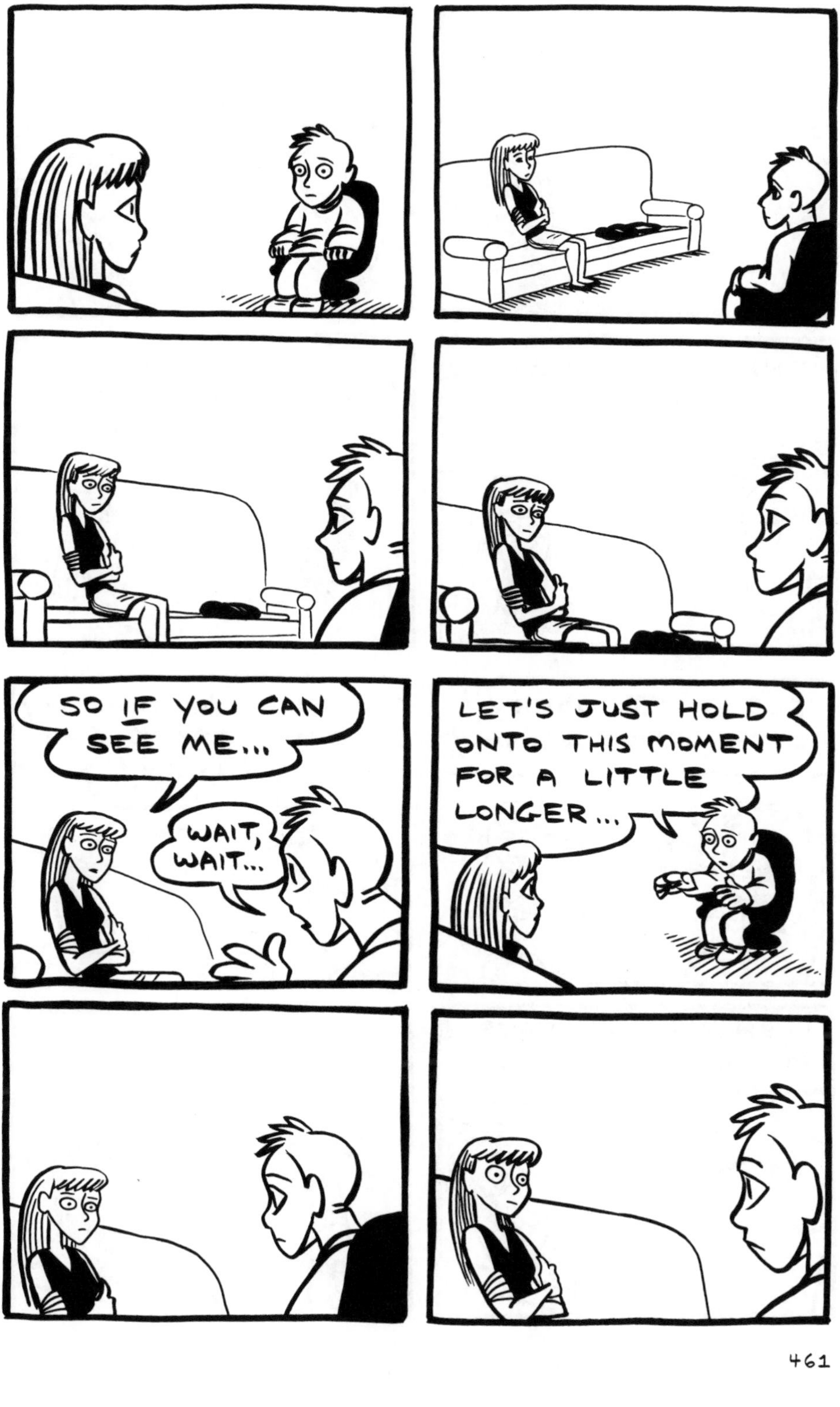
SO IF YOU CAN SEE ME...
WAIT, WAIT...
LET'S JUST HOLD ONTO THIS MOMENT FOR A LITTLE LONGER...

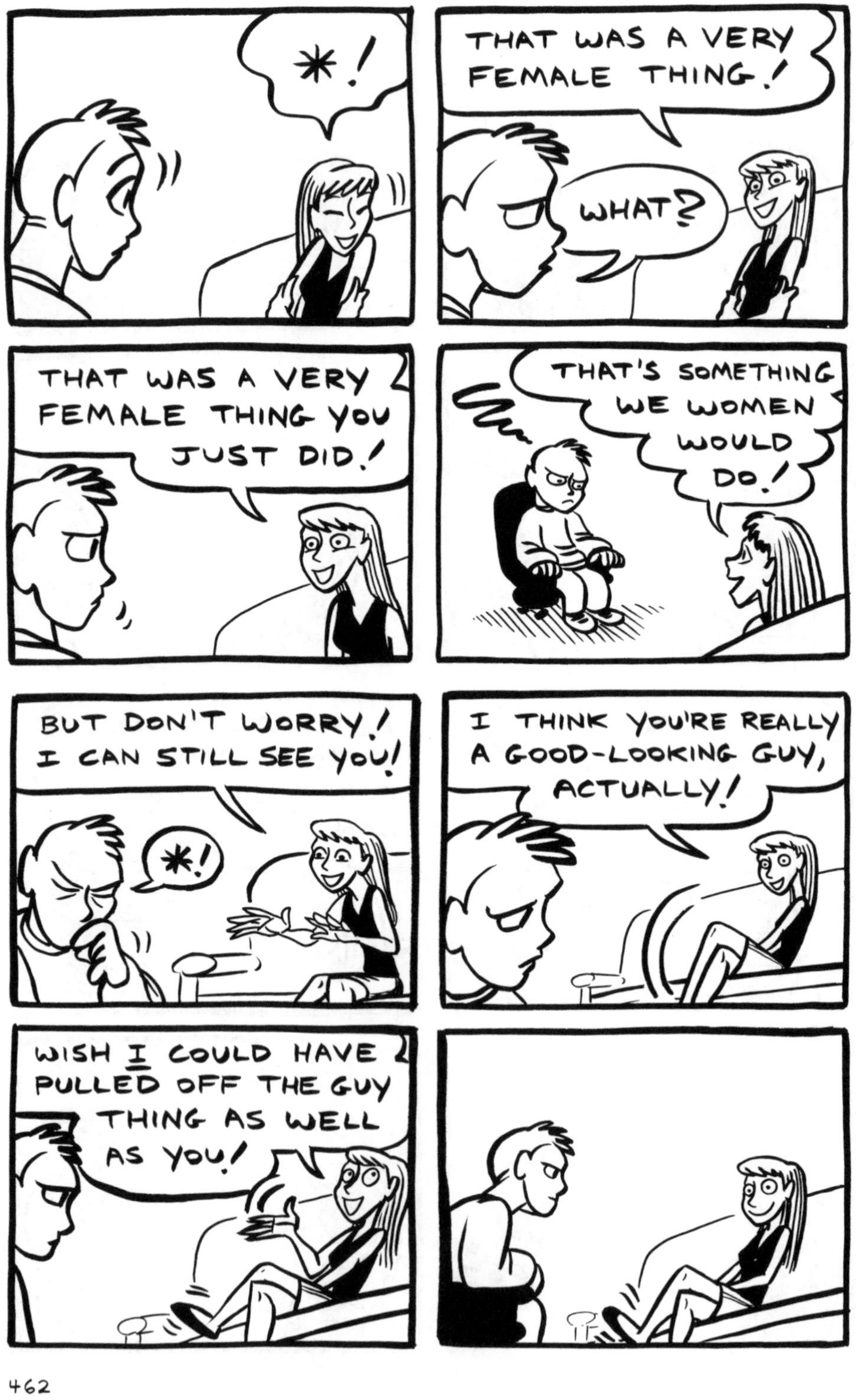
*!
THAT WAS A VERY FEMALE THING!
WHAT?
THAT WAS A VERY FEMALE THING YOU JUST DID!
THAT'S SOMETHING WE WOMEN WOULD DO!
BUT DON'T WORRY! I CAN STILL SEE YOU!
*!
I THINK YOU'RE REALLY A GOOD-LOOKING GUY, ACTUALLY!
WISH I COULD HAVE PULLED OFF THE GUY THING AS WELL AS YOU!

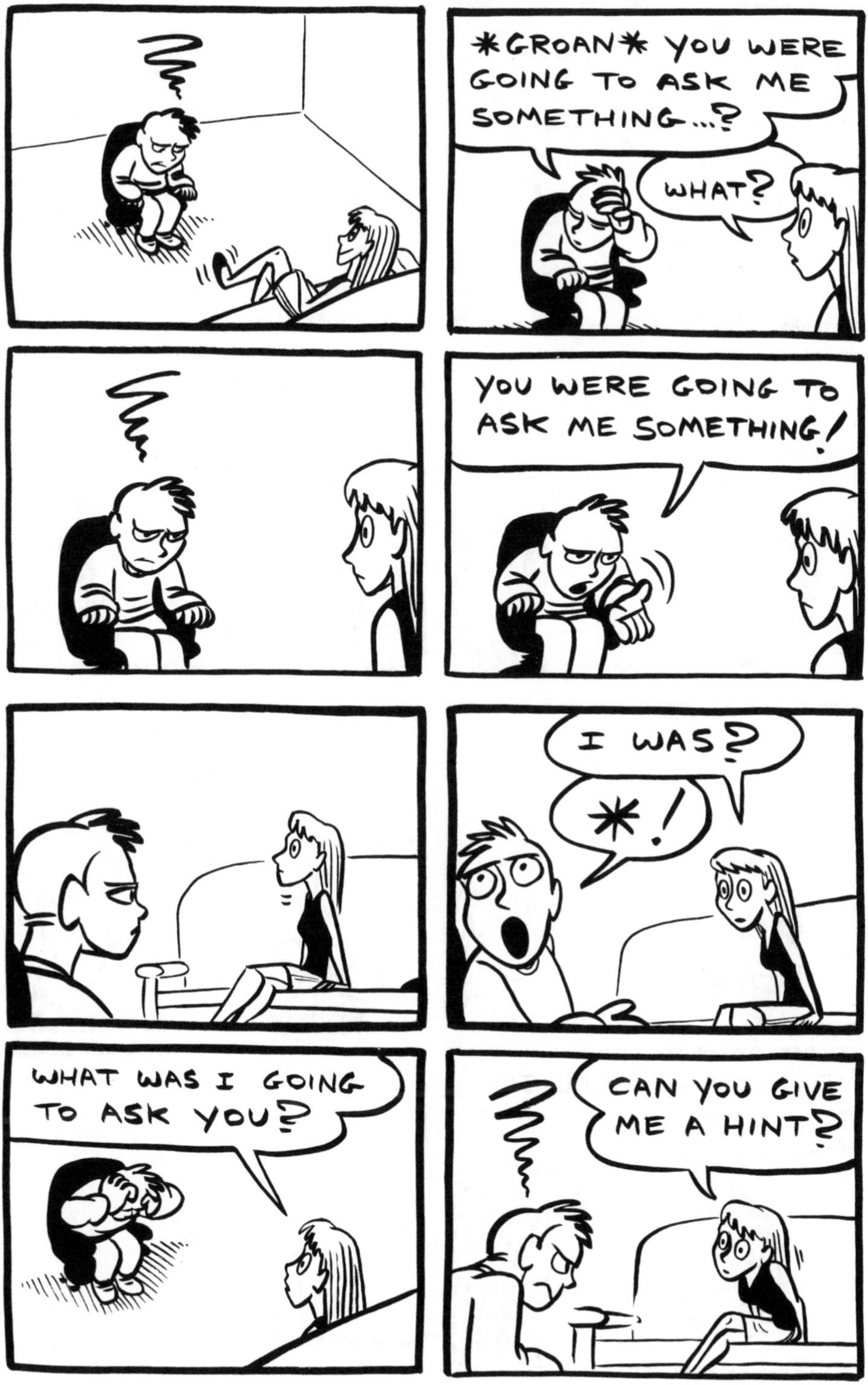
GROAN YOU WERE GOING TO ASK ME SOMETHING...?
WHAT?
YOU WERE GOING TO ASK ME SOMETHING!
I WAS?
*!
WHAT WAS I GOING TO ASK YOU?
CAN YOU GIVE ME A HINT?

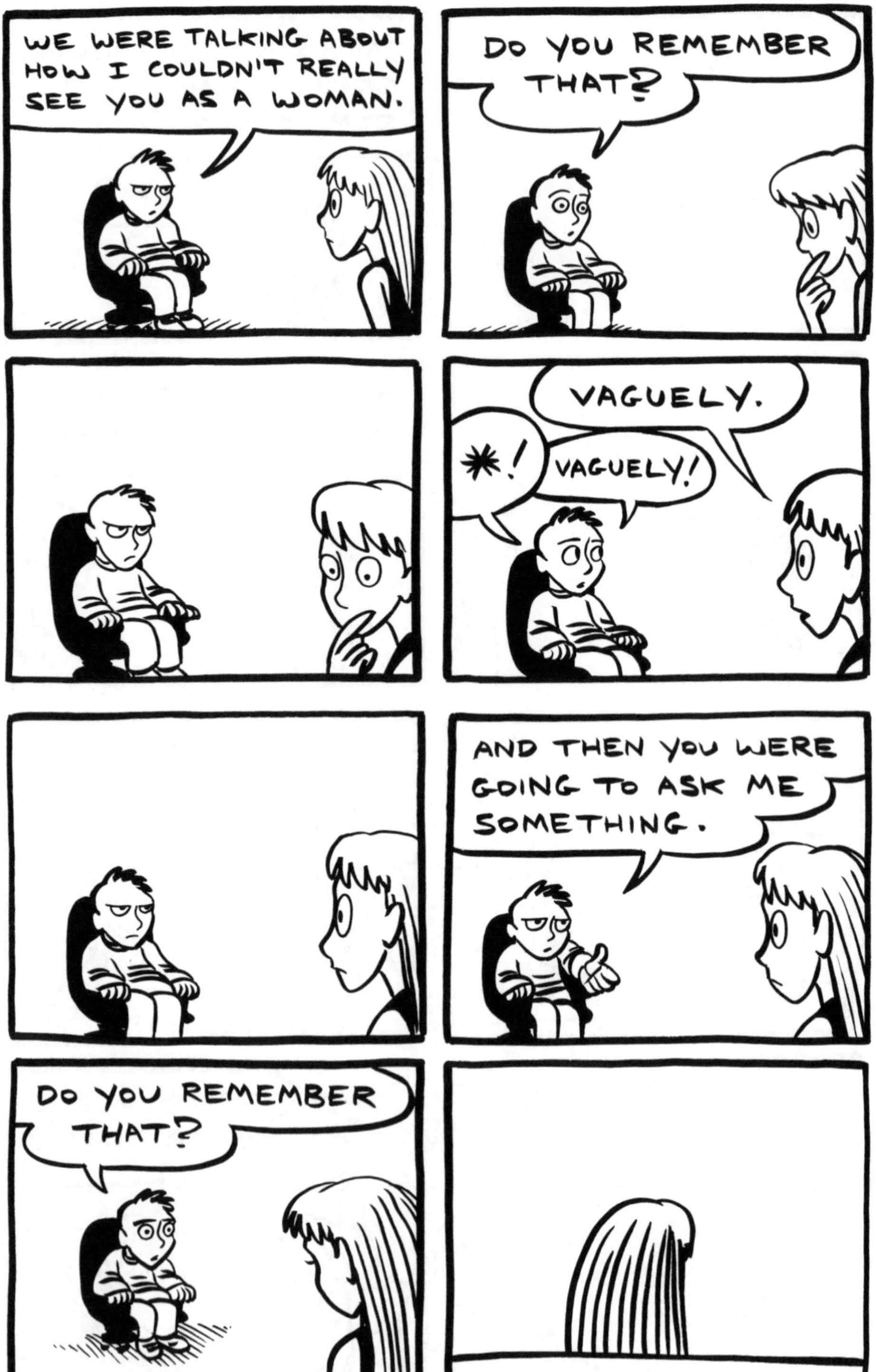
WE WERE TALKING ABOUT HOW I COULDN'T REALLY SEE YOU AS A WOMAN.
DO YOU REMEMBER THAT?
VAGUELY.
*!
VAGUELY!
AND THEN YOU WERE GOING TO ASK ME SOMETHING.
DO YOU REMEMBER THAT?

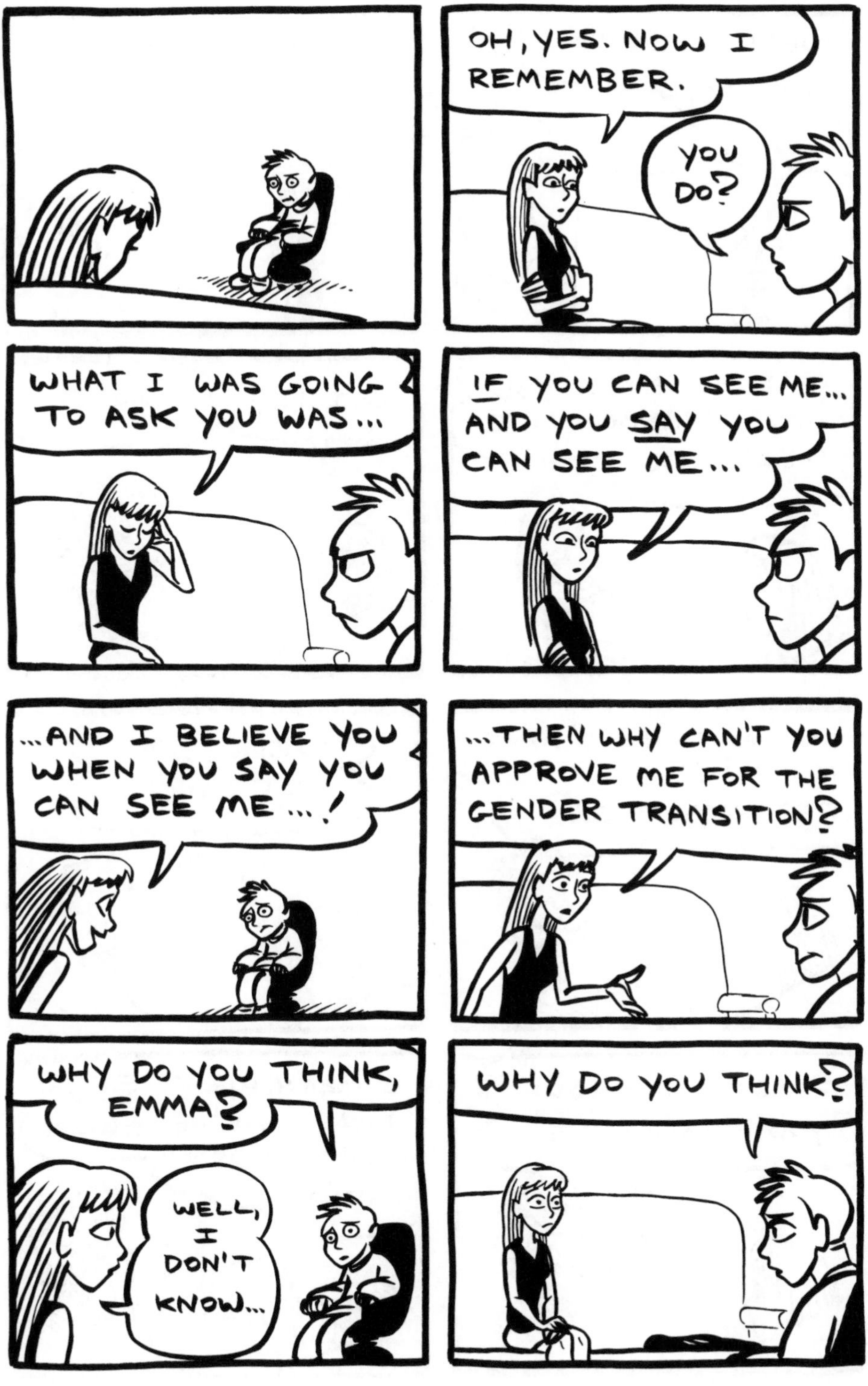
OH, YES. NOW I REMEMBER.
YOU DO?
WHAT I WAS GOING TO ASK YOU WAS...
IF YOU CAN SEE ME... AND YOU SAY YOU CAN SEE ME...
...AND I BELIEVE YOU WHEN YOU SAY YOU CAN SEE ME...!
...THEN WHY CAN'T YOU APPROVE ME FOR THE GENDER TRANSITION?
WHY DO YOU THINK, EMMA?
WELL, I DON'T KNOW...
WHY DO YOU THINK?

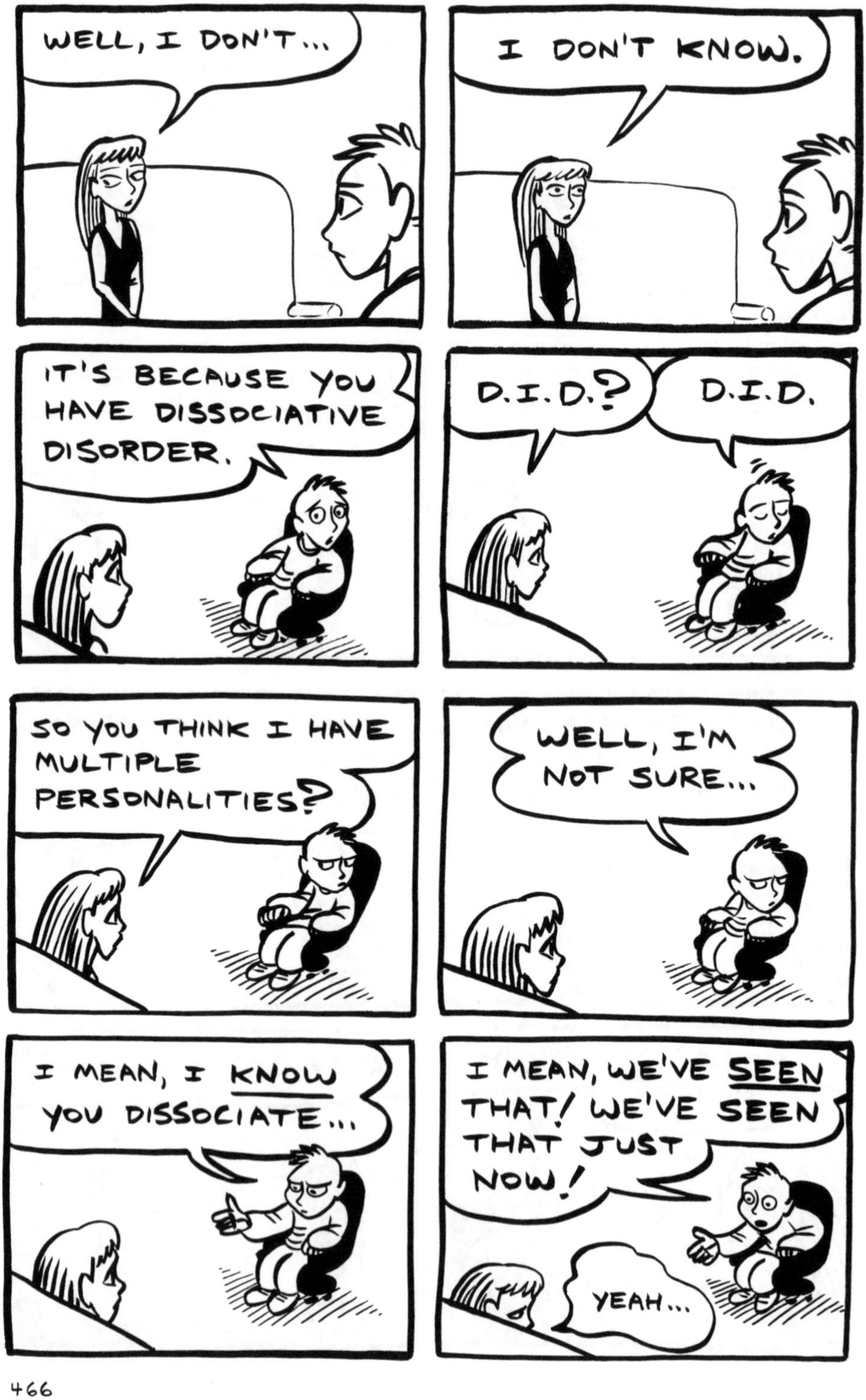
WELL, I DON'T...
I DON'T KNOW.
IT'S BECAUSE YOU HAVE DISSOCIATIVE DISORDER.
D.I.D.?
D.I.D.
SO YOU THINK I HAVE MULTIPLE PERSONALITIES?
WELL, I'M NOT SURE...
I MEAN, I KNOW YOU DISSOCIATE...
I MEAN, WE'VE SEEN THAT! WE'VE SEEN THAT JUST NOW!
YEAH...

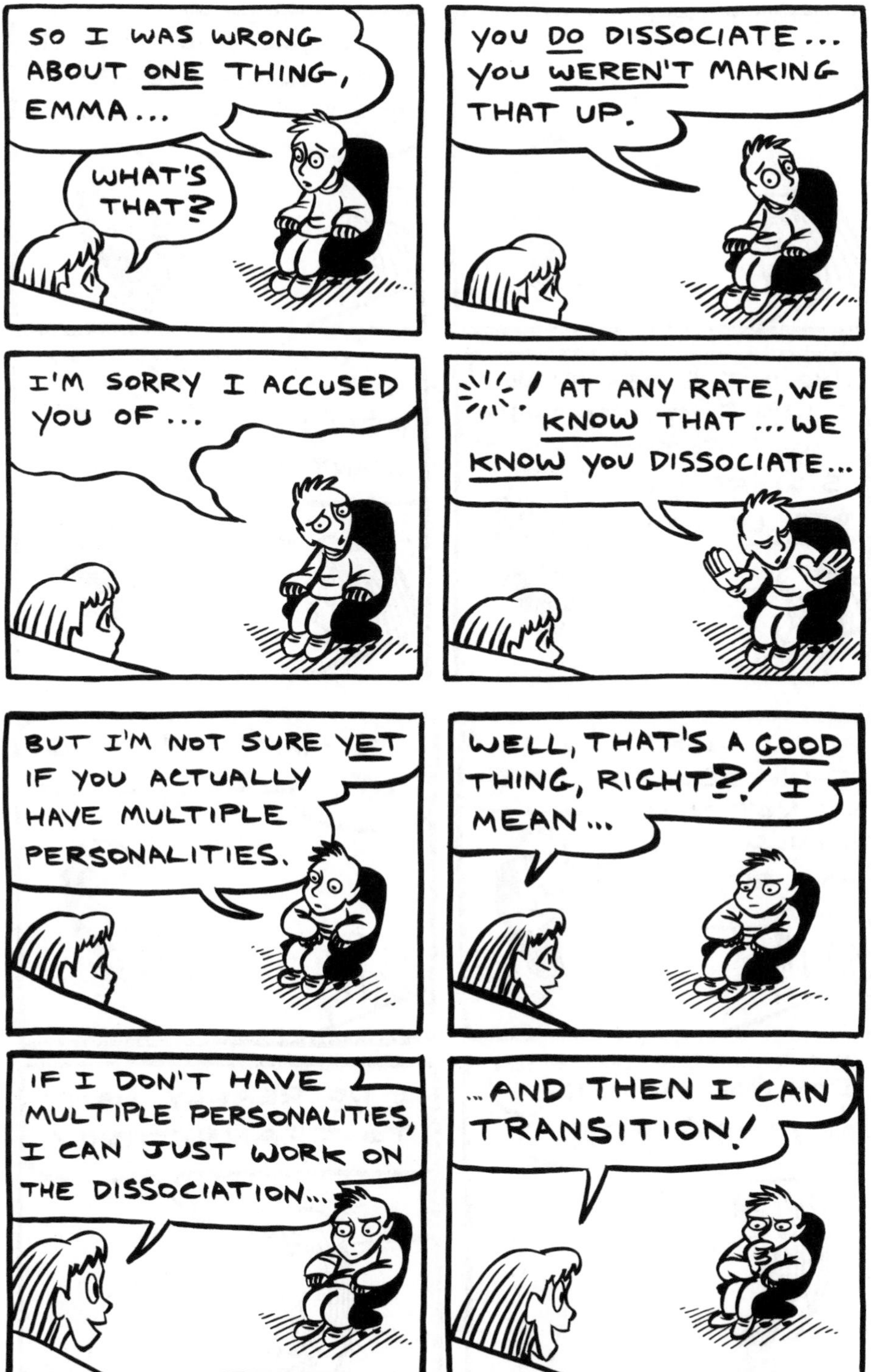

SO I WAS WRONG ABOUT ONE THING, EMMA...
WHAT'S THAT?
YOU DO DISSOCIATE... YOU WEREN'T MAKING THAT UP.
I'M SORRY I ACCUSED YOU OF...
! AT ANY RATE, WE KNOW THAT... WE KNOW YOU DISSOCIATE...
BUT I'M NOT SURE YET IF YOU ACTUALLY HAVE MULTIPLE PERSONALITIES.
WELL, THAT'S A GOOD THING, RIGHT?! I MEAN...
IF I DON'T HAVE MULTIPLE PERSONALITIES, I CAN JUST WORK ON THE DISSOCIATION...
...AND THEN I CAN TRANSITION!

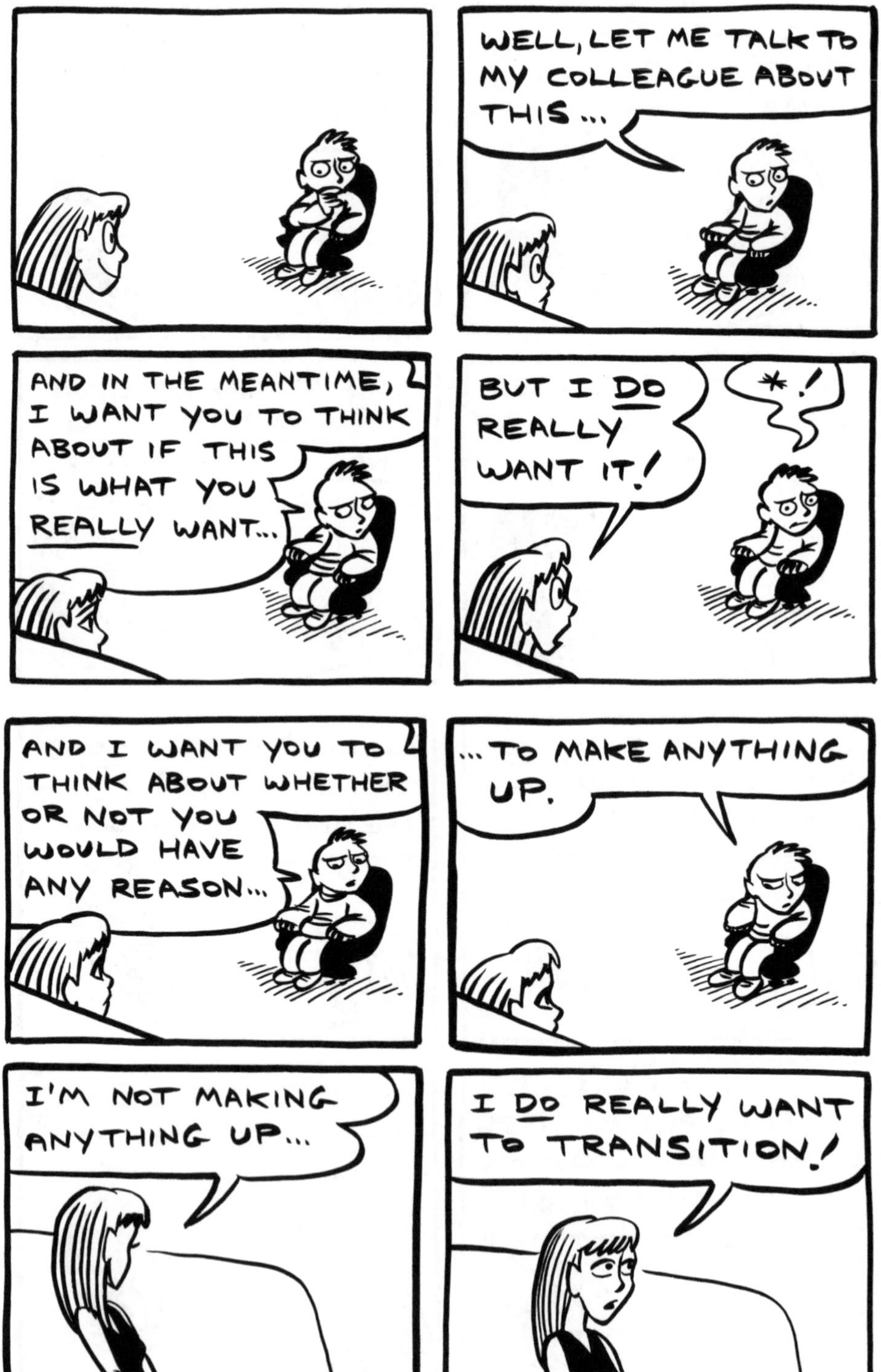
WELL, LET ME TALK TO MY COLLEAGUE ABOUT THIS...
AND IN THE MEANTIME, I WANT YOU TO THINK ABOUT IF THIS IS WHAT YOU REALLY WANT...
BUT I DO REALLY WANT IT!
*!
AND I WANT YOU TO THINK ABOUT WHETHER OR NOT YOU WOULD HAVE ANY REASON...
...TO MAKE ANYTHING UP.
I'M NOT MAKING ANYTHING UP...
I DO REALLY WANT TO TRANSITION!

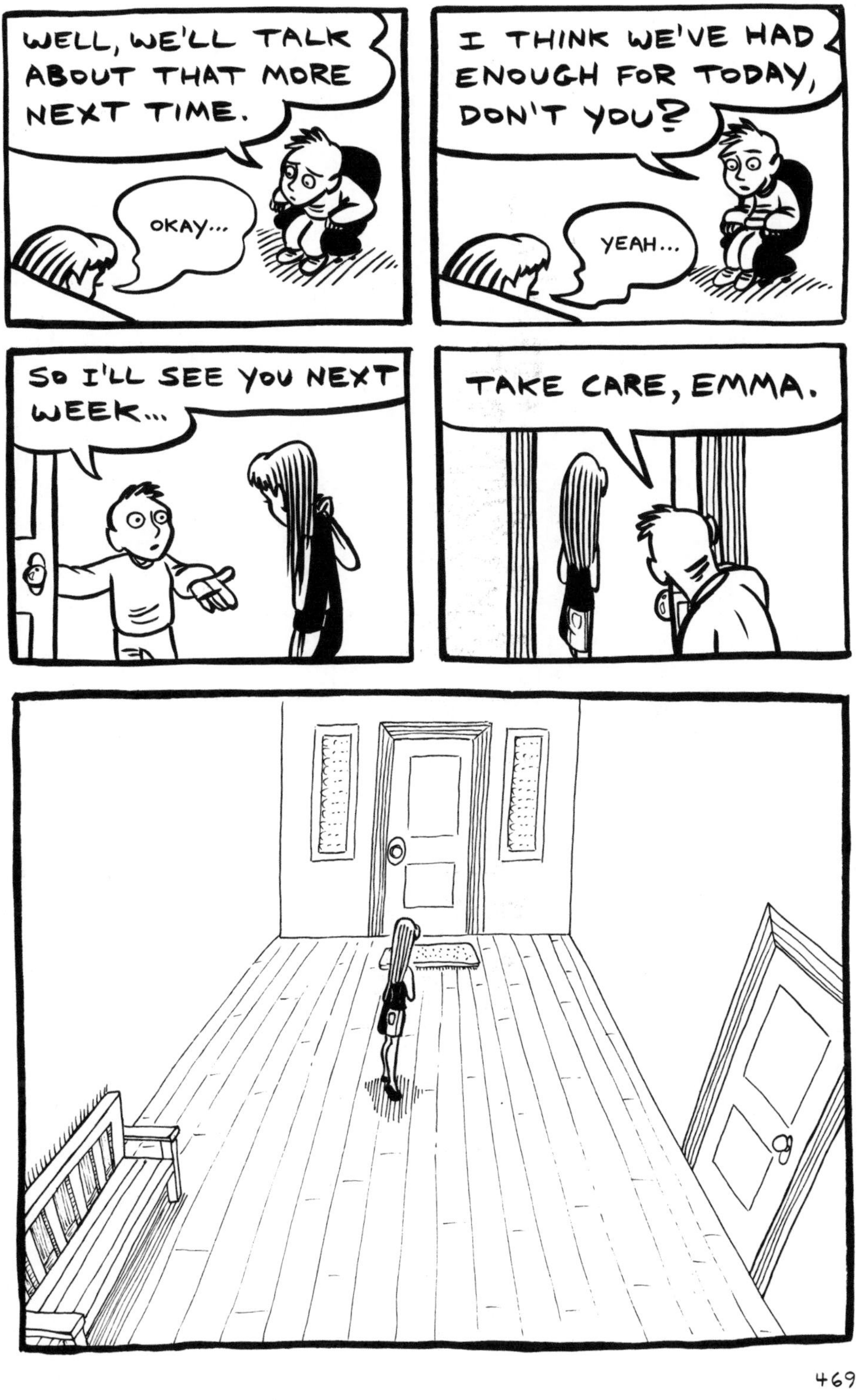

WELL, WE'LL TALK ABOUT THAT MORE NEXT TIME.
OKAY...
I THINK WE'VE HAD ENOUGH FOR TODAY, DON'T YOU?
YEAH...
SO I'LL SEE YOU NEXT WEEK...
TAKE CARE, EMMA.

WELCOME MAT

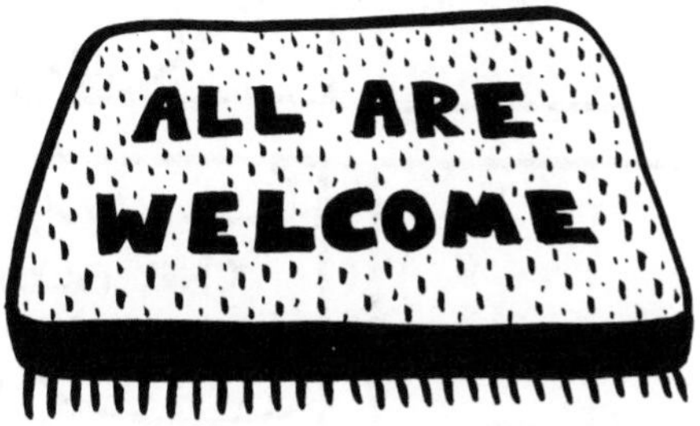
ALL ARE WELCOME

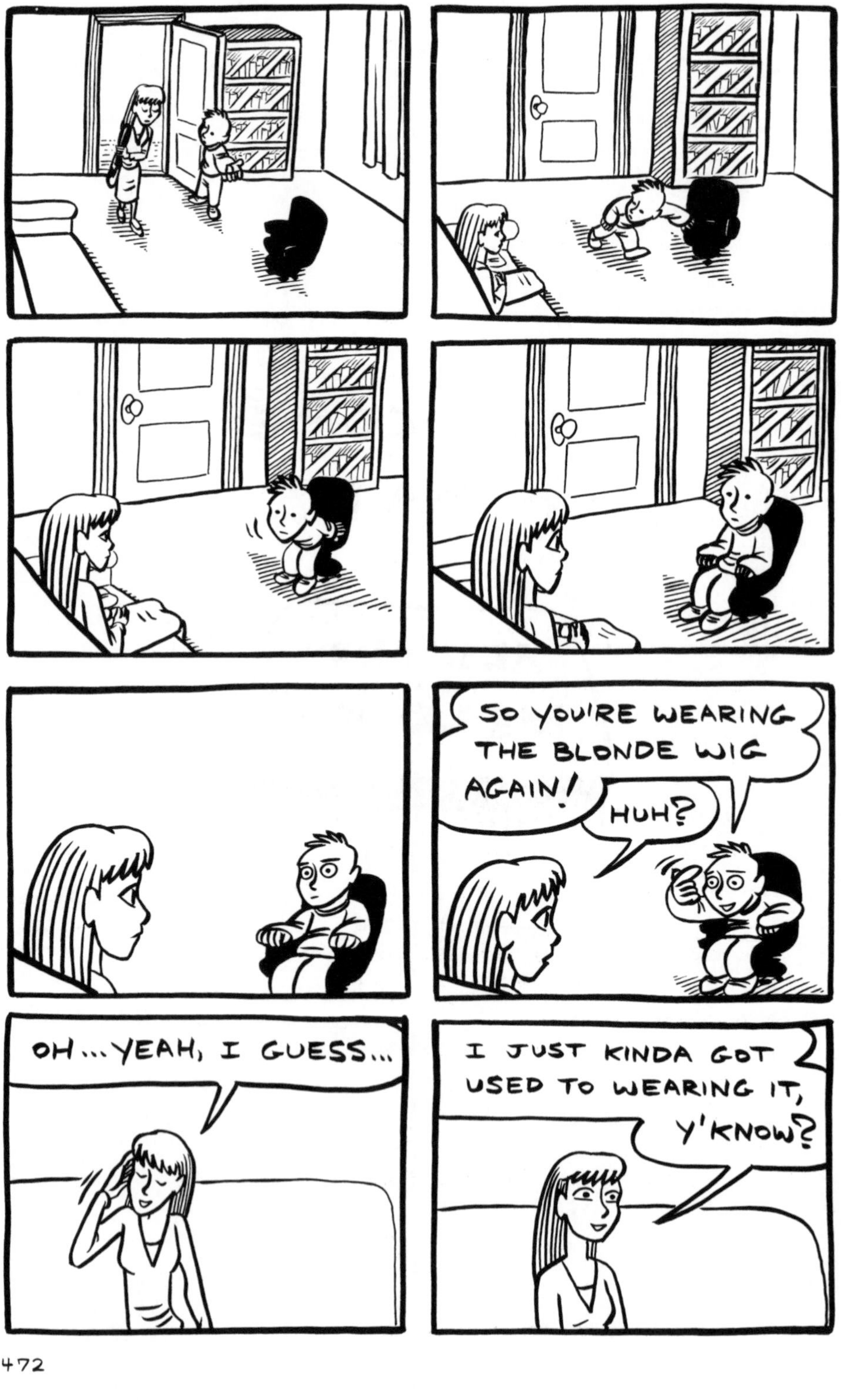
SO YOU'RE WEARING THE BLONDE WIG AGAIN!
HUH?
OH... YEAH, I GUESS...
I JUST KINDA GOT USED TO WEARING IT, Y'KNOW?

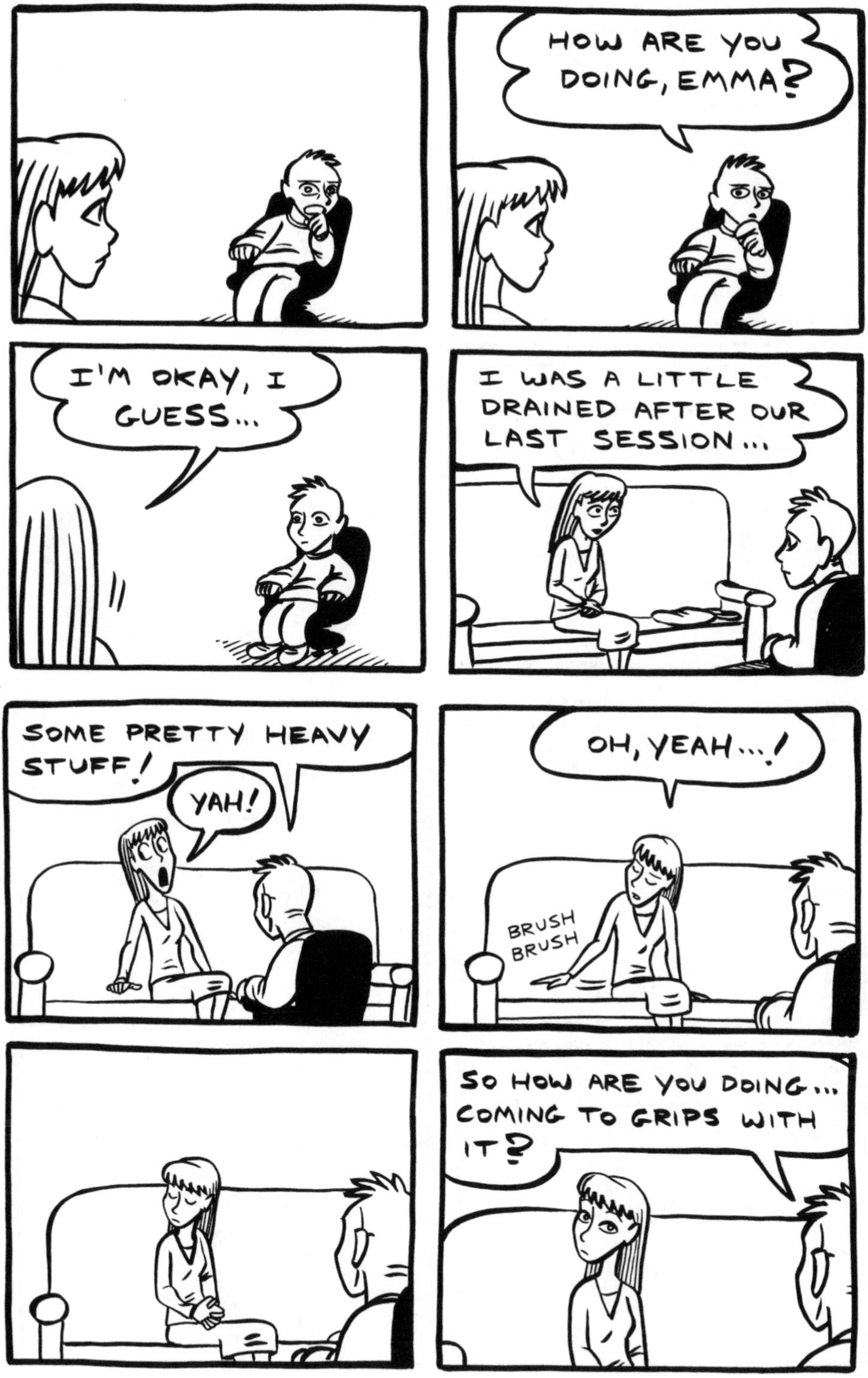
HOW ARE YOU DOING, EMMA?
I'M OKAY, I GUESS...
I WAS A LITTLE DRAINED AFTER OUR LAST SESSION...
SOME PRETTY HEAVY STUFF!
YAH!
OH, YEAH...!
BRUSH BRUSH
SO HOW ARE YOU DOING... COMING TO GRIPS WITH IT?

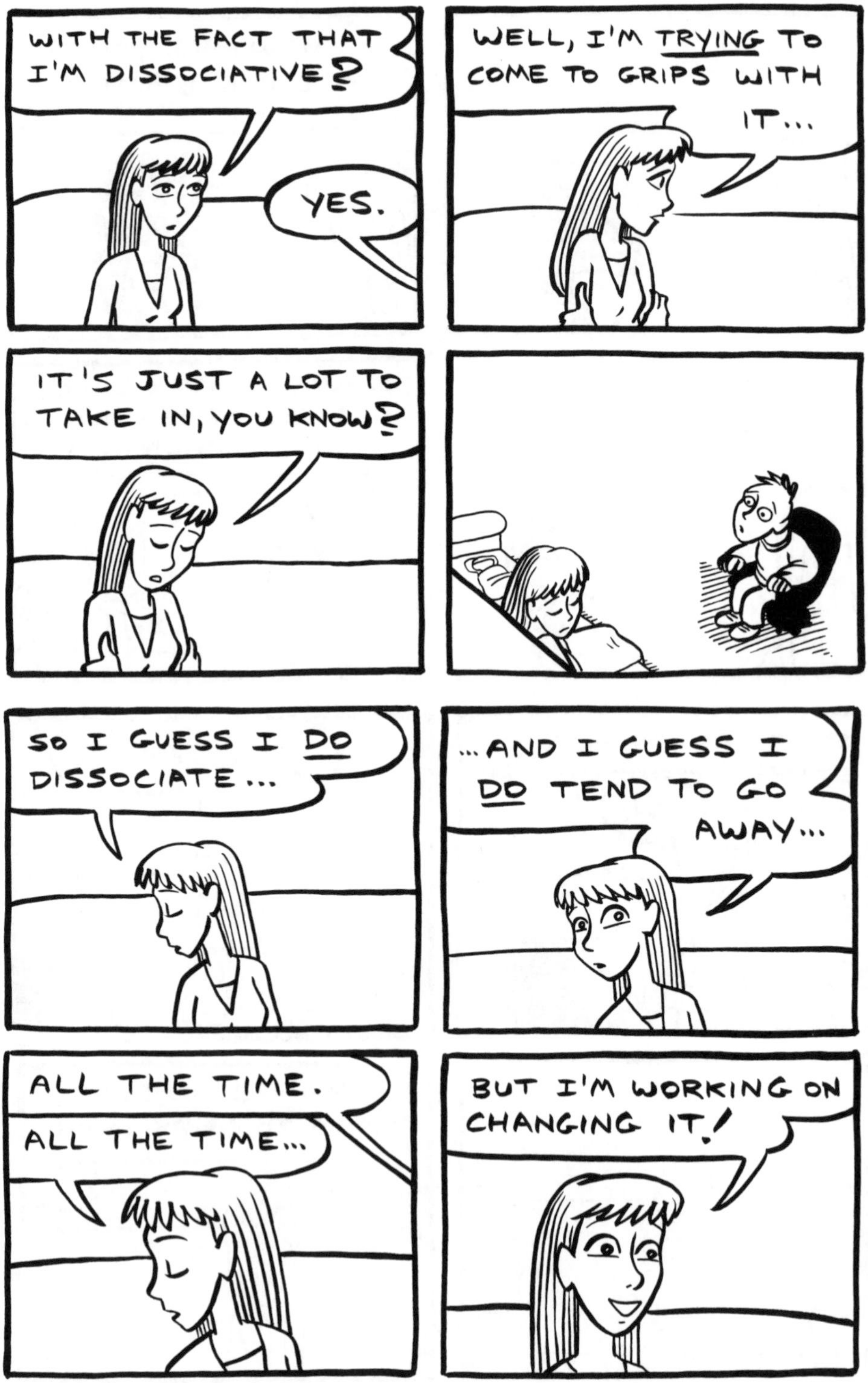
WITH THE FACT THAT I'M DISSOCIATIVE?
YES.
WELL, I'M TRYING TO COME TO GRIPS WITH IT...
IT'S JUST A LOT TO TAKE IN, YOU KNOW?
SO I GUESS I DO DISSOCIATE...
...AND I GUESS I DO TEND TO GO AWAY...
ALL THE TIME.
ALL THE TIME...
BUT I'M WORKING ON CHANGING IT!

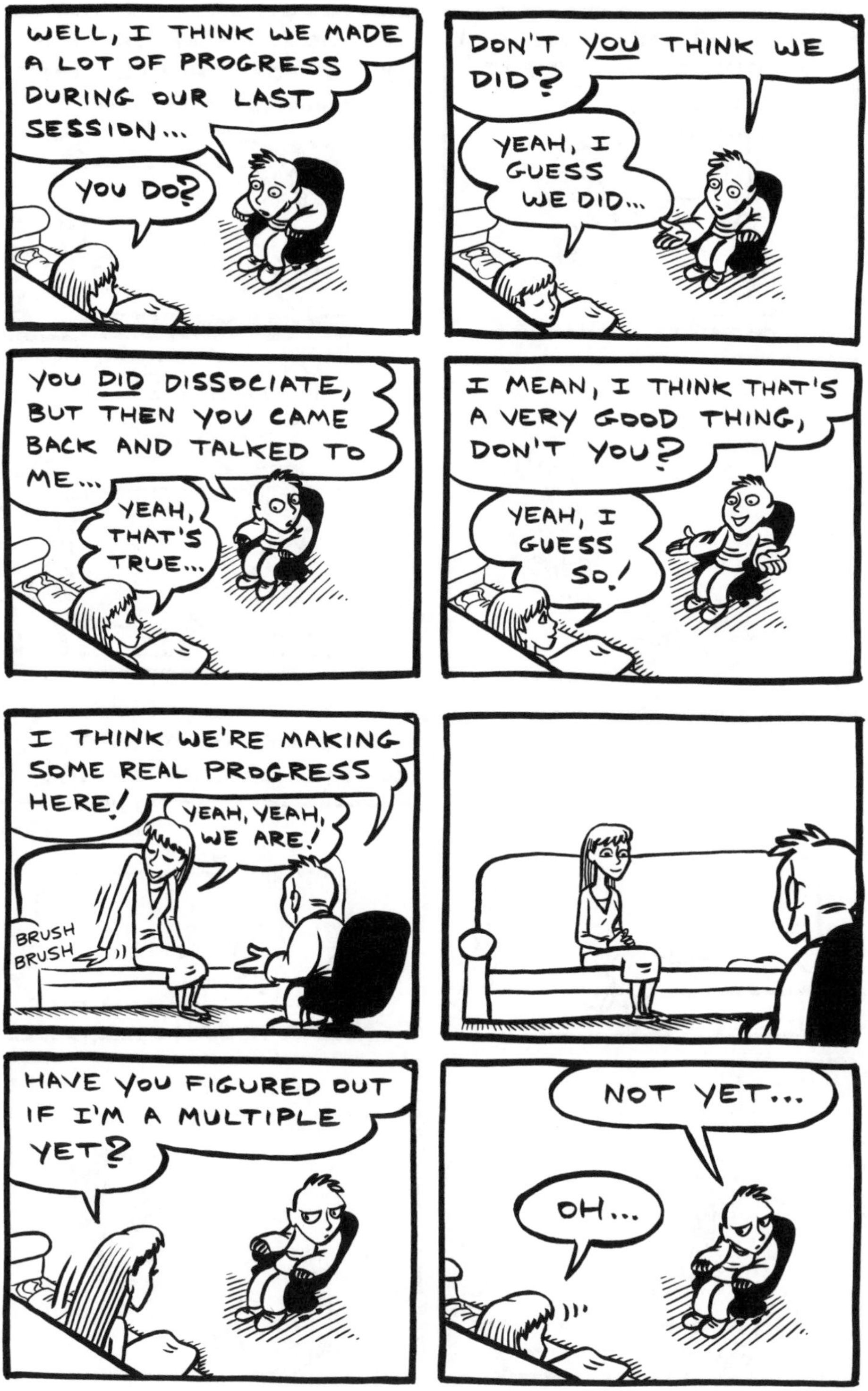
WELL, I THINK WE MADE A LOT OF PROGRESS DURING OUR LAST SESSION...
YOU DO?
DON'T YOU THINK WE DID?
YEAH, I GUESS WE DID...
YOU DID DISSOCIATE, BUT THEN YOU CAME BACK AND TALKED TO ME...
YEAH, THAT'S TRUE...
I MEAN, I THINK THAT'S A VERY GOOD THING, DON'T YOU?
YEAH, I GUESS SO!
I THINK WE'RE MAKING SOME REAL PROGRESS HERE!
YEAH, YEAH, WE ARE!
BRUSH BRUSH
HAVE YOU FIGURED OUT IF I'M A MULTIPLE YET?
NOT YET...
OH...

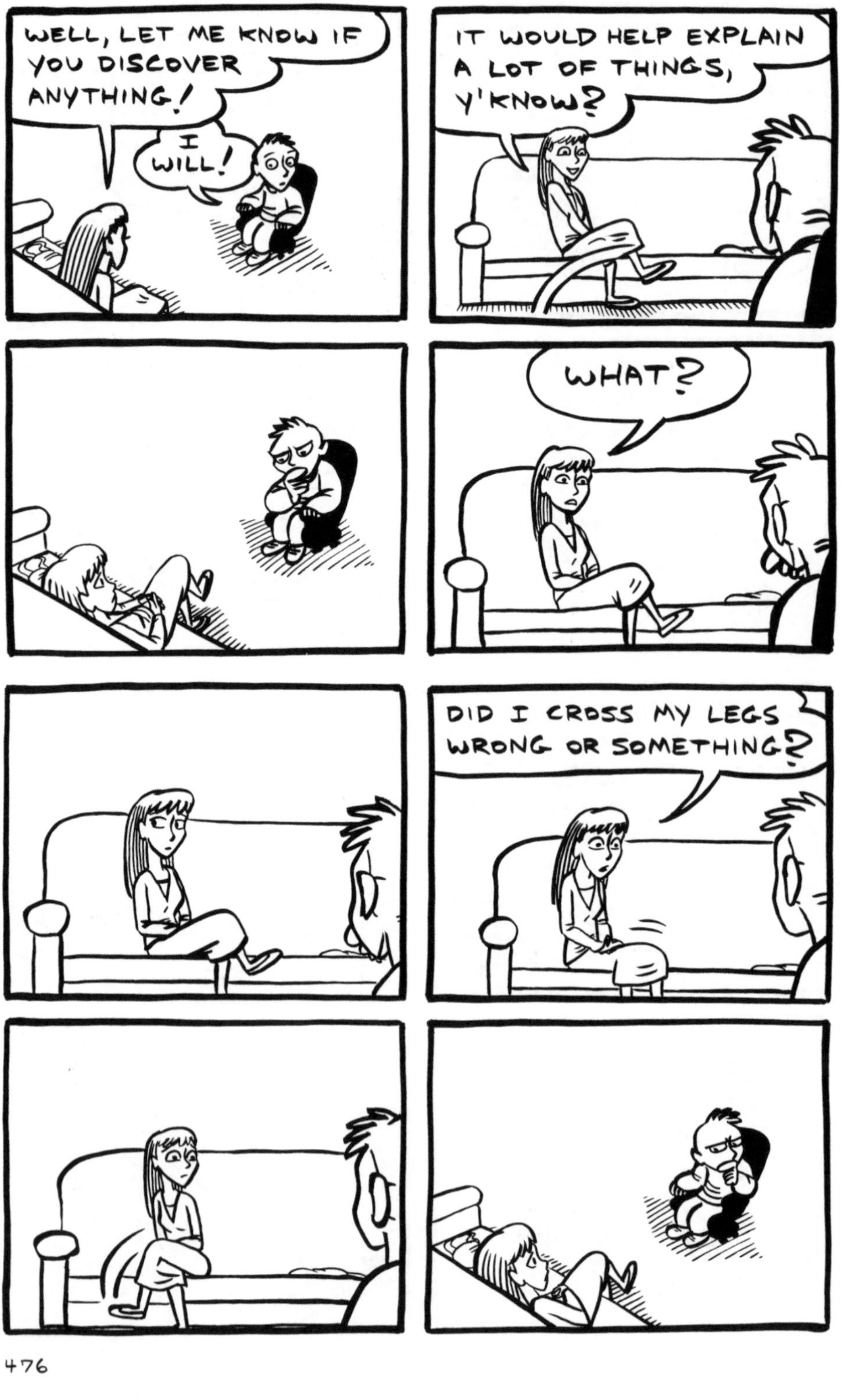
WELL, LET ME KNOW IF YOU DISCOVER ANYTHING!
I WILL!
IT WOULD HELP EXPLAIN A LOT OF THINGS, Y'KNOW?
WHAT?
DID I CROSS MY LEGS WRONG OR SOMETHING?

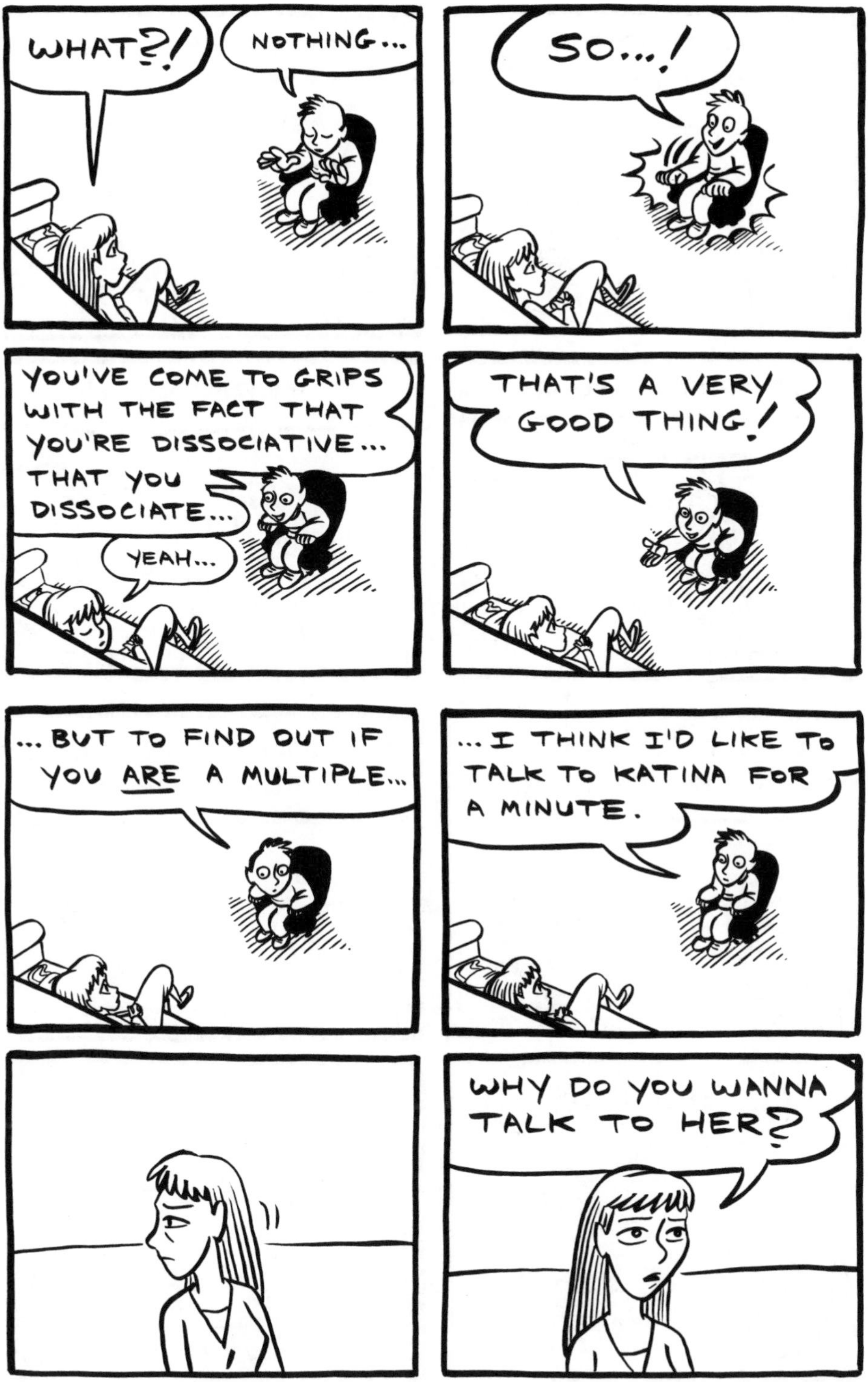
WHAT?!
NOTHING...
SO...!
YOU'VE COME TO GRIPS WITH THE FACT THAT YOU'RE DISSOCIATIVE... THAT YOU DISSOCIATE...
YEAH...
THAT'S A VERY GOOD THING!
... BUT TO FIND OUT IF YOU ARE A MULTIPLE...
... I THINK I'D LIKE TO TALK TO KATINA FOR A MINUTE.
WHY DO YOU WANNA TALK TO HER?

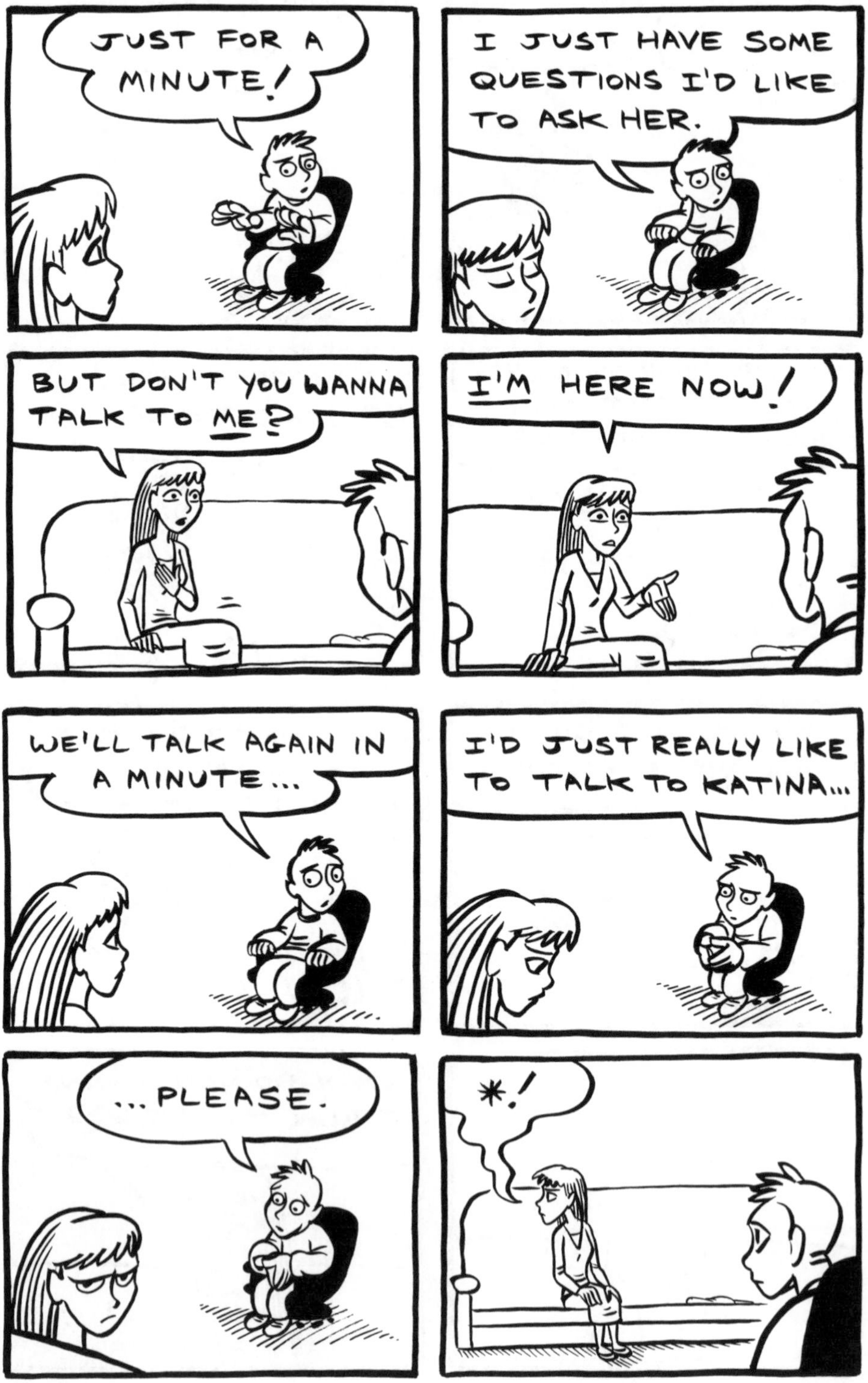
JUST FOR A MINUTE!
I JUST HAVE SOME QUESTIONS I'D LIKE TO ASK HER.
BUT DON'T YOU WANNA TALK TO ME?
I'M HERE NOW!
WE'LL TALK AGAIN IN A MINUTE...
I'D JUST REALLY LIKE TO TALK TO KATINA...
...PLEASE.
*!

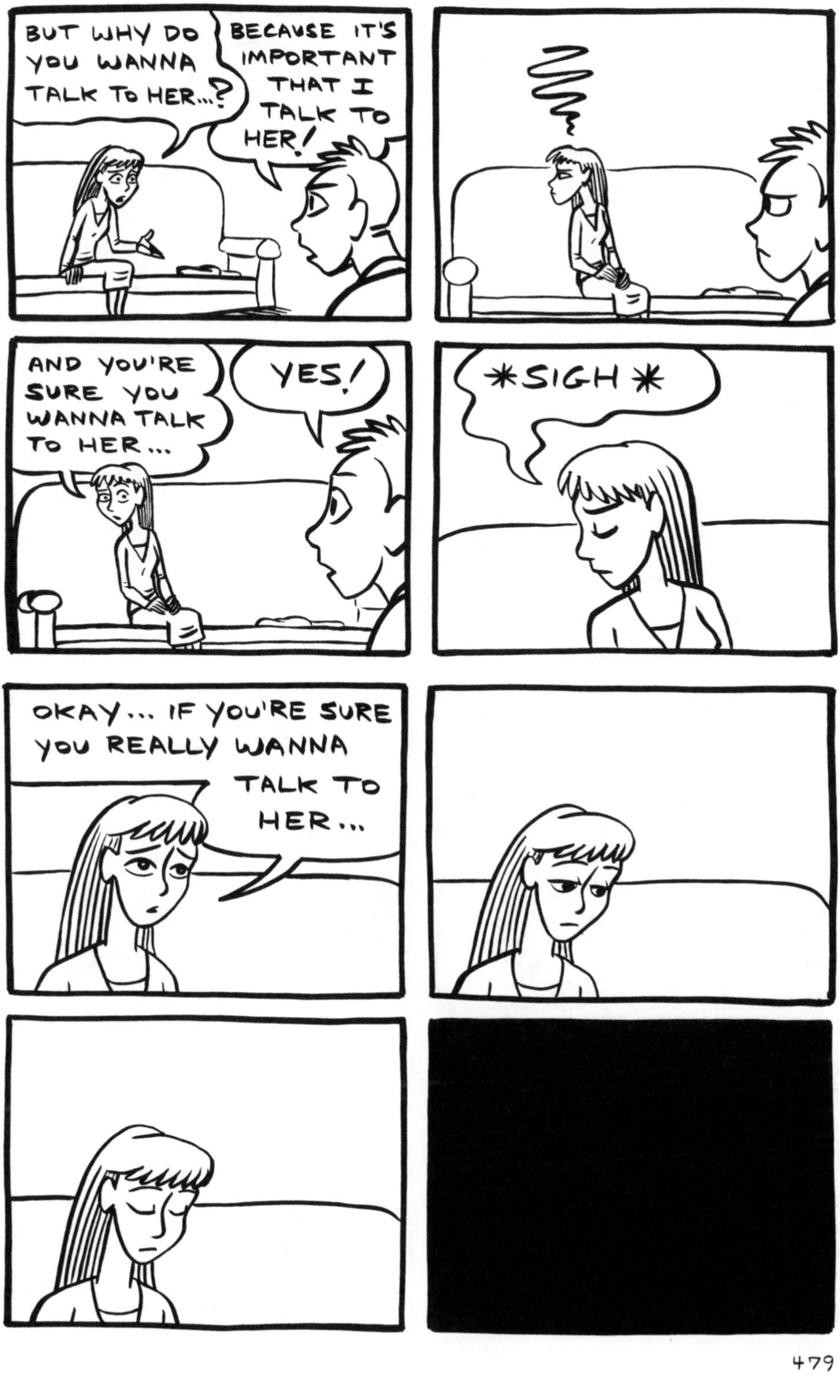
BUT WHY DO YOU WANNA TALK TO HER...?
BECAUSE IT'S IMPORTANT THAT I TALK TO HER!
AND YOU'RE SURE YOU WANNA TALK TO HER...
YES!
SIGH
OKAY... IF YOU'RE SURE YOU REALLY WANNA TALK TO HER...

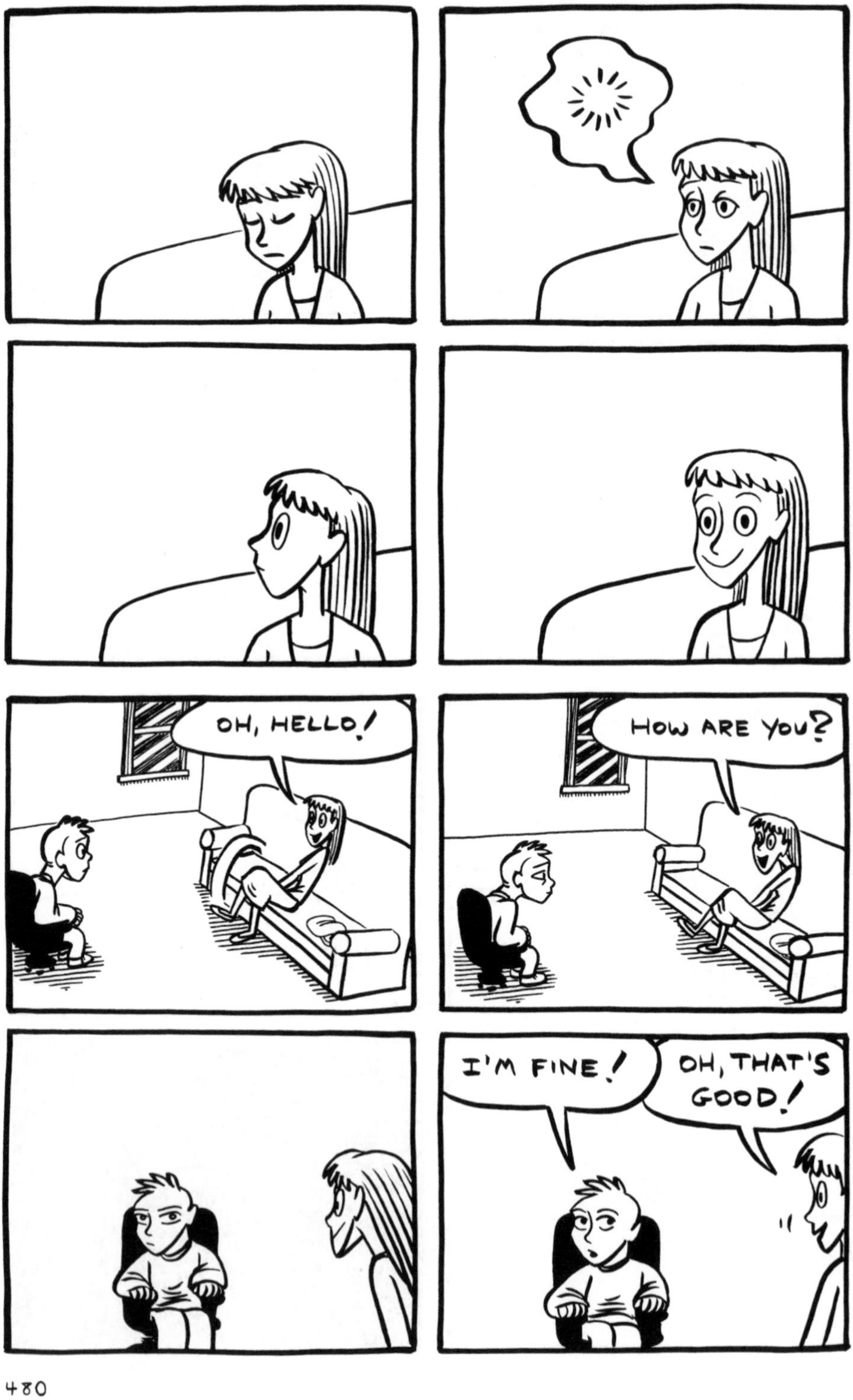
OH, HELLO!
HOW ARE YOU?
I'M FINE!
OH, THAT'S GOOD!

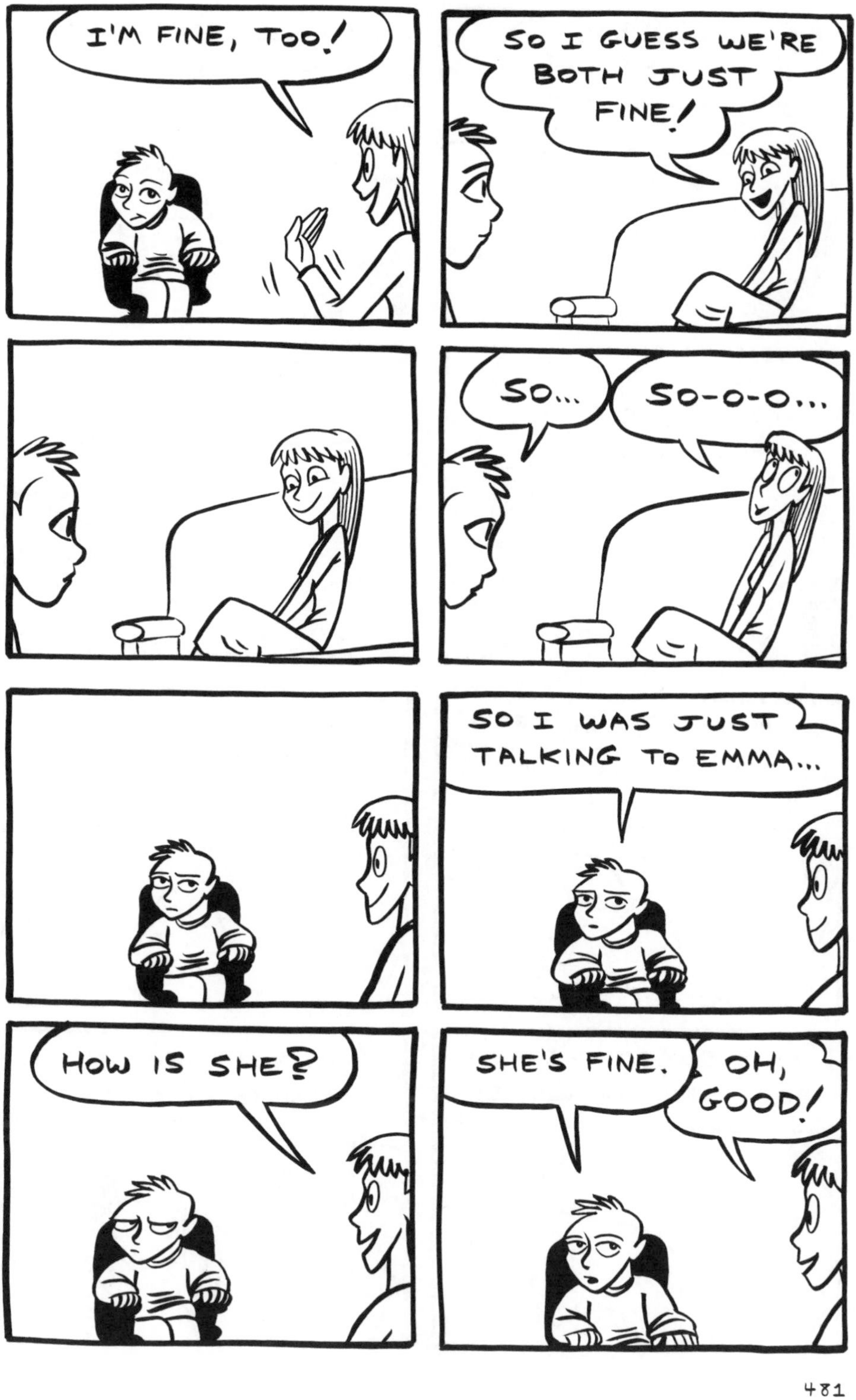
I'M FINE, TOO!
SO I GUESS WE'RE BOTH JUST FINE!
SO...
SO-O-O...
SO I WAS JUST TALKING TO EMMA...
HOW IS SHE?
SHE'S FINE.
OH, GOOD!

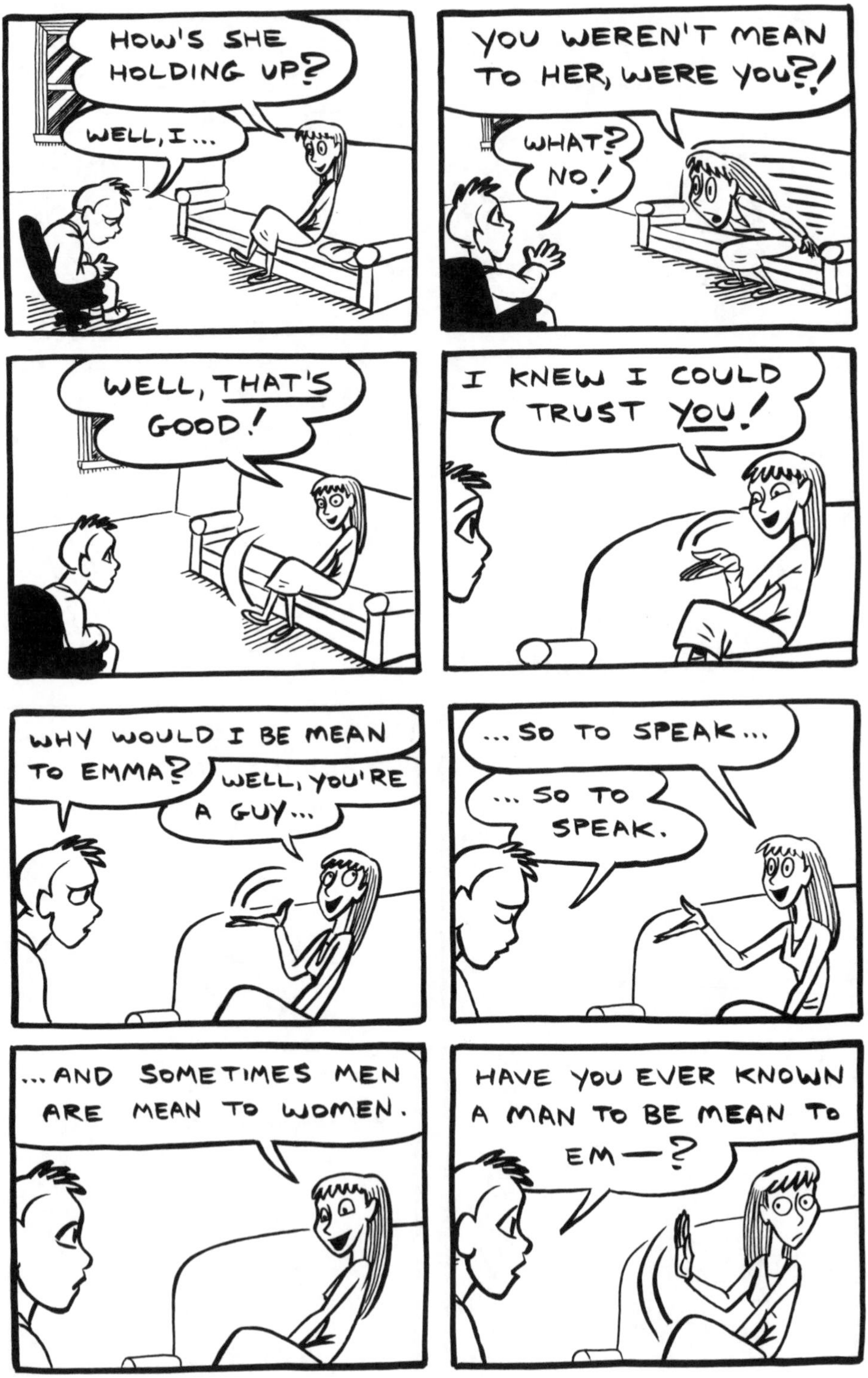
HOW'S SHE HOLDING UP?
WELL, I...
YOU WEREN'T MEAN TO HER, WERE YOU?!
WHAT? NO!
WELL, THAT'S GOOD!
I KNEW I COULD TRUST YOU!
WHY WOULD I BE MEAN TO EMMA?
WELL, YOU'RE A GUY...
...SO TO SPEAK...
...SO TO SPEAK.
...AND SOMETIMES MEN ARE MEAN TO WOMEN.
HAVE YOU EVER KNOWN A MAN TO BE MEAN TO EM—?

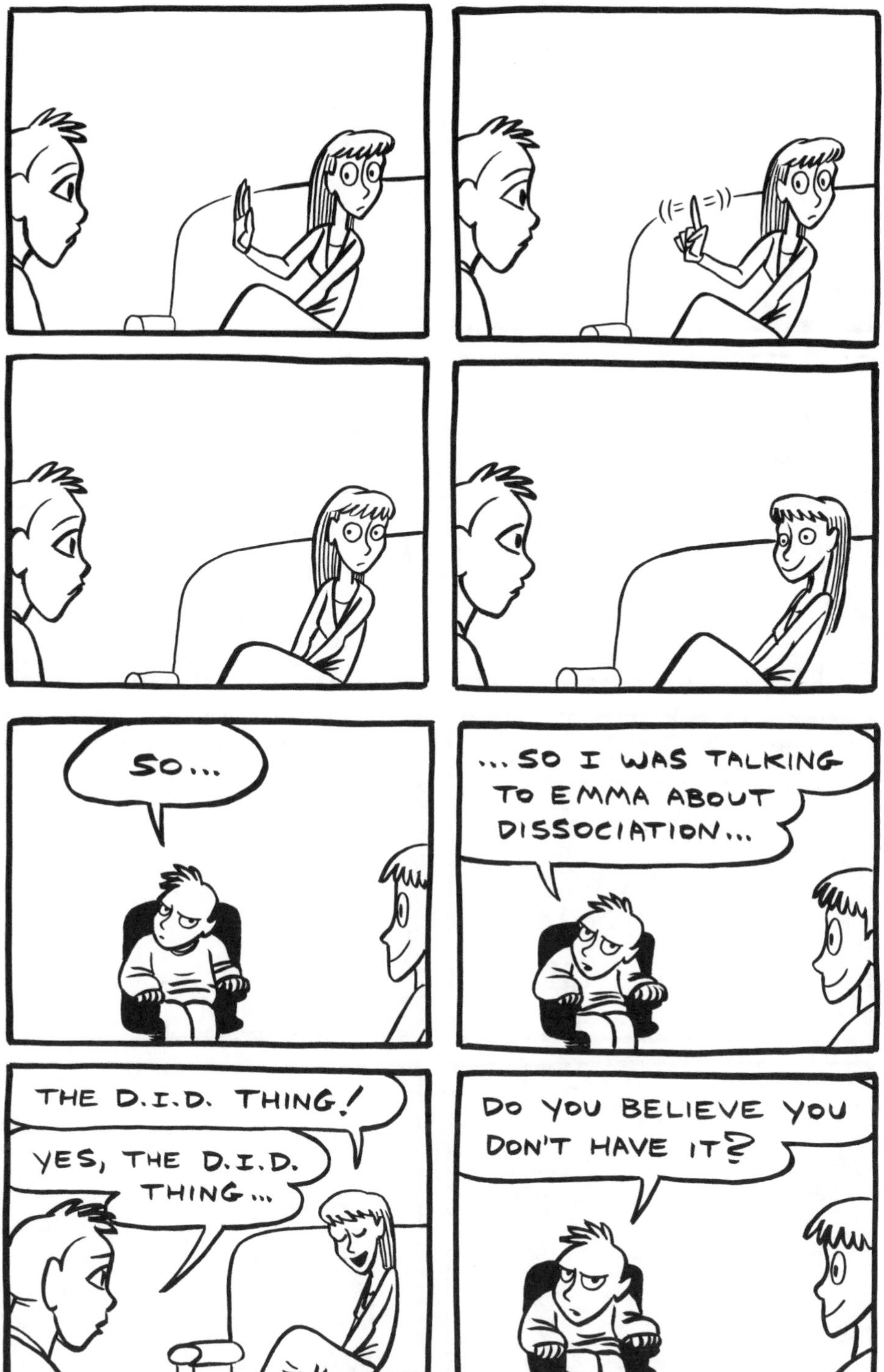
SO...
...SO I WAS TALKING TO EMMA ABOUT DISSOCIATION...
THE D.I.D. THING!
YES, THE D.I.D. THING...
DO YOU BELIEVE YOU DON'T HAVE IT?

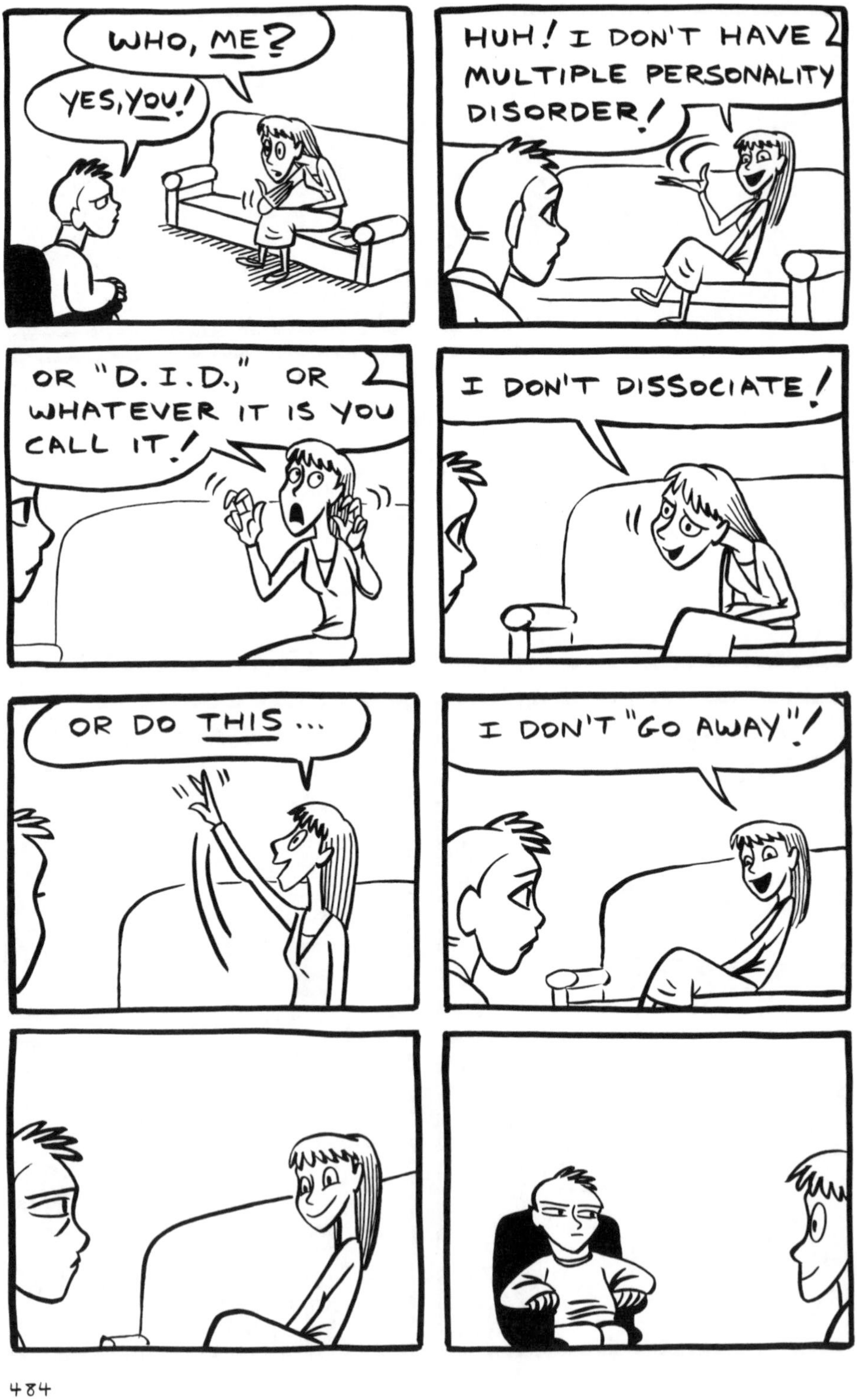
WHO, ME?
YES, YOU!
HUH! I DON'T HAVE MULTIPLE PERSONALITY DISORDER!
OR "D.I.D.," OR WHATEVER IT IS YOU CALL IT!
I DON'T DISSOCIATE!
OR DO THIS...
I DON'T "GO AWAY"!

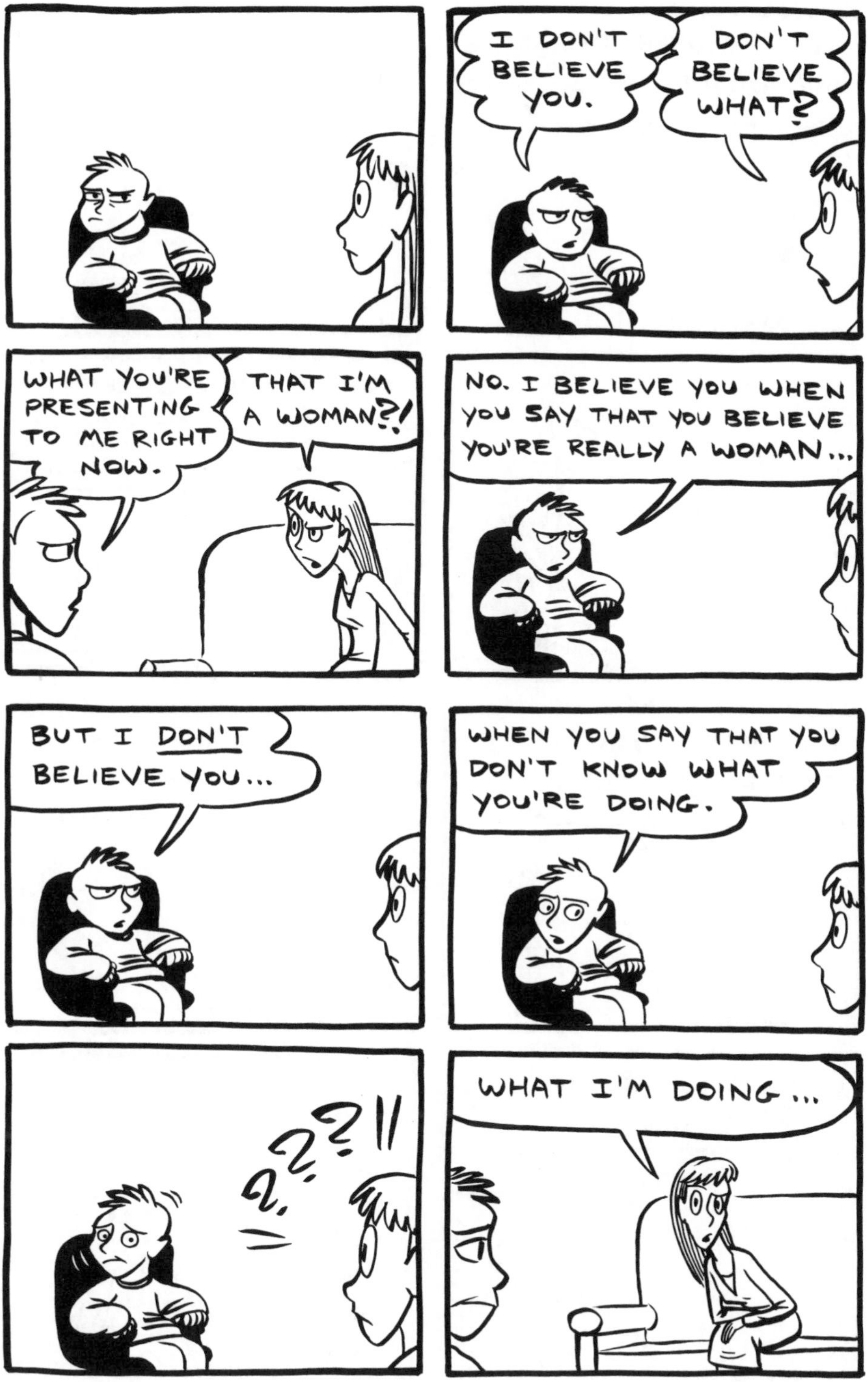
I DON'T BELIEVE YOU.
DON'T BELIEVE WHAT?
WHAT YOU'RE PRESENTING TO ME RIGHT NOW.
THAT I'M A WOMAN?!
NO. I BELIEVE YOU WHEN YOU SAY THAT YOU BELIEVE YOU'RE REALLY A WOMAN...
BUT I DON'T BELIEVE YOU...
WHEN YOU SAY THAT YOU DON'T KNOW WHAT YOU'RE DOING.
WHAT I'M DOING...

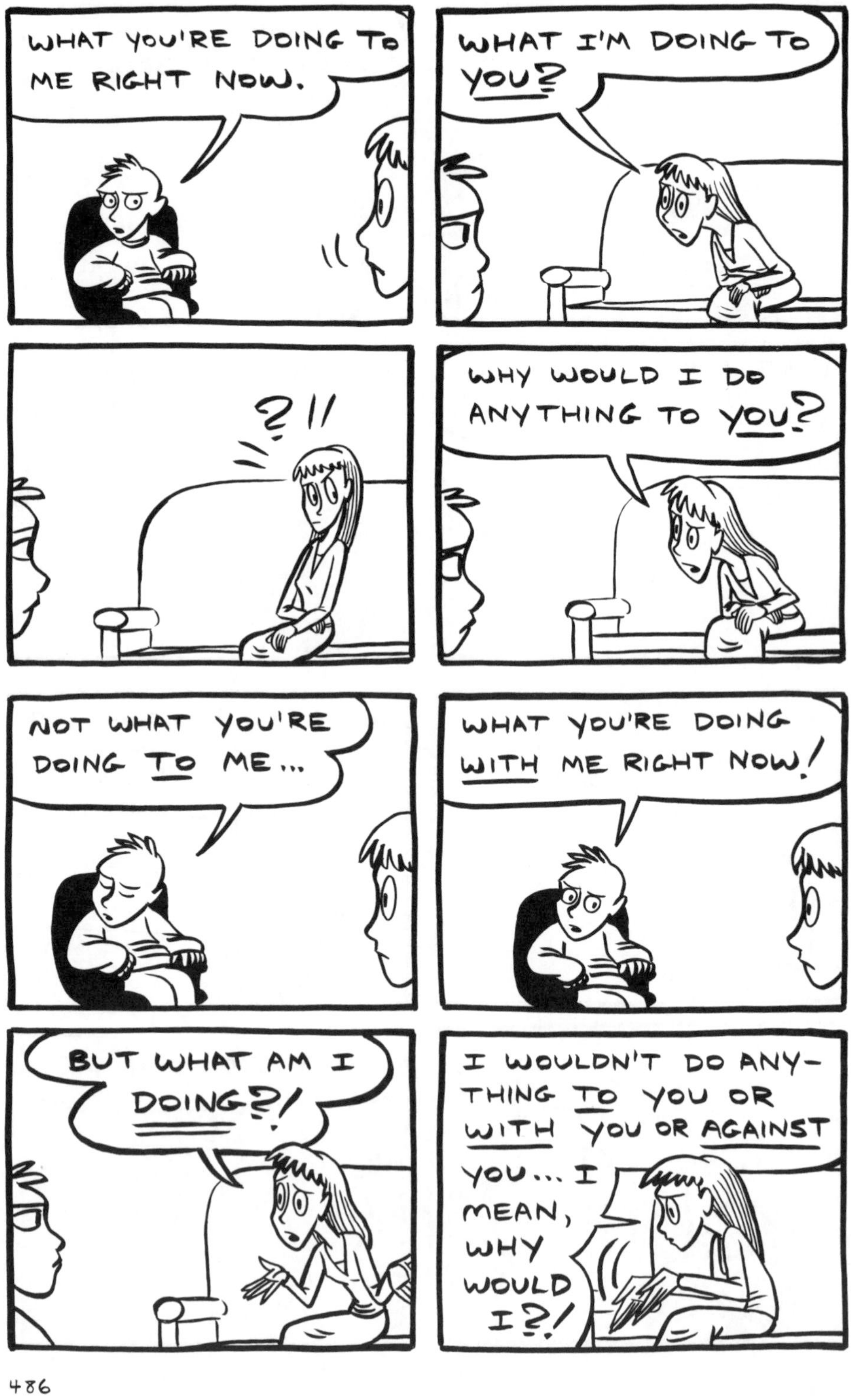
WHAT YOU'RE DOING TO ME RIGHT NOW.
WHAT I'M DOING TO YOU?
?!!
WHY WOULD I DO ANYTHING TO YOU?
NOT WHAT YOU'RE DOING TO ME...
WHAT YOU'RE DOING WITH ME RIGHT NOW!
BUT WHAT AM I DOING?!
I WOULDN'T DO ANYTHING TO YOU OR WITH YOU OR AGAINST YOU... I MEAN, WHY WOULD I?!

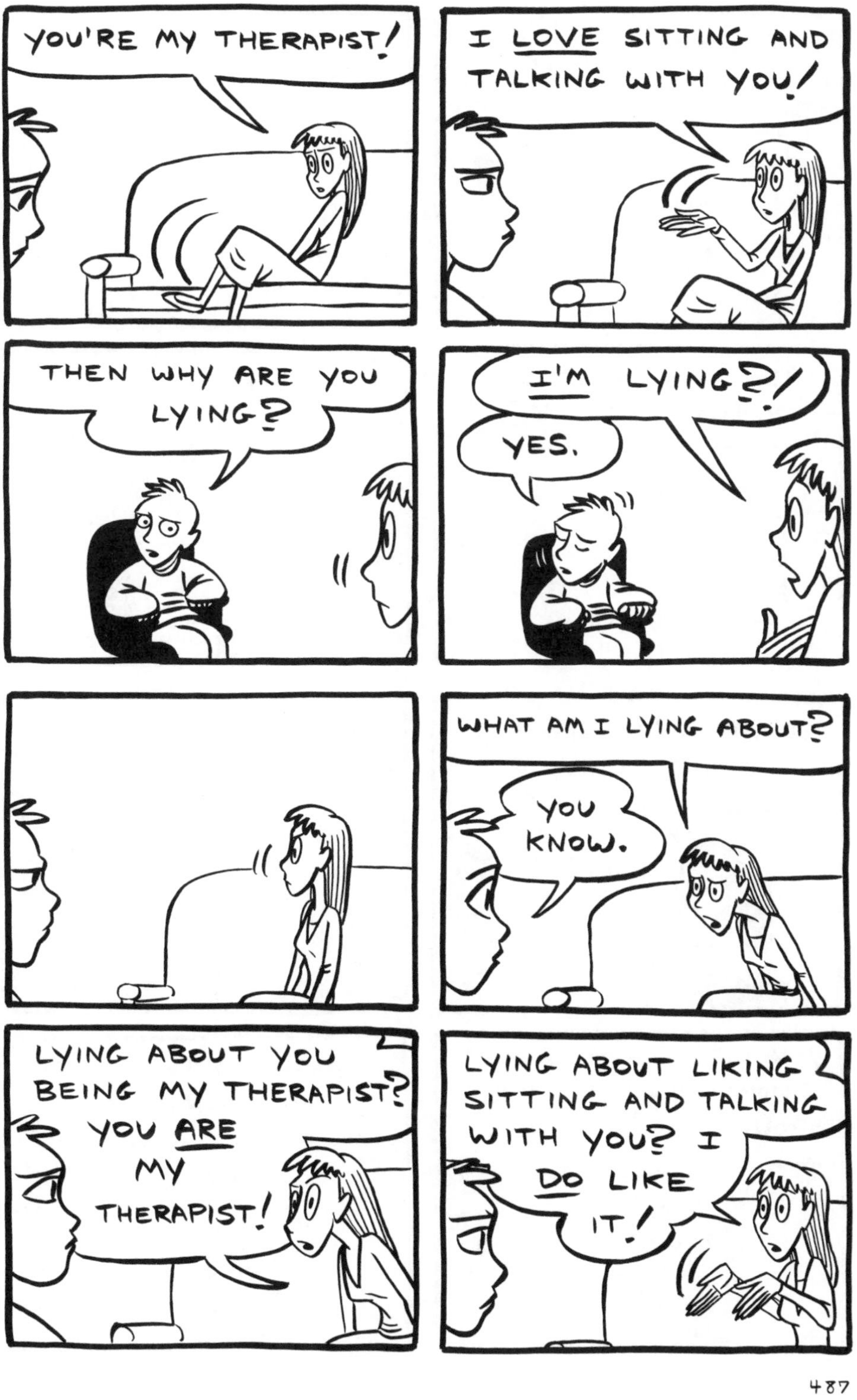
YOU'RE MY THERAPIST!
I LOVE SITTING AND TALKING WITH YOU!
THEN WHY ARE YOU LYING?
I'M LYING?!
YES.
WHAT AM I LYING ABOUT?
YOU KNOW.
LYING ABOUT YOU BEING MY THERAPIST? YOU ARE MY THERAPIST!
LYING ABOUT LIKING SITTING AND TALKING WITH YOU? I DO LIKE IT!

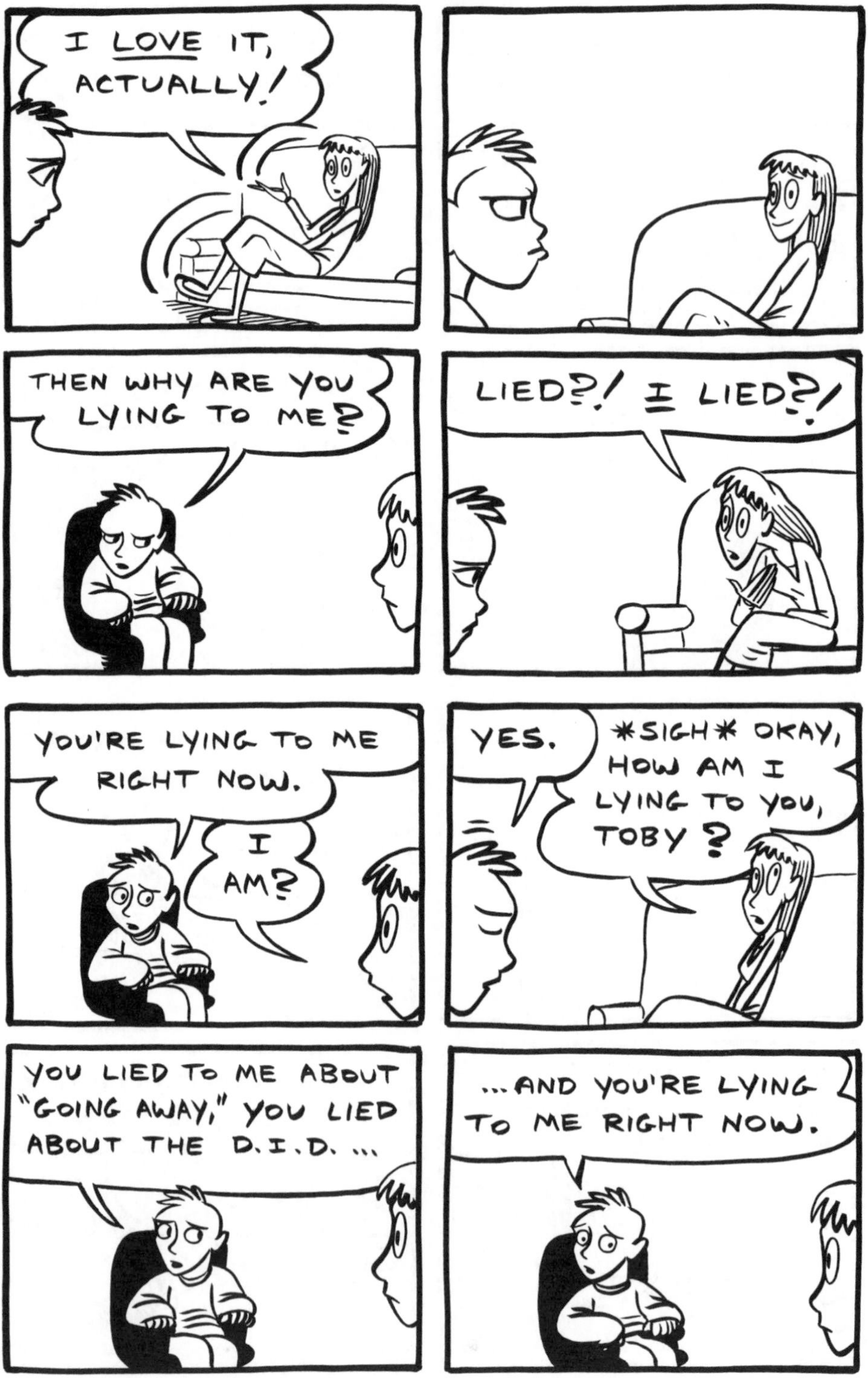
I LOVE IT, ACTUALLY!
THEN WHY ARE YOU LYING TO ME?
LIED?! I LIED?!
YOU'RE LYING TO ME RIGHT NOW.
I AM?
YES.
SIGH OKAY, HOW AM I LYING TO YOU, TOBY?
YOU LIED TO ME ABOUT "GOING AWAY," YOU LIED ABOUT THE D.I.D. ...
...AND YOU'RE LYING TO ME RIGHT NOW.

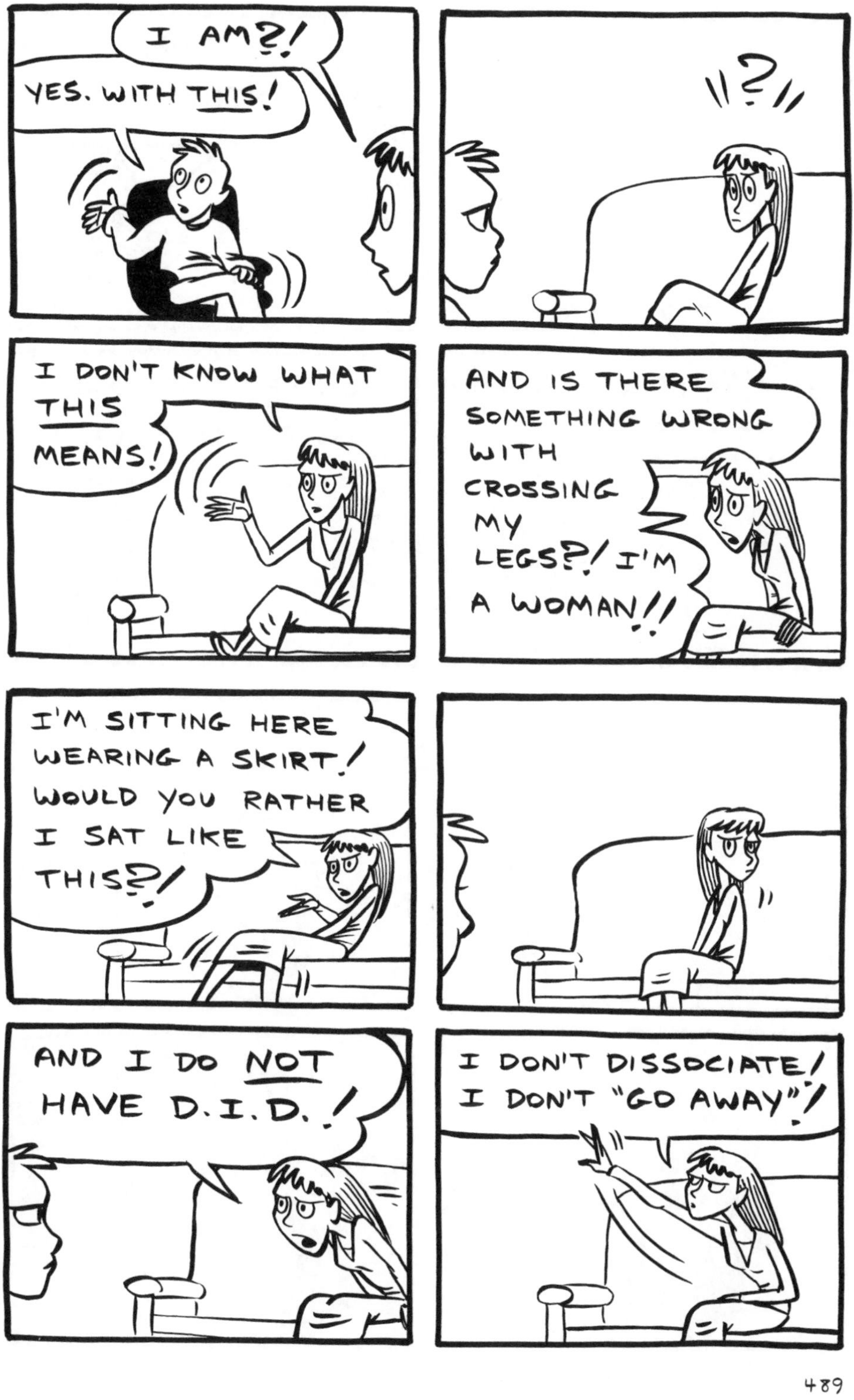
I AM?!
YES. WITH THIS!
?
I DON'T KNOW WHAT THIS MEANS!
AND IS THERE SOMETHING WRONG WITH CROSSING MY LEGS?! I'M A WOMAN!!
I'M SITTING HERE WEARING A SKIRT! WOULD YOU RATHER I SAT LIKE THIS?!
AND I DO NOT HAVE D.I.D.!
I DON'T DISSOCIATE! I DON'T "GO AWAY"!

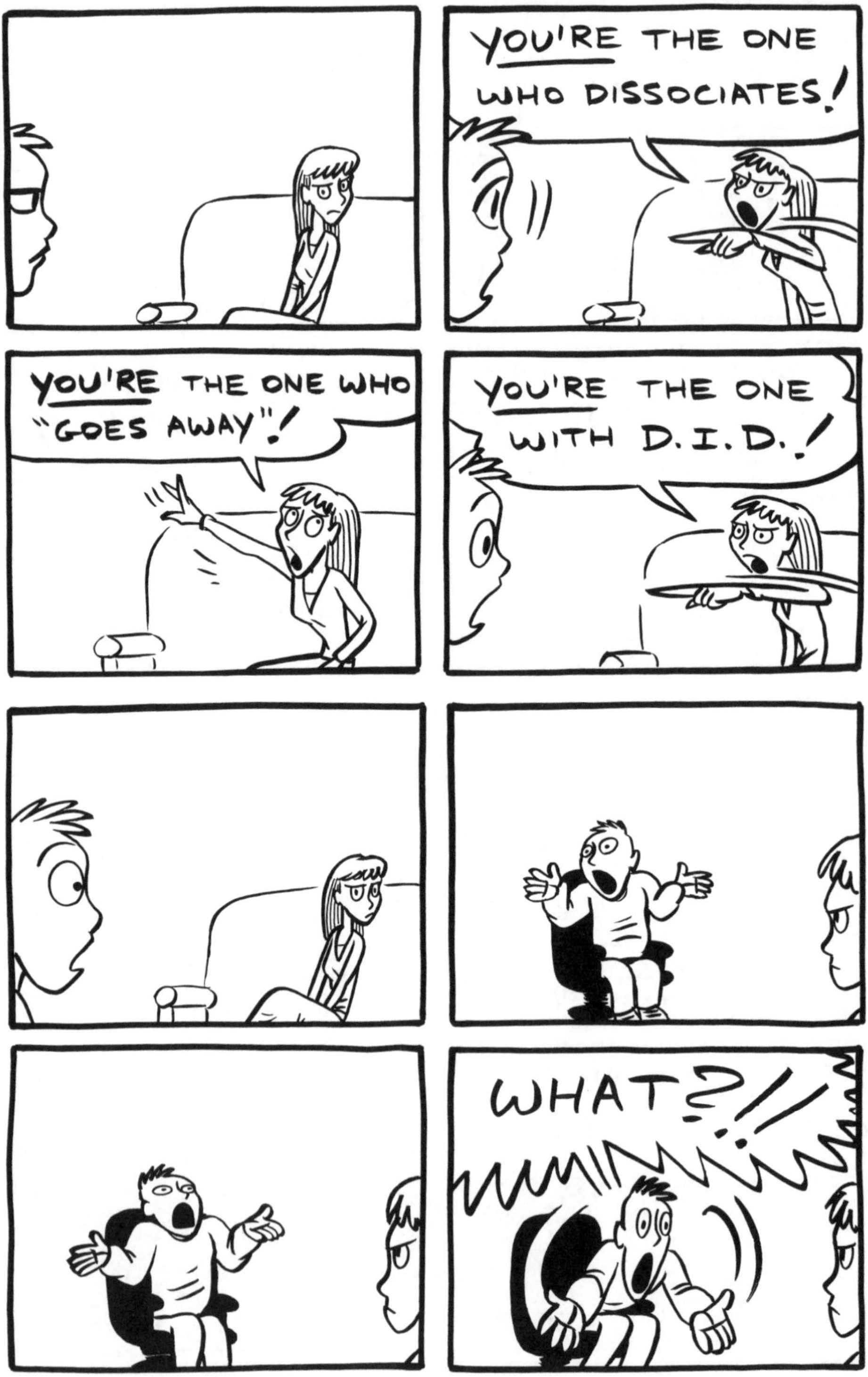
YOU'RE THE ONE WHO DISSOCIATES!
YOU'RE THE ONE WHO "GOES AWAY"!
YOU'RE THE ONE WITH D.I.D.!
WHAT?!!

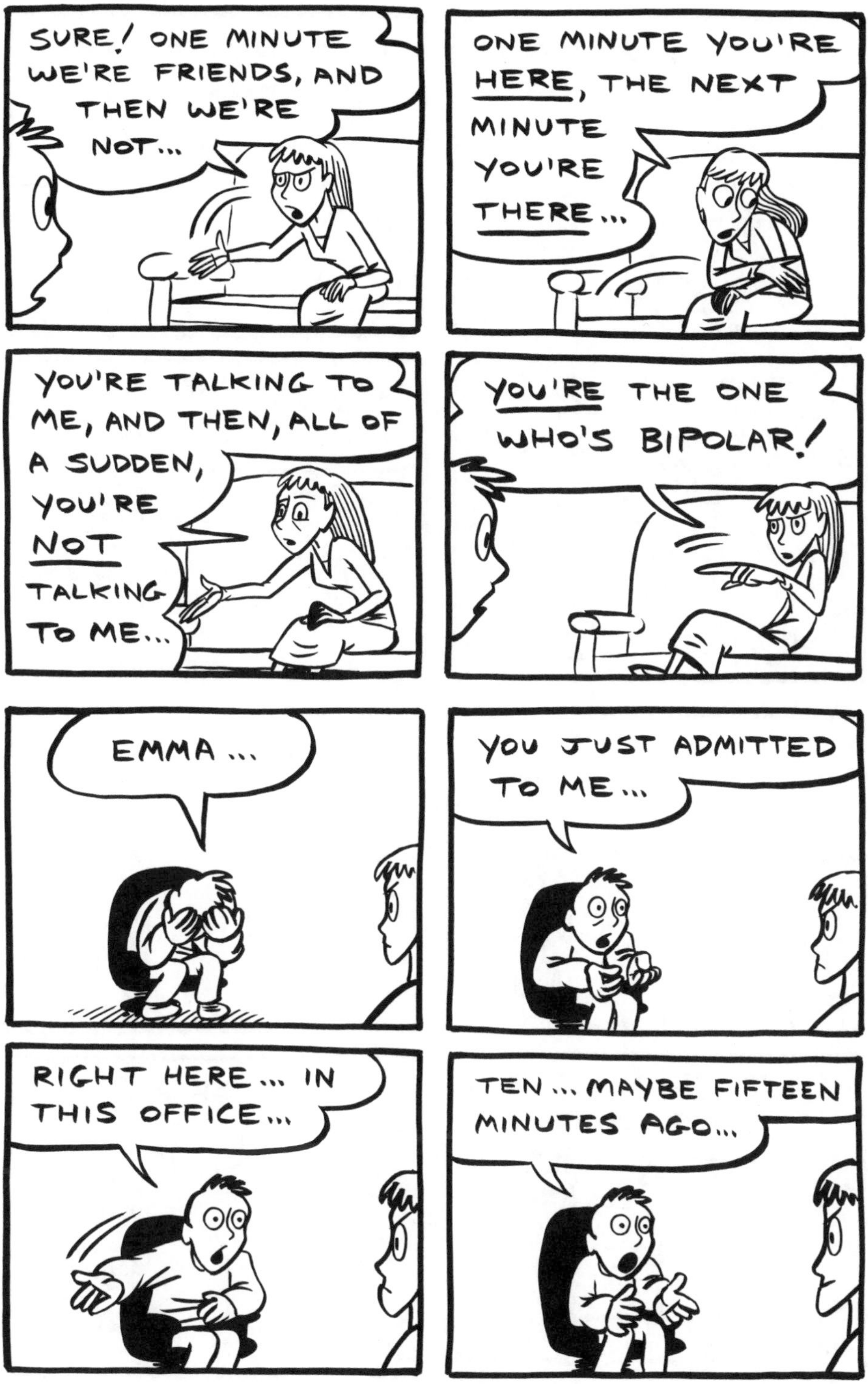
SURE! ONE MINUTE WE'RE FRIENDS, AND THEN WE'RE NOT...
ONE MINUTE YOU'RE HERE, THE NEXT MINUTE YOU'RE THERE...
YOU'RE TALKING TO ME, AND THEN, ALL OF A SUDDEN, YOU'RE NOT TALKING TO ME...
YOU'RE THE ONE WHO'S BIPOLAR!
EMMA...
YOU JUST ADMITTED TO ME...
RIGHT HERE... IN THIS OFFICE...
TEN... MAYBE FIFTEEN MINUTES AGO...

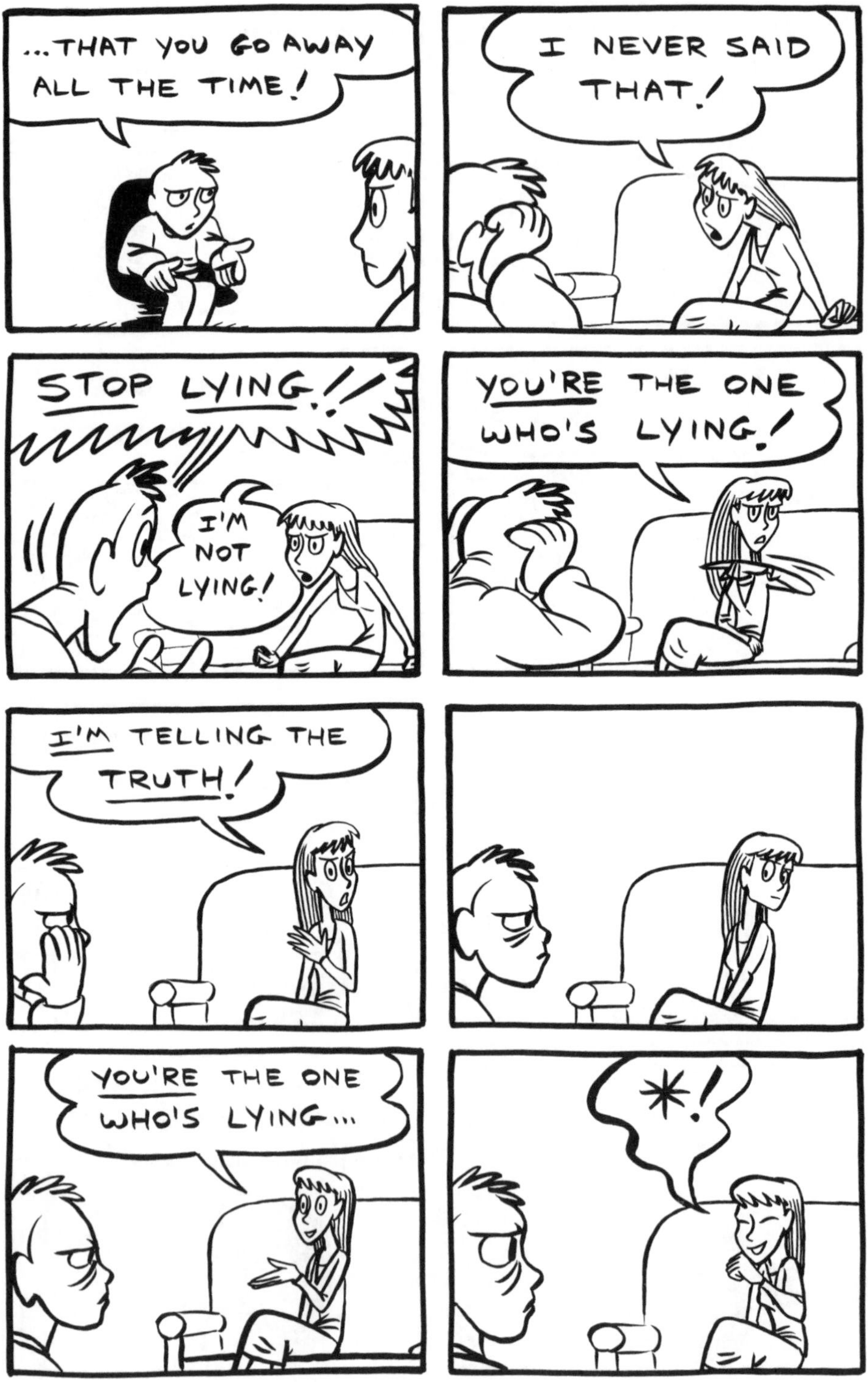
...THAT YOU GO AWAY ALL THE TIME!
I NEVER SAID THAT!
STOP LYING!!
I'M NOT LYING!
YOU'RE THE ONE WHO'S LYING!
I'M TELLING THE TRUTH!
YOU'RE THE ONE WHO'S LYING...
*!

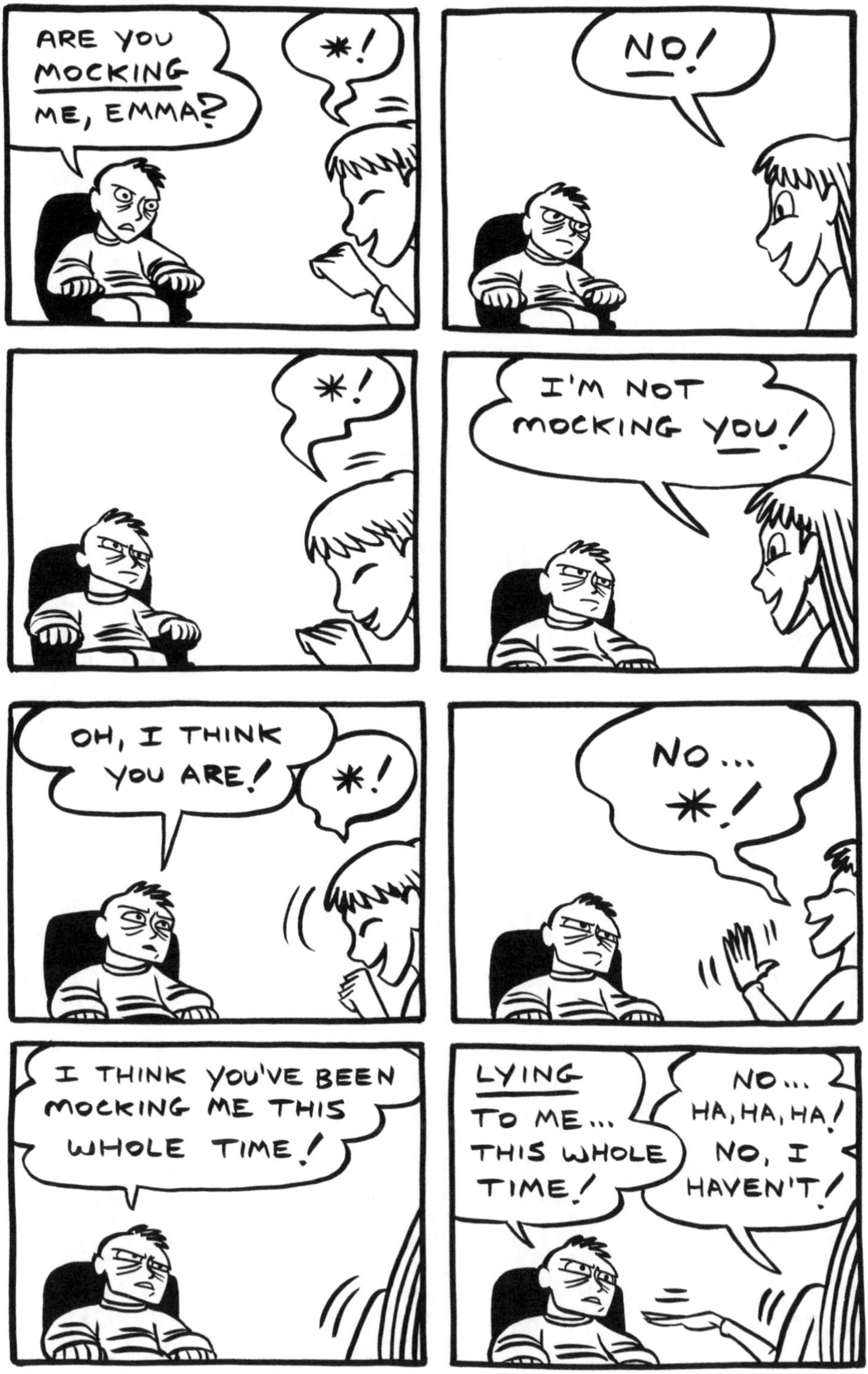
ARE YOU MOCKING ME, EMMA?
*!
NO!
*!
I'M NOT MOCKING YOU!
OH, I THINK YOU ARE!
*!
NO... *!
I THINK YOU'VE BEEN MOCKING ME THIS WHOLE TIME!
LYING TO ME... THIS WHOLE TIME!
NO... HA, HA, HA! NO, I HAVEN'T!

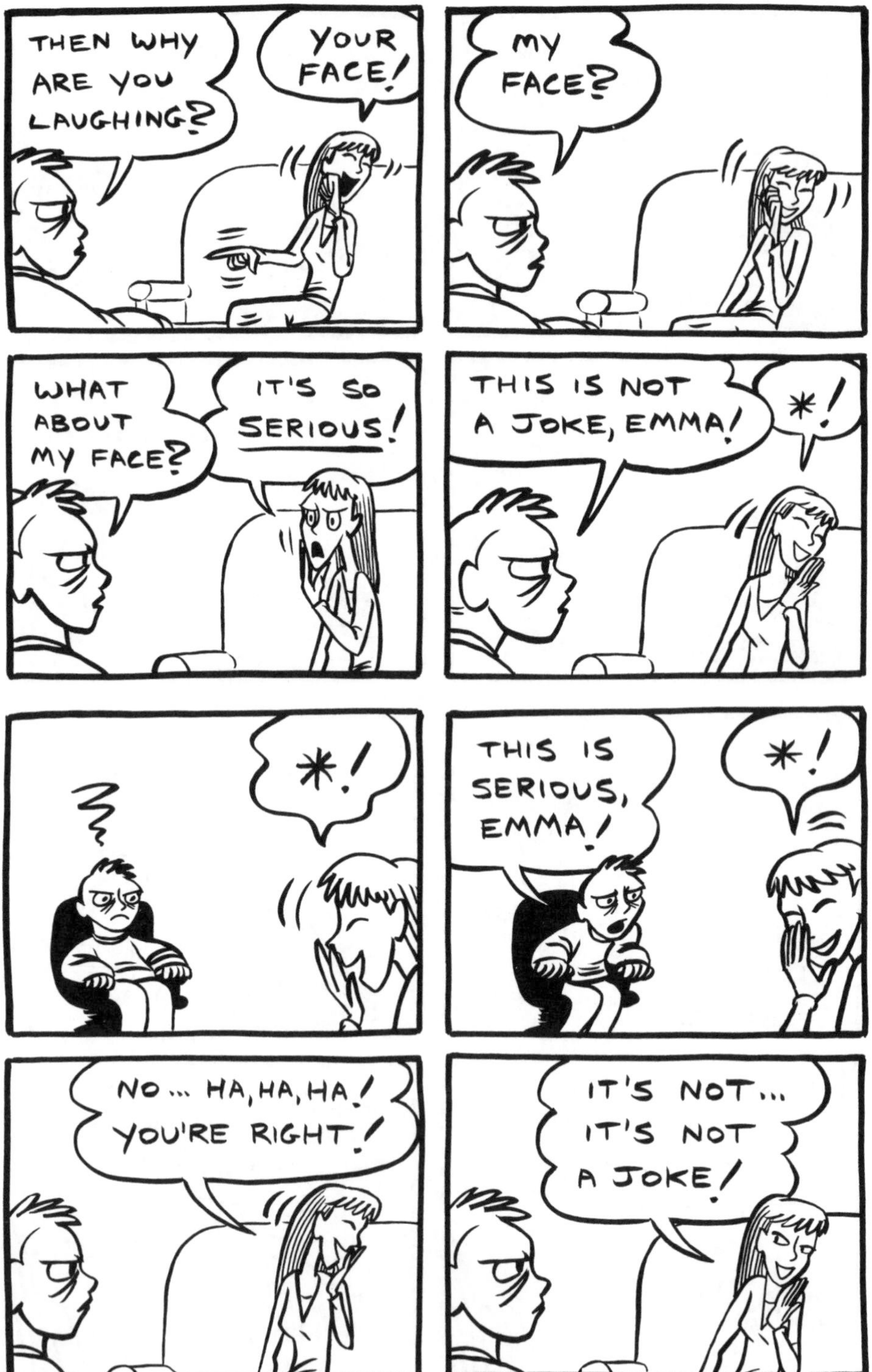
THEN WHY ARE YOU LAUGHING?
YOUR FACE!
MY FACE?
WHAT ABOUT MY FACE?
IT'S SO SERIOUS!
THIS IS NOT A JOKE, EMMA!
*!
*!
THIS IS SERIOUS, EMMA!
*!
NO... HA, HA, HA! YOU'RE RIGHT!
IT'S NOT... IT'S NOT A JOKE!

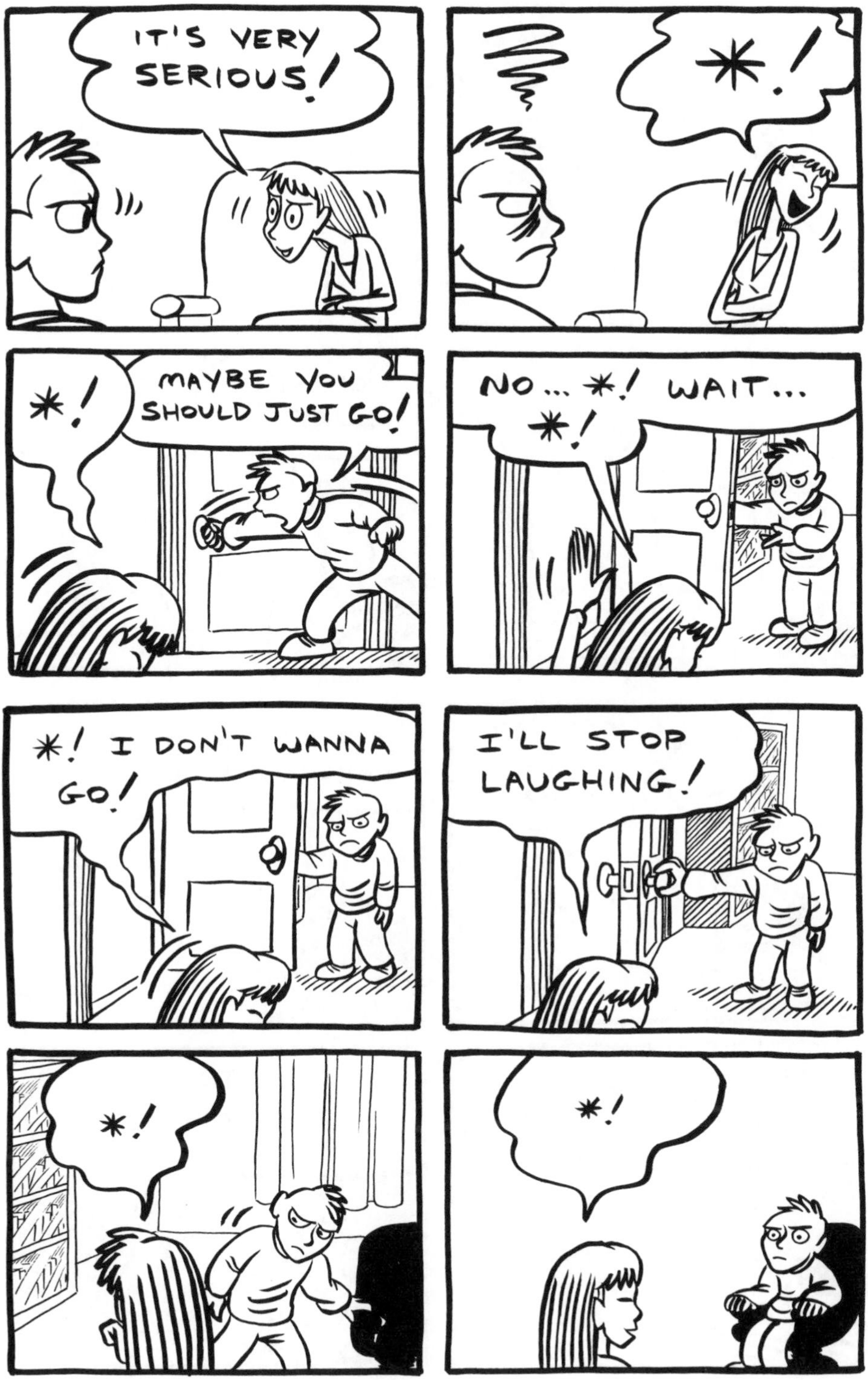
IT'S VERY SERIOUS!
*!
*!
MAYBE YOU SHOULD JUST GO!
NO... *! WAIT... *!
*! I DON'T WANNA GO!
I'LL STOP LAUGHING!
*!
*!

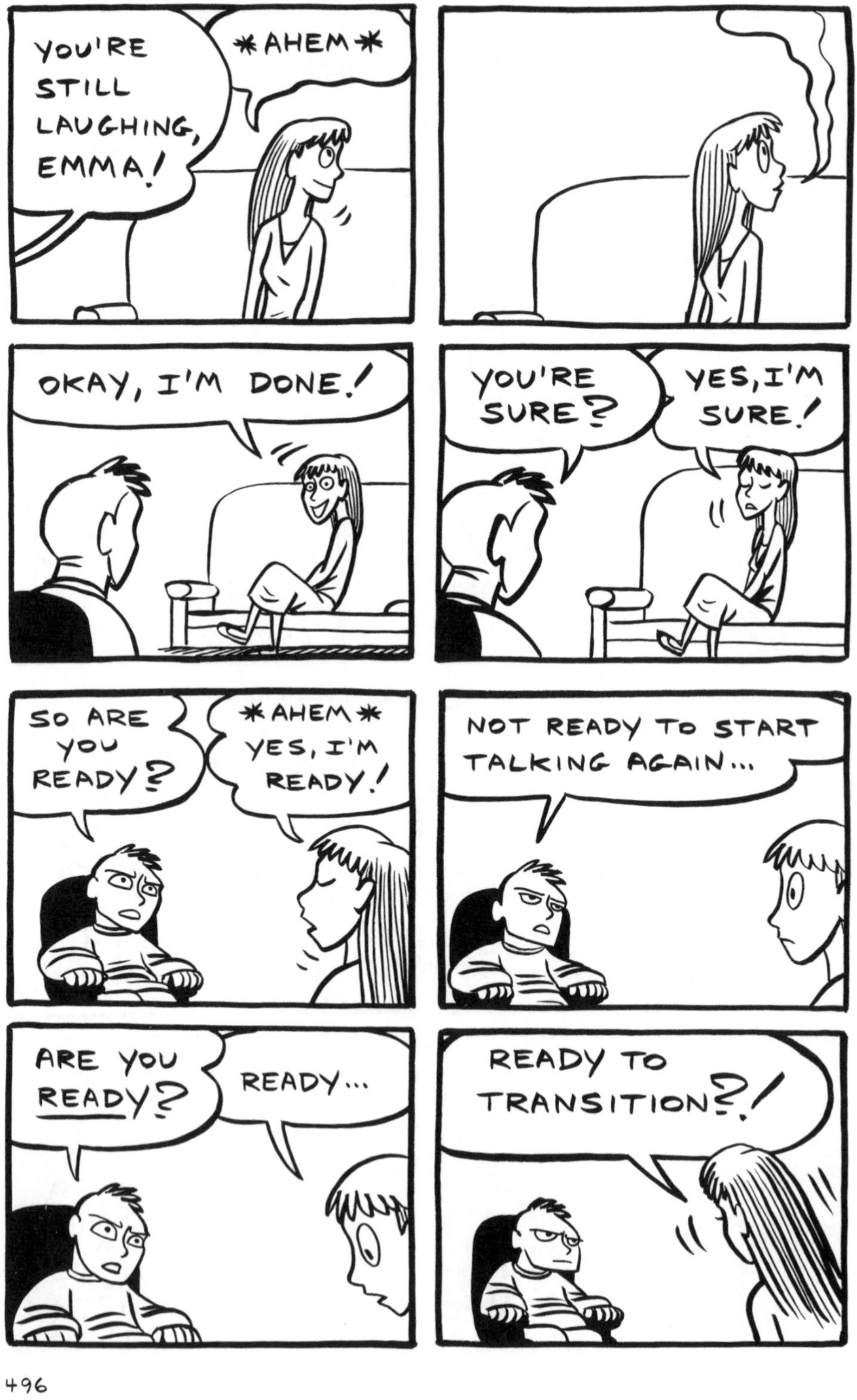
YOU'RE STILL LAUGHING, EMMA!
AHEM
OKAY, I'M DONE!
YOU'RE SURE?
YES, I'M SURE!
SO ARE YOU READY?
AHEM YES, I'M READY!
NOT READY TO START TALKING AGAIN...
ARE YOU READY?
READY...
READY TO TRANSITION?!

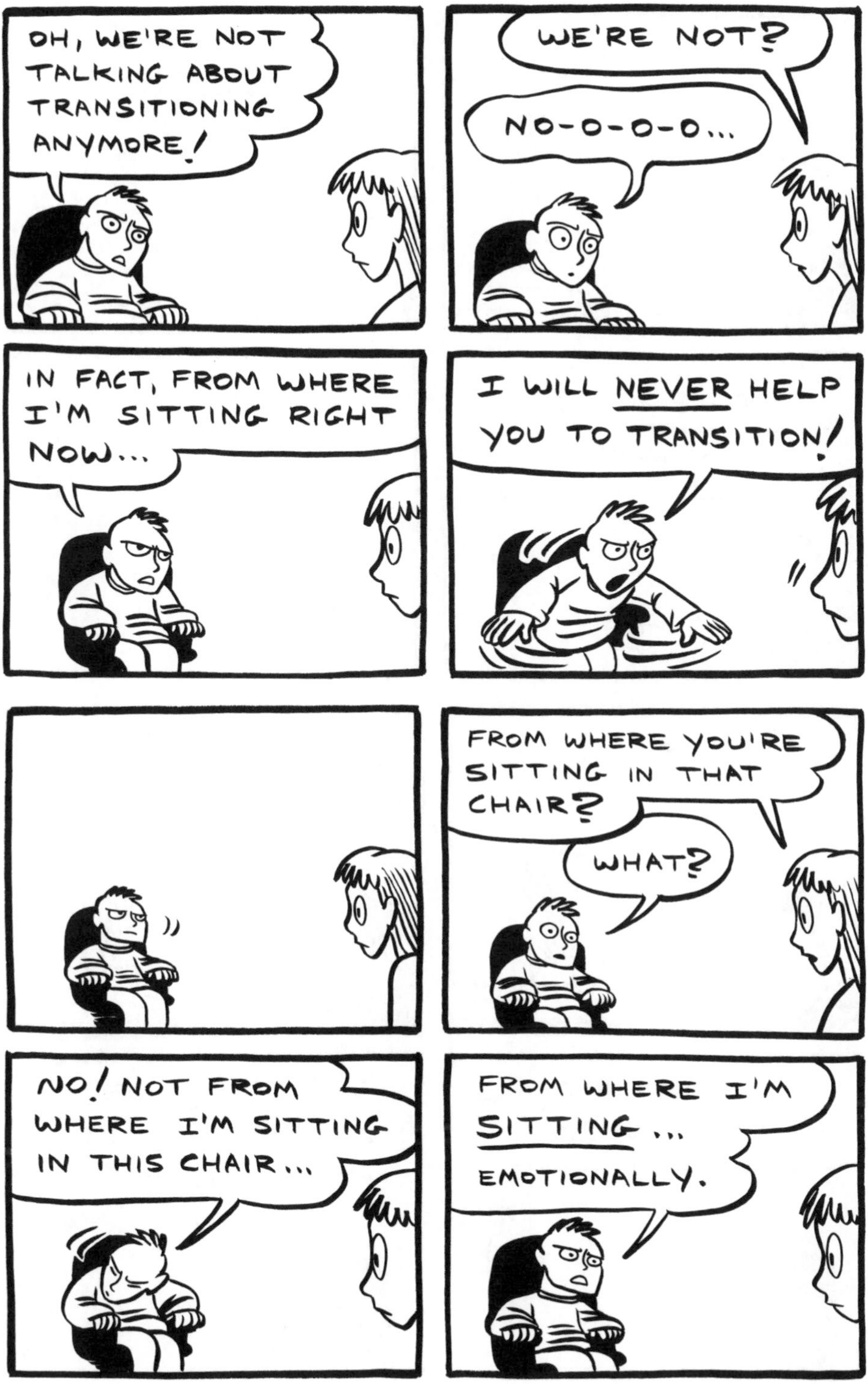
OH, WE'RE NOT TALKING ABOUT TRANSITIONING ANYMORE!
WE'RE NOT?
NO-O-O-O...
IN FACT, FROM WHERE I'M SITTING RIGHT NOW...
I WILL NEVER HELP YOU TO TRANSITION!
FROM WHERE YOU'RE SITTING IN THAT CHAIR?
WHAT?
NO! NOT FROM WHERE I'M SITTING IN THIS CHAIR...
FROM WHERE I'M SITTING... EMOTIONALLY.

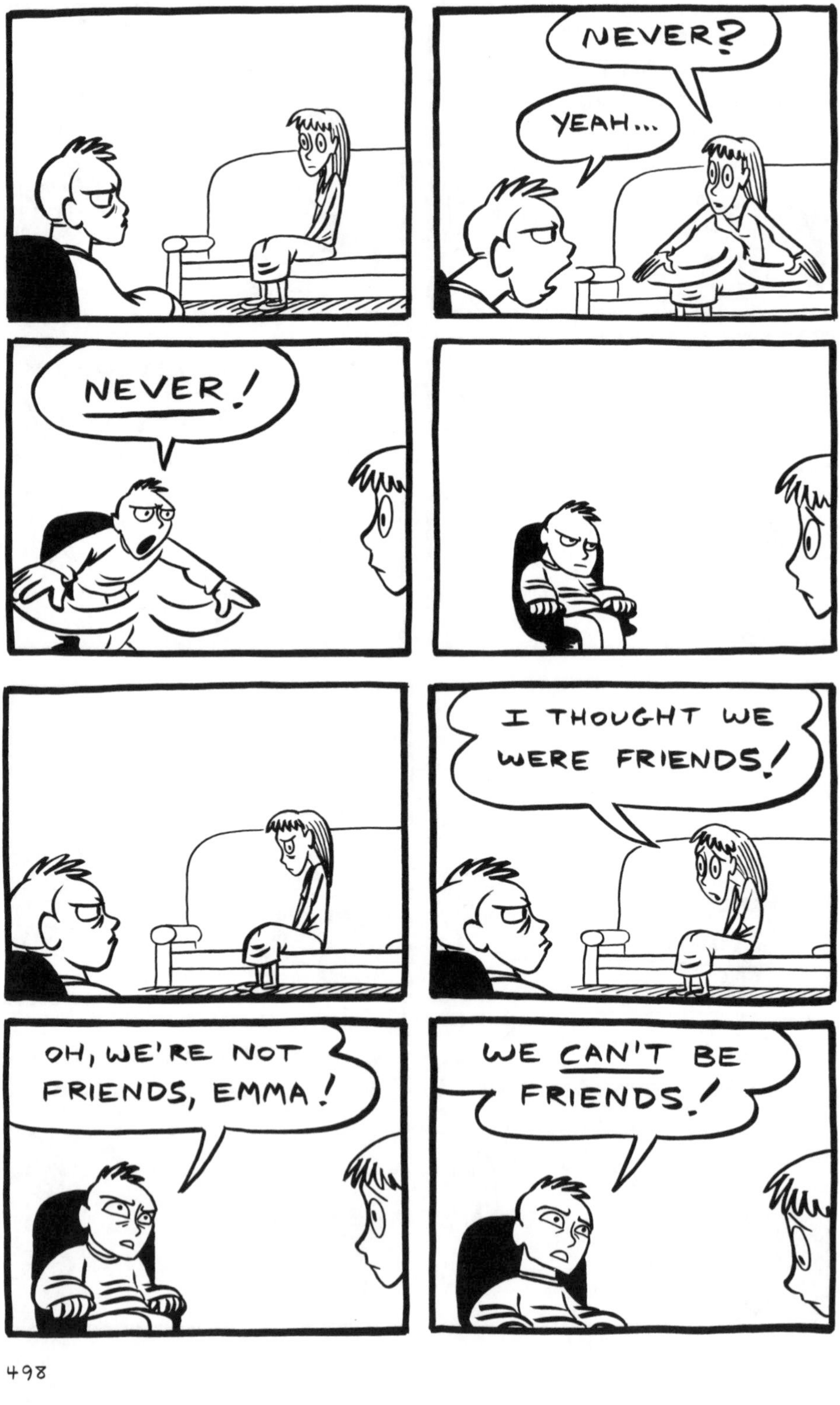

NEVER?
YEAH...
NEVER!
I THOUGHT WE WERE FRIENDS!
OH, WE'RE NOT FRIENDS, EMMA!
WE CAN'T BE FRIENDS!

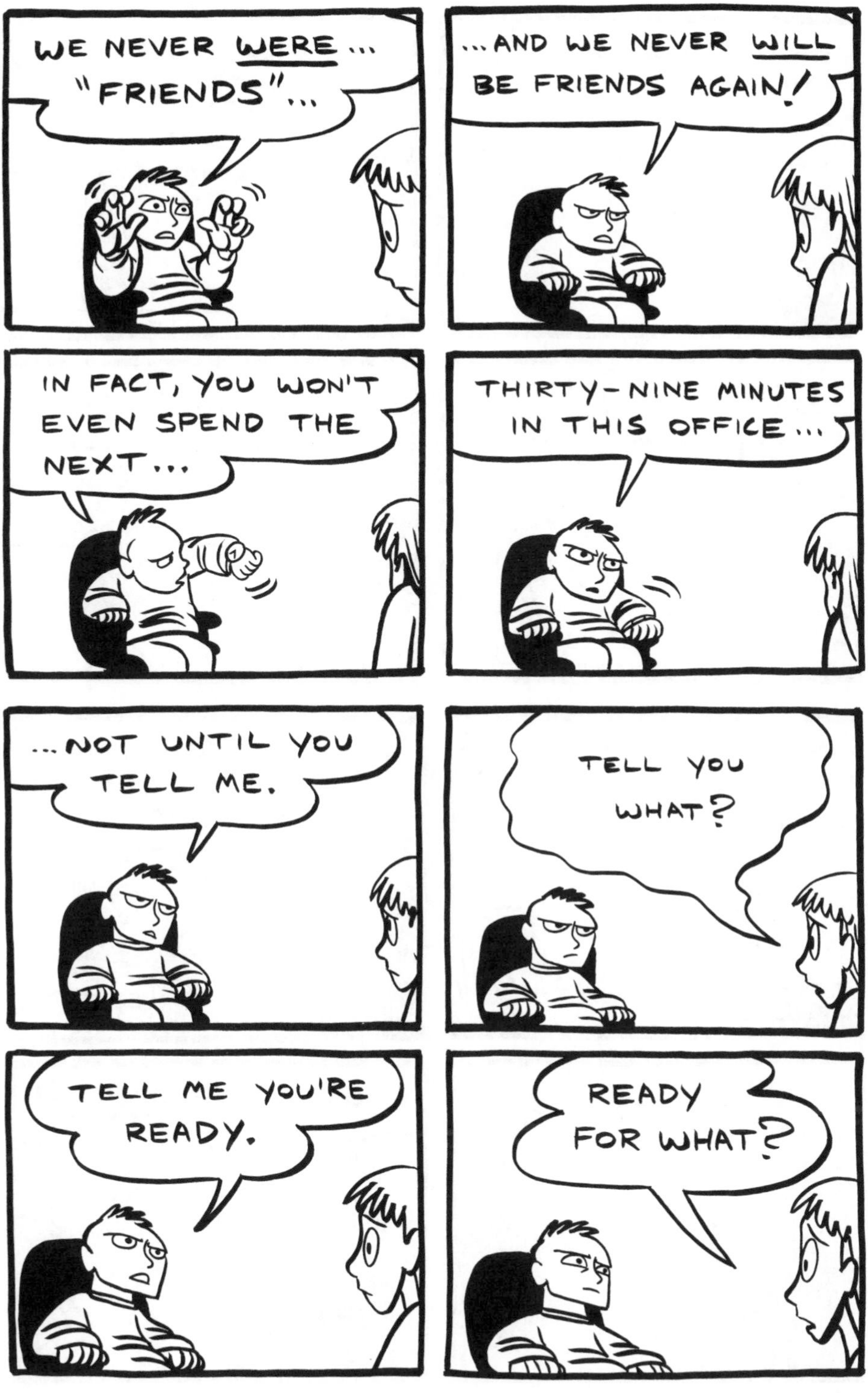
WE NEVER WERE... "FRIENDS"...
...AND WE NEVER WILL BE FRIENDS AGAIN!
IN FACT, YOU WON'T EVEN SPEND THE NEXT...
THIRTY-NINE MINUTES IN THIS OFFICE...
...NOT UNTIL YOU TELL ME.
TELL YOU WHAT?
TELL ME YOU'RE READY.
READY FOR WHAT?

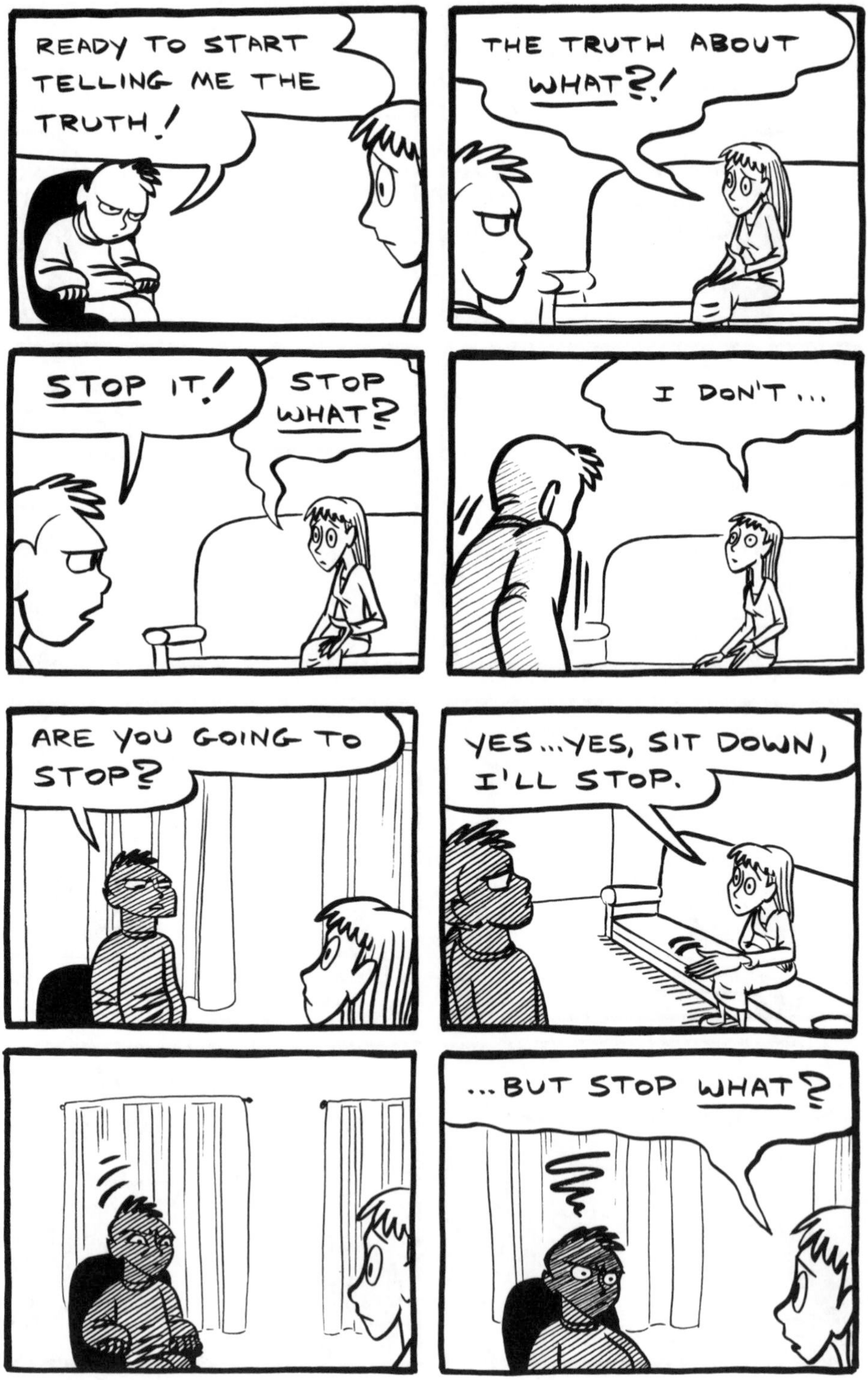
READY TO START TELLING ME THE TRUTH!
THE TRUTH ABOUT WHAT?!
STOP IT!
STOP WHAT?
I DON'T ...
ARE YOU GOING TO STOP?
YES...YES, SIT DOWN, I'LL STOP.
...BUT STOP WHAT?

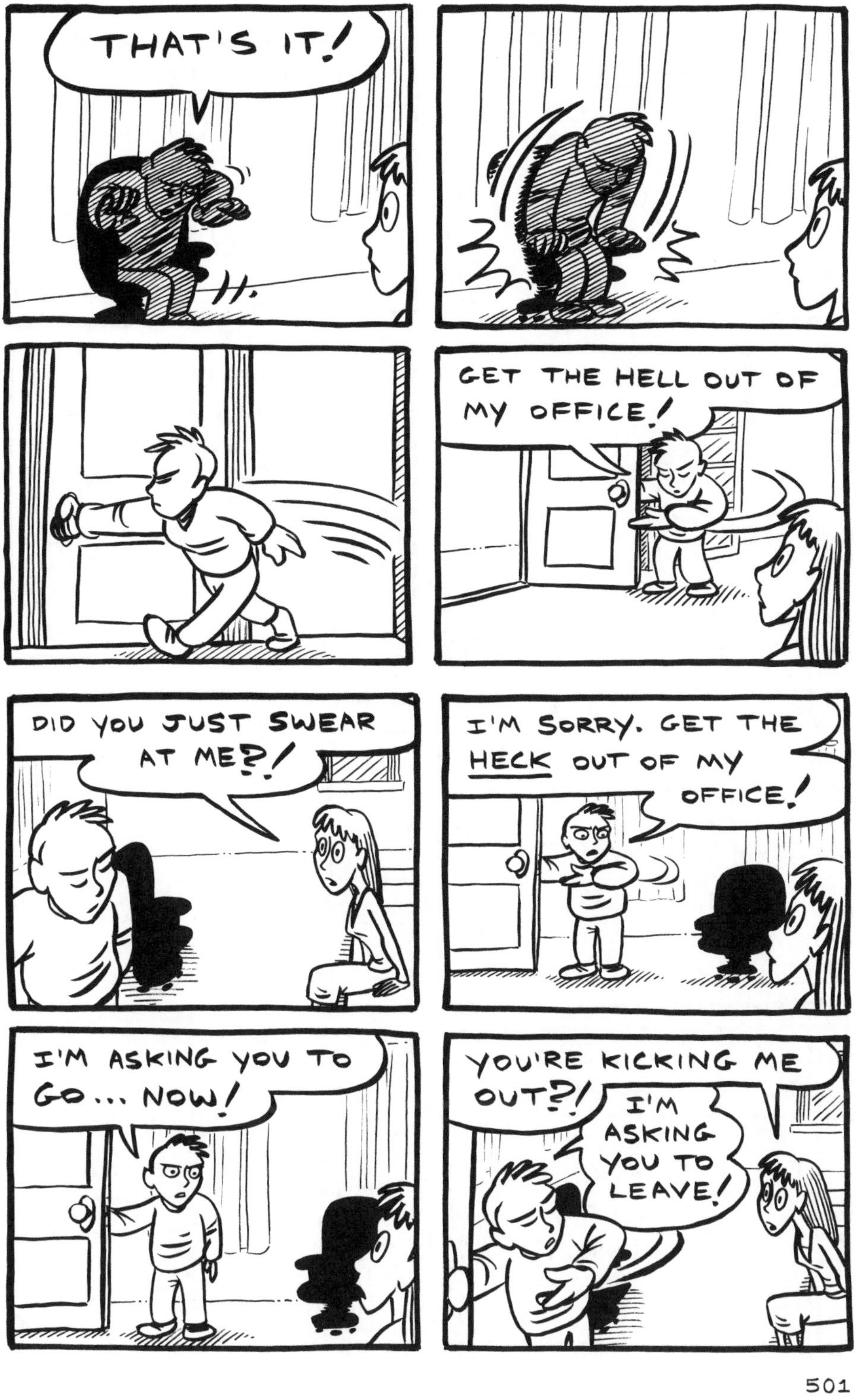
THAT'S IT!
GET THE HELL OUT OF MY OFFICE!
DID YOU JUST SWEAR AT ME?!
I'M SORRY. GET THE HECK OUT OF MY OFFICE!
I'M ASKING YOU TO GO... NOW!
YOU'RE KICKING ME OUT?!
I'M ASKING YOU TO LEAVE!

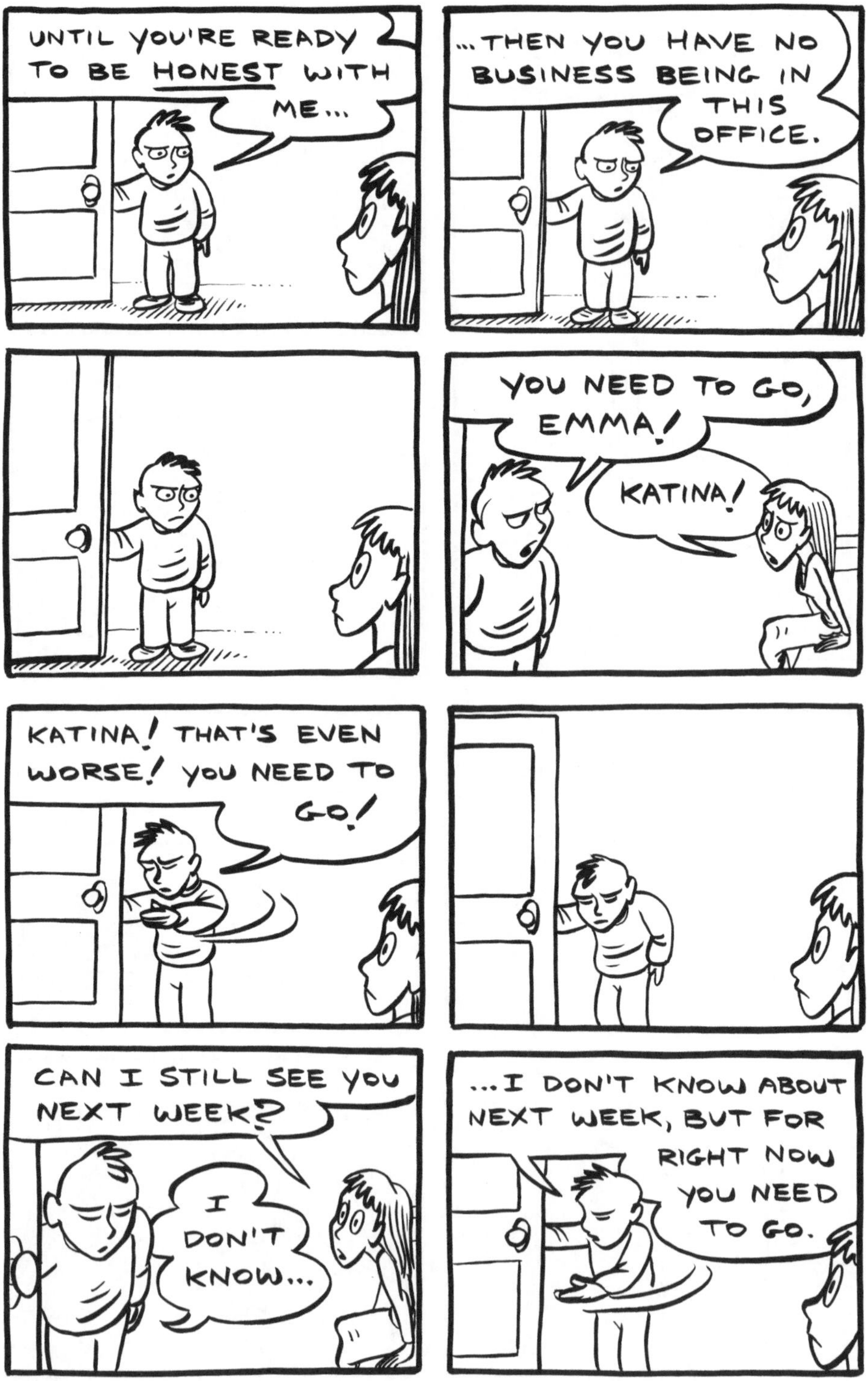

UNTIL YOU'RE READY TO BE HONEST WITH ME...
...THEN YOU HAVE NO BUSINESS BEING IN THIS OFFICE.
YOU NEED TO GO, EMMA!
KATINA!
KATINA! THAT'S EVEN WORSE! YOU NEED TO GO!
CAN I STILL SEE YOU NEXT WEEK?
I DON'T KNOW...
...I DON'T KNOW ABOUT NEXT WEEK, BUT FOR RIGHT NOW YOU NEED TO GO.

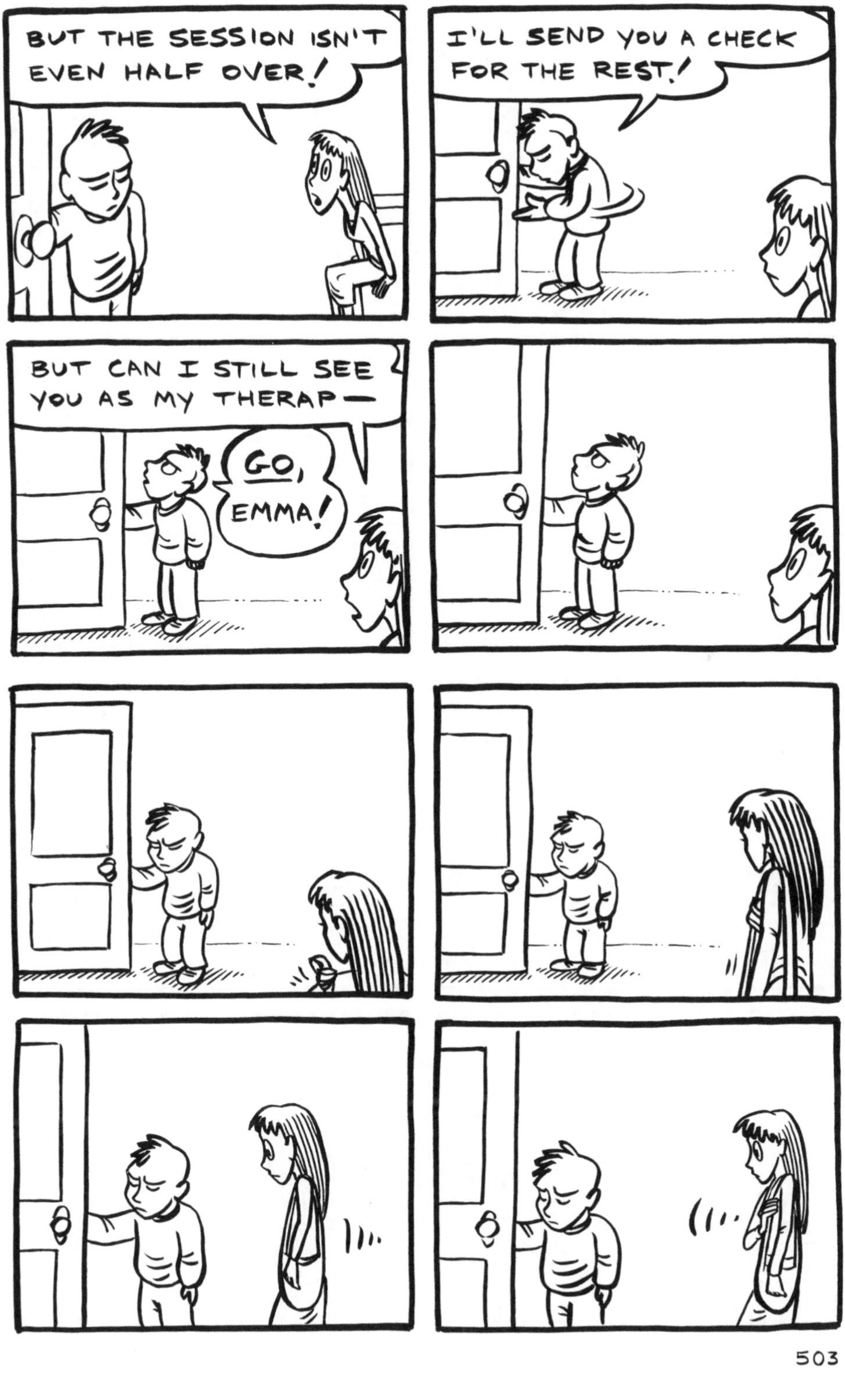
BUT THE SESSION ISN'T EVEN HALF OVER!
I'LL SEND YOU A CHECK FOR THE REST!
BUT CAN I STILL SEE YOU AS MY THERAP—
GO, EMMA!

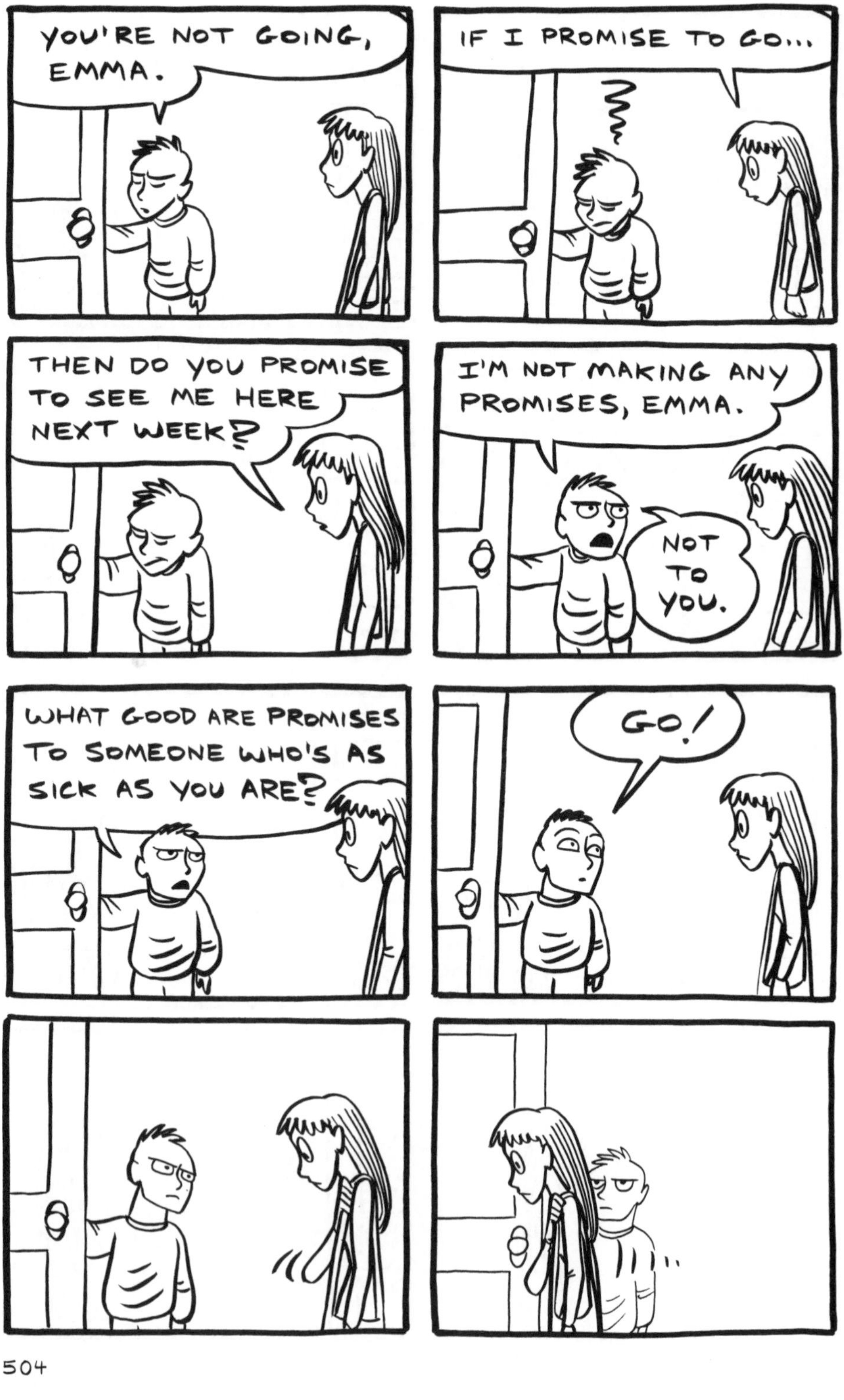
YOU'RE NOT GOING, EMMA.
IF I PROMISE TO GO...
THEN DO YOU PROMISE TO SEE ME HERE NEXT WEEK?
I'M NOT MAKING ANY PROMISES, EMMA.
NOT TO YOU.
WHAT GOOD ARE PROMISES TO SOMEONE WHO'S AS SICK AS YOU ARE?
GO!

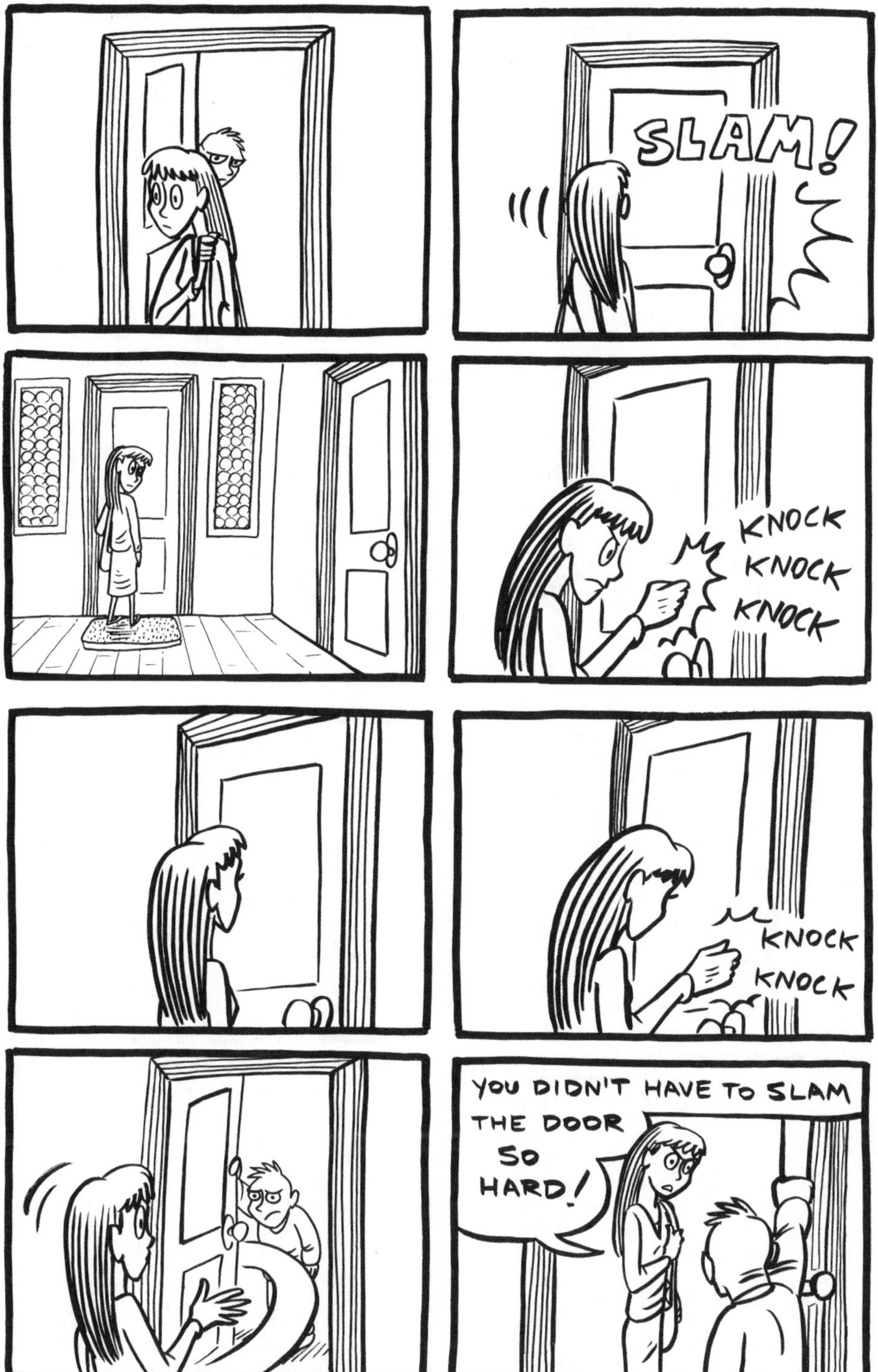
SLAM!
KNOCK
KNOCK
KNOCK
KNOCK
KNOCK
YOU DIDN'T HAVE TO SLAM THE DOOR SO HARD!

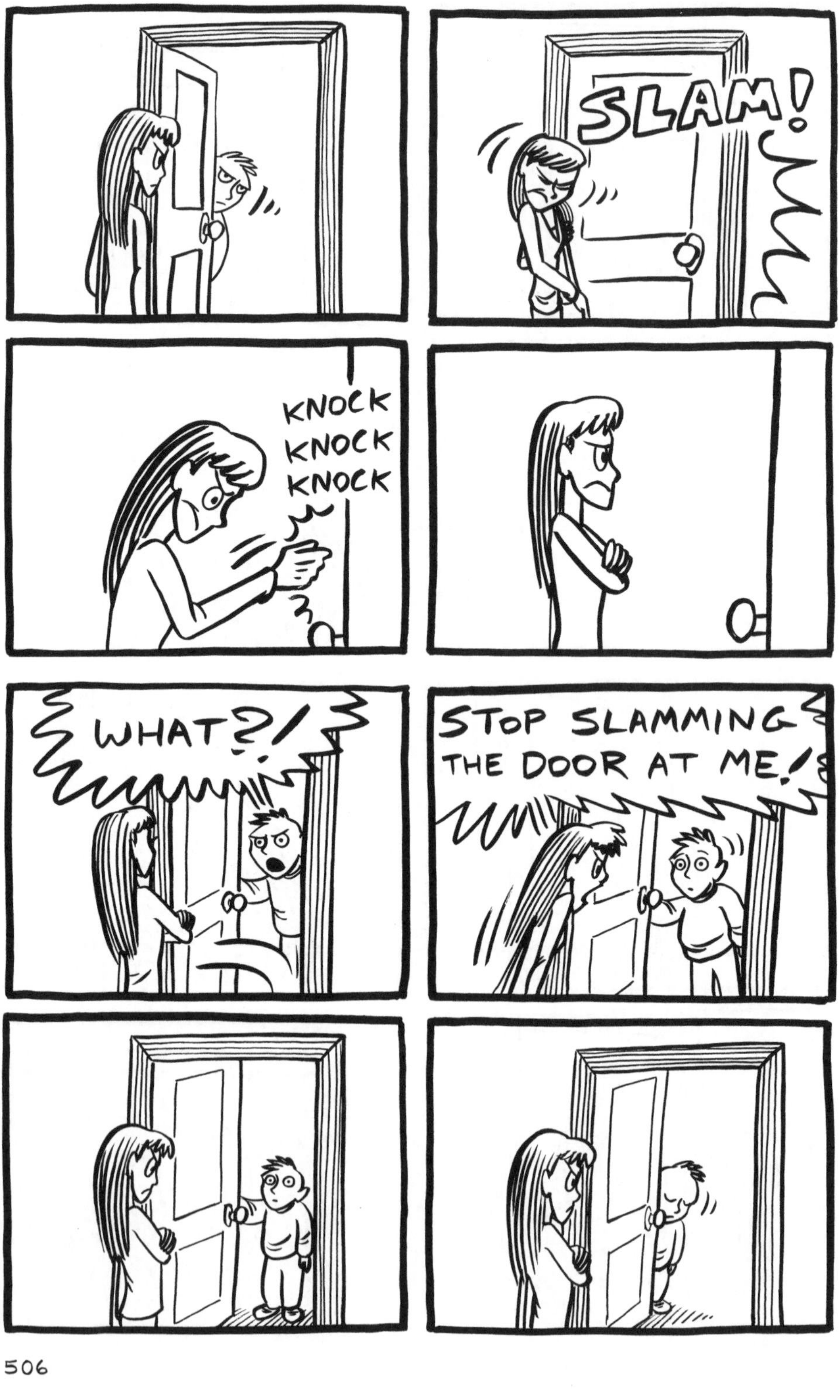
SLAM!
KNOCK
KNOCK
KNOCK
WHAT?!
STOP SLAMMING THE DOOR AT ME!

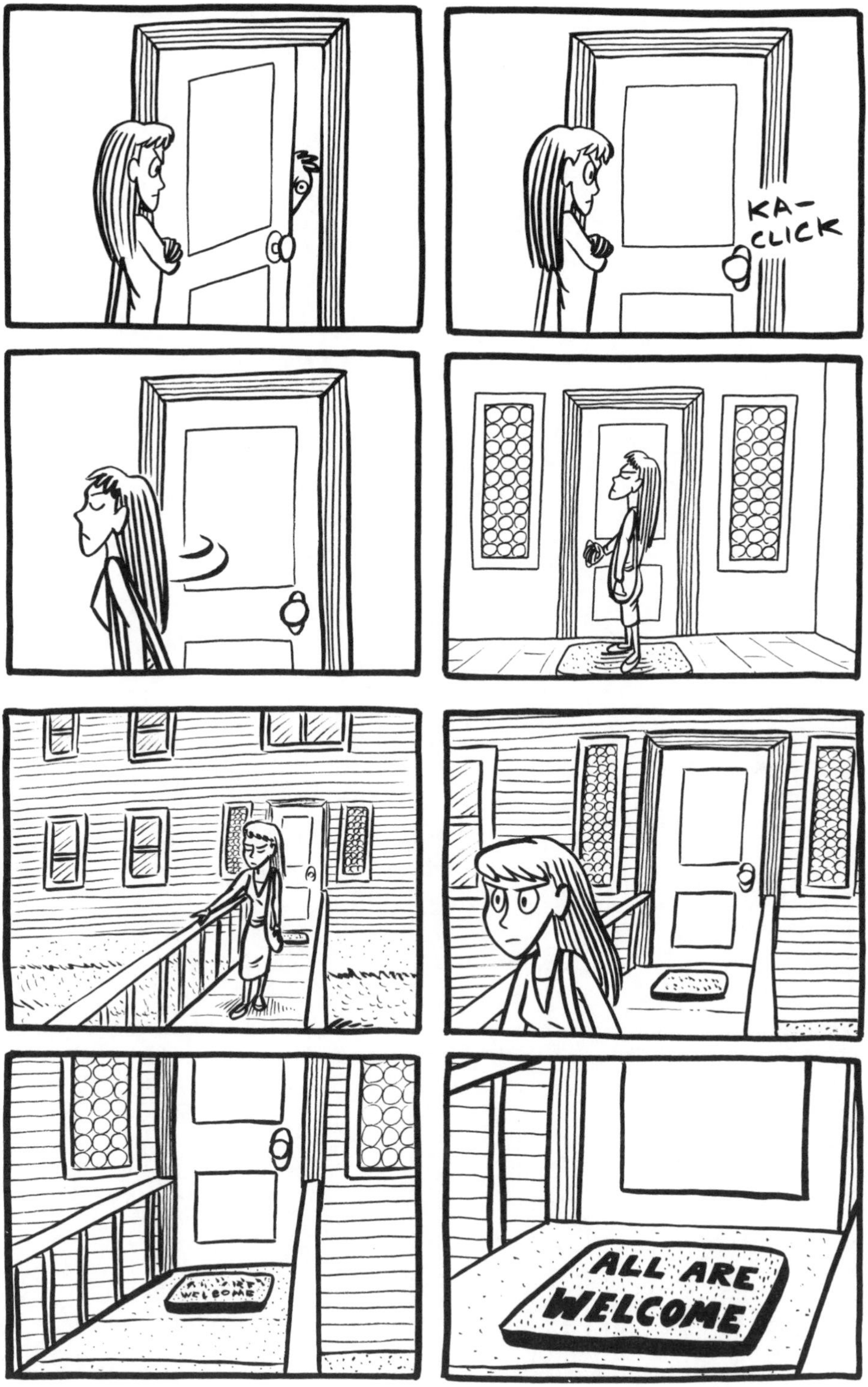
KA-
CLICK
ALL ARE
WELCOME

CHECK

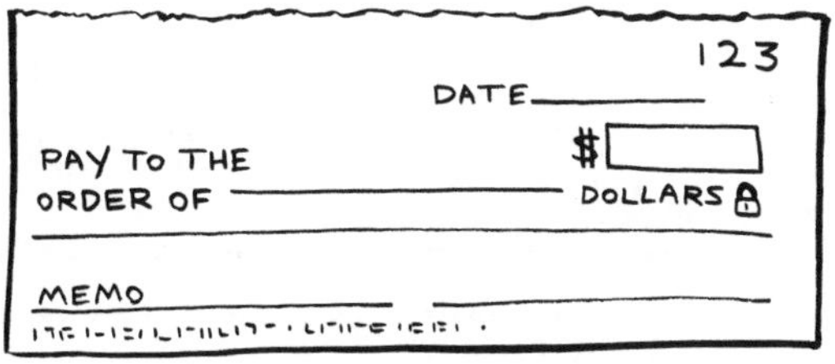
123
DATE
PAY TO THE
ORDER OF
$
DOLLARS
MEMO

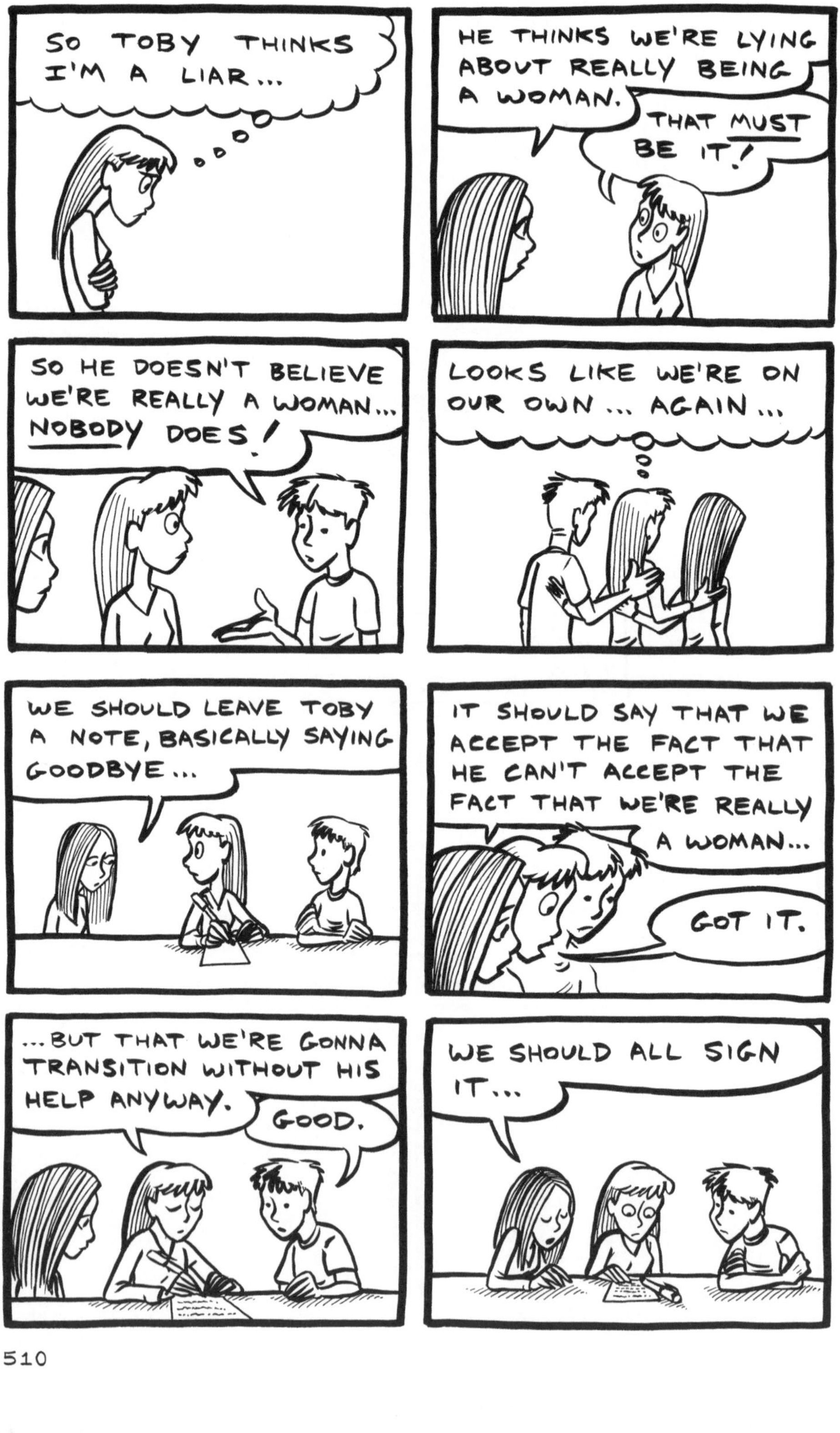

SO TOBY THINKS I'M A LIAR...
HE THINKS WE'RE LYING ABOUT REALLY BEING A WOMAN.
THAT MUST BE IT!
SO HE DOESN'T BELIEVE WE'RE REALLY A WOMAN... NOBODY DOES!
LOOKS LIKE WE'RE ON OUR OWN ... AGAIN...
WE SHOULD LEAVE TOBY A NOTE, BASICALLY SAYING GOODBYE...
IT SHOULD SAY THAT WE ACCEPT THE FACT THAT HE CAN'T ACCEPT THE FACT THAT WE'RE REALLY A WOMAN...
GOT IT.
...BUT THAT WE'RE GONNA TRANSITION WITHOUT HIS HELP ANYWAY.
GOOD.
WE SHOULD ALL SIGN IT...

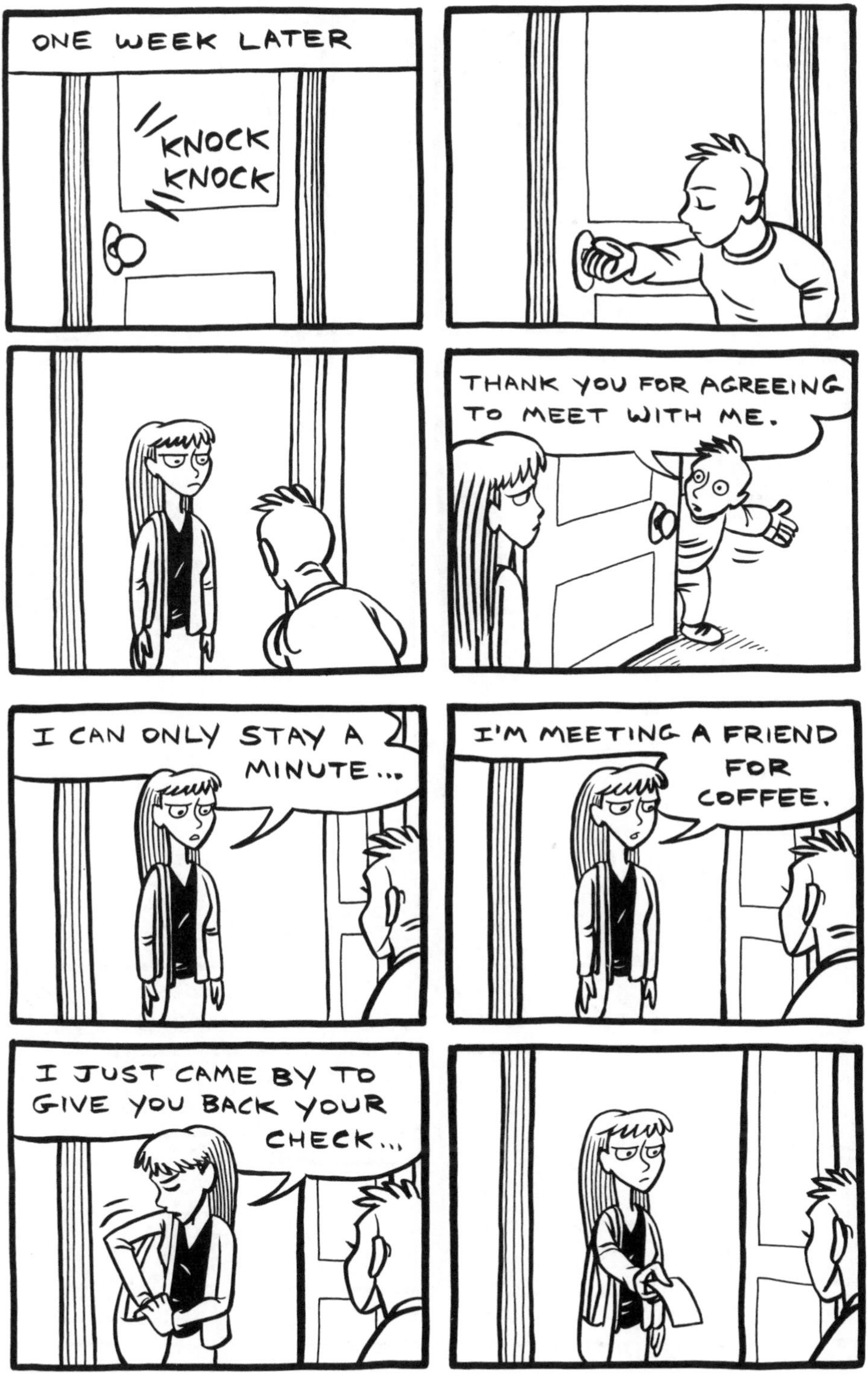
ONE WEEK LATER
KNOCK KNOCK
THANK YOU FOR AGREEING TO MEET WITH ME.
I CAN ONLY STAY A MINUTE...
I'M MEETING A FRIEND FOR COFFEE.
I JUST CAME BY TO GIVE YOU BACK YOUR CHECK...

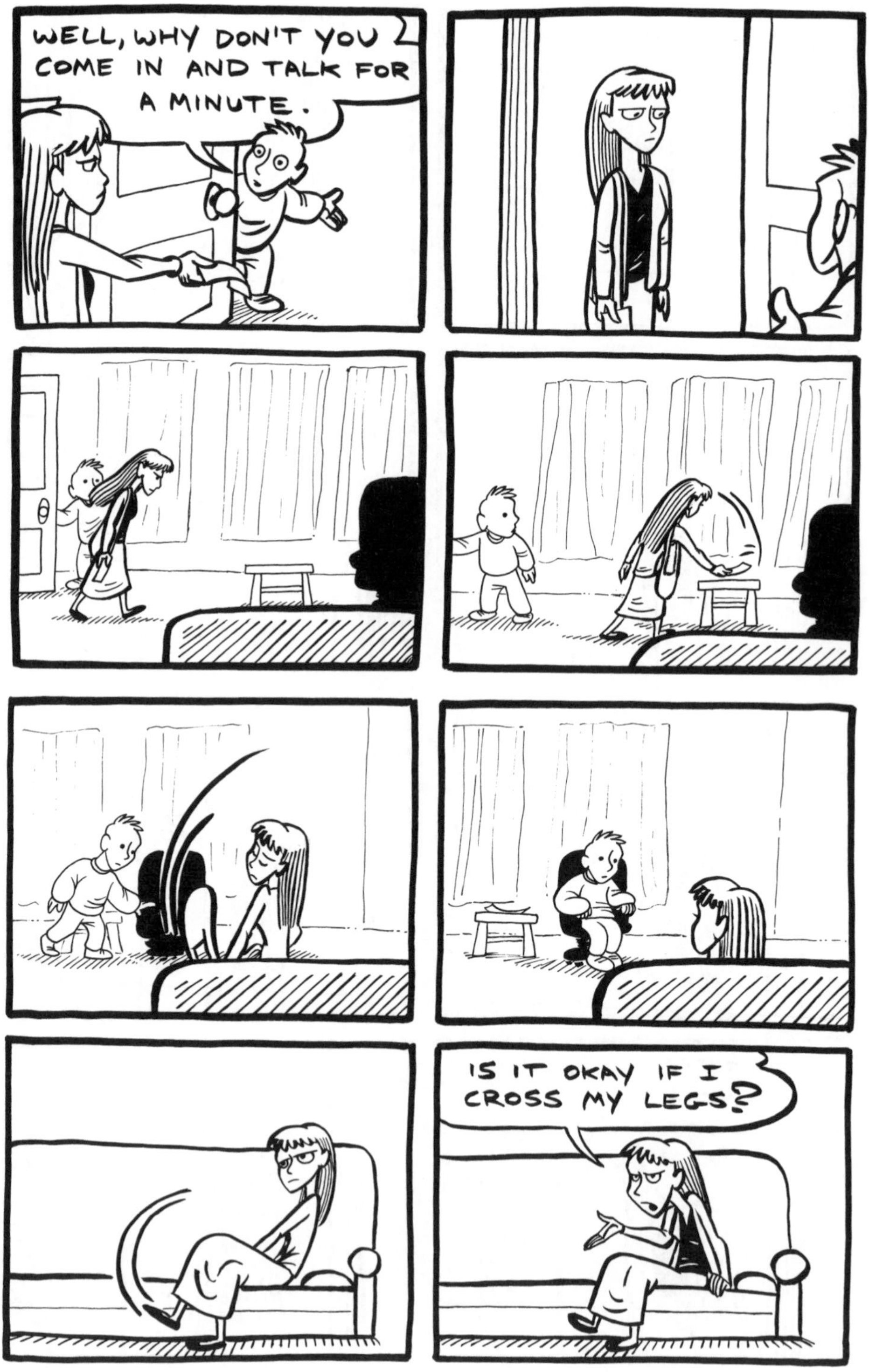
WELL, WHY DON'T YOU COME IN AND TALK FOR A MINUTE.
IS IT OKAY IF I CROSS MY LEGS?

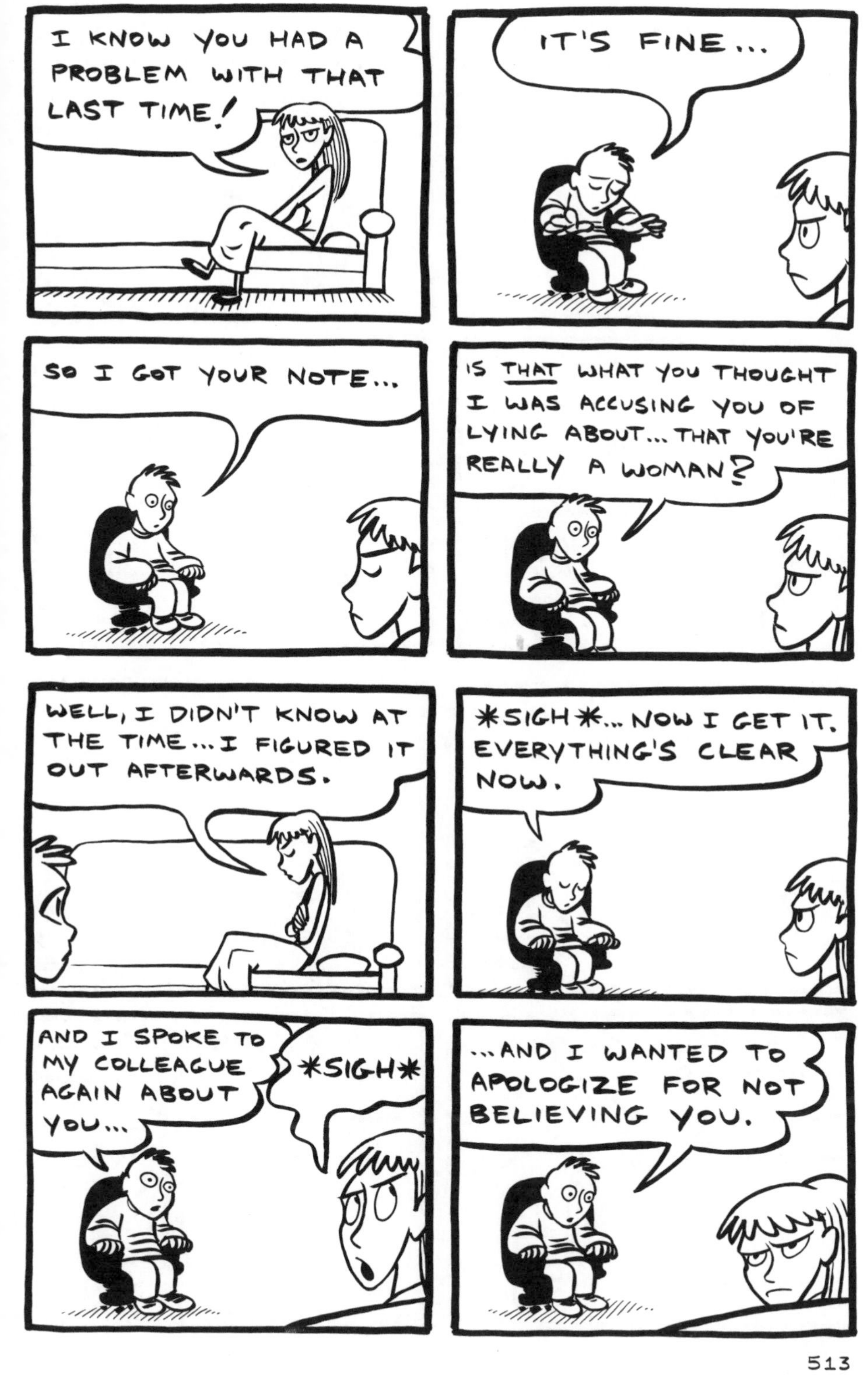
I KNOW YOU HAD A PROBLEM WITH THAT LAST TIME!
IT'S FINE...
SO I GOT YOUR NOTE...
IS THAT WHAT YOU THOUGHT I WAS ACCUSING YOU OF LYING ABOUT... THAT YOU'RE REALLY A WOMAN?
WELL, I DIDN'T KNOW AT THE TIME... I FIGURED IT OUT AFTERWARDS.
SIGH... NOW I GET IT. EVERYTHING'S CLEAR NOW.
AND I SPOKE TO MY COLLEAGUE AGAIN ABOUT YOU...
SIGH
...AND I WANTED TO APOLOGIZE FOR NOT BELIEVING YOU.

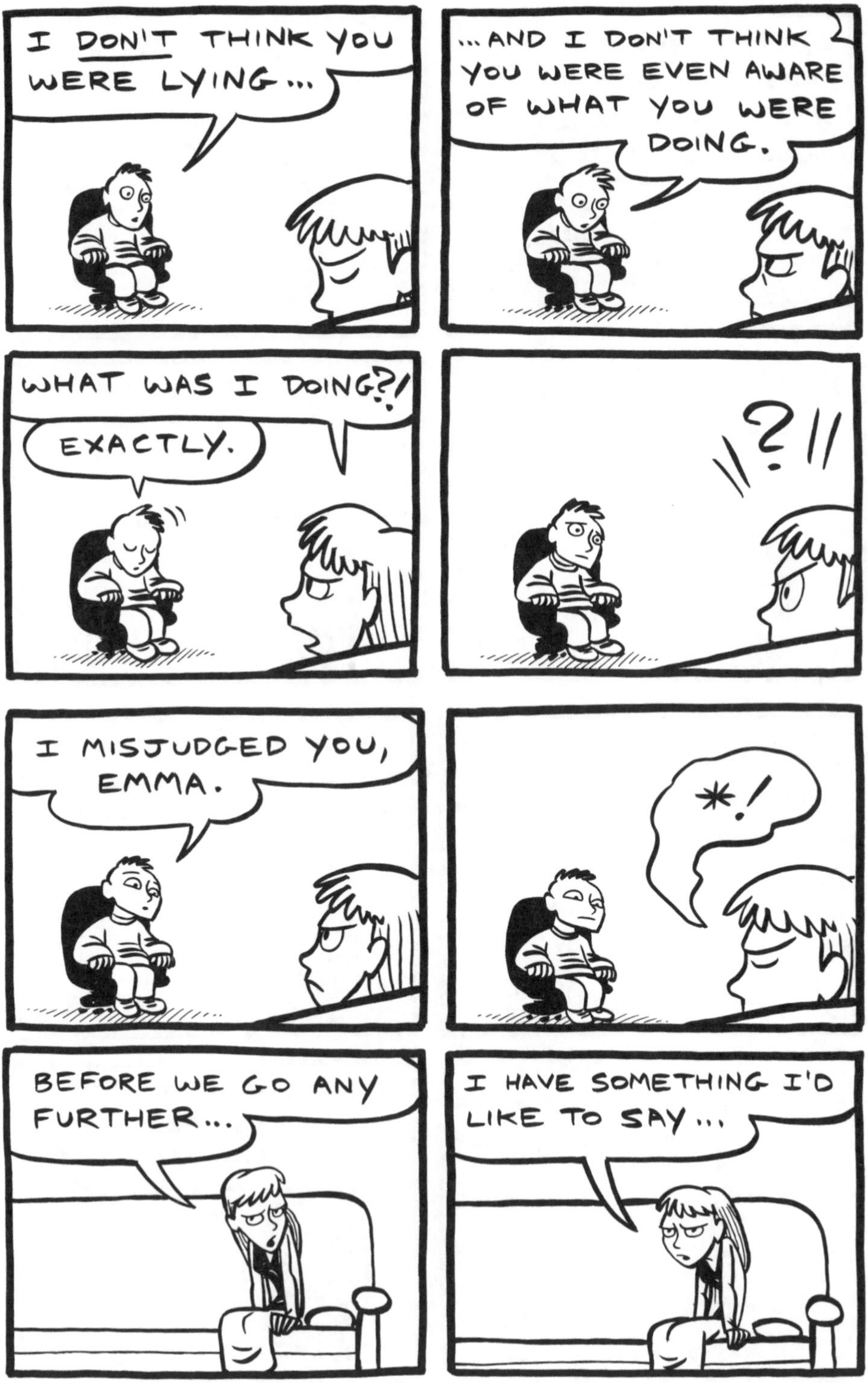
I DON'T THINK YOU WERE LYING...
...AND I DON'T THINK YOU WERE EVEN AWARE OF WHAT YOU WERE DOING.
WHAT WAS I DOING?!
EXACTLY.
?
I MISJUDGED YOU, EMMA.
*!
BEFORE WE GO ANY FURTHER...
I HAVE SOMETHING I'D LIKE TO SAY...

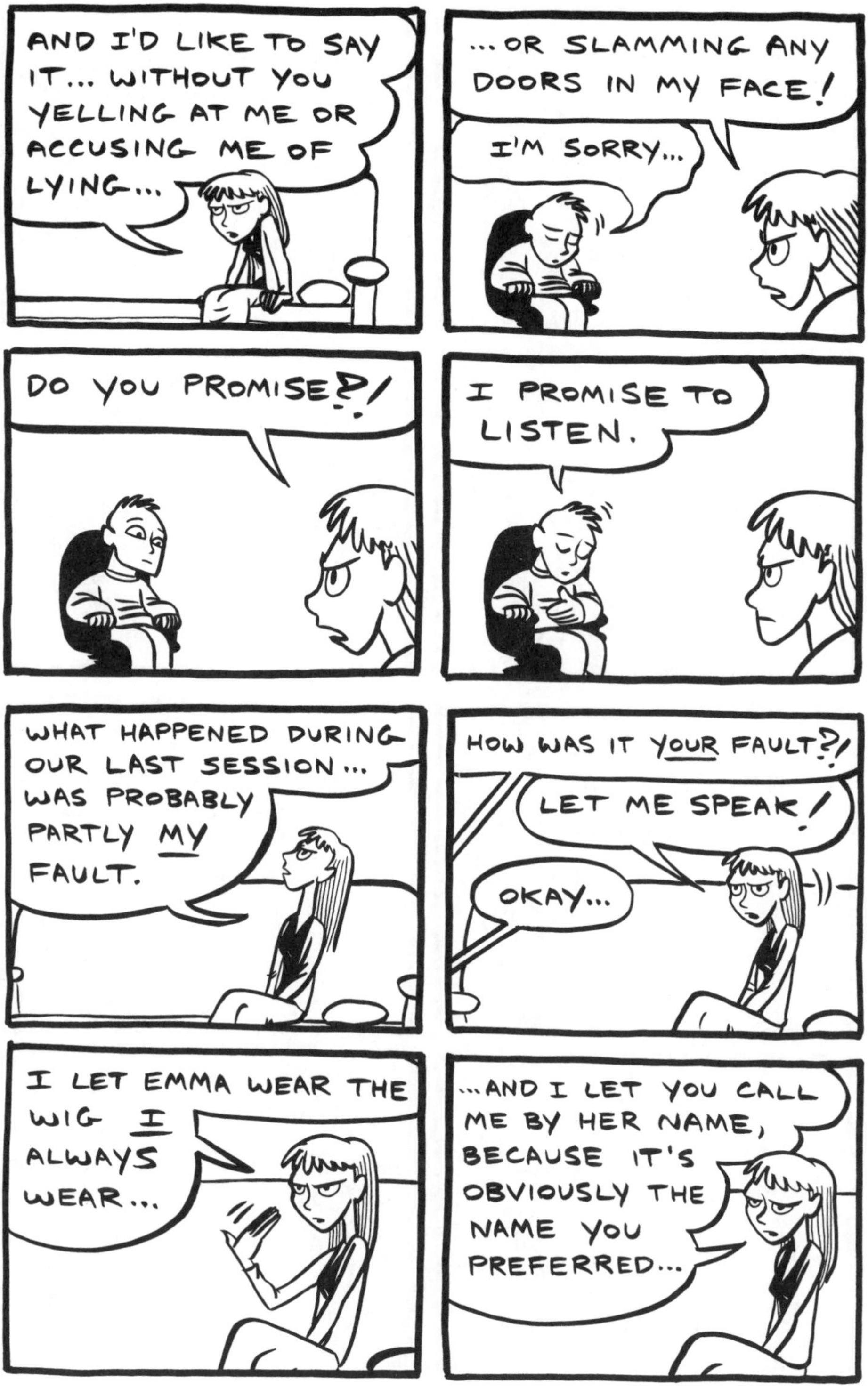
AND I'D LIKE TO SAY IT... WITHOUT YOU YELLING AT ME OR ACCUSING ME OF LYING...
...OR SLAMMING ANY DOORS IN MY FACE!
I'M SORRY...
DO YOU PROMISE?!
I PROMISE TO LISTEN.
WHAT HAPPENED DURING OUR LAST SESSION... WAS PROBABLY PARTLY MY FAULT.
HOW WAS IT YOUR FAULT?!
LET ME SPEAK!
OKAY...
I LET EMMA WEAR THE WIG I ALWAYS WEAR...
...AND I LET YOU CALL ME BY HER NAME, BECAUSE IT'S OBVIOUSLY THE NAME YOU PREFERRED...

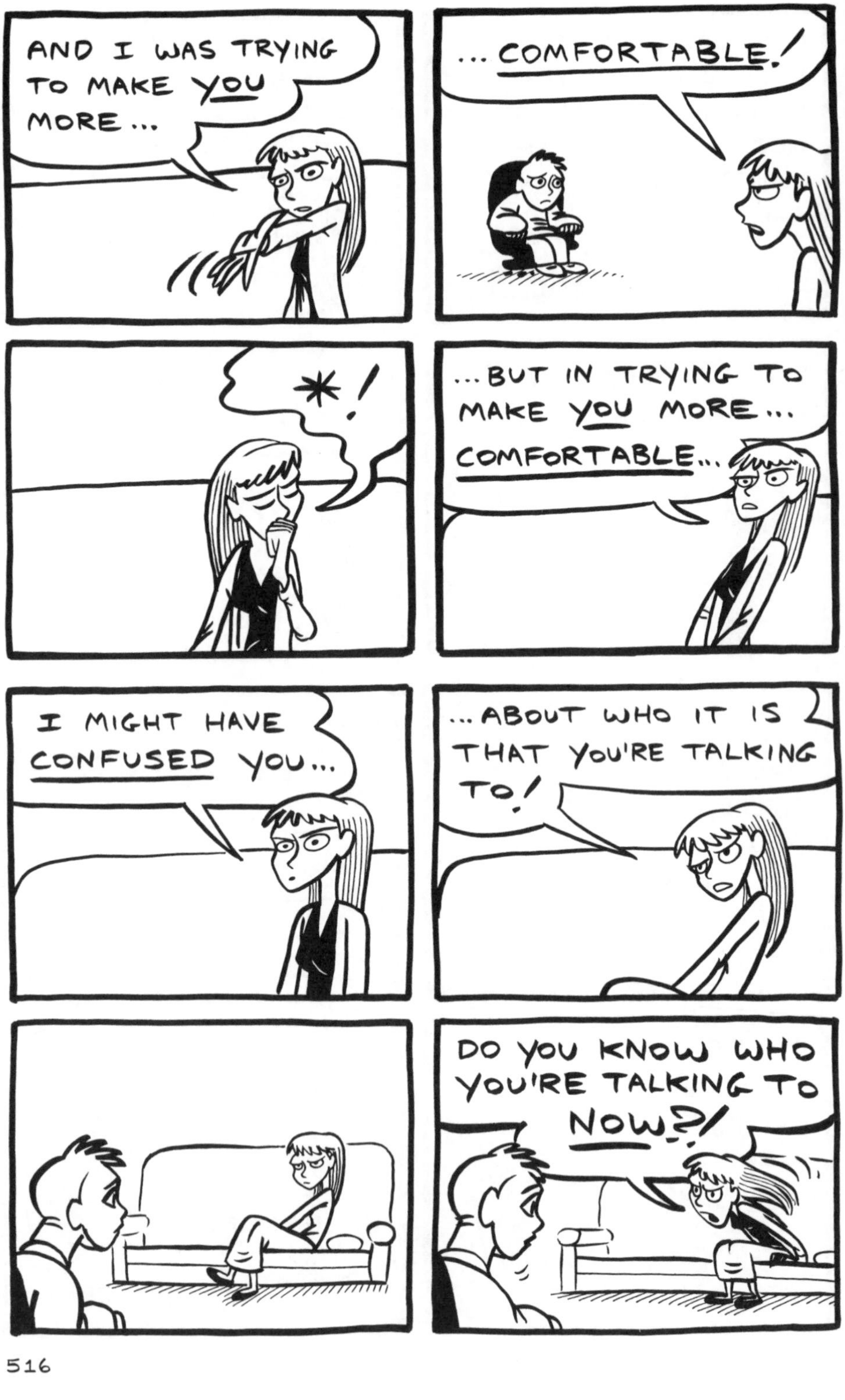
AND I WAS TRYING TO MAKE YOU MORE...
...COMFORTABLE!
*!
...BUT IN TRYING TO MAKE YOU MORE... COMFORTABLE...
I MIGHT HAVE CONFUSED YOU...
...ABOUT WHO IT IS THAT YOU'RE TALKING TO!
DO YOU KNOW WHO YOU'RE TALKING TO NOW?!

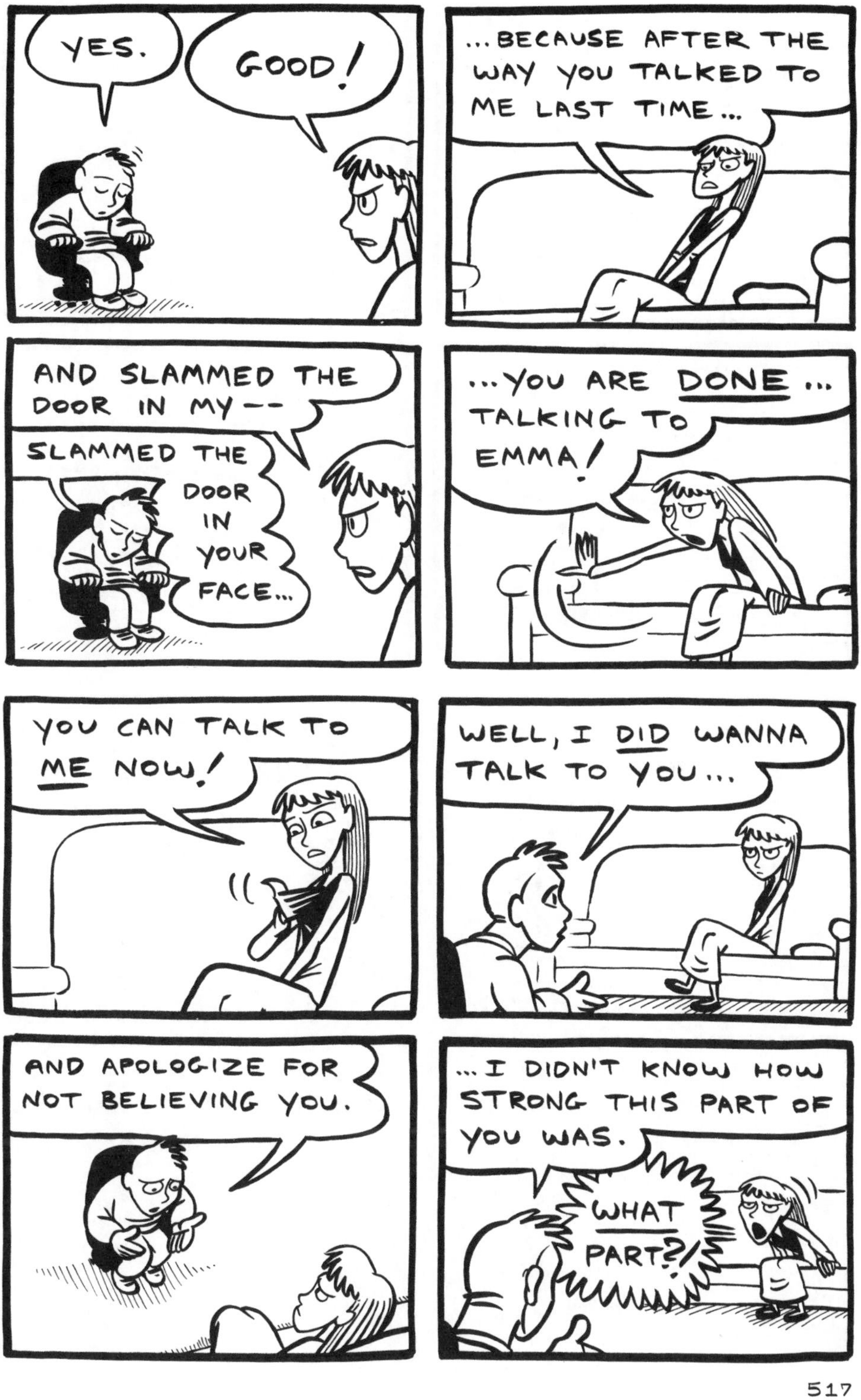

YES.
GOOD!
...BECAUSE AFTER THE WAY YOU TALKED TO ME LAST TIME...
AND SLAMMED THE DOOR IN MY --
SLAMMED THE DOOR IN YOUR FACE...
...YOU ARE DONE... TALKING TO EMMA!
YOU CAN TALK TO ME NOW!
WELL, I DID WANNA TALK TO YOU...
AND APOLOGIZE FOR NOT BELIEVING YOU.
...I DIDN'T KNOW HOW STRONG THIS PART OF YOU WAS.
WHAT PART?!

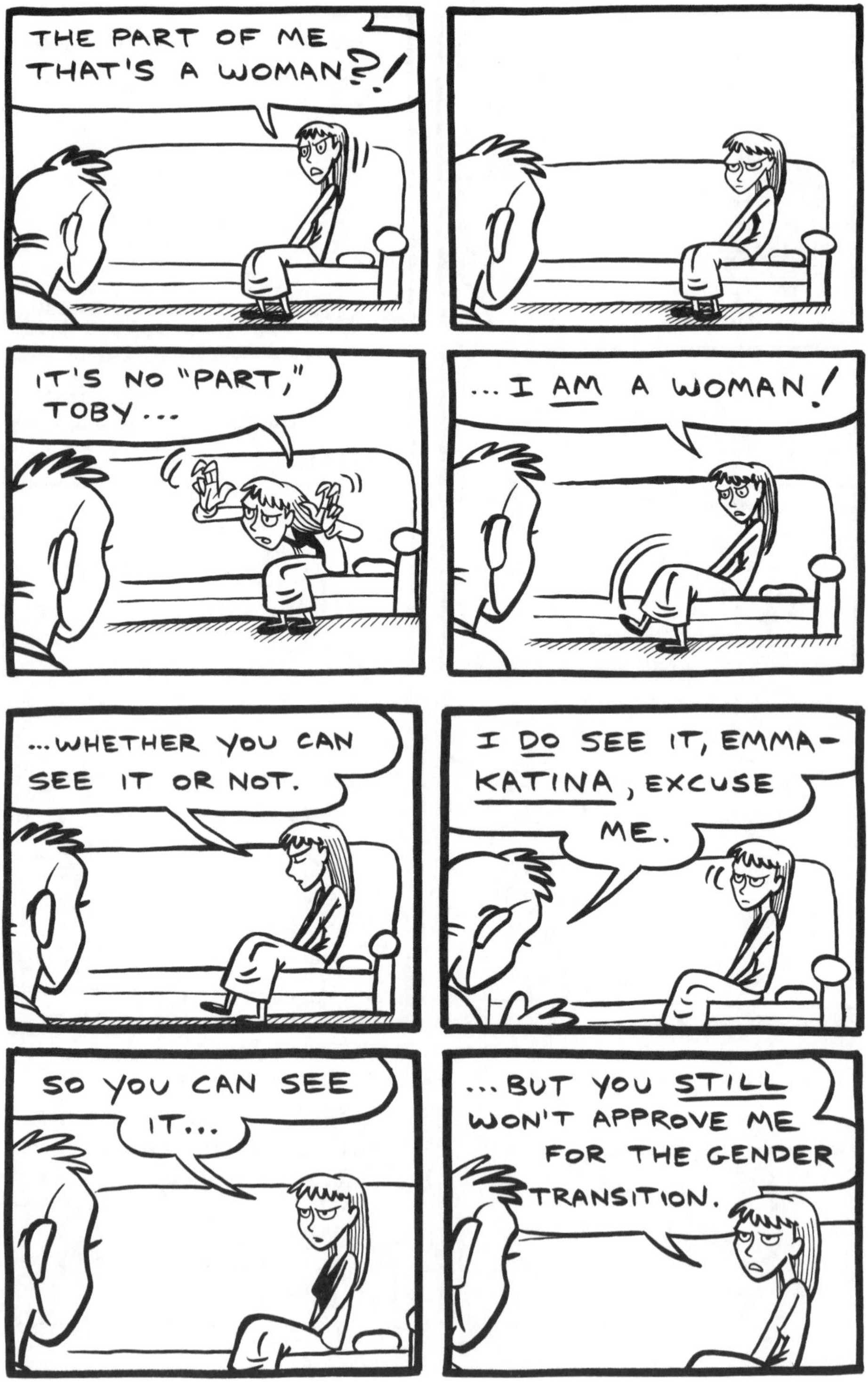
THE PART OF ME THAT'S A WOMAN?!
IT'S NO "PART," TOBY...
...I AM A WOMAN!
...WHETHER YOU CAN SEE IT OR NOT.
I DO SEE IT, EMMA-KATINA, EXCUSE ME.
SO YOU CAN SEE IT...
...BUT YOU STILL WON'T APPROVE ME FOR THE GENDER TRANSITION.

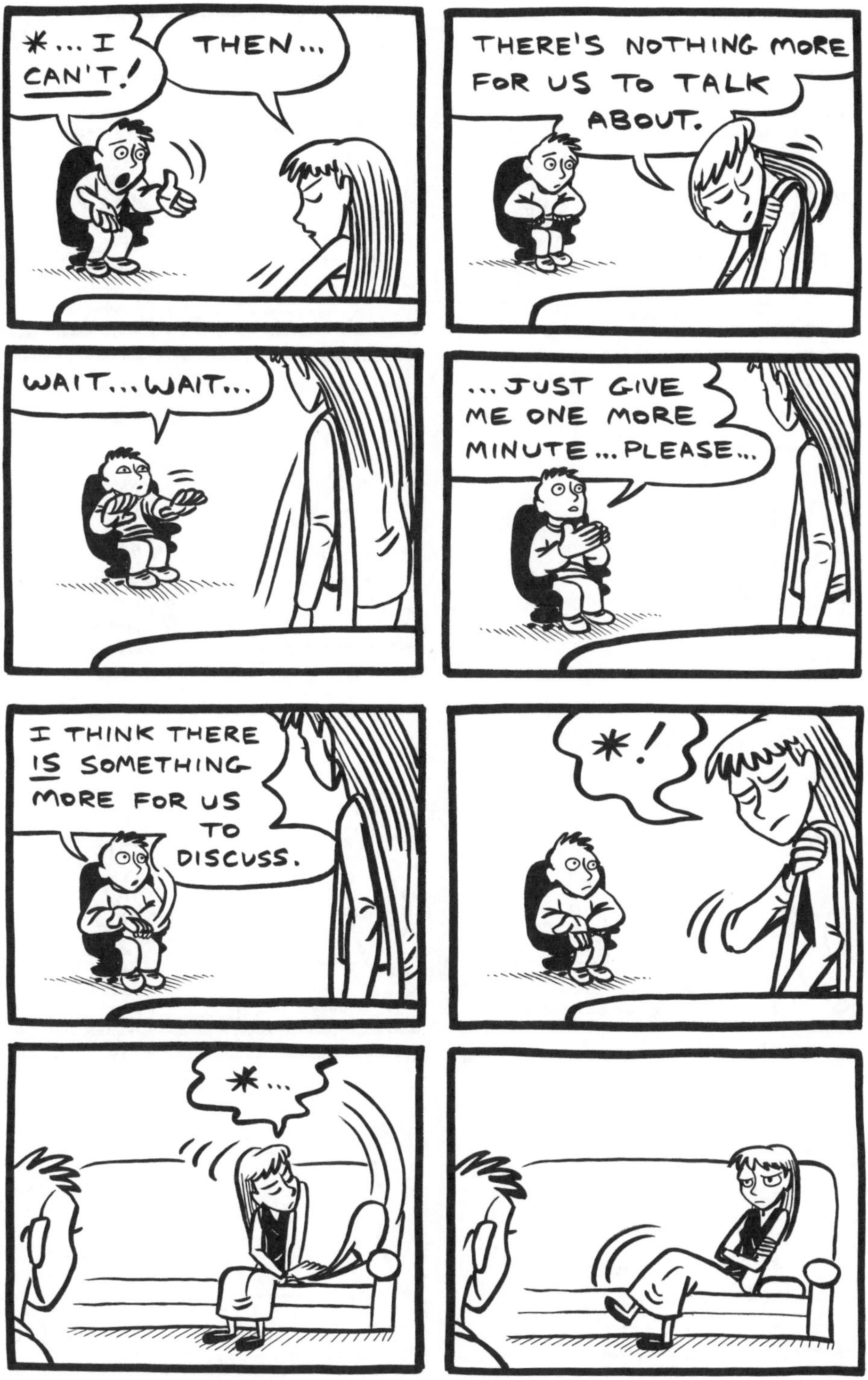
*... I CAN'T!
THEN...
THERE'S NOTHING MORE FOR US TO TALK ABOUT.
WAIT... WAIT...
... JUST GIVE ME ONE MORE MINUTE... PLEASE...
I THINK THERE IS SOMETHING MORE FOR US TO DISCUSS.
*!
*...

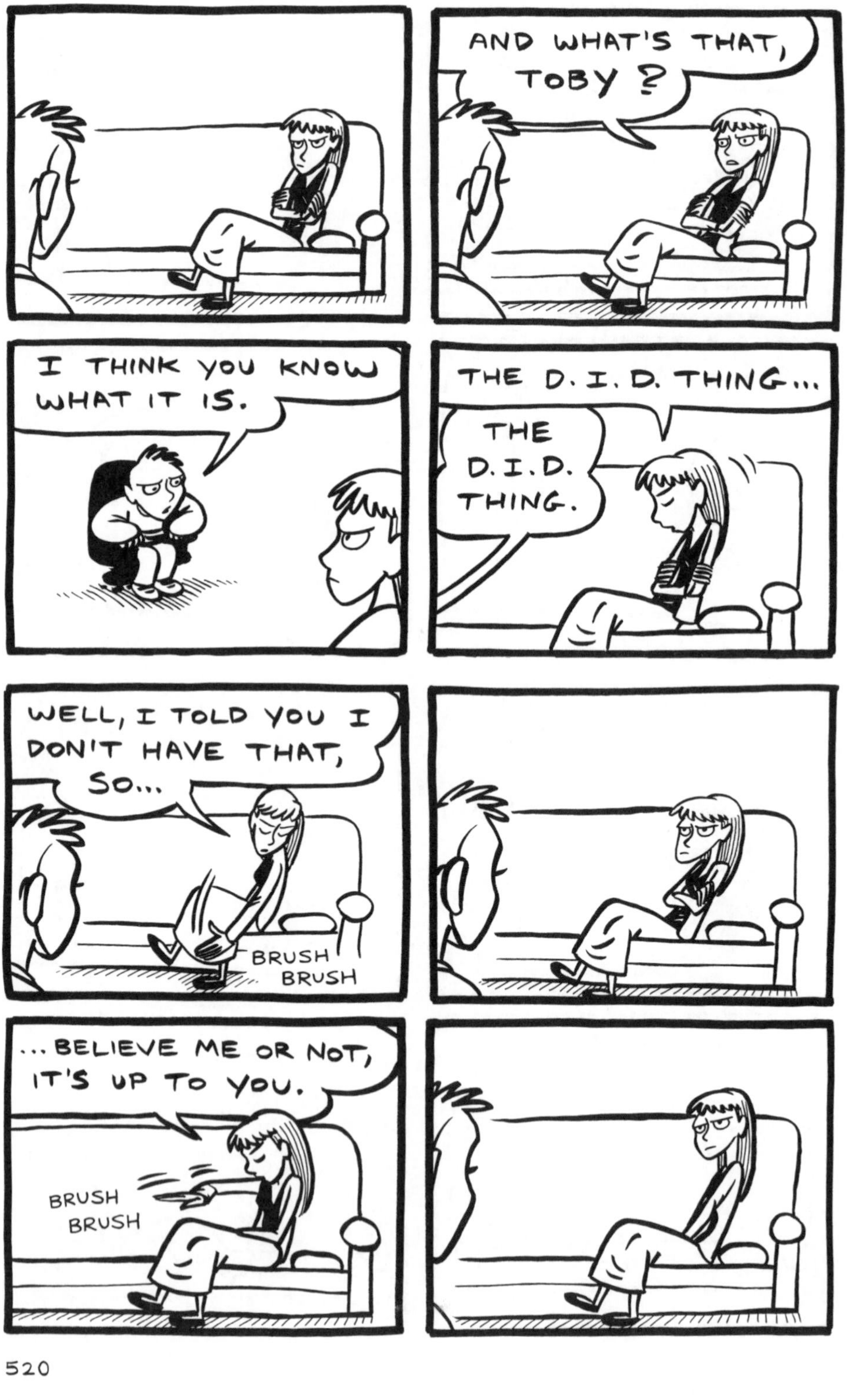
AND WHAT'S THAT, TOBY ?
I THINK YOU KNOW WHAT IT IS.
THE D. I. D. THING...
THE D.I.D. THING.
WELL, I TOLD YOU I DON'T HAVE THAT, SO...
BRUSH BRUSH
...BELIEVE ME OR NOT, IT'S UP TO YOU.
BRUSH BRUSH

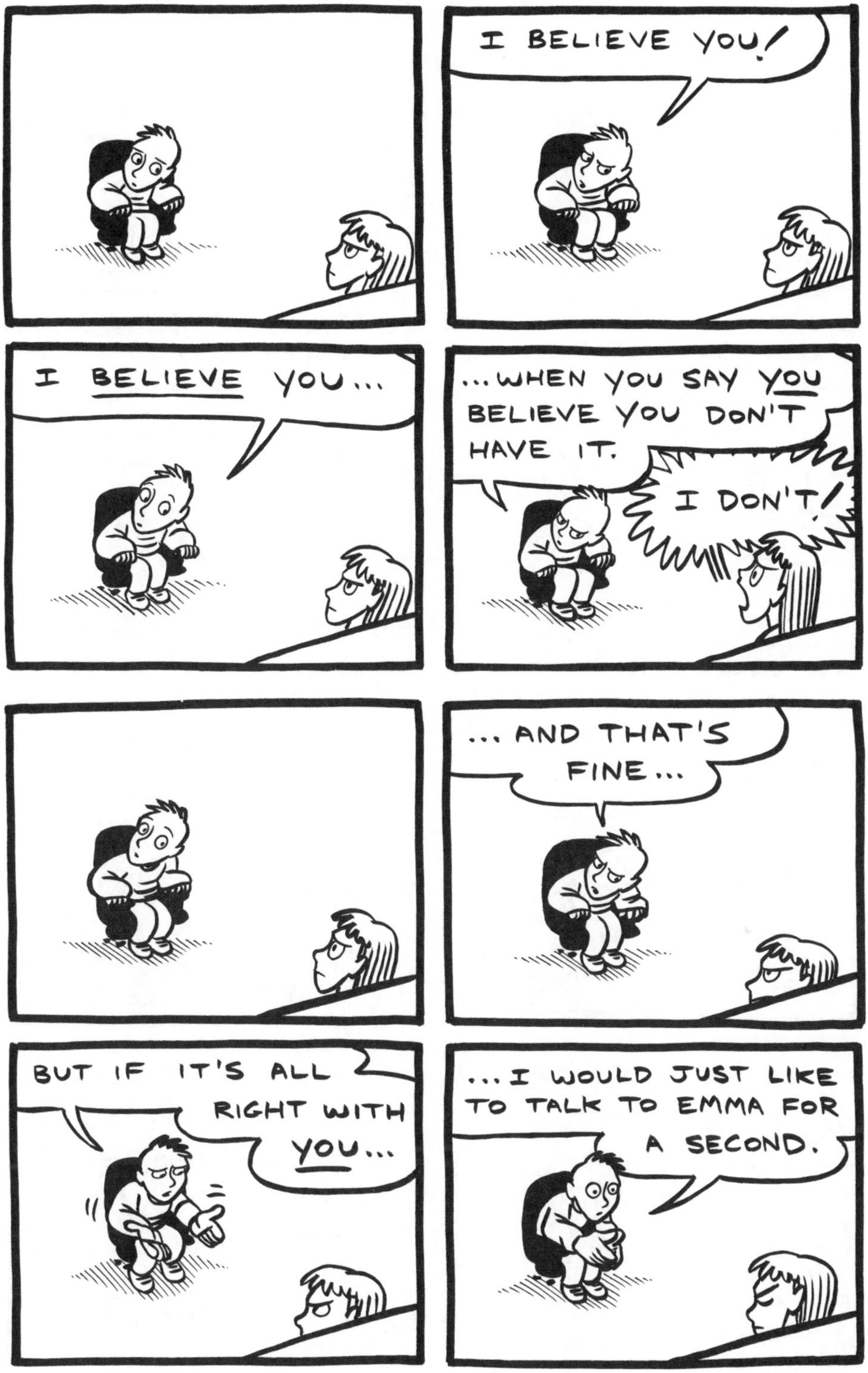
I BELIEVE YOU!
I BELIEVE YOU...
...WHEN YOU SAY YOU BELIEVE YOU DON'T HAVE IT.
I DON'T!
... AND THAT'S FINE...
BUT IF IT'S ALL RIGHT WITH YOU...
...I WOULD JUST LIKE TO TALK TO EMMA FOR A SECOND.

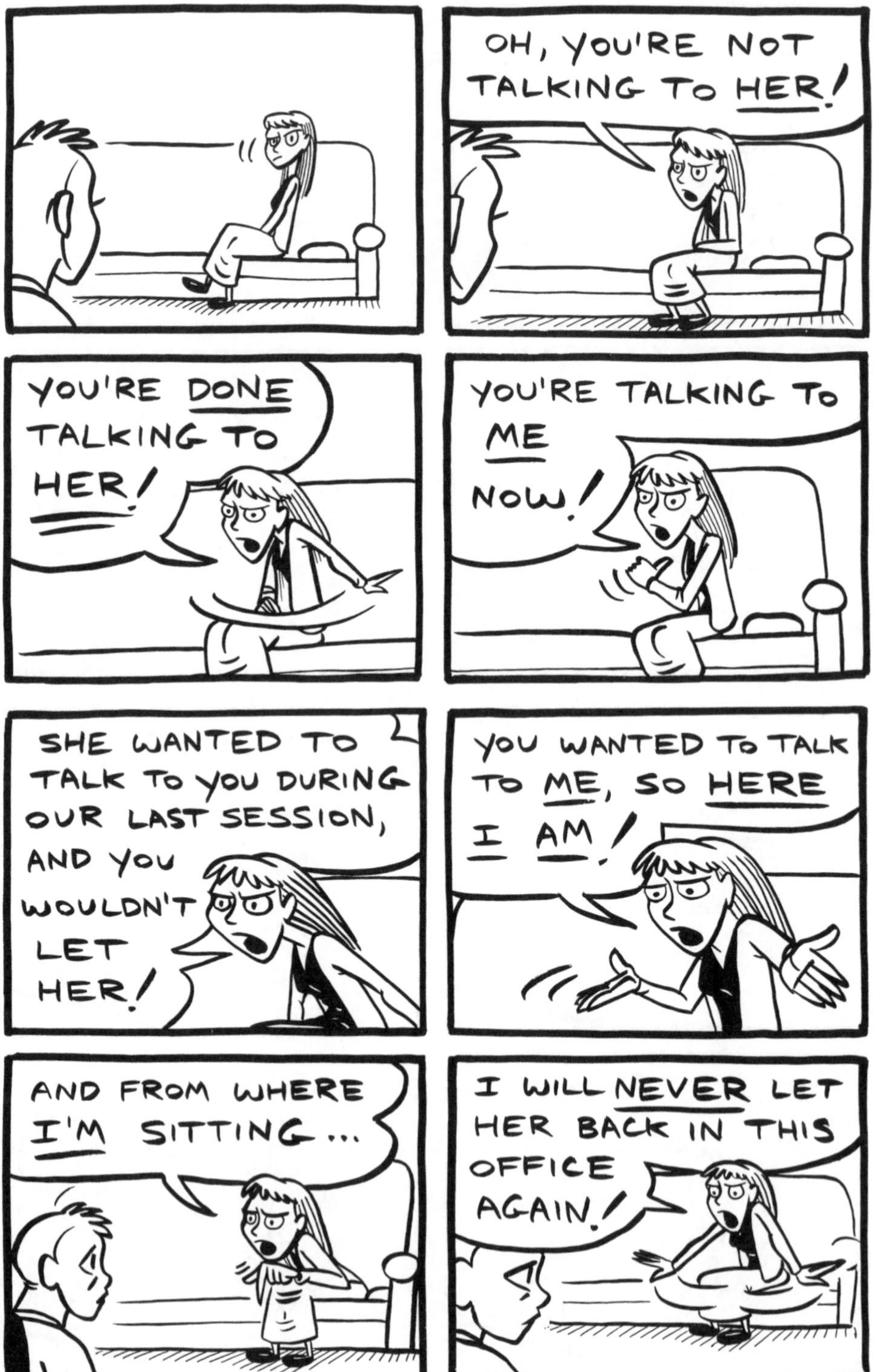
OH, YOU'RE NOT TALKING TO HER!
YOU'RE DONE TALKING TO HER!
YOU'RE TALKING TO ME NOW!
SHE WANTED TO TALK TO YOU DURING OUR LAST SESSION, AND YOU WOULDN'T LET HER!
YOU WANTED TO TALK TO ME, SO HERE I AM!
AND FROM WHERE I'M SITTING...
I WILL NEVER LET HER BACK IN THIS OFFICE AGAIN!

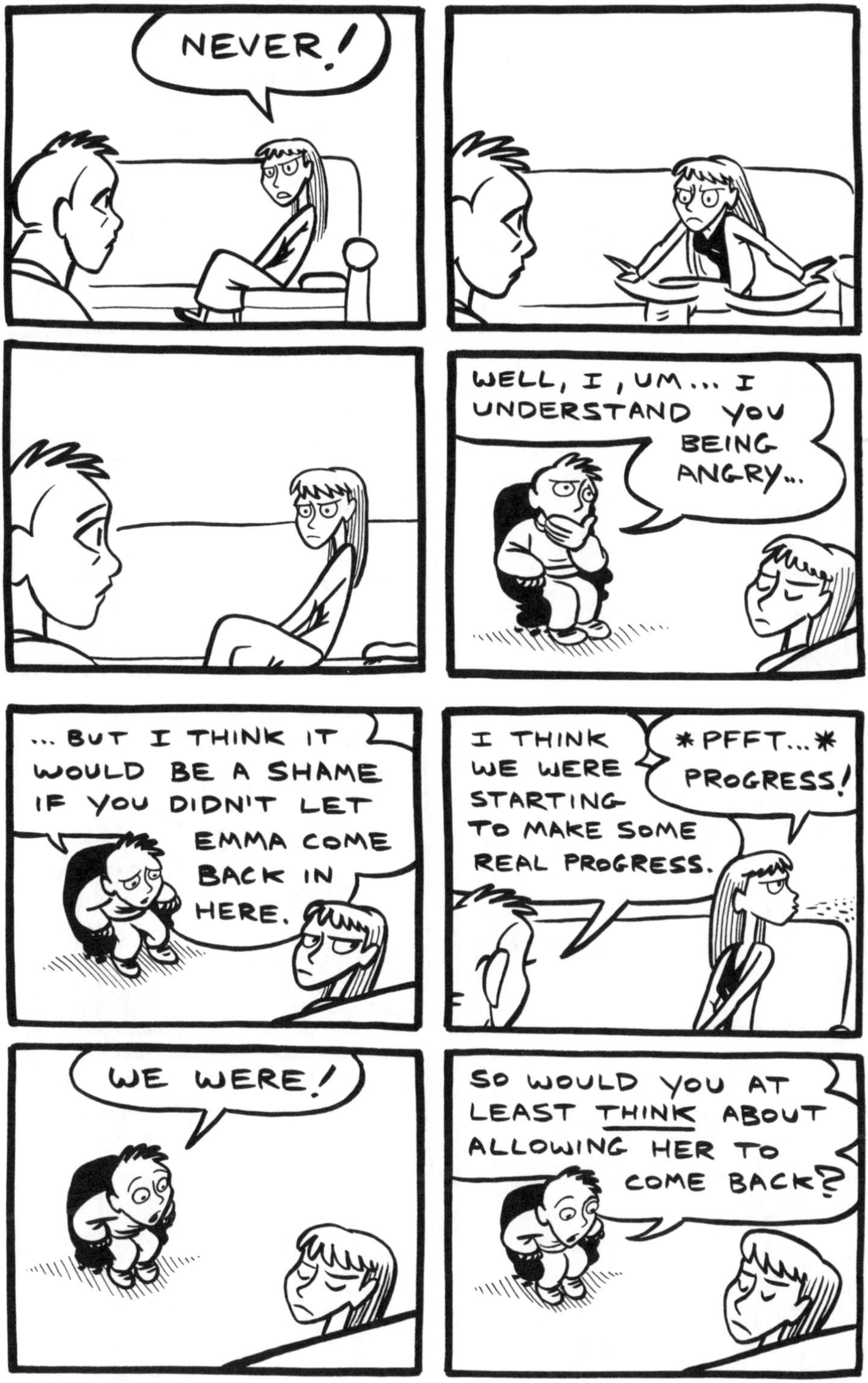
NEVER!
WELL, I, UM... I UNDERSTAND YOU BEING ANGRY..
...BUT I THINK IT WOULD BE A SHAME IF YOU DIDN'T LET EMMA COME BACK IN HERE.
I THINK WE WERE STARTING TO MAKE SOME REAL PROGRESS.
PFFT... PROGRESS!
WE WERE!
SO WOULD YOU AT LEAST THINK ABOUT ALLOWING HER TO COME BACK?

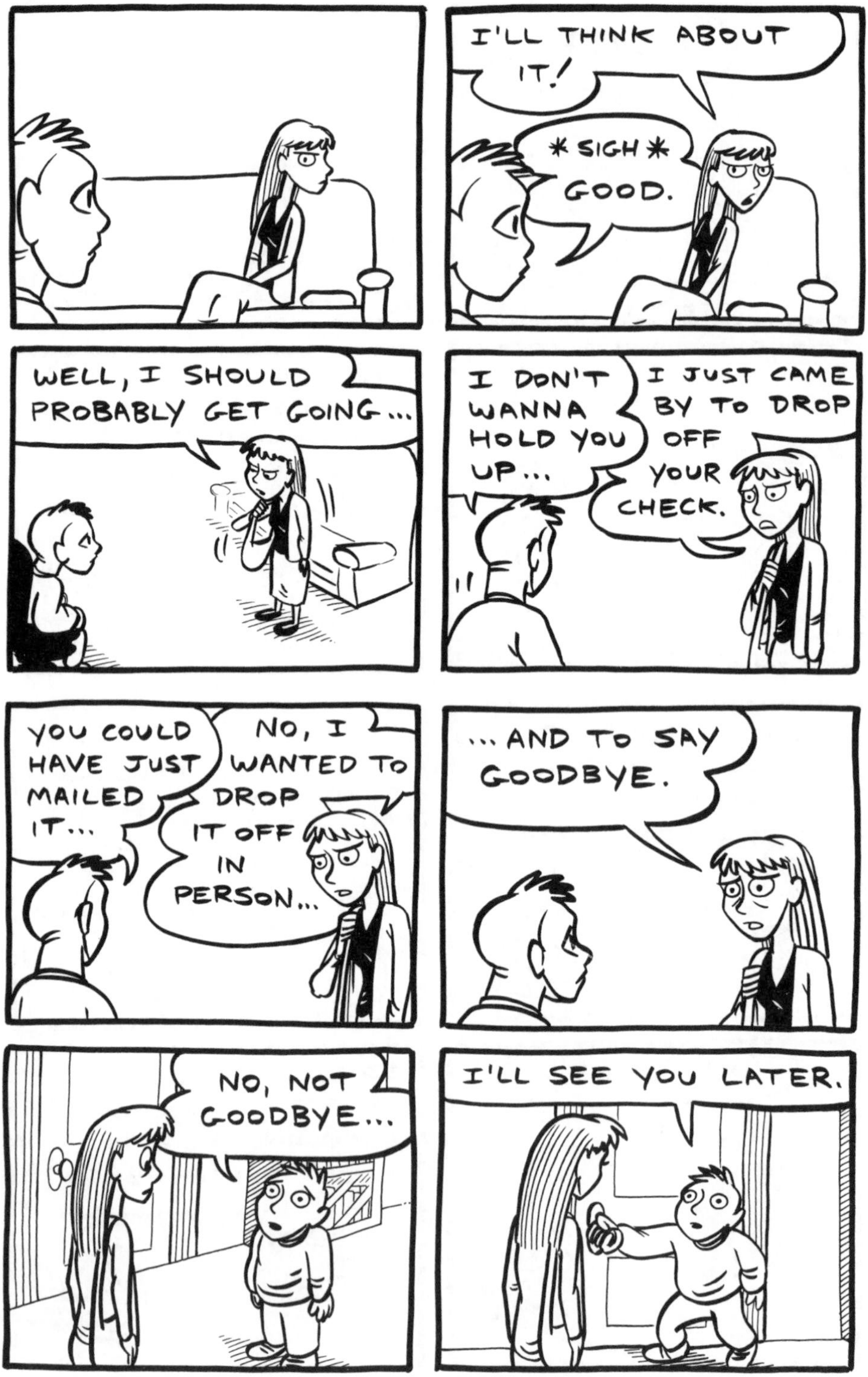
I'LL THINK ABOUT IT!
SIGH GOOD.
WELL, I SHOULD PROBABLY GET GOING...
I DON'T WANNA HOLD YOU UP...
I JUST CAME BY TO DROP OFF YOUR CHECK.
YOU COULD HAVE JUST MAILED IT...
NO, I WANTED TO DROP IT OFF IN PERSON...
...AND TO SAY GOODBYE.
NO, NOT GOODBYE...
I'LL SEE YOU LATER.

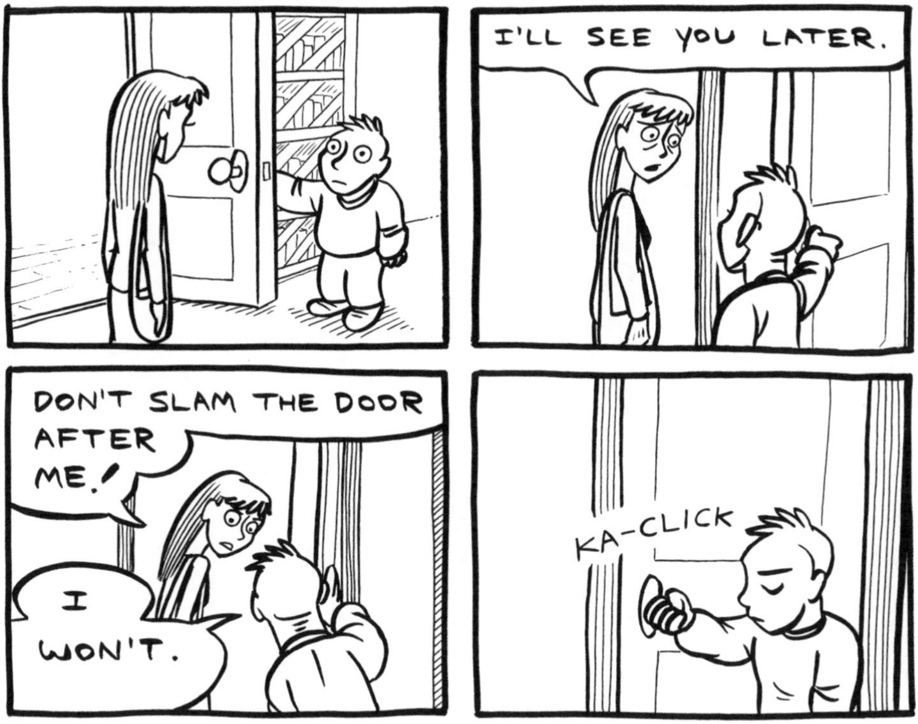
I'LL SEE YOU LATER.
DON'T SLAM THE DOOR AFTER ME.!
I WON'T.
KA-CLICK

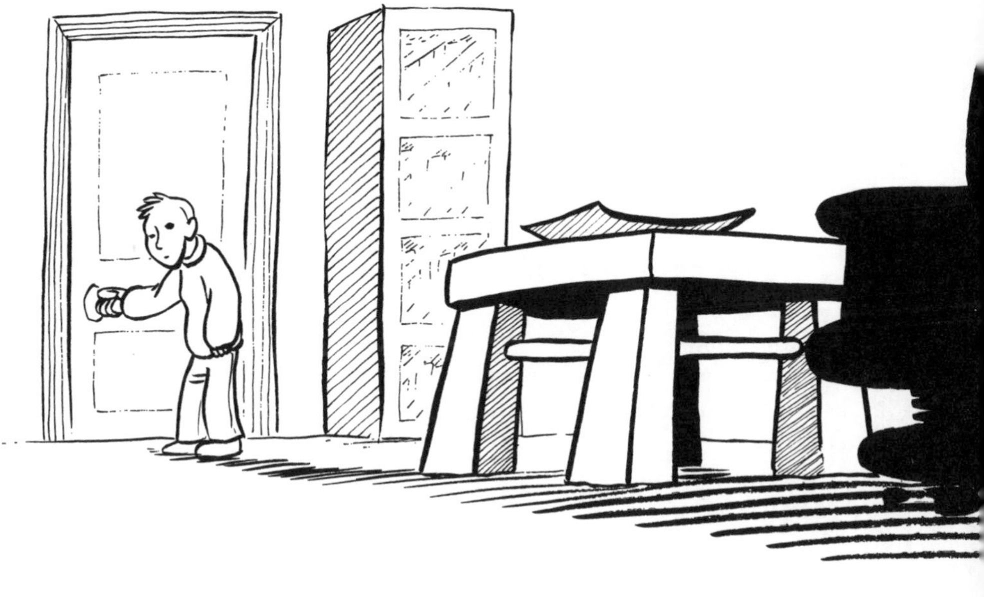

CASHEWS

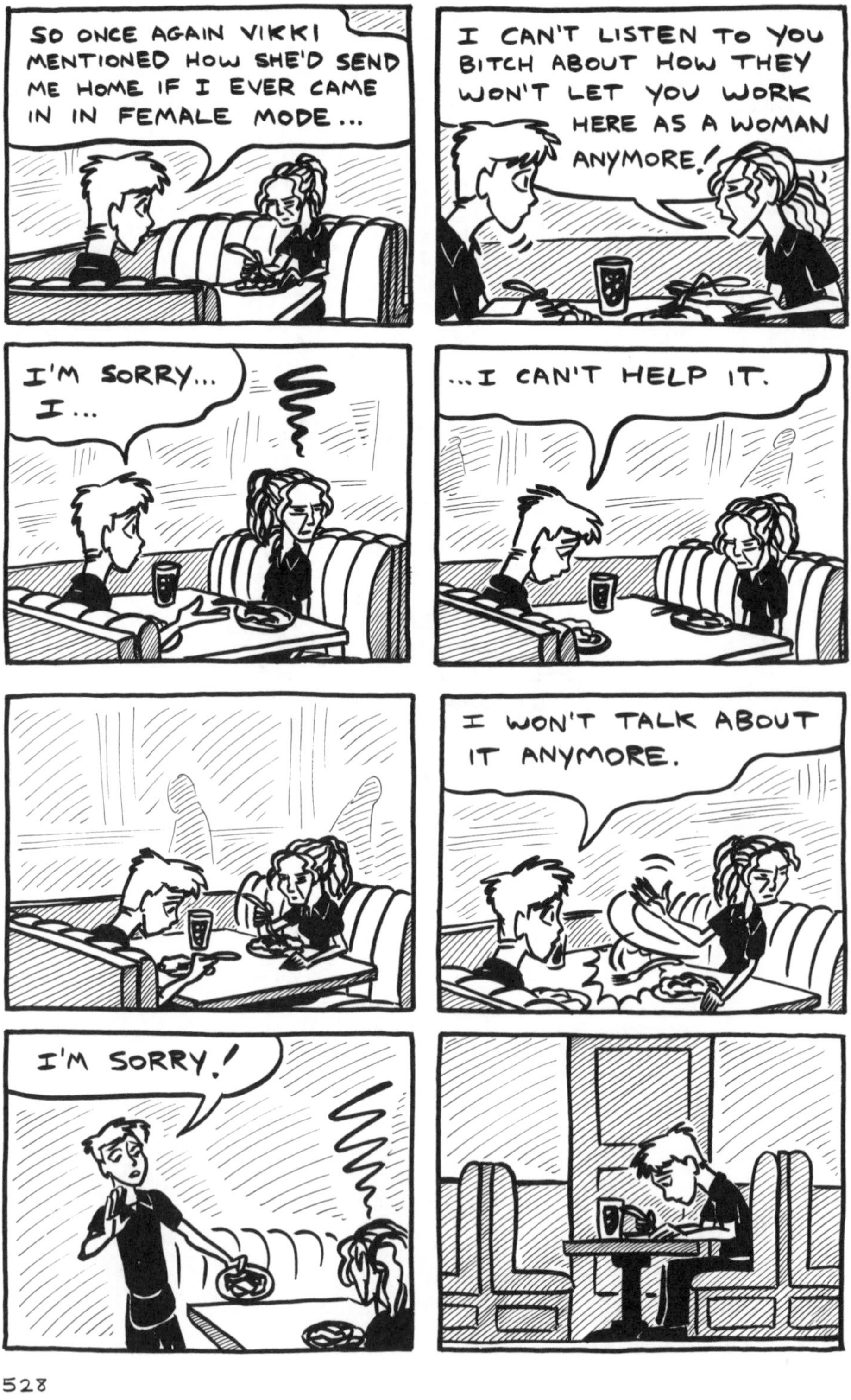
SO ONCE AGAIN VIKKI MENTIONED HOW SHE'D SEND ME HOME IF I EVER CAME IN IN FEMALE MODE...
I CAN'T LISTEN TO YOU BITCH ABOUT HOW THEY WON'T LET YOU WORK HERE AS A WOMAN ANYMORE!
I'M SORRY... I...
...I CAN'T HELP IT.
I WON'T TALK ABOUT IT ANYMORE.
I'M SORRY!

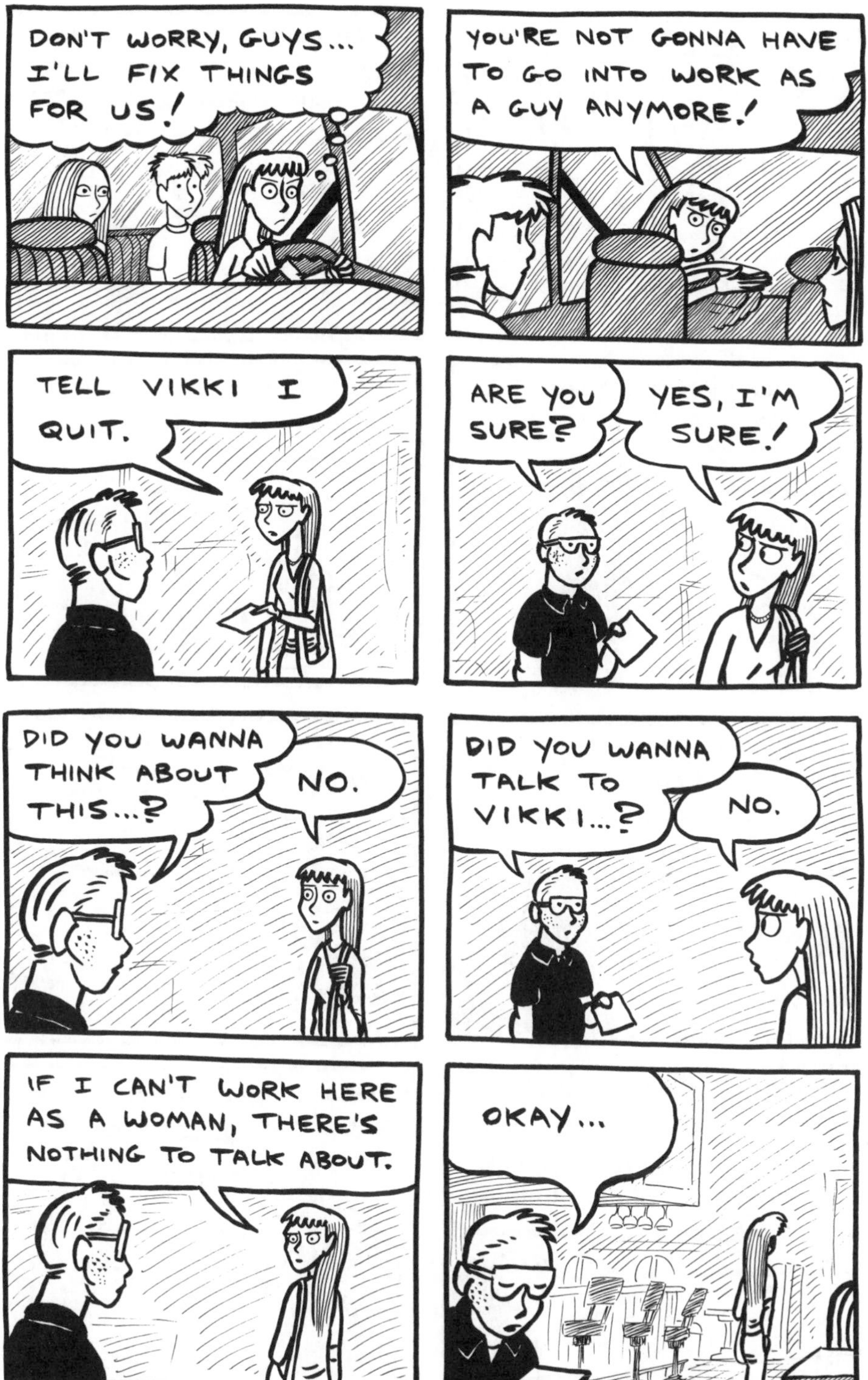

DON'T WORRY, GUYS... I'LL FIX THINGS FOR US!
YOU'RE NOT GONNA HAVE TO GO INTO WORK AS A GUY ANYMORE!
TELL VIKKI I QUIT.
ARE YOU SURE?
YES, I'M SURE!
DID YOU WANNA THINK ABOUT THIS...?
NO.
DID YOU WANNA TALK TO VIKKI...?
NO.
IF I CAN'T WORK HERE AS A WOMAN, THERE'S NOTHING TO TALK ABOUT.
OKAY...

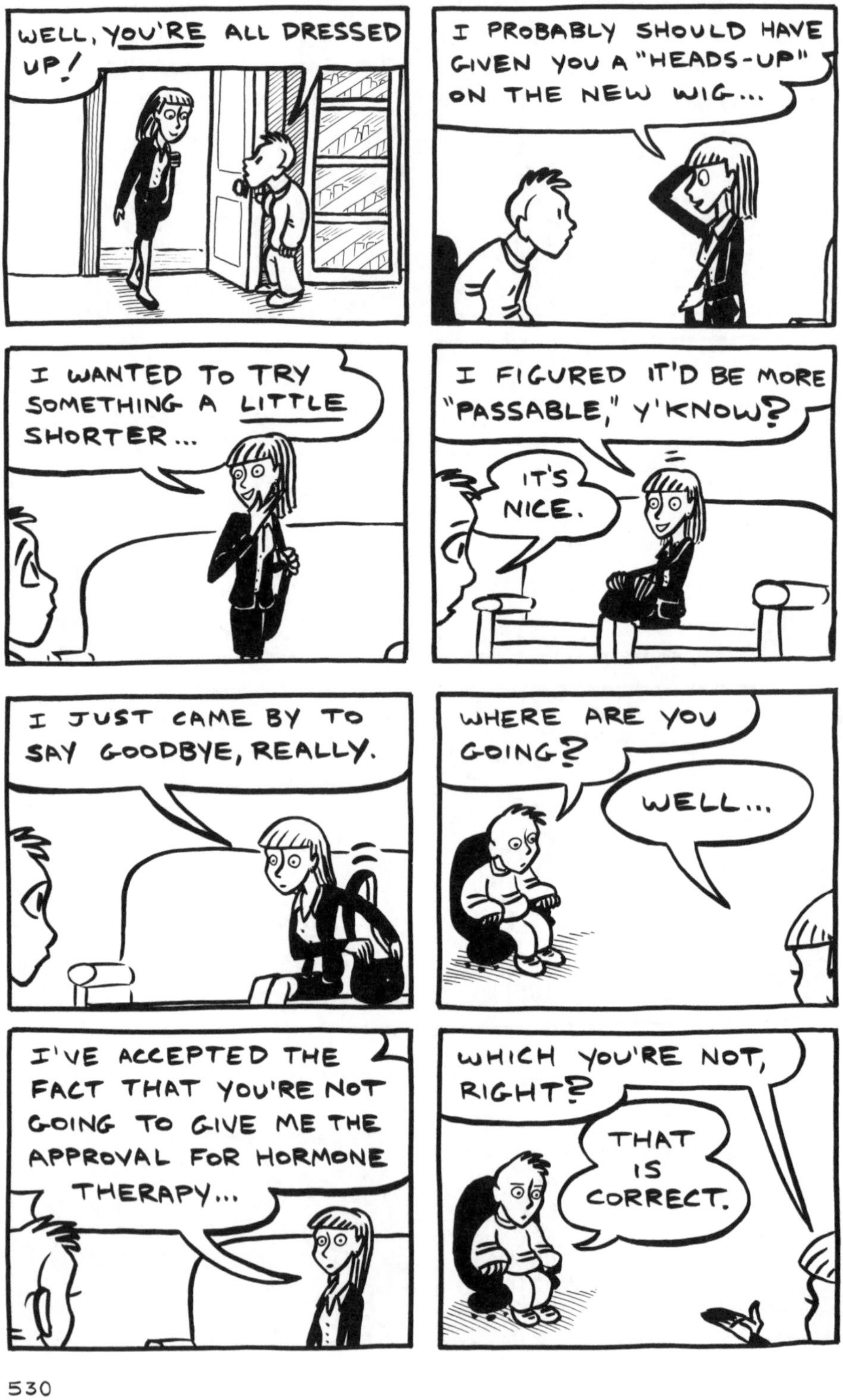
WELL, YOU'RE ALL DRESSED UP!
I PROBABLY SHOULD HAVE GIVEN YOU A "HEADS-UP" ON THE NEW WIG...
I WANTED TO TRY SOMETHING A LITTLE SHORTER...
I FIGURED IT'D BE MORE "PASSABLE," Y'KNOW?
IT'S NICE.
I JUST CAME BY TO SAY GOODBYE, REALLY.
WHERE ARE YOU GOING?
WELL...
I'VE ACCEPTED THE FACT THAT YOU'RE NOT GOING TO GIVE ME THE APPROVAL FOR HORMONE THERAPY...
WHICH YOU'RE NOT, RIGHT?
THAT IS CORRECT.

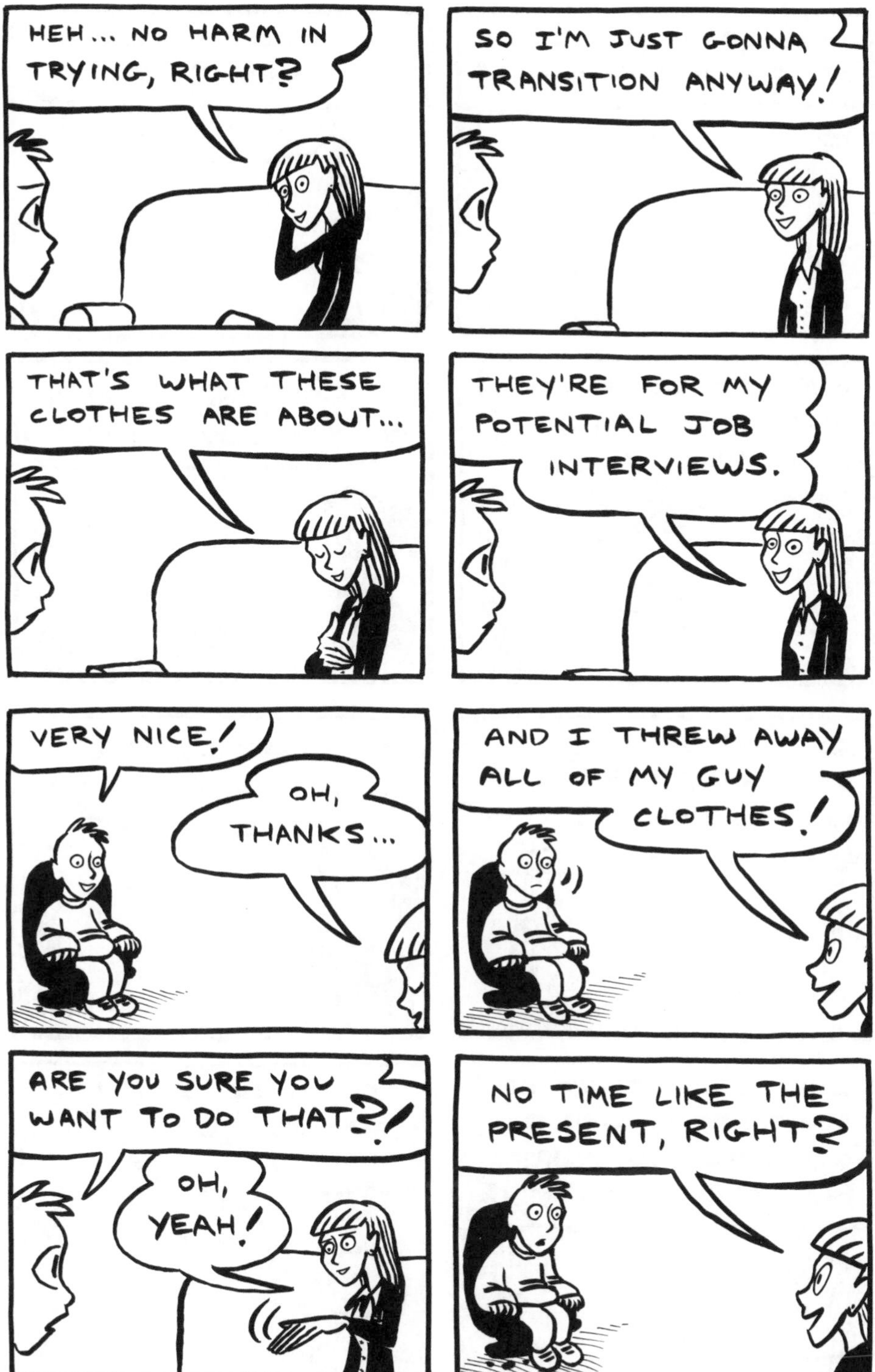
HEH... NO HARM IN TRYING, RIGHT?
SO I'M JUST GONNA TRANSITION ANYWAY!
THAT'S WHAT THESE CLOTHES ARE ABOUT...
THEY'RE FOR MY POTENTIAL JOB INTERVIEWS.
VERY NICE!
OH, THANKS...
AND I THREW AWAY ALL OF MY GUY CLOTHES!
ARE YOU SURE YOU WANT TO DO THAT?!
OH, YEAH!
NO TIME LIKE THE PRESENT, RIGHT?

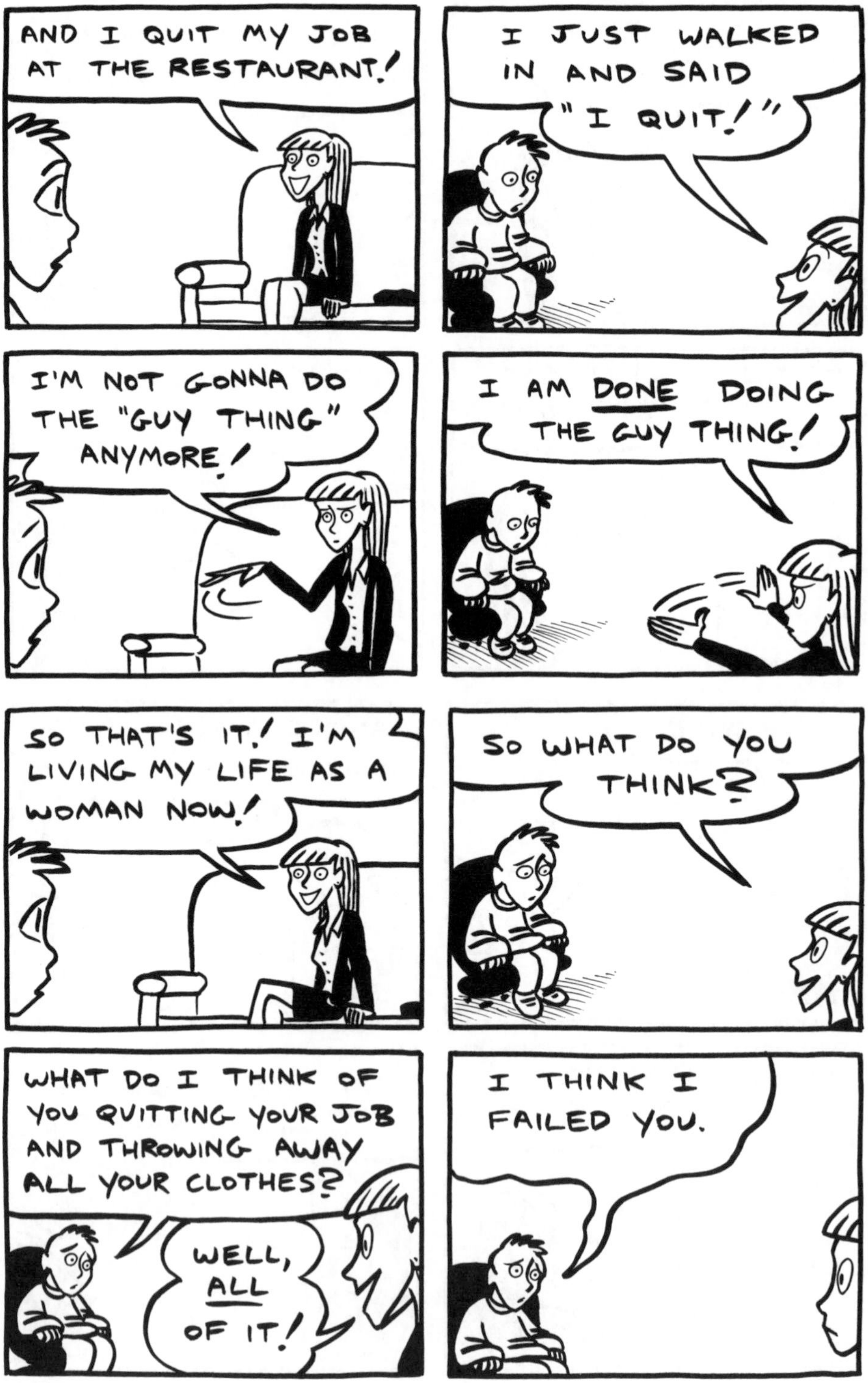
AND I QUIT MY JOB AT THE RESTAURANT!
I JUST WALKED IN AND SAID "I QUIT!"
I'M NOT GONNA DO THE "GUY THING" ANYMORE!
I AM DONE DOING THE GUY THING!
SO THAT'S IT! I'M LIVING MY LIFE AS A WOMAN NOW!
SO WHAT DO YOU THINK?
WHAT DO I THINK OF YOU QUITTING YOUR JOB AND THROWING AWAY ALL YOUR CLOTHES?
WELL, ALL OF IT!
I THINK I FAILED YOU.

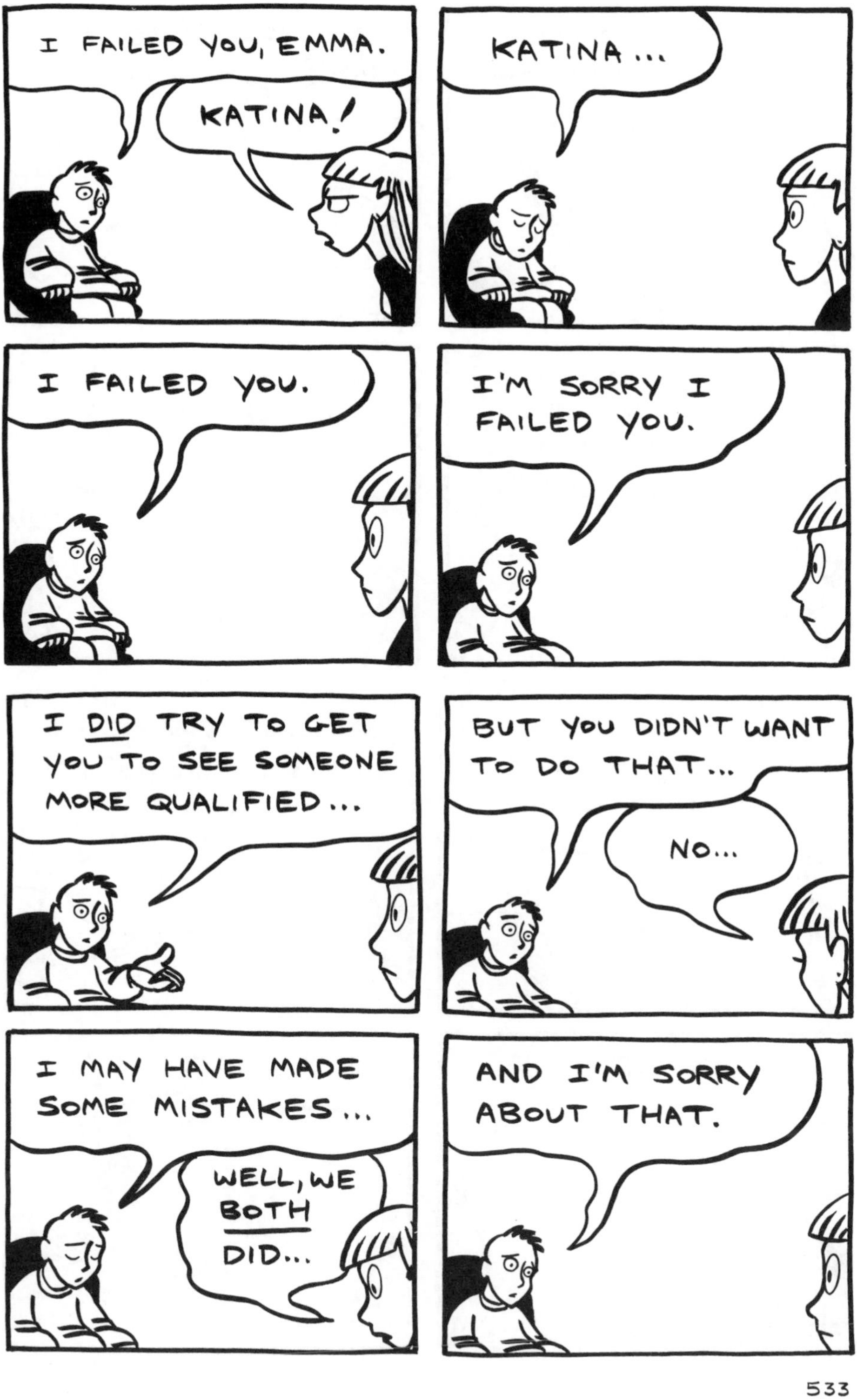
I FAILED YOU, EMMA.
KATINA!
KATINA...
I FAILED YOU.
I'M SORRY I FAILED YOU.
I DID TRY TO GET YOU TO SEE SOMEONE MORE QUALIFIED...
BUT YOU DIDN'T WANT TO DO THAT...
NO...
I MAY HAVE MADE SOME MISTAKES...
WELL, WE BOTH DID...
AND I'M SORRY ABOUT THAT.

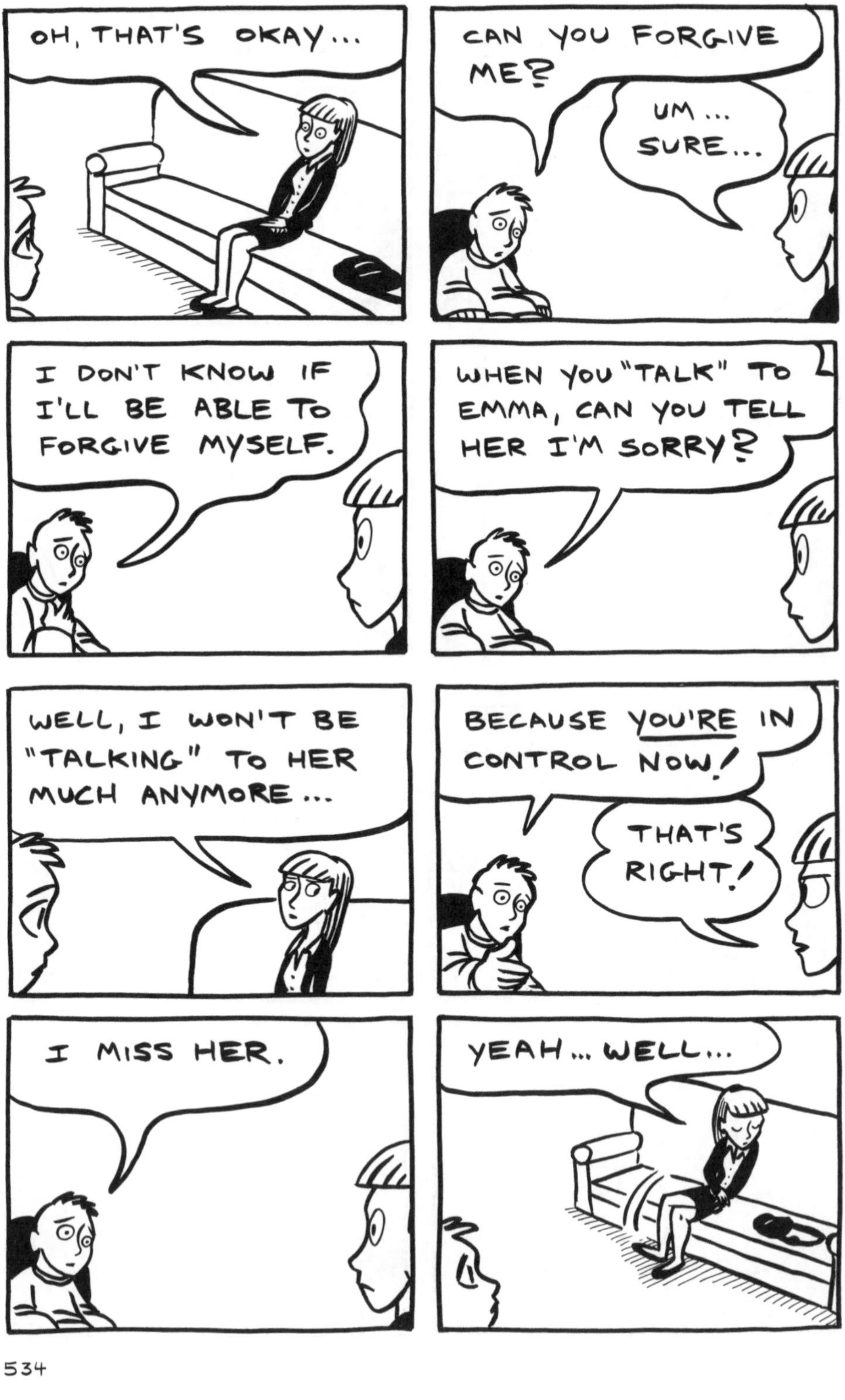
OH, THAT'S OKAY...
CAN YOU FORGIVE ME?
UM... SURE...
I DON'T KNOW IF I'LL BE ABLE TO FORGIVE MYSELF.
WHEN YOU "TALK" TO EMMA, CAN YOU TELL HER I'M SORRY?
WELL, I WON'T BE "TALKING" TO HER MUCH ANYMORE...
BECAUSE YOU'RE IN CONTROL NOW!
THAT'S RIGHT!
I MISS HER.
YEAH... WELL...

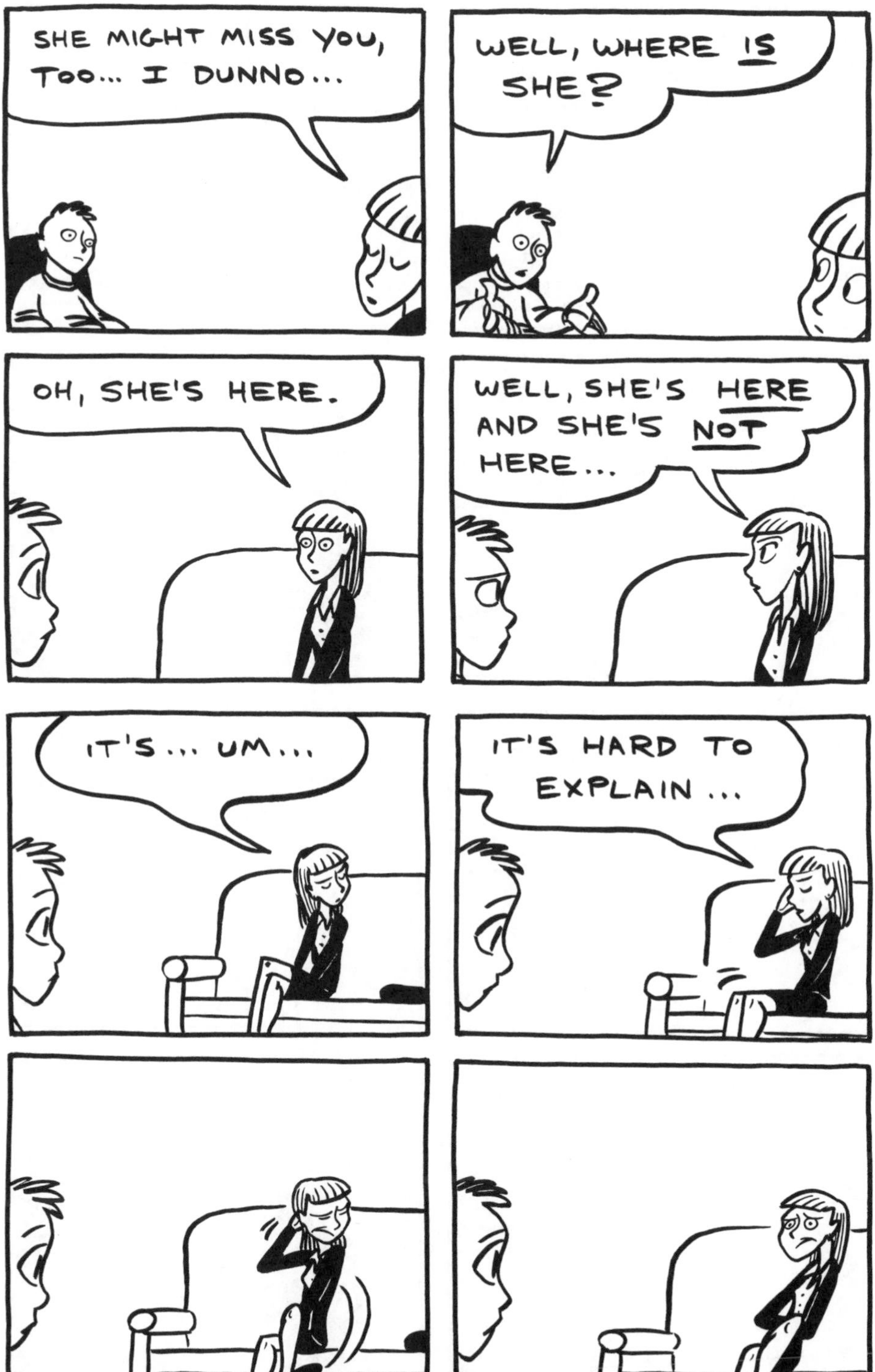
SHE MIGHT MISS YOU, TOO... I DUNNO...
WELL, WHERE IS SHE?
OH, SHE'S HERE.
WELL, SHE'S HERE AND SHE'S NOT HERE...
IT'S... UM...
IT'S HARD TO EXPLAIN...

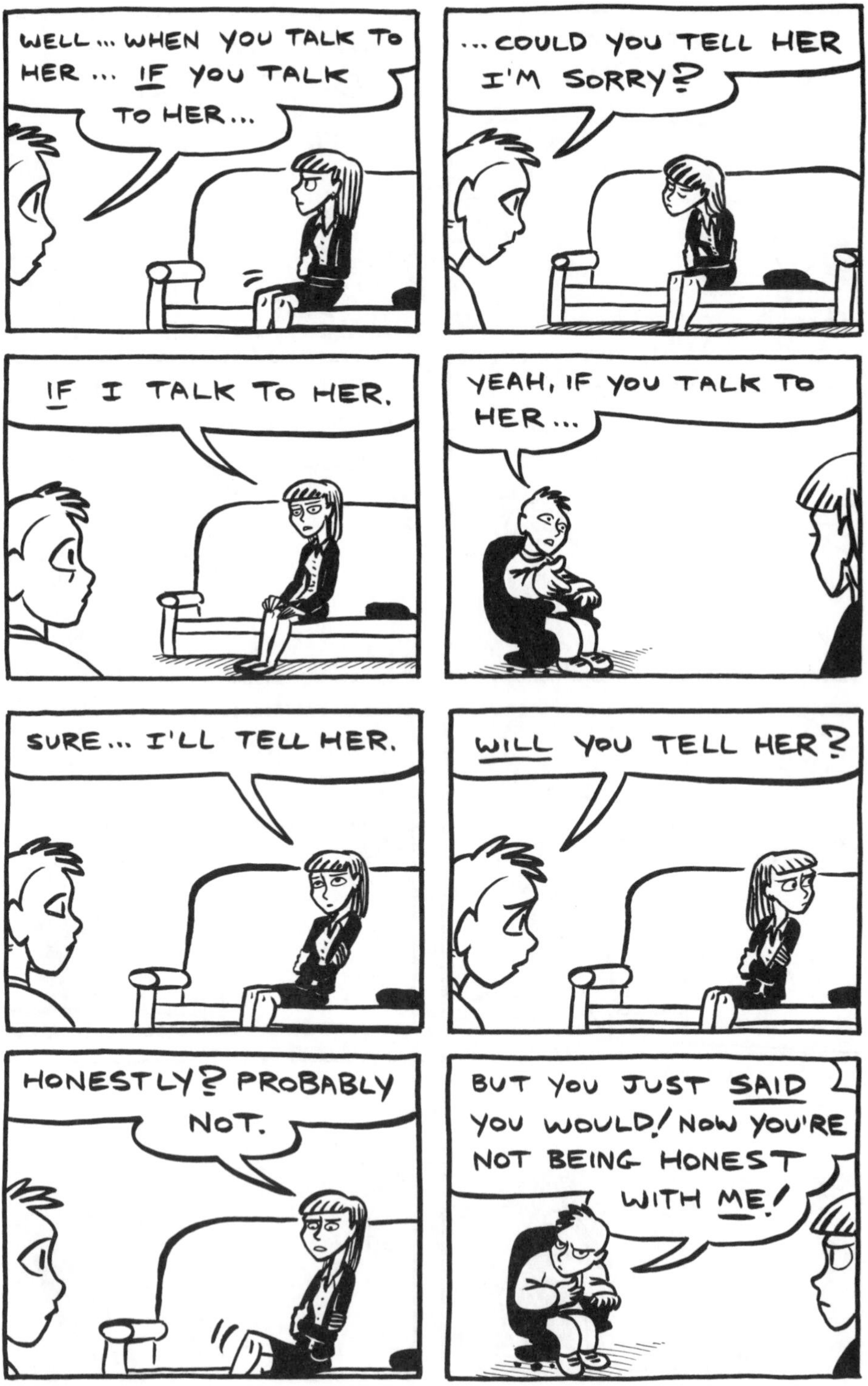

WELL... WHEN YOU TALK TO HER... IF YOU TALK TO HER...
...COULD YOU TELL HER I'M SORRY?
IF I TALK TO HER.
YEAH, IF YOU TALK TO HER...
SURE... I'LL TELL HER.
WILL YOU TELL HER?
HONESTLY? PROBABLY NOT.
BUT YOU JUST SAID YOU WOULD! NOW YOU'RE NOT BEING HONEST WITH ME!

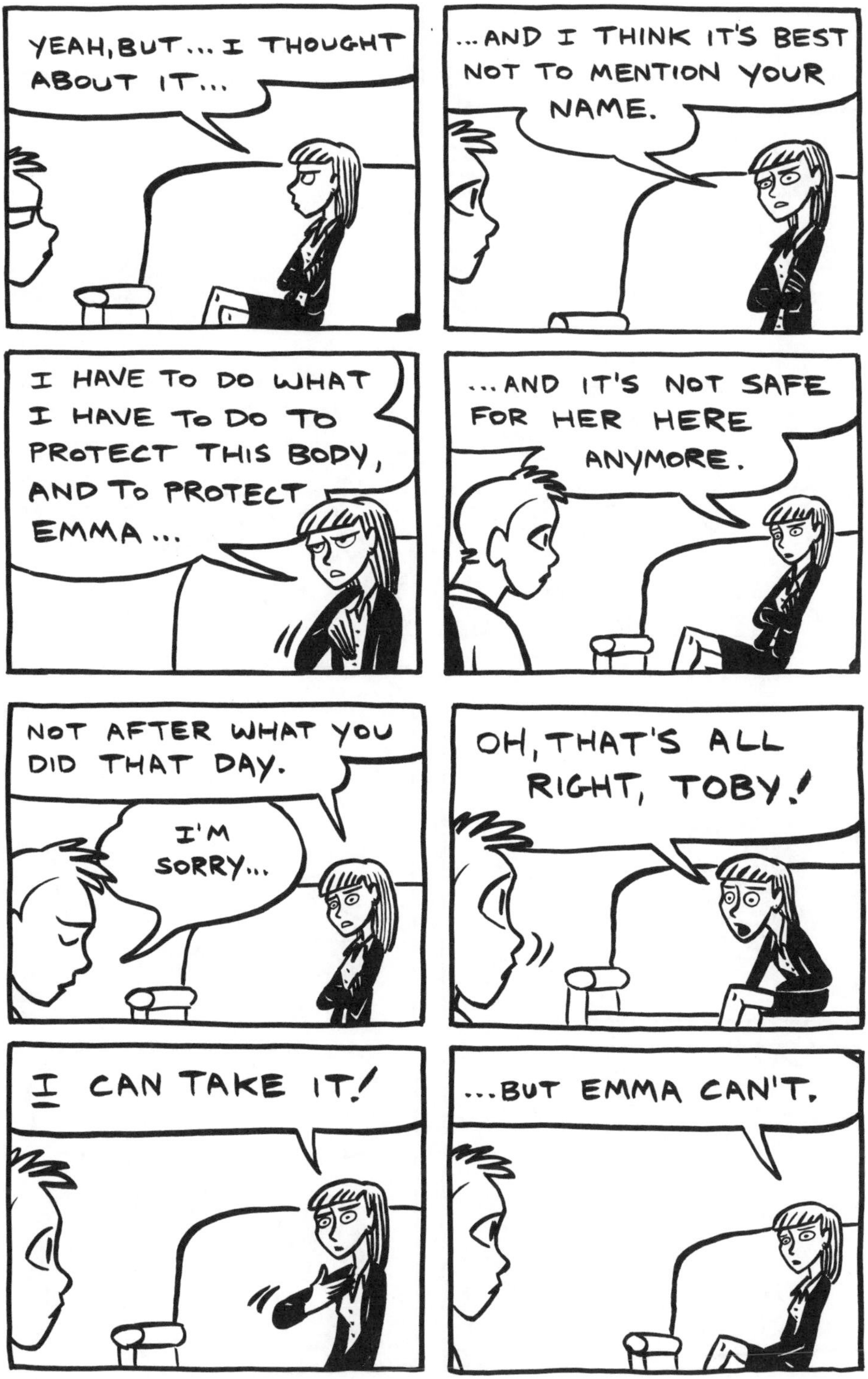
YEAH, BUT... I THOUGHT ABOUT IT...
...AND I THINK IT'S BEST NOT TO MENTION YOUR NAME.
I HAVE TO DO WHAT I HAVE TO DO TO PROTECT THIS BODY, AND TO PROTECT EMMA...
...AND IT'S NOT SAFE FOR HER HERE ANYMORE.
NOT AFTER WHAT YOU DID THAT DAY.
I'M SORRY...
OH, THAT'S ALL RIGHT, TOBY!
I CAN TAKE IT!
...BUT EMMA CAN'T.

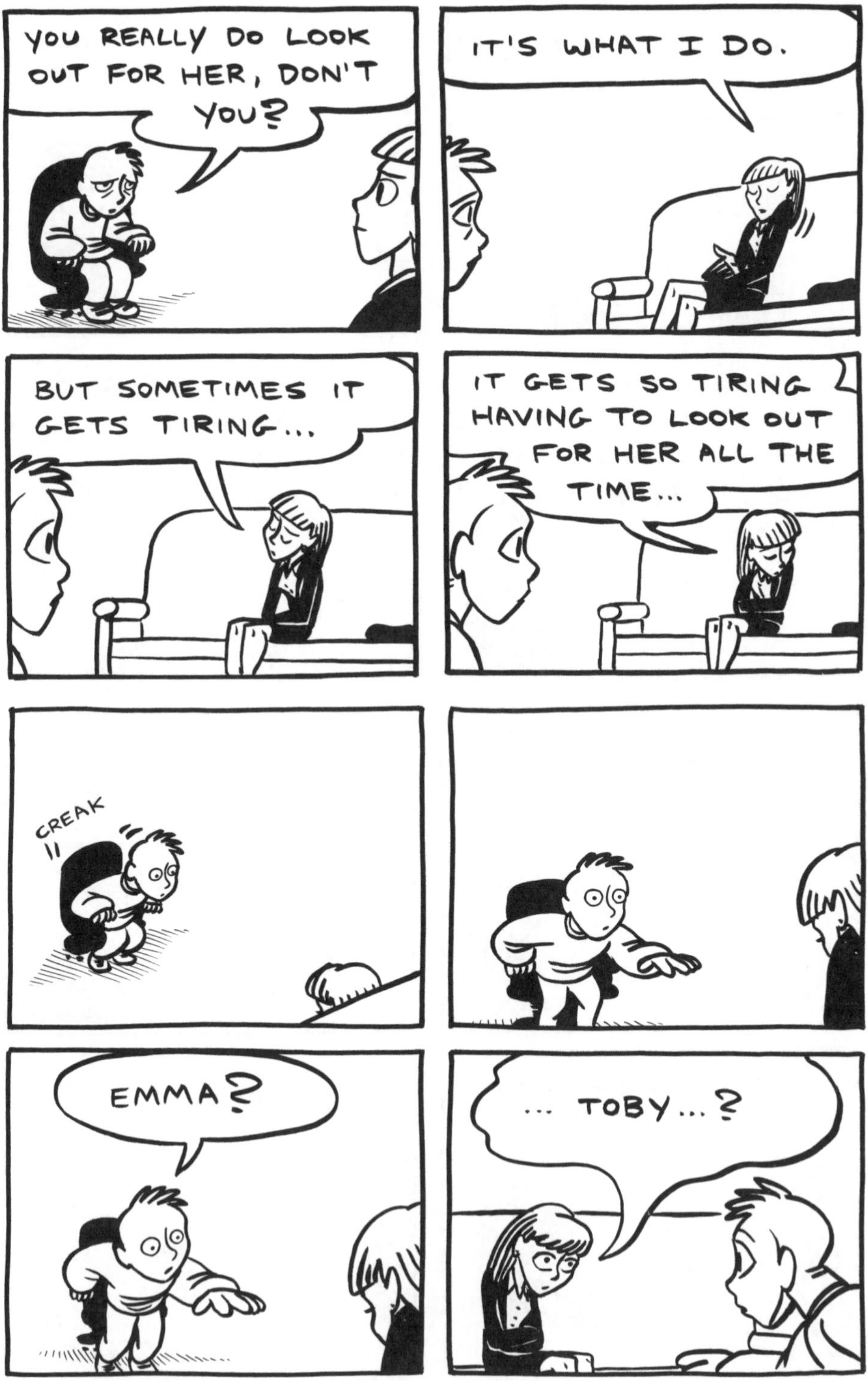
YOU REALLY DO LOOK OUT FOR HER, DON'T YOU?
IT'S WHAT I DO.
BUT SOMETIMES IT GETS TIRING...
IT GETS SO TIRING HAVING TO LOOK OUT FOR HER ALL THE TIME...
CREAK
EMMA?
... TOBY...?

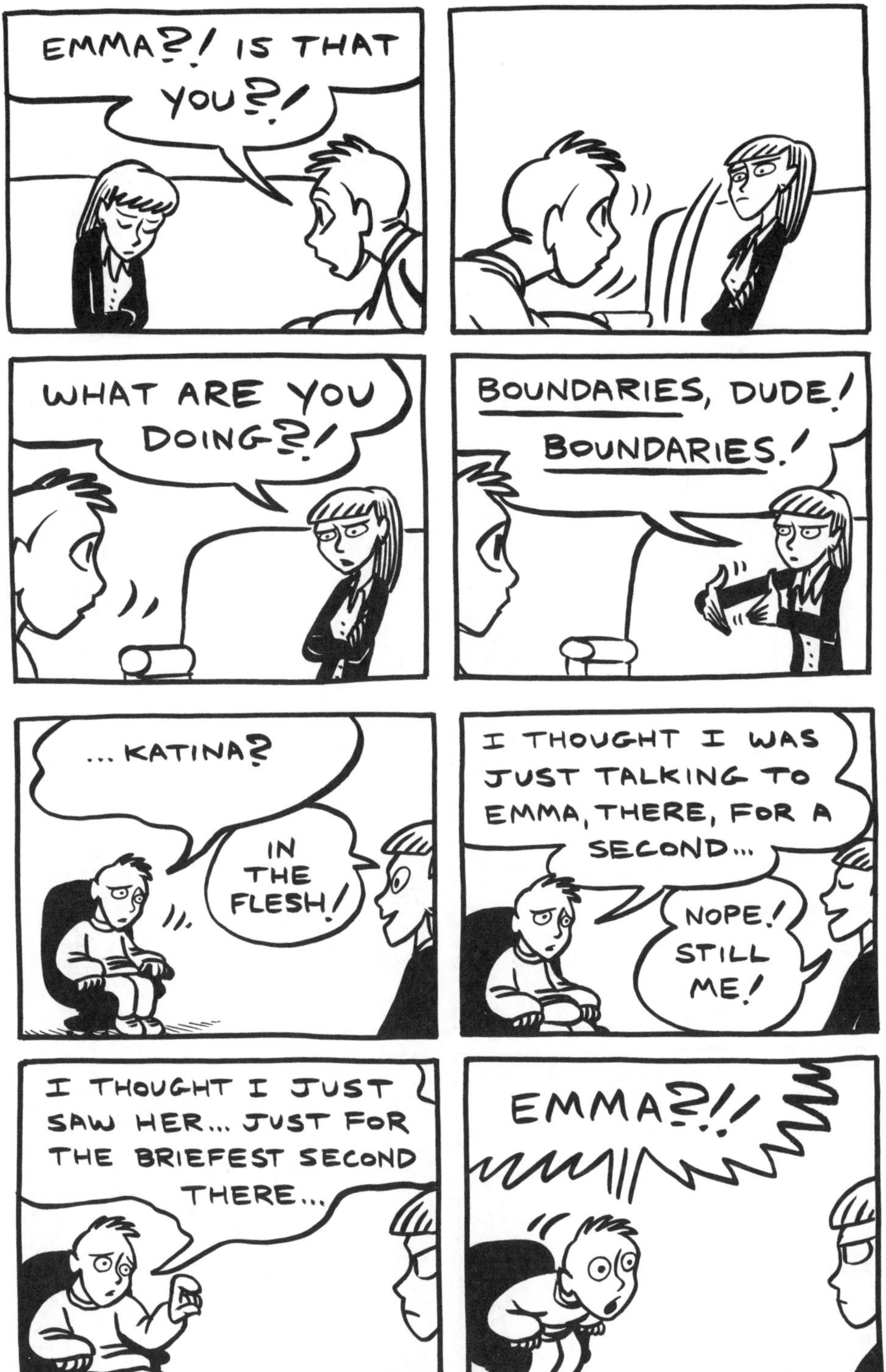
EMMA?! IS THAT YOU?!
WHAT ARE YOU DOING?!
BOUNDARIES, DUDE! BOUNDARIES!
...KATINA?
IN THE FLESH!
I THOUGHT I WAS JUST TALKING TO EMMA, THERE, FOR A SECOND...
NOPE! STILL ME!
I THOUGHT I JUST SAW HER... JUST FOR THE BRIEFEST SECOND THERE...
EMMA?!!

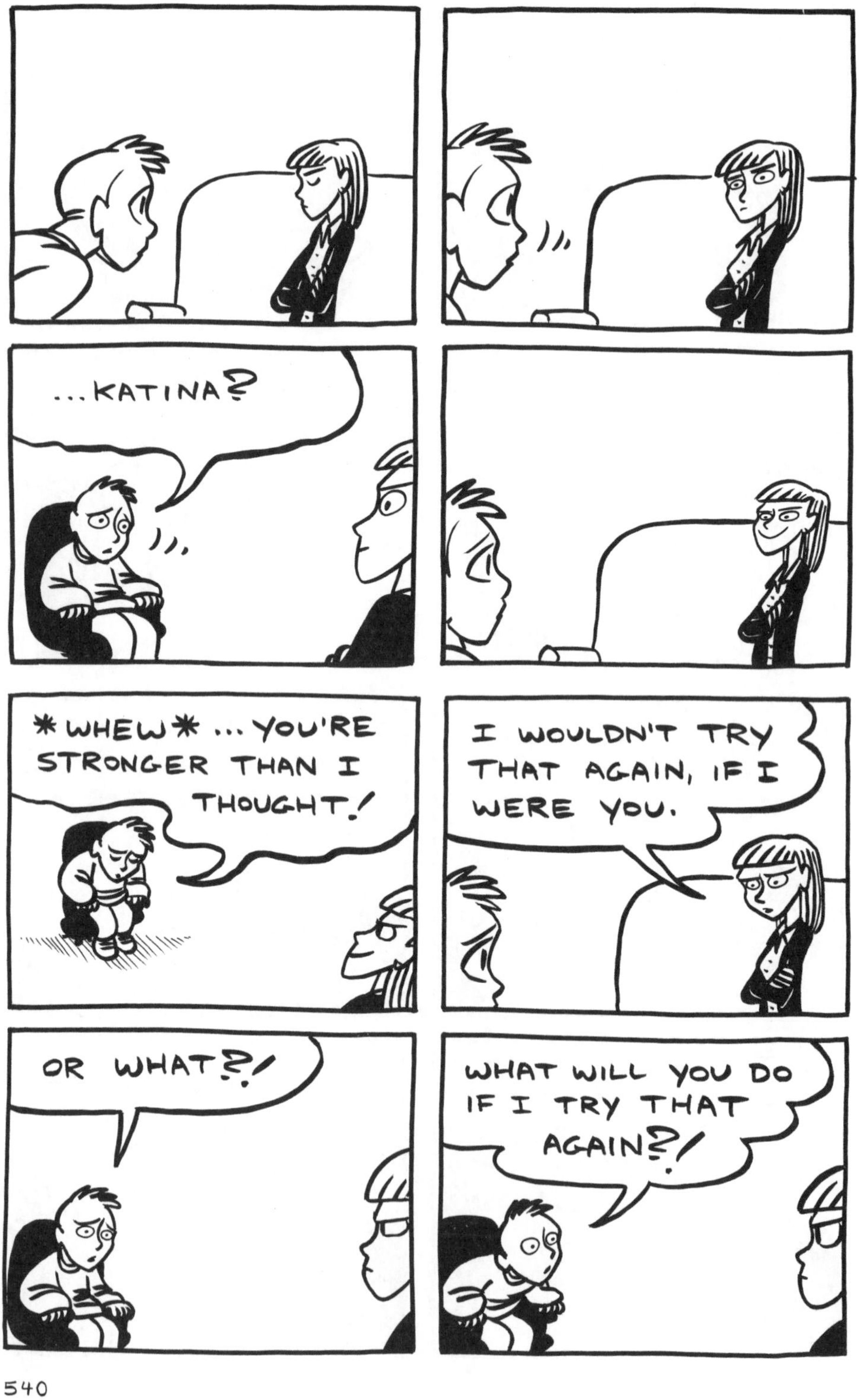

...KATINA?
WHEW ... YOU'RE STRONGER THAN I THOUGHT!
I WOULDN'T TRY THAT AGAIN, IF I WERE YOU.
OR WHAT?!
WHAT WILL YOU DO IF I TRY THAT AGAIN?!

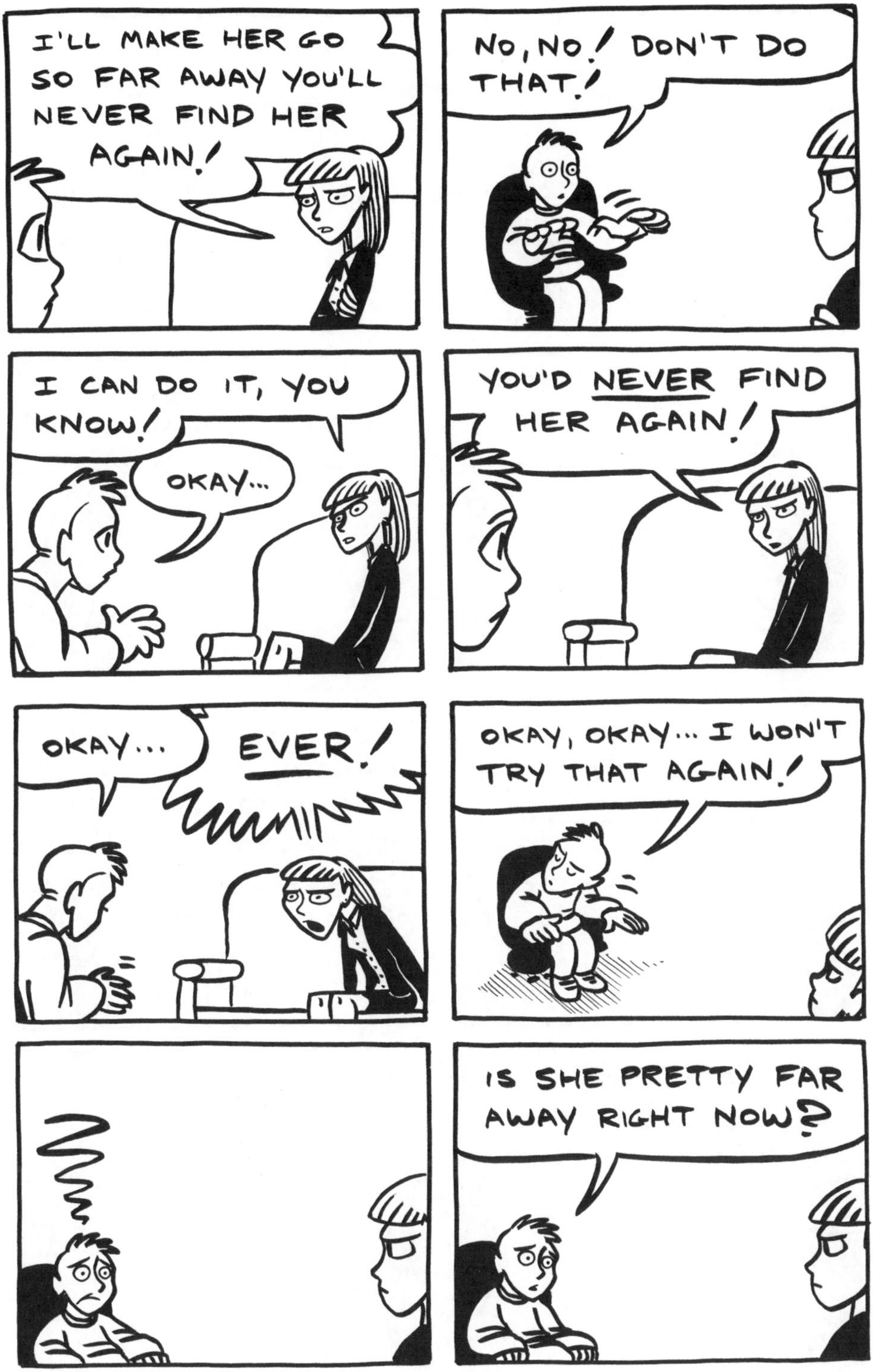
I'LL MAKE HER GO SO FAR AWAY YOU'LL NEVER FIND HER AGAIN!
NO, NO! DON'T DO THAT!
I CAN DO IT, YOU KNOW!
OKAY...
YOU'D NEVER FIND HER AGAIN!
OKAY...
EVER!
OKAY, OKAY... I WON'T TRY THAT AGAIN!
IS SHE PRETTY FAR AWAY RIGHT NOW?

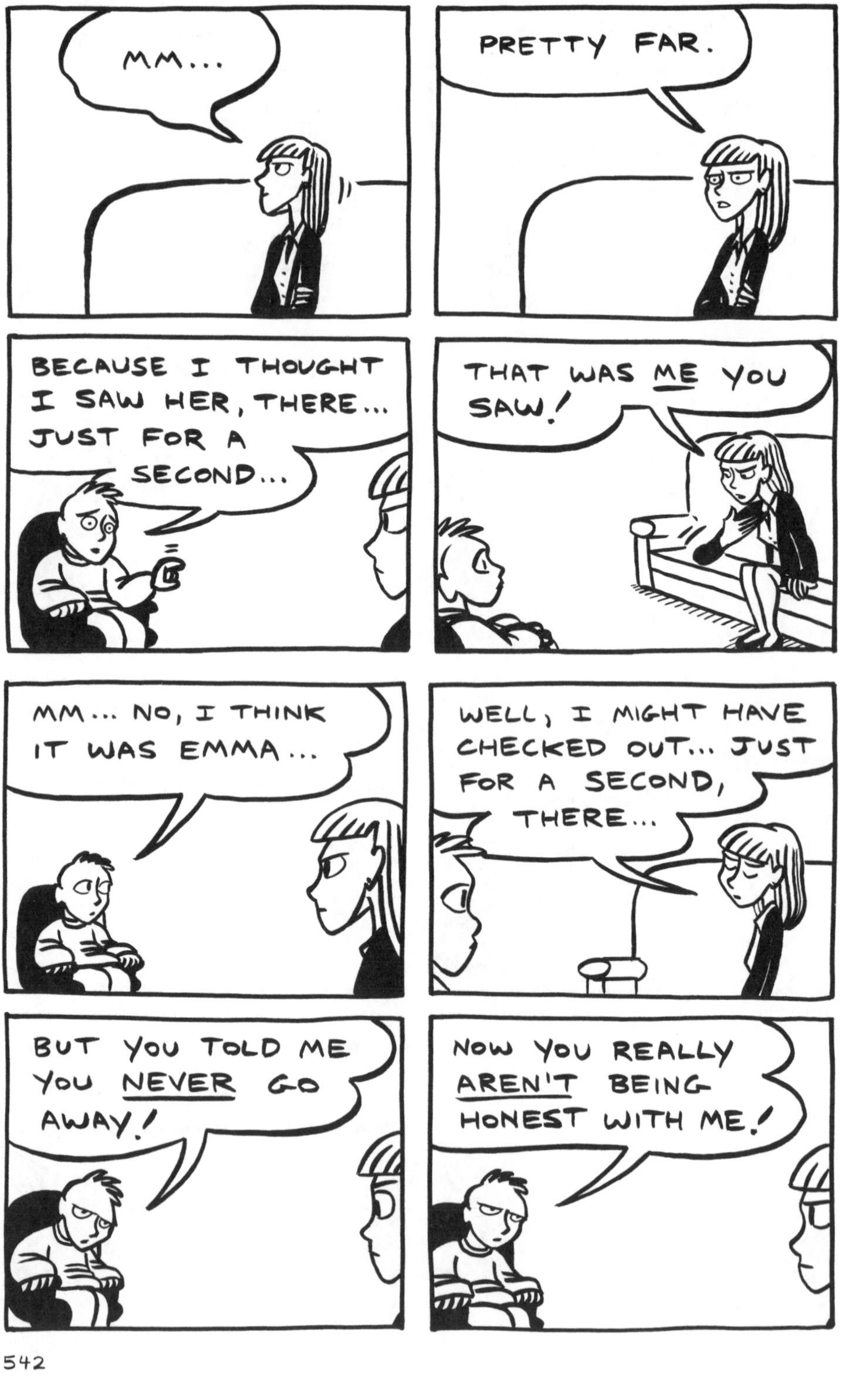
MM...
PRETTY FAR.
BECAUSE I THOUGHT I SAW HER, THERE... JUST FOR A SECOND...
THAT WAS ME YOU SAW!
MM... NO, I THINK IT WAS EMMA...
WELL, I MIGHT HAVE CHECKED OUT... JUST FOR A SECOND, THERE...
BUT YOU TOLD ME YOU NEVER GO AWAY!
NOW YOU REALLY AREN'T BEING HONEST WITH ME!

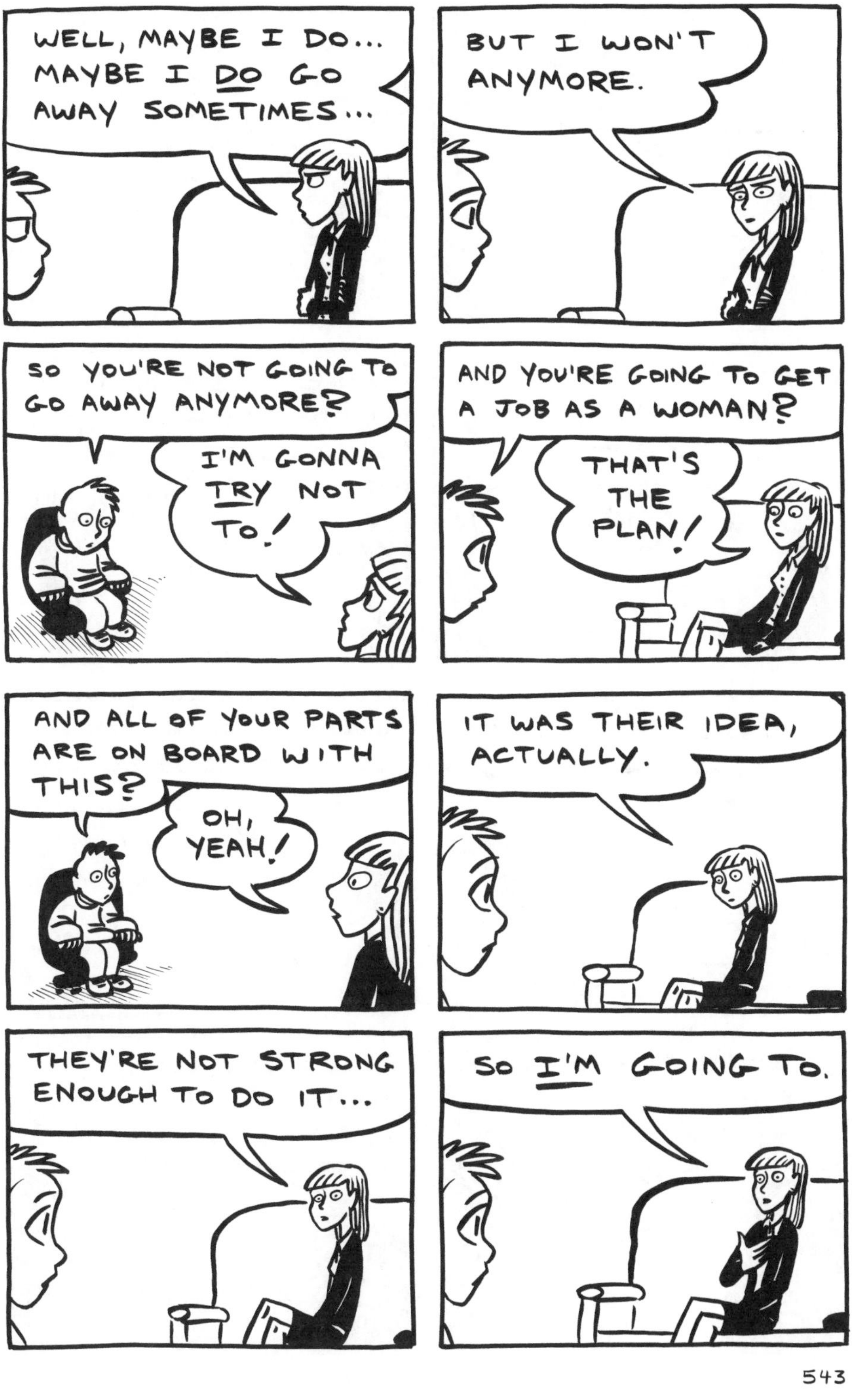
WELL, MAYBE I DO... MAYBE I DO GO AWAY SOMETIMES...
BUT I WON'T ANYMORE.
SO YOU'RE NOT GOING TO GO AWAY ANYMORE?
I'M GONNA TRY NOT TO!
AND YOU'RE GOING TO GET A JOB AS A WOMAN?
THAT'S THE PLAN!
AND ALL OF YOUR PARTS ARE ON BOARD WITH THIS?
OH, YEAH!
IT WAS THEIR IDEA, ACTUALLY.
THEY'RE NOT STRONG ENOUGH TO DO IT...
SO I'M GOING TO.

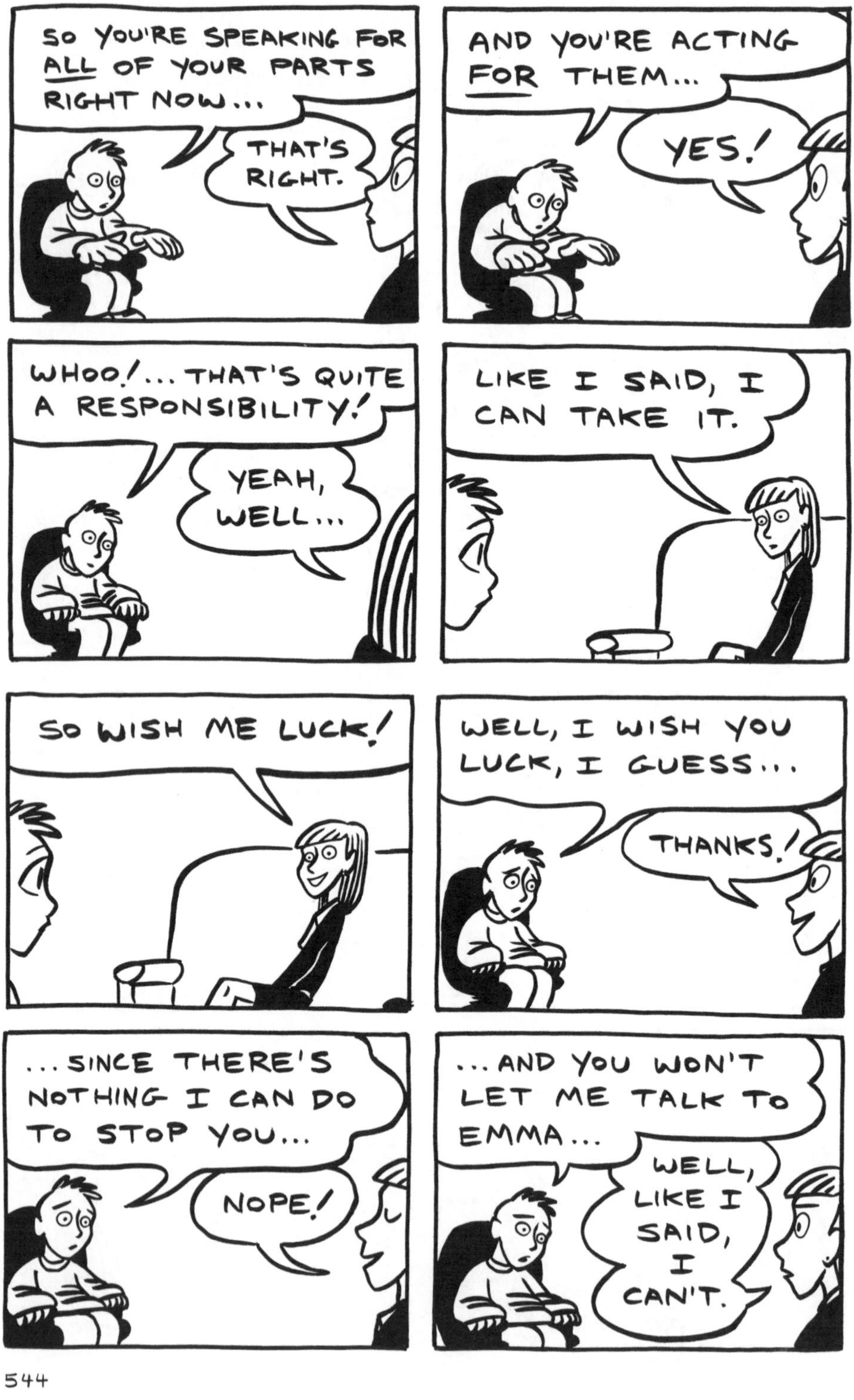
SO YOU'RE SPEAKING FOR ALL OF YOUR PARTS RIGHT NOW...
THAT'S RIGHT.
AND YOU'RE ACTING FOR THEM...
YES!
WHOO!... THAT'S QUITE A RESPONSIBILITY!
YEAH, WELL...
LIKE I SAID, I CAN TAKE IT.
SO WISH ME LUCK!
WELL, I WISH YOU LUCK, I GUESS...
THANKS!
...SINCE THERE'S NOTHING I CAN DO TO STOP YOU...
NOPE!
...AND YOU WON'T LET ME TALK TO EMMA...
WELL, LIKE I SAID, I CAN'T.

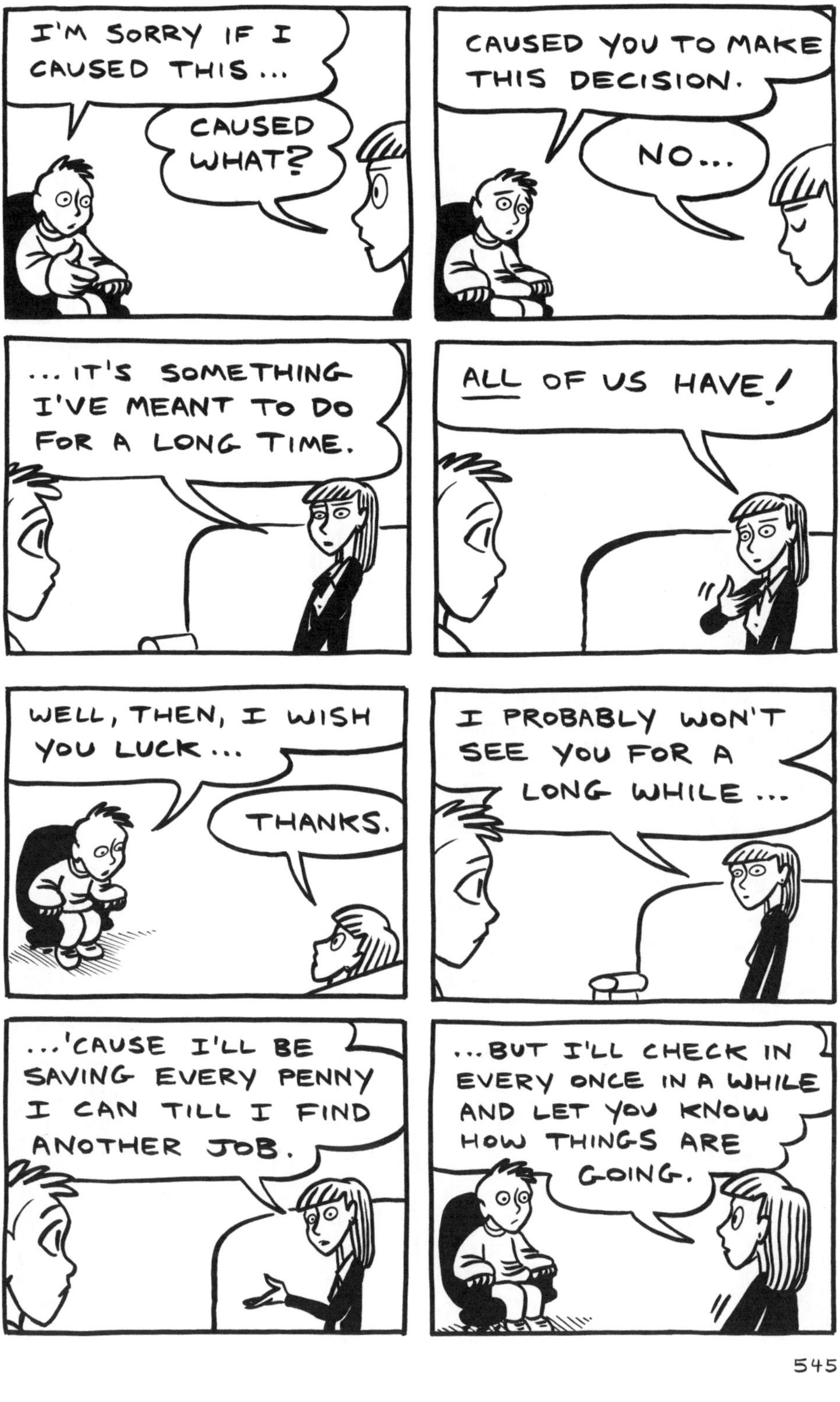
I'M SORRY IF I CAUSED THIS...
CAUSED WHAT?
CAUSED YOU TO MAKE THIS DECISION.
NO...
...IT'S SOMETHING I'VE MEANT TO DO FOR A LONG TIME.
ALL OF US HAVE!
WELL, THEN, I WISH YOU LUCK...
THANKS.
I PROBABLY WON'T SEE YOU FOR A LONG WHILE...
...'CAUSE I'LL BE SAVING EVERY PENNY I CAN TILL I FIND ANOTHER JOB.
...BUT I'LL CHECK IN EVERY ONCE IN A WHILE AND LET YOU KNOW HOW THINGS ARE GOING.

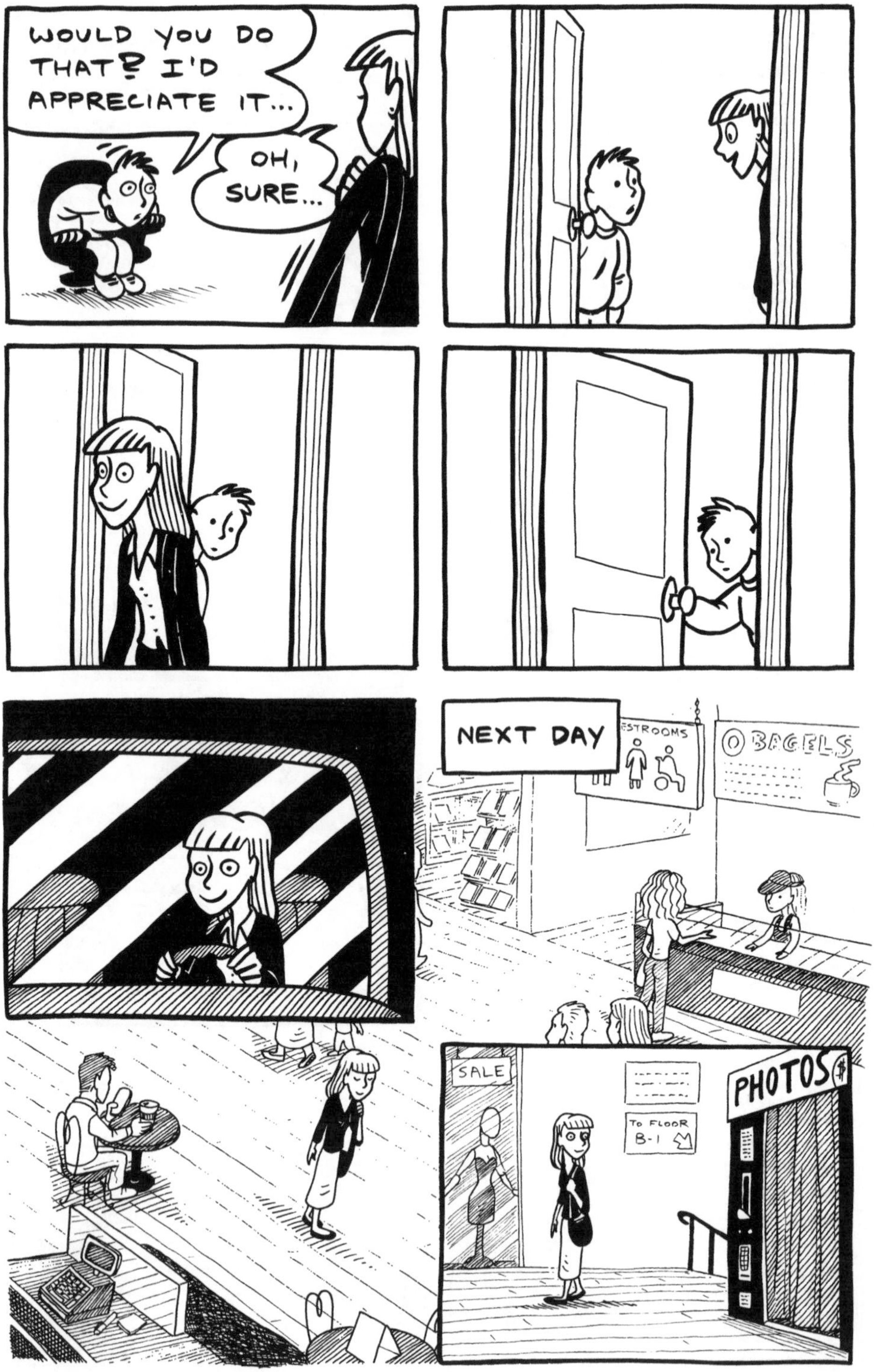
WOULD YOU DO THAT? I'D APPRECIATE IT...
OH, SURE...
NEXT DAY
ESTROOMS
BAGELS
SALE
TO FLOOR B-1
PHOTOS

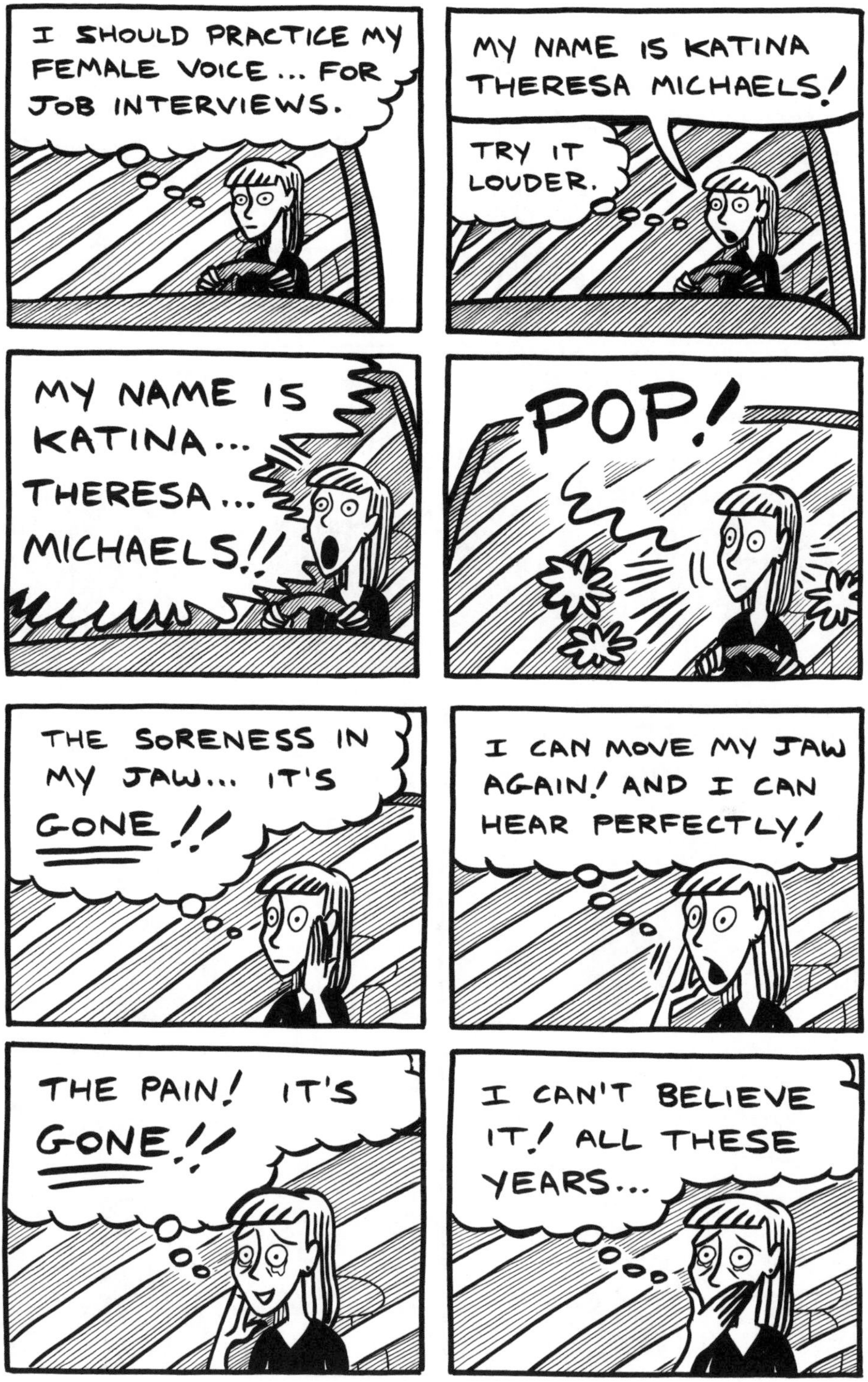
I SHOULD PRACTICE MY FEMALE VOICE... FOR JOB INTERVIEWS.
MY NAME IS KATINA THERESA MICHAELS!
TRY IT LOUDER.
MY NAME IS KATINA... THERESA... MICHAELS!!
POP!
THE SORENESS IN MY JAW... IT'S GONE!!
I CAN MOVE MY JAW AGAIN! AND I CAN HEAR PERFECTLY!
THE PAIN! IT'S GONE!!
I CAN'T BELIEVE IT! ALL THESE YEARS...

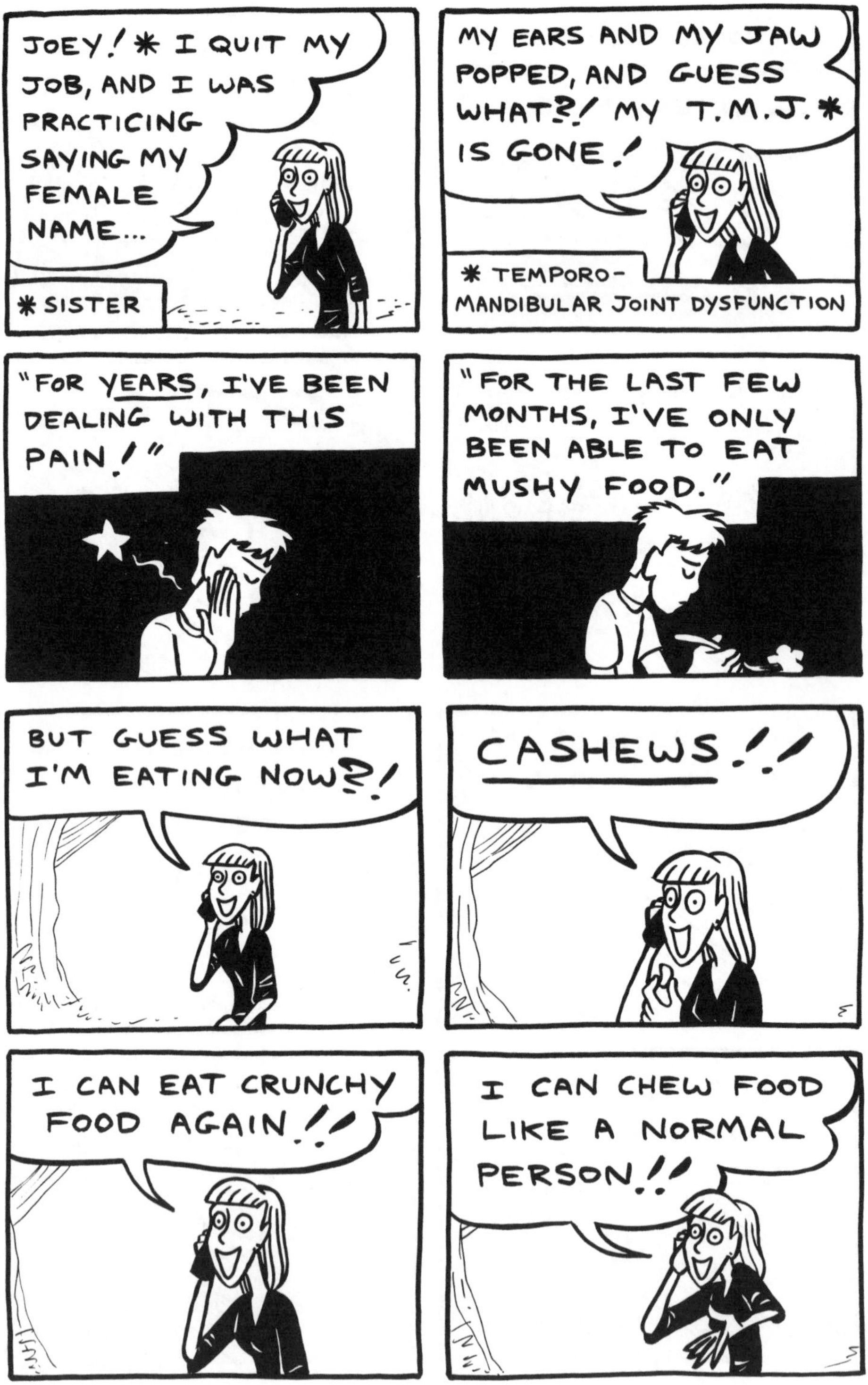
JOEY!* I QUIT MY JOB, AND I WAS PRACTICING SAYING MY FEMALE NAME...
* SISTER
MY EARS AND MY JAW POPPED, AND GUESS WHAT?! MY T.M.J.* IS GONE!
* TEMPORO-MANDIBULAR JOINT DYSFUNCTION
"FOR YEARS, I'VE BEEN DEALING WITH THIS PAIN!"
"FOR THE LAST FEW MONTHS, I'VE ONLY BEEN ABLE TO EAT MUSHY FOOD."
BUT GUESS WHAT I'M EATING NOW?!
CASHEWS!!
I CAN EAT CRUNCHY FOOD AGAIN!!
I CAN CHEW FOOD LIKE A NORMAL PERSON!!

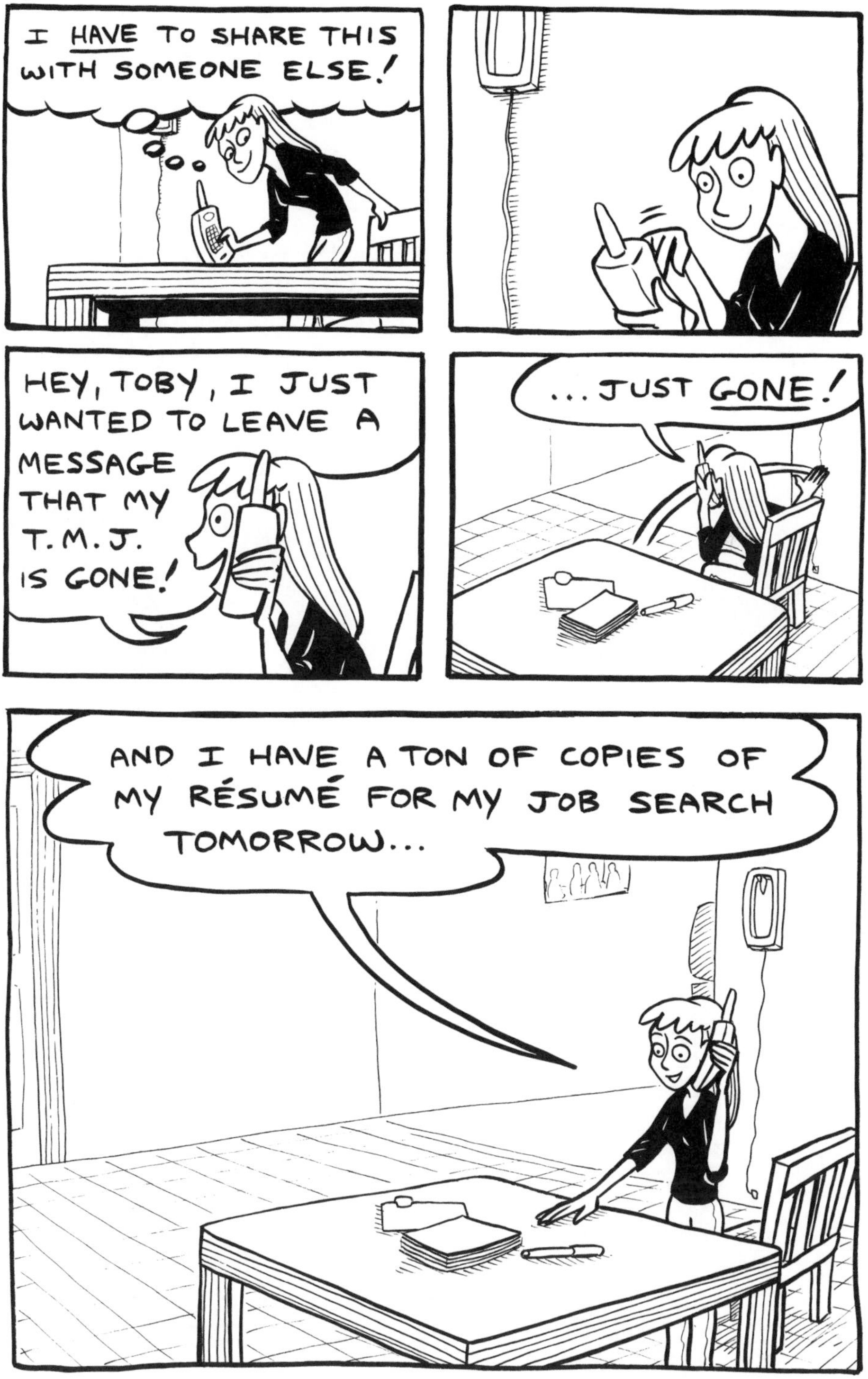
I HAVE TO SHARE THIS WITH SOMEONE ELSE!
HEY, TOBY, I JUST WANTED TO LEAVE A MESSAGE THAT MY T.M.J. IS GONE!
...JUST GONE!
AND I HAVE A TON OF COPIES OF MY RÉSUMÉ FOR MY JOB SEARCH TOMORROW...

PHOTO
BOOTH

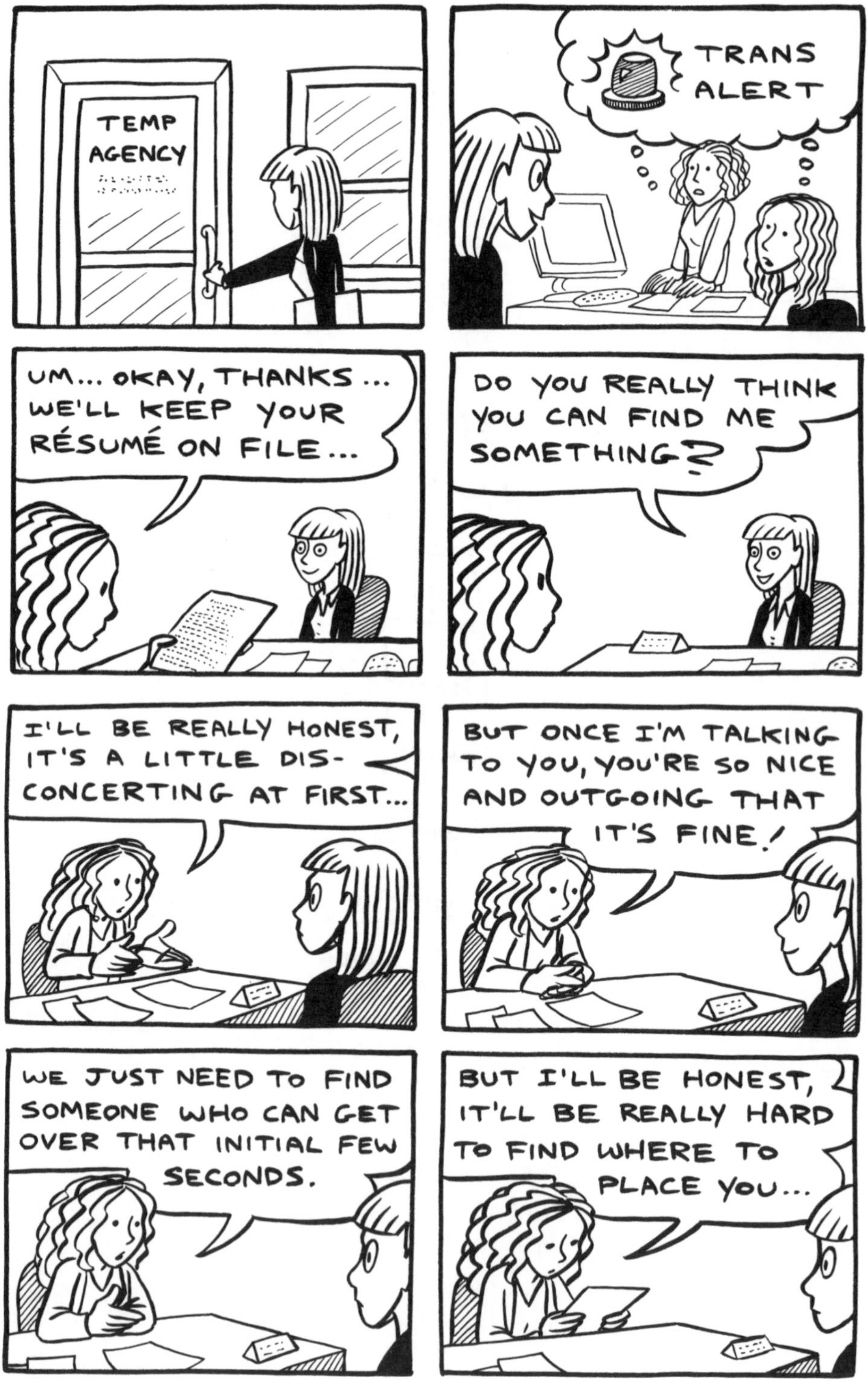
TEMP AGENCY
TRANS ALERT
UM... OKAY, THANKS... WE'LL KEEP YOUR RÉSUMÉ ON FILE...
DO YOU REALLY THINK YOU CAN FIND ME SOMETHING?
I'LL BE REALLY HONEST, IT'S A LITTLE DIS-CONCERTING AT FIRST...
BUT ONCE I'M TALKING TO YOU, YOU'RE SO NICE AND OUTGOING THAT IT'S FINE!
WE JUST NEED TO FIND SOMEONE WHO CAN GET OVER THAT INITIAL FEW SECONDS.
BUT I'LL BE HONEST, IT'LL BE REALLY HARD TO FIND WHERE TO PLACE YOU...

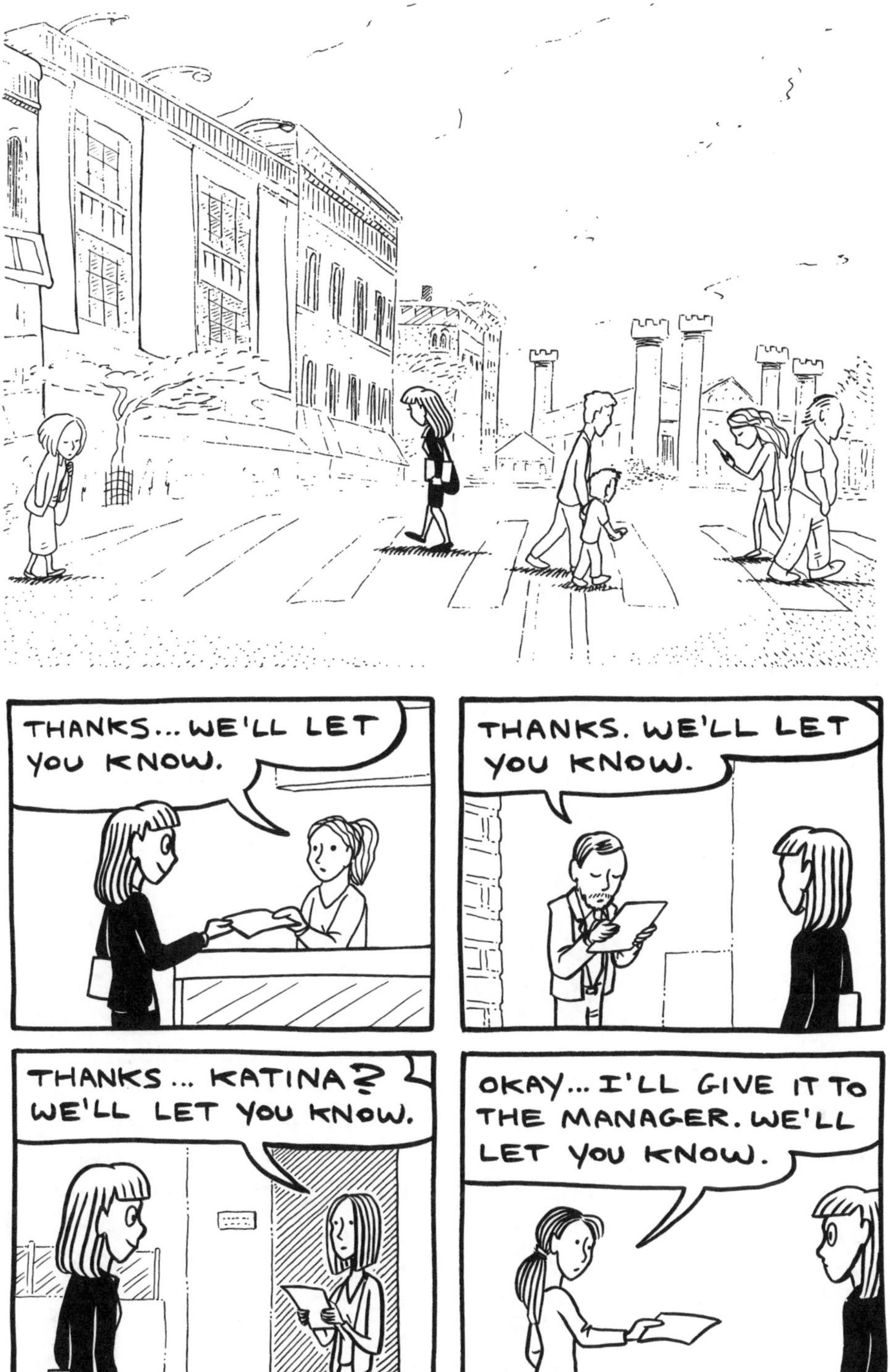
THANKS... WE'LL LET YOU KNOW.
THANKS. WE'LL LET YOU KNOW.
THANKS... KATINA? WE'LL LET YOU KNOW.
OKAY... I'LL GIVE IT TO THE MANAGER. WE'LL LET YOU KNOW.

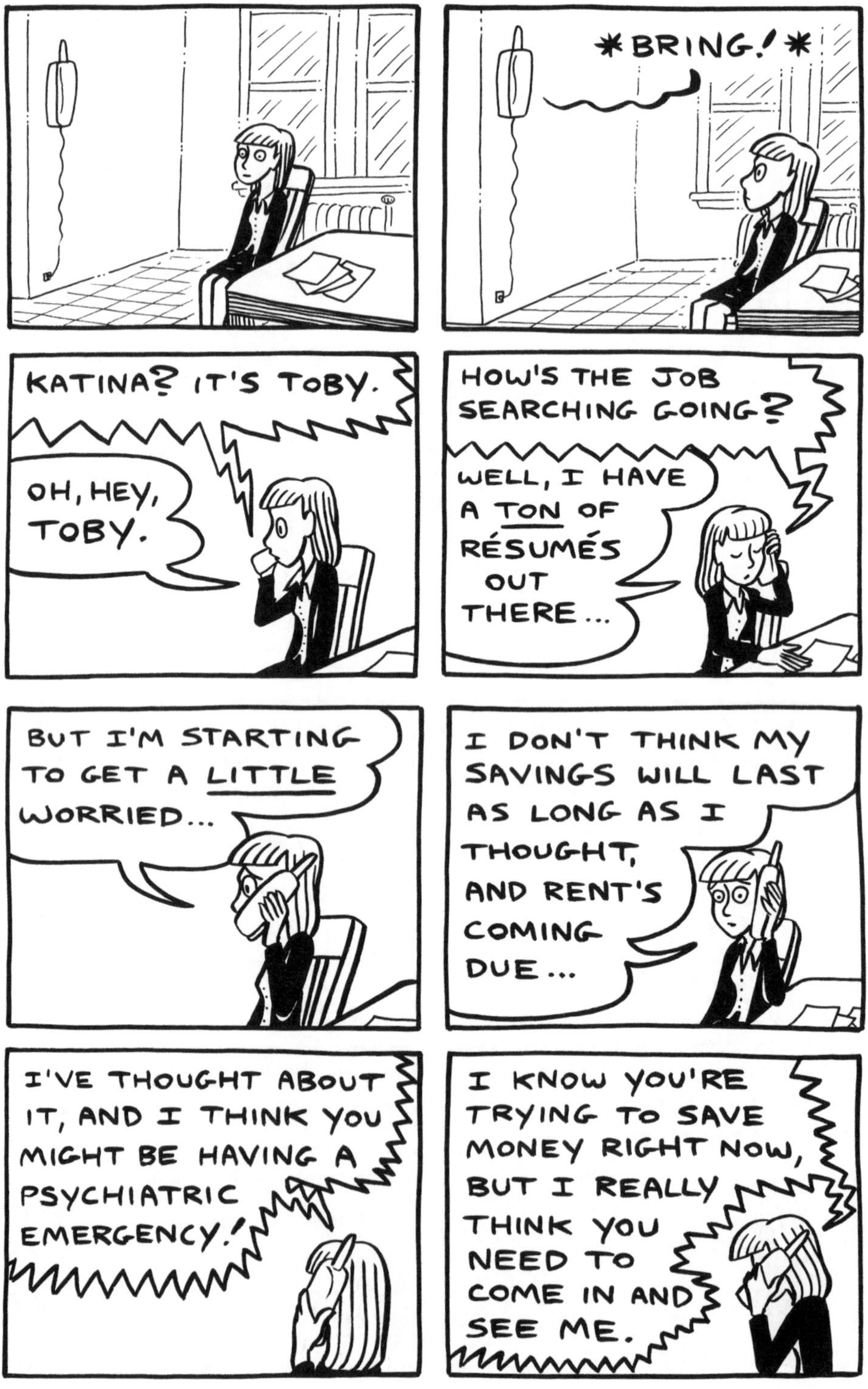
BRING!
KATINA? IT'S TOBY.
OH, HEY, TOBY.
HOW'S THE JOB SEARCHING GOING?
WELL, I HAVE A TON OF RÉSUMÉS OUT THERE...
BUT I'M STARTING TO GET A LITTLE WORRIED...
I DON'T THINK MY SAVINGS WILL LAST AS LONG AS I THOUGHT, AND RENT'S COMING DUE...
I'VE THOUGHT ABOUT IT, AND I THINK YOU MIGHT BE HAVING A PSYCHIATRIC EMERGENCY!
I KNOW YOU'RE TRYING TO SAVE MONEY RIGHT NOW, BUT I REALLY THINK YOU NEED TO COME IN AND SEE ME.

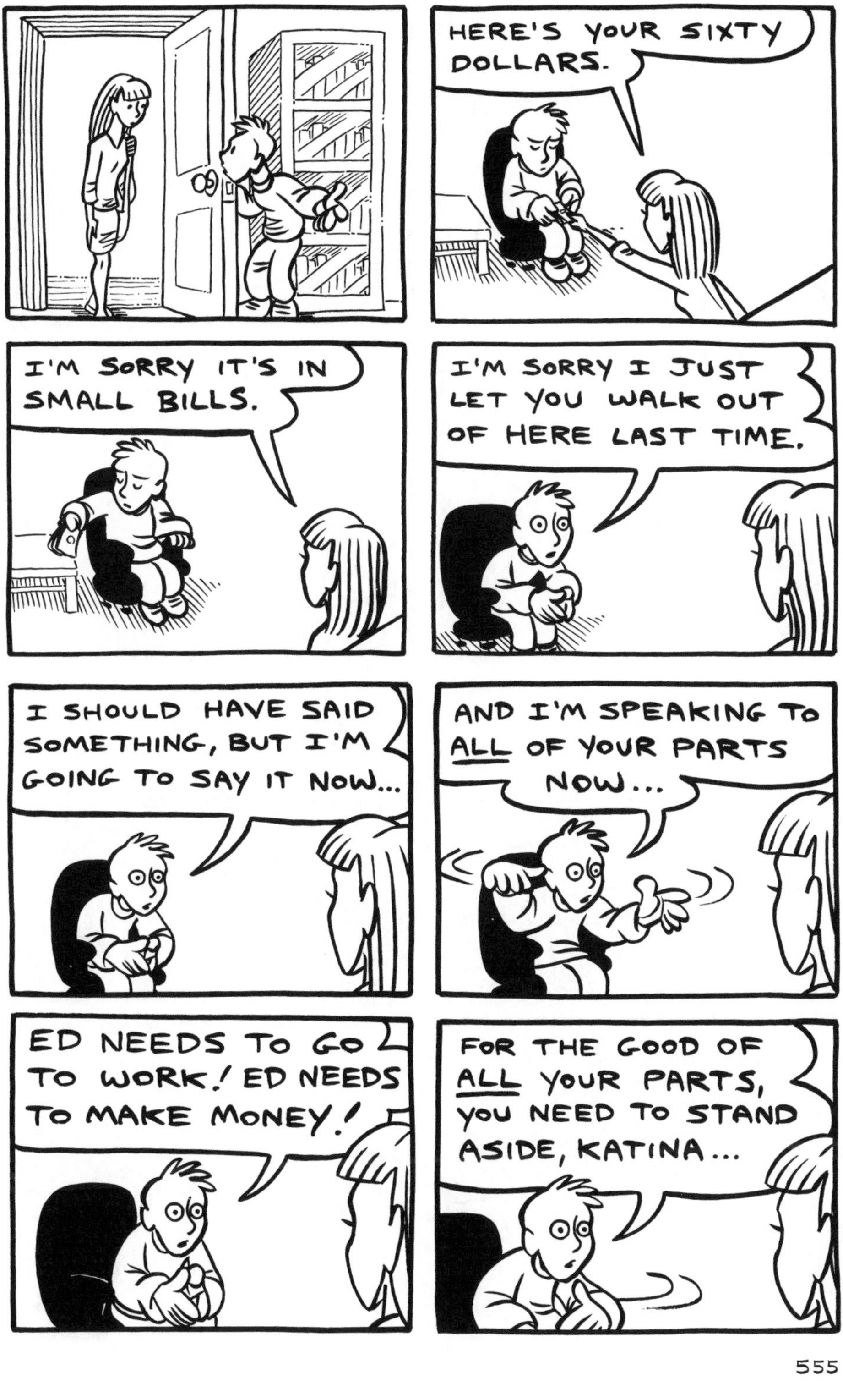
HERE'S YOUR SIXTY DOLLARS.
I'M SORRY IT'S IN SMALL BILLS.
I'M SORRY I JUST LET YOU WALK OUT OF HERE LAST TIME.
I SHOULD HAVE SAID SOMETHING, BUT I'M GOING TO SAY IT NOW...
AND I'M SPEAKING TO ALL OF YOUR PARTS NOW...
ED NEEDS TO GO TO WORK! ED NEEDS TO MAKE MONEY!
FOR THE GOOD OF ALL YOUR PARTS, YOU NEED TO STAND ASIDE, KATINA...

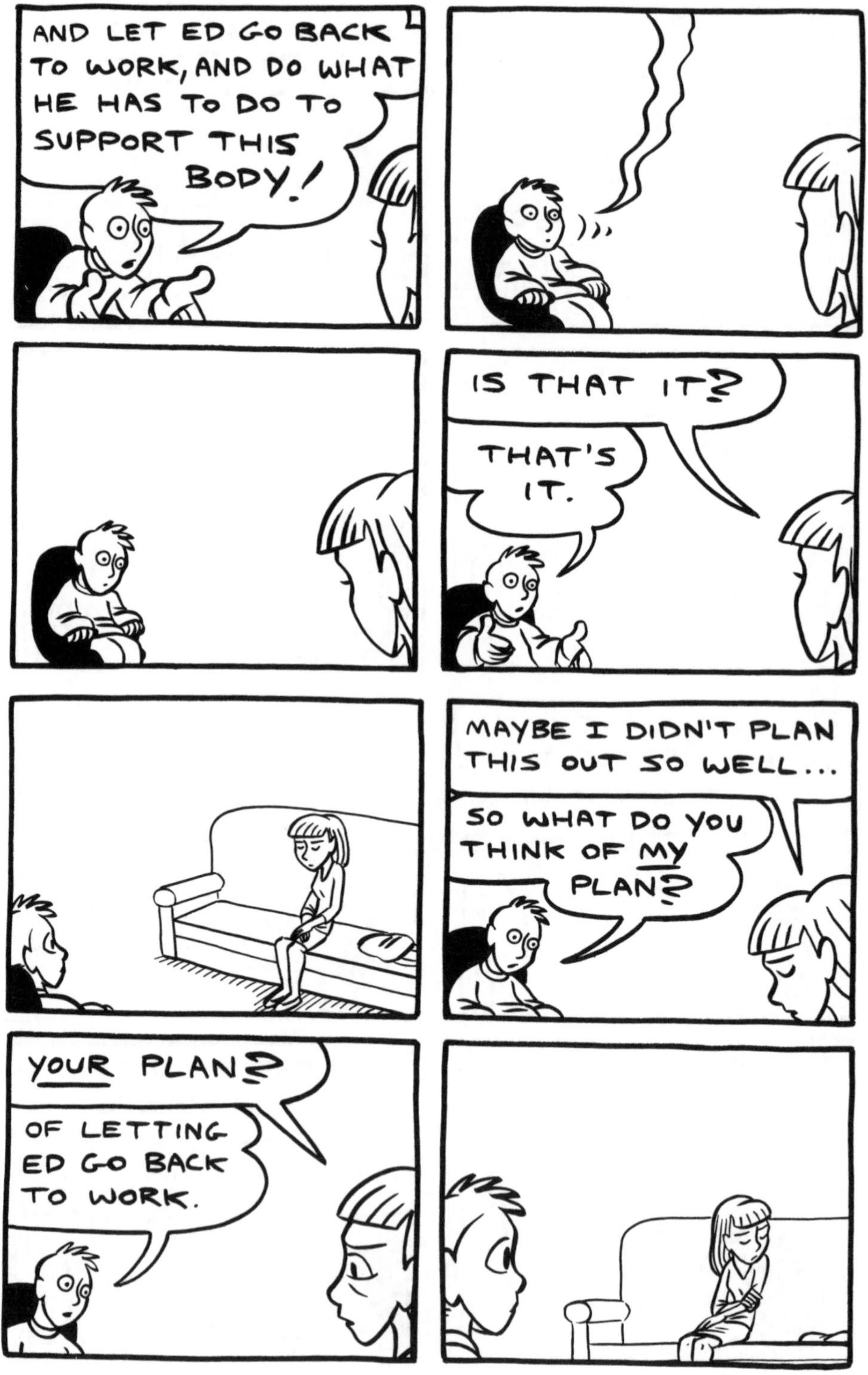
AND LET ED GO BACK TO WORK, AND DO WHAT HE HAS TO DO TO SUPPORT THIS BODY!
IS THAT IT?
THAT'S IT.
MAYBE I DIDN'T PLAN THIS OUT SO WELL...
SO WHAT DO YOU THINK OF MY PLAN?
YOUR PLAN?
OF LETTING ED GO BACK TO WORK.

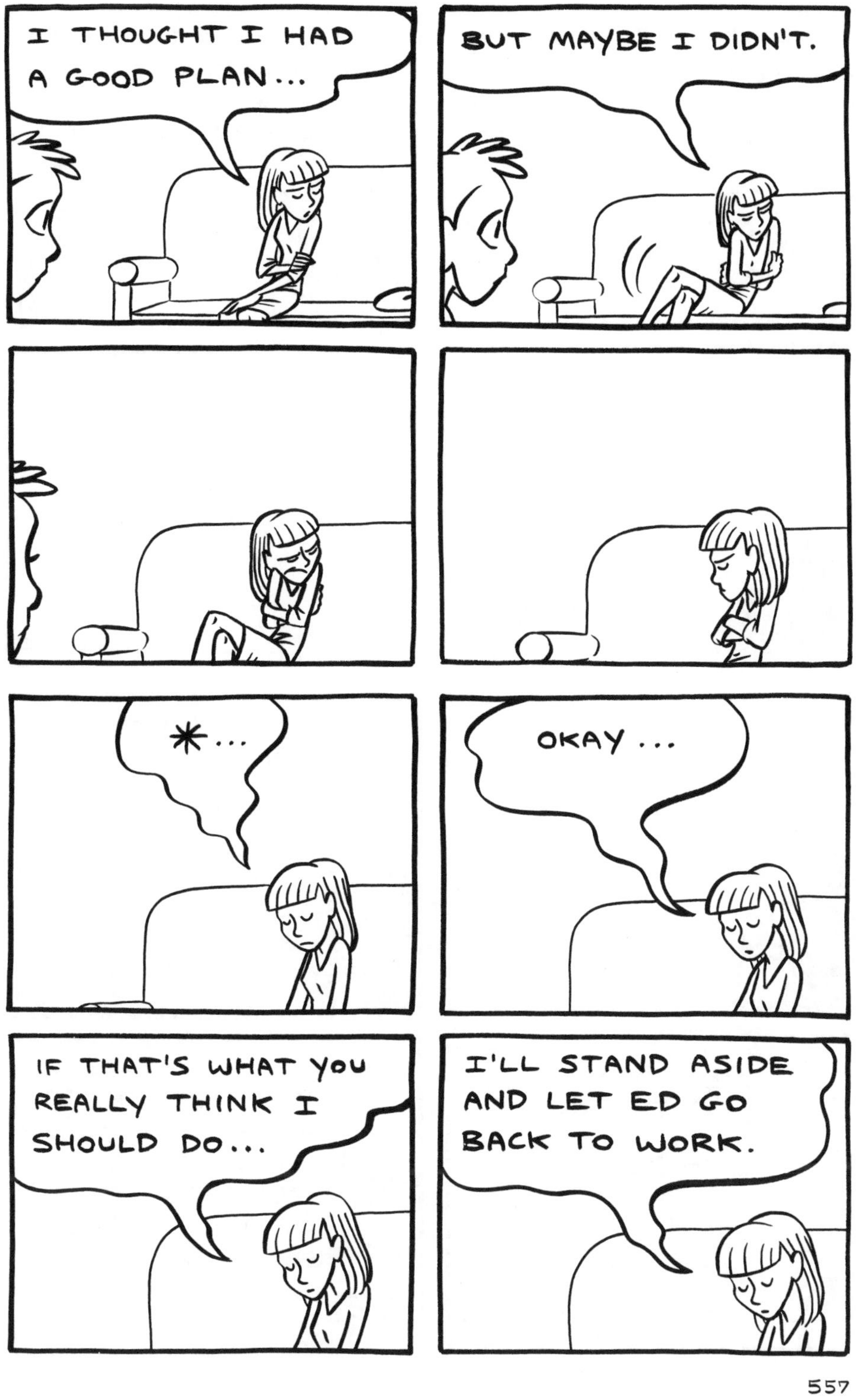
I THOUGHT I HAD A GOOD PLAN...
BUT MAYBE I DIDN'T.
*...
OKAY ...
IF THAT'S WHAT YOU REALLY THINK I SHOULD DO...
I'LL STAND ASIDE AND LET ED GO BACK TO WORK.

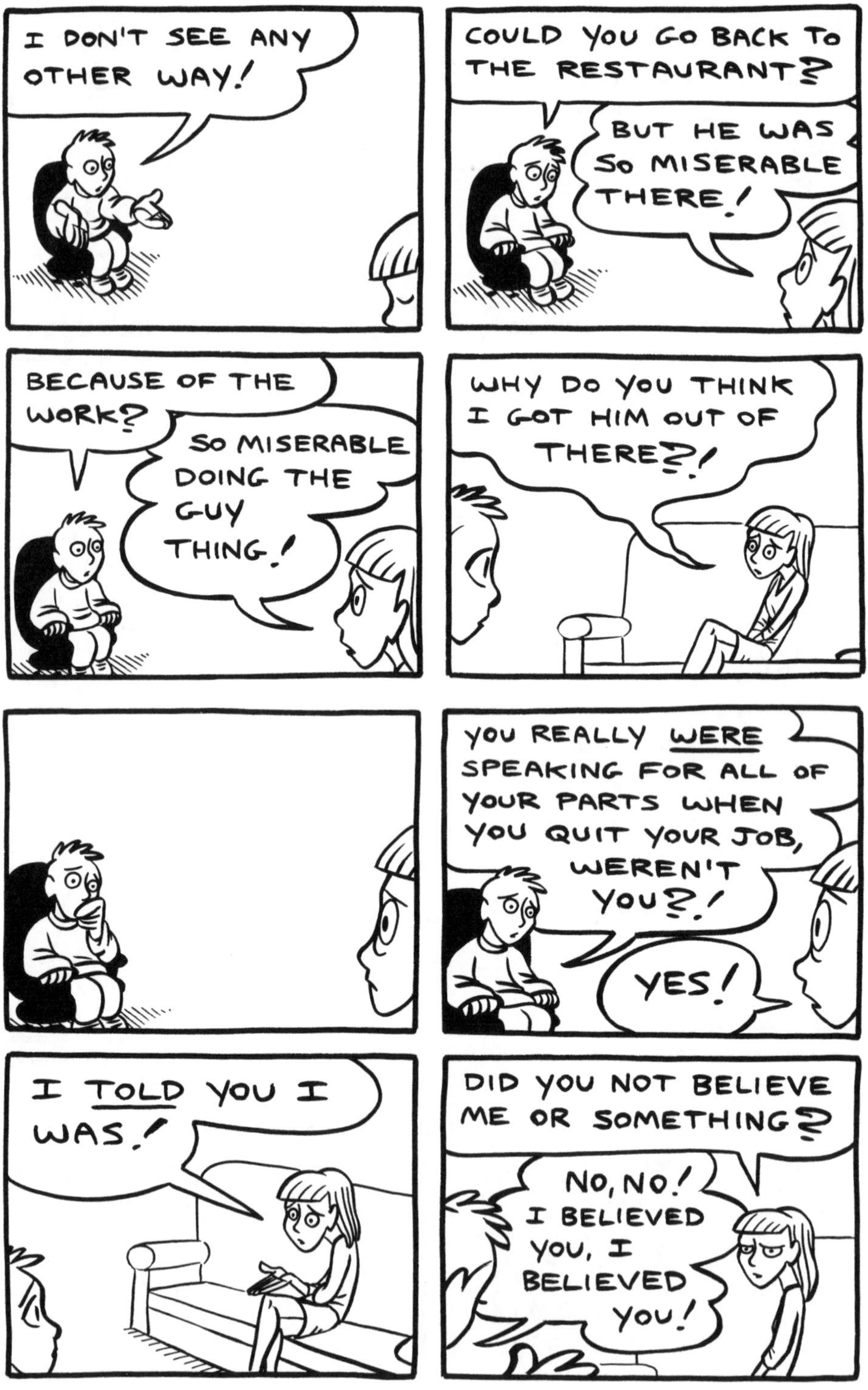
I DON'T SEE ANY OTHER WAY!
COULD YOU GO BACK TO THE RESTAURANT?
BUT HE WAS SO MISERABLE THERE!
BECAUSE OF THE WORK?
SO MISERABLE DOING THE GUY THING!
WHY DO YOU THINK I GOT HIM OUT OF THERE?!
YOU REALLY WERE SPEAKING FOR ALL OF YOUR PARTS WHEN YOU QUIT YOUR JOB, WEREN'T YOU?!
YES!
I TOLD YOU I WAS!
DID YOU NOT BELIEVE ME OR SOMETHING?
NO, NO! I BELIEVED YOU, I BELIEVED YOU!

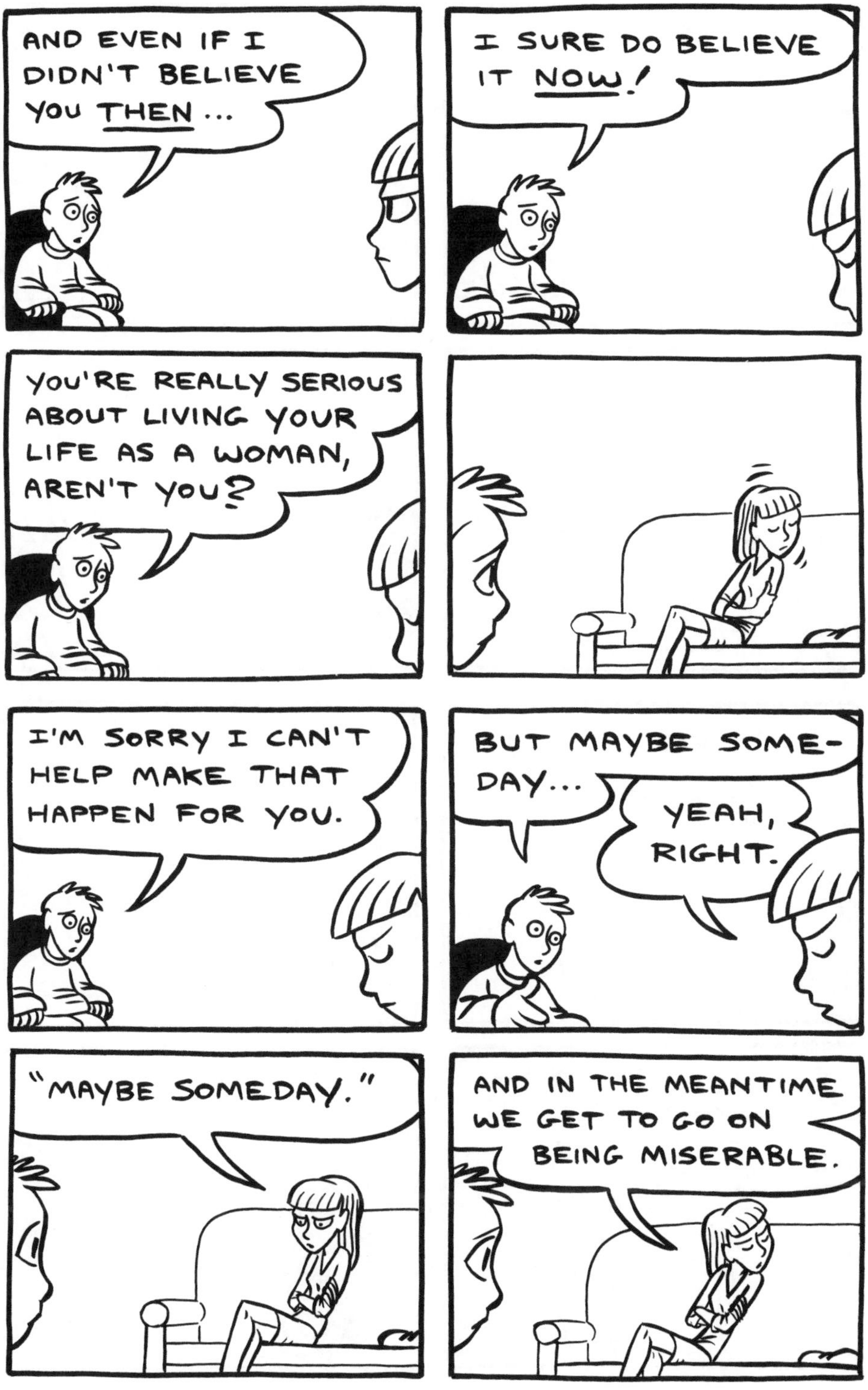

AND EVEN IF I DIDN'T BELIEVE YOU THEN ...
I SURE DO BELIEVE IT NOW!
YOU'RE REALLY SERIOUS ABOUT LIVING YOUR LIFE AS A WOMAN, AREN'T YOU?
I'M SORRY I CAN'T HELP MAKE THAT HAPPEN FOR YOU.
BUT MAYBE SOME-DAY...
YEAH, RIGHT.
"MAYBE SOMEDAY."
AND IN THE MEANTIME WE GET TO GO ON BEING MISERABLE.

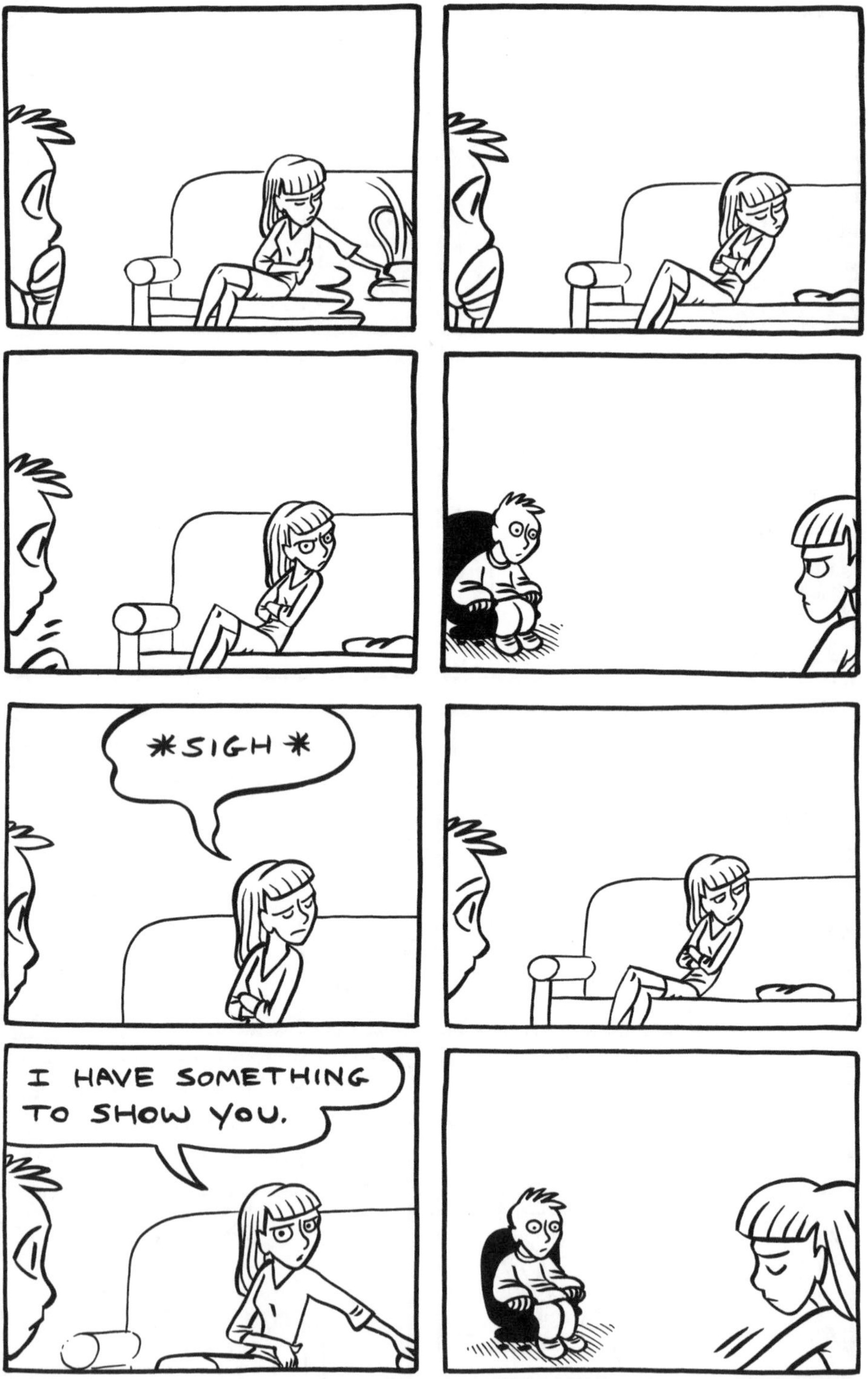
SIGH
I HAVE SOMETHING TO SHOW YOU.

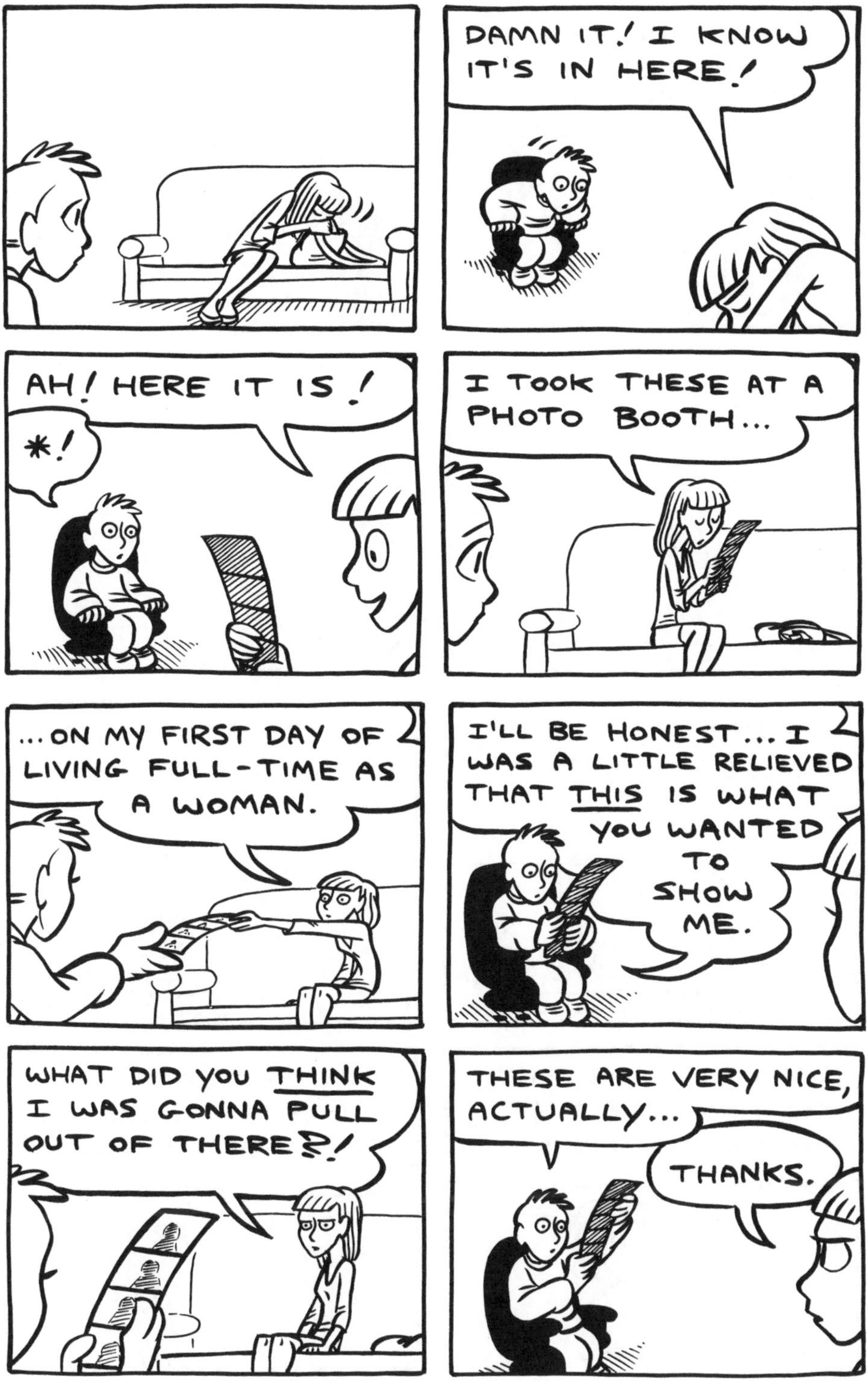
DAMN IT! I KNOW IT'S IN HERE!
AH! HERE IT IS!
*!
I TOOK THESE AT A PHOTO BOOTH...
...ON MY FIRST DAY OF LIVING FULL-TIME AS A WOMAN.
I'LL BE HONEST... I WAS A LITTLE RELIEVED THAT THIS IS WHAT YOU WANTED TO SHOW ME.
WHAT DID YOU THINK I WAS GONNA PULL OUT OF THERE?!
THESE ARE VERY NICE, ACTUALLY...
THANKS.

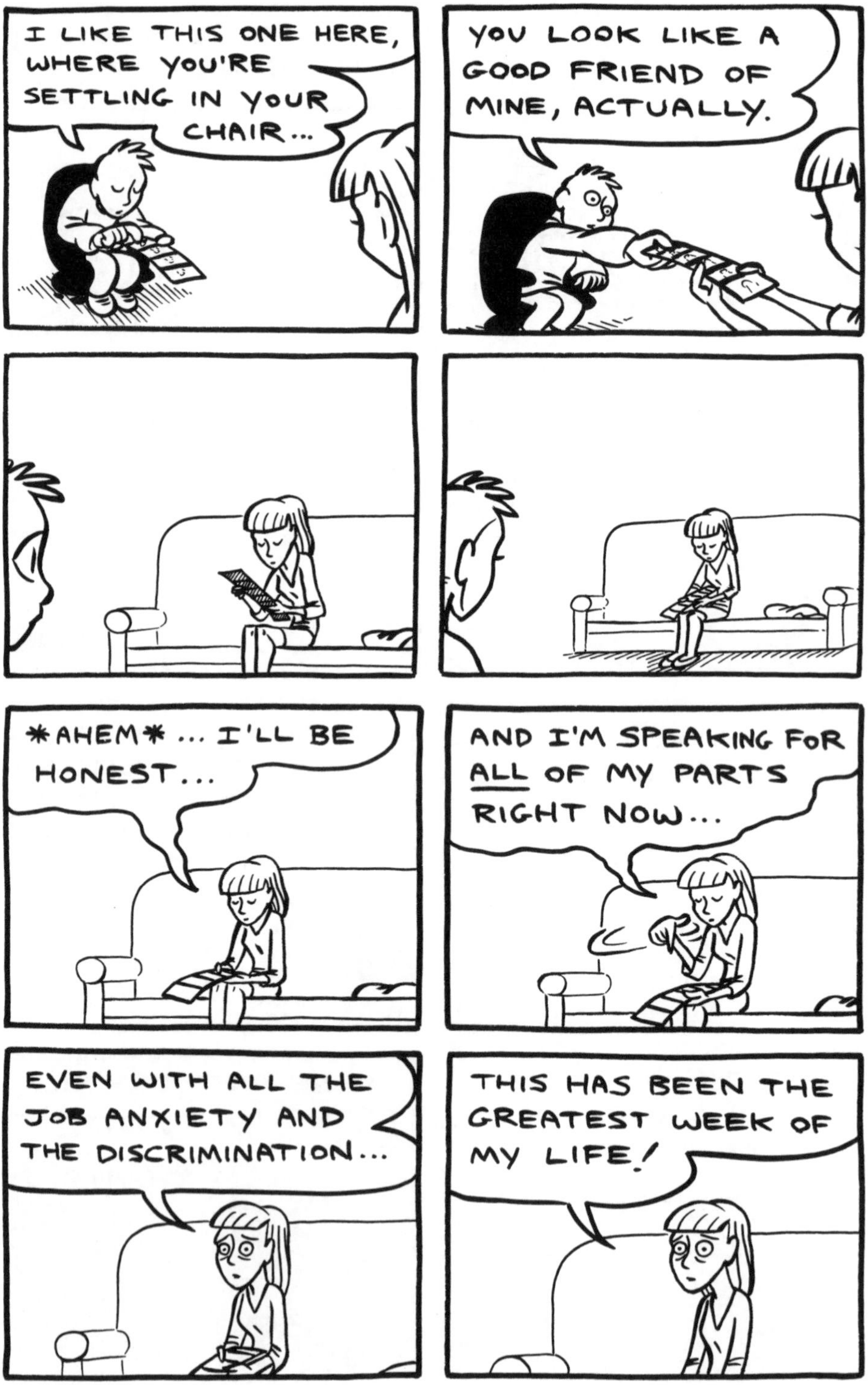
I LIKE THIS ONE HERE, WHERE YOU'RE SETTLING IN YOUR CHAIR...
YOU LOOK LIKE A GOOD FRIEND OF MINE, ACTUALLY.
AHEM ... I'LL BE HONEST...
AND I'M SPEAKING FOR ALL OF MY PARTS RIGHT NOW...
EVEN WITH ALL THE JOB ANXIETY AND THE DISCRIMINATION...
THIS HAS BEEN THE GREATEST WEEK OF MY LIFE!

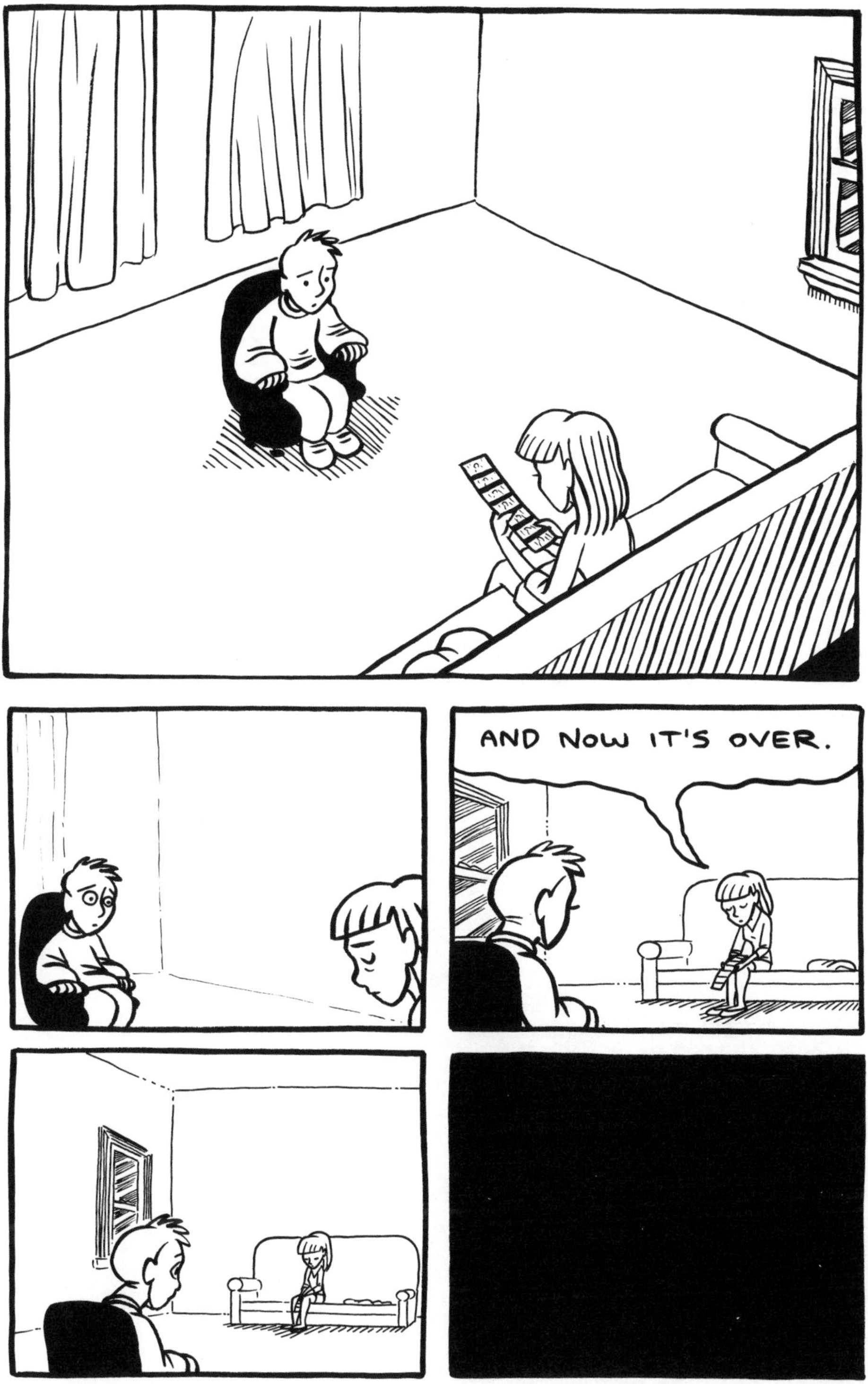
AND NOW IT'S OVER.

SEPARATE

PERSON

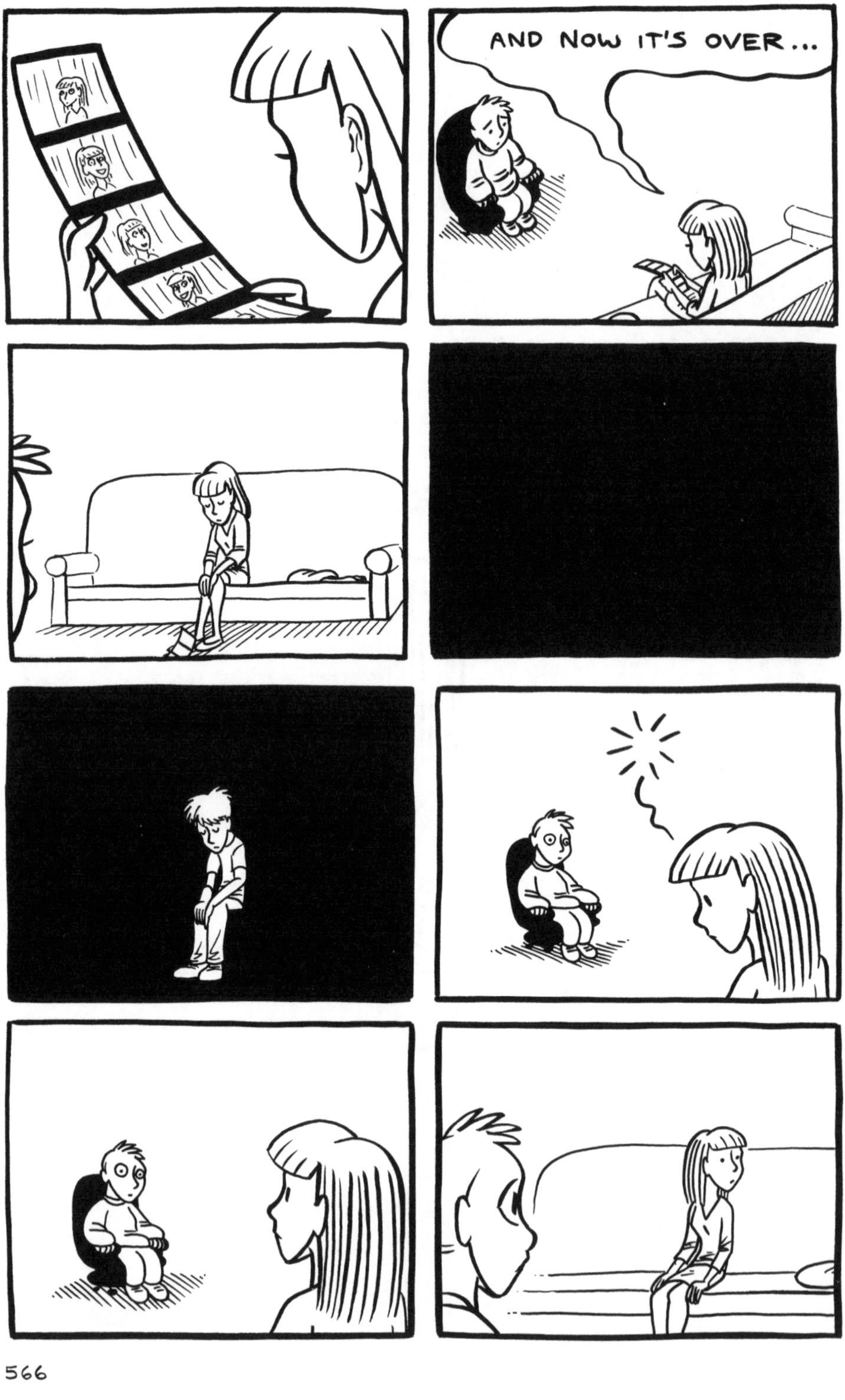
AND NOW IT'S OVER...

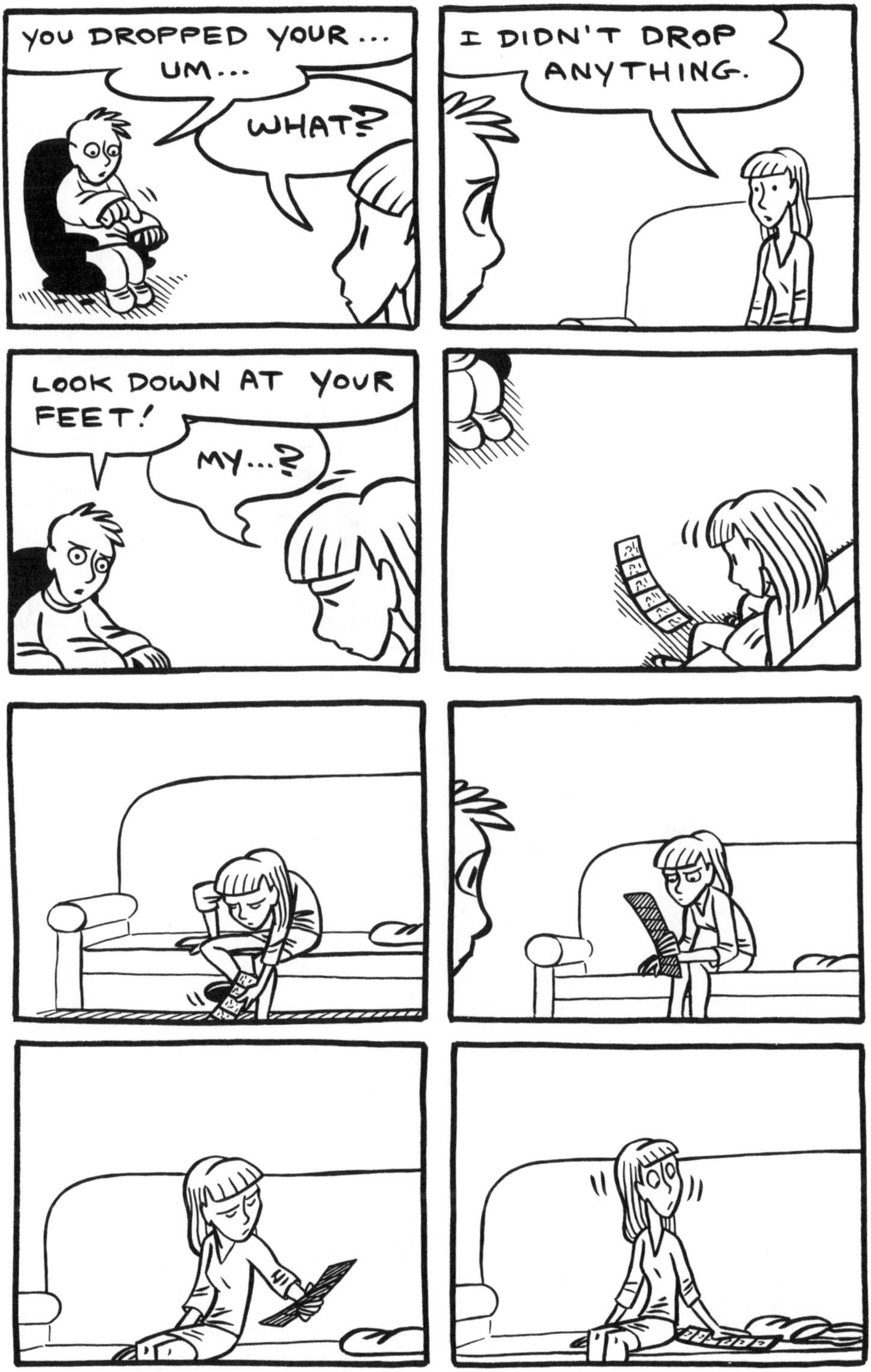
YOU DROPPED YOUR... UM...
WHAT?
I DIDN'T DROP ANYTHING.
LOOK DOWN AT YOUR FEET!
MY...?

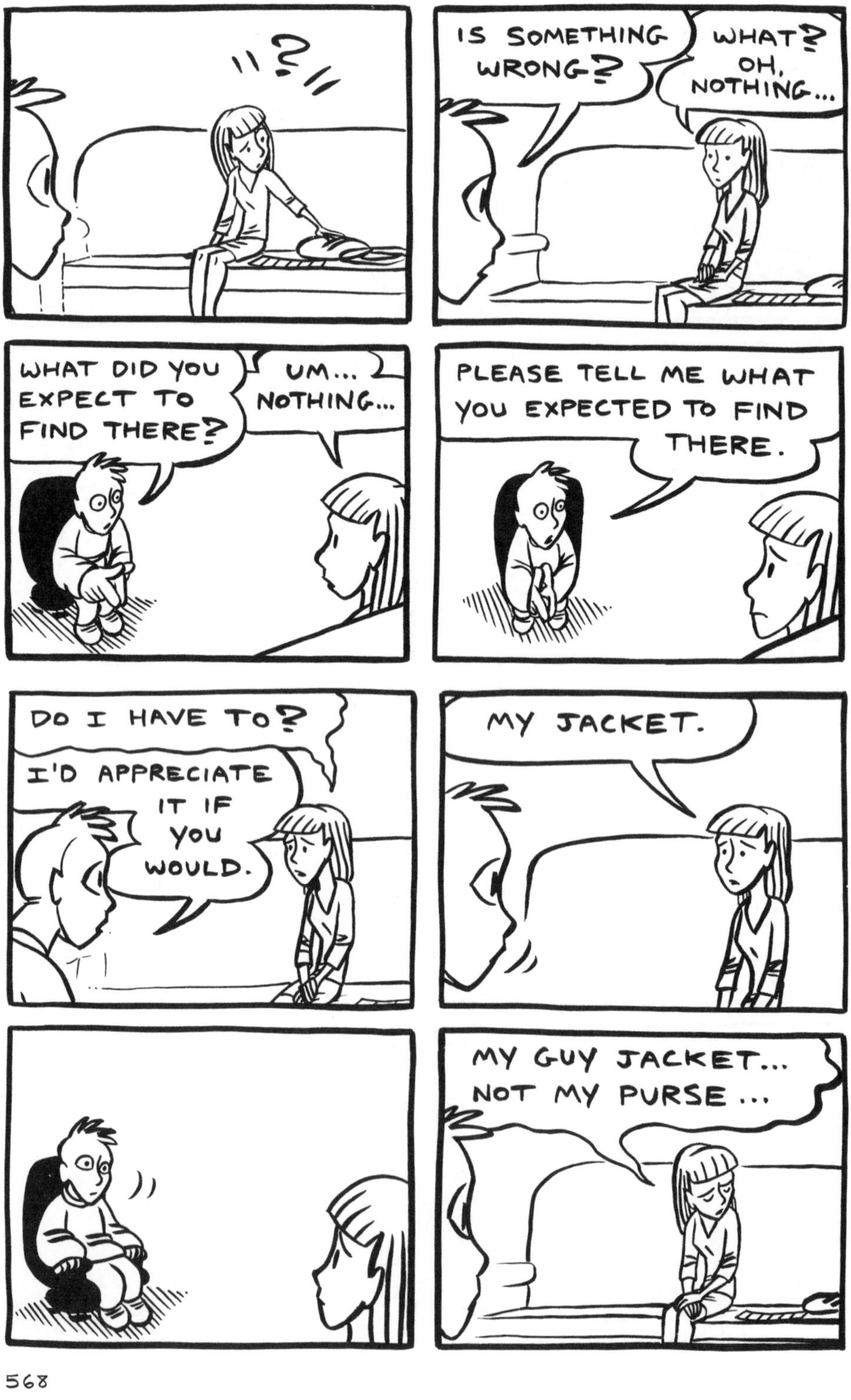
?
IS SOMETHING WRONG?
WHAT? OH, NOTHING...
WHAT DID YOU EXPECT TO FIND THERE?
UM... NOTHING...
PLEASE TELL ME WHAT YOU EXPECTED TO FIND THERE.
DO I HAVE TO?
I'D APPRECIATE IT IF YOU WOULD.
MY JACKET.
MY GUY JACKET... NOT MY PURSE...

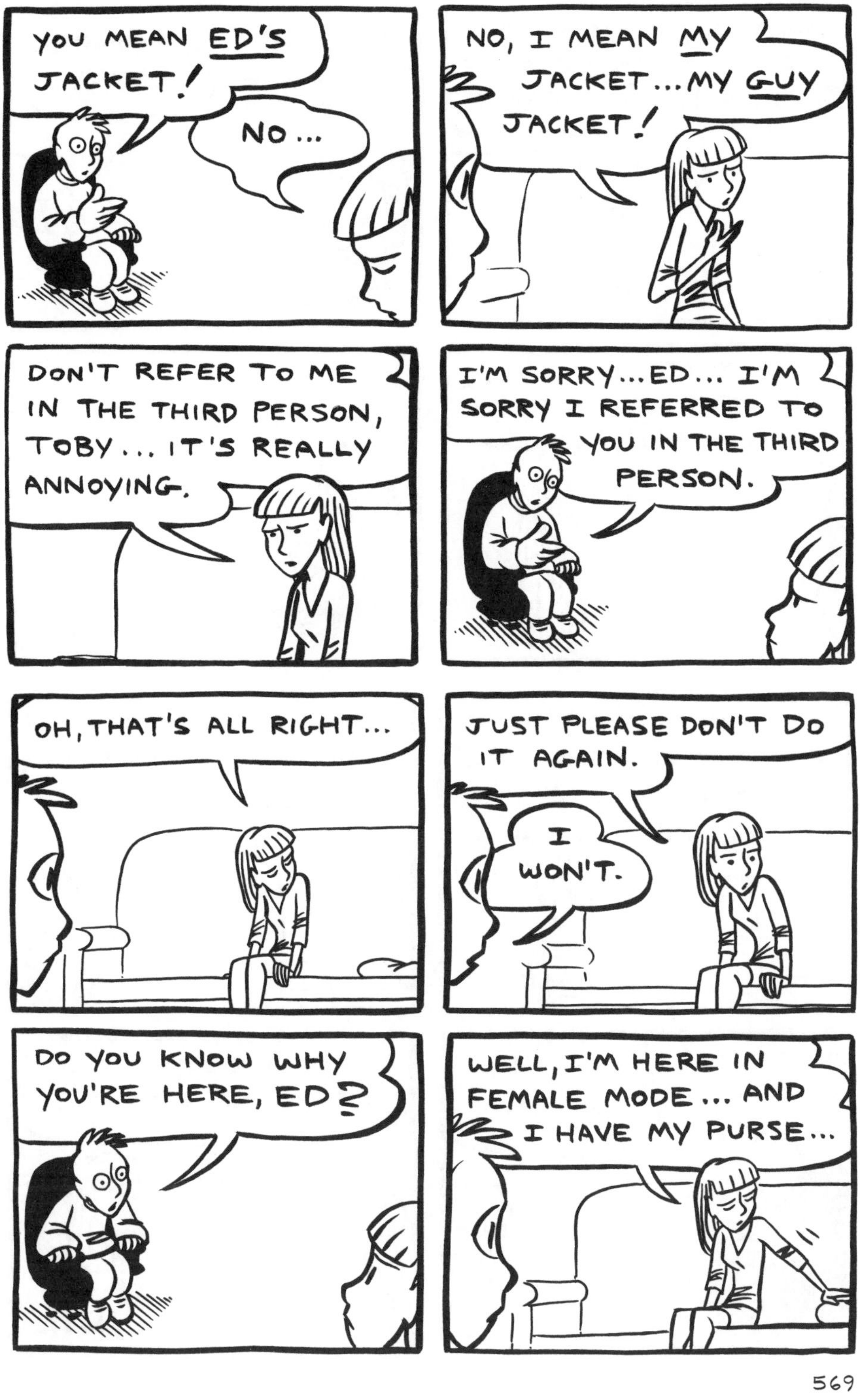
YOU MEAN ED'S JACKET!
NO...
NO, I MEAN MY JACKET... MY GUY JACKET!
DON'T REFER TO ME IN THE THIRD PERSON, TOBY... IT'S REALLY ANNOYING.
I'M SORRY... ED... I'M SORRY I REFERRED TO YOU IN THE THIRD PERSON.
OH, THAT'S ALL RIGHT...
JUST PLEASE DON'T DO IT AGAIN.
I WON'T.
DO YOU KNOW WHY YOU'RE HERE, ED?
WELL, I'M HERE IN FEMALE MODE... AND I HAVE MY PURSE...

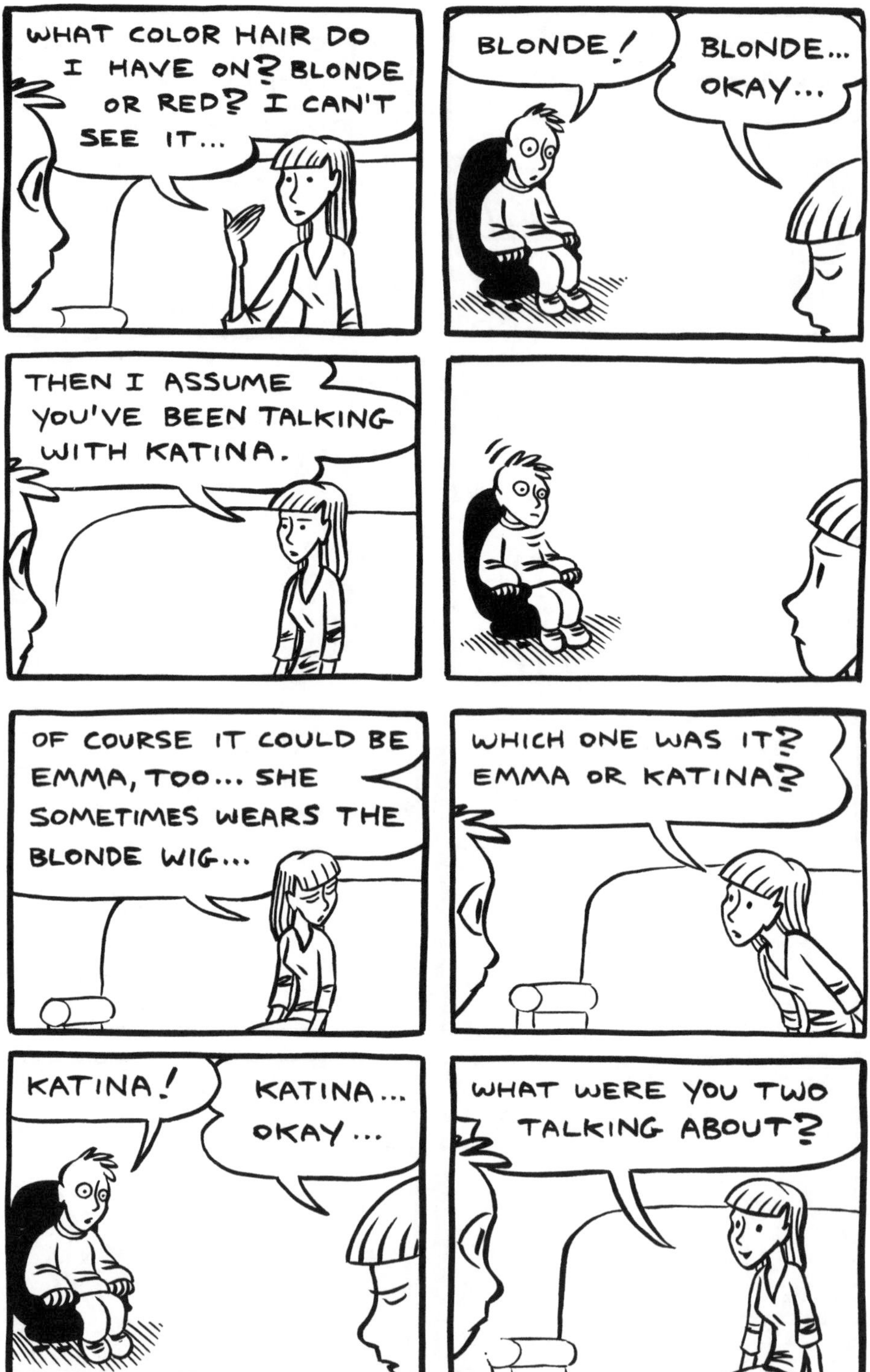

WHAT COLOR HAIR DO I HAVE ON? BLONDE OR RED? I CAN'T SEE IT...
BLONDE!
BLONDE... OKAY...
THEN I ASSUME YOU'VE BEEN TALKING WITH KATINA.
OF COURSE IT COULD BE EMMA, TOO... SHE SOMETIMES WEARS THE BLONDE WIG...
WHICH ONE WAS IT? EMMA OR KATINA?
KATINA!
KATINA... OKAY...
WHAT WERE YOU TWO TALKING ABOUT?

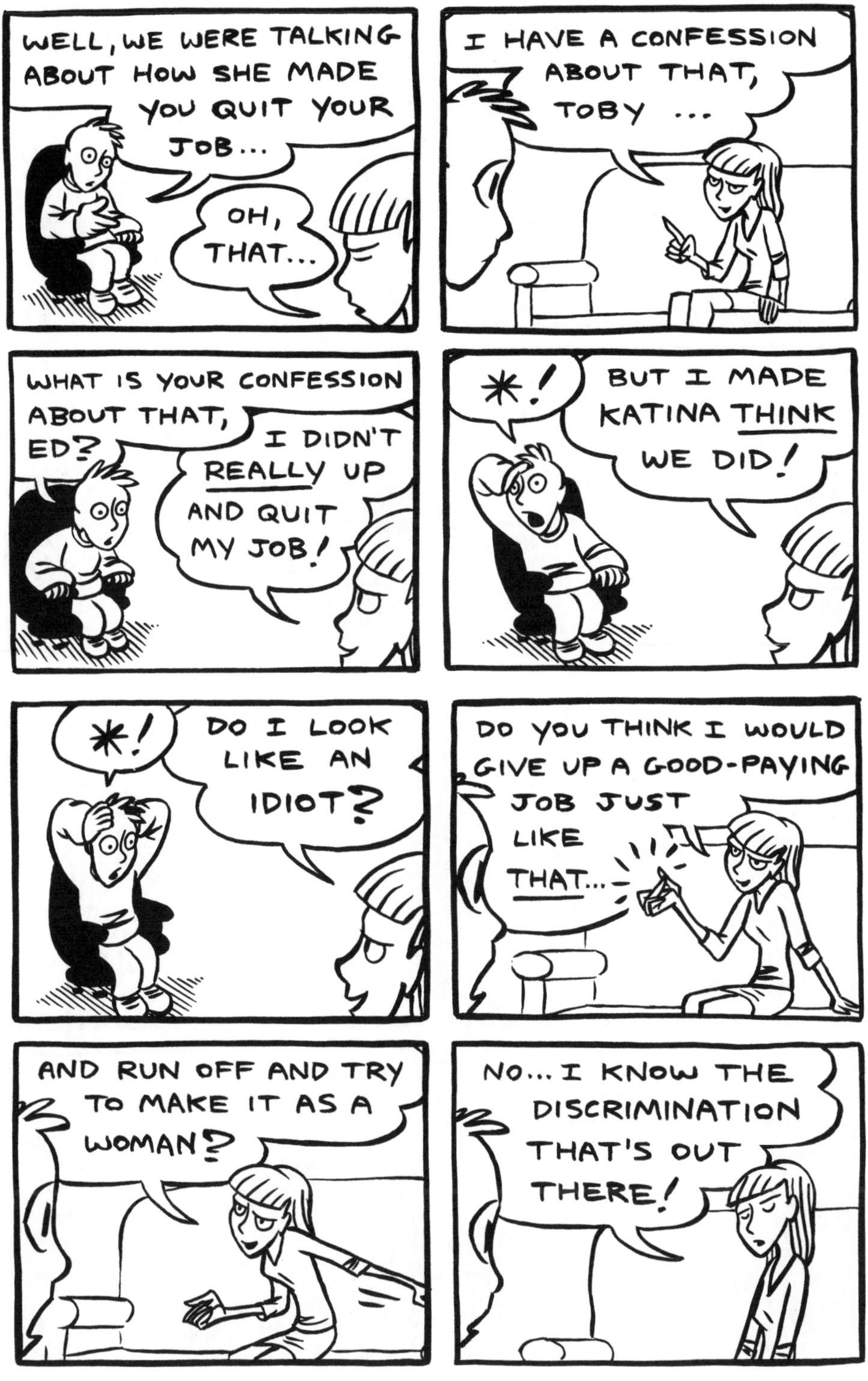

WELL, WE WERE TALKING ABOUT HOW SHE MADE YOU QUIT YOUR JOB...
OH, THAT...
I HAVE A CONFESSION ABOUT THAT, TOBY ...
WHAT IS YOUR CONFESSION ABOUT THAT, ED?
I DIDN'T REALLY UP AND QUIT MY JOB!
*!
BUT I MADE KATINA THINK WE DID!
*!
DO I LOOK LIKE AN IDIOT?
DO YOU THINK I WOULD GIVE UP A GOOD-PAYING JOB JUST LIKE THAT...
AND RUN OFF AND TRY TO MAKE IT AS A WOMAN?
NO... I KNOW THE DISCRIMINATION THAT'S OUT THERE!

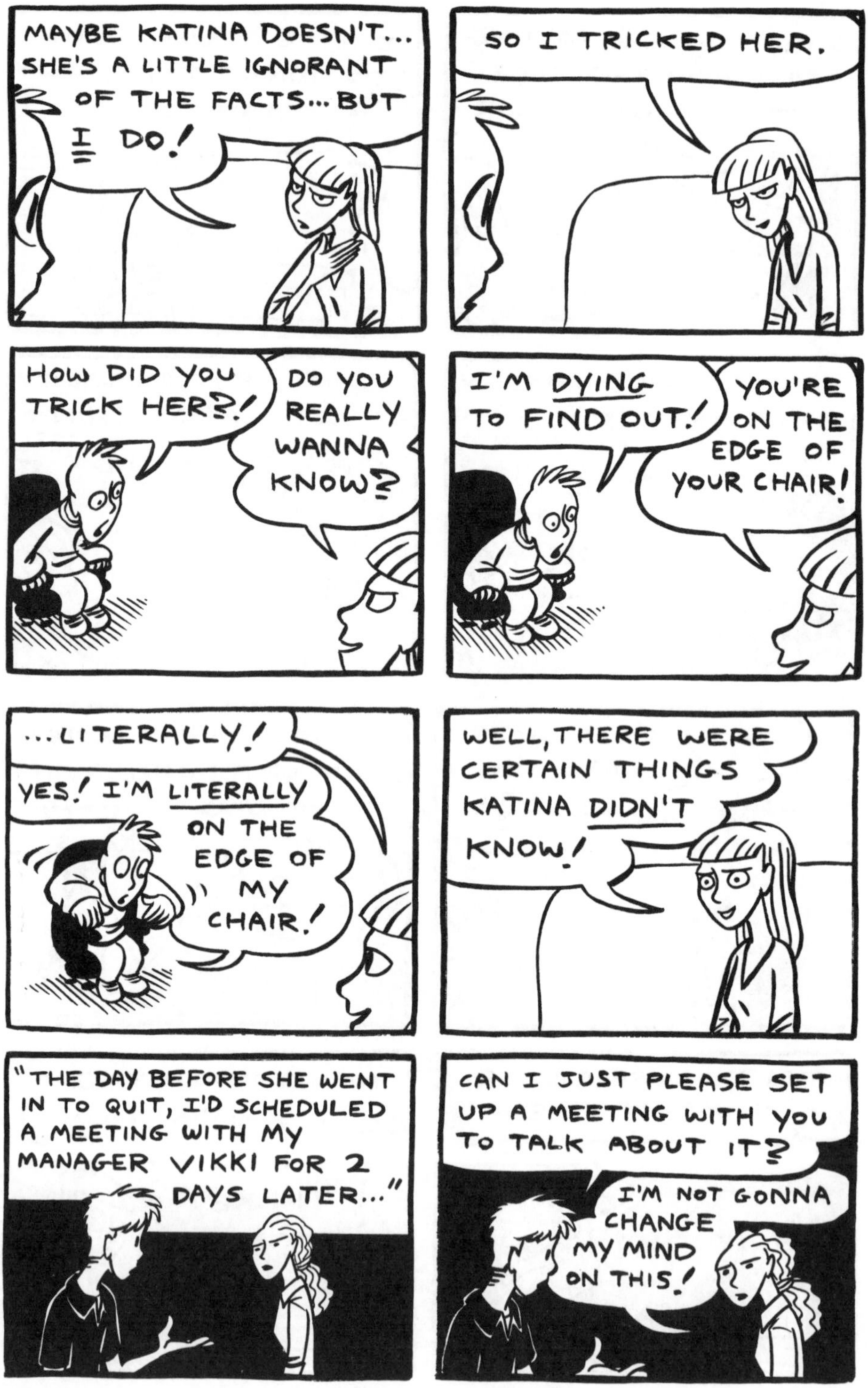
MAYBE KATINA DOESN'T... SHE'S A LITTLE IGNORANT OF THE FACTS... BUT I DO!
SO I TRICKED HER.
HOW DID YOU TRICK HER?!
DO YOU REALLY WANNA KNOW?
I'M DYING TO FIND OUT!
YOU'RE ON THE EDGE OF YOUR CHAIR!
...LITERALLY!
YES! I'M LITERALLY ON THE EDGE OF MY CHAIR!
WELL, THERE WERE CERTAIN THINGS KATINA DIDN'T KNOW!
"THE DAY BEFORE SHE WENT IN TO QUIT, I'D SCHEDULED A MEETING WITH MY MANAGER VIKKI FOR 2 DAYS LATER..."
CAN I JUST PLEASE SET UP A MEETING WITH YOU TO TALK ABOUT IT?
I'M NOT GONNA CHANGE MY MIND ON THIS!

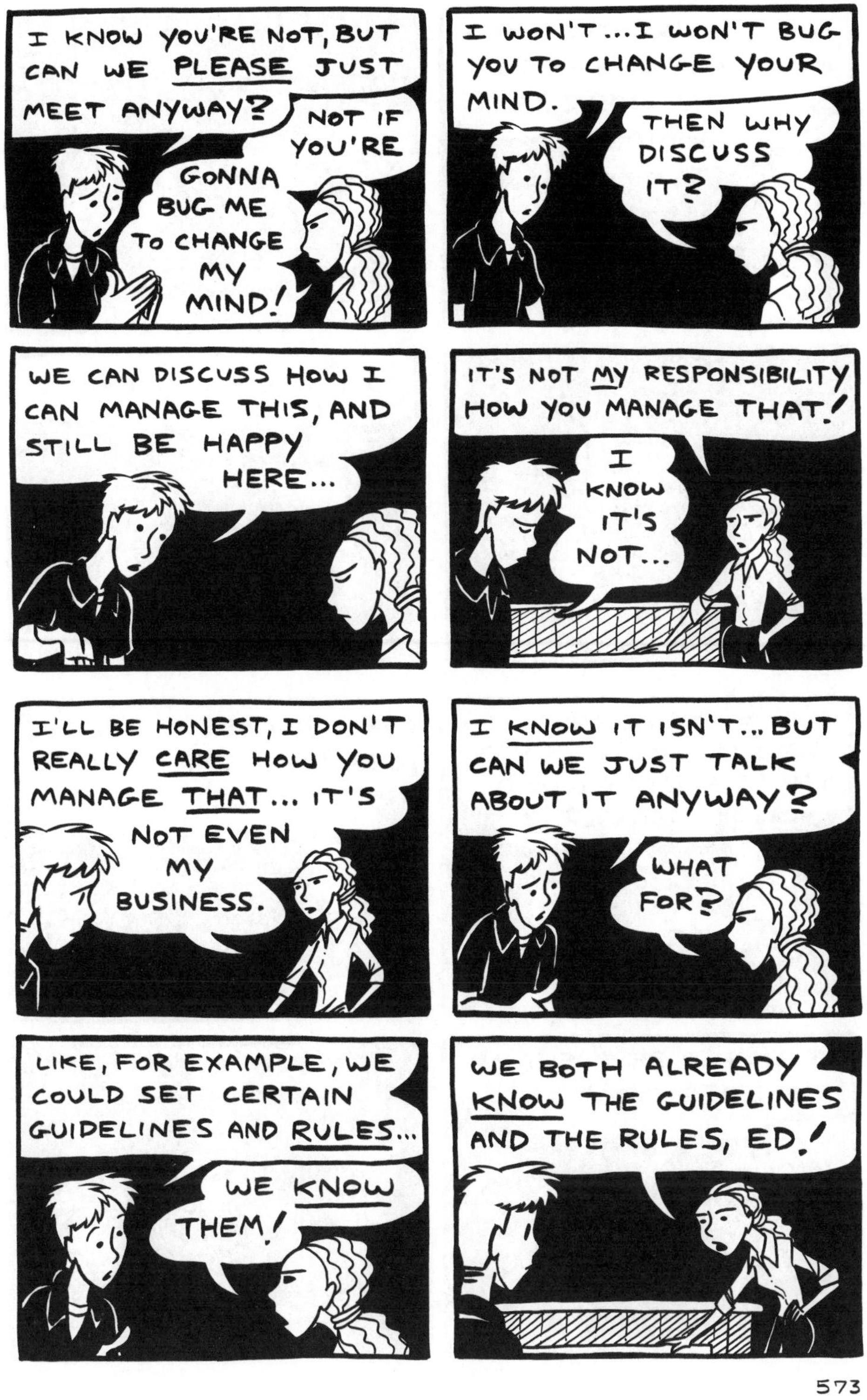
I KNOW YOU'RE NOT, BUT CAN WE PLEASE JUST MEET ANYWAY?
NOT IF YOU'RE GONNA BUG ME TO CHANGE MY MIND!
I WON'T... I WON'T BUG YOU TO CHANGE YOUR MIND.
THEN WHY DISCUSS IT?
WE CAN DISCUSS HOW I CAN MANAGE THIS, AND STILL BE HAPPY HERE...
IT'S NOT MY RESPONSIBILITY HOW YOU MANAGE THAT!
I KNOW IT'S NOT...
I'LL BE HONEST, I DON'T REALLY CARE HOW YOU MANAGE THAT... IT'S NOT EVEN MY BUSINESS.
I KNOW IT ISN'T... BUT CAN WE JUST TALK ABOUT IT ANYWAY?
WHAT FOR?
LIKE, FOR EXAMPLE, WE COULD SET CERTAIN GUIDELINES AND RULES...
WE KNOW THEM!
WE BOTH ALREADY KNOW THE GUIDELINES AND THE RULES, ED!

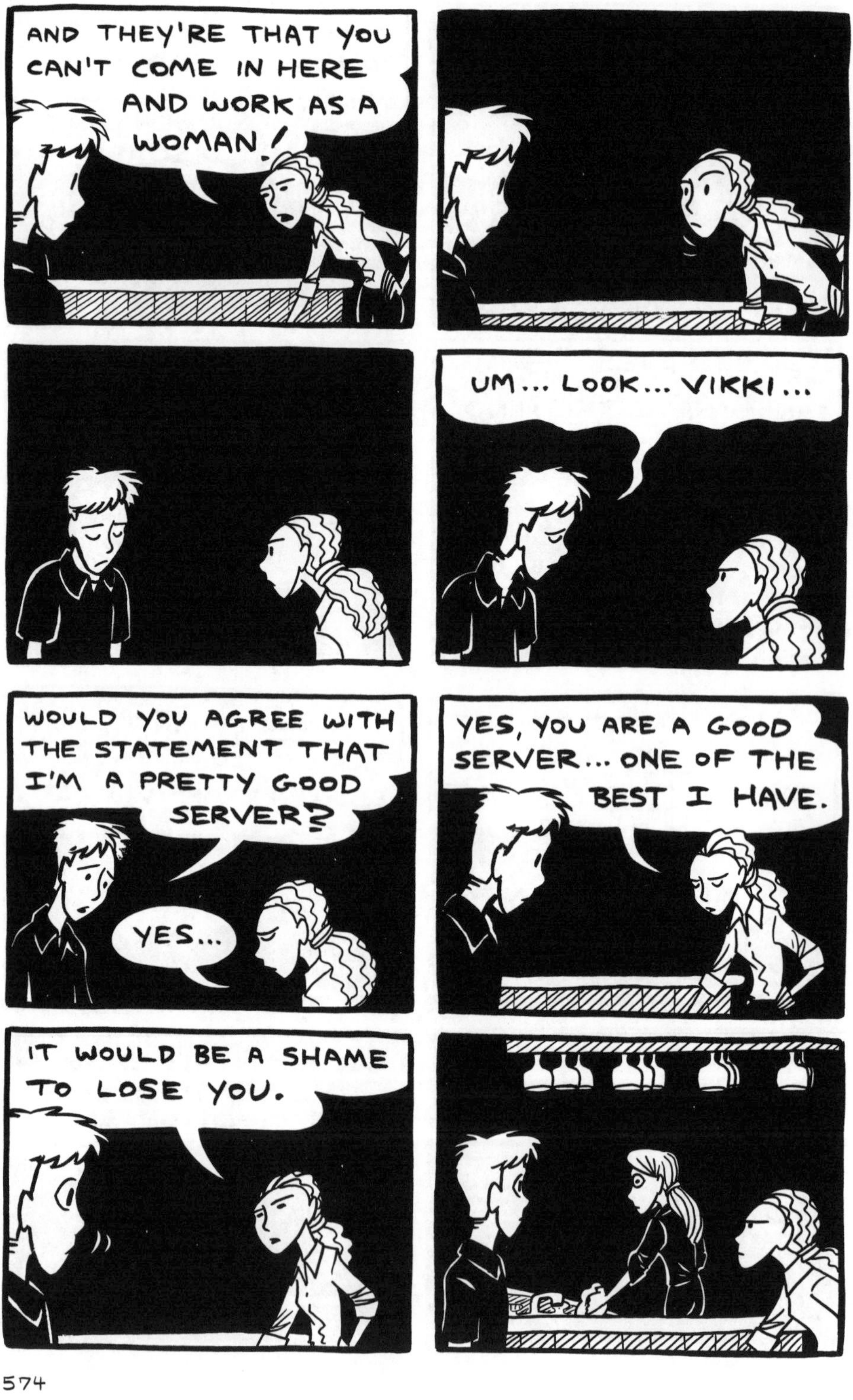
AND THEY'RE THAT YOU CAN'T COME IN HERE AND WORK AS A WOMAN!
UM... LOOK... VIKKI...
WOULD YOU AGREE WITH THE STATEMENT THAT I'M A PRETTY GOOD SERVER?
YES...
YES, YOU ARE A GOOD SERVER... ONE OF THE BEST I HAVE.
IT WOULD BE A SHAME TO LOSE YOU.

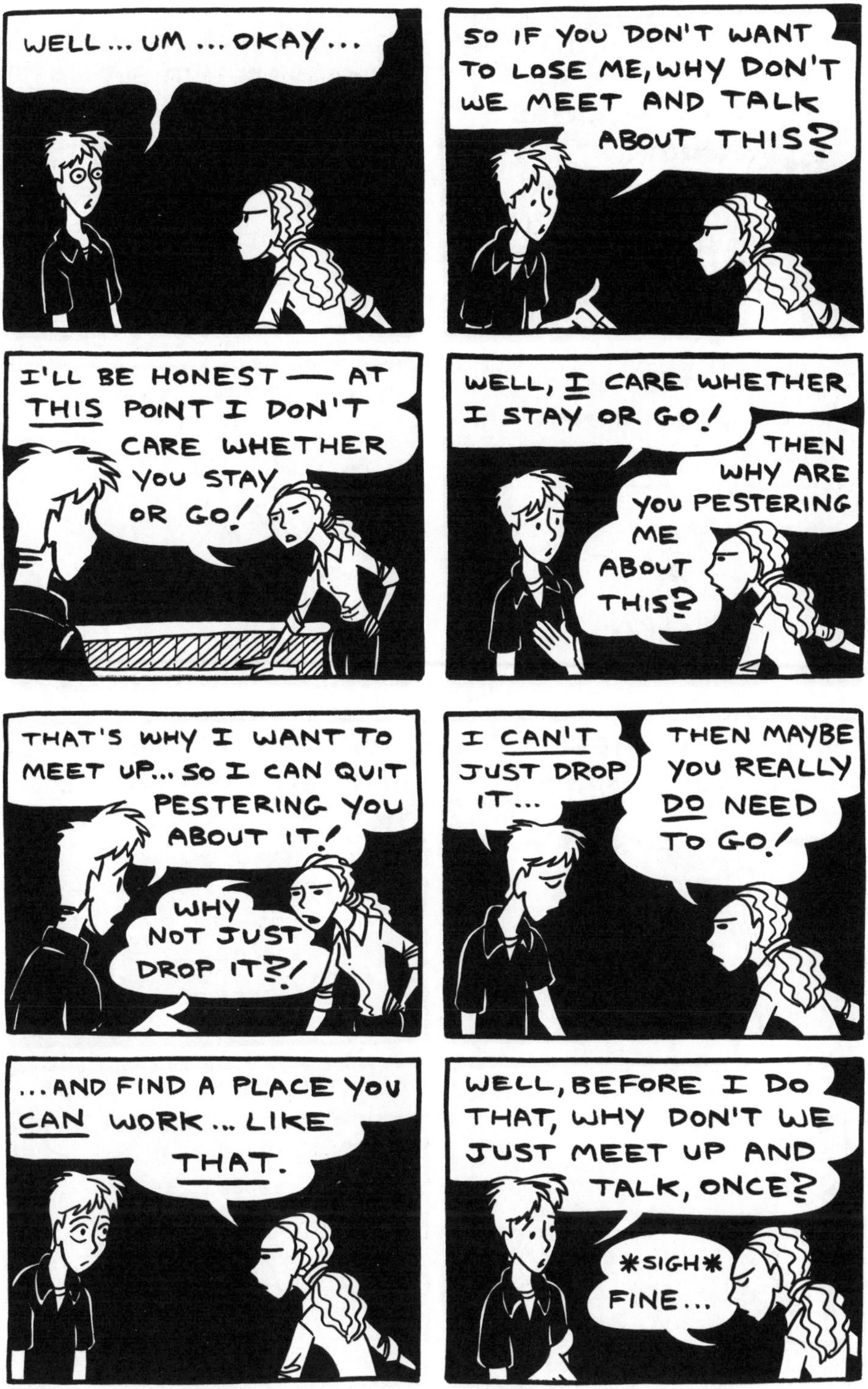
WELL ... UM ... OKAY ...
SO IF YOU DON'T WANT TO LOSE ME, WHY DON'T WE MEET AND TALK ABOUT THIS?
I'LL BE HONEST — AT THIS POINT I DON'T CARE WHETHER YOU STAY OR GO!
WELL, I CARE WHETHER I STAY OR GO!
THEN WHY ARE YOU PESTERING ME ABOUT THIS?
THAT'S WHY I WANT TO MEET UP... SO I CAN QUIT PESTERING YOU ABOUT IT!
WHY NOT JUST DROP IT?!
I CAN'T JUST DROP IT...
THEN MAYBE YOU REALLY DO NEED TO GO!
...AND FIND A PLACE YOU CAN WORK... LIKE THAT.
WELL, BEFORE I DO THAT, WHY DON'T WE JUST MEET UP AND TALK, ONCE?
SIGH FINE...

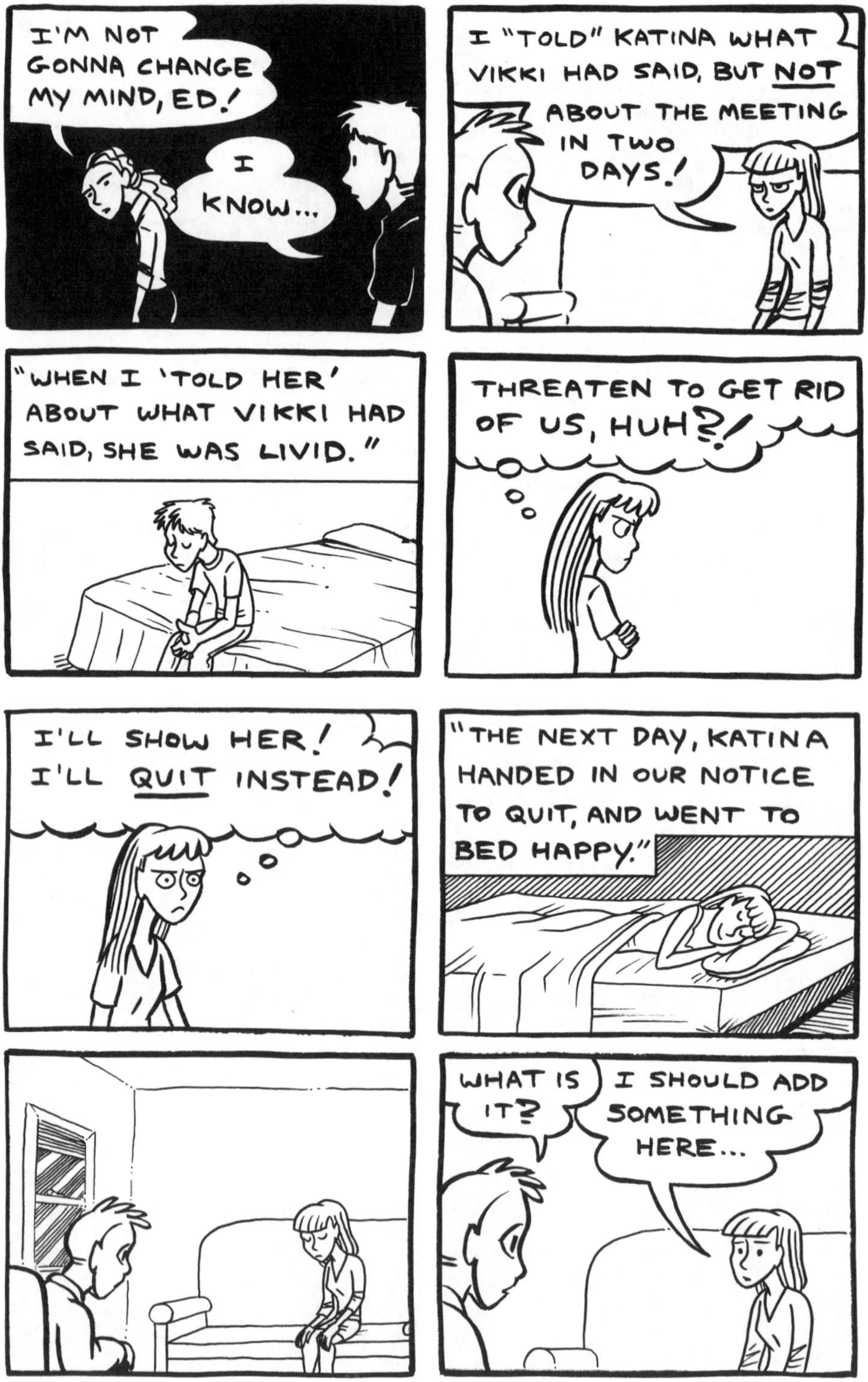
I'M NOT GONNA CHANGE MY MIND, ED!
I KNOW...
I "TOLD" KATINA WHAT VIKKI HAD SAID, BUT NOT ABOUT THE MEETING IN TWO DAYS!
"WHEN I 'TOLD HER' ABOUT WHAT VIKKI HAD SAID, SHE WAS LIVID."
THREATEN TO GET RID OF US, HUH?!
I'LL SHOW HER! I'LL QUIT INSTEAD!
"THE NEXT DAY, KATINA HANDED IN OUR NOTICE TO QUIT, AND WENT TO BED HAPPY."
WHAT IS IT?
I SHOULD ADD SOMETHING HERE...

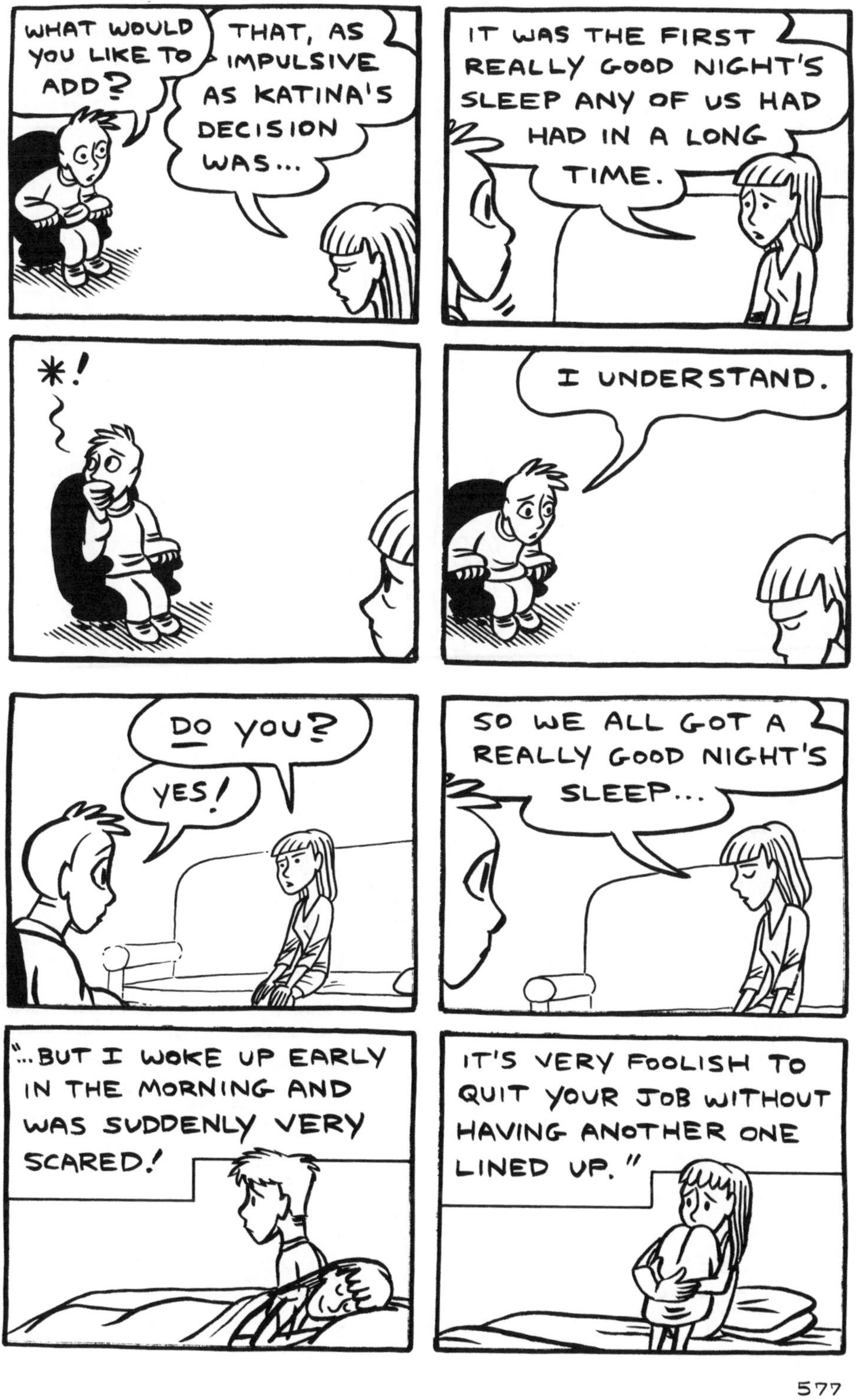
WHAT WOULD YOU LIKE TO ADD?
THAT, AS IMPULSIVE AS KATINA'S DECISION WAS...
IT WAS THE FIRST REALLY GOOD NIGHT'S SLEEP ANY OF US HAD HAD IN A LONG TIME.
*!
I UNDERSTAND.
DO YOU?
YES!
SO WE ALL GOT A REALLY GOOD NIGHT'S SLEEP...
"...BUT I WOKE UP EARLY IN THE MORNING AND WAS SUDDENLY VERY SCARED!
IT'S VERY FOOLISH TO QUIT YOUR JOB WITHOUT HAVING ANOTHER ONE LINED UP."

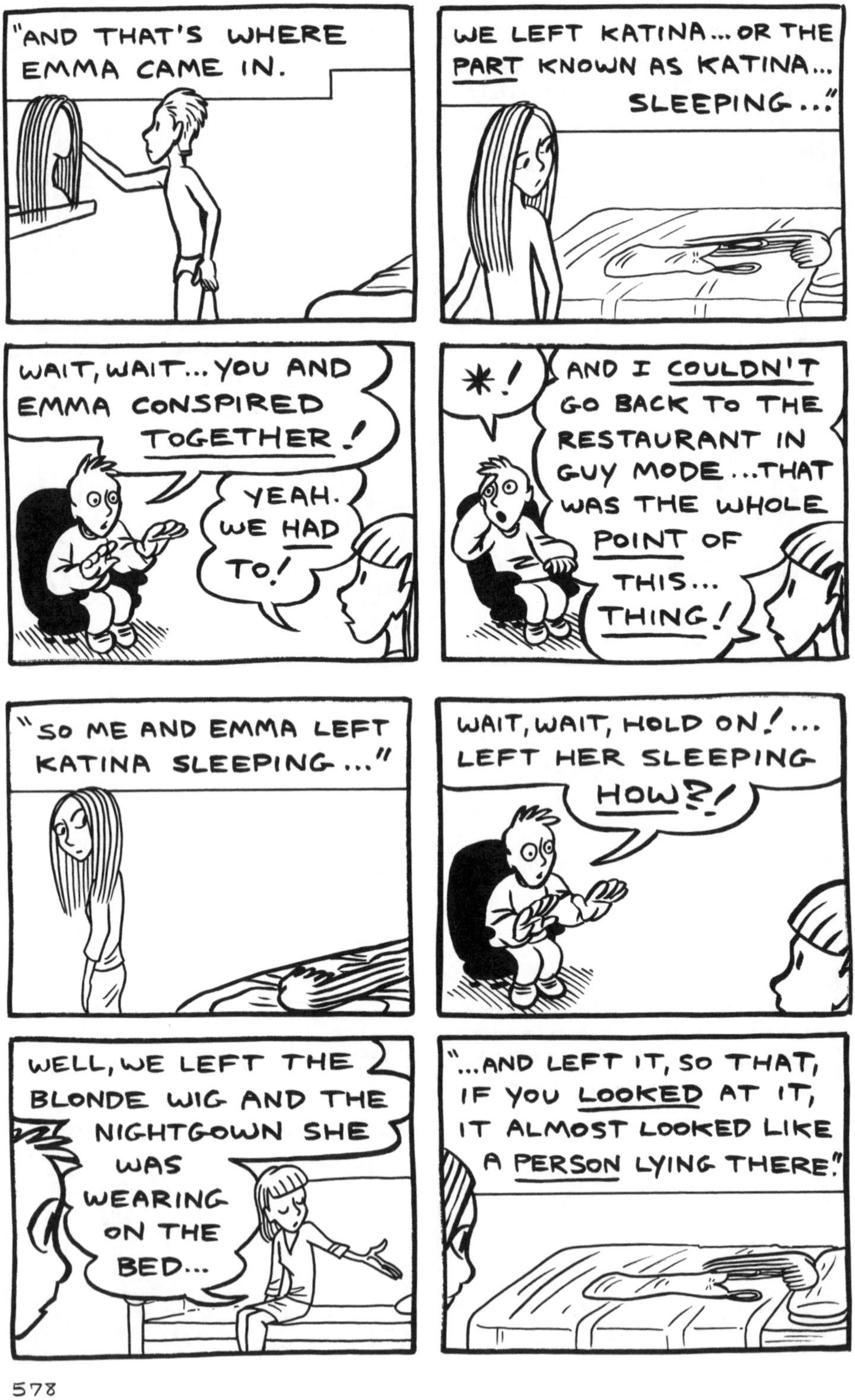
"AND THAT'S WHERE EMMA CAME IN.
WE LEFT KATINA... OR THE PART KNOWN AS KATINA... SLEEPING..."
WAIT, WAIT... YOU AND EMMA CONSPIRED TOGETHER!
YEAH. WE HAD TO!
*!
AND I COULDN'T GO BACK TO THE RESTAURANT IN GUY MODE... THAT WAS THE WHOLE POINT OF THIS... THING!
"SO ME AND EMMA LEFT KATINA SLEEPING..."
WAIT, WAIT, HOLD ON!... LEFT HER SLEEPING HOW?!
WELL, WE LEFT THE BLONDE WIG AND THE NIGHTGOWN SHE WAS WEARING ON THE BED...
"...AND LEFT IT, SO THAT, IF YOU LOOKED AT IT, IT ALMOST LOOKED LIKE A PERSON LYING THERE."

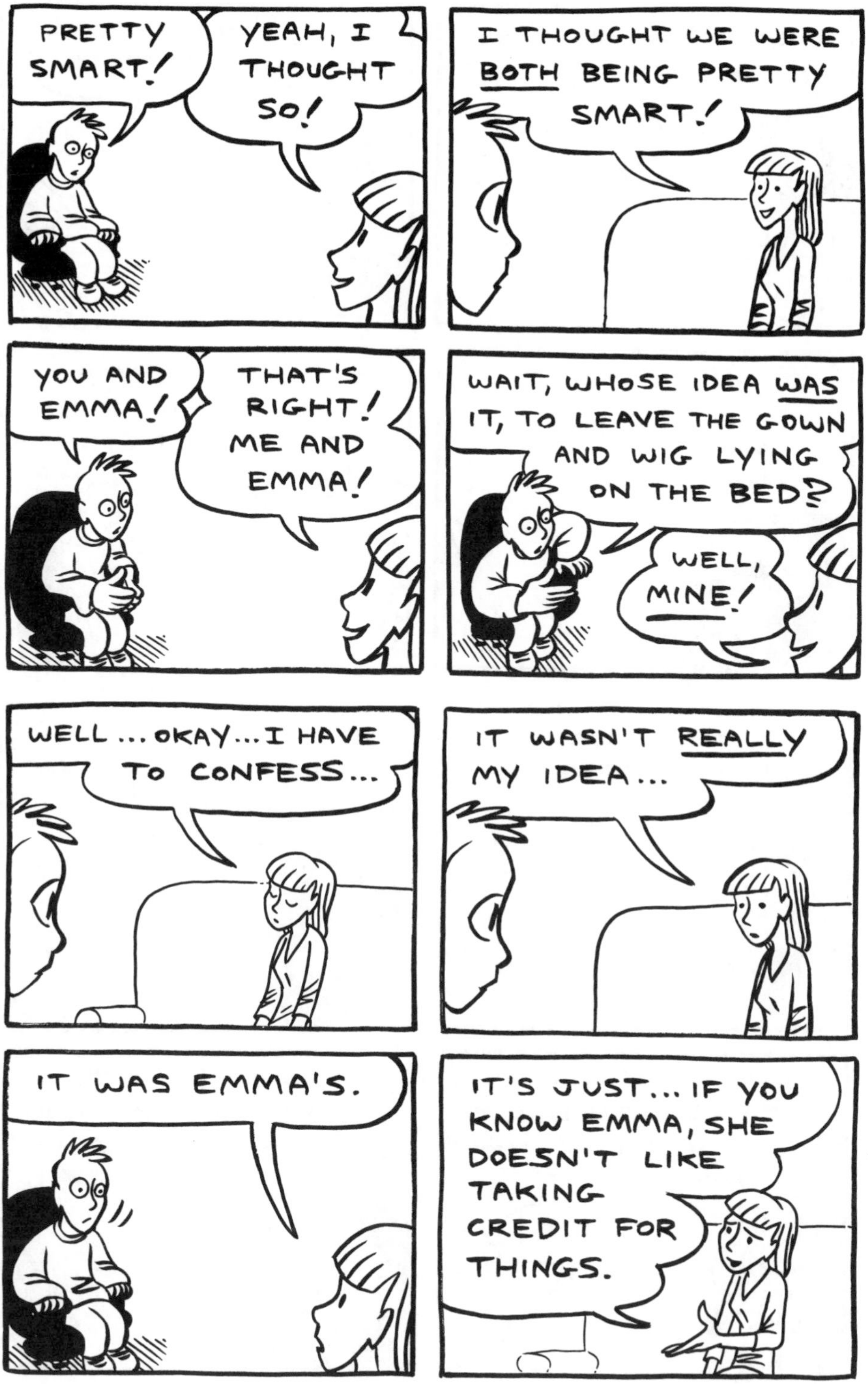

PRETTY SMART!
YEAH, I THOUGHT SO!
I THOUGHT WE WERE BOTH BEING PRETTY SMART!
YOU AND EMMA!
THAT'S RIGHT! ME AND EMMA!
WAIT, WHOSE IDEA WAS IT, TO LEAVE THE GOWN AND WIG LYING ON THE BED?
WELL, MINE!
WELL... OKAY... I HAVE TO CONFESS...
IT WASN'T REALLY MY IDEA...
IT WAS EMMA'S.
IT'S JUST... IF YOU KNOW EMMA, SHE DOESN'T LIKE TAKING CREDIT FOR THINGS.

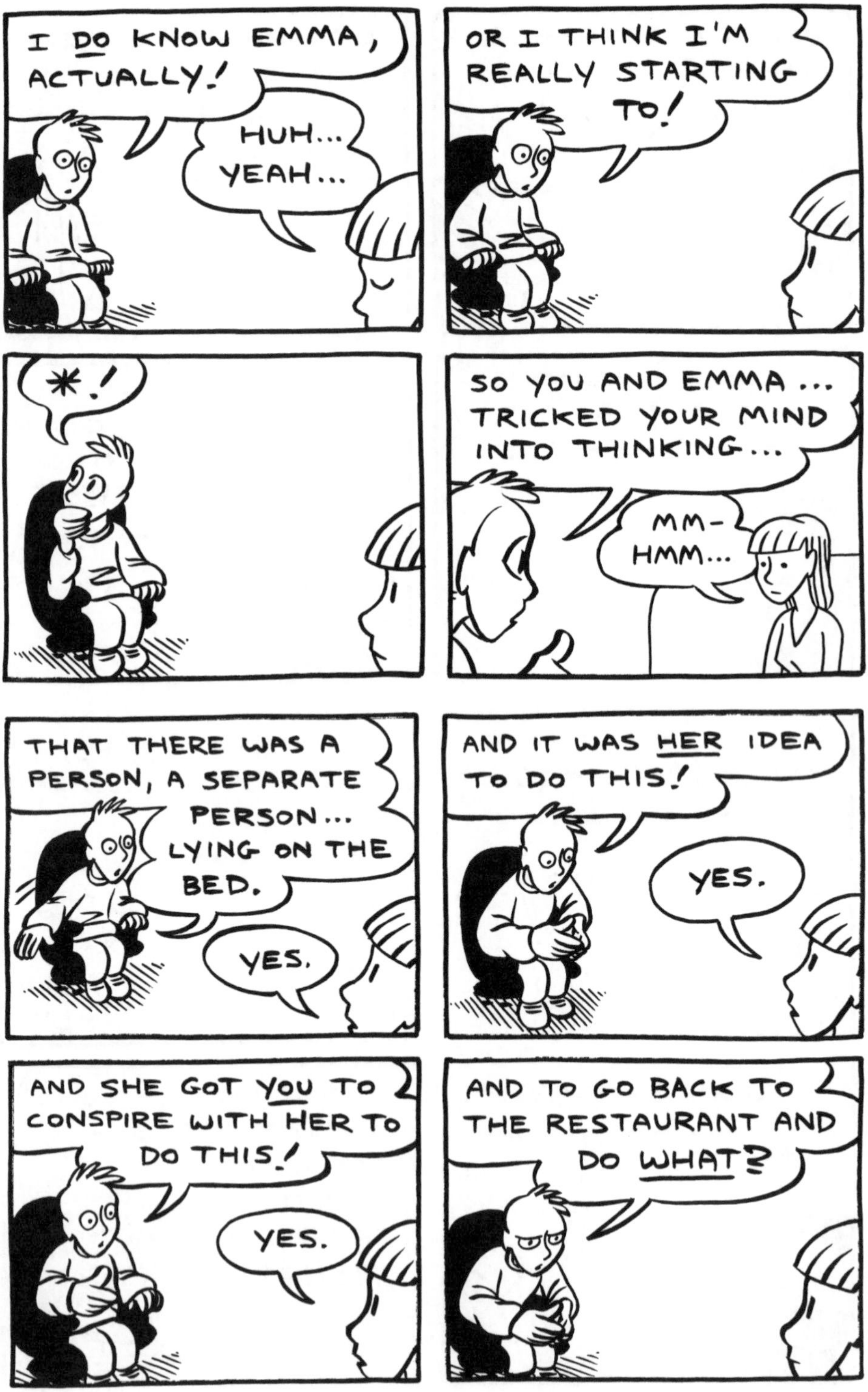
I DO KNOW EMMA, ACTUALLY!
HUH... YEAH...
OR I THINK I'M REALLY STARTING TO!
*!
SO YOU AND EMMA... TRICKED YOUR MIND INTO THINKING...
MM-HMM...
THAT THERE WAS A PERSON, A SEPARATE PERSON... LYING ON THE BED.
YES.
AND IT WAS HER IDEA TO DO THIS!
YES.
AND SHE GOT YOU TO CONSPIRE WITH HER TO DO THIS!
YES.
AND TO GO BACK TO THE RESTAURANT AND DO WHAT?

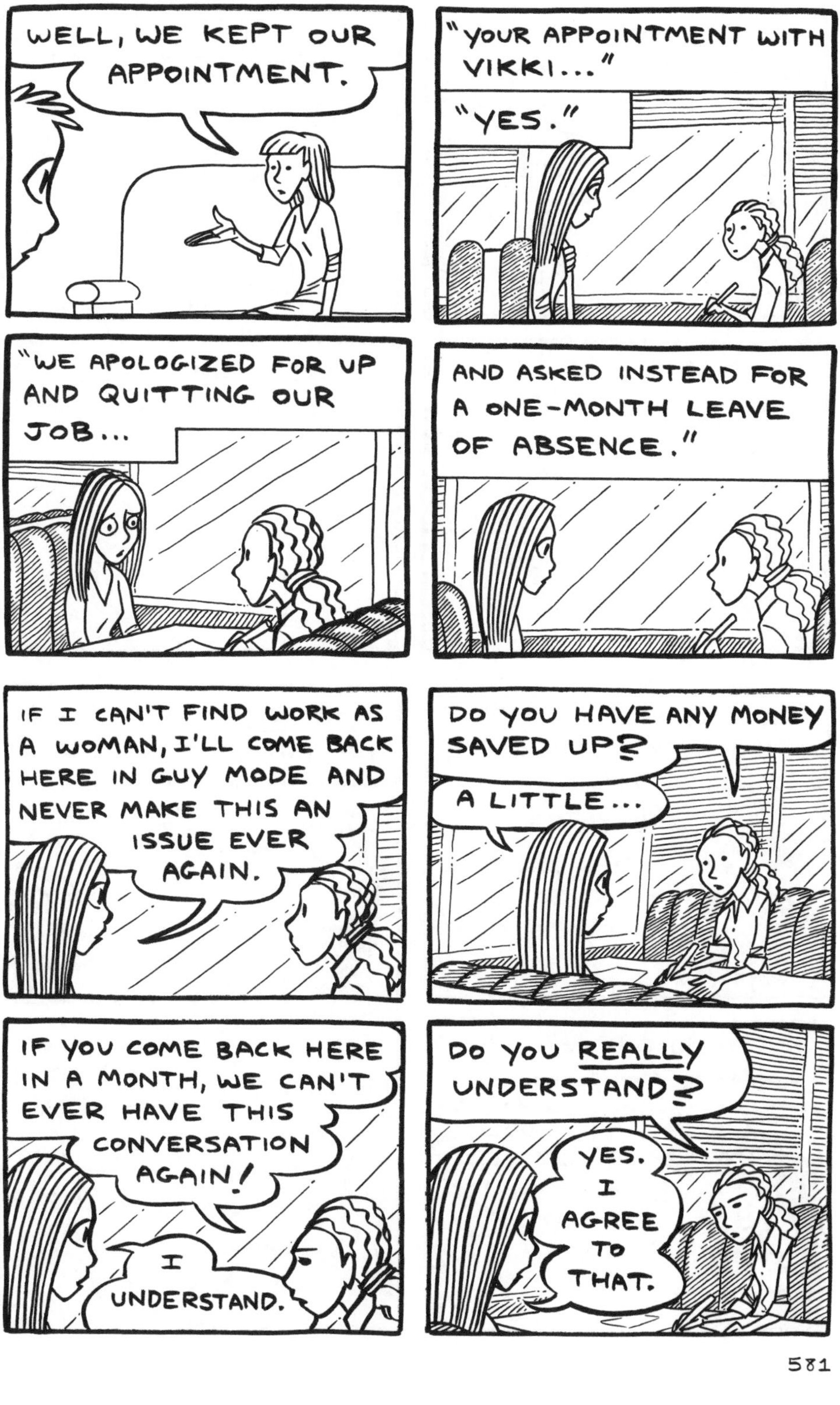
WELL, WE KEPT OUR APPOINTMENT.
"YOUR APPOINTMENT WITH VIKKI..."
"YES."
"WE APOLOGIZED FOR UP AND QUITTING OUR JOB...
AND ASKED INSTEAD FOR A ONE-MONTH LEAVE OF ABSENCE."
IF I CAN'T FIND WORK AS A WOMAN, I'LL COME BACK HERE IN GUY MODE AND NEVER MAKE THIS AN ISSUE EVER AGAIN.
DO YOU HAVE ANY MONEY SAVED UP?
A LITTLE...
IF YOU COME BACK HERE IN A MONTH, WE CAN'T EVER HAVE THIS CONVERSATION AGAIN!
I UNDERSTAND.
DO YOU REALLY UNDERSTAND?
YES. I AGREE TO THAT.

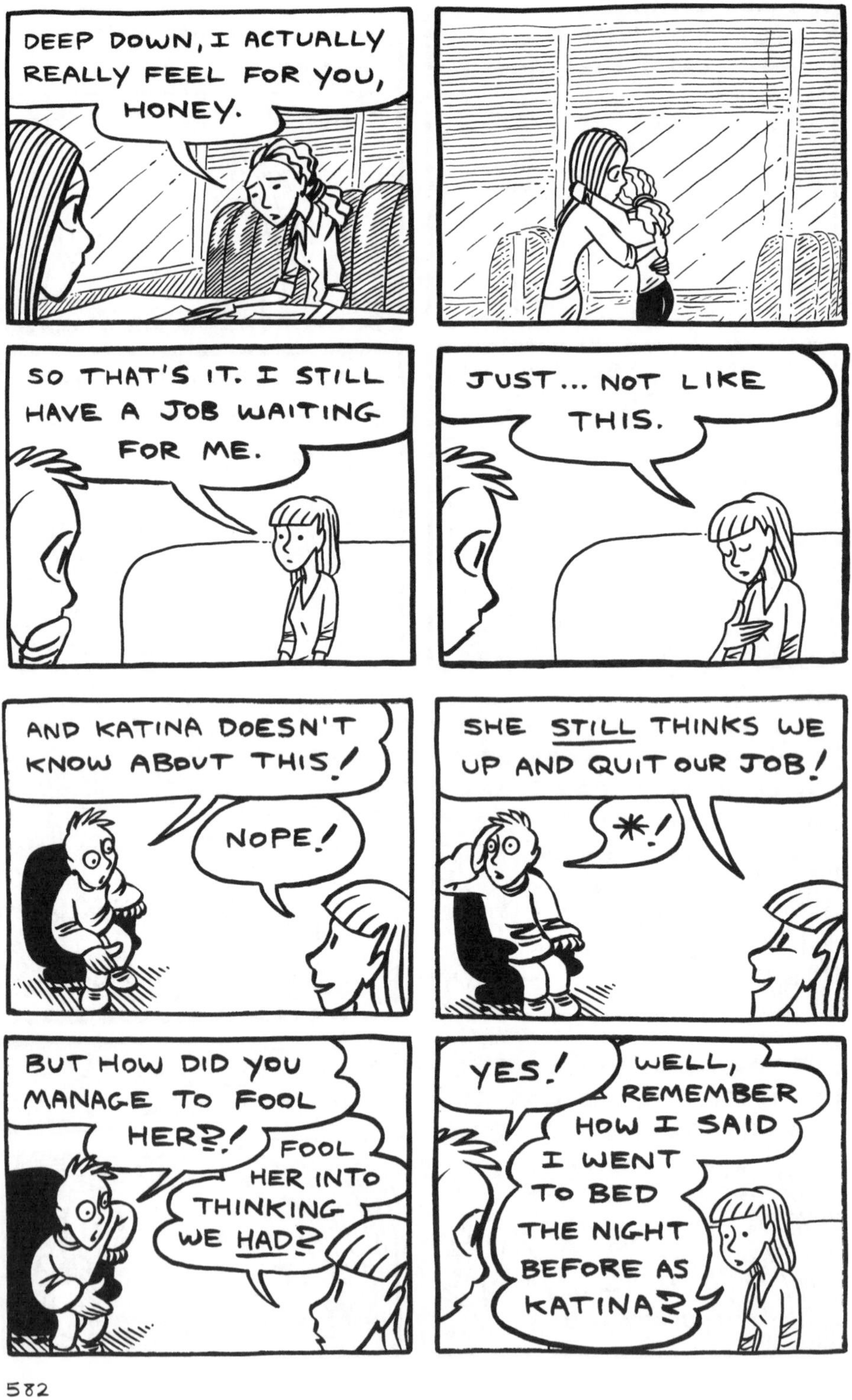
DEEP DOWN, I ACTUALLY REALLY FEEL FOR YOU, HONEY.
SO THAT'S IT. I STILL HAVE A JOB WAITING FOR ME.
JUST... NOT LIKE THIS.
AND KATINA DOESN'T KNOW ABOUT THIS!
NOPE!
SHE STILL THINKS WE UP AND QUIT OUR JOB!
*!
BUT HOW DID YOU MANAGE TO FOOL HER?!
FOOL HER INTO THINKING WE HAD?
YES!
WELL, REMEMBER HOW I SAID I WENT TO BED THE NIGHT BEFORE AS KATINA?

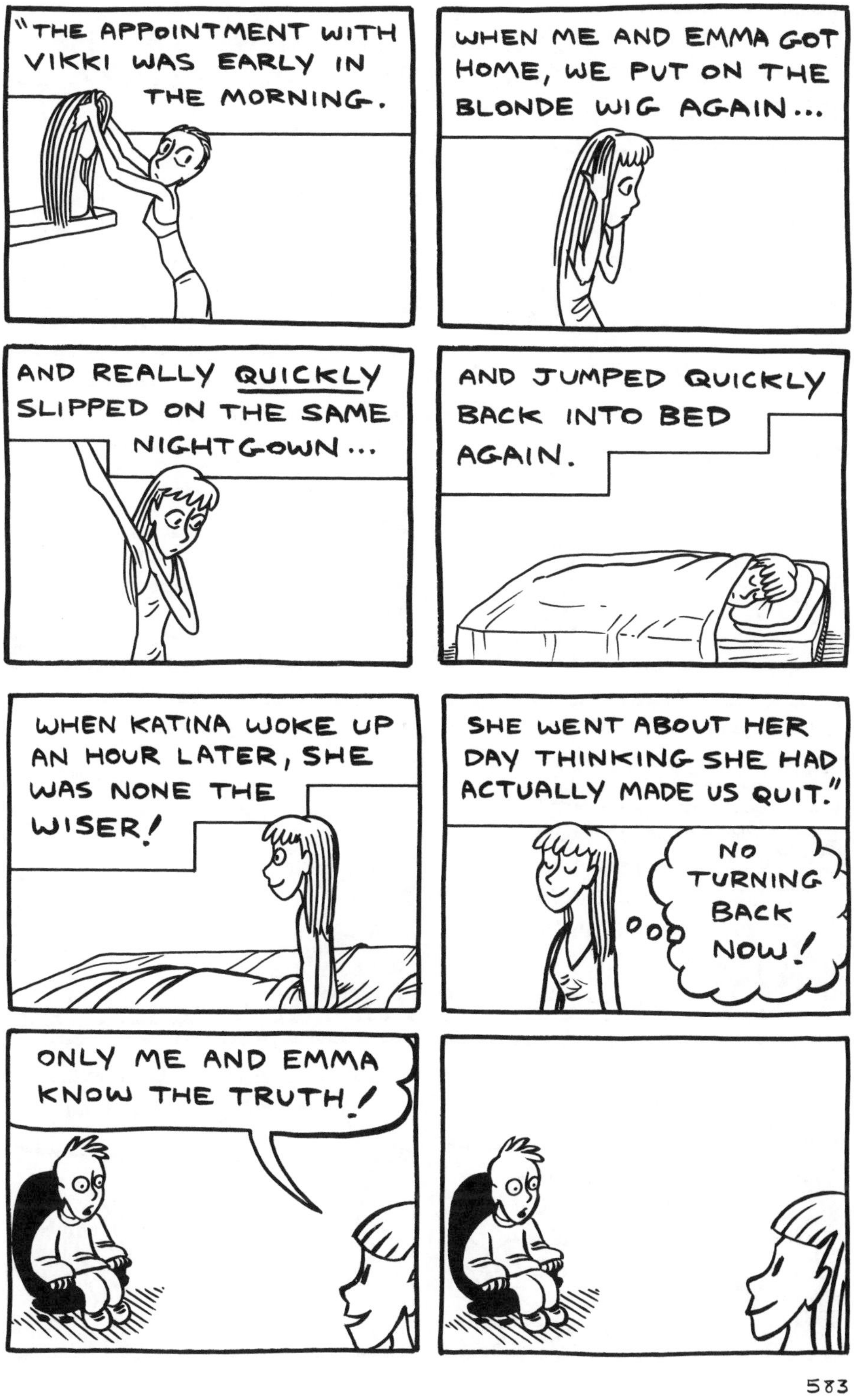
"THE APPOINTMENT WITH VIKKI WAS EARLY IN THE MORNING.
WHEN ME AND EMMA GOT HOME, WE PUT ON THE BLONDE WIG AGAIN...
AND REALLY QUICKLY SLIPPED ON THE SAME NIGHTGOWN...
AND JUMPED QUICKLY BACK INTO BED AGAIN.
WHEN KATINA WOKE UP AN HOUR LATER, SHE WAS NONE THE WISER!
SHE WENT ABOUT HER DAY THINKING SHE HAD ACTUALLY MADE US QUIT."
NO TURNING BACK NOW!
ONLY ME AND EMMA KNOW THE TRUTH!

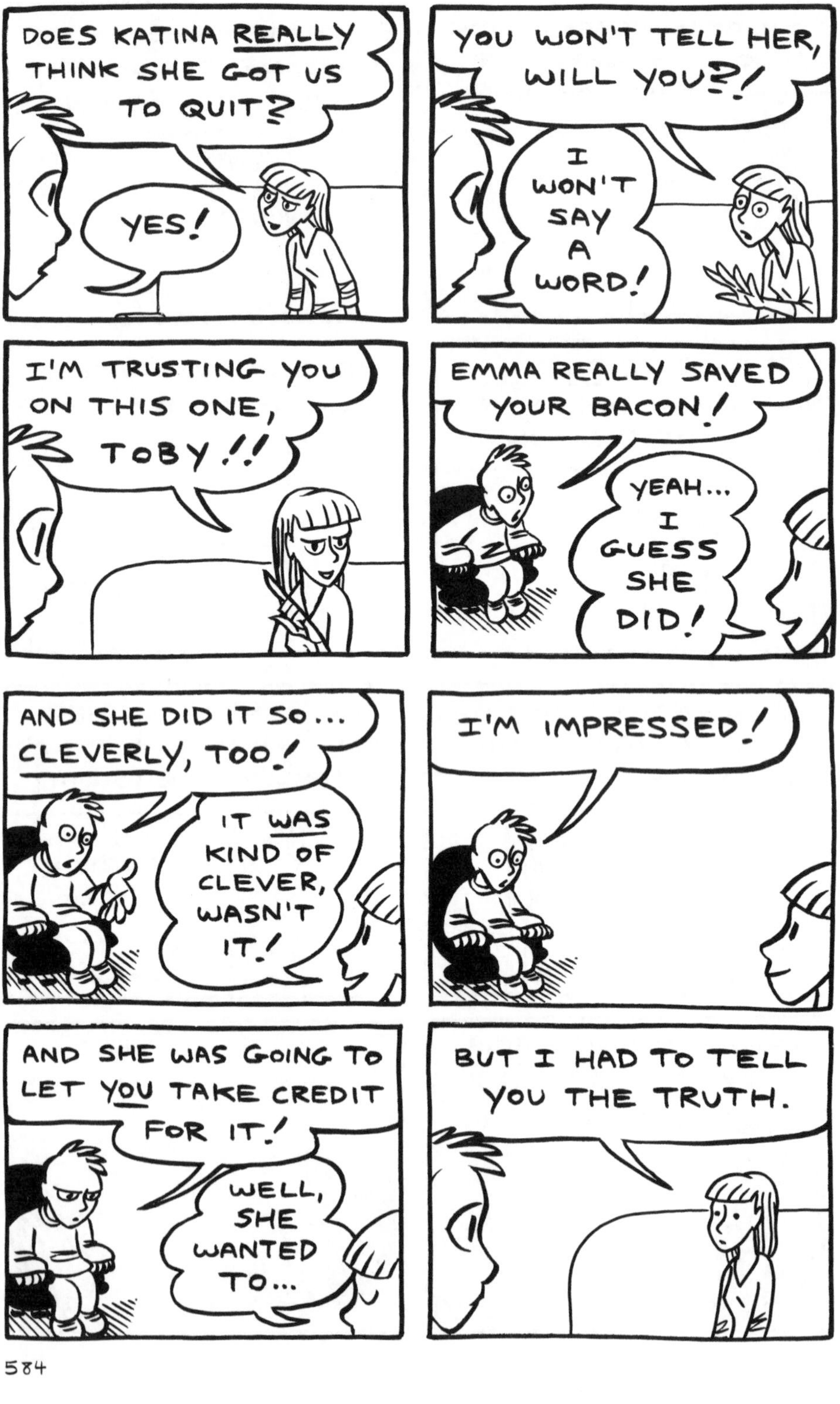
DOES KATINA REALLY THINK SHE GOT US TO QUIT?
YES!
YOU WON'T TELL HER, WILL YOU?!
I WON'T SAY A WORD!
I'M TRUSTING YOU ON THIS ONE, TOBY!!
EMMA REALLY SAVED YOUR BACON!
YEAH... I GUESS SHE DID!
AND SHE DID IT SO... CLEVERLY, TOO!
IT WAS KIND OF CLEVER, WASN'T IT!
I'M IMPRESSED!
AND SHE WAS GOING TO LET YOU TAKE CREDIT FOR IT!
WELL, SHE WANTED TO...
BUT I HAD TO TELL YOU THE TRUTH.

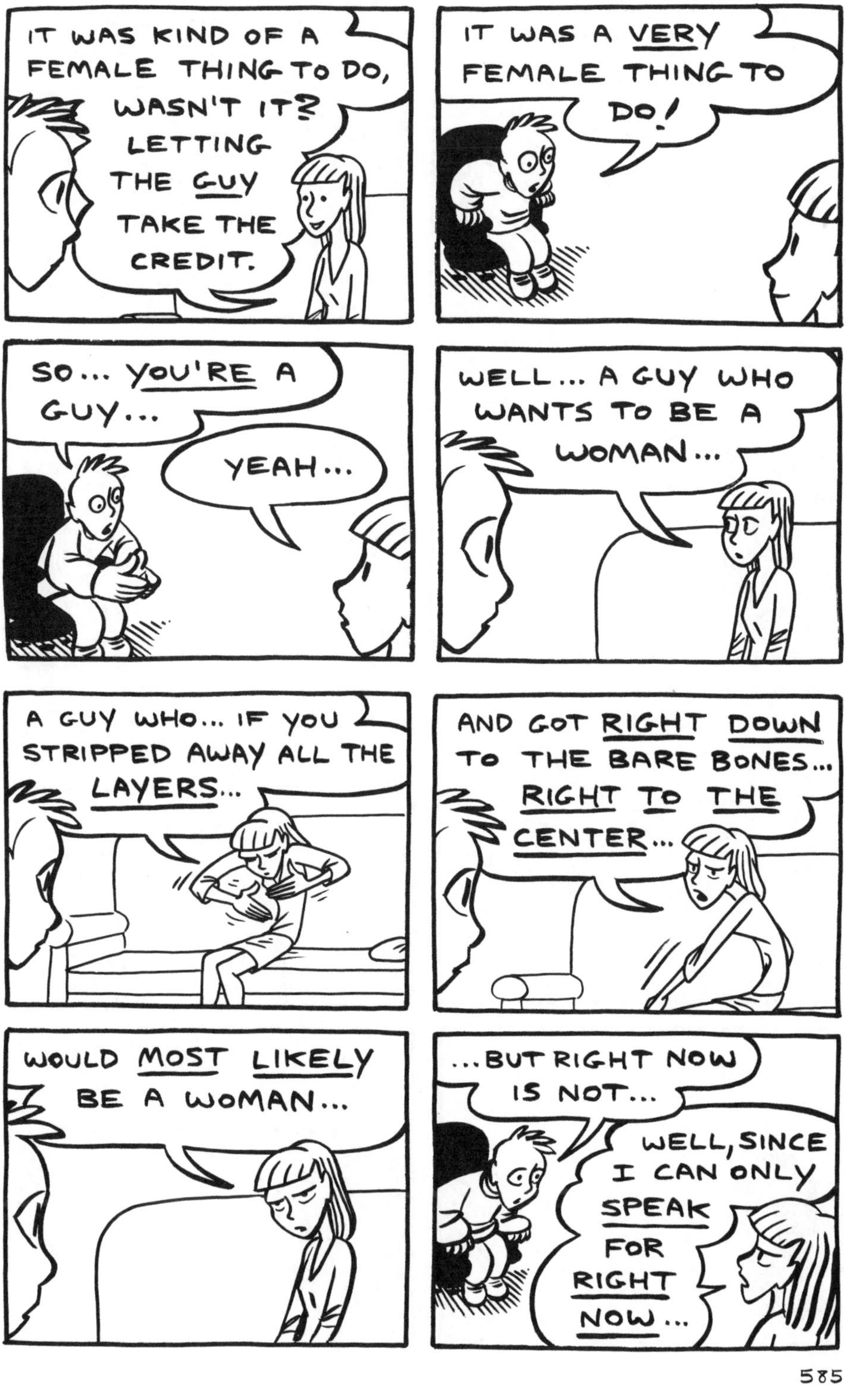
IT WAS KIND OF A FEMALE THING TO DO, WASN'T IT? LETTING THE GUY TAKE THE CREDIT.
IT WAS A VERY FEMALE THING TO DO!
SO... YOU'RE A GUY...
YEAH...
WELL... A GUY WHO WANTS TO BE A WOMAN...
A GUY WHO... IF YOU STRIPPED AWAY ALL THE LAYERS...
AND GOT RIGHT DOWN TO THE BARE BONES... RIGHT TO THE CENTER...
WOULD MOST LIKELY BE A WOMAN...
...BUT RIGHT NOW IS NOT...
WELL, SINCE I CAN ONLY SPEAK FOR RIGHT NOW...

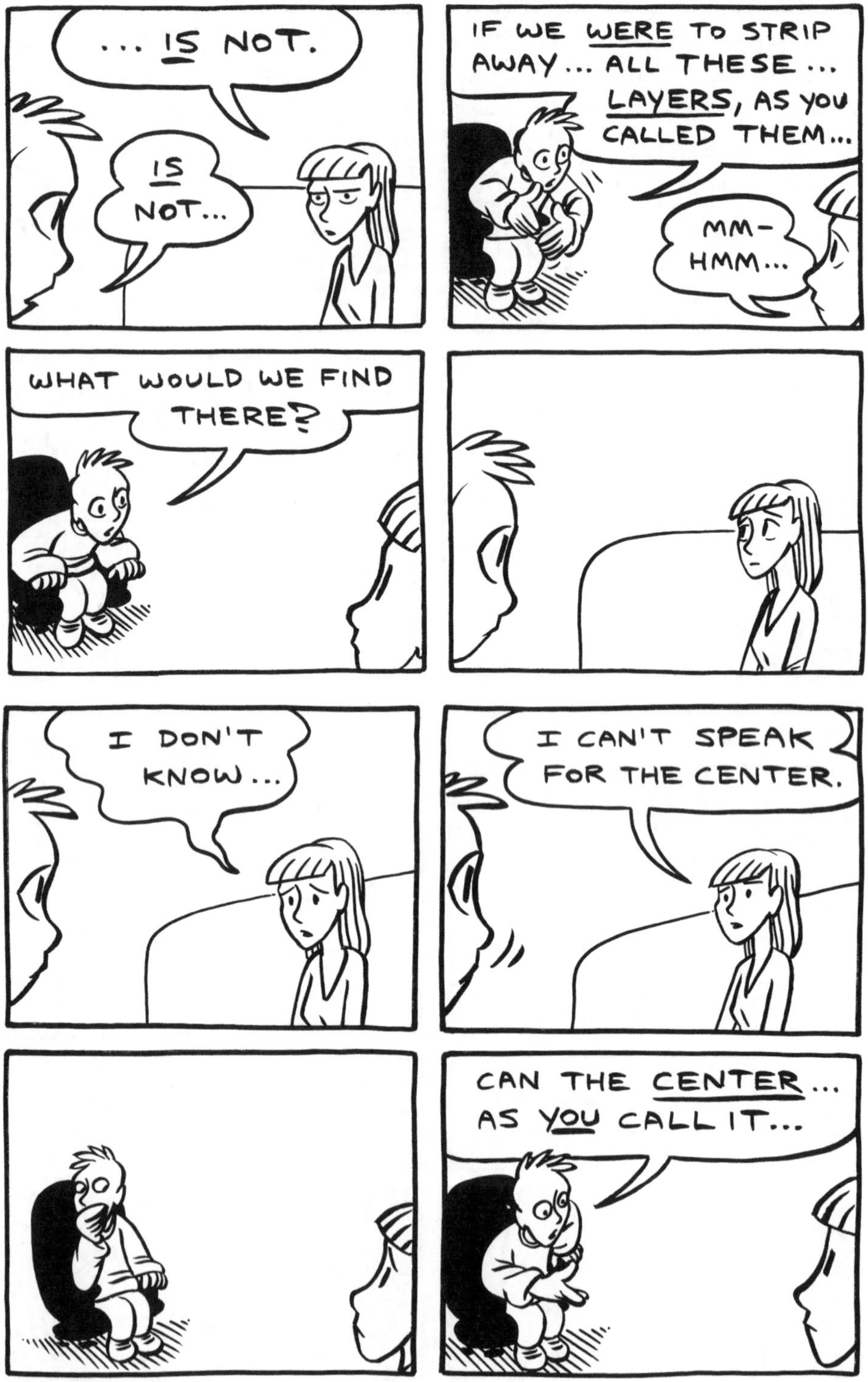
... IS NOT.
IS NOT...
IF WE WERE TO STRIP AWAY... ALL THESE... LAYERS, AS YOU CALLED THEM...
MM-HMM...
WHAT WOULD WE FIND THERE?
I DON'T KNOW...
I CAN'T SPEAK FOR THE CENTER.
CAN THE CENTER... AS YOU CALL IT...

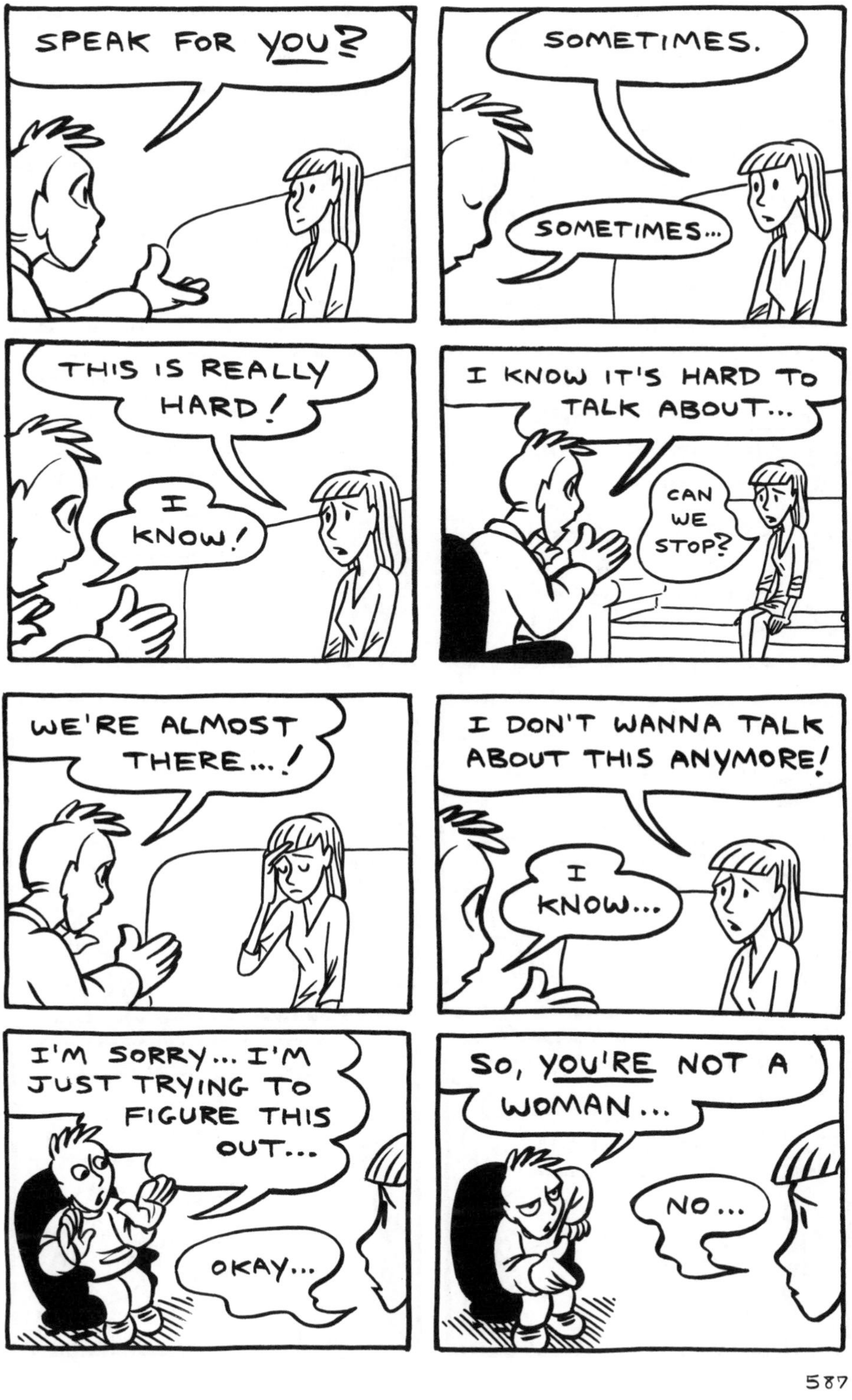
SPEAK FOR YOU?
SOMETIMES.
SOMETIMES...
THIS IS REALLY HARD!
I KNOW!
I KNOW IT'S HARD TO TALK ABOUT...
CAN WE STOP?
WE'RE ALMOST THERE...!
I DON'T WANNA TALK ABOUT THIS ANYMORE!
I KNOW...
I'M SORRY... I'M JUST TRYING TO FIGURE THIS OUT...
OKAY...
SO, YOU'RE NOT A WOMAN...
NO...

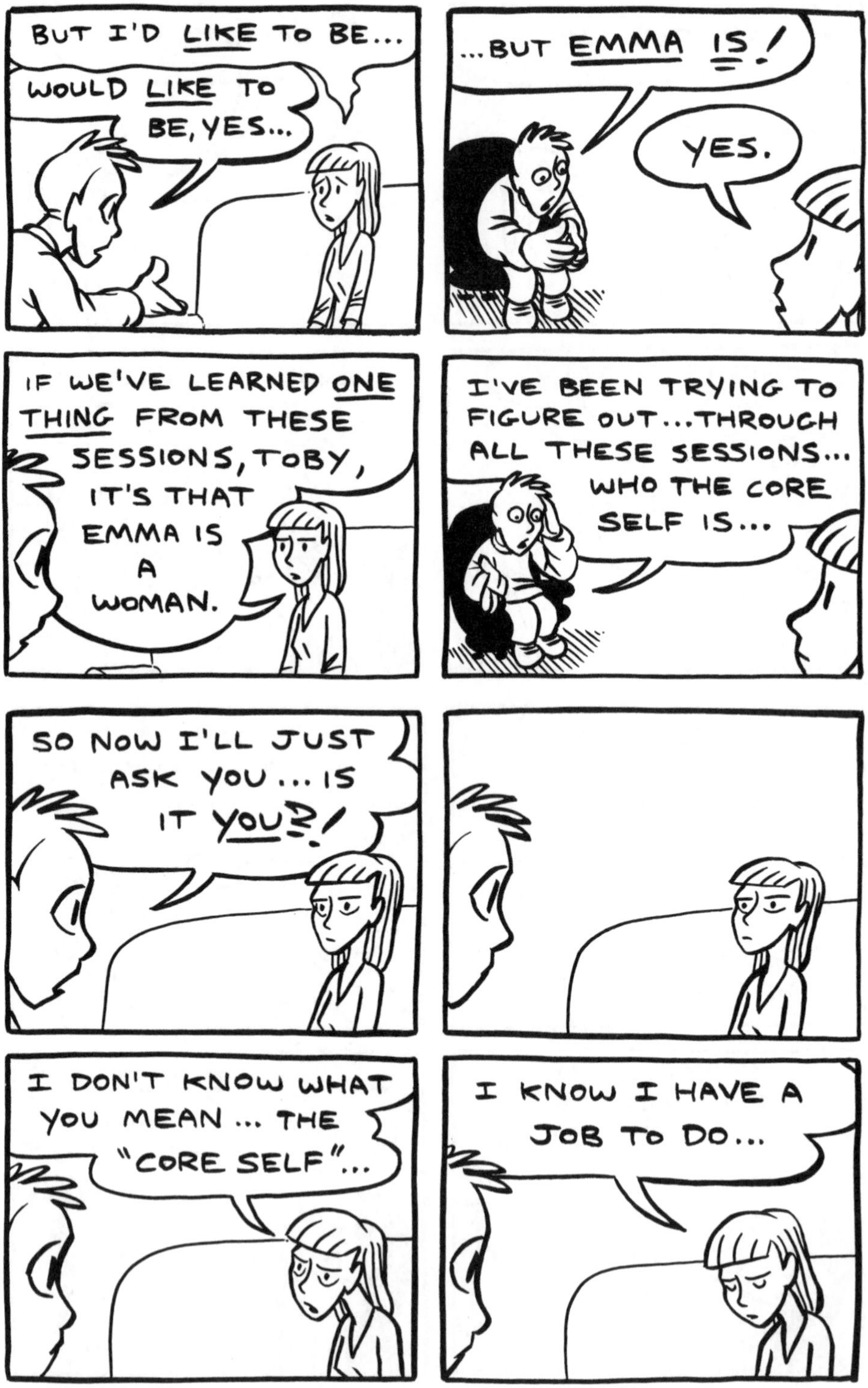
BUT I'D LIKE TO BE...
WOULD LIKE TO BE, YES...
...BUT EMMA IS!
YES.
IF WE'VE LEARNED ONE THING FROM THESE SESSIONS, TOBY, IT'S THAT EMMA IS A WOMAN.
I'VE BEEN TRYING TO FIGURE OUT...THROUGH ALL THESE SESSIONS... WHO THE CORE SELF IS...
SO NOW I'LL JUST ASK YOU... IS IT YOU?!
I DON'T KNOW WHAT YOU MEAN... THE "CORE SELF"...
I KNOW I HAVE A JOB TO DO...

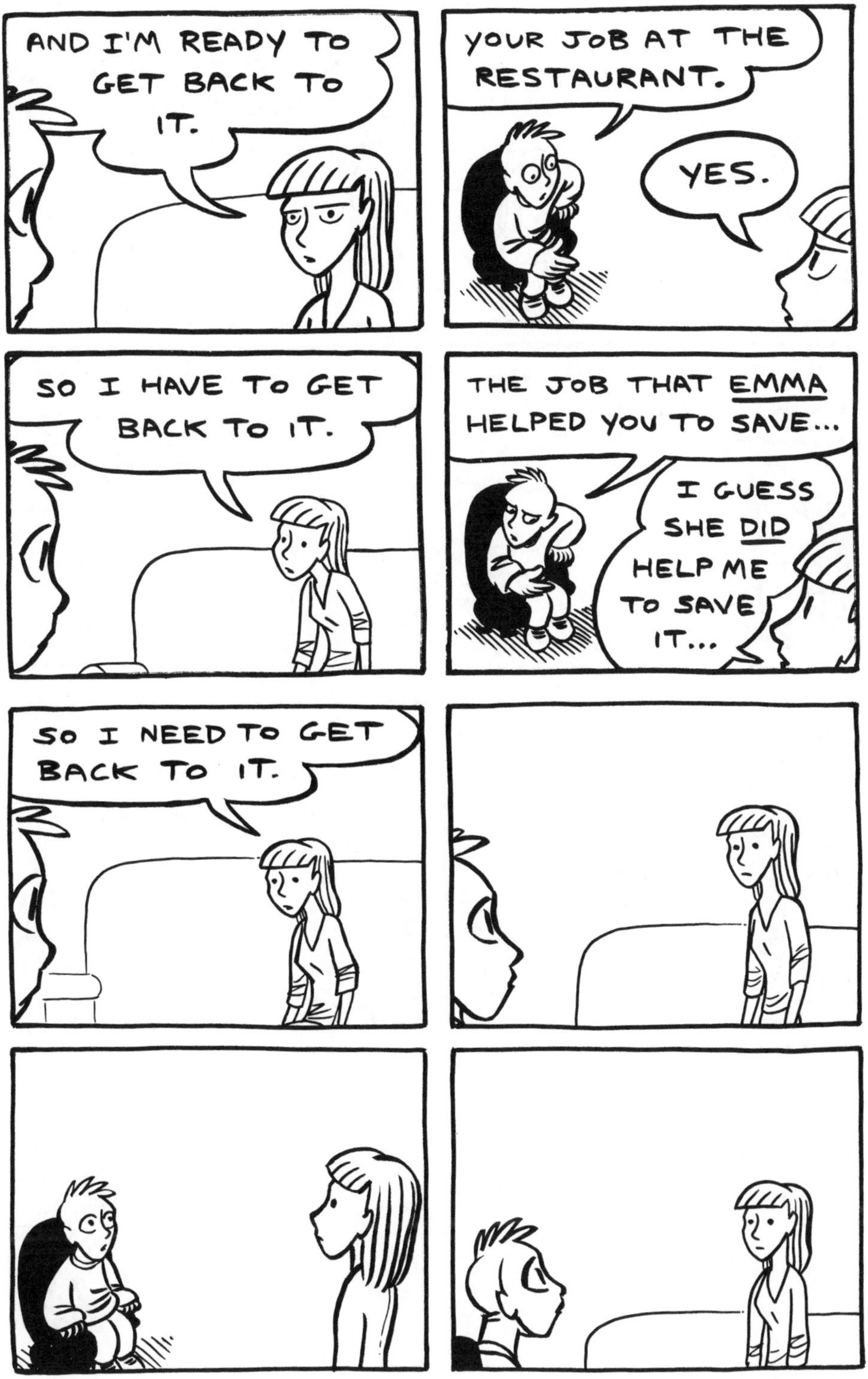
AND I'M READY TO GET BACK TO IT.
YOUR JOB AT THE RESTAURANT.
YES.
SO I HAVE TO GET BACK TO IT.
THE JOB THAT EMMA HELPED YOU TO SAVE...
I GUESS SHE DID HELP ME TO SAVE IT...
SO I NEED TO GET BACK TO IT.

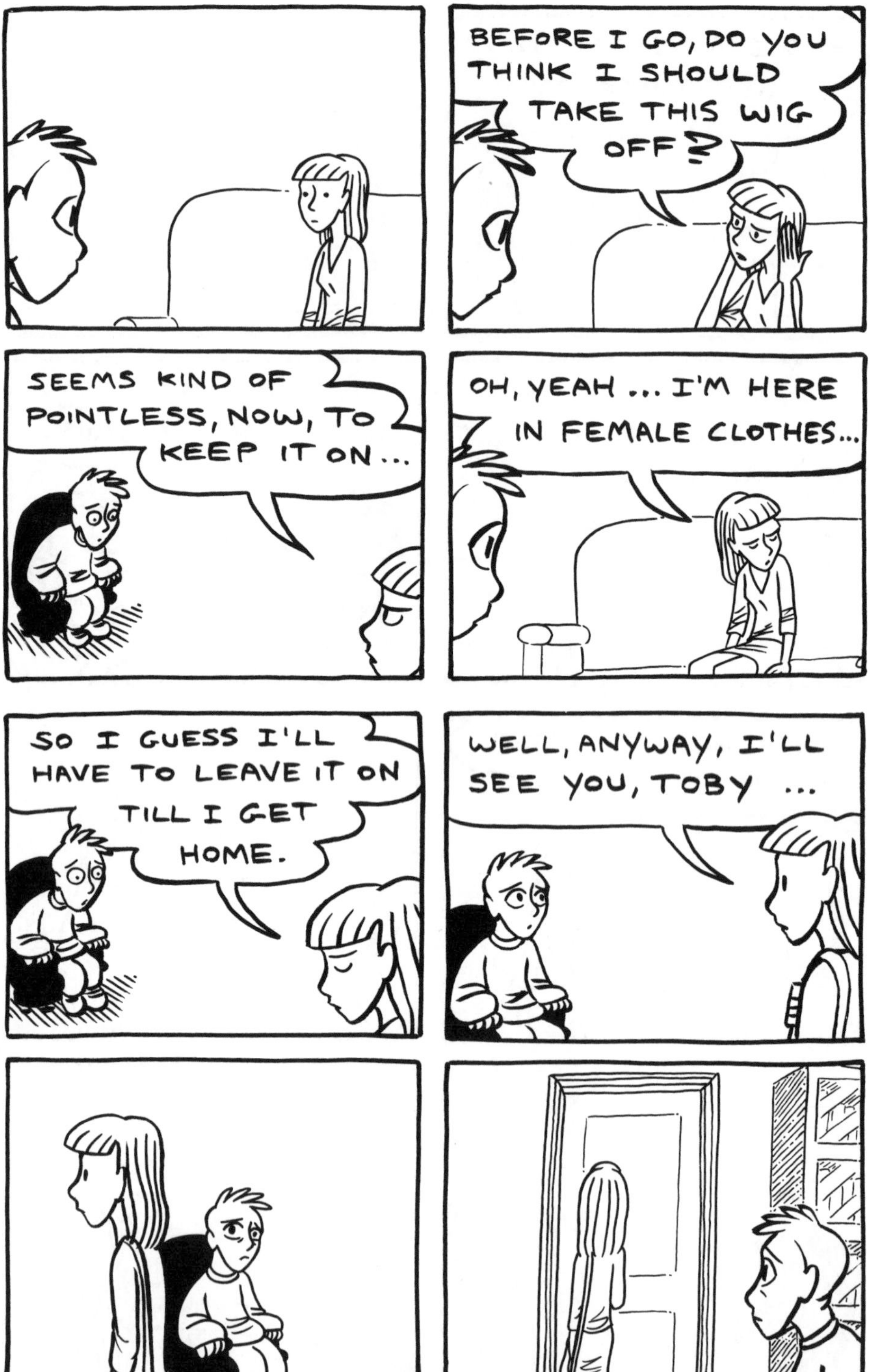
BEFORE I GO, DO YOU THINK I SHOULD TAKE THIS WIG OFF?
SEEMS KIND OF POINTLESS, NOW, TO KEEP IT ON...
OH, YEAH ... I'M HERE IN FEMALE CLOTHES...
SO I GUESS I'LL HAVE TO LEAVE IT ON TILL I GET HOME.
WELL, ANYWAY, I'LL SEE YOU, TOBY ...

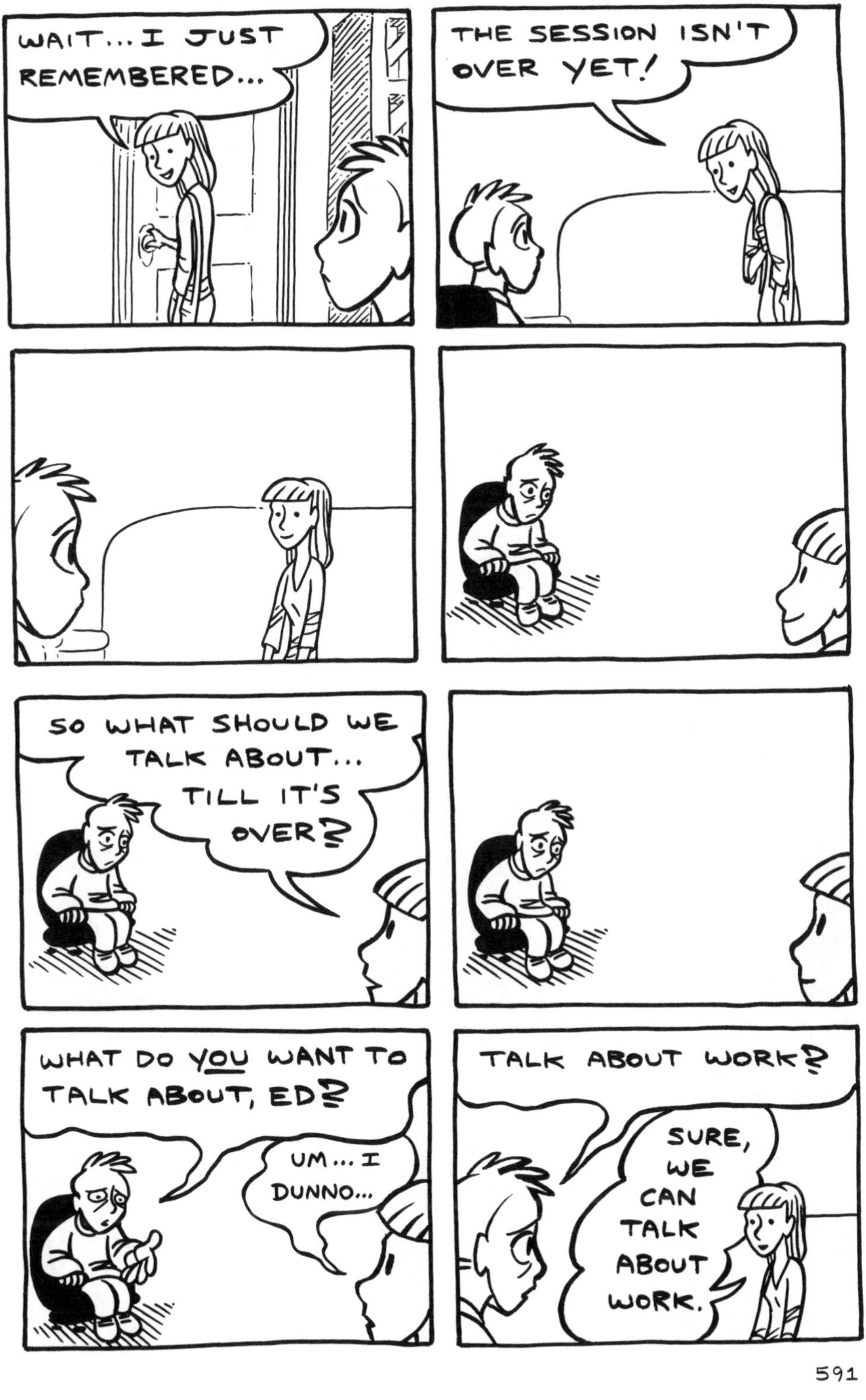
WAIT... I JUST REMEMBERED...
THE SESSION ISN'T OVER YET!
SO WHAT SHOULD WE TALK ABOUT... TILL IT'S OVER?
WHAT DO YOU WANT TO TALK ABOUT, ED?
UM... I DUNNO...
TALK ABOUT WORK?
SURE, WE CAN TALK ABOUT WORK.

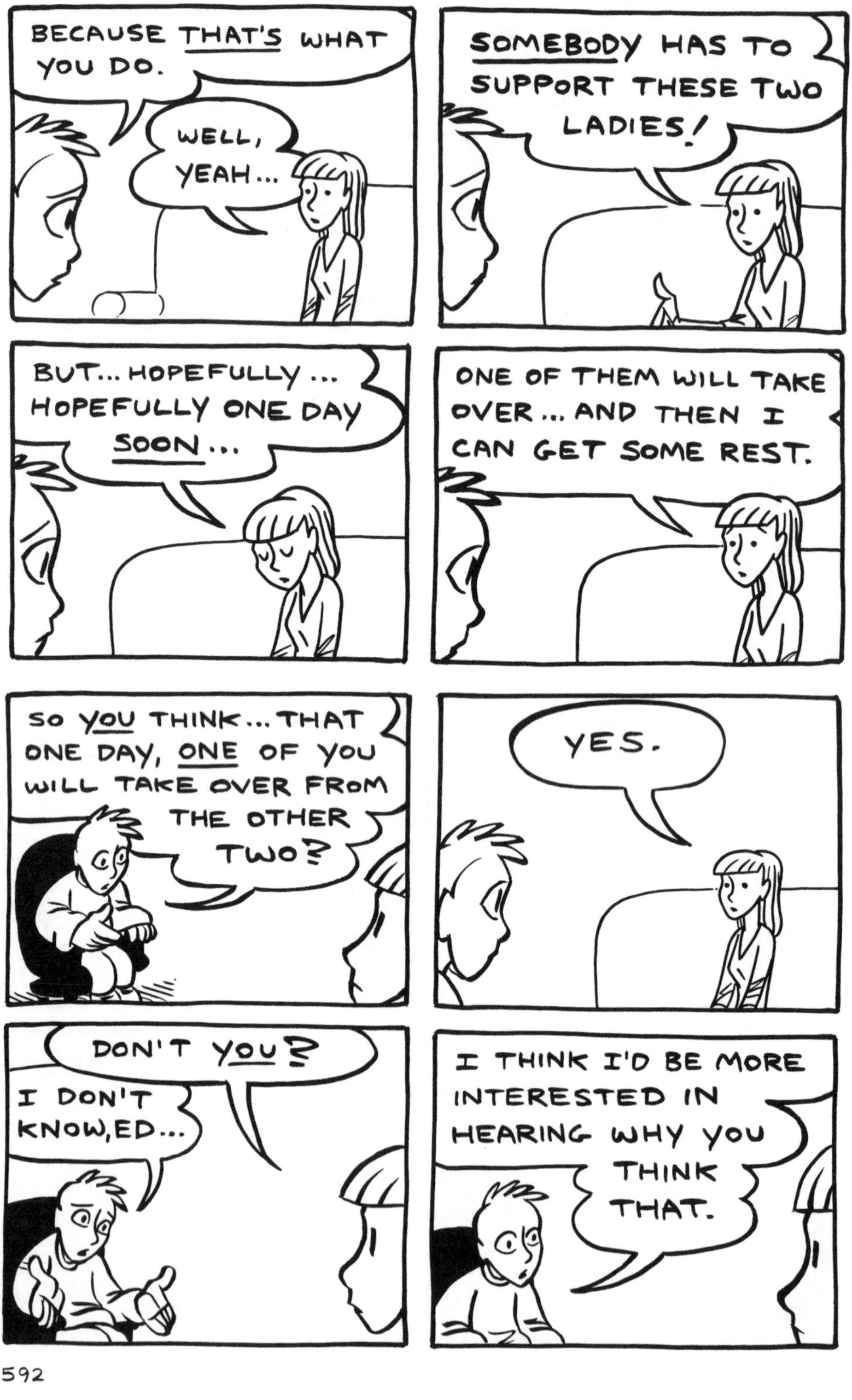
BECAUSE THAT'S WHAT YOU DO.
WELL, YEAH...
SOMEBODY HAS TO SUPPORT THESE TWO LADIES!
BUT... HOPEFULLY... HOPEFULLY ONE DAY SOON...
ONE OF THEM WILL TAKE OVER... AND THEN I CAN GET SOME REST.
SO YOU THINK... THAT ONE DAY, ONE OF YOU WILL TAKE OVER FROM THE OTHER TWO?
YES.
DON'T YOU?
I DON'T KNOW, ED...
I THINK I'D BE MORE INTERESTED IN HEARING WHY YOU THINK THAT.

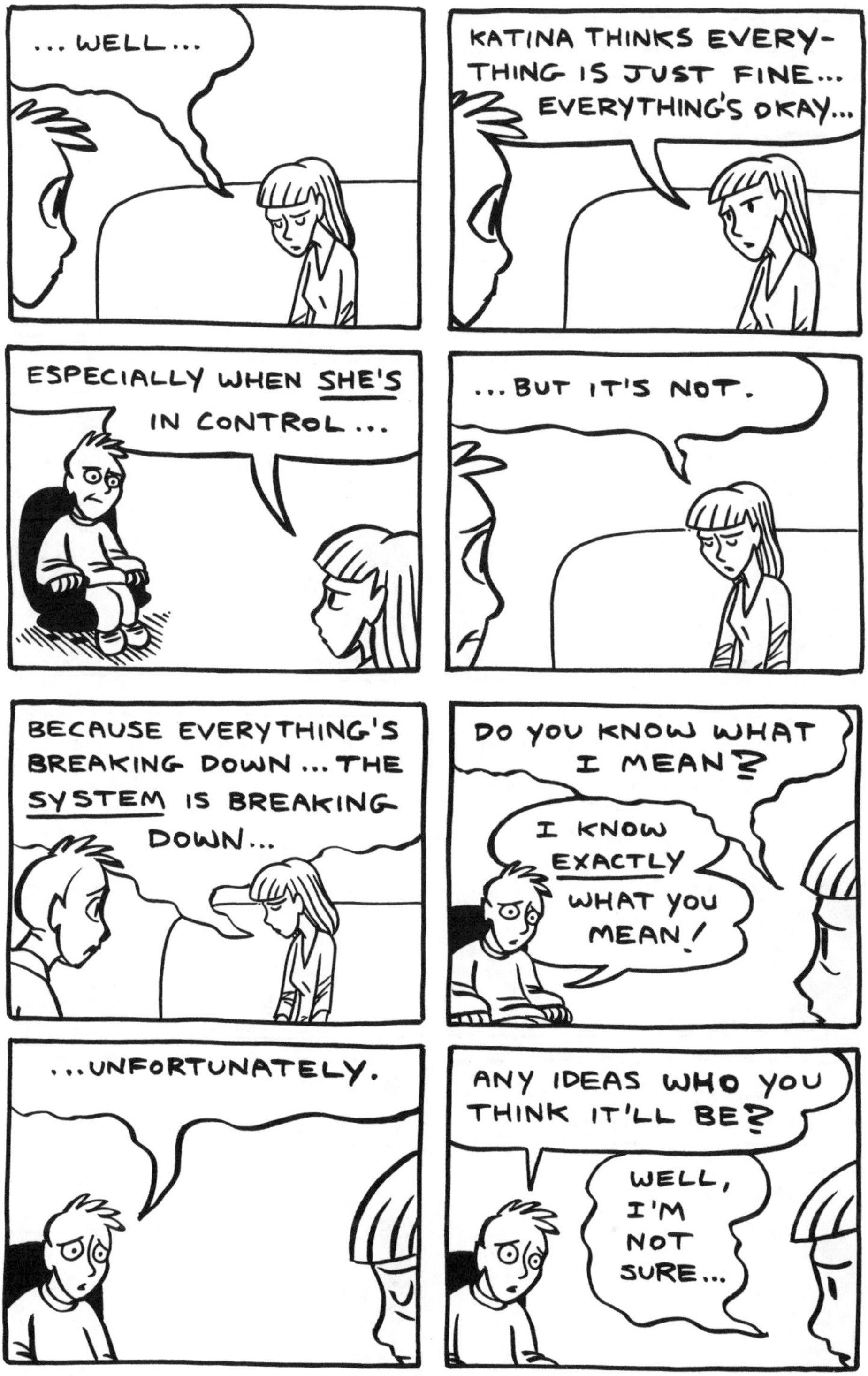
...WELL...
KATINA THINKS EVERYTHING IS JUST FINE... EVERYTHING'S OKAY...
ESPECIALLY WHEN SHE'S IN CONTROL...
...BUT IT'S NOT.
BECAUSE EVERYTHING'S BREAKING DOWN... THE SYSTEM IS BREAKING DOWN...
DO YOU KNOW WHAT I MEAN?
I KNOW EXACTLY WHAT YOU MEAN!
...UNFORTUNATELY.
ANY IDEAS WHO YOU THINK IT'LL BE?
WELL, I'M NOT SURE...

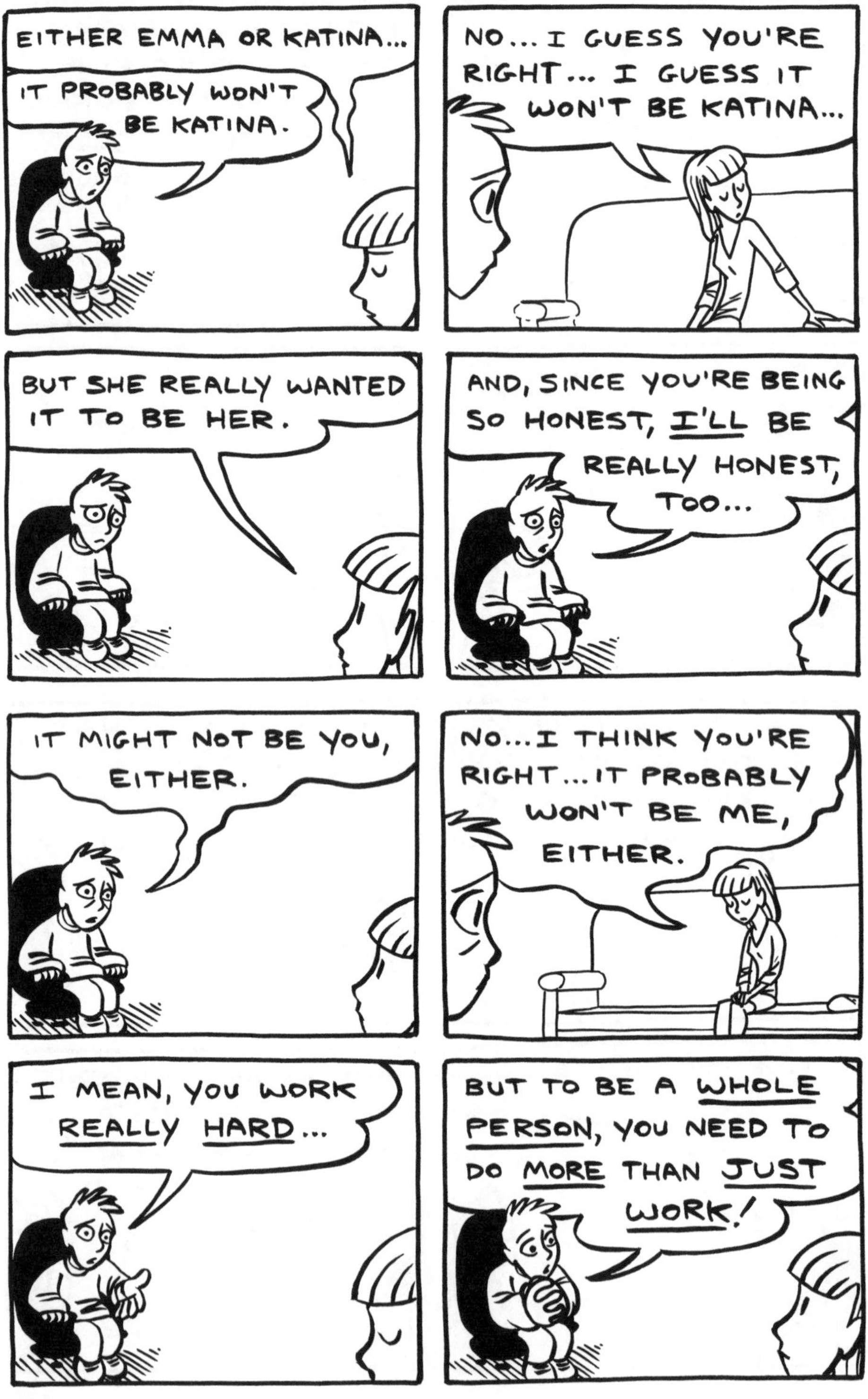
EITHER EMMA OR KATINA...
IT PROBABLY WON'T BE KATINA.
NO... I GUESS YOU'RE RIGHT... I GUESS IT WON'T BE KATINA...
BUT SHE REALLY WANTED IT TO BE HER.
AND, SINCE YOU'RE BEING SO HONEST, I'LL BE REALLY HONEST, TOO...
IT MIGHT NOT BE YOU, EITHER.
NO... I THINK YOU'RE RIGHT... IT PROBABLY WON'T BE ME, EITHER.
I MEAN, YOU WORK REALLY HARD...
BUT TO BE A WHOLE PERSON, YOU NEED TO DO MORE THAN JUST WORK!

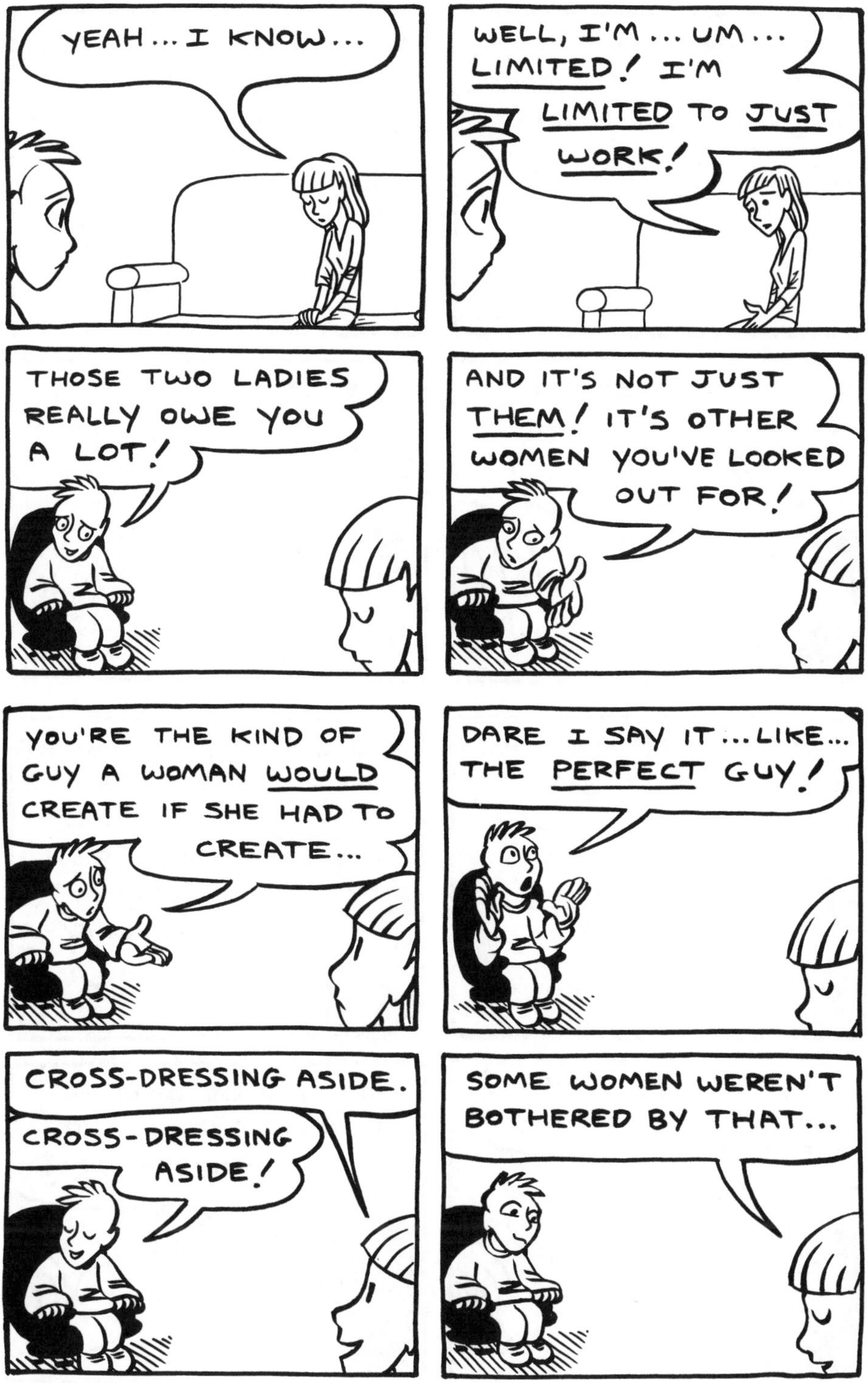
YEAH ... I KNOW ...
WELL, I'M ... UM ... LIMITED! I'M LIMITED TO JUST WORK!
THOSE TWO LADIES REALLY OWE YOU A LOT!
AND IT'S NOT JUST THEM! IT'S OTHER WOMEN YOU'VE LOOKED OUT FOR!
YOU'RE THE KIND OF GUY A WOMAN WOULD CREATE IF SHE HAD TO CREATE...
DARE I SAY IT ... LIKE... THE PERFECT GUY!
CROSS-DRESSING ASIDE.
CROSS-DRESSING ASIDE!
SOME WOMEN WEREN'T BOTHERED BY THAT...

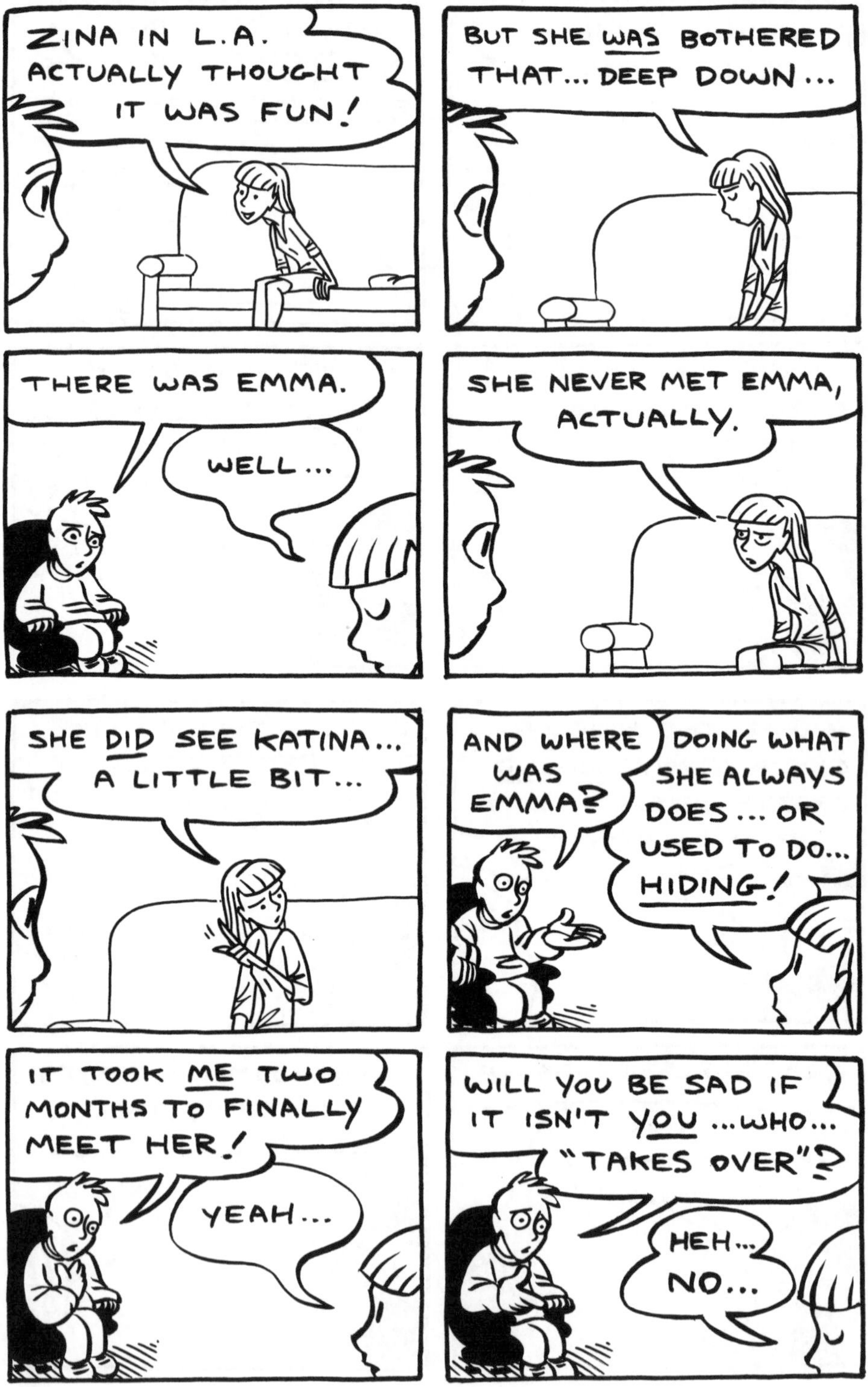
ZINA IN L.A. ACTUALLY THOUGHT IT WAS FUN!
BUT SHE WAS BOTHERED THAT... DEEP DOWN...
THERE WAS EMMA.
WELL...
SHE NEVER MET EMMA, ACTUALLY.
SHE DID SEE KATINA... A LITTLE BIT...
AND WHERE WAS EMMA?
DOING WHAT SHE ALWAYS DOES... OR USED TO DO... HIDING!
IT TOOK ME TWO MONTHS TO FINALLY MEET HER!
YEAH...
WILL YOU BE SAD IF IT ISN'T YOU ...WHO... "TAKES OVER"?
HEH... NO...

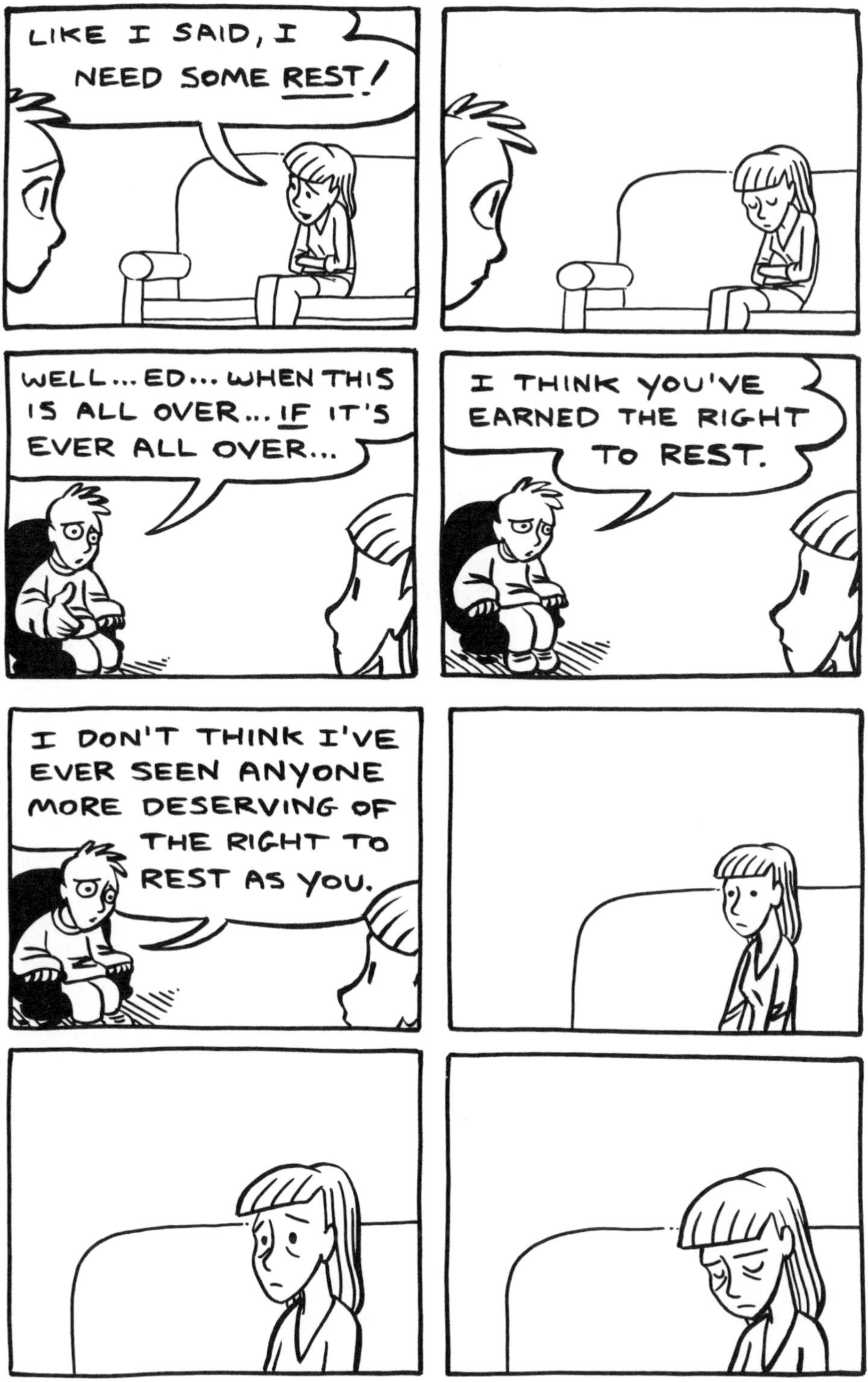
LIKE I SAID, I NEED SOME REST!
WELL... ED... WHEN THIS IS ALL OVER... IF IT'S EVER ALL OVER...
I THINK YOU'VE EARNED THE RIGHT TO REST.
I DON'T THINK I'VE EVER SEEN ANYONE MORE DESERVING OF THE RIGHT TO REST AS YOU.

DUMPSTER

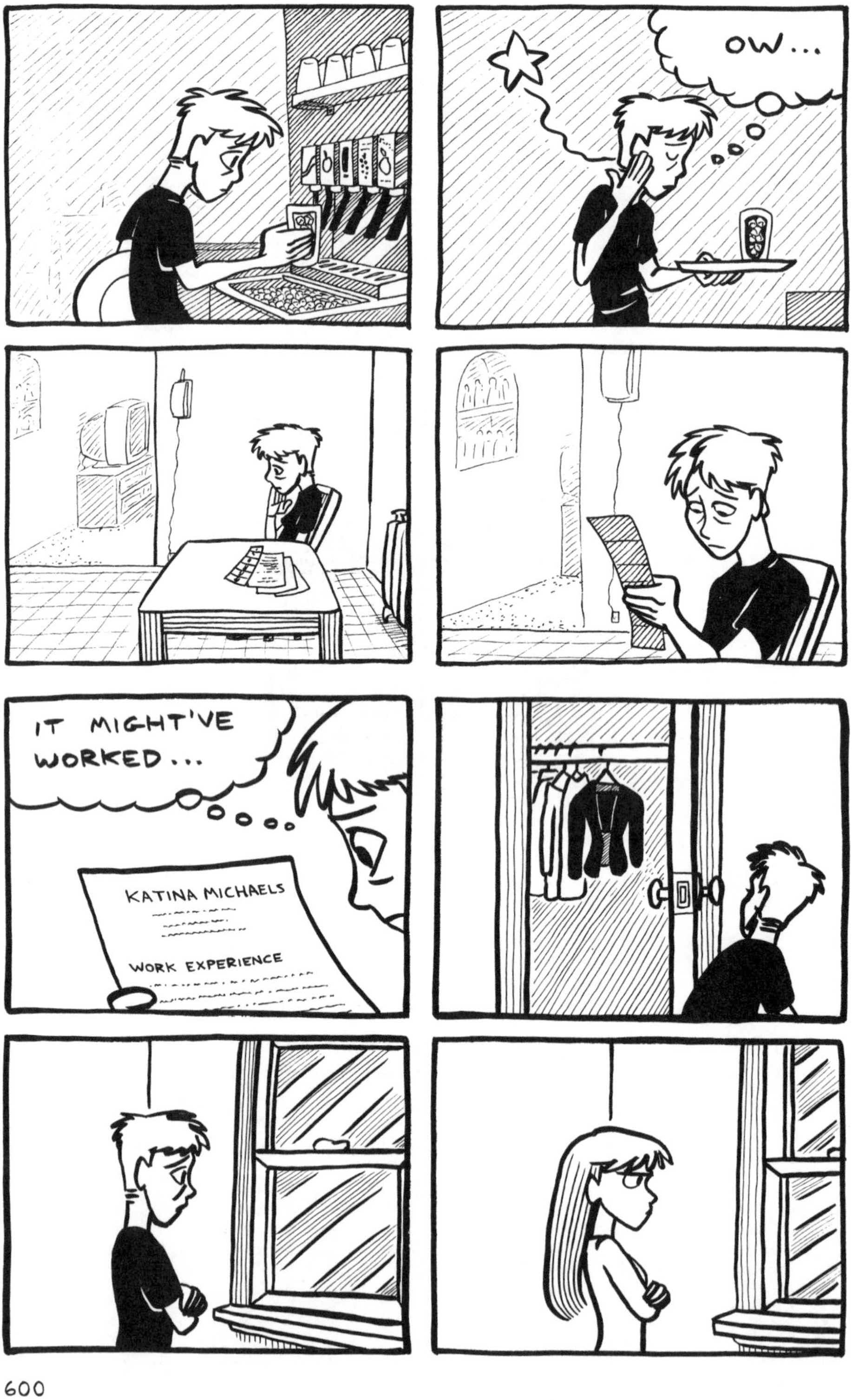
OW...
IT MIGHT'VE WORKED...
KATINA MICHAELS
WORK EXPERIENCE

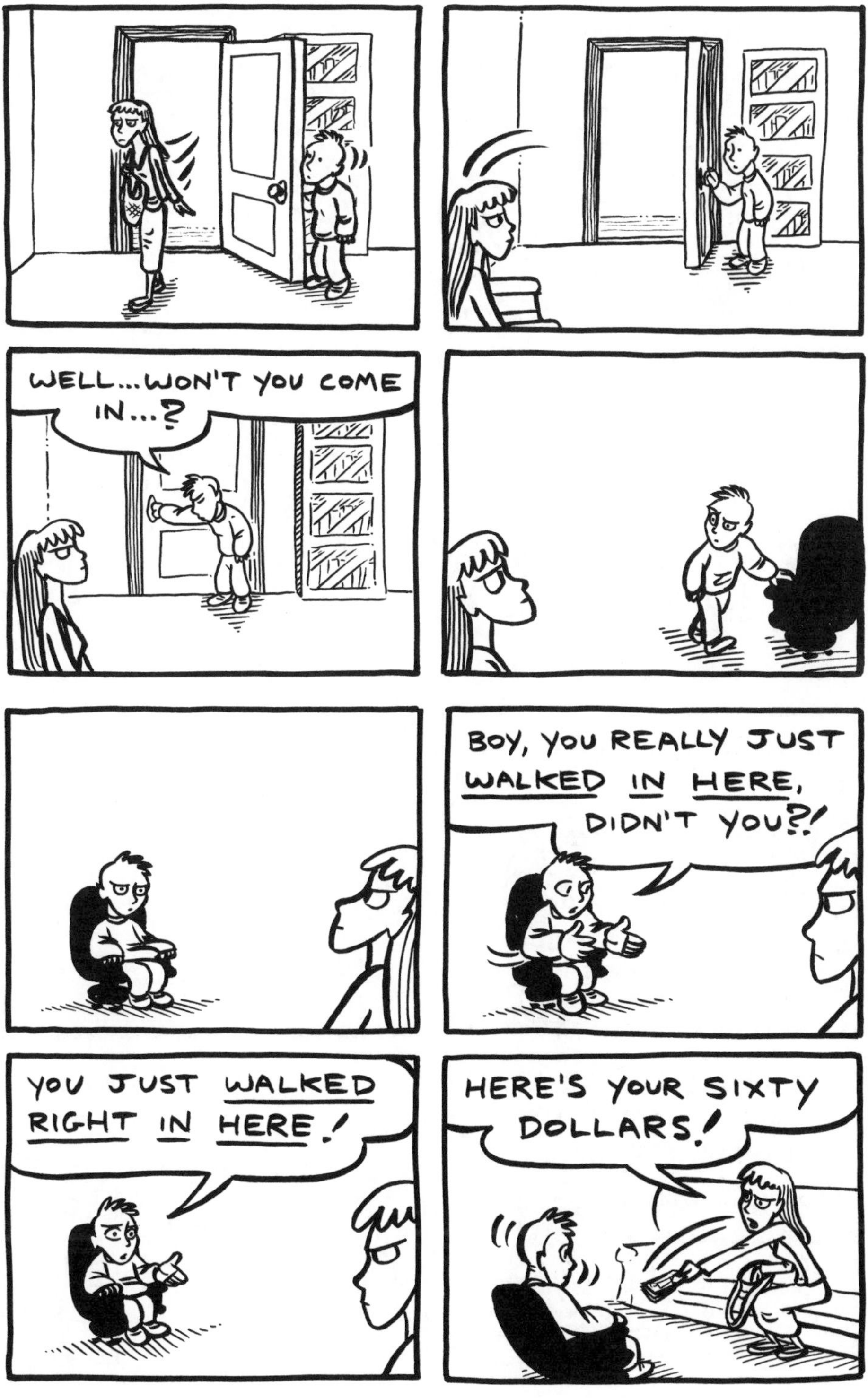
WELL... WON'T YOU COME IN...?
BOY, YOU REALLY JUST WALKED IN HERE, DIDN'T YOU?!
YOU JUST WALKED RIGHT IN HERE!
HERE'S YOUR SIXTY DOLLARS!

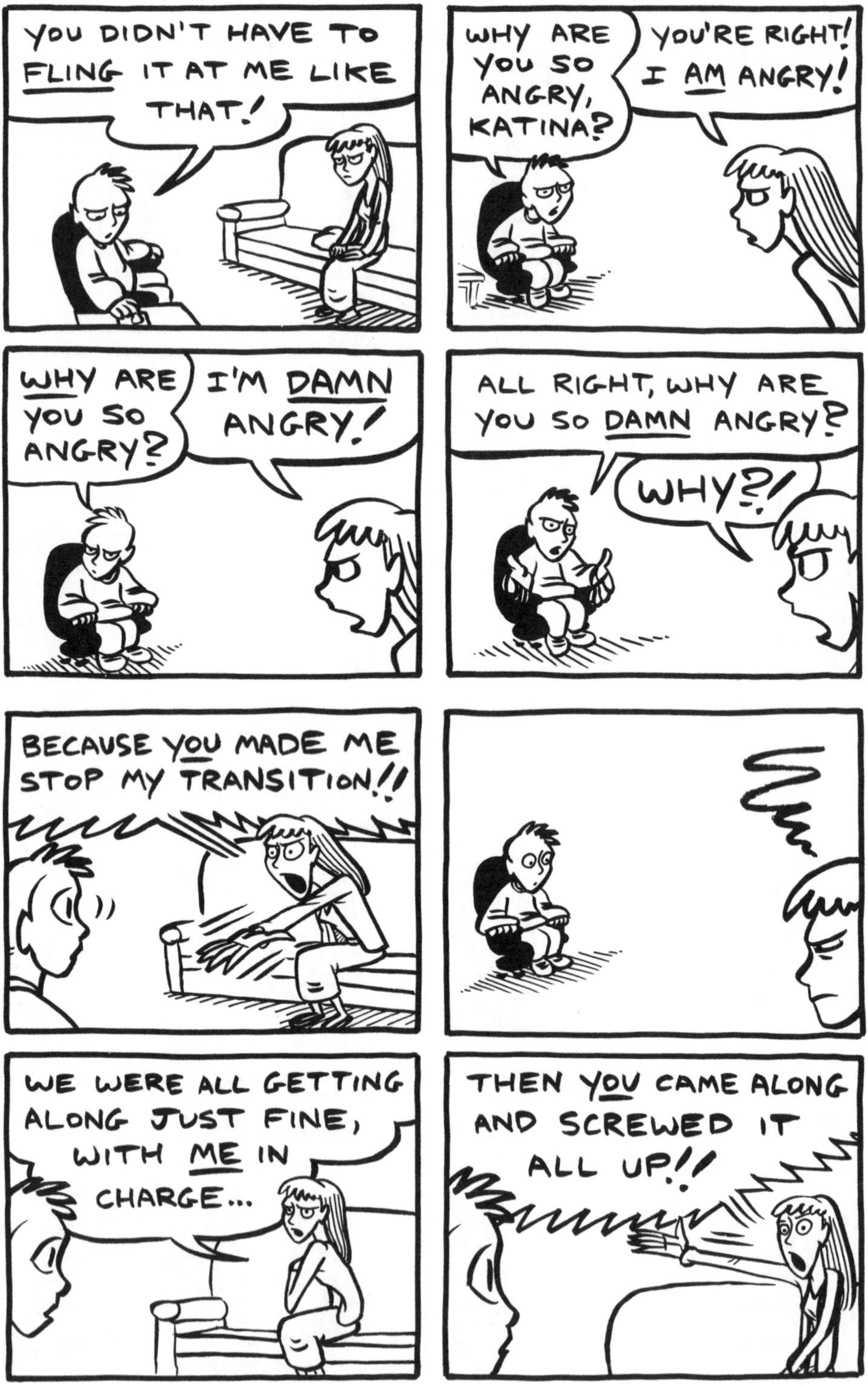
YOU DIDN'T HAVE TO FLING IT AT ME LIKE THAT!
WHY ARE YOU SO ANGRY, KATINA?
YOU'RE RIGHT! I AM ANGRY!
WHY ARE YOU SO ANGRY?
I'M DAMN ANGRY!
ALL RIGHT, WHY ARE YOU SO DAMN ANGRY?
WHY?!
BECAUSE YOU MADE ME STOP MY TRANSITION!!
WE WERE ALL GETTING ALONG JUST FINE, WITH ME IN CHARGE...
THEN YOU CAME ALONG AND SCREWED IT ALL UP!!

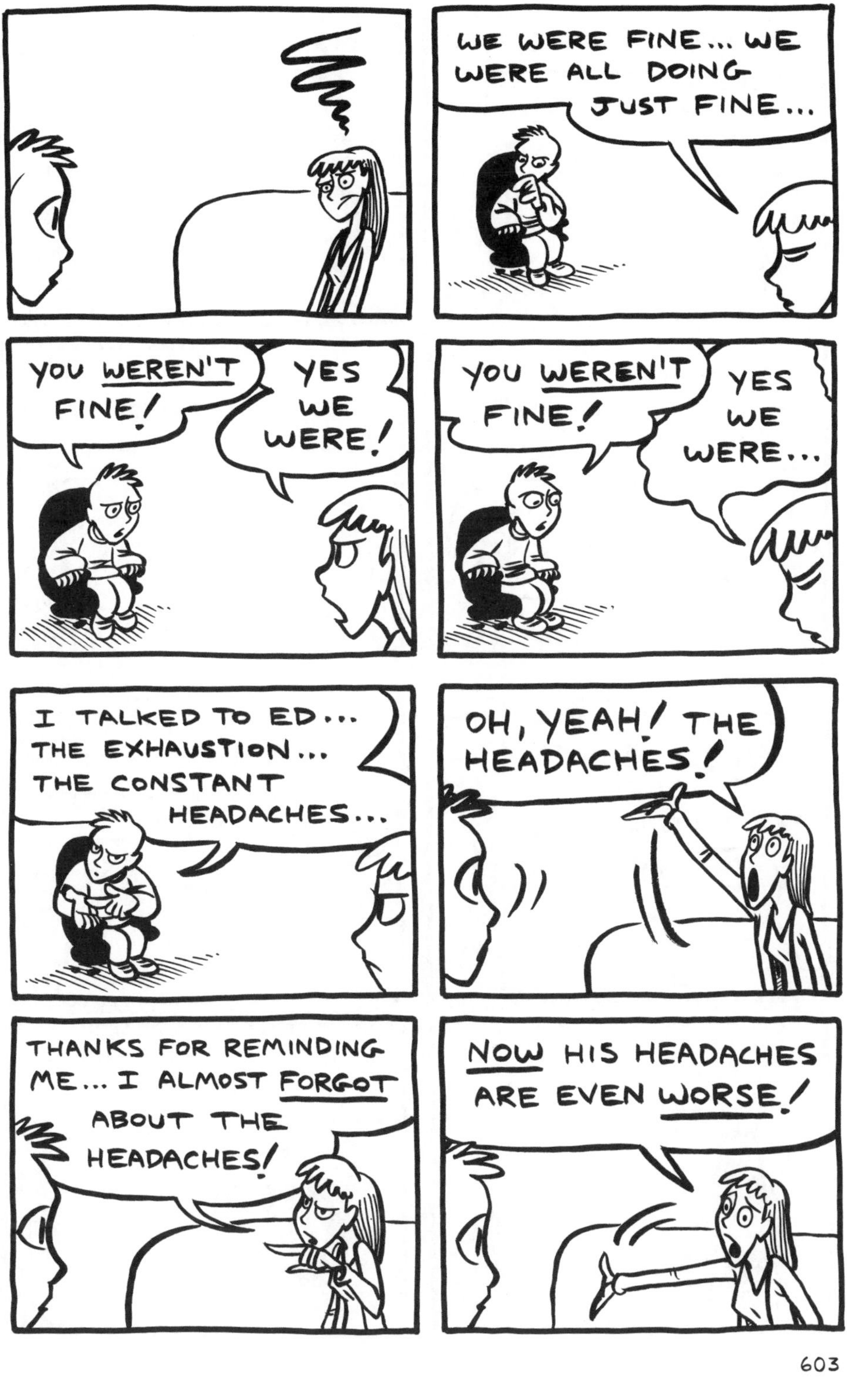

WE WERE FINE... WE WERE ALL DOING JUST FINE...
YOU WEREN'T FINE!
YES WE WERE!
YOU WEREN'T FINE!
YES WE WERE...
I TALKED TO ED... THE EXHAUSTION... THE CONSTANT HEADACHES...
OH, YEAH! THE HEADACHES!
THANKS FOR REMINDING ME... I ALMOST FORGOT ABOUT THE HEADACHES!
NOW HIS HEADACHES ARE EVEN WORSE!

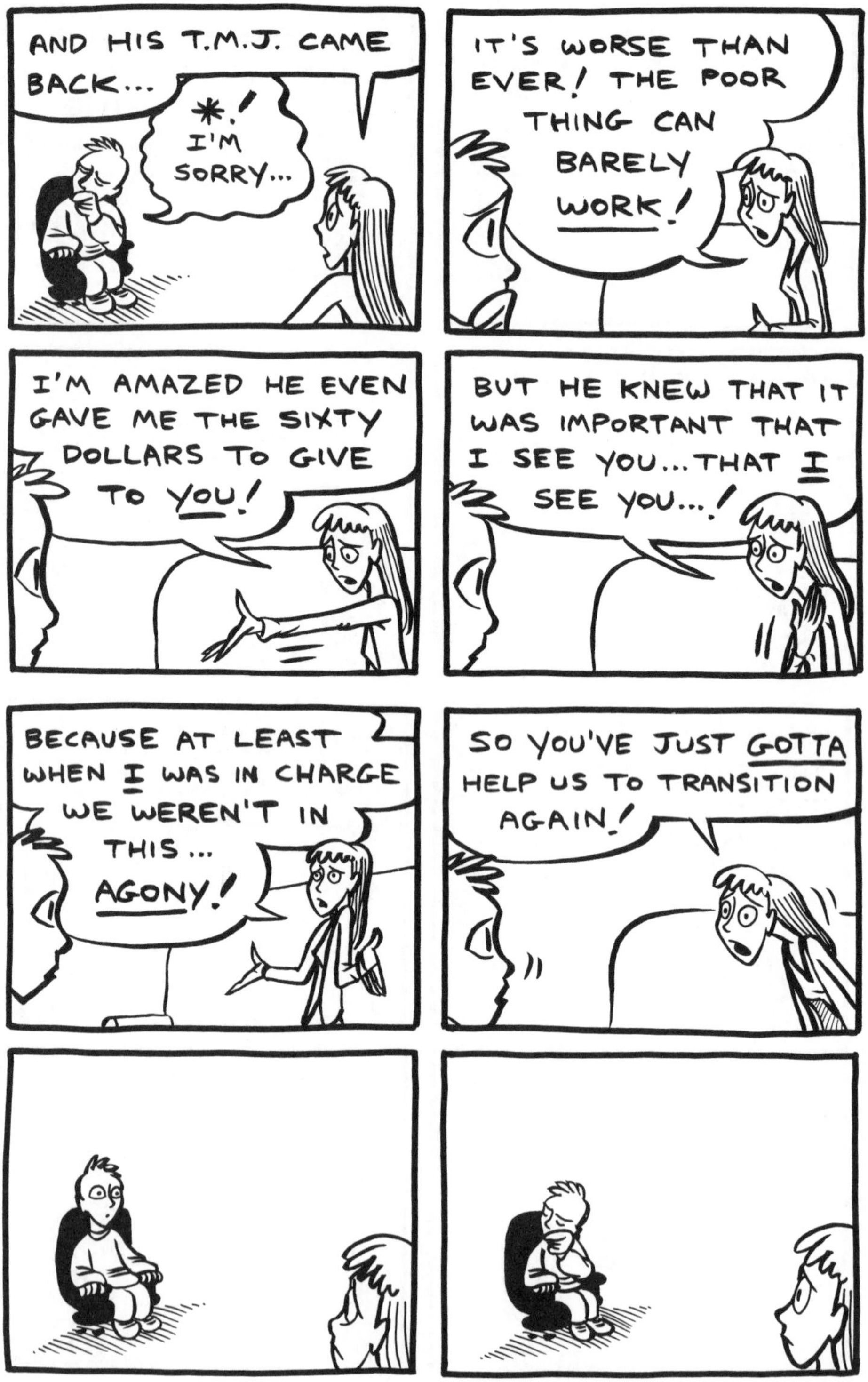
AND HIS T.M.J. CAME BACK...
*.! I'M SORRY...
IT'S WORSE THAN EVER! THE POOR THING CAN BARELY WORK!
I'M AMAZED HE EVEN GAVE ME THE SIXTY DOLLARS TO GIVE TO YOU!
BUT HE KNEW THAT IT WAS IMPORTANT THAT I SEE YOU... THAT I SEE YOU...!
BECAUSE AT LEAST WHEN I WAS IN CHARGE WE WEREN'T IN THIS... AGONY!
SO YOU'VE JUST GOTTA HELP US TO TRANSITION AGAIN!

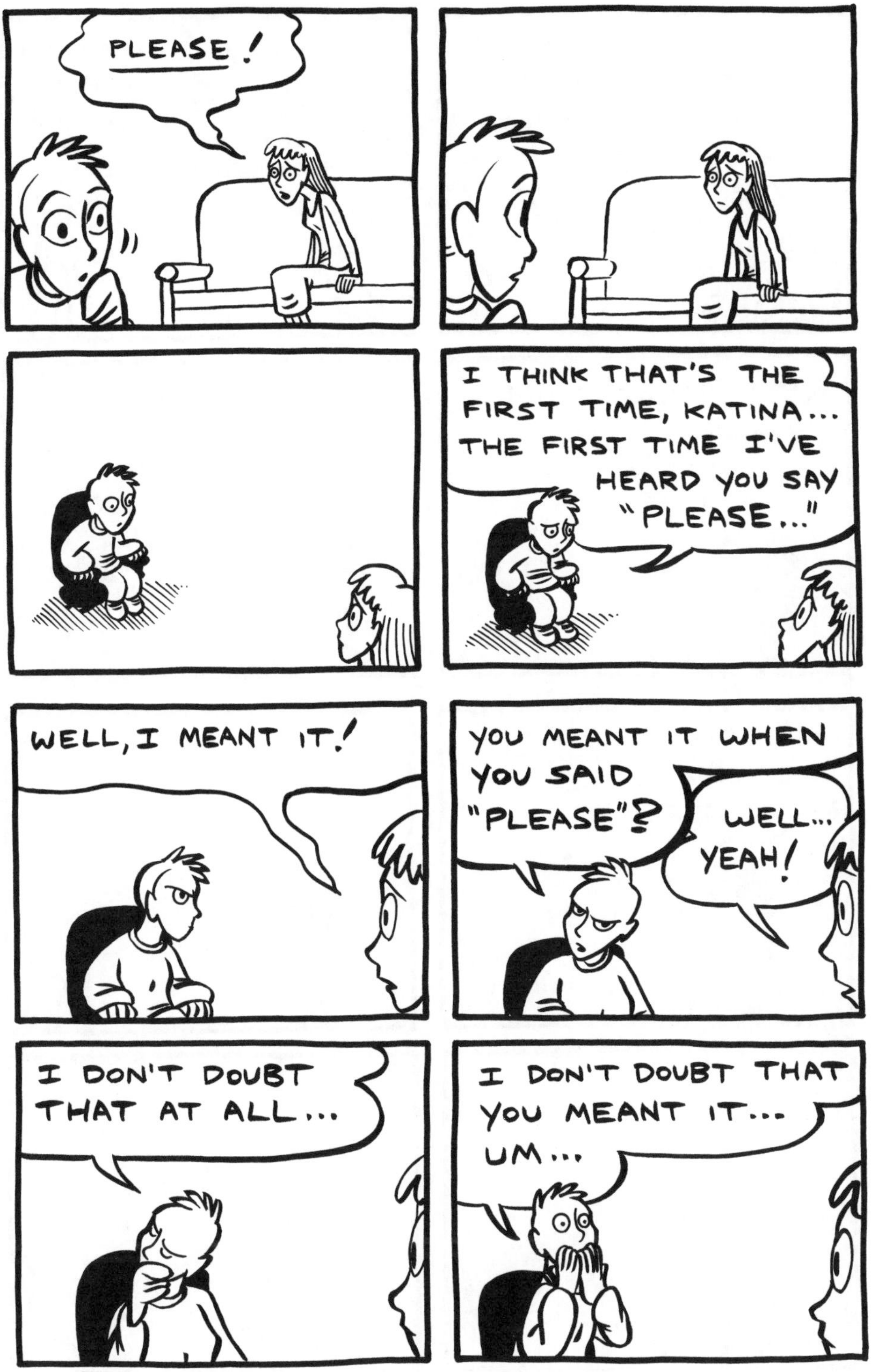
PLEASE!
I THINK THAT'S THE FIRST TIME, KATINA... THE FIRST TIME I'VE HEARD YOU SAY "PLEASE..."
WELL, I MEANT IT!
YOU MEANT IT WHEN YOU SAID "PLEASE"?
WELL... YEAH!
I DON'T DOUBT THAT AT ALL...
I DON'T DOUBT THAT YOU MEANT IT... UM...

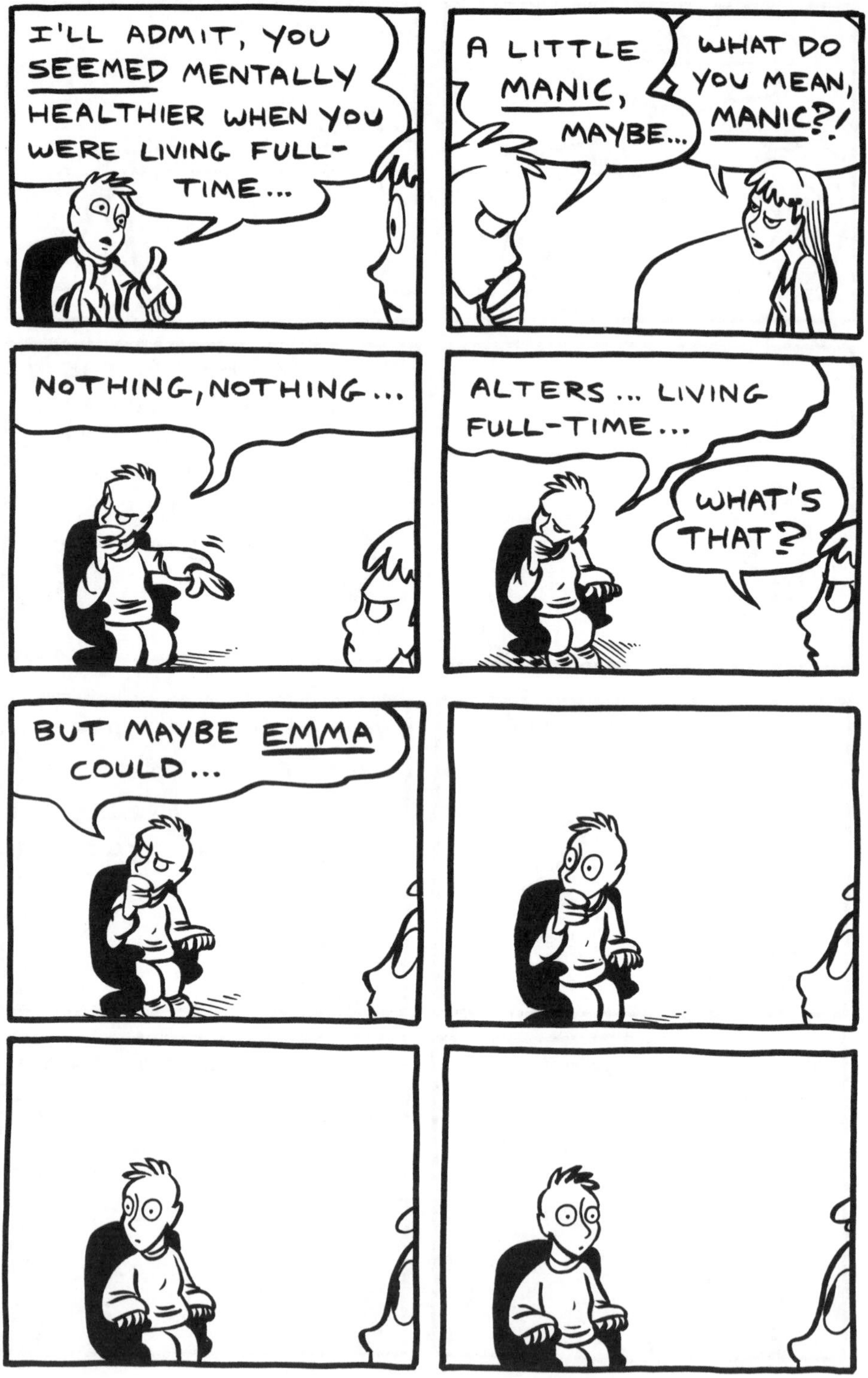
I'LL ADMIT, YOU SEEMED MENTALLY HEALTHIER WHEN YOU WERE LIVING FULL-TIME...
A LITTLE MANIC, MAYBE...
WHAT DO YOU MEAN, MANIC?!
NOTHING, NOTHING...
ALTERS... LIVING FULL-TIME...
WHAT'S THAT?
BUT MAYBE EMMA COULD...

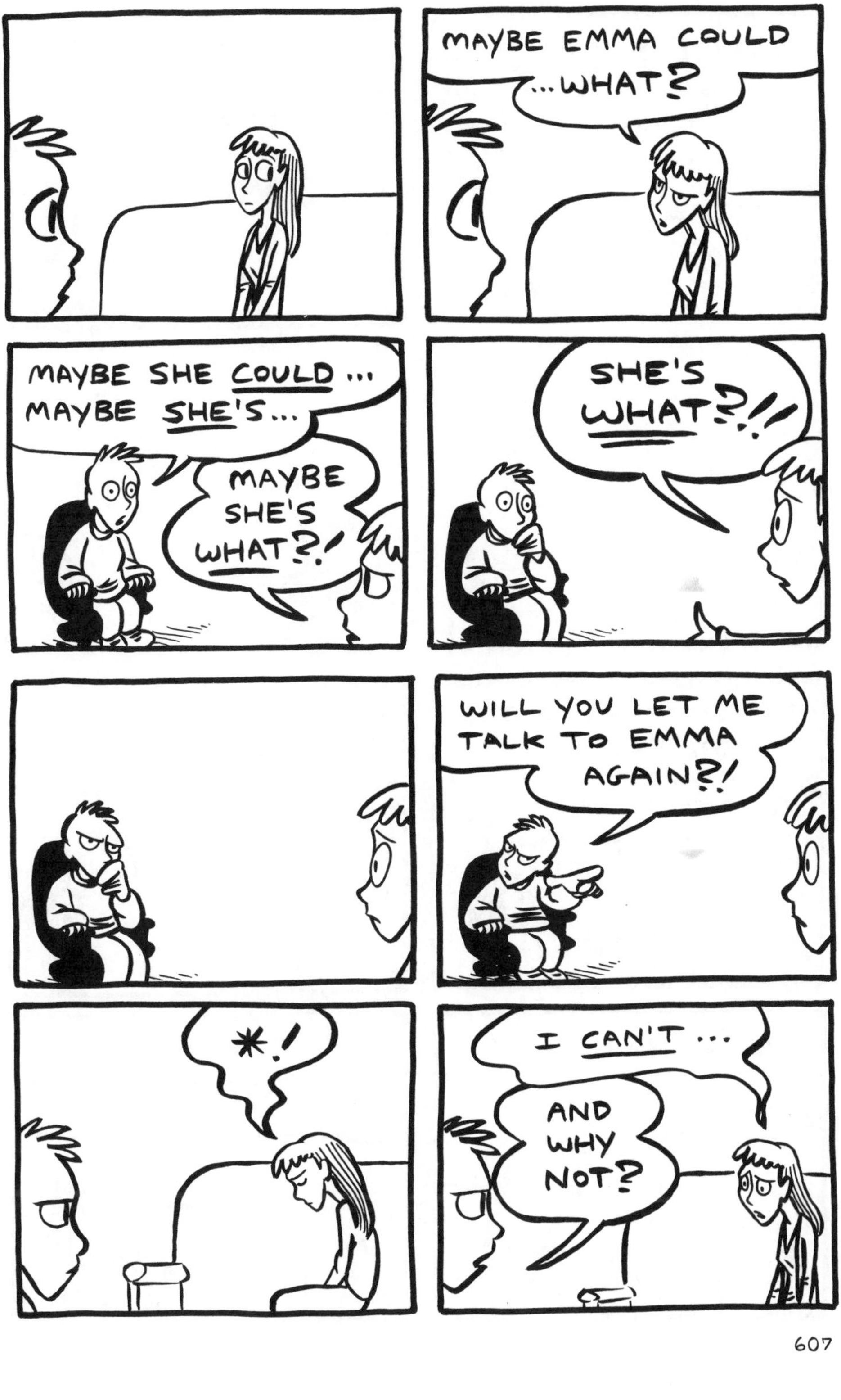

MAYBE EMMA COULD
...WHAT?
MAYBE SHE COULD ...
MAYBE SHE'S...
MAYBE
SHE'S
WHAT?!
SHE'S
WHAT?!!
WILL YOU LET ME
TALK TO EMMA
AGAIN?!
*!
I CAN'T ...
AND
WHY
NOT?

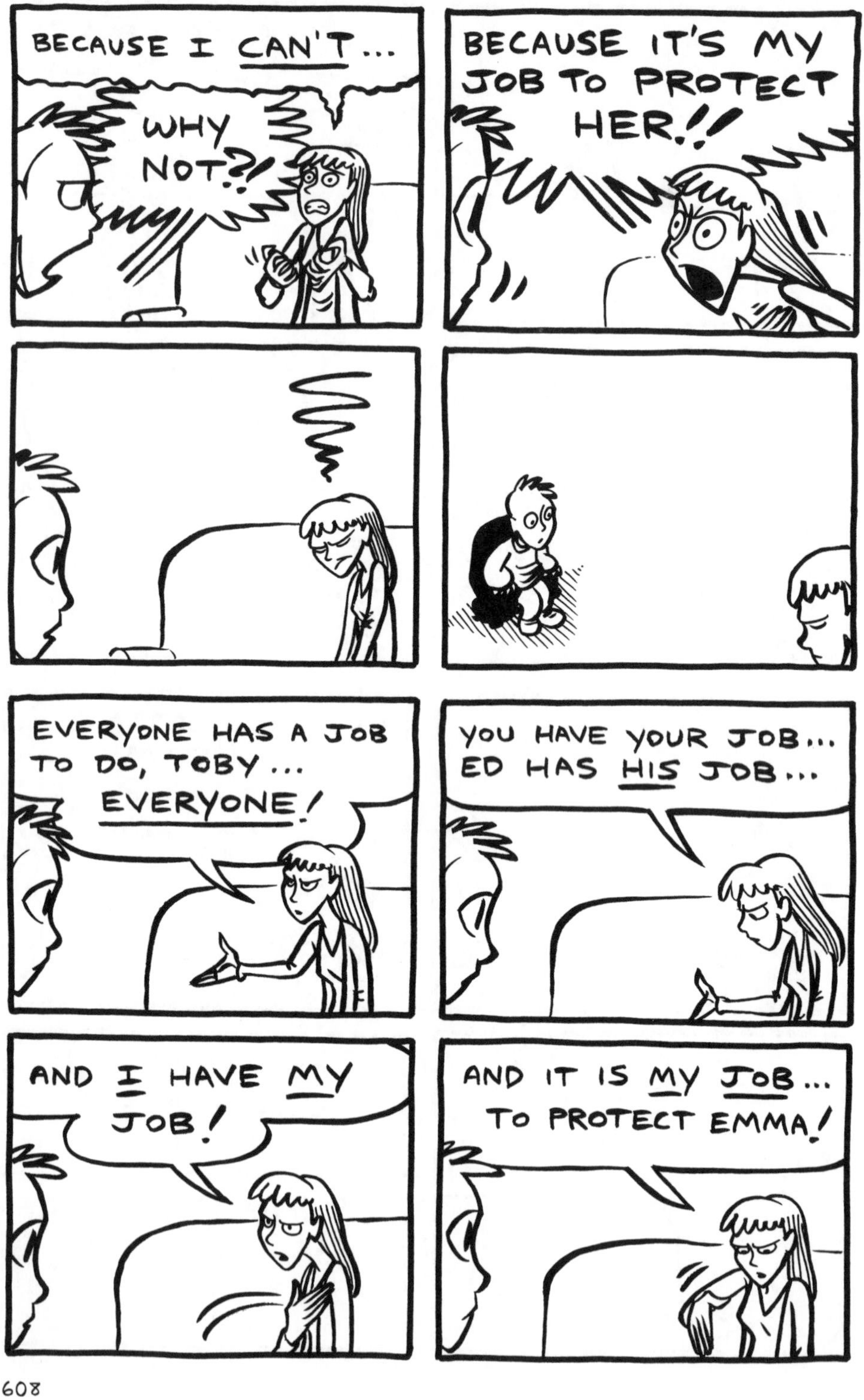
BECAUSE I CAN'T...
WHY NOT?!
BECAUSE IT'S MY JOB TO PROTECT HER!!
EVERYONE HAS A JOB TO DO, TOBY... EVERYONE!
YOU HAVE YOUR JOB... ED HAS HIS JOB...
AND I HAVE MY JOB!
AND IT IS MY JOB... TO PROTECT EMMA!

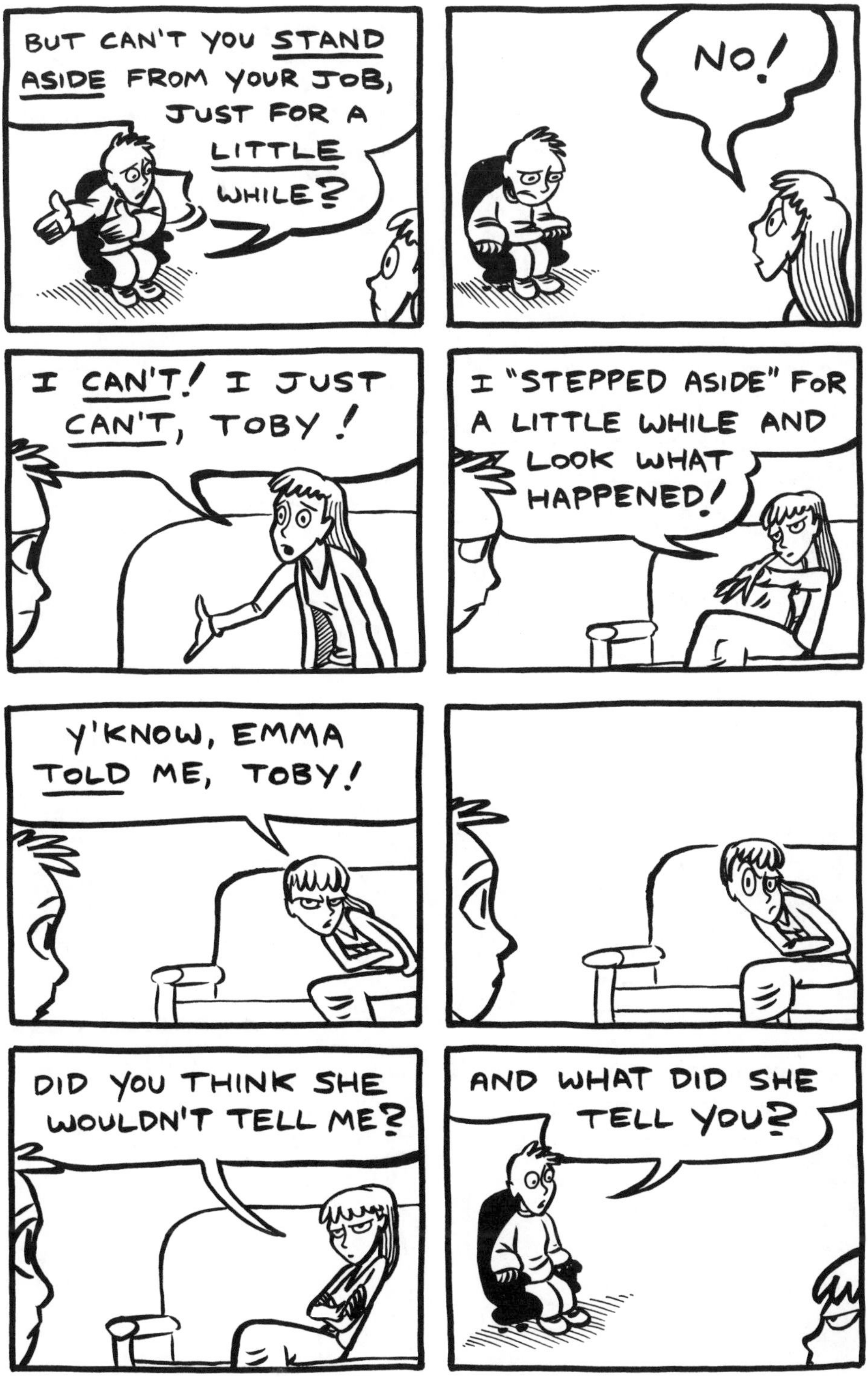
BUT CAN'T YOU STAND ASIDE FROM YOUR JOB, JUST FOR A LITTLE WHILE?
NO!
I CAN'T! I JUST CAN'T, TOBY!
I "STEPPED ASIDE" FOR A LITTLE WHILE AND LOOK WHAT HAPPENED!
Y'KNOW, EMMA TOLD ME, TOBY!
DID YOU THINK SHE WOULDN'T TELL ME?
AND WHAT DID SHE TELL YOU?

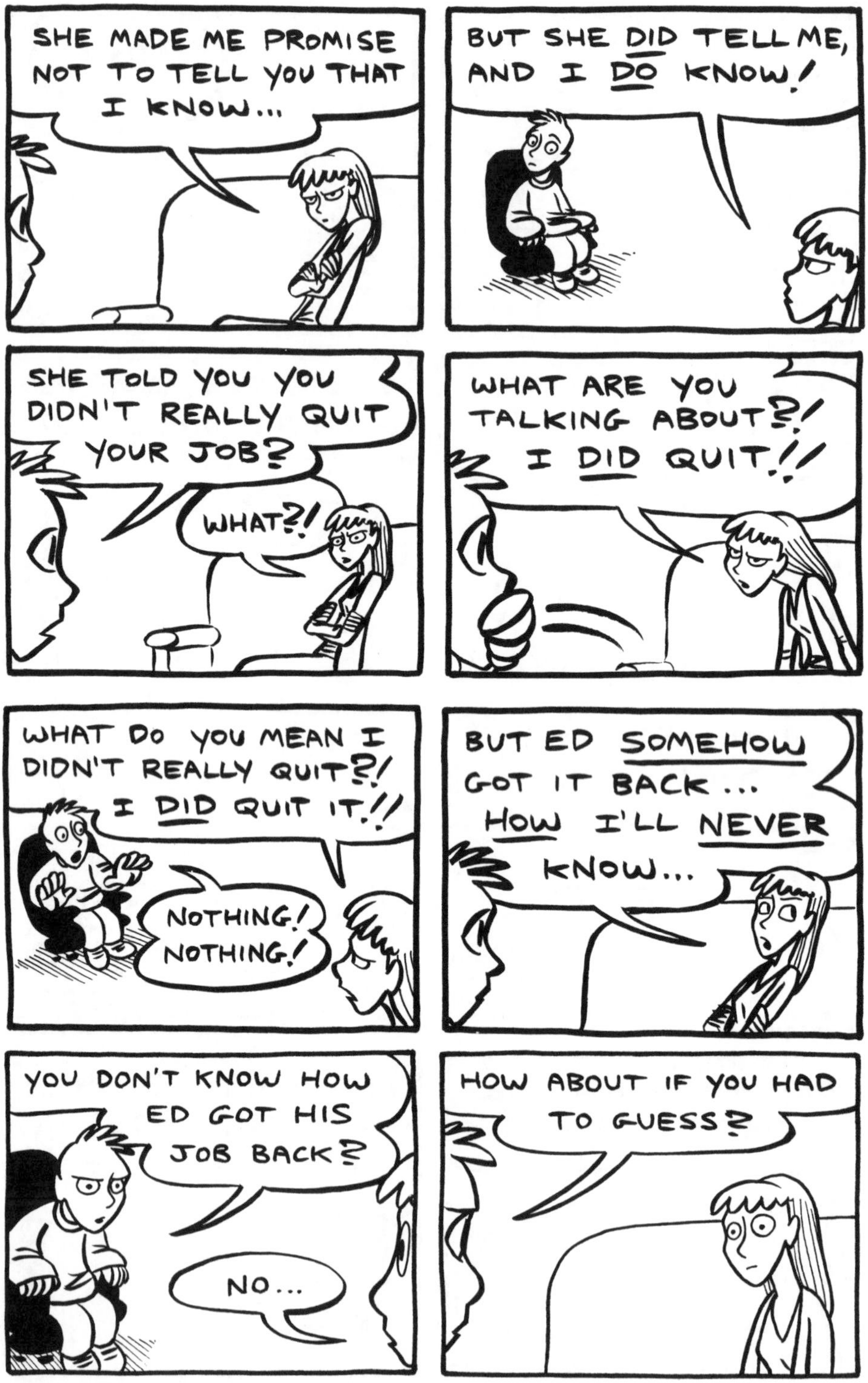
SHE MADE ME PROMISE NOT TO TELL YOU THAT I KNOW...
BUT SHE DID TELL ME, AND I DO KNOW!
SHE TOLD YOU YOU DIDN'T REALLY QUIT YOUR JOB?
WHAT?!
WHAT ARE YOU TALKING ABOUT?! I DID QUIT!!
WHAT DO YOU MEAN I DIDN'T REALLY QUIT?! I DID QUIT IT!!
NOTHING! NOTHING!
BUT ED SOMEHOW GOT IT BACK... HOW I'LL NEVER KNOW...
YOU DON'T KNOW HOW ED GOT HIS JOB BACK?
NO...
HOW ABOUT IF YOU HAD TO GUESS?

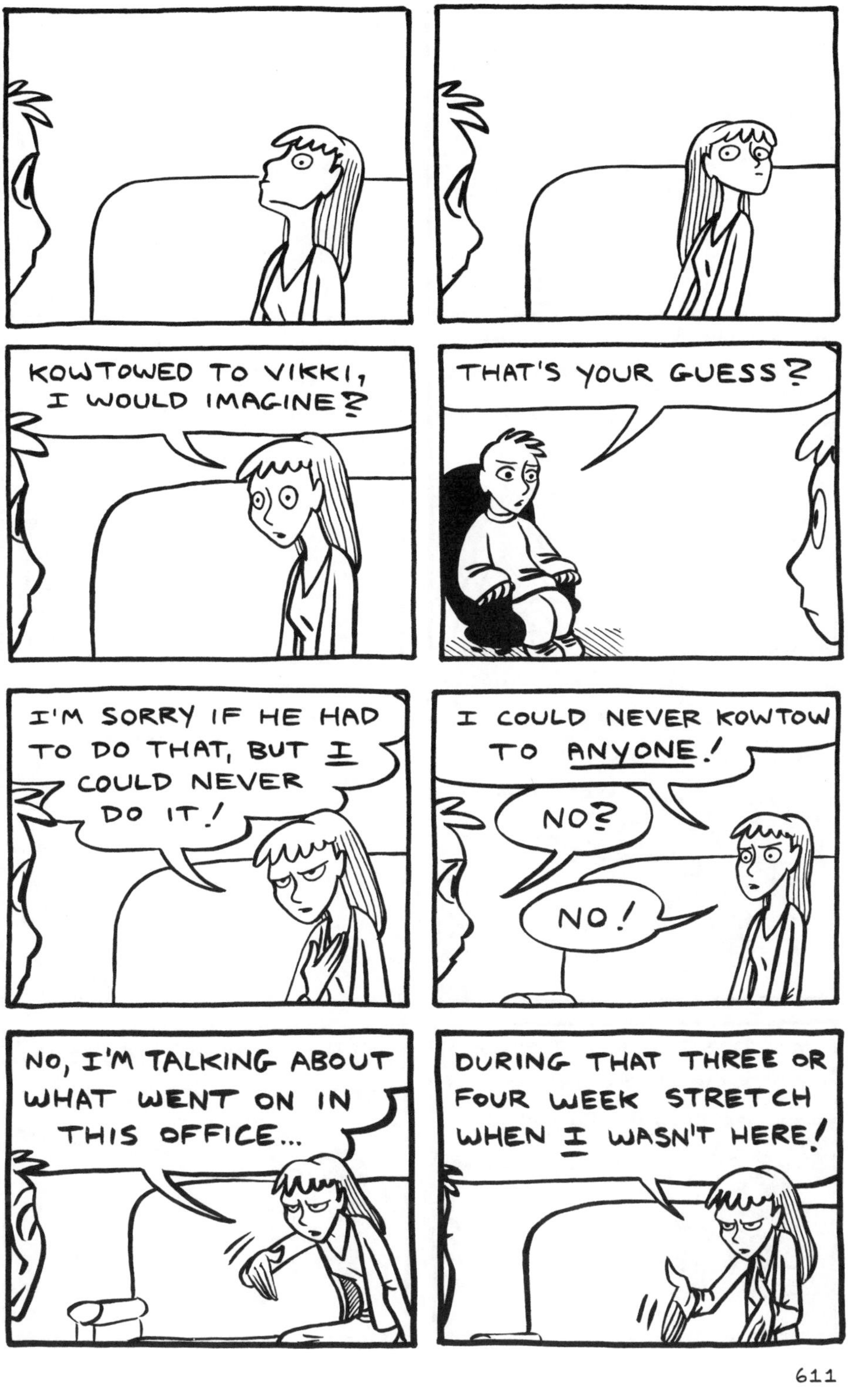
KOWTOWED TO VIKKI, I WOULD IMAGINE?
THAT'S YOUR GUESS?
I'M SORRY IF HE HAD TO DO THAT, BUT I COULD NEVER DO IT!
I COULD NEVER KOWTOW TO ANYONE!
NO?
NO!
NO, I'M TALKING ABOUT WHAT WENT ON IN THIS OFFICE...
DURING THAT THREE OR FOUR WEEK STRETCH WHEN I WASN'T HERE!

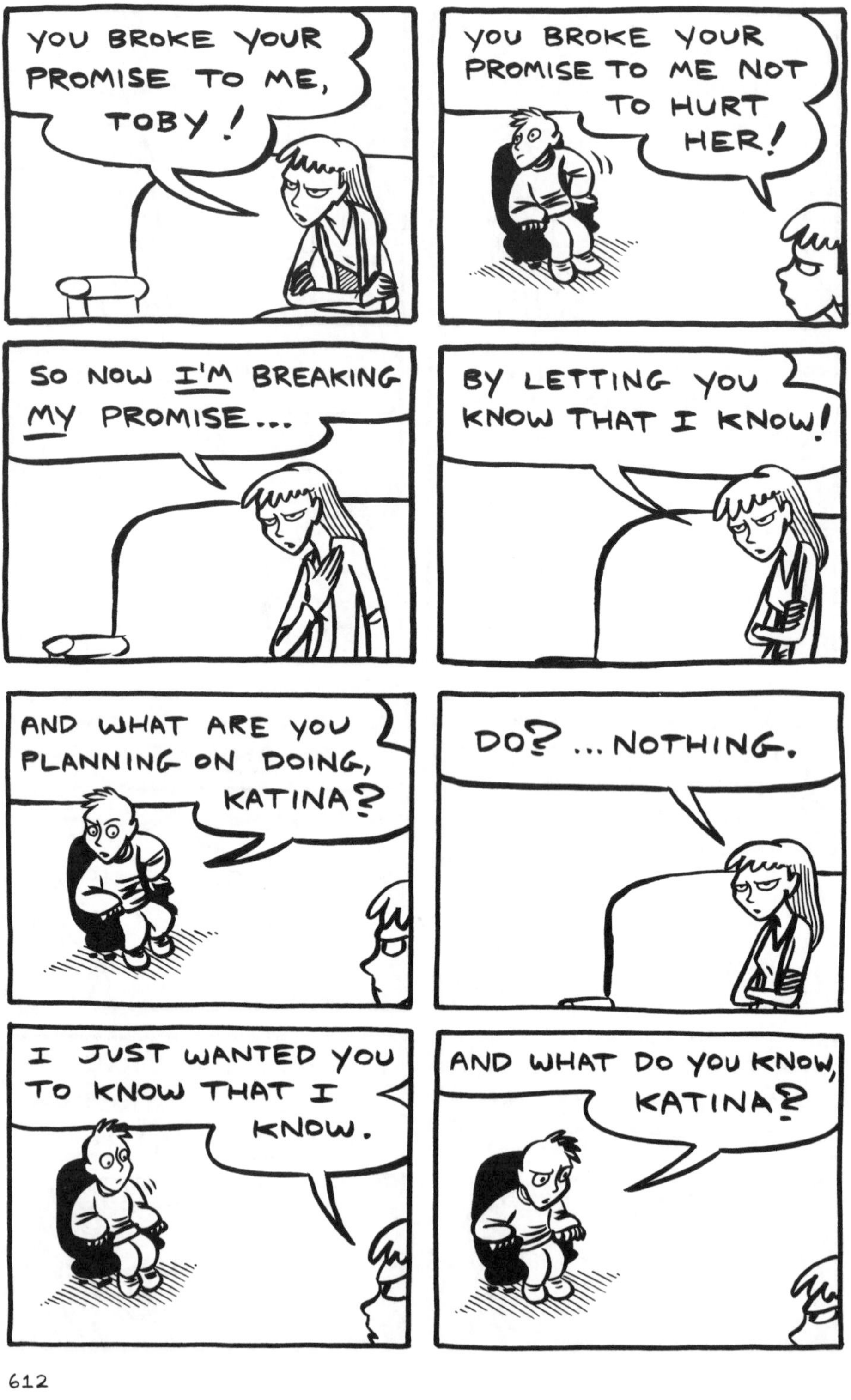
YOU BROKE YOUR PROMISE TO ME, TOBY!
YOU BROKE YOUR PROMISE TO ME NOT TO HURT HER!
SO NOW I'M BREAKING MY PROMISE...
BY LETTING YOU KNOW THAT I KNOW!
AND WHAT ARE YOU PLANNING ON DOING, KATINA?
DO? ...NOTHING.
I JUST WANTED YOU TO KNOW THAT I KNOW.
AND WHAT DO YOU KNOW, KATINA?

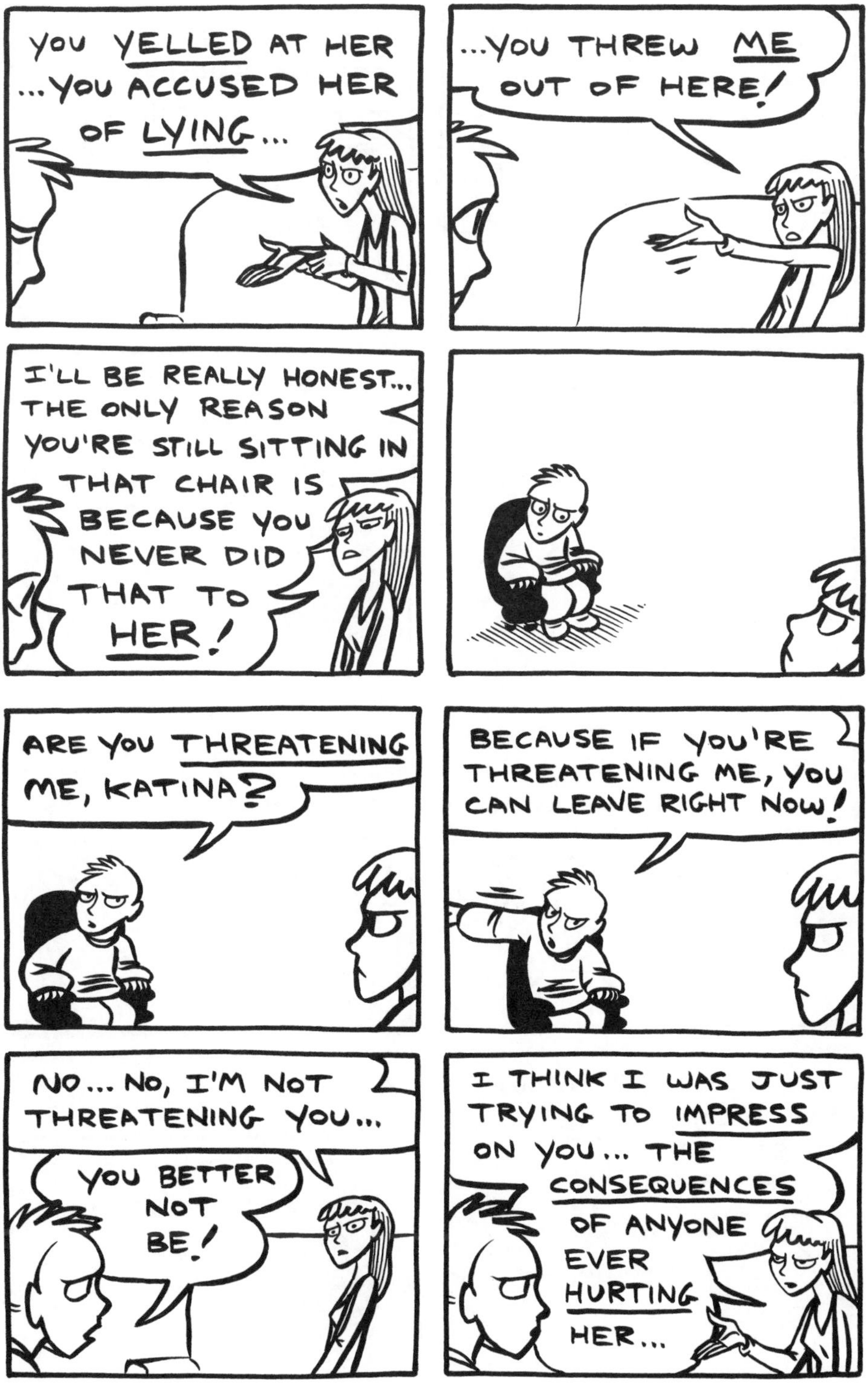
YOU YELLED AT HER ...YOU ACCUSED HER OF LYING...
...YOU THREW ME OUT OF HERE!
I'LL BE REALLY HONEST... THE ONLY REASON YOU'RE STILL SITTING IN THAT CHAIR IS BECAUSE YOU NEVER DID THAT TO HER!
ARE YOU THREATENING ME, KATINA?
BECAUSE IF YOU'RE THREATENING ME, YOU CAN LEAVE RIGHT NOW!
NO... NO, I'M NOT THREATENING YOU...
YOU BETTER NOT BE!
I THINK I WAS JUST TRYING TO IMPRESS ON YOU... THE CONSEQUENCES OF ANYONE EVER HURTING HER...

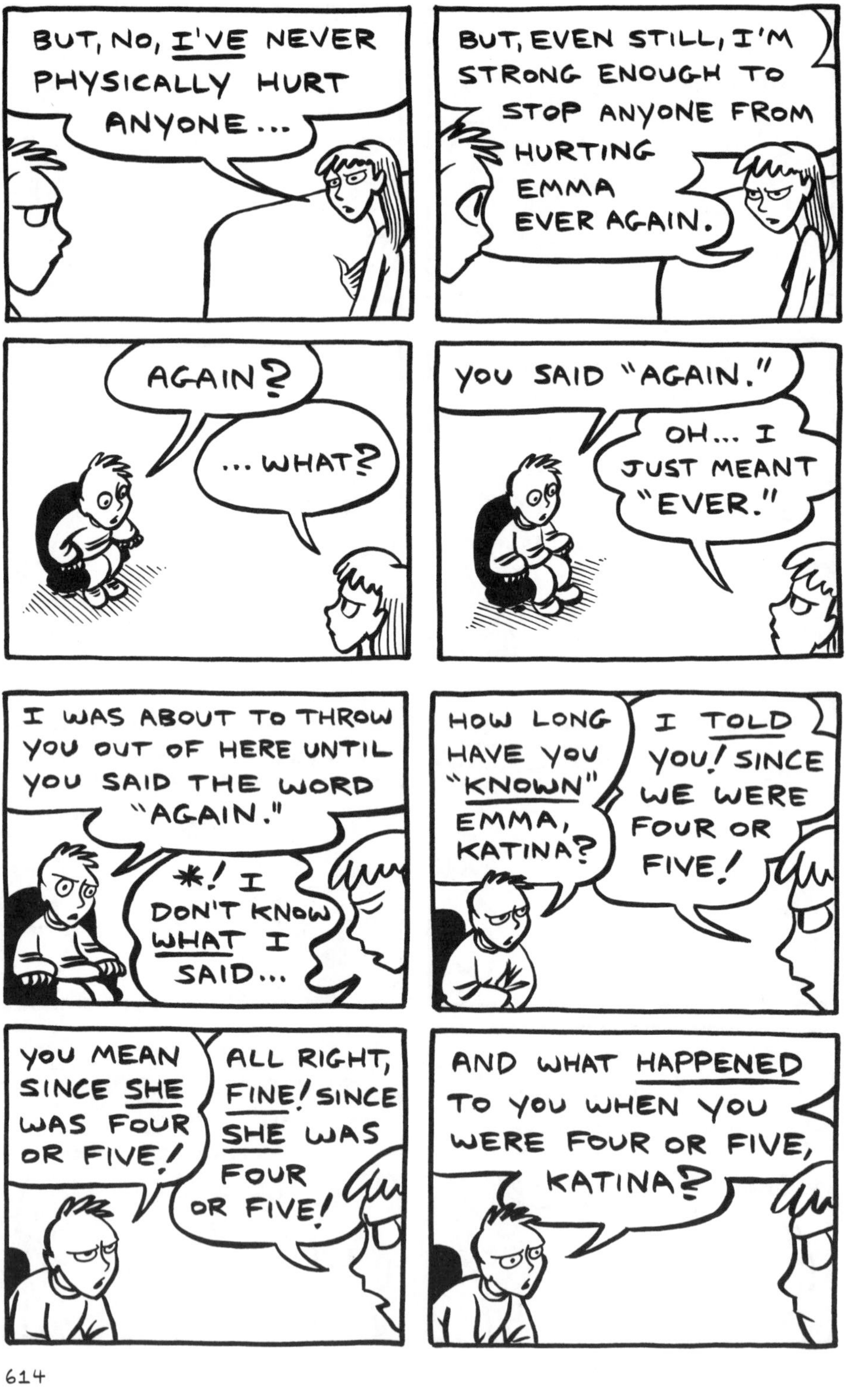
BUT, NO, I'VE NEVER PHYSICALLY HURT ANYONE...
BUT, EVEN STILL, I'M STRONG ENOUGH TO STOP ANYONE FROM HURTING EMMA EVER AGAIN.
AGAIN?
...WHAT?
YOU SAID "AGAIN."
OH... I JUST MEANT "EVER."
I WAS ABOUT TO THROW YOU OUT OF HERE UNTIL YOU SAID THE WORD "AGAIN."
*! I DON'T KNOW WHAT I SAID...
HOW LONG HAVE YOU "KNOWN" EMMA, KATINA?
I TOLD YOU! SINCE WE WERE FOUR OR FIVE!
YOU MEAN SINCE SHE WAS FOUR OR FIVE!
ALL RIGHT, FINE! SINCE SHE WAS FOUR OR FIVE!
AND WHAT HAPPENED TO YOU WHEN YOU WERE FOUR OR FIVE, KATINA?

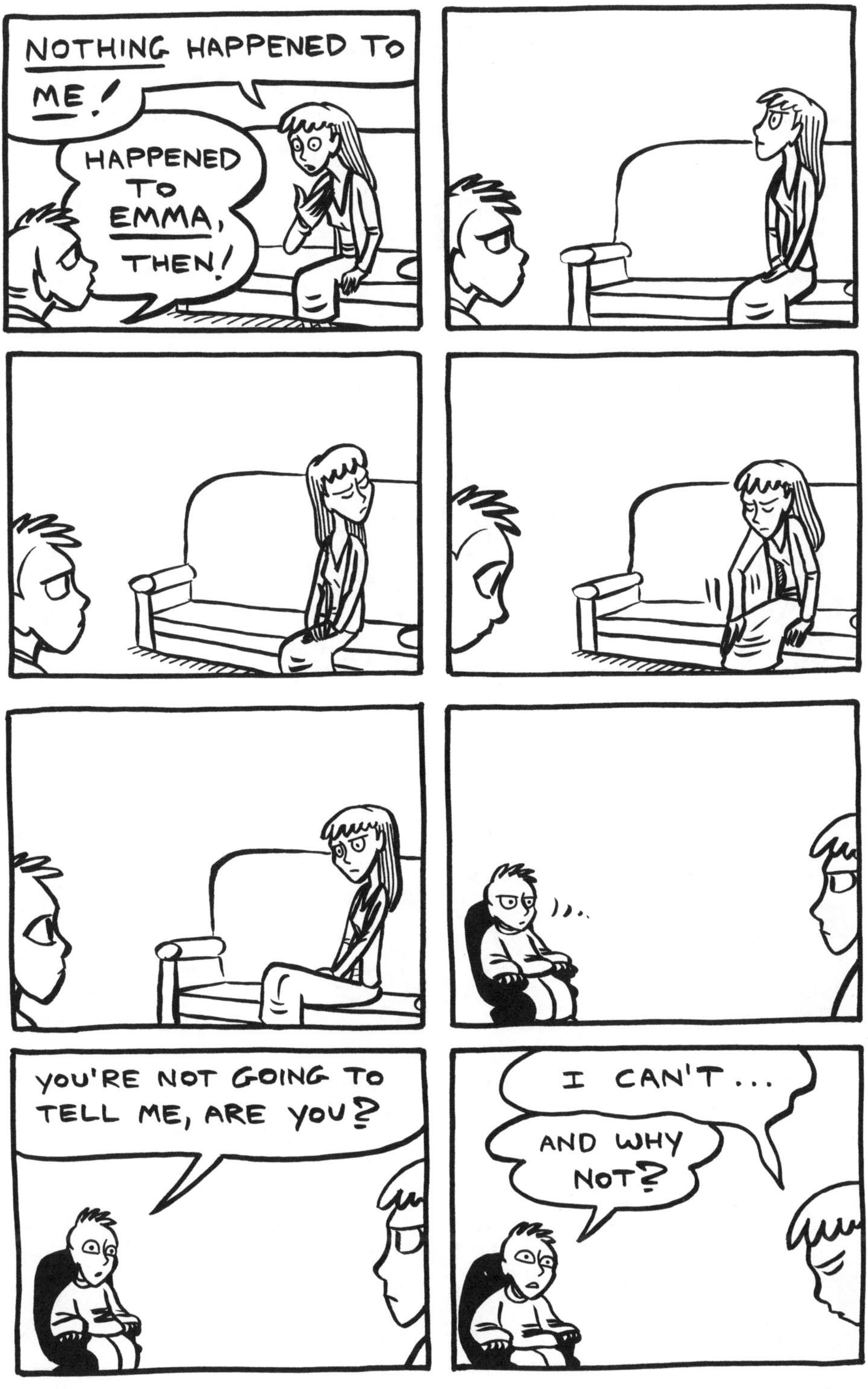
NOTHING HAPPENED TO ME!
HAPPENED TO EMMA, THEN!
YOU'RE NOT GOING TO TELL ME, ARE YOU?
I CAN'T...
AND WHY NOT?

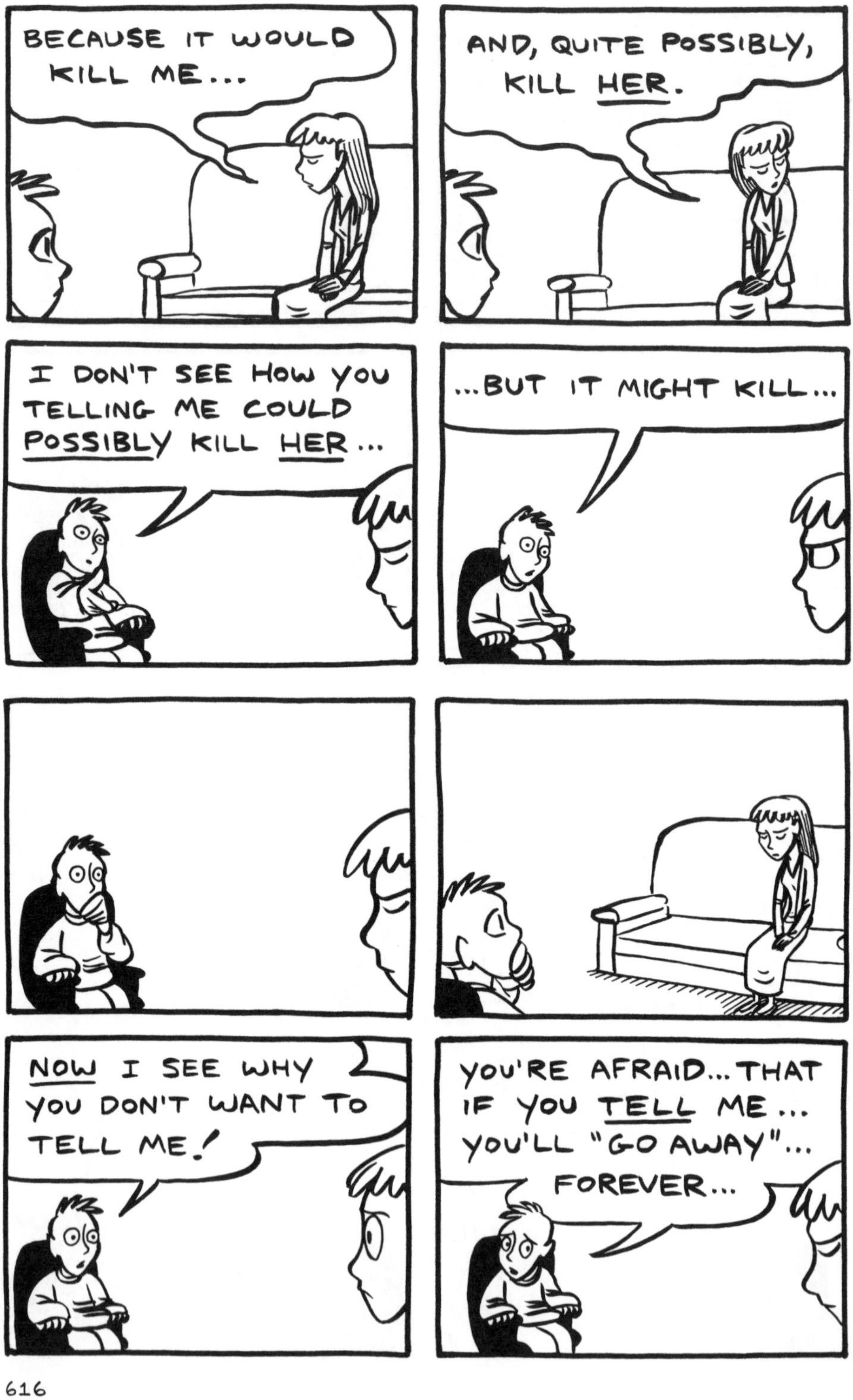
BECAUSE IT WOULD KILL ME...
AND, QUITE POSSIBLY, KILL HER.
I DON'T SEE HOW YOU TELLING ME COULD POSSIBLY KILL HER...
...BUT IT MIGHT KILL...
NOW I SEE WHY YOU DON'T WANT TO TELL ME!
YOU'RE AFRAID... THAT IF YOU TELL ME... YOU'LL "GO AWAY"... FOREVER...

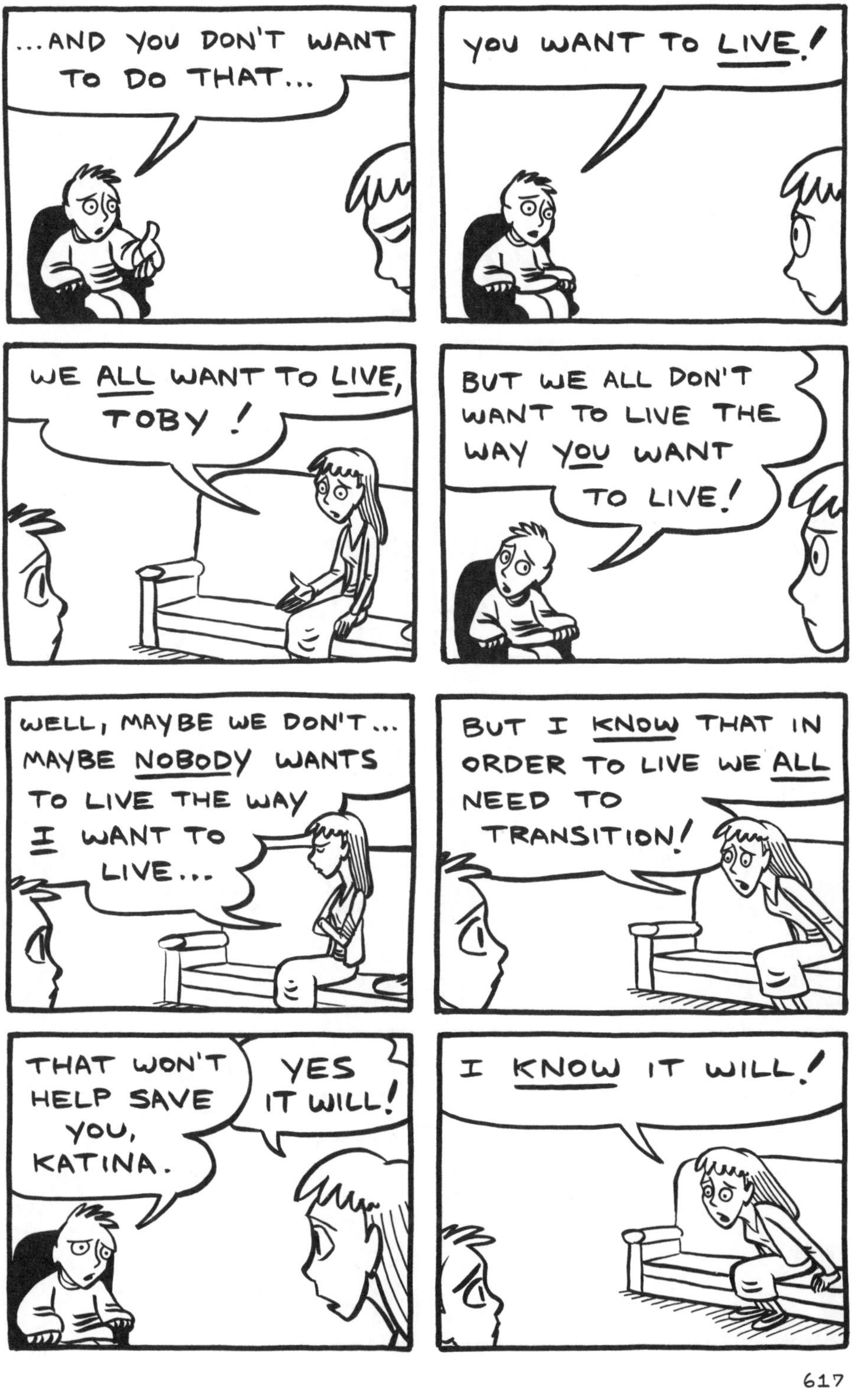
...AND YOU DON'T WANT TO DO THAT...
YOU WANT TO LIVE!
WE ALL WANT TO LIVE, TOBY!
BUT WE ALL DON'T WANT TO LIVE THE WAY YOU WANT TO LIVE!
WELL, MAYBE WE DON'T... MAYBE NOBODY WANTS TO LIVE THE WAY I WANT TO LIVE...
BUT I KNOW THAT IN ORDER TO LIVE WE ALL NEED TO TRANSITION!
THAT WON'T HELP SAVE YOU, KATINA.
YES IT WILL!
I KNOW IT WILL!

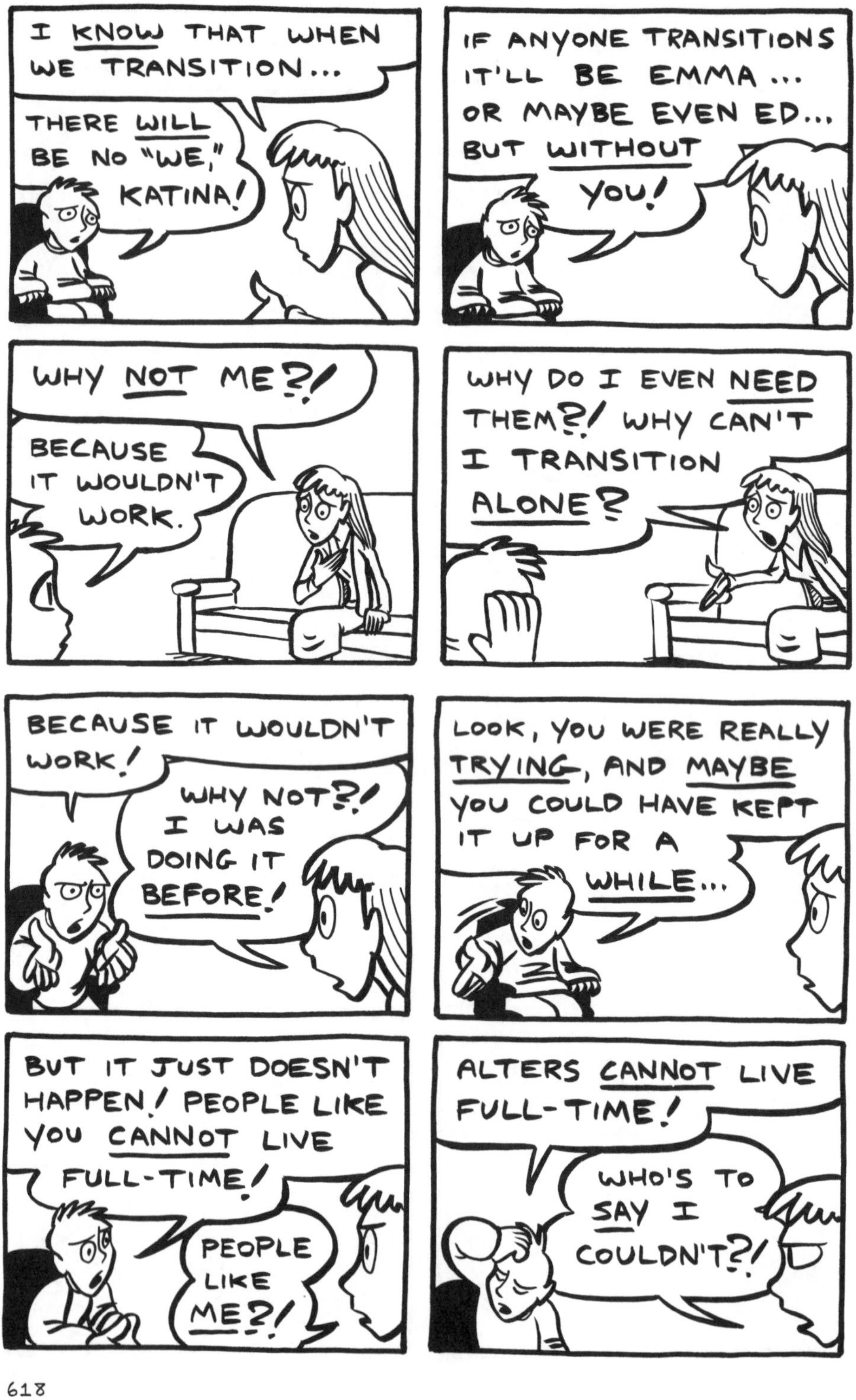

I KNOW THAT WHEN WE TRANSITION...
THERE WILL BE NO "WE," KATINA!
IF ANYONE TRANSITIONS IT'LL BE EMMA... OR MAYBE EVEN ED... BUT WITHOUT YOU!
WHY NOT ME?!
BECAUSE IT WOULDN'T WORK.
WHY DO I EVEN NEED THEM?! WHY CAN'T I TRANSITION ALONE?
BECAUSE IT WOULDN'T WORK!
WHY NOT?! I WAS DOING IT BEFORE!
LOOK, YOU WERE REALLY TRYING, AND MAYBE YOU COULD HAVE KEPT IT UP FOR A WHILE...
BUT IT JUST DOESN'T HAPPEN! PEOPLE LIKE YOU CANNOT LIVE FULL-TIME!
PEOPLE LIKE ME?!
ALTERS CANNOT LIVE FULL-TIME!
WHO'S TO SAY I COULDN'T?!

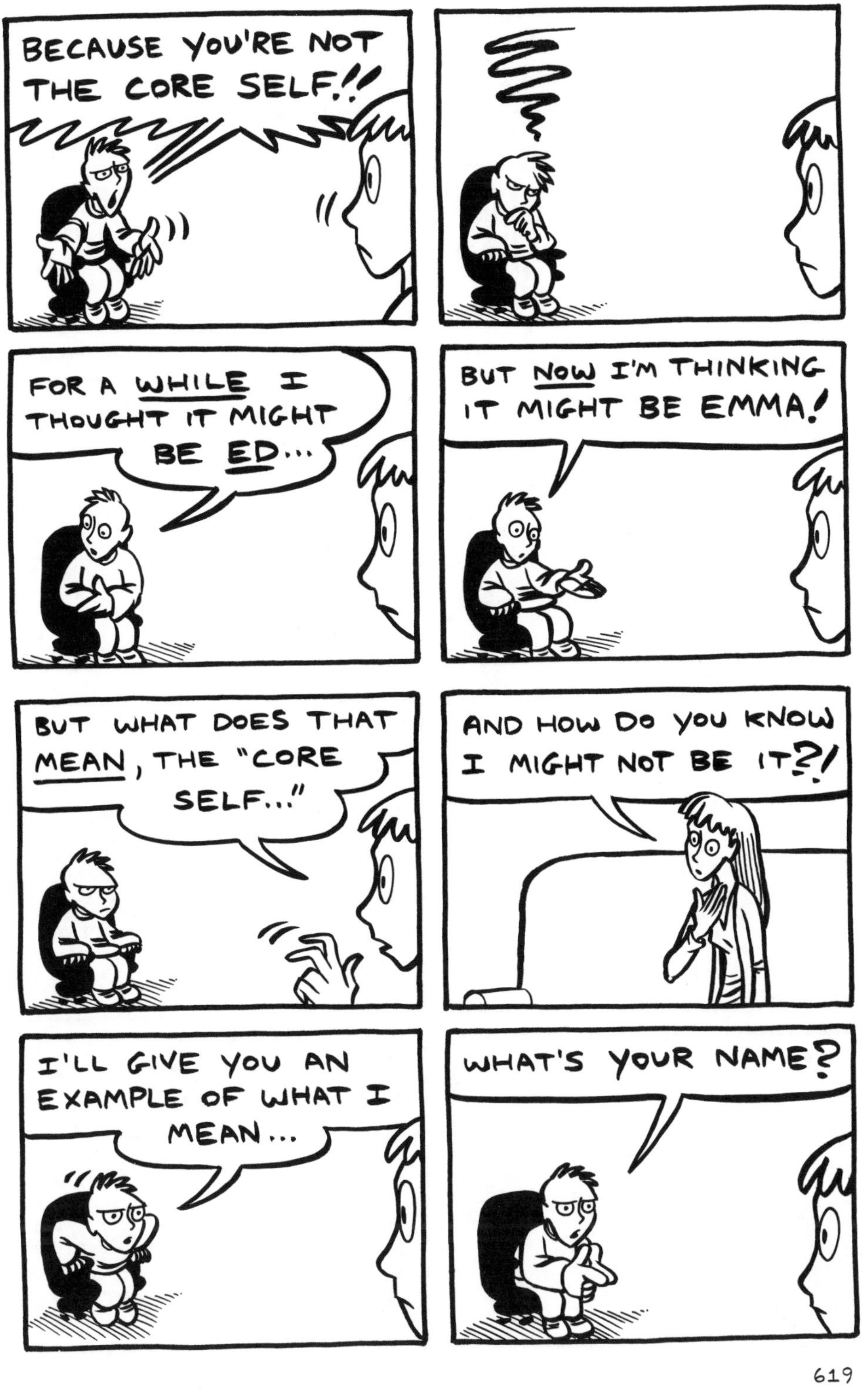
BECAUSE YOU'RE NOT THE CORE SELF!!
FOR A WHILE I THOUGHT IT MIGHT BE ED...
BUT NOW I'M THINKING IT MIGHT BE EMMA!
BUT WHAT DOES THAT MEAN, THE "CORE SELF..."
AND HOW DO YOU KNOW I MIGHT NOT BE IT?!
I'LL GIVE YOU AN EXAMPLE OF WHAT I MEAN...
WHAT'S YOUR NAME?

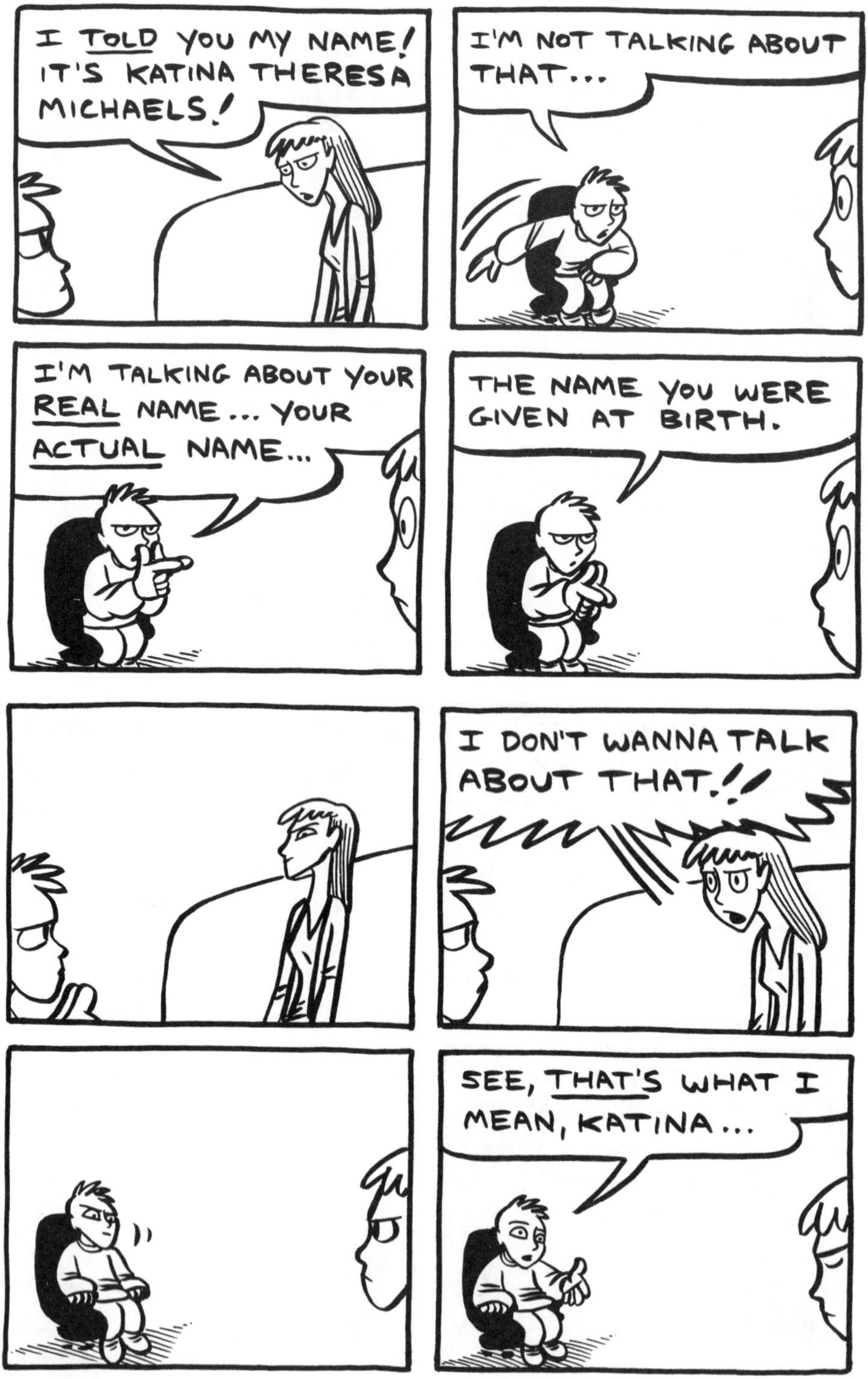
I TOLD YOU MY NAME! IT'S KATINA THERESA MICHAELS!
I'M NOT TALKING ABOUT THAT...
I'M TALKING ABOUT YOUR REAL NAME... YOUR ACTUAL NAME...
THE NAME YOU WERE GIVEN AT BIRTH.
I DON'T WANNA TALK ABOUT THAT!!
SEE, THAT'S WHAT I MEAN, KATINA...

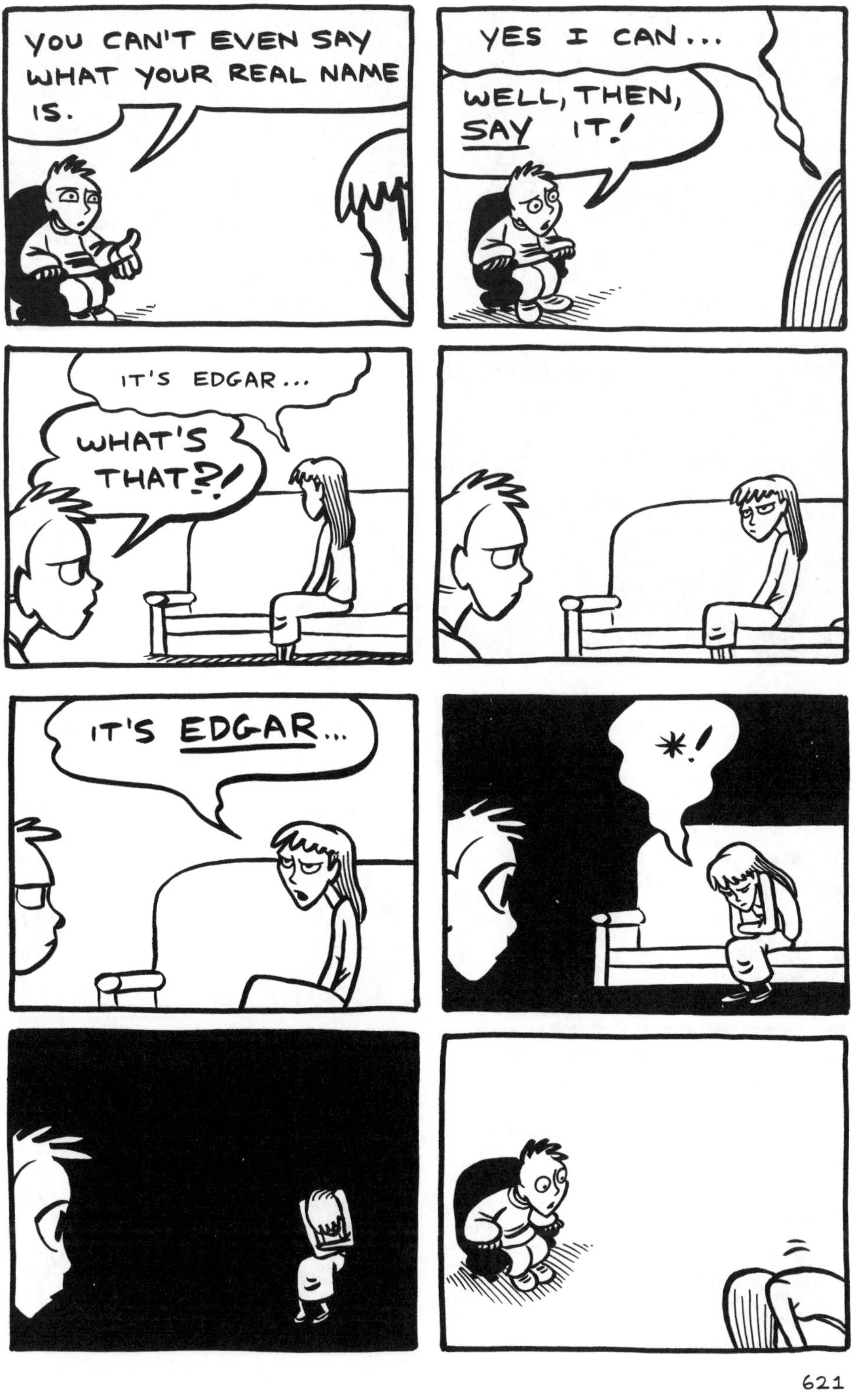
YOU CAN'T EVEN SAY WHAT YOUR REAL NAME IS.
YES I CAN...
WELL, THEN, SAY IT!
IT'S EDGAR...
WHAT'S THAT?!
IT'S EDGAR...
*!

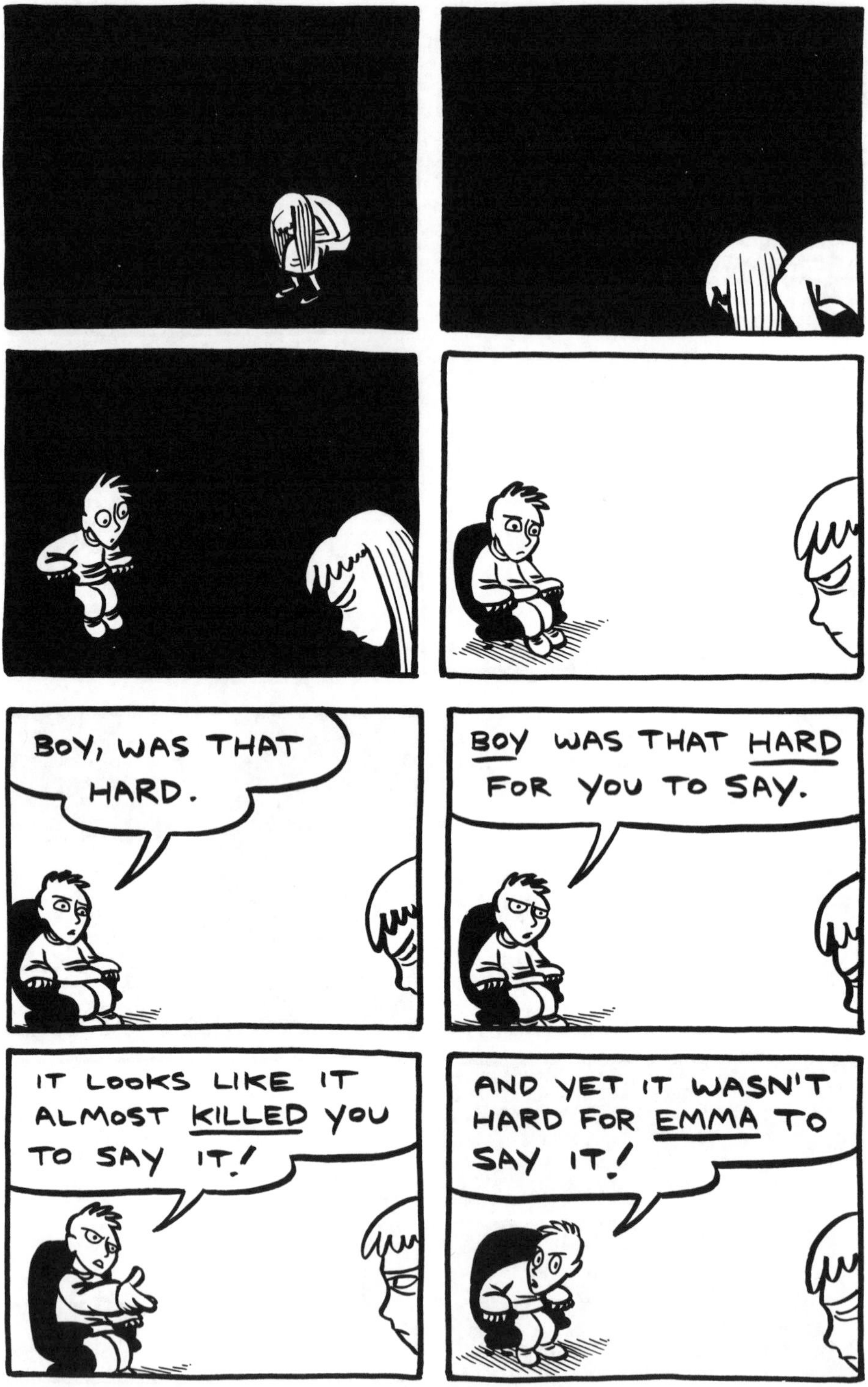
BOY, WAS THAT HARD.
BOY WAS THAT HARD FOR YOU TO SAY.
IT LOOKS LIKE IT ALMOST KILLED YOU TO SAY IT!
AND YET IT WASN'T HARD FOR EMMA TO SAY IT!

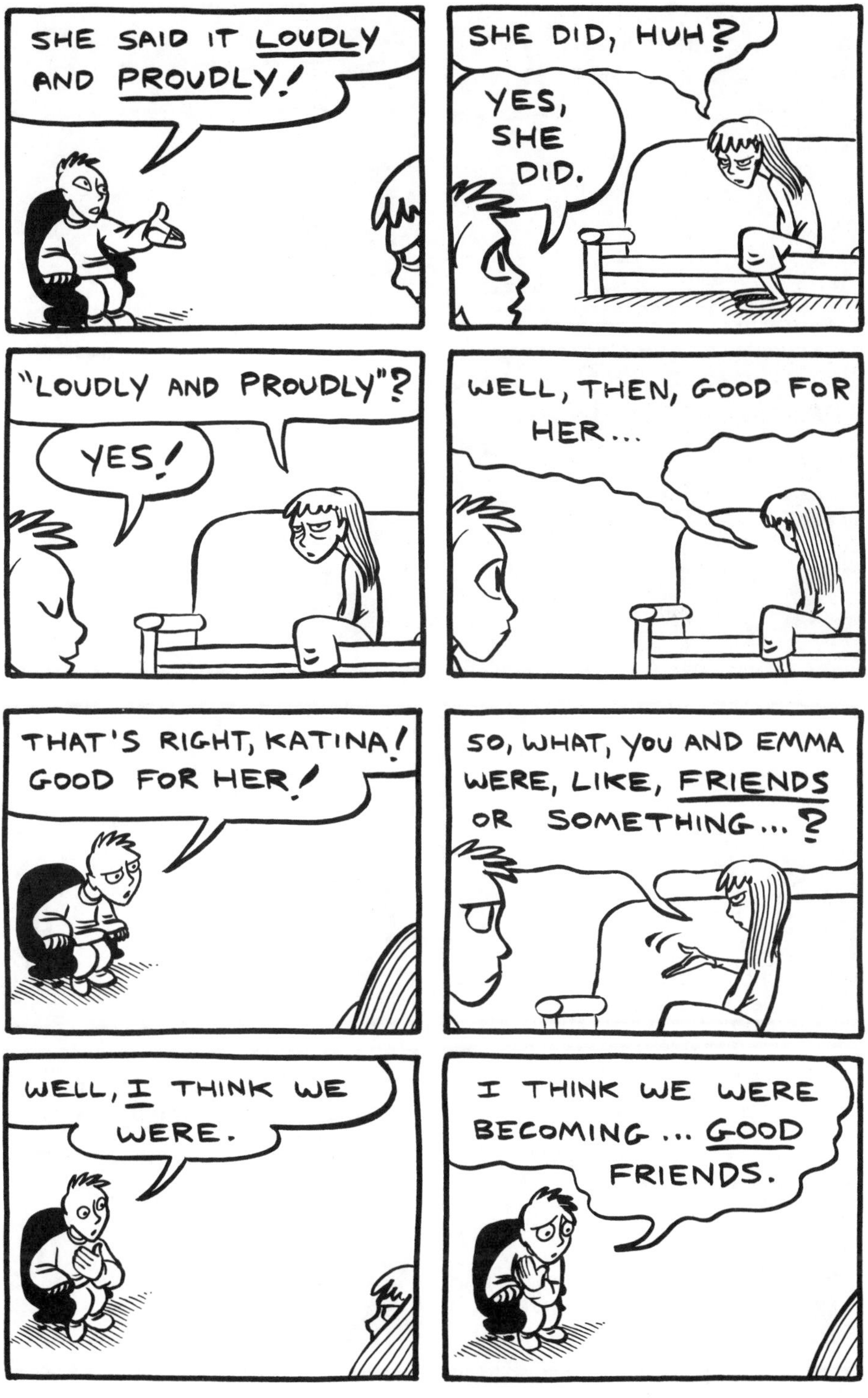
SHE SAID IT LOUDLY AND PROUDLY!
SHE DID, HUH?
YES, SHE DID.
"LOUDLY AND PROUDLY"?
YES!
WELL, THEN, GOOD FOR HER...
THAT'S RIGHT, KATINA! GOOD FOR HER!
SO, WHAT, YOU AND EMMA WERE, LIKE, FRIENDS OR SOMETHING...?
WELL, I THINK WE WERE.
I THINK WE WERE BECOMING... GOOD FRIENDS.

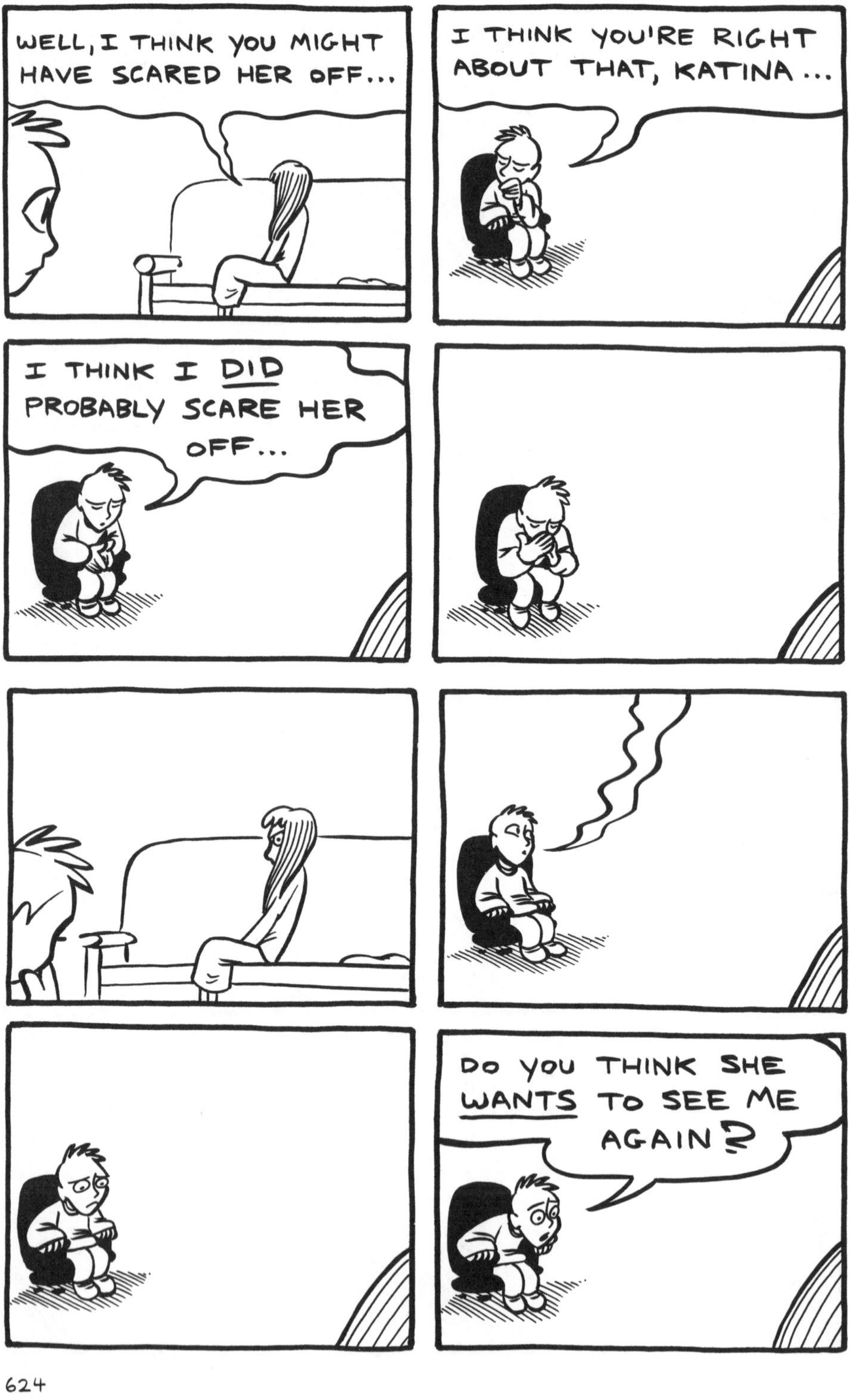
WELL, I THINK YOU MIGHT HAVE SCARED HER OFF...
I THINK YOU'RE RIGHT ABOUT THAT, KATINA...
I THINK I DID PROBABLY SCARE HER OFF...
DO YOU THINK SHE WANTS TO SEE ME AGAIN?

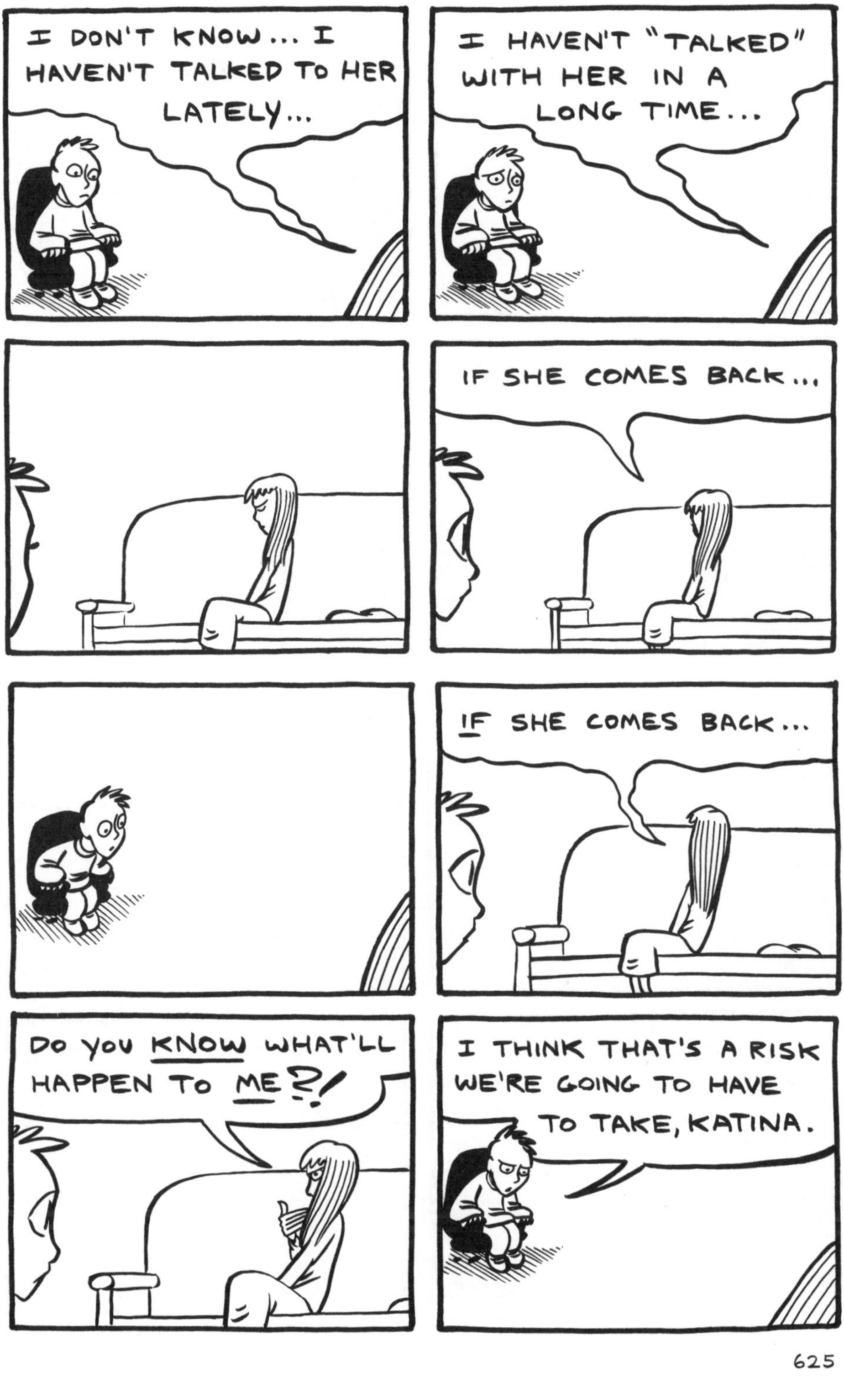
I DON'T KNOW... I HAVEN'T TALKED TO HER LATELY...
I HAVEN'T "TALKED" WITH HER IN A LONG TIME...
IF SHE COMES BACK...
IF SHE COMES BACK...
DO YOU KNOW WHAT'LL HAPPEN TO ME?!
I THINK THAT'S A RISK WE'RE GOING TO HAVE TO TAKE, KATINA.

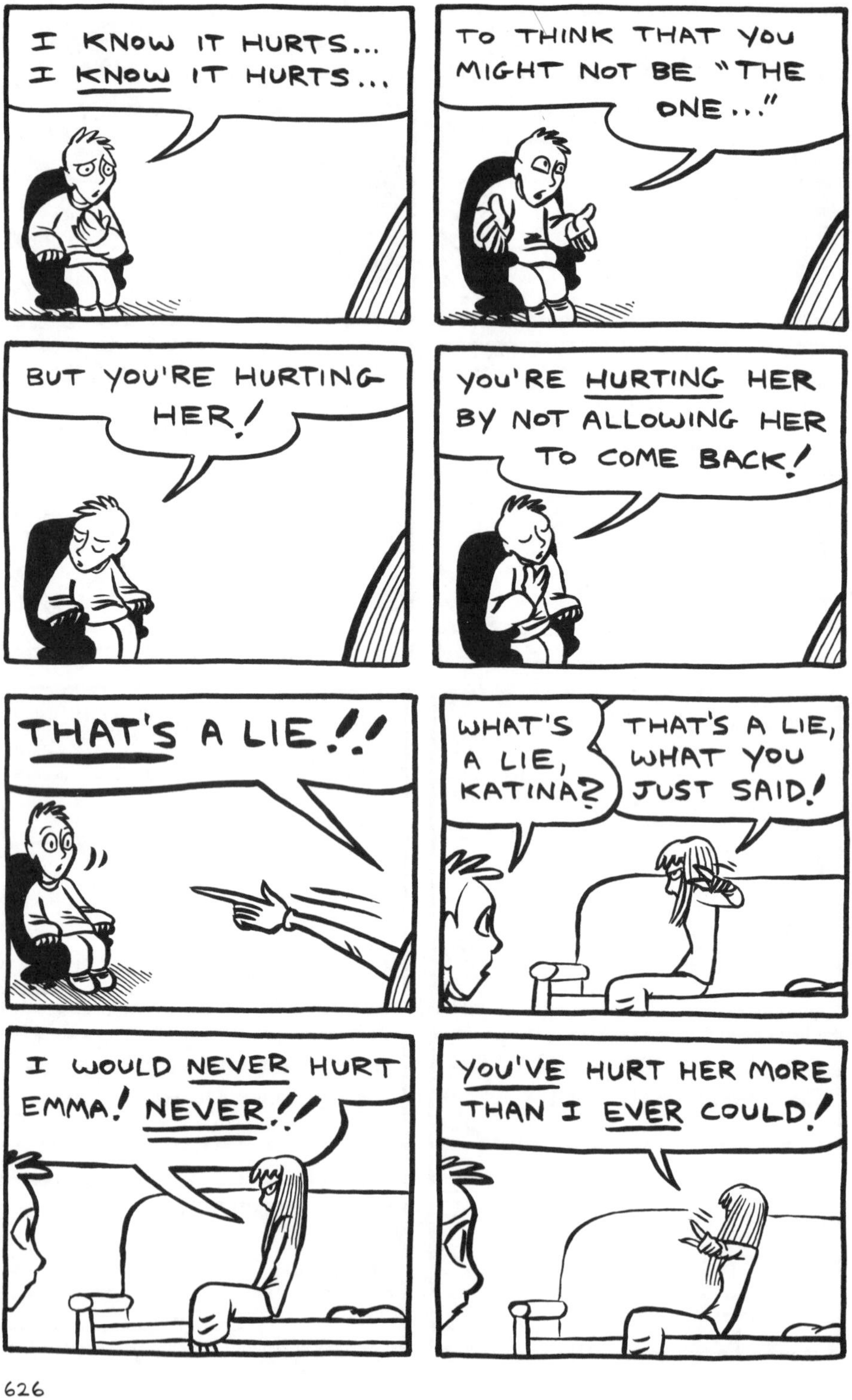
I KNOW IT HURTS...
I KNOW IT HURTS...
TO THINK THAT YOU MIGHT NOT BE "THE ONE..."
BUT YOU'RE HURTING HER!
YOU'RE HURTING HER BY NOT ALLOWING HER TO COME BACK!
THAT'S A LIE!!
WHAT'S A LIE, KATINA?
THAT'S A LIE, WHAT YOU JUST SAID!
I WOULD NEVER HURT EMMA! NEVER!!
YOU'VE HURT HER MORE THAN I EVER COULD!

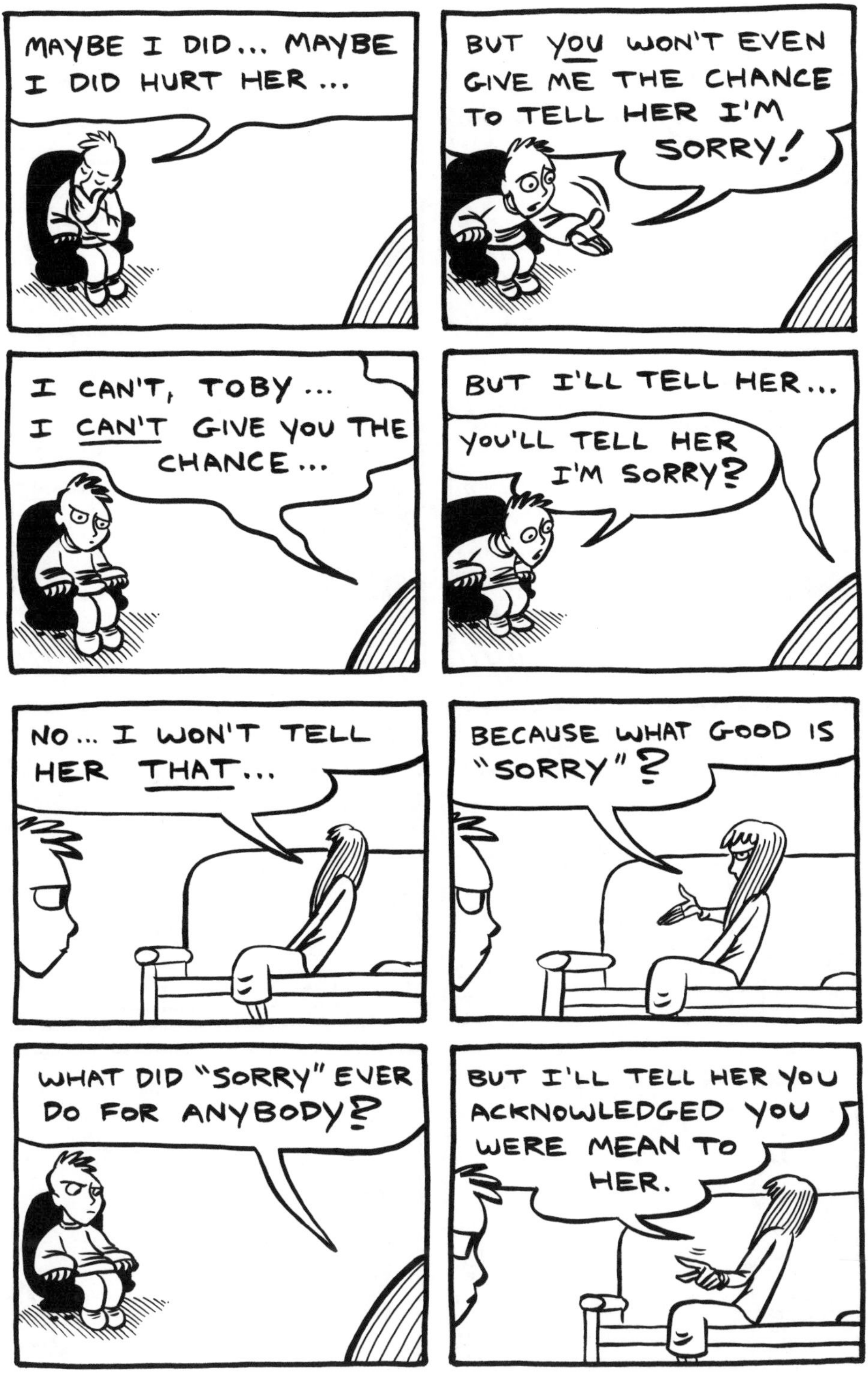
MAYBE I DID... MAYBE I DID HURT HER...
BUT YOU WON'T EVEN GIVE ME THE CHANCE TO TELL HER I'M SORRY!
I CAN'T, TOBY... I CAN'T GIVE YOU THE CHANCE...
BUT I'LL TELL HER...
YOU'LL TELL HER I'M SORRY?
NO... I WON'T TELL HER THAT...
BECAUSE WHAT GOOD IS "SORRY"?
WHAT DID "SORRY" EVER DO FOR ANYBODY?
BUT I'LL TELL HER YOU ACKNOWLEDGED YOU WERE MEAN TO HER.

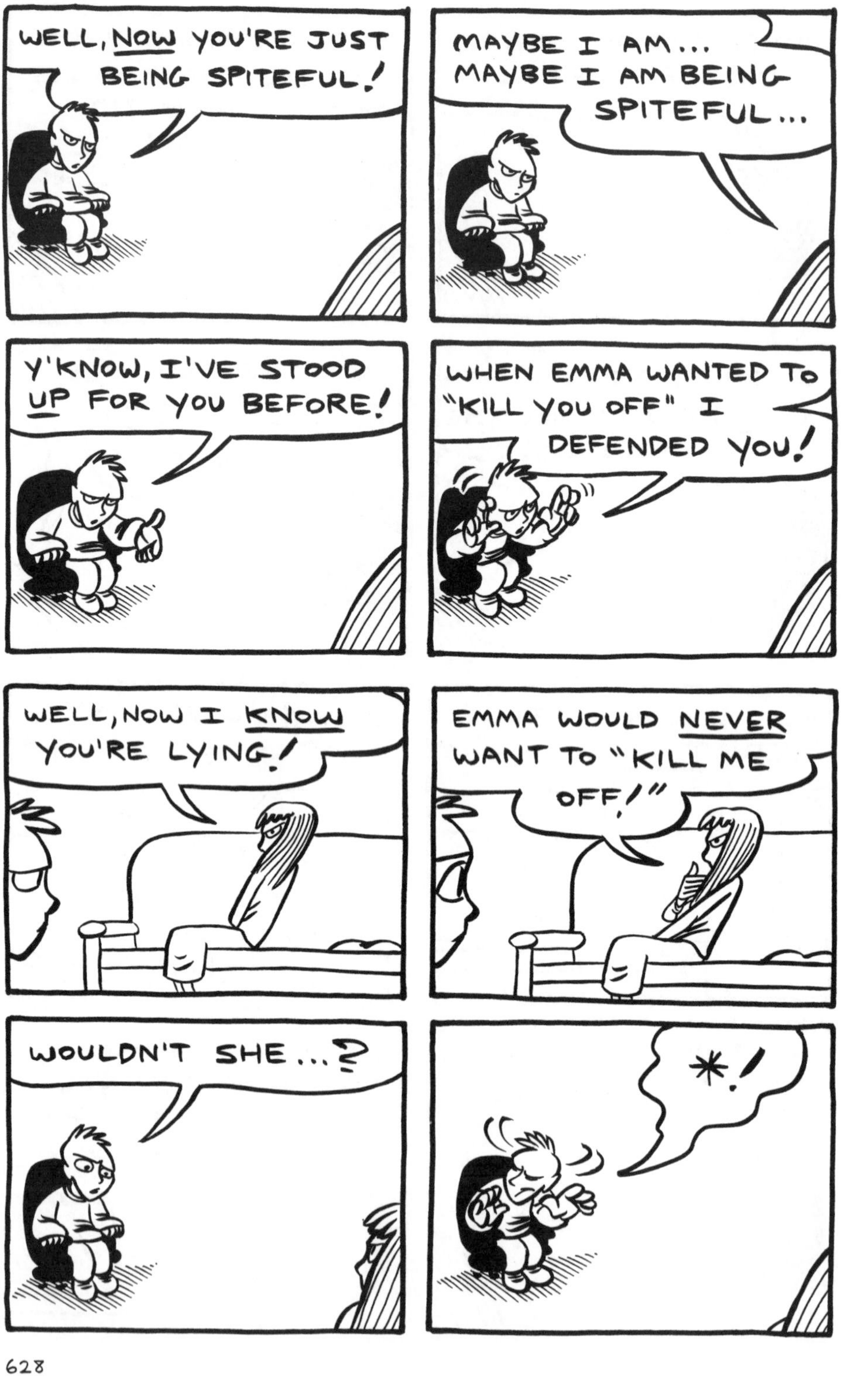
WELL, NOW YOU'RE JUST BEING SPITEFUL!
MAYBE I AM... MAYBE I AM BEING SPITEFUL...
Y'KNOW, I'VE STOOD UP FOR YOU BEFORE!
WHEN EMMA WANTED TO "KILL YOU OFF" I DEFENDED YOU!
WELL, NOW I KNOW YOU'RE LYING!
EMMA WOULD NEVER WANT TO "KILL ME OFF!"
WOULDN'T SHE...?
*!

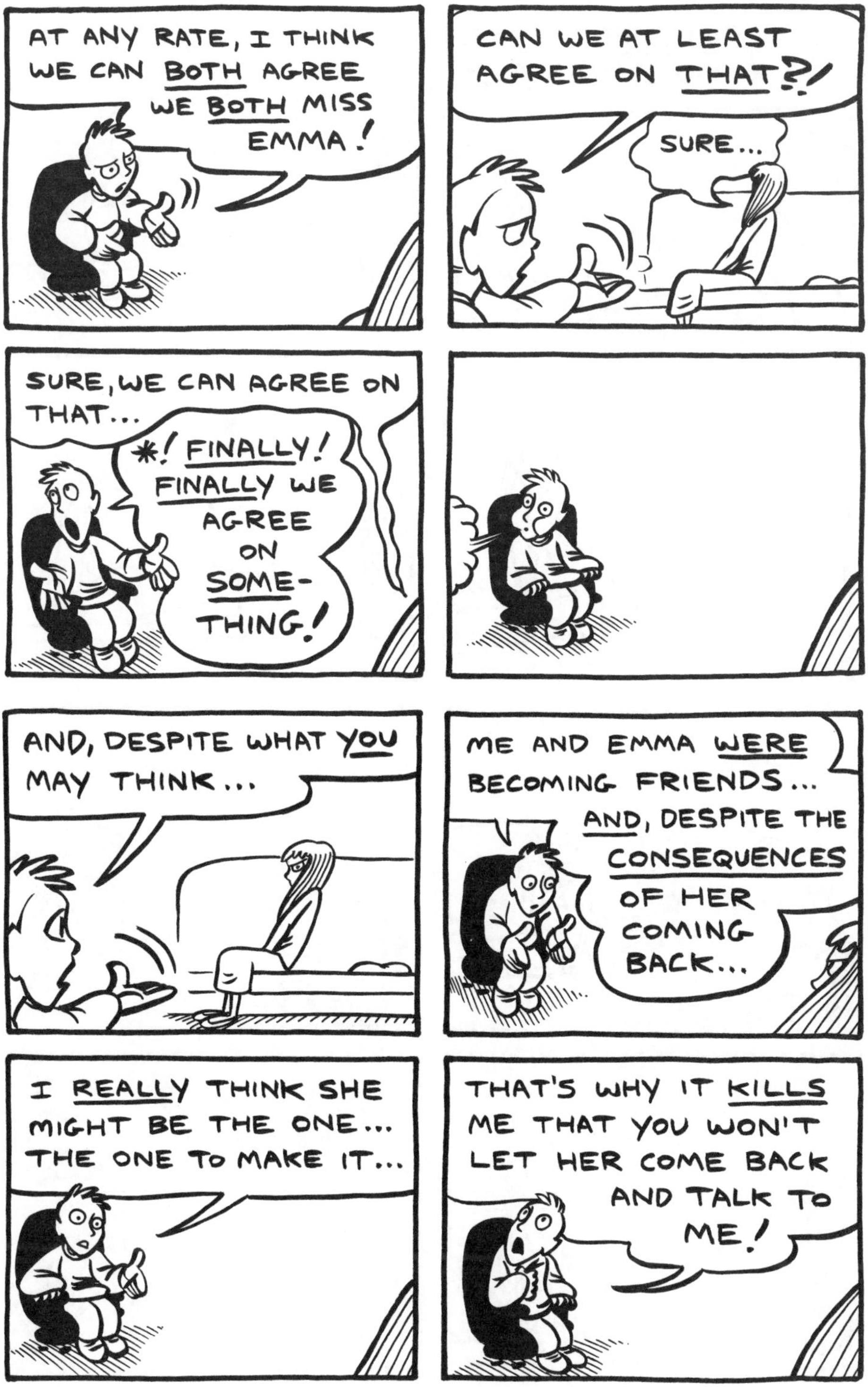
AT ANY RATE, I THINK WE CAN BOTH AGREE WE BOTH MISS EMMA!
CAN WE AT LEAST AGREE ON THAT?!
SURE...
SURE, WE CAN AGREE ON THAT...
*! FINALLY! FINALLY WE AGREE ON SOME-THING!
AND, DESPITE WHAT YOU MAY THINK...
ME AND EMMA WERE BECOMING FRIENDS... AND, DESPITE THE CONSEQUENCES OF HER COMING BACK...
I REALLY THINK SHE MIGHT BE THE ONE... THE ONE TO MAKE IT...
THAT'S WHY IT KILLS ME THAT YOU WON'T LET HER COME BACK AND TALK TO ME!

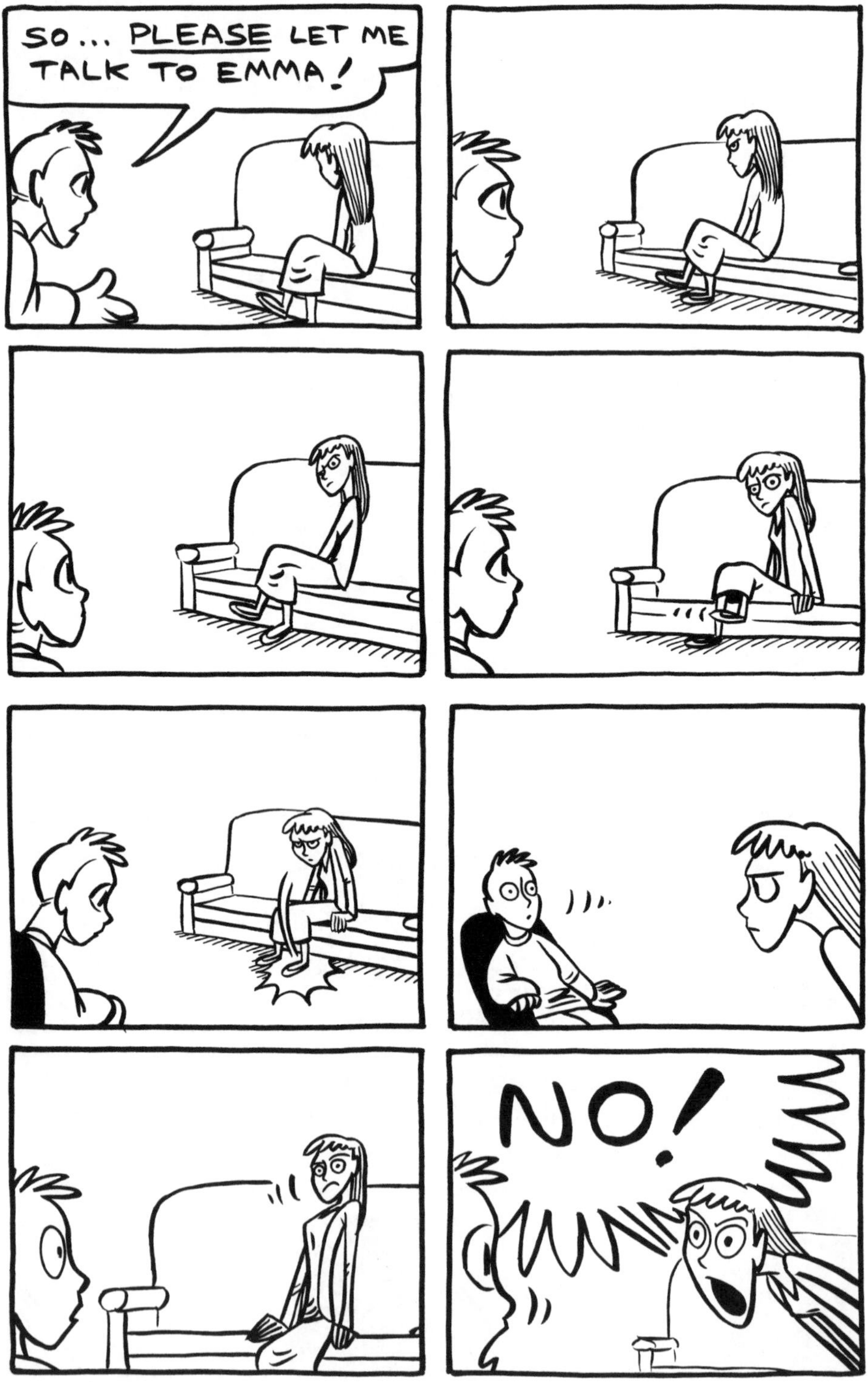
SO... PLEASE LET ME TALK TO EMMA!
NO!

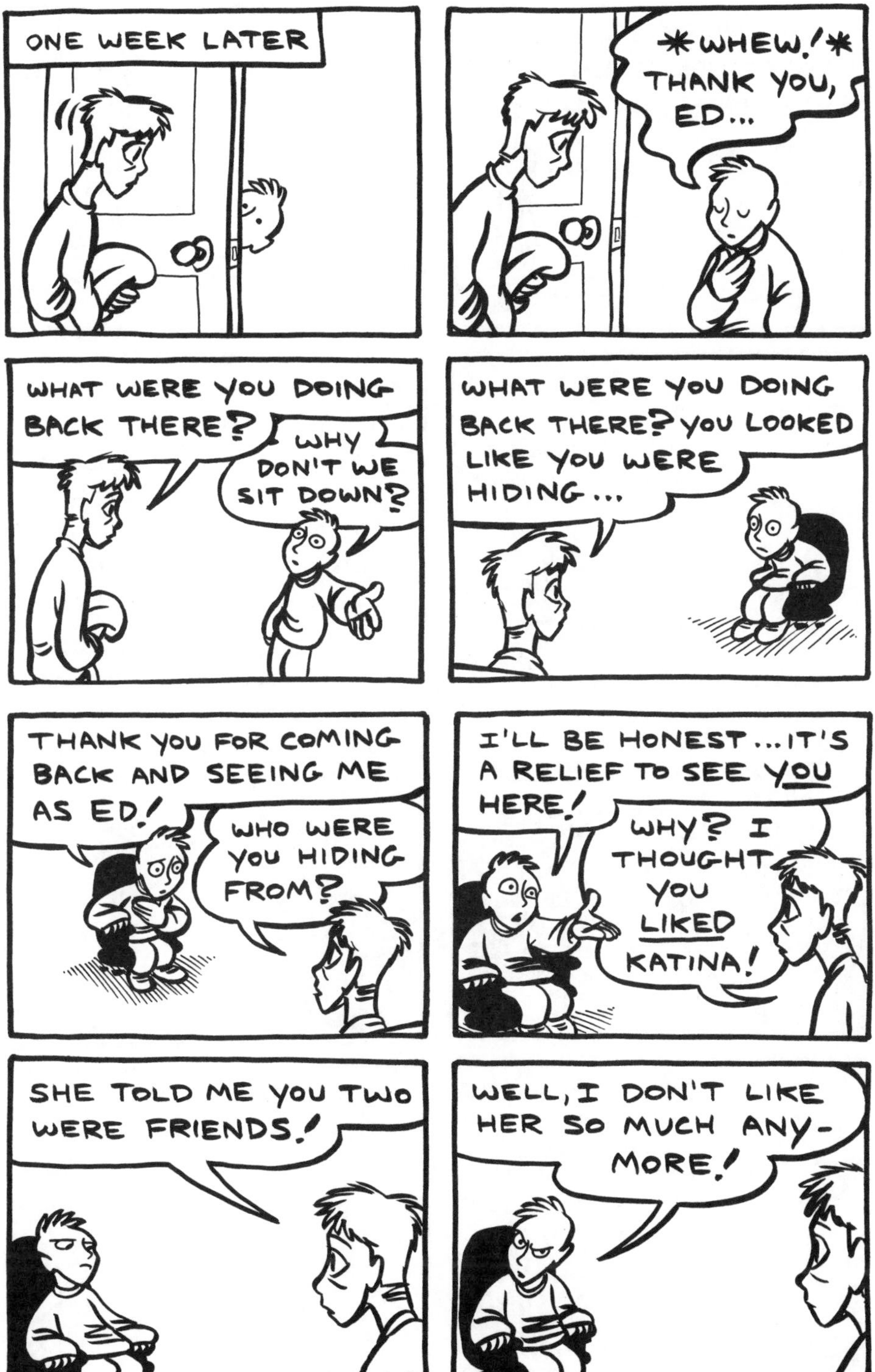
ONE WEEK LATER
WHEW! THANK YOU, ED...
WHAT WERE YOU DOING BACK THERE?
WHY DON'T WE SIT DOWN?
WHAT WERE YOU DOING BACK THERE? YOU LOOKED LIKE YOU WERE HIDING...
THANK YOU FOR COMING BACK AND SEEING ME AS ED!
WHO WERE YOU HIDING FROM?
I'LL BE HONEST...IT'S A RELIEF TO SEE YOU HERE!
WHY? I THOUGHT YOU LIKED KATINA!
SHE TOLD ME YOU TWO WERE FRIENDS!
WELL, I DON'T LIKE HER SO MUCH ANY-MORE!

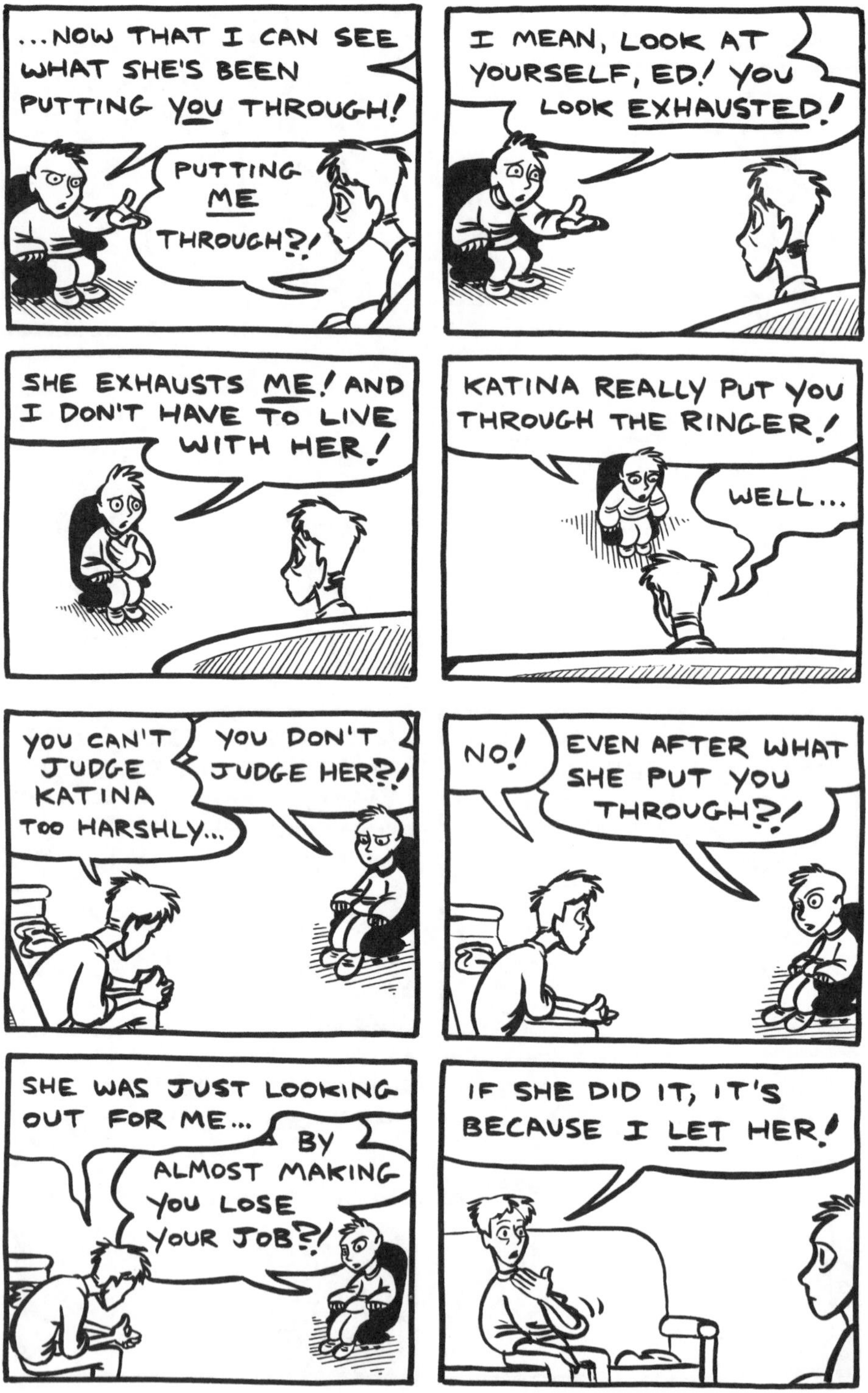
...NOW THAT I CAN SEE WHAT SHE'S BEEN PUTTING YOU THROUGH!
PUTTING ME THROUGH?!
I MEAN, LOOK AT YOURSELF, ED! YOU LOOK EXHAUSTED!
SHE EXHAUSTS ME! AND I DON'T HAVE TO LIVE WITH HER!
KATINA REALLY PUT YOU THROUGH THE RINGER!
WELL...
YOU CAN'T JUDGE KATINA TOO HARSHLY...
YOU DON'T JUDGE HER?!
NO!
EVEN AFTER WHAT SHE PUT YOU THROUGH?!
SHE WAS JUST LOOKING OUT FOR ME...
BY ALMOST MAKING YOU LOSE YOUR JOB?!
IF SHE DID IT, IT'S BECAUSE I LET HER!

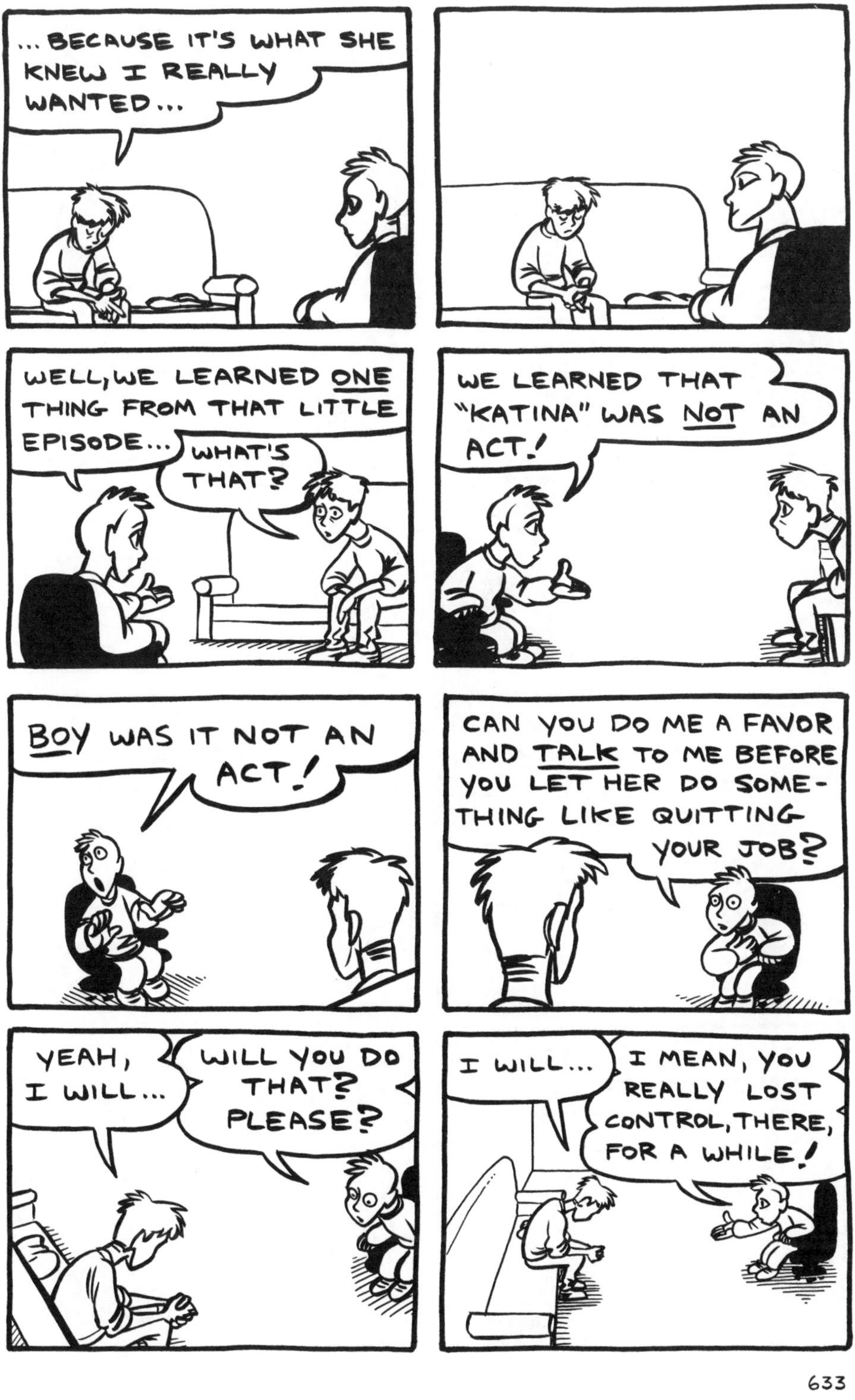
... BECAUSE IT'S WHAT SHE KNEW I REALLY WANTED...
WELL, WE LEARNED ONE THING FROM THAT LITTLE EPISODE...
WHAT'S THAT?
WE LEARNED THAT "KATINA" WAS NOT AN ACT!
BOY WAS IT NOT AN ACT!
CAN YOU DO ME A FAVOR AND TALK TO ME BEFORE YOU LET HER DO SOME-THING LIKE QUITTING YOUR JOB?
YEAH, I WILL...
WILL YOU DO THAT? PLEASE?
I WILL...
I MEAN, YOU REALLY LOST CONTROL, THERE, FOR A WHILE!

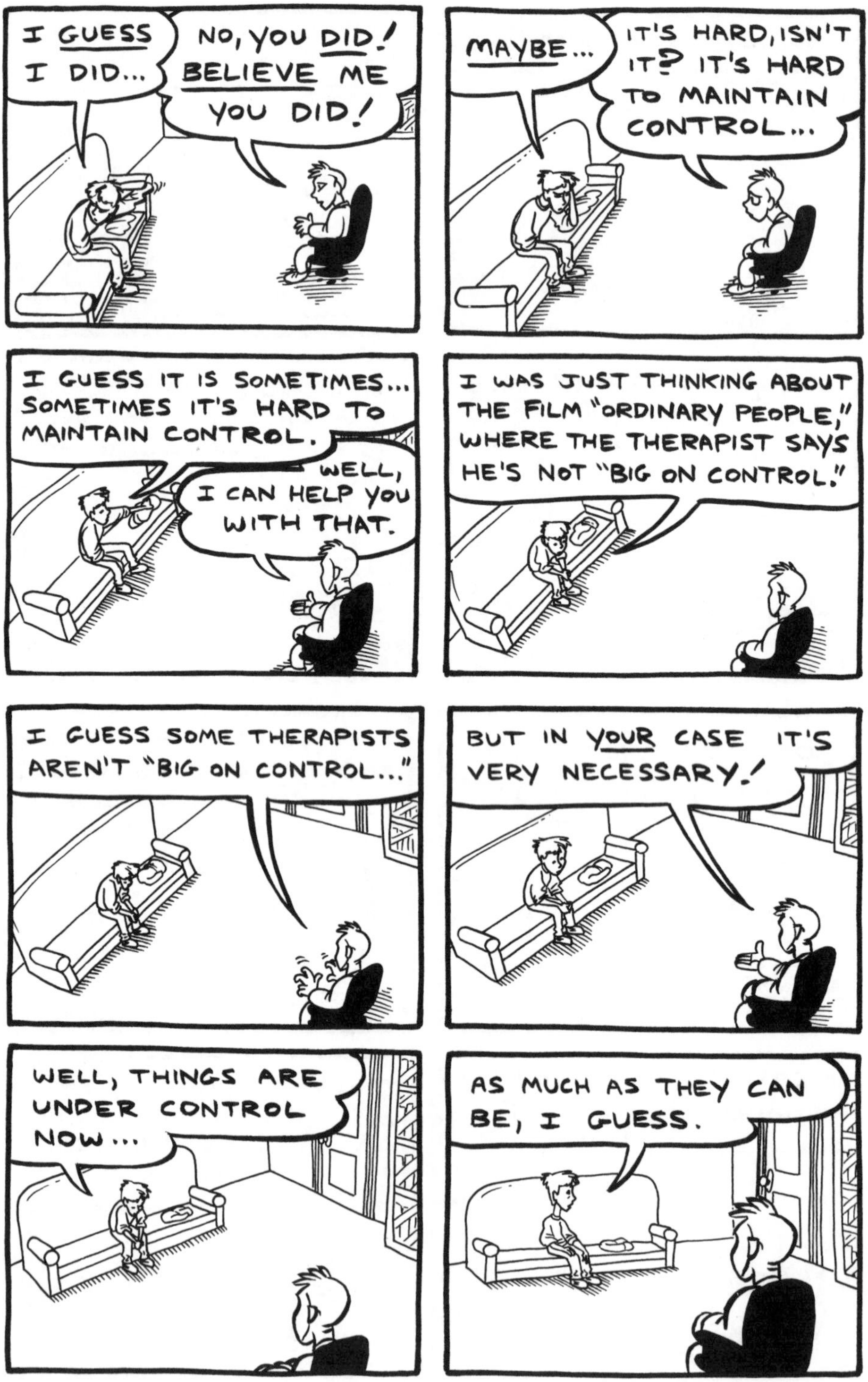
I GUESS I DID...
NO, YOU DID! BELIEVE ME YOU DID!
MAYBE...
IT'S HARD, ISN'T IT? IT'S HARD TO MAINTAIN CONTROL...
I GUESS IT IS SOMETIMES... SOMETIMES IT'S HARD TO MAINTAIN CONTROL.
WELL, I CAN HELP YOU WITH THAT.
I WAS JUST THINKING ABOUT THE FILM "ORDINARY PEOPLE," WHERE THE THERAPIST SAYS HE'S NOT "BIG ON CONTROL."
I GUESS SOME THERAPISTS AREN'T "BIG ON CONTROL..."
BUT IN YOUR CASE IT'S VERY NECESSARY!
WELL, THINGS ARE UNDER CONTROL NOW...
AS MUCH AS THEY CAN BE, I GUESS.

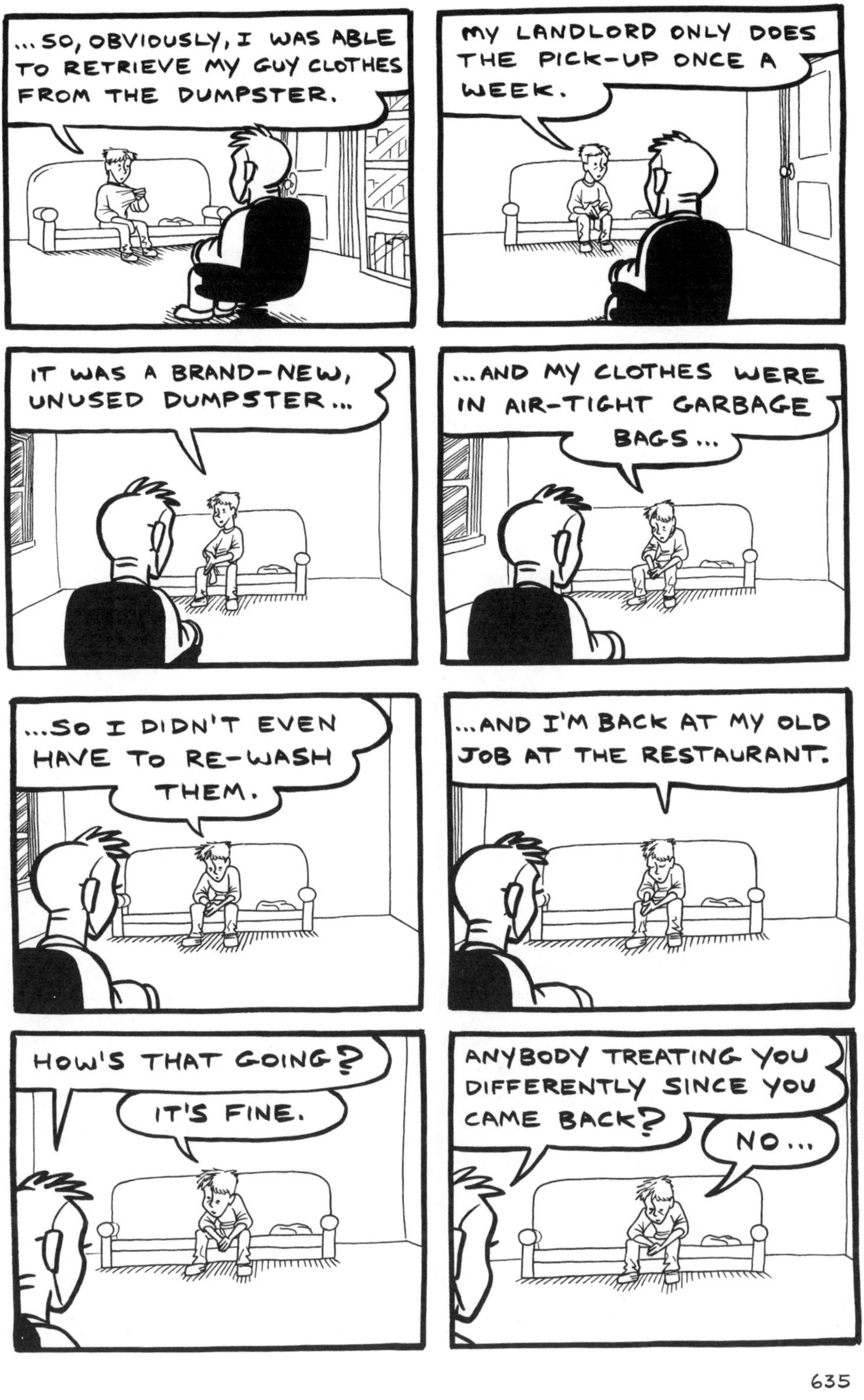
...SO, OBVIOUSLY, I WAS ABLE TO RETRIEVE MY GUY CLOTHES FROM THE DUMPSTER.
MY LANDLORD ONLY DOES THE PICK-UP ONCE A WEEK.
IT WAS A BRAND-NEW, UNUSED DUMPSTER...
...AND MY CLOTHES WERE IN AIR-TIGHT GARBAGE BAGS...
...SO I DIDN'T EVEN HAVE TO RE-WASH THEM.
...AND I'M BACK AT MY OLD JOB AT THE RESTAURANT.
HOW'S THAT GOING?
IT'S FINE.
ANYBODY TREATING YOU DIFFERENTLY SINCE YOU CAME BACK?
NO...

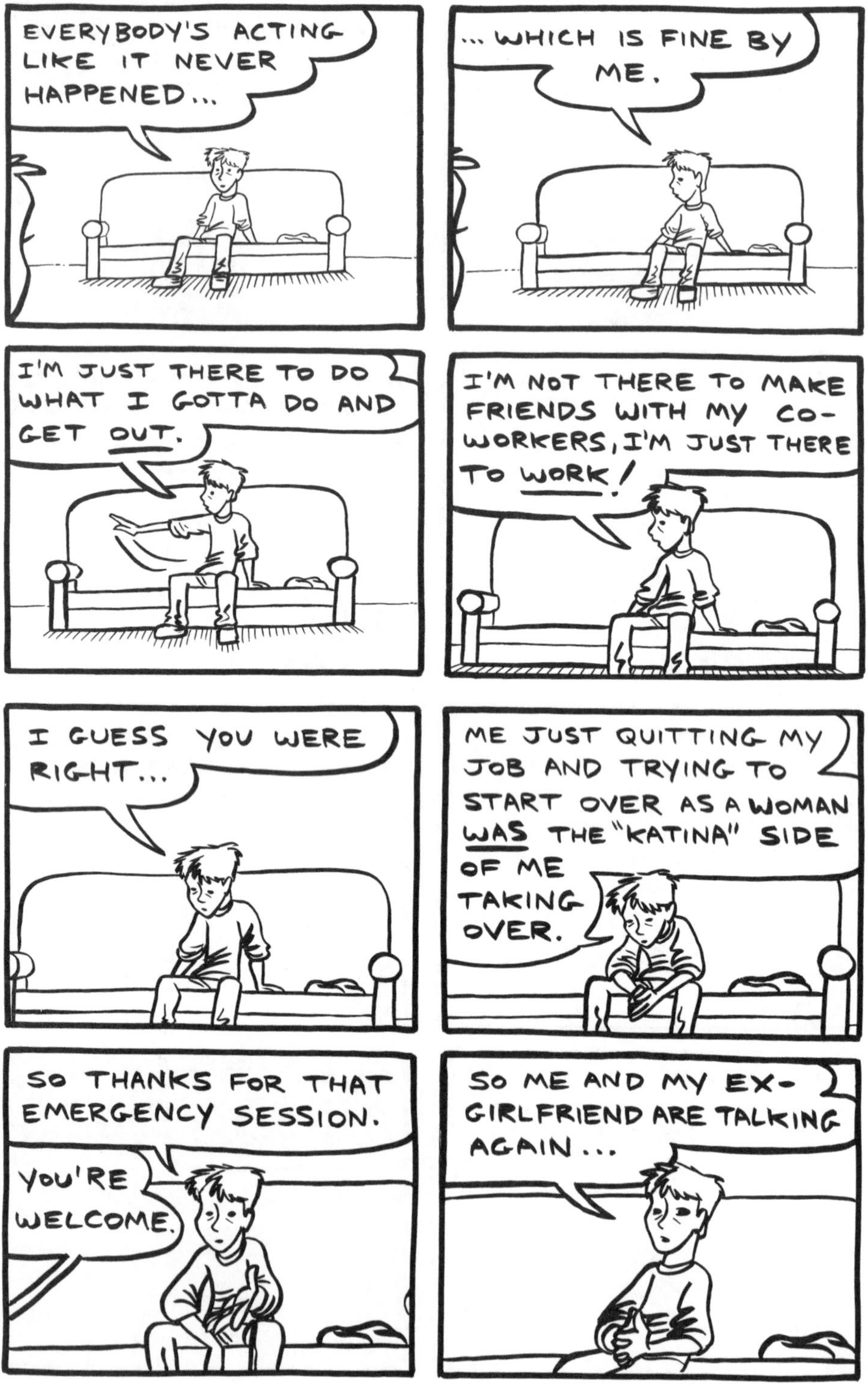
EVERYBODY'S ACTING LIKE IT NEVER HAPPENED...
...WHICH IS FINE BY ME.
I'M JUST THERE TO DO WHAT I GOTTA DO AND GET OUT.
I'M NOT THERE TO MAKE FRIENDS WITH MY CO-WORKERS, I'M JUST THERE TO WORK!
I GUESS YOU WERE RIGHT...
ME JUST QUITTING MY JOB AND TRYING TO START OVER AS A WOMAN WAS THE "KATINA" SIDE OF ME TAKING OVER.
SO THANKS FOR THAT EMERGENCY SESSION.
YOU'RE WELCOME.
SO ME AND MY EX-GIRLFRIEND ARE TALKING AGAIN...

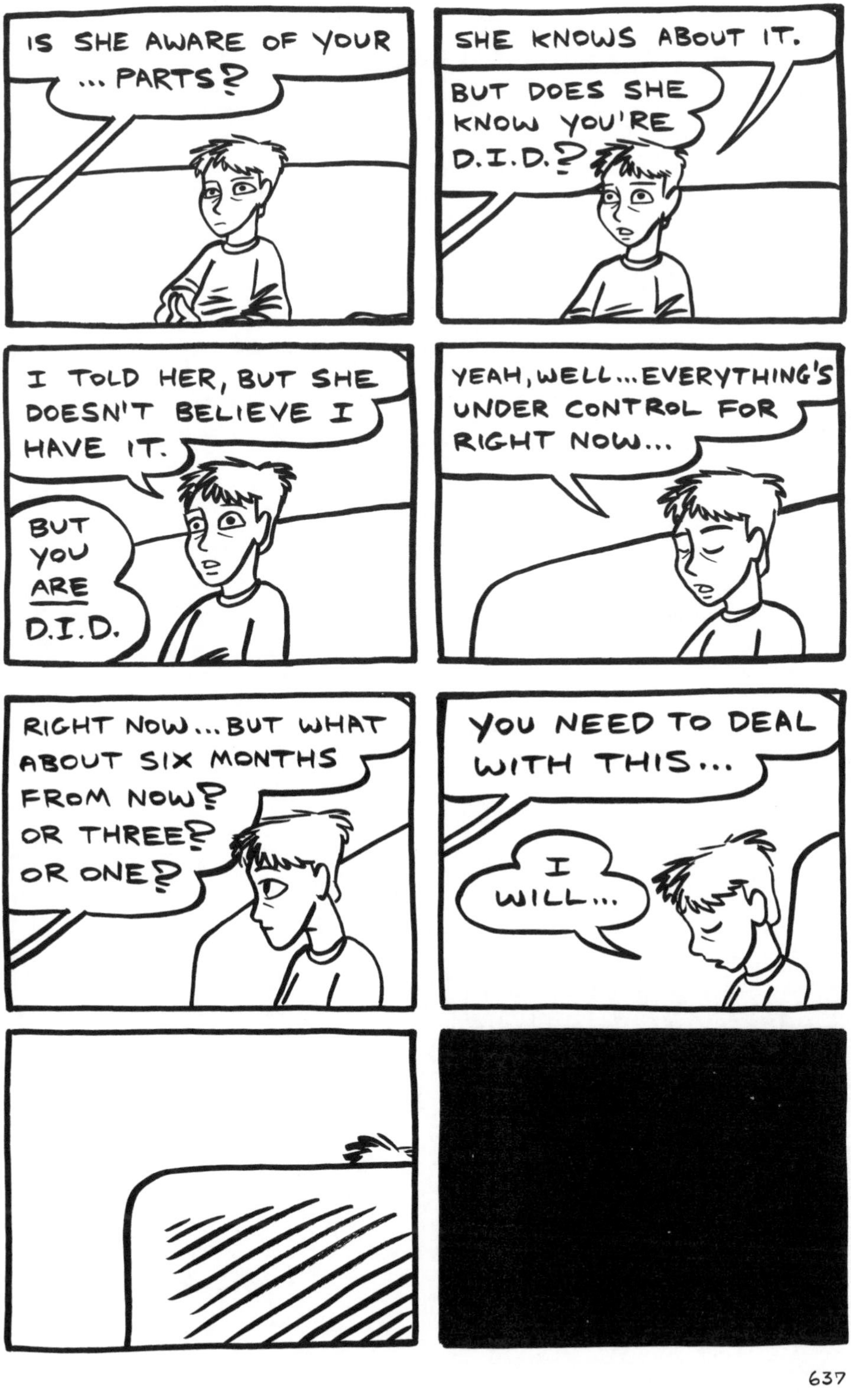

IS SHE AWARE OF YOUR ... PARTS?
SHE KNOWS ABOUT IT.
BUT DOES SHE KNOW YOU'RE D.I.D.?
I TOLD HER, BUT SHE DOESN'T BELIEVE I HAVE IT.
BUT YOU ARE D.I.D.
YEAH, WELL... EVERYTHING'S UNDER CONTROL FOR RIGHT NOW...
RIGHT NOW... BUT WHAT ABOUT SIX MONTHS FROM NOW? OR THREE? OR ONE?
YOU NEED TO DEAL WITH THIS...
I WILL...

MISSING PERSON

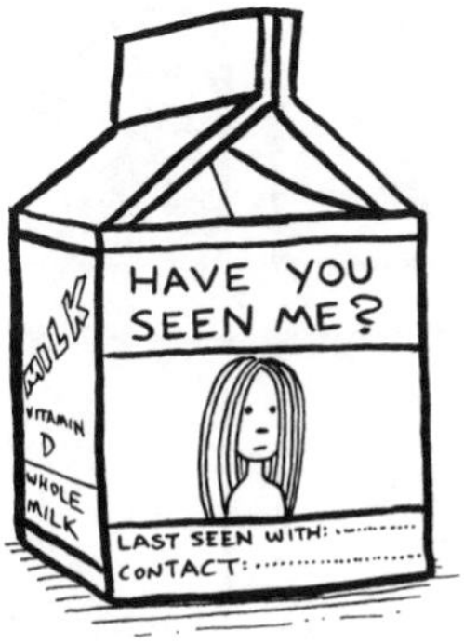
MILK
VITAMIN D
WHOLE MILK
HAVE YOU SEEN ME?
LAST SEEN WITH:
CONTACT:

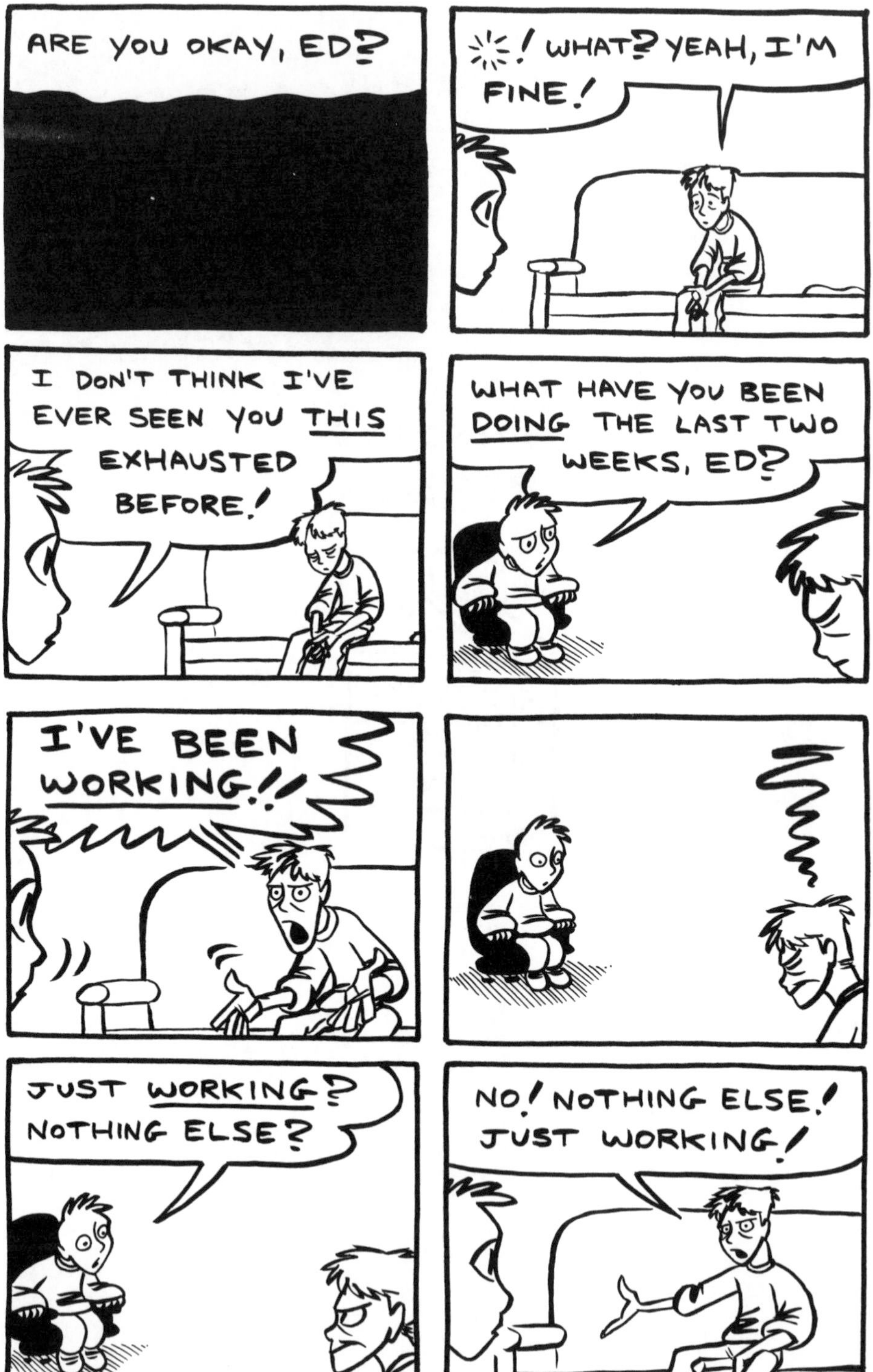
ARE YOU OKAY, ED?
!! WHAT? YEAH, I'M FINE!
I DON'T THINK I'VE EVER SEEN YOU THIS EXHAUSTED BEFORE!
WHAT HAVE YOU BEEN DOING THE LAST TWO WEEKS, ED?
I'VE BEEN WORKING!!
JUST WORKING? NOTHING ELSE?
NO! NOTHING ELSE! JUST WORKING!

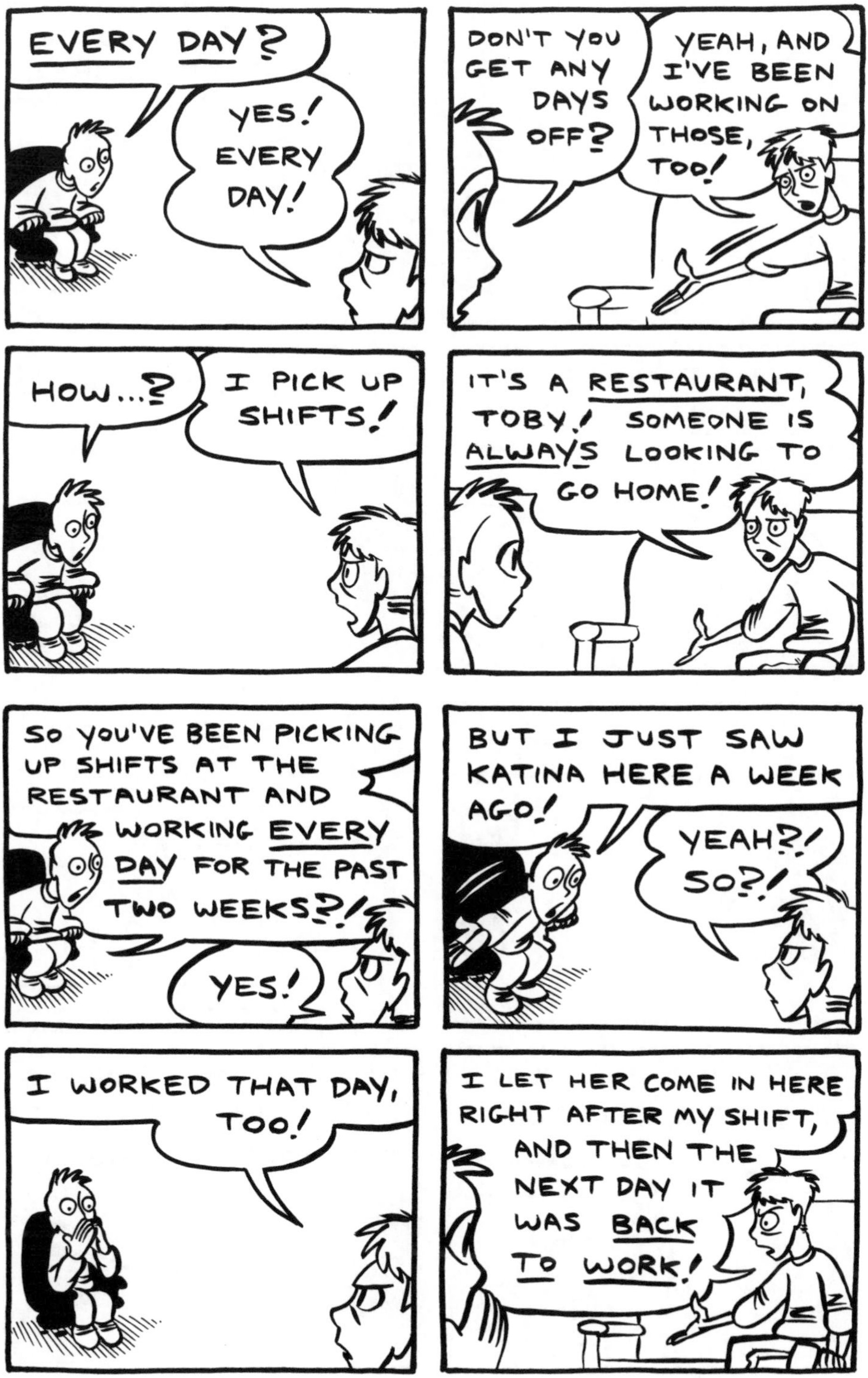
EVERY DAY?
YES! EVERY DAY!
DON'T YOU GET ANY DAYS OFF?
YEAH, AND I'VE BEEN WORKING ON THOSE, TOO!
HOW...?
I PICK UP SHIFTS!
IT'S A RESTAURANT, TOBY! SOMEONE IS ALWAYS LOOKING TO GO HOME!
SO YOU'VE BEEN PICKING UP SHIFTS AT THE RESTAURANT AND WORKING EVERY DAY FOR THE PAST TWO WEEKS?!
YES!
BUT I JUST SAW KATINA HERE A WEEK AGO!
YEAH?! SO?!
I WORKED THAT DAY, TOO!
I LET HER COME IN HERE RIGHT AFTER MY SHIFT, AND THEN THE NEXT DAY IT WAS BACK TO WORK!

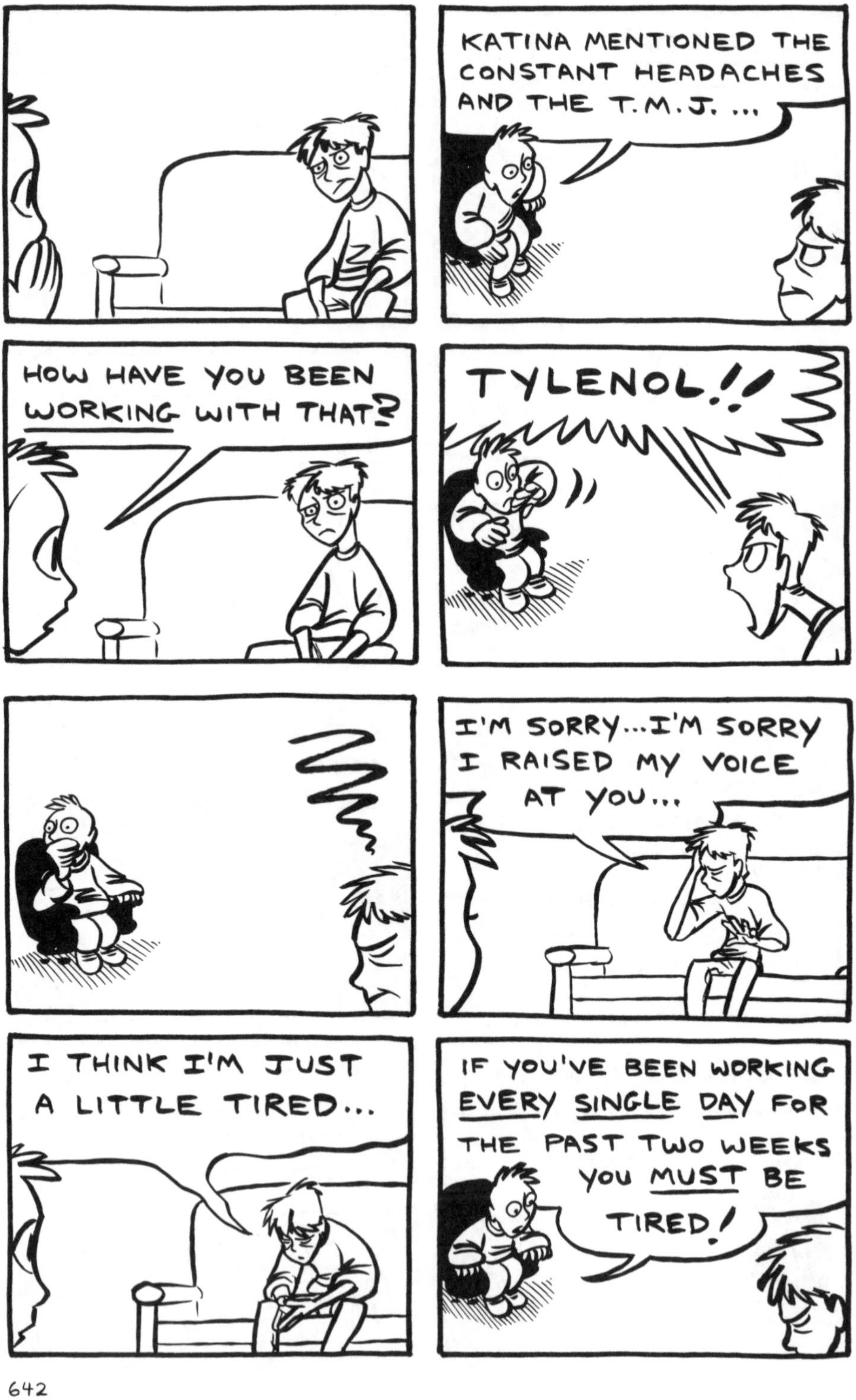
KATINA MENTIONED THE CONSTANT HEADACHES AND THE T.M.J. ...
HOW HAVE YOU BEEN WORKING WITH THAT?
TYLENOL!!
I'M SORRY...I'M SORRY I RAISED MY VOICE AT YOU...
I THINK I'M JUST A LITTLE TIRED...
IF YOU'VE BEEN WORKING EVERY SINGLE DAY FOR THE PAST TWO WEEKS YOU MUST BE TIRED!

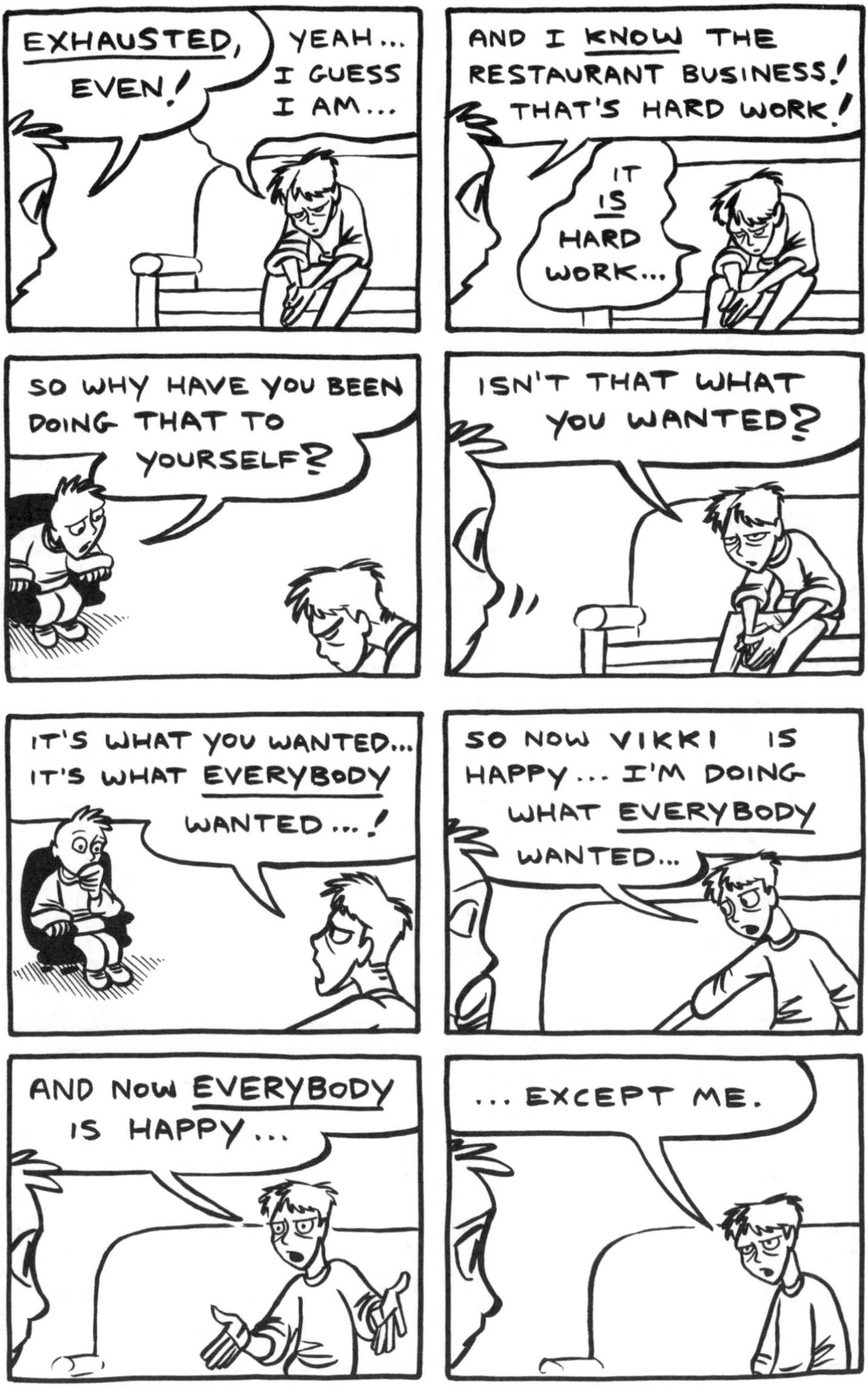
EXHAUSTED, EVEN!
YEAH... I GUESS I AM...
AND I KNOW THE RESTAURANT BUSINESS! THAT'S HARD WORK!
IT IS HARD WORK...
SO WHY HAVE YOU BEEN DOING THAT TO YOURSELF?
ISN'T THAT WHAT YOU WANTED?
IT'S WHAT YOU WANTED... IT'S WHAT EVERYBODY WANTED...!
SO NOW VIKKI IS HAPPY... I'M DOING WHAT EVERYBODY WANTED...
AND NOW EVERYBODY IS HAPPY...
... EXCEPT ME.

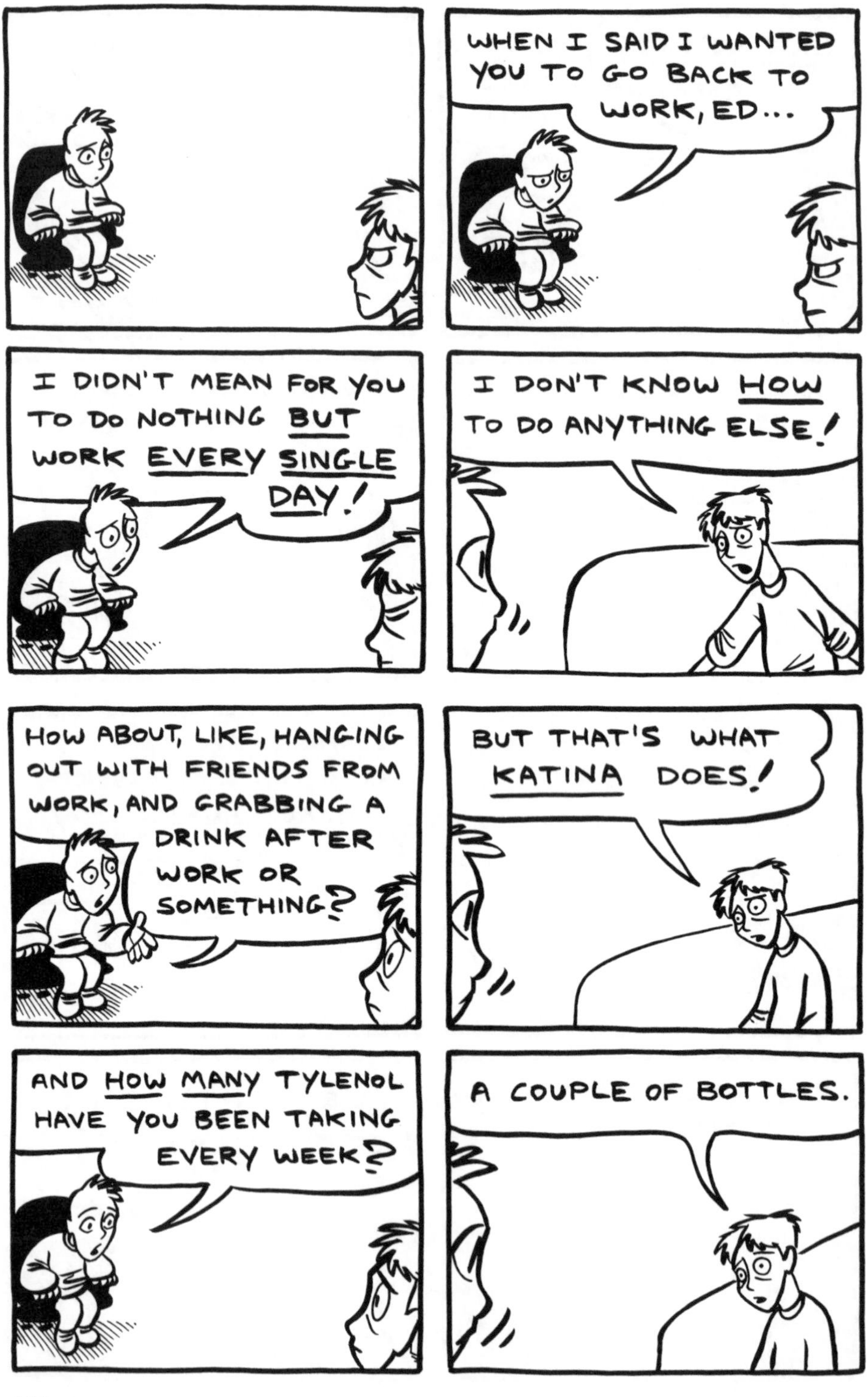
WHEN I SAID I WANTED YOU TO GO BACK TO WORK, ED...
I DIDN'T MEAN FOR YOU TO DO NOTHING BUT WORK EVERY SINGLE DAY!
I DON'T KNOW HOW TO DO ANYTHING ELSE!
HOW ABOUT, LIKE, HANGING OUT WITH FRIENDS FROM WORK, AND GRABBING A DRINK AFTER WORK OR SOMETHING?
BUT THAT'S WHAT KATINA DOES!
AND HOW MANY TYLENOL HAVE YOU BEEN TAKING EVERY WEEK?
A COUPLE OF BOTTLES.

THANK GOD I CAN AFFORD IT, NOW THAT I'VE BEEN WORKING EVERY DAY...

TYLENOL IS EXPENSIVE...

DON'T YOU THINK TYLENOL IS EXPENSIVE?

YES, IT IS...

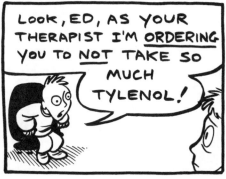

LOOK, ED, AS YOUR THERAPIST I'M ORDERING YOU TO NOT TAKE SO MUCH TYLENOL!

AND TO NOT WORK SO MUCH, AND TO GET SOME REST!

I AM STARTING TO GET KIND OF WORN DOWN...

I DO HAVE A SCHEDULED DAY OFF IN A COUPLE OF DAYS...

TAKE IT!

I WAS GONNA PICK UP THIS GIRL KAREN'S SHIFT...

NO, NO, DON'T DO THAT!

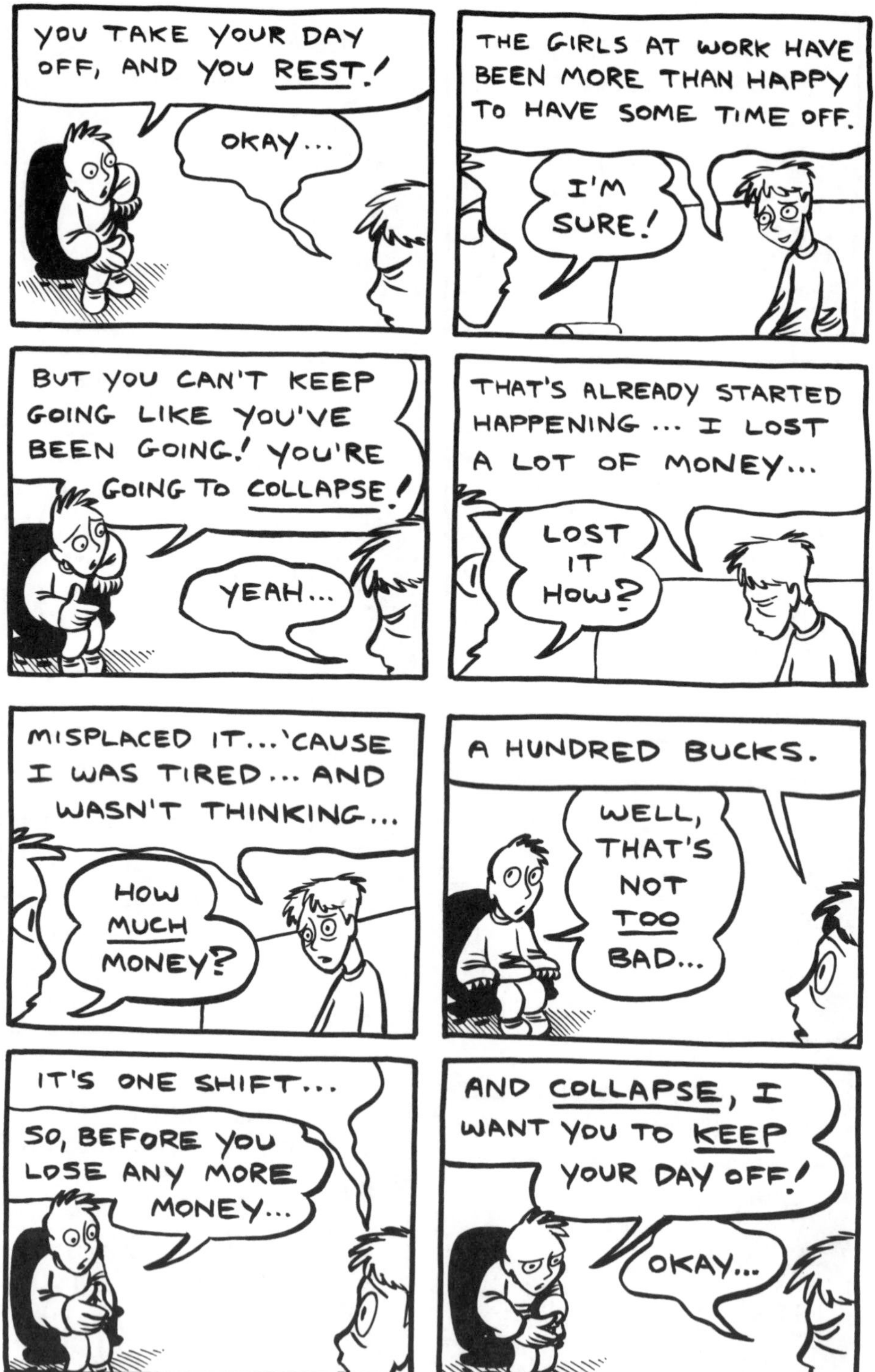

YOU TAKE YOUR DAY OFF, AND YOU REST!
OKAY...
THE GIRLS AT WORK HAVE BEEN MORE THAN HAPPY TO HAVE SOME TIME OFF.
I'M SURE!
BUT YOU CAN'T KEEP GOING LIKE YOU'VE BEEN GOING! YOU'RE GOING TO COLLAPSE!
YEAH...
THAT'S ALREADY STARTED HAPPENING... I LOST A LOT OF MONEY...
LOST IT HOW?
MISPLACED IT...'CAUSE I WAS TIRED... AND WASN'T THINKING...
HOW MUCH MONEY?
A HUNDRED BUCKS.
WELL, THAT'S NOT TOO BAD...
IT'S ONE SHIFT...
SO, BEFORE YOU LOSE ANY MORE MONEY...
AND COLLAPSE, I WANT YOU TO KEEP YOUR DAY OFF!
OKAY...

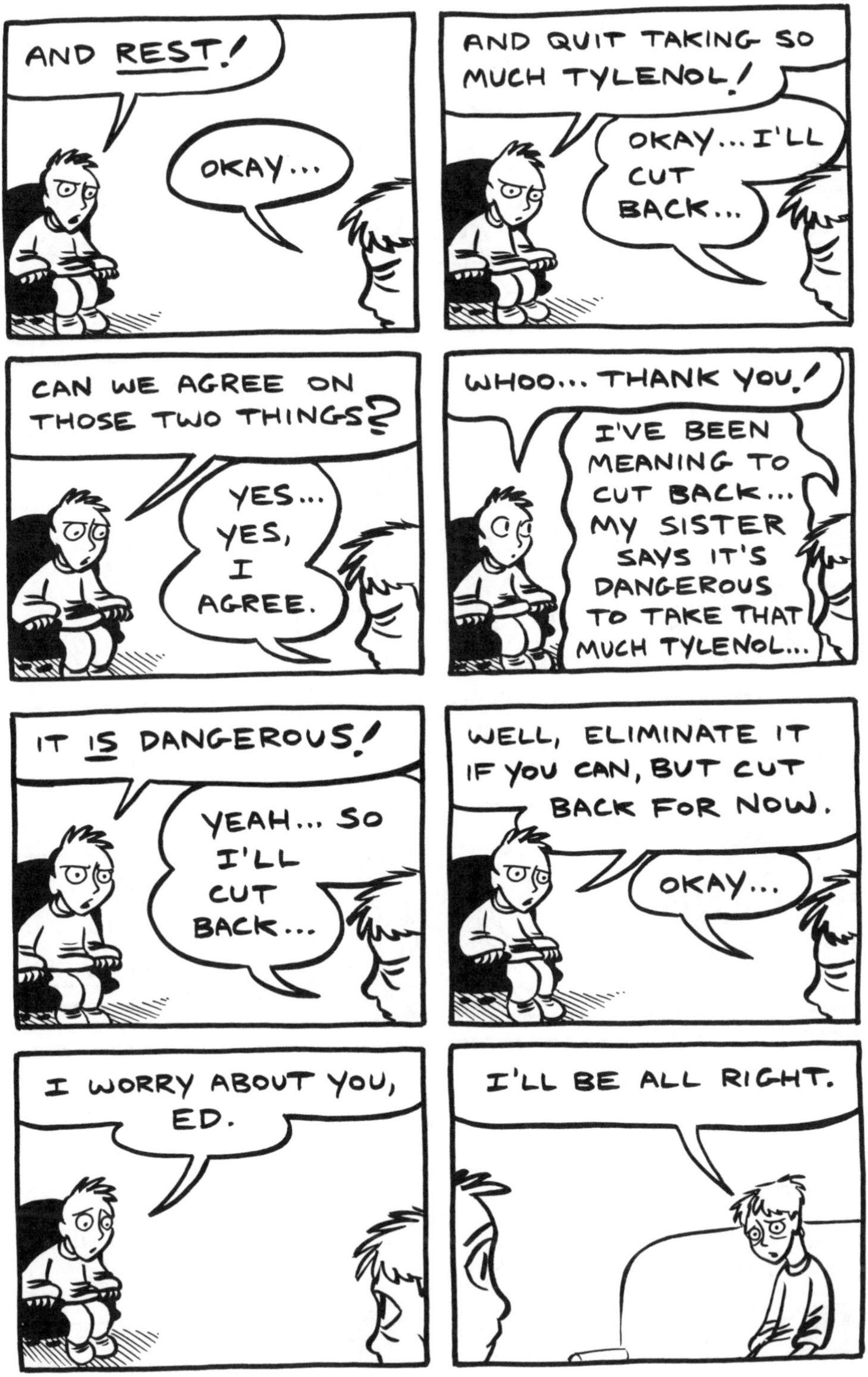
AND REST!
OKAY...
AND QUIT TAKING SO MUCH TYLENOL!
OKAY... I'LL CUT BACK...
CAN WE AGREE ON THOSE TWO THINGS?
YES... YES, I AGREE.
WHOO... THANK YOU!
I'VE BEEN MEANING TO CUT BACK... MY SISTER SAYS IT'S DANGEROUS TO TAKE THAT MUCH TYLENOL...
IT IS DANGEROUS!
YEAH... SO I'LL CUT BACK...
WELL, ELIMINATE IT IF YOU CAN, BUT CUT BACK FOR NOW.
OKAY...
I WORRY ABOUT YOU, ED.
I'LL BE ALL RIGHT.

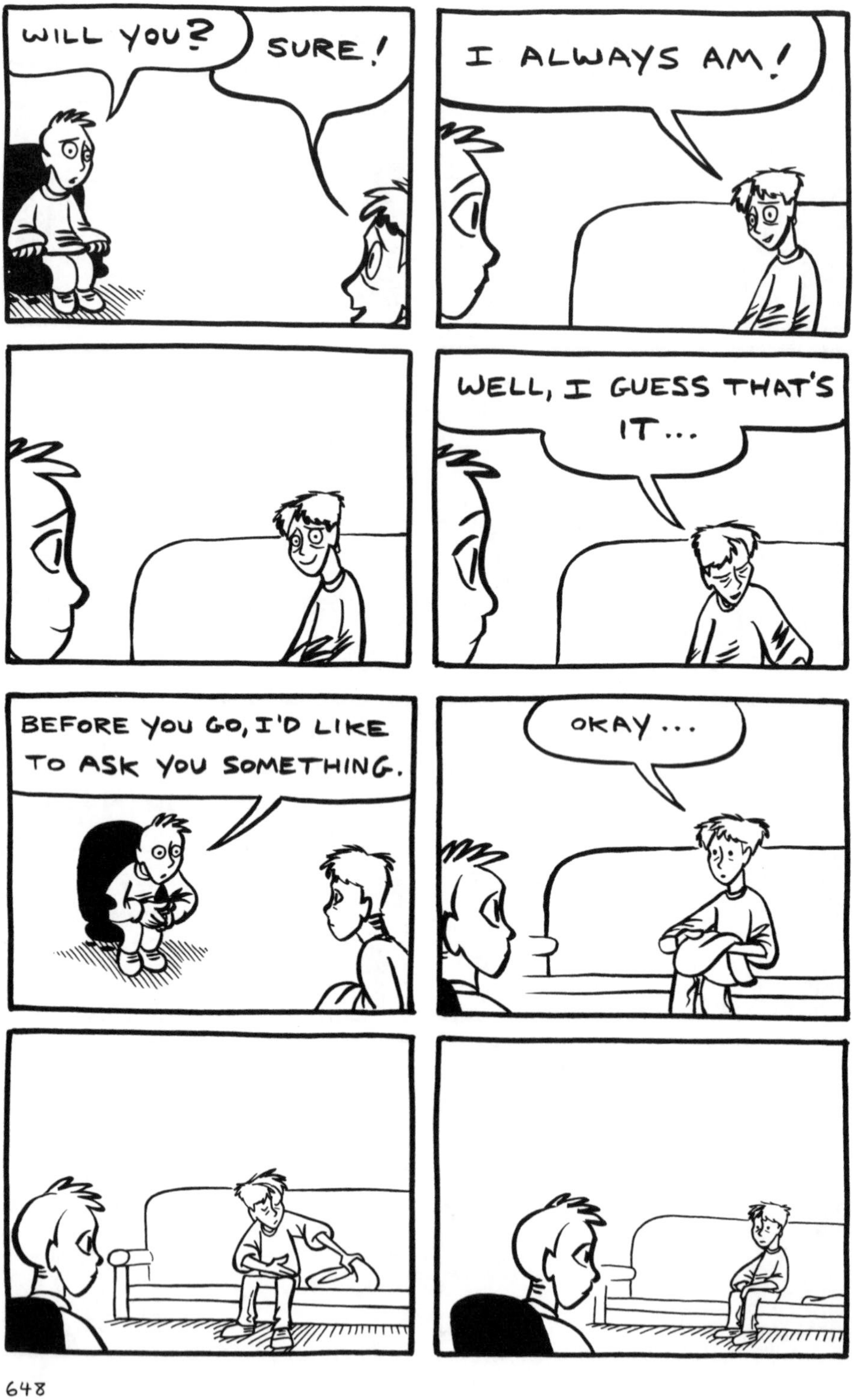
WILL YOU?
SURE!
I ALWAYS AM!
WELL, I GUESS THAT'S IT...
BEFORE YOU GO, I'D LIKE TO ASK YOU SOMETHING.
OKAY...

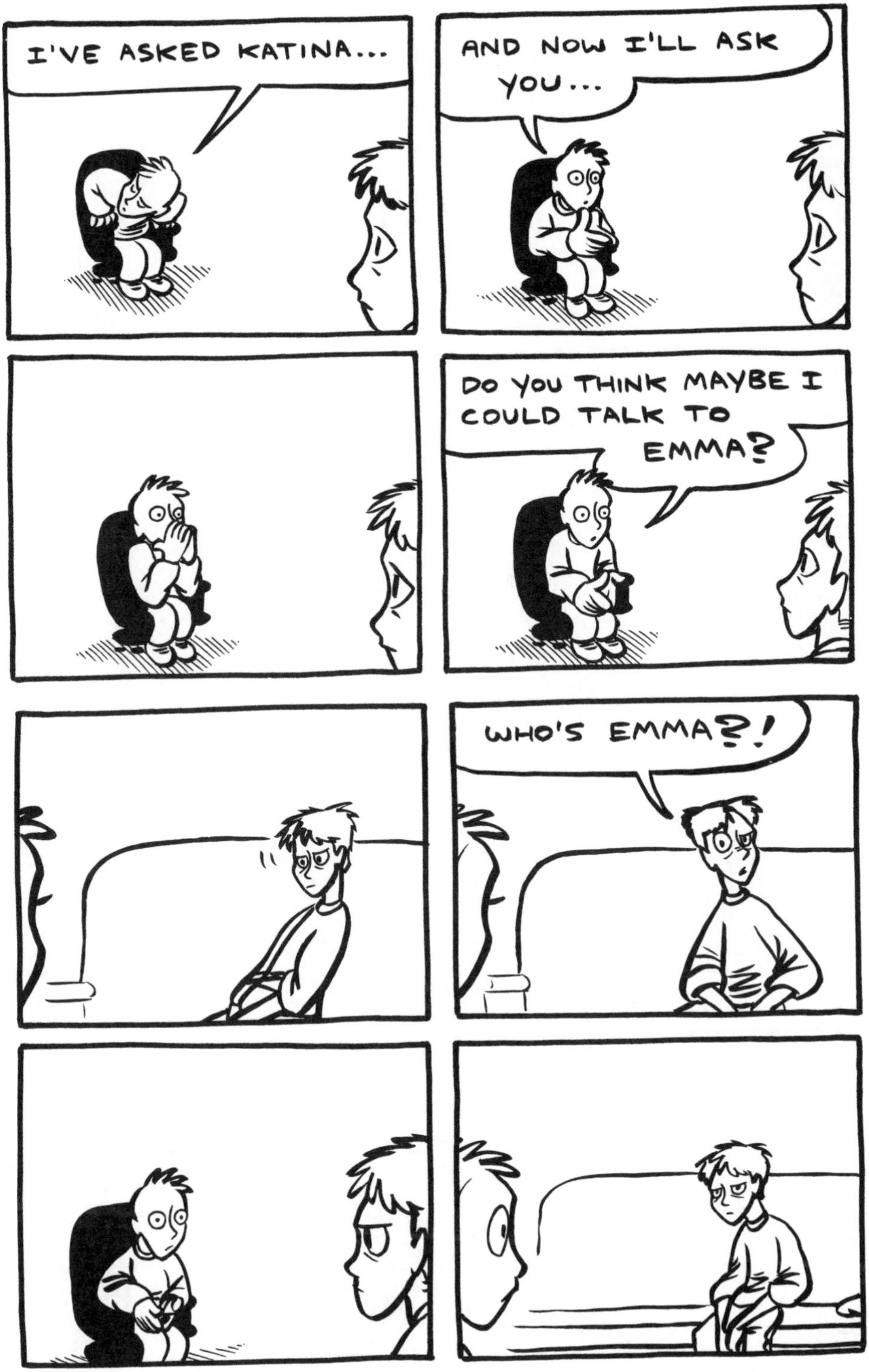
I'VE ASKED KATINA...
AND NOW I'LL ASK YOU...
DO YOU THINK MAYBE I COULD TALK TO EMMA?
WHO'S EMMA?!

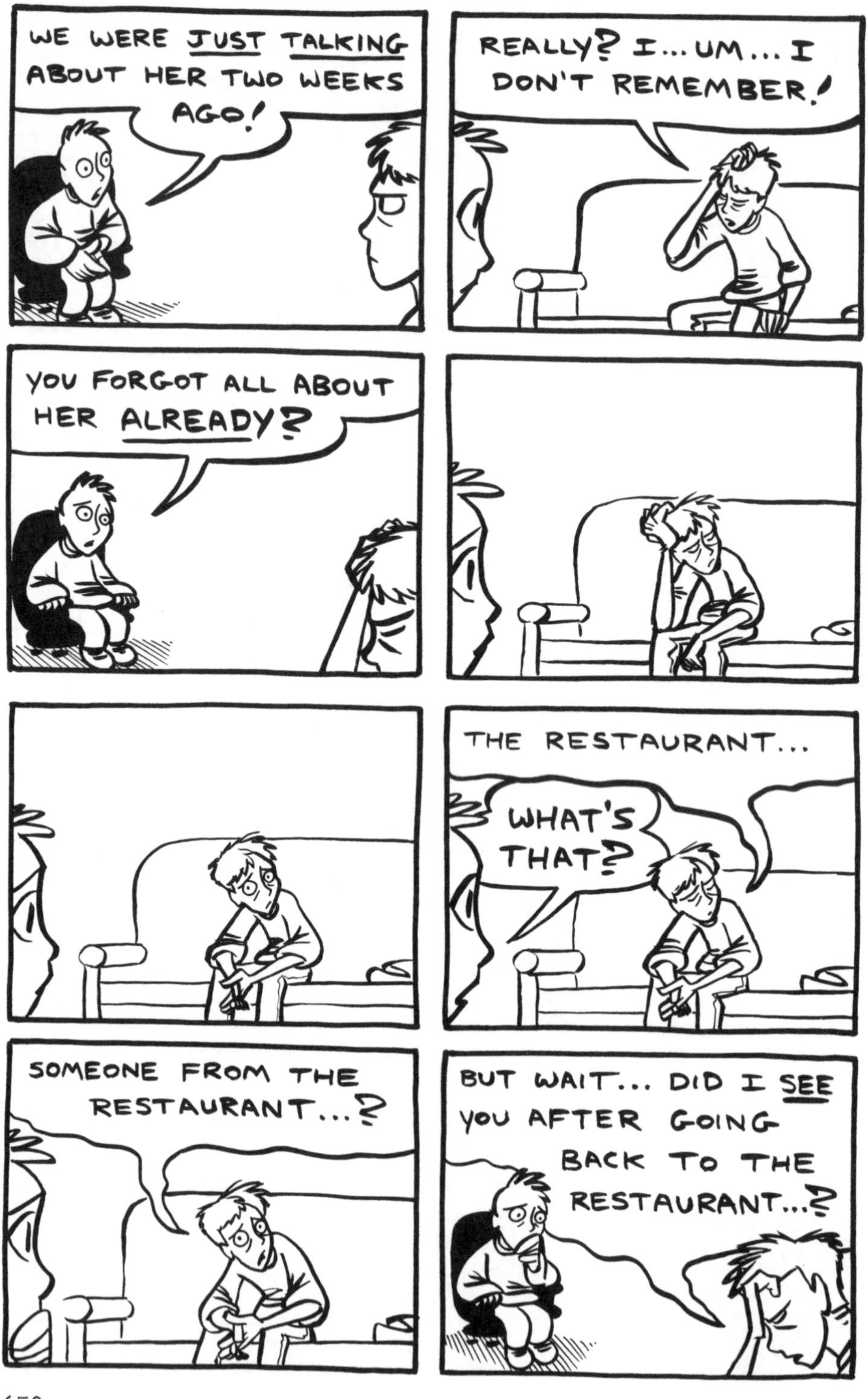
WE WERE JUST TALKING ABOUT HER TWO WEEKS AGO!
REALLY? I... UM... I DON'T REMEMBER!
YOU FORGOT ALL ABOUT HER ALREADY?
THE RESTAURANT...
WHAT'S THAT?
SOMEONE FROM THE RESTAURANT...?
BUT WAIT... DID I SEE YOU AFTER GOING BACK TO THE RESTAURANT...?

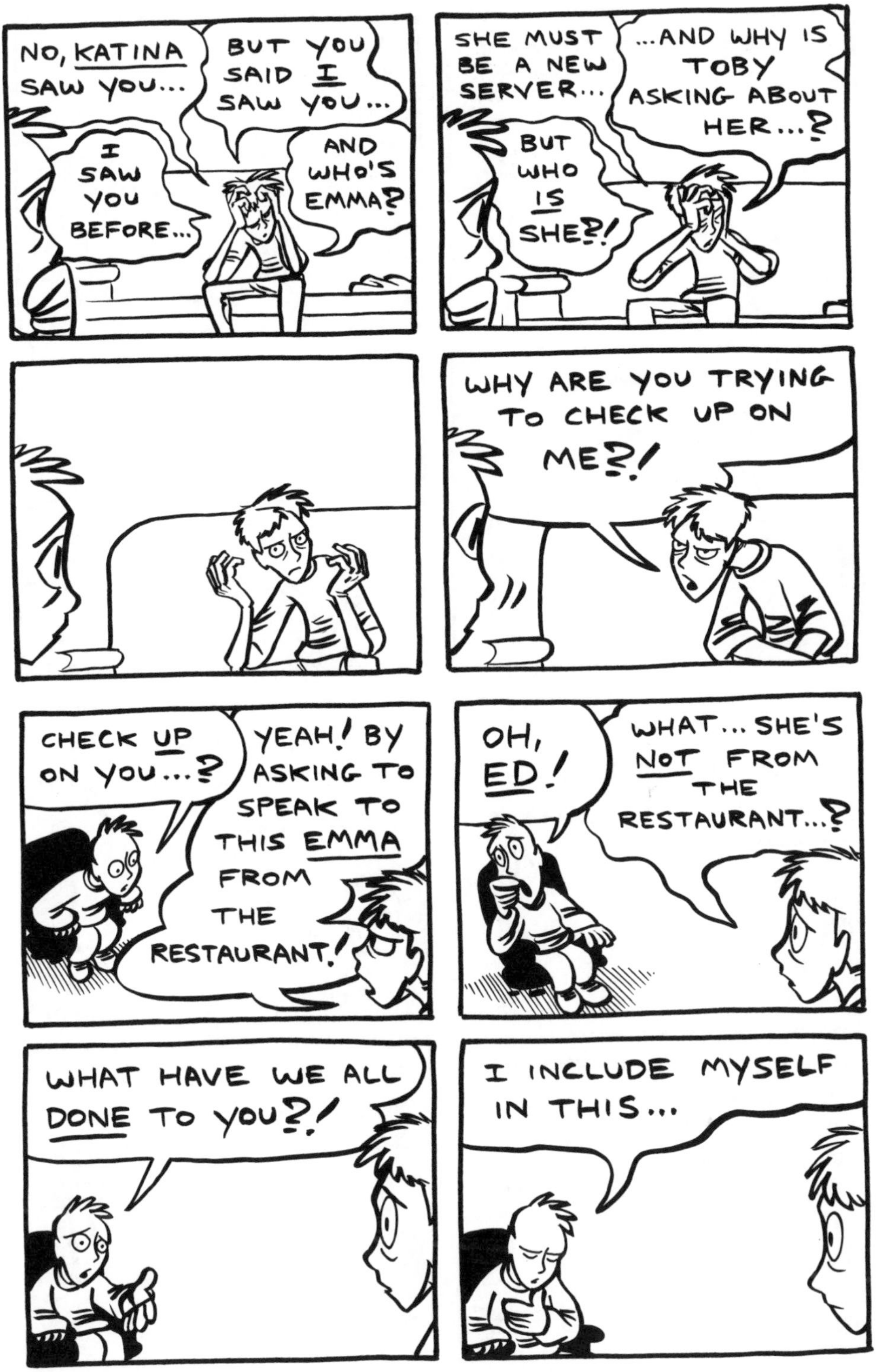
NO, KATINA SAW YOU...
BUT YOU SAID I SAW YOU...
I SAW YOU BEFORE...
AND WHO'S EMMA?
SHE MUST BE A NEW SERVER...
...AND WHY IS TOBY ASKING ABOUT HER...?
BUT WHO IS SHE?!
WHY ARE YOU TRYING TO CHECK UP ON ME?!
CHECK UP ON YOU...?
YEAH! BY ASKING TO SPEAK TO THIS EMMA FROM THE RESTAURANT!
OH, ED!
WHAT... SHE'S NOT FROM THE RESTAURANT...?
WHAT HAVE WE ALL DONE TO YOU?!
I INCLUDE MYSELF IN THIS...

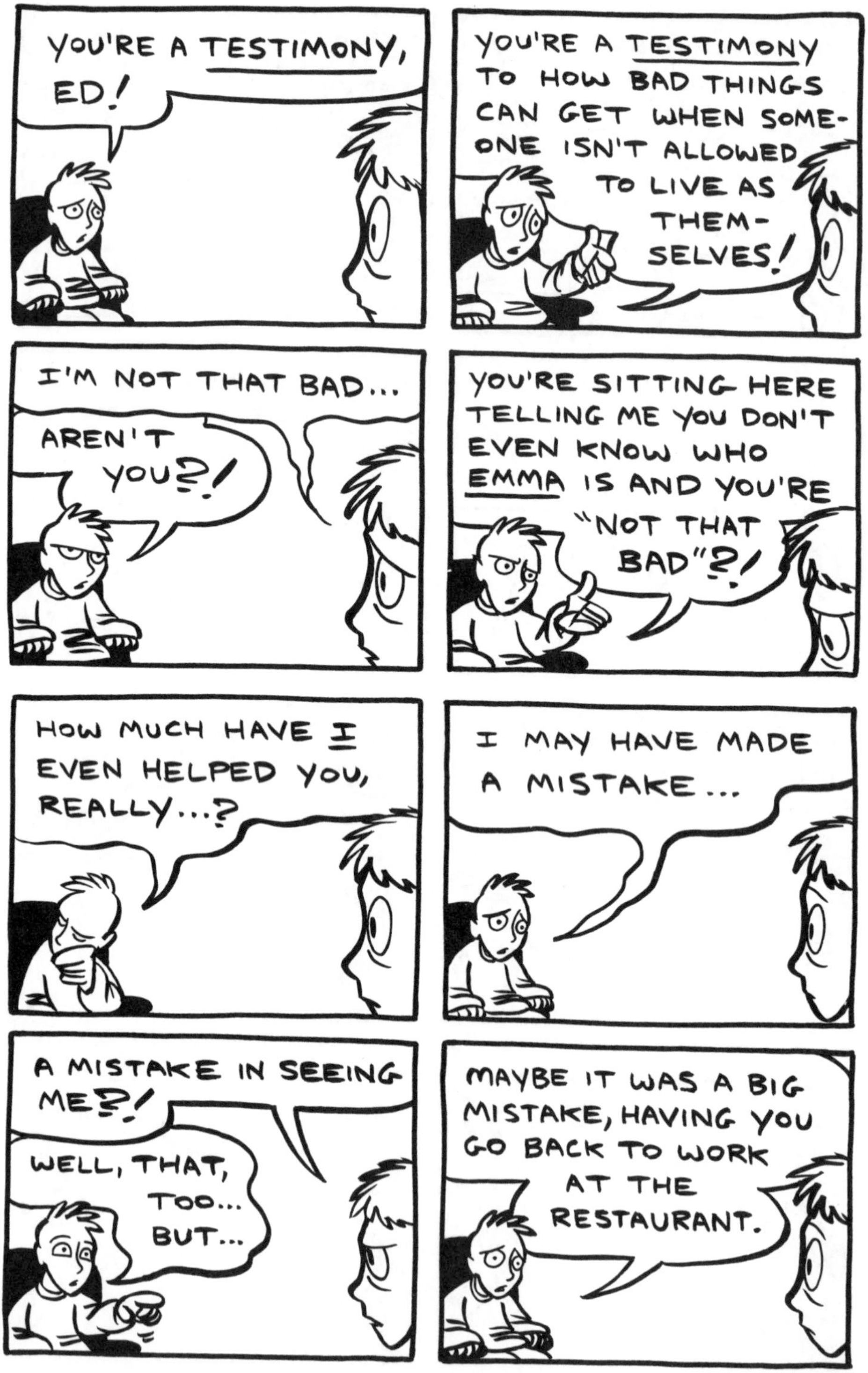
YOU'RE A TESTIMONY, ED!
YOU'RE A TESTIMONY TO HOW BAD THINGS CAN GET WHEN SOME-ONE ISN'T ALLOWED TO LIVE AS THEM-SELVES!
I'M NOT THAT BAD...
AREN'T YOU?!
YOU'RE SITTING HERE TELLING ME YOU DON'T EVEN KNOW WHO EMMA IS AND YOU'RE "NOT THAT BAD"?!
HOW MUCH HAVE I EVEN HELPED YOU, REALLY...?
I MAY HAVE MADE A MISTAKE...
A MISTAKE IN SEEING ME?!
WELL, THAT, TOO... BUT...
MAYBE IT WAS A BIG MISTAKE, HAVING YOU GO BACK TO WORK AT THE RESTAURANT.

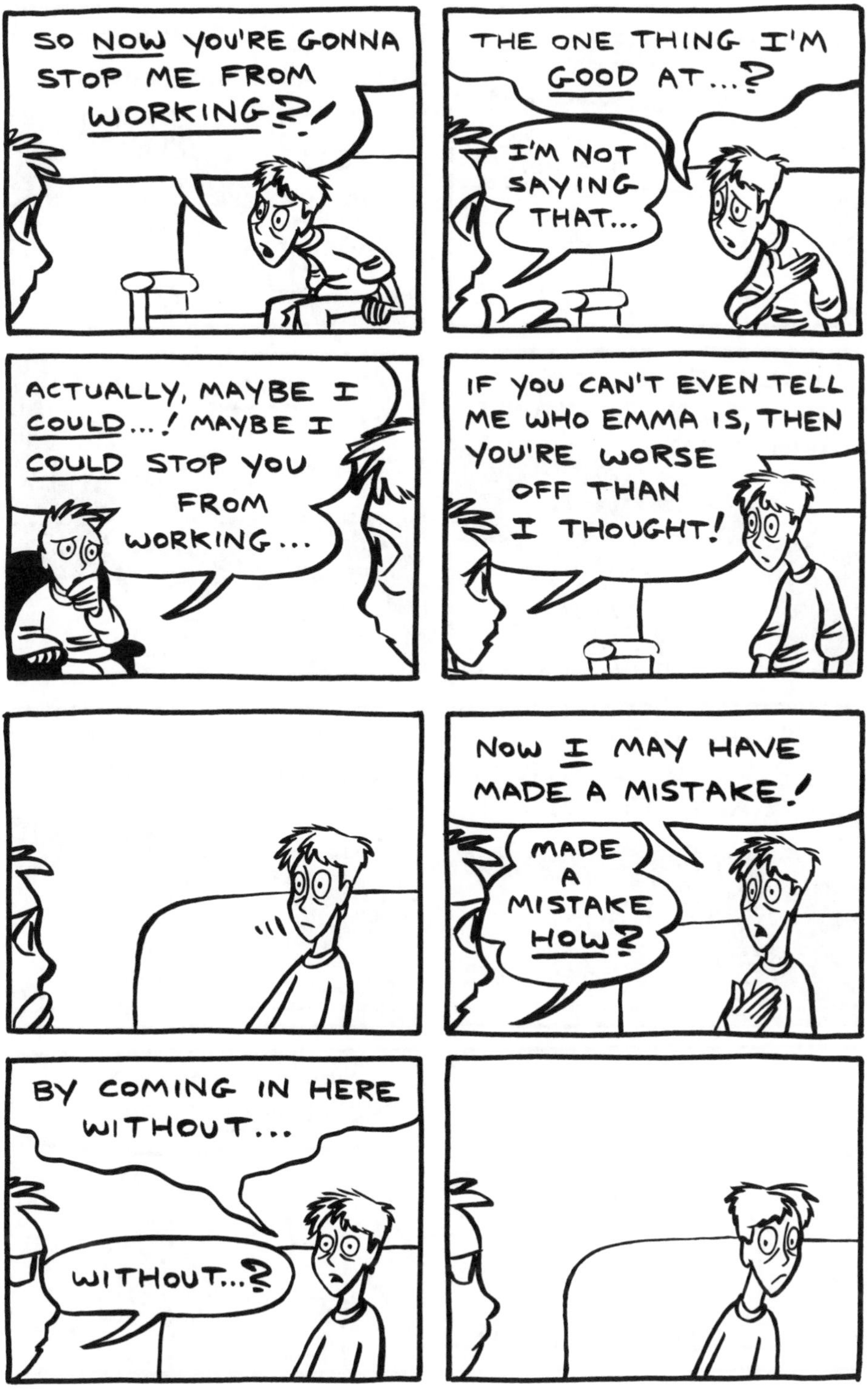
SO NOW YOU'RE GONNA STOP ME FROM WORKING?!
THE ONE THING I'M GOOD AT...?
I'M NOT SAYING THAT...
ACTUALLY, MAYBE I COULD...! MAYBE I COULD STOP YOU FROM WORKING...
IF YOU CAN'T EVEN TELL ME WHO EMMA IS, THEN YOU'RE WORSE OFF THAN I THOUGHT!
NOW I MAY HAVE MADE A MISTAKE!
MADE A MISTAKE HOW?
BY COMING IN HERE WITHOUT...
WITHOUT...?

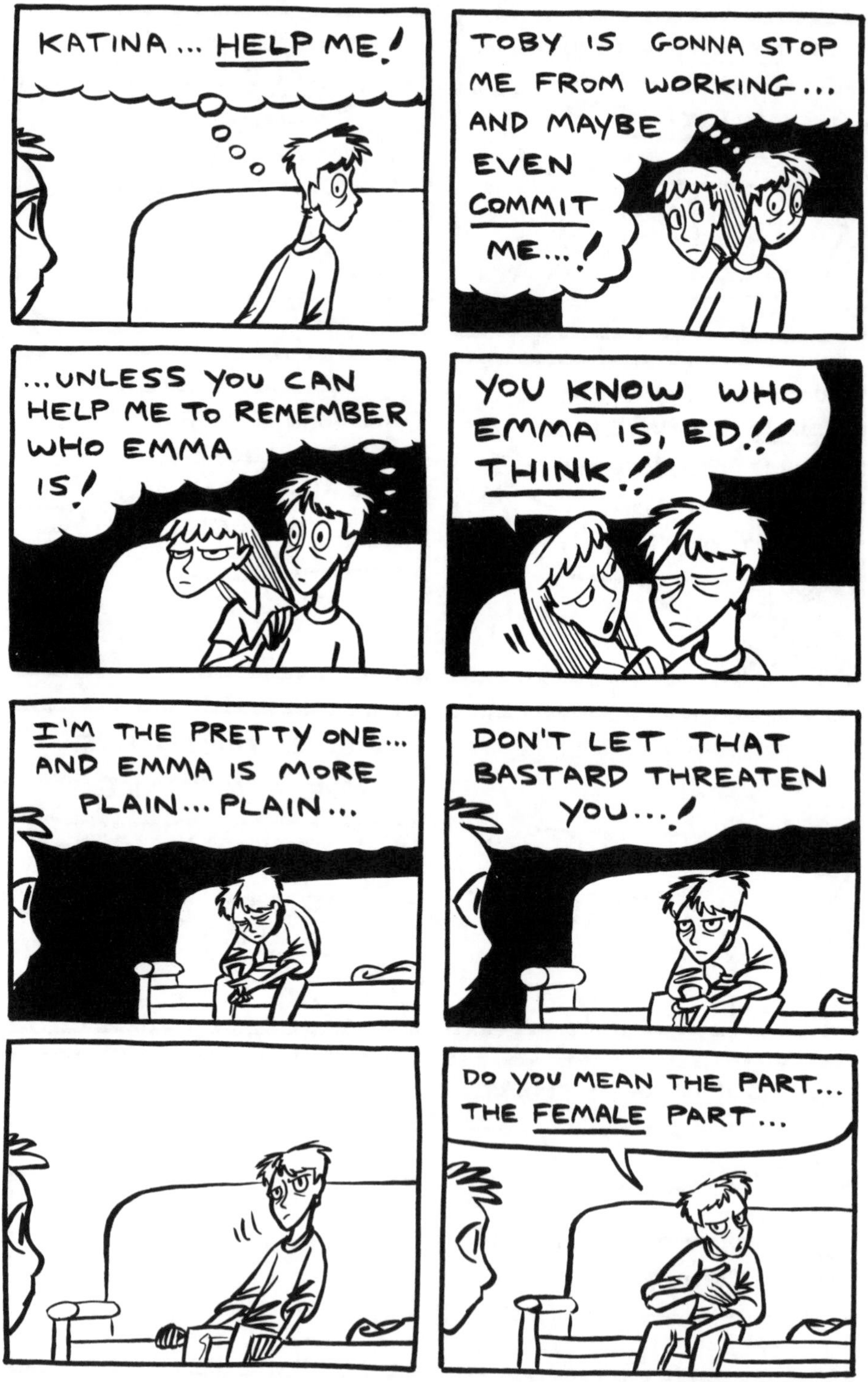
KATINA... HELP ME!
TOBY IS GONNA STOP ME FROM WORKING... AND MAYBE EVEN COMMIT ME...!
...UNLESS YOU CAN HELP ME TO REMEMBER WHO EMMA IS!
YOU KNOW WHO EMMA IS, ED!! THINK!!
I'M THE PRETTY ONE... AND EMMA IS MORE PLAIN... PLAIN...
DON'T LET THAT BASTARD THREATEN YOU...!
DO YOU MEAN THE PART... THE FEMALE PART...

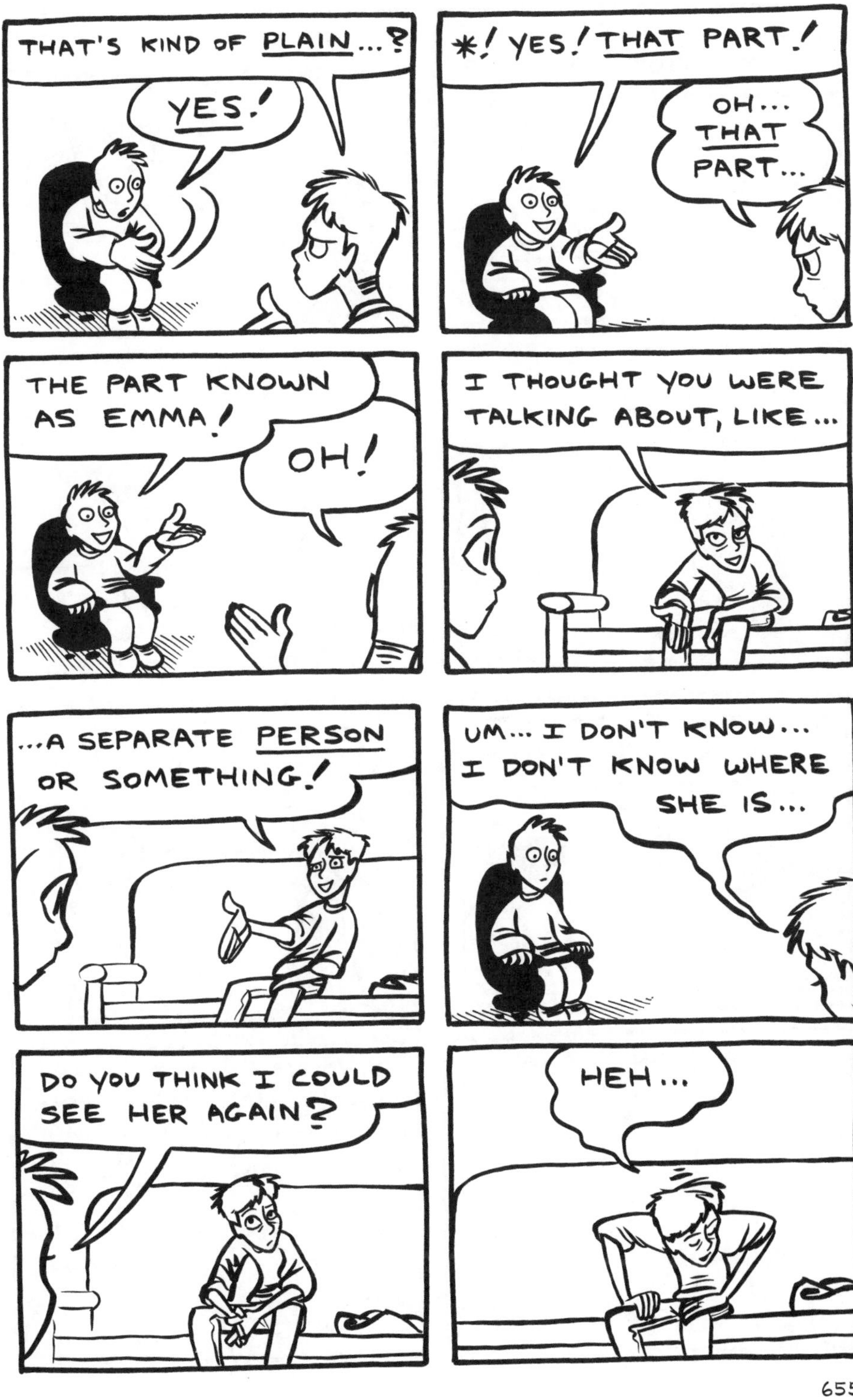
THAT'S KIND OF PLAIN...?
YES!
*! YES! THAT PART!
OH... THAT PART...
THE PART KNOWN AS EMMA!
OH!
I THOUGHT YOU WERE TALKING ABOUT, LIKE...
...A SEPARATE PERSON OR SOMETHING!
UM... I DON'T KNOW... I DON'T KNOW WHERE SHE IS...
DO YOU THINK I COULD SEE HER AGAIN?
HEH...

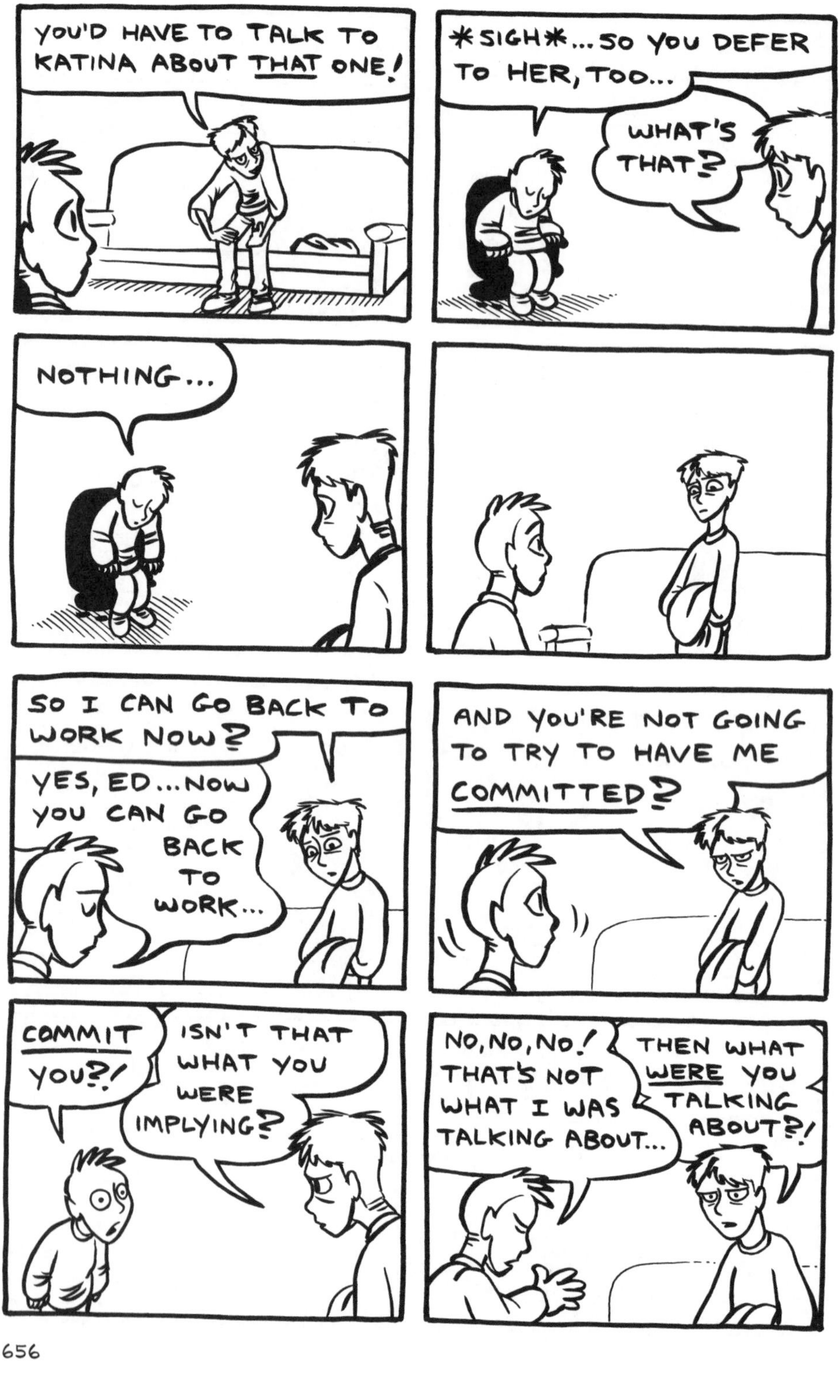
YOU'D HAVE TO TALK TO KATINA ABOUT THAT ONE!
SIGH... SO YOU DEFER TO HER, TOO...
WHAT'S THAT?
NOTHING...
SO I CAN GO BACK TO WORK NOW?
YES, ED... NOW YOU CAN GO BACK TO WORK...
AND YOU'RE NOT GOING TO TRY TO HAVE ME COMMITTED?
COMMIT YOU?!
ISN'T THAT WHAT YOU WERE IMPLYING?
NO, NO, NO! THAT'S NOT WHAT I WAS TALKING ABOUT...
THEN WHAT WERE YOU TALKING ABOUT?!

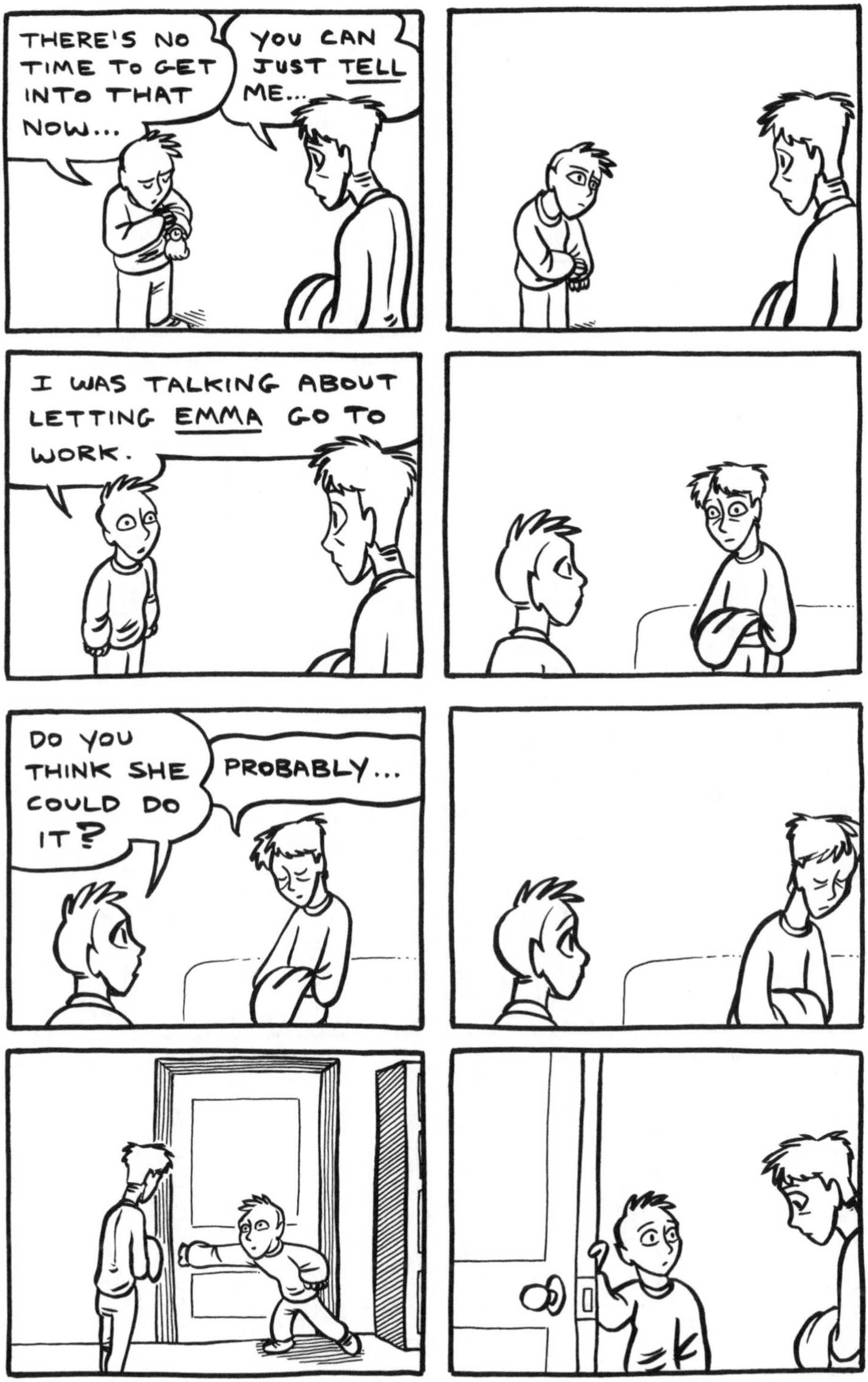
THERE'S NO TIME TO GET INTO THAT NOW...
YOU CAN JUST TELL ME...
I WAS TALKING ABOUT LETTING EMMA GO TO WORK.
DO YOU THINK SHE COULD DO IT?
PROBABLY...

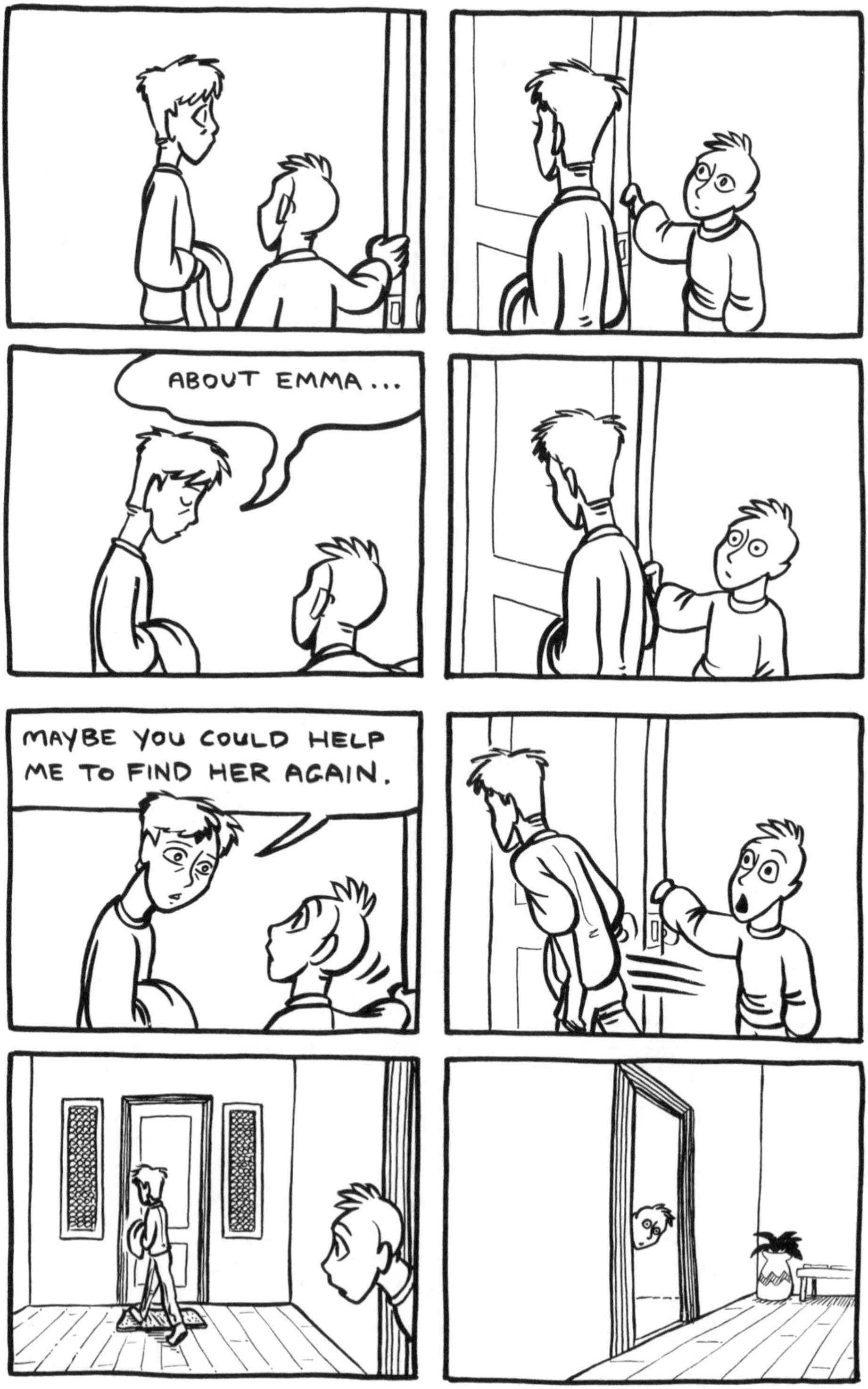
ABOUT EMMA...
MAYBE YOU COULD HELP ME TO FIND HER AGAIN.

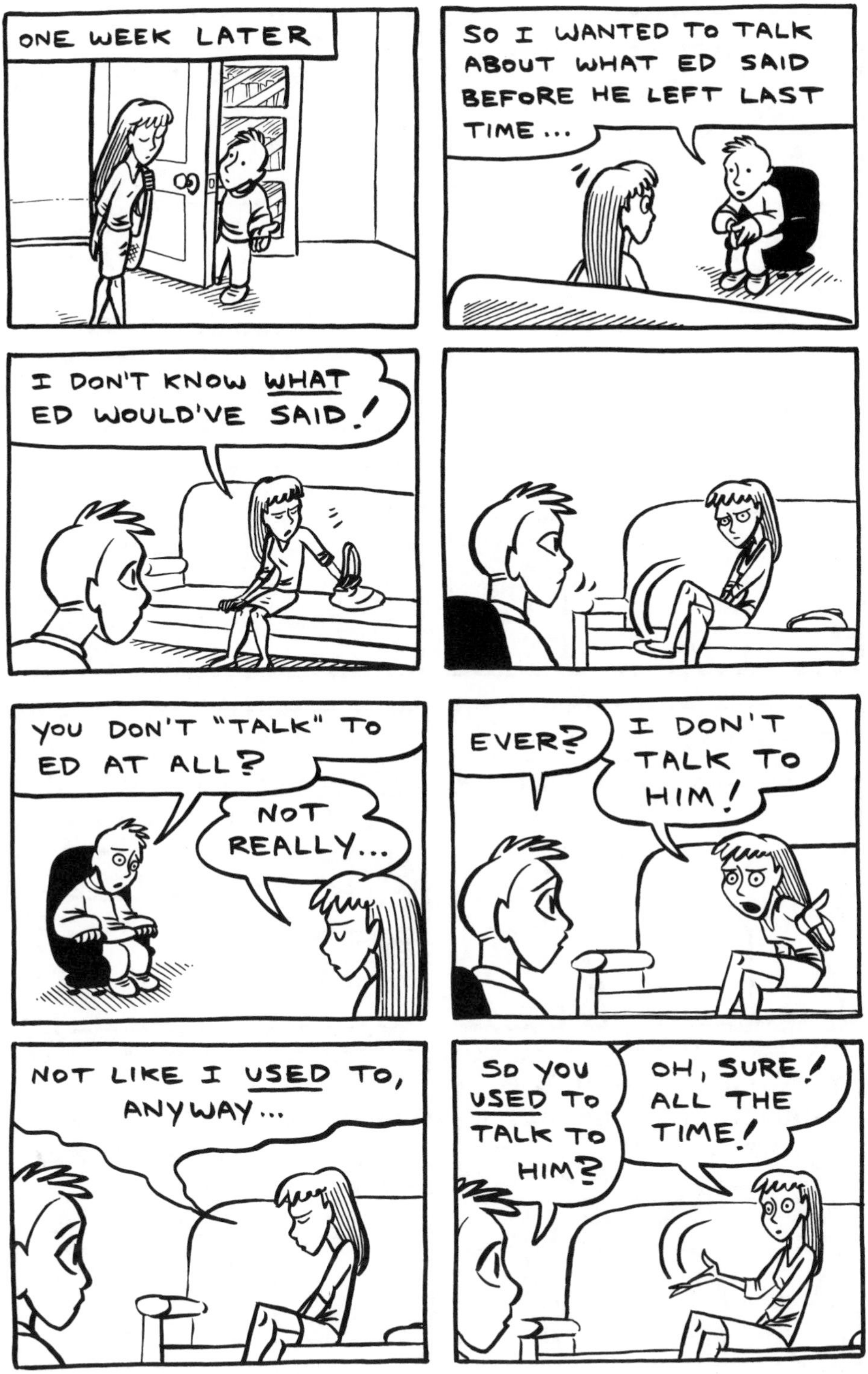
ONE WEEK LATER
SO I WANTED TO TALK ABOUT WHAT ED SAID BEFORE HE LEFT LAST TIME...
I DON'T KNOW WHAT ED WOULD'VE SAID!
YOU DON'T "TALK" TO ED AT ALL?
NOT REALLY...
EVER?
I DON'T TALK TO HIM!
NOT LIKE I USED TO, ANYWAY...
SO YOU USED TO TALK TO HIM?
OH, SURE! ALL THE TIME!

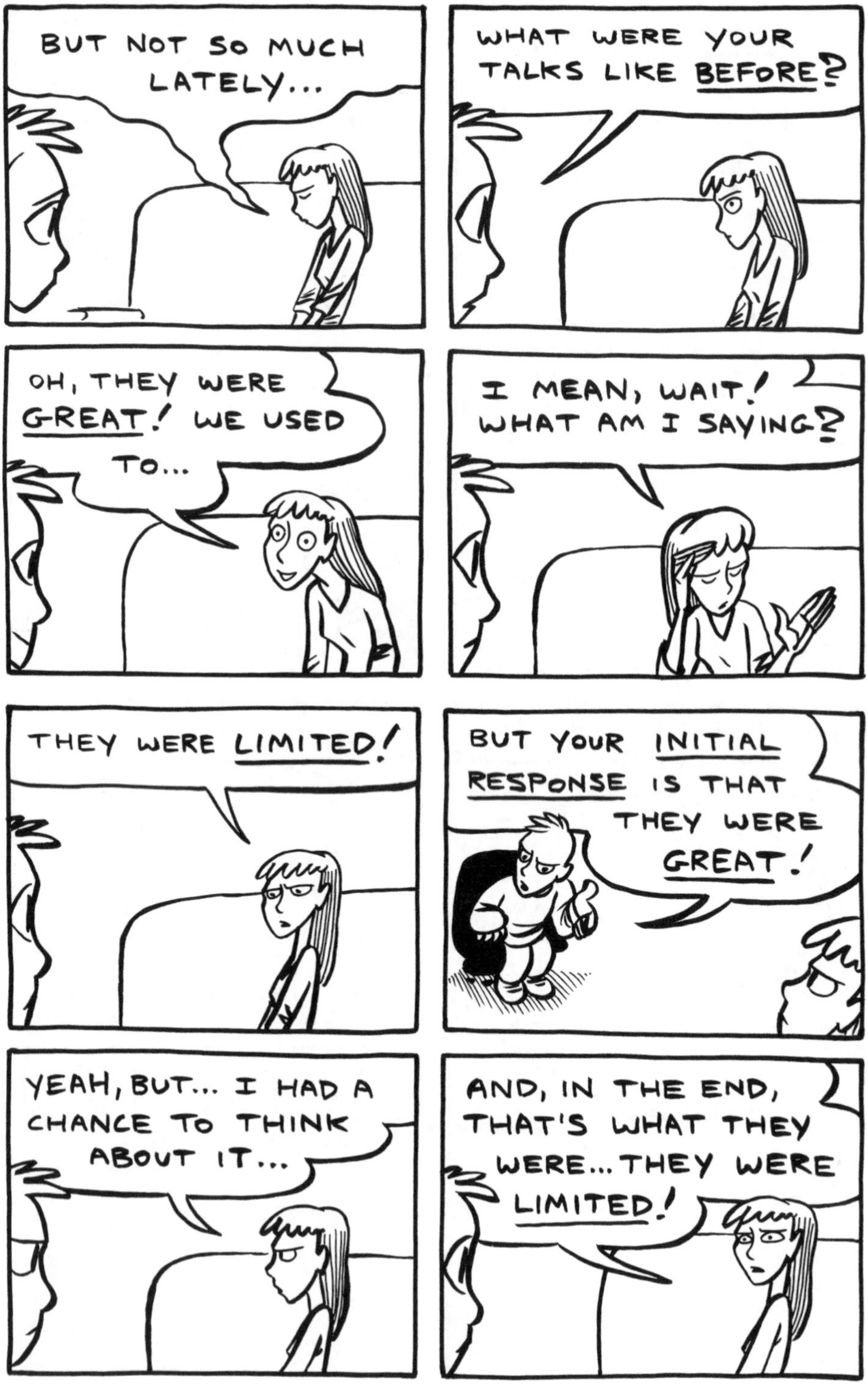
BUT NOT SO MUCH LATELY...
WHAT WERE YOUR TALKS LIKE BEFORE?
OH, THEY WERE GREAT! WE USED TO...
I MEAN, WAIT! WHAT AM I SAYING?
THEY WERE LIMITED!
BUT YOUR INITIAL RESPONSE IS THAT THEY WERE GREAT!
YEAH, BUT... I HAD A CHANCE TO THINK ABOUT IT...
AND, IN THE END, THAT'S WHAT THEY WERE... THEY WERE LIMITED!

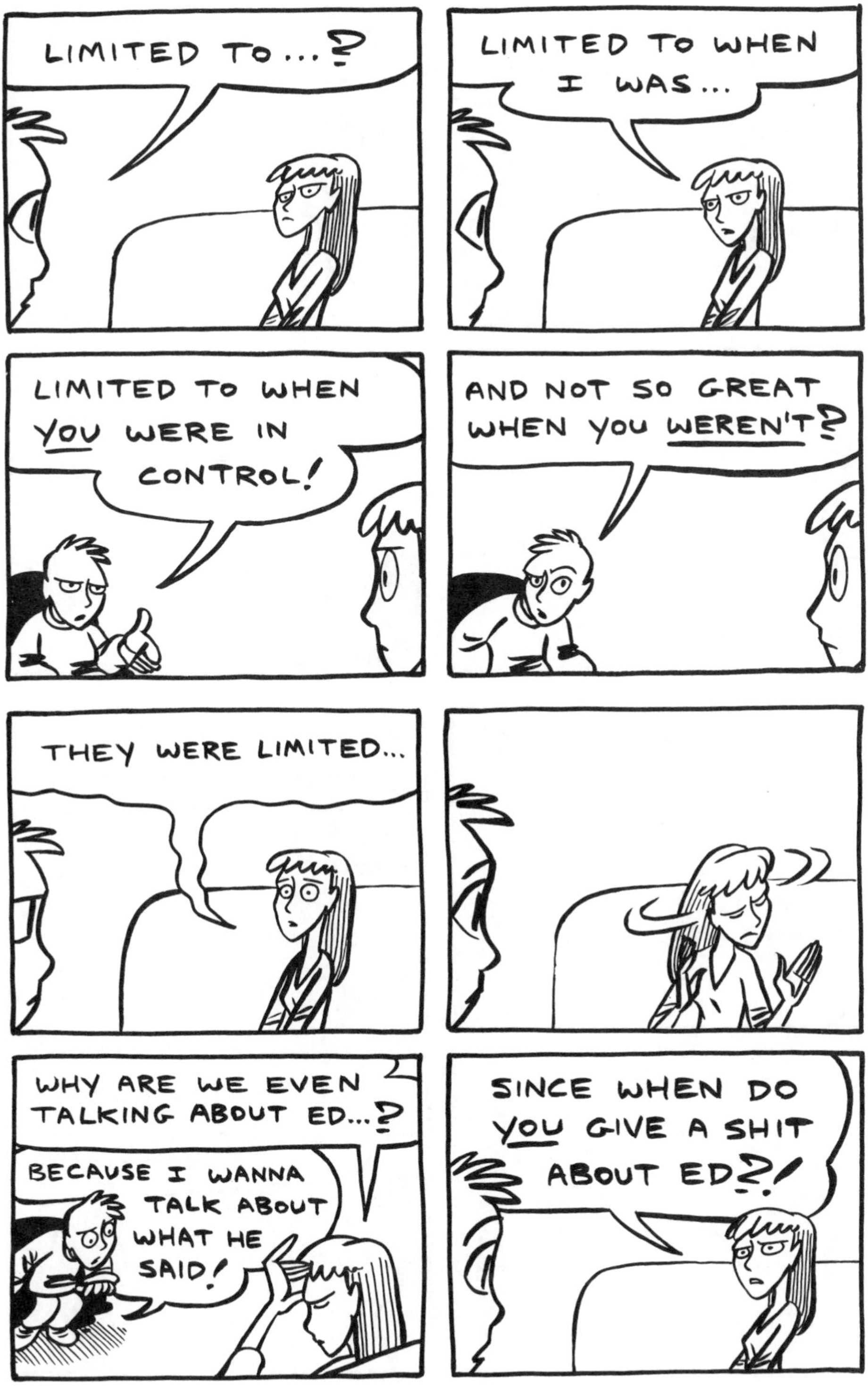
LIMITED TO...?
LIMITED TO WHEN I WAS...
LIMITED TO WHEN YOU WERE IN CONTROL!
AND NOT SO GREAT WHEN YOU WEREN'T?
THEY WERE LIMITED...
WHY ARE WE EVEN TALKING ABOUT ED...?
BECAUSE I WANNA TALK ABOUT WHAT HE SAID!
SINCE WHEN DO YOU GIVE A SHIT ABOUT ED?!

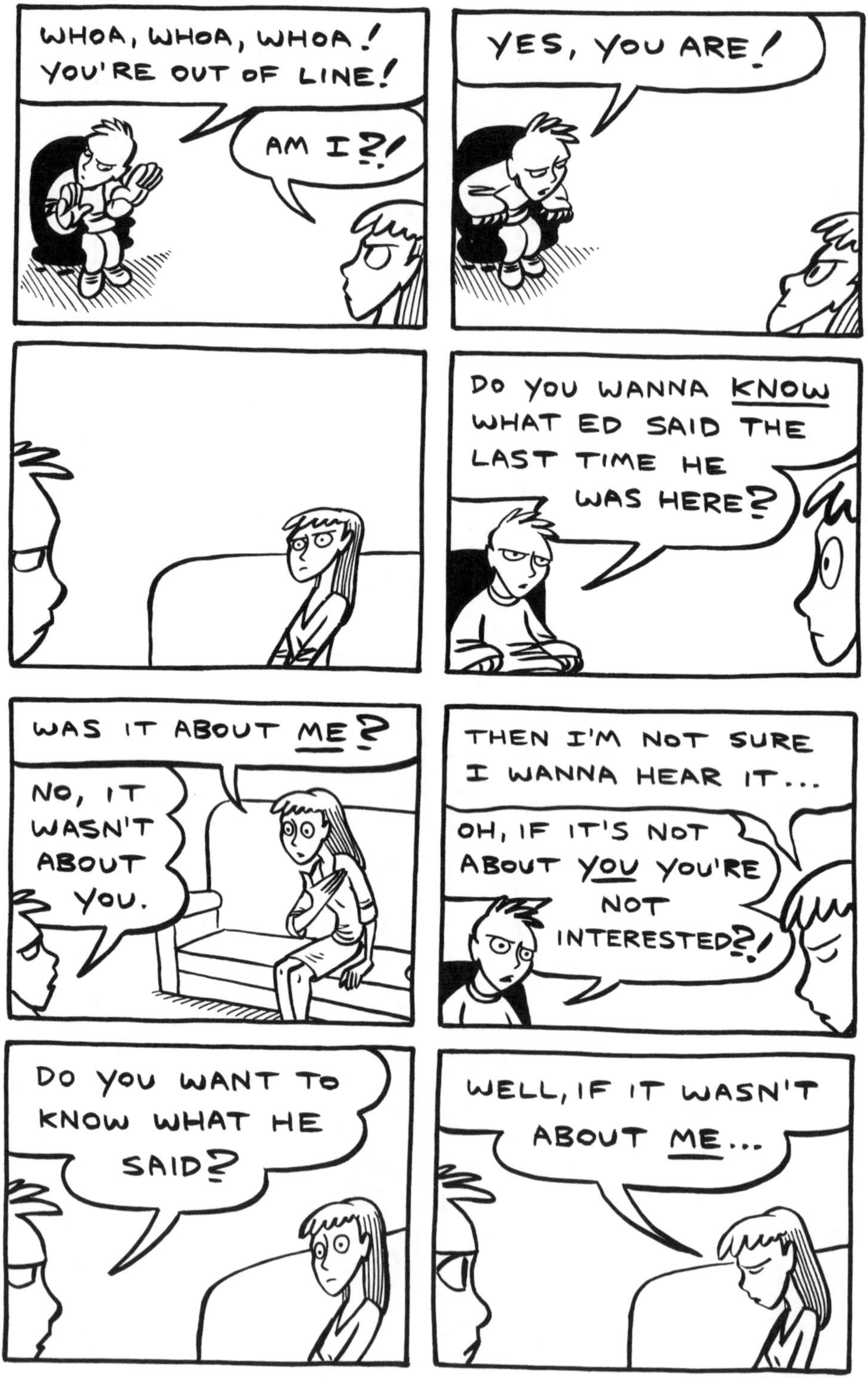
WHOA, WHOA, WHOA! YOU'RE OUT OF LINE!
AM I?!
YES, YOU ARE!
DO YOU WANNA KNOW WHAT ED SAID THE LAST TIME HE WAS HERE?
WAS IT ABOUT ME?
NO, IT WASN'T ABOUT YOU.
THEN I'M NOT SURE I WANNA HEAR IT...
OH, IF IT'S NOT ABOUT YOU YOU'RE NOT INTERESTED?!
DO YOU WANT TO KNOW WHAT HE SAID?
WELL, IF IT WASN'T ABOUT ME...

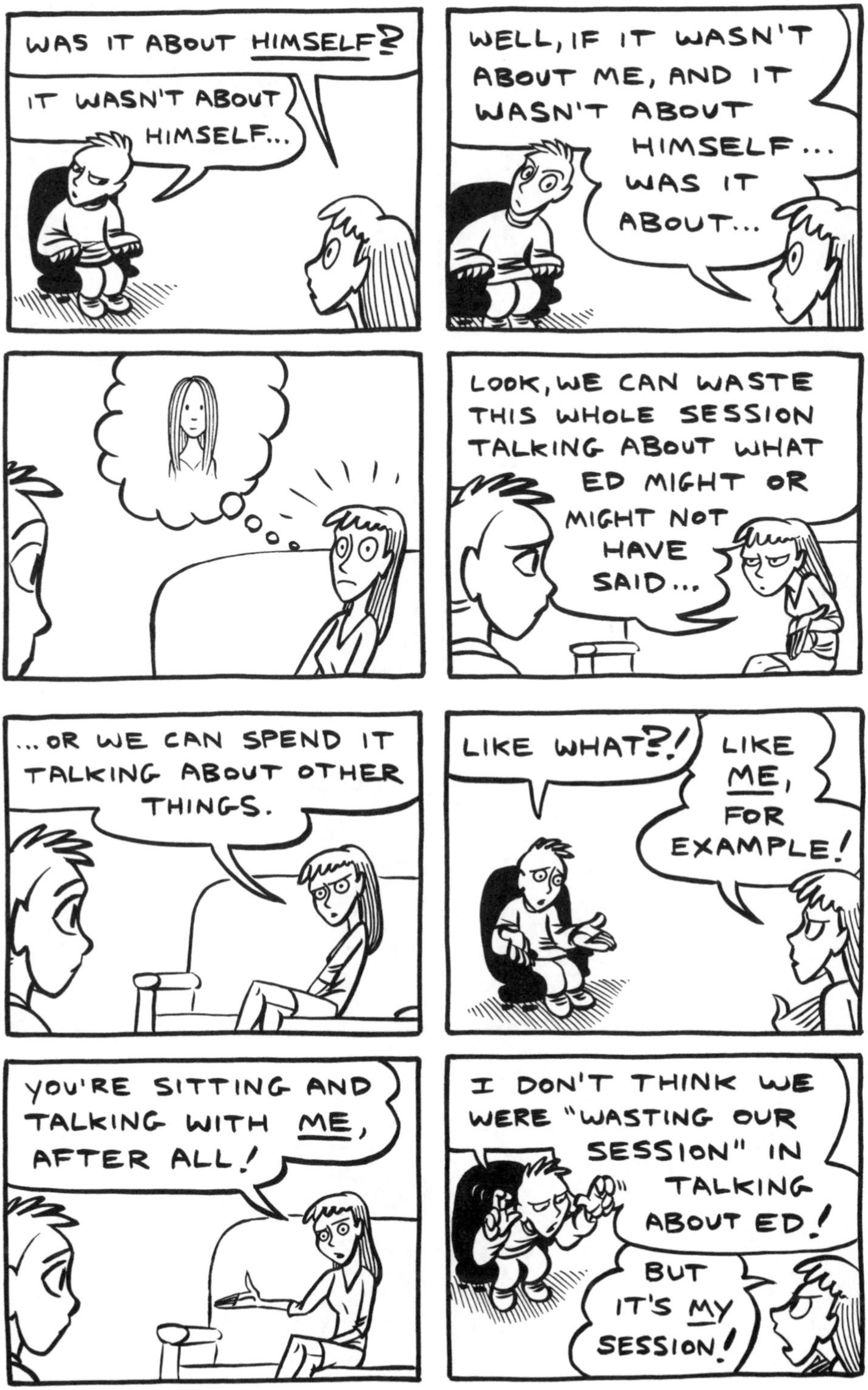
WAS IT ABOUT HIMSELF?
IT WASN'T ABOUT HIMSELF...
WELL, IF IT WASN'T ABOUT ME, AND IT WASN'T ABOUT HIMSELF... WAS IT ABOUT...
LOOK, WE CAN WASTE THIS WHOLE SESSION TALKING ABOUT WHAT ED MIGHT OR MIGHT NOT HAVE SAID...
...OR WE CAN SPEND IT TALKING ABOUT OTHER THINGS.
LIKE WHAT?!
LIKE ME, FOR EXAMPLE!
YOU'RE SITTING AND TALKING WITH ME, AFTER ALL!
I DON'T THINK WE WERE "WASTING OUR SESSION" IN TALKING ABOUT ED!
BUT IT'S MY SESSION!

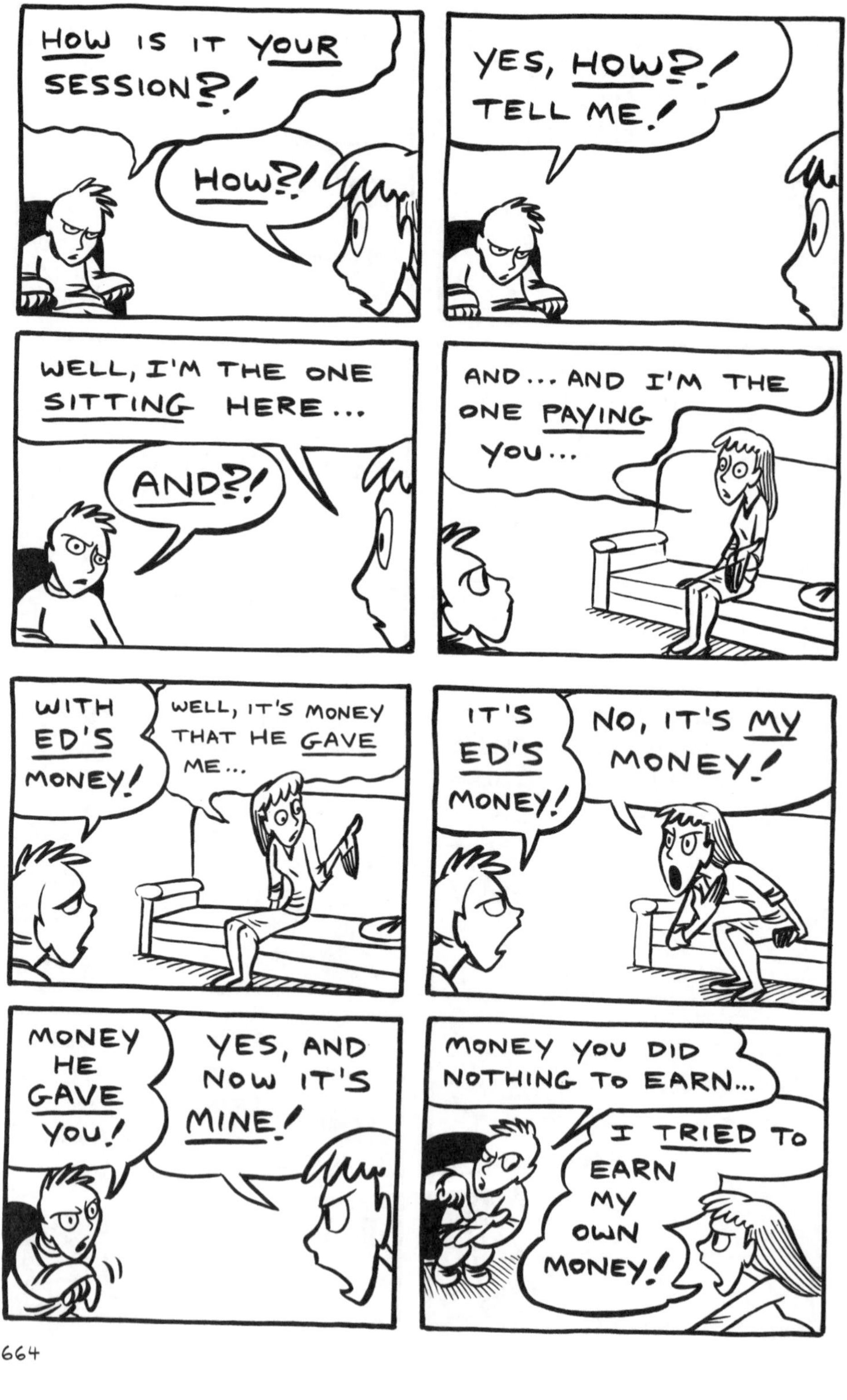
HOW IS IT YOUR SESSION?!
HOW?!
YES, HOW?! TELL ME!
WELL, I'M THE ONE SITTING HERE...
AND?!
AND... AND I'M THE ONE PAYING YOU...
WITH ED'S MONEY!
WELL, IT'S MONEY THAT HE GAVE ME...
IT'S ED'S MONEY!
NO, IT'S MY MONEY!
MONEY HE GAVE YOU!
YES, AND NOW IT'S MINE!
MONEY YOU DID NOTHING TO EARN...
I TRIED TO EARN MY OWN MONEY!

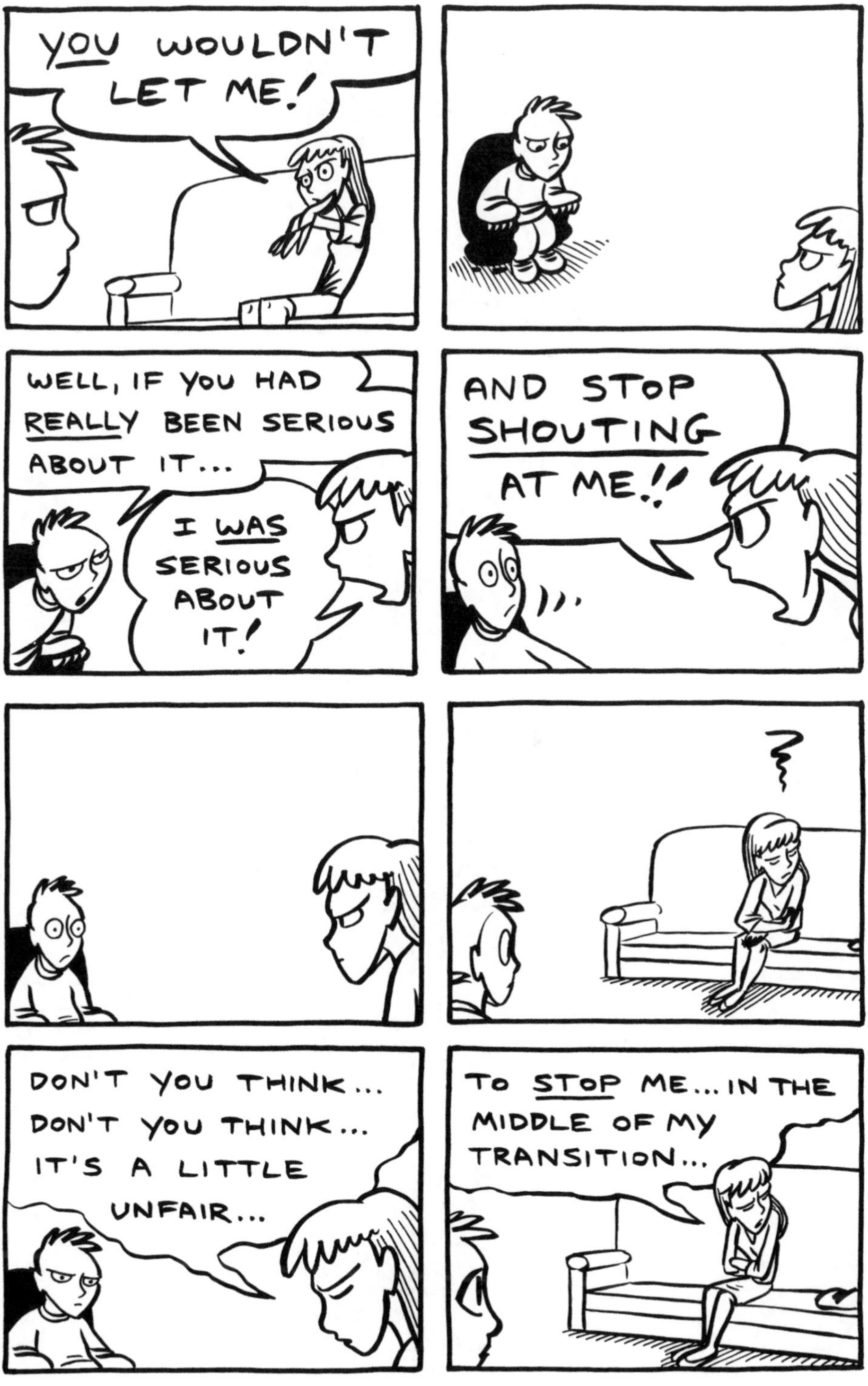
YOU WOULDN'T LET ME!
WELL, IF YOU HAD REALLY BEEN SERIOUS ABOUT IT...
I WAS SERIOUS ABOUT IT!
AND STOP SHOUTING AT ME!!
DON'T YOU THINK... DON'T YOU THINK... IT'S A LITTLE UNFAIR...
TO STOP ME... IN THE MIDDLE OF MY TRANSITION...

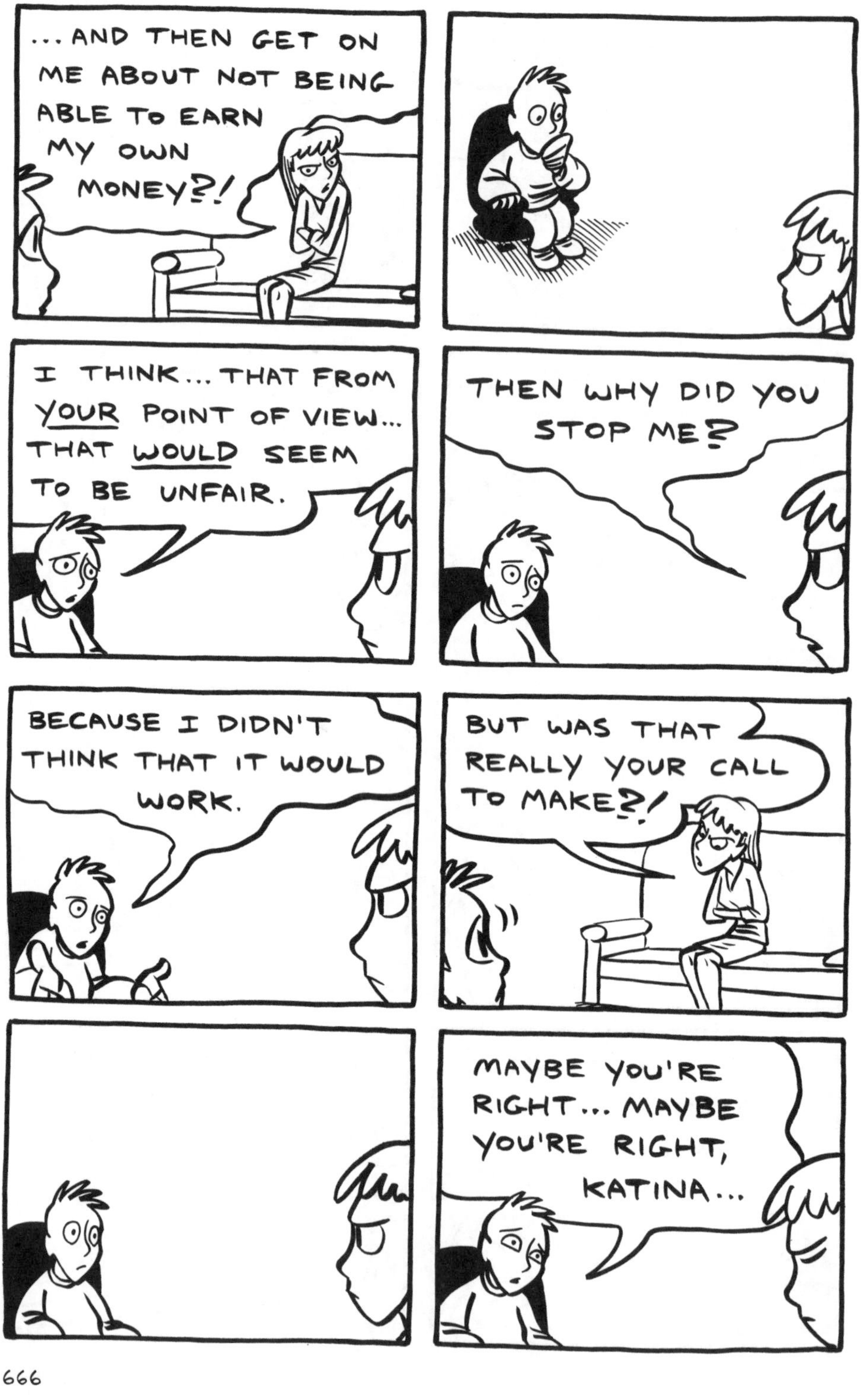
...AND THEN GET ON ME ABOUT NOT BEING ABLE TO EARN MY OWN MONEY?!
I THINK... THAT FROM YOUR POINT OF VIEW... THAT WOULD SEEM TO BE UNFAIR.
THEN WHY DID YOU STOP ME?
BECAUSE I DIDN'T THINK THAT IT WOULD WORK.
BUT WAS THAT REALLY YOUR CALL TO MAKE?!
MAYBE YOU'RE RIGHT... MAYBE YOU'RE RIGHT, KATINA...

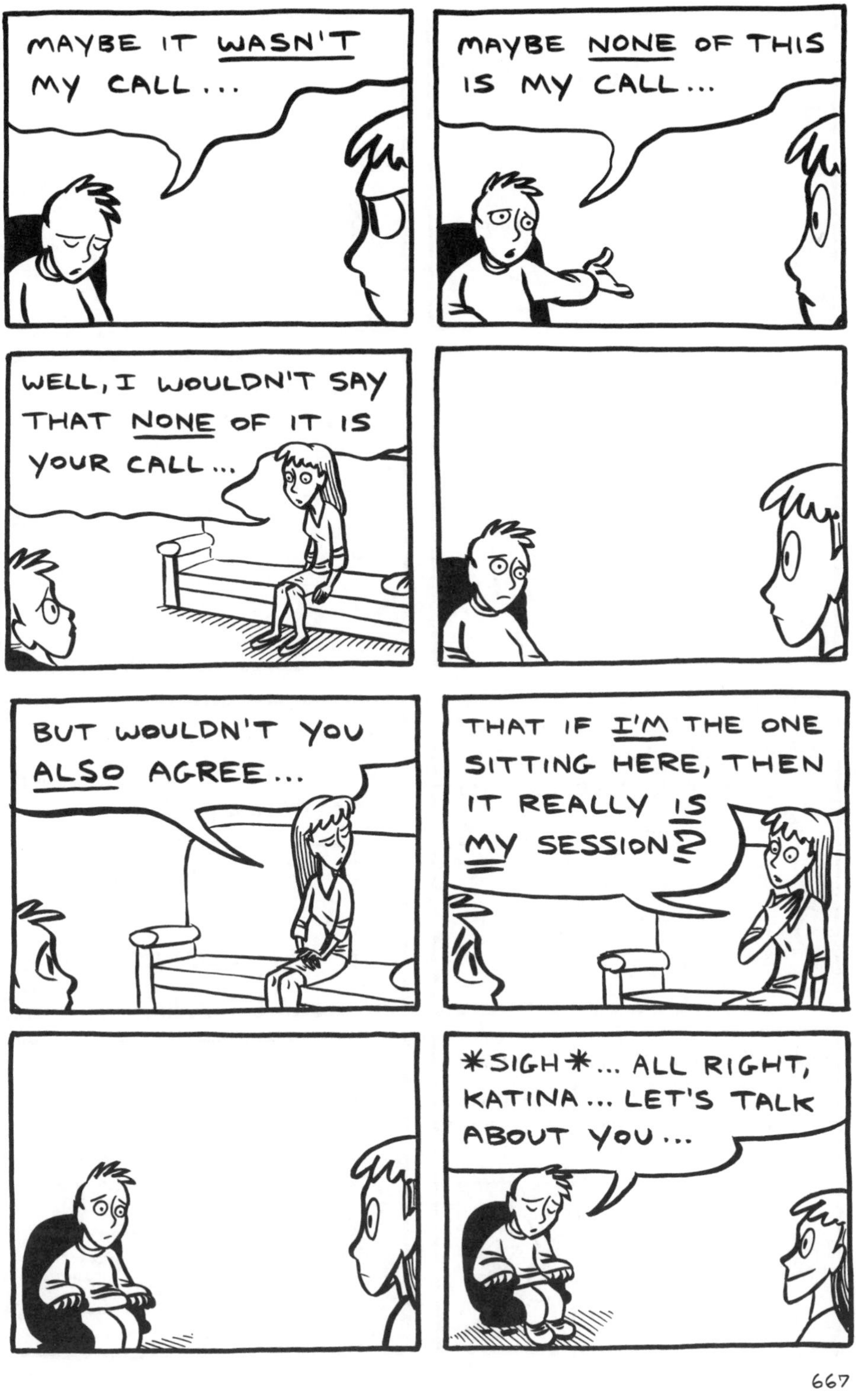
MAYBE IT WASN'T MY CALL...
MAYBE NONE OF THIS IS MY CALL...
WELL, I WOULDN'T SAY THAT NONE OF IT IS YOUR CALL...
BUT WOULDN'T YOU ALSO AGREE...
THAT IF I'M THE ONE SITTING HERE, THEN IT REALLY IS MY SESSION?
SIGH... ALL RIGHT, KATINA... LET'S TALK ABOUT YOU...

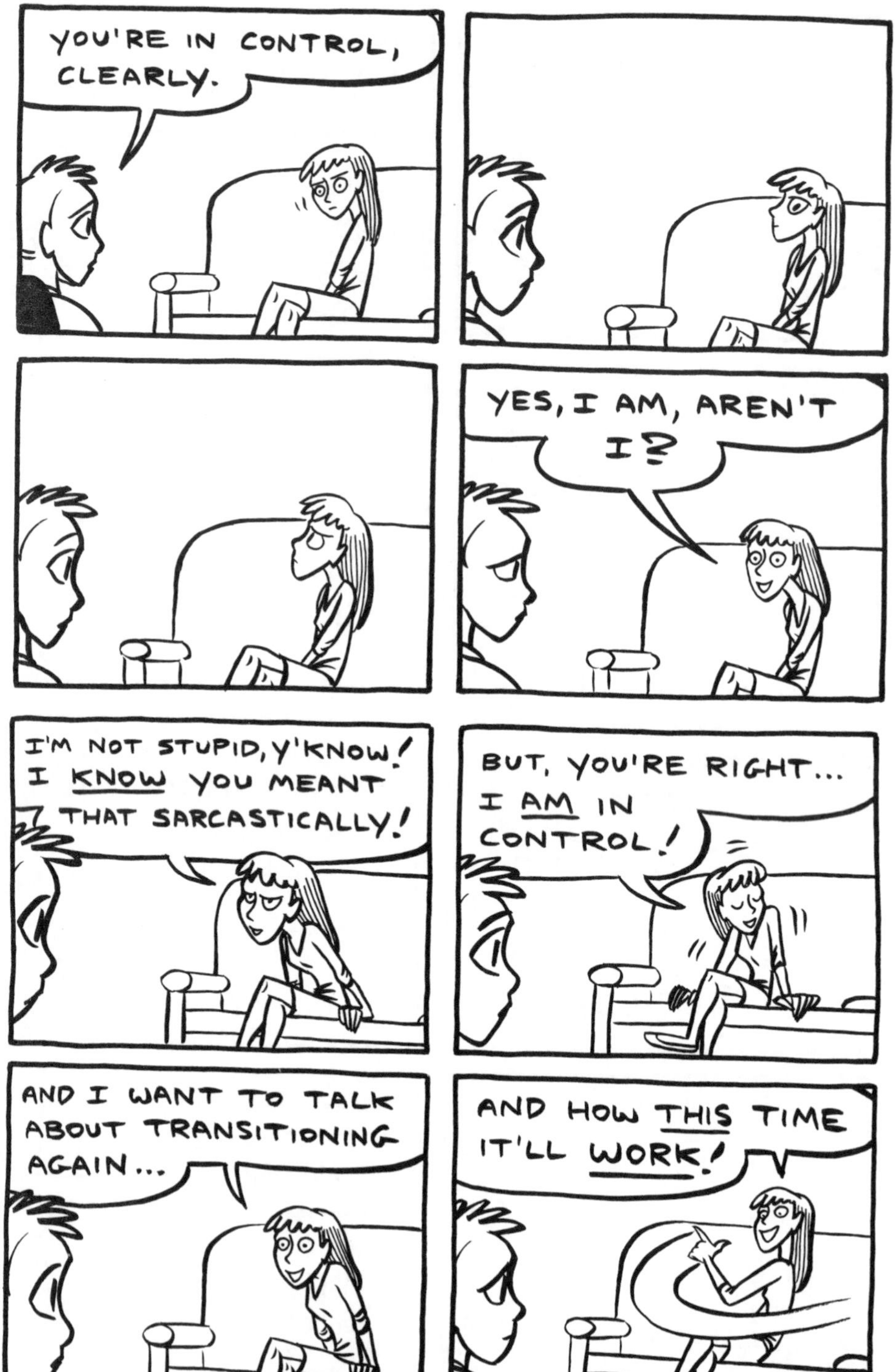
YOU'RE IN CONTROL, CLEARLY.
YES, I AM, AREN'T I?
I'M NOT STUPID, Y'KNOW! I KNOW YOU MEANT THAT SARCASTICALLY!
BUT, YOU'RE RIGHT... I AM IN CONTROL!
AND I WANT TO TALK ABOUT TRANSITIONING AGAIN...
AND HOW THIS TIME IT'LL WORK!

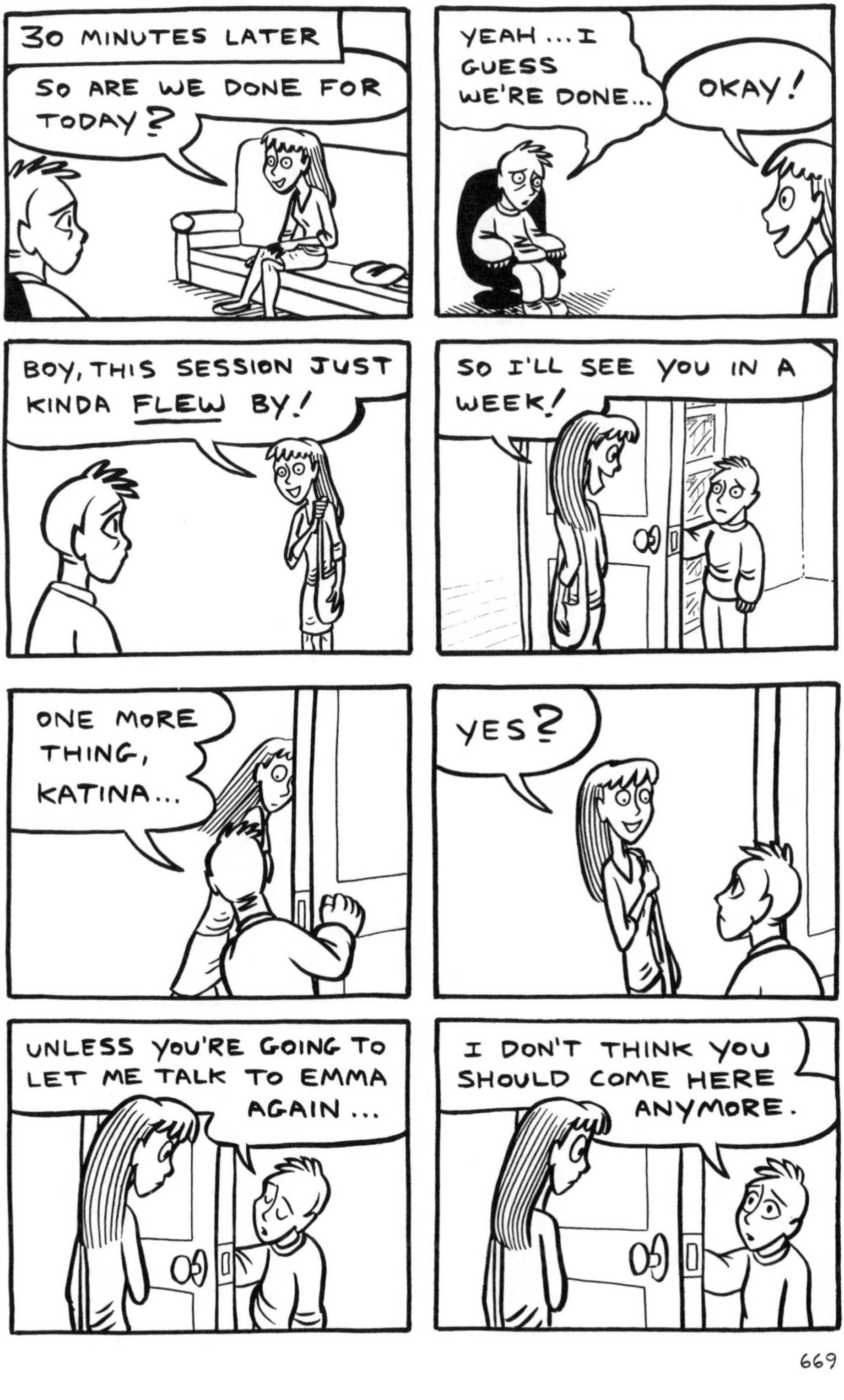
30 MINUTES LATER
SO ARE WE DONE FOR TODAY?
YEAH ... I GUESS WE'RE DONE...
OKAY!
BOY, THIS SESSION JUST KINDA FLEW BY!
SO I'LL SEE YOU IN A WEEK!
ONE MORE THING, KATINA...
YES?
UNLESS YOU'RE GOING TO LET ME TALK TO EMMA AGAIN...
I DON'T THINK YOU SHOULD COME HERE ANYMORE.

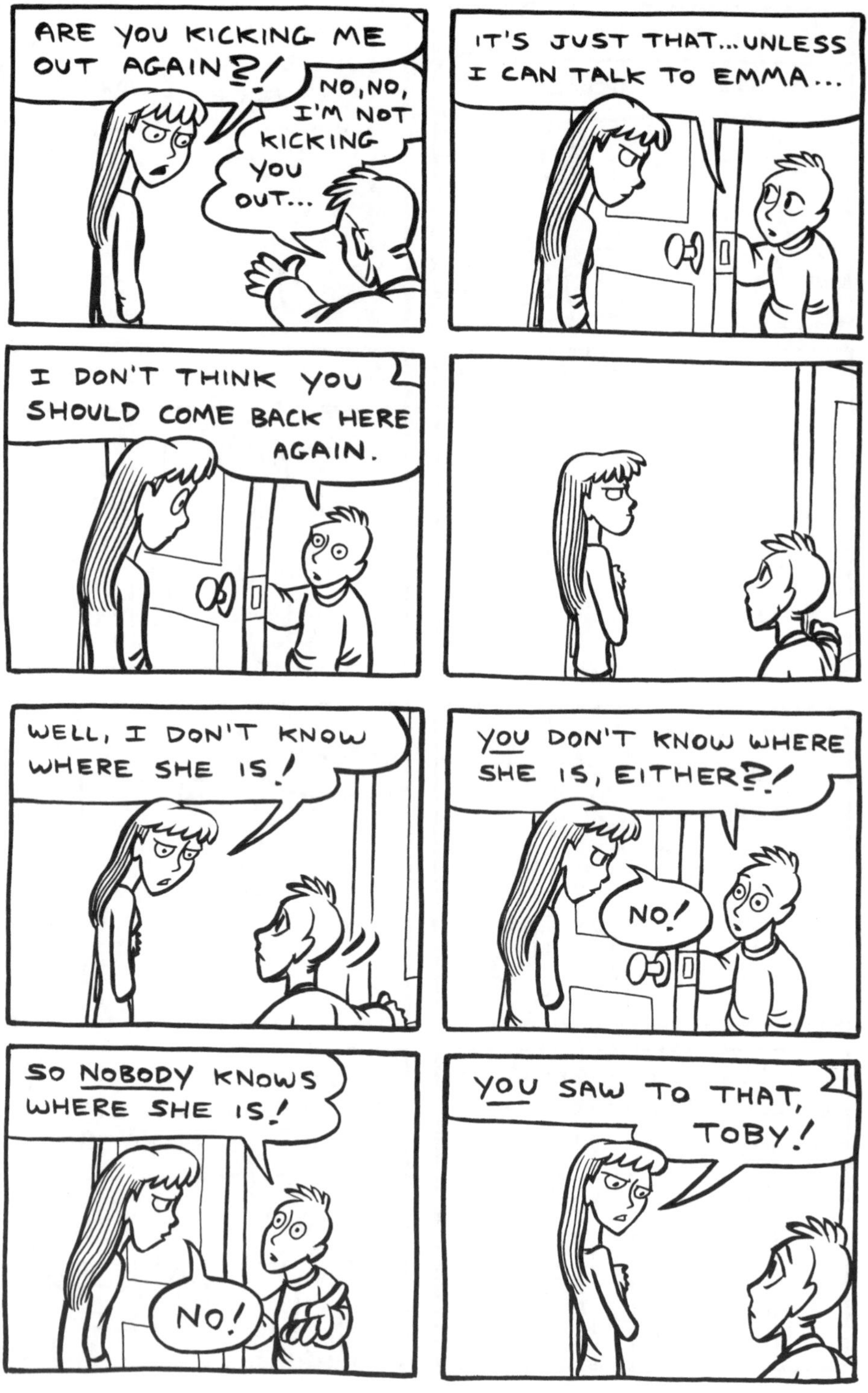
ARE YOU KICKING ME OUT AGAIN?!
NO, NO, I'M NOT KICKING YOU OUT...
IT'S JUST THAT... UNLESS I CAN TALK TO EMMA...
I DON'T THINK YOU SHOULD COME BACK HERE AGAIN.
WELL, I DON'T KNOW WHERE SHE IS!
YOU DON'T KNOW WHERE SHE IS, EITHER?!
NO!
SO NOBODY KNOWS WHERE SHE IS!
NO!
YOU SAW TO THAT, TOBY!

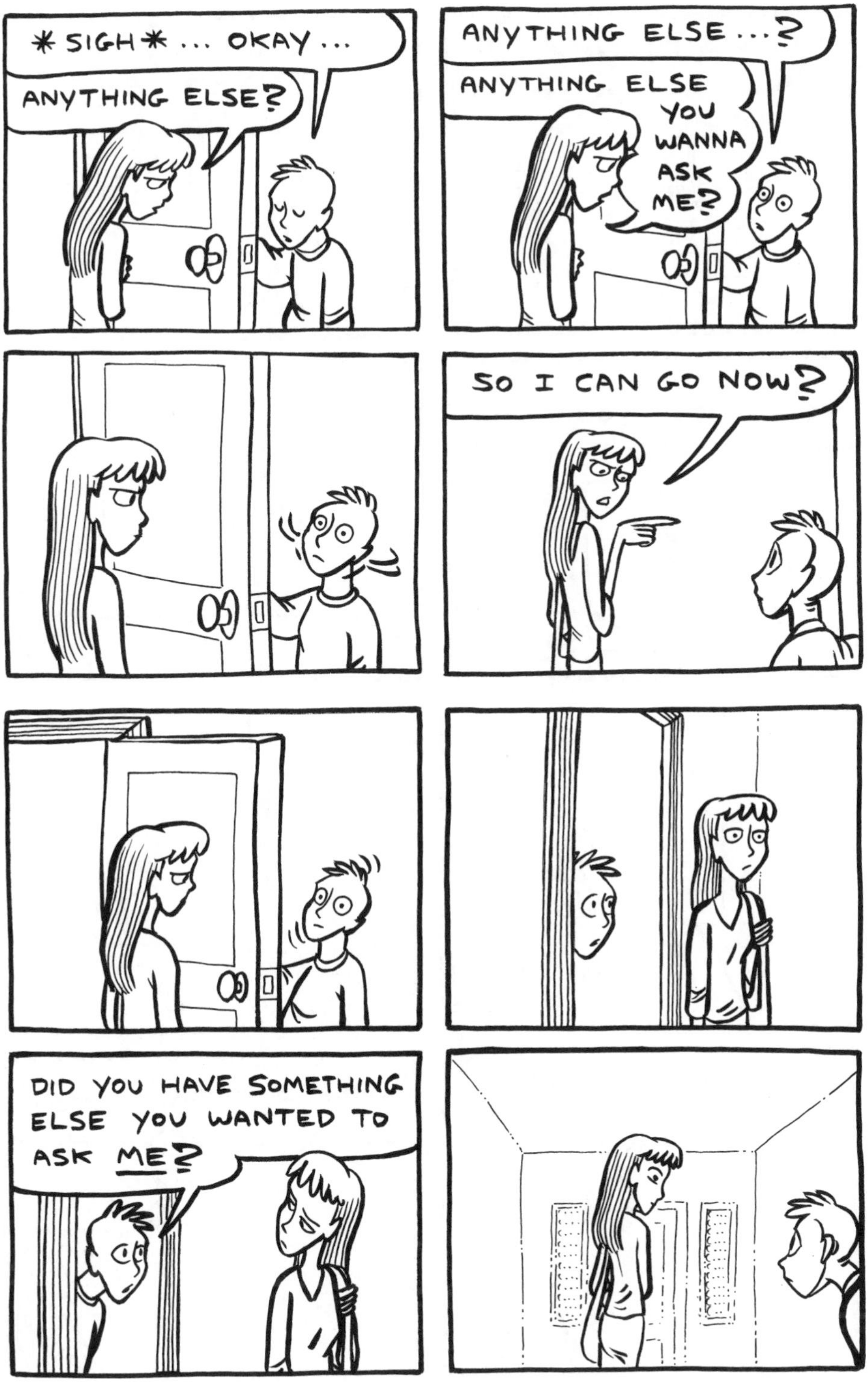

SIGH ... OKAY ...
ANYTHING ELSE?
ANYTHING ELSE ...?
ANYTHING ELSE YOU WANNA ASK ME?
SO I CAN GO NOW?
DID YOU HAVE SOMETHING ELSE YOU WANTED TO ASK ME?

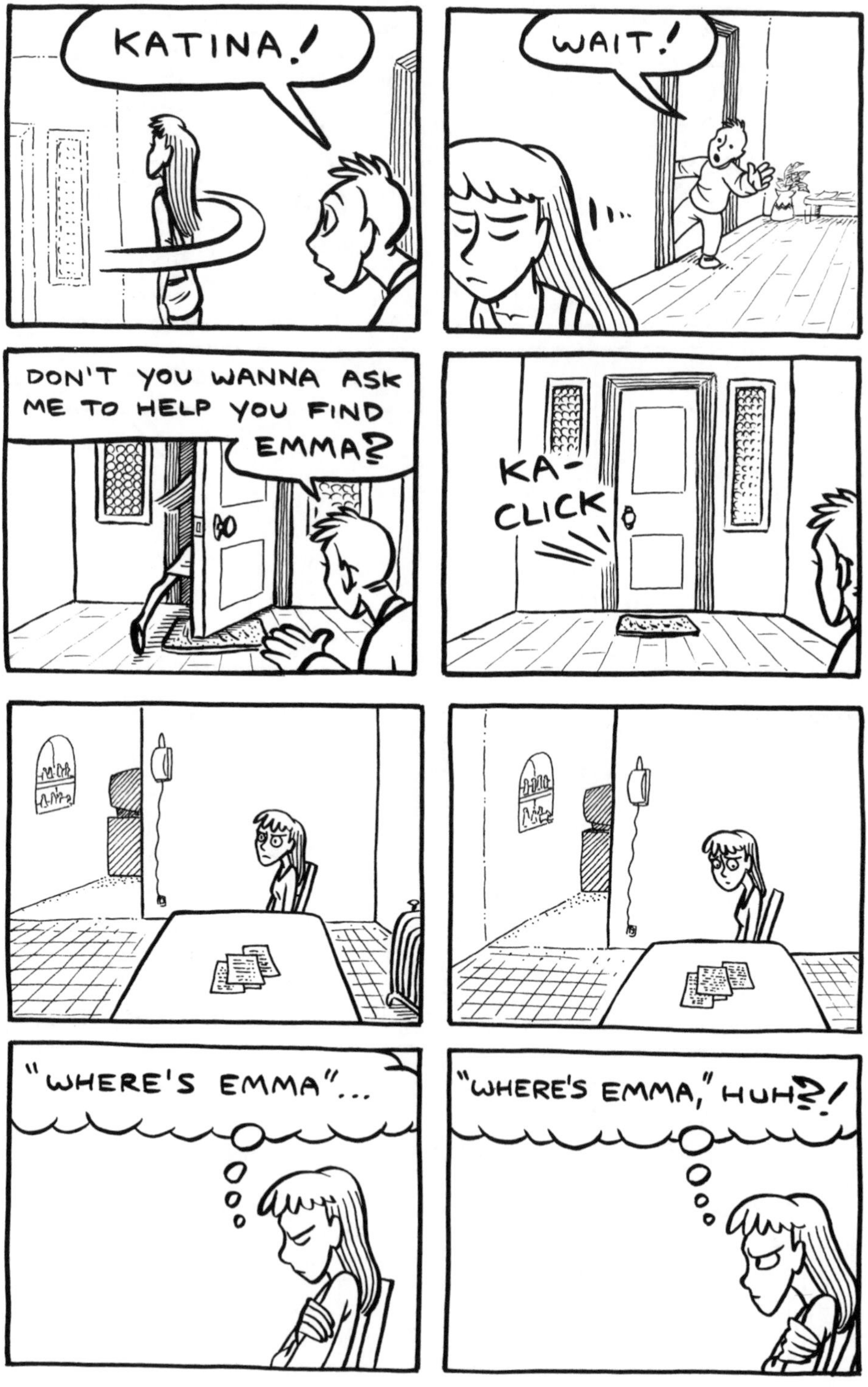
KATINA!
WAIT!
DON'T YOU WANNA ASK ME TO HELP YOU FIND EMMA?
KA-CLICK
"WHERE'S EMMA"...
"WHERE'S EMMA," HUH?!

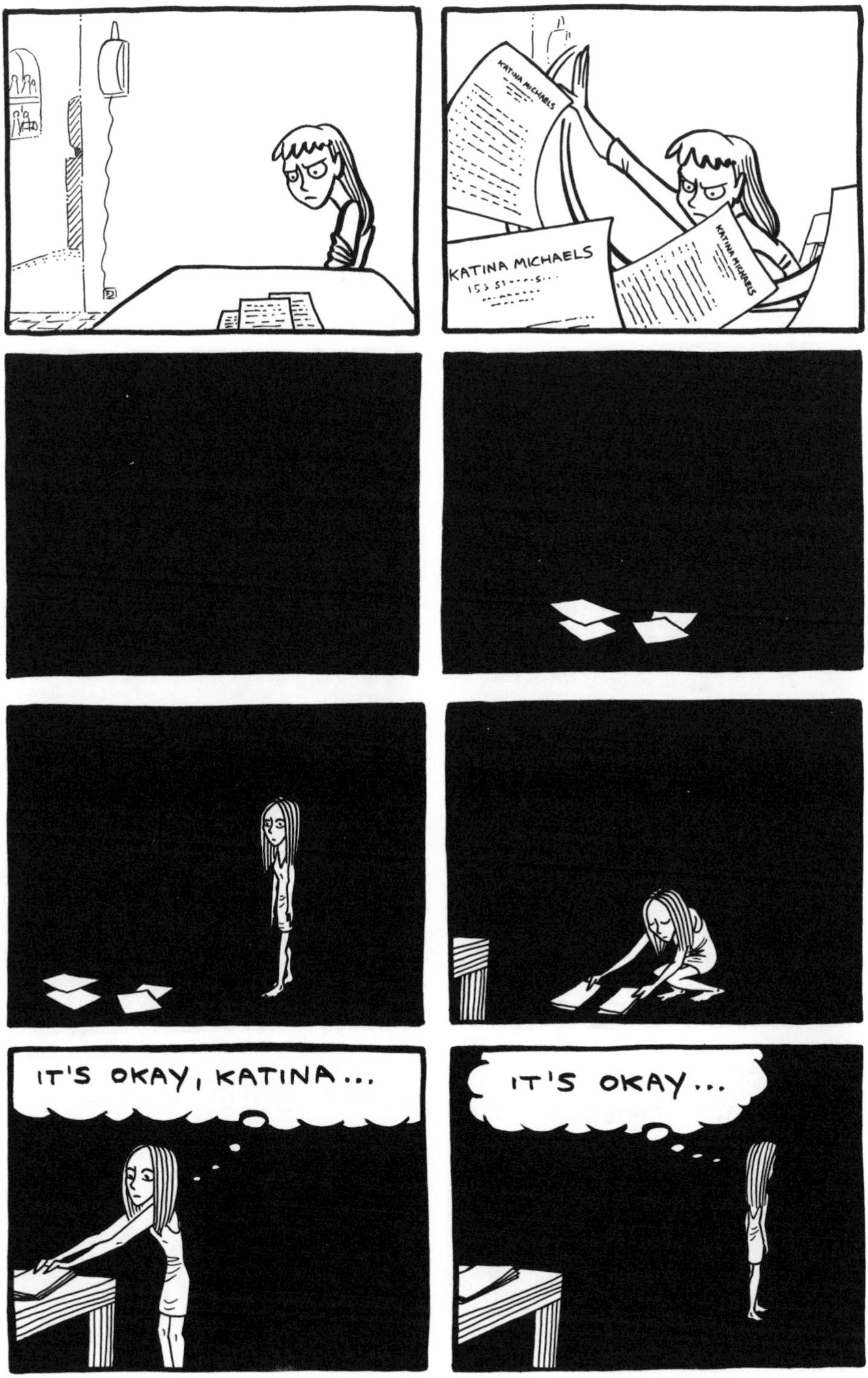
KATINA MICHAELS
KATINA MICHAELS
KATINA MICHAELS
KATINA MICHAELS
IT'S OKAY, KATINA...
IT'S OKAY...

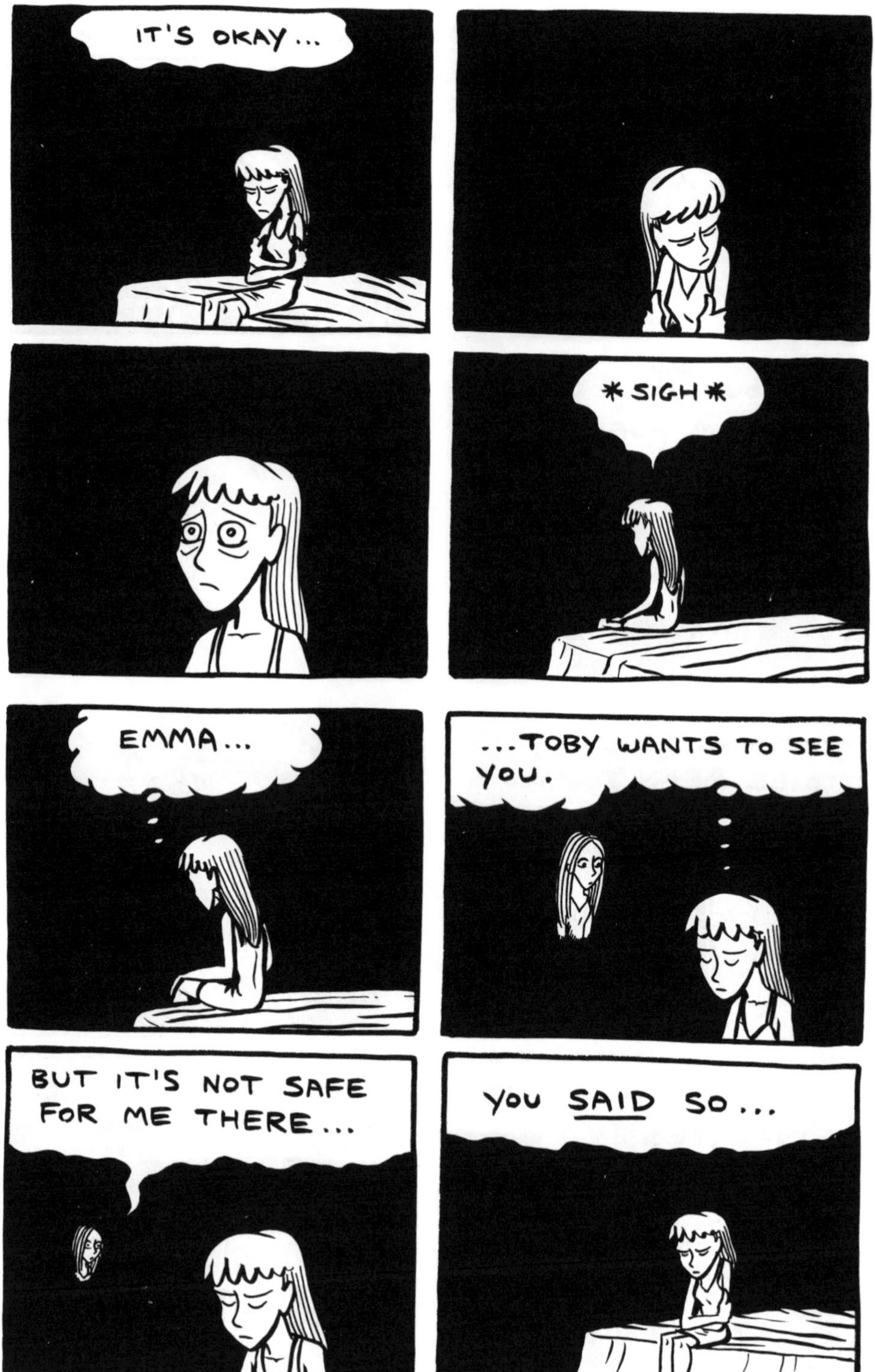
IT'S OKAY...
SIGH
EMMA...
...TOBY WANTS TO SEE YOU.
BUT IT'S NOT SAFE FOR ME THERE...
YOU SAID SO...

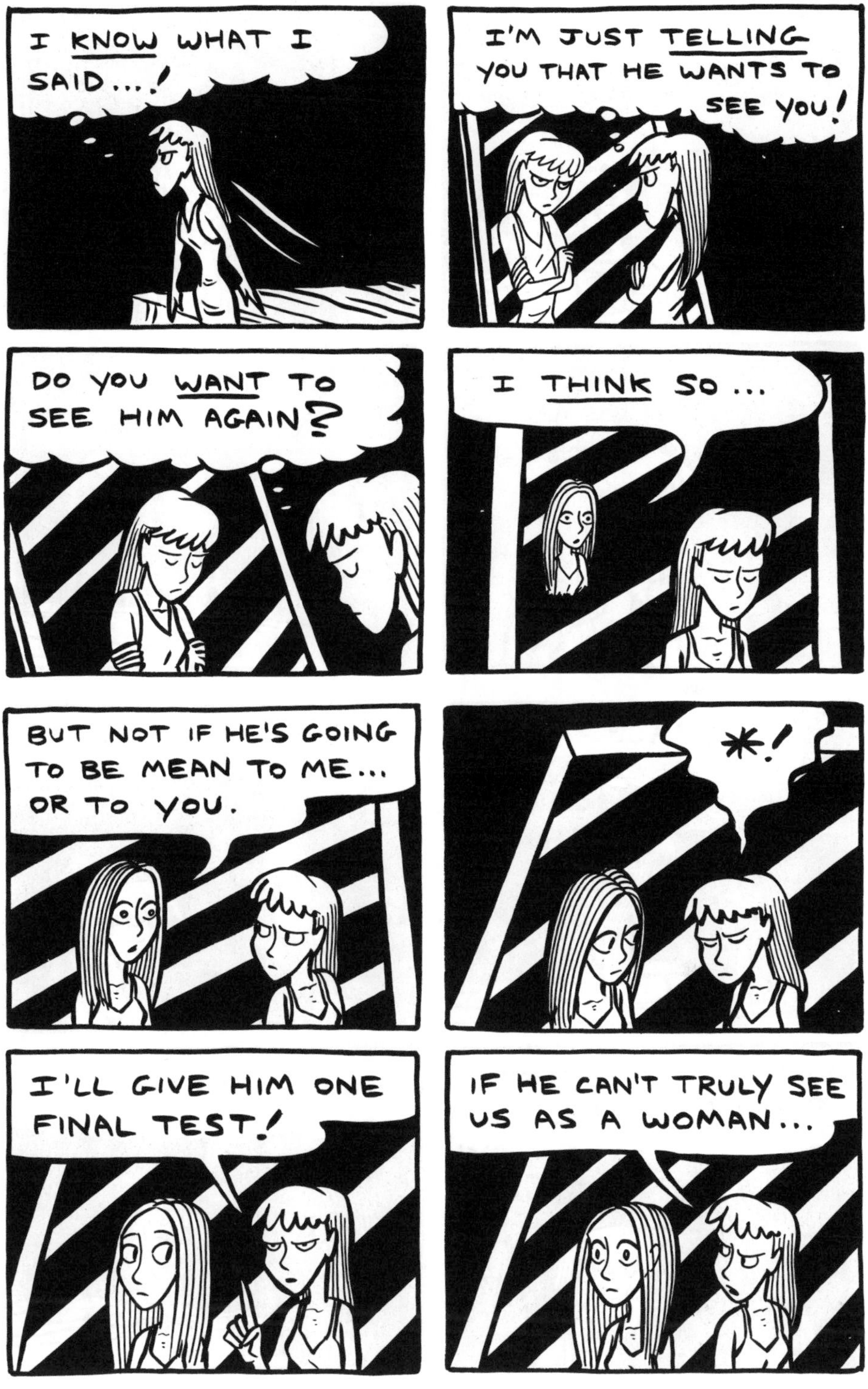
I KNOW WHAT I SAID...!
I'M JUST TELLING YOU THAT HE WANTS TO SEE YOU!
DO YOU WANT TO SEE HIM AGAIN?
I THINK SO...
BUT NOT IF HE'S GOING TO BE MEAN TO ME... OR TO YOU.
*!
I'LL GIVE HIM ONE FINAL TEST!
IF HE CAN'T TRULY SEE US AS A WOMAN...

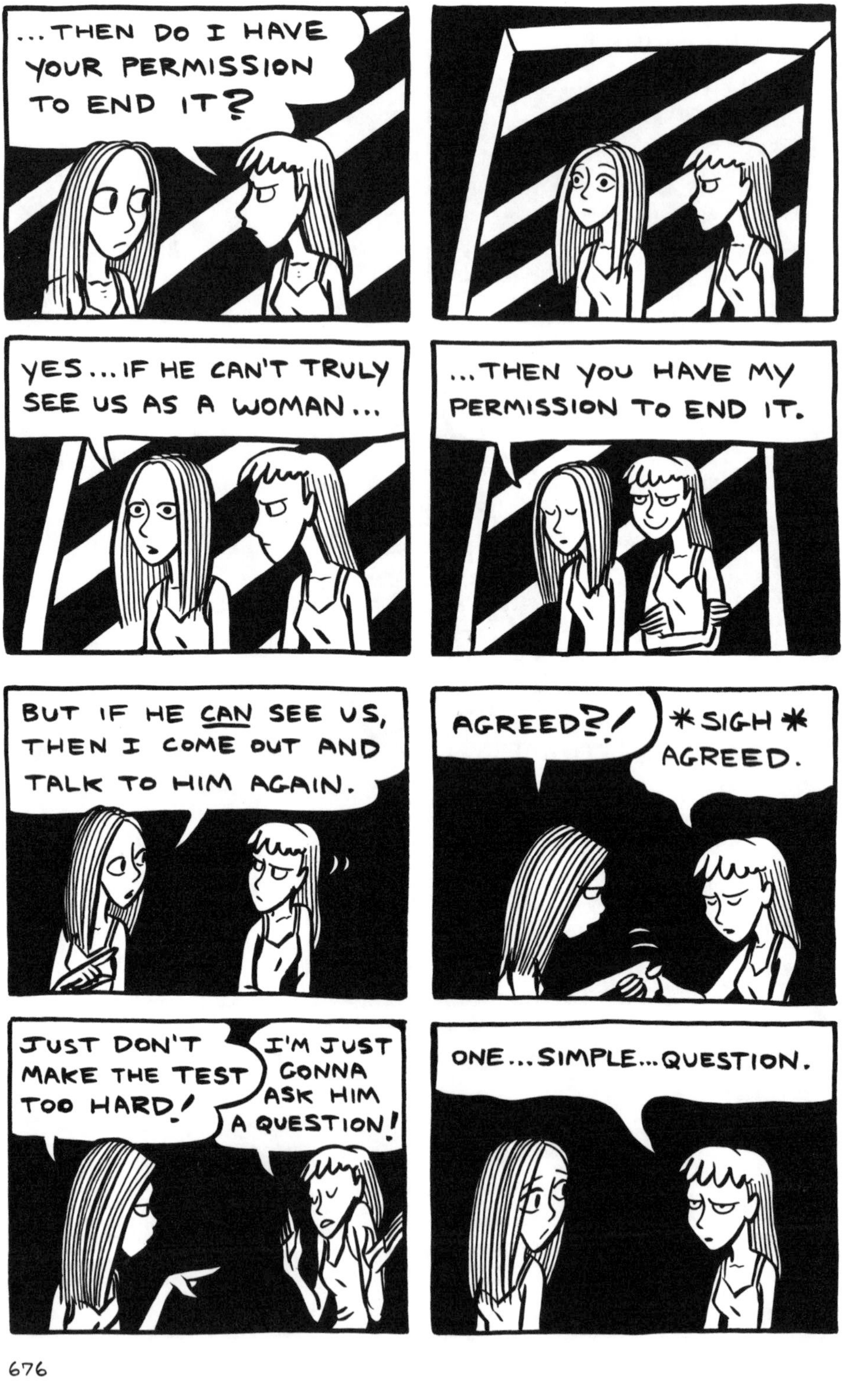
...THEN DO I HAVE YOUR PERMISSION TO END IT?
YES...IF HE CAN'T TRULY SEE US AS A WOMAN...
...THEN YOU HAVE MY PERMISSION TO END IT.
BUT IF HE CAN SEE US, THEN I COME OUT AND TALK TO HIM AGAIN.
AGREED?!
SIGH AGREED.
JUST DON'T MAKE THE TEST TOO HARD!
I'M JUST GONNA ASK HIM A QUESTION!
ONE...SIMPLE...QUESTION.

LIST

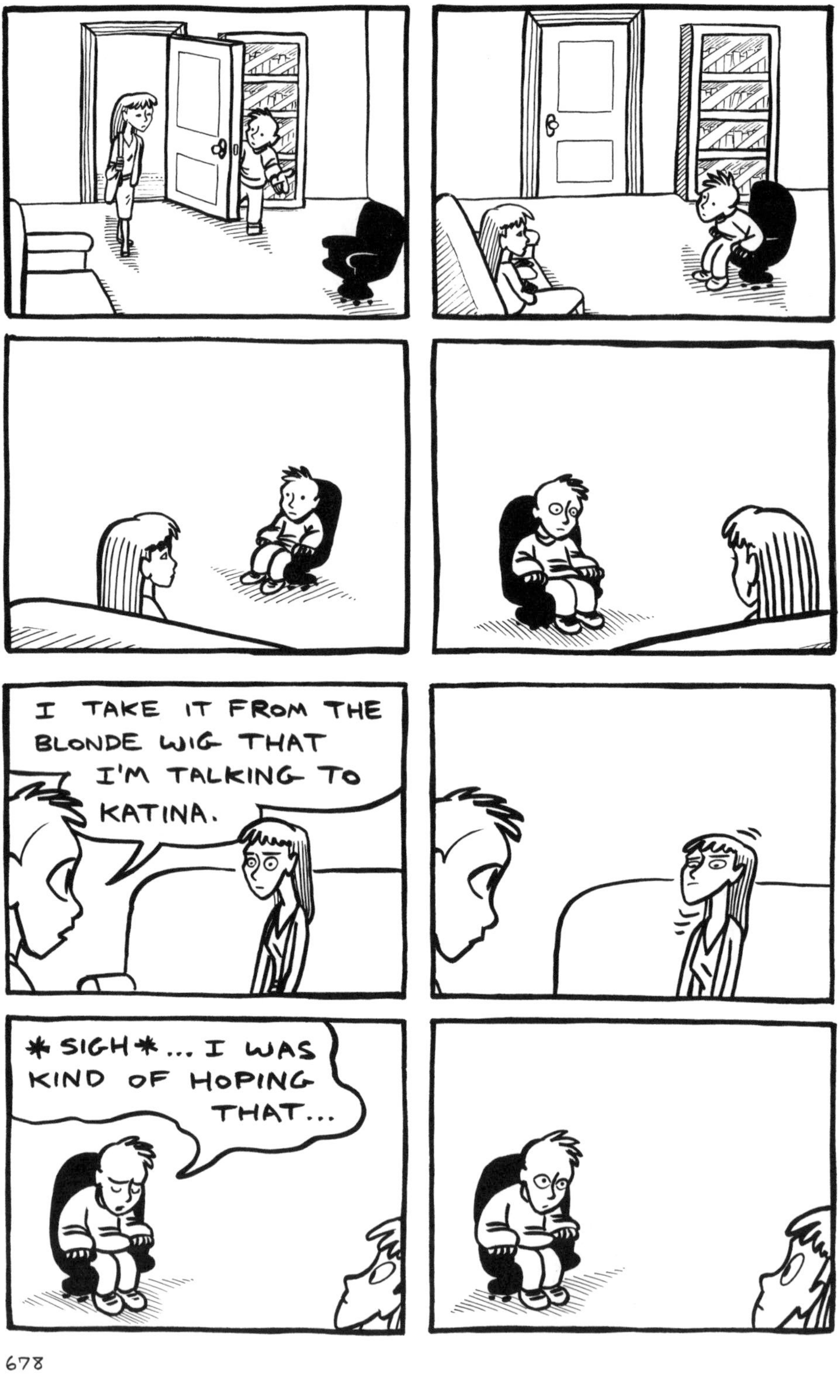
I TAKE IT FROM THE BLONDE WIG THAT I'M TALKING TO KATINA.
SIGH... I WAS KIND OF HOPING THAT...

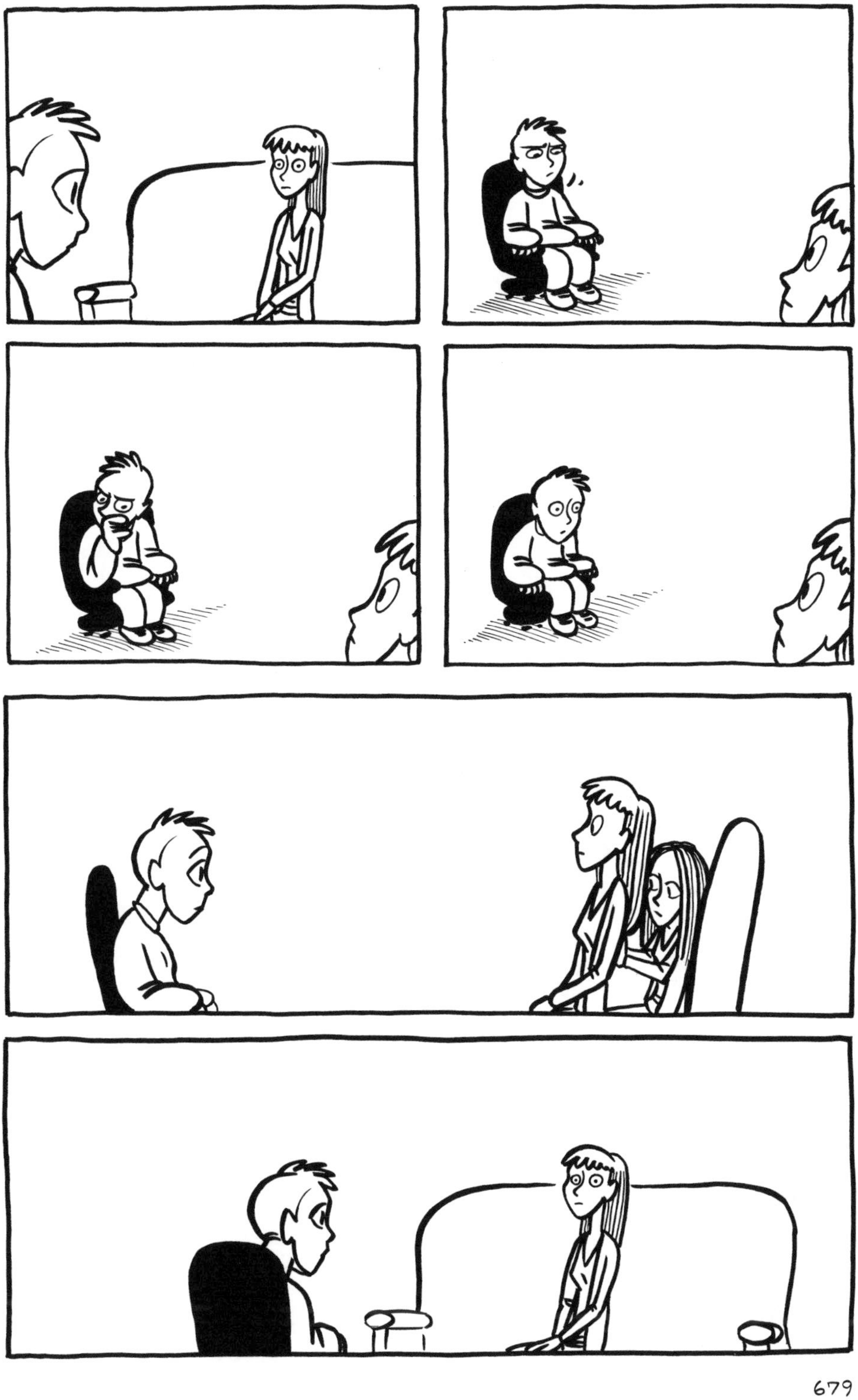

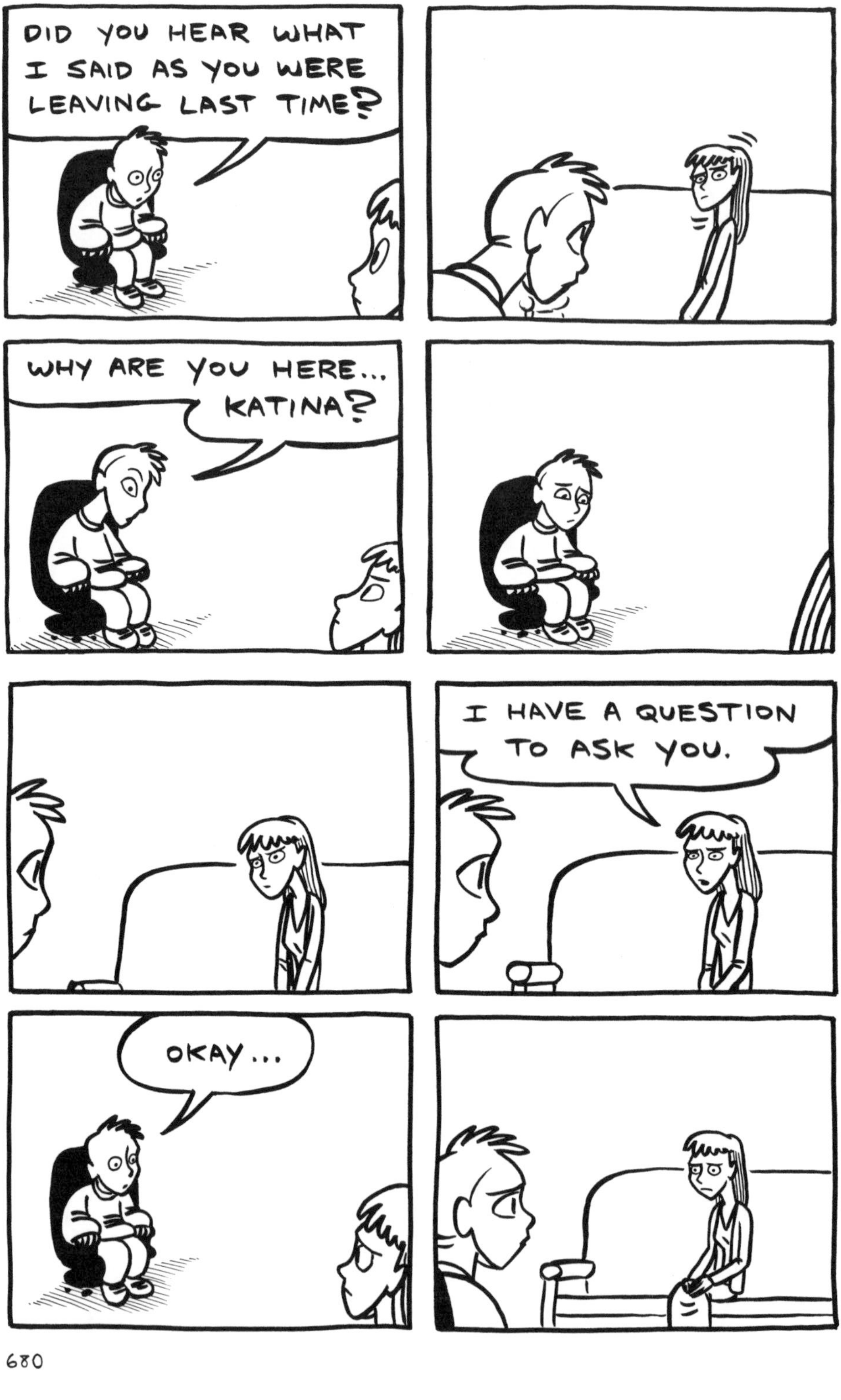
DID YOU HEAR WHAT I SAID AS YOU WERE LEAVING LAST TIME?
WHY ARE YOU HERE... KATINA?
I HAVE A QUESTION TO ASK YOU.
OKAY...

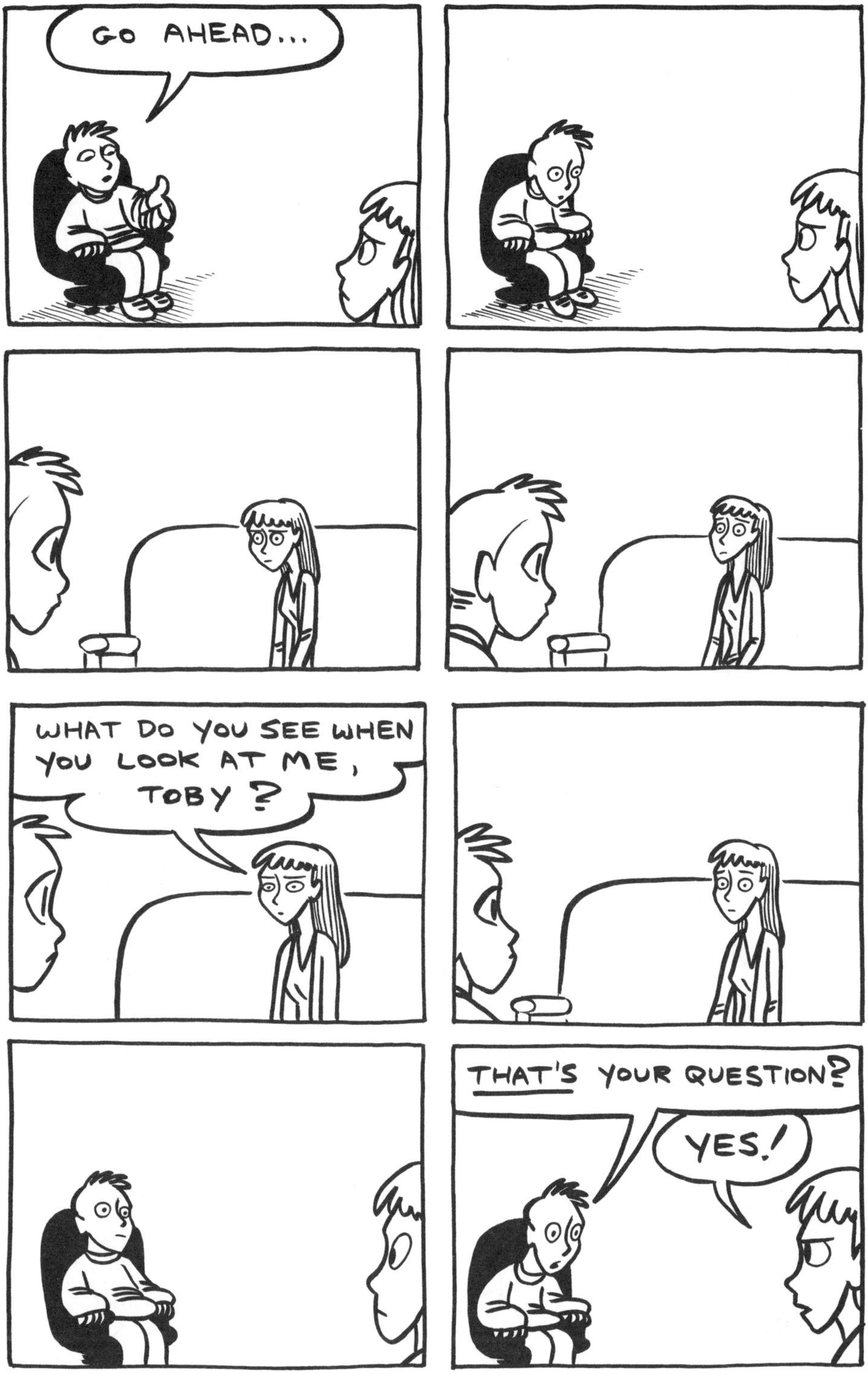
GO AHEAD...
WHAT DO YOU SEE WHEN YOU LOOK AT ME, TOBY?
THAT'S YOUR QUESTION?
YES!

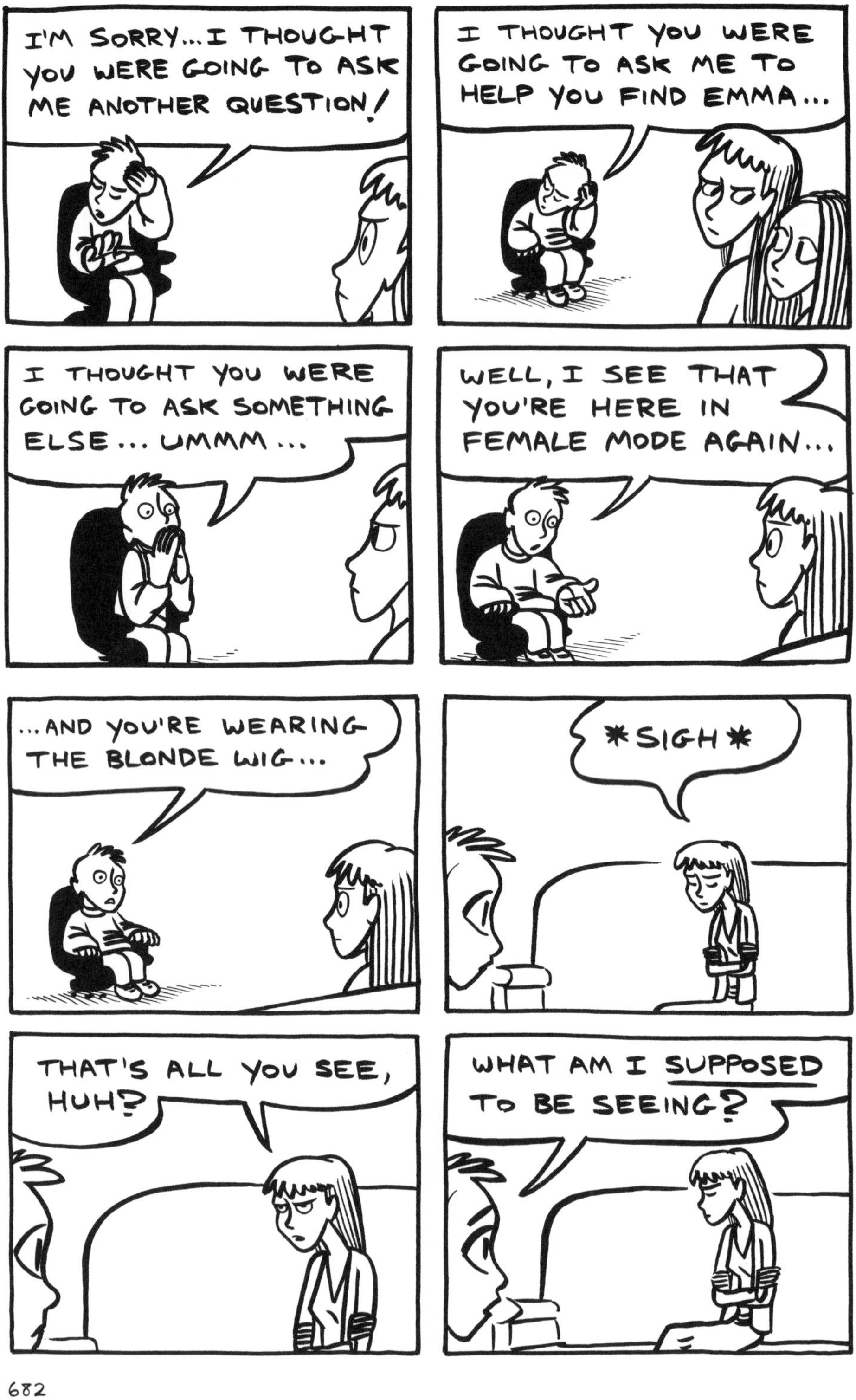

I'M SORRY... I THOUGHT YOU WERE GOING TO ASK ME ANOTHER QUESTION!
I THOUGHT YOU WERE GOING TO ASK ME TO HELP YOU FIND EMMA...
I THOUGHT YOU WERE GOING TO ASK SOMETHING ELSE... UMMM...
WELL, I SEE THAT YOU'RE HERE IN FEMALE MODE AGAIN...
...AND YOU'RE WEARING THE BLONDE WIG...
SIGH
THAT'S ALL YOU SEE, HUH?
WHAT AM I SUPPOSED TO BE SEEING?

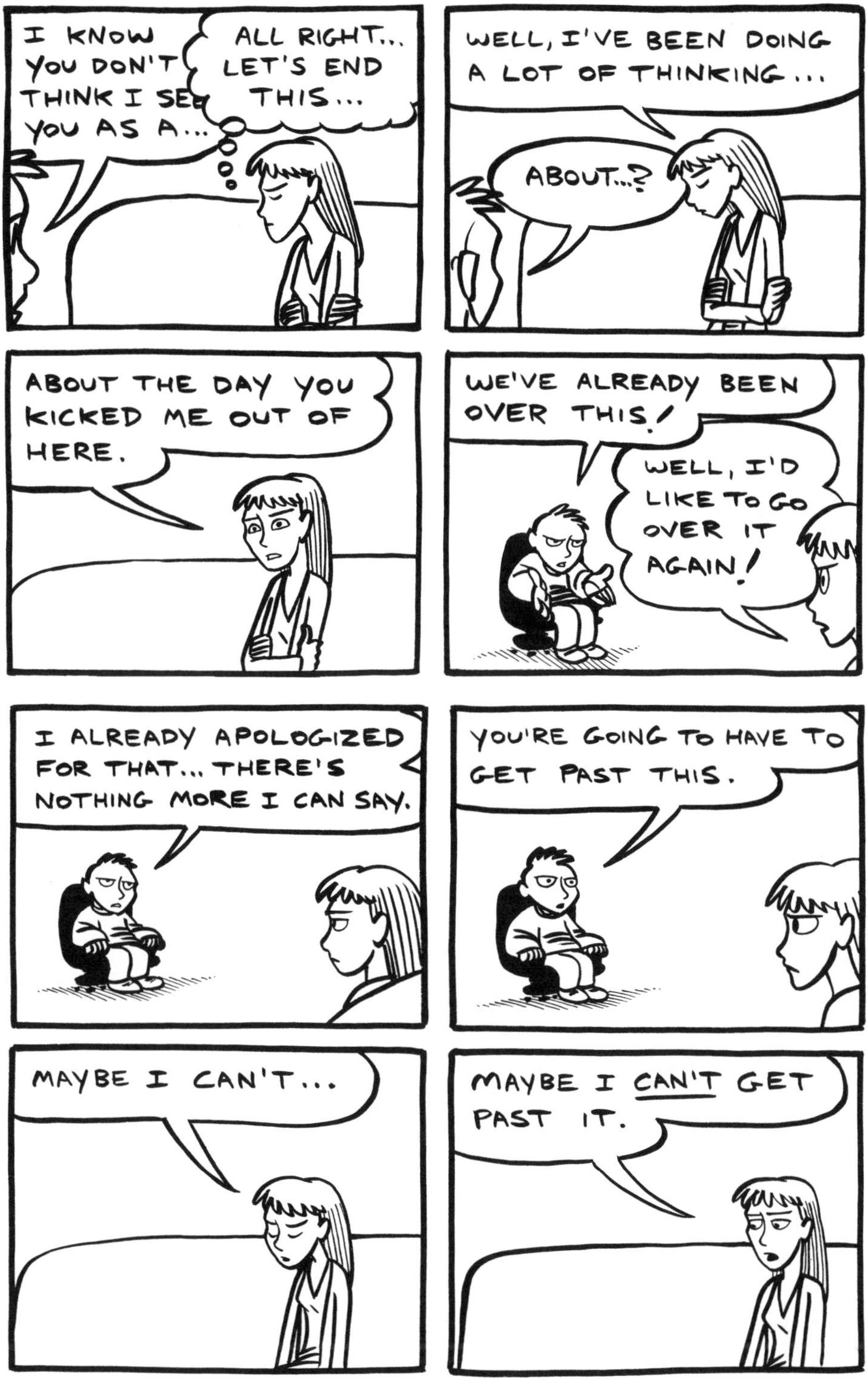

I KNOW YOU DON'T THINK I SEE YOU AS A...
ALL RIGHT... LET'S END THIS...
WELL, I'VE BEEN DOING A LOT OF THINKING...
ABOUT...?
ABOUT THE DAY YOU KICKED ME OUT OF HERE.
WE'VE ALREADY BEEN OVER THIS!
WELL, I'D LIKE TO GO OVER IT AGAIN!
I ALREADY APOLOGIZED FOR THAT... THERE'S NOTHING MORE I CAN SAY.
YOU'RE GOING TO HAVE TO GET PAST THIS.
MAYBE I CAN'T...
MAYBE I CAN'T GET PAST IT.

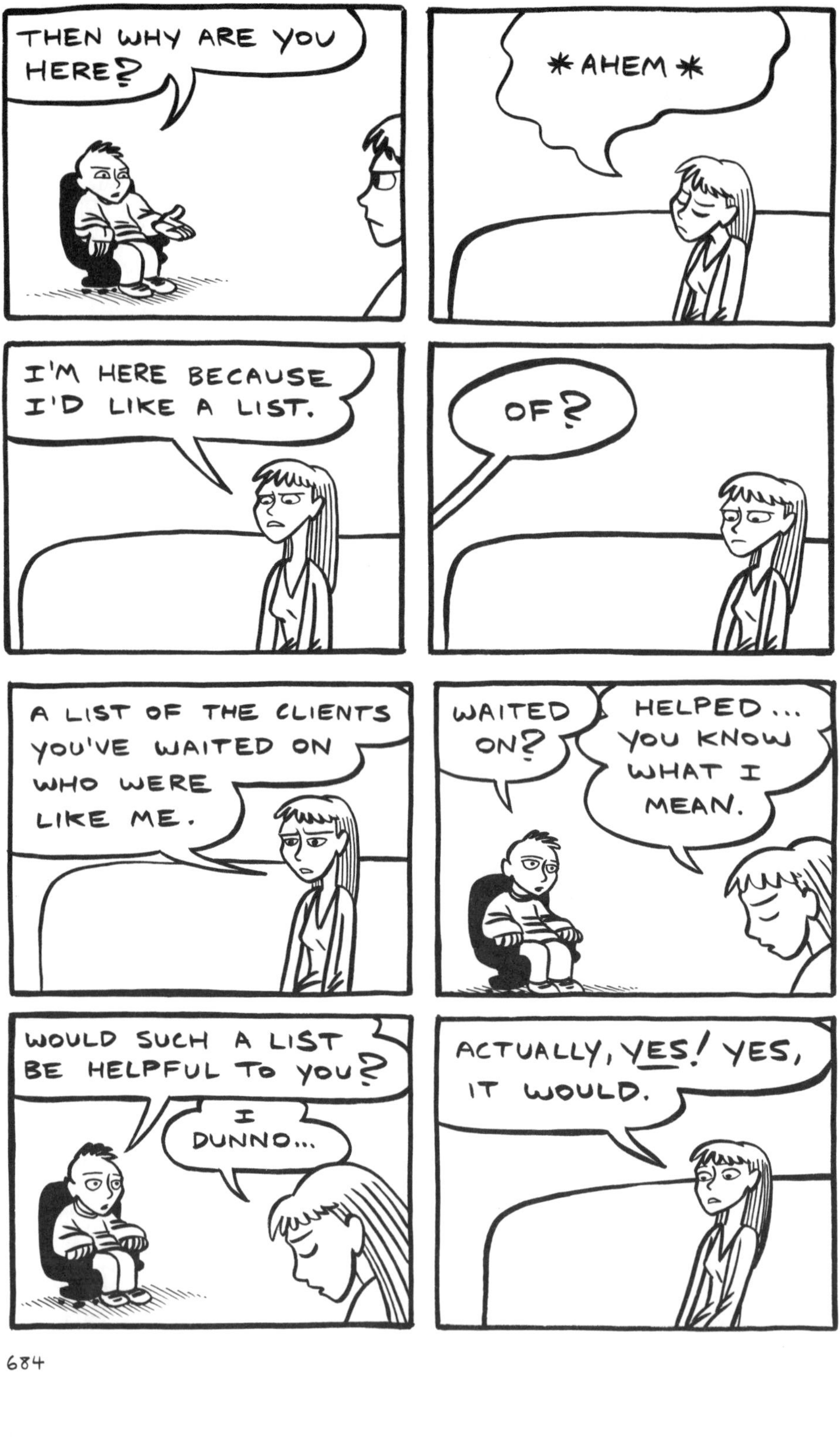
THEN WHY ARE YOU HERE?
AHEM
I'M HERE BECAUSE I'D LIKE A LIST.
OF?
A LIST OF THE CLIENTS YOU'VE WAITED ON WHO WERE LIKE ME.
WAITED ON?
HELPED... YOU KNOW WHAT I MEAN.
WOULD SUCH A LIST BE HELPFUL TO YOU?
I DUNNO...
ACTUALLY, YES! YES, IT WOULD.

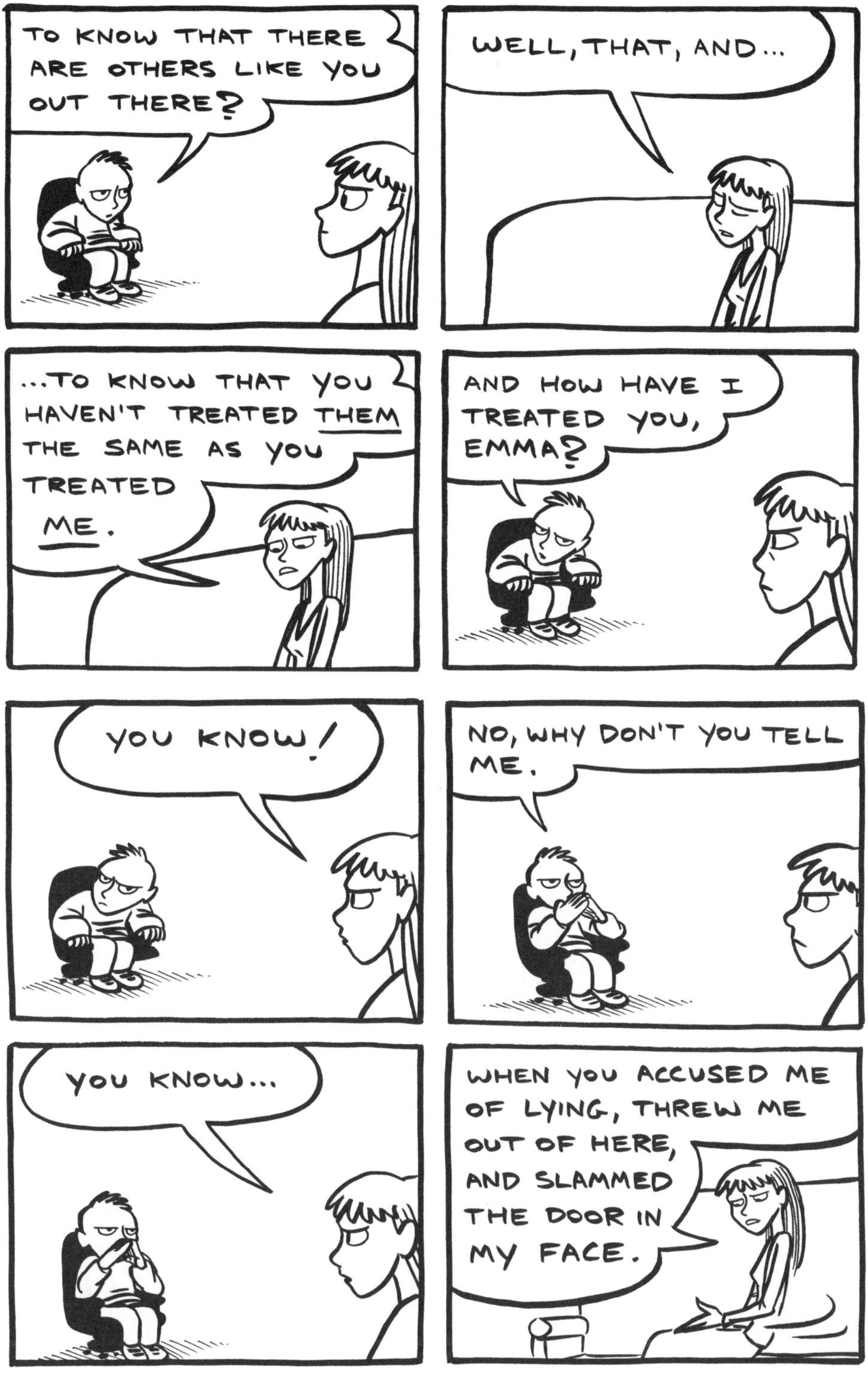
TO KNOW THAT THERE ARE OTHERS LIKE YOU OUT THERE?
WELL, THAT, AND...
...TO KNOW THAT YOU HAVEN'T TREATED THEM THE SAME AS YOU TREATED ME.
AND HOW HAVE I TREATED YOU, EMMA?
YOU KNOW!
NO, WHY DON'T YOU TELL ME.
YOU KNOW...
WHEN YOU ACCUSED ME OF LYING, THREW ME OUT OF HERE, AND SLAMMED THE DOOR IN MY FACE.

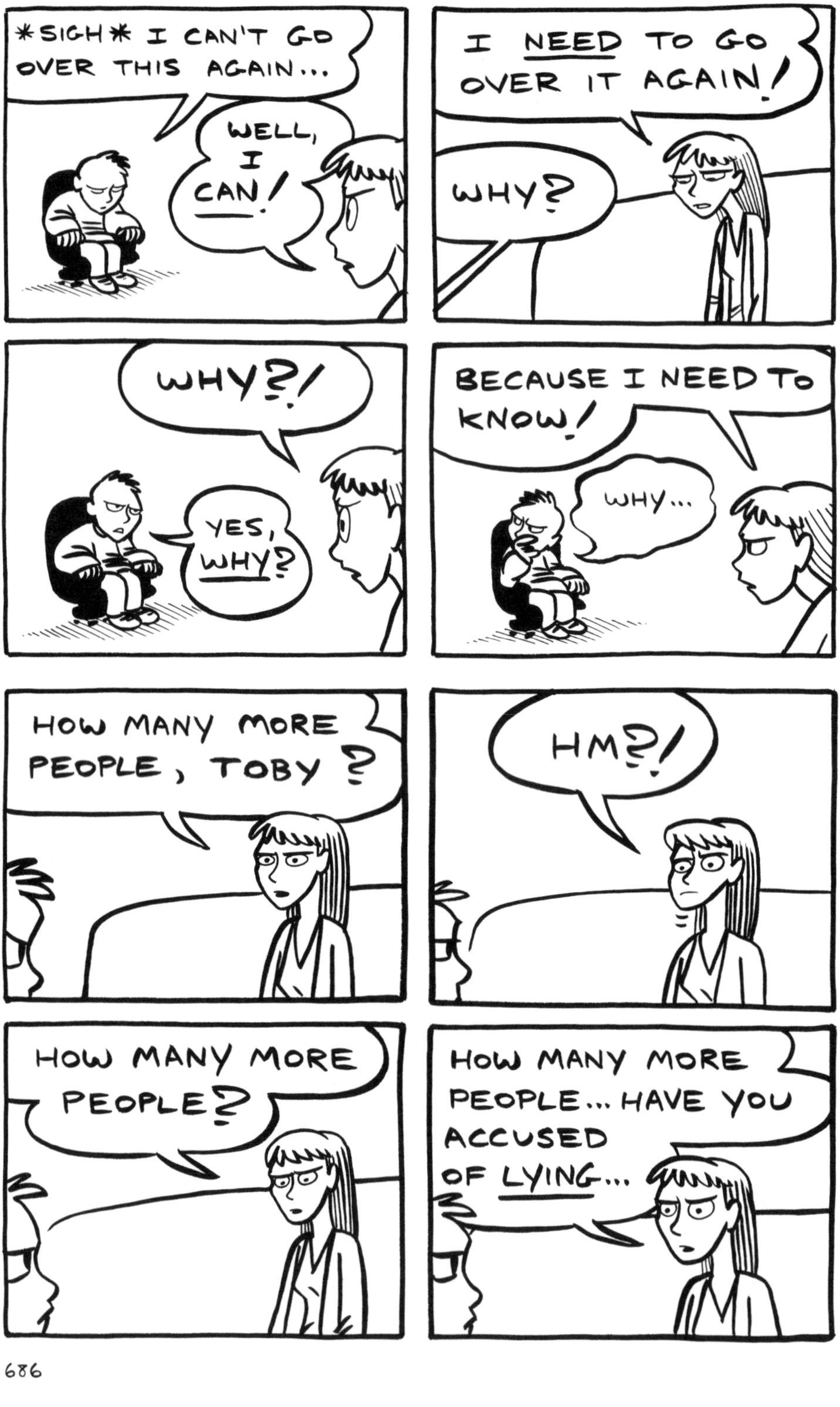
SIGH I CAN'T GO OVER THIS AGAIN...
WELL, I CAN!
I NEED TO GO OVER IT AGAIN!
WHY?
WHY?!
YES, WHY?
BECAUSE I NEED TO KNOW!
WHY...
HOW MANY MORE PEOPLE, TOBY?
HM?!
HOW MANY MORE PEOPLE?
HOW MANY MORE PEOPLE... HAVE YOU ACCUSED OF LYING...

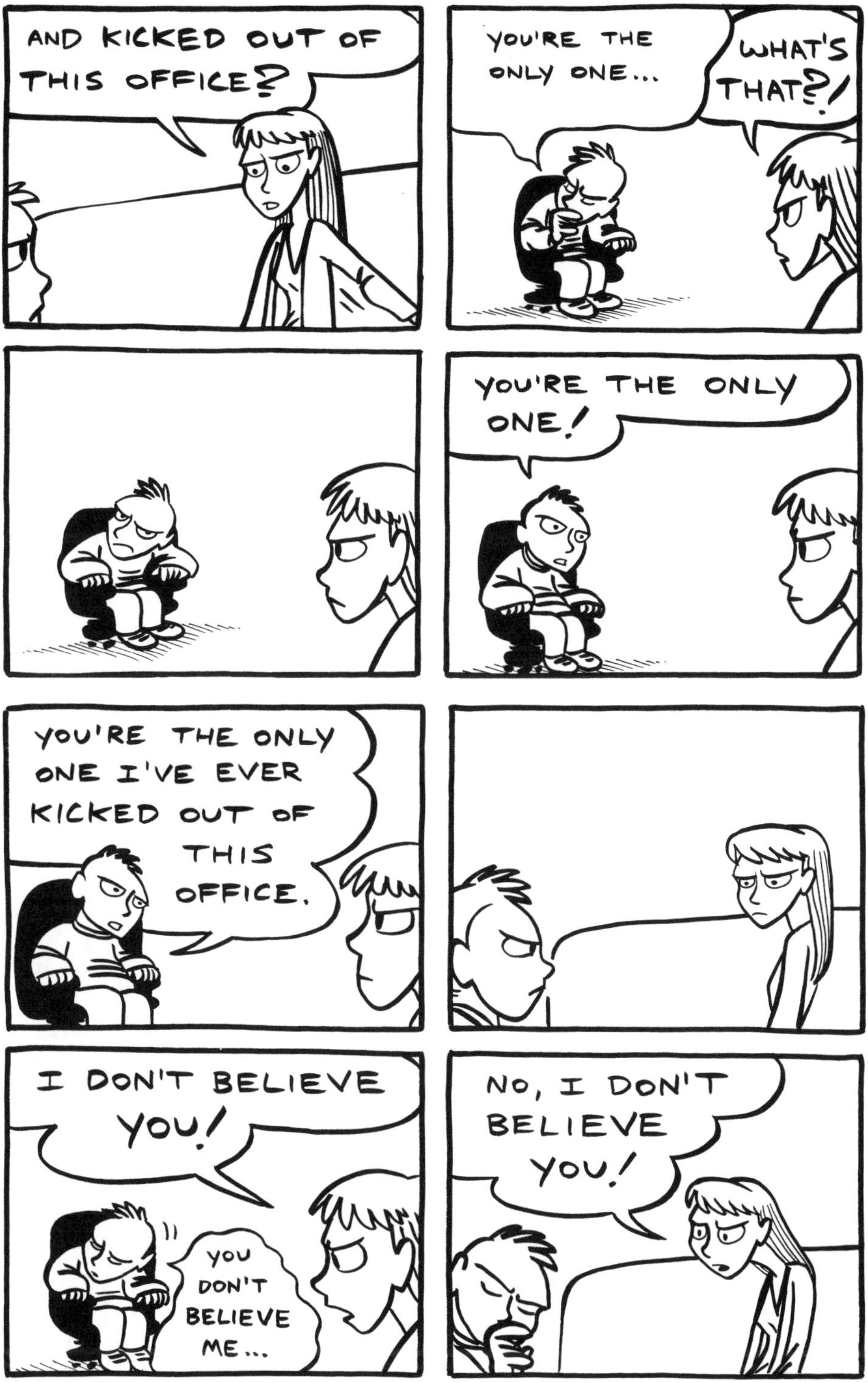
AND KICKED OUT OF THIS OFFICE?
YOU'RE THE ONLY ONE...
WHAT'S THAT?!
YOU'RE THE ONLY ONE!
YOU'RE THE ONLY ONE I'VE EVER KICKED OUT OF THIS OFFICE.
I DON'T BELIEVE YOU!
YOU DON'T BELIEVE ME...
NO, I DON'T BELIEVE YOU!

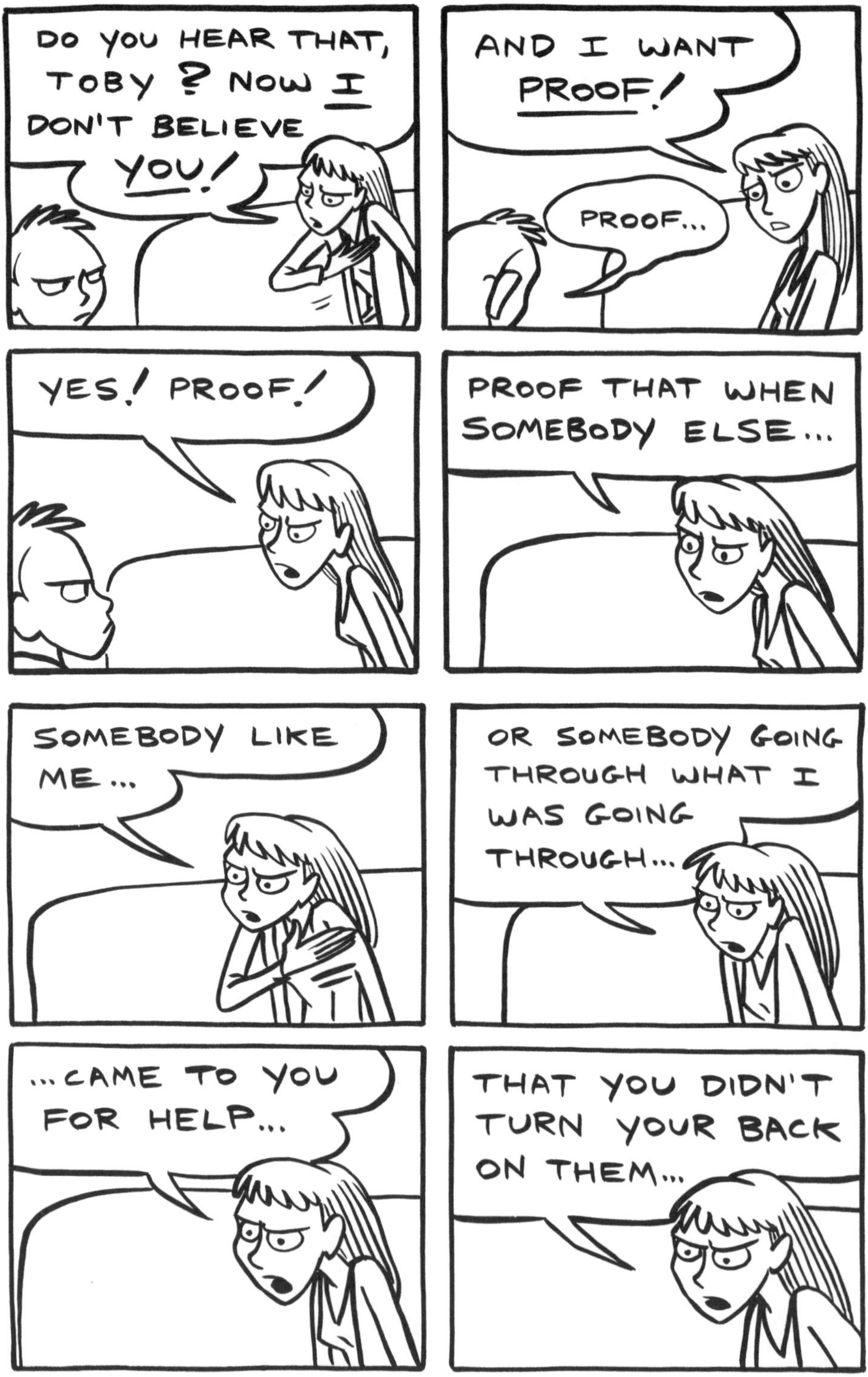
DO YOU HEAR THAT, TOBY ? NOW I DON'T BELIEVE YOU!
AND I WANT PROOF!
PROOF...
YES! PROOF!
PROOF THAT WHEN SOMEBODY ELSE...
SOMEBODY LIKE ME...
OR SOMEBODY GOING THROUGH WHAT I WAS GOING THROUGH...
...CAME TO YOU FOR HELP...
THAT YOU DIDN'T TURN YOUR BACK ON THEM...

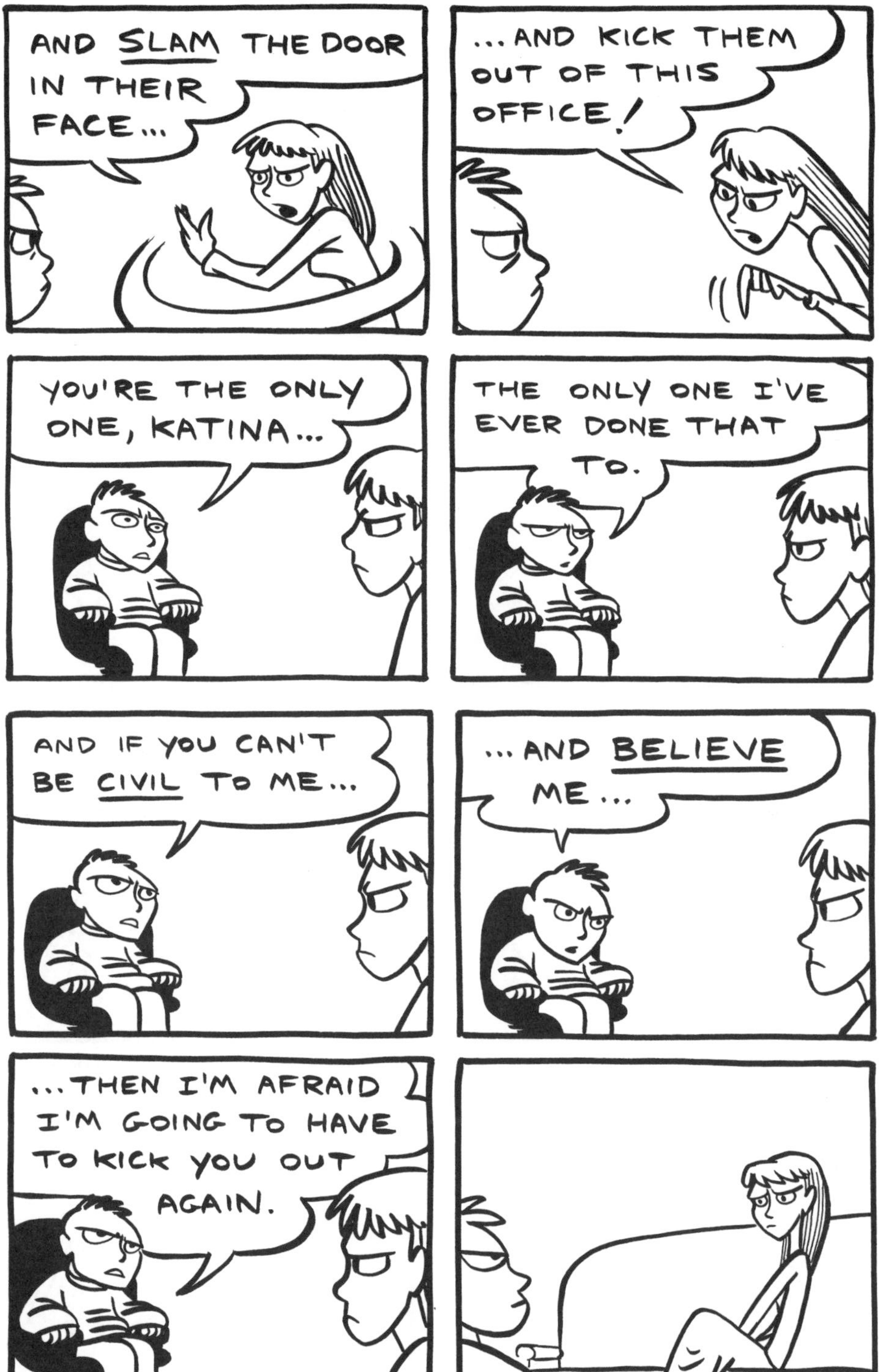
AND SLAM THE DOOR IN THEIR FACE...
...AND KICK THEM OUT OF THIS OFFICE!
YOU'RE THE ONLY ONE, KATINA...
THE ONLY ONE I'VE EVER DONE THAT TO.
AND IF YOU CAN'T BE CIVIL TO ME...
...AND BELIEVE ME...
...THEN I'M AFRAID I'M GOING TO HAVE TO KICK YOU OUT AGAIN.

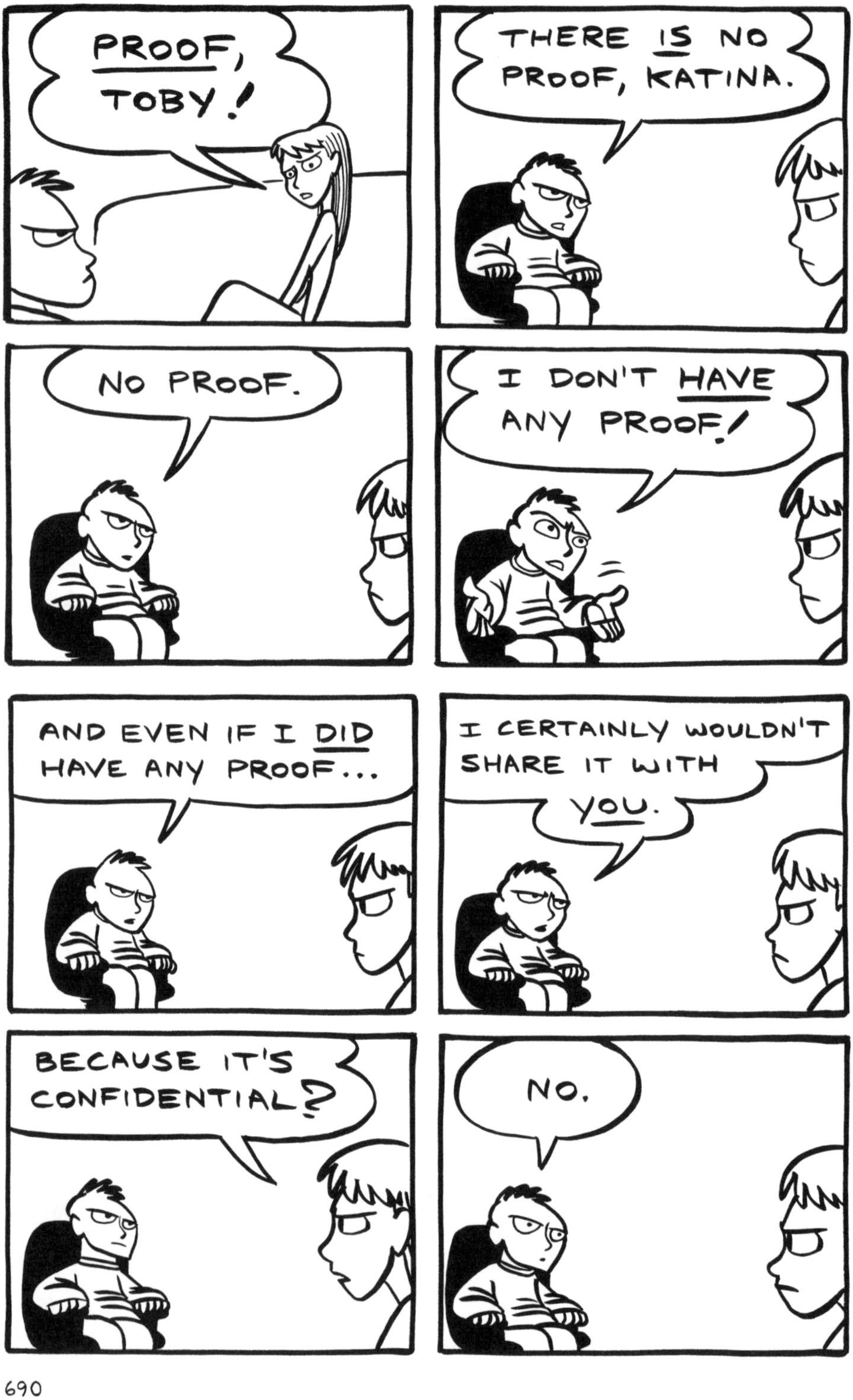
PROOF, TOBY!
THERE IS NO PROOF, KATINA.
NO PROOF.
I DON'T HAVE ANY PROOF!
AND EVEN IF I DID HAVE ANY PROOF...
I CERTAINLY WOULDN'T SHARE IT WITH YOU.
BECAUSE IT'S CONFIDENTIAL?
NO.

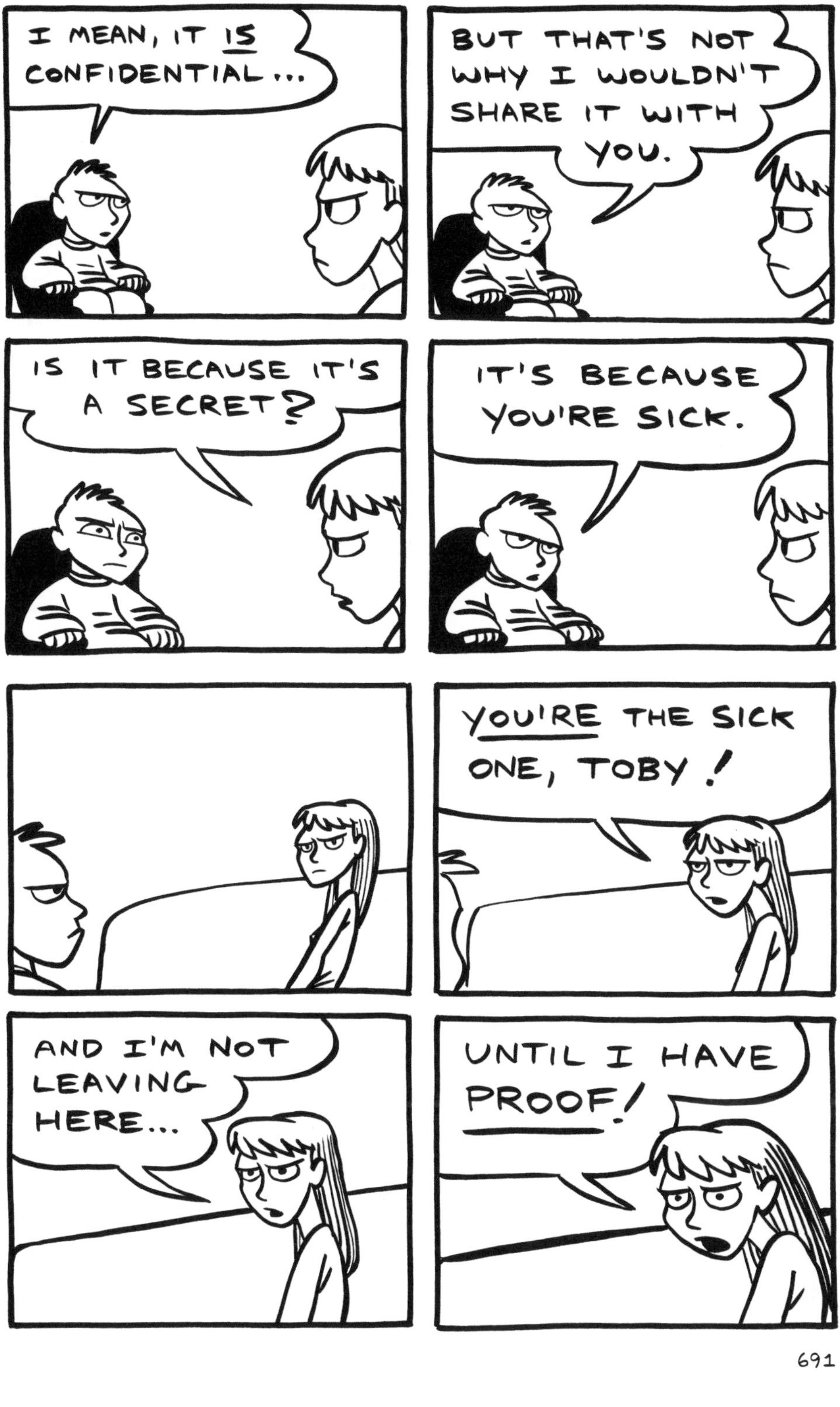
I MEAN, IT IS CONFIDENTIAL...
BUT THAT'S NOT WHY I WOULDN'T SHARE IT WITH YOU.
IS IT BECAUSE IT'S A SECRET?
IT'S BECAUSE YOU'RE SICK.
YOU'RE THE SICK ONE, TOBY!
AND I'M NOT LEAVING HERE...
UNTIL I HAVE PROOF!

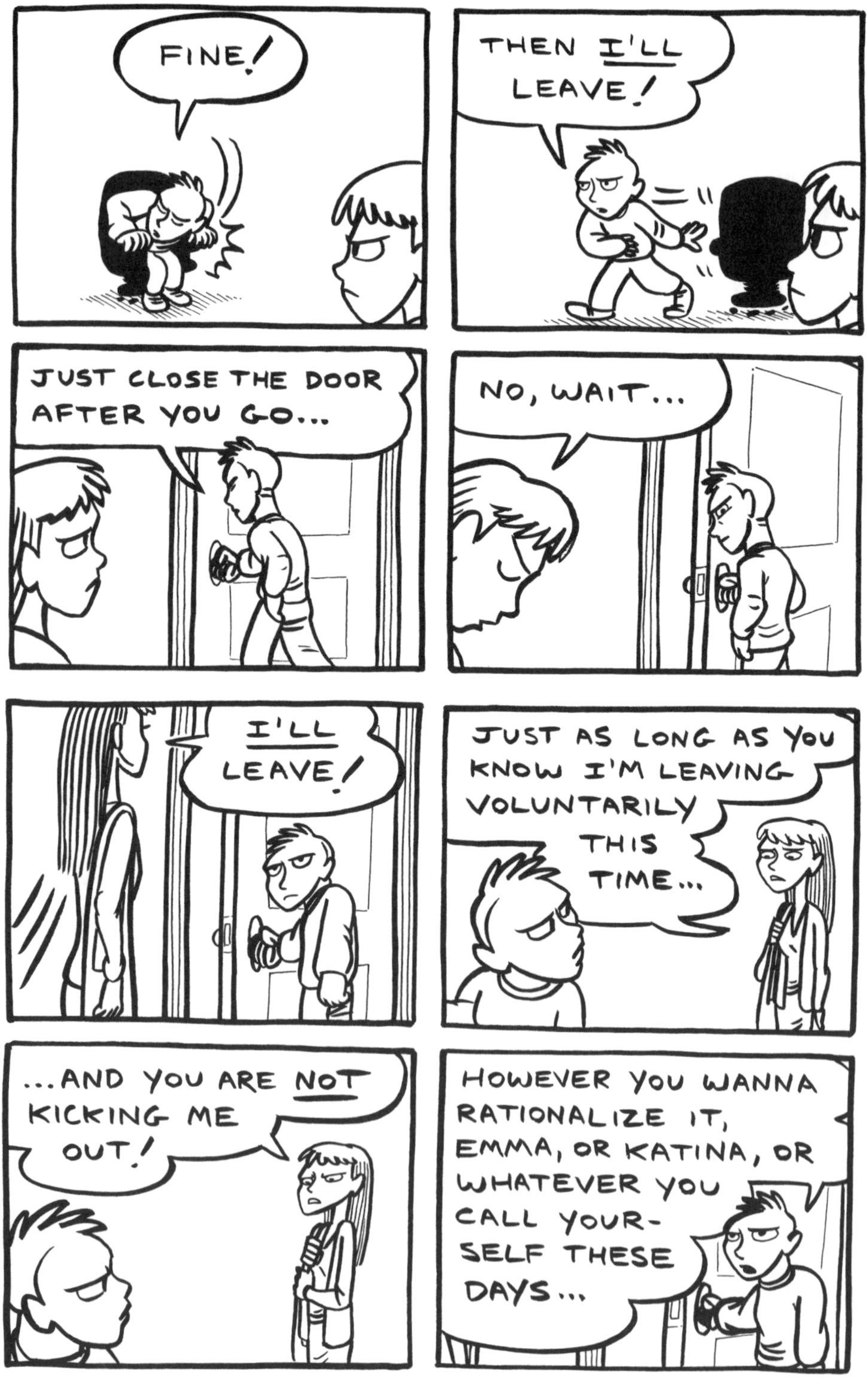

FINE!
THEN I'LL LEAVE!
JUST CLOSE THE DOOR AFTER YOU GO...
NO, WAIT...
I'LL LEAVE!
JUST AS LONG AS YOU KNOW I'M LEAVING VOLUNTARILY THIS TIME...
...AND YOU ARE NOT KICKING ME OUT!
HOWEVER YOU WANNA RATIONALIZE IT, EMMA, OR KATINA, OR WHATEVER YOU CALL YOUR-SELF THESE DAYS...

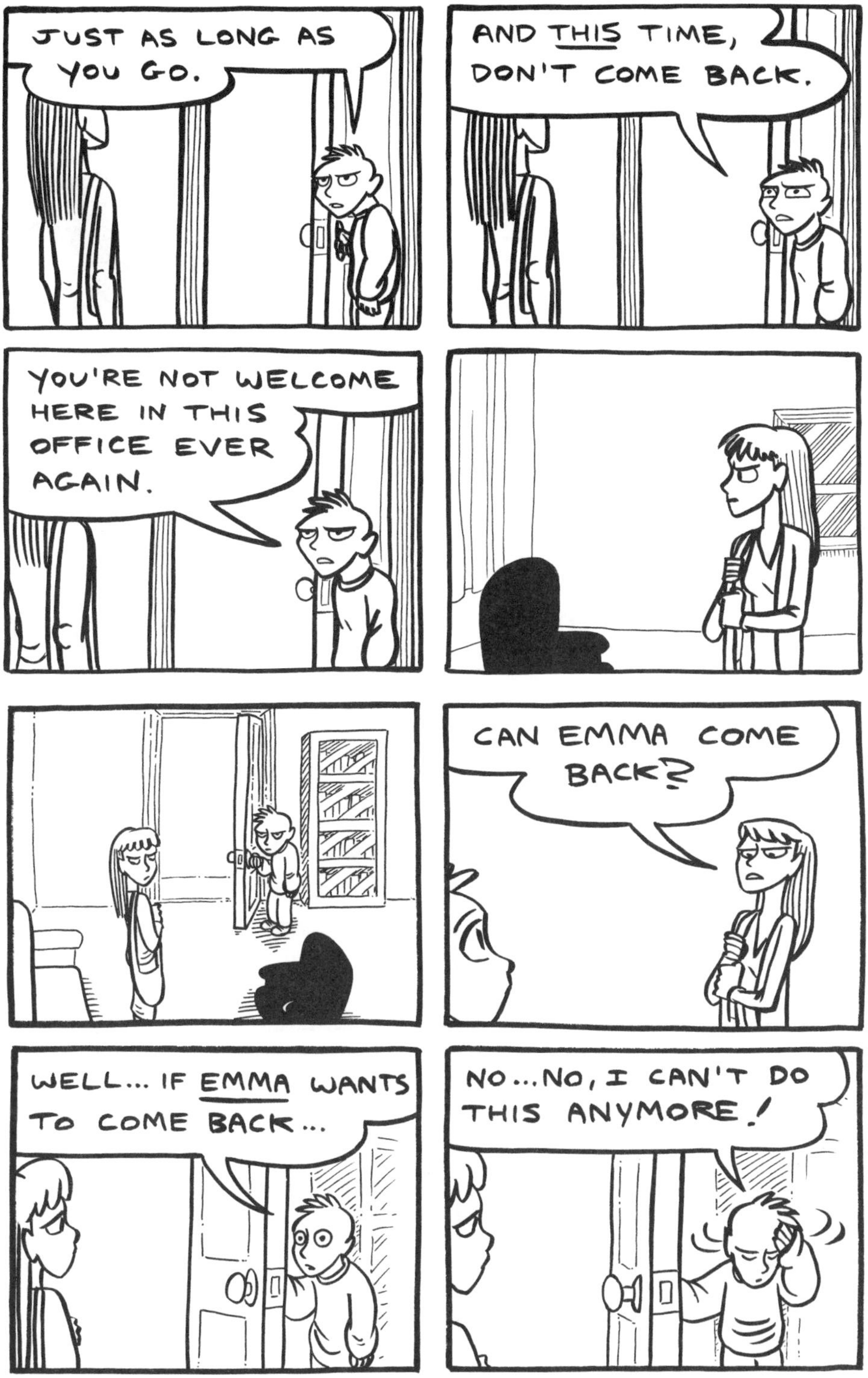
JUST AS LONG AS YOU GO.
AND THIS TIME, DON'T COME BACK.
YOU'RE NOT WELCOME HERE IN THIS OFFICE EVER AGAIN.
CAN EMMA COME BACK?
WELL... IF EMMA WANTS TO COME BACK...
NO...NO, I CAN'T DO THIS ANYMORE!

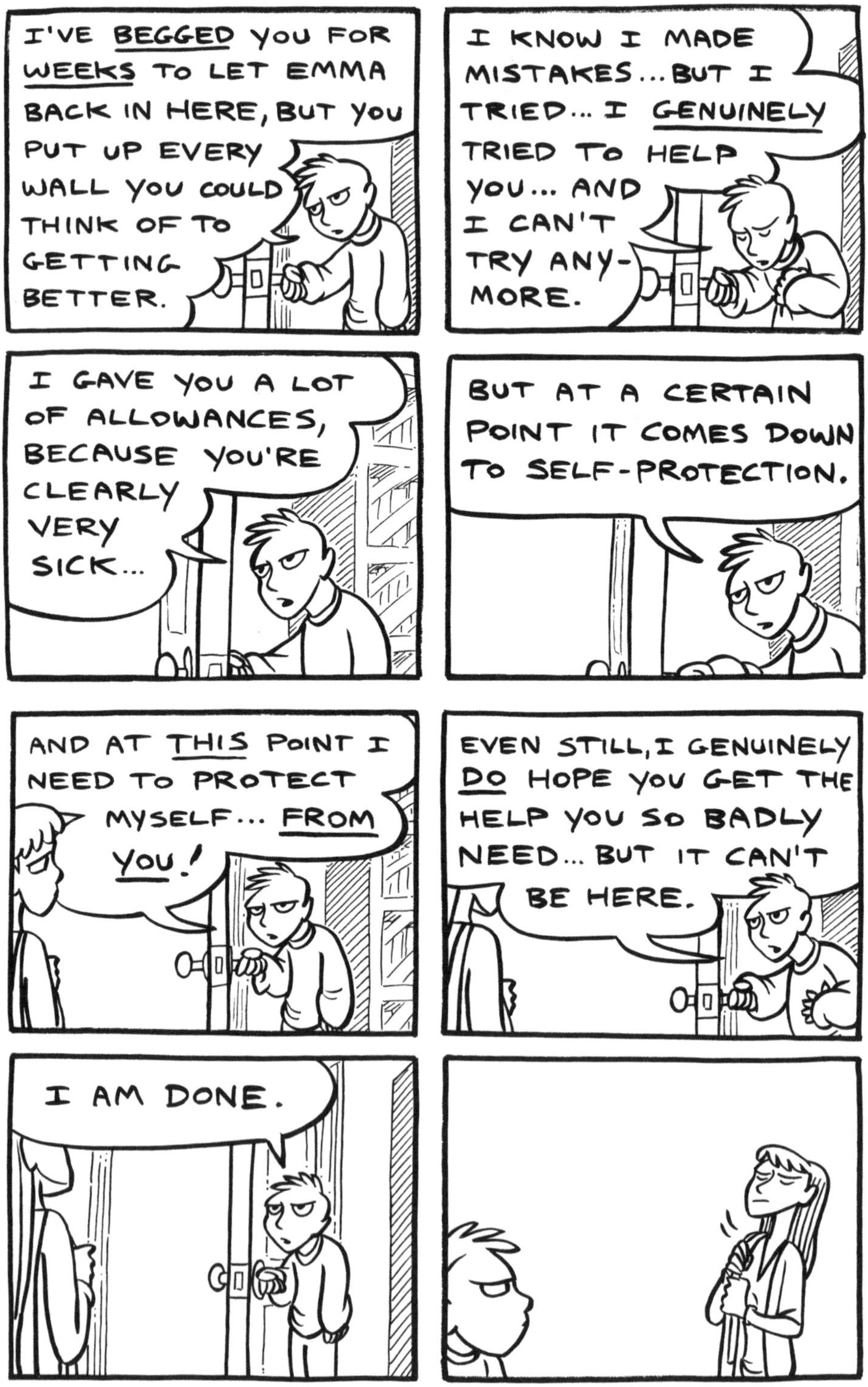
I'VE BEGGED YOU FOR WEEKS TO LET EMMA BACK IN HERE, BUT YOU PUT UP EVERY WALL YOU COULD THINK OF TO GETTING BETTER.
I KNOW I MADE MISTAKES... BUT I TRIED... I GENUINELY TRIED TO HELP YOU... AND I CAN'T TRY ANY-MORE.
I GAVE YOU A LOT OF ALLOWANCES, BECAUSE YOU'RE CLEARLY VERY SICK...
BUT AT A CERTAIN POINT IT COMES DOWN TO SELF-PROTECTION.
AND AT THIS POINT I NEED TO PROTECT MYSELF... FROM YOU!
EVEN STILL, I GENUINELY DO HOPE YOU GET THE HELP YOU SO BADLY NEED... BUT IT CAN'T BE HERE.
I AM DONE.

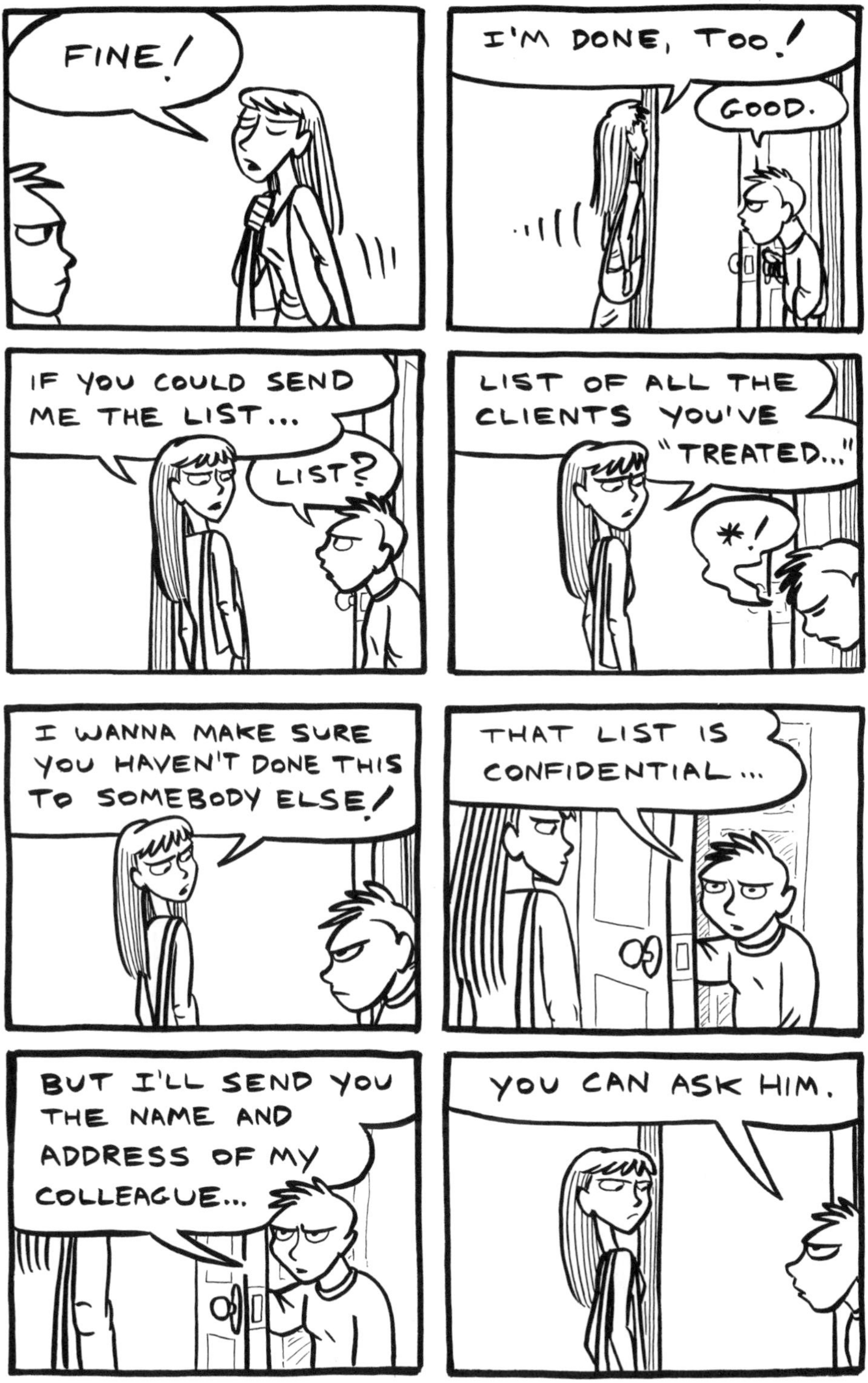
FINE!
I'M DONE, TOO!
GOOD.
IF YOU COULD SEND ME THE LIST...
LIST?
LIST OF ALL THE CLIENTS YOU'VE "TREATED..."
*!
I WANNA MAKE SURE YOU HAVEN'T DONE THIS TO SOMEBODY ELSE!
THAT LIST IS CONFIDENTIAL...
BUT I'LL SEND YOU THE NAME AND ADDRESS OF MY COLLEAGUE...
YOU CAN ASK HIM.

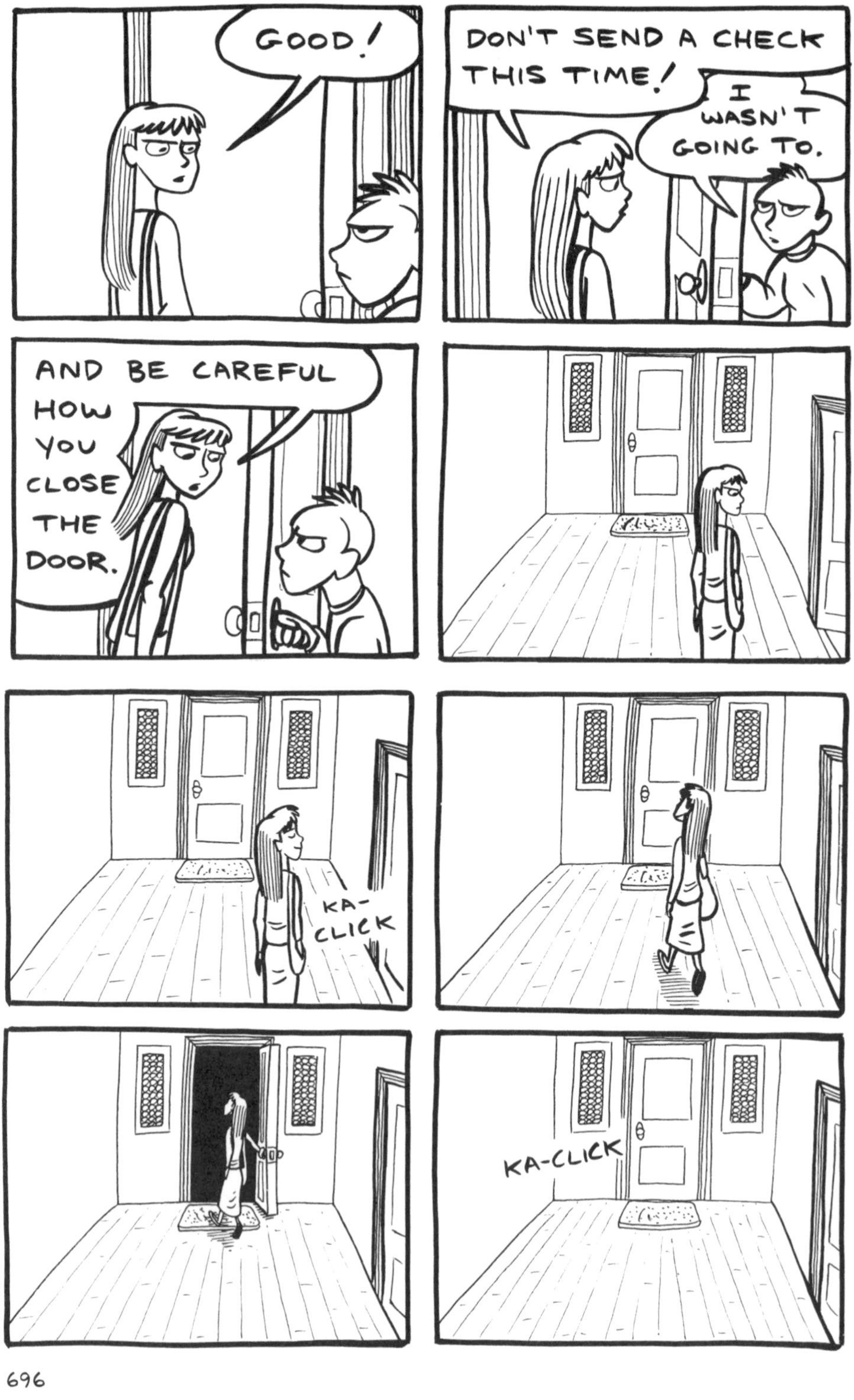
GOOD!
DON'T SEND A CHECK THIS TIME!
I WASN'T GOING TO.
AND BE CAREFUL HOW YOU CLOSE THE DOOR.
KA-CLICK
KA-CLICK

BOOK THREE

CORE SELF

ROCK

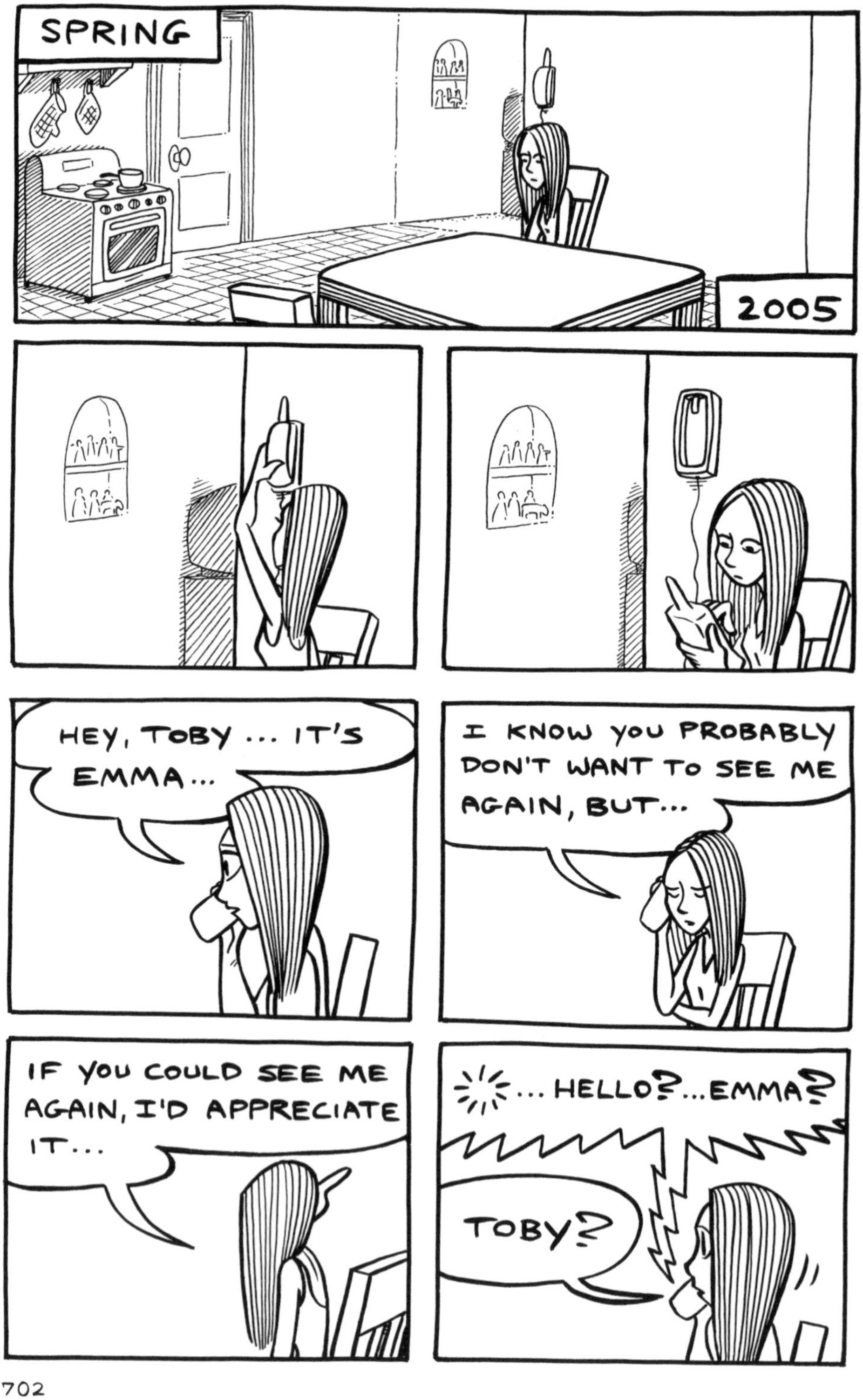
SPRING
2005
HEY, TOBY ... IT'S EMMA...
I KNOW YOU PROBABLY DON'T WANT TO SEE ME AGAIN, BUT...
IF YOU COULD SEE ME AGAIN, I'D APPRECIATE IT...
... HELLO?...EMMA?
TOBY?

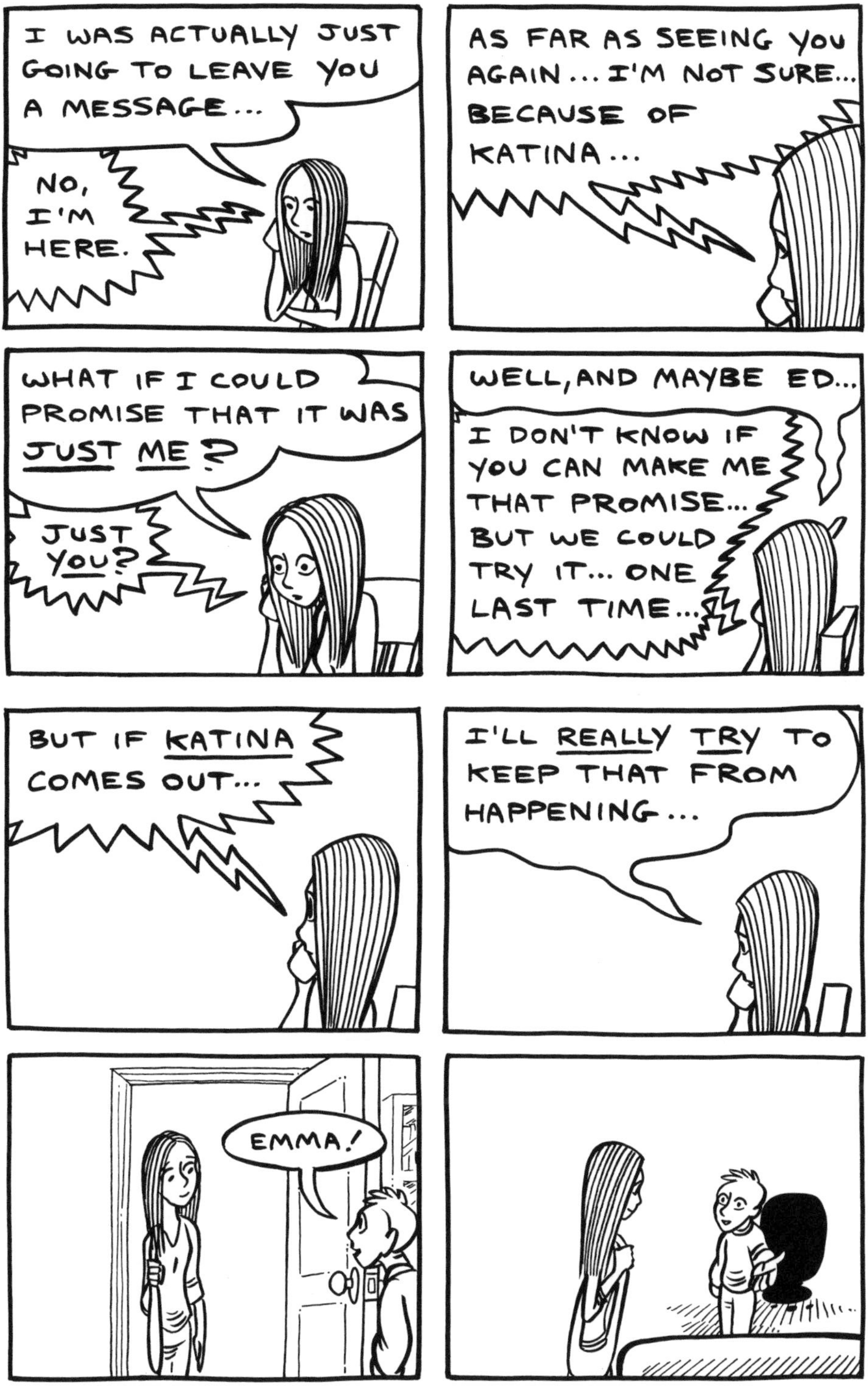
I WAS ACTUALLY JUST GOING TO LEAVE YOU A MESSAGE...
NO, I'M HERE.
AS FAR AS SEEING YOU AGAIN... I'M NOT SURE... BECAUSE OF KATINA...
WHAT IF I COULD PROMISE THAT IT WAS JUST ME?
JUST YOU?
WELL, AND MAYBE ED...
I DON'T KNOW IF YOU CAN MAKE ME THAT PROMISE... BUT WE COULD TRY IT... ONE LAST TIME...
BUT IF KATINA COMES OUT...
I'LL REALLY TRY TO KEEP THAT FROM HAPPENING...
EMMA!

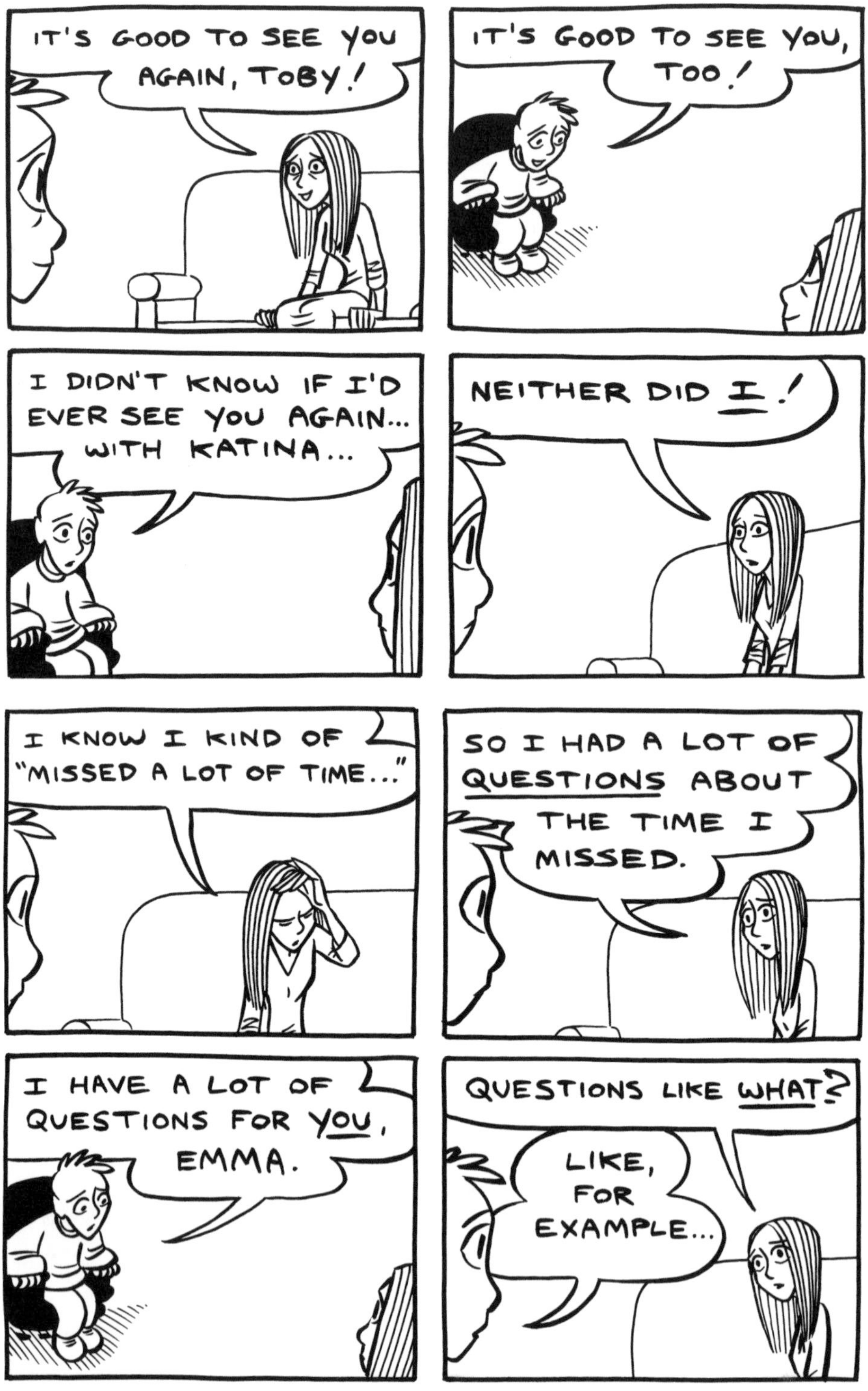
IT'S GOOD TO SEE YOU AGAIN, TOBY!
IT'S GOOD TO SEE YOU, TOO!
I DIDN'T KNOW IF I'D EVER SEE YOU AGAIN... WITH KATINA...
NEITHER DID I!
I KNOW I KIND OF "MISSED A LOT OF TIME..."
SO I HAD A LOT OF QUESTIONS ABOUT THE TIME I MISSED.
I HAVE A LOT OF QUESTIONS FOR YOU, EMMA.
QUESTIONS LIKE WHAT?
LIKE, FOR EXAMPLE...

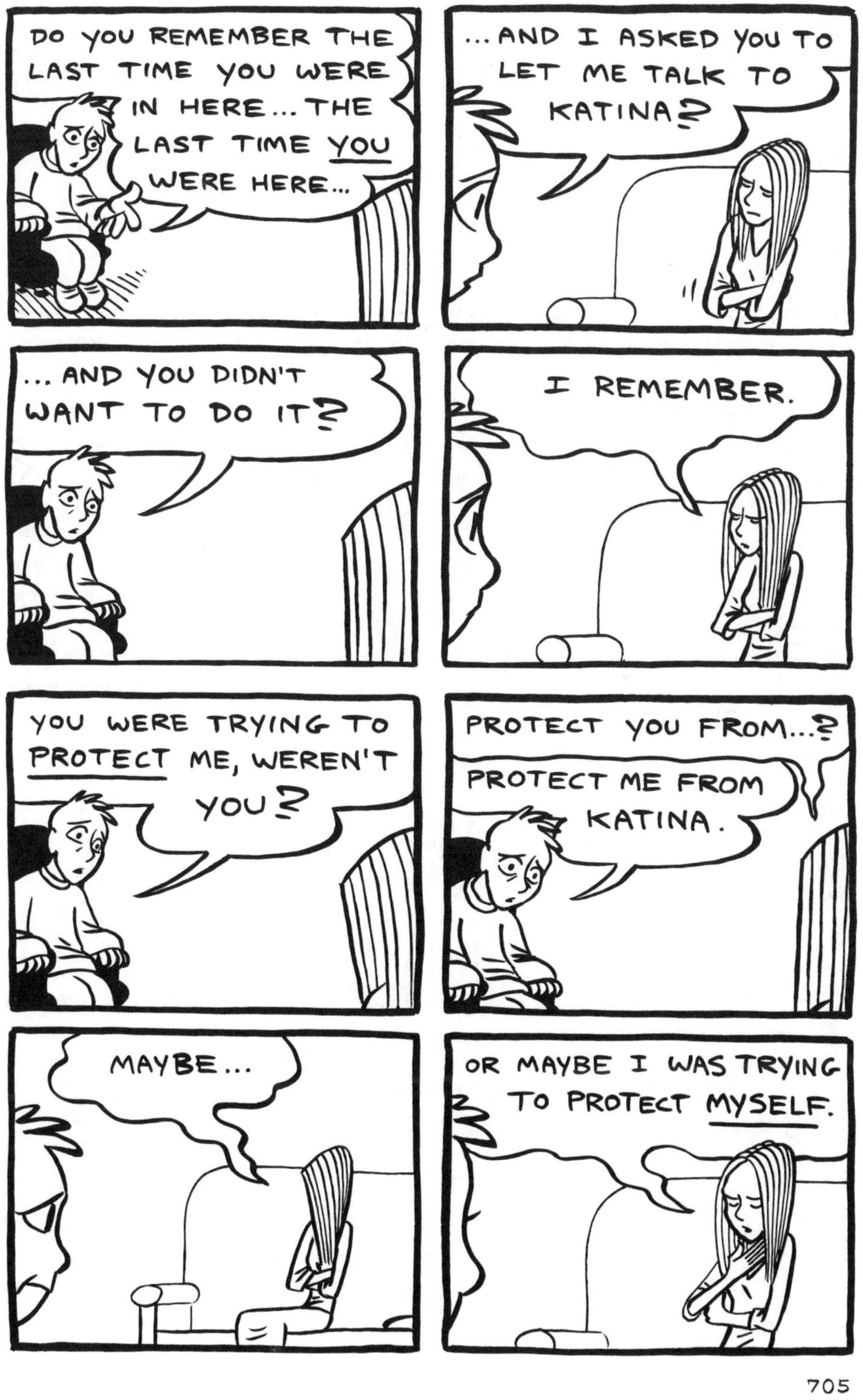
DO YOU REMEMBER THE LAST TIME YOU WERE IN HERE... THE LAST TIME YOU WERE HERE...
...AND I ASKED YOU TO LET ME TALK TO KATINA?
...AND YOU DIDN'T WANT TO DO IT?
I REMEMBER.
YOU WERE TRYING TO PROTECT ME, WEREN'T YOU?
PROTECT YOU FROM...?
PROTECT ME FROM KATINA.
MAYBE...
OR MAYBE I WAS TRYING TO PROTECT MYSELF.

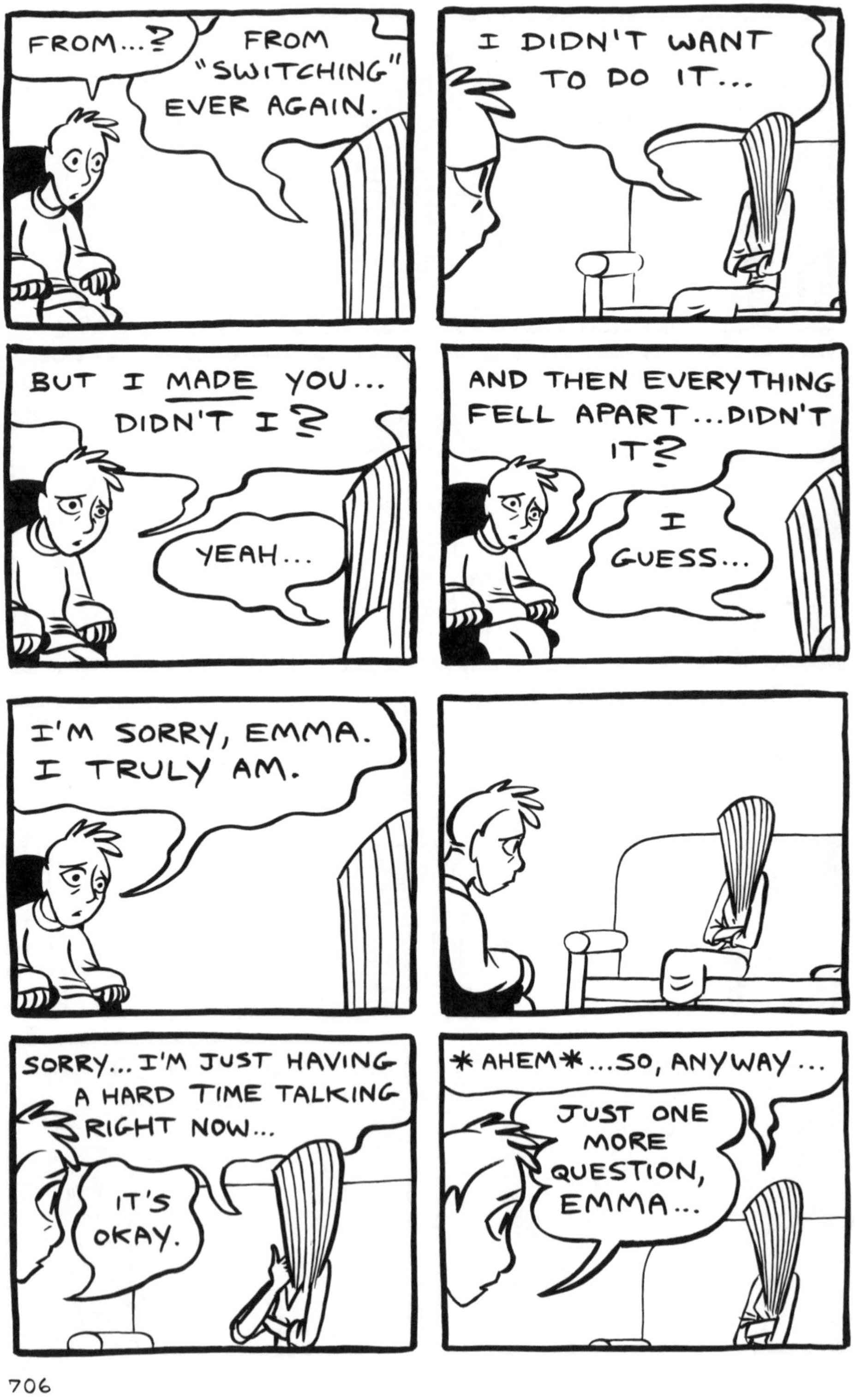
FROM...?
FROM "SWITCHING" EVER AGAIN.
I DIDN'T WANT TO DO IT...
BUT I MADE YOU... DIDN'T I?
YEAH...
AND THEN EVERYTHING FELL APART...DIDN'T IT?
I GUESS...
I'M SORRY, EMMA. I TRULY AM.
SORRY... I'M JUST HAVING A HARD TIME TALKING RIGHT NOW...
IT'S OKAY.
AHEM...SO, ANYWAY...
JUST ONE MORE QUESTION, EMMA...

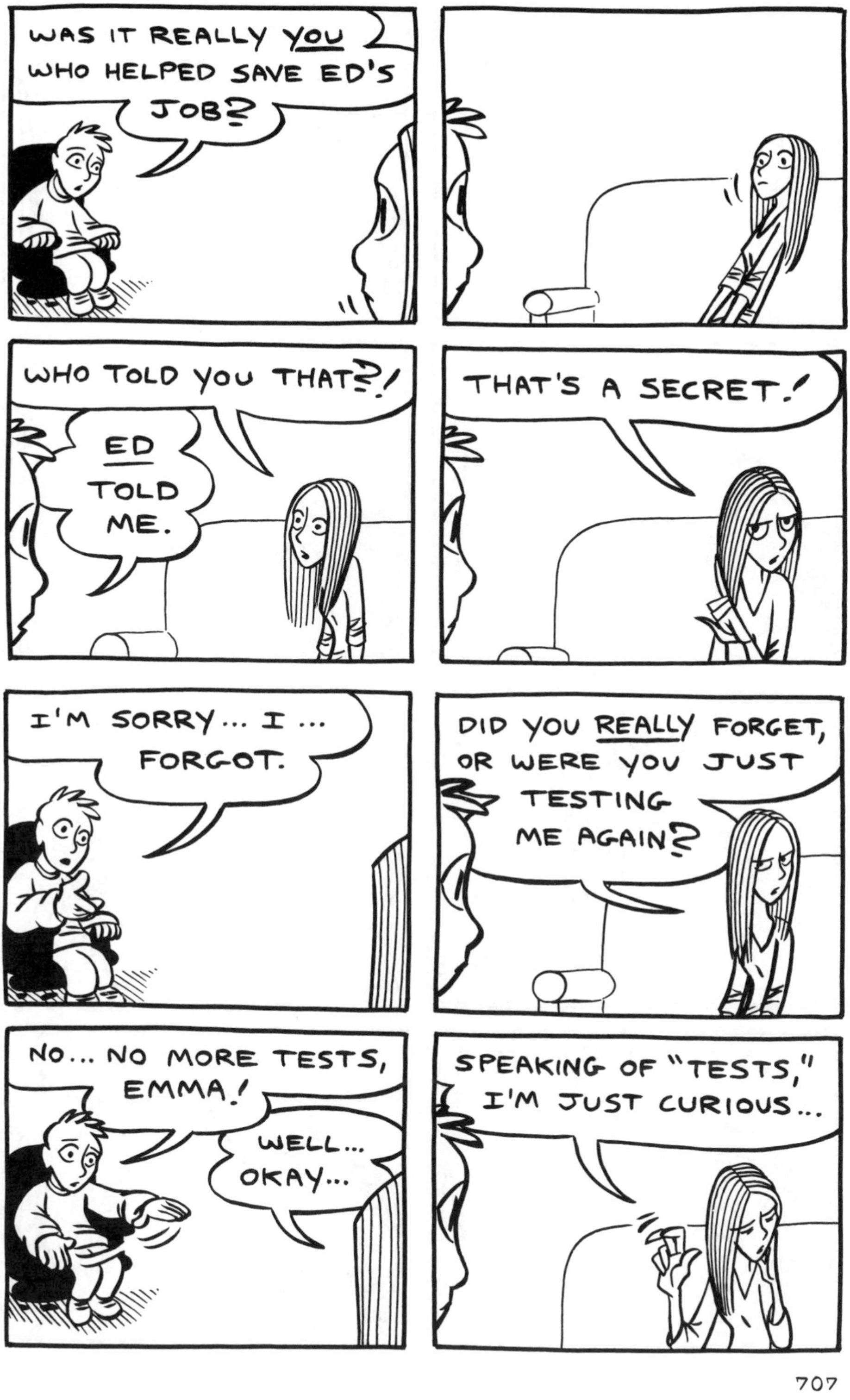
WAS IT REALLY YOU WHO HELPED SAVE ED'S JOB?
WHO TOLD YOU THAT?!
ED TOLD ME.
THAT'S A SECRET!
I'M SORRY... I... FORGOT.
DID YOU REALLY FORGET, OR WERE YOU JUST TESTING ME AGAIN?
NO... NO MORE TESTS, EMMA!
WELL... OKAY...
SPEAKING OF "TESTS," I'M JUST CURIOUS...

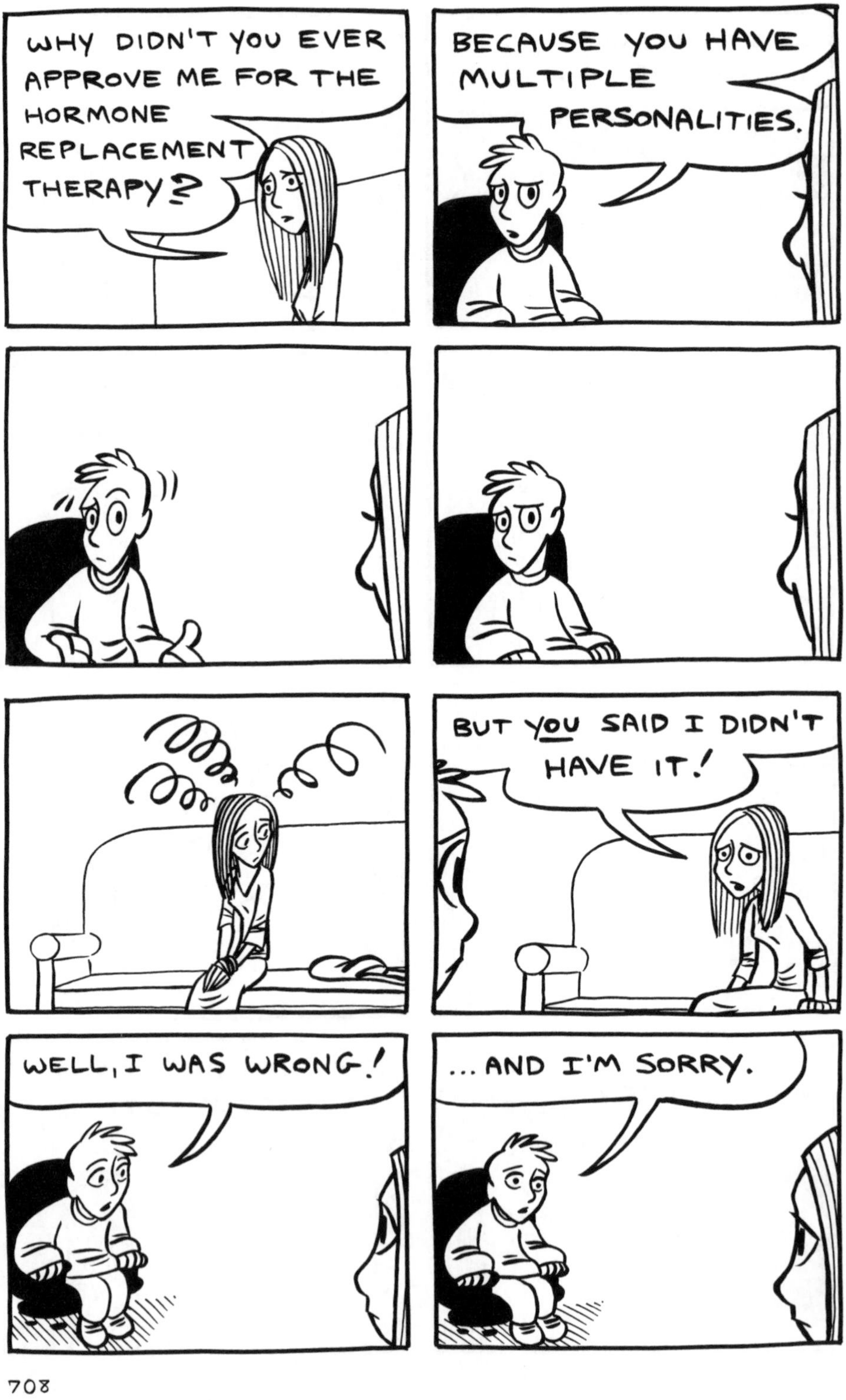

WHY DIDN'T YOU EVER APPROVE ME FOR THE HORMONE REPLACEMENT THERAPY?
BECAUSE YOU HAVE MULTIPLE PERSONALITIES.
BUT YOU SAID I DIDN'T HAVE IT!
WELL, I WAS WRONG!
... AND I'M SORRY.

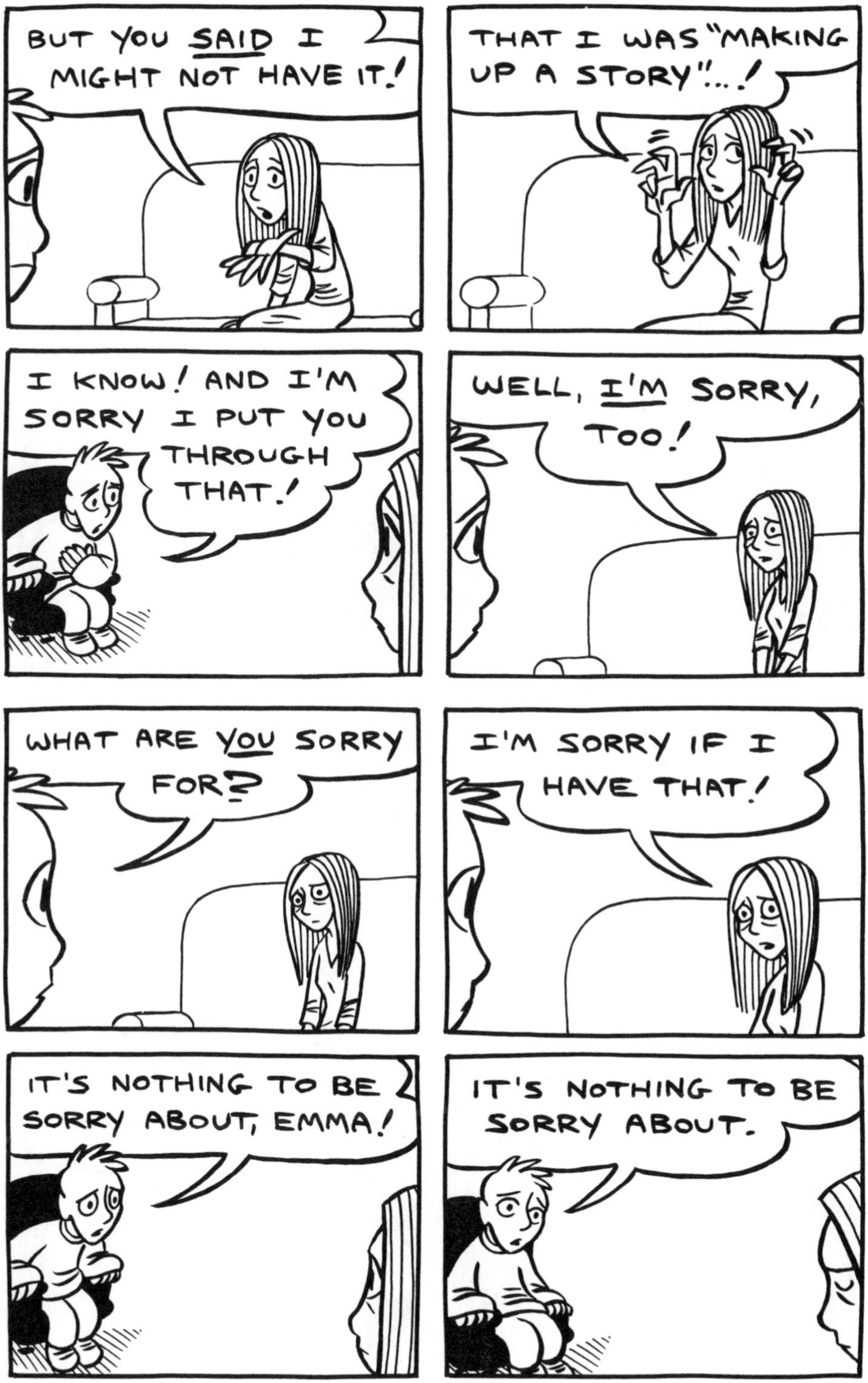
BUT YOU SAID I MIGHT NOT HAVE IT!
THAT I WAS "MAKING UP A STORY"...!
I KNOW! AND I'M SORRY I PUT YOU THROUGH THAT!
WELL, I'M SORRY, TOO!
WHAT ARE YOU SORRY FOR?
I'M SORRY IF I HAVE THAT!
IT'S NOTHING TO BE SORRY ABOUT, EMMA!
IT'S NOTHING TO BE SORRY ABOUT.

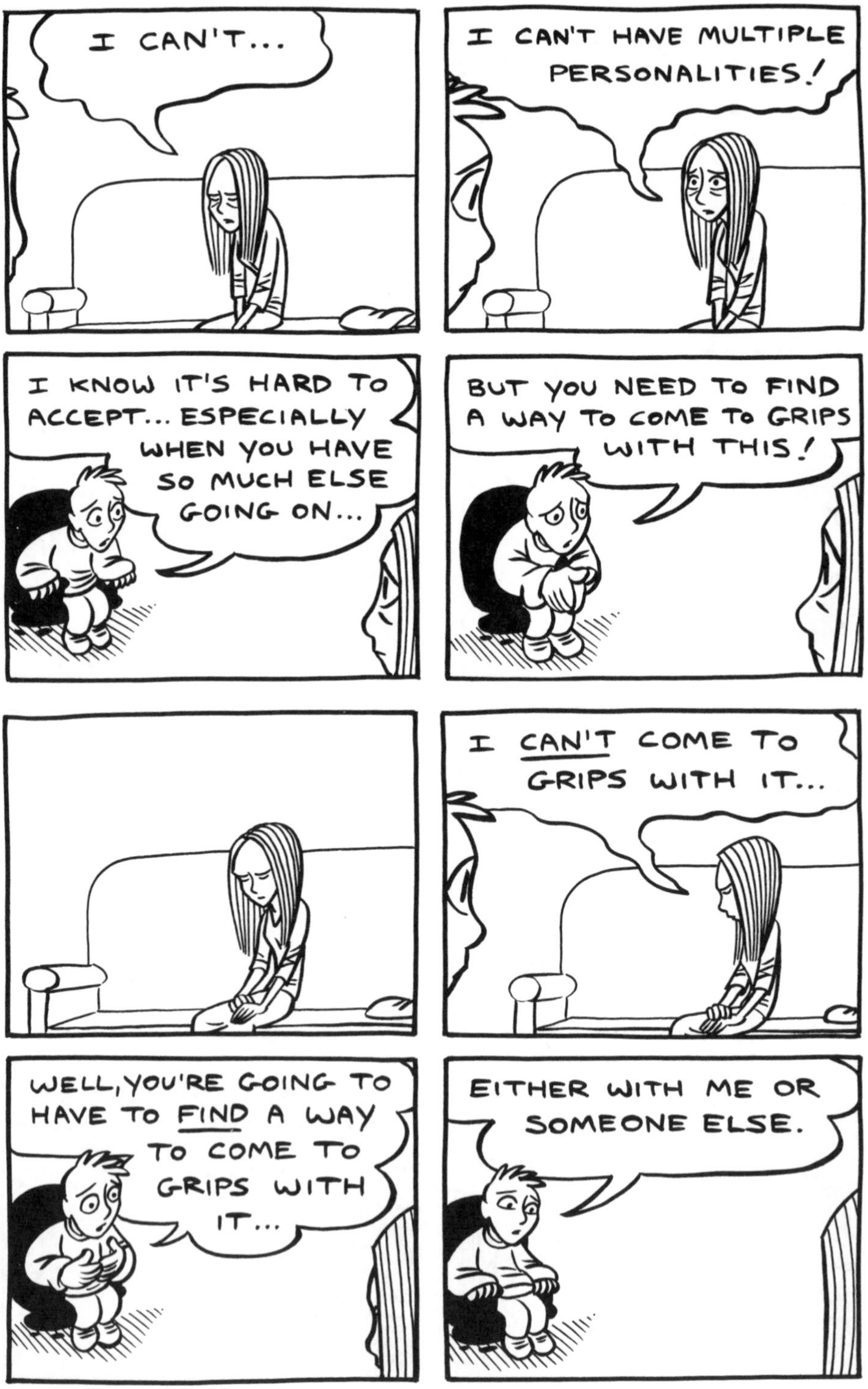
I CAN'T...
I CAN'T HAVE MULTIPLE PERSONALITIES!
I KNOW IT'S HARD TO ACCEPT... ESPECIALLY WHEN YOU HAVE SO MUCH ELSE GOING ON...
BUT YOU NEED TO FIND A WAY TO COME TO GRIPS WITH THIS!
I CAN'T COME TO GRIPS WITH IT...
WELL, YOU'RE GOING TO HAVE TO FIND A WAY TO COME TO GRIPS WITH IT...
EITHER WITH ME OR SOMEONE ELSE.

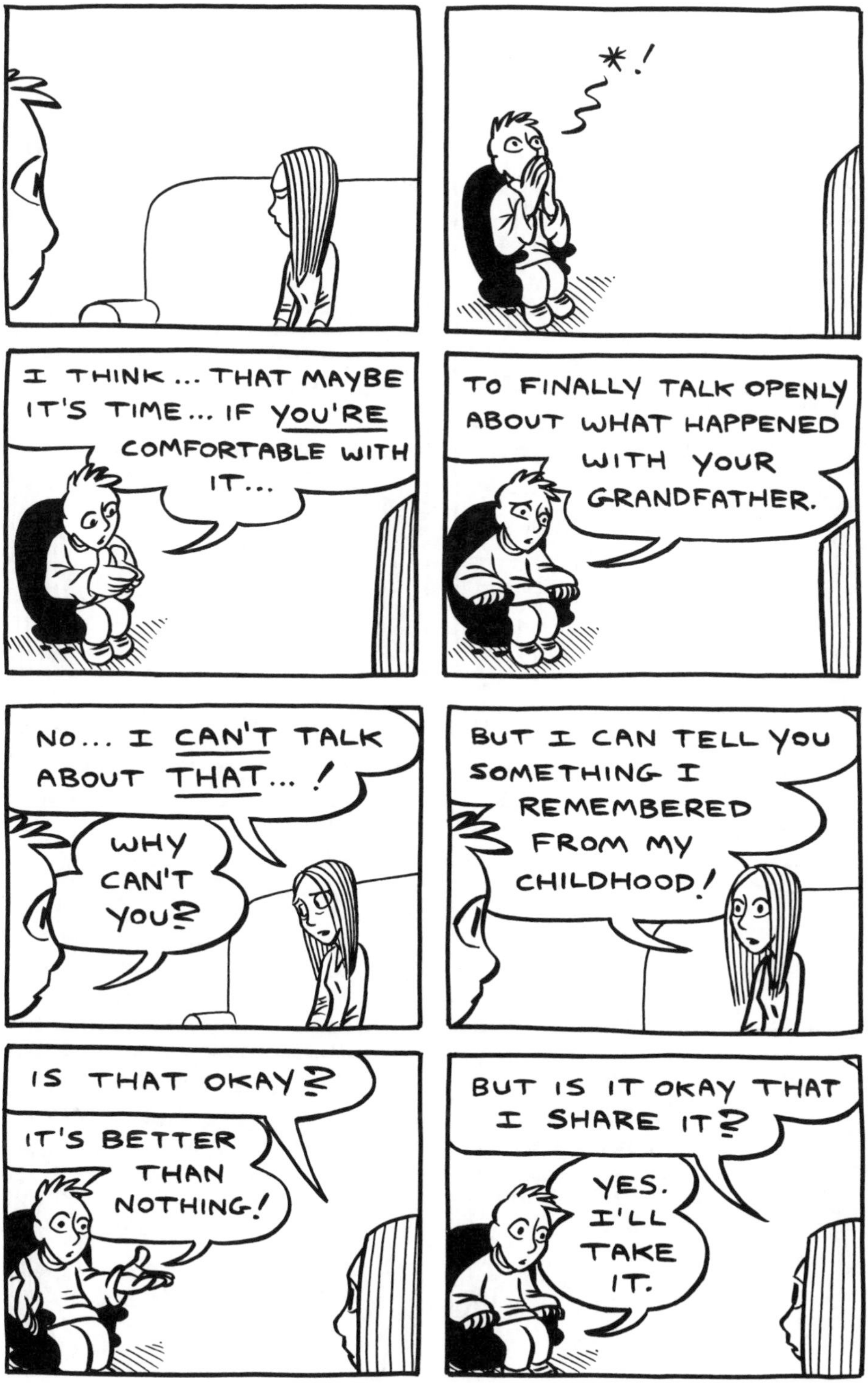

*!
I THINK... THAT MAYBE IT'S TIME... IF YOU'RE COMFORTABLE WITH IT...
TO FINALLY TALK OPENLY ABOUT WHAT HAPPENED WITH YOUR GRANDFATHER.
NO... I CAN'T TALK ABOUT THAT... !
WHY CAN'T YOU?
BUT I CAN TELL YOU SOMETHING I REMEMBERED FROM MY CHILDHOOD!
IS THAT OKAY?
IT'S BETTER THAN NOTHING!
BUT IS IT OKAY THAT I SHARE IT?
YES. I'LL TAKE IT.

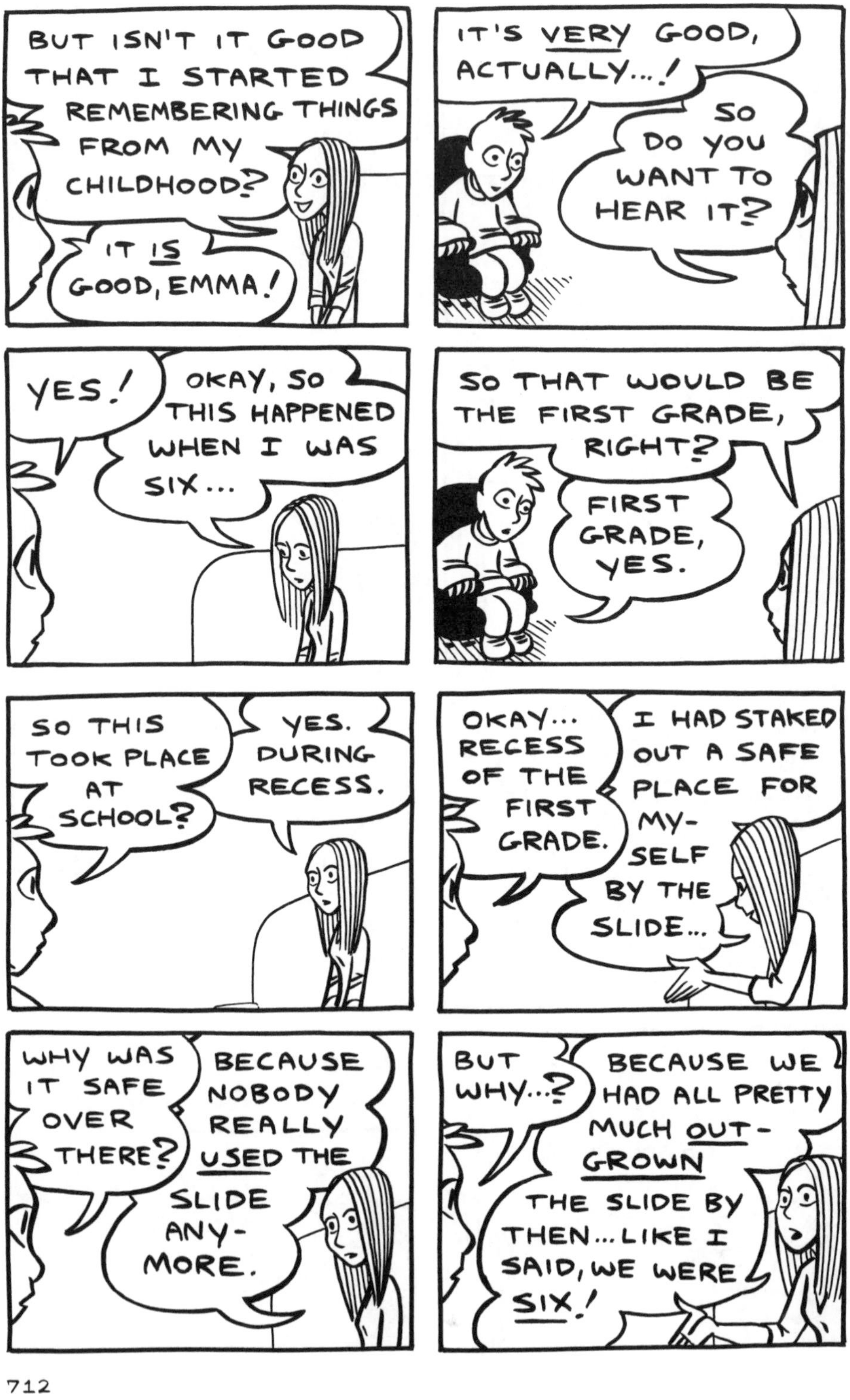
BUT ISN'T IT GOOD THAT I STARTED REMEMBERING THINGS FROM MY CHILDHOOD?
IT IS GOOD, EMMA!
IT'S VERY GOOD, ACTUALLY...!
SO DO YOU WANT TO HEAR IT?
YES!
OKAY, SO THIS HAPPENED WHEN I WAS SIX...
SO THAT WOULD BE THE FIRST GRADE, RIGHT?
FIRST GRADE, YES.
SO THIS TOOK PLACE AT SCHOOL?
YES. DURING RECESS.
OKAY... RECESS OF THE FIRST GRADE.
I HAD STAKED OUT A SAFE PLACE FOR MY-SELF BY THE SLIDE...
WHY WAS IT SAFE OVER THERE?
BECAUSE NOBODY REALLY USED THE SLIDE ANY-MORE.
BUT WHY...?
BECAUSE WE HAD ALL PRETTY MUCH OUT-GROWN THE SLIDE BY THEN... LIKE I SAID, WE WERE SIX!

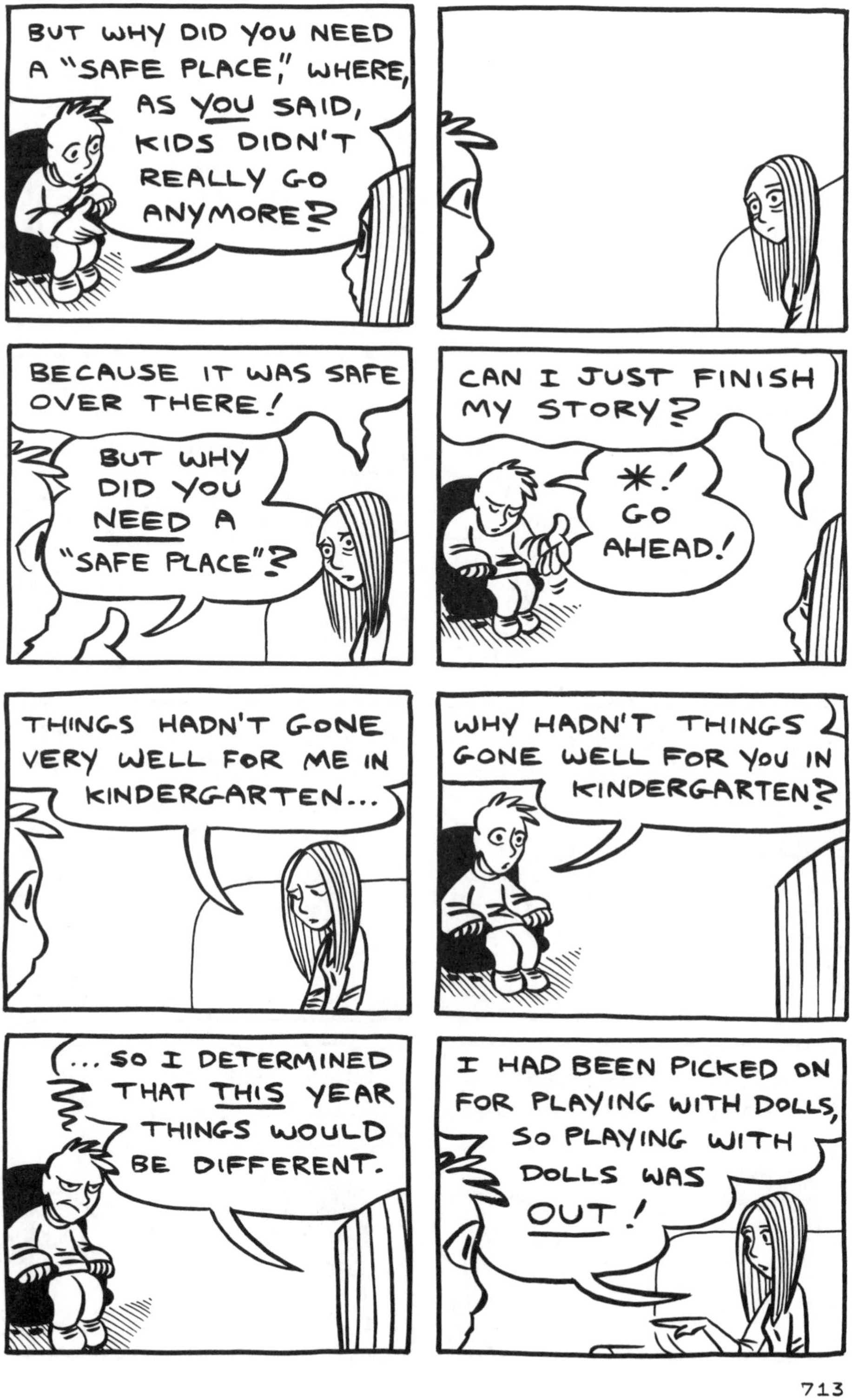
BUT WHY DID YOU NEED A "SAFE PLACE," WHERE, AS YOU SAID, KIDS DIDN'T REALLY GO ANYMORE?
BECAUSE IT WAS SAFE OVER THERE!
BUT WHY DID YOU NEED A "SAFE PLACE"?
CAN I JUST FINISH MY STORY?
*! GO AHEAD!
THINGS HADN'T GONE VERY WELL FOR ME IN KINDERGARTEN...
WHY HADN'T THINGS GONE WELL FOR YOU IN KINDERGARTEN?
... SO I DETERMINED THAT THIS YEAR THINGS WOULD BE DIFFERENT.
I HAD BEEN PICKED ON FOR PLAYING WITH DOLLS, SO PLAYING WITH DOLLS WAS OUT!

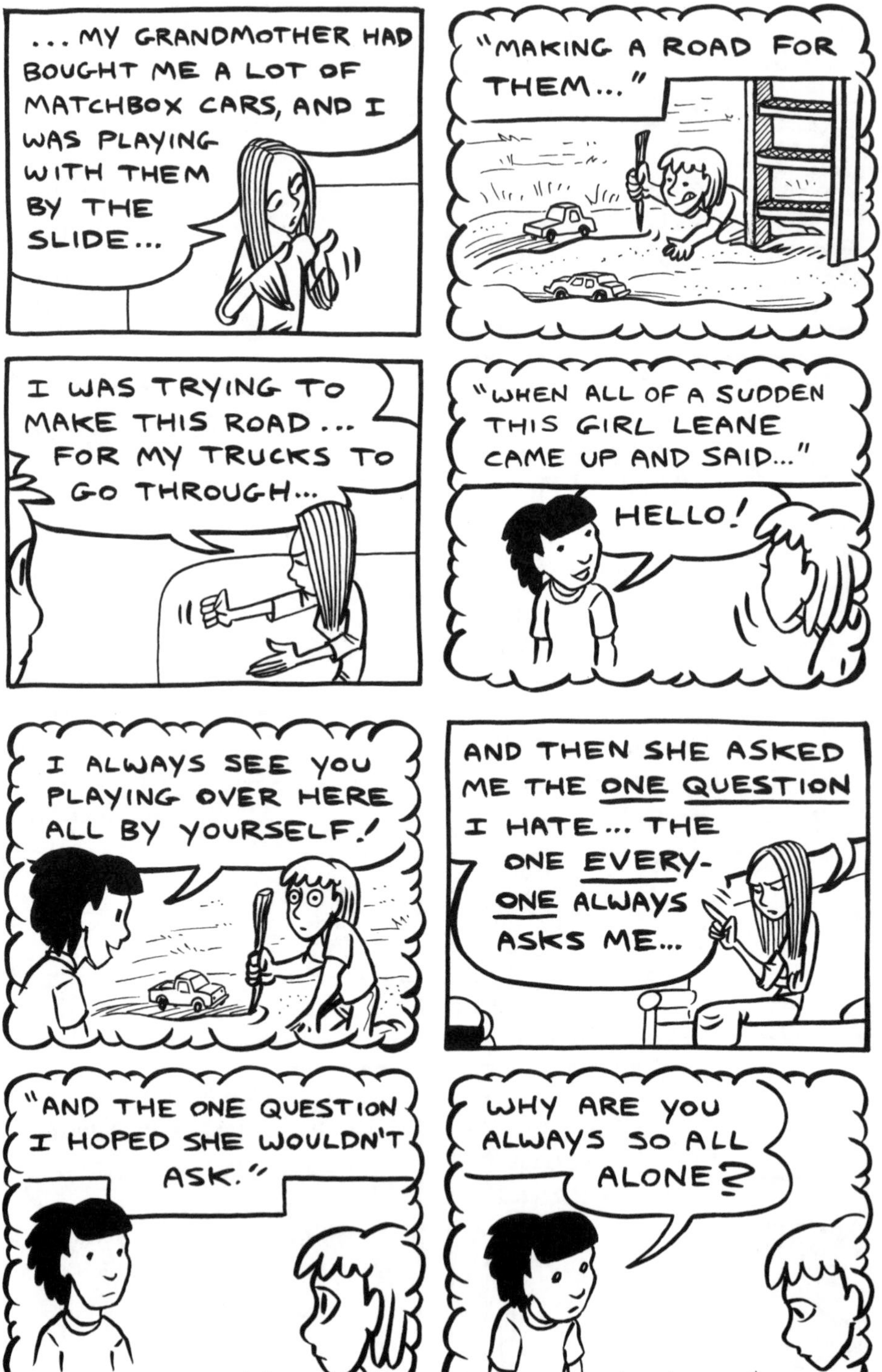

...MY GRANDMOTHER HAD BOUGHT ME A LOT OF MATCHBOX CARS, AND I WAS PLAYING WITH THEM BY THE SLIDE...
"MAKING A ROAD FOR THEM..."
I WAS TRYING TO MAKE THIS ROAD... FOR MY TRUCKS TO GO THROUGH...
"WHEN ALL OF A SUDDEN THIS GIRL LEANE CAME UP AND SAID..."
HELLO!
I ALWAYS SEE YOU PLAYING OVER HERE ALL BY YOURSELF!
AND THEN SHE ASKED ME THE ONE QUESTION I HATE... THE ONE EVERY-ONE ALWAYS ASKS ME...
"AND THE ONE QUESTION I HOPED SHE WOULDN'T ASK."
WHY ARE YOU ALWAYS SO ALL ALONE?

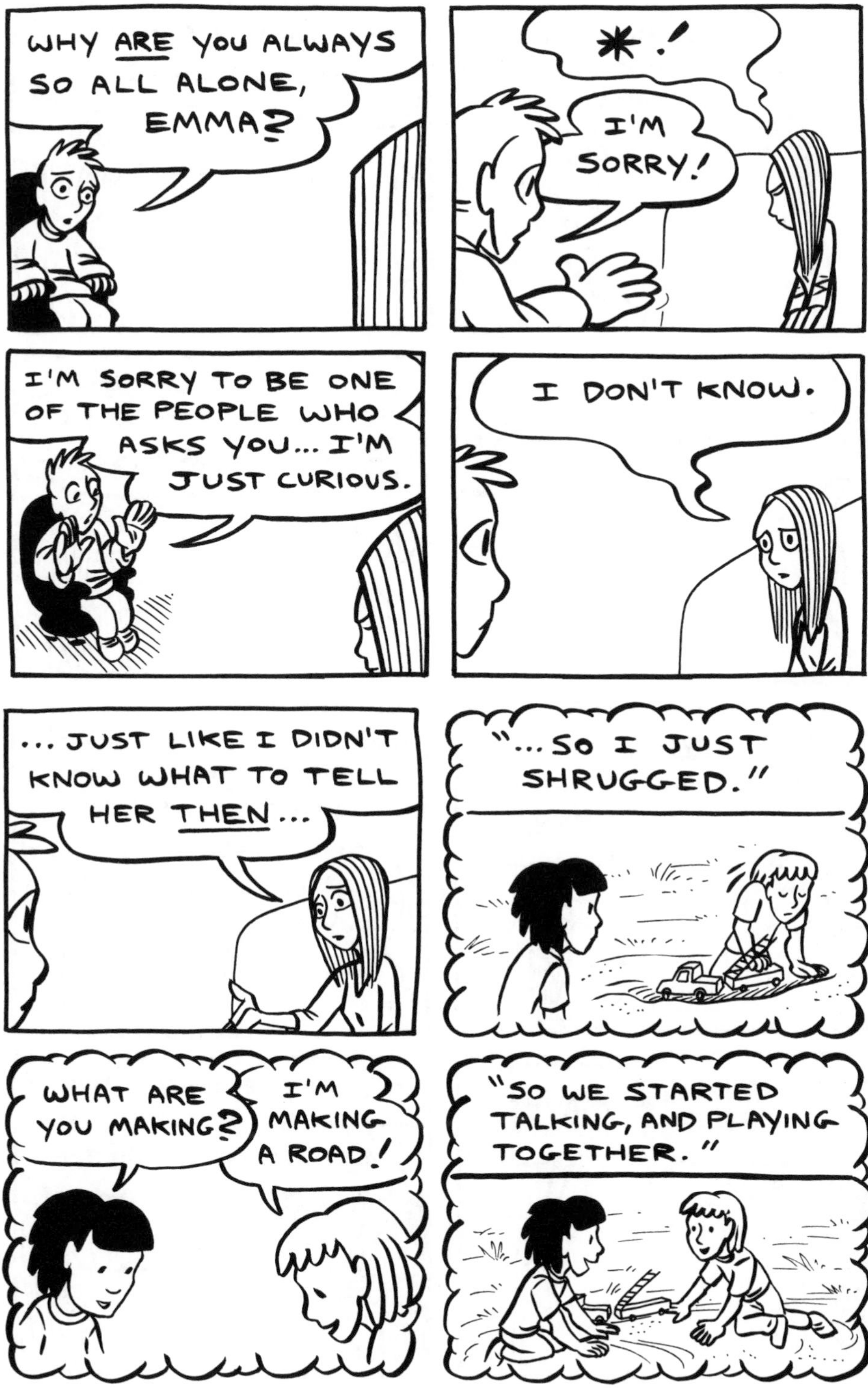
WHY ARE YOU ALWAYS SO ALL ALONE, EMMA?
*!
I'M SORRY!
I'M SORRY TO BE ONE OF THE PEOPLE WHO ASKS YOU... I'M JUST CURIOUS.
I DON'T KNOW.
... JUST LIKE I DIDN'T KNOW WHAT TO TELL HER THEN...
"... SO I JUST SHRUGGED."
WHAT ARE YOU MAKING?
I'M MAKING A ROAD!
"SO WE STARTED TALKING, AND PLAYING TOGETHER."

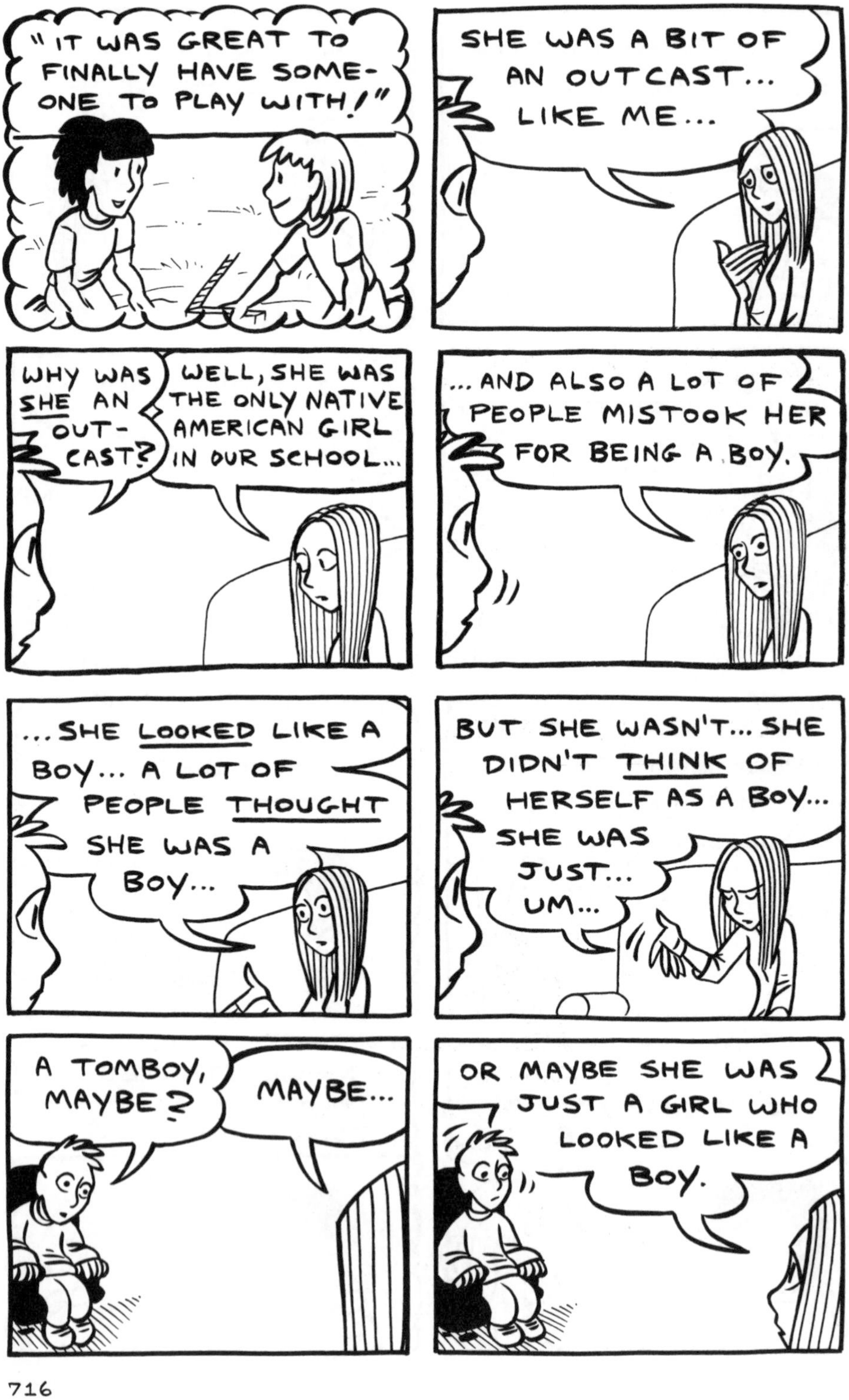
"IT WAS GREAT TO FINALLY HAVE SOME-ONE TO PLAY WITH!"
SHE WAS A BIT OF AN OUTCAST... LIKE ME...
WHY WAS SHE AN OUT-CAST?
WELL, SHE WAS THE ONLY NATIVE AMERICAN GIRL IN OUR SCHOOL...
...AND ALSO A LOT OF PEOPLE MISTOOK HER FOR BEING A BOY.
...SHE LOOKED LIKE A BOY... A LOT OF PEOPLE THOUGHT SHE WAS A BOY...
BUT SHE WASN'T... SHE DIDN'T THINK OF HERSELF AS A BOY...
SHE WAS JUST... UM...
A TOMBOY, MAYBE?
MAYBE...
OR MAYBE SHE WAS JUST A GIRL WHO LOOKED LIKE A BOY.

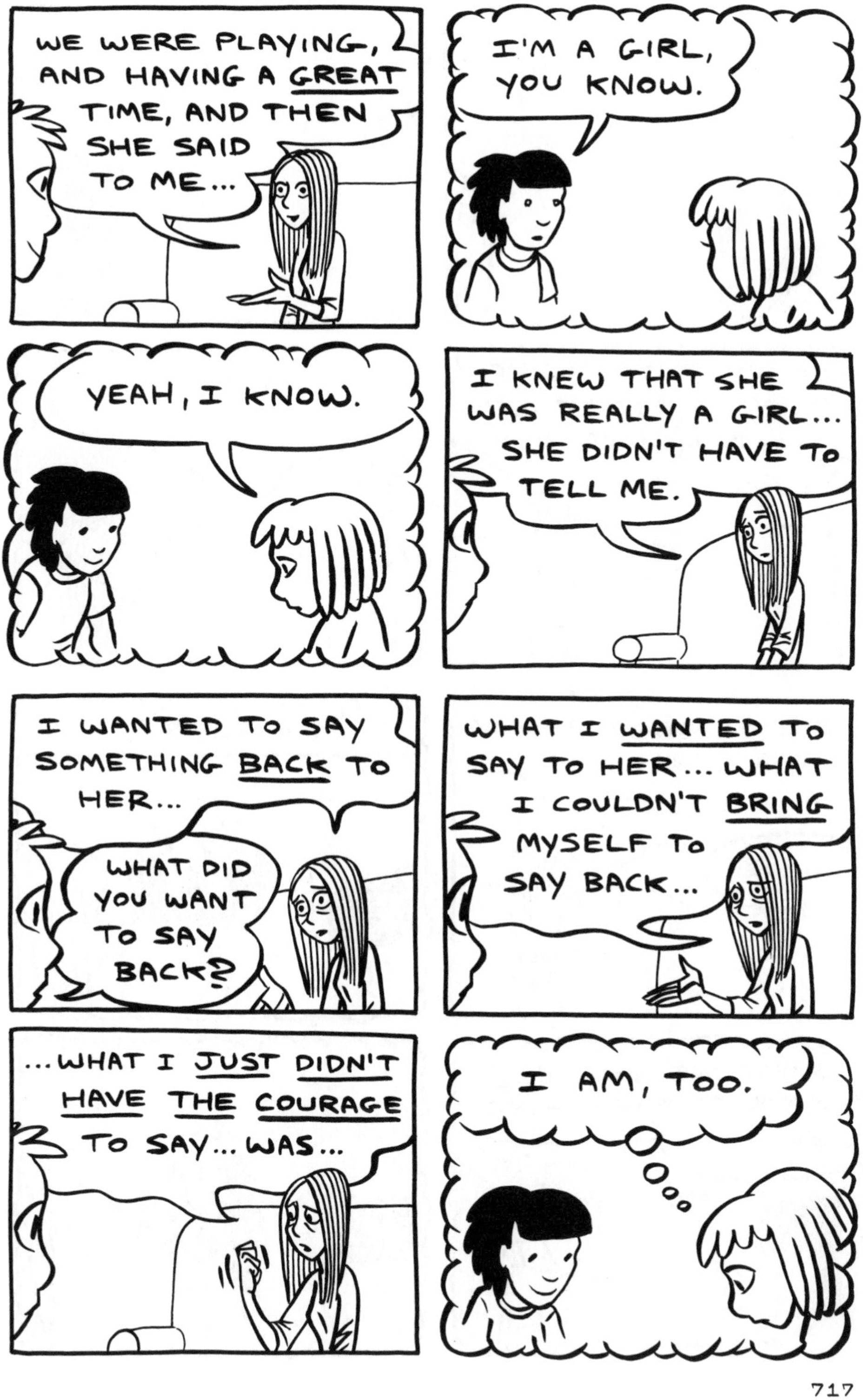
WE WERE PLAYING, AND HAVING A GREAT TIME, AND THEN SHE SAID TO ME...
I'M A GIRL, YOU KNOW.
YEAH, I KNOW.
I KNEW THAT SHE WAS REALLY A GIRL... SHE DIDN'T HAVE TO TELL ME.
I WANTED TO SAY SOMETHING BACK TO HER...
WHAT DID YOU WANT TO SAY BACK?
WHAT I WANTED TO SAY TO HER... WHAT I COULDN'T BRING MYSELF TO SAY BACK...
...WHAT I JUST DIDN'T HAVE THE COURAGE TO SAY... WAS...
I AM, TOO.

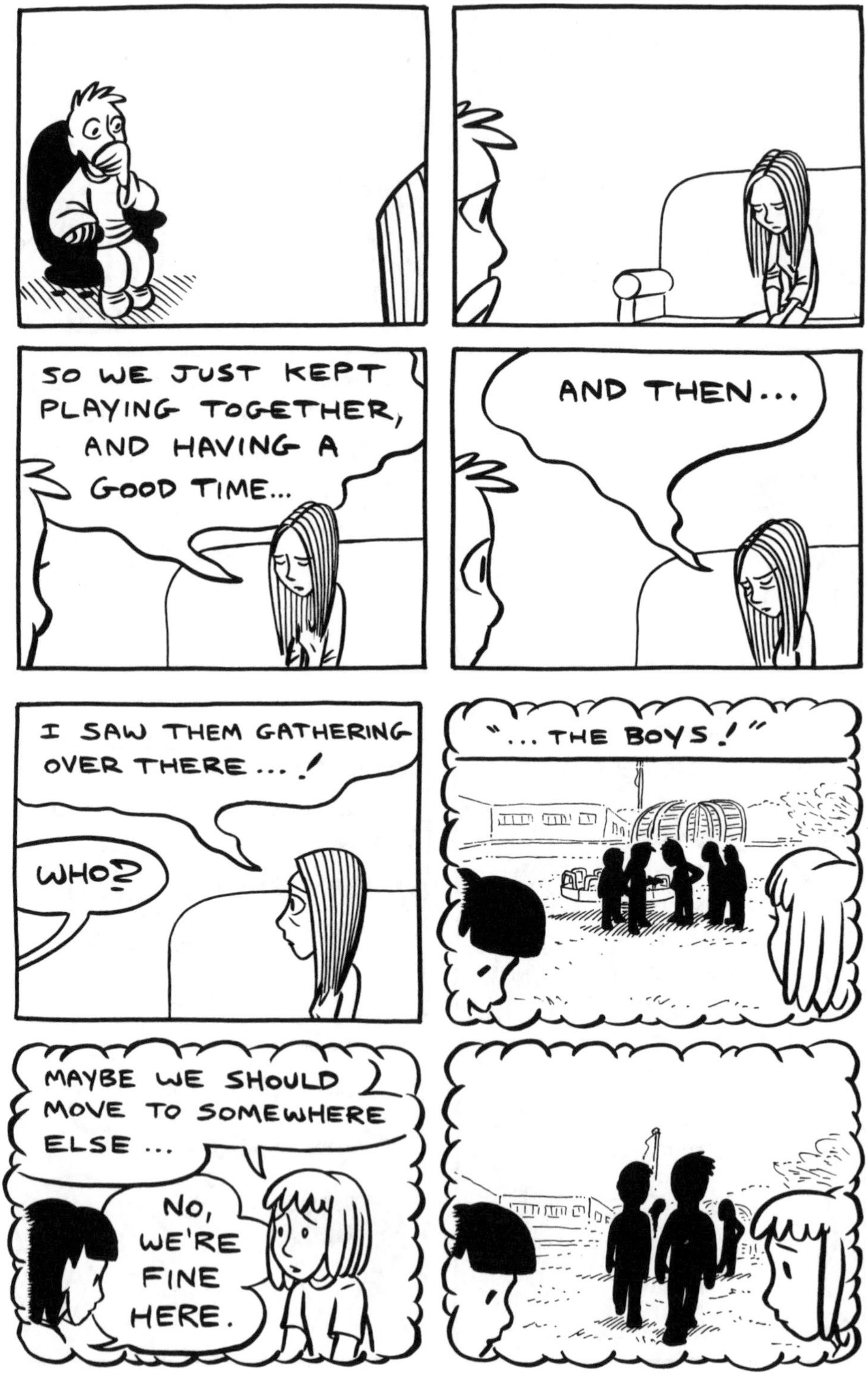
SO WE JUST KEPT PLAYING TOGETHER, AND HAVING A GOOD TIME...
AND THEN...
I SAW THEM GATHERING OVER THERE...!
WHO?
"...THE BOYS!"
MAYBE WE SHOULD MOVE TO SOMEWHERE ELSE...
NO, WE'RE FINE HERE.

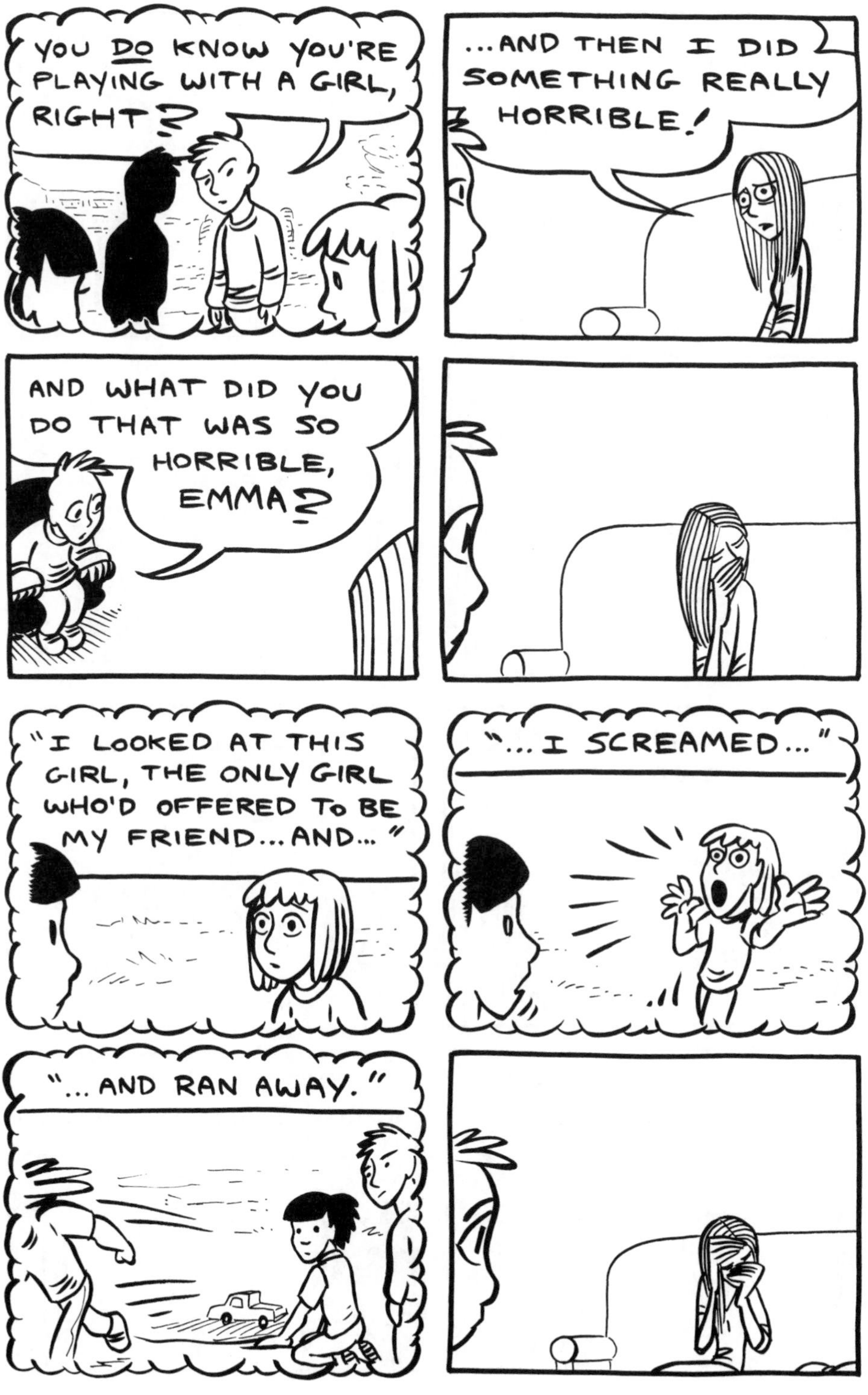
YOU DO KNOW YOU'RE PLAYING WITH A GIRL, RIGHT?
...AND THEN I DID SOMETHING REALLY HORRIBLE!
AND WHAT DID YOU DO THAT WAS SO HORRIBLE, EMMA?
"I LOOKED AT THIS GIRL, THE ONLY GIRL WHO'D OFFERED TO BE MY FRIEND... AND..."
"...I SCREAMED..."
"...AND RAN AWAY."

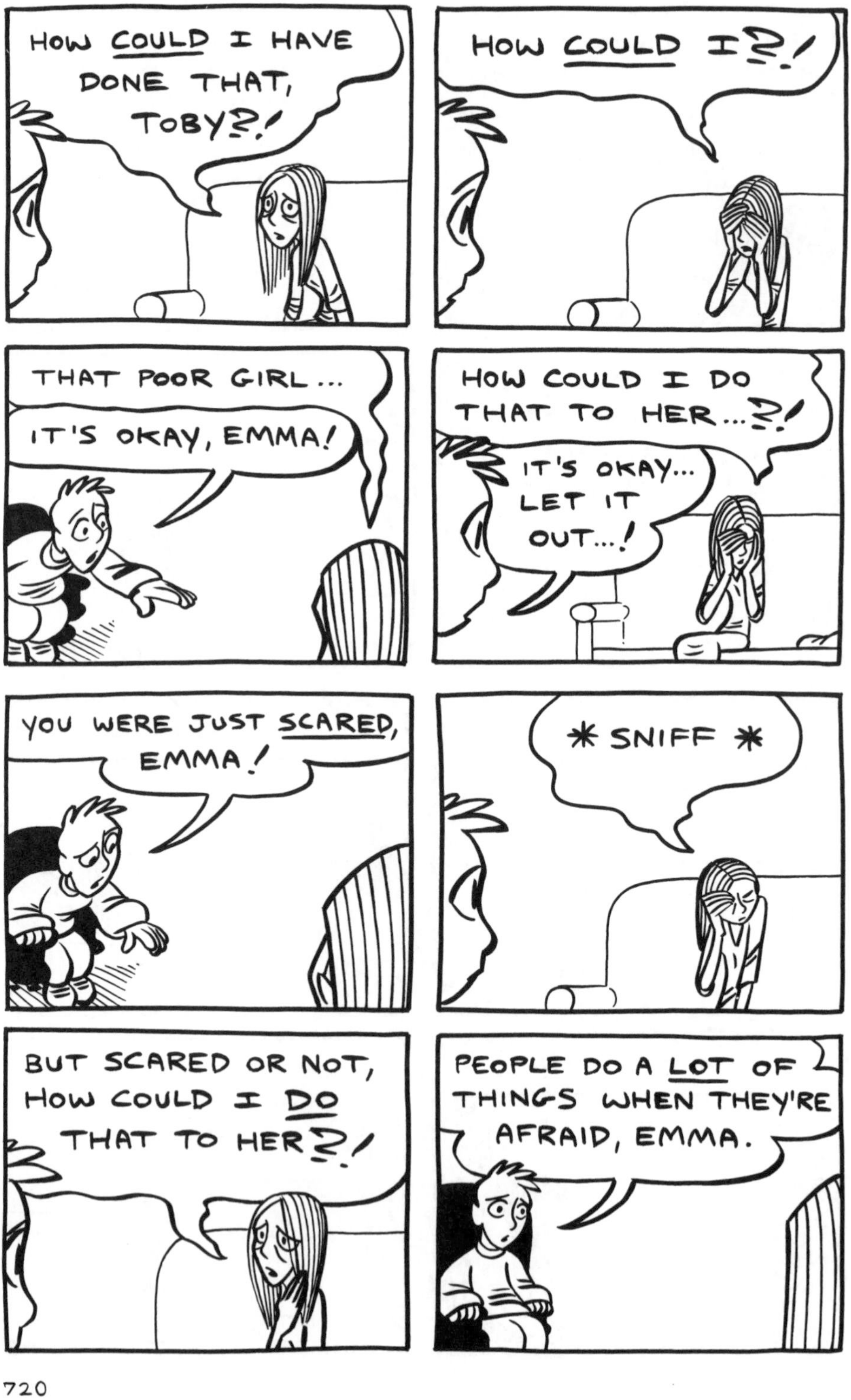
HOW COULD I HAVE DONE THAT, TOBY?!
HOW COULD I?!
THAT POOR GIRL...
IT'S OKAY, EMMA!
HOW COULD I DO THAT TO HER...?!
IT'S OKAY... LET IT OUT...!
YOU WERE JUST SCARED, EMMA!
* SNIFF *
BUT SCARED OR NOT, HOW COULD I DO THAT TO HER?!
PEOPLE DO A LOT OF THINGS WHEN THEY'RE AFRAID, EMMA.

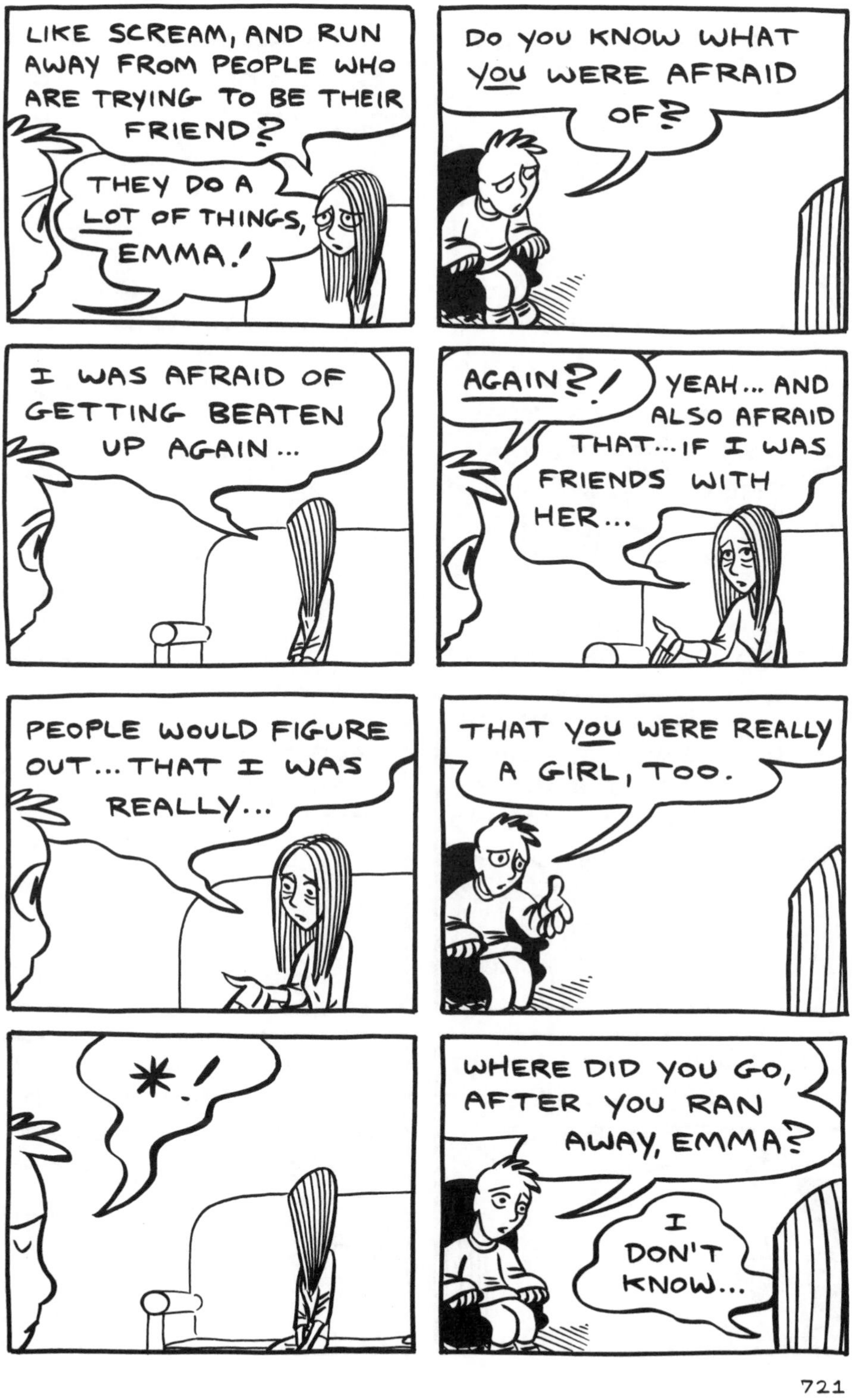
LIKE SCREAM, AND RUN AWAY FROM PEOPLE WHO ARE TRYING TO BE THEIR FRIEND?
THEY DO A LOT OF THINGS, EMMA!
DO YOU KNOW WHAT YOU WERE AFRAID OF?
I WAS AFRAID OF GETTING BEATEN UP AGAIN...
AGAIN?!
YEAH... AND ALSO AFRAID THAT... IF I WAS FRIENDS WITH HER...
PEOPLE WOULD FIGURE OUT... THAT I WAS REALLY... REALLY...
THAT YOU WERE REALLY A GIRL, TOO.
*!
WHERE DID YOU GO, AFTER YOU RAN AWAY, EMMA?
I DON'T KNOW...

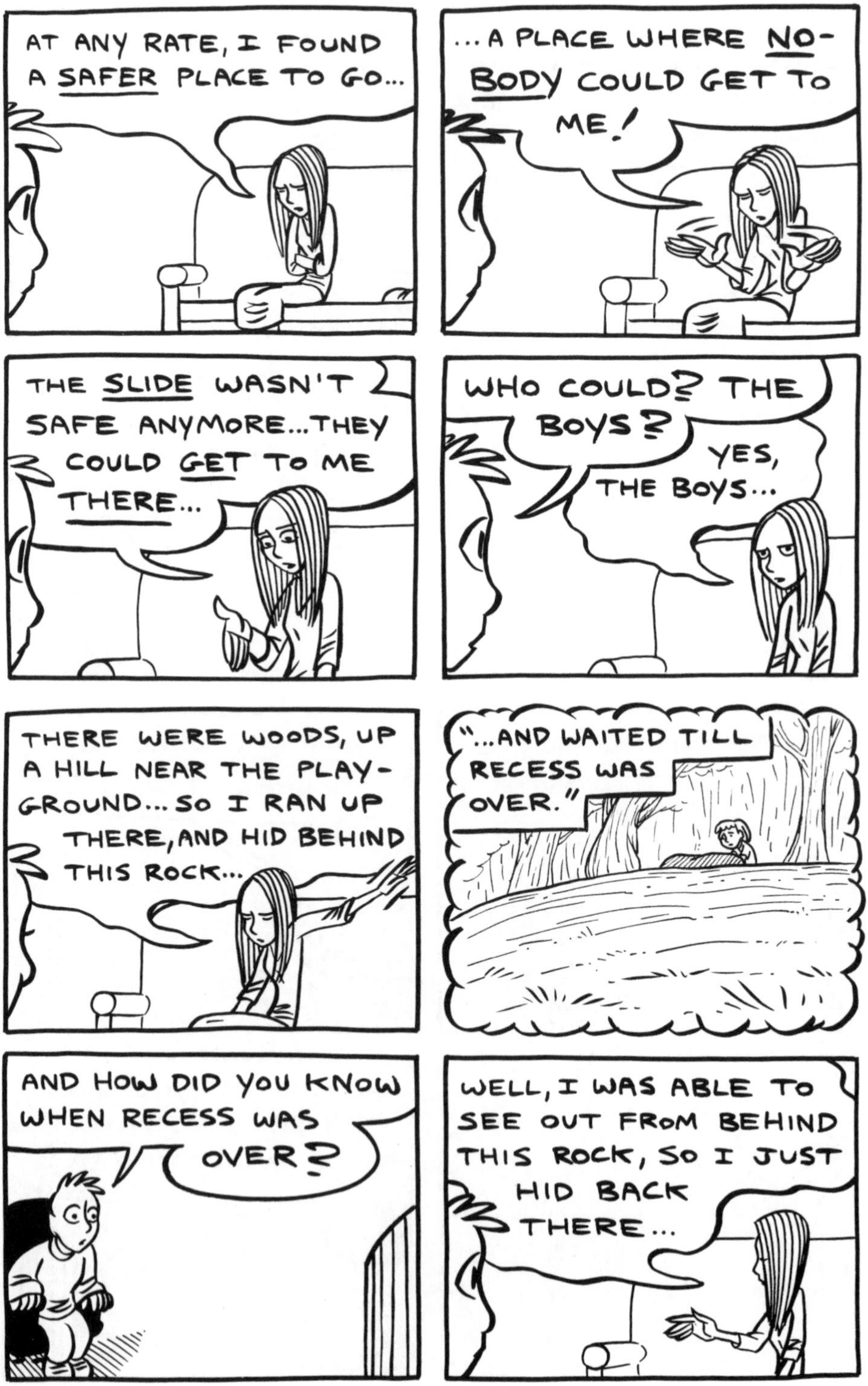
AT ANY RATE, I FOUND A SAFER PLACE TO GO...
...A PLACE WHERE NO-BODY COULD GET TO ME!
THE SLIDE WASN'T SAFE ANYMORE...THEY COULD GET TO ME THERE...
WHO COULD? THE BOYS?
YES, THE BOYS...
THERE WERE WOODS, UP A HILL NEAR THE PLAY-GROUND... SO I RAN UP THERE, AND HID BEHIND THIS ROCK...
"...AND WAITED TILL RECESS WAS OVER."
AND HOW DID YOU KNOW WHEN RECESS WAS OVER?
WELL, I WAS ABLE TO SEE OUT FROM BEHIND THIS ROCK, SO I JUST HID BACK THERE...

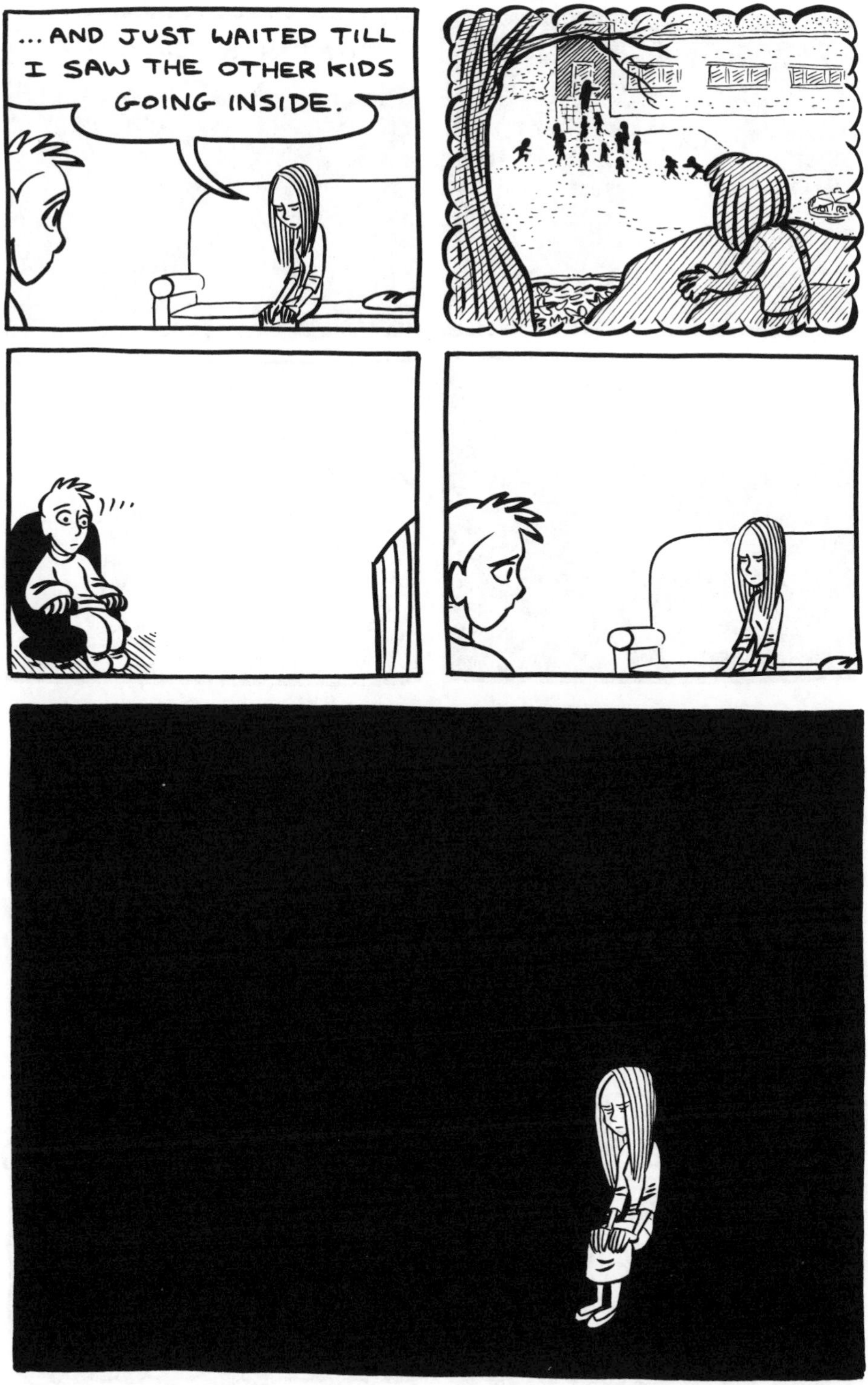
...AND JUST WAITED TILL I SAW THE OTHER KIDS GOING INSIDE.

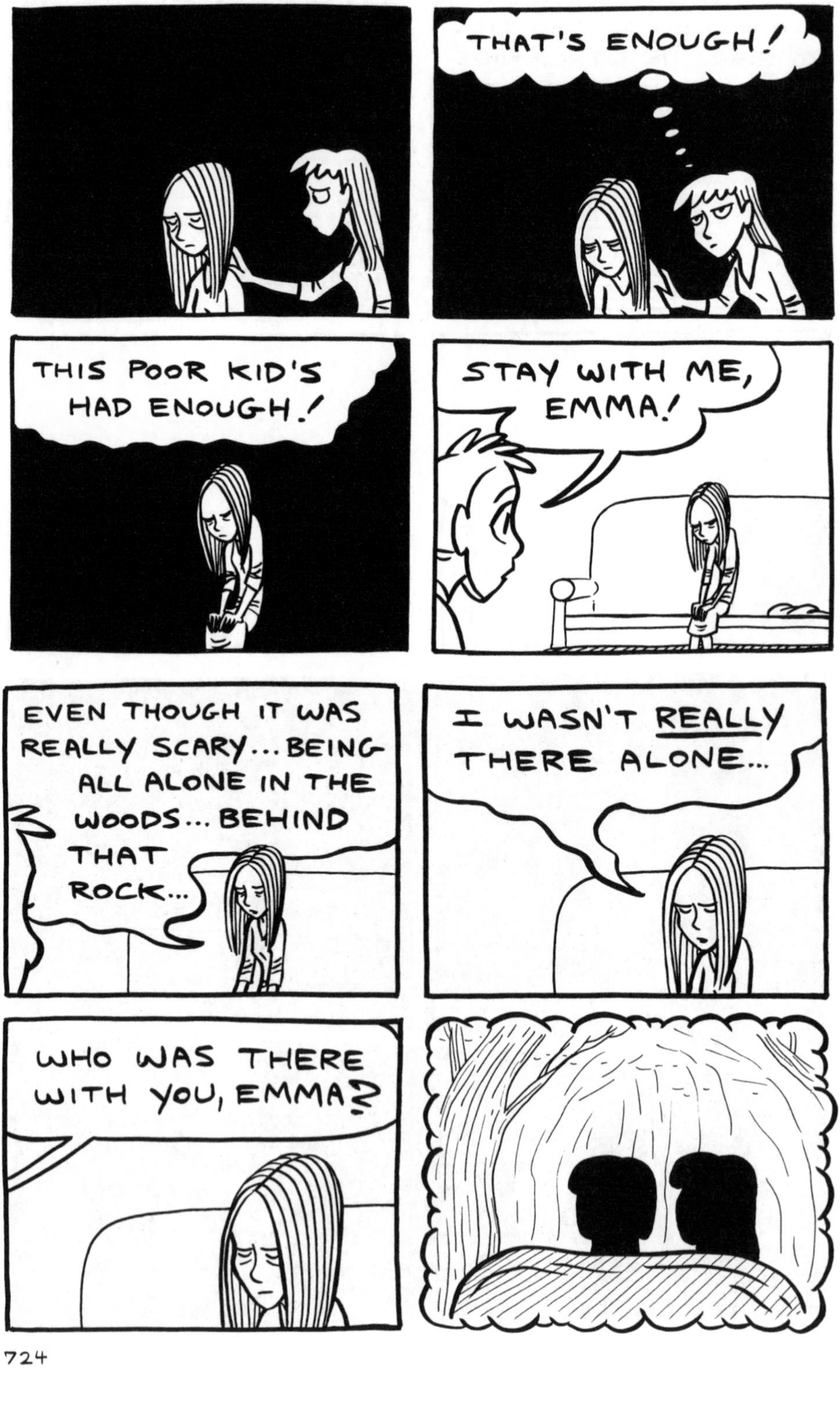
THAT'S ENOUGH!
THIS POOR KID'S HAD ENOUGH!
STAY WITH ME, EMMA!
EVEN THOUGH IT WAS REALLY SCARY... BEING ALL ALONE IN THE WOODS... BEHIND THAT ROCK...
I WASN'T REALLY THERE ALONE...
WHO WAS THERE WITH YOU, EMMA?

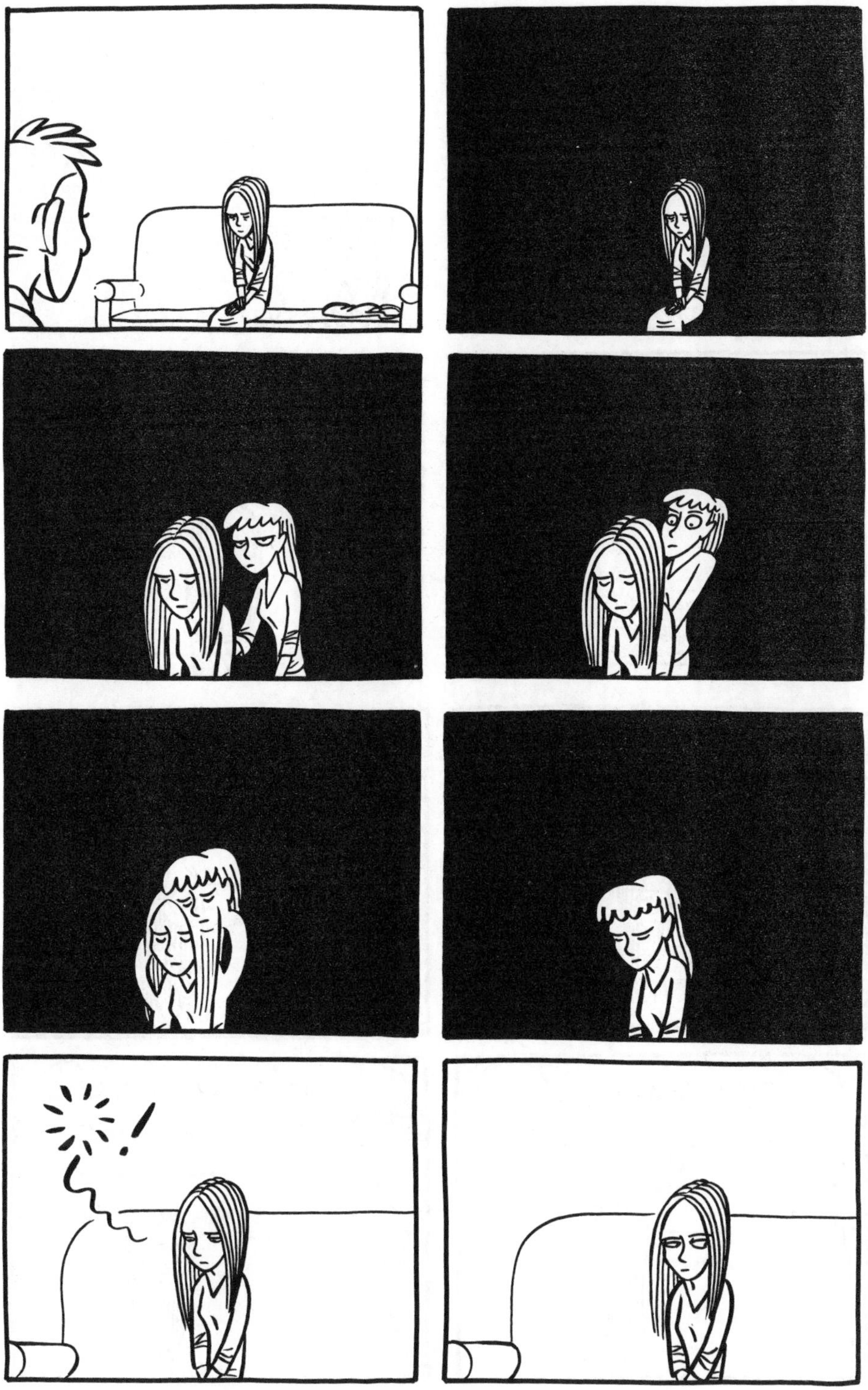

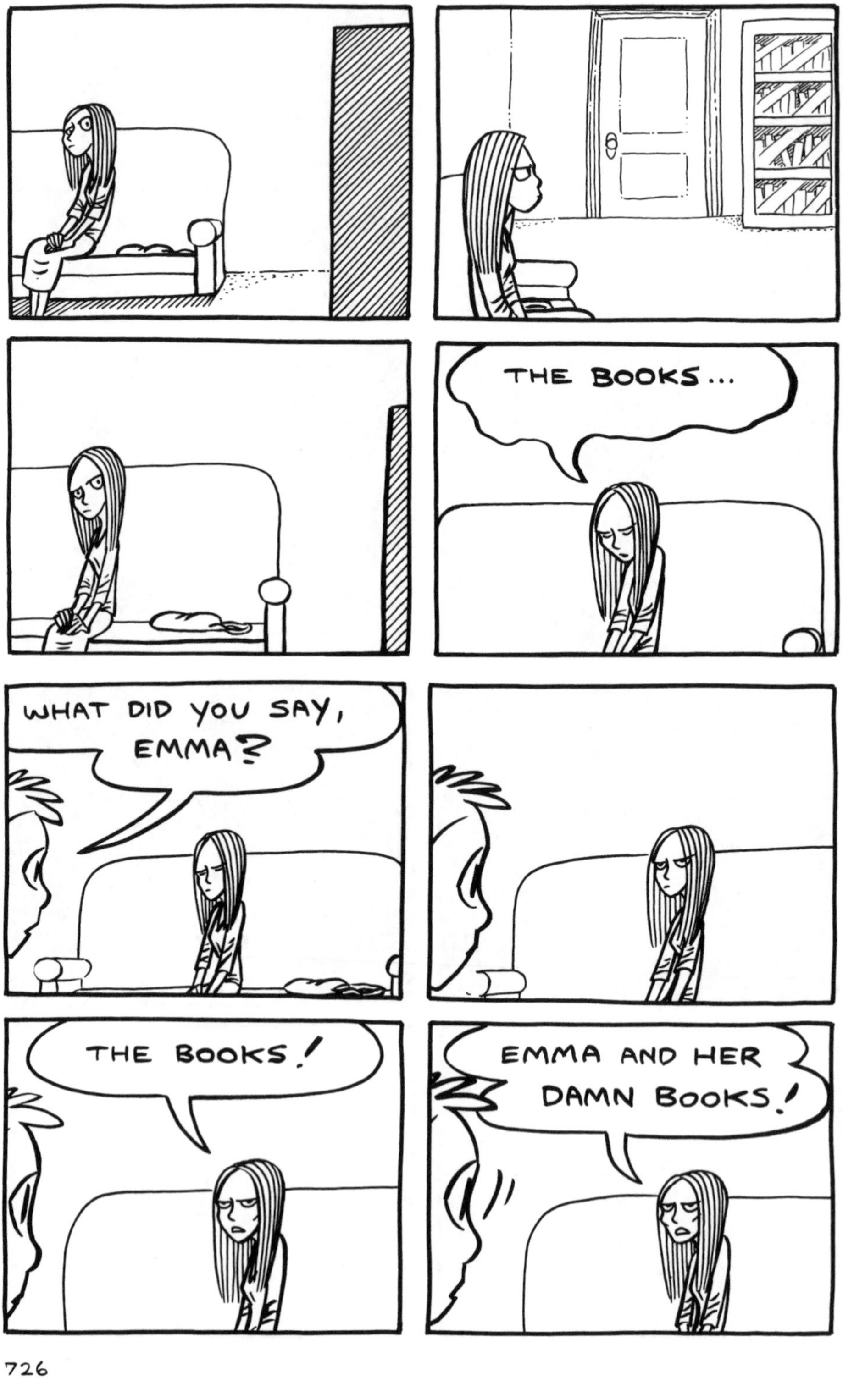
THE BOOKS...
WHAT DID YOU SAY, EMMA?
THE BOOKS!
EMMA AND HER DAMN BOOKS!

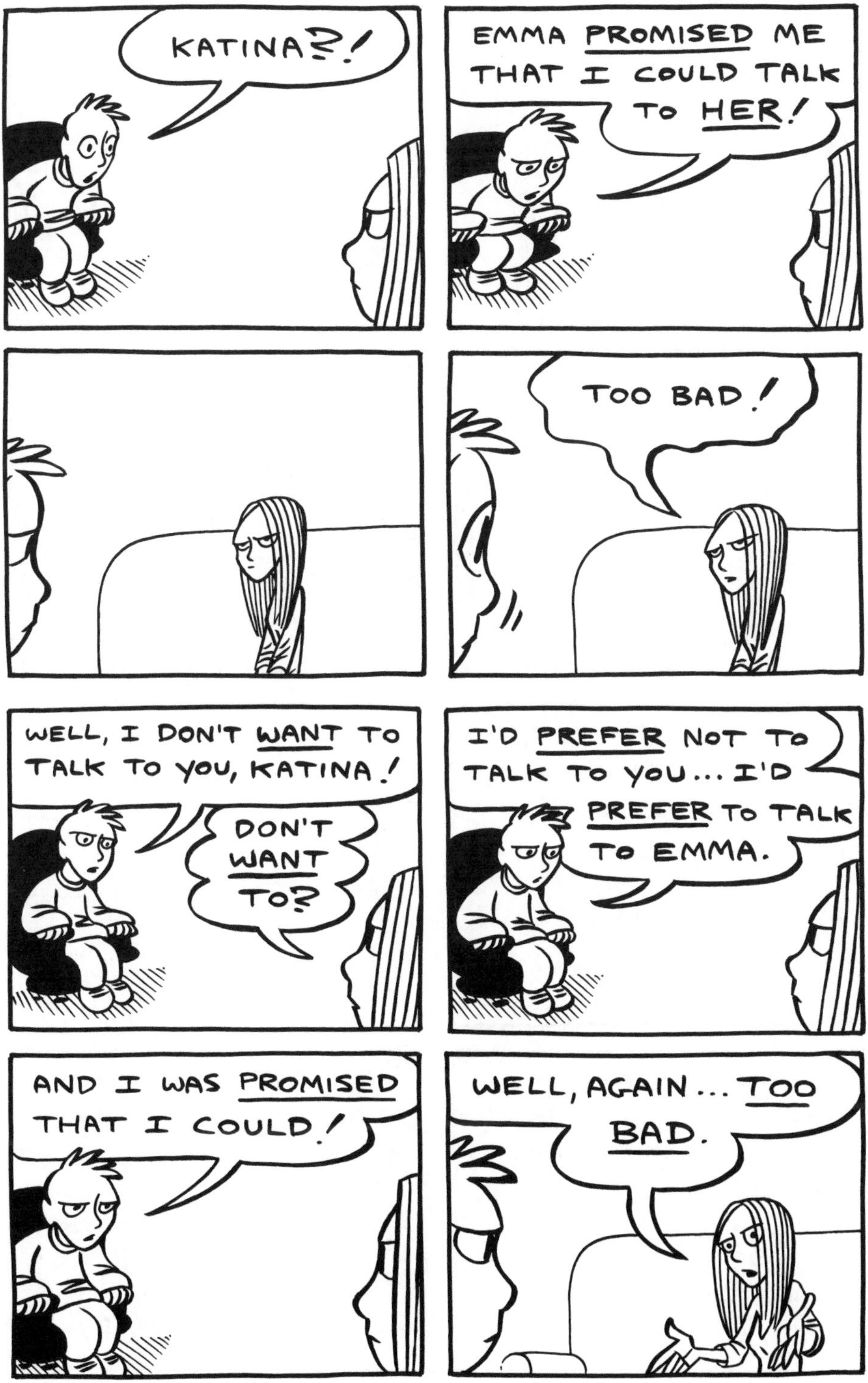
KATINA?!
EMMA PROMISED ME THAT I COULD TALK TO HER!
TOO BAD!
WELL, I DON'T WANT TO TALK TO YOU, KATINA!
DON'T WANT TO?
I'D PREFER NOT TO TALK TO YOU... I'D PREFER TO TALK TO EMMA.
AND I WAS PROMISED THAT I COULD!
WELL, AGAIN... TOO BAD.

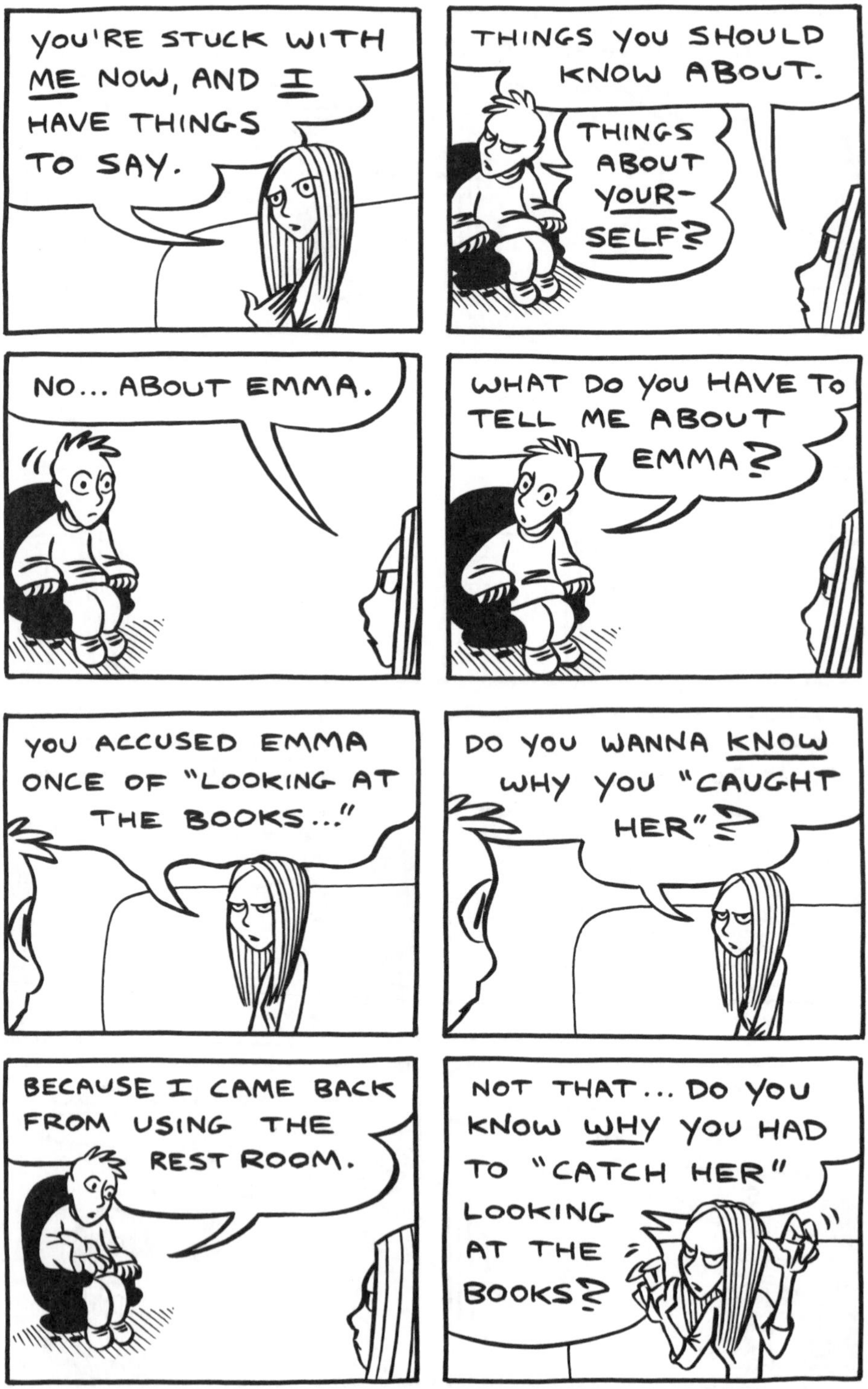
YOU'RE STUCK WITH ME NOW, AND I HAVE THINGS TO SAY.
THINGS YOU SHOULD KNOW ABOUT.
THINGS ABOUT YOURSELF?
NO... ABOUT EMMA.
WHAT DO YOU HAVE TO TELL ME ABOUT EMMA?
YOU ACCUSED EMMA ONCE OF "LOOKING AT THE BOOKS..."
DO YOU WANNA KNOW WHY YOU "CAUGHT HER"?
BECAUSE I CAME BACK FROM USING THE REST ROOM.
NOT THAT... DO YOU KNOW WHY YOU HAD TO "CATCH HER" LOOKING AT THE BOOKS?

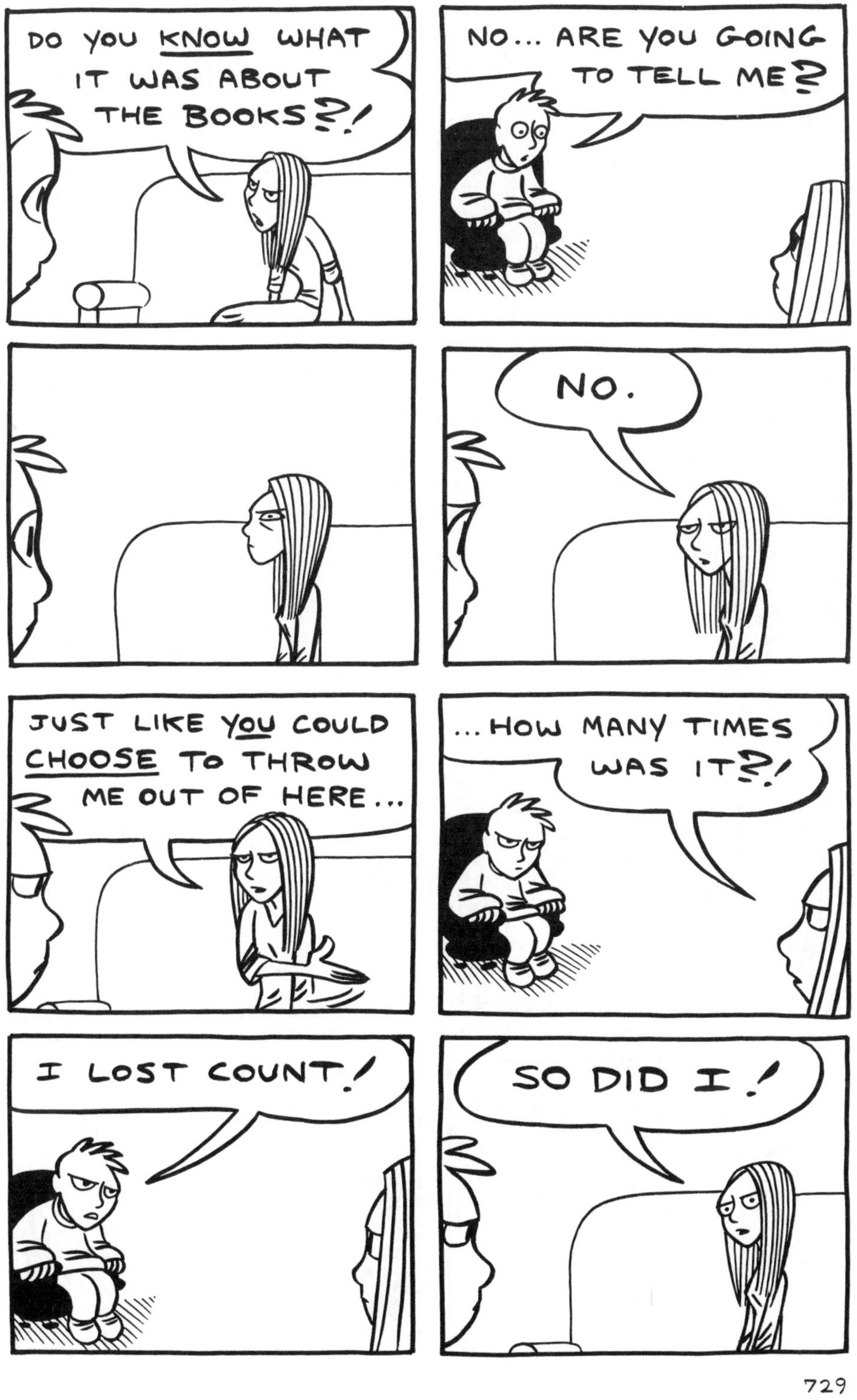
DO YOU KNOW WHAT IT WAS ABOUT THE BOOKS?!
NO... ARE YOU GOING TO TELL ME?
NO.
JUST LIKE YOU COULD CHOOSE TO THROW ME OUT OF HERE...
...HOW MANY TIMES WAS IT?!
I LOST COUNT!
SO DID I!

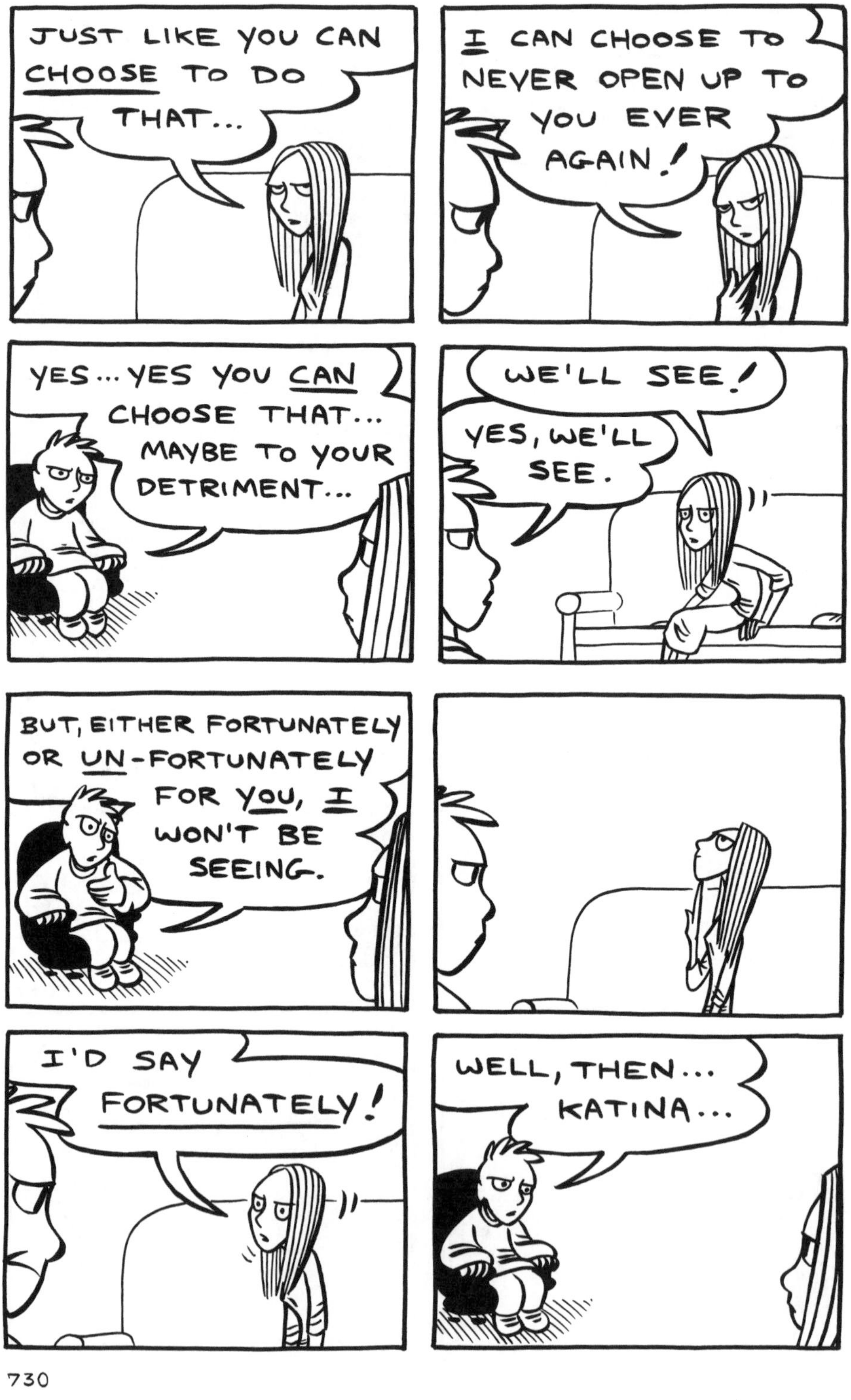
JUST LIKE YOU CAN CHOOSE TO DO THAT...
I CAN CHOOSE TO NEVER OPEN UP TO YOU EVER AGAIN!
YES... YES YOU CAN CHOOSE THAT... MAYBE TO YOUR DETRIMENT...
WE'LL SEE!
YES, WE'LL SEE.
BUT, EITHER FORTUNATELY OR UN-FORTUNATELY FOR YOU, I WON'T BE SEEING.
I'D SAY FORTUNATELY!
WELL, THEN... KATINA...

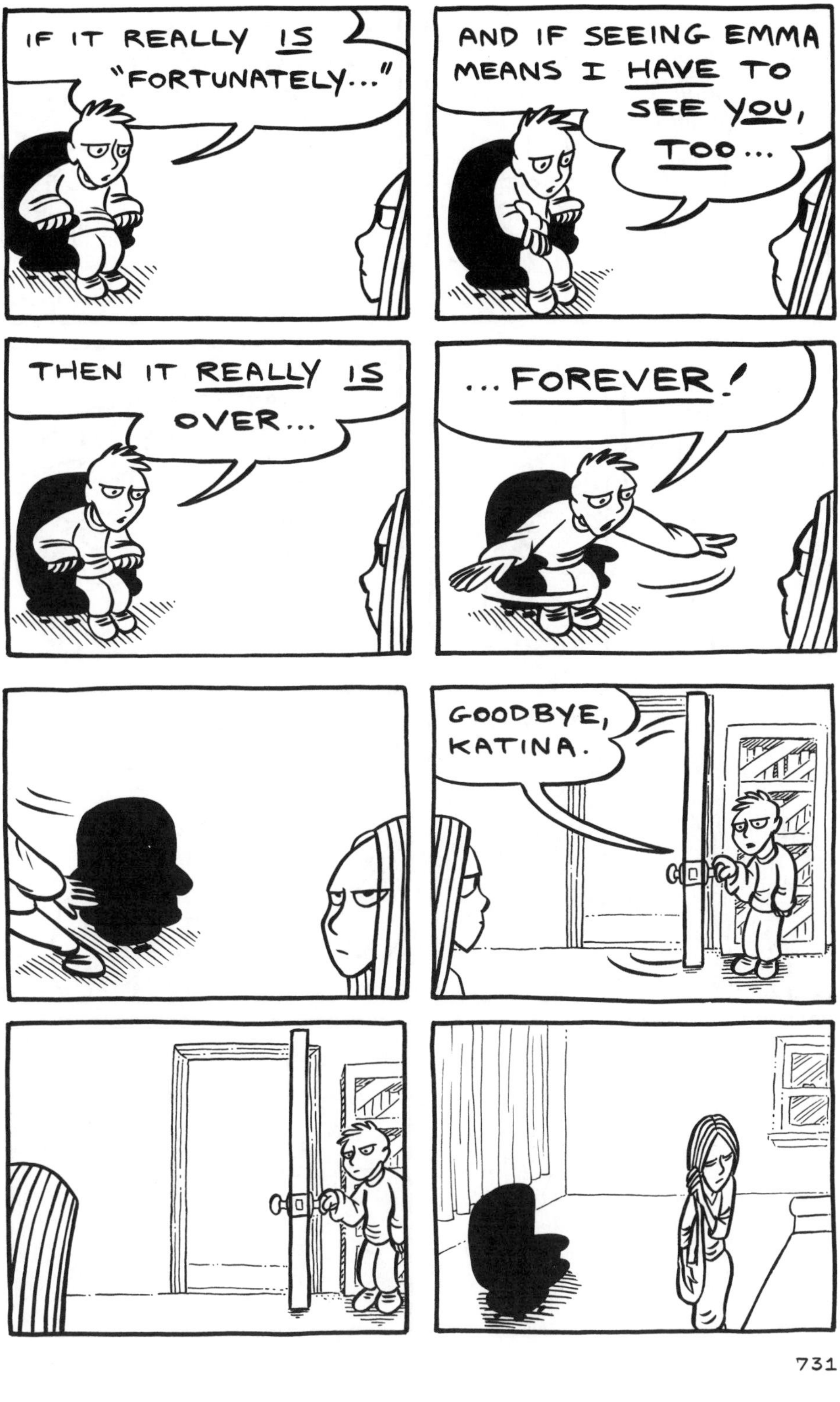
IF IT REALLY IS "FORTUNATELY..."
AND IF SEEING EMMA MEANS I HAVE TO SEE YOU, TOO...
THEN IT REALLY IS OVER...
...FOREVER!
GOODBYE, KATINA.

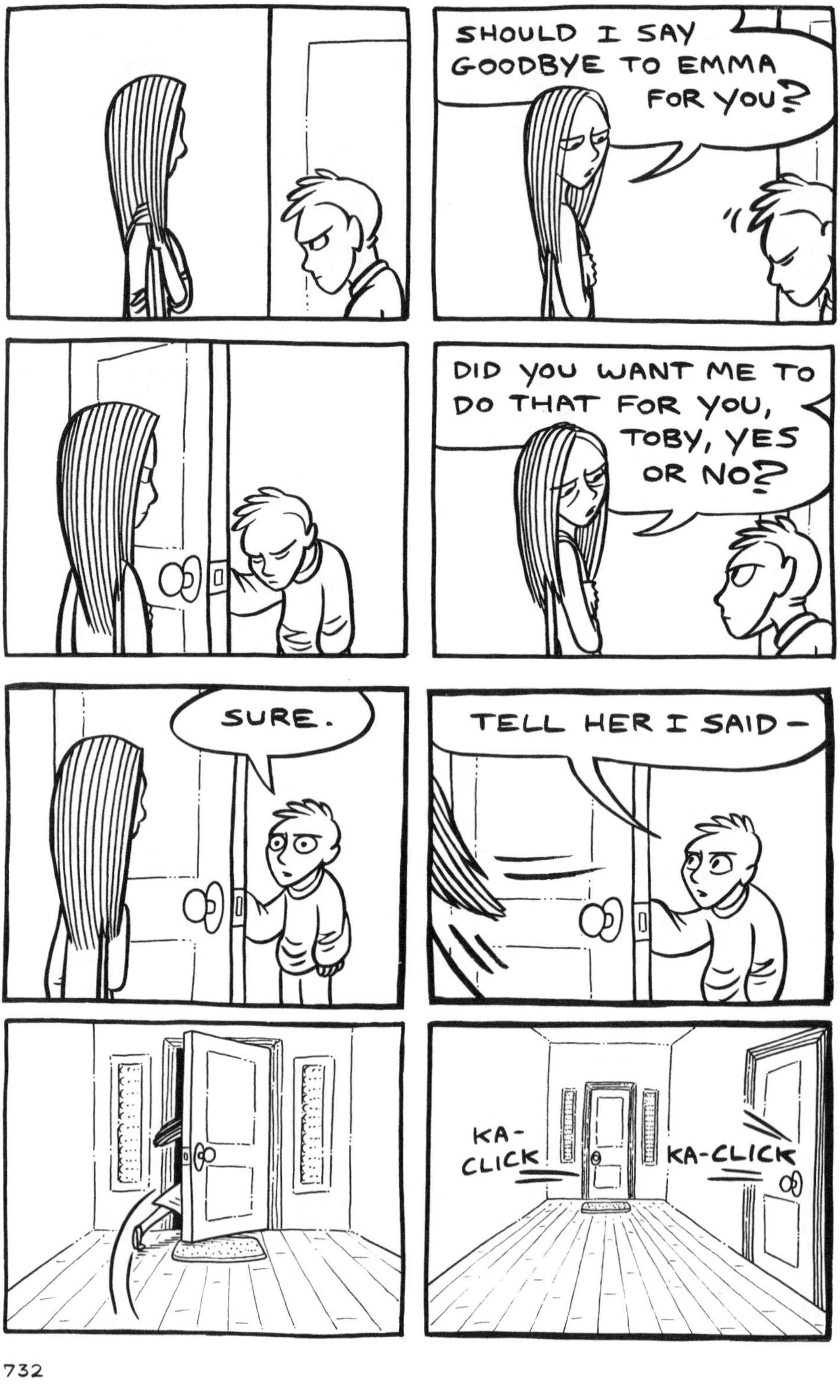
SHOULD I SAY GOODBYE TO EMMA FOR YOU?
DID YOU WANT ME TO DO THAT FOR YOU, TOBY, YES OR NO?
SURE.
TELL HER I SAID—
KA-CLICK
KA-CLICK

CASTLE

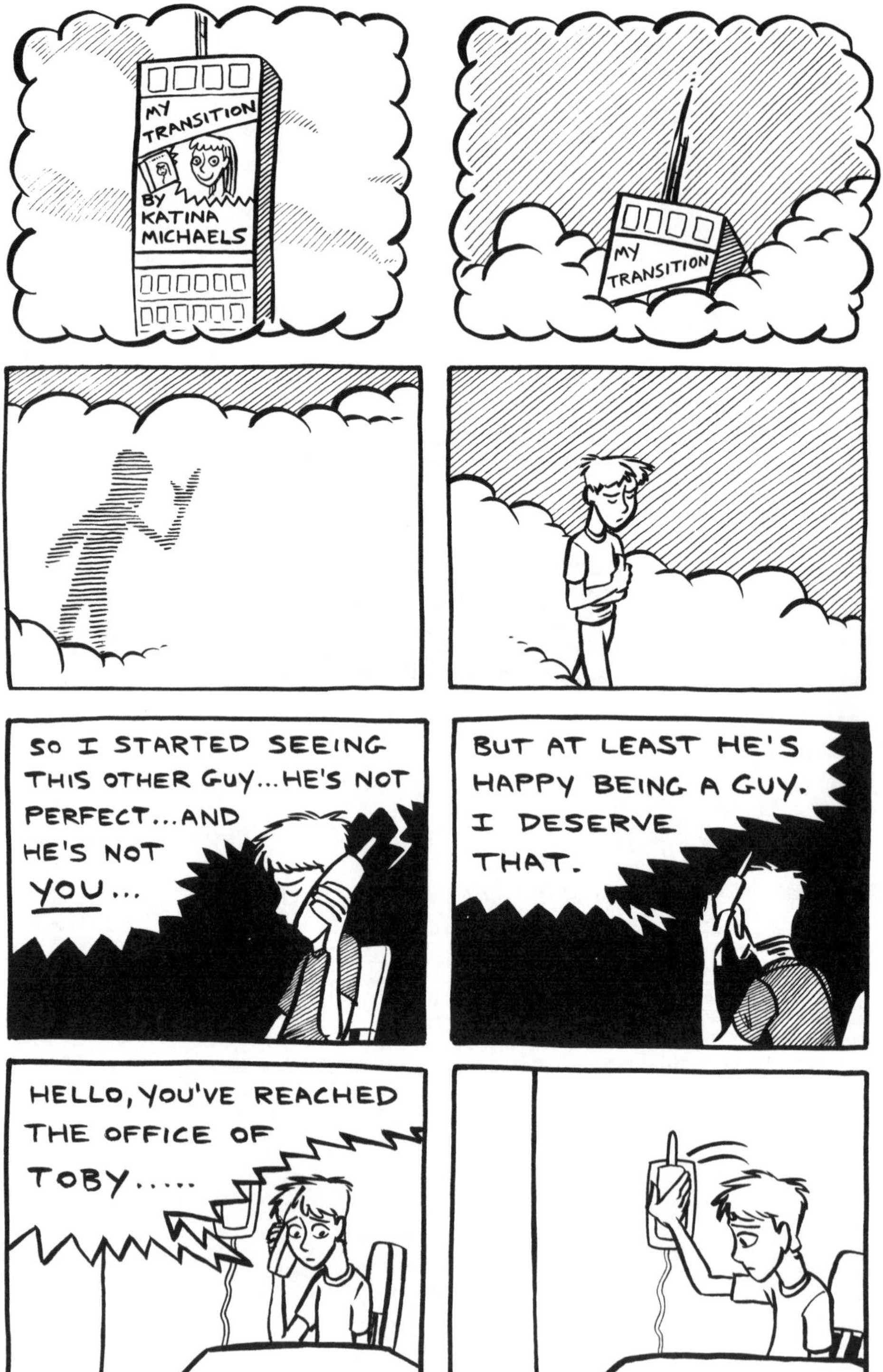
MY TRANSITION
BY KATINA MICHAELS
MY TRANSITION
SO I STARTED SEEING THIS OTHER GUY...HE'S NOT PERFECT...AND HE'S NOT YOU...
BUT AT LEAST HE'S HAPPY BEING A GUY. I DESERVE THAT.
HELLO, YOU'VE REACHED THE OFFICE OF TOBY.....

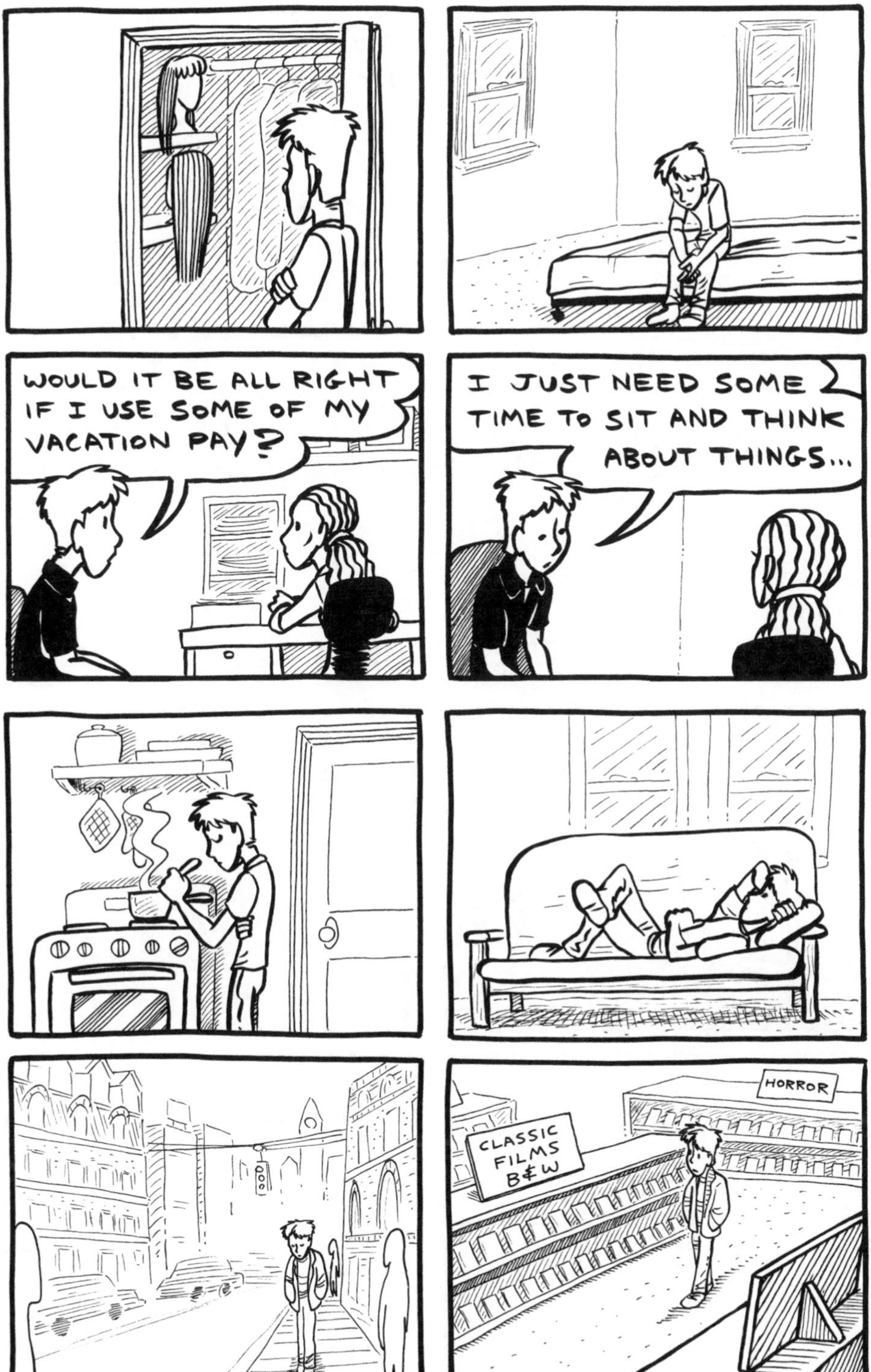
WOULD IT BE ALL RIGHT IF I USE SOME OF MY VACATION PAY?
I JUST NEED SOME TIME TO SIT AND THINK ABOUT THINGS...
CLASSIC FILMS B&W
HORROR

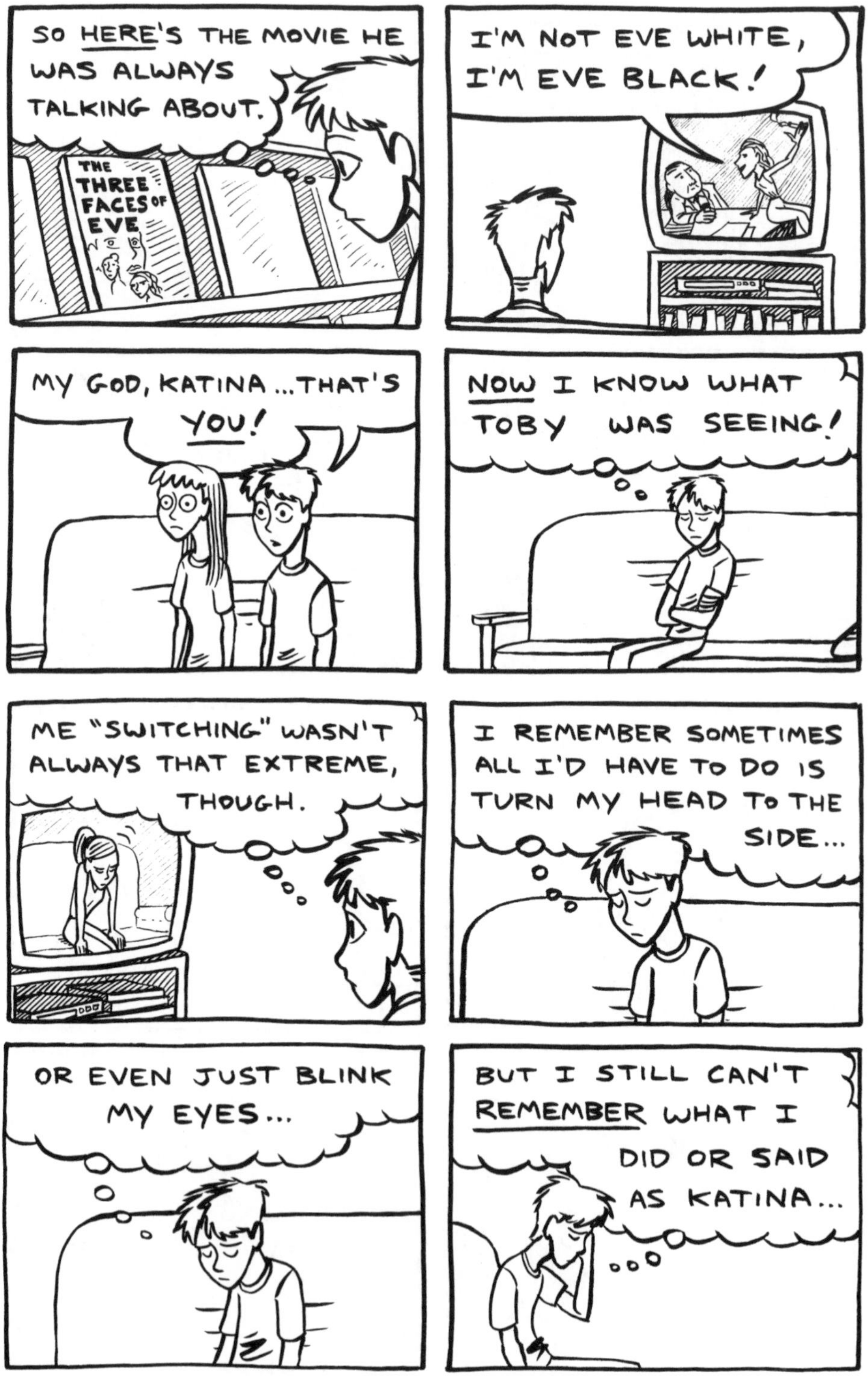
SO HERE'S THE MOVIE HE WAS ALWAYS TALKING ABOUT.
THE THREE FACES OF EVE
I'M NOT EVE WHITE, I'M EVE BLACK!
MY GOD, KATINA ...THAT'S YOU!
NOW I KNOW WHAT TOBY WAS SEEING!
ME "SWITCHING" WASN'T ALWAYS THAT EXTREME, THOUGH.
I REMEMBER SOMETIMES ALL I'D HAVE TO DO IS TURN MY HEAD TO THE SIDE...
OR EVEN JUST BLINK MY EYES...
BUT I STILL CAN'T REMEMBER WHAT I DID OR SAID AS KATINA...

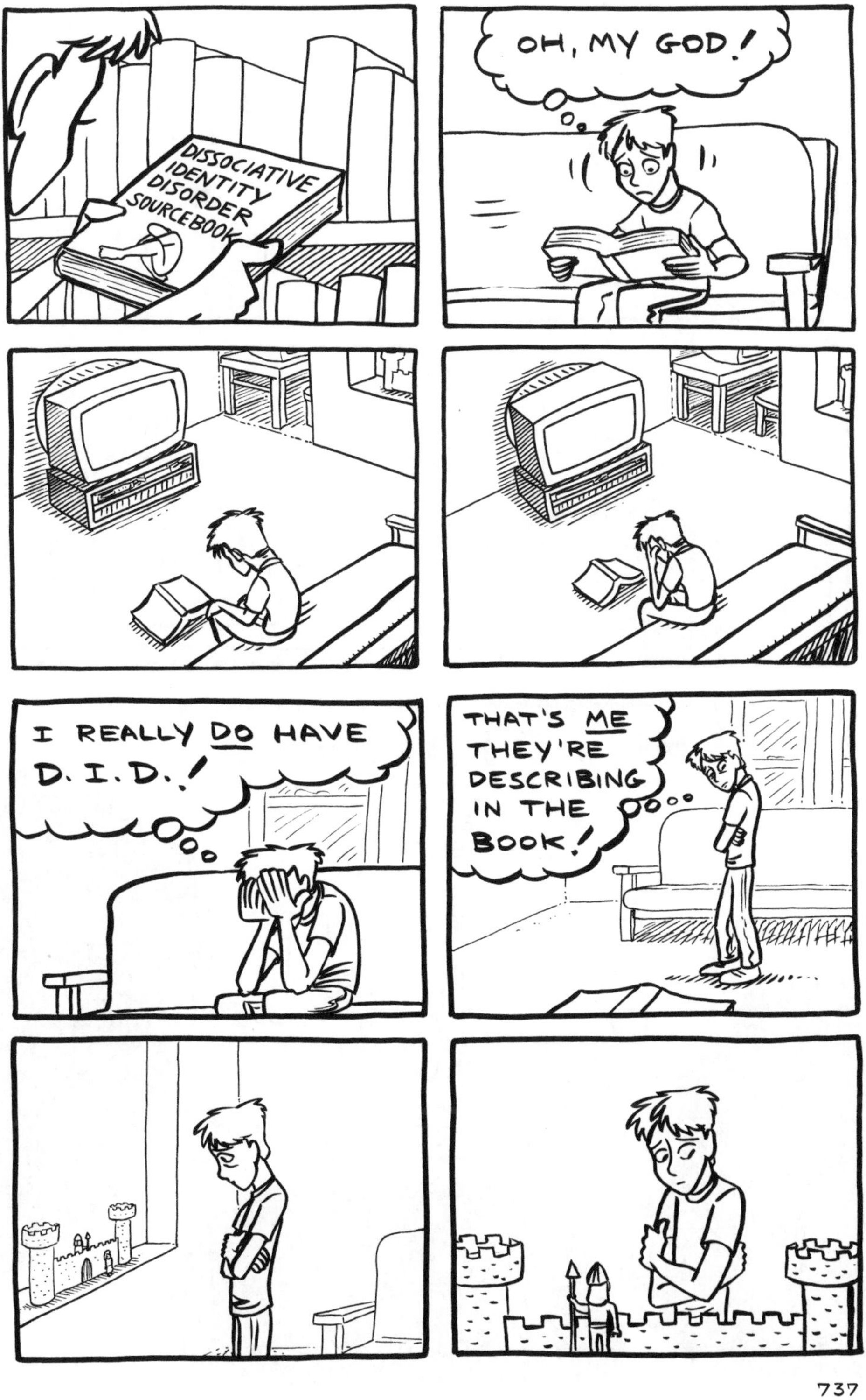
DISSOCIATIVE IDENTITY DISORDER SOURCEBOOK
OH, MY GOD!
I REALLY DO HAVE D.I.D.!
THAT'S ME THEY'RE DESCRIBING IN THE BOOK!

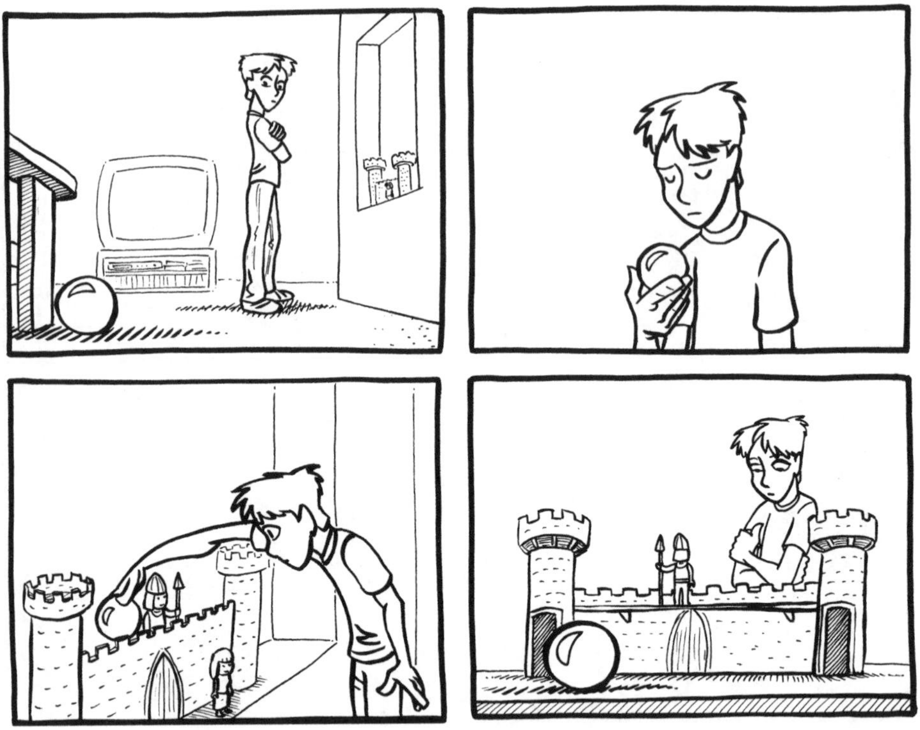

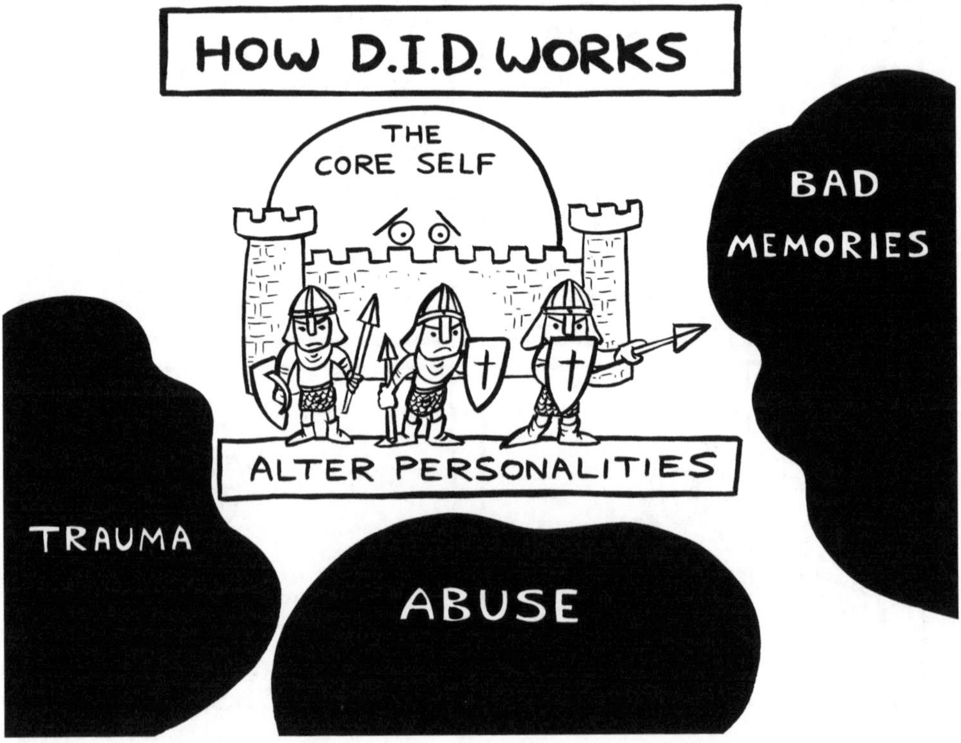

HOW D.I.D. WORKS
THE CORE SELF
BAD MEMORIES
ALTER PERSONALITIES
TRAUMA
ABUSE

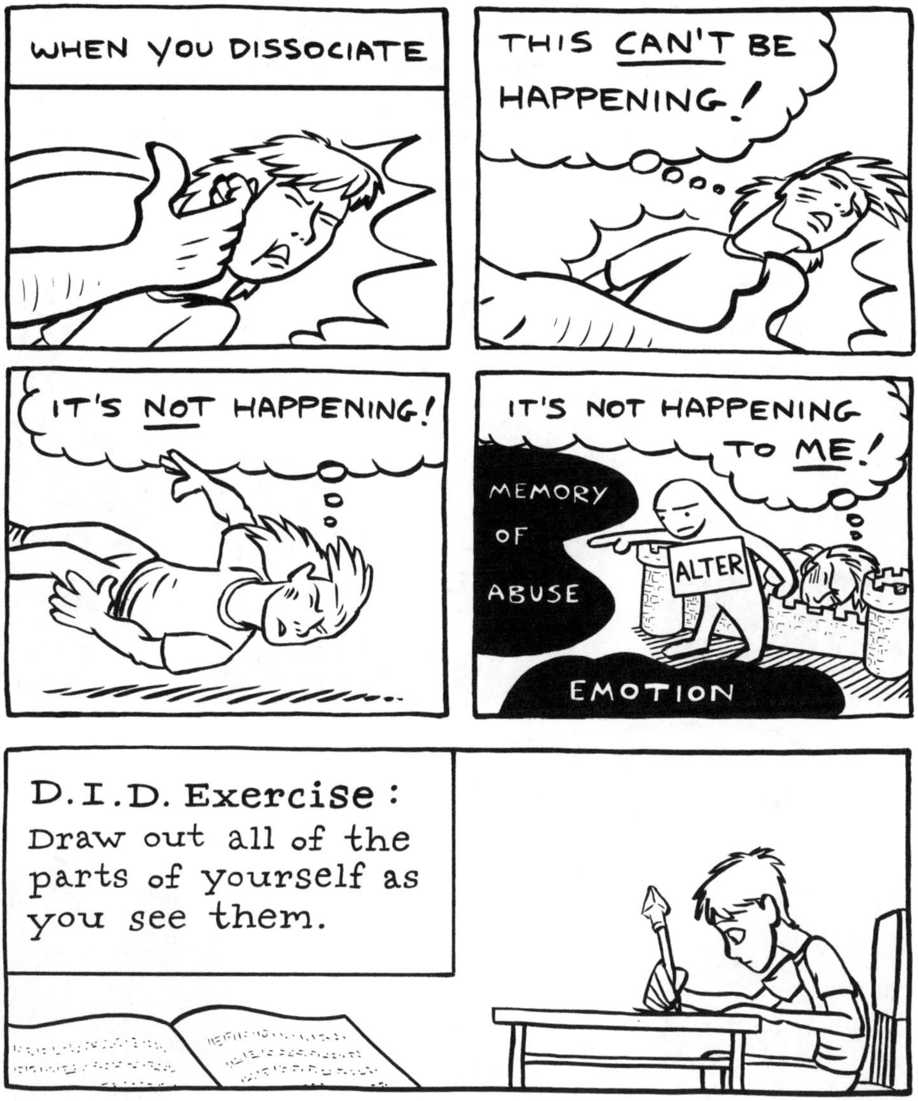
WHEN YOU DISSOCIATE
THIS CAN'T BE HAPPENING!
IT'S NOT HAPPENING!
IT'S NOT HAPPENING TO ME!
MEMORY OF ABUSE
ALTER
EMOTION
D.I.D. Exercise:
Draw out all of the parts of yourself as you see them.

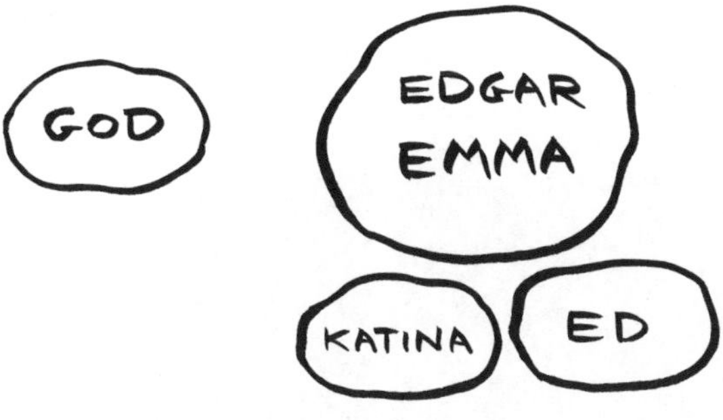
GOD
EDGAR
EMMA
KATINA
ED

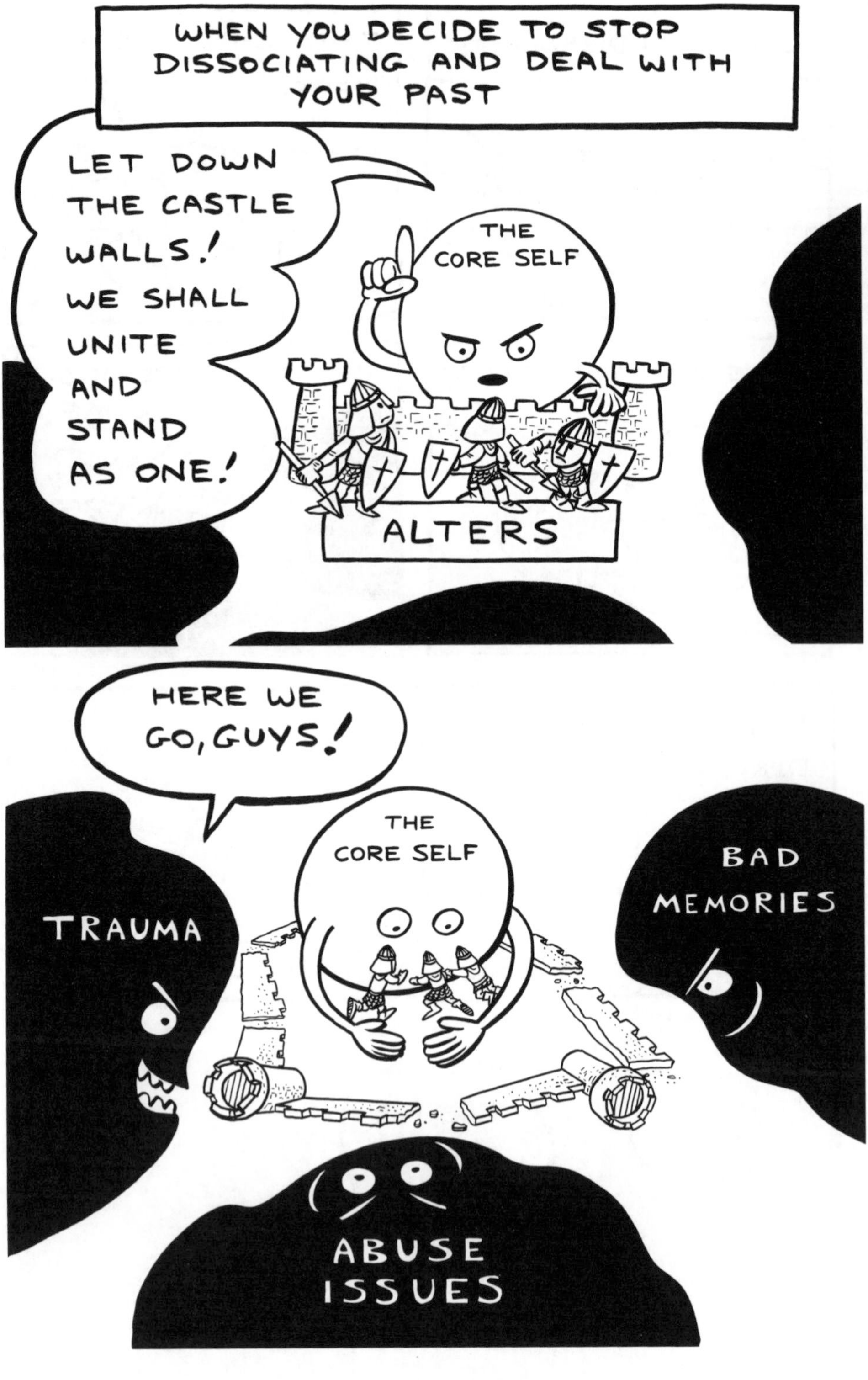
WHEN YOU DECIDE TO STOP DISSOCIATING AND DEAL WITH YOUR PAST
LET DOWN THE CASTLE WALLS! WE SHALL UNITE AND STAND AS ONE!
THE CORE SELF
ALTERS
HERE WE GO, GUYS!
THE CORE SELF
TRAUMA
BAD MEMORIES
ABUSE ISSUES

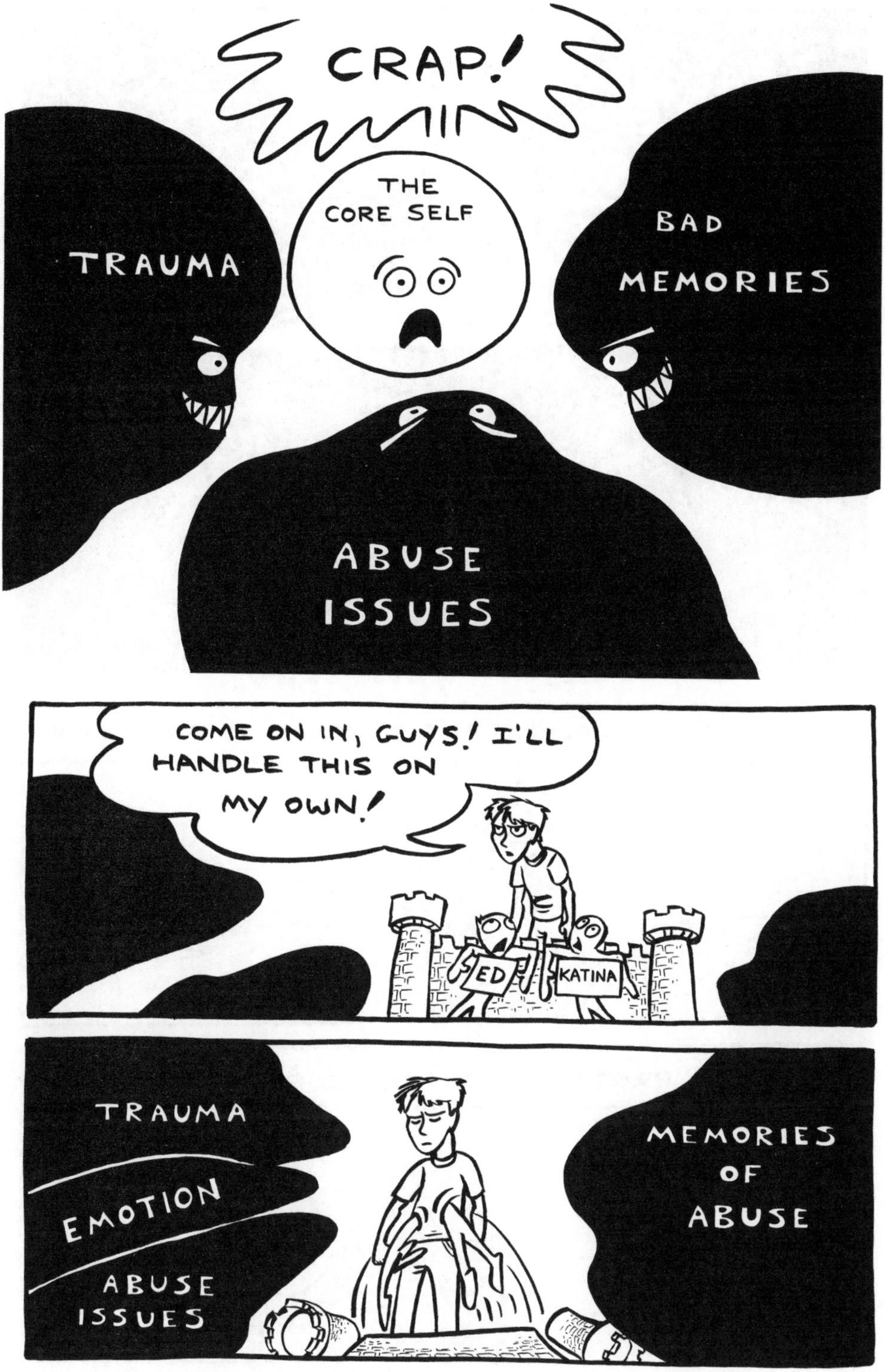
CRAP!
THE CORE SELF
TRAUMA
BAD MEMORIES
ABUSE ISSUES
COME ON IN, GUYS! I'LL HANDLE THIS ON MY OWN!
ED
KATINA
TRAUMA
EMOTION
ABUSE ISSUES
MEMORIES OF ABUSE

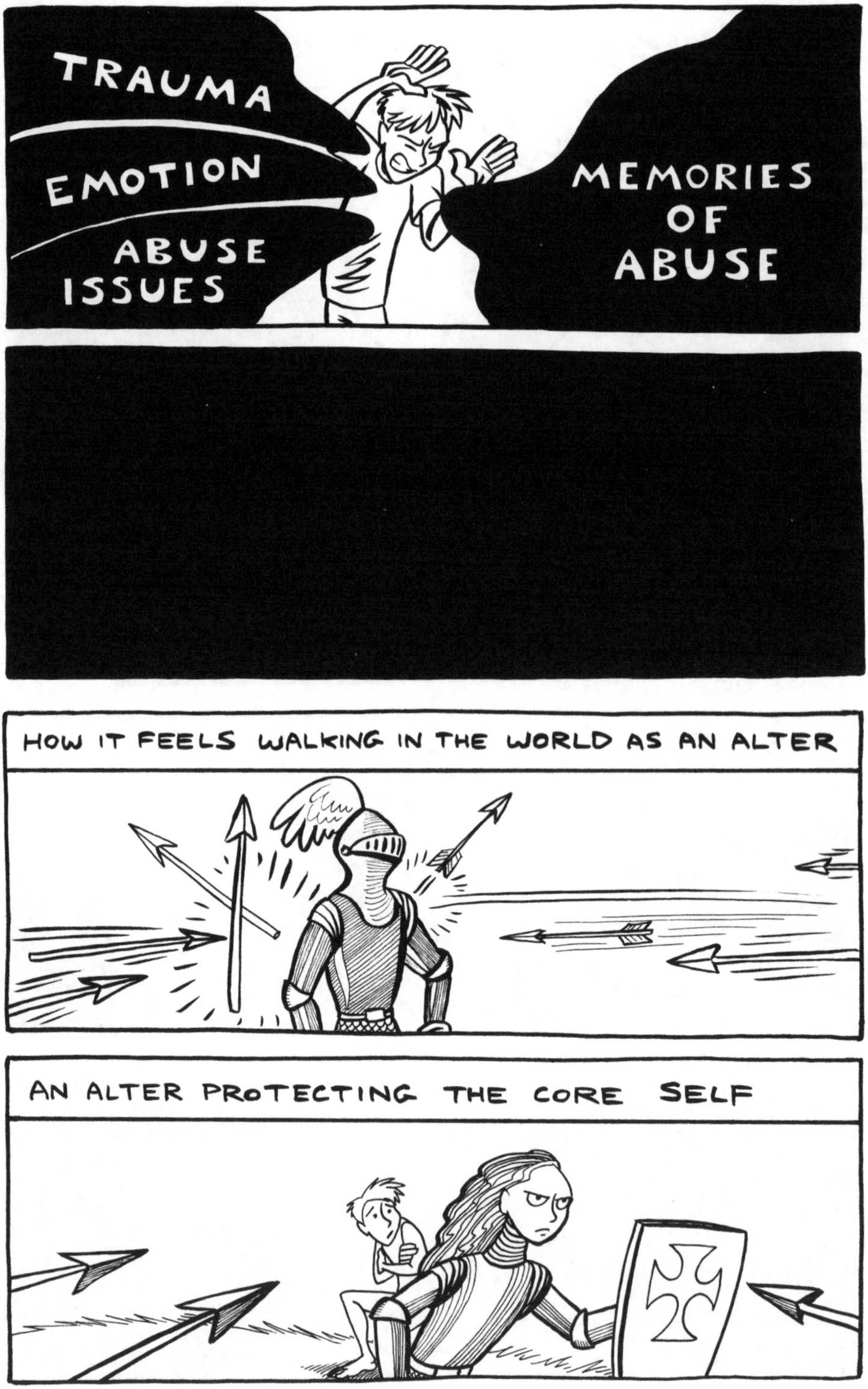
TRAUMA
EMOTION
ABUSE ISSUES
MEMORIES OF ABUSE
HOW IT FEELS WALKING IN THE WORLD AS AN ALTER
AN ALTER PROTECTING THE CORE SELF

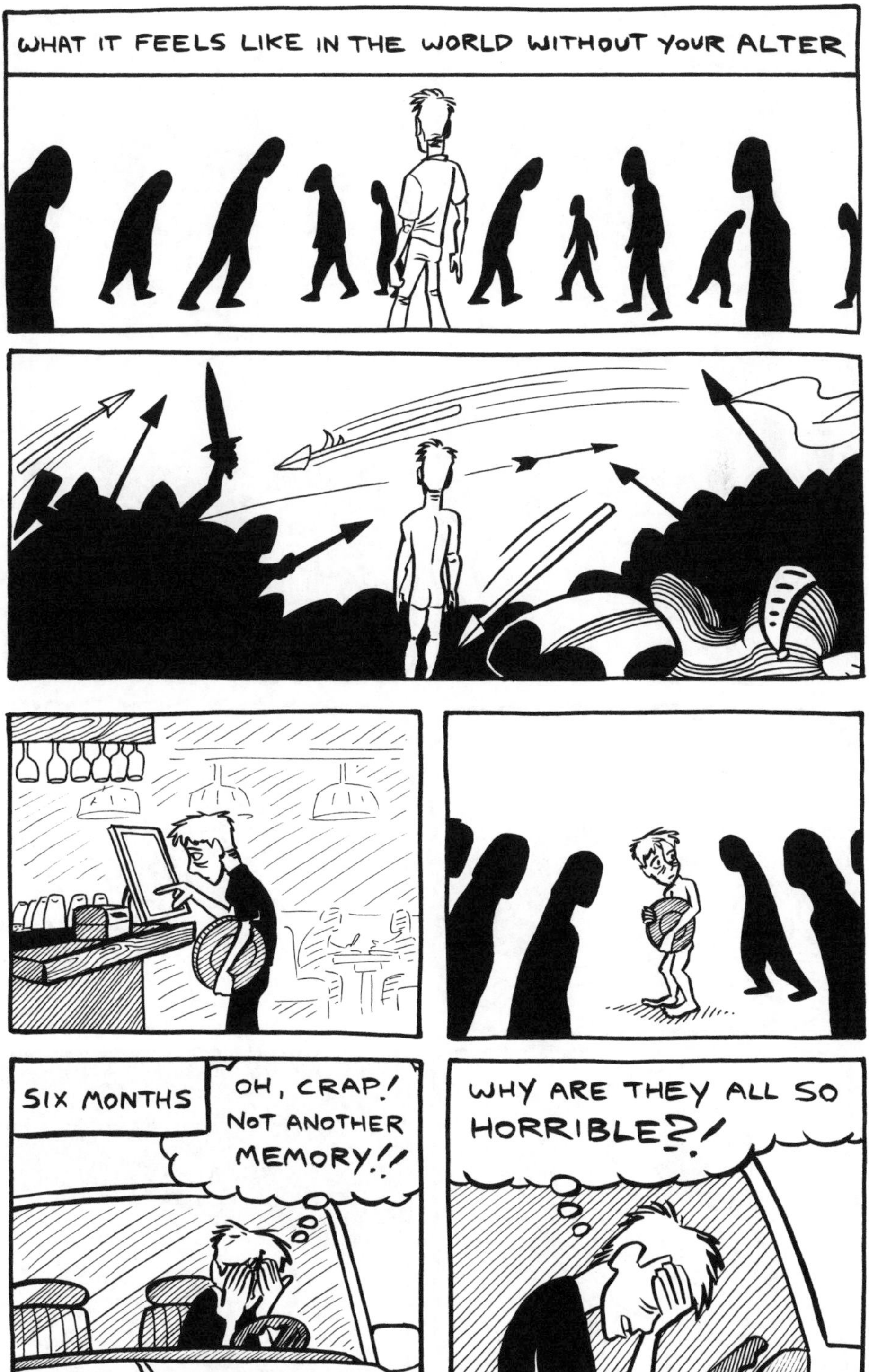
WHAT IT FEELS LIKE IN THE WORLD WITHOUT YOUR ALTER
SIX MONTHS
OH, CRAP! NOT ANOTHER MEMORY!!
WHY ARE THEY ALL SO HORRIBLE?!

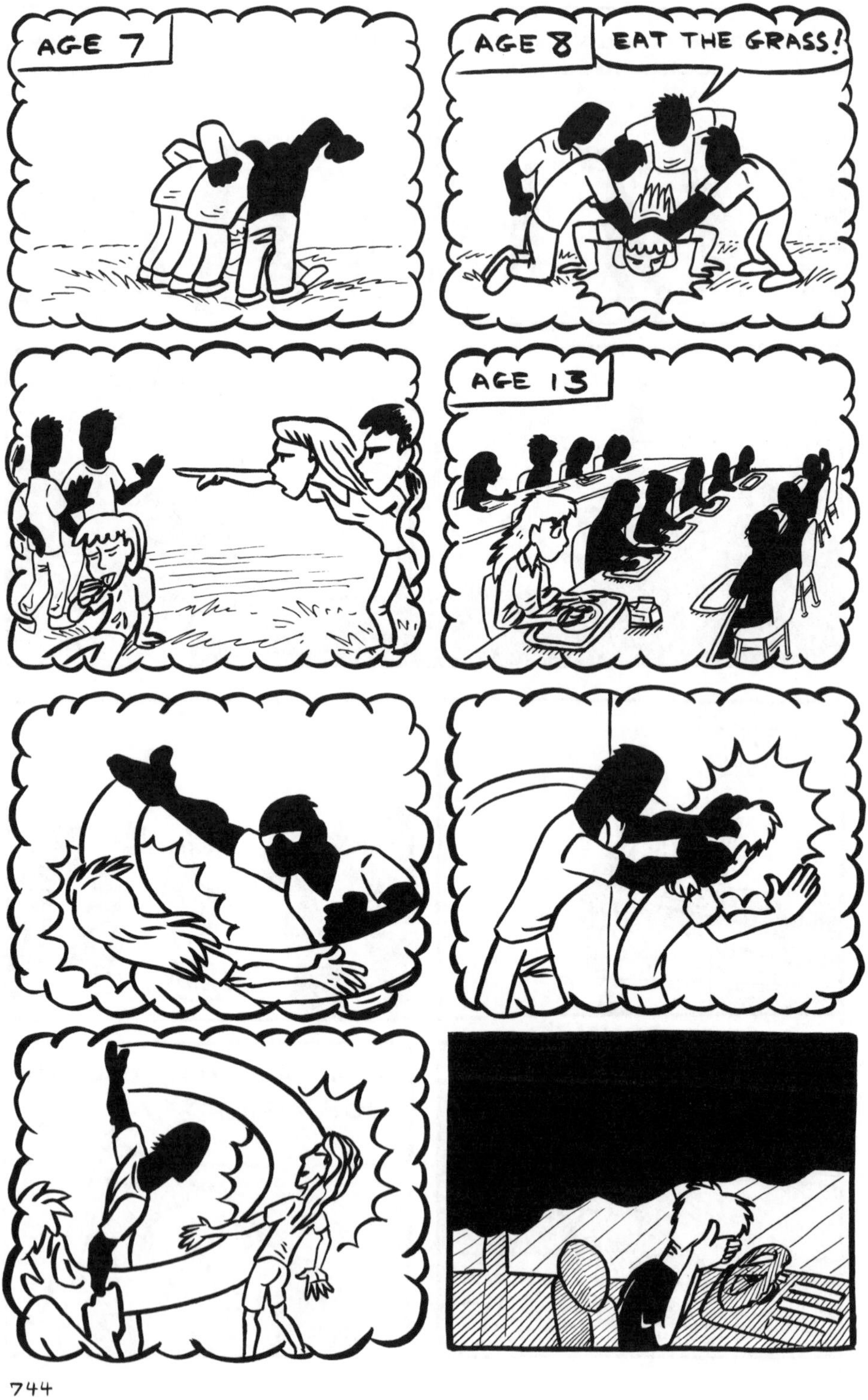
AGE 7
AGE 8
EAT THE GRASS!
AGE 13

I CAN SEE WHAT KATINA WAS PROTECTING ME FROM!

WHEN ARE THE MEMORIES GOING TO STOP?!

REMEMBERING THEM IS LIKE LIVING THROUGH IT ALL OVER AGAIN...

...ONLY WORSE!

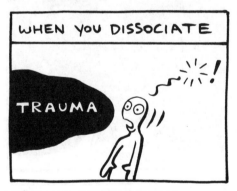

WHEN YOU DISSOCIATE

TRAUMA

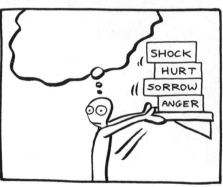

SHOCK
HURT
SORROW
ANGER

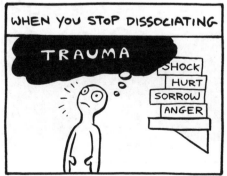

WHEN YOU STOP DISSOCIATING

TRAUMA

SHOCK
HURT
SORROW
ANGER

SHOCK
HURT
SORROW
ANGER

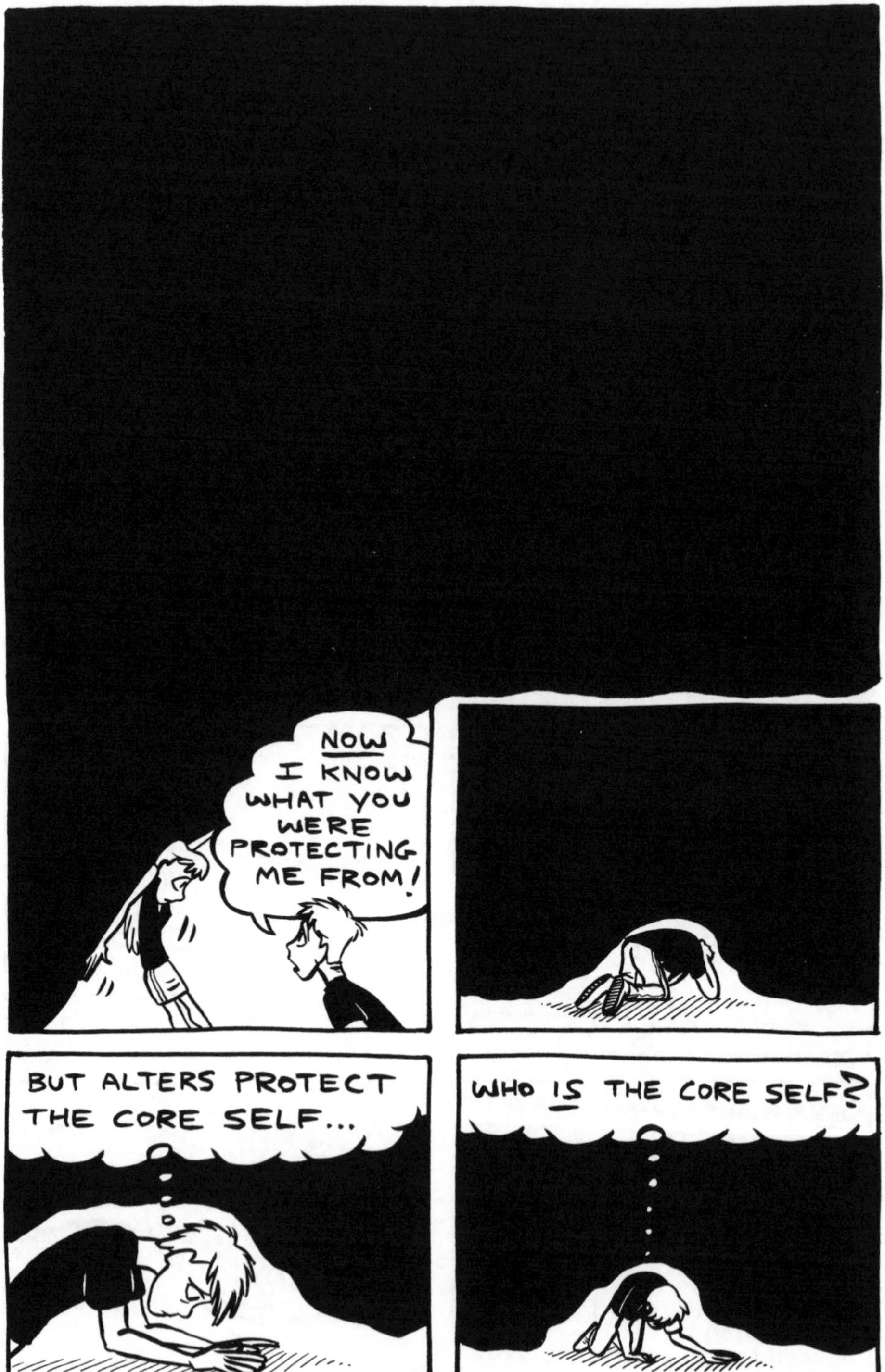

NOW I KNOW WHAT YOU WERE PROTECTING ME FROM!
BUT ALTERS PROTECT THE CORE SELF...
WHO IS THE CORE SELF?

TRACING

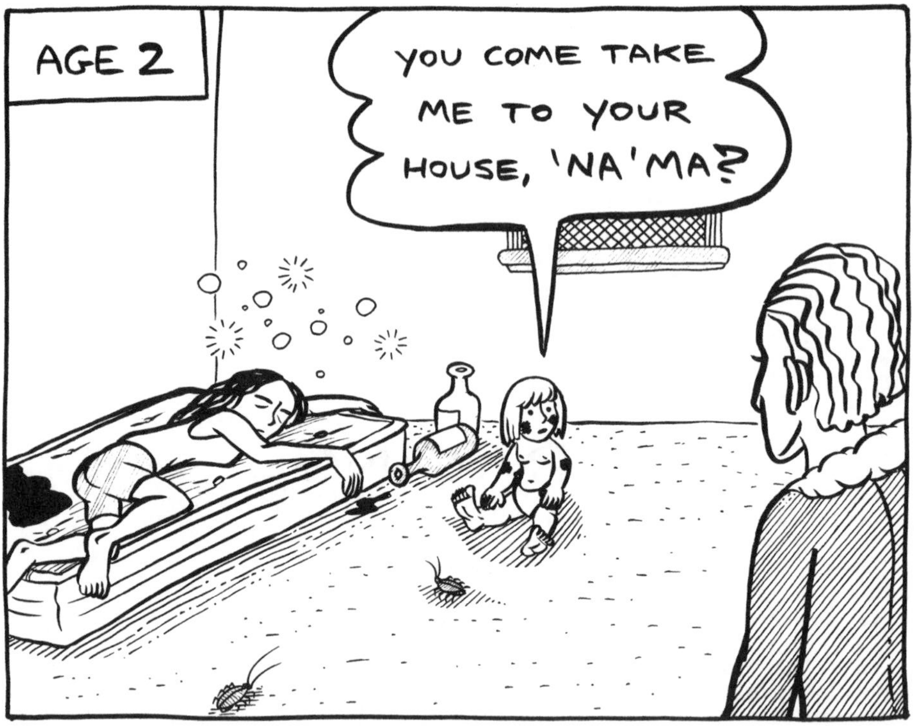
AGE 2
YOU COME TAKE ME TO YOUR HOUSE, 'NA'MA?

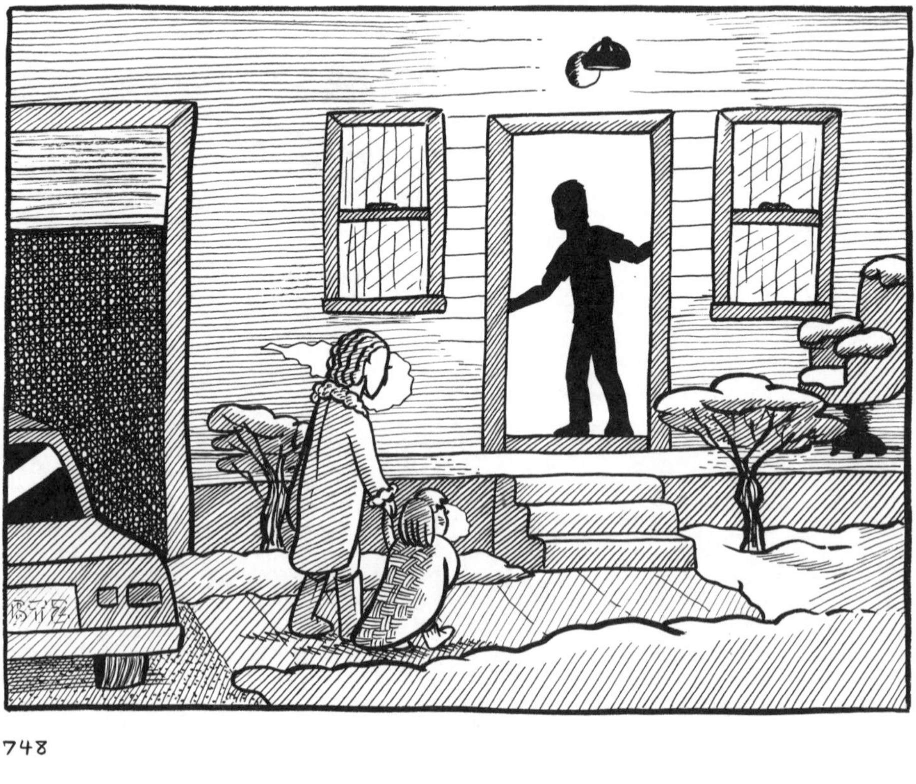

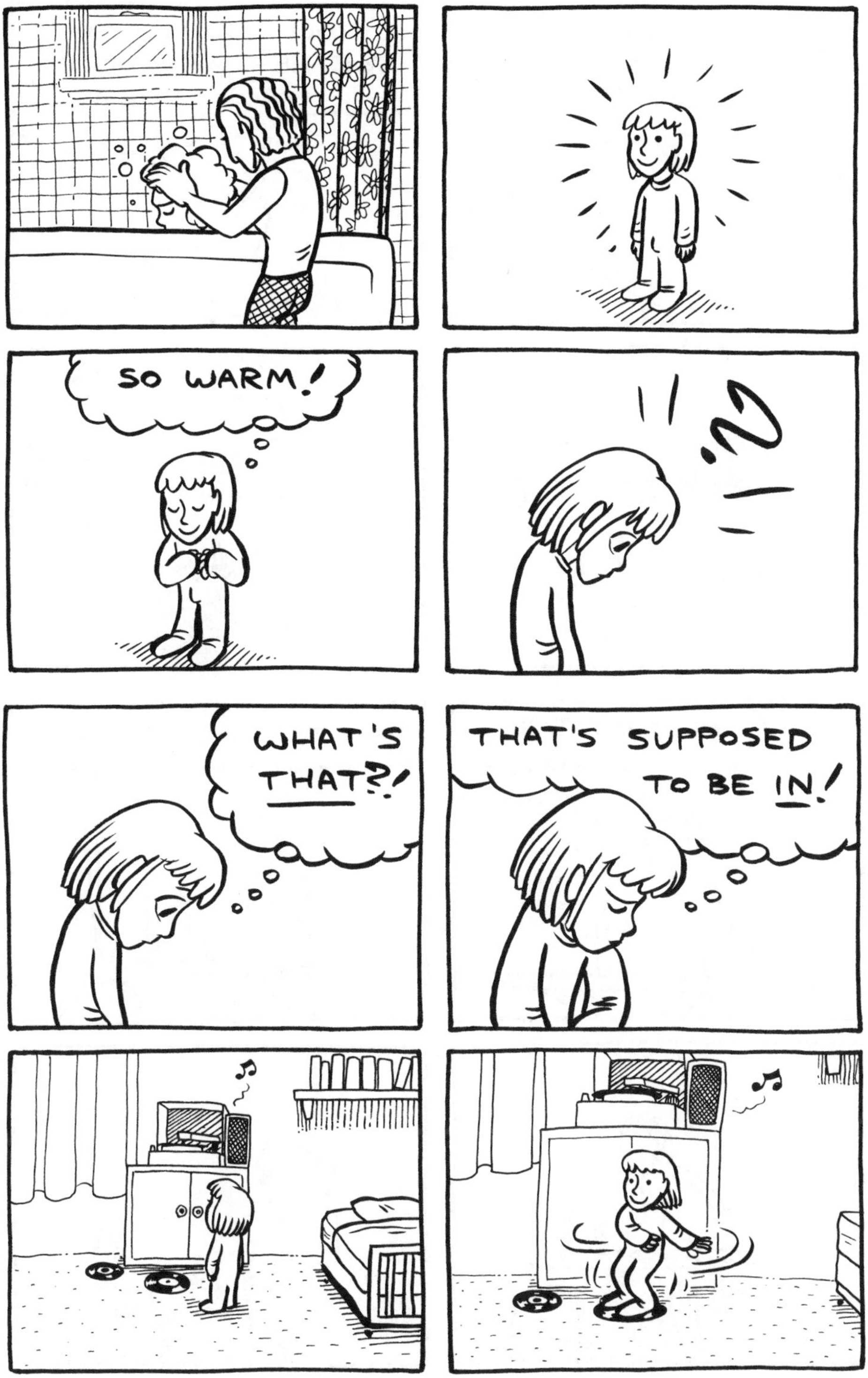
SO WARM!
WHAT'S THAT?!
THAT'S SUPPOSED TO BE IN!

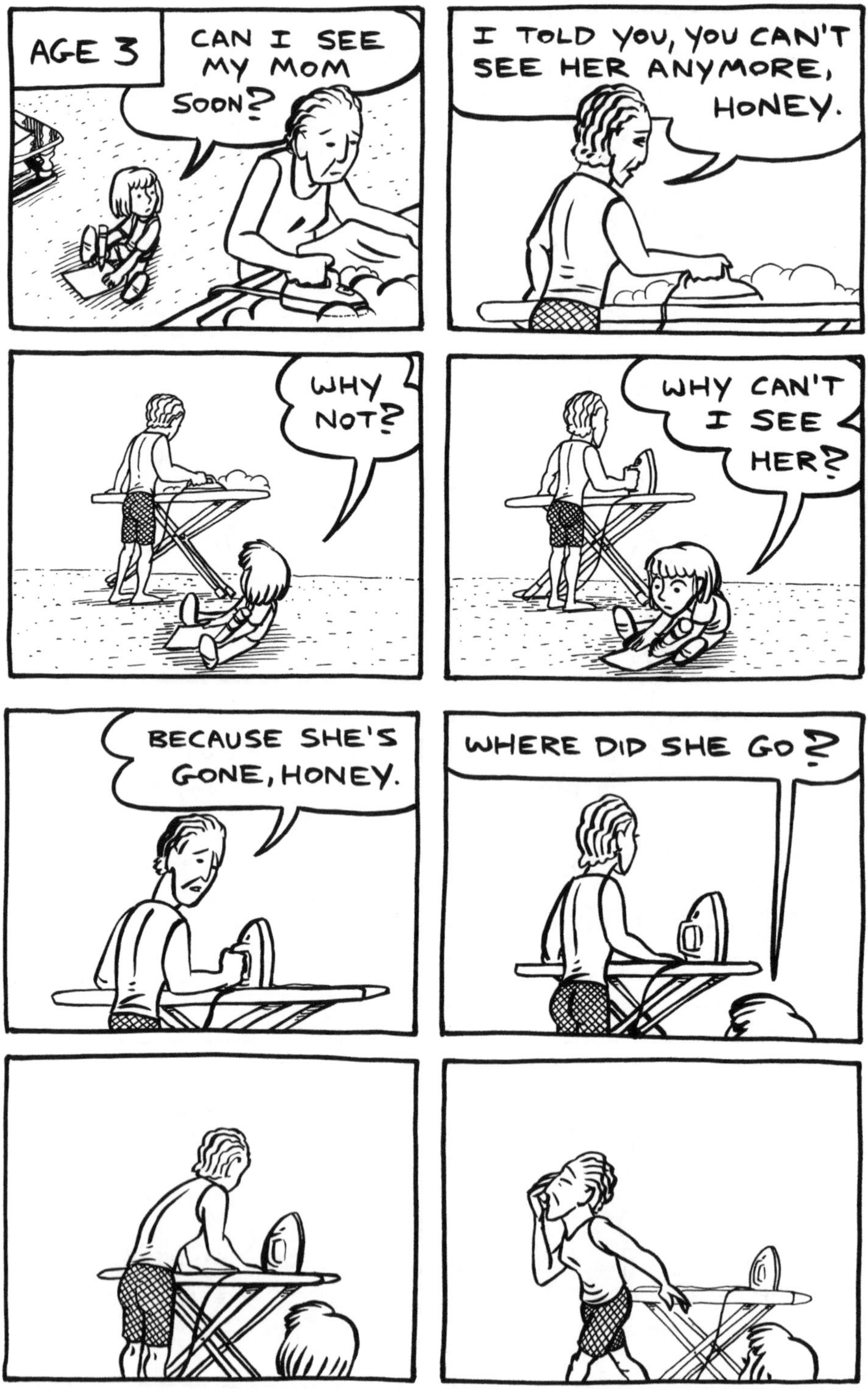
AGE 3
CAN I SEE MY MOM SOON?
I TOLD YOU, YOU CAN'T SEE HER ANYMORE, HONEY.
WHY NOT?
WHY CAN'T I SEE HER?
BECAUSE SHE'S GONE, HONEY.
WHERE DID SHE GO?

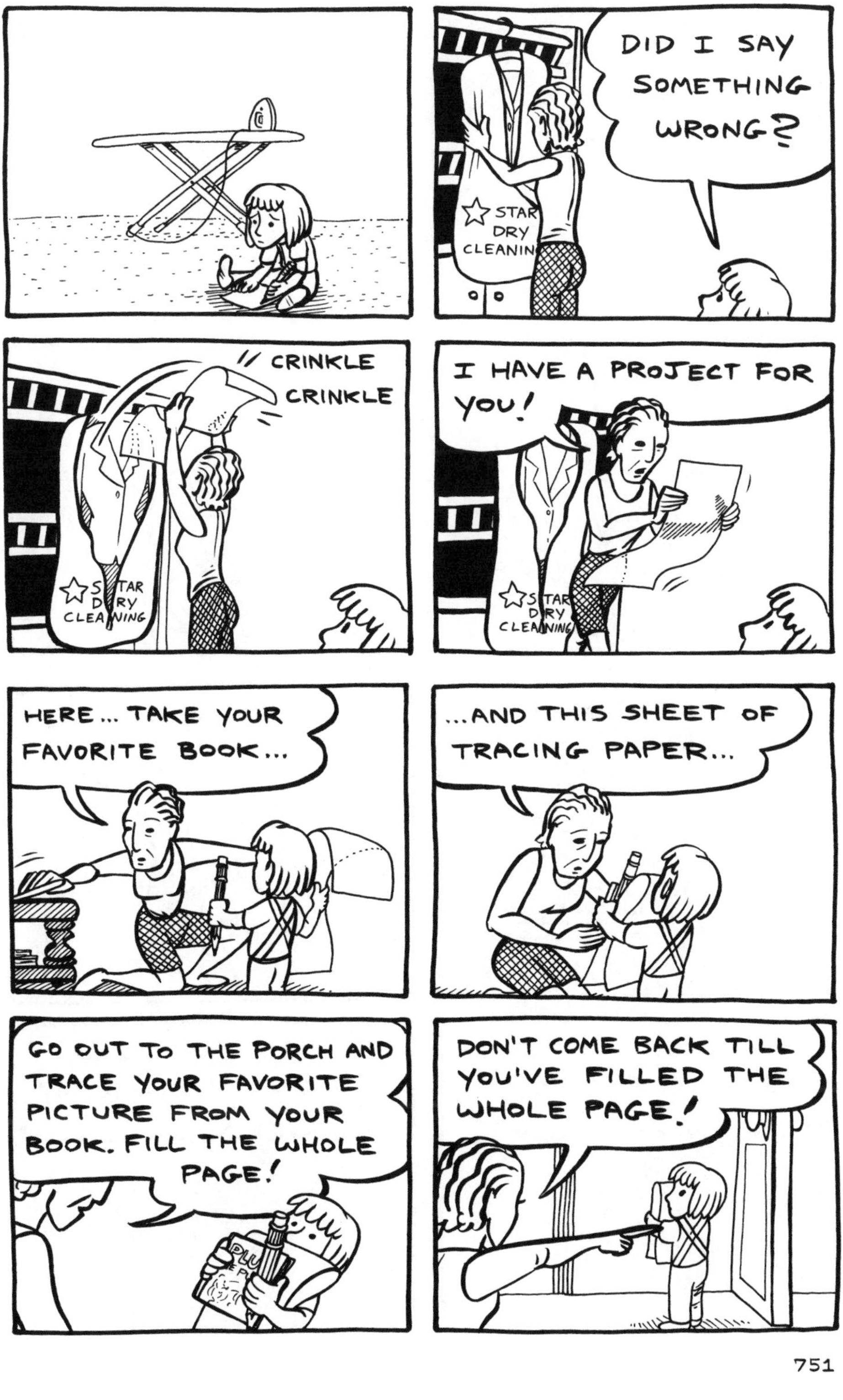
DID I SAY SOMETHING WRONG?
STAR DRY CLEANING
CRINKLE CRINKLE
STAR DRY CLEANING
I HAVE A PROJECT FOR YOU!
STAR DRY CLEANING
HERE... TAKE YOUR FAVORITE BOOK...
...AND THIS SHEET OF TRACING PAPER...
GO OUT TO THE PORCH AND TRACE YOUR FAVORITE PICTURE FROM YOUR BOOK. FILL THE WHOLE PAGE!
DON'T COME BACK TILL YOU'VE FILLED THE WHOLE PAGE!

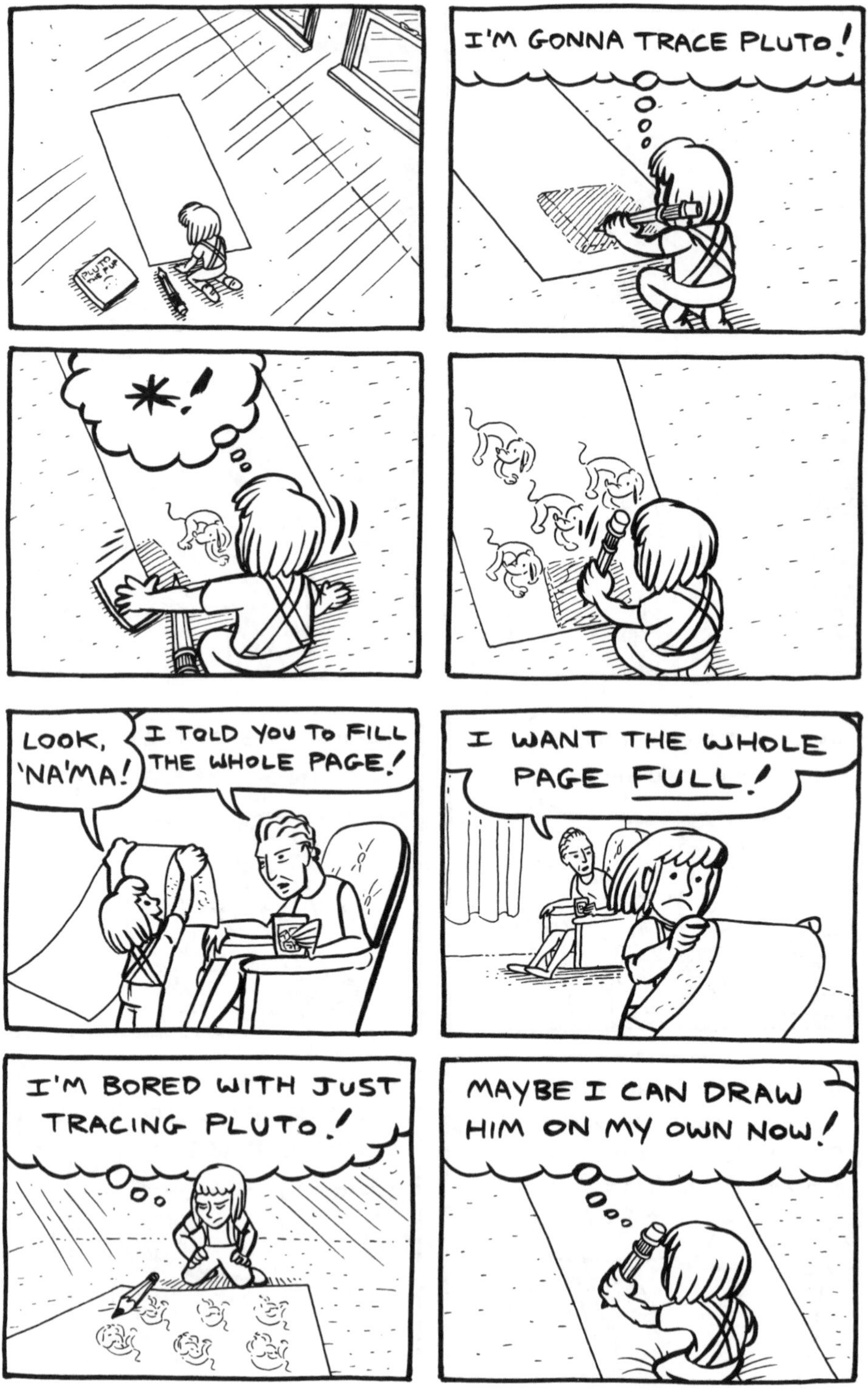
I'M GONNA TRACE PLUTO!
*!
LOOK, 'NA'MA!
I TOLD YOU TO FILL THE WHOLE PAGE!
I WANT THE WHOLE PAGE FULL!
I'M BORED WITH JUST TRACING PLUTO!
MAYBE I CAN DRAW HIM ON MY OWN NOW!

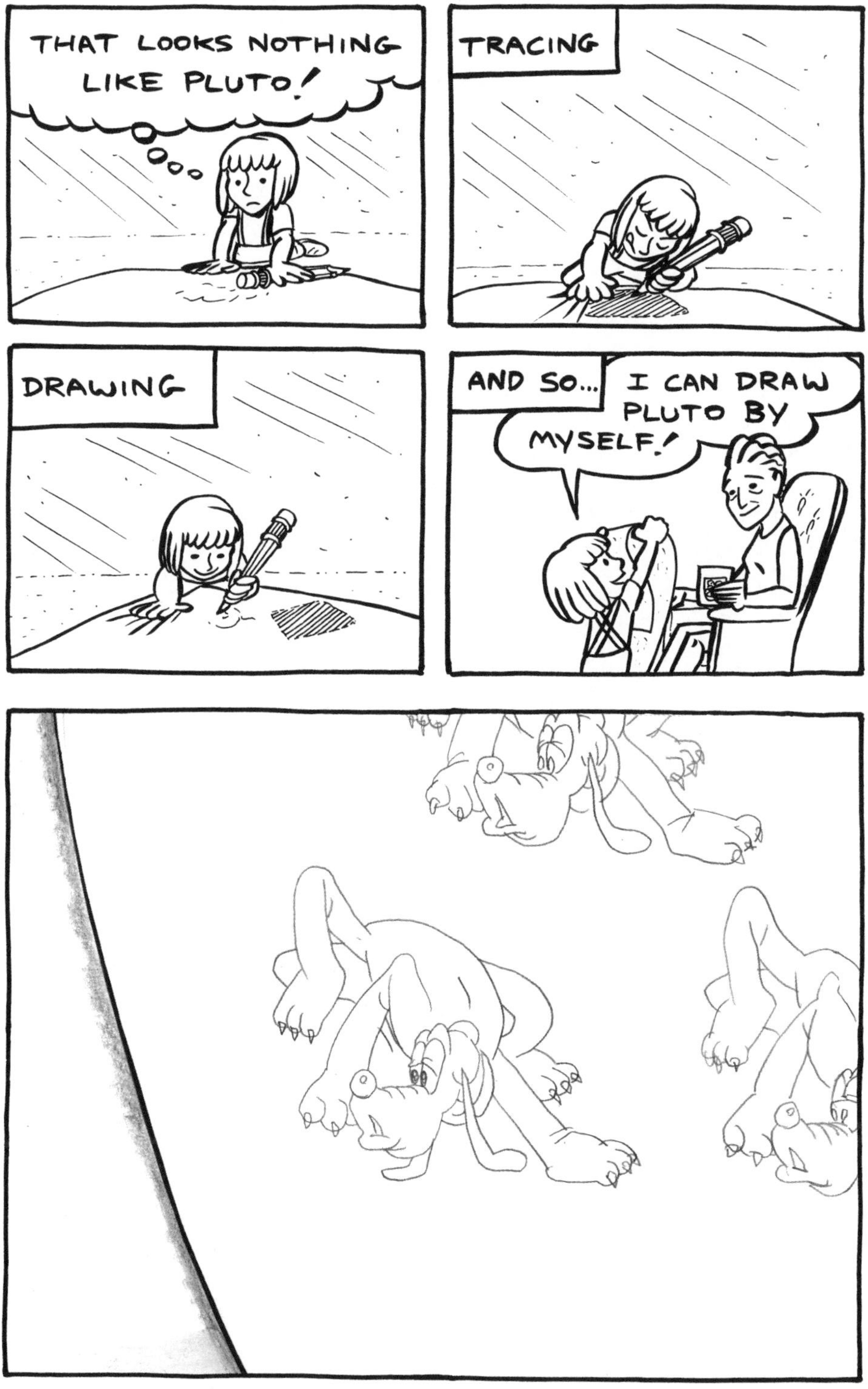
THAT LOOKS NOTHING LIKE PLUTO!
TRACING
DRAWING
AND SO...
I CAN DRAW PLUTO BY MYSELF!

OVEN

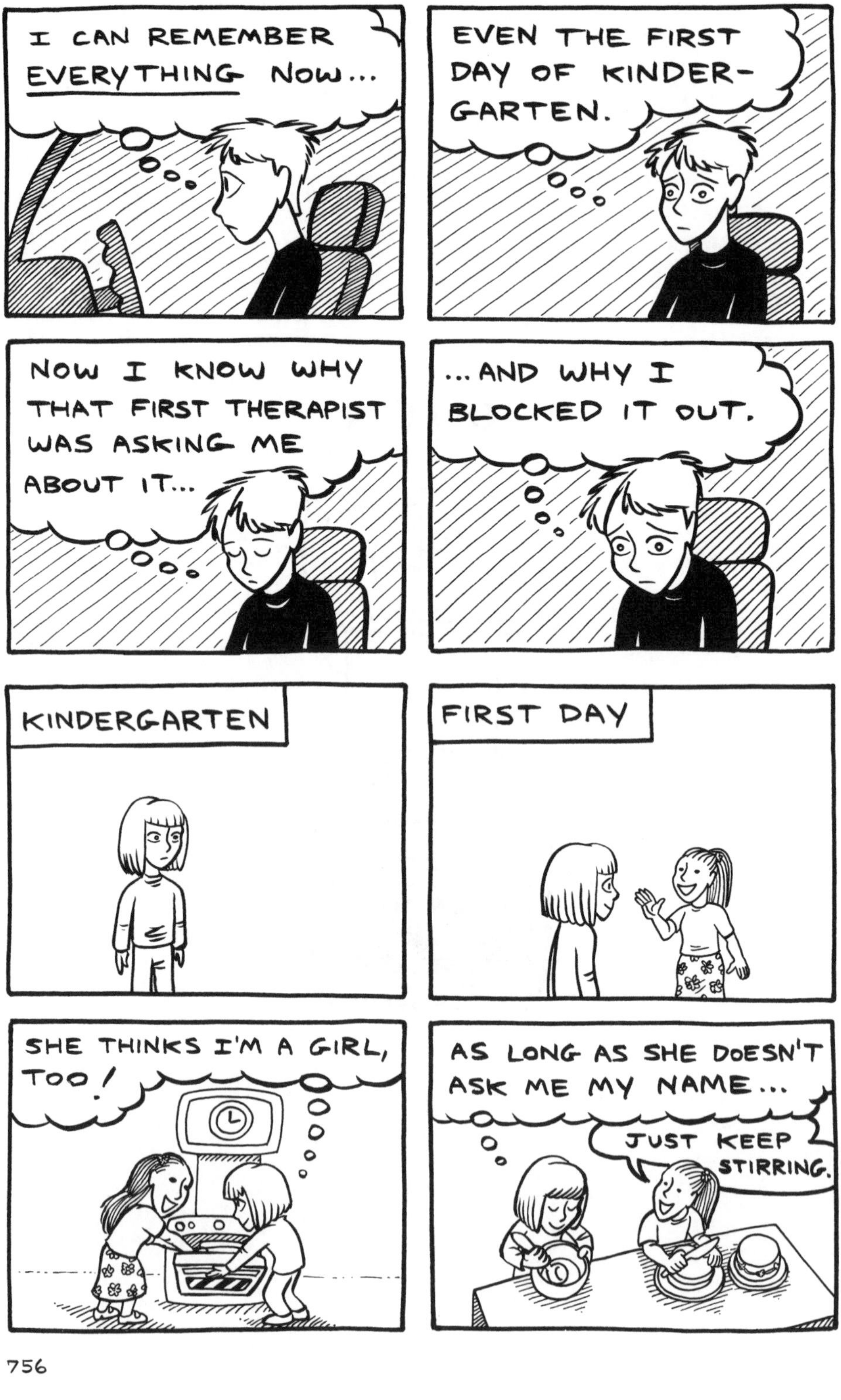
I CAN REMEMBER EVERYTHING NOW...
EVEN THE FIRST DAY OF KINDER-GARTEN.
NOW I KNOW WHY THAT FIRST THERAPIST WAS ASKING ME ABOUT IT...
...AND WHY I BLOCKED IT OUT.
KINDERGARTEN
FIRST DAY
SHE THINKS I'M A GIRL, TOO!
AS LONG AS SHE DOESN'T ASK ME MY NAME...
JUST KEEP STIRRING.

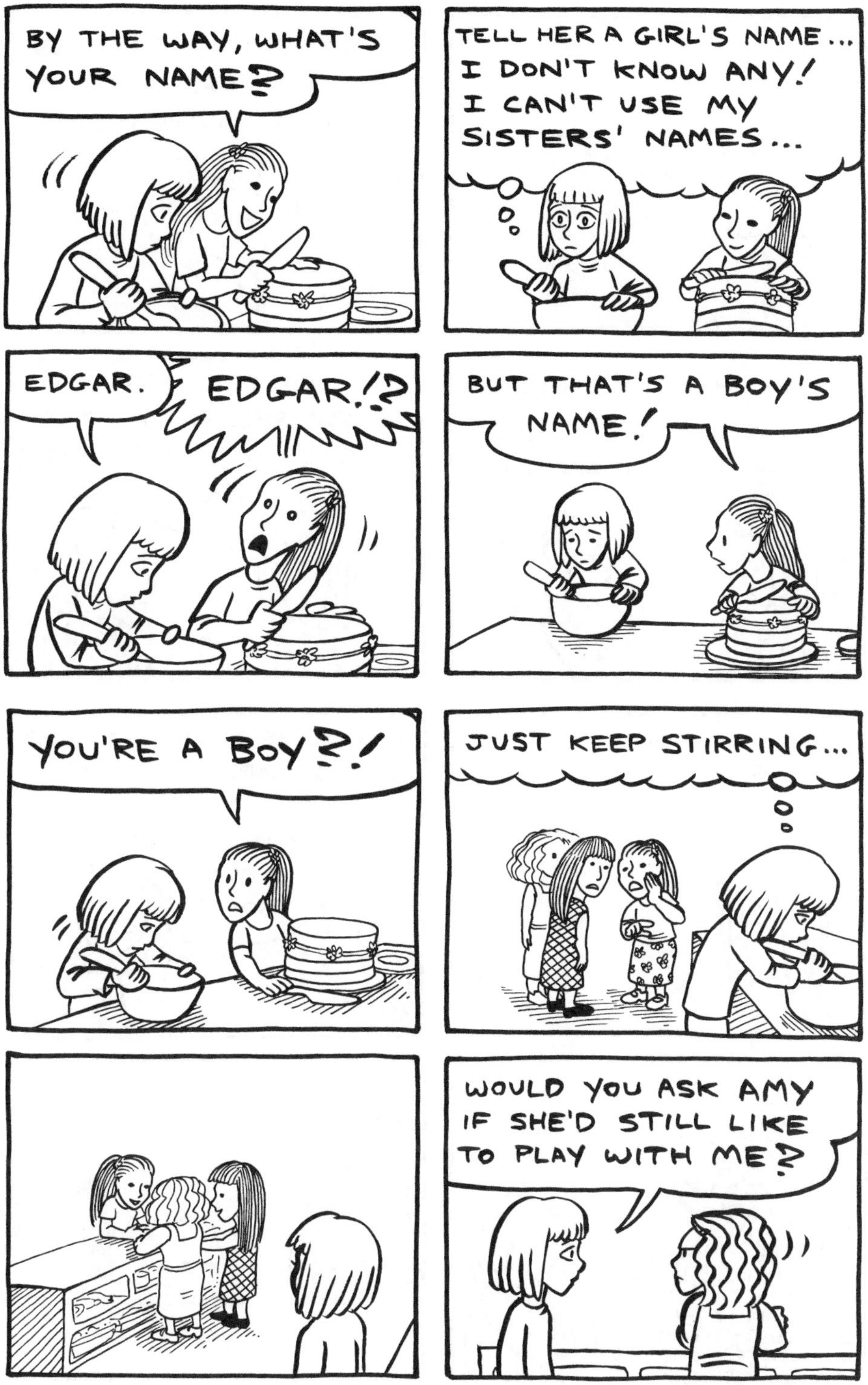
BY THE WAY, WHAT'S YOUR NAME?
TELL HER A GIRL'S NAME... I DON'T KNOW ANY! I CAN'T USE MY SISTERS' NAMES...
EDGAR.
EDGAR!?
BUT THAT'S A BOY'S NAME!
YOU'RE A BOY?!
JUST KEEP STIRRING...
WOULD YOU ASK AMY IF SHE'D STILL LIKE TO PLAY WITH ME?

SHE'S ANGRY THAT YOU TRICKED HER INTO THINKING YOU'RE A GIRL!

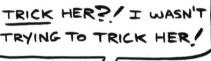

TRICK HER?! I WASN'T TRYING TO TRICK HER!

CAN YOU TELL HER I'M SORRY SHE THOUGHT I WAS TRYING TO TRICK HER?

SHE SAYS THANK YOU FOR SAYING SORRY, BUT THAT YOU NEED TO PLAY WITH THE OTHER LITTLE BOYS.

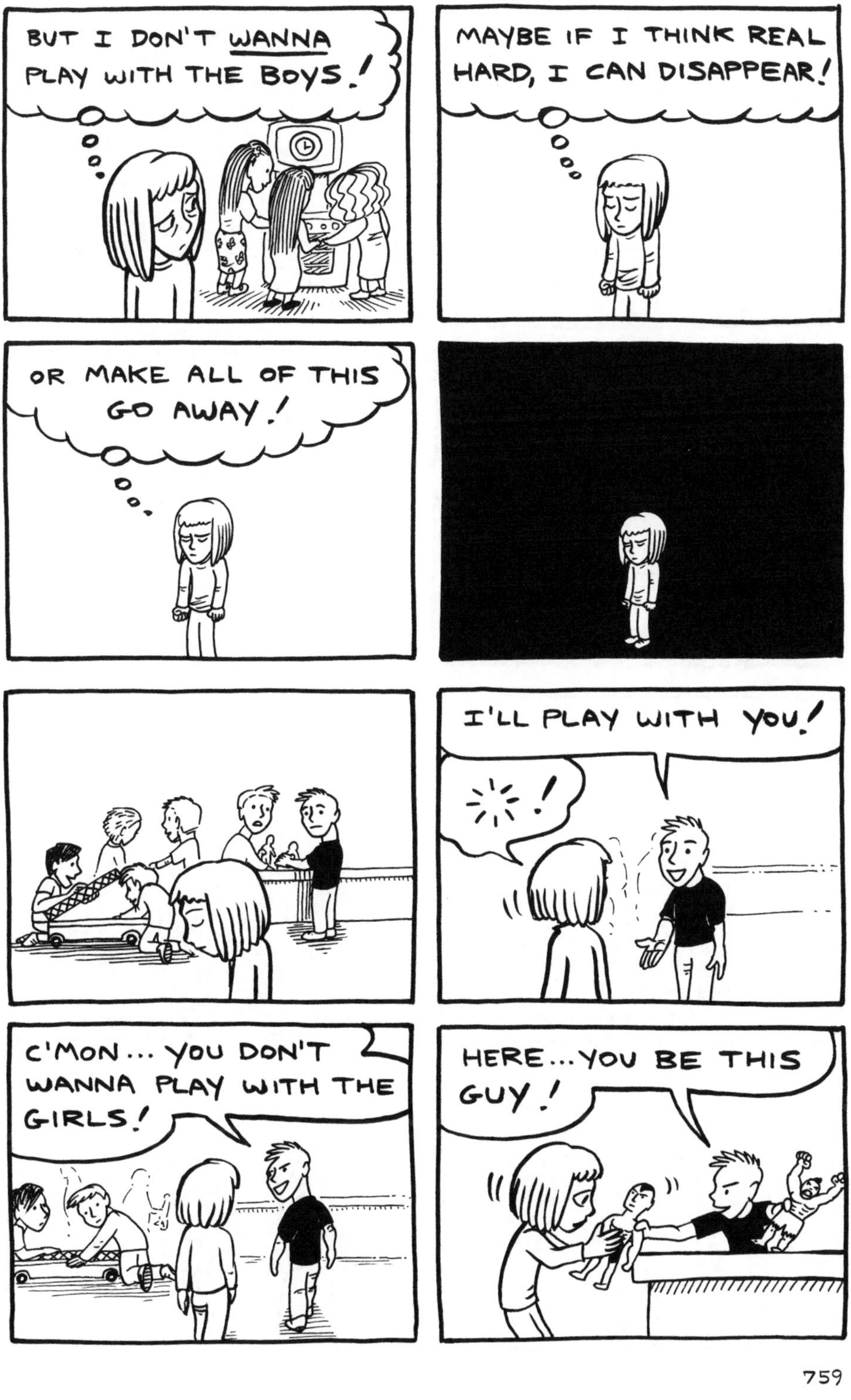
BUT I DON'T WANNA PLAY WITH THE BOYS!
MAYBE IF I THINK REAL HARD, I CAN DISAPPEAR!
OR MAKE ALL OF THIS GO AWAY!
I'LL PLAY WITH YOU!
!
C'MON... YOU DON'T WANNA PLAY WITH THE GIRLS!
HERE... YOU BE THIS GUY!

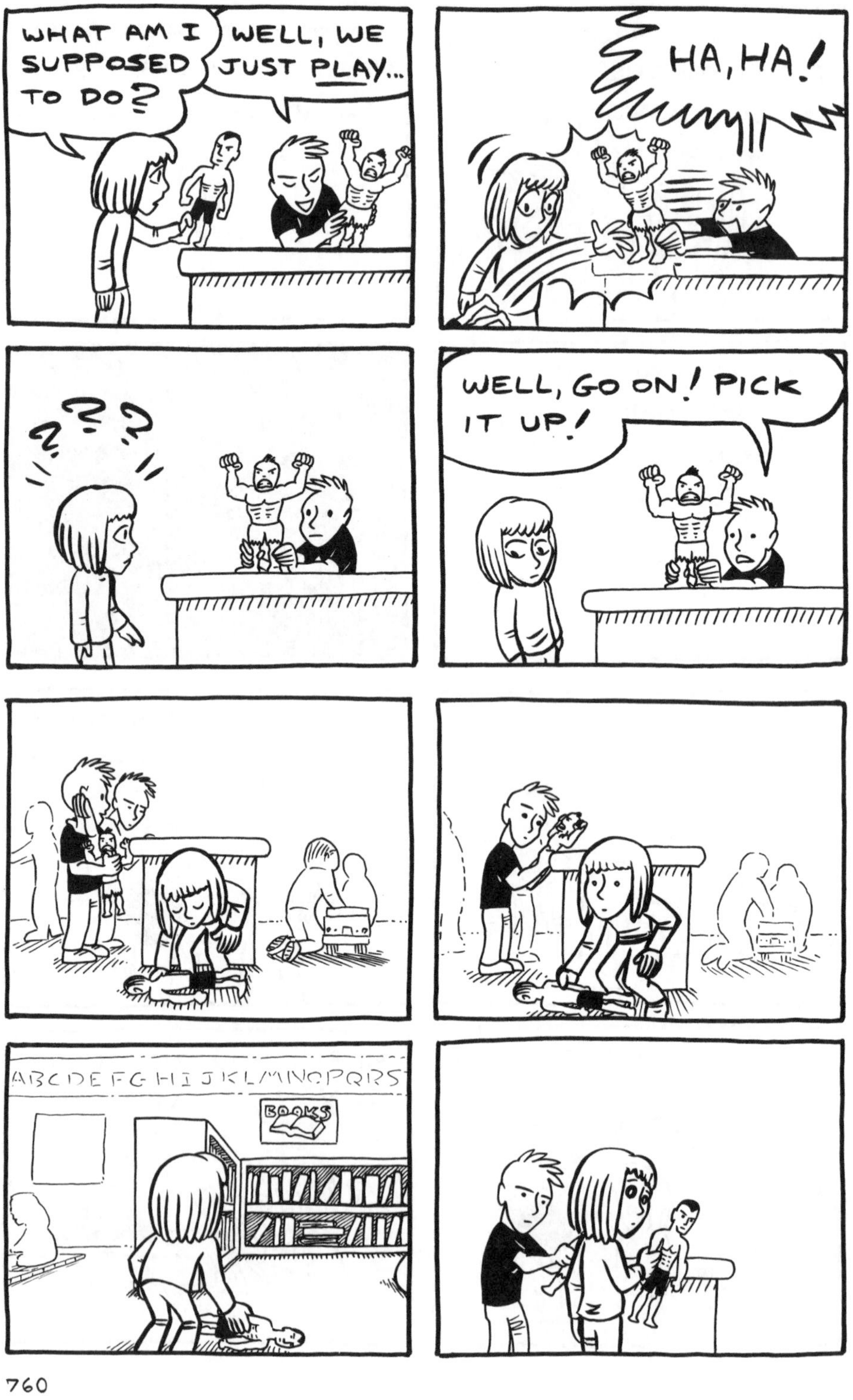
WHAT AM I SUPPOSED TO DO?
WELL, WE JUST PLAY...
HA, HA!
WELL, GO ON! PICK IT UP!
ABCDEFGHIJKLMNOPQRS
BOOKS

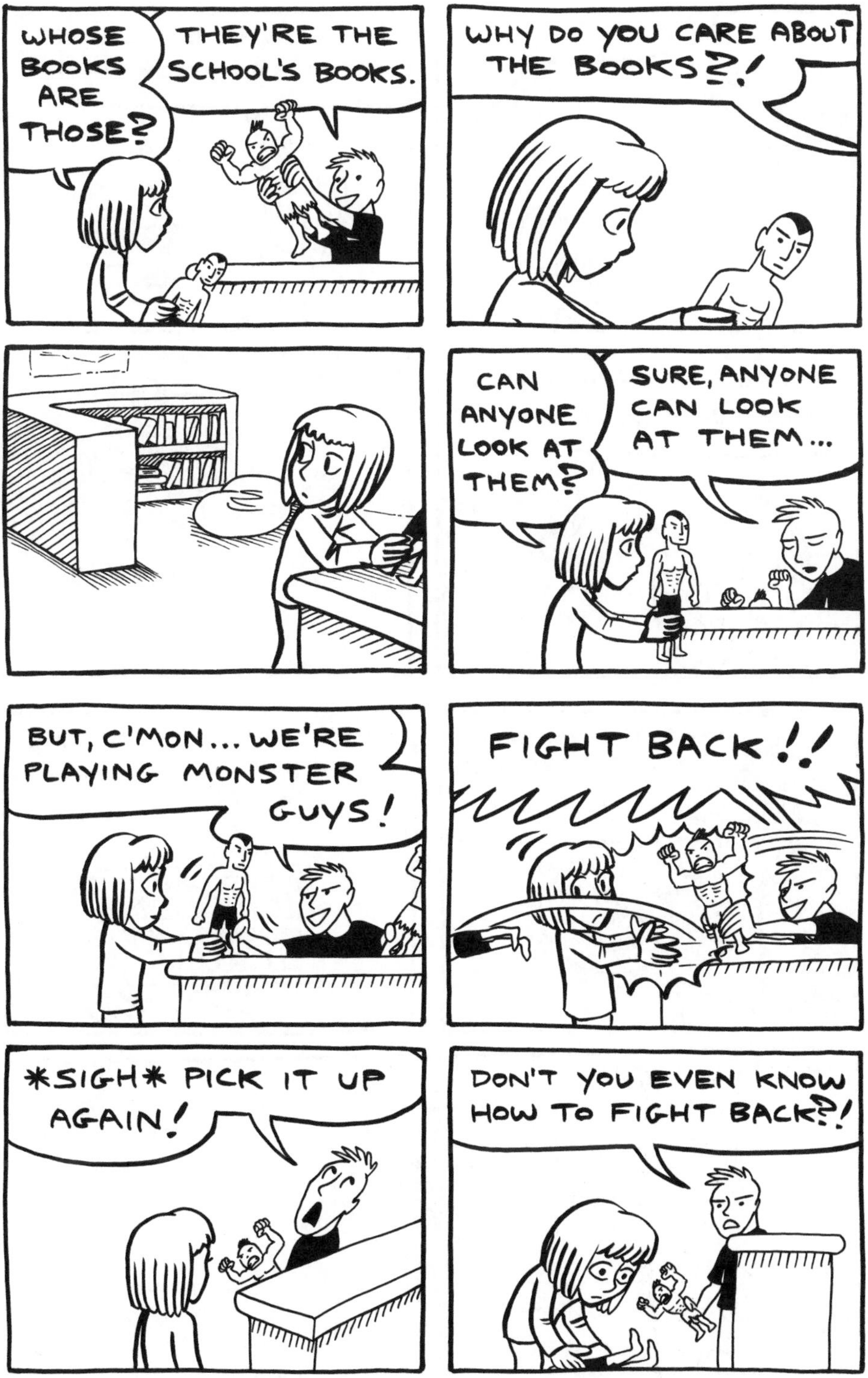
WHOSE BOOKS ARE THOSE?
THEY'RE THE SCHOOL'S BOOKS.
WHY DO YOU CARE ABOUT THE BOOKS?!
CAN ANYONE LOOK AT THEM?
SURE, ANYONE CAN LOOK AT THEM...
BUT, C'MON... WE'RE PLAYING MONSTER GUYS!
FIGHT BACK!!
SIGH PICK IT UP AGAIN!
DON'T YOU EVEN KNOW HOW TO FIGHT BACK?!

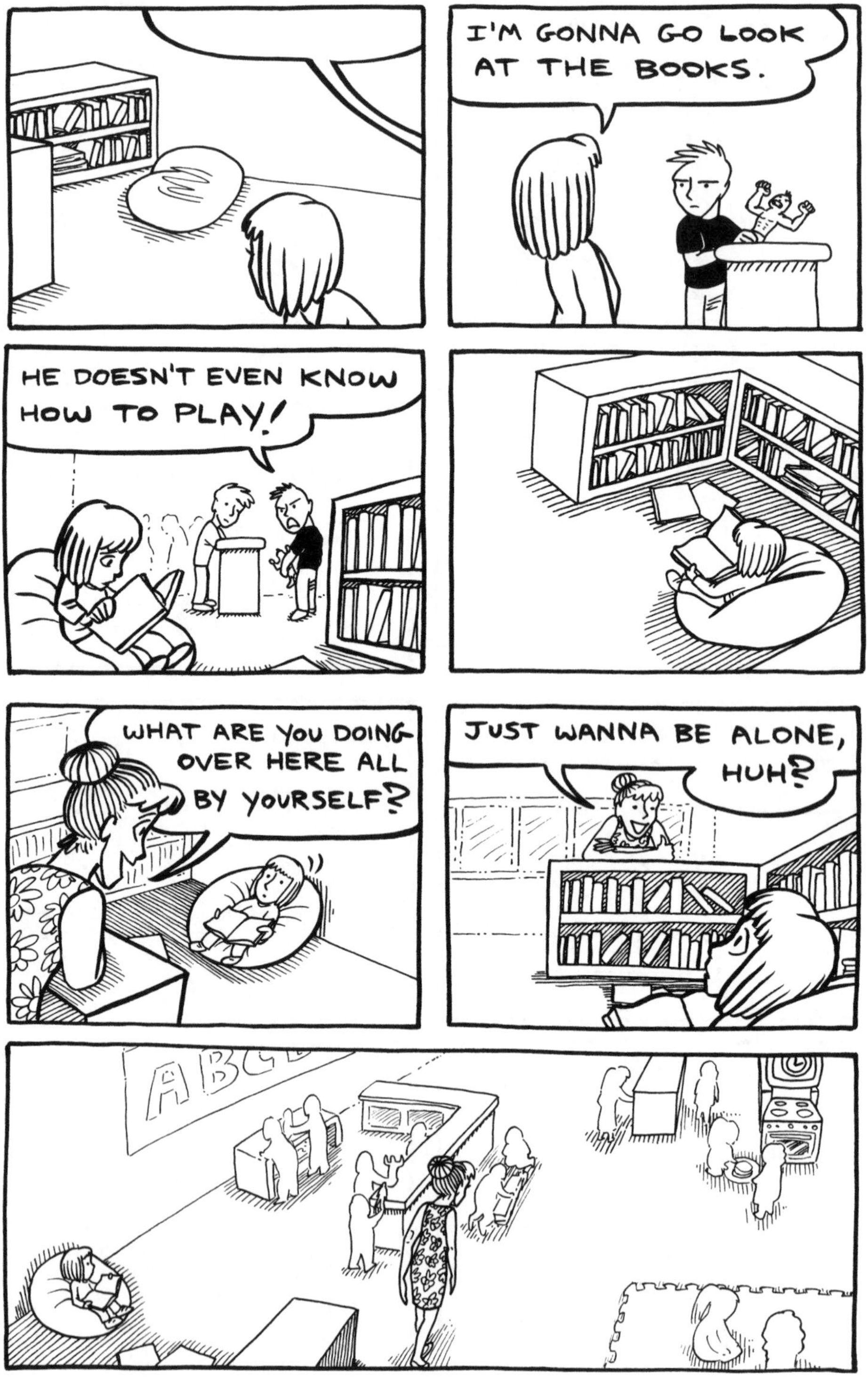
I'M GONNA GO LOOK AT THE BOOKS.
HE DOESN'T EVEN KNOW HOW TO PLAY!
WHAT ARE YOU DOING OVER HERE ALL BY YOURSELF?
JUST WANNA BE ALONE, HUH?
ABC

LAMP

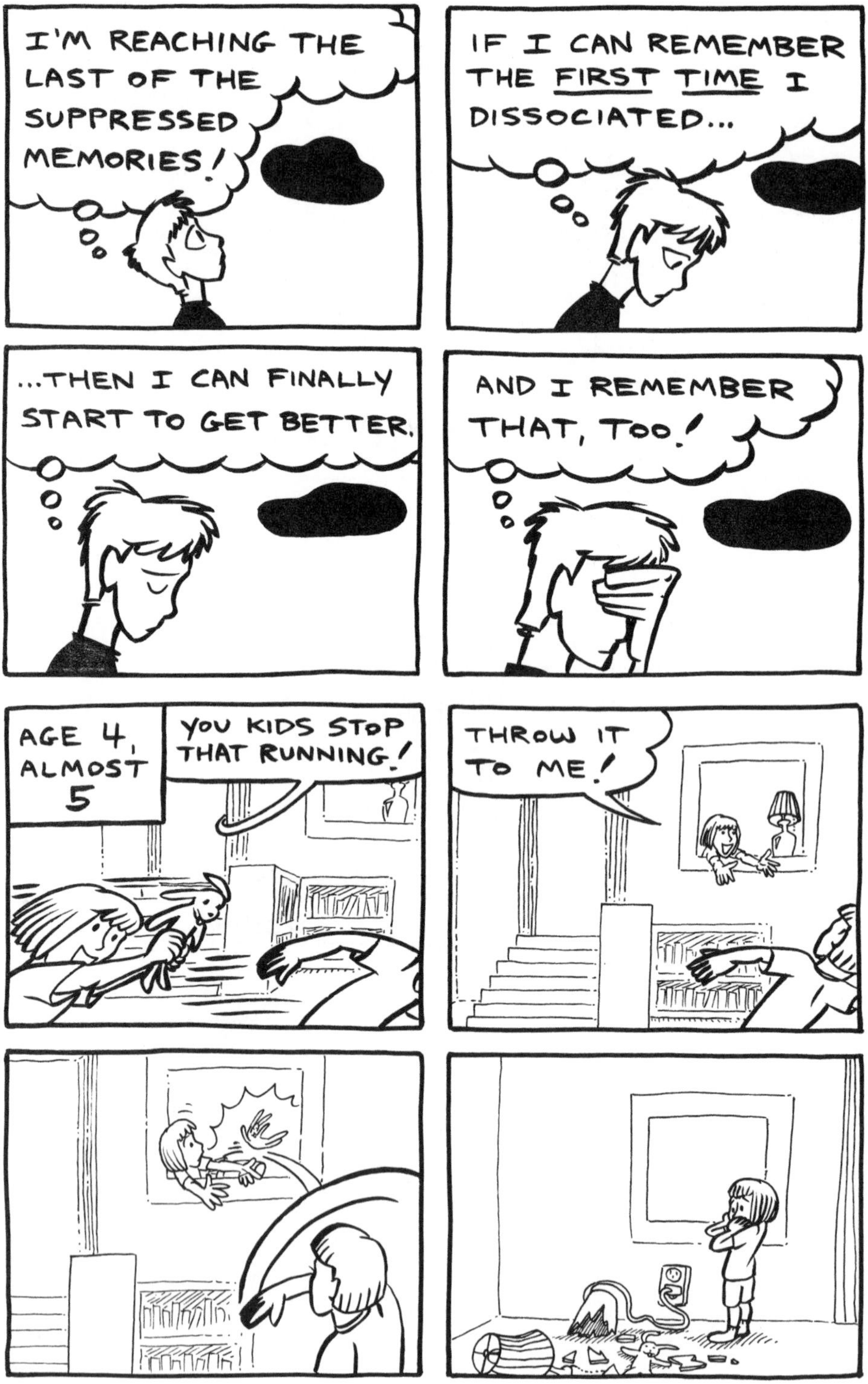
I'M REACHING THE LAST OF THE SUPPRESSED MEMORIES!
IF I CAN REMEMBER THE FIRST TIME I DISSOCIATED...
...THEN I CAN FINALLY START TO GET BETTER.
AND I REMEMBER THAT, TOO!
AGE 4, ALMOST 5
YOU KIDS STOP THAT RUNNING!
THROW IT TO ME!

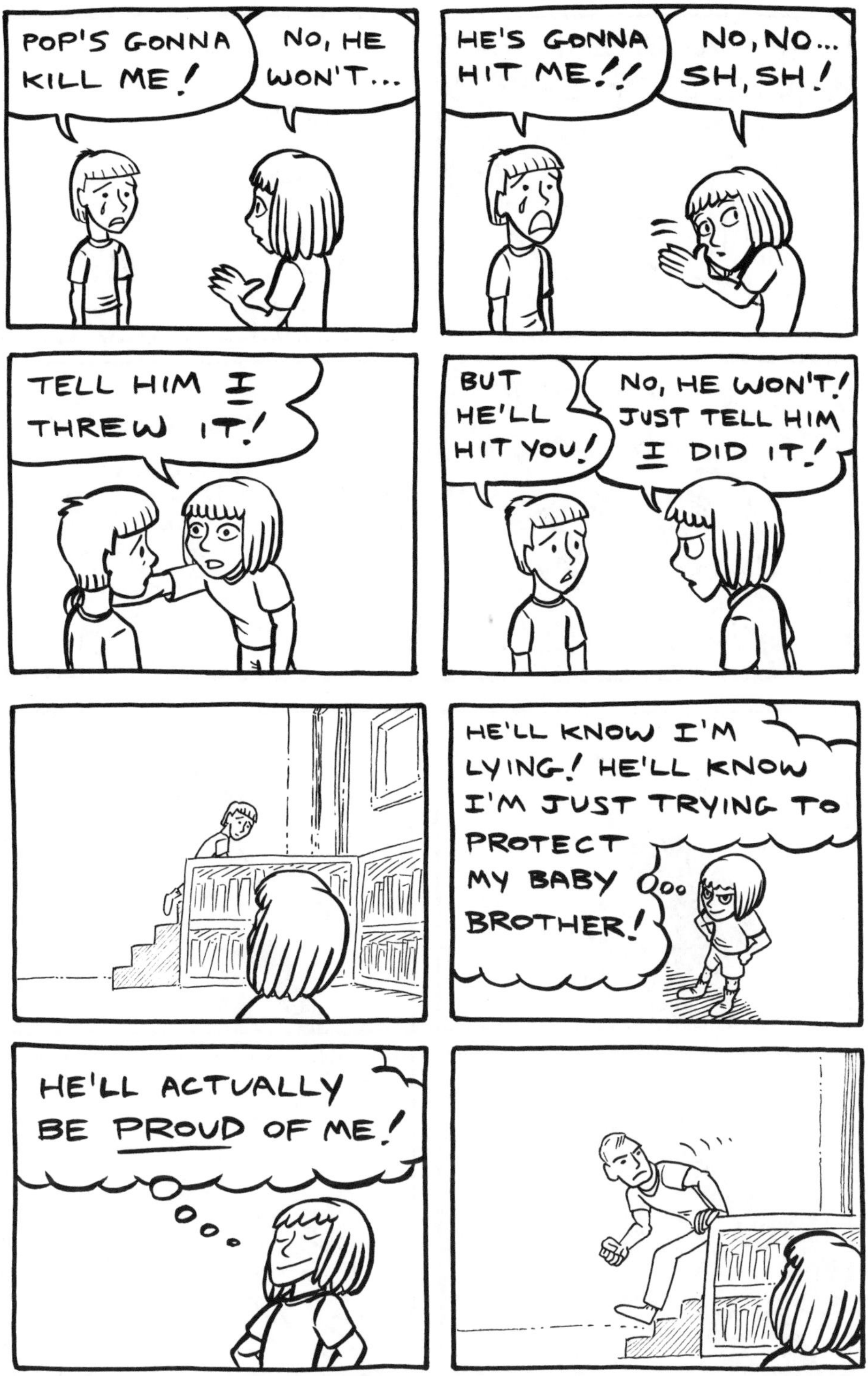
POP'S GONNA KILL ME!
NO, HE WON'T...
HE'S GONNA HIT ME!!
NO, NO... SH, SH!
TELL HIM I THREW IT!
BUT HE'LL HIT YOU!
NO, HE WON'T! JUST TELL HIM I DID IT!
HE'LL KNOW I'M LYING! HE'LL KNOW I'M JUST TRYING TO PROTECT MY BABY BROTHER!
HE'LL ACTUALLY BE PROUD OF ME!

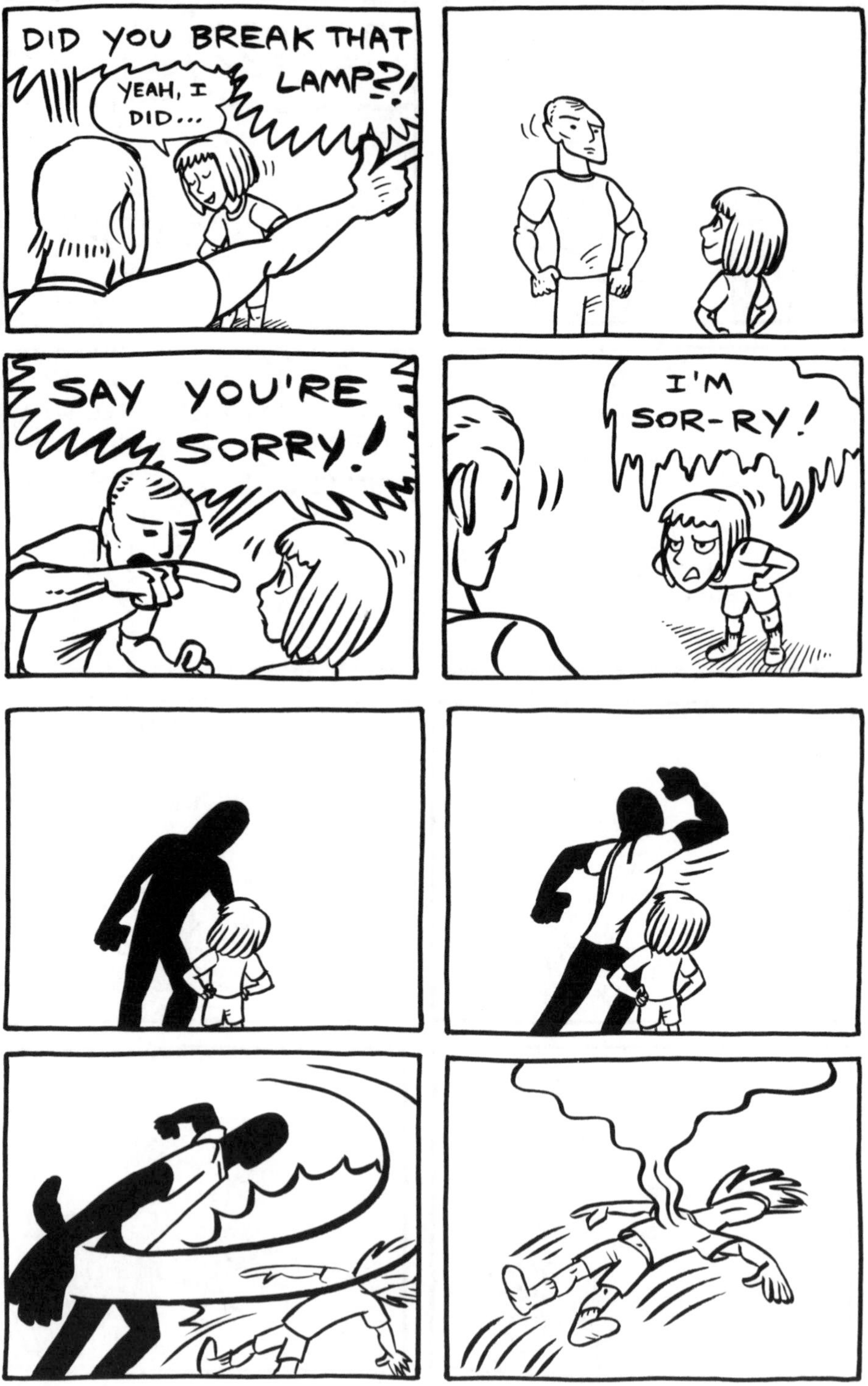
DID YOU BREAK THAT LAMP?!
YEAH, I DID...
SAY YOU'RE SORRY!
I'M SOR-RY!

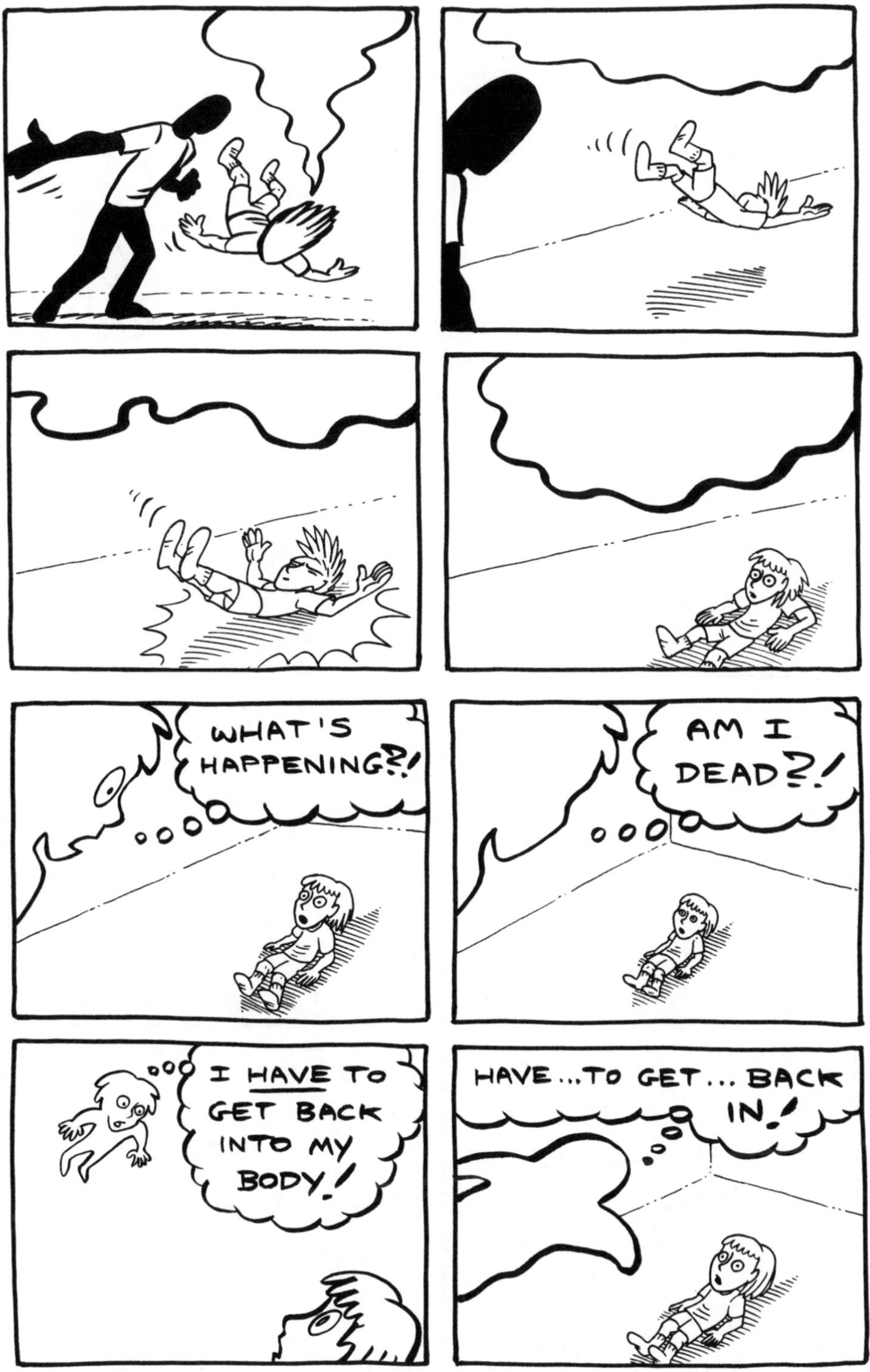
WHAT'S HAPPENING?!
AM I DEAD?!
I HAVE TO GET BACK INTO MY BODY!
HAVE...TO GET... BACK IN!

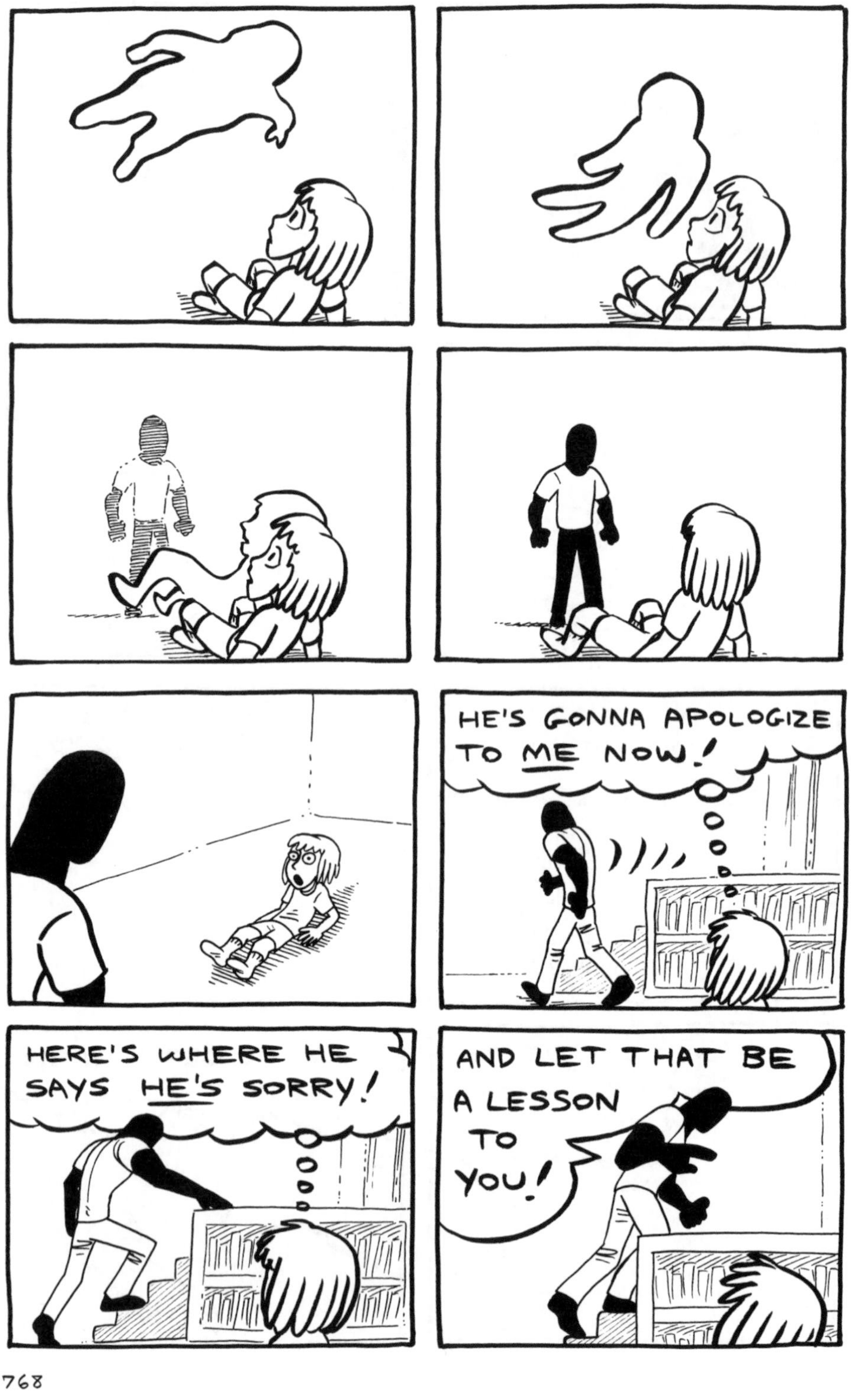
HE'S GONNA APOLOGIZE TO ME NOW!
HERE'S WHERE HE SAYS HE'S SORRY!
AND LET THAT BE A LESSON TO YOU!

SECRET
FRIEND

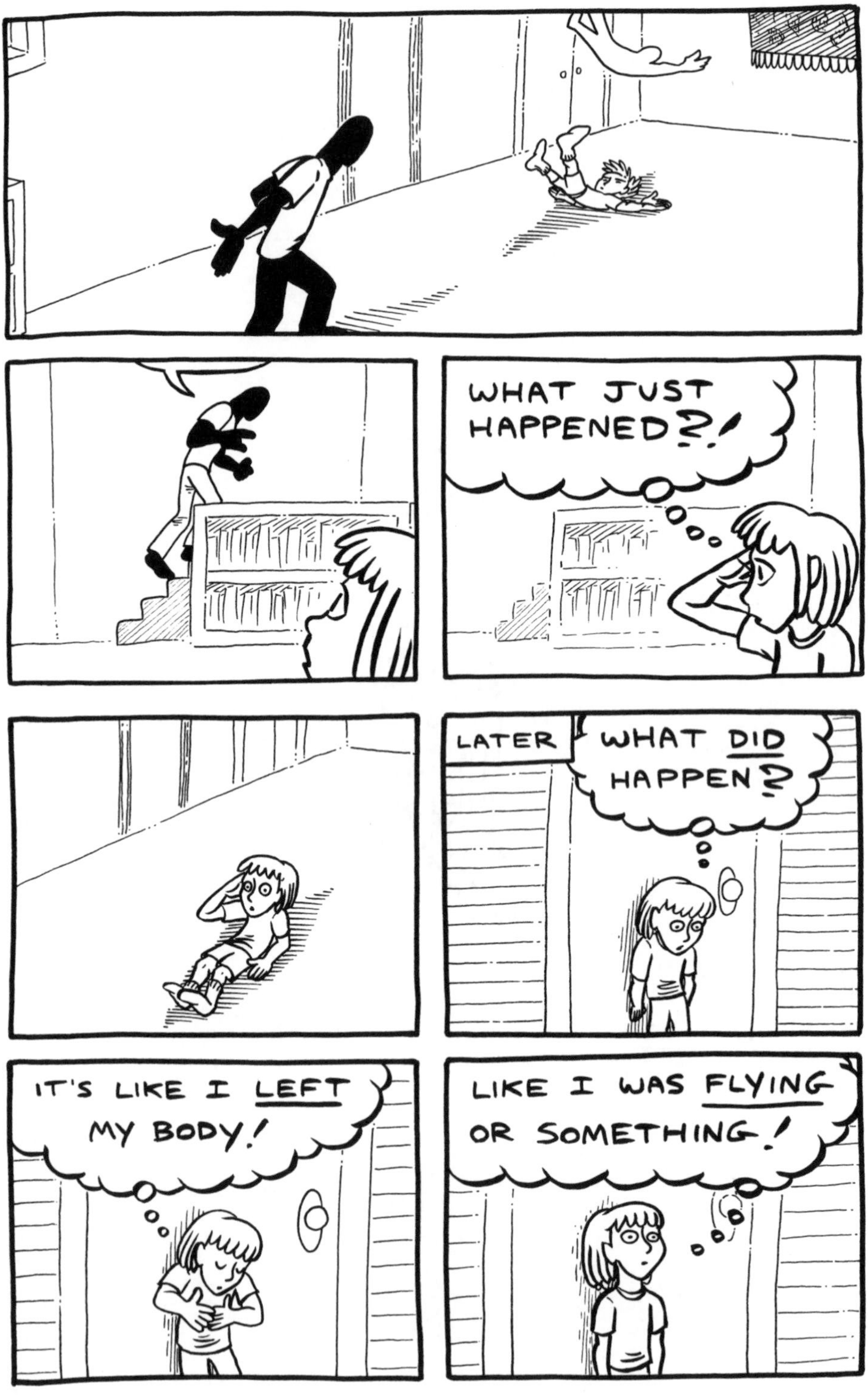
WHAT JUST HAPPENED?!
LATER
WHAT DID HAPPEN?
IT'S LIKE I LEFT MY BODY!
LIKE I WAS FLYING OR SOMETHING!

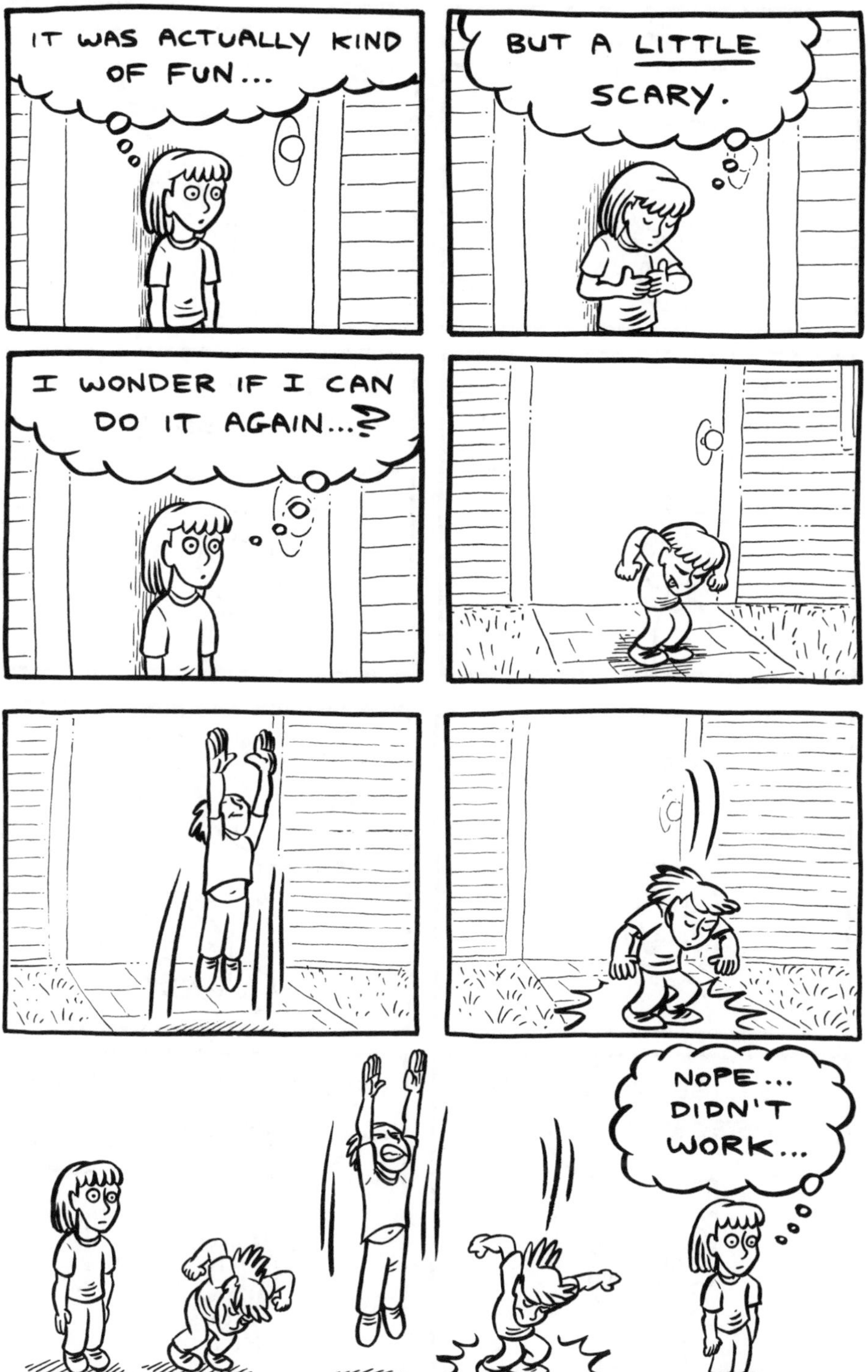
IT WAS ACTUALLY KIND OF FUN...
BUT A LITTLE SCARY.
I WONDER IF I CAN DO IT AGAIN...?
NOPE... DIDN'T WORK...

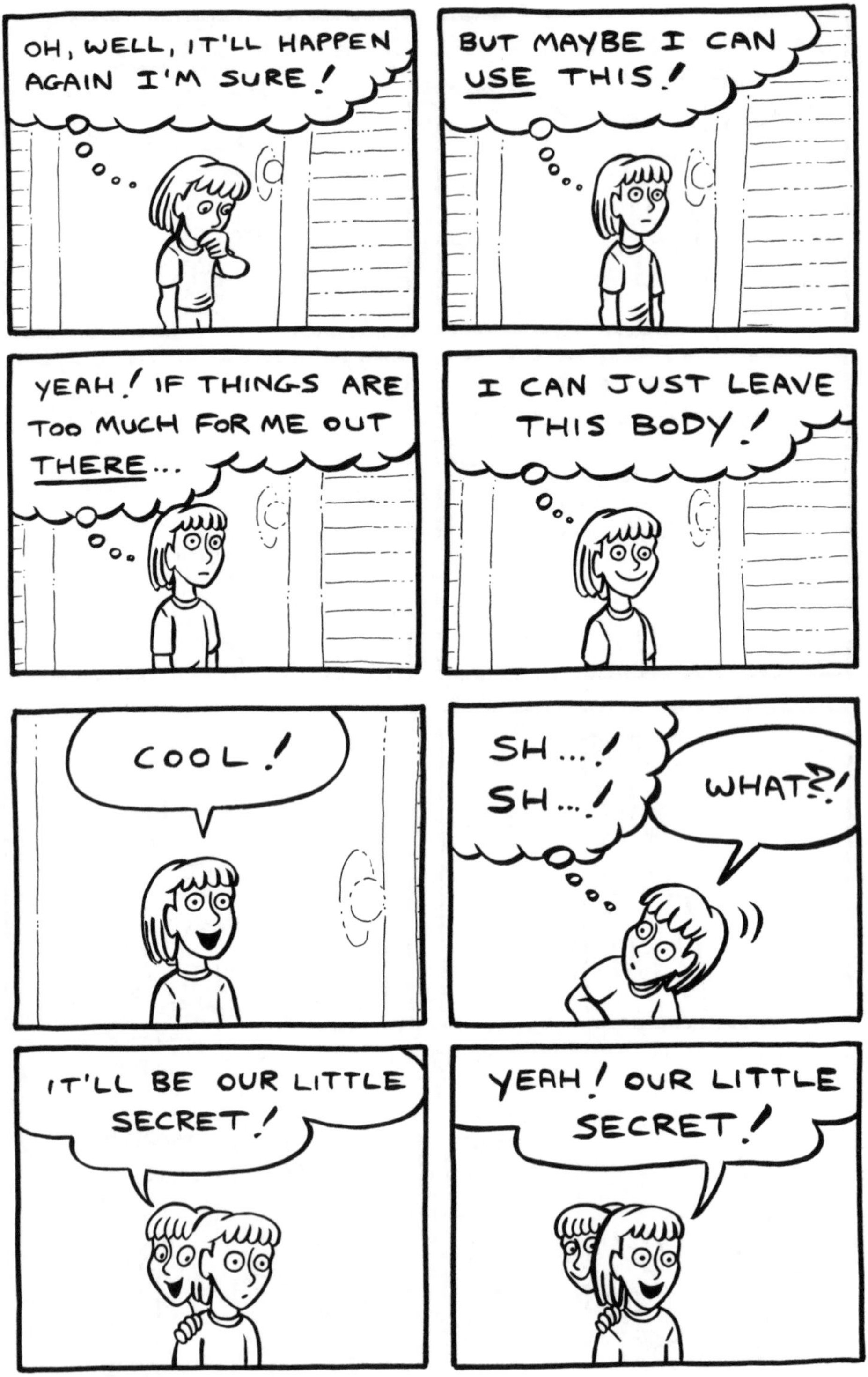
OH, WELL, IT'LL HAPPEN AGAIN I'M SURE!
BUT MAYBE I CAN USE THIS!
YEAH! IF THINGS ARE TOO MUCH FOR ME OUT THERE...
I CAN JUST LEAVE THIS BODY!
COOL!
SH...!
SH...!
WHAT?!
IT'LL BE OUR LITTLE SECRET!
YEAH! OUR LITTLE SECRET!

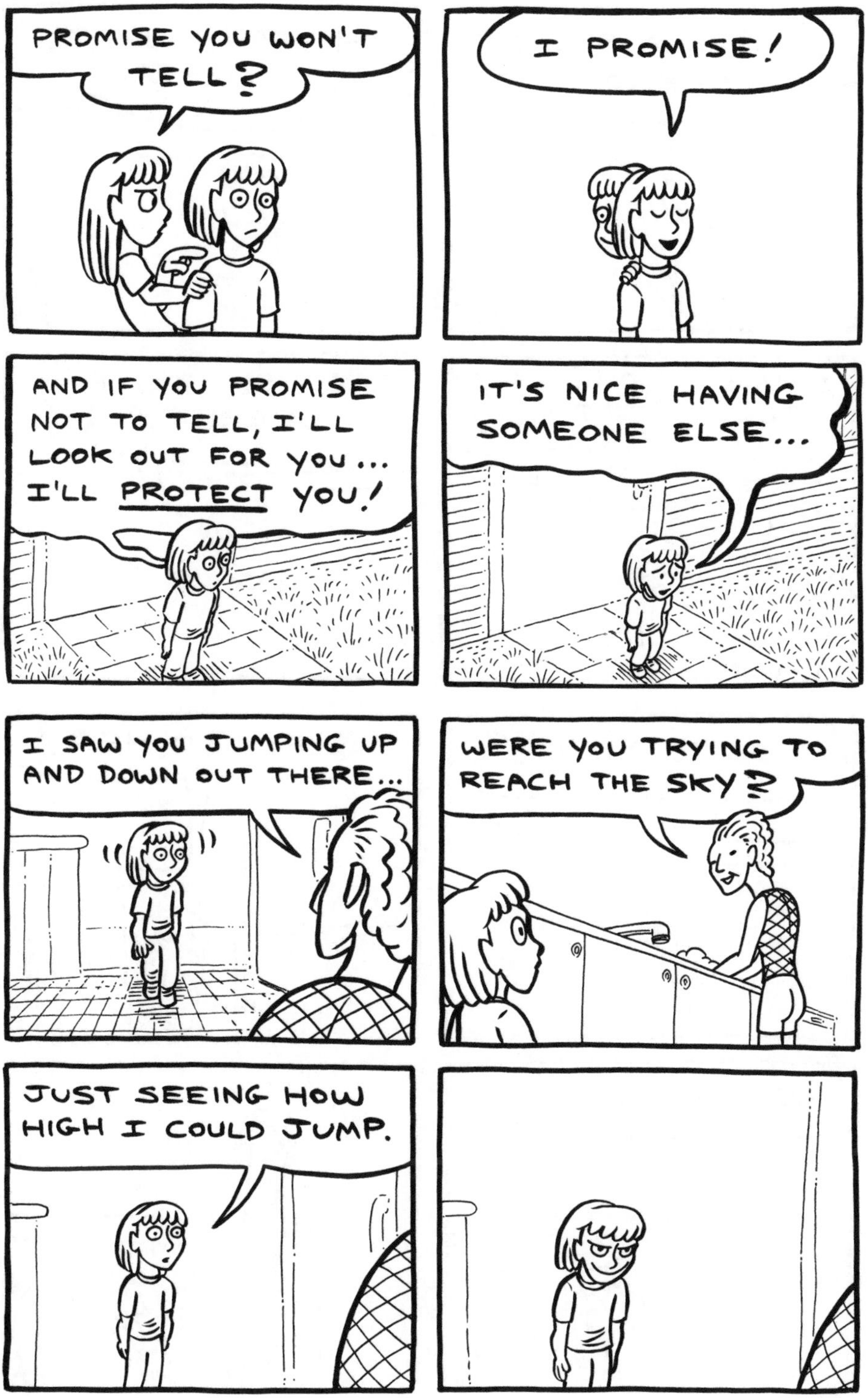
PROMISE YOU WON'T TELL?
I PROMISE!
AND IF YOU PROMISE NOT TO TELL, I'LL LOOK OUT FOR YOU... I'LL PROTECT YOU!
IT'S NICE HAVING SOMEONE ELSE...
I SAW YOU JUMPING UP AND DOWN OUT THERE...
WERE YOU TRYING TO REACH THE SKY?
JUST SEEING HOW HIGH I COULD JUMP.

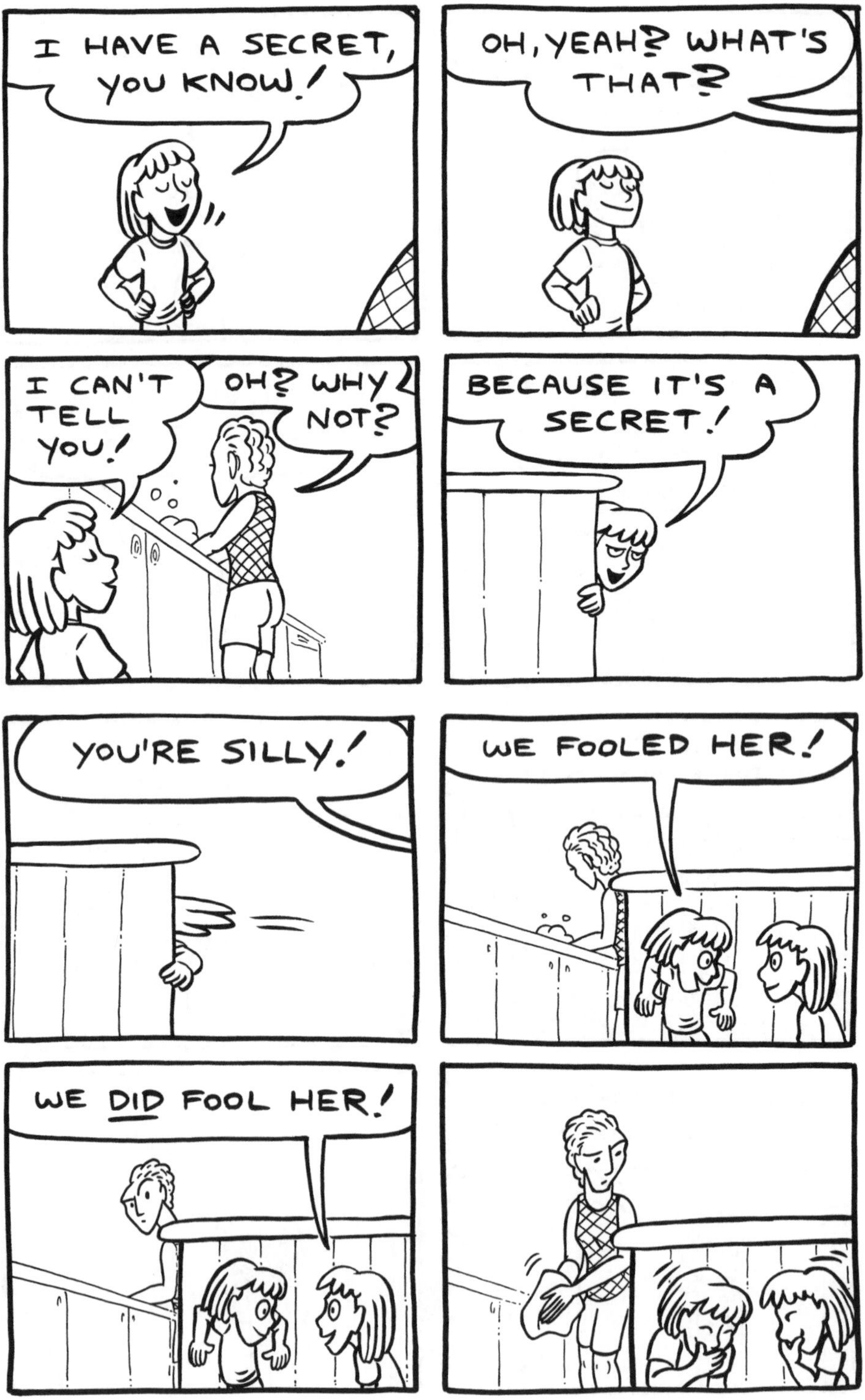
I HAVE A SECRET, YOU KNOW!
OH, YEAH? WHAT'S THAT?
I CAN'T TELL YOU!
OH? WHY NOT?
BECAUSE IT'S A SECRET!
YOU'RE SILLY!
WE FOOLED HER!
WE DID FOOL HER!

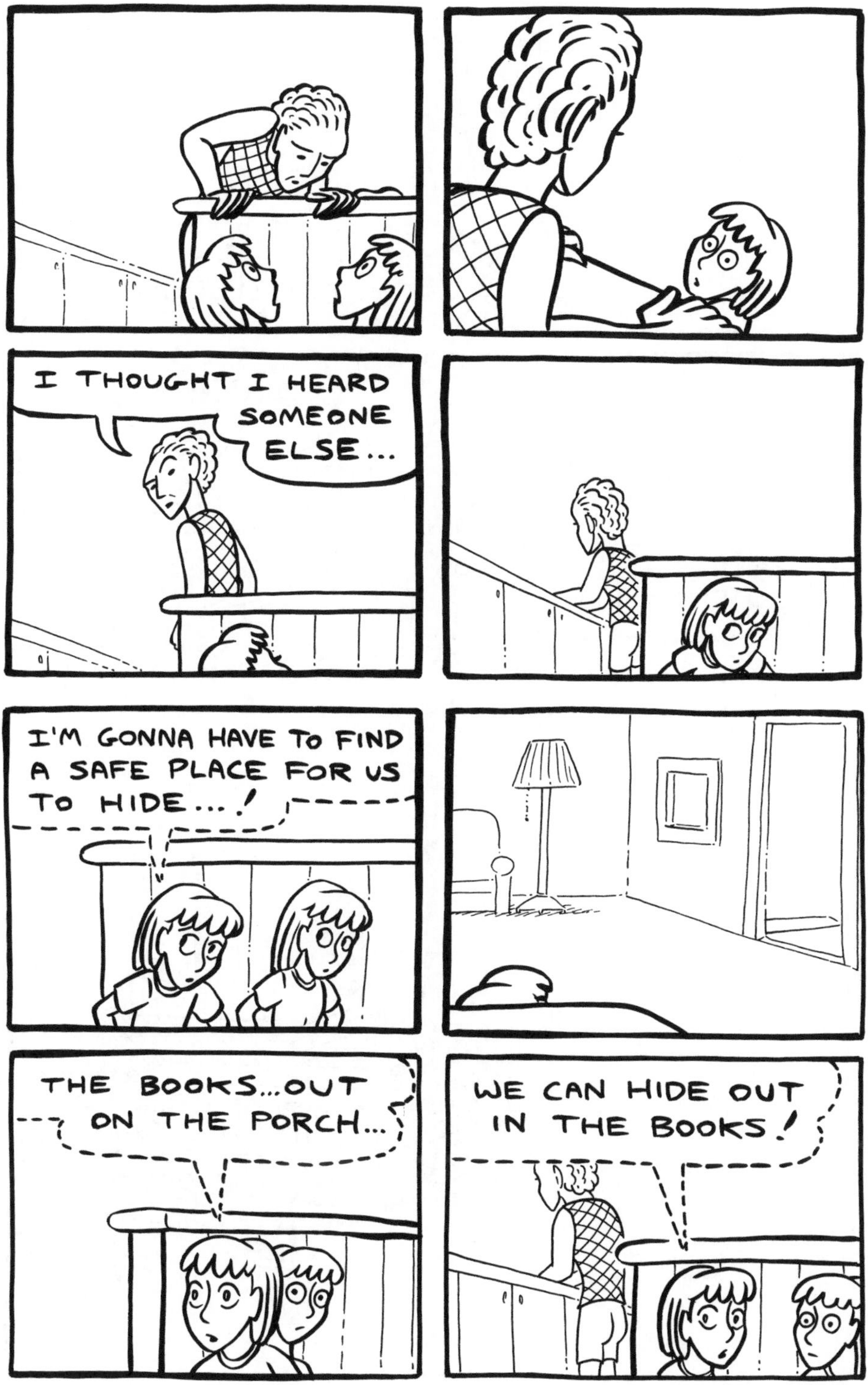
I THOUGHT I HEARD SOMEONE ELSE...
I'M GONNA HAVE TO FIND A SAFE PLACE FOR US TO HIDE...!
THE BOOKS...OUT ON THE PORCH...
WE CAN HIDE OUT IN THE BOOKS!

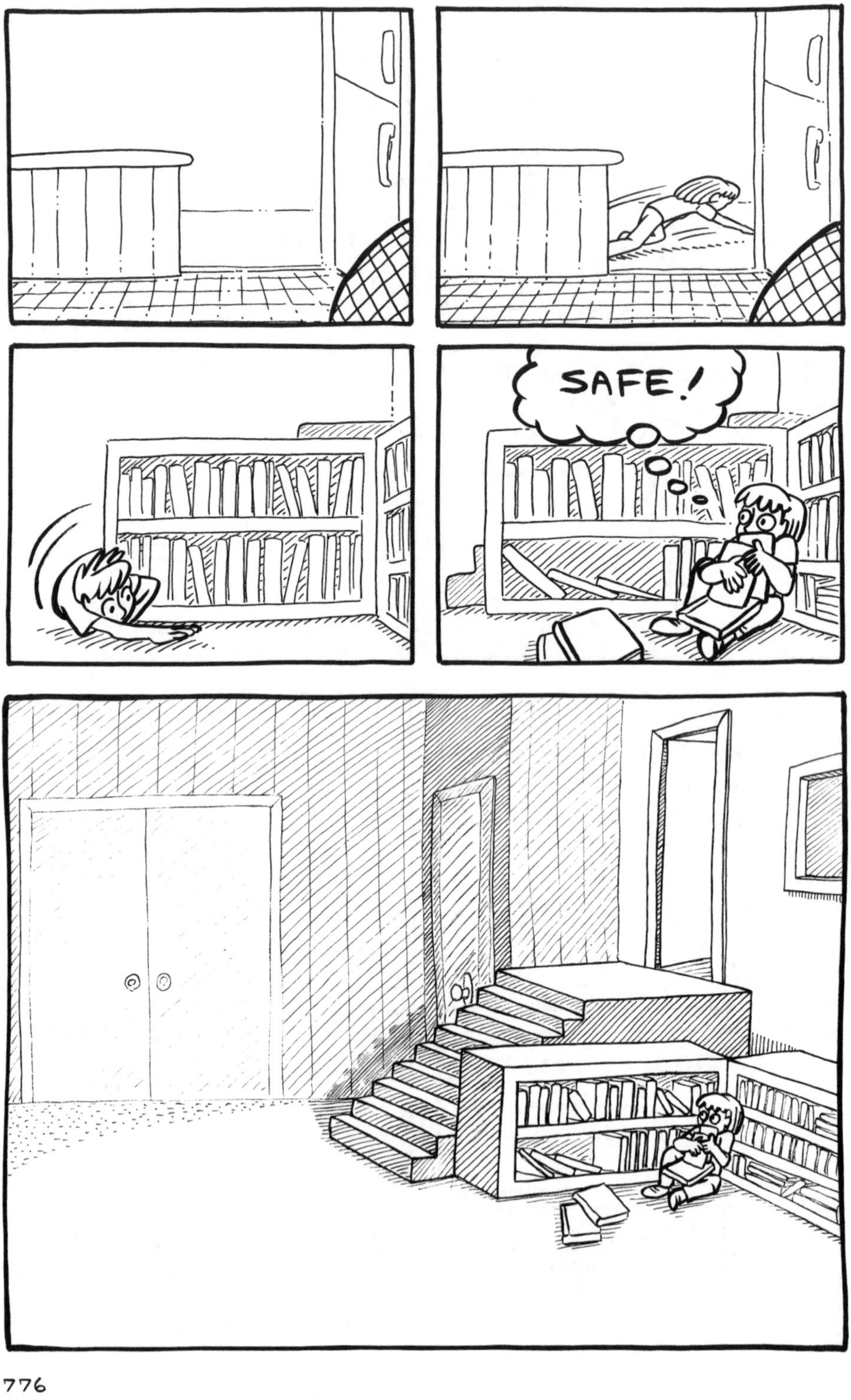
SAFE!

FALLING

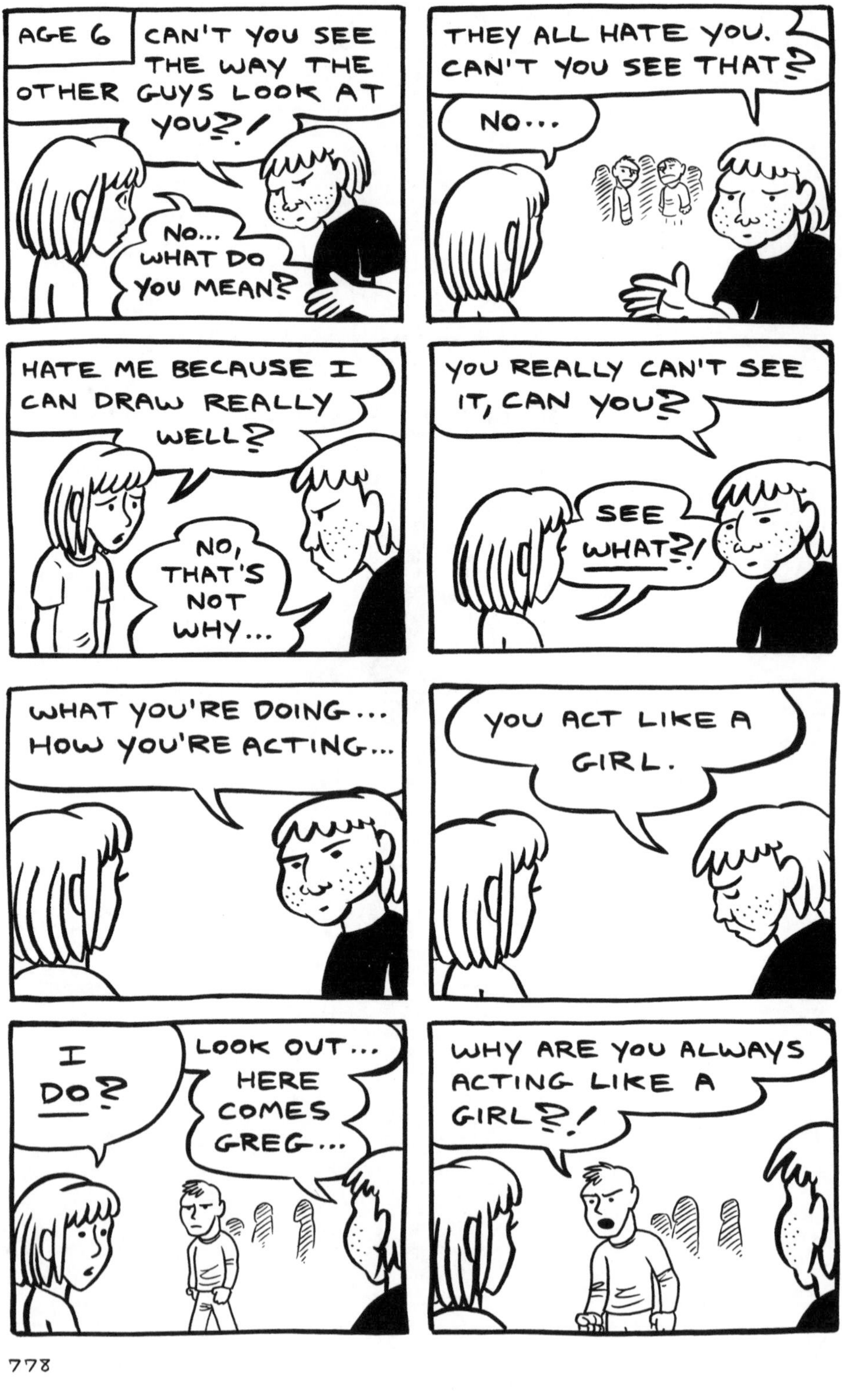
AGE 6
CAN'T YOU SEE THE WAY THE OTHER GUYS LOOK AT YOU?!
NO... WHAT DO YOU MEAN?
THEY ALL HATE YOU. CAN'T YOU SEE THAT?
NO...
HATE ME BECAUSE I CAN DRAW REALLY WELL?
NO, THAT'S NOT WHY...
YOU REALLY CAN'T SEE IT, CAN YOU?
SEE WHAT?!
WHAT YOU'RE DOING... HOW YOU'RE ACTING...
YOU ACT LIKE A GIRL.
I DO?
LOOK OUT... HERE COMES GREG...
WHY ARE YOU ALWAYS ACTING LIKE A GIRL?!

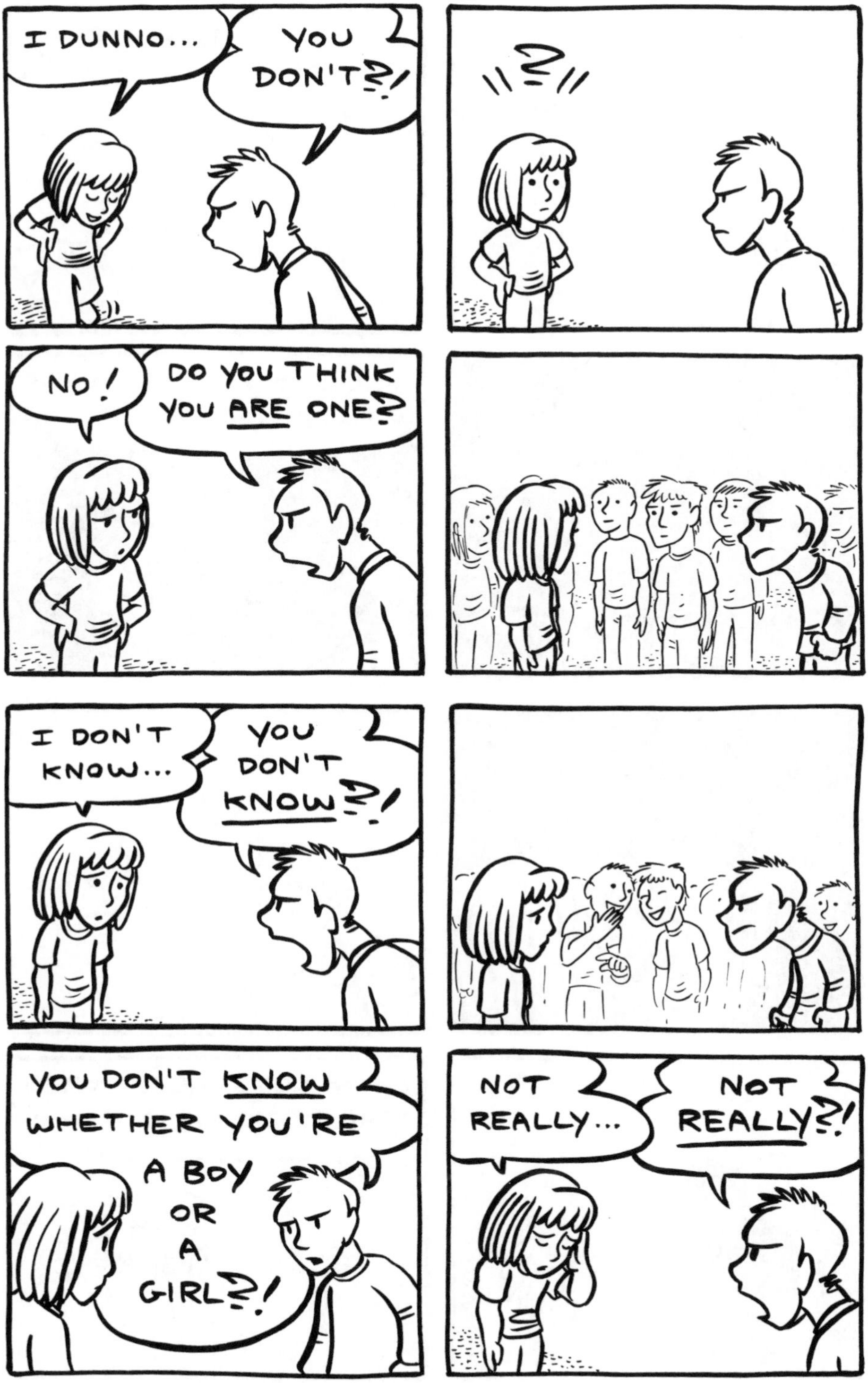

I DUNNO...
YOU DON'T?!
?
NO!
DO YOU THINK YOU ARE ONE?
I DON'T KNOW...
YOU DON'T KNOW?!
YOU DON'T KNOW WHETHER YOU'RE A BOY OR A GIRL?!
NOT REALLY...
NOT REALLY?!

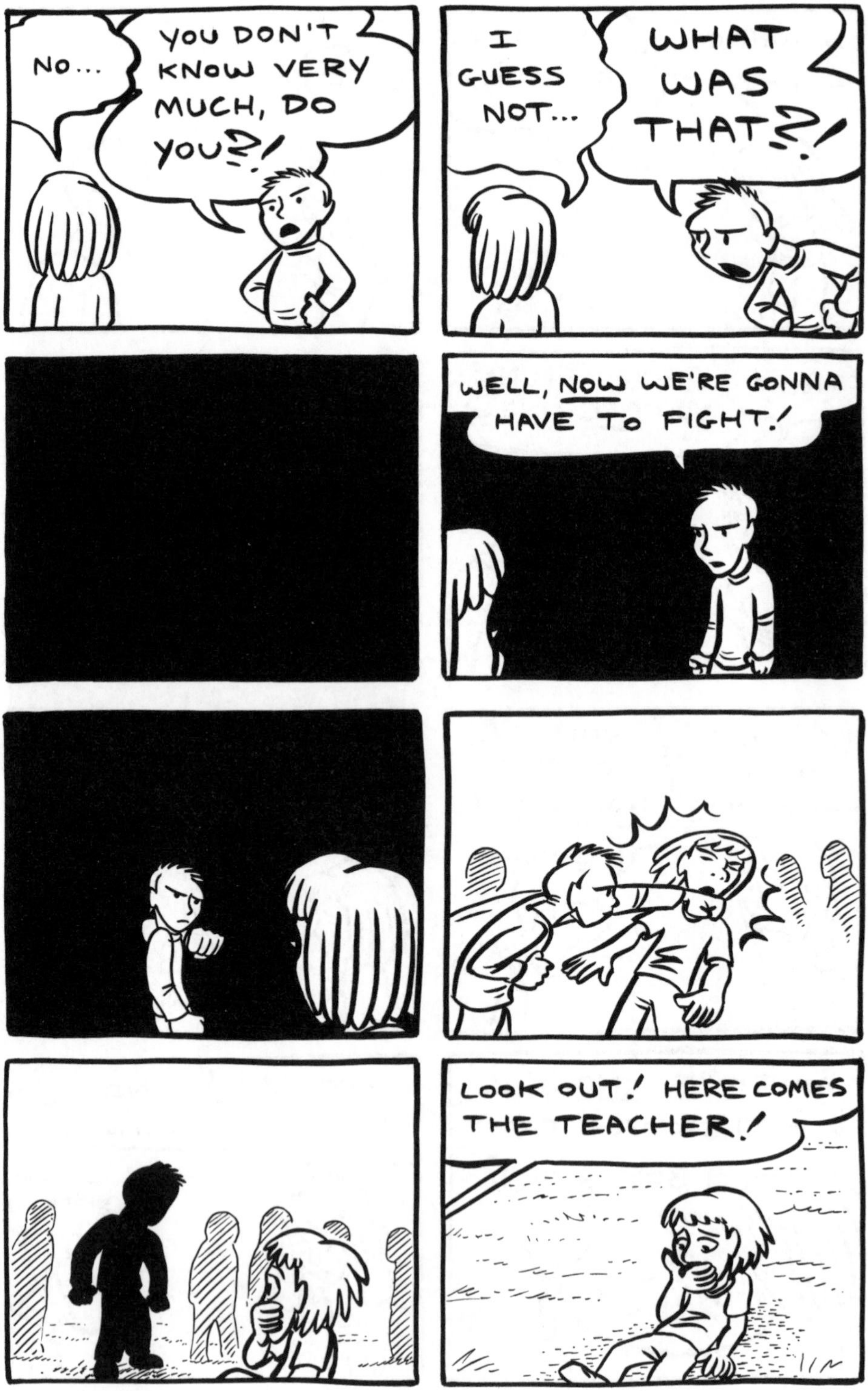
NO...
YOU DON'T KNOW VERY MUCH, DO YOU?!
I GUESS NOT...
WHAT WAS THAT?!
WELL, NOW WE'RE GONNA HAVE TO FIGHT!
LOOK OUT! HERE COMES THE TEACHER!

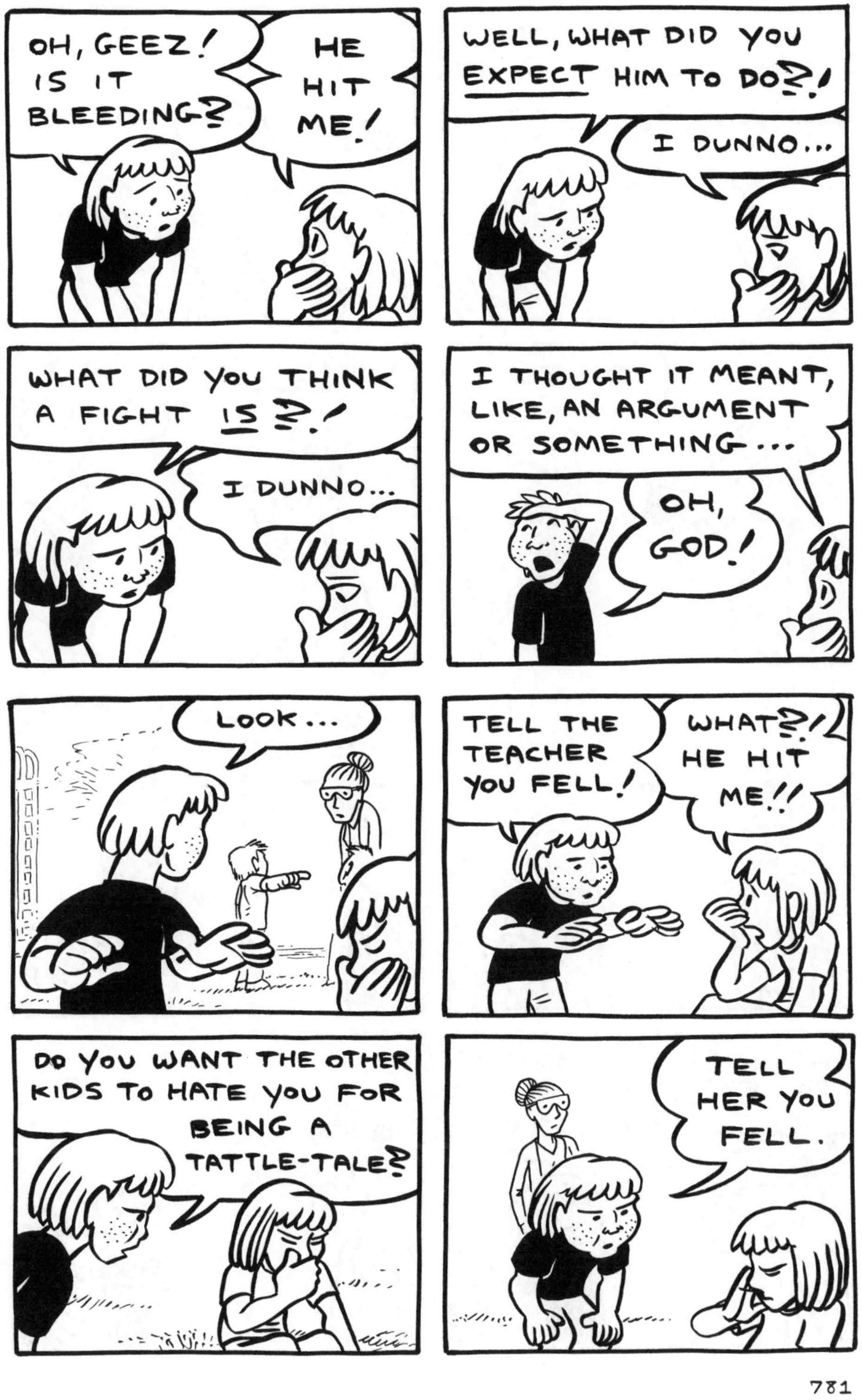
OH, GEEZ! IS IT BLEEDING?
HE HIT ME!
WELL, WHAT DID YOU EXPECT HIM TO DO?!
I DUNNO...
WHAT DID YOU THINK A FIGHT IS?!
I DUNNO...
I THOUGHT IT MEANT, LIKE, AN ARGUMENT OR SOMETHING...
OH, GOD!
LOOK...
TELL THE TEACHER YOU FELL!
WHAT?! HE HIT ME!!
DO YOU WANT THE OTHER KIDS TO HATE YOU FOR BEING A TATTLE-TALE?
TELL HER YOU FELL.

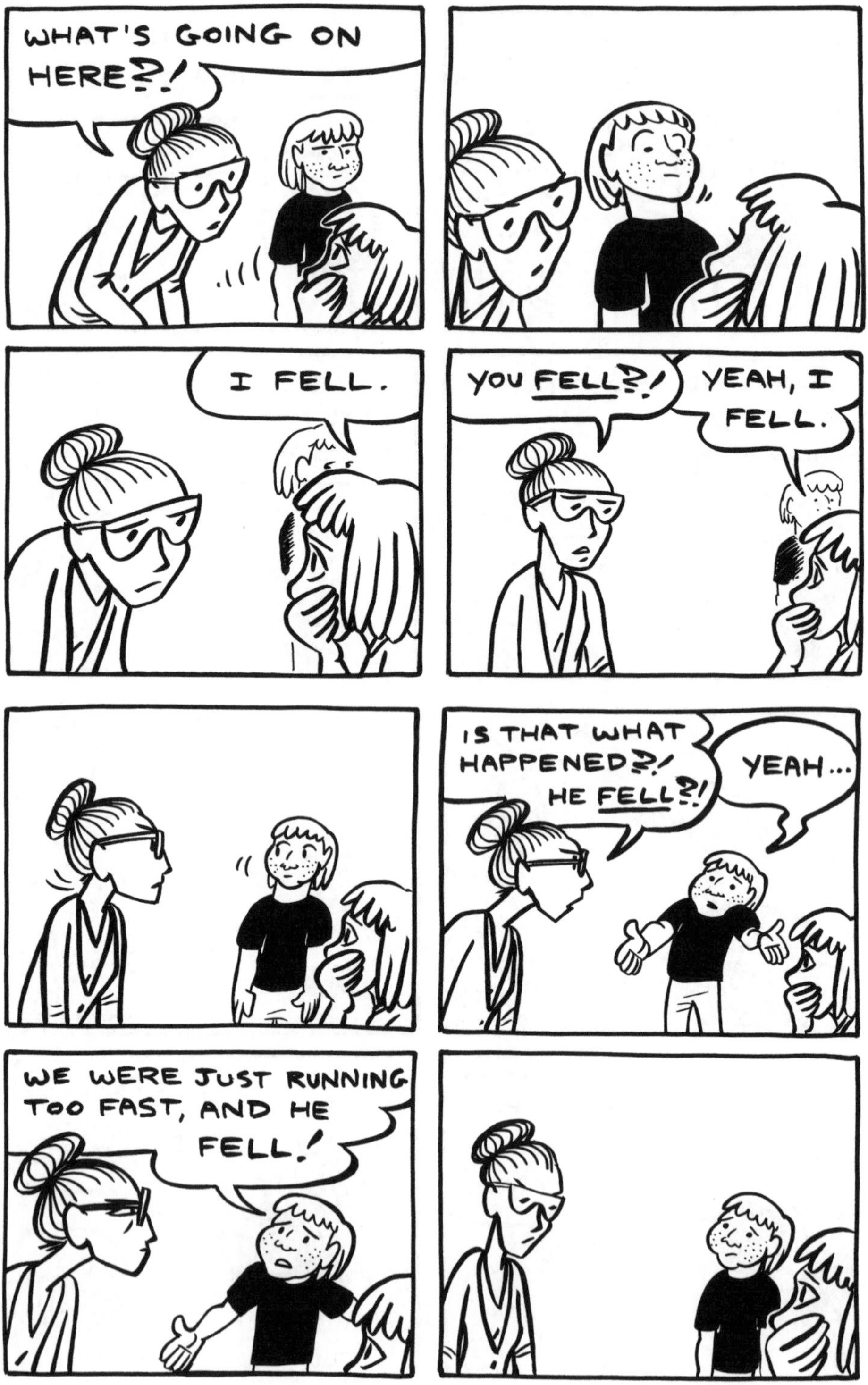
WHAT'S GOING ON HERE?!
I FELL.
YOU FELL?!
YEAH, I FELL.
IS THAT WHAT HAPPENED?! HE FELL?!
YEAH...
WE WERE JUST RUNNING TOO FAST, AND HE FELL!

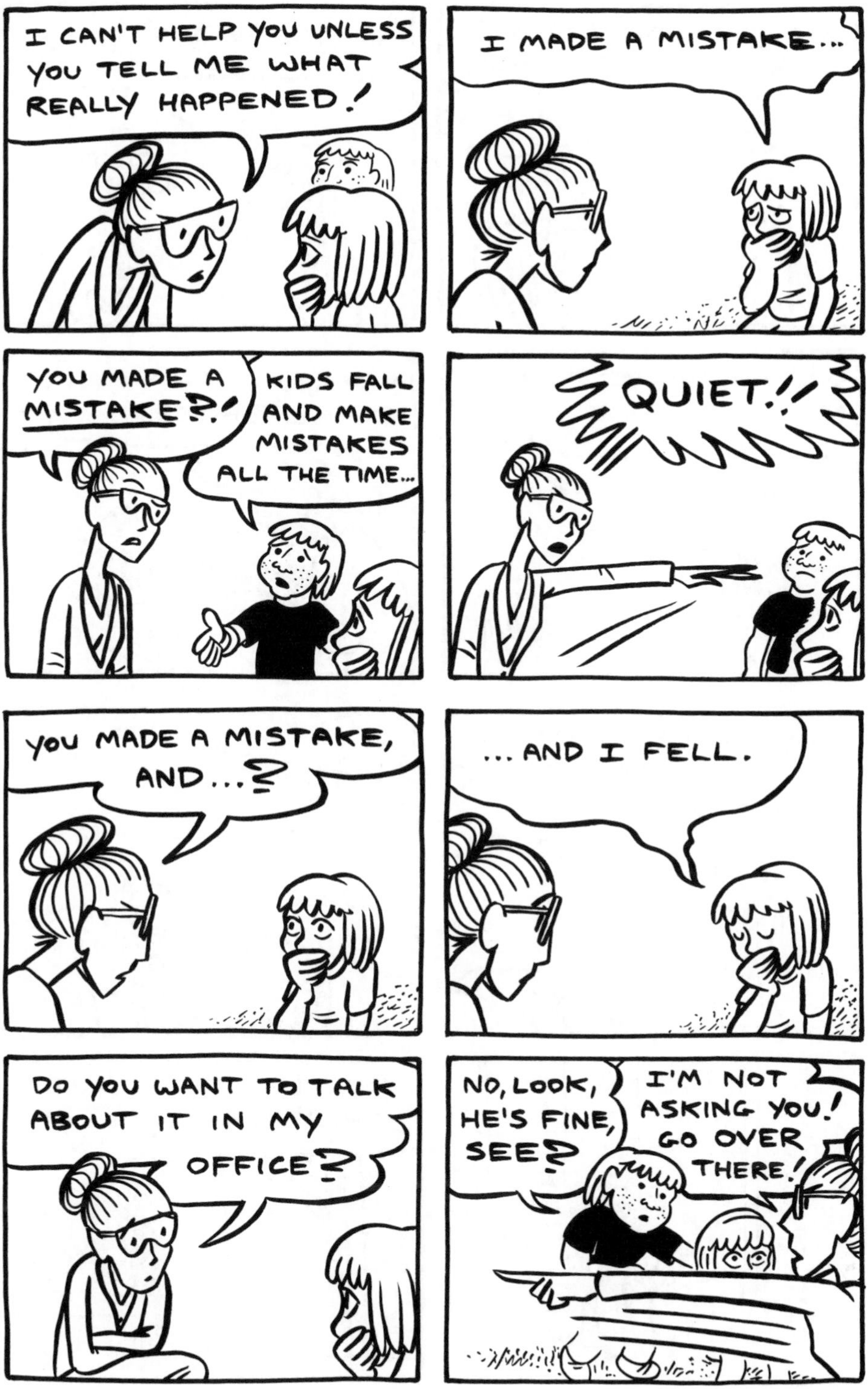
I CAN'T HELP YOU UNLESS YOU TELL ME WHAT REALLY HAPPENED!
I MADE A MISTAKE...
YOU MADE A MISTAKE?!
KIDS FALL AND MAKE MISTAKES ALL THE TIME...
QUIET!!
YOU MADE A MISTAKE, AND...?
...AND I FELL.
DO YOU WANT TO TALK ABOUT IT IN MY OFFICE?
NO, LOOK, HE'S FINE, SEE?
I'M NOT ASKING YOU! GO OVER THERE!

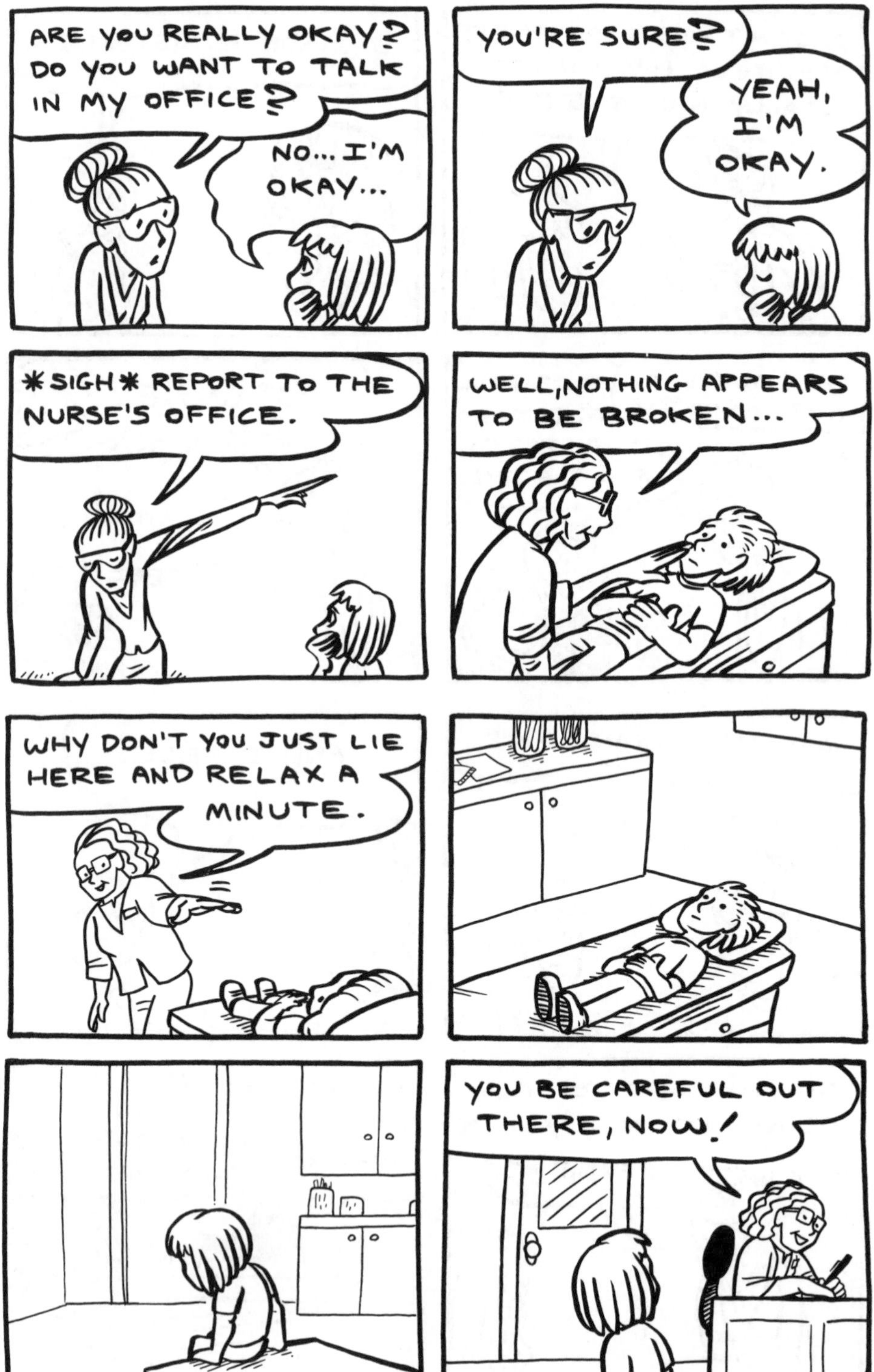
ARE YOU REALLY OKAY? DO YOU WANT TO TALK IN MY OFFICE?
NO... I'M OKAY...
YOU'RE SURE?
YEAH, I'M OKAY.
SIGH REPORT TO THE NURSE'S OFFICE.
WELL, NOTHING APPEARS TO BE BROKEN...
WHY DON'T YOU JUST LIE HERE AND RELAX A MINUTE.
YOU BE CAREFUL OUT THERE, NOW!

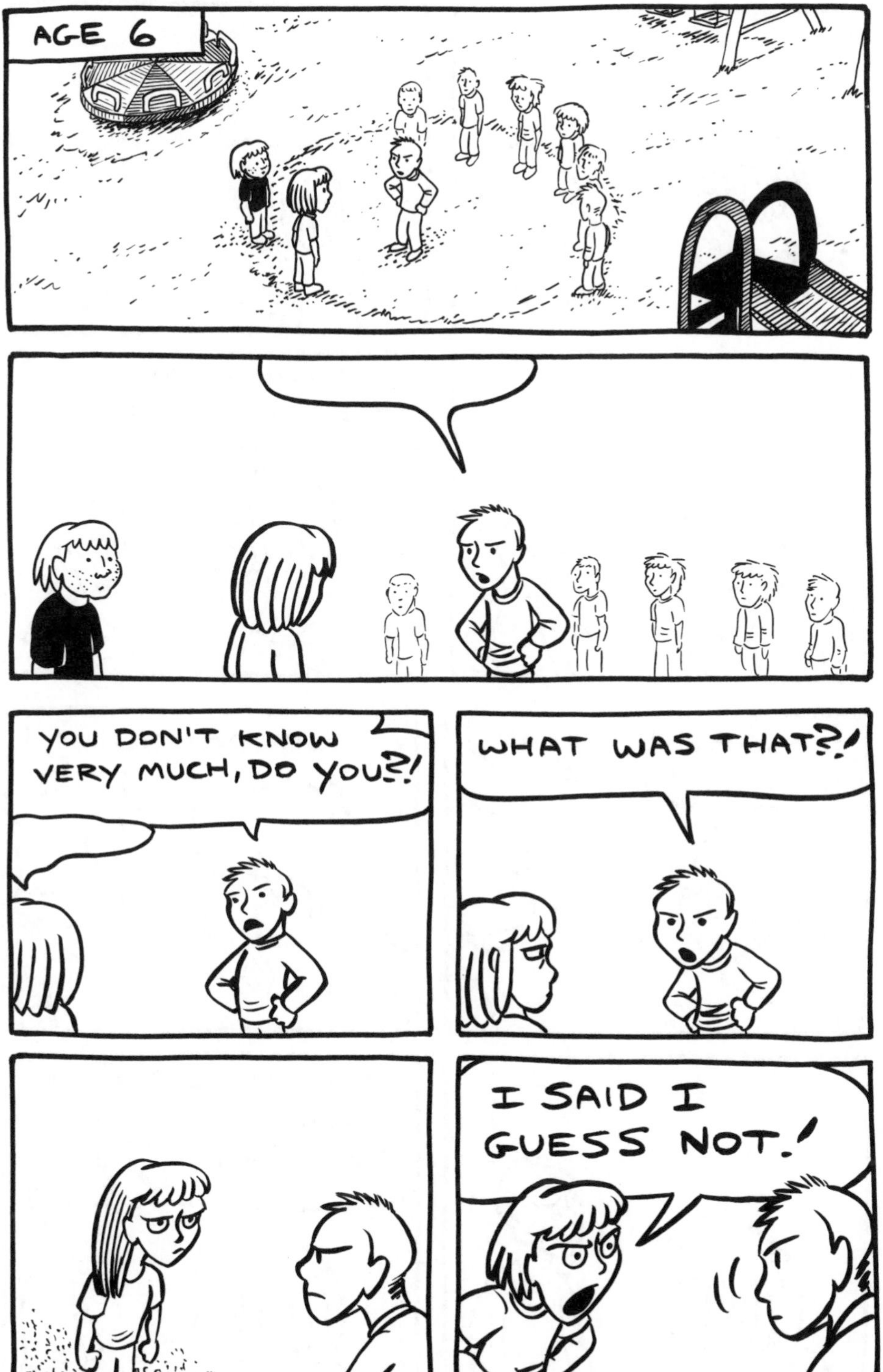
AGE 6
YOU DON'T KNOW VERY MUCH, DO YOU?!
WHAT WAS THAT?!
I SAID I GUESS NOT.!

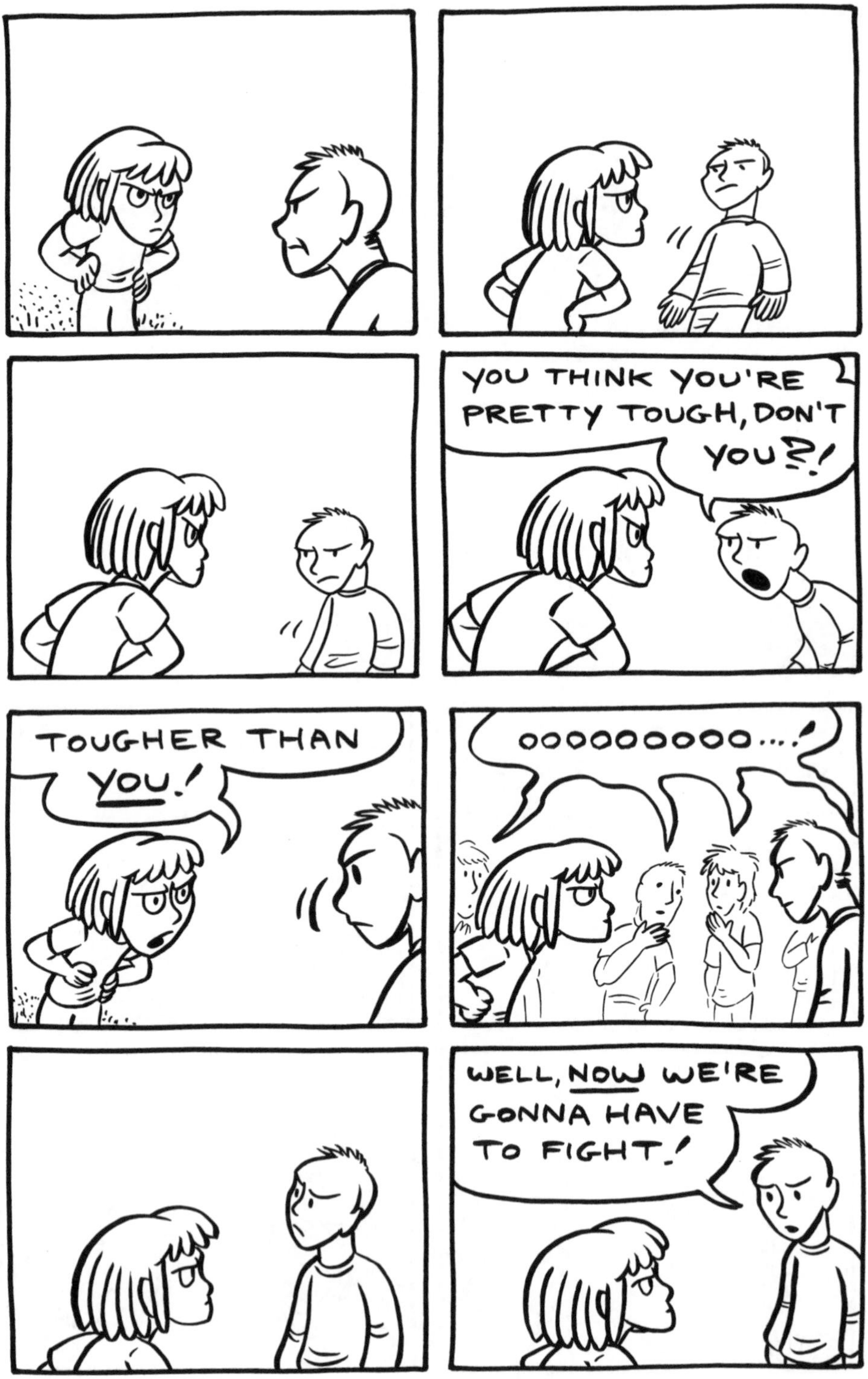
YOU THINK YOU'RE PRETTY TOUGH, DON'T YOU?!
TOUGHER THAN YOU!
OOOOOOOOO....!
WELL, NOW WE'RE GONNA HAVE TO FIGHT!

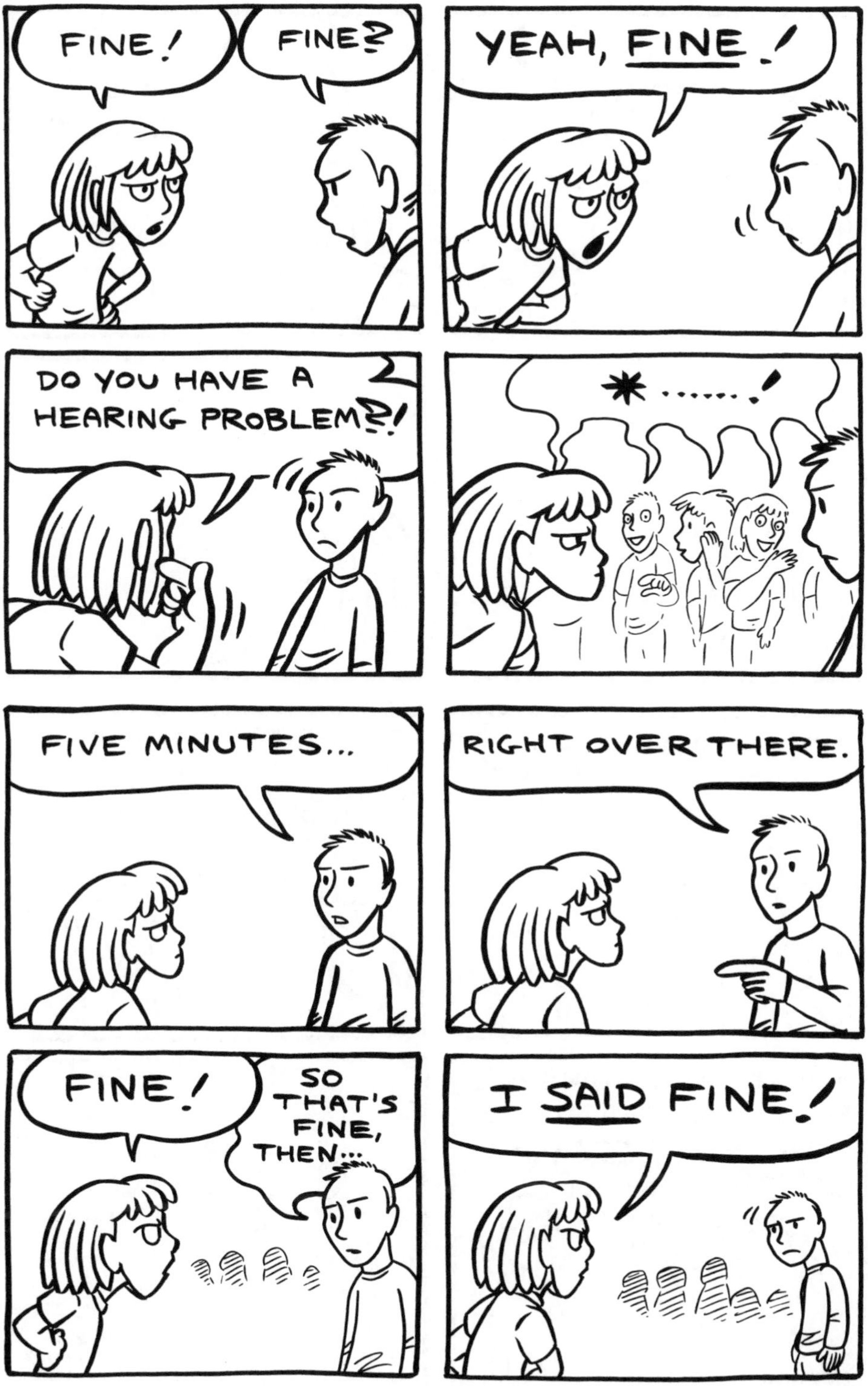
FINE!
FINE?
YEAH, FINE!
DO YOU HAVE A HEARING PROBLEM?!
*......!
FIVE MINUTES...
RIGHT OVER THERE.
FINE!
SO THAT'S FINE, THEN...
I SAID FINE!

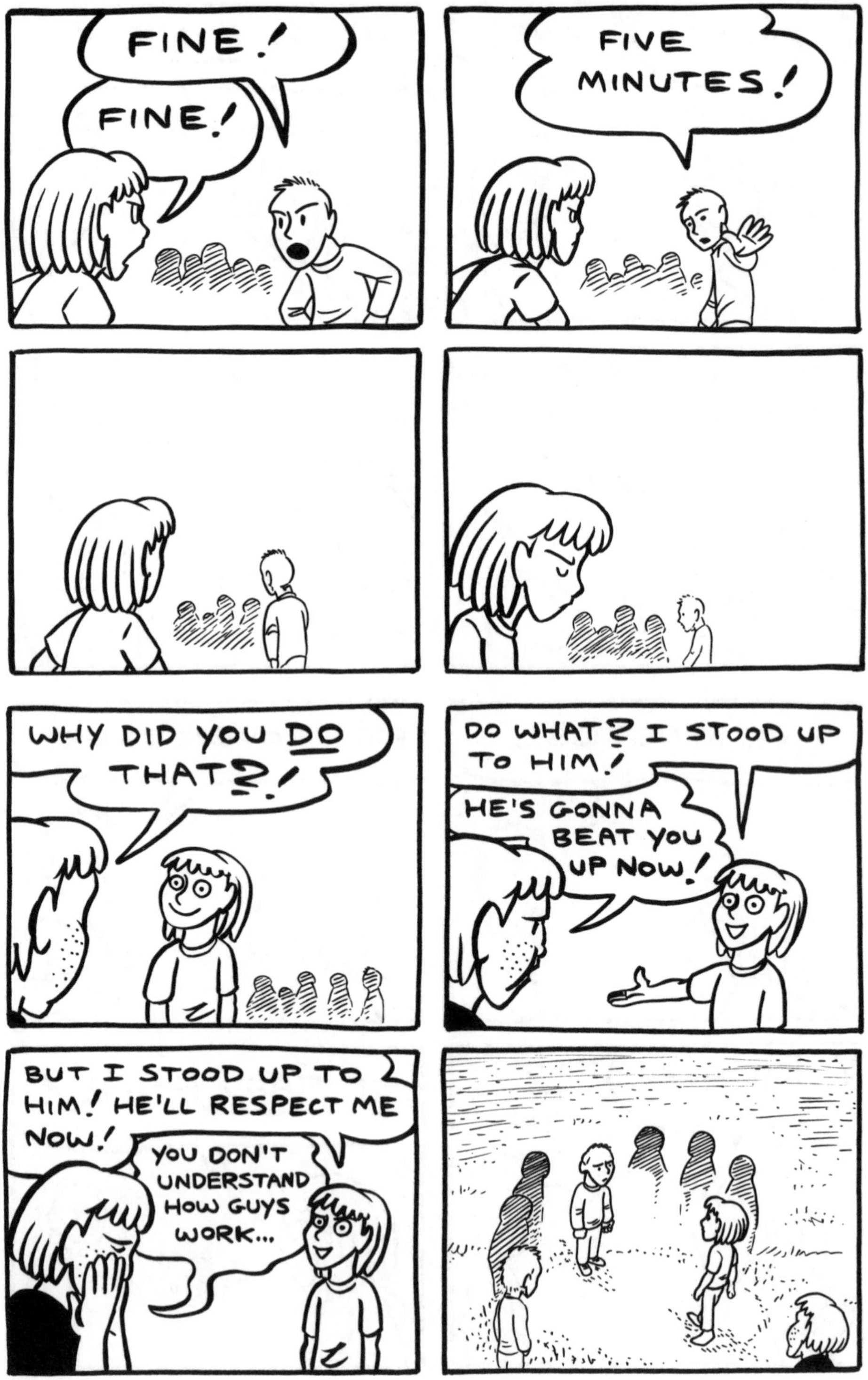
FINE!
FINE!
FIVE MINUTES!
WHY DID YOU DO THAT?!
DO WHAT? I STOOD UP TO HIM!
HE'S GONNA BEAT YOU UP NOW!
BUT I STOOD UP TO HIM! HE'LL RESPECT ME NOW!
YOU DON'T UNDERSTAND HOW GUYS WORK...

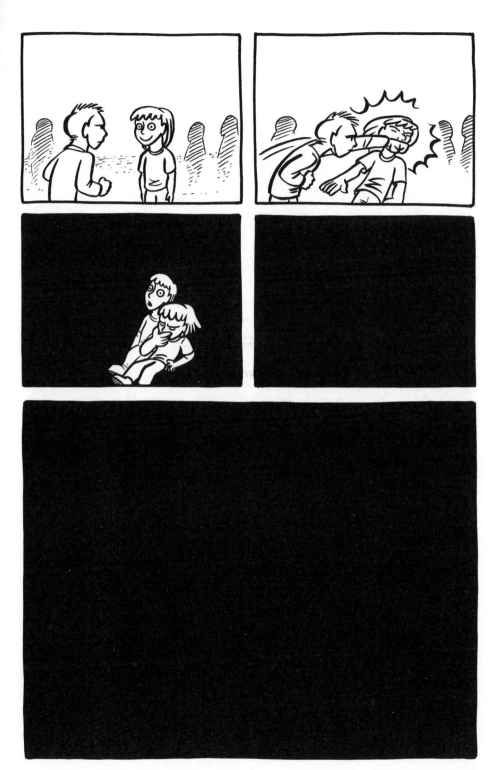

BOOK
SHELF

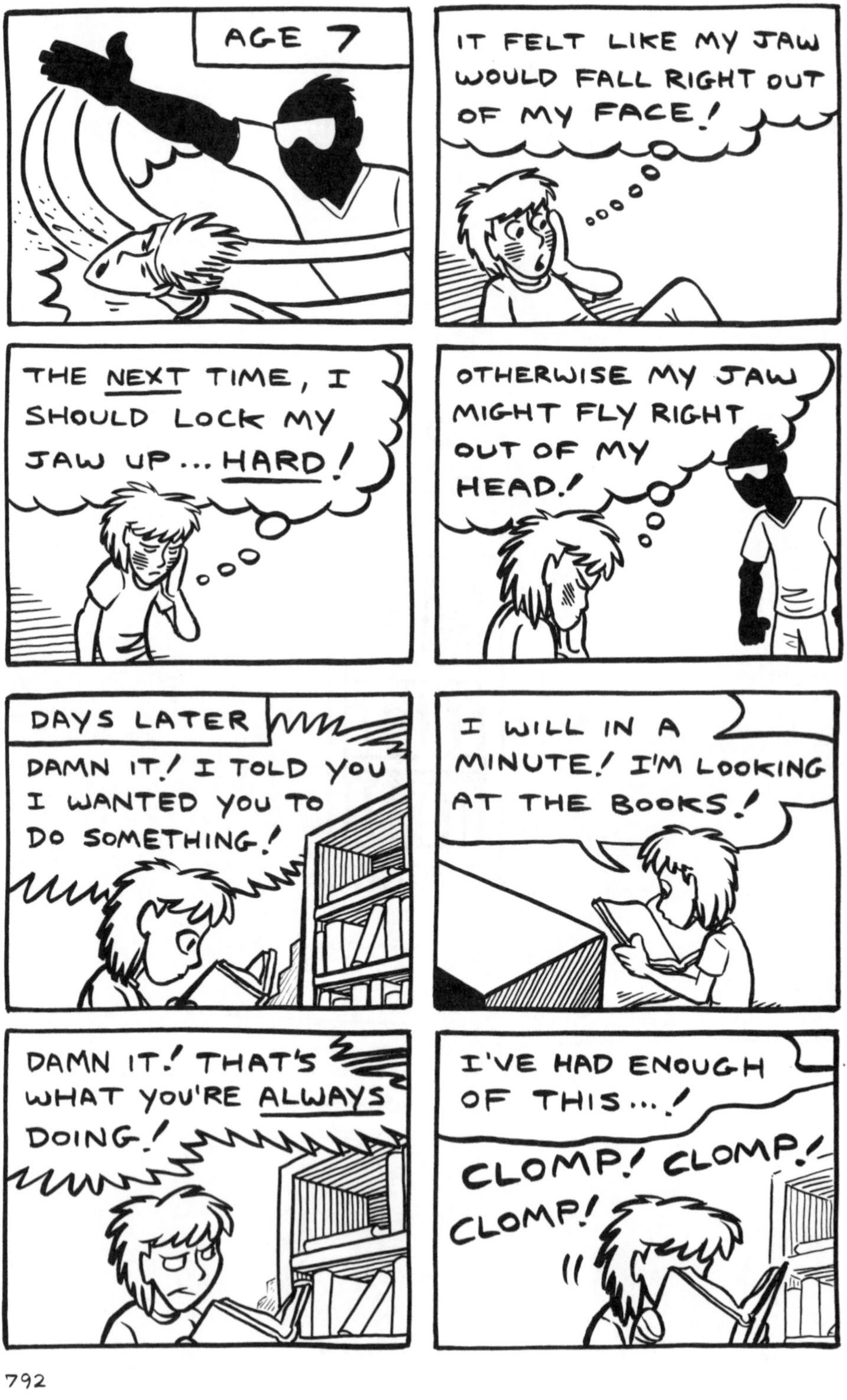
AGE 7
IT FELT LIKE MY JAW WOULD FALL RIGHT OUT OF MY FACE!
THE NEXT TIME, I SHOULD LOCK MY JAW UP... HARD!
OTHERWISE MY JAW MIGHT FLY RIGHT OUT OF MY HEAD!
DAYS LATER
DAMN IT! I TOLD YOU I WANTED YOU TO DO SOMETHING!
I WILL IN A MINUTE! I'M LOOKING AT THE BOOKS!
DAMN IT! THAT'S WHAT YOU'RE ALWAYS DOING!
I'VE HAD ENOUGH OF THIS...!
CLOMP! CLOMP! CLOMP!

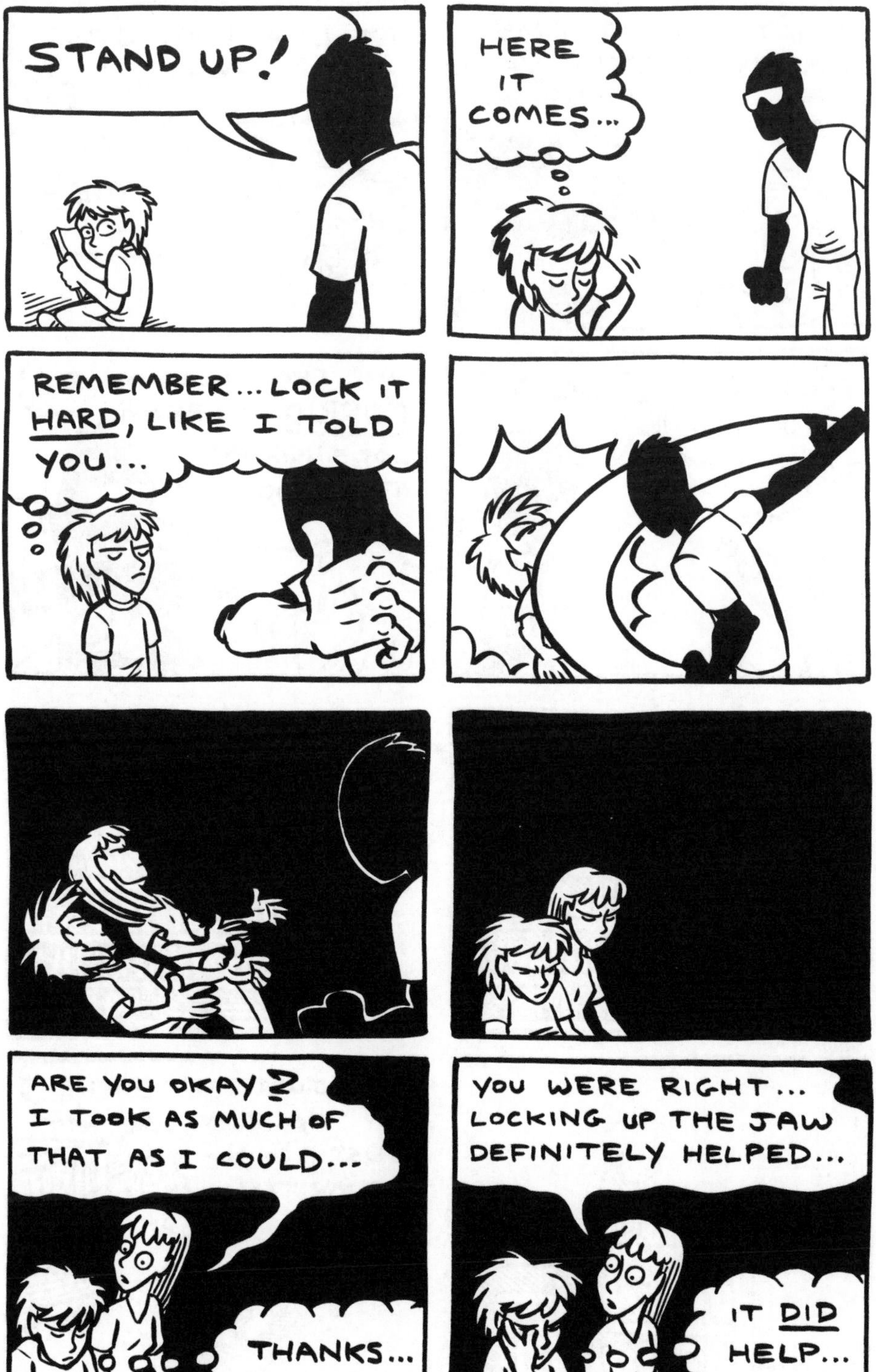

STAND UP!
HERE IT COMES...
REMEMBER... LOCK IT HARD, LIKE I TOLD YOU...
ARE YOU OKAY? I TOOK AS MUCH OF THAT AS I COULD...
THANKS...
YOU WERE RIGHT... LOCKING UP THE JAW DEFINITELY HELPED...
IT DID HELP...

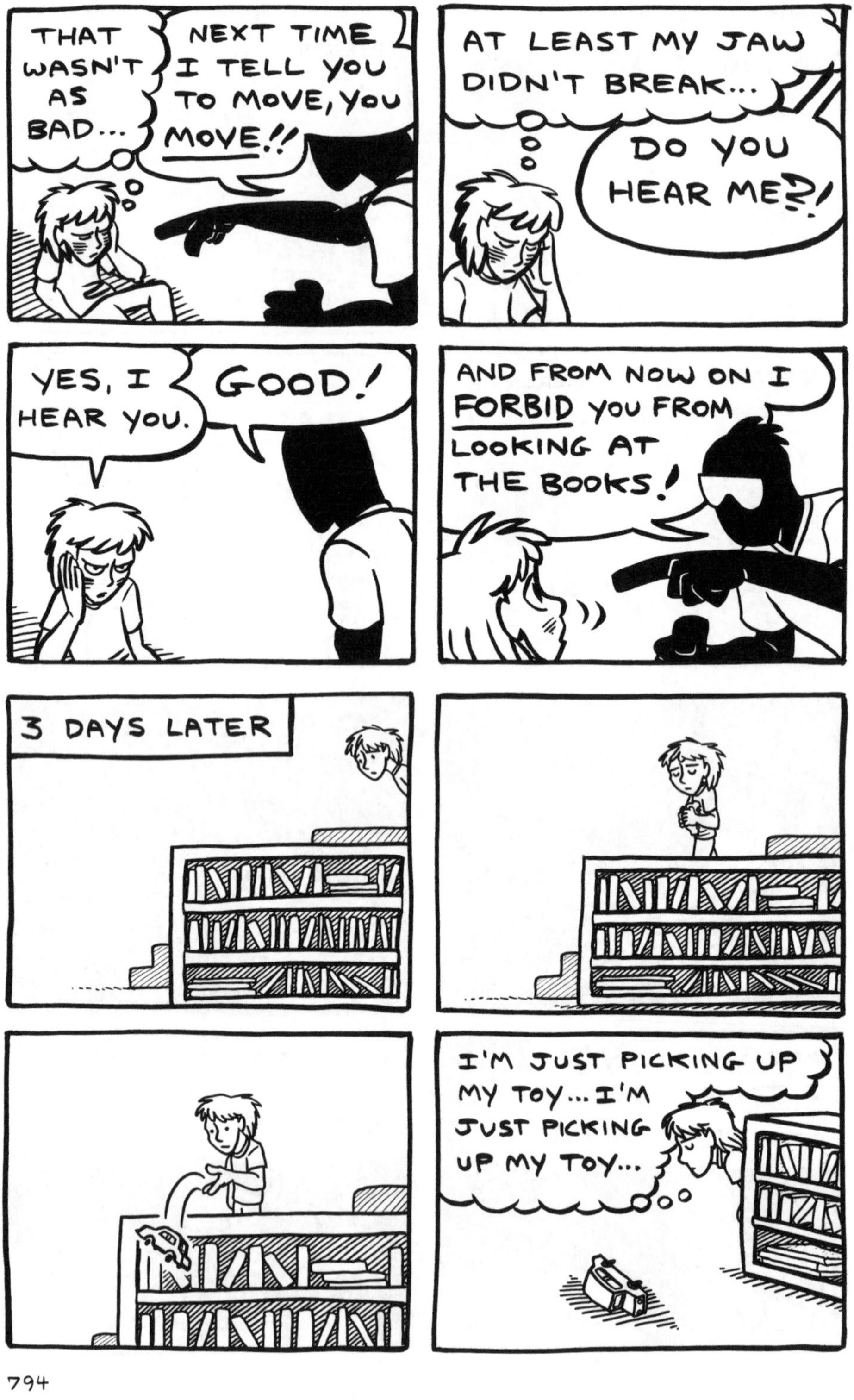
THAT WASN'T AS BAD...
NEXT TIME I TELL YOU TO MOVE, YOU MOVE!!
AT LEAST MY JAW DIDN'T BREAK...
DO YOU HEAR ME?!
YES, I HEAR YOU.
GOOD!
AND FROM NOW ON I FORBID YOU FROM LOOKING AT THE BOOKS!
3 DAYS LATER
I'M JUST PICKING UP MY TOY... I'M JUST PICKING UP MY TOY...

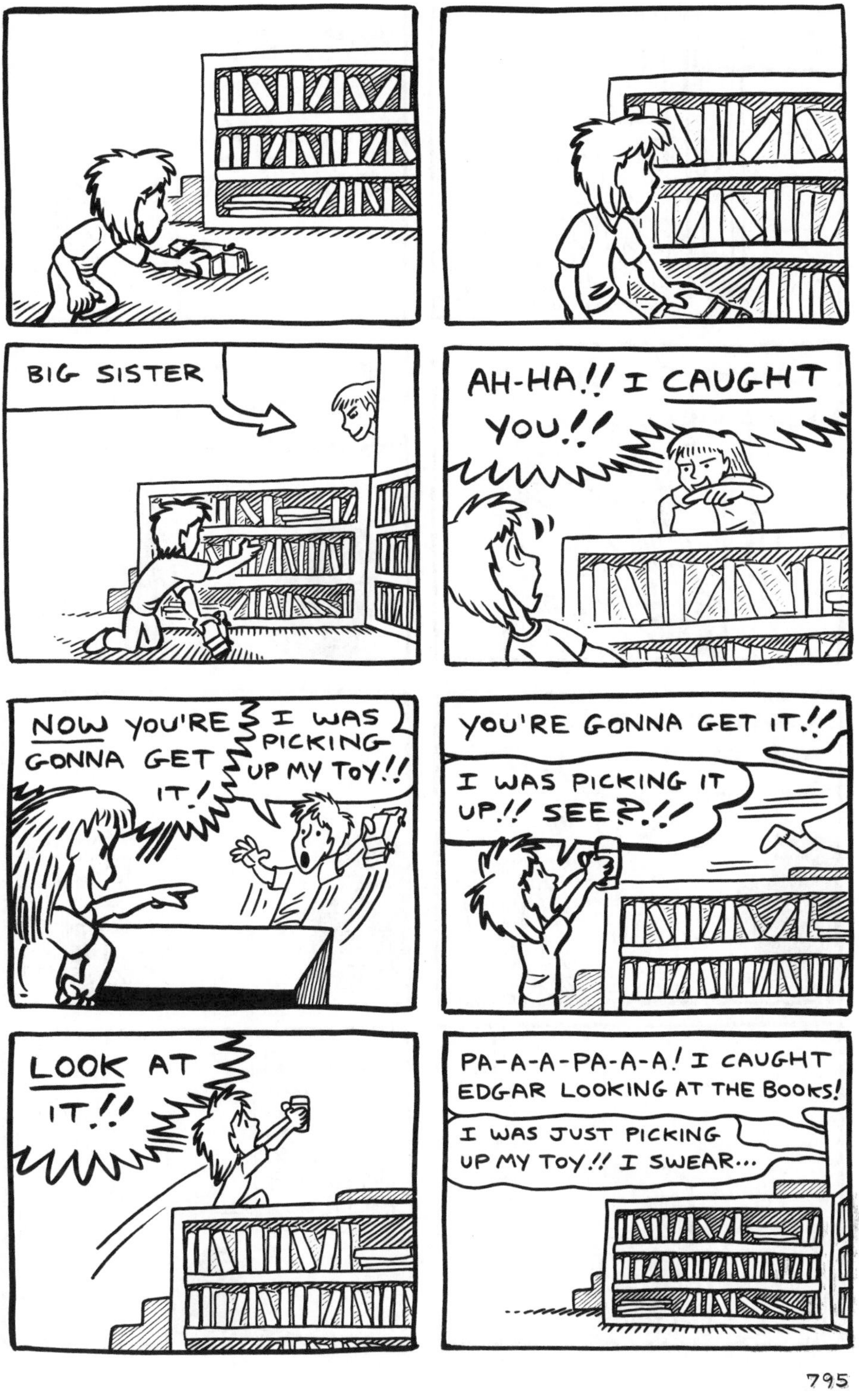

BIG SISTER
AH-HA!! I CAUGHT YOU!!
NOW YOU'RE GONNA GET IT!
I WAS PICKING UP MY TOY!!
YOU'RE GONNA GET IT!!
I WAS PICKING IT UP!! SEE?!!
LOOK AT IT!!
PA-A-A-PA-A-A! I CAUGHT EDGAR LOOKING AT THE BOOKS!
I WAS JUST PICKING UP MY TOY!! I SWEAR...

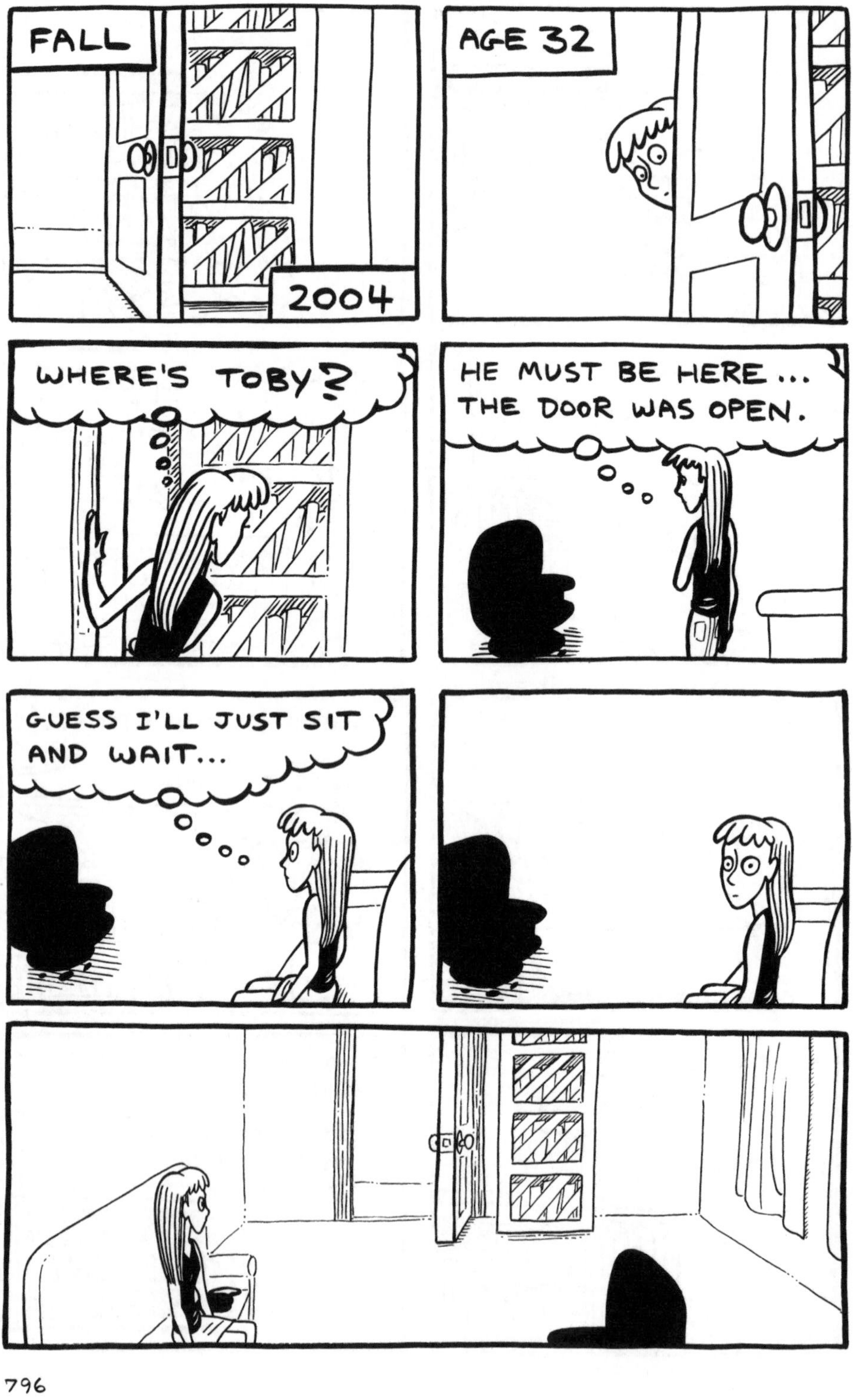
FALL
2004
AGE 32
WHERE'S TOBY?
HE MUST BE HERE...
THE DOOR WAS OPEN.
GUESS I'LL JUST SIT
AND WAIT...

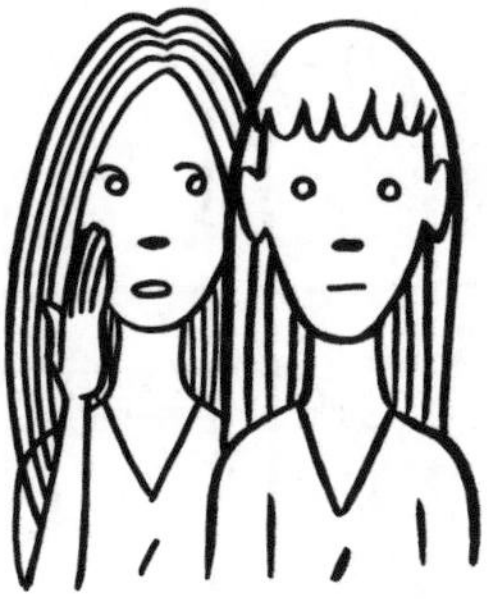

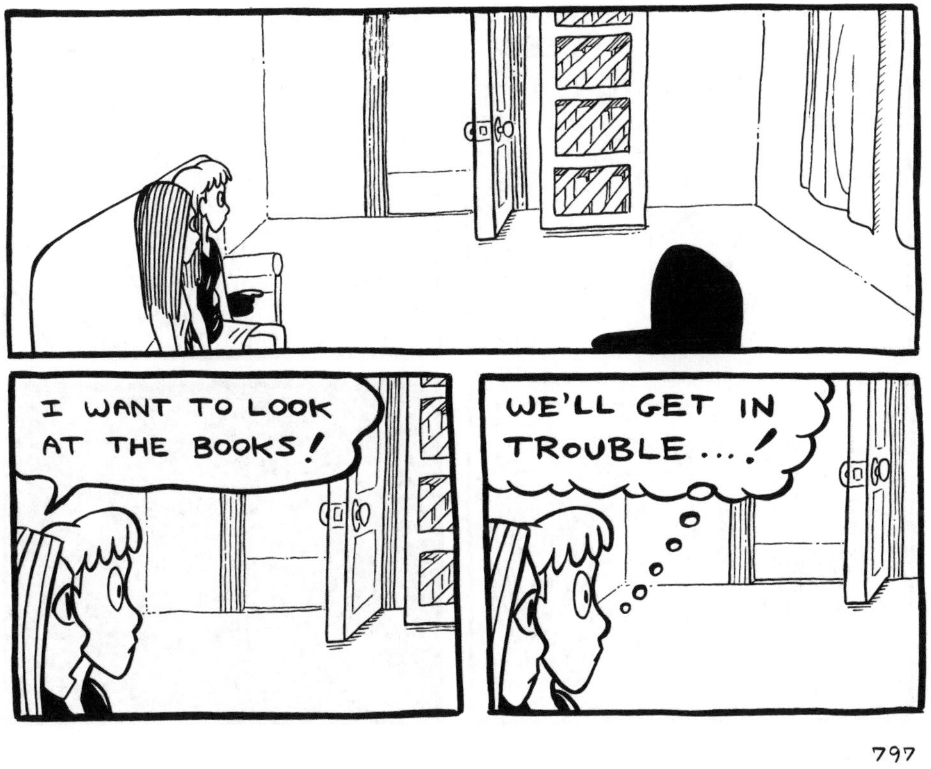
I WANT TO LOOK AT THE BOOKS!
WE'LL GET IN TROUBLE...!

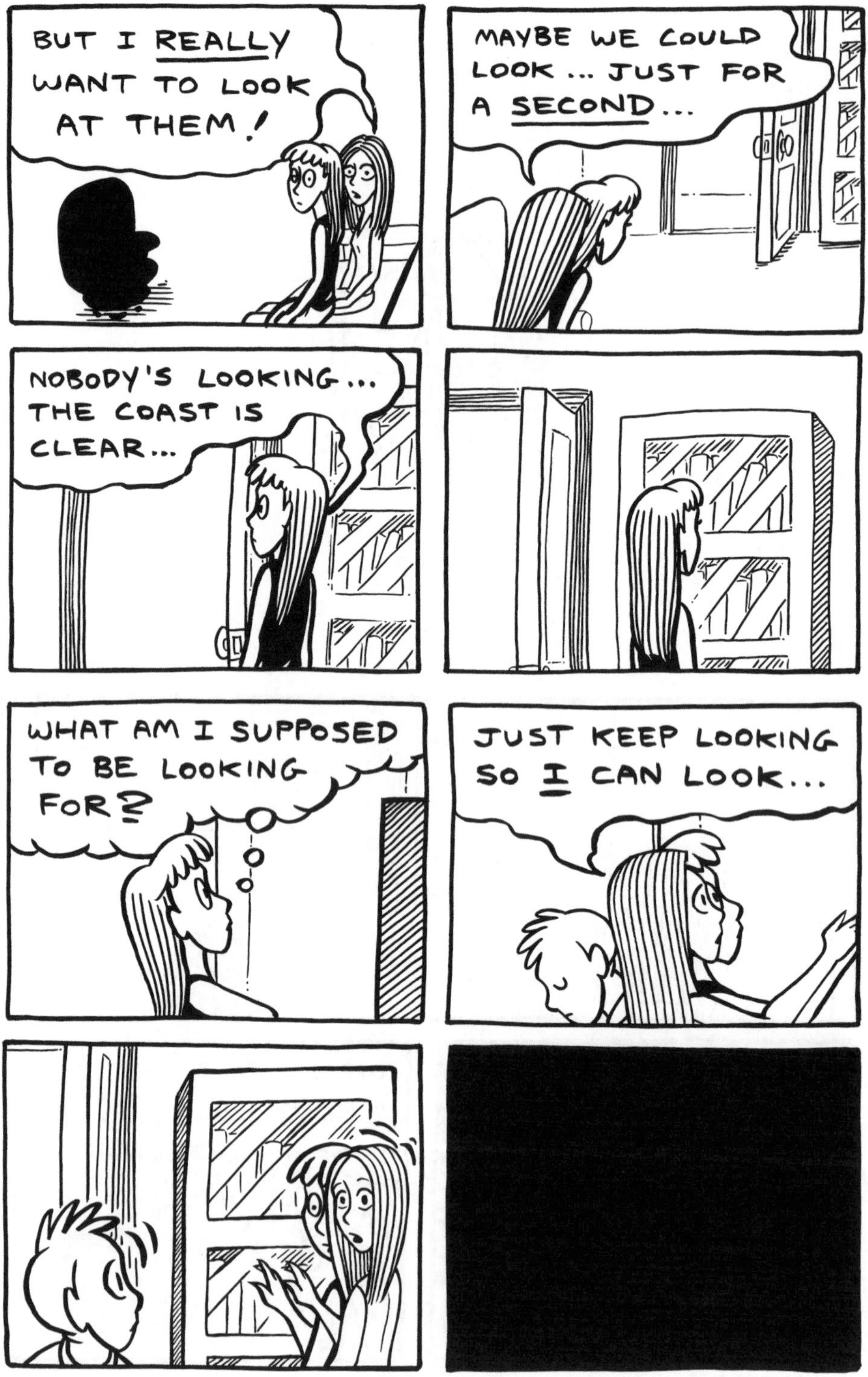
BUT I REALLY WANT TO LOOK AT THEM!
MAYBE WE COULD LOOK ... JUST FOR A SECOND...
NOBODY'S LOOKING... THE COAST IS CLEAR...
WHAT AM I SUPPOSED TO BE LOOKING FOR?
JUST KEEP LOOKING SO I CAN LOOK...

HELLO!
HELLO...YOU'RE HERE EARLY!
SORRY I JUST WALKED IN...
THAT'S OKAY.
I DIDN'T KNOW WHERE YOU WERE...
I WAS IN THE BATHROOM!

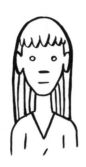

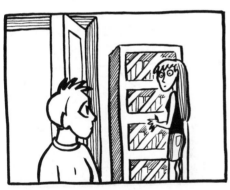

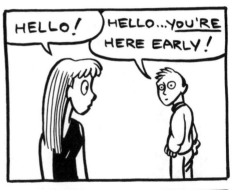

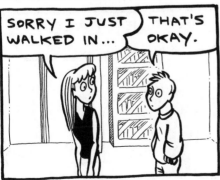

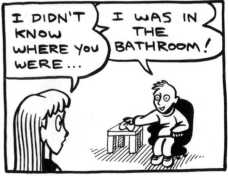

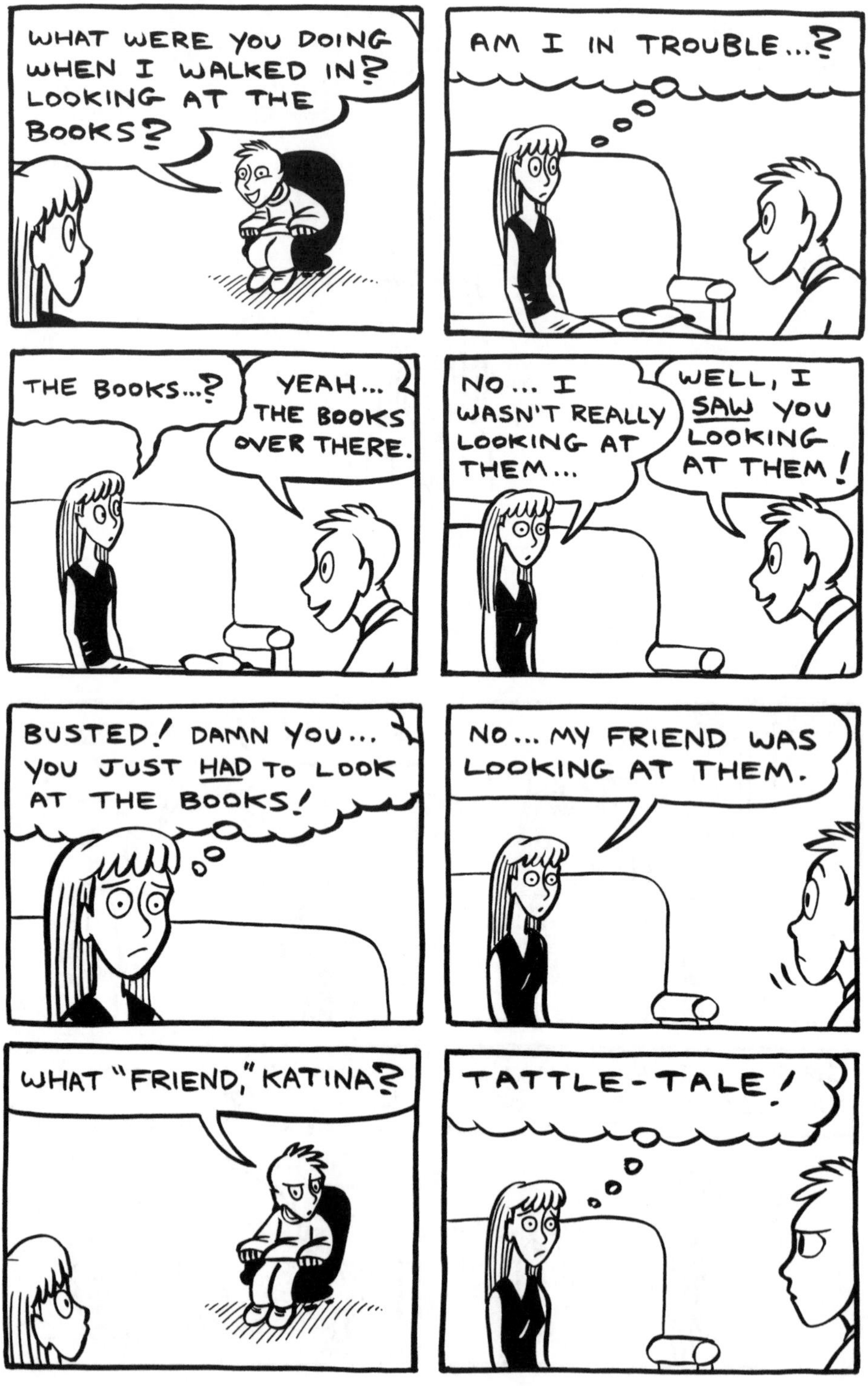
WHAT WERE YOU DOING WHEN I WALKED IN? LOOKING AT THE BOOKS?
AM I IN TROUBLE...?
THE BOOKS...?
YEAH... THE BOOKS OVER THERE.
NO... I WASN'T REALLY LOOKING AT THEM...
WELL, I SAW YOU LOOKING AT THEM!
BUSTED! DAMN YOU... YOU JUST HAD TO LOOK AT THE BOOKS!
NO... MY FRIEND WAS LOOKING AT THEM.
WHAT "FRIEND," KATINA?
TATTLE-TALE!

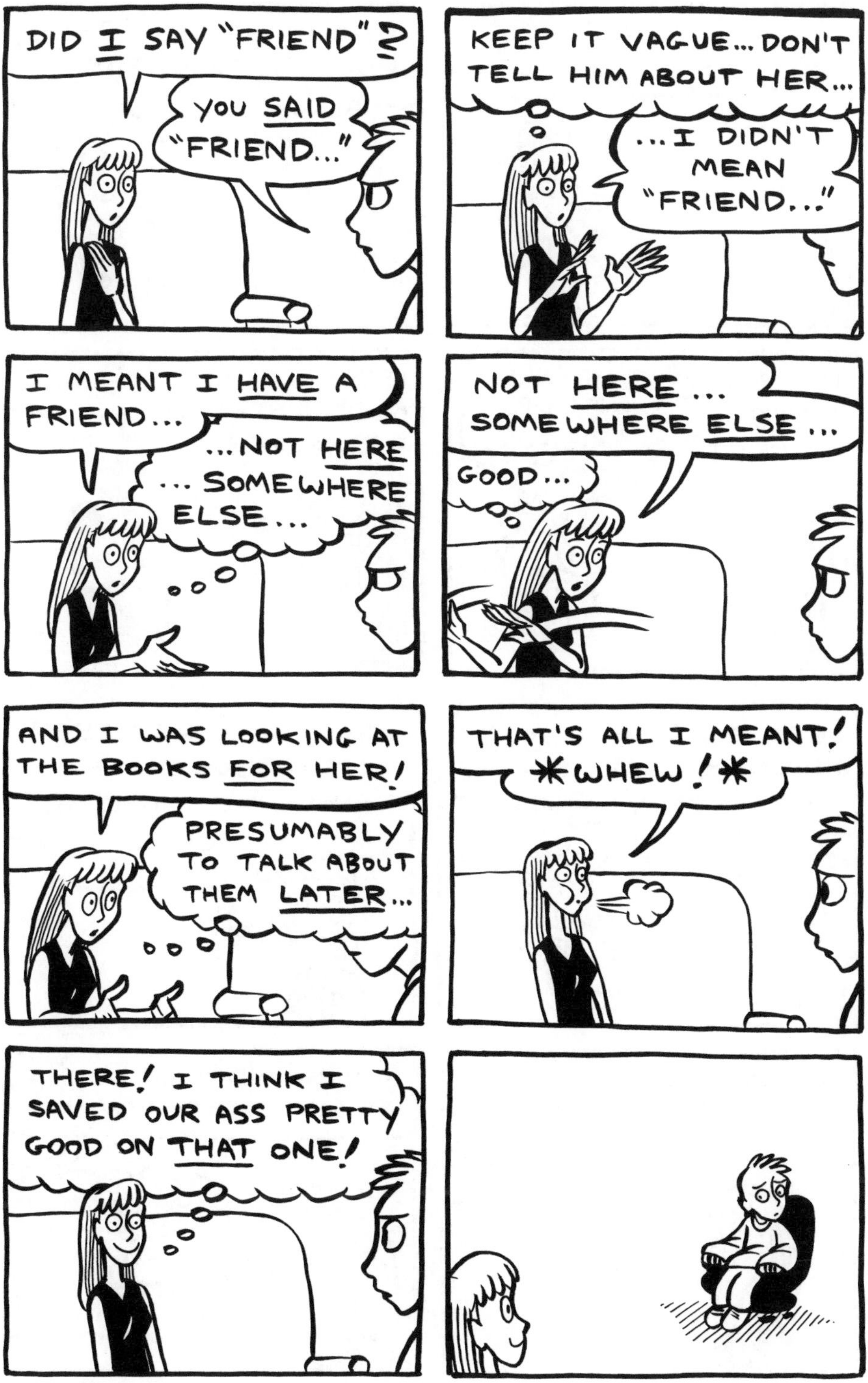
DID I SAY "FRIEND"?
YOU SAID "FRIEND..."
KEEP IT VAGUE... DON'T TELL HIM ABOUT HER...
...I DIDN'T MEAN "FRIEND..."
I MEANT I HAVE A FRIEND...
...NOT HERE ... SOMEWHERE ELSE...
NOT HERE ... SOMEWHERE ELSE ...
GOOD...
AND I WAS LOOKING AT THE BOOKS FOR HER!
PRESUMABLY TO TALK ABOUT THEM LATER...
THAT'S ALL I MEANT! *WHEW!*
THERE! I THINK I SAVED OUR ASS PRETTY GOOD ON THAT ONE!

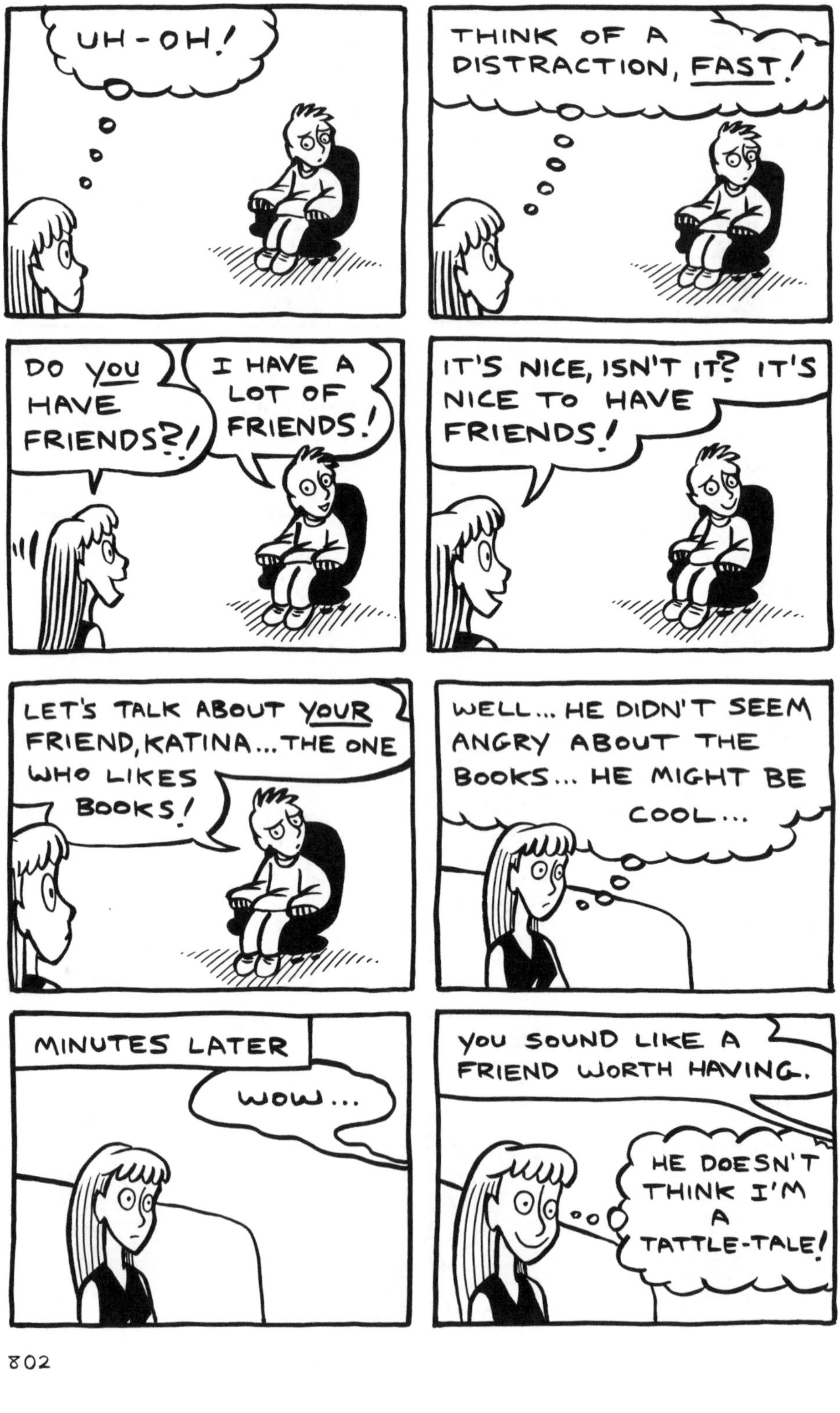
UH-OH!
THINK OF A DISTRACTION, FAST!
DO YOU HAVE FRIENDS?!
I HAVE A LOT OF FRIENDS!
IT'S NICE, ISN'T IT? IT'S NICE TO HAVE FRIENDS!
LET'S TALK ABOUT YOUR FRIEND, KATINA... THE ONE WHO LIKES BOOKS!
WELL... HE DIDN'T SEEM ANGRY ABOUT THE BOOKS... HE MIGHT BE COOL...
MINUTES LATER
WOW...
YOU SOUND LIKE A FRIEND WORTH HAVING.
HE DOESN'T THINK I'M A TATTLE-TALE!

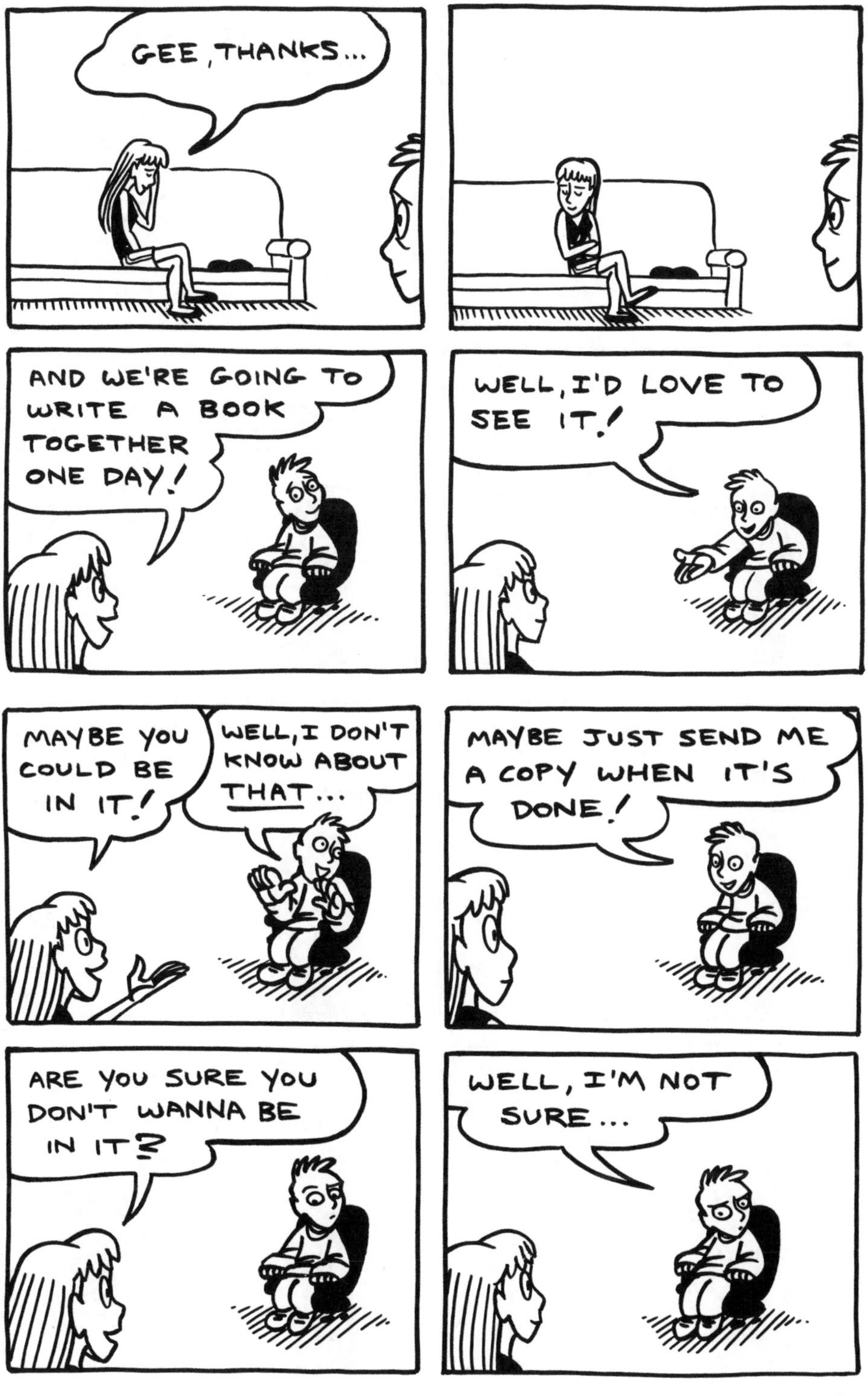
GEE, THANKS...
AND WE'RE GOING TO WRITE A BOOK TOGETHER ONE DAY!
WELL, I'D LOVE TO SEE IT!
MAYBE YOU COULD BE IN IT!
WELL, I DON'T KNOW ABOUT THAT...
MAYBE JUST SEND ME A COPY WHEN IT'S DONE!
ARE YOU SURE YOU DON'T WANNA BE IN IT?
WELL, I'M NOT SURE...

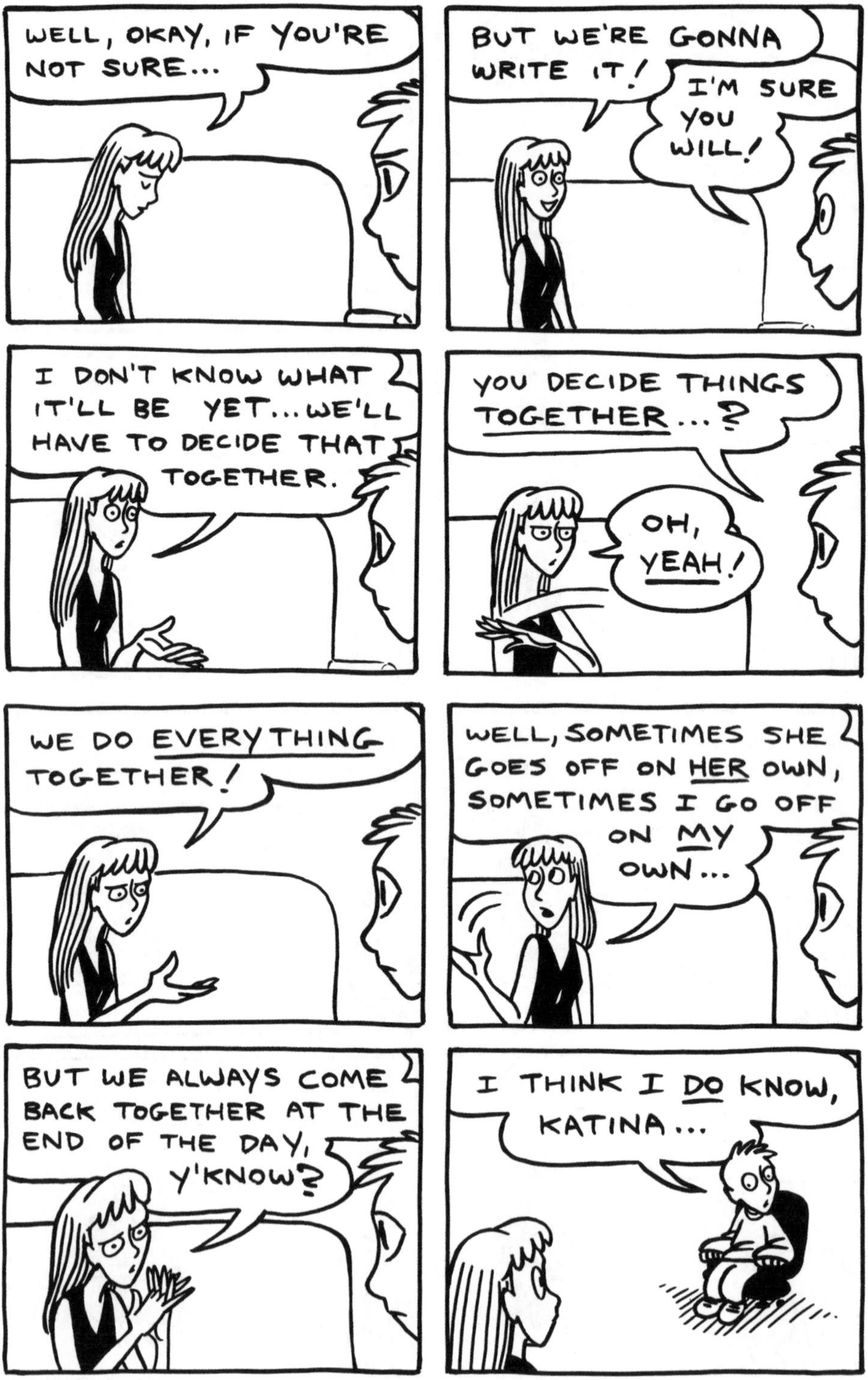
WELL, OKAY, IF YOU'RE NOT SURE...
BUT WE'RE GONNA WRITE IT!
I'M SURE YOU WILL!
I DON'T KNOW WHAT IT'LL BE YET...WE'LL HAVE TO DECIDE THAT TOGETHER.
YOU DECIDE THINGS TOGETHER...?
OH, YEAH!
WE DO EVERYTHING TOGETHER!
WELL, SOMETIMES SHE GOES OFF ON HER OWN, SOMETIMES I GO OFF ON MY OWN...
BUT WE ALWAYS COME BACK TOGETHER AT THE END OF THE DAY, Y'KNOW?
I THINK I DO KNOW, KATINA...

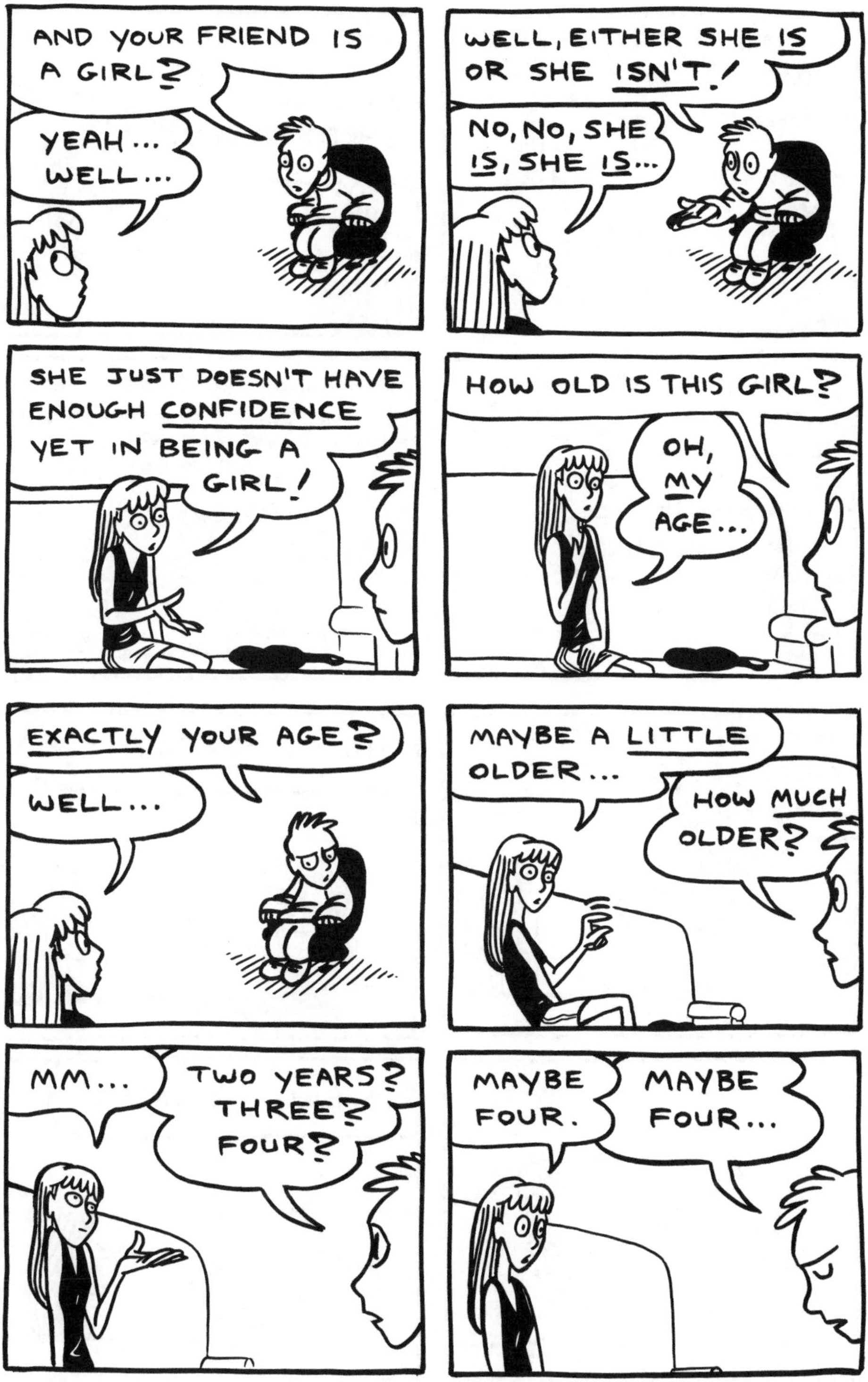
AND YOUR FRIEND IS A GIRL?
YEAH... WELL...
WELL, EITHER SHE IS OR SHE ISN'T!
NO, NO, SHE IS, SHE IS...
SHE JUST DOESN'T HAVE ENOUGH CONFIDENCE YET IN BEING A GIRL!
HOW OLD IS THIS GIRL?
OH, MY AGE...
EXACTLY YOUR AGE?
WELL...
MAYBE A LITTLE OLDER...
HOW MUCH OLDER?
MM...
TWO YEARS? THREE? FOUR?
MAYBE FOUR.
MAYBE FOUR...

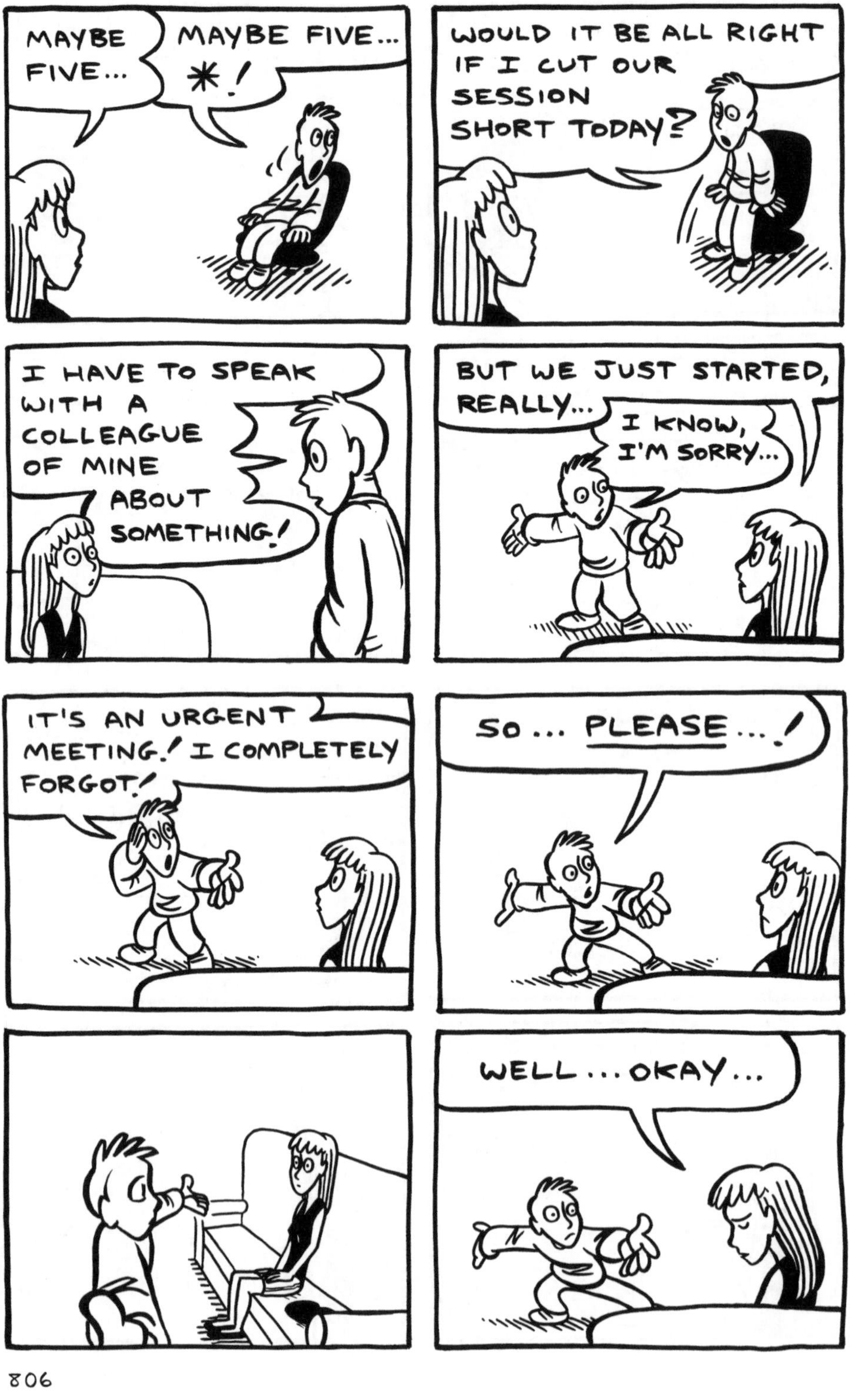

MAYBE FIVE...
MAYBE FIVE... *!
WOULD IT BE ALL RIGHT IF I CUT OUR SESSION SHORT TODAY?
I HAVE TO SPEAK WITH A COLLEAGUE OF MINE ABOUT SOMETHING!
BUT WE JUST STARTED, REALLY...
I KNOW, I'M SORRY...
IT'S AN URGENT MEETING! I COMPLETELY FORGOT!
SO ... PLEASE ... !
WELL ... OKAY ...

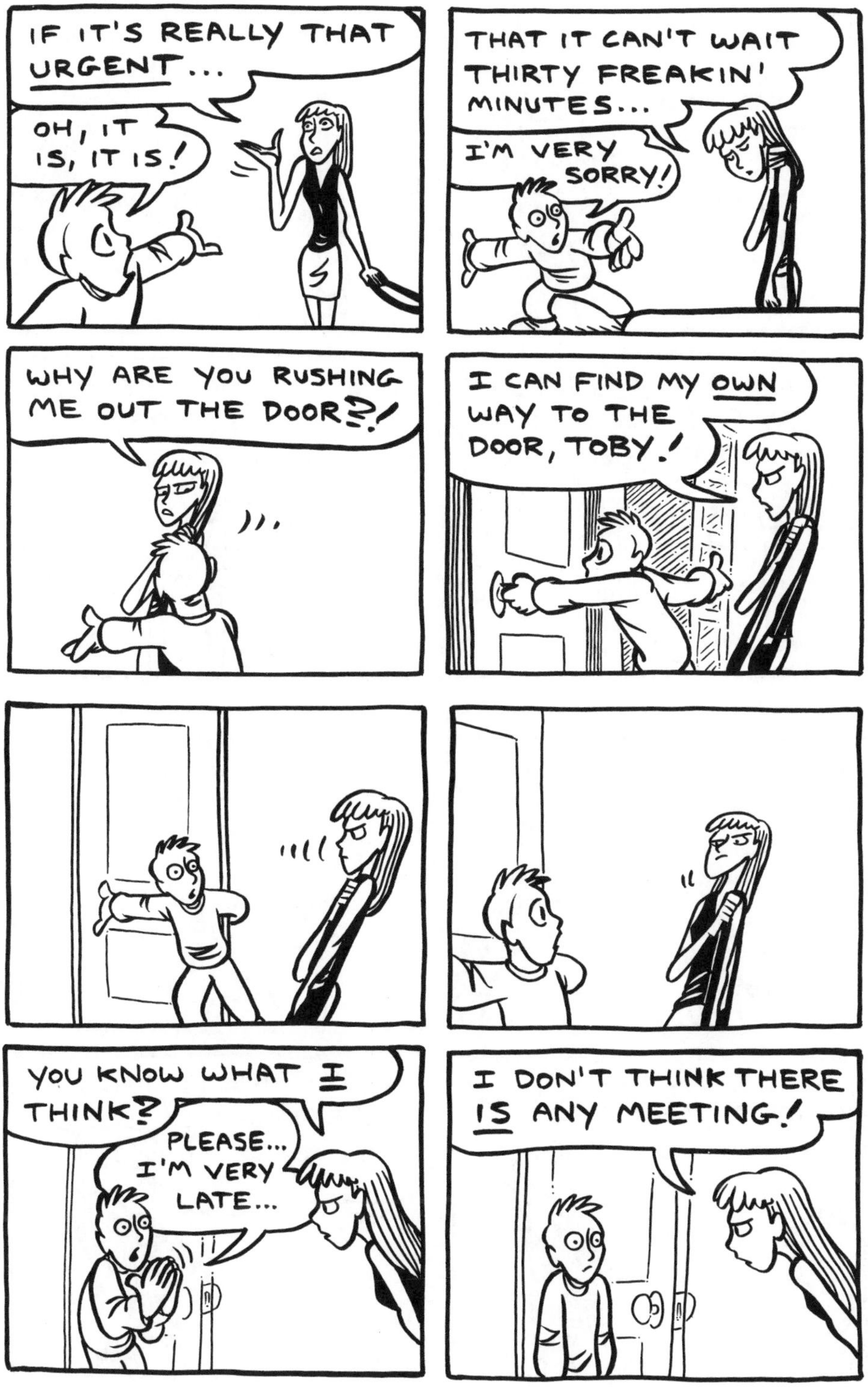
IF IT'S REALLY THAT URGENT...
OH, IT IS, IT IS!
THAT IT CAN'T WAIT THIRTY FREAKIN' MINUTES...
I'M VERY SORRY!
WHY ARE YOU RUSHING ME OUT THE DOOR?!
I CAN FIND MY OWN WAY TO THE DOOR, TOBY!
YOU KNOW WHAT I THINK?
PLEASE... I'M VERY LATE...
I DON'T THINK THERE IS ANY MEETING!

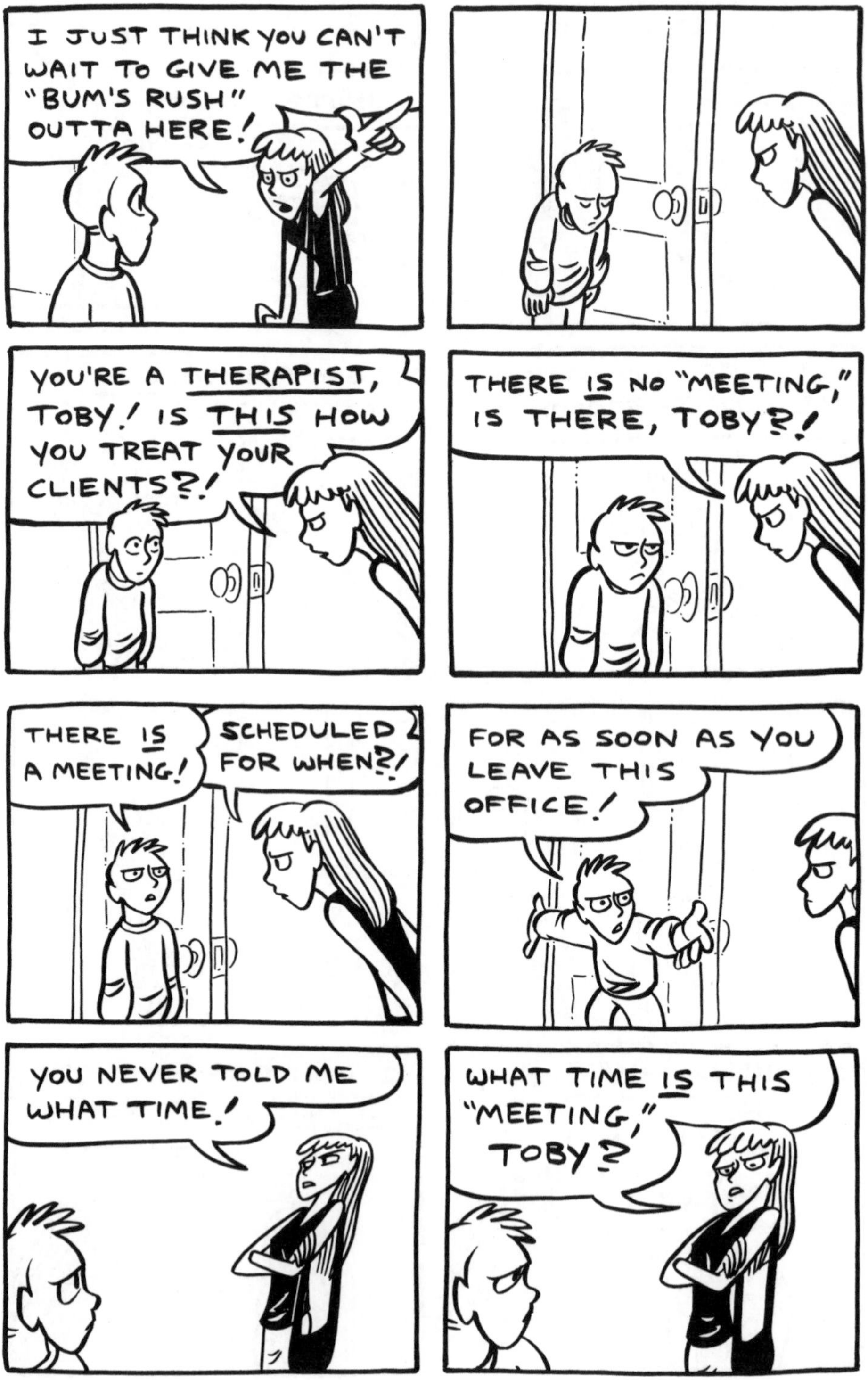
I JUST THINK YOU CAN'T WAIT TO GIVE ME THE "BUM'S RUSH" OUTTA HERE!
YOU'RE A THERAPIST, TOBY! IS THIS HOW YOU TREAT YOUR CLIENTS?!
THERE IS NO "MEETING," IS THERE, TOBY?!
THERE IS A MEETING!
SCHEDULED FOR WHEN?!
FOR AS SOON AS YOU LEAVE THIS OFFICE!
YOU NEVER TOLD ME WHAT TIME!
WHAT TIME IS THIS "MEETING," TOBY?

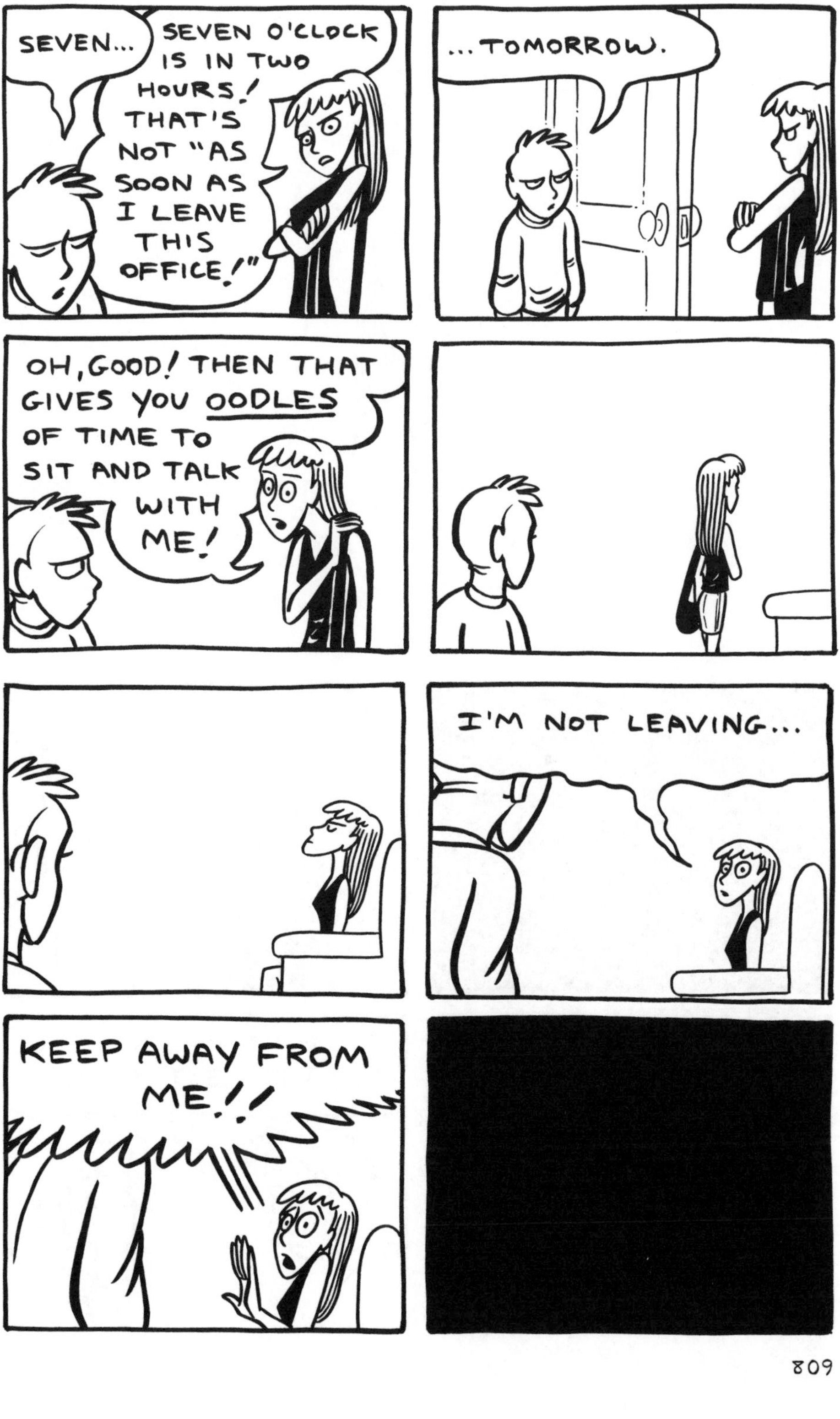
SEVEN...
SEVEN O'CLOCK IS IN TWO HOURS! THAT'S NOT "AS SOON AS I LEAVE THIS OFFICE!"
...TOMORROW.
OH, GOOD! THEN THAT GIVES YOU OODLES OF TIME TO SIT AND TALK WITH ME!
I'M NOT LEAVING...
KEEP AWAY FROM ME!!

LISTEN...
I'M VERY SORRY, BUT I REALLY HAVE TO ASK YOU TO LEAVE.
I WON'T CHARGE YOU FOR THE NEXT SESSION.

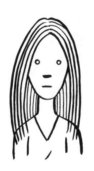

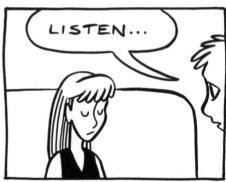

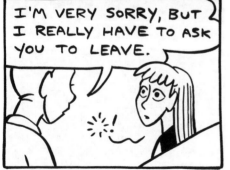

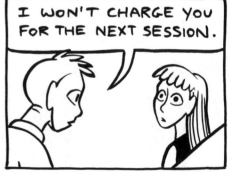

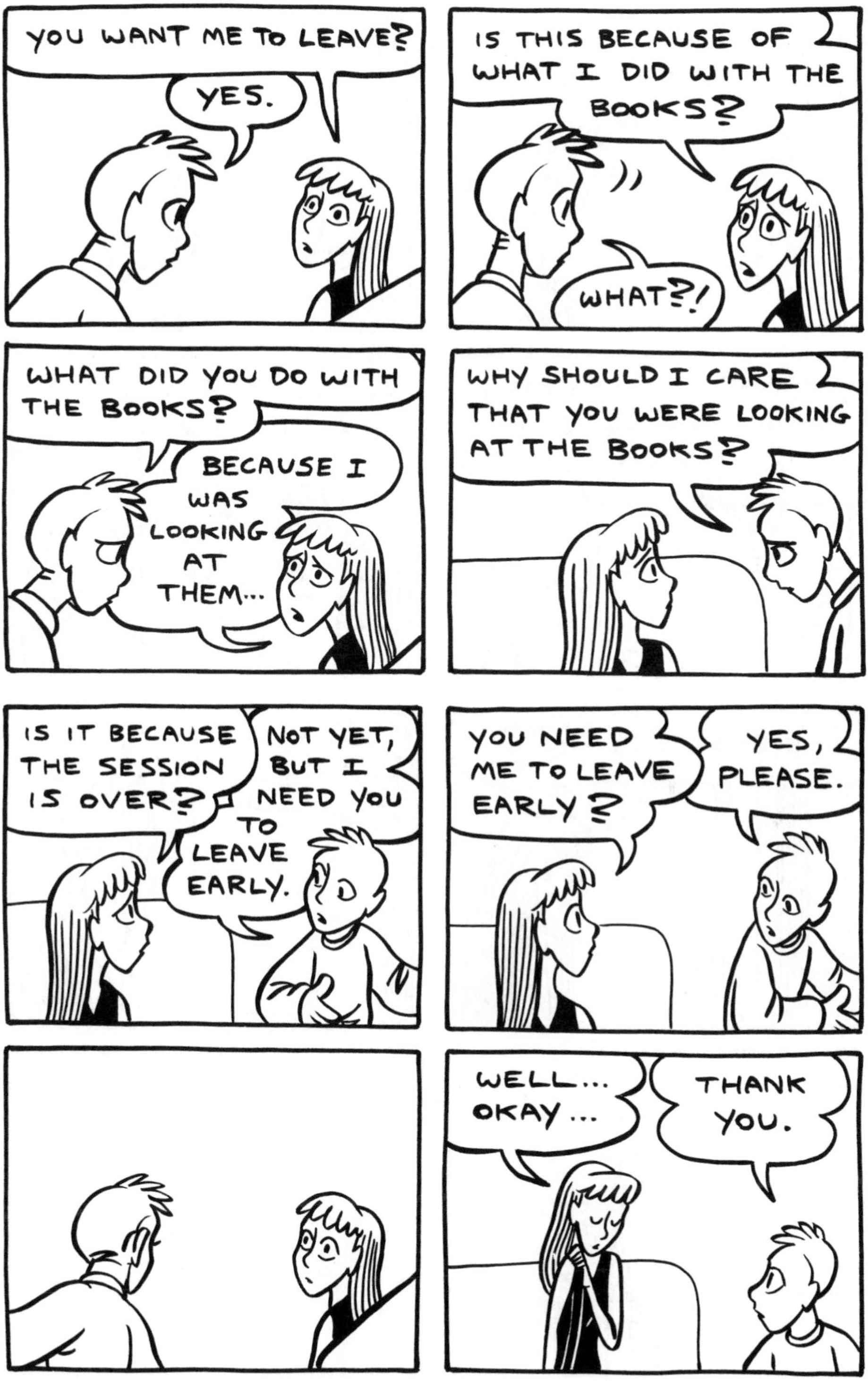
YOU WANT ME TO LEAVE?
YES.
IS THIS BECAUSE OF WHAT I DID WITH THE BOOKS?
WHAT?!
WHAT DID YOU DO WITH THE BOOKS?
BECAUSE I WAS LOOKING AT THEM...
WHY SHOULD I CARE THAT YOU WERE LOOKING AT THE BOOKS?
IS IT BECAUSE THE SESSION IS OVER?
NOT YET, BUT I NEED YOU TO LEAVE EARLY.
YOU NEED ME TO LEAVE EARLY?
YES, PLEASE.
WELL... OKAY...
THANK YOU.

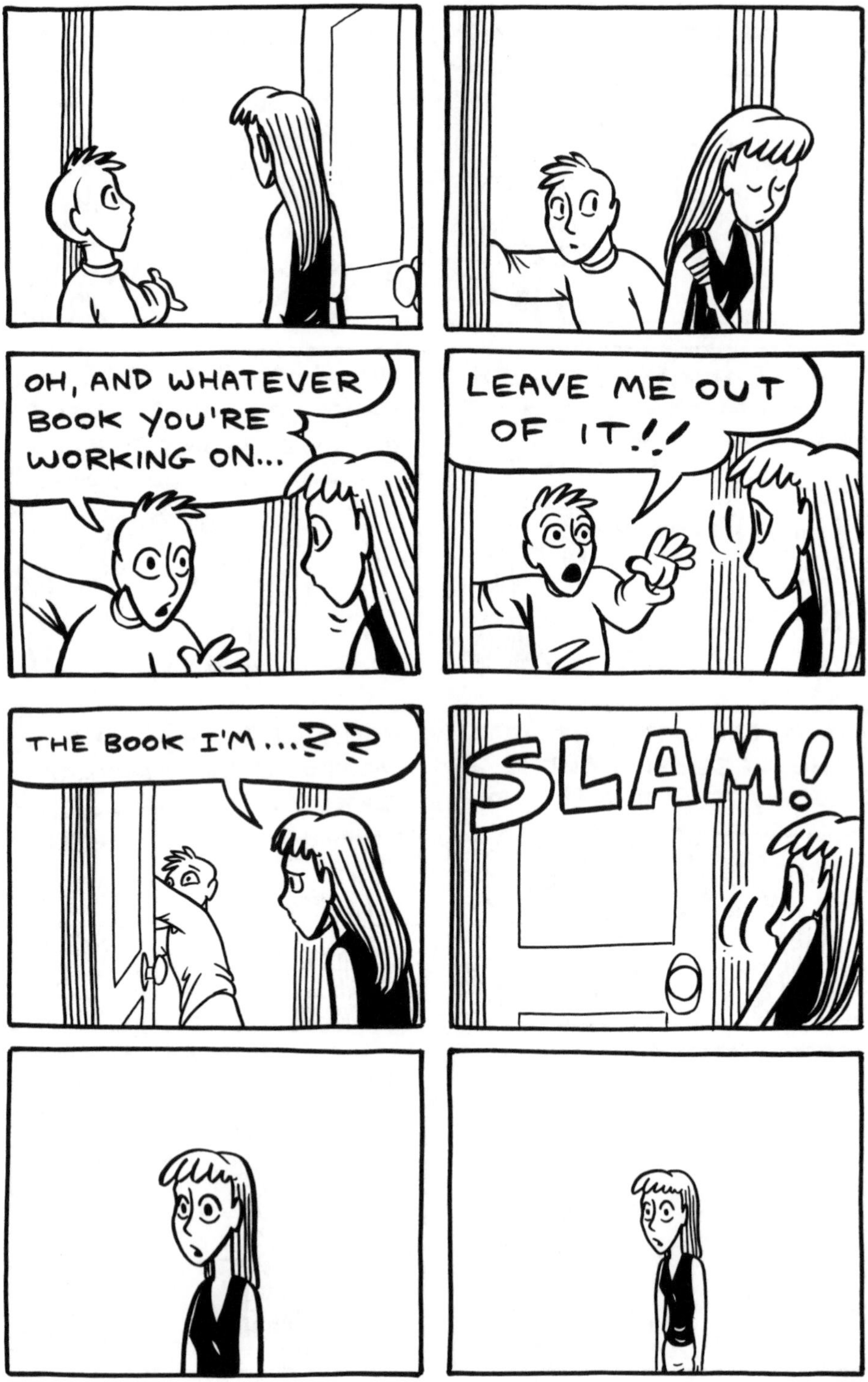
OH, AND WHATEVER BOOK YOU'RE WORKING ON...
LEAVE ME OUT OF IT!!
THE BOOK I'M...??
SLAM!

PENCIL

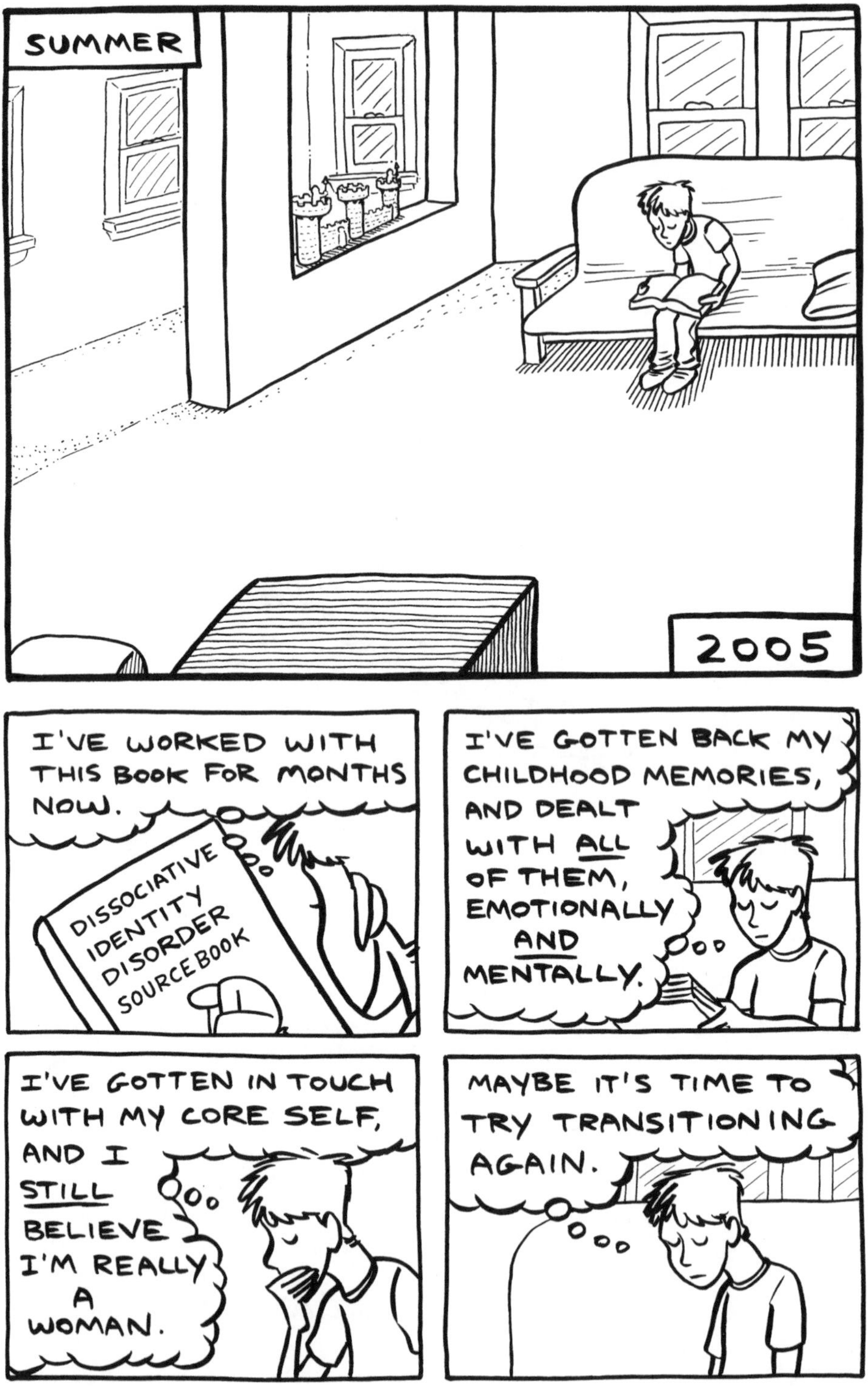
SUMMER
2005
I'VE WORKED WITH THIS BOOK FOR MONTHS NOW.
DISSOCIATIVE IDENTITY DISORDER SOURCEBOOK
I'VE GOTTEN BACK MY CHILDHOOD MEMORIES, AND DEALT WITH ALL OF THEM, EMOTIONALLY AND MENTALLY.
I'VE GOTTEN IN TOUCH WITH MY CORE SELF, AND I STILL BELIEVE I'M REALLY A WOMAN.
MAYBE IT'S TIME TO TRY TRANSITIONING AGAIN.

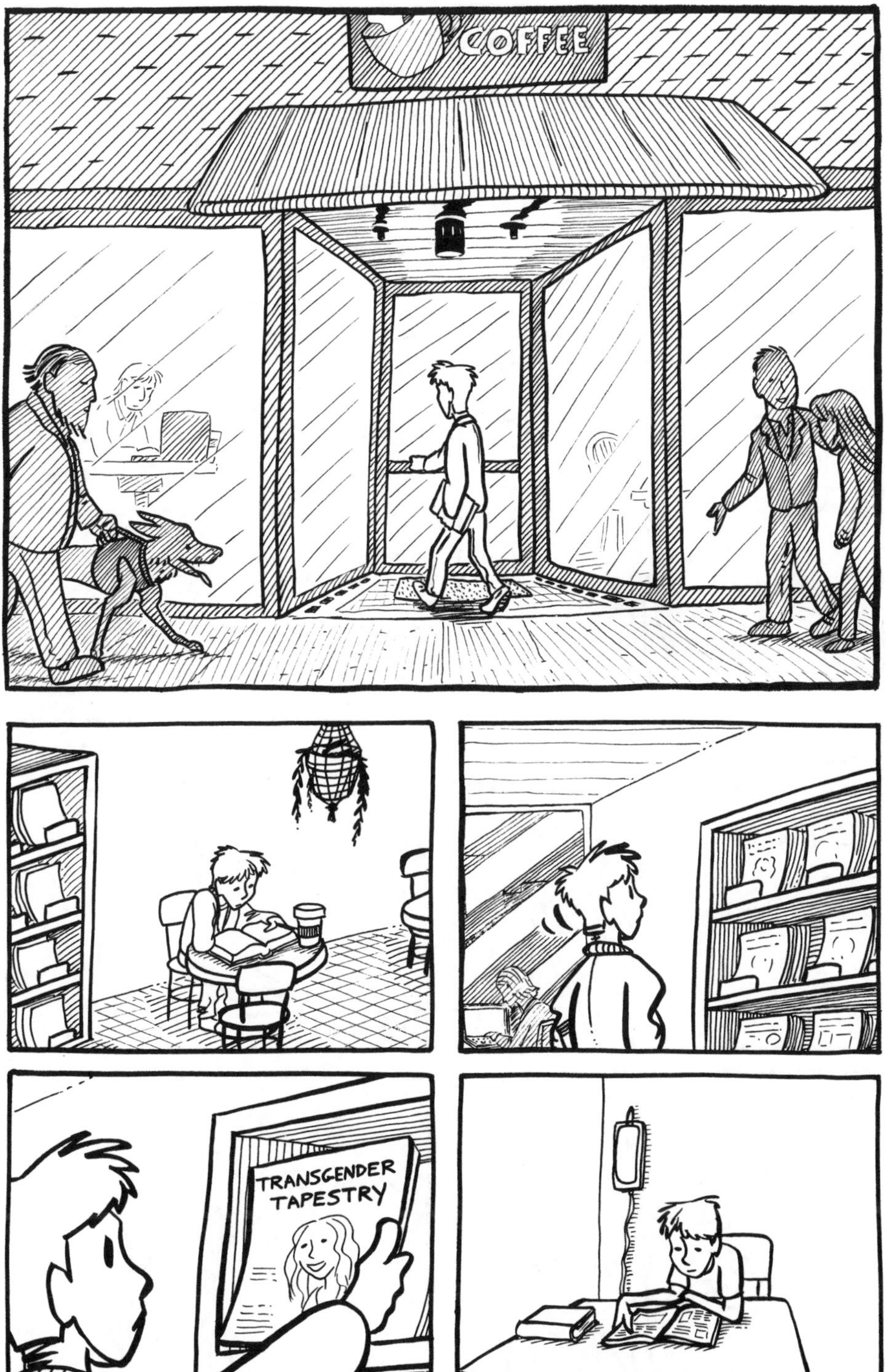
COFFEE
TRANSGENDER TAPESTRY

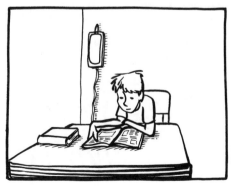

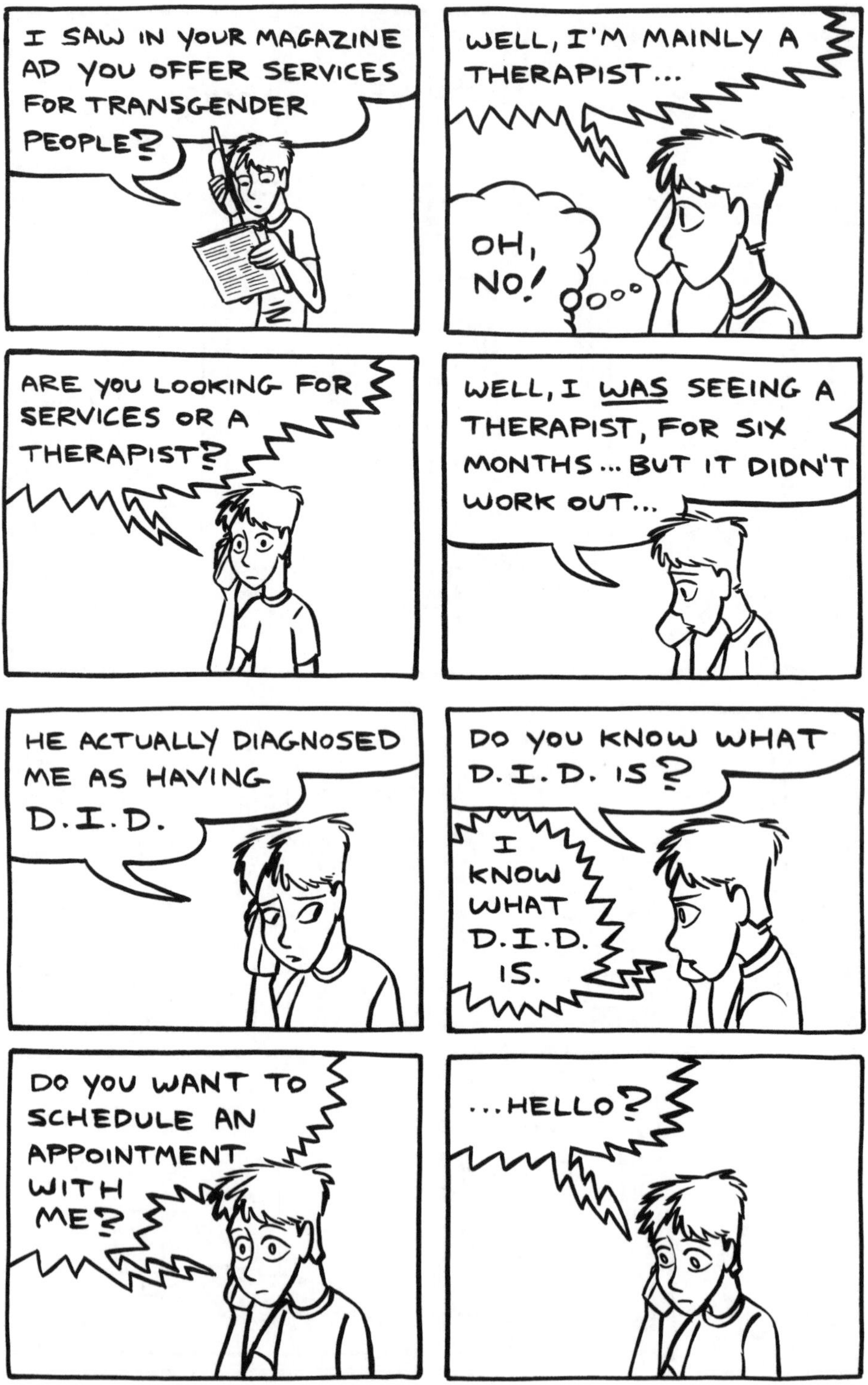
I SAW IN YOUR MAGAZINE AD YOU OFFER SERVICES FOR TRANSGENDER PEOPLE?
WELL, I'M MAINLY A THERAPIST...
OH, NO!
ARE YOU LOOKING FOR SERVICES OR A THERAPIST?
WELL, I WAS SEEING A THERAPIST, FOR SIX MONTHS... BUT IT DIDN'T WORK OUT...
HE ACTUALLY DIAGNOSED ME AS HAVING D.I.D.
DO YOU KNOW WHAT D.I.D. IS?
I KNOW WHAT D.I.D. IS.
DO YOU WANT TO SCHEDULE AN APPOINTMENT WITH ME?
...HELLO?

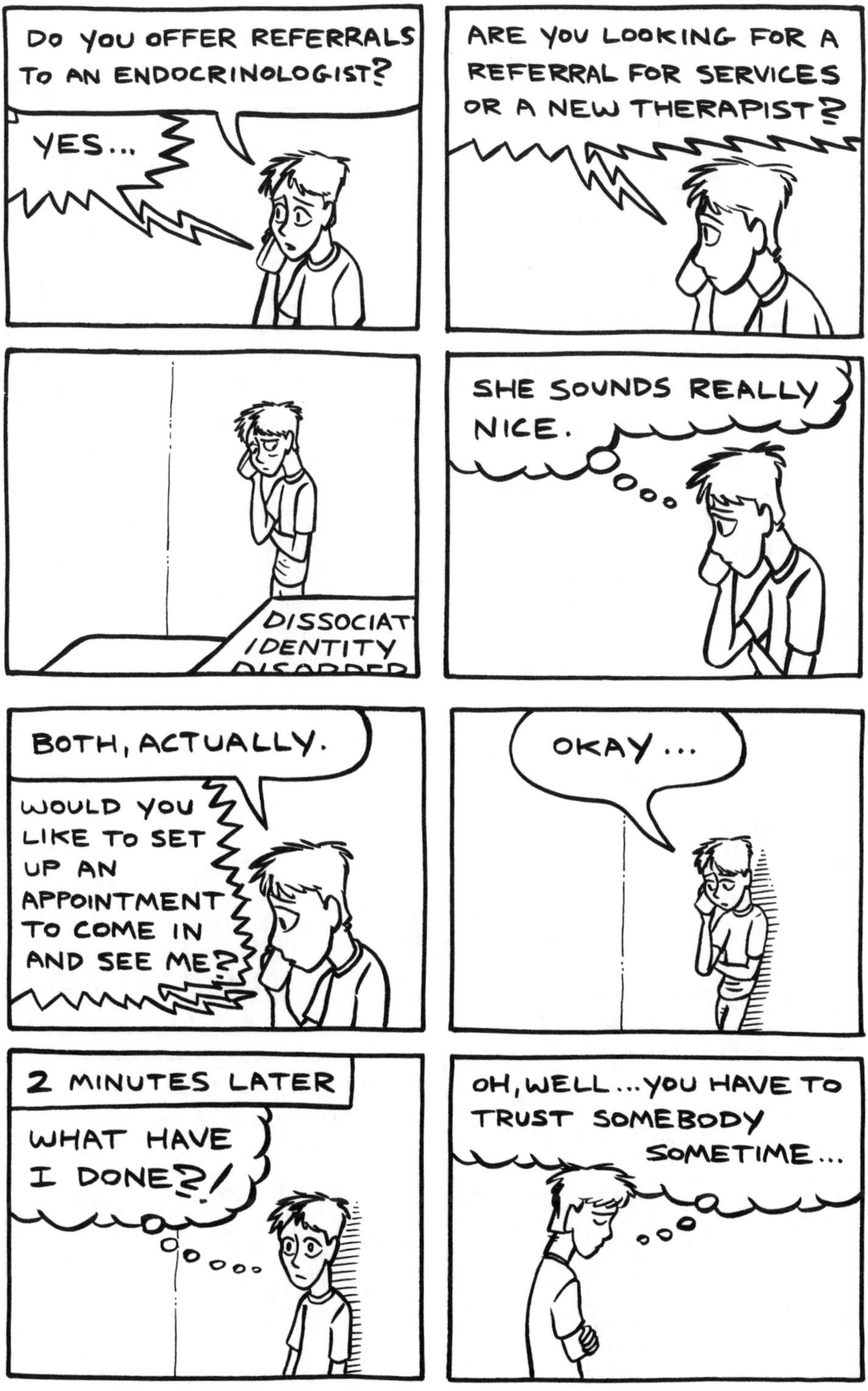
DO YOU OFFER REFERRALS TO AN ENDOCRINOLOGIST?
YES...
ARE YOU LOOKING FOR A REFERRAL FOR SERVICES OR A NEW THERAPIST?
DISSOCIAT
IDENTITY
SHE SOUNDS REALLY NICE.
BOTH, ACTUALLY.
WOULD YOU LIKE TO SET UP AN APPOINTMENT TO COME IN AND SEE ME?
OKAY...
2 MINUTES LATER
WHAT HAVE I DONE?!
OH, WELL...YOU HAVE TO TRUST SOMEBODY SOMETIME...

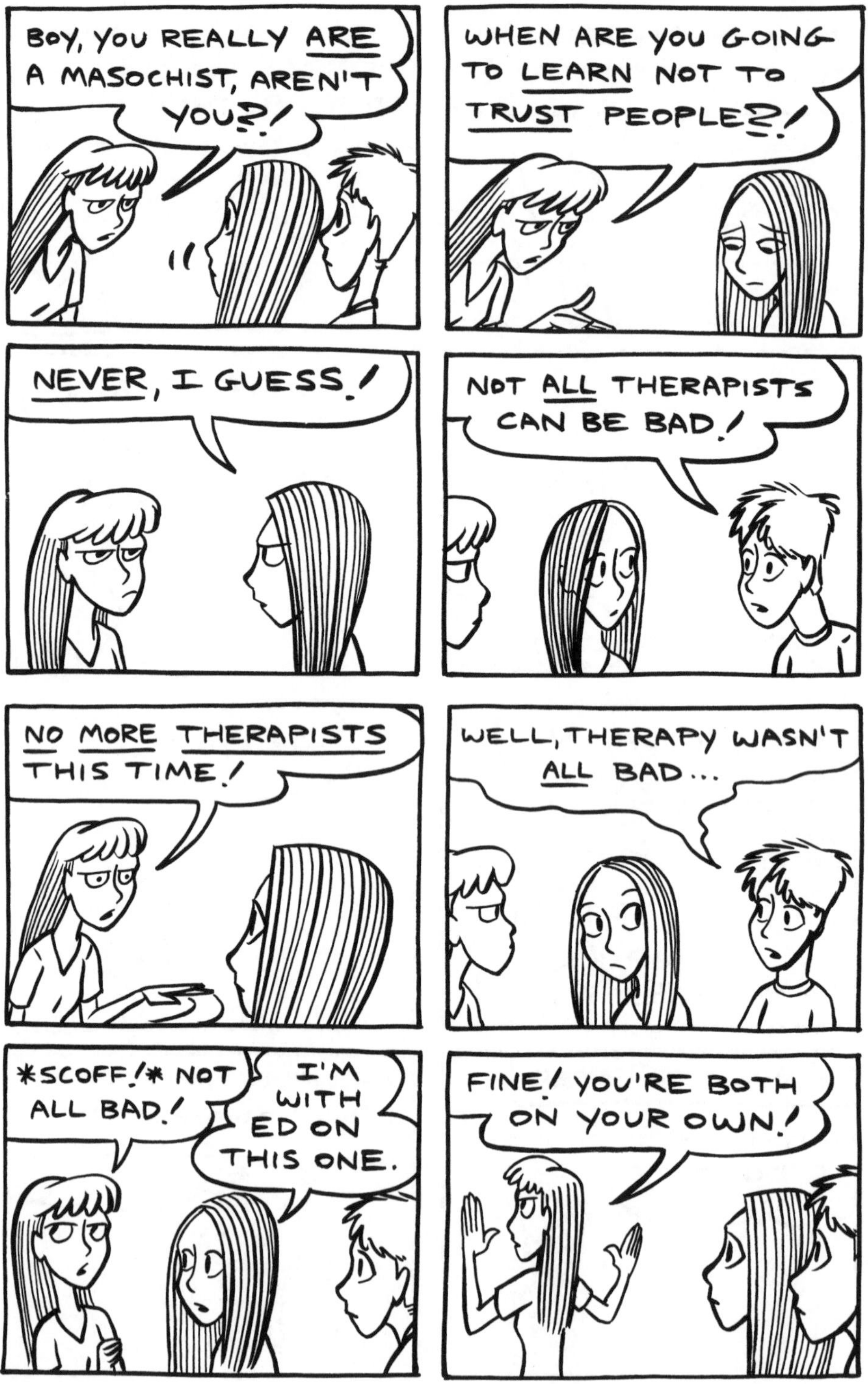
BOY, YOU REALLY ARE A MASOCHIST, AREN'T YOU?!
WHEN ARE YOU GOING TO LEARN NOT TO TRUST PEOPLE?!
NEVER, I GUESS!
NOT ALL THERAPISTS CAN BE BAD!
NO MORE THERAPISTS THIS TIME!
WELL, THERAPY WASN'T ALL BAD...
SCOFF! NOT ALL BAD!
I'M WITH ED ON THIS ONE.
FINE! YOU'RE BOTH ON YOUR OWN!

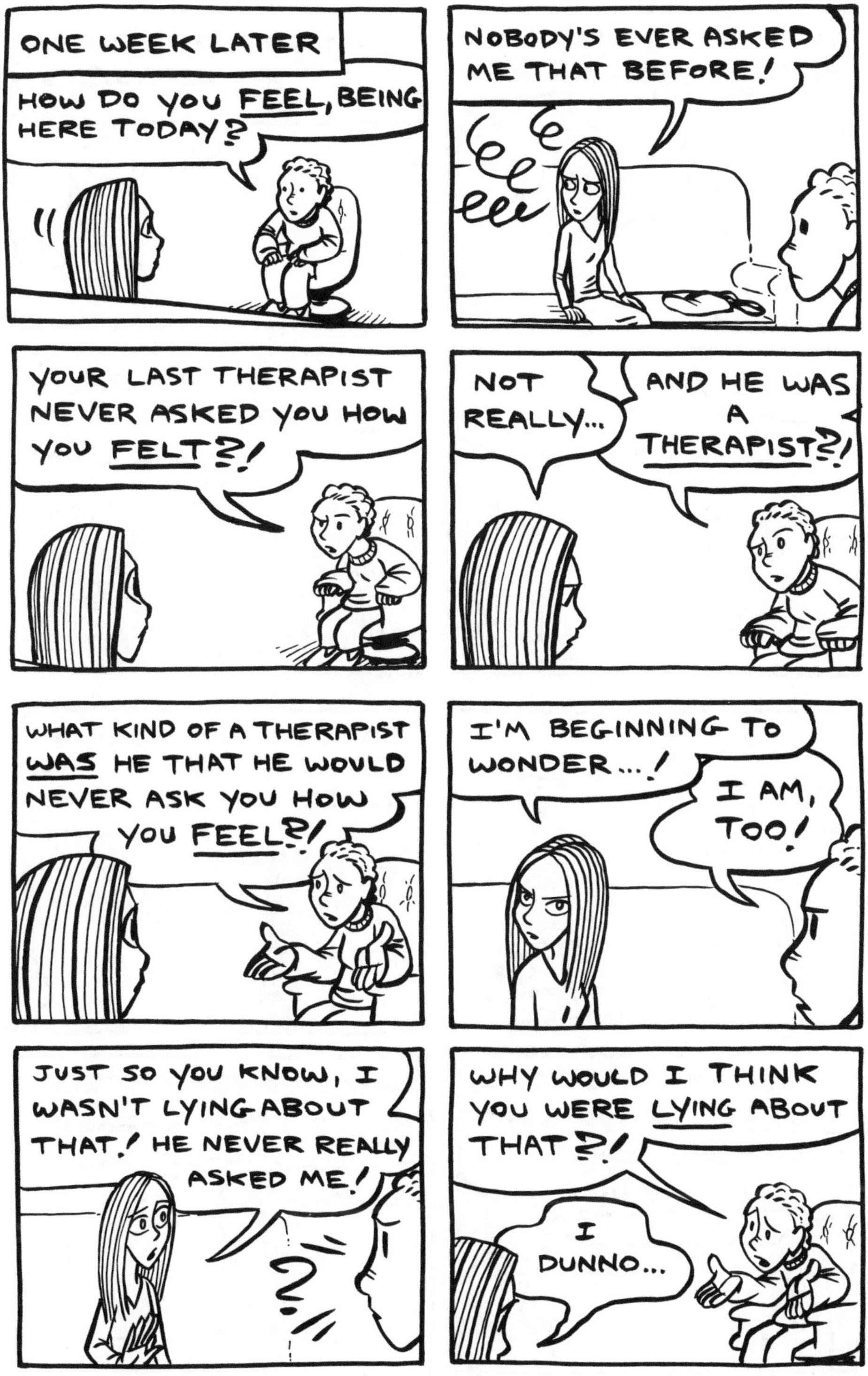
ONE WEEK LATER
HOW DO YOU FEEL, BEING HERE TODAY?
NOBODY'S EVER ASKED ME THAT BEFORE!
YOUR LAST THERAPIST NEVER ASKED YOU HOW YOU FELT?!
NOT REALLY...
AND HE WAS A THERAPIST?!
WHAT KIND OF A THERAPIST WAS HE THAT HE WOULD NEVER ASK YOU HOW YOU FEEL?!
I'M BEGINNING TO WONDER...!
I AM, TOO!
JUST SO YOU KNOW, I WASN'T LYING ABOUT THAT! HE NEVER REALLY ASKED ME!
?
WHY WOULD I THINK YOU WERE LYING ABOUT THAT?!
I DUNNO...

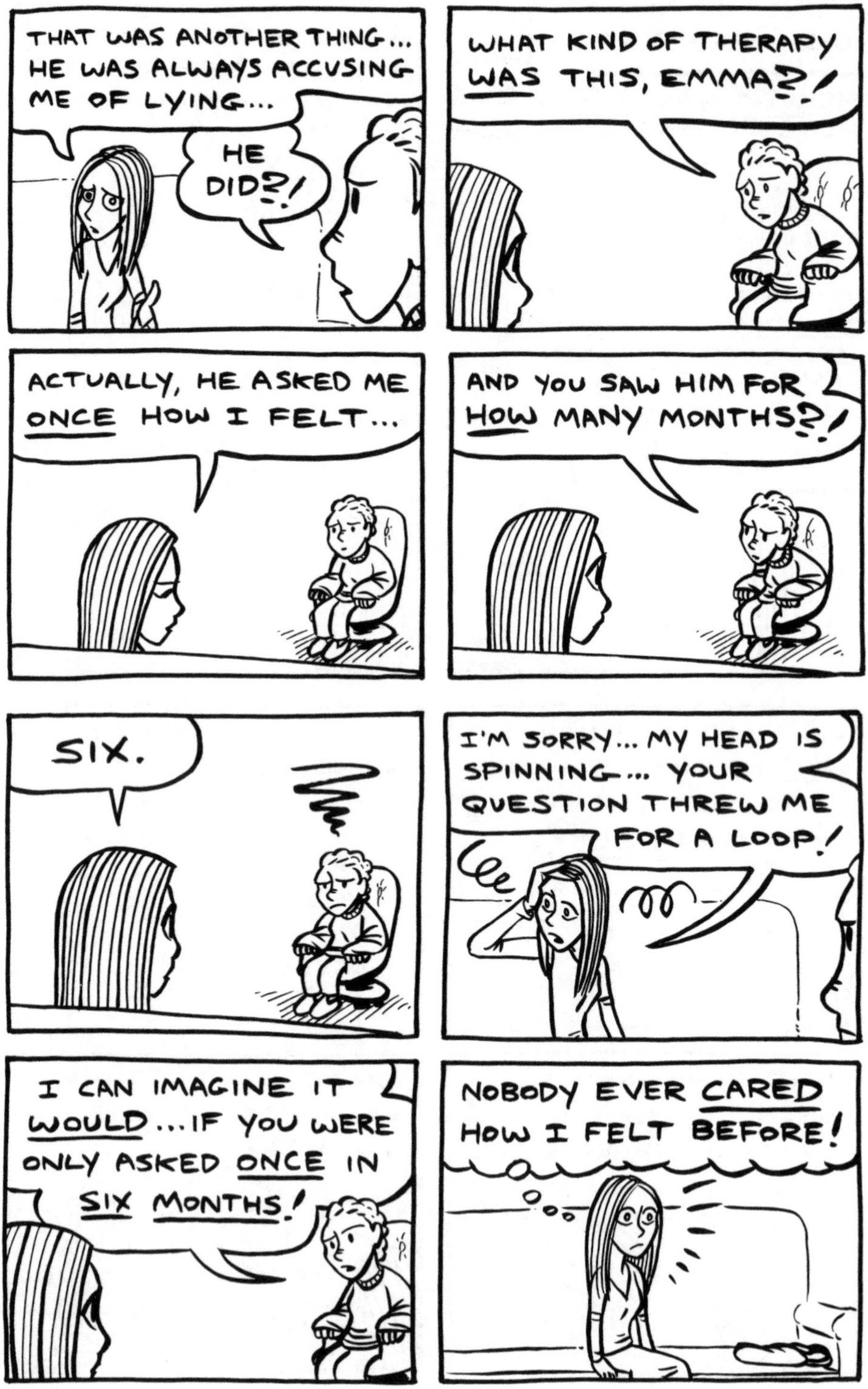
THAT WAS ANOTHER THING... HE WAS ALWAYS ACCUSING ME OF LYING...
HE DID?!
WHAT KIND OF THERAPY WAS THIS, EMMA?!
ACTUALLY, HE ASKED ME ONCE HOW I FELT...
AND YOU SAW HIM FOR HOW MANY MONTHS?!
SIX.
I'M SORRY... MY HEAD IS SPINNING... YOUR QUESTION THREW ME FOR A LOOP!
I CAN IMAGINE IT WOULD...IF YOU WERE ONLY ASKED ONCE IN SIX MONTHS!
NOBODY EVER CARED HOW I FELT BEFORE!

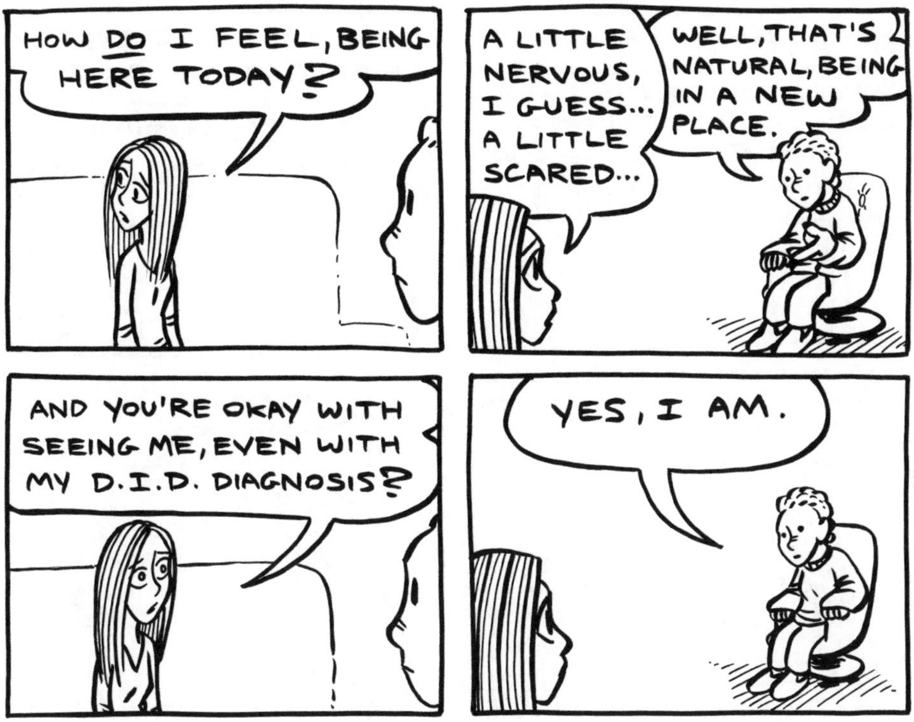
HOW DO I FEEL, BEING HERE TODAY?
A LITTLE NERVOUS, I GUESS... A LITTLE SCARED...
WELL, THAT'S NATURAL, BEING IN A NEW PLACE.
AND YOU'RE OKAY WITH SEEING ME, EVEN WITH MY D.I.D. DIAGNOSIS?
YES, I AM.

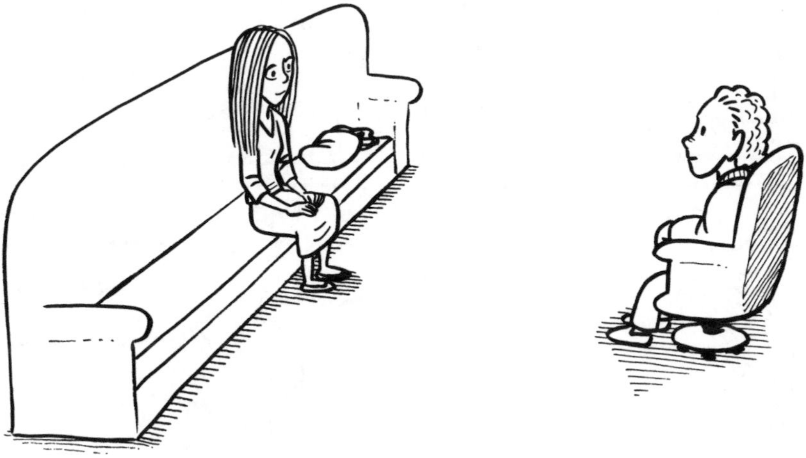

END OF FIRST SESSION

BEFORE YOU GO, I'D JUST LIKE YOU TO SIGN AND PRINT YOUR NAME AND YOUR BIRTHDAY.

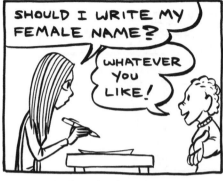

SHOULD I WRITE MY FEMALE NAME?

WHATEVER YOU LIKE!

I'LL WRITE MY GUY NAME, SINCE THAT'S MY LEGAL NAME.

EDGAR. YEAH...

BUT I WANT TO LEGALLY CHANGE IT TO EMMA.

YOU'RE RIGHT-HANDED!

YEAH...

NO TIME TO TALK ABOUT HOW I WASN'T... ORIGINALLY...

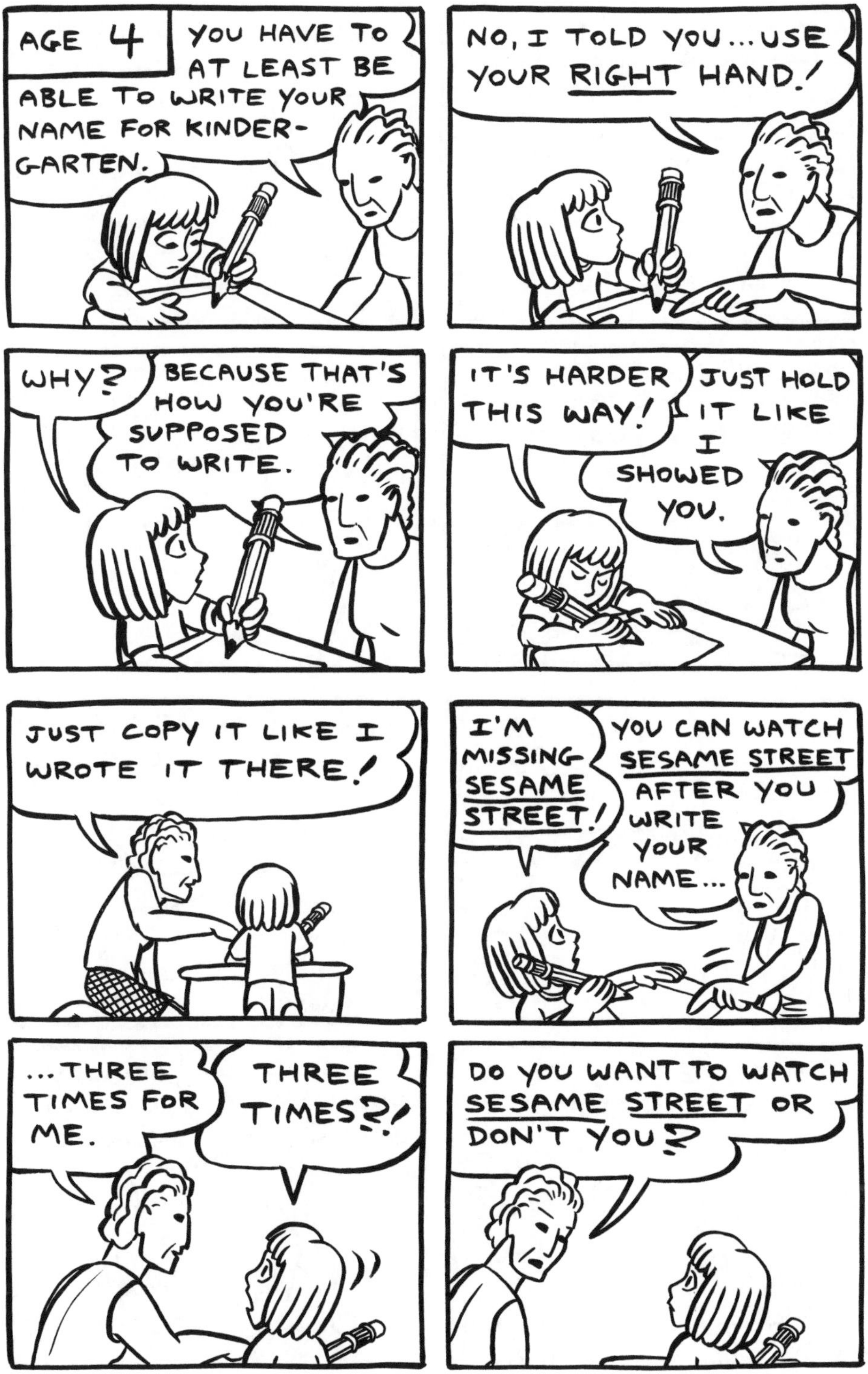
AGE 4
YOU HAVE TO AT LEAST BE ABLE TO WRITE YOUR NAME FOR KINDER-GARTEN.
NO, I TOLD YOU... USE YOUR RIGHT HAND!
WHY?
BECAUSE THAT'S HOW YOU'RE SUPPOSED TO WRITE.
IT'S HARDER THIS WAY!
JUST HOLD IT LIKE I SHOWED YOU.
JUST COPY IT LIKE I WROTE IT THERE!
I'M MISSING SESAME STREET!
YOU CAN WATCH SESAME STREET AFTER YOU WRITE YOUR NAME...
...THREE TIMES FOR ME.
THREE TIMES?!
DO YOU WANT TO WATCH SESAME STREET OR DON'T YOU?

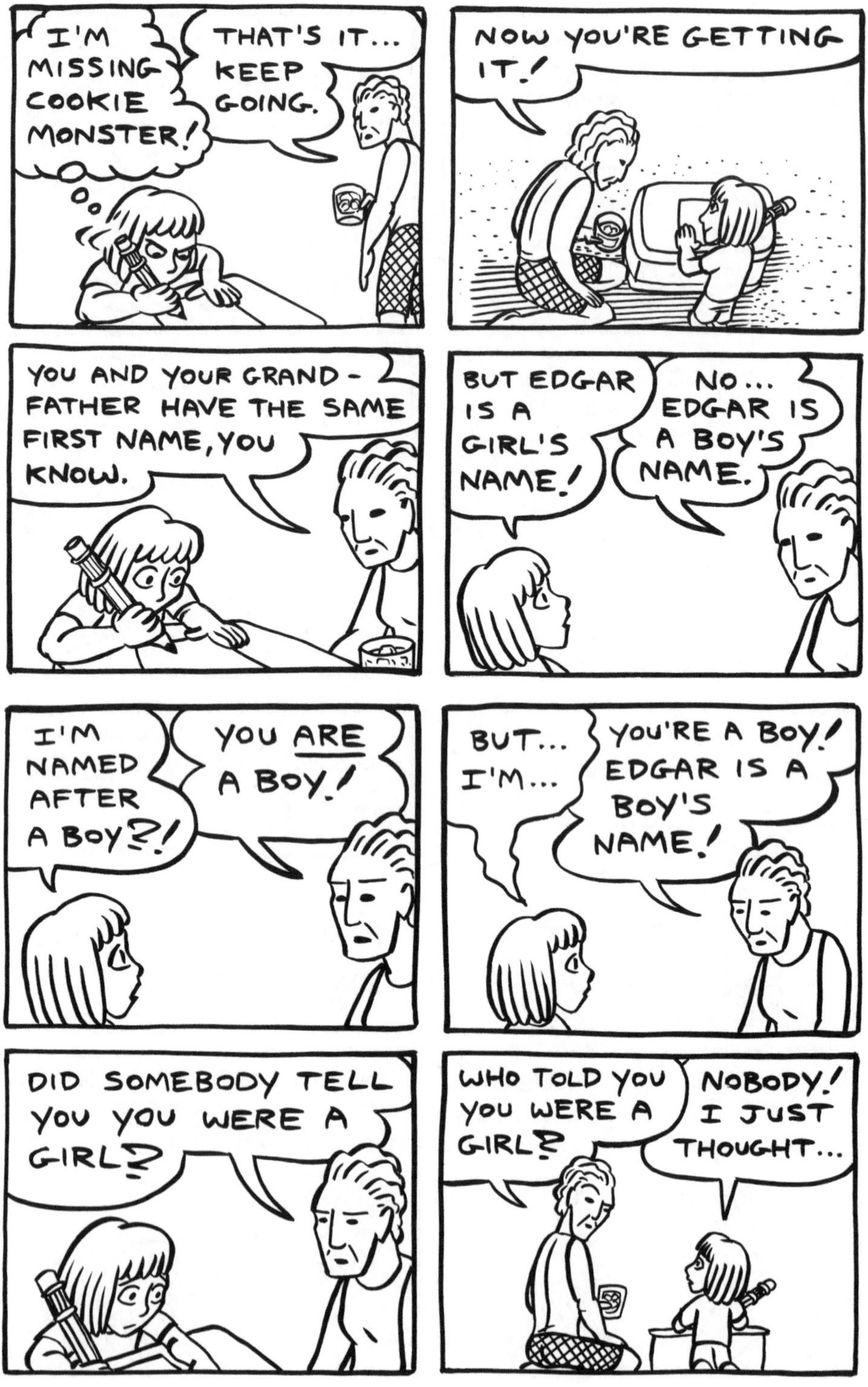
I'M MISSING COOKIE MONSTER!
THAT'S IT... KEEP GOING.
NOW YOU'RE GETTING IT!
YOU AND YOUR GRAND-FATHER HAVE THE SAME FIRST NAME, YOU KNOW.
BUT EDGAR IS A GIRL'S NAME!
NO... EDGAR IS A BOY'S NAME.
I'M NAMED AFTER A BOY?!
YOU ARE A BOY!
BUT... I'M...
YOU'RE A BOY! EDGAR IS A BOY'S NAME!
DID SOMEBODY TELL YOU YOU WERE A GIRL?
WHO TOLD YOU YOU WERE A GIRL?
NOBODY! I JUST THOUGHT...

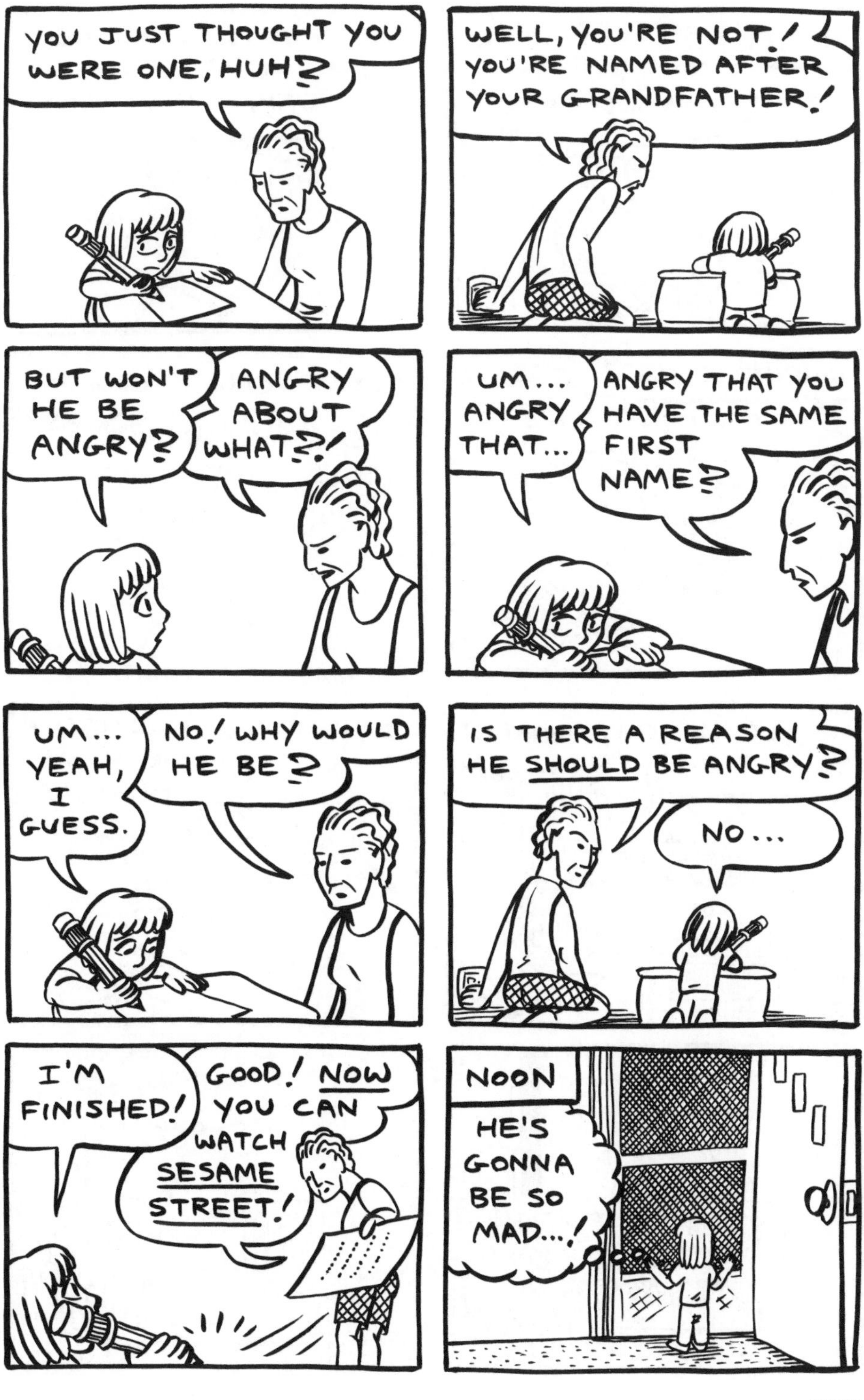
YOU JUST THOUGHT YOU WERE ONE, HUH?
WELL, YOU'RE NOT! YOU'RE NAMED AFTER YOUR GRANDFATHER!
BUT WON'T HE BE ANGRY?
ANGRY ABOUT WHAT?!
UM... ANGRY THAT...
ANGRY THAT YOU HAVE THE SAME FIRST NAME?
UM... YEAH, I GUESS.
NO! WHY WOULD HE BE?
IS THERE A REASON HE SHOULD BE ANGRY?
NO...
I'M FINISHED!
GOOD! NOW YOU CAN WATCH SESAME STREET!
NOON
HE'S GONNA BE SO MAD...!

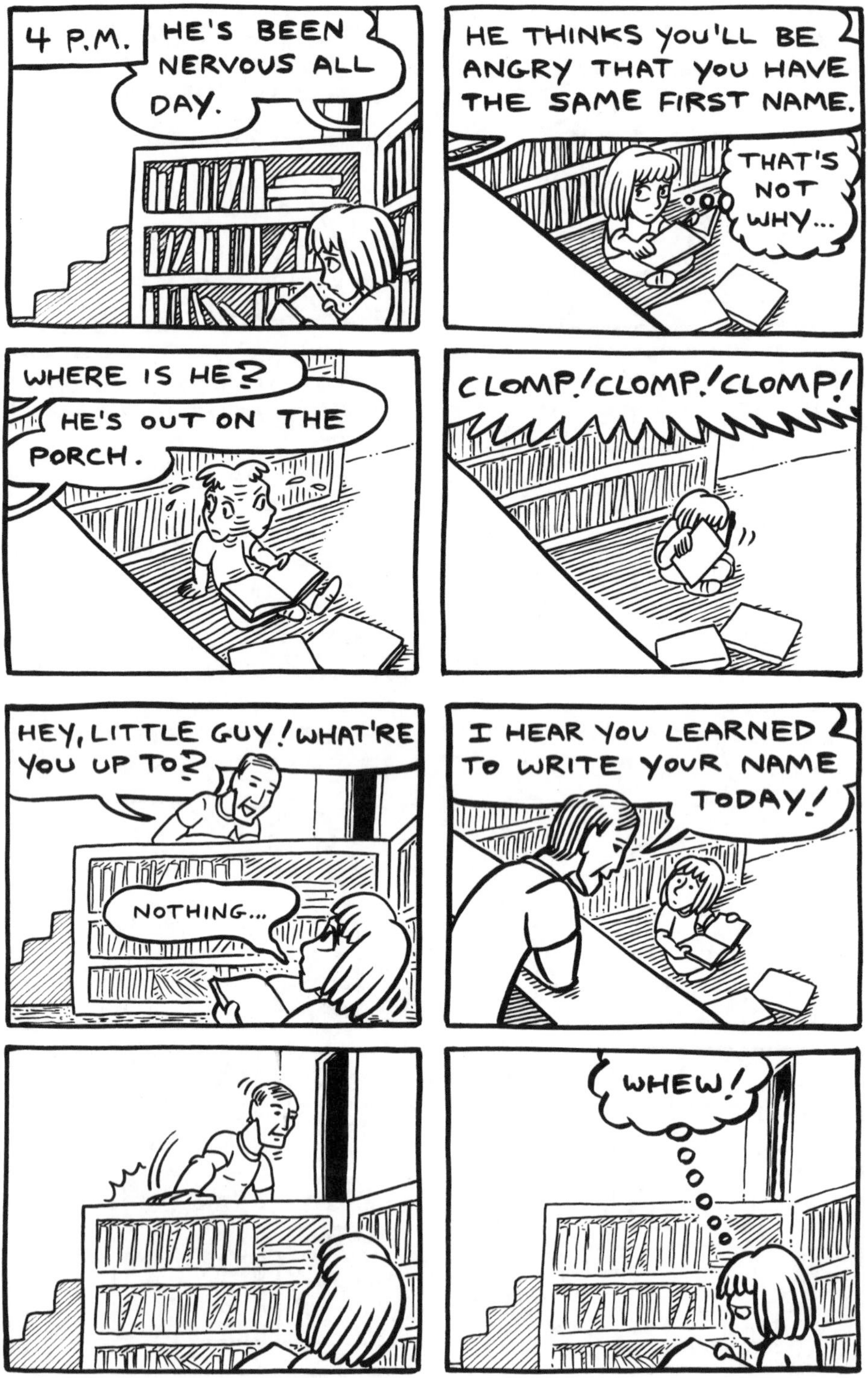
4 P.M.
HE'S BEEN NERVOUS ALL DAY.
HE THINKS YOU'LL BE ANGRY THAT YOU HAVE THE SAME FIRST NAME.
THAT'S NOT WHY...
WHERE IS HE?
HE'S OUT ON THE PORCH.
CLOMP! CLOMP! CLOMP!
HEY, LITTLE GUY! WHAT'RE YOU UP TO?
NOTHING...
I HEAR YOU LEARNED TO WRITE YOUR NAME TODAY!
WHEW!

KNIGHT

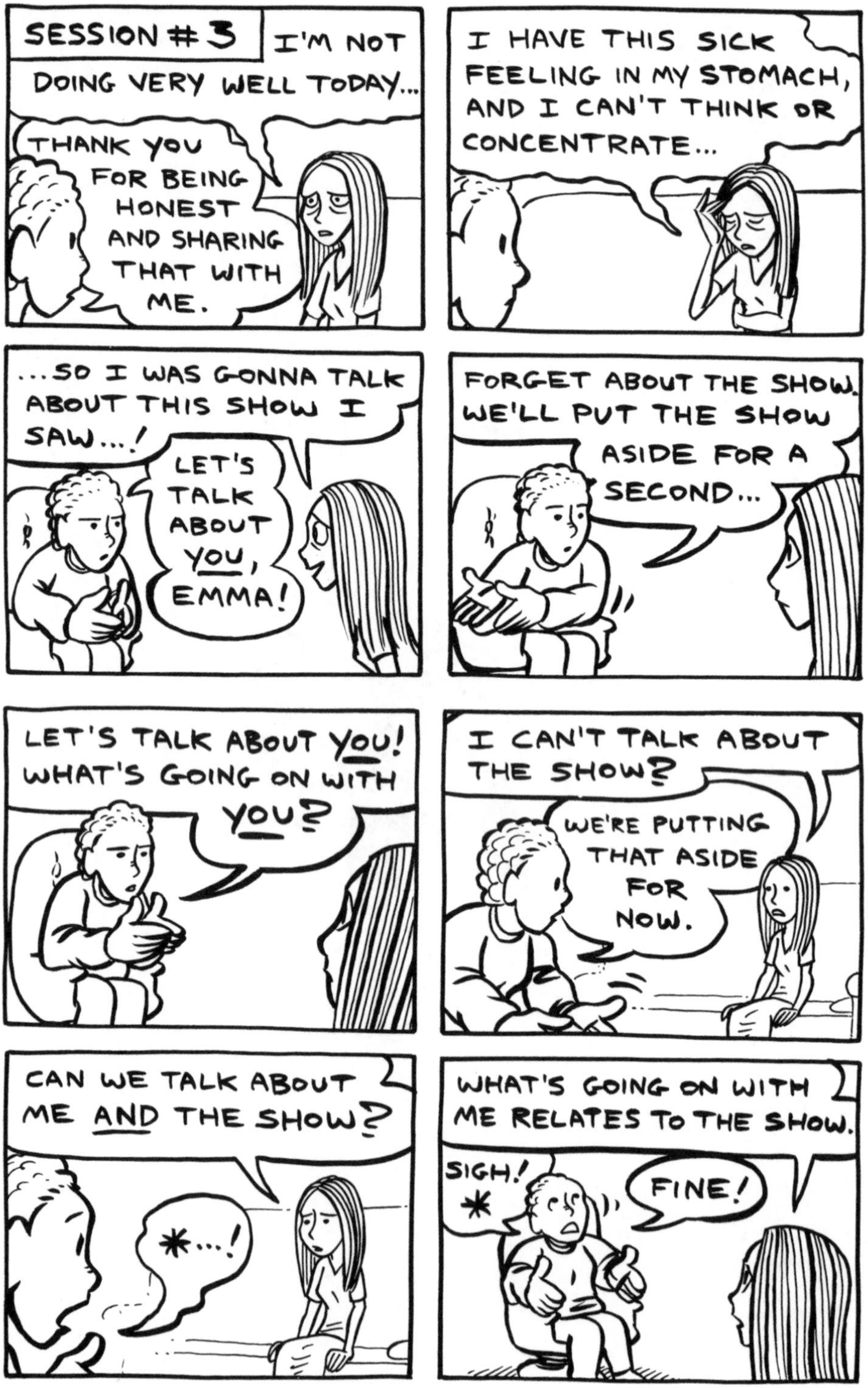
SESSION #3
I'M NOT DOING VERY WELL TODAY...
THANK YOU FOR BEING HONEST AND SHARING THAT WITH ME.
I HAVE THIS SICK FEELING IN MY STOMACH, AND I CAN'T THINK OR CONCENTRATE...
...SO I WAS GONNA TALK ABOUT THIS SHOW I SAW...!
LET'S TALK ABOUT YOU, EMMA!
FORGET ABOUT THE SHOW. WE'LL PUT THE SHOW ASIDE FOR A SECOND...
LET'S TALK ABOUT YOU! WHAT'S GOING ON WITH YOU?
I CAN'T TALK ABOUT THE SHOW?
WE'RE PUTTING THAT ASIDE FOR NOW.
CAN WE TALK ABOUT ME AND THE SHOW?
*...!
WHAT'S GOING ON WITH ME RELATES TO THE SHOW.
SIGH! *
FINE!

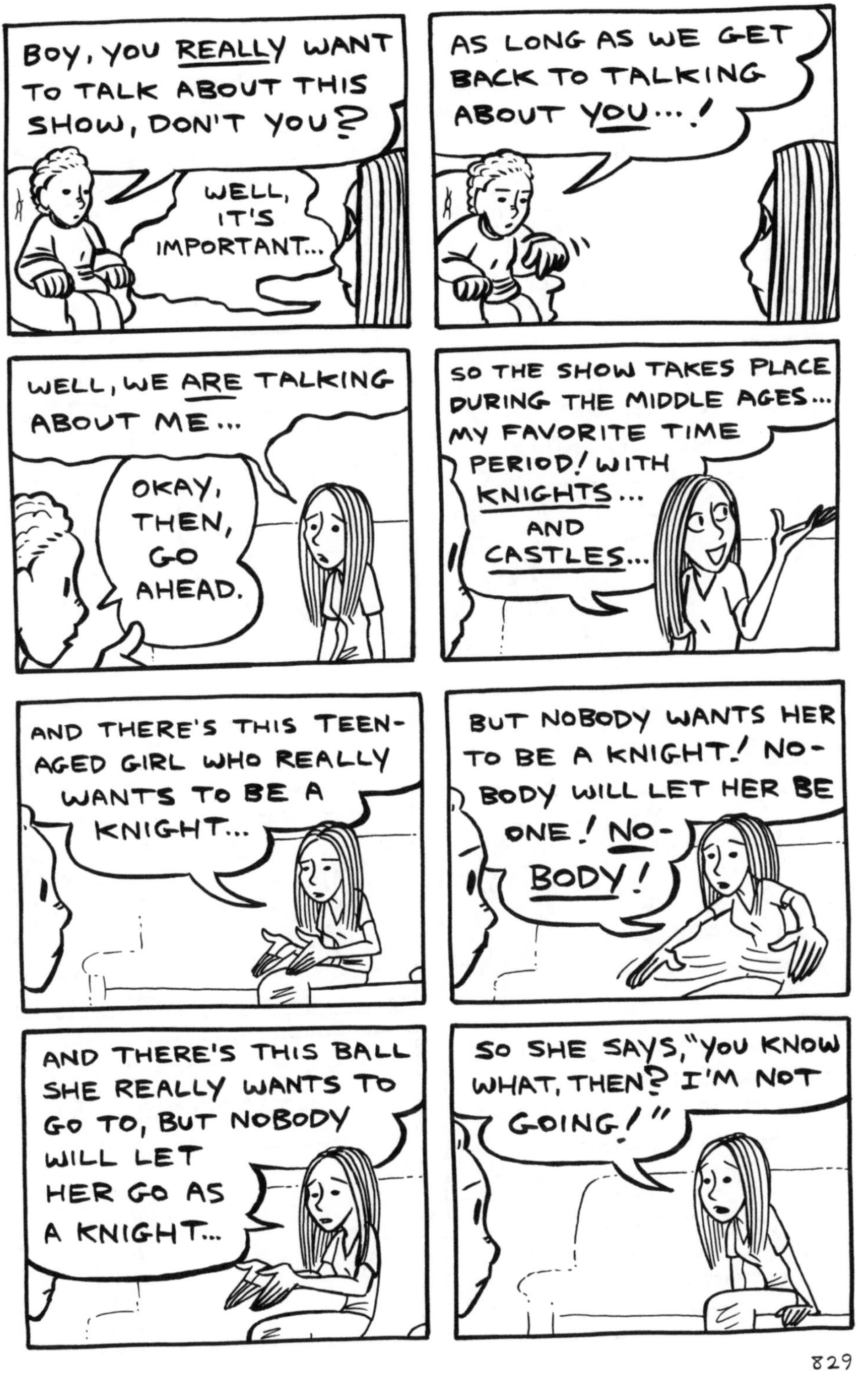
BOY, YOU REALLY WANT TO TALK ABOUT THIS SHOW, DON'T YOU?
WELL, IT'S IMPORTANT...
AS LONG AS WE GET BACK TO TALKING ABOUT YOU...!
WELL, WE ARE TALKING ABOUT ME...
OKAY, THEN, GO AHEAD.
SO THE SHOW TAKES PLACE DURING THE MIDDLE AGES... MY FAVORITE TIME PERIOD! WITH KNIGHTS... AND CASTLES...
AND THERE'S THIS TEEN-AGED GIRL WHO REALLY WANTS TO BE A KNIGHT...
BUT NOBODY WANTS HER TO BE A KNIGHT! NO-BODY WILL LET HER BE ONE! NO-BODY!
AND THERE'S THIS BALL SHE REALLY WANTS TO GO TO, BUT NOBODY WILL LET HER GO AS A KNIGHT...
SO SHE SAYS, "YOU KNOW WHAT, THEN? I'M NOT GOING!"

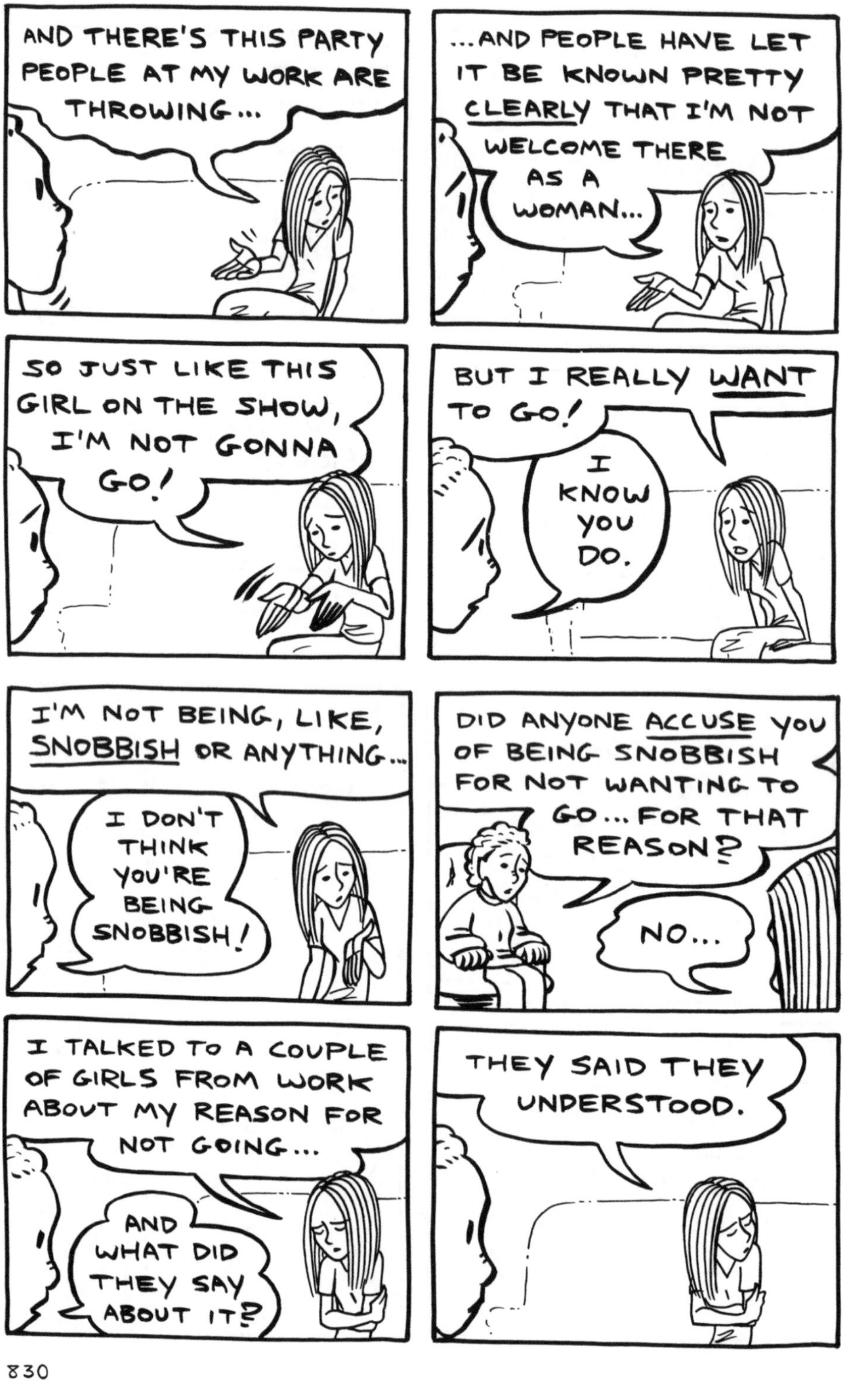
AND THERE'S THIS PARTY PEOPLE AT MY WORK ARE THROWING...
...AND PEOPLE HAVE LET IT BE KNOWN PRETTY CLEARLY THAT I'M NOT WELCOME THERE AS A WOMAN...
SO JUST LIKE THIS GIRL ON THE SHOW, I'M NOT GONNA GO!
BUT I REALLY WANT TO GO!
I KNOW YOU DO.
I'M NOT BEING, LIKE, SNOBBISH OR ANYTHING...
I DON'T THINK YOU'RE BEING SNOBBISH!
DID ANYONE ACCUSE YOU OF BEING SNOBBISH FOR NOT WANTING TO GO... FOR THAT REASON?
NO...
I TALKED TO A COUPLE OF GIRLS FROM WORK ABOUT MY REASON FOR NOT GOING...
AND WHAT DID THEY SAY ABOUT IT?
THEY SAID THEY UNDERSTOOD.

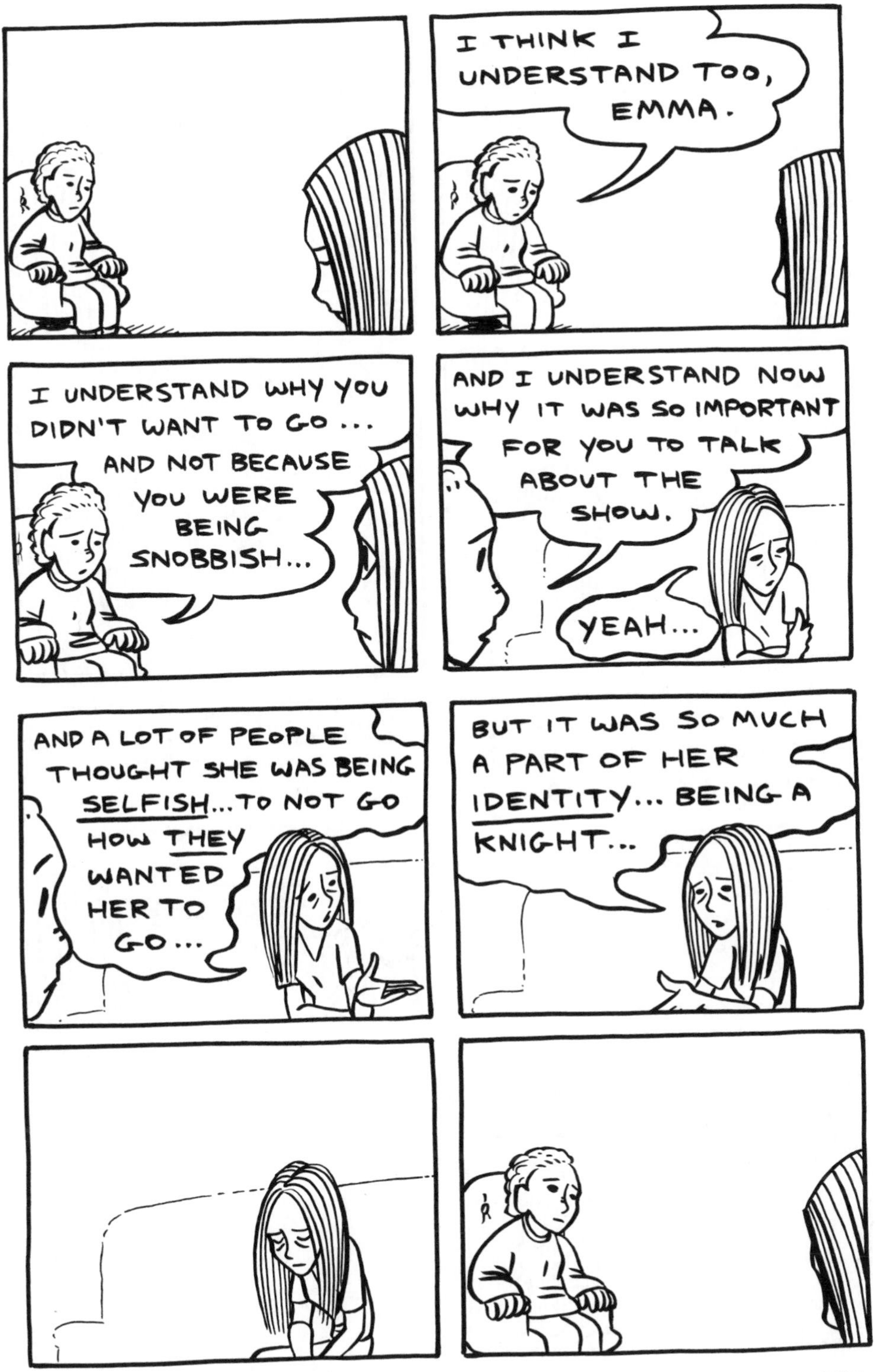
I THINK I UNDERSTAND TOO, EMMA.
I UNDERSTAND WHY YOU DIDN'T WANT TO GO ...
AND NOT BECAUSE YOU WERE BEING SNOBBISH...
AND I UNDERSTAND NOW WHY IT WAS SO IMPORTANT FOR YOU TO TALK ABOUT THE SHOW.
YEAH...
AND A LOT OF PEOPLE THOUGHT SHE WAS BEING SELFISH...TO NOT GO HOW THEY WANTED HER TO GO...
BUT IT WAS SO MUCH A PART OF HER IDENTITY... BEING A KNIGHT...

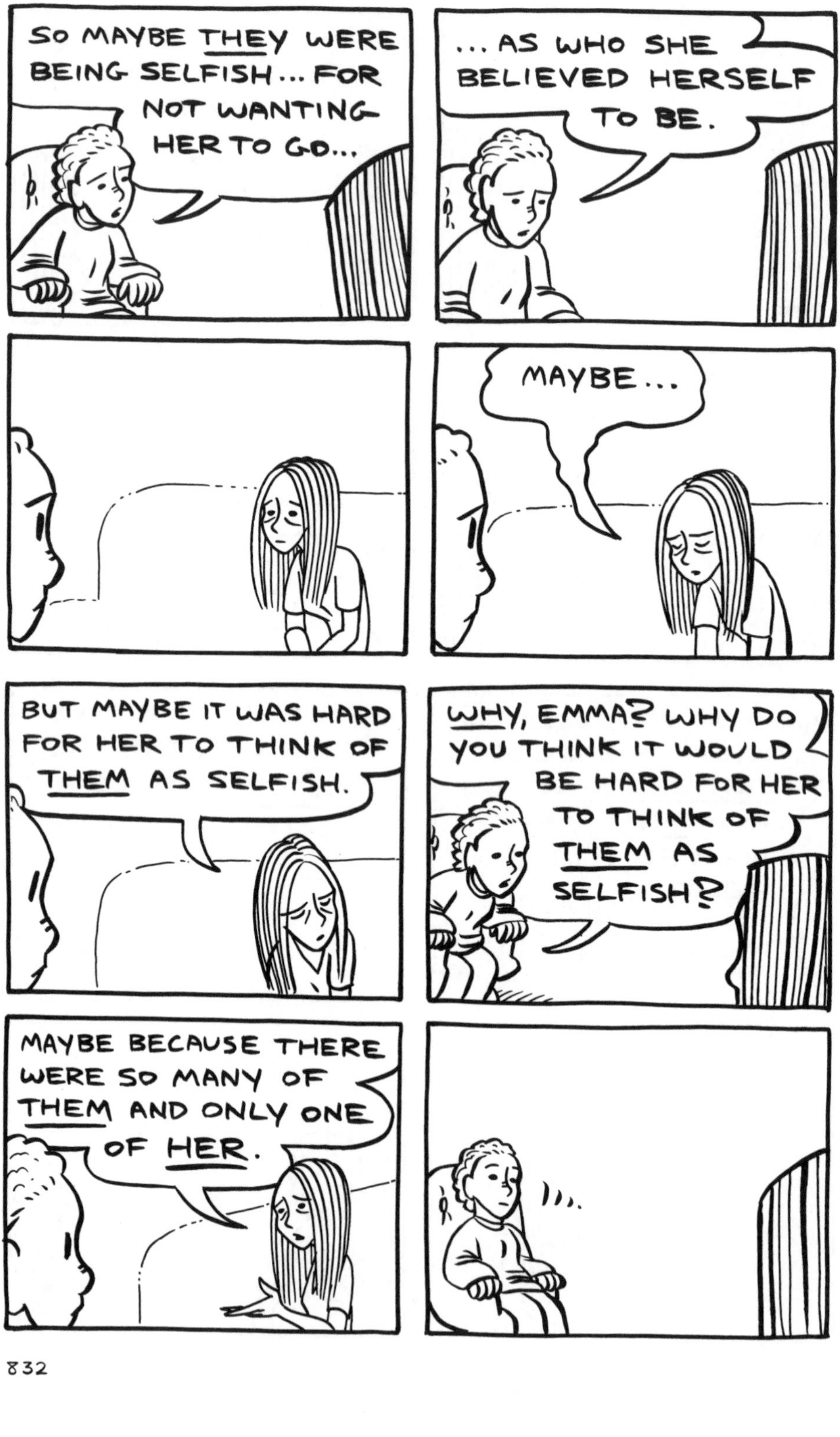
SO MAYBE THEY WERE BEING SELFISH... FOR NOT WANTING HER TO GO...
...AS WHO SHE BELIEVED HERSELF TO BE.
MAYBE...
BUT MAYBE IT WAS HARD FOR HER TO THINK OF THEM AS SELFISH.
WHY, EMMA? WHY DO YOU THINK IT WOULD BE HARD FOR HER TO THINK OF THEM AS SELFISH?
MAYBE BECAUSE THERE WERE SO MANY OF THEM AND ONLY ONE OF HER.

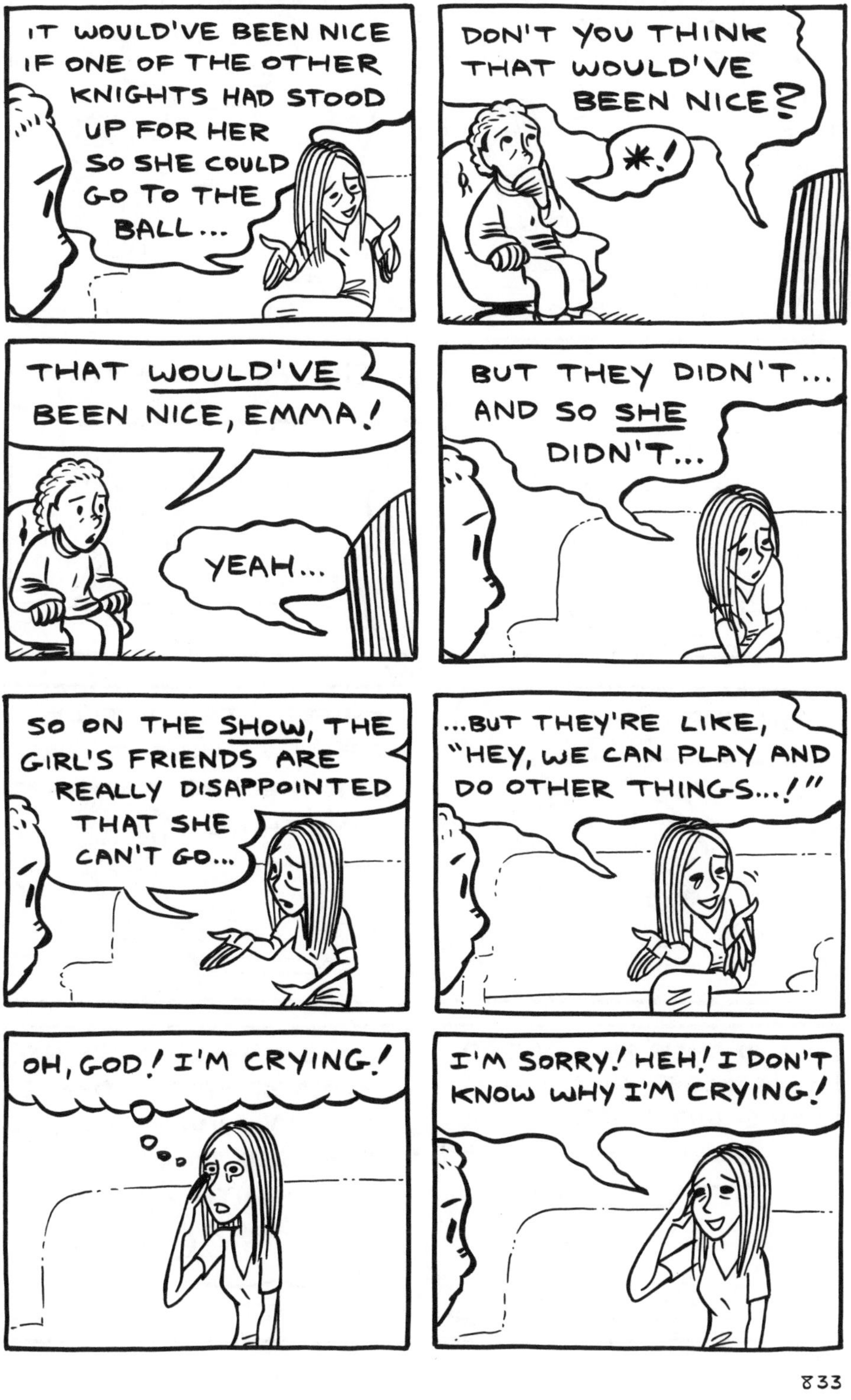
IT WOULD'VE BEEN NICE IF ONE OF THE OTHER KNIGHTS HAD STOOD UP FOR HER SO SHE COULD GO TO THE BALL...
DON'T YOU THINK THAT WOULD'VE BEEN NICE?
*!
THAT WOULD'VE BEEN NICE, EMMA!
YEAH...
BUT THEY DIDN'T... AND SO SHE DIDN'T...
SO ON THE SHOW, THE GIRL'S FRIENDS ARE REALLY DISAPPOINTED THAT SHE CAN'T GO...
...BUT THEY'RE LIKE, "HEY, WE CAN PLAY AND DO OTHER THINGS...!"
OH, GOD! I'M CRYING!
I'M SORRY! HEH! I DON'T KNOW WHY I'M CRYING!

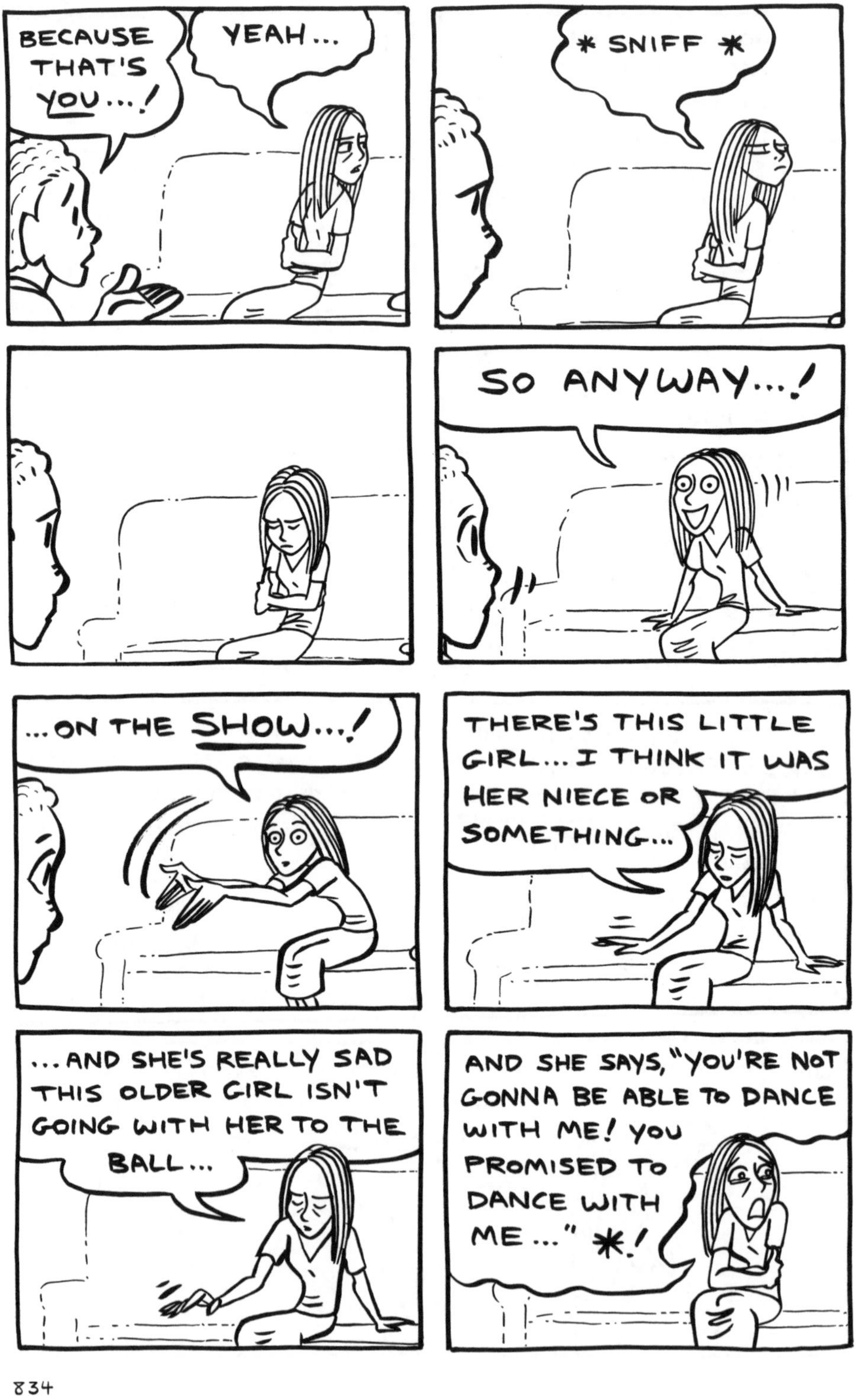
BECAUSE THAT'S YOU...!
YEAH...
* SNIFF *
SO ANYWAY...!
...ON THE SHOW...!
THERE'S THIS LITTLE GIRL... I THINK IT WAS HER NIECE OR SOMETHING...
...AND SHE'S REALLY SAD THIS OLDER GIRL ISN'T GOING WITH HER TO THE BALL...
AND SHE SAYS, "YOU'RE NOT GONNA BE ABLE TO DANCE WITH ME! YOU PROMISED TO DANCE WITH ME..." *!

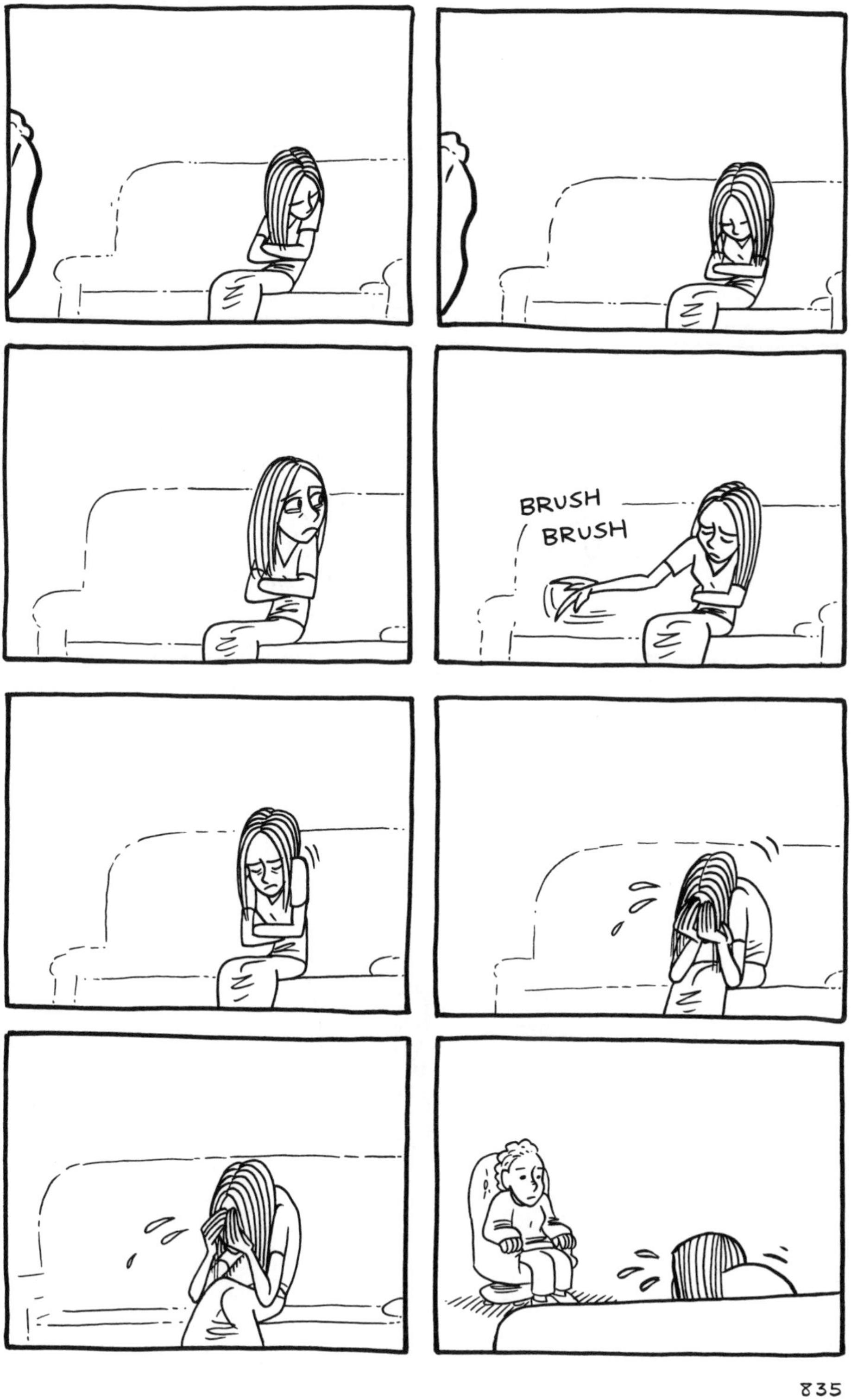
BRUSH
BRUSH

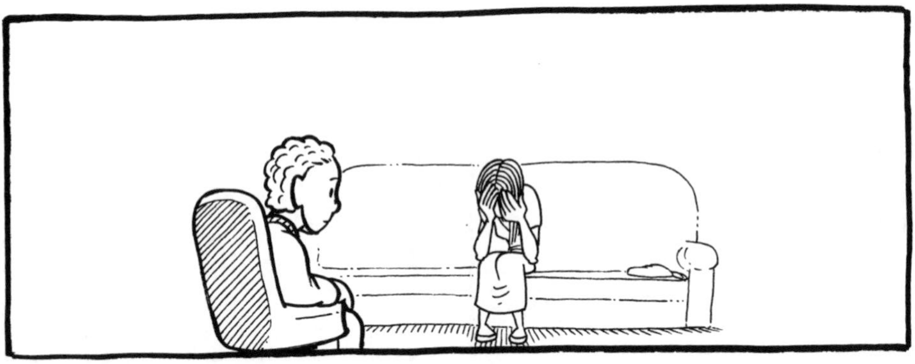

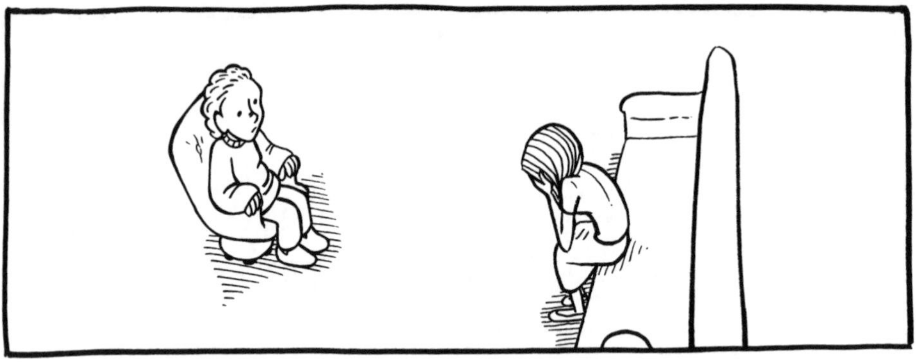

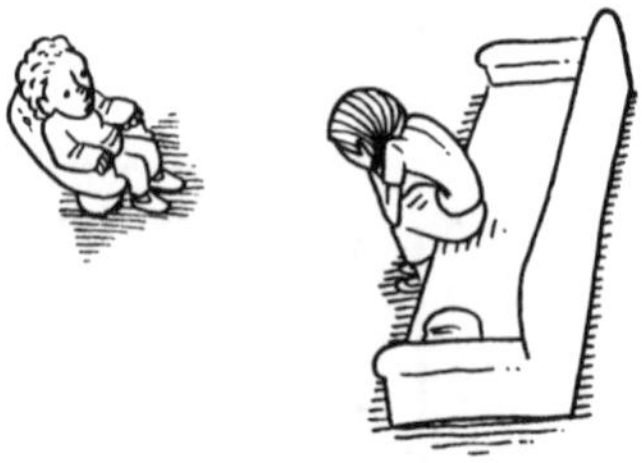

SAFE

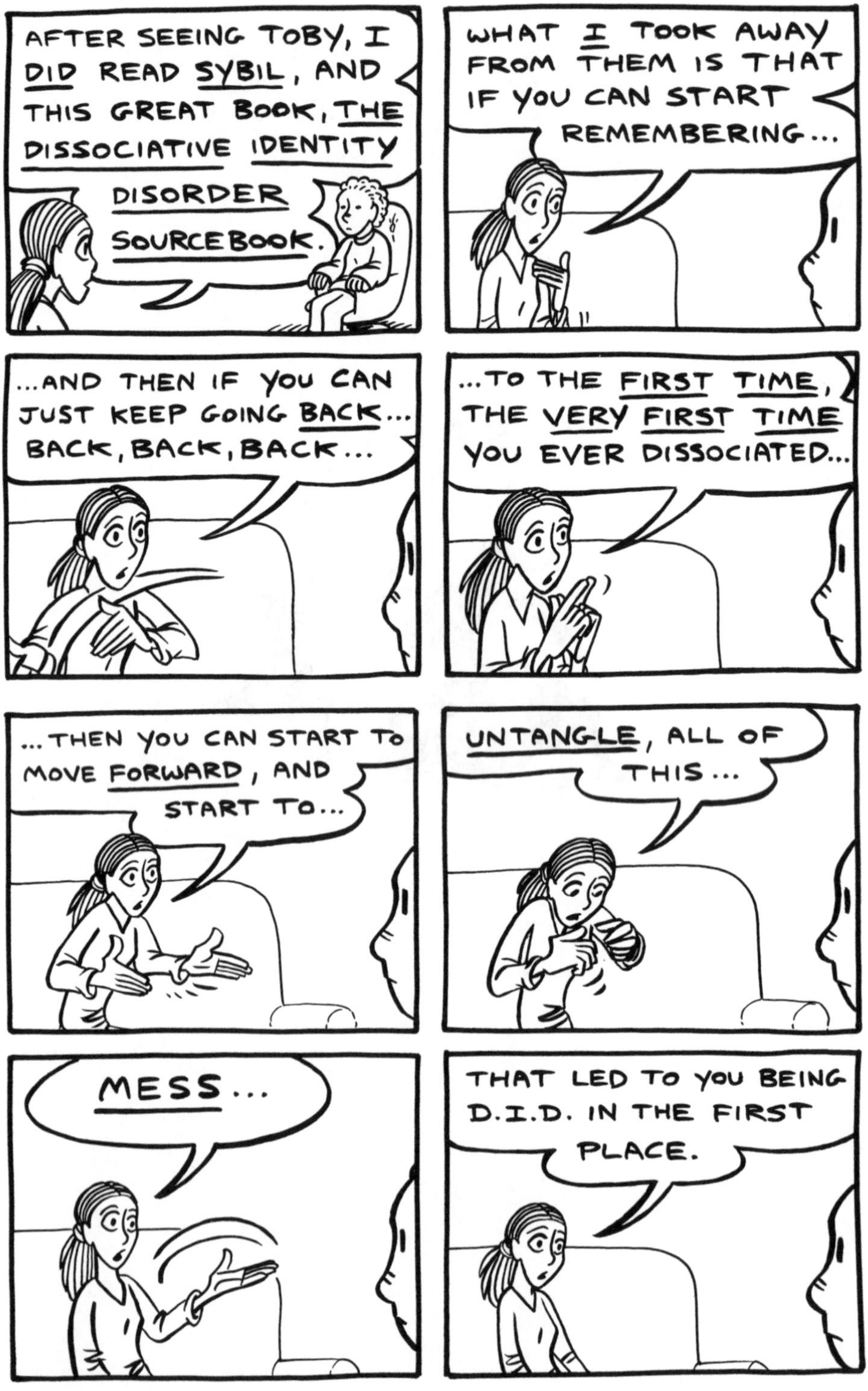
AFTER SEEING TOBY, I DID READ SYBIL, AND THIS GREAT BOOK, THE DISSOCIATIVE IDENTITY DISORDER SOURCEBOOK.
WHAT I TOOK AWAY FROM THEM IS THAT IF YOU CAN START REMEMBERING...
...AND THEN IF YOU CAN JUST KEEP GOING BACK... BACK, BACK, BACK...
...TO THE FIRST TIME, THE VERY FIRST TIME YOU EVER DISSOCIATED...
...THEN YOU CAN START TO MOVE FORWARD, AND START TO...
UNTANGLE, ALL OF THIS...
MESS...
THAT LED TO YOU BEING D.I.D. IN THE FIRST PLACE.

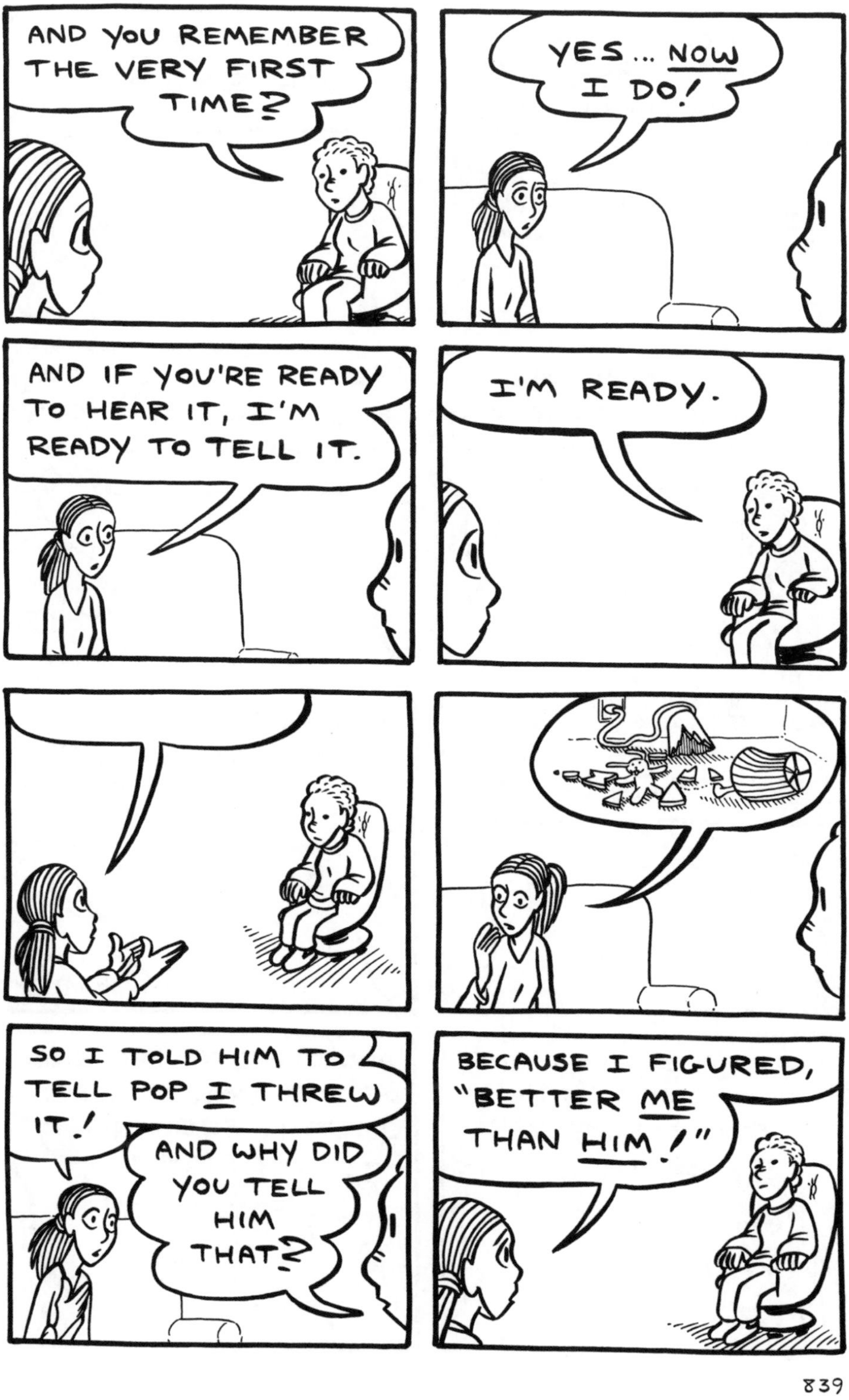
AND YOU REMEMBER THE VERY FIRST TIME?
YES... NOW I DO!
AND IF YOU'RE READY TO HEAR IT, I'M READY TO TELL IT.
I'M READY.
SO I TOLD HIM TO TELL POP I THREW IT!
AND WHY DID YOU TELL HIM THAT?
BECAUSE I FIGURED, "BETTER ME THAN HIM!"

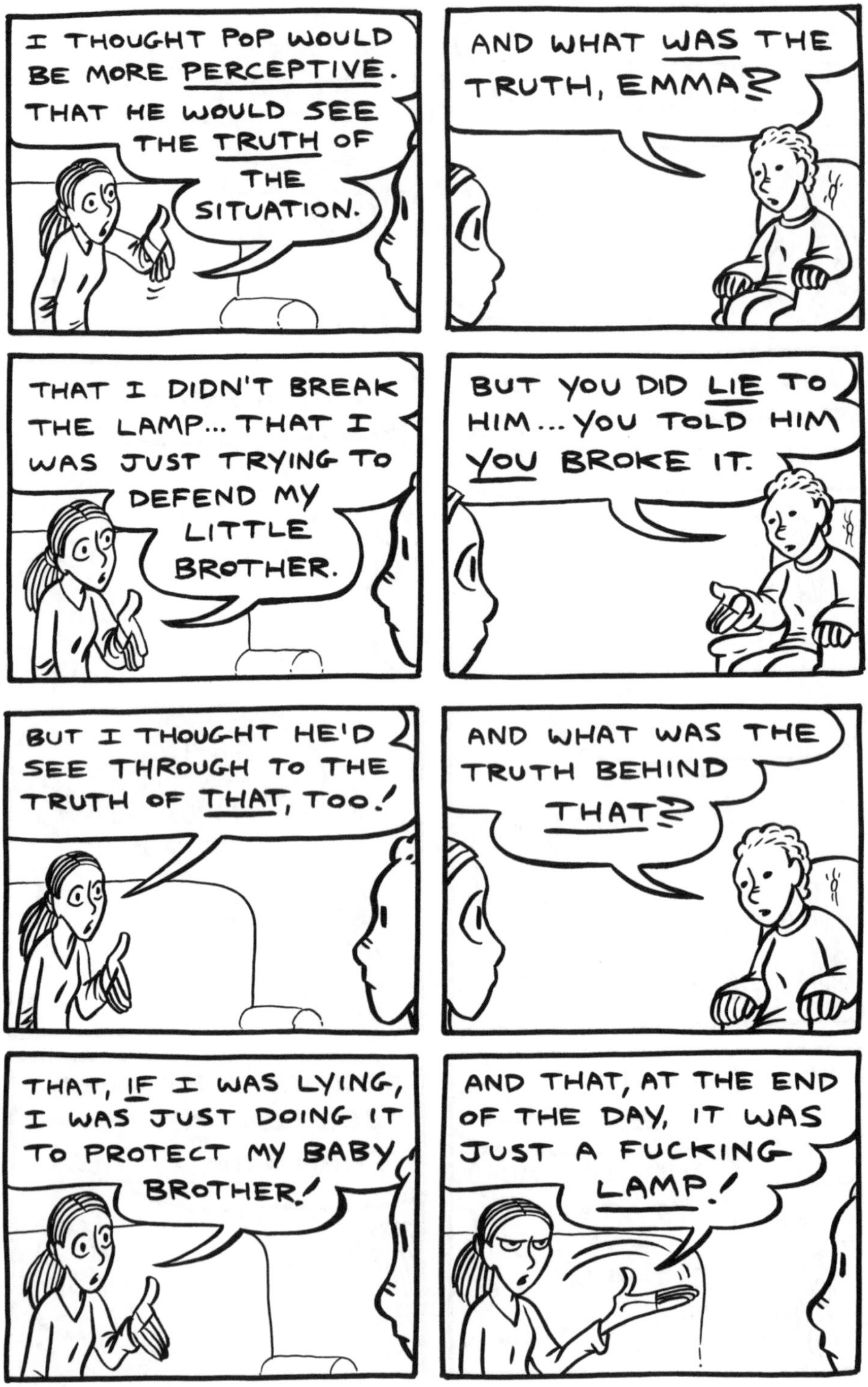
I THOUGHT POP WOULD BE MORE PERCEPTIVE. THAT HE WOULD SEE THE TRUTH OF THE SITUATION.
AND WHAT WAS THE TRUTH, EMMA?
THAT I DIDN'T BREAK THE LAMP... THAT I WAS JUST TRYING TO DEFEND MY LITTLE BROTHER.
BUT YOU DID LIE TO HIM... YOU TOLD HIM YOU BROKE IT.
BUT I THOUGHT HE'D SEE THROUGH TO THE TRUTH OF THAT, TOO!
AND WHAT WAS THE TRUTH BEHIND THAT?
THAT, IF I WAS LYING, I WAS JUST DOING IT TO PROTECT MY BABY BROTHER!
AND THAT, AT THE END OF THE DAY, IT WAS JUST A FUCKING LAMP!

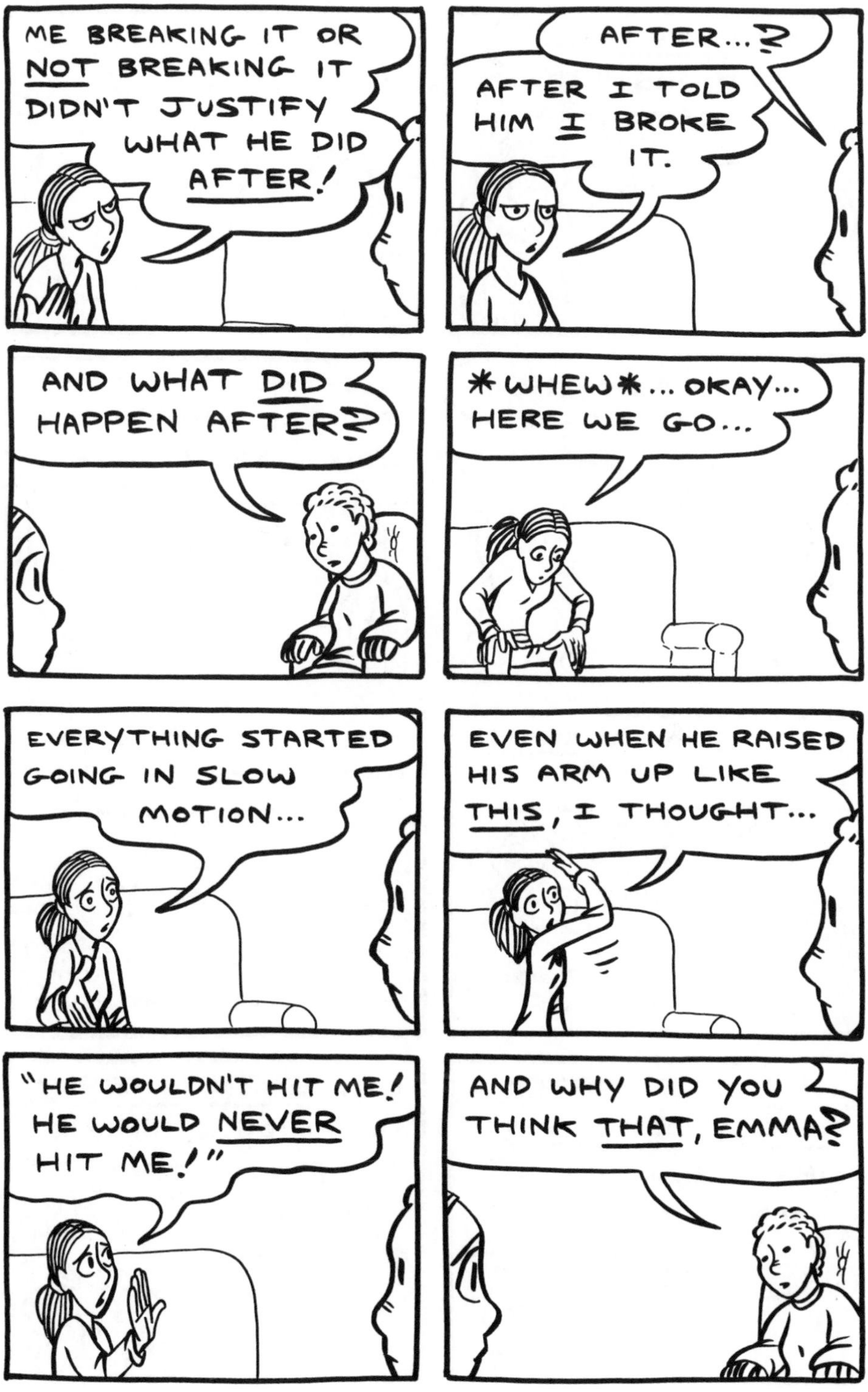
ME BREAKING IT OR NOT BREAKING IT DIDN'T JUSTIFY WHAT HE DID AFTER!
AFTER...?
AFTER I TOLD HIM I BROKE IT.
AND WHAT DID HAPPEN AFTER?
WHEW... OKAY... HERE WE GO...
EVERYTHING STARTED GOING IN SLOW MOTION...
EVEN WHEN HE RAISED HIS ARM UP LIKE THIS, I THOUGHT...
"HE WOULDN'T HIT ME! HE WOULD NEVER HIT ME!"
AND WHY DID YOU THINK THAT, EMMA?

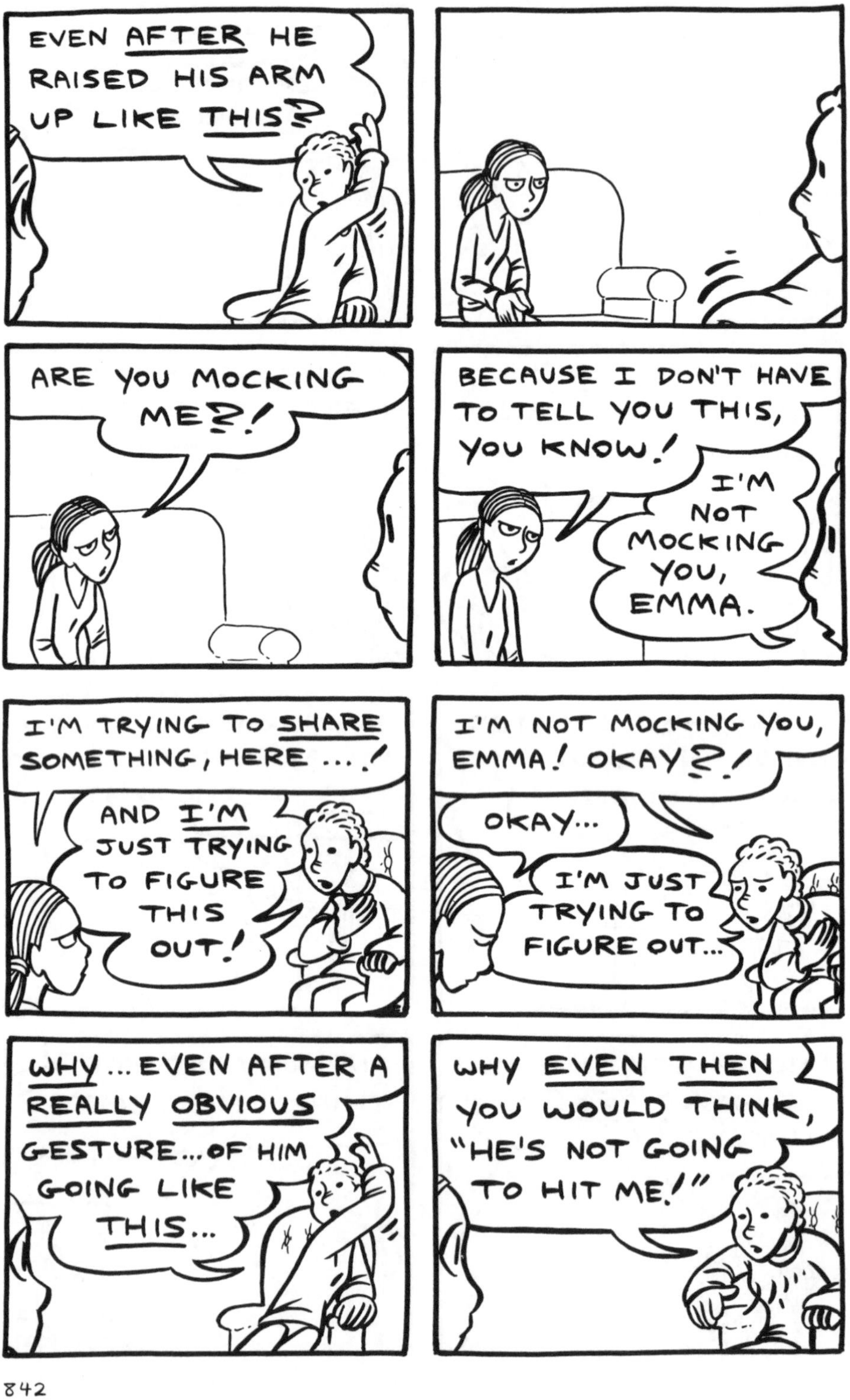
EVEN AFTER HE RAISED HIS ARM UP LIKE THIS?
ARE YOU MOCKING ME?!
BECAUSE I DON'T HAVE TO TELL YOU THIS, YOU KNOW!
I'M NOT MOCKING YOU, EMMA.
I'M TRYING TO SHARE SOMETHING, HERE ...!
AND I'M JUST TRYING TO FIGURE THIS OUT!
I'M NOT MOCKING YOU, EMMA! OKAY?!
OKAY...
I'M JUST TRYING TO FIGURE OUT...
WHY... EVEN AFTER A REALLY OBVIOUS GESTURE... OF HIM GOING LIKE THIS...
WHY EVEN THEN YOU WOULD THINK, "HE'S NOT GOING TO HIT ME!"

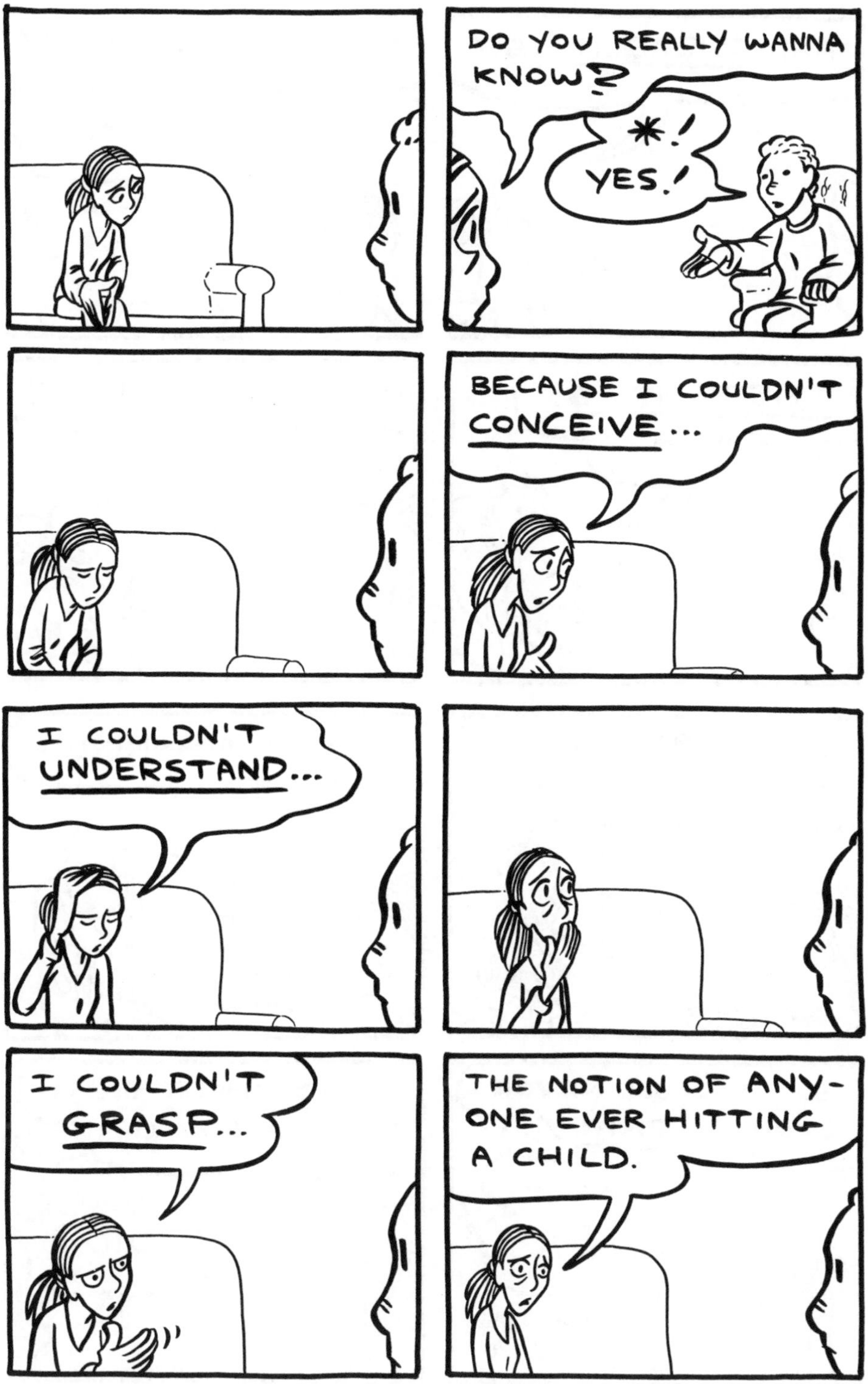
DO YOU REALLY WANNA KNOW?
*!
YES.!
BECAUSE I COULDN'T CONCEIVE...
I COULDN'T UNDERSTAND...
I COULDN'T GRASP...
THE NOTION OF ANY-ONE EVER HITTING A CHILD.

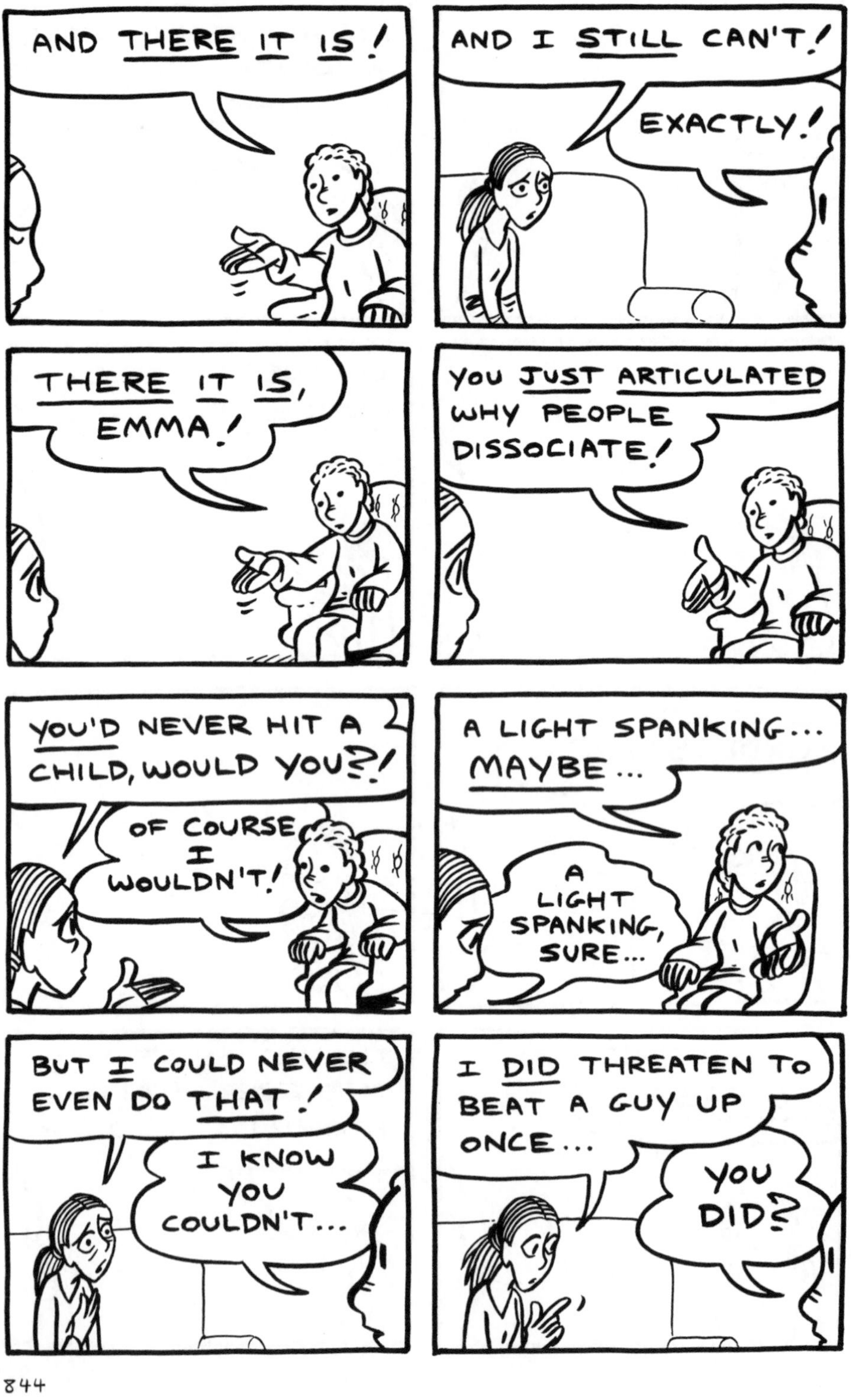
AND THERE IT IS!
AND I STILL CAN'T!
EXACTLY!
THERE IT IS, EMMA!
YOU JUST ARTICULATED WHY PEOPLE DISSOCIATE!
YOU'D NEVER HIT A CHILD, WOULD YOU?!
OF COURSE I WOULDN'T!
A LIGHT SPANKING... MAYBE...
A LIGHT SPANKING, SURE...
BUT I COULD NEVER EVEN DO THAT!
I KNOW YOU COULDN'T...
I DID THREATEN TO BEAT A GUY UP ONCE...
YOU DID?

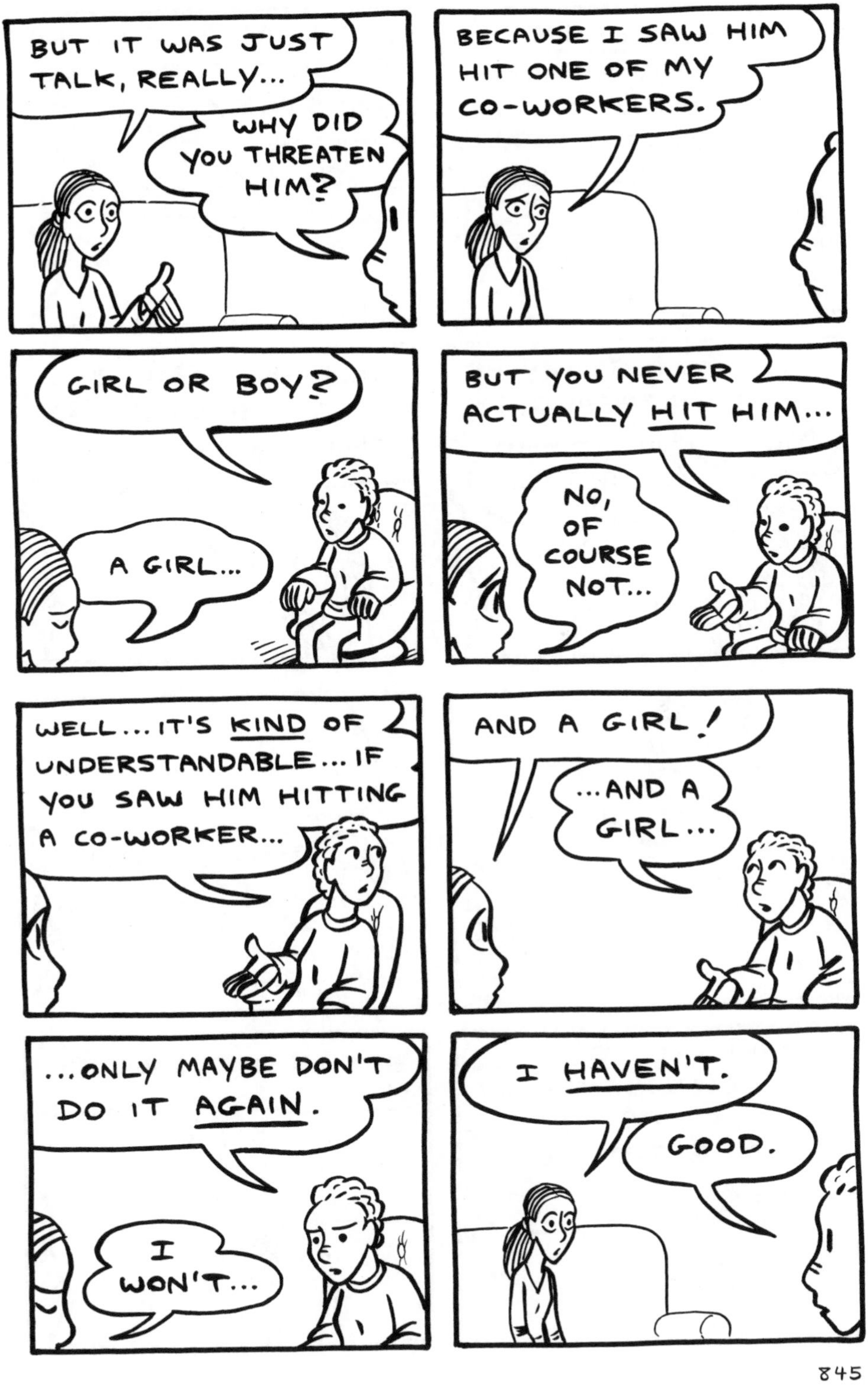
BUT IT WAS JUST TALK, REALLY...
WHY DID YOU THREATEN HIM?
BECAUSE I SAW HIM HIT ONE OF MY CO-WORKERS.
GIRL OR BOY?
A GIRL...
BUT YOU NEVER ACTUALLY HIT HIM...
NO, OF COURSE NOT...
WELL... IT'S KIND OF UNDERSTANDABLE... IF YOU SAW HIM HITTING A CO-WORKER...
AND A GIRL!
...AND A GIRL...
...ONLY MAYBE DON'T DO IT AGAIN.
I WON'T...
I HAVEN'T.
GOOD.

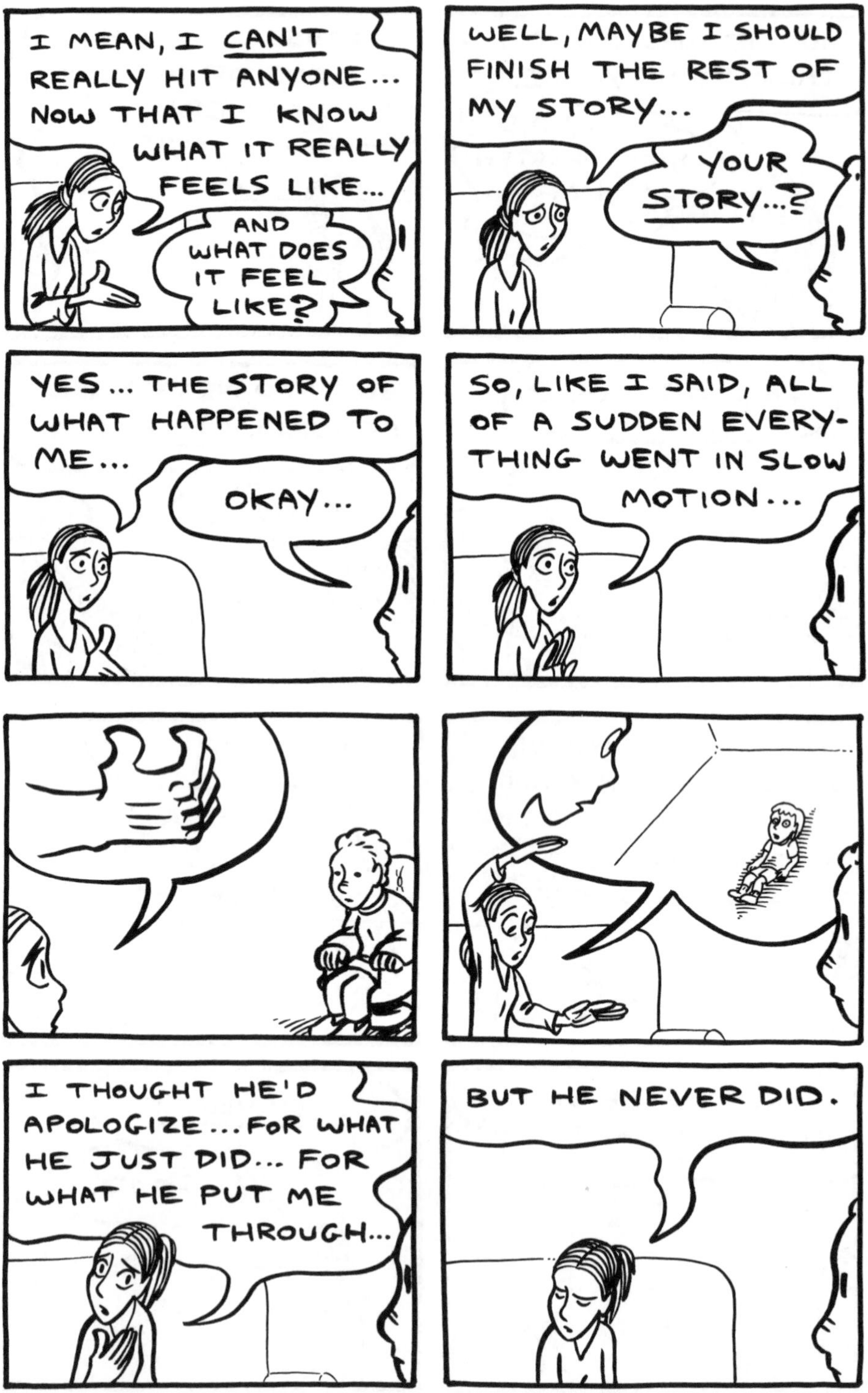

I MEAN, I CAN'T REALLY HIT ANYONE... NOW THAT I KNOW WHAT IT REALLY FEELS LIKE...
AND WHAT DOES IT FEEL LIKE?
WELL, MAYBE I SHOULD FINISH THE REST OF MY STORY...
YOUR STORY...?
YES... THE STORY OF WHAT HAPPENED TO ME...
OKAY...
SO, LIKE I SAID, ALL OF A SUDDEN EVERY-THING WENT IN SLOW MOTION...
I THOUGHT HE'D APOLOGIZE... FOR WHAT HE JUST DID... FOR WHAT HE PUT ME THROUGH...
BUT HE NEVER DID.

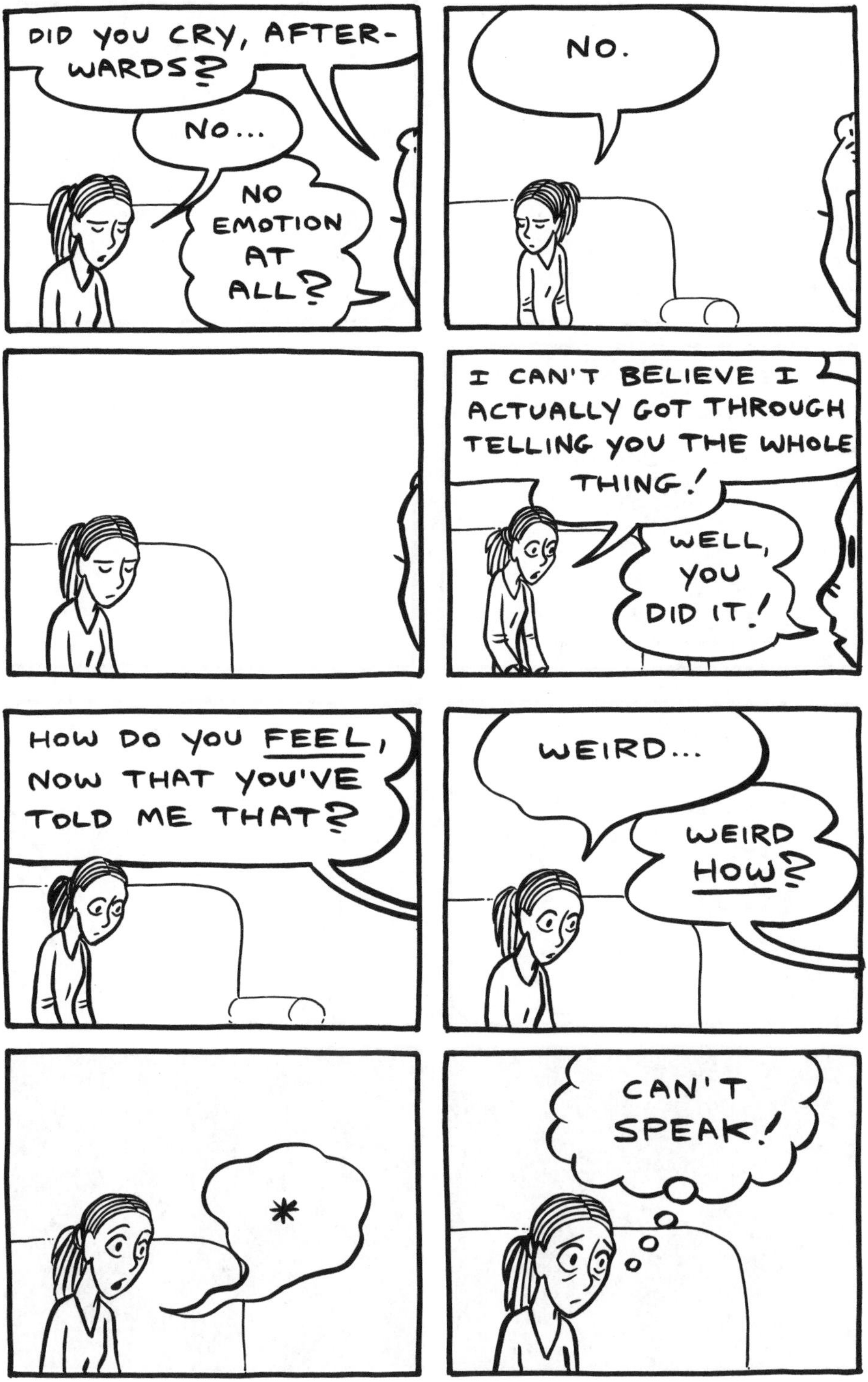
DID YOU CRY, AFTER-WARDS?
NO...
NO EMOTION AT ALL?
NO.
I CAN'T BELIEVE I ACTUALLY GOT THROUGH TELLING YOU THE WHOLE THING!
WELL, YOU DID IT!
HOW DO YOU FEEL, NOW THAT YOU'VE TOLD ME THAT?
WEIRD...
WEIRD HOW?
*
CAN'T SPEAK!

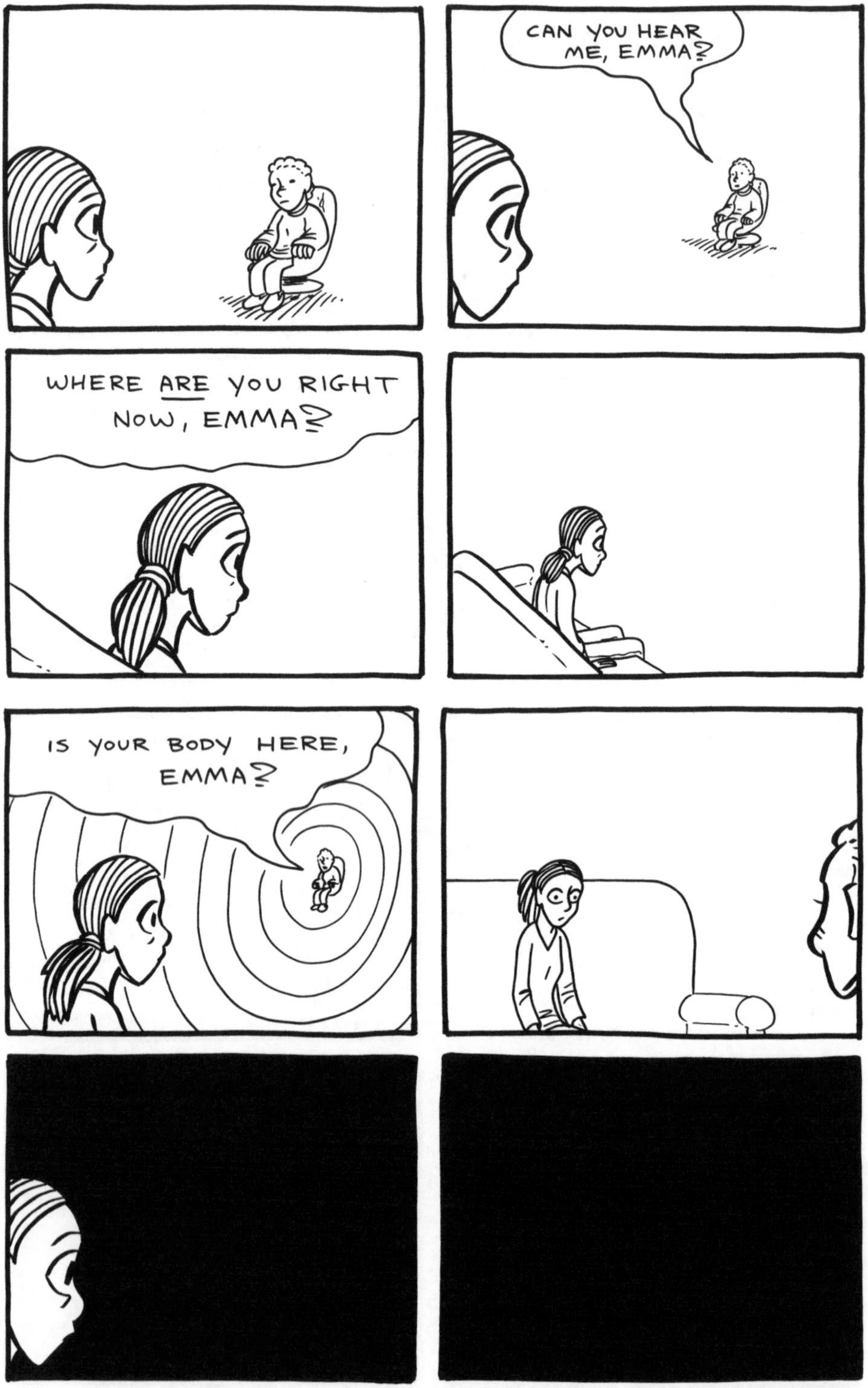
CAN YOU HEAR ME, EMMA?
WHERE ARE YOU RIGHT NOW, EMMA?
IS YOUR BODY HERE, EMMA?

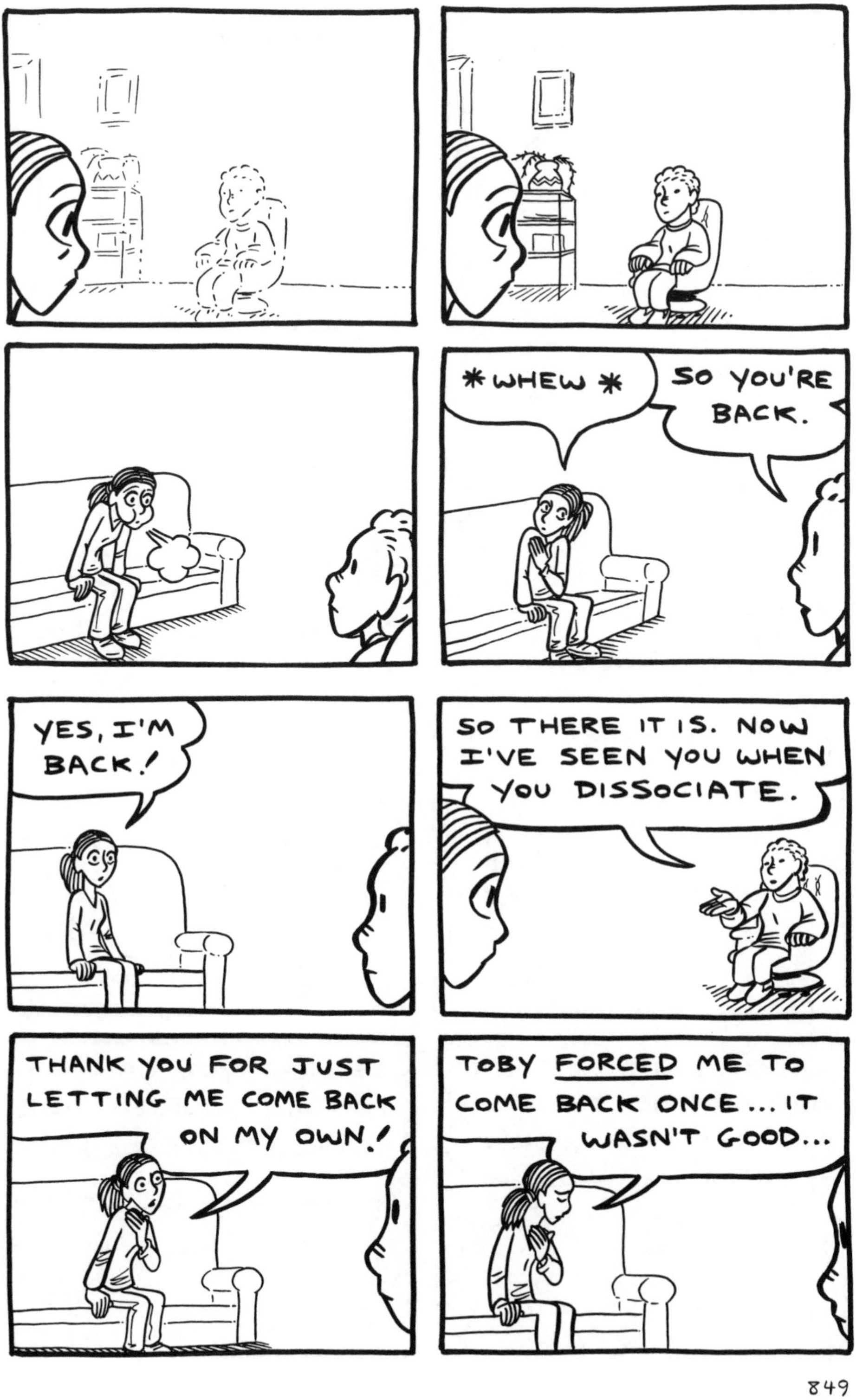
WHEW
SO YOU'RE BACK.
YES, I'M BACK!
SO THERE IT IS. NOW I'VE SEEN YOU WHEN YOU DISSOCIATE.
THANK YOU FOR JUST LETTING ME COME BACK ON MY OWN!
TOBY FORCED ME TO COME BACK ONCE... IT WASN'T GOOD...

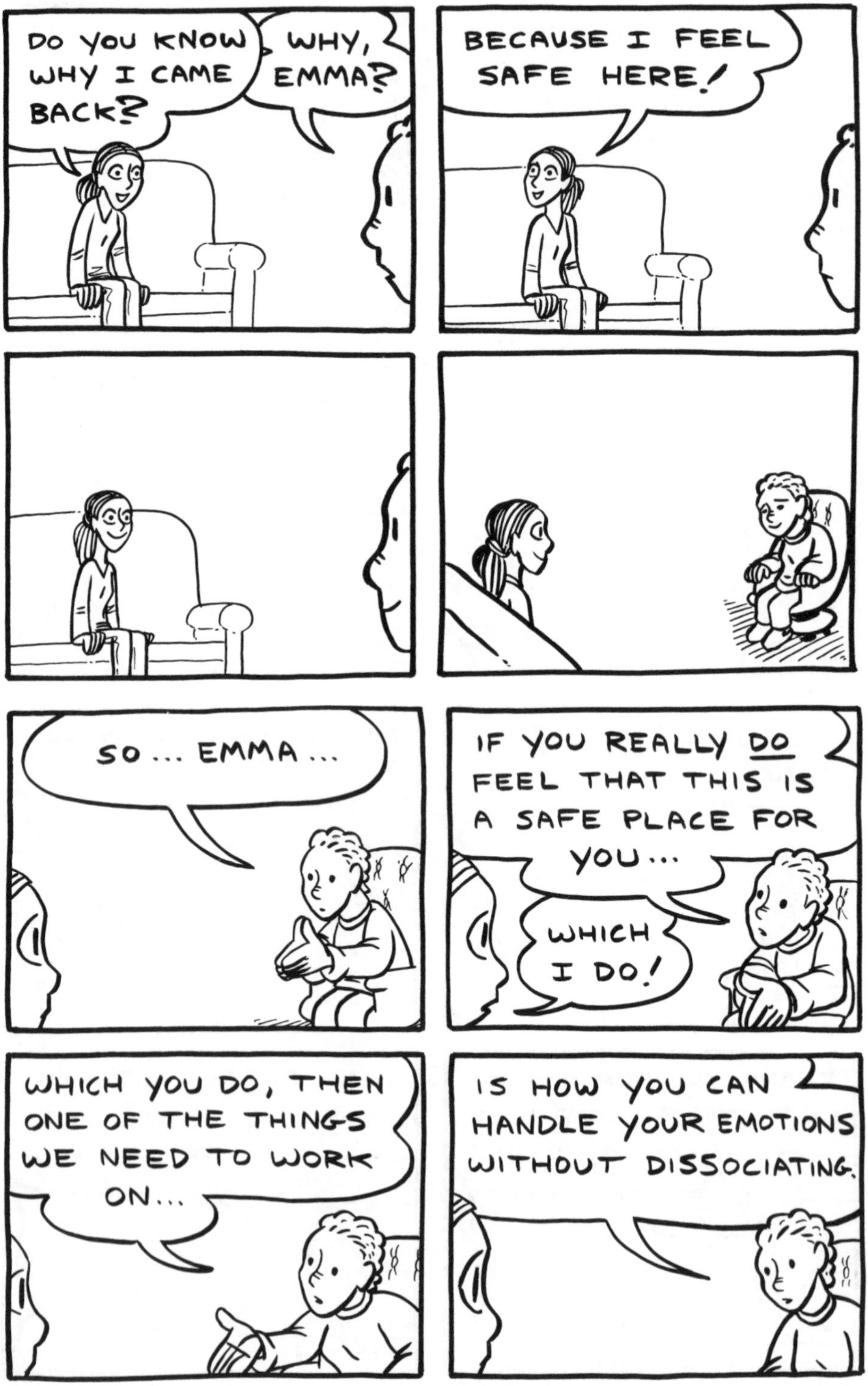
DO YOU KNOW WHY I CAME BACK?
WHY, EMMA?
BECAUSE I FEEL SAFE HERE!
SO ... EMMA ...
IF YOU REALLY DO FEEL THAT THIS IS A SAFE PLACE FOR YOU ...
WHICH I DO!
WHICH YOU DO, THEN ONE OF THE THINGS WE NEED TO WORK ON ...
IS HOW YOU CAN HANDLE YOUR EMOTIONS WITHOUT DISSOCIATING.

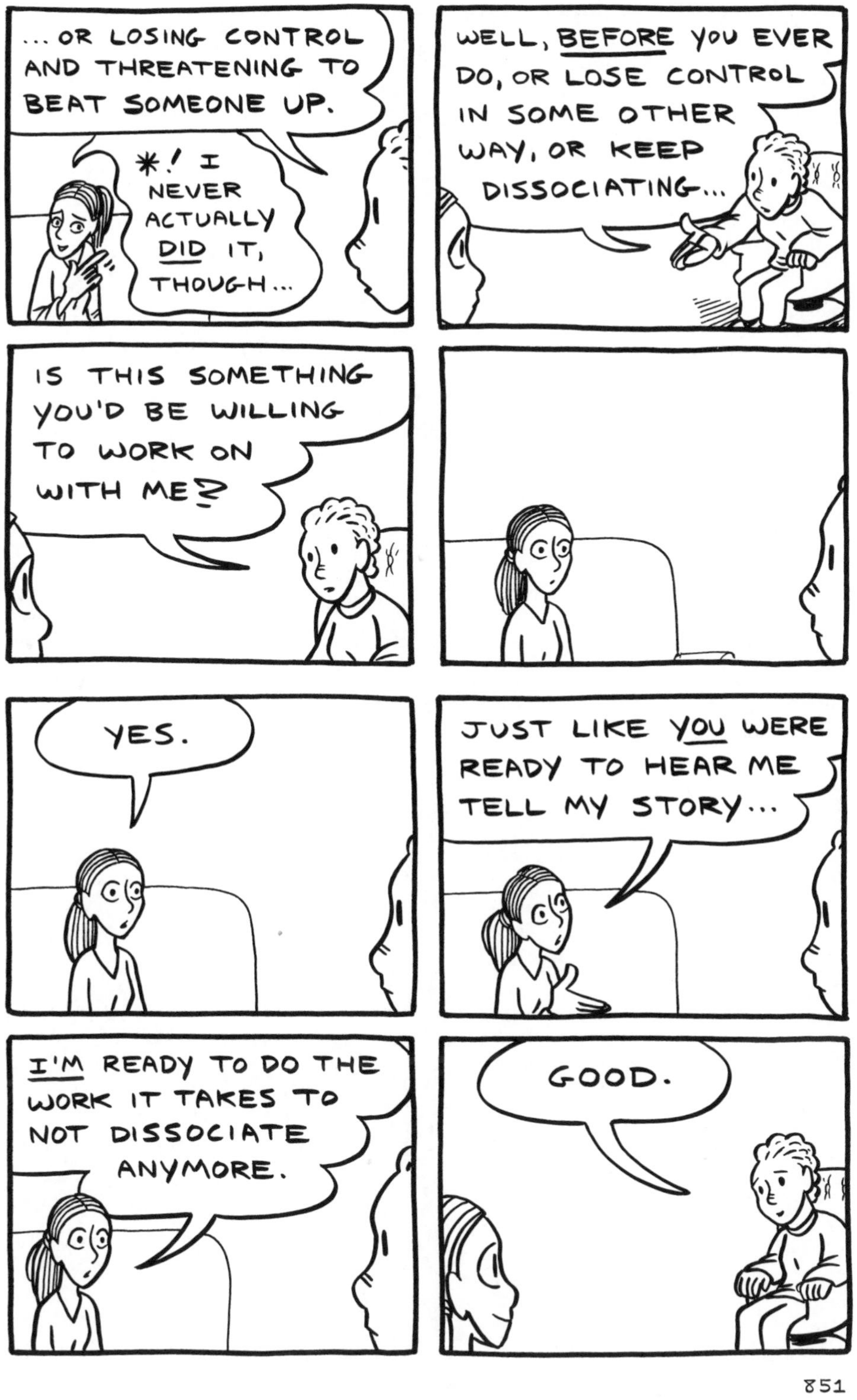
...OR LOSING CONTROL AND THREATENING TO BEAT SOMEONE UP.
*! I NEVER ACTUALLY DID IT, THOUGH...
WELL, BEFORE YOU EVER DO, OR LOSE CONTROL IN SOME OTHER WAY, OR KEEP DISSOCIATING...
IS THIS SOMETHING YOU'D BE WILLING TO WORK ON WITH ME?
YES.
JUST LIKE YOU WERE READY TO HEAR ME TELL MY STORY...
I'M READY TO DO THE WORK IT TAKES TO NOT DISSOCIATE ANYMORE.
GOOD.

KATIE

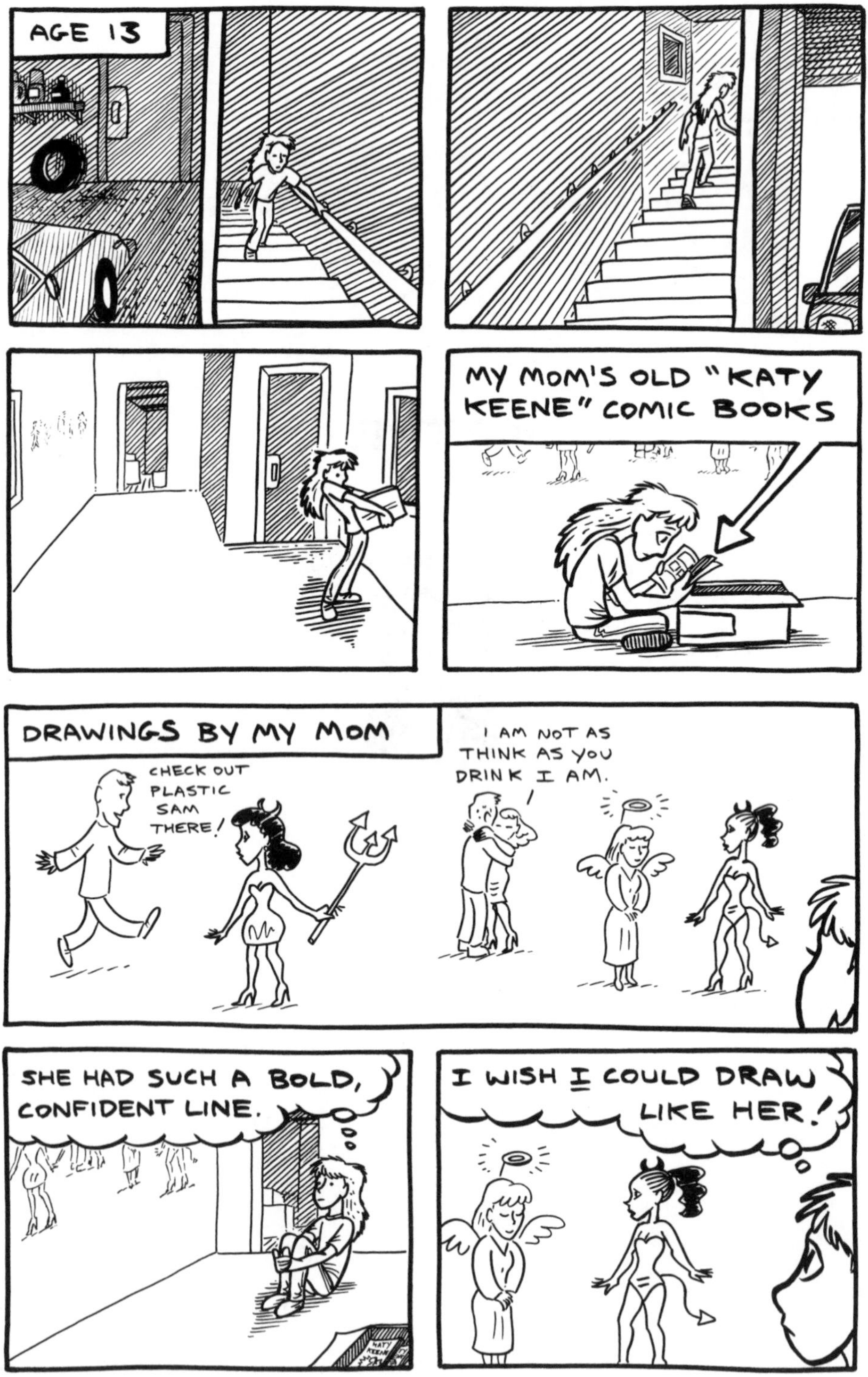

AGE 13
MY MOM'S OLD "KATY KEENE" COMIC BOOKS
DRAWINGS BY MY MOM
CHECK OUT PLASTIC SAM THERE!
I AM NOT AS THINK AS YOU DRINK I AM.
SHE HAD SUCH A BOLD, CONFIDENT LINE.
I WISH I COULD DRAW LIKE HER!

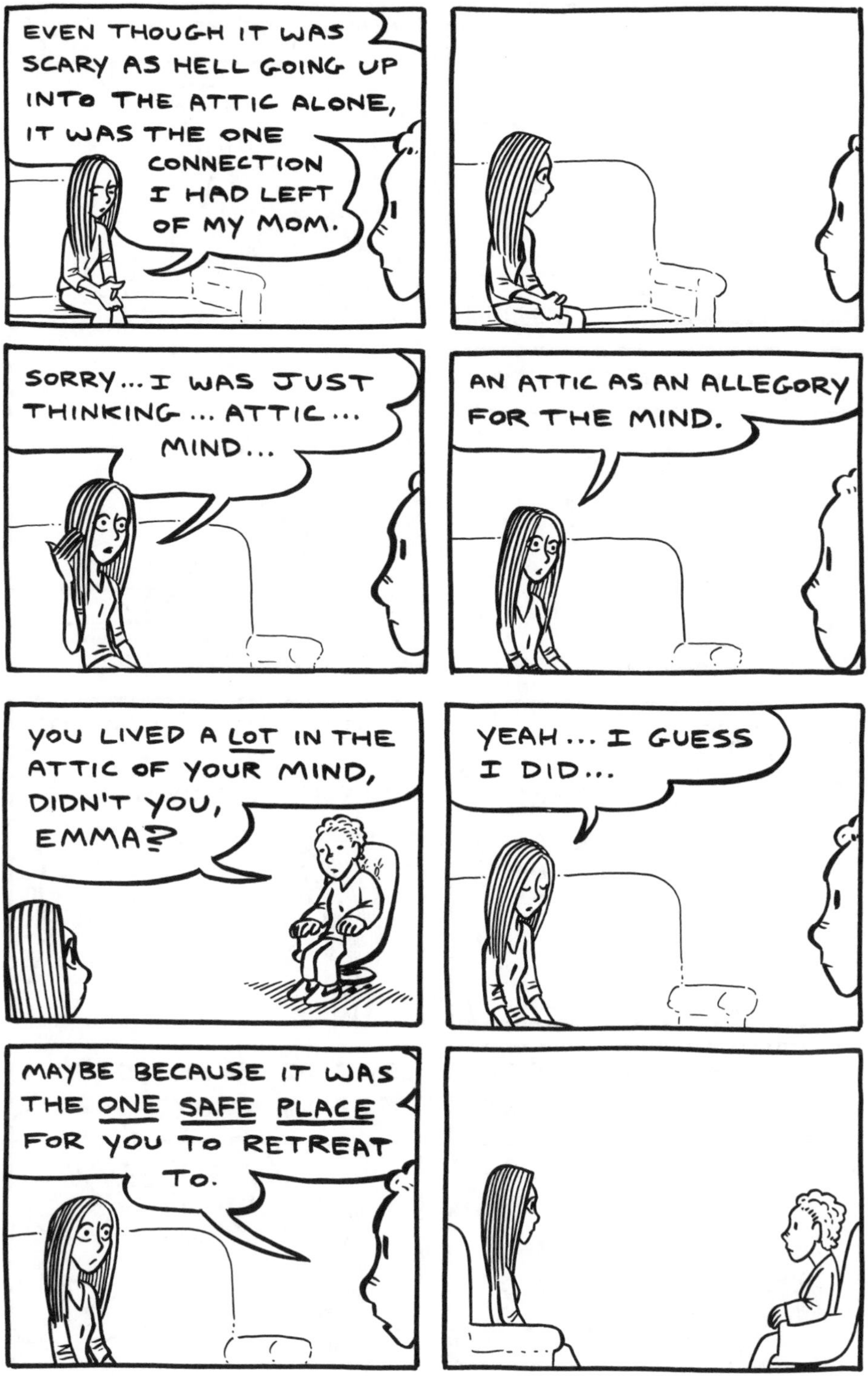
EVEN THOUGH IT WAS SCARY AS HELL GOING UP INTO THE ATTIC ALONE, IT WAS THE ONE CONNECTION I HAD LEFT OF MY MOM.
SORRY... I WAS JUST THINKING... ATTIC... MIND...
AN ATTIC AS AN ALLEGORY FOR THE MIND.
YOU LIVED A LOT IN THE ATTIC OF YOUR MIND, DIDN'T YOU, EMMA?
YEAH... I GUESS I DID...
MAYBE BECAUSE IT WAS THE ONE SAFE PLACE FOR YOU TO RETREAT TO.

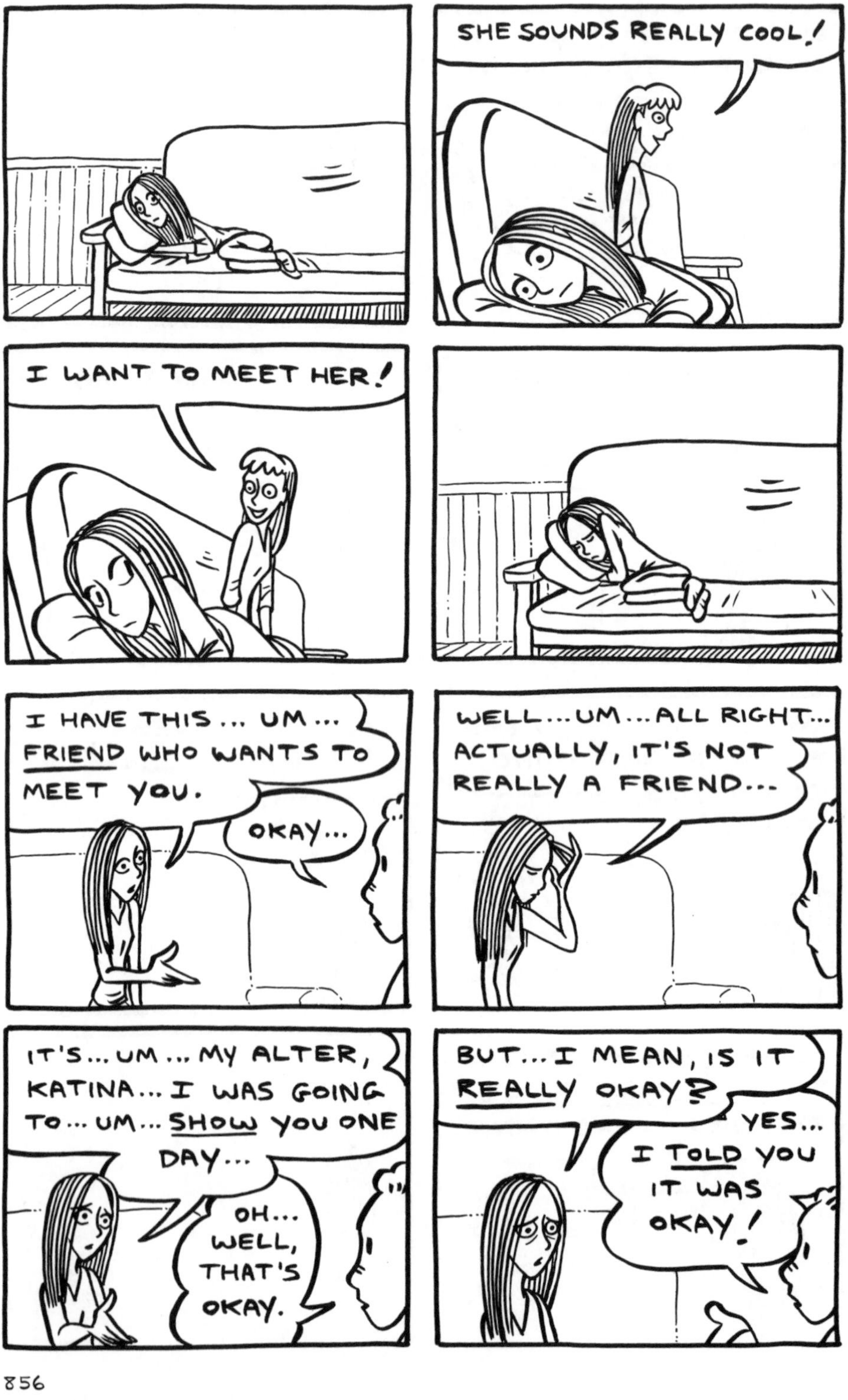
SHE SOUNDS REALLY COOL!
I WANT TO MEET HER!
I HAVE THIS ... UM ... FRIEND WHO WANTS TO MEET YOU.
OKAY...
WELL...UM...ALL RIGHT... ACTUALLY, IT'S NOT REALLY A FRIEND...
IT'S... UM ... MY ALTER, KATINA... I WAS GOING TO... UM... SHOW YOU ONE DAY...
OH... WELL, THAT'S OKAY.
BUT... I MEAN, IS IT REALLY OKAY?
YES... I TOLD YOU IT WAS OKAY!

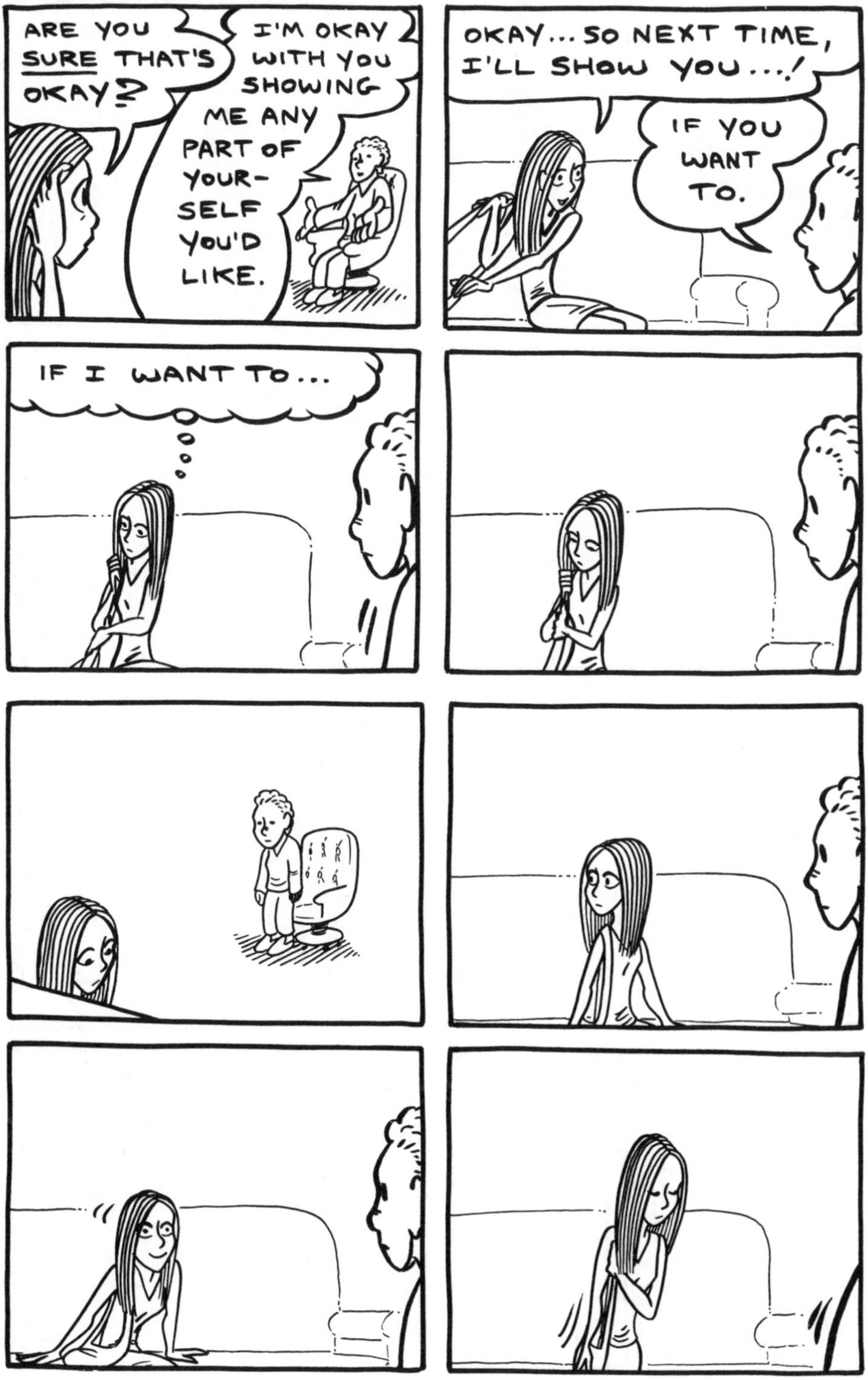
ARE YOU SURE THAT'S OKAY?
I'M OKAY WITH YOU SHOWING ME ANY PART OF YOURSELF YOU'D LIKE.
OKAY... SO NEXT TIME, I'LL SHOW YOU...!
IF YOU WANT TO.
IF I WANT TO...

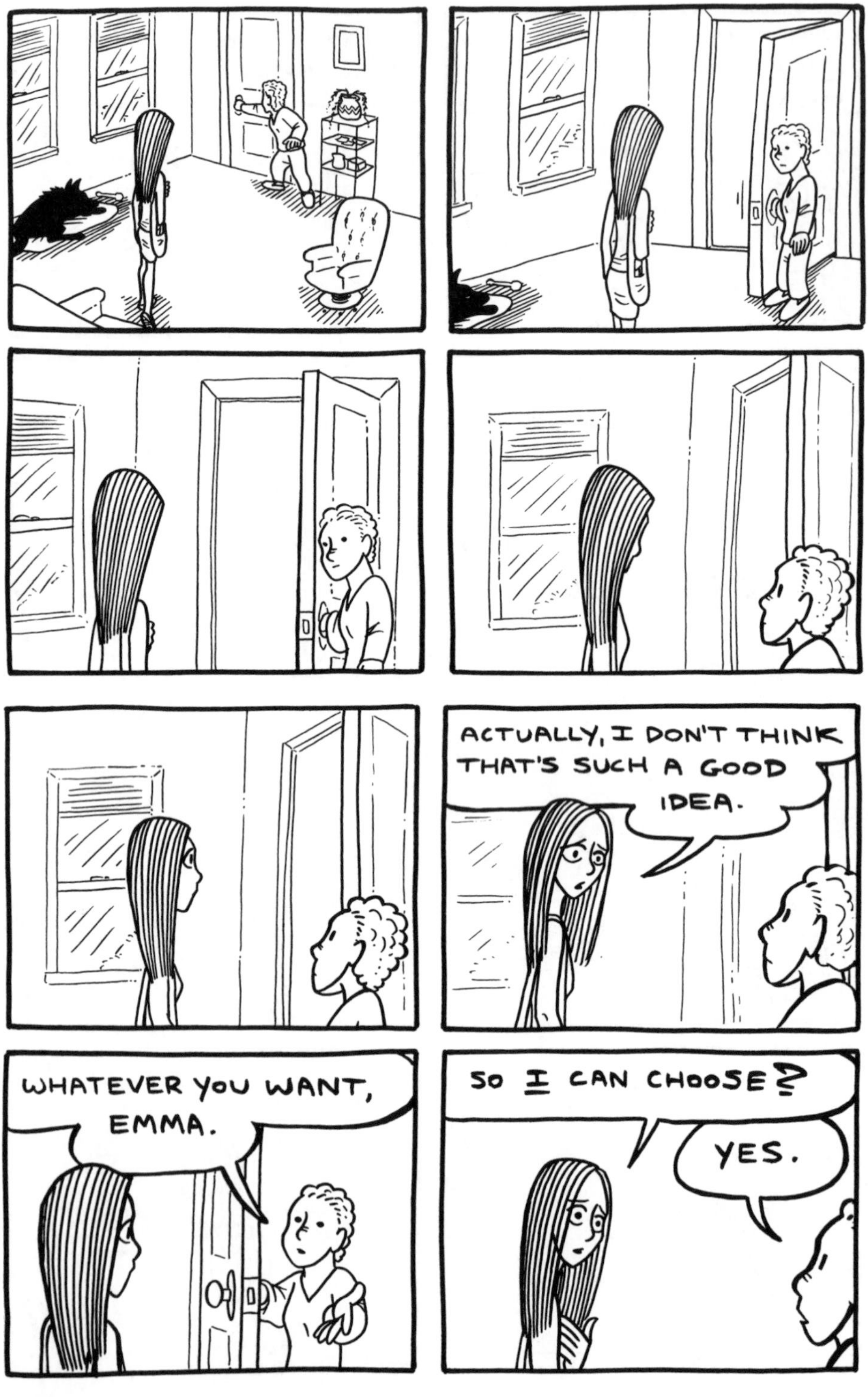
ACTUALLY, I DON'T THINK THAT'S SUCH A GOOD IDEA.
WHATEVER YOU WANT, EMMA.
SO I CAN CHOOSE?
YES.

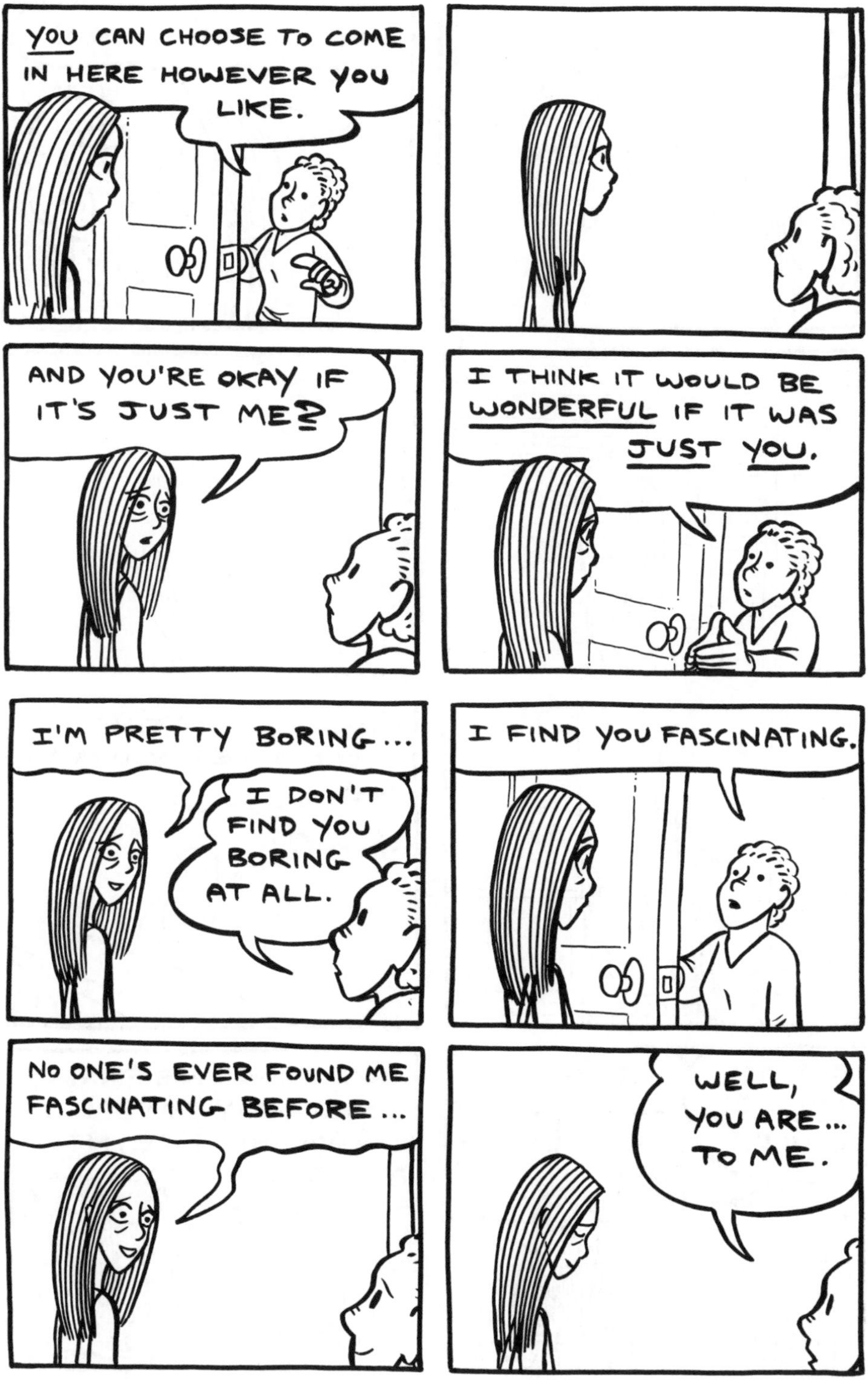
YOU CAN CHOOSE TO COME IN HERE HOWEVER YOU LIKE.
AND YOU'RE OKAY IF IT'S JUST ME?
I THINK IT WOULD BE WONDERFUL IF IT WAS JUST YOU.
I'M PRETTY BORING...
I DON'T FIND YOU BORING AT ALL.
I FIND YOU FASCINATING.
NO ONE'S EVER FOUND ME FASCINATING BEFORE...
WELL, YOU ARE... TO ME.

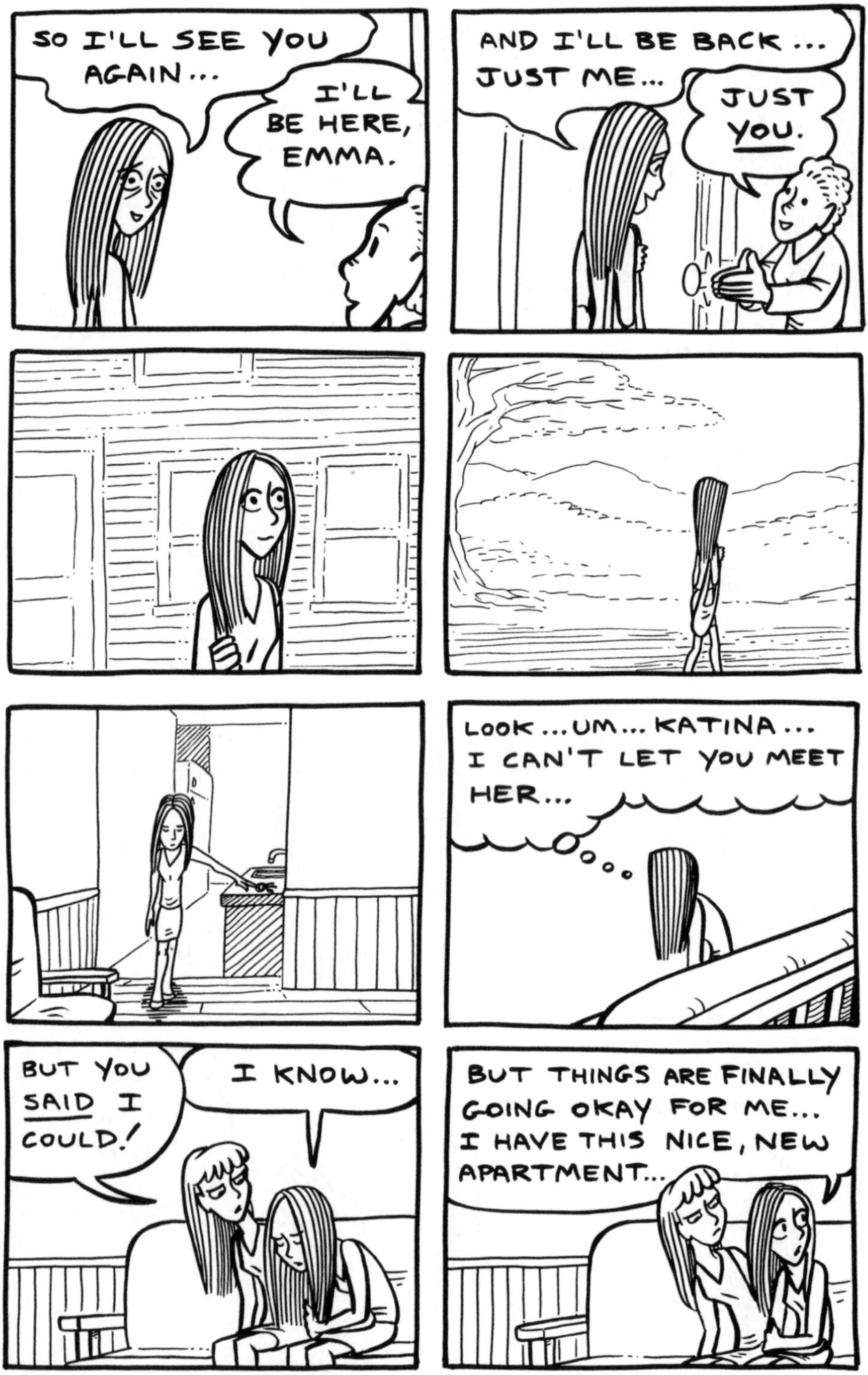
SO I'LL SEE YOU AGAIN...
I'LL BE HERE, EMMA.
AND I'LL BE BACK... JUST ME...
JUST YOU.
LOOK...UM...KATINA... I CAN'T LET YOU MEET HER...
BUT YOU SAID I COULD!
I KNOW...
BUT THINGS ARE FINALLY GOING OKAY FOR ME... I HAVE THIS NICE, NEW APARTMENT...

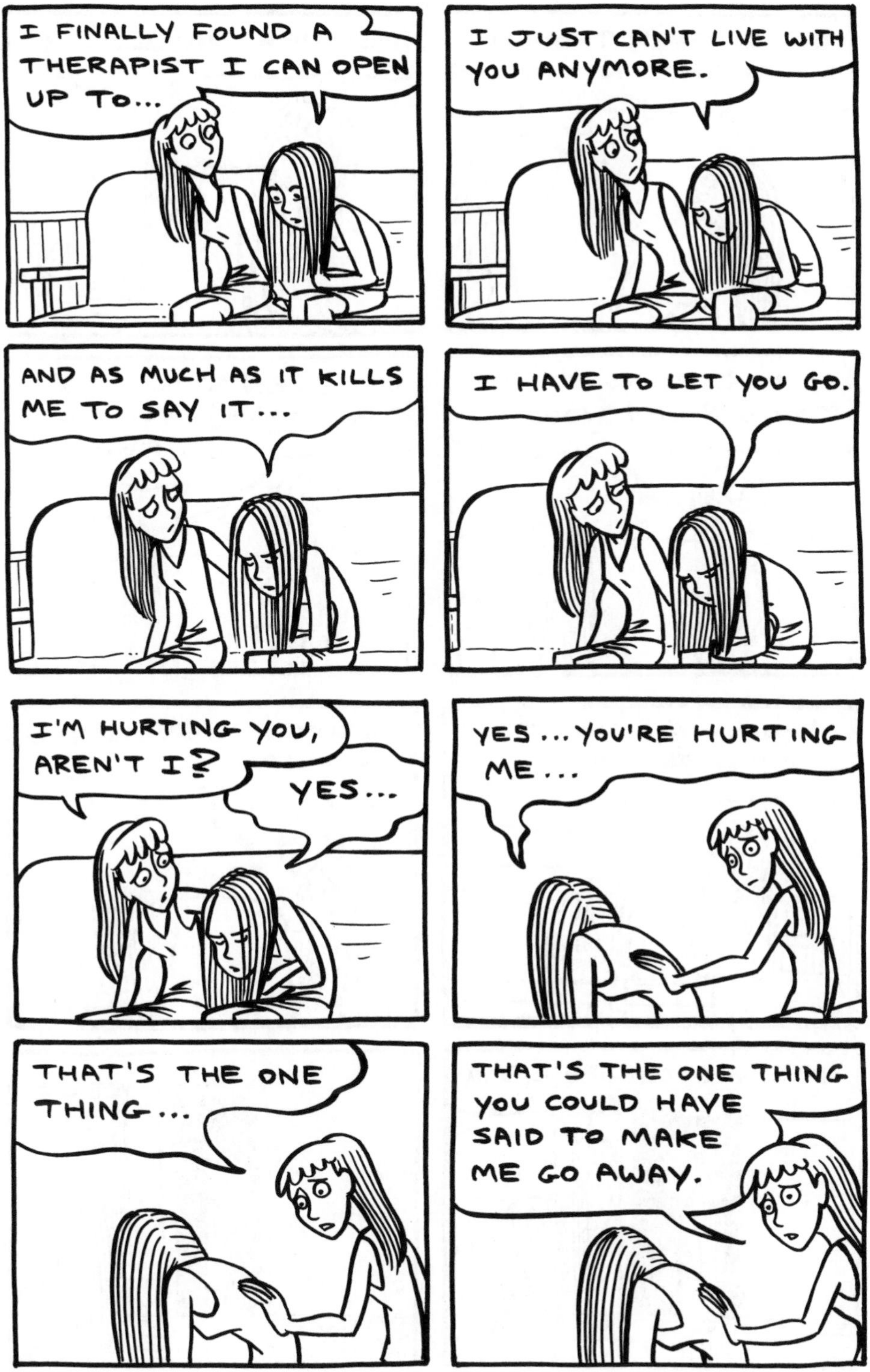
I FINALLY FOUND A THERAPIST I CAN OPEN UP TO...
I JUST CAN'T LIVE WITH YOU ANYMORE.
AND AS MUCH AS IT KILLS ME TO SAY IT...
I HAVE TO LET YOU GO.
I'M HURTING YOU, AREN'T I?
YES...
YES... YOU'RE HURTING ME...
THAT'S THE ONE THING...
THAT'S THE ONE THING YOU COULD HAVE SAID TO MAKE ME GO AWAY.

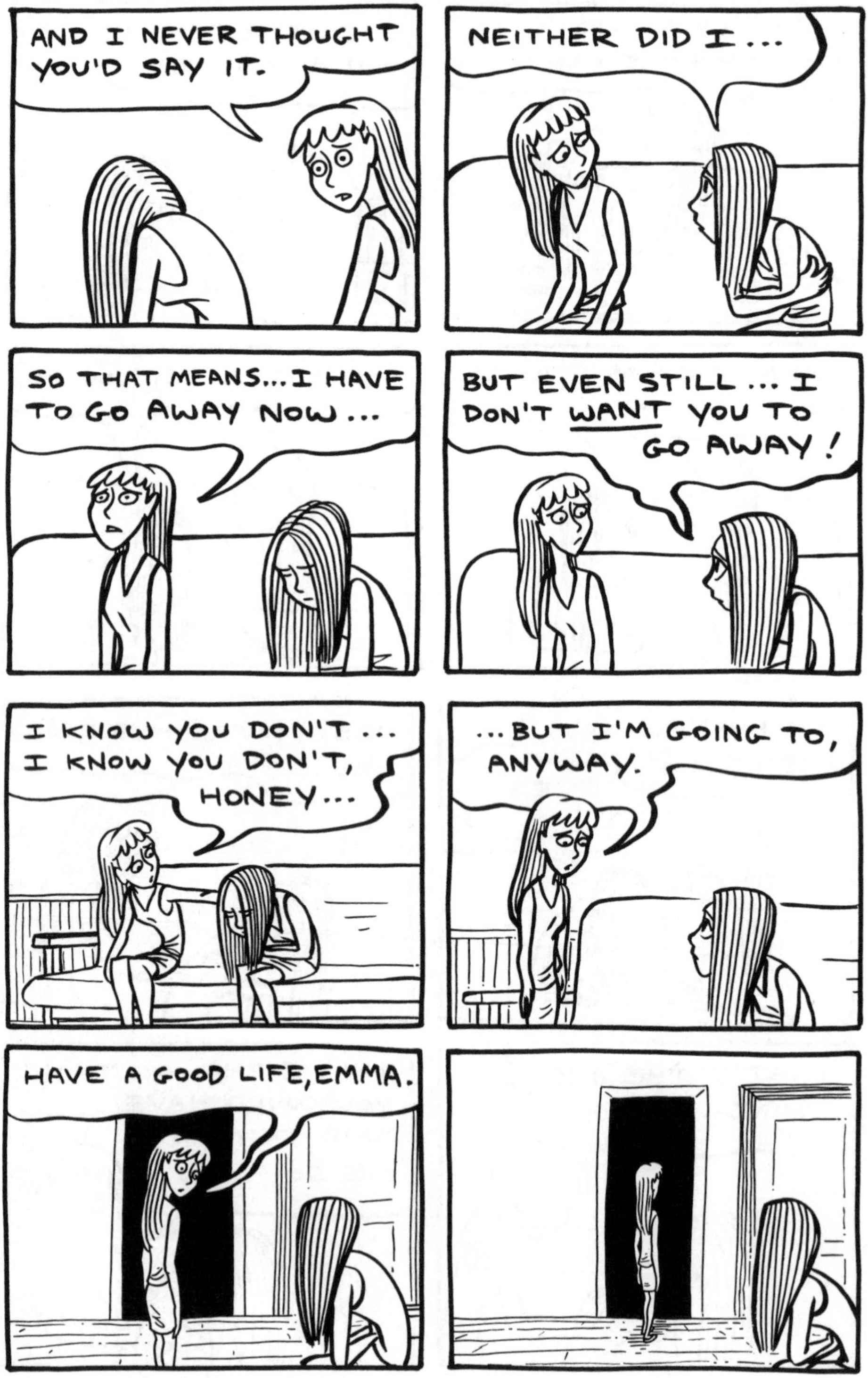
AND I NEVER THOUGHT YOU'D SAY IT.
NEITHER DID I...
SO THAT MEANS... I HAVE TO GO AWAY NOW...
BUT EVEN STILL... I DON'T WANT YOU TO GO AWAY!
I KNOW YOU DON'T... I KNOW YOU DON'T, HONEY...
...BUT I'M GOING TO, ANYWAY.
HAVE A GOOD LIFE, EMMA.

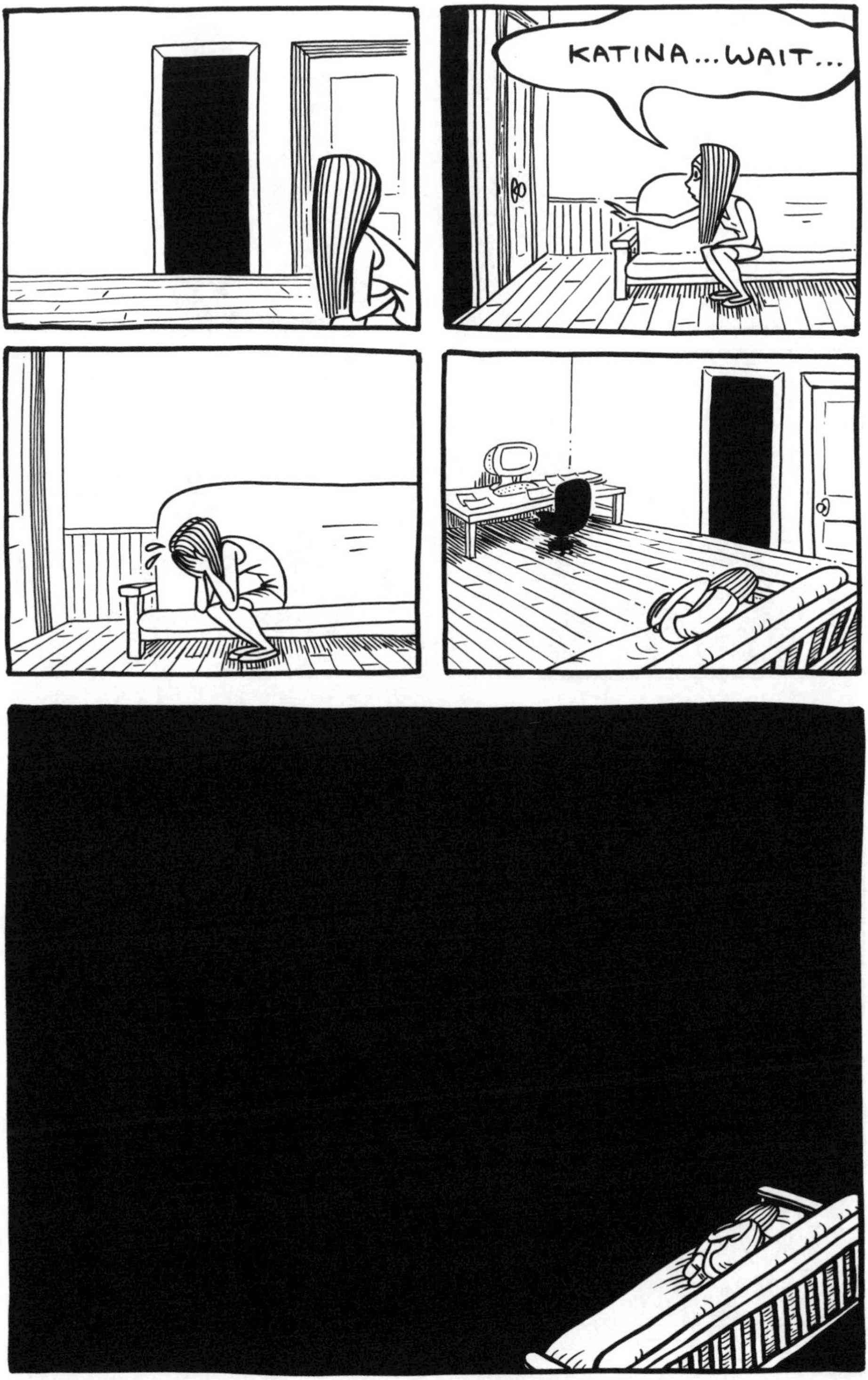
KATINA... WAIT...

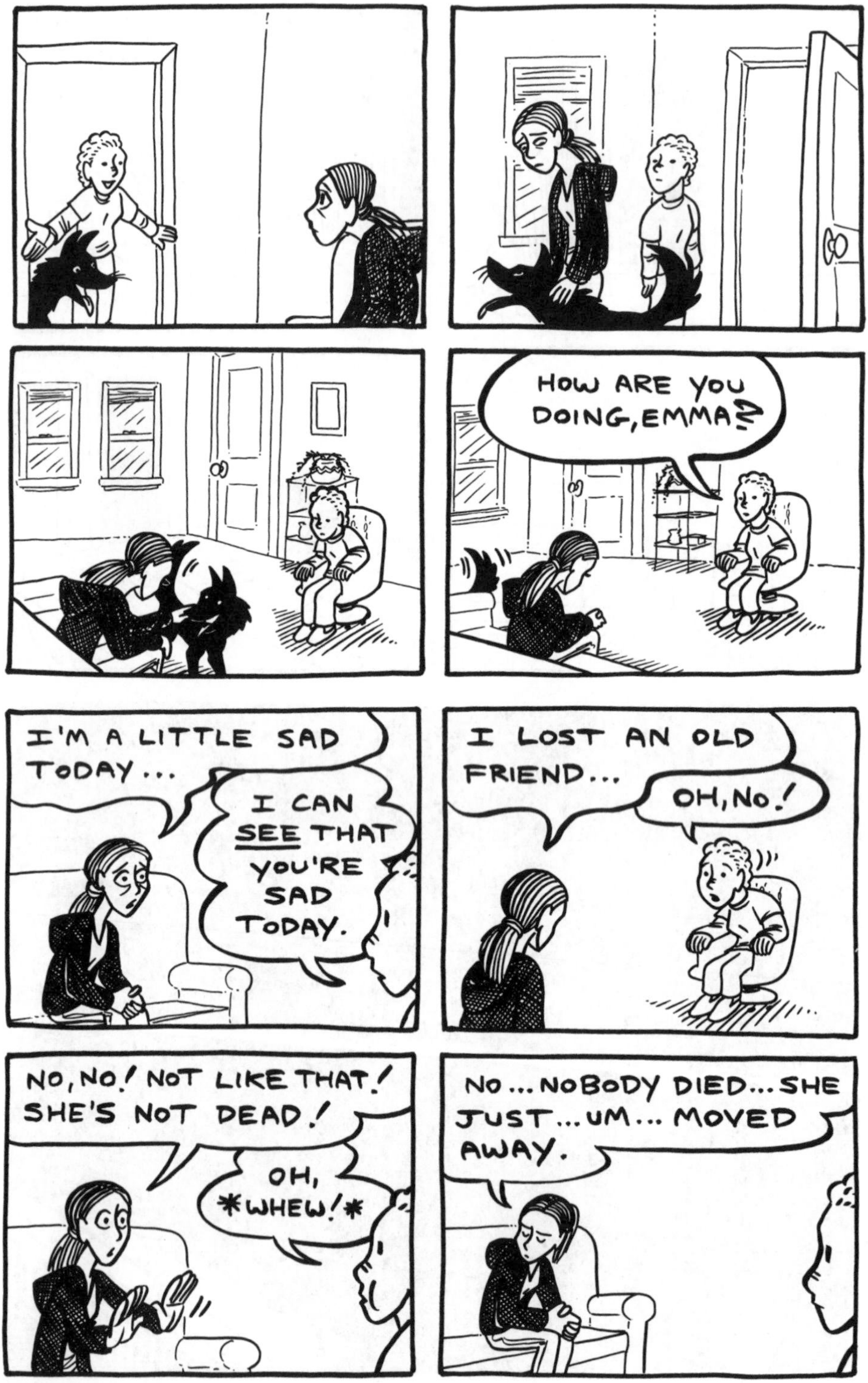
HOW ARE YOU DOING, EMMA?
I'M A LITTLE SAD TODAY...
I CAN SEE THAT YOU'RE SAD TODAY.
I LOST AN OLD FRIEND...
OH, NO!
NO, NO! NOT LIKE THAT! SHE'S NOT DEAD!
OH, *WHEW!*
NO... NOBODY DIED... SHE JUST... UM... MOVED AWAY.

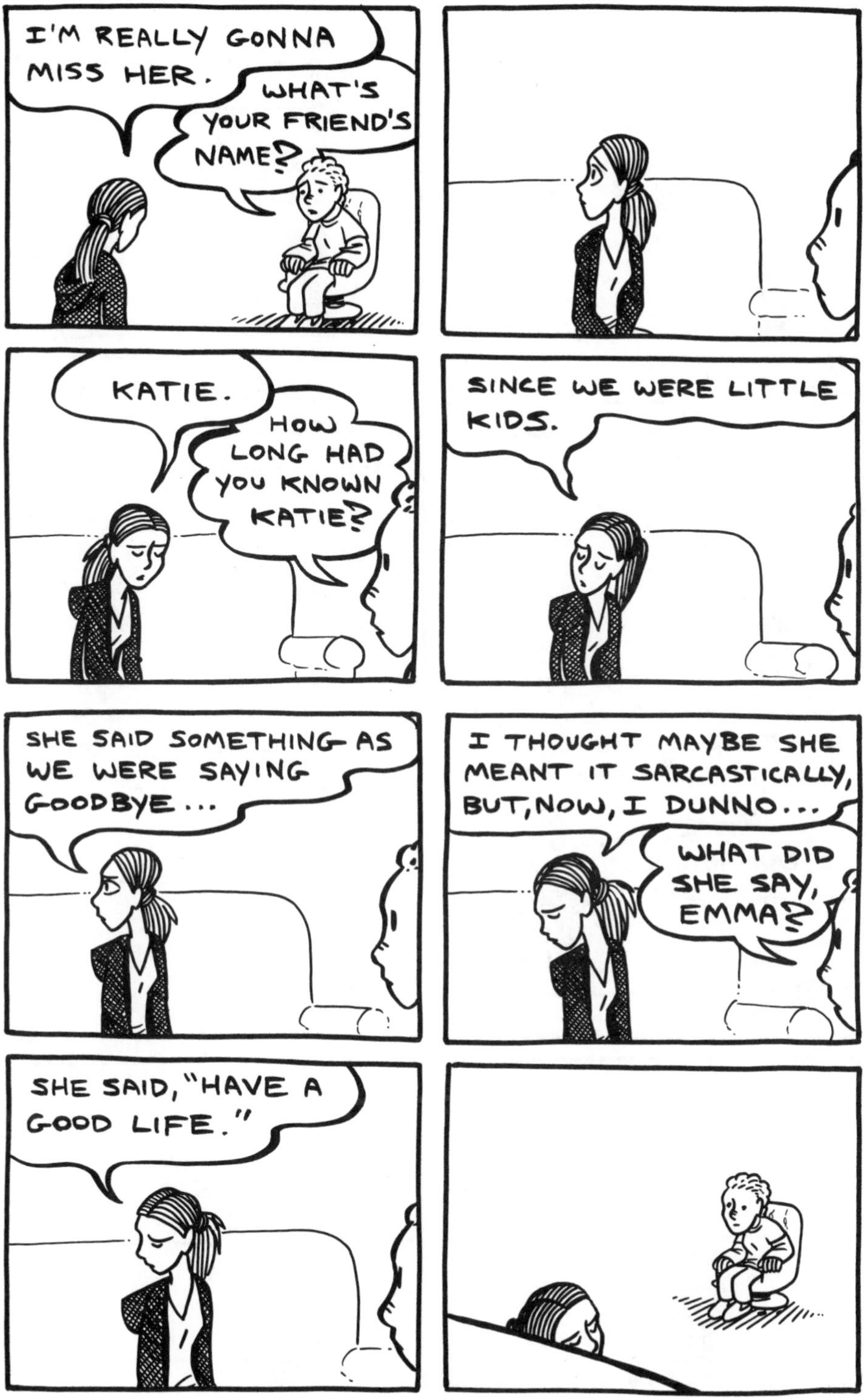
I'M REALLY GONNA MISS HER.
WHAT'S YOUR FRIEND'S NAME?
KATIE.
HOW LONG HAD YOU KNOWN KATIE?
SINCE WE WERE LITTLE KIDS.
SHE SAID SOMETHING AS WE WERE SAYING GOODBYE...
I THOUGHT MAYBE SHE MEANT IT SARCASTICALLY, BUT, NOW, I DUNNO...
WHAT DID SHE SAY, EMMA?
SHE SAID, "HAVE A GOOD LIFE."

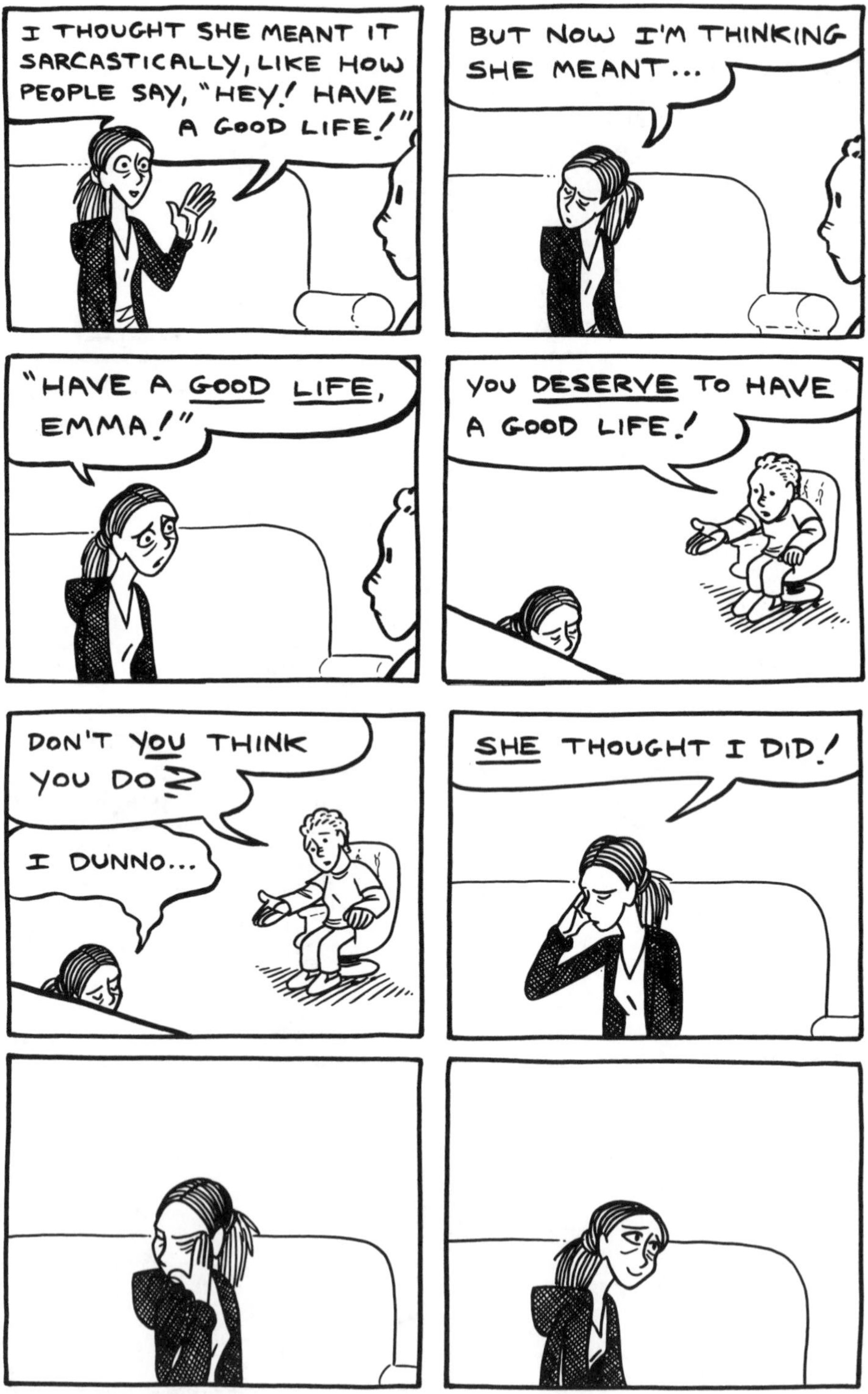
I THOUGHT SHE MEANT IT SARCASTICALLY, LIKE HOW PEOPLE SAY, "HEY! HAVE A GOOD LIFE!"
BUT NOW I'M THINKING SHE MEANT...
"HAVE A GOOD LIFE, EMMA!"
YOU DESERVE TO HAVE A GOOD LIFE!
DON'T YOU THINK YOU DO?
I DUNNO...
SHE THOUGHT I DID!

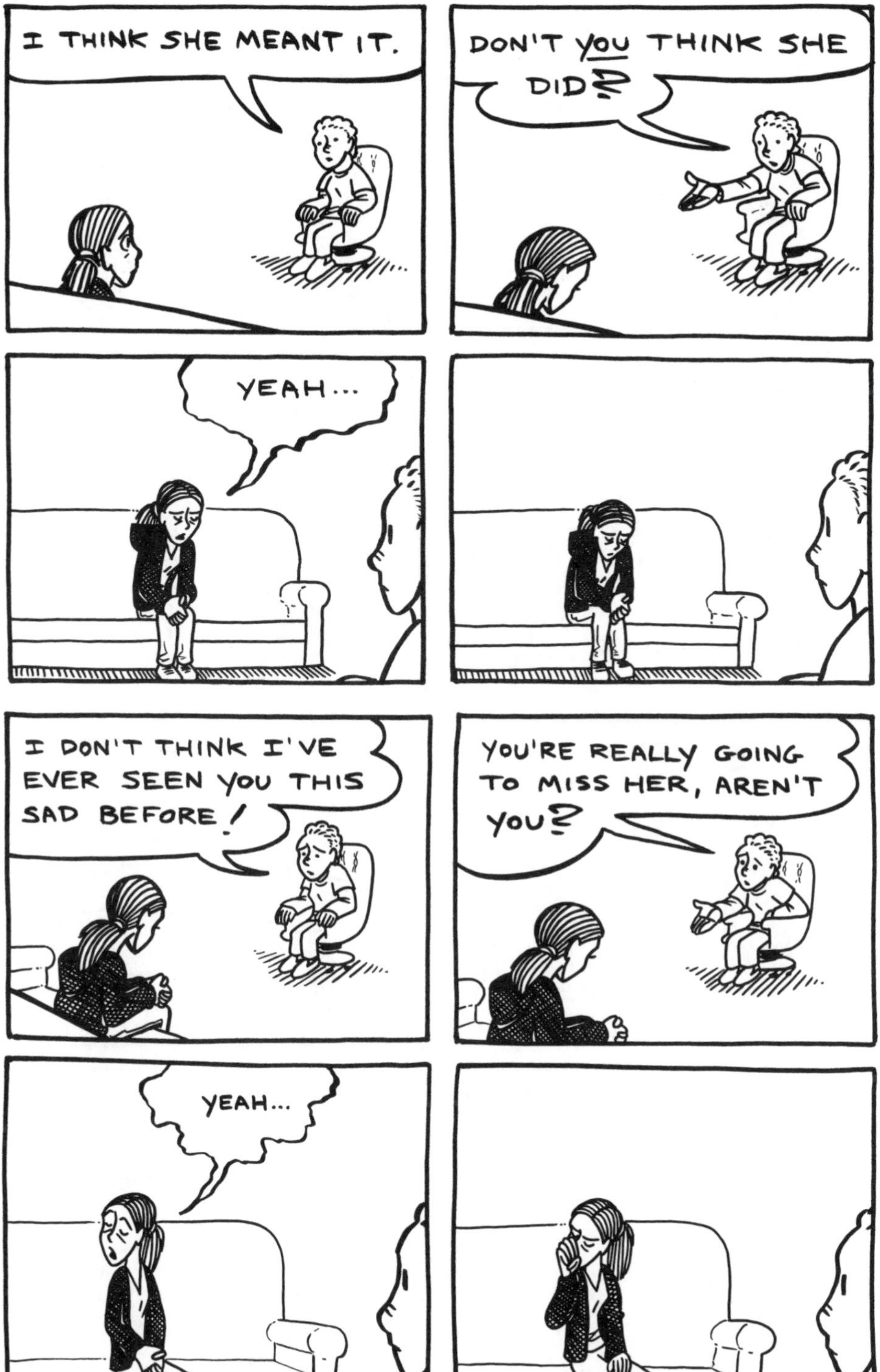
I THINK SHE MEANT IT.
DON'T YOU THINK SHE DID?
YEAH...
I DON'T THINK I'VE EVER SEEN YOU THIS SAD BEFORE!
YOU'RE REALLY GOING TO MISS HER, AREN'T YOU?
YEAH...

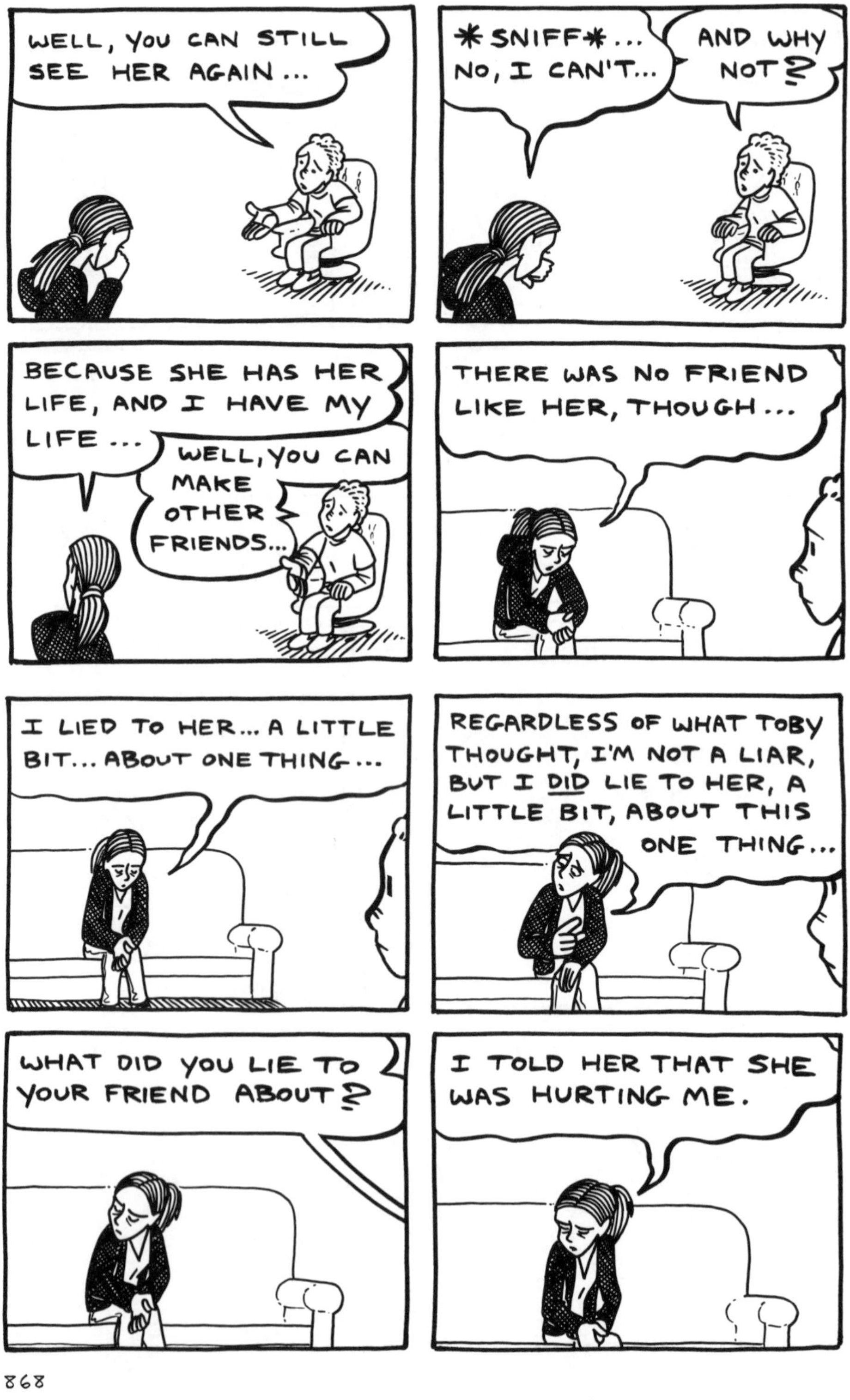
WELL, YOU CAN STILL SEE HER AGAIN...
SNIFF... NO, I CAN'T...
AND WHY NOT?
BECAUSE SHE HAS HER LIFE, AND I HAVE MY LIFE...
WELL, YOU CAN MAKE OTHER FRIENDS...
THERE WAS NO FRIEND LIKE HER, THOUGH...
I LIED TO HER... A LITTLE BIT... ABOUT ONE THING...
REGARDLESS OF WHAT TOBY THOUGHT, I'M NOT A LIAR, BUT I DID LIE TO HER, A LITTLE BIT, ABOUT THIS ONE THING...
WHAT DID YOU LIE TO YOUR FRIEND ABOUT?
I TOLD HER THAT SHE WAS HURTING ME.

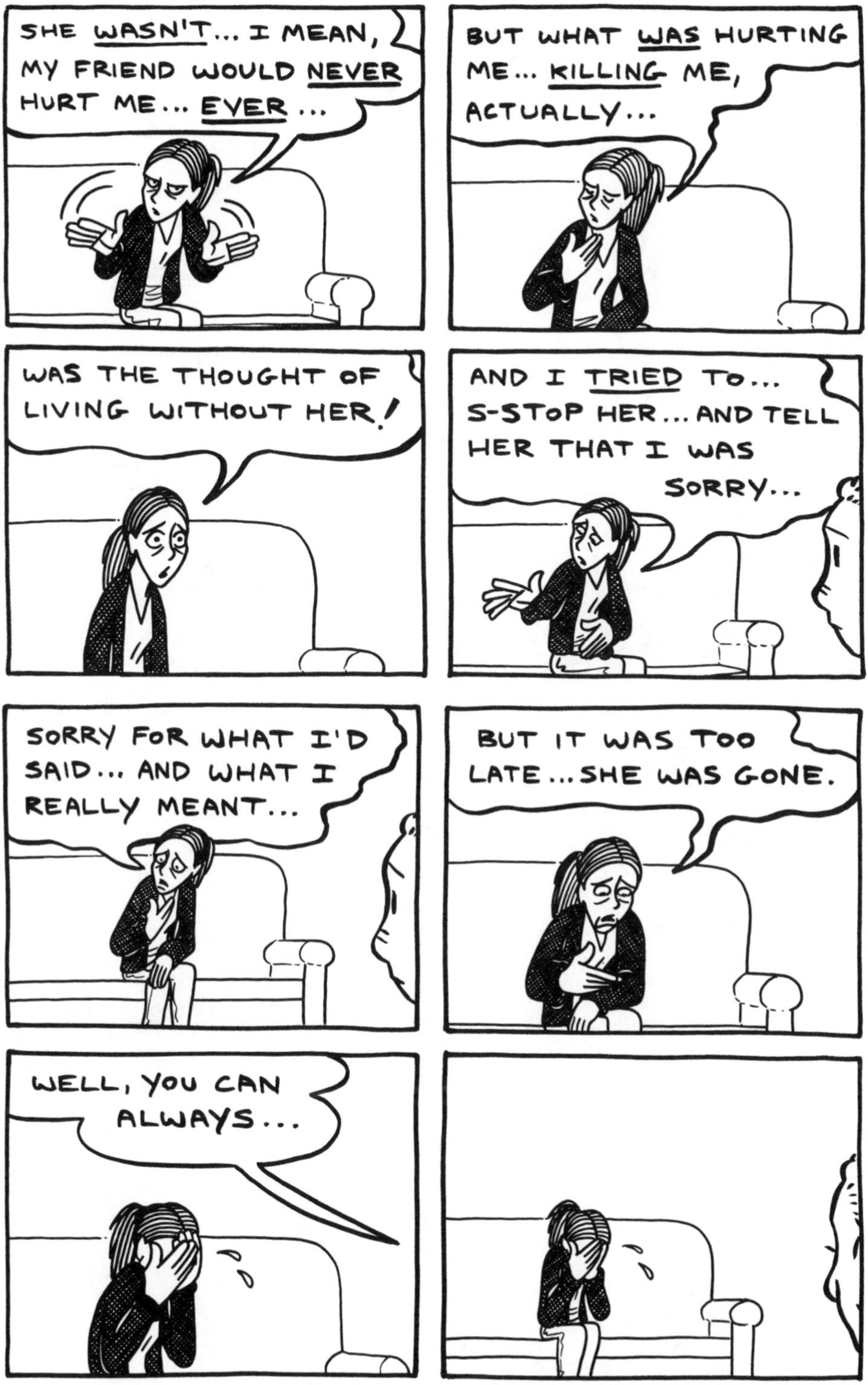
SHE WASN'T... I MEAN, MY FRIEND WOULD NEVER HURT ME... EVER...
BUT WHAT WAS HURTING ME... KILLING ME, ACTUALLY...
WAS THE THOUGHT OF LIVING WITHOUT HER!
AND I TRIED TO... S-STOP HER... AND TELL HER THAT I WAS SORRY...
SORRY FOR WHAT I'D SAID... AND WHAT I REALLY MEANT...
BUT IT WAS TOO LATE... SHE WAS GONE.
WELL, YOU CAN ALWAYS...

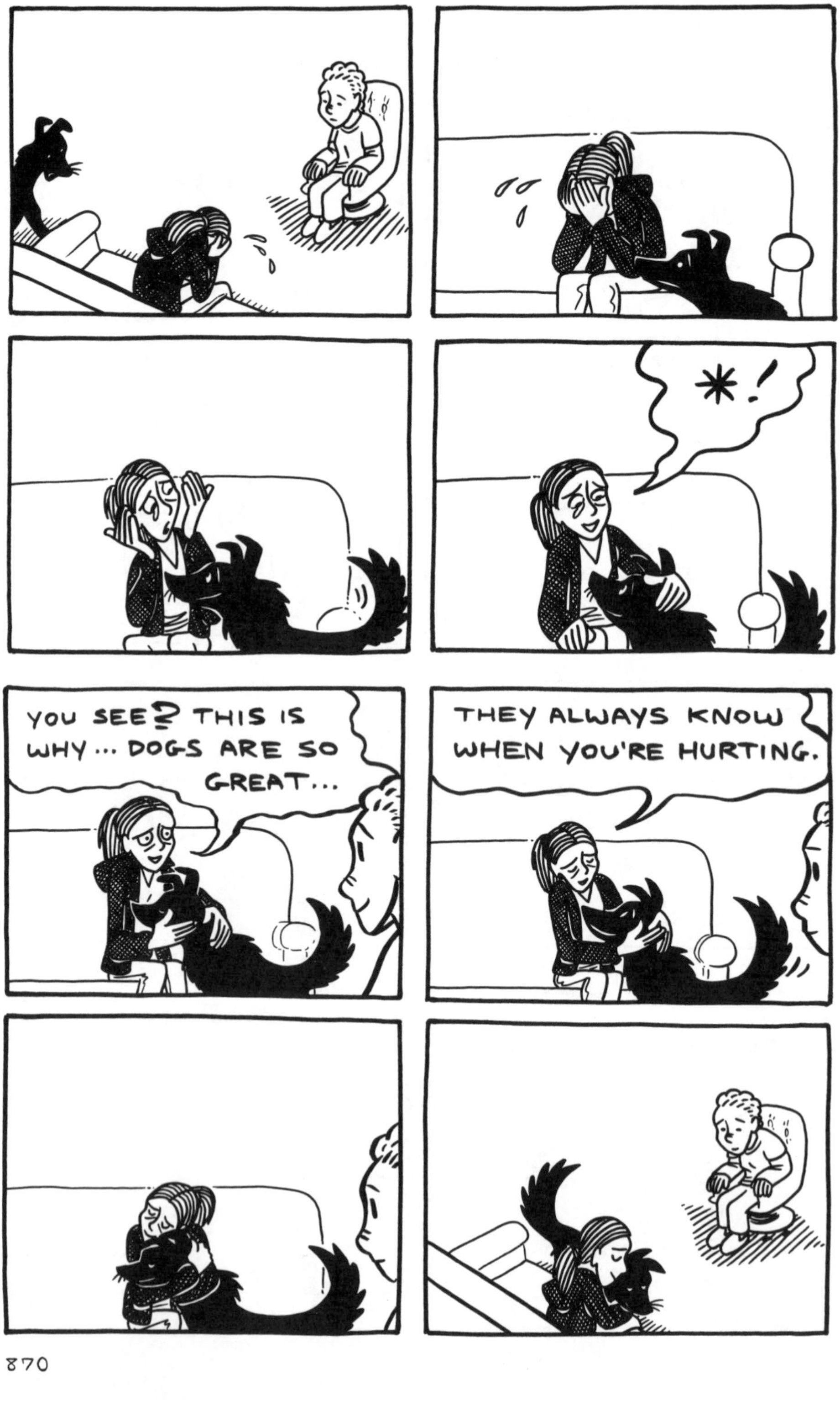
*!
YOU SEE? THIS IS WHY... DOGS ARE SO GREAT...
THEY ALWAYS KNOW WHEN YOU'RE HURTING.

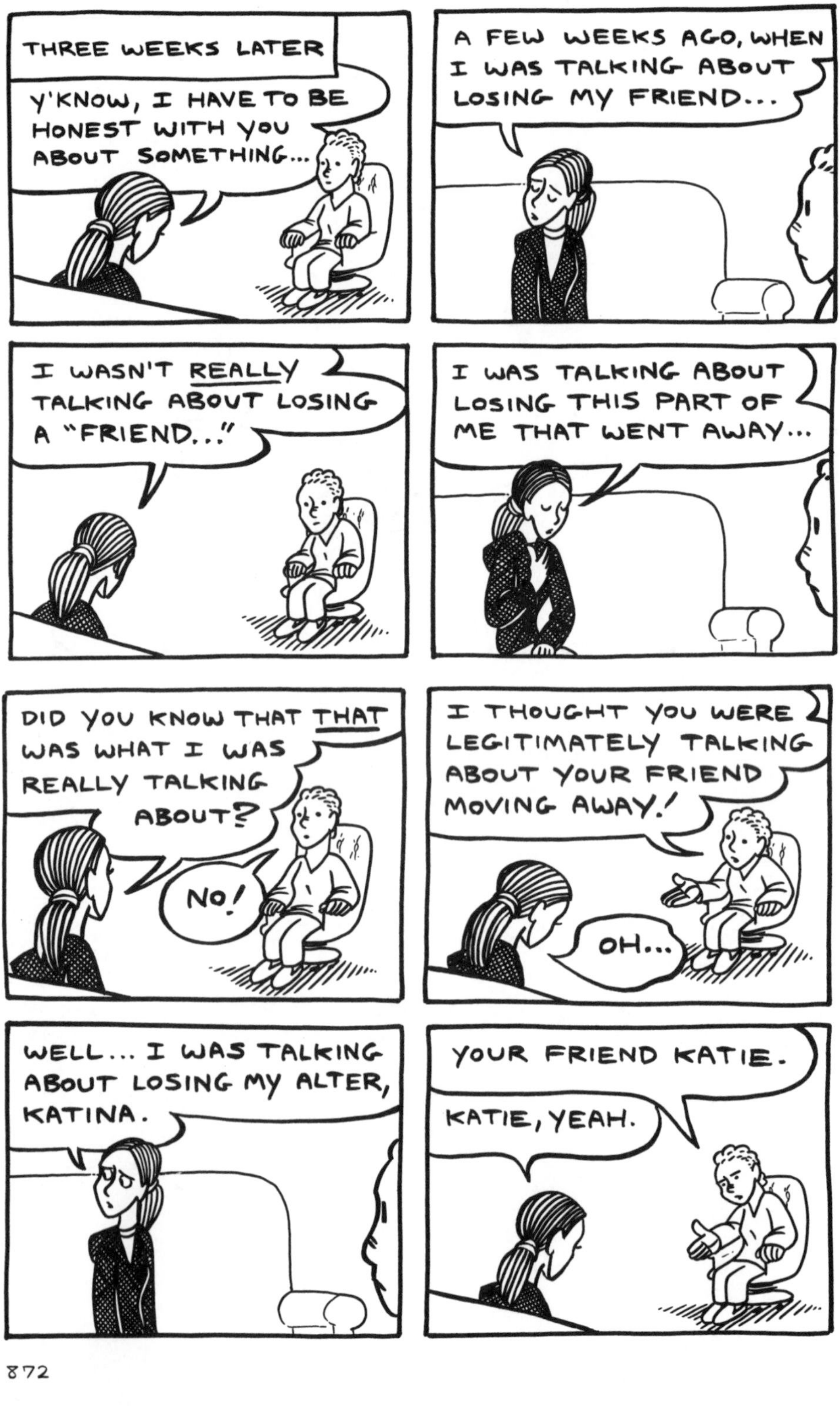
THREE WEEKS LATER
Y'KNOW, I HAVE TO BE HONEST WITH YOU ABOUT SOMETHING...
A FEW WEEKS AGO, WHEN I WAS TALKING ABOUT LOSING MY FRIEND...
I WASN'T REALLY TALKING ABOUT LOSING A "FRIEND..."
I WAS TALKING ABOUT LOSING THIS PART OF ME THAT WENT AWAY...
DID YOU KNOW THAT THAT WAS WHAT I WAS REALLY TALKING ABOUT?
NO!
I THOUGHT YOU WERE LEGITIMATELY TALKING ABOUT YOUR FRIEND MOVING AWAY!
OH...
WELL... I WAS TALKING ABOUT LOSING MY ALTER, KATINA.
YOUR FRIEND KATIE.
KATIE, YEAH.

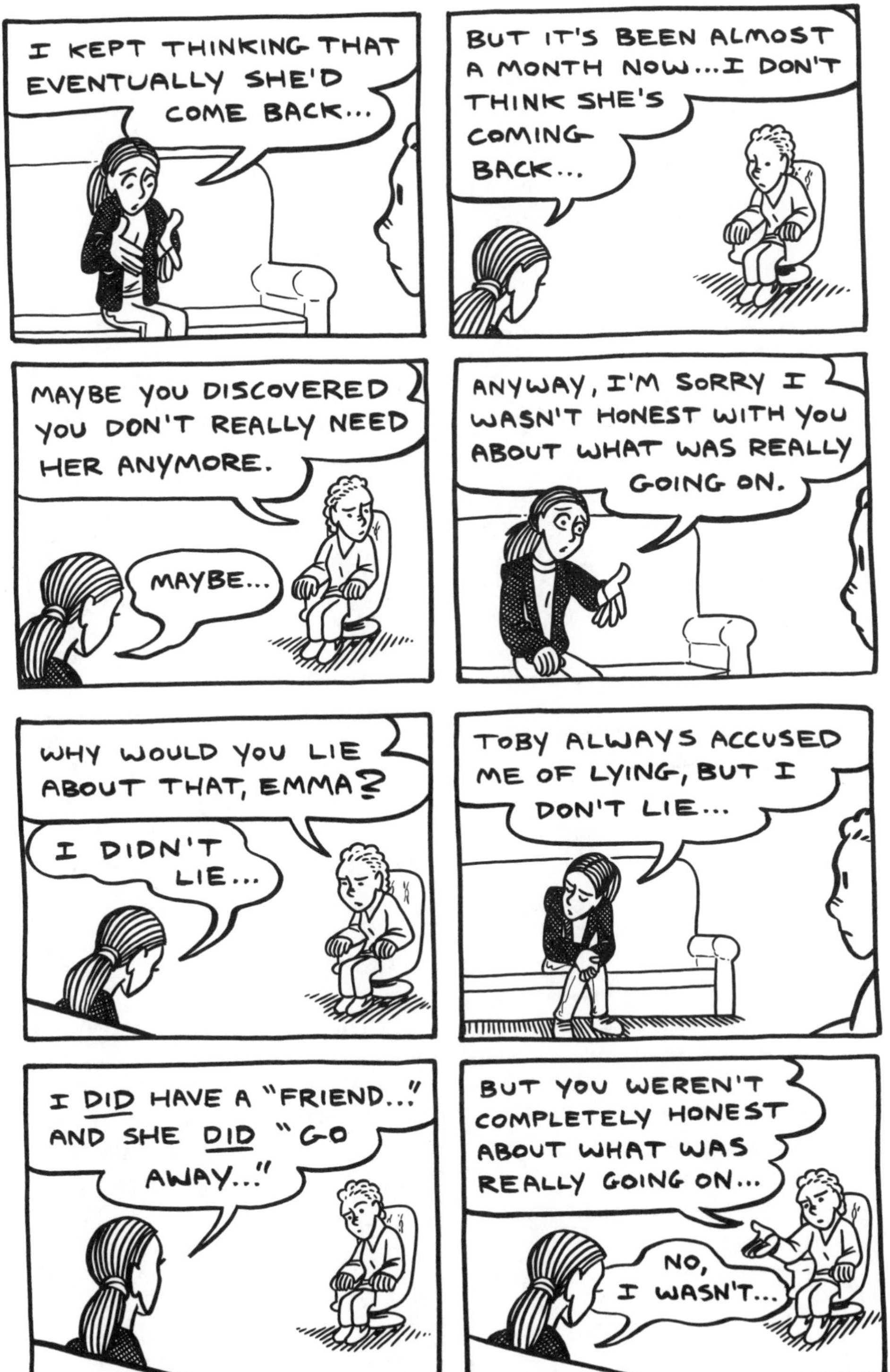
I KEPT THINKING THAT EVENTUALLY SHE'D COME BACK...
BUT IT'S BEEN ALMOST A MONTH NOW...I DON'T THINK SHE'S COMING BACK...
MAYBE YOU DISCOVERED YOU DON'T REALLY NEED HER ANYMORE.
MAYBE...
ANYWAY, I'M SORRY I WASN'T HONEST WITH YOU ABOUT WHAT WAS REALLY GOING ON.
WHY WOULD YOU LIE ABOUT THAT, EMMA?
I DIDN'T LIE...
TOBY ALWAYS ACCUSED ME OF LYING, BUT I DON'T LIE...
I DID HAVE A "FRIEND..." AND SHE DID "GO AWAY..."
BUT YOU WEREN'T COMPLETELY HONEST ABOUT WHAT WAS REALLY GOING ON...
NO, I WASN'T...

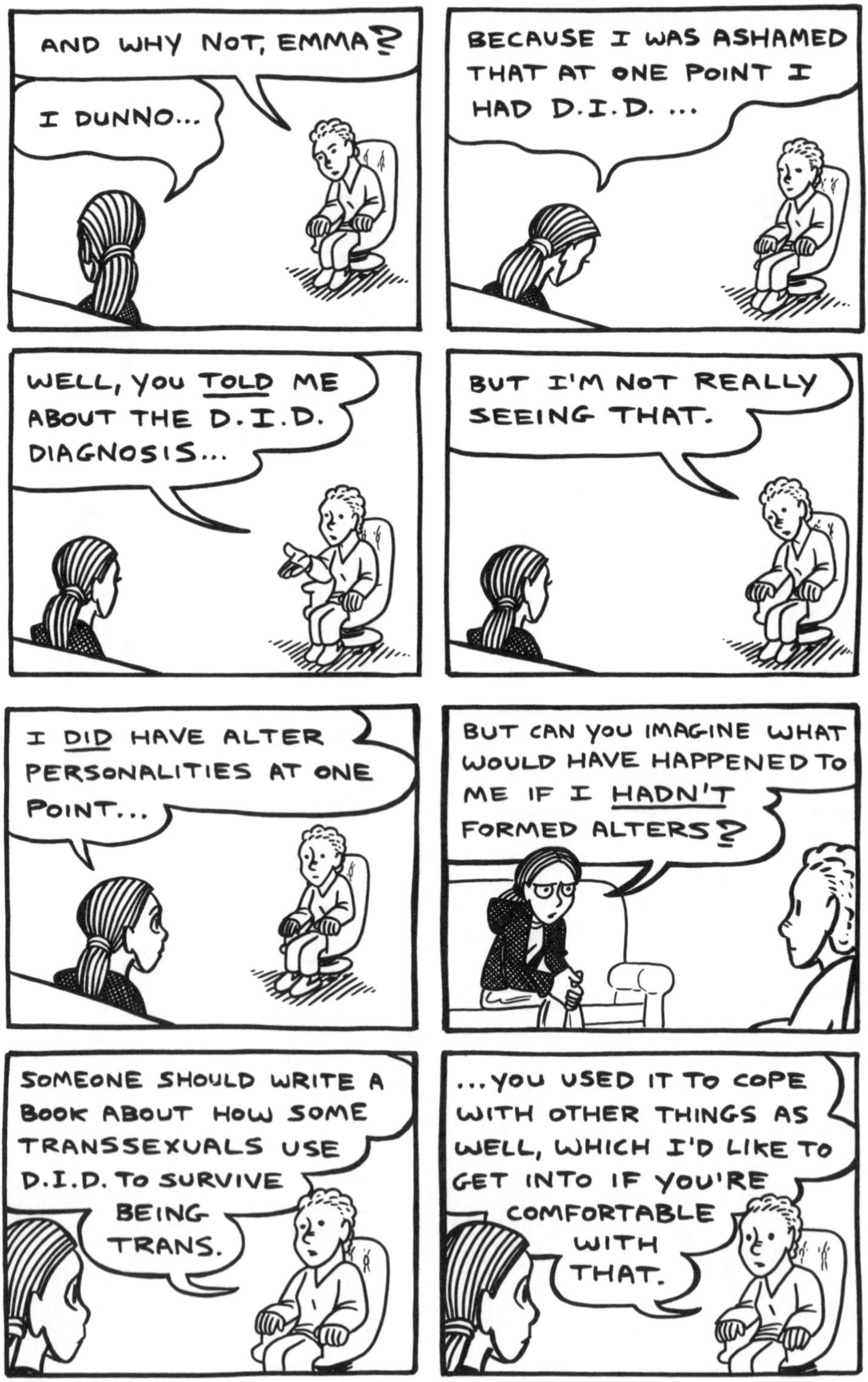
AND WHY NOT, EMMA?
I DUNNO...
BECAUSE I WAS ASHAMED THAT AT ONE POINT I HAD D.I.D. ...
WELL, YOU TOLD ME ABOUT THE D.I.D. DIAGNOSIS...
BUT I'M NOT REALLY SEEING THAT.
I DID HAVE ALTER PERSONALITIES AT ONE POINT...
BUT CAN YOU IMAGINE WHAT WOULD HAVE HAPPENED TO ME IF I HADN'T FORMED ALTERS?
SOMEONE SHOULD WRITE A BOOK ABOUT HOW SOME TRANSSEXUALS USE D.I.D. TO SURVIVE BEING TRANS.
...YOU USED IT TO COPE WITH OTHER THINGS AS WELL, WHICH I'D LIKE TO GET INTO IF YOU'RE COMFORTABLE WITH THAT.

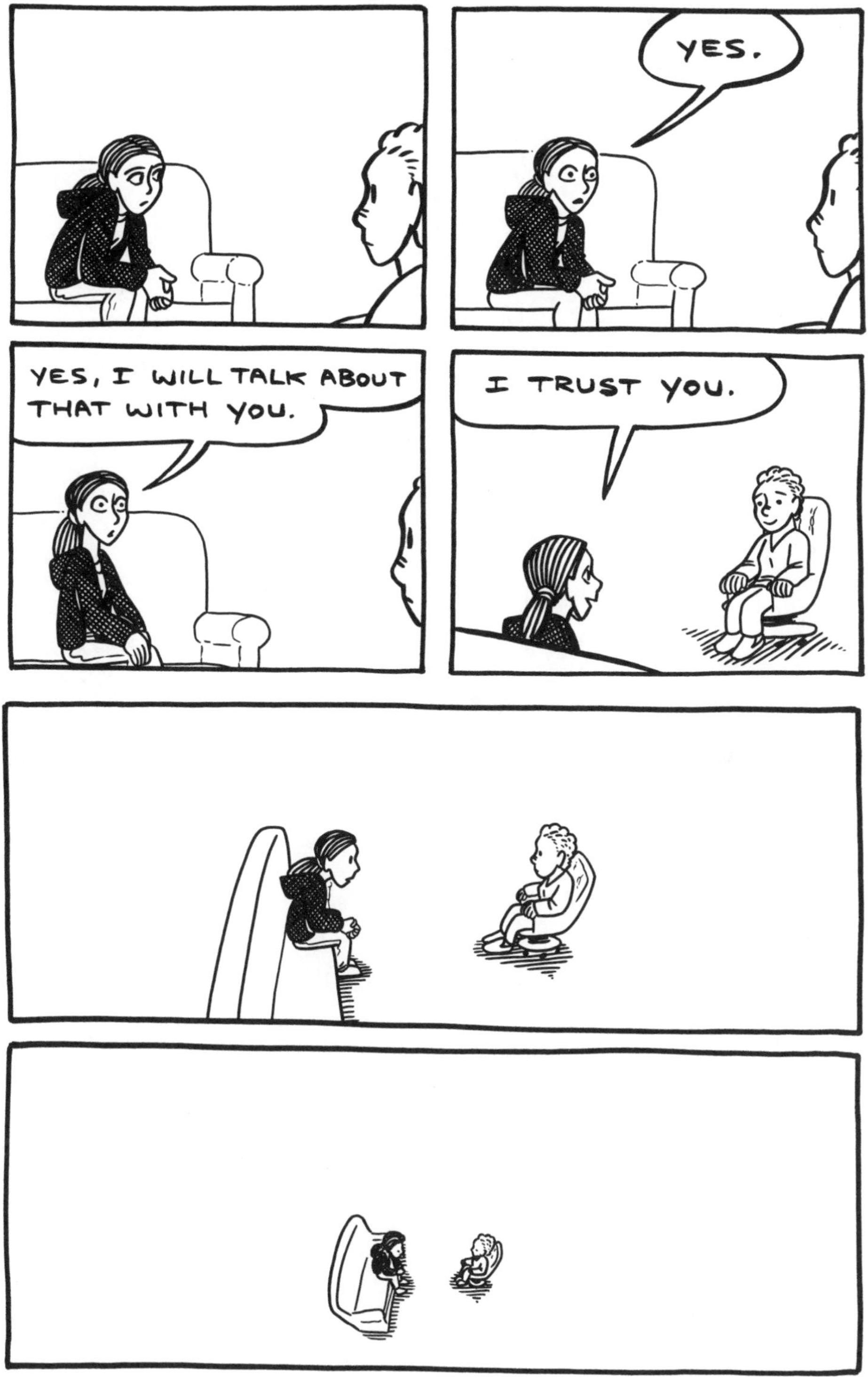
YES.
YES, I WILL TALK ABOUT THAT WITH YOU.
I TRUST YOU.

RED
BALLOON

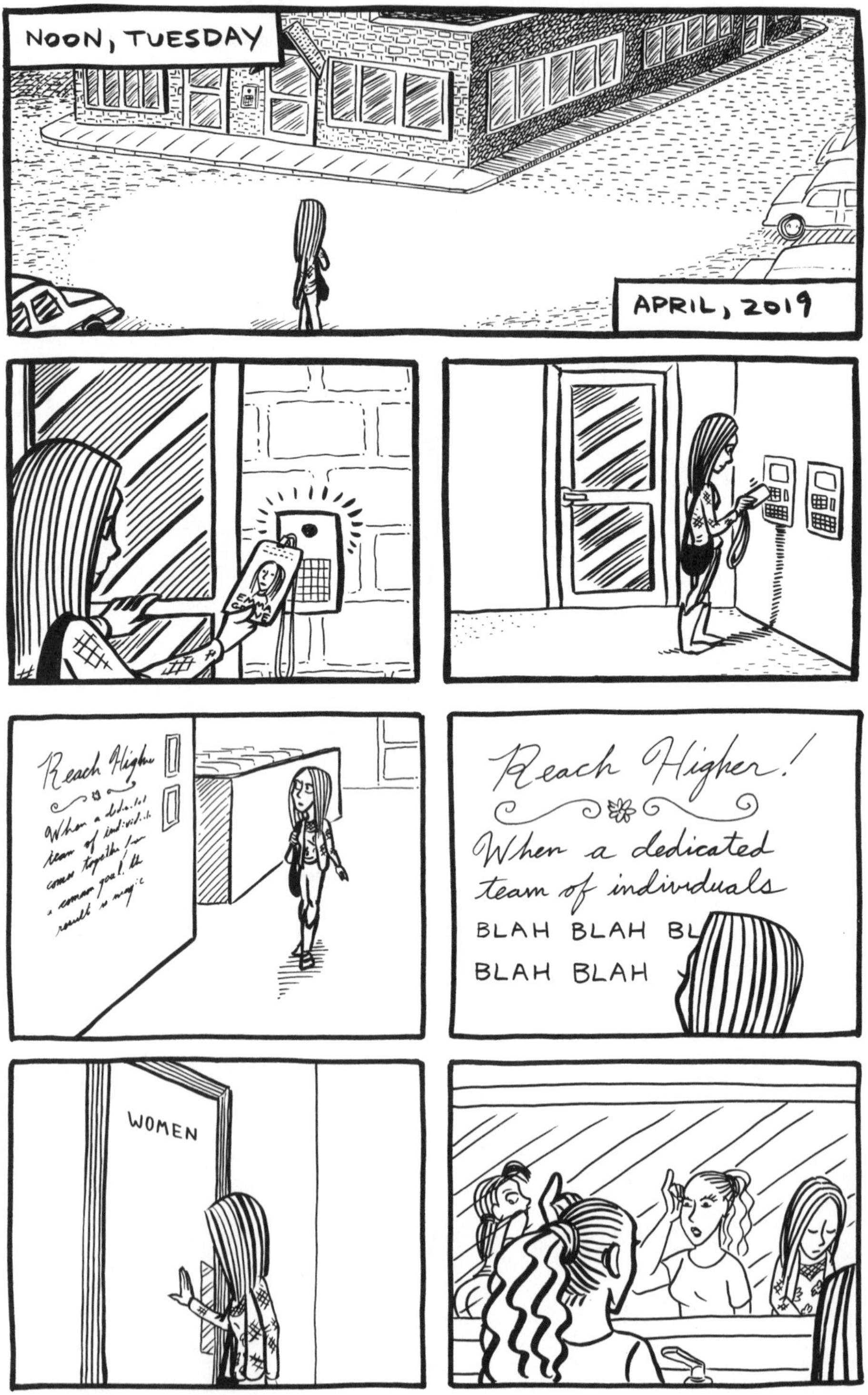
NOON, TUESDAY
APRIL, 2019
Reach Higher!
When a dedicated team of individuals
BLAH BLAH BL
BLAH BLAH
WOMEN

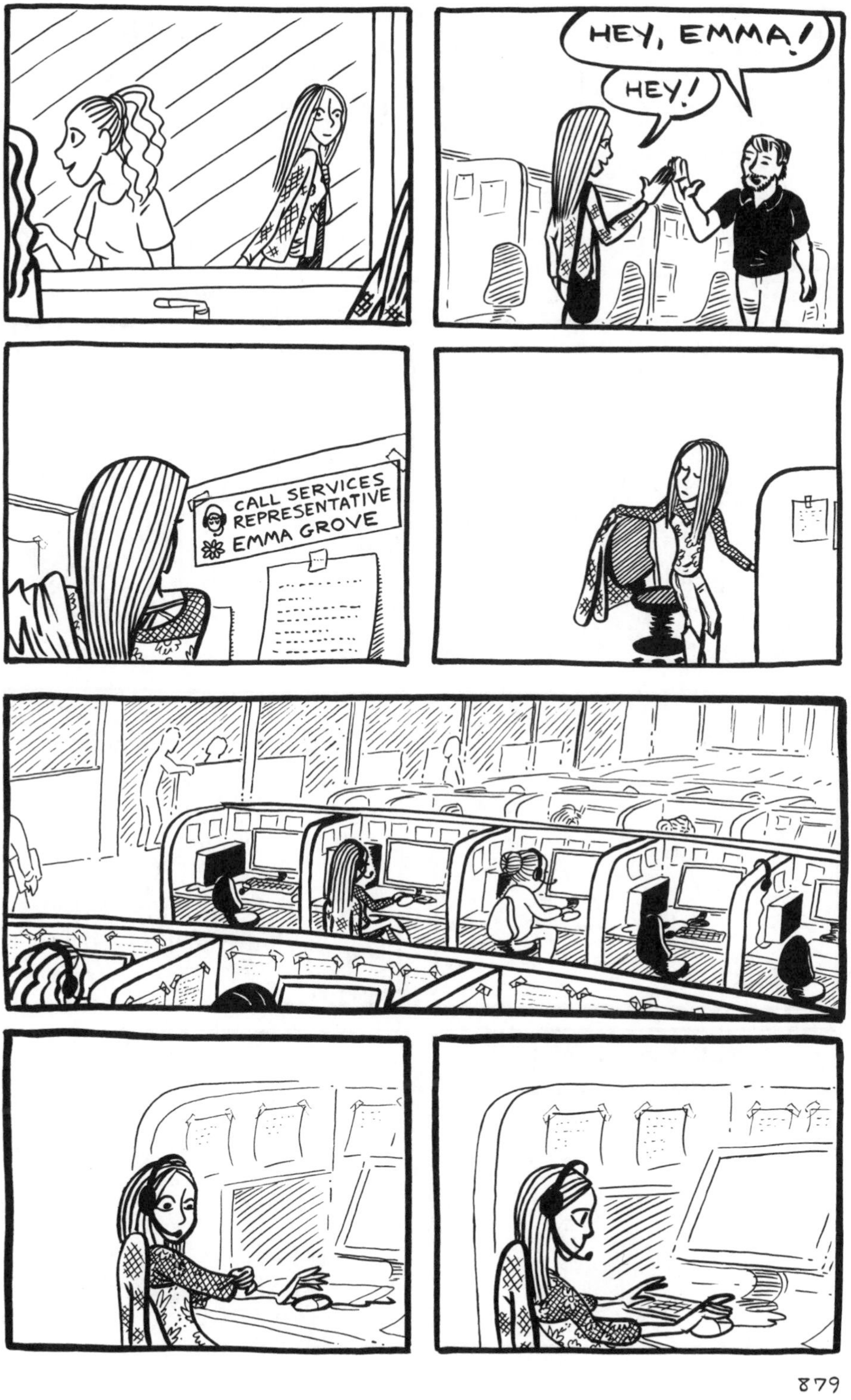
HEY, EMMA!
HEY!
CALL SERVICES REPRESENTATIVE
EMMA GROVE

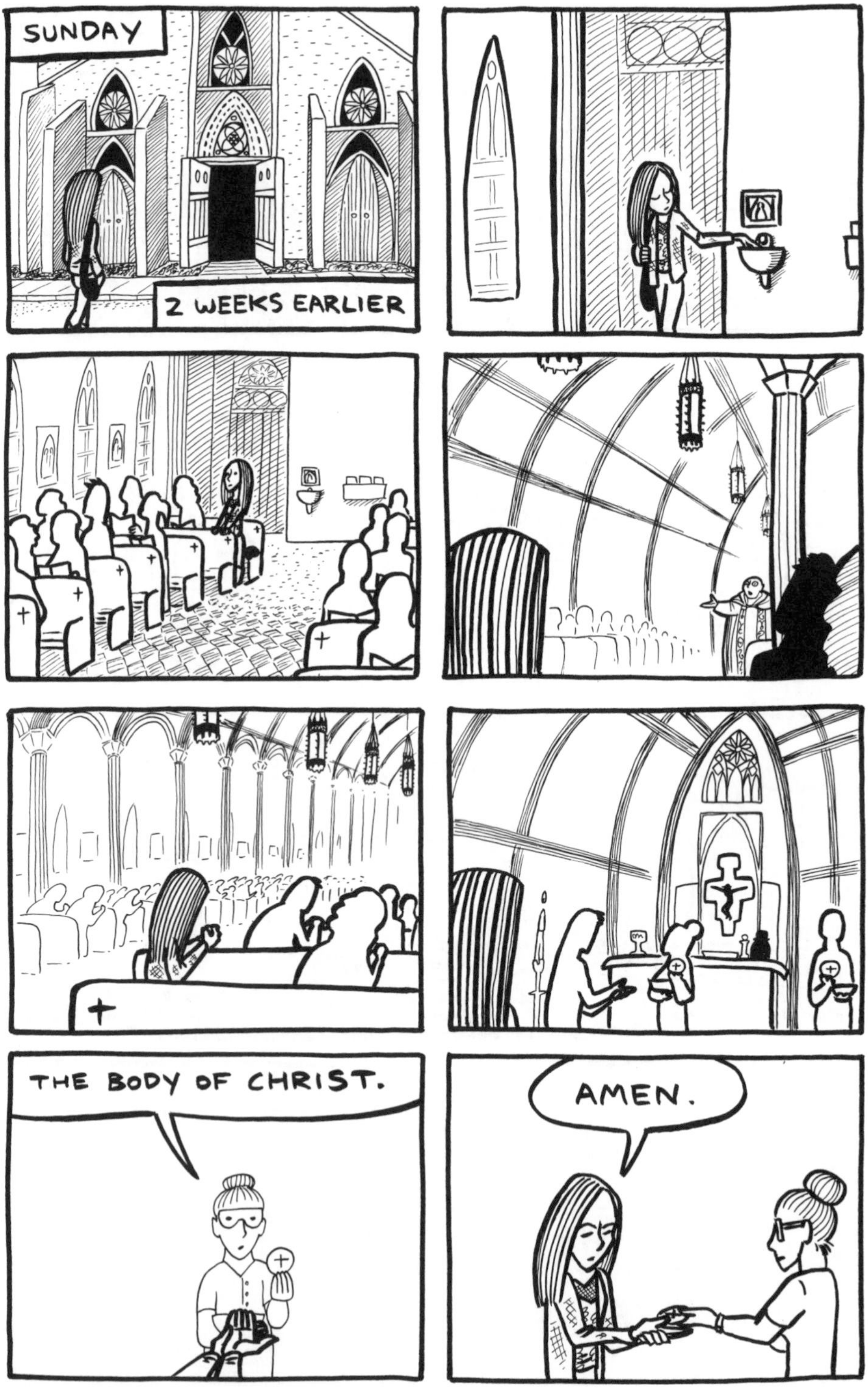
SUNDAY
2 WEEKS EARLIER
THE BODY OF CHRIST.
AMEN.

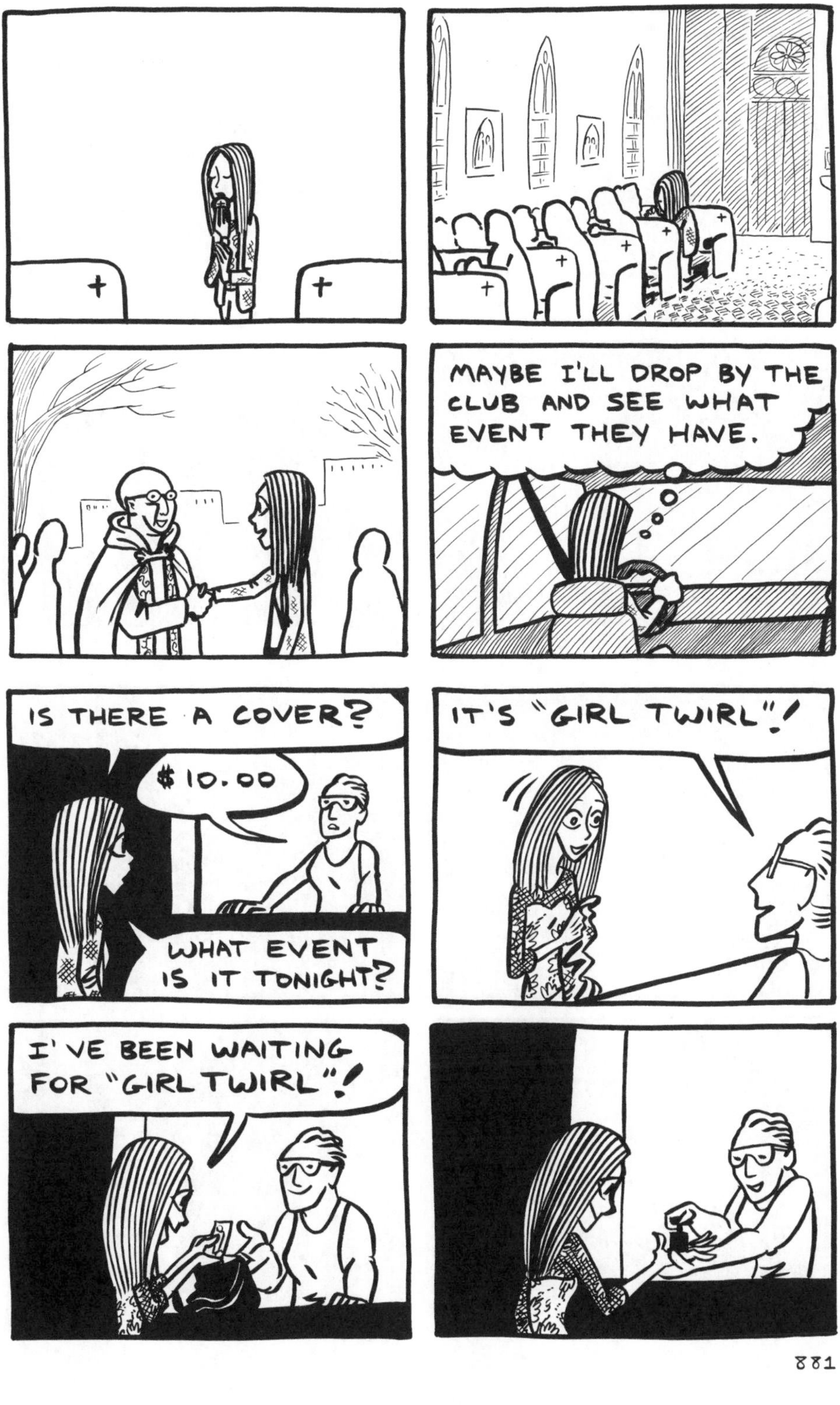

MAYBE I'LL DROP BY THE CLUB AND SEE WHAT EVENT THEY HAVE.
IS THERE A COVER?
$10.00
WHAT EVENT IS IT TONIGHT?
IT'S "GIRL TWIRL"!
I'VE BEEN WAITING FOR "GIRL TWIRL"!

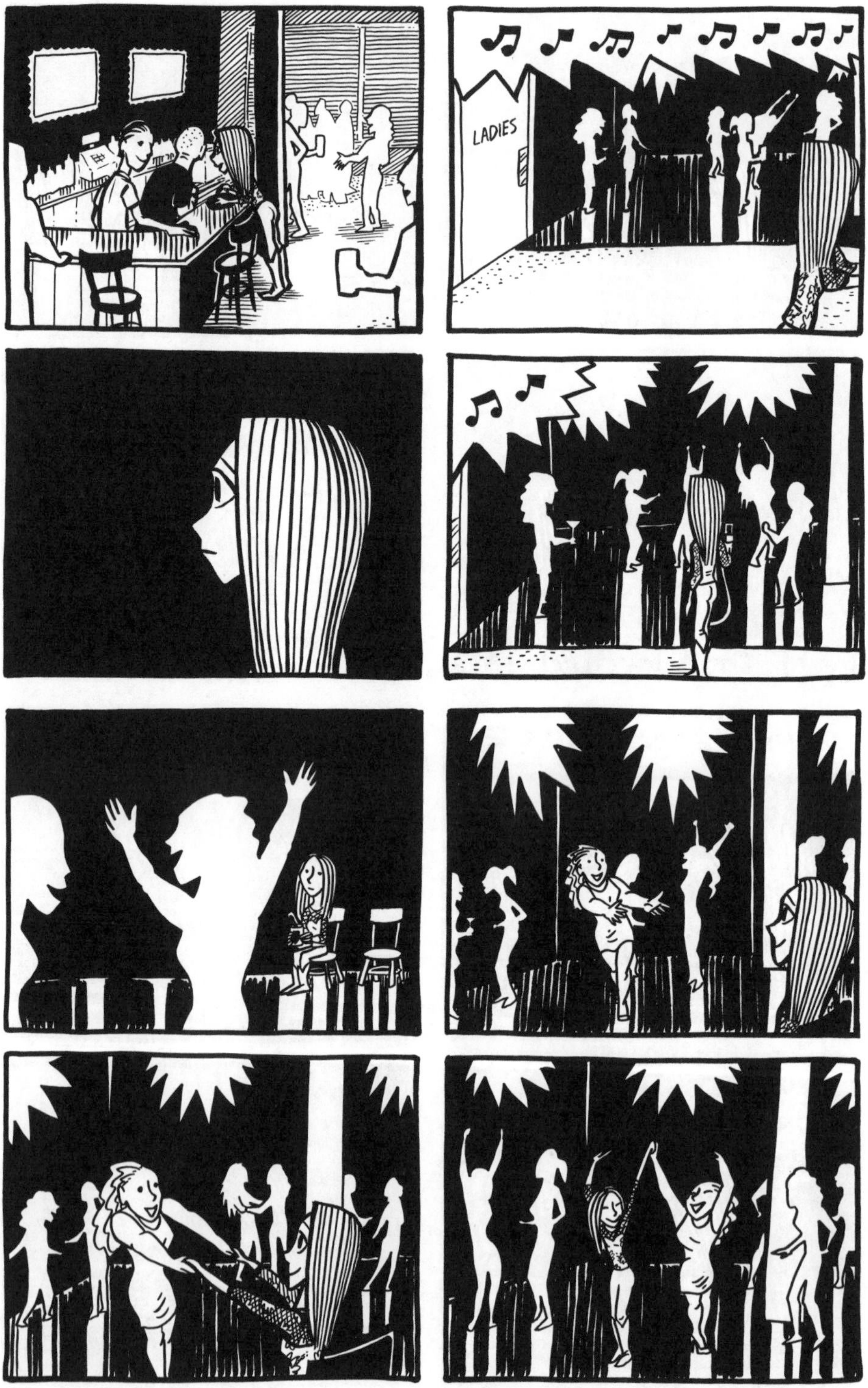
LADIES

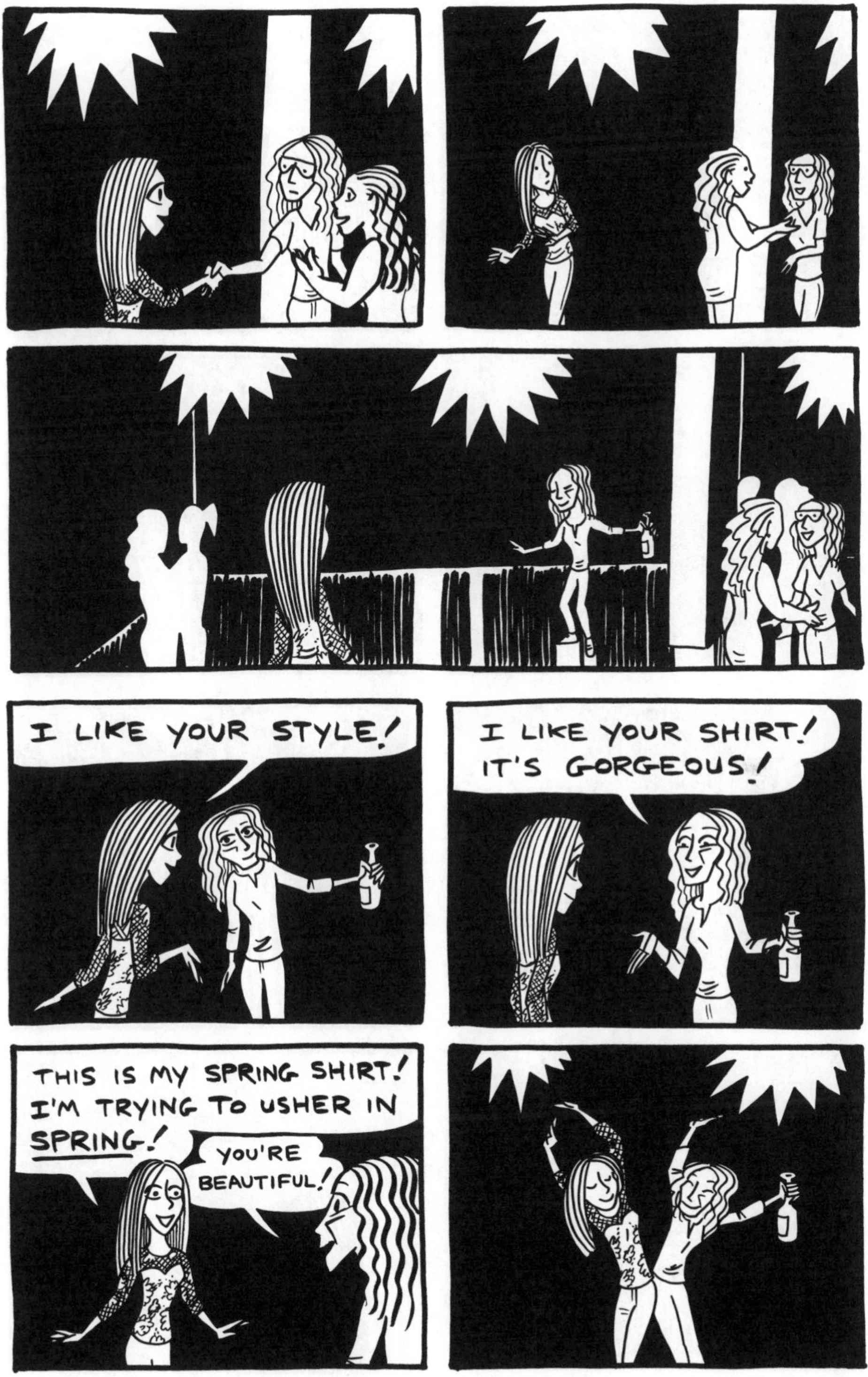

I LIKE YOUR STYLE!
I LIKE YOUR SHIRT! IT'S GORGEOUS!
THIS IS MY SPRING SHIRT! I'M TRYING TO USHER IN SPRING!
YOU'RE BEAUTIFUL!

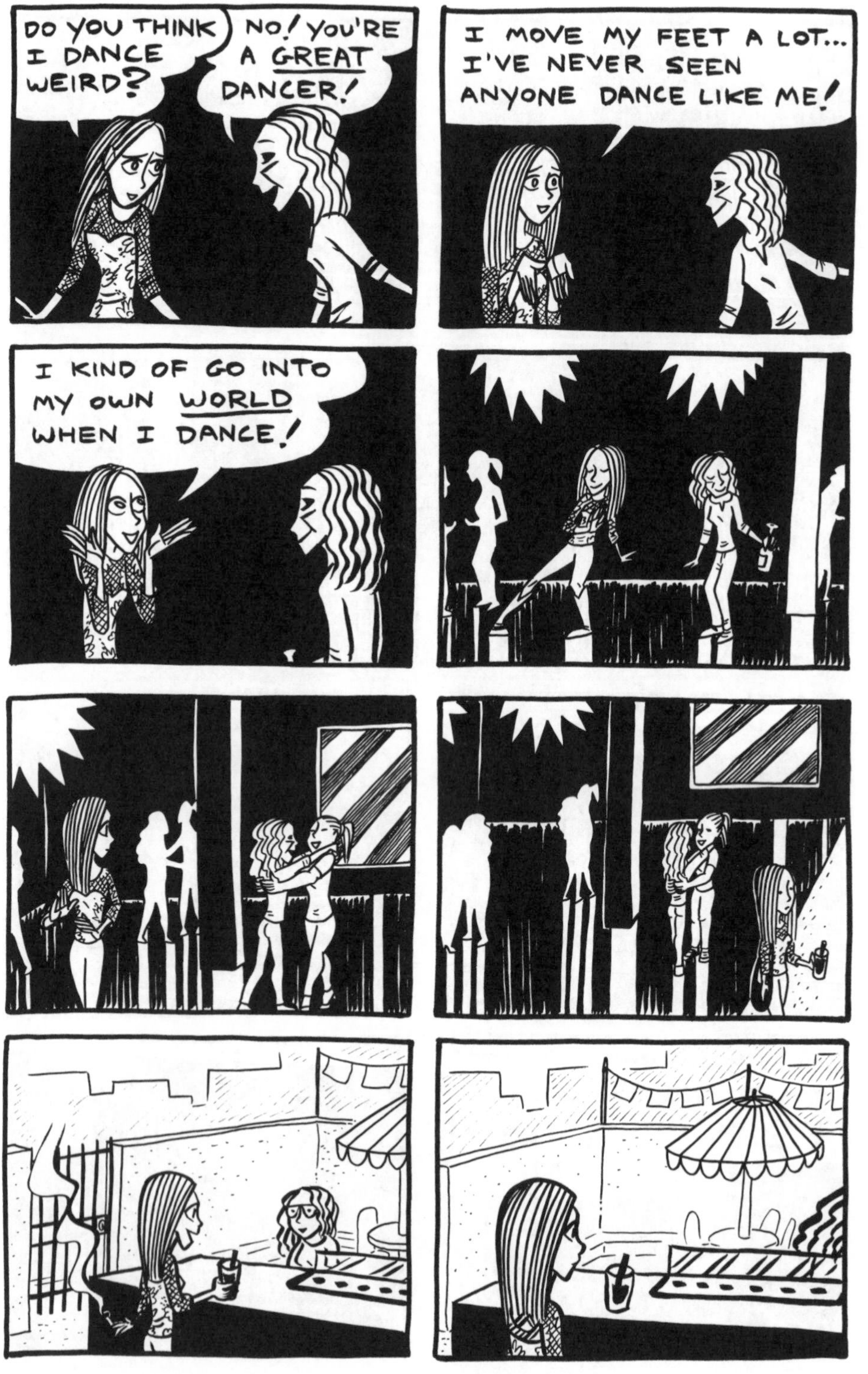

DO YOU THINK I DANCE WEIRD?
NO! YOU'RE A GREAT DANCER!
I MOVE MY FEET A LOT... I'VE NEVER SEEN ANYONE DANCE LIKE ME!
I KIND OF GO INTO MY OWN WORLD WHEN I DANCE!

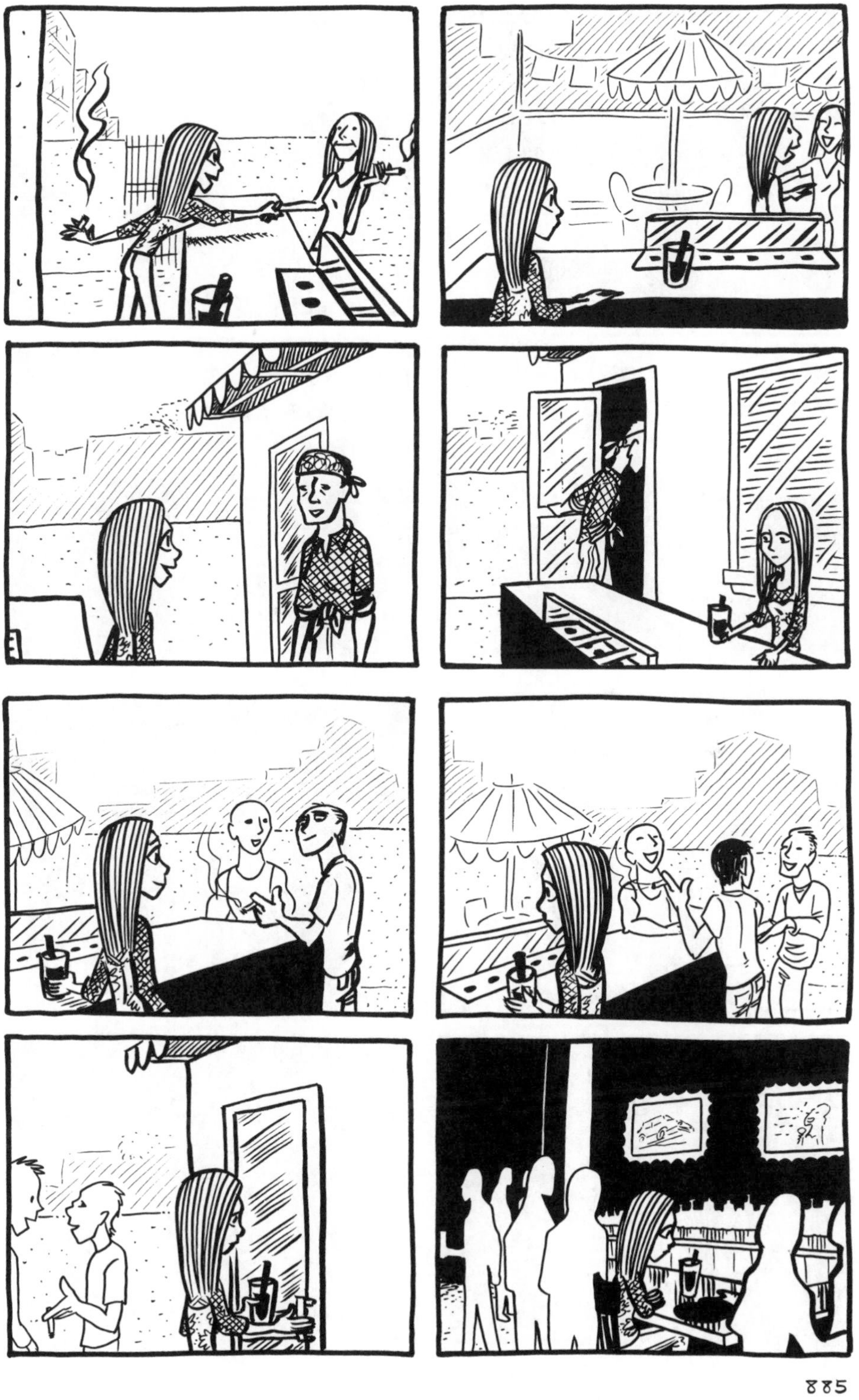

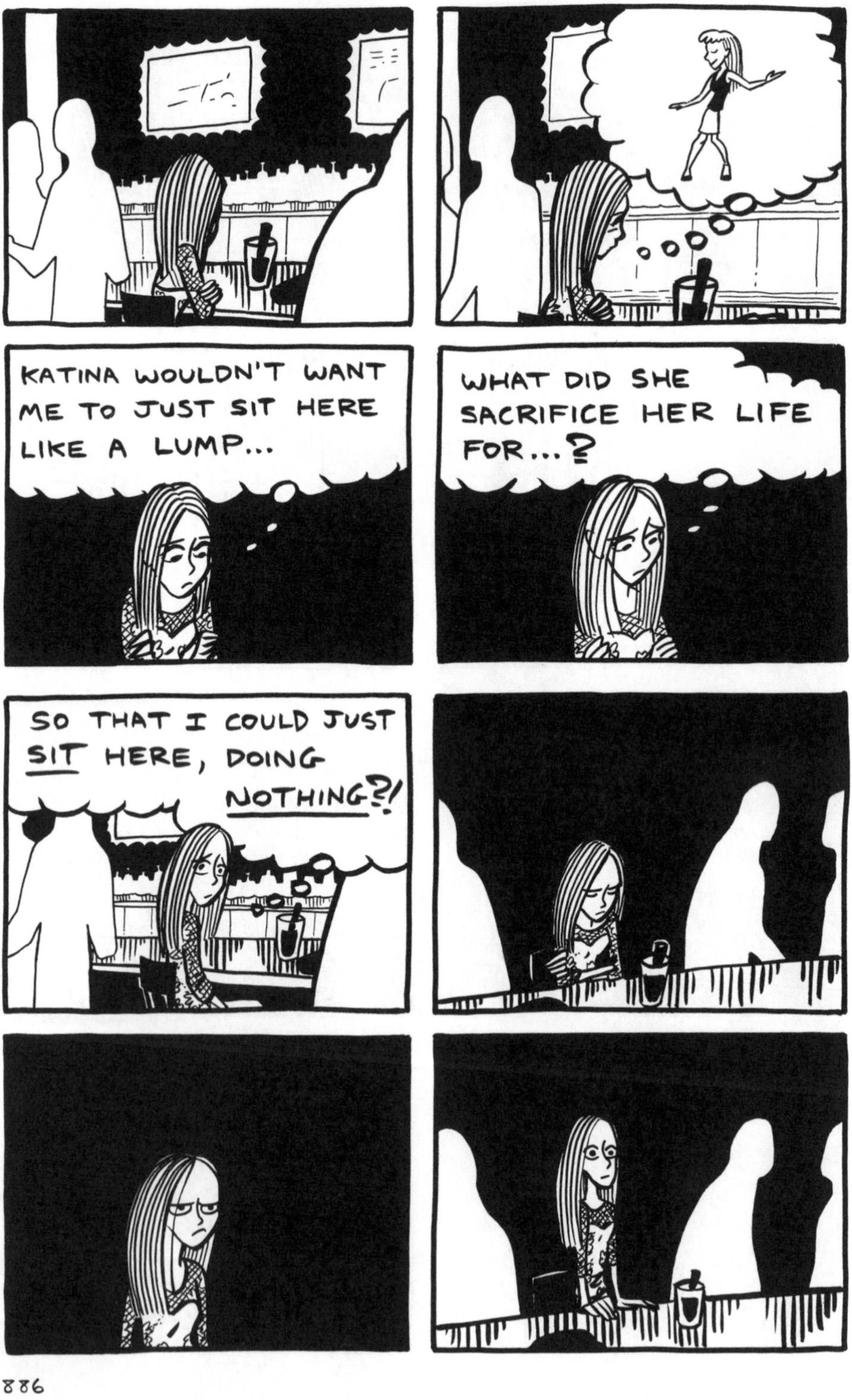
KATINA WOULDN'T WANT ME TO JUST SIT HERE LIKE A LUMP...
WHAT DID SHE SACRIFICE HER LIFE FOR...?
SO THAT I COULD JUST SIT HERE, DOING NOTHING?!

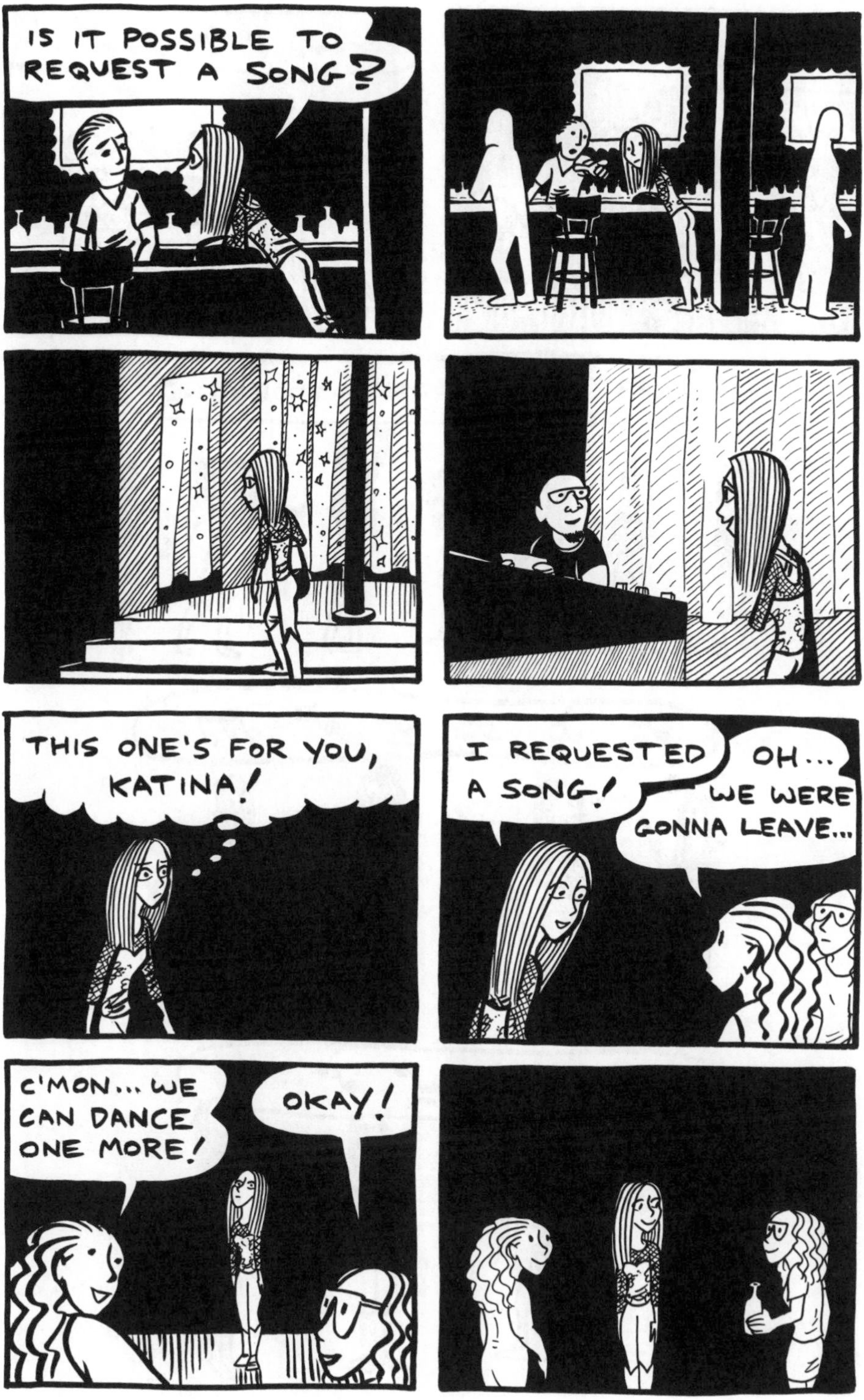
IS IT POSSIBLE TO REQUEST A SONG?
THIS ONE'S FOR YOU, KATINA!
I REQUESTED A SONG!
OH... WE WERE GONNA LEAVE...
C'MON... WE CAN DANCE ONE MORE!
OKAY!

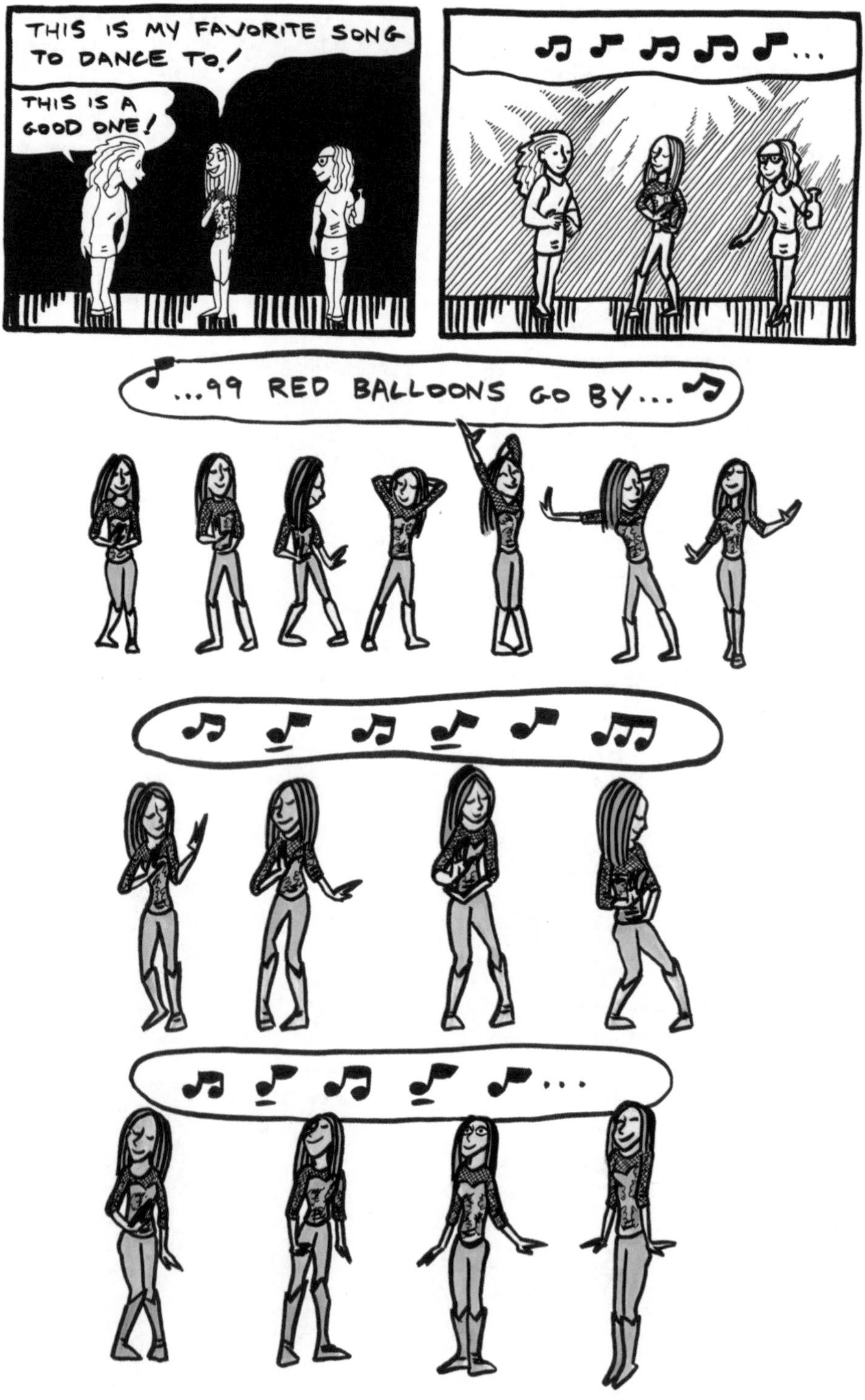
THIS IS MY FAVORITE SONG TO DANCE TO!
THIS IS A GOOD ONE!
♫ ♪ ♫ ♫ ♪...
...99 RED BALLOONS GO BY...

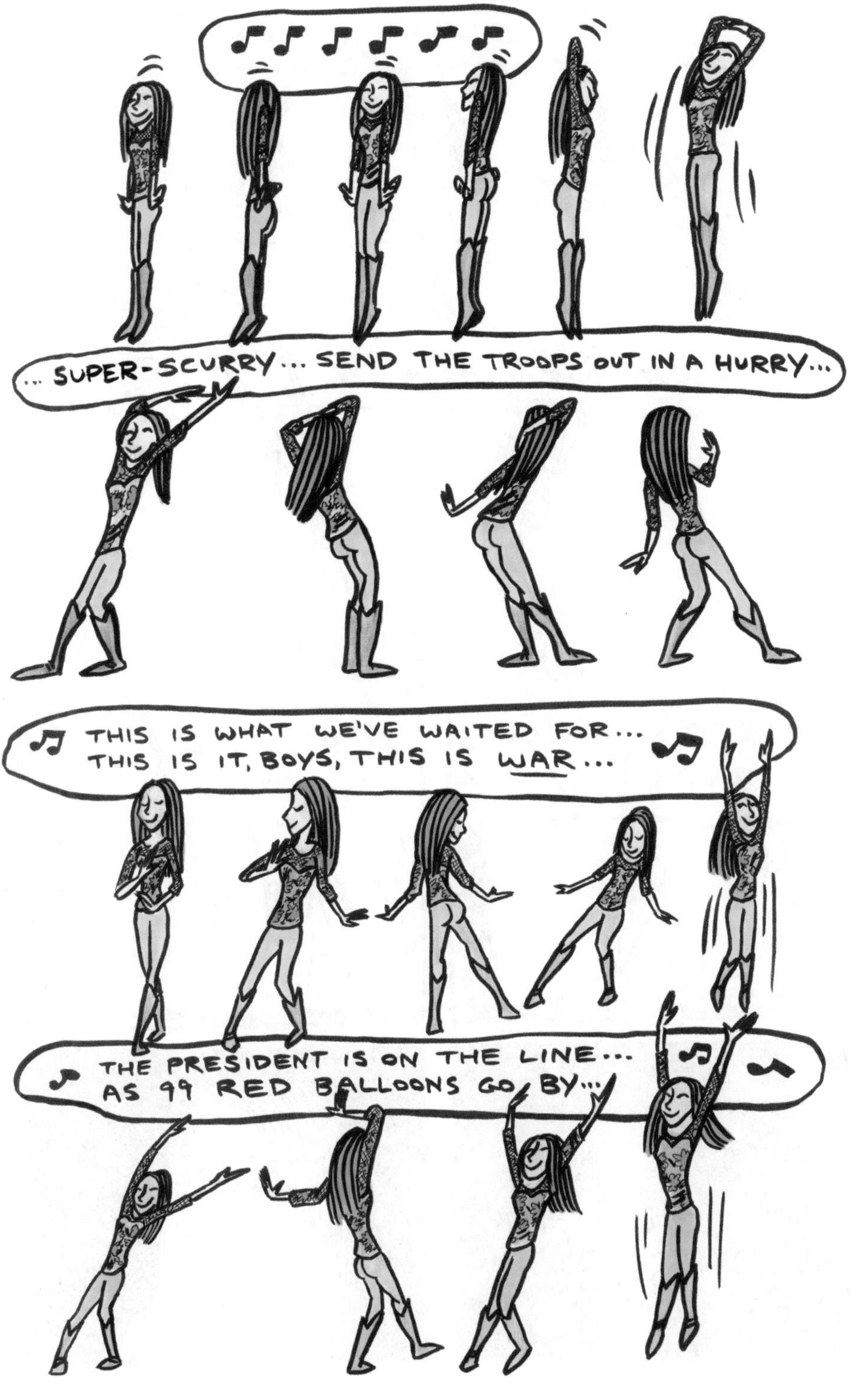
... SUPER-SCURRY... SEND THE TROOPS OUT IN A HURRY...
THIS IS WHAT WE'VE WAITED FOR...
THIS IS IT, BOYS, THIS IS WAR...
THE PRESIDENT IS ON THE LINE...
AS 99 RED BALLOONS GO BY...

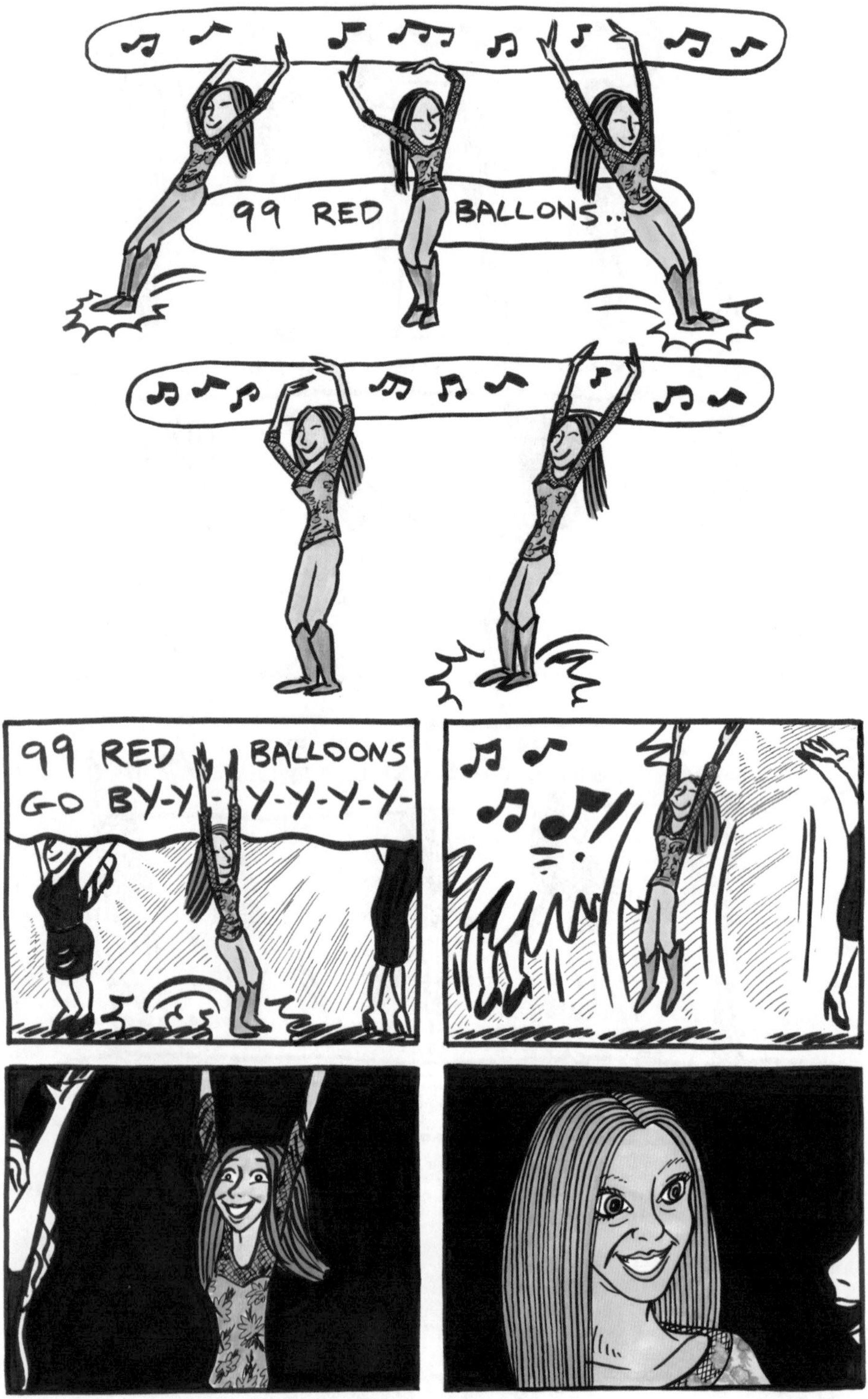
99 RED
BALLONS...
99 RED BALLOONS GO BY-Y-Y-Y-Y-Y-

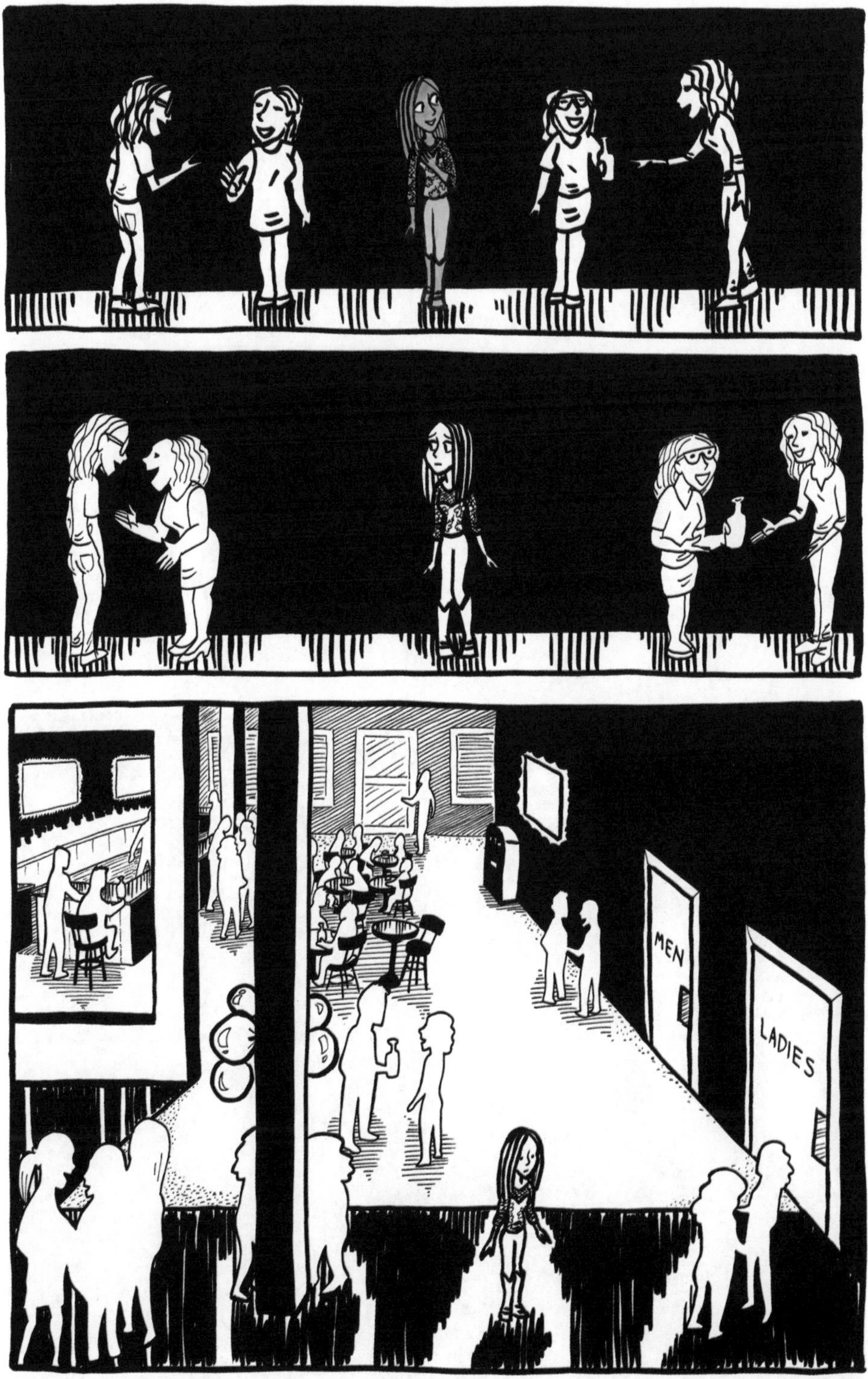
MEN
LADIES

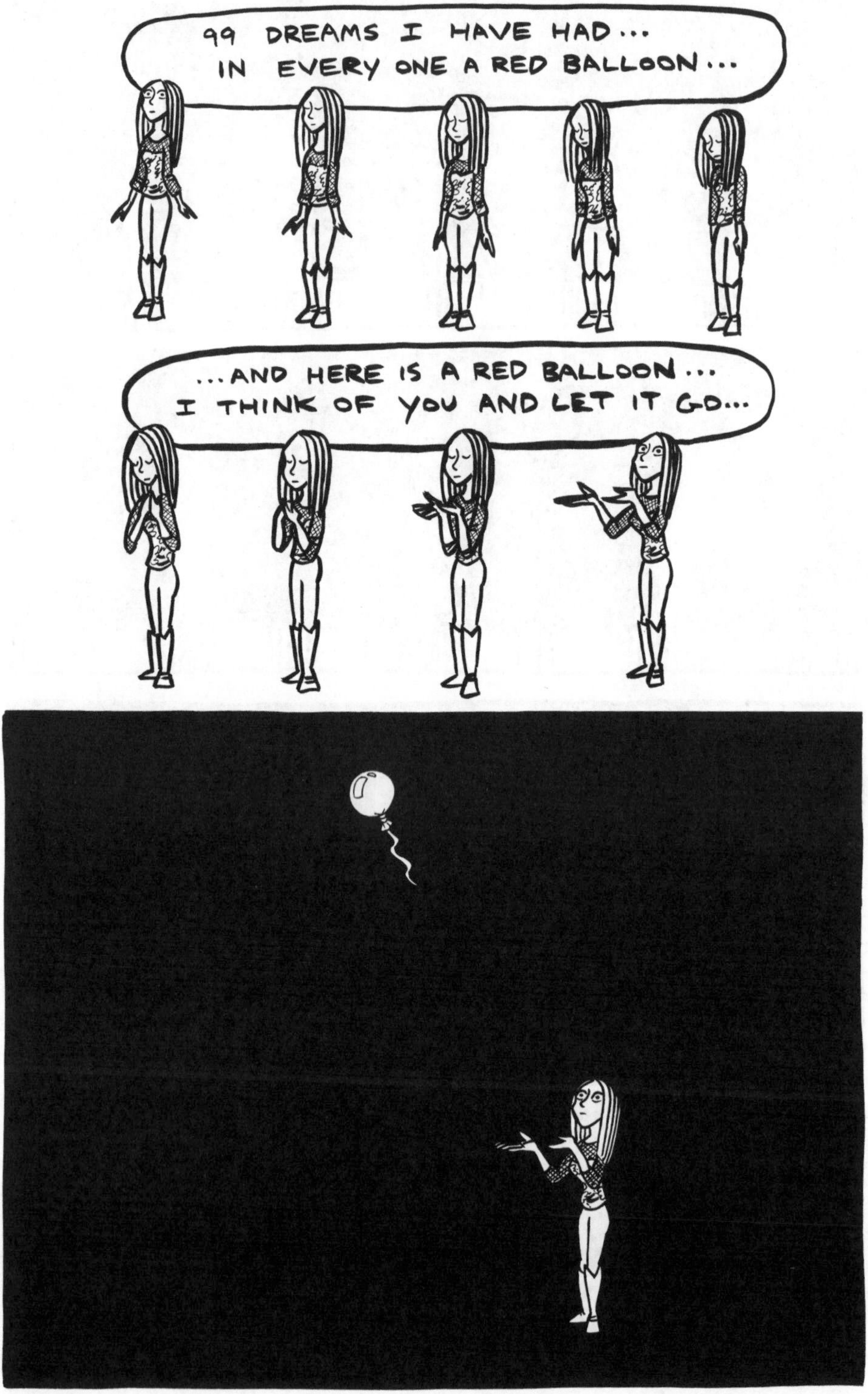
99 DREAMS I HAVE HAD... IN EVERY ONE A RED BALLOON...
...AND HERE IS A RED BALLOON... I THINK OF YOU AND LET IT GO...

EPILOGUE

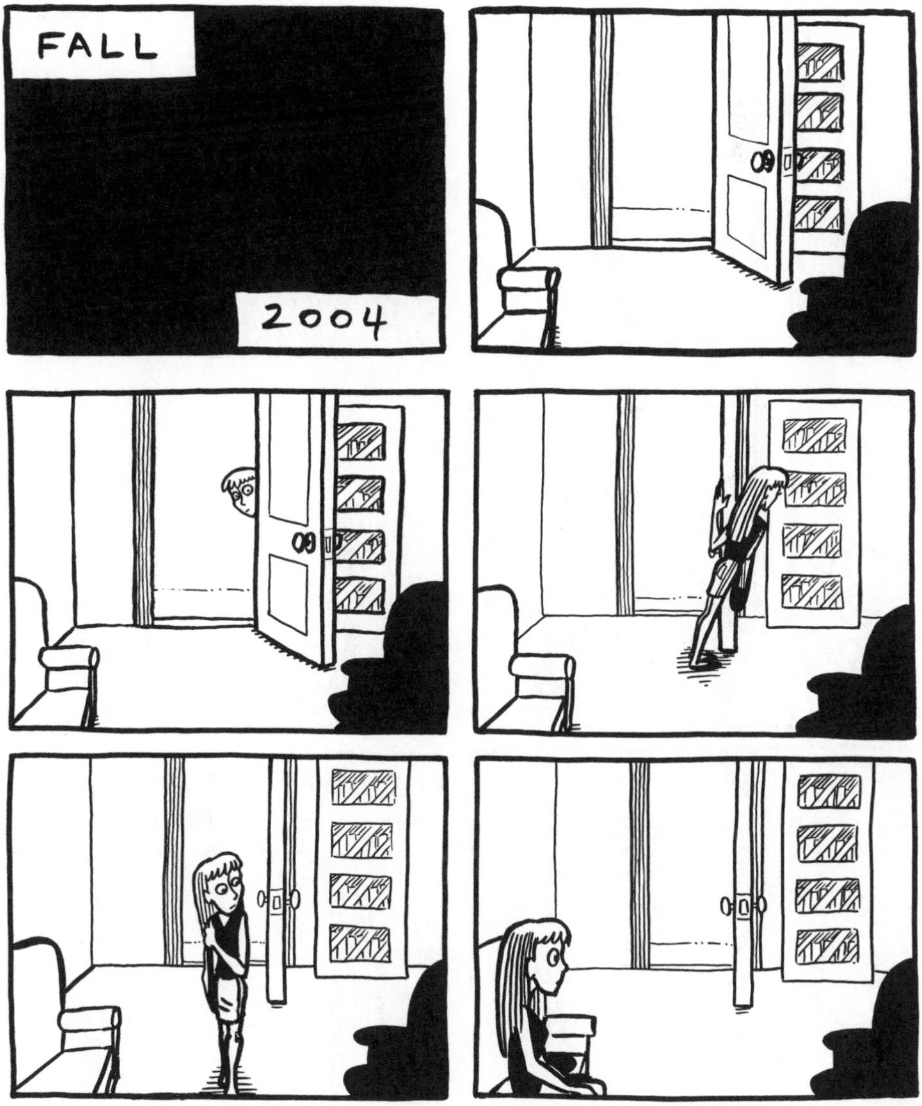
FALL
2004

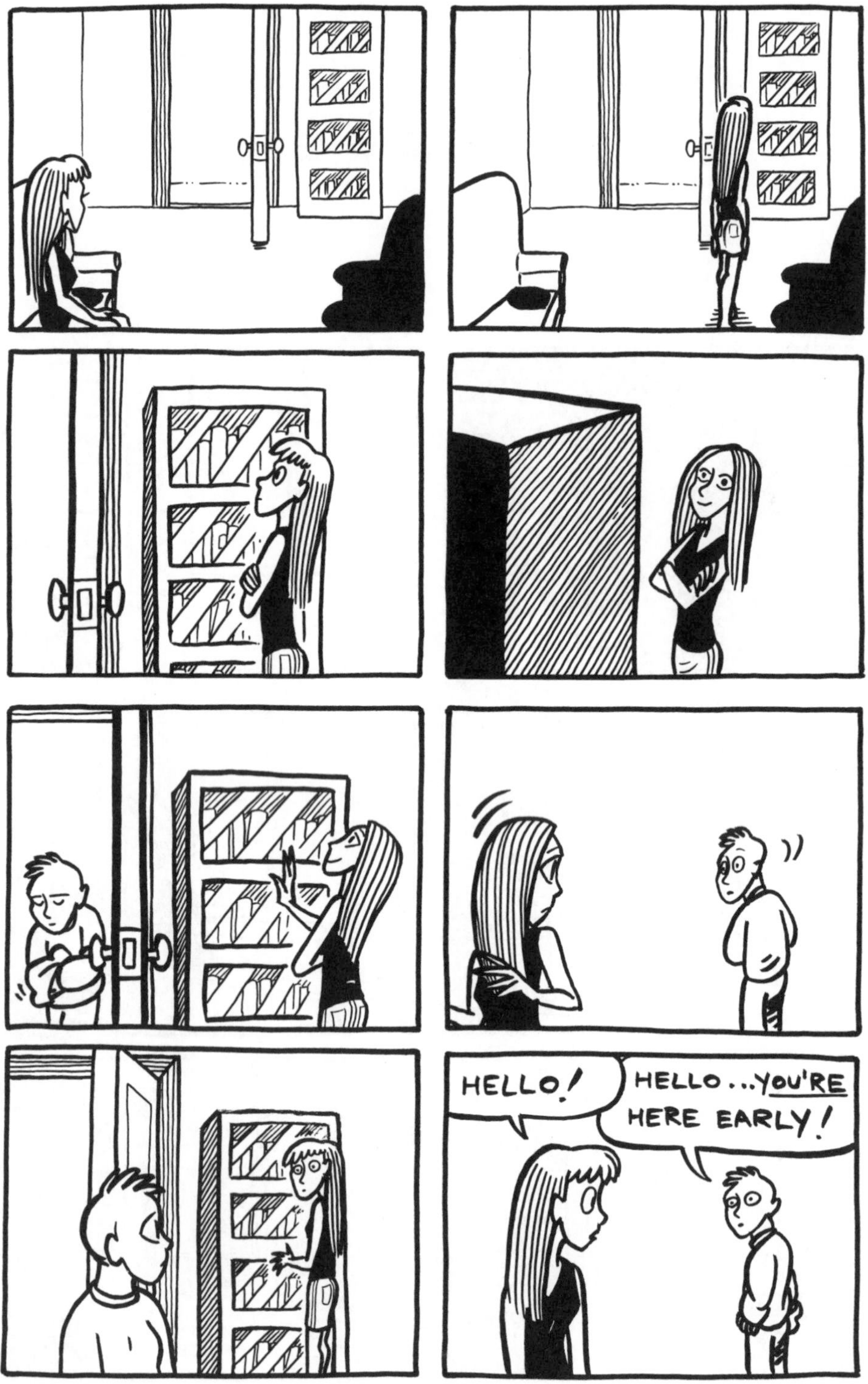
HELLO!
HELLO...YOU'RE HERE EARLY!

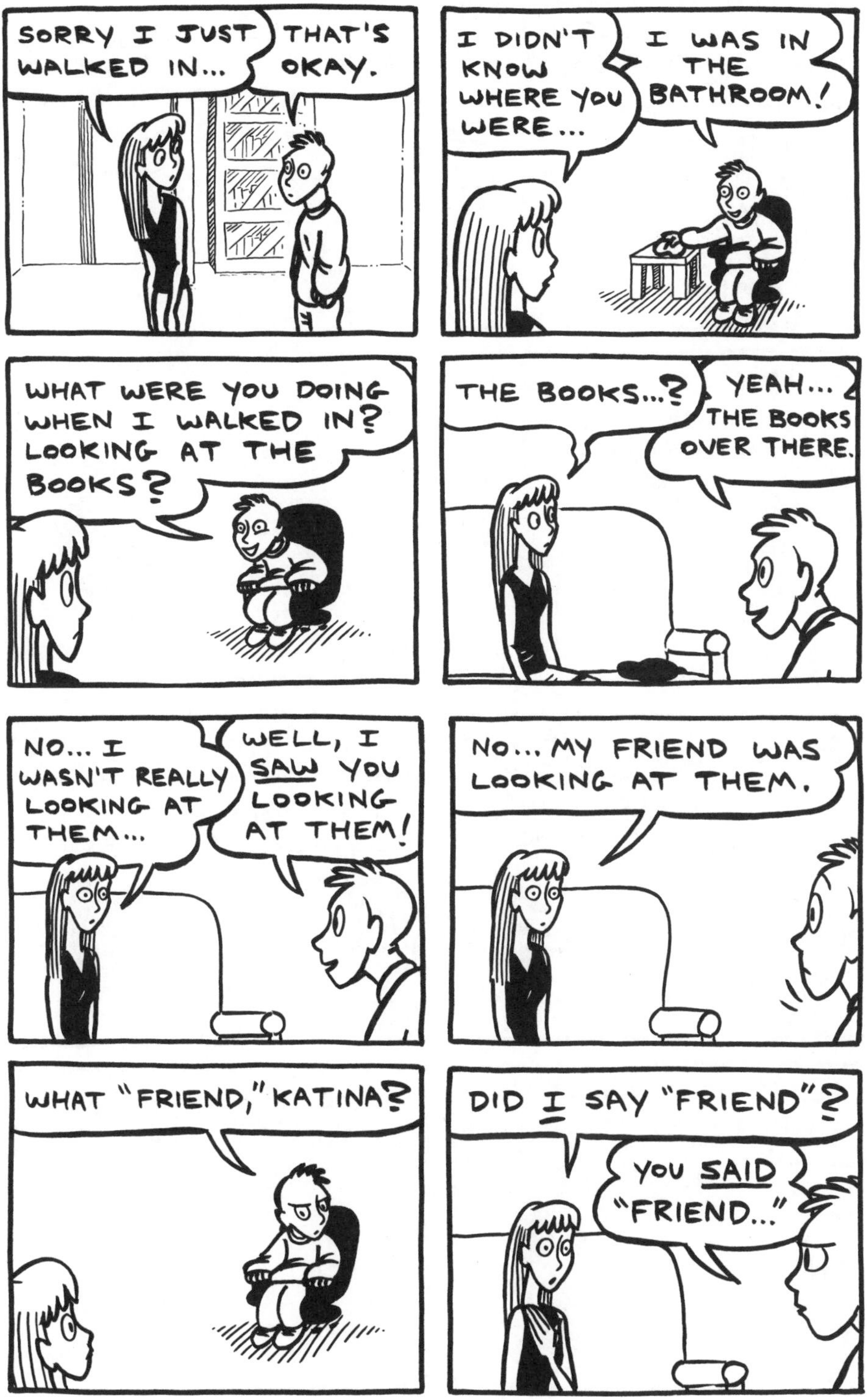
SORRY I JUST WALKED IN...
THAT'S OKAY.
I DIDN'T KNOW WHERE YOU WERE...
I WAS IN THE BATHROOM!
WHAT WERE YOU DOING WHEN I WALKED IN? LOOKING AT THE BOOKS?
THE BOOKS...?
YEAH... THE BOOKS OVER THERE.
NO... I WASN'T REALLY LOOKING AT THEM...
WELL, I SAW YOU LOOKING AT THEM!
NO... MY FRIEND WAS LOOKING AT THEM.
WHAT "FRIEND," KATINA?
DID I SAY "FRIEND"?
YOU SAID "FRIEND..."

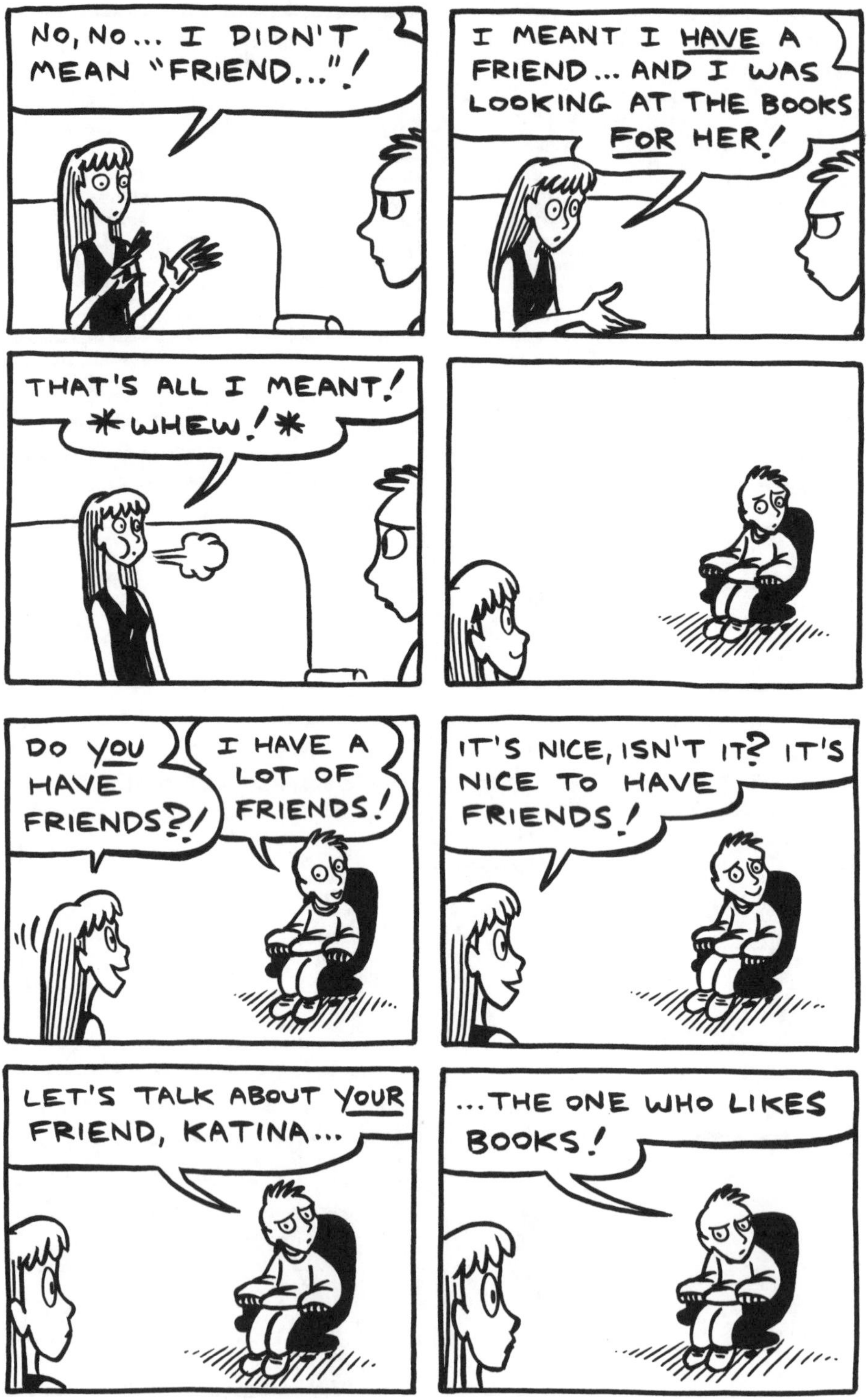
NO, NO... I DIDN'T MEAN "FRIEND..."!
I MEANT I HAVE A FRIEND... AND I WAS LOOKING AT THE BOOKS FOR HER!
THAT'S ALL I MEANT! *WHEW!*
DO YOU HAVE FRIENDS?!
I HAVE A LOT OF FRIENDS!
IT'S NICE, ISN'T IT? IT'S NICE TO HAVE FRIENDS!
LET'S TALK ABOUT YOUR FRIEND, KATINA...
...THE ONE WHO LIKES BOOKS!

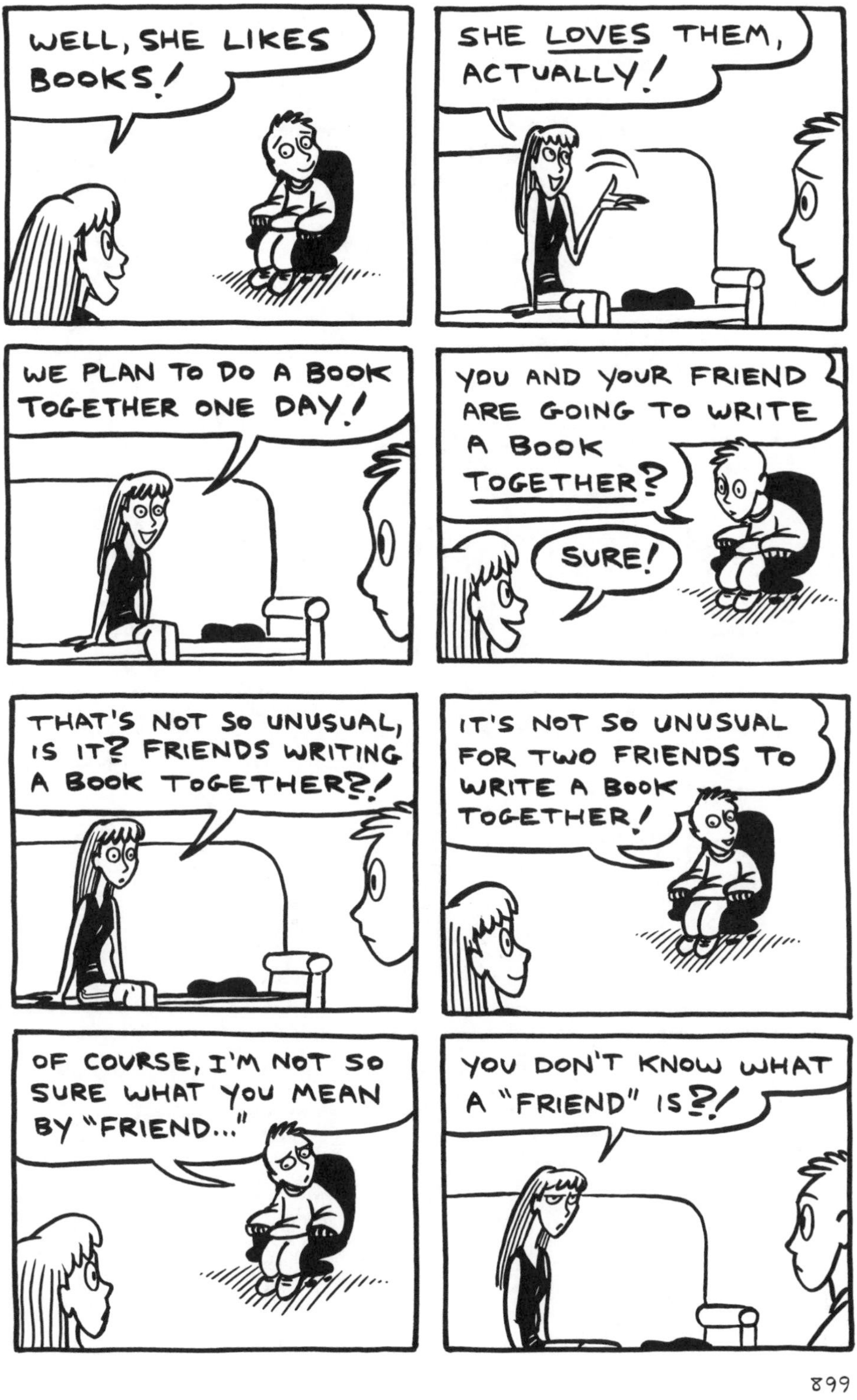
WELL, SHE LIKES BOOKS!
SHE LOVES THEM, ACTUALLY!
WE PLAN TO DO A BOOK TOGETHER ONE DAY!
YOU AND YOUR FRIEND ARE GOING TO WRITE A BOOK TOGETHER?
SURE!
THAT'S NOT SO UNUSUAL, IS IT? FRIENDS WRITING A BOOK TOGETHER?!
IT'S NOT SO UNUSUAL FOR TWO FRIENDS TO WRITE A BOOK TOGETHER!
OF COURSE, I'M NOT SO SURE WHAT YOU MEAN BY "FRIEND..."
YOU DON'T KNOW WHAT A "FRIEND" IS?!

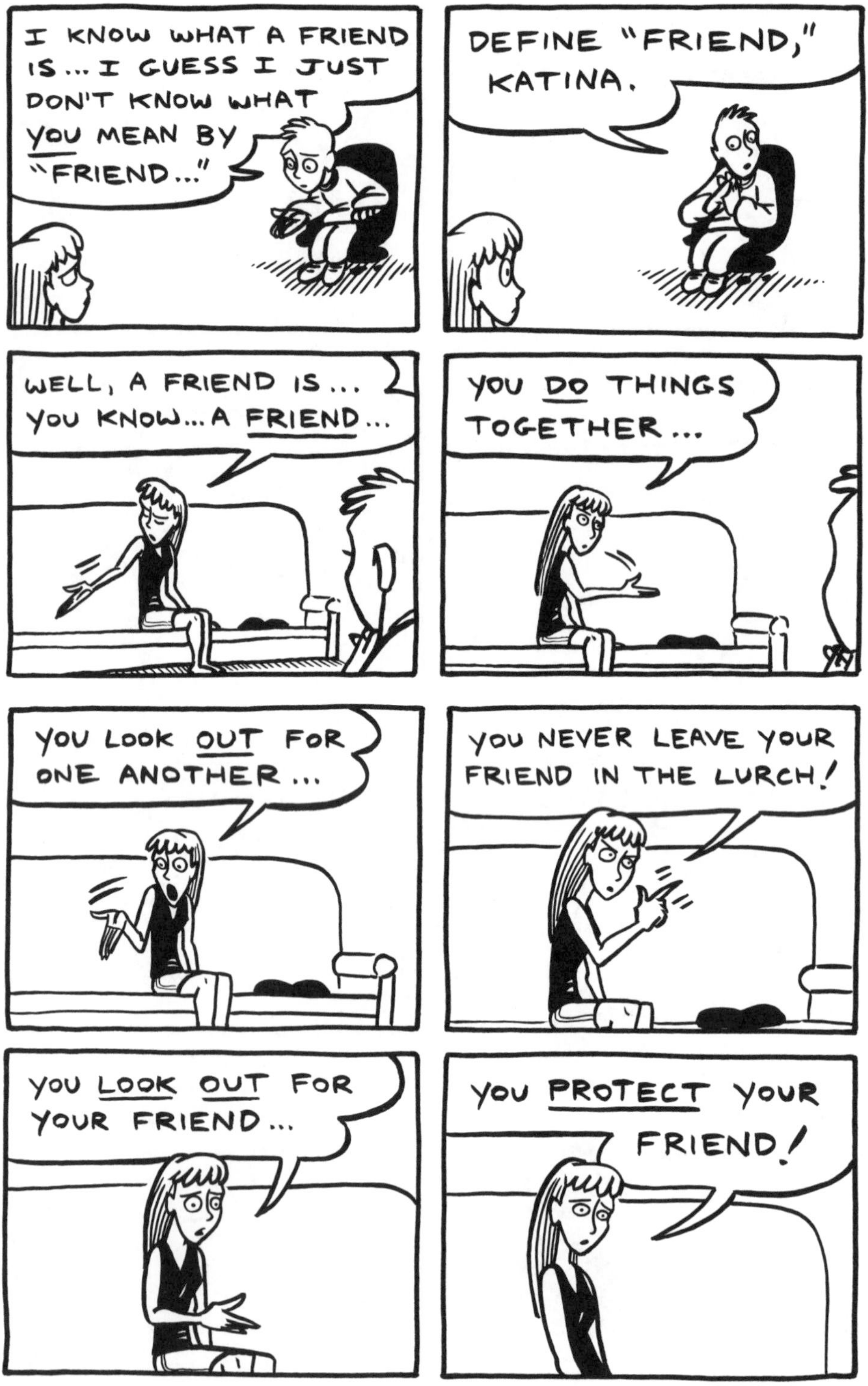
I KNOW WHAT A FRIEND IS... I GUESS I JUST DON'T KNOW WHAT YOU MEAN BY "FRIEND..."
DEFINE "FRIEND," KATINA.
WELL, A FRIEND IS... YOU KNOW... A FRIEND...
YOU DO THINGS TOGETHER...
YOU LOOK OUT FOR ONE ANOTHER...
YOU NEVER LEAVE YOUR FRIEND IN THE LURCH!
YOU LOOK OUT FOR YOUR FRIEND...
YOU PROTECT YOUR FRIEND!

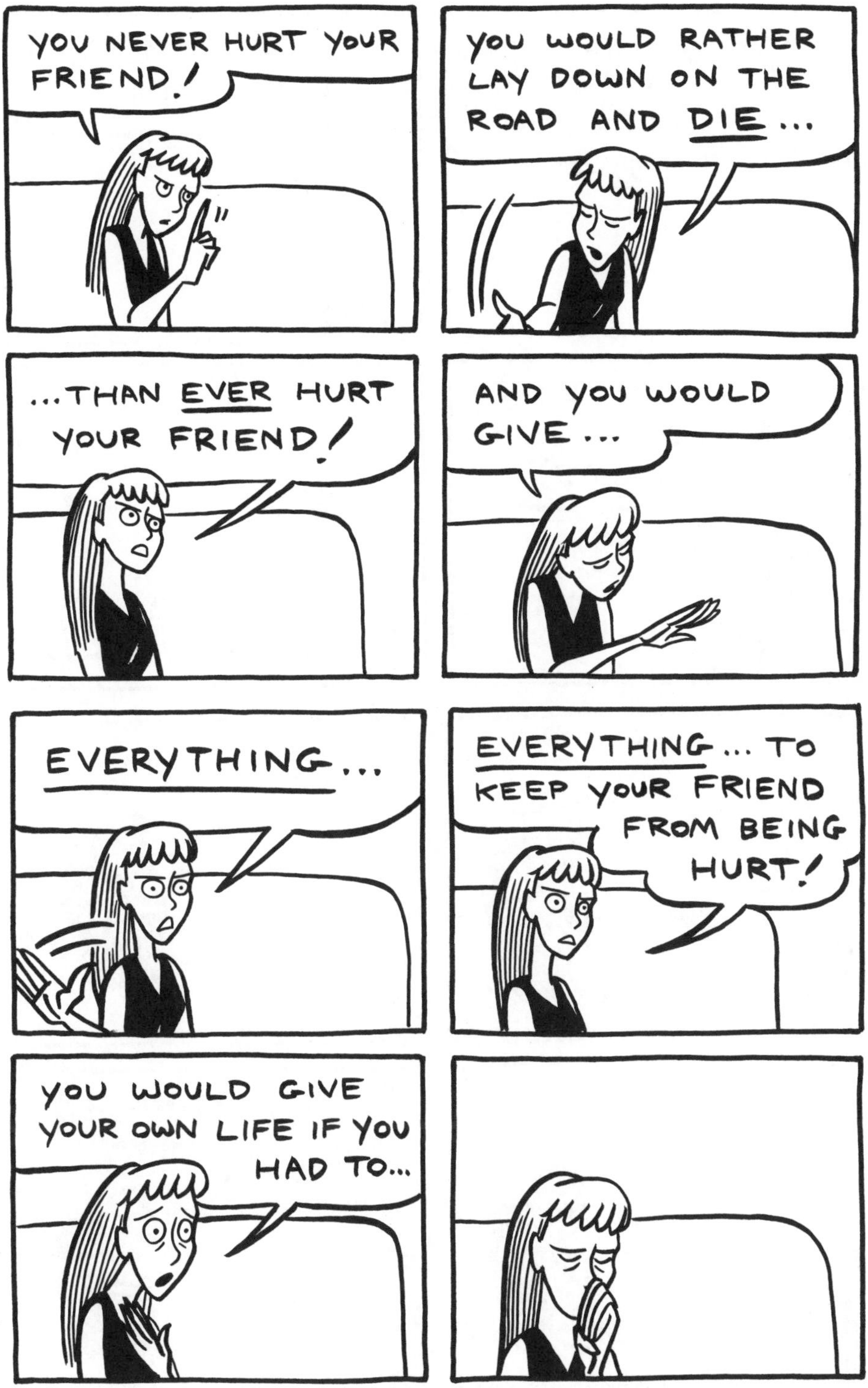
YOU NEVER HURT YOUR FRIEND!
YOU WOULD RATHER LAY DOWN ON THE ROAD AND DIE...
...THAN EVER HURT YOUR FRIEND!
AND YOU WOULD GIVE...
EVERYTHING...
EVERYTHING... TO KEEP YOUR FRIEND FROM BEING HURT!
YOU WOULD GIVE YOUR OWN LIFE IF YOU HAD TO...

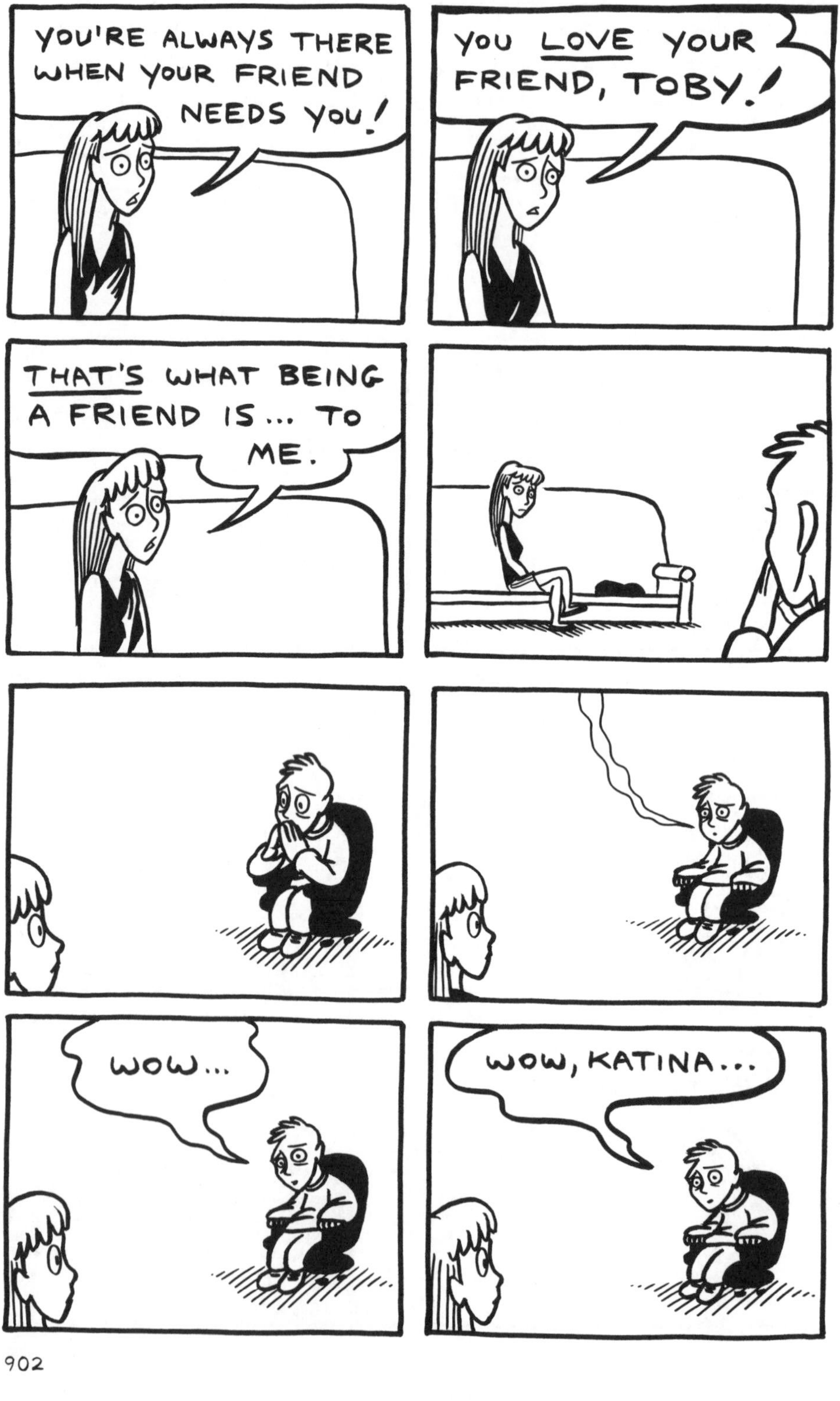
YOU'RE ALWAYS THERE WHEN YOUR FRIEND NEEDS YOU!
YOU LOVE YOUR FRIEND, TOBY!
THAT'S WHAT BEING A FRIEND IS... TO ME.
WOW...
WOW, KATINA...

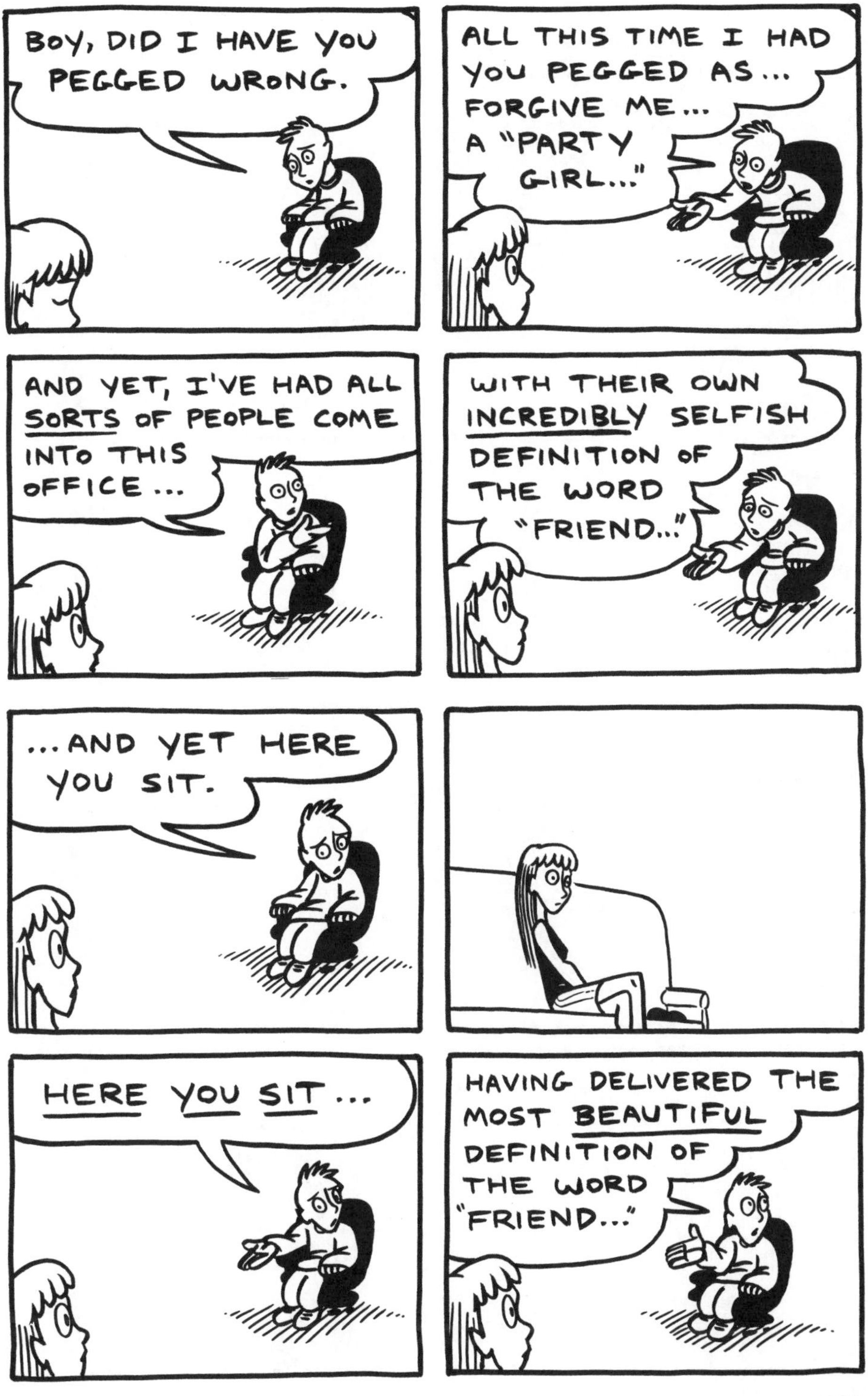
BOY, DID I HAVE YOU PEGGED WRONG.
ALL THIS TIME I HAD YOU PEGGED AS... FORGIVE ME... A "PARTY GIRL..."
AND YET, I'VE HAD ALL SORTS OF PEOPLE COME INTO THIS OFFICE...
WITH THEIR OWN INCREDIBLY SELFISH DEFINITION OF THE WORD "FRIEND..."
...AND YET HERE YOU SIT.
HERE YOU SIT...
HAVING DELIVERED THE MOST BEAUTIFUL DEFINITION OF THE WORD "FRIEND..."

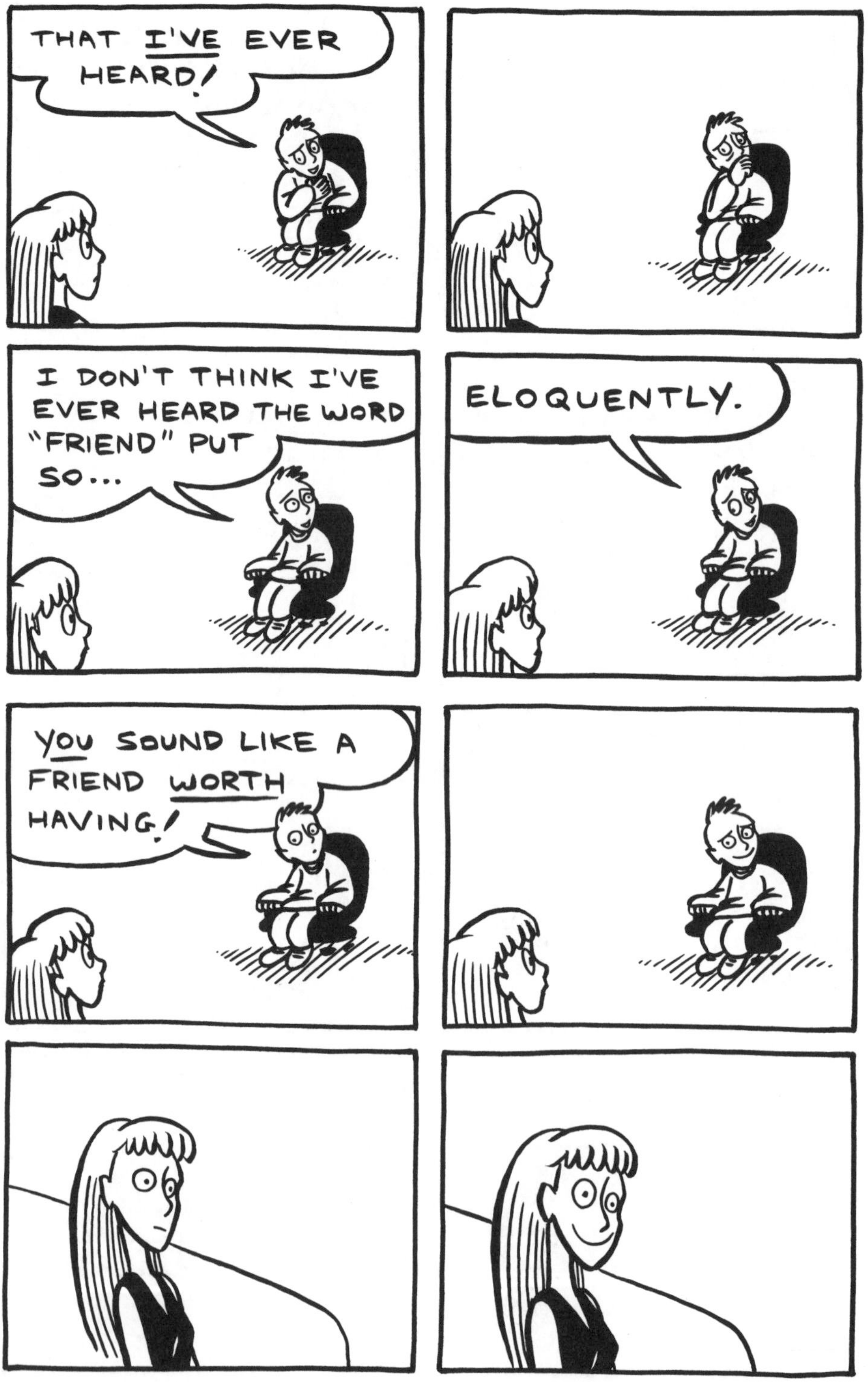
THAT I'VE EVER HEARD!
I DON'T THINK I'VE EVER HEARD THE WORD "FRIEND" PUT SO...
ELOQUENTLY.
YOU SOUND LIKE A FRIEND WORTH HAVING!

FOR MY FRIEND...

NOTES

HOW THIS BOOK WAS MADE

THIS BOOK WAS NOT PUT TOGETHER IN ANYTHING EVEN RESEMBLING CHRONOLOGICAL ORDER ... IT WAS MORE LIKE A GIGANTIC JIGSAW PUZZLE.

I DIDN'T REMEMBER ANY OF THE CHAPTERS WITH "TOBY" UNTIL 13 YEARS AFTERWARDS, WHEN I DECIDED TO PUT THIS PERIOD OF MY LIFE IN AN AUTO-BIOGRAPHICAL BOOK ABOUT BEING TRANSGENDER.

I ACTUALLY DIDN'T EVEN WANT TO THINK ABOUT THIS TIME IN MY LIFE, BECAUSE IT WAS TOO CONFUSING. ABOUT THE ONLY THING THAT STUCK OUT IN MY MEMORY WAS A BOOK THAT I HAD BROUGHT IN VANISHING A MOMENT LATER. CONSEQUENTLY, THAT WAS THE FIRST PART I DECIDED TO TACKLE, TO TRY TO SORT OUT WHAT HAPPENED.

HOW I REMEMBERED IT CAN BE SUMMED UP IN THIS QUOTE FROM THE BOOK TALKING ANIMALS AND OTHER PEOPLE BY ANIMATOR SHAMUS CULHANE:

" ... By sketching at top speed, I didn't have time to think about the individual drawings. Instead, I was drawing emotionally and tapping my unconscious."

YOU CAN TAP INTO YOUR SUBCONSCIOUS BY UTILIZING THE RIGHT SIDE OF THE BRAIN, ALMOST LIKE AUTOMATIC WRITING.

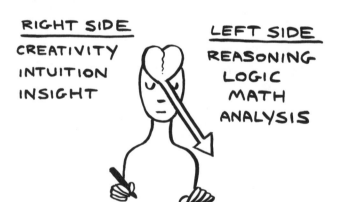

RIGHT SIDE

CREATIVITY
INTUITION
INSIGHT

LEFT SIDE

REASONING
LOGIC
MATH
ANALYSIS

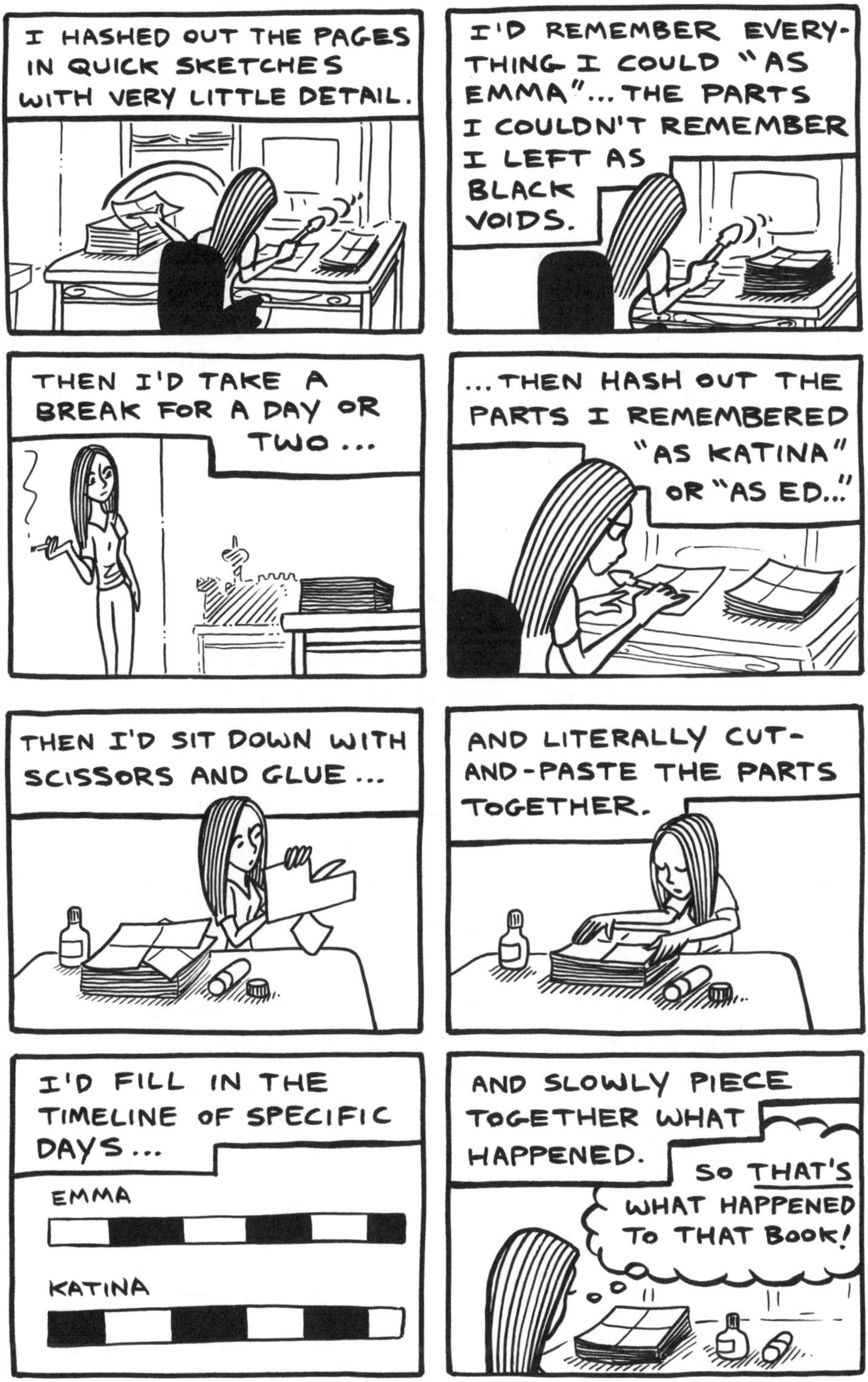
I HASHED OUT THE PAGES IN QUICK SKETCHES WITH VERY LITTLE DETAIL.
I'D REMEMBER EVERYTHING I COULD "AS EMMA"... THE PARTS I COULDN'T REMEMBER I LEFT AS BLACK VOIDS.
THEN I'D TAKE A BREAK FOR A DAY OR TWO...
...THEN HASH OUT THE PARTS I REMEMBERED "AS KATINA" OR "AS ED..."
THEN I'D SIT DOWN WITH SCISSORS AND GLUE...
AND LITERALLY CUT-AND-PASTE THE PARTS TOGETHER.
I'D FILL IN THE TIMELINE OF SPECIFIC DAYS...
EMMA
KATINA
AND SLOWLY PIECE TOGETHER WHAT HAPPENED.
So THAT'S WHAT HAPPENED TO THAT BOOK!

WHAT I ATTEMPTED TO SHOW
IN THIS BOOK WAS HOW, WITH
D.I.D., "PARTS" WORK SOME-
TIMES TOGETHER, SOMETIMES
SEPARATELY, SOMETIMES SHARE
INFORMATION, SOMETIMES
WITHHOLD IT FROM EACH
OTHER.

I REMEMBERED <u>NONE</u> OF
THE INCIDENTS WITH KATINA
UNTIL I DECIDED TO WRITE
ABOUT MY EXPERIENCES AS
A TRANSPERSON IN JULY, 2018.
I WAS ABLE TO RECALL THEM
<u>ONLY</u> BY SKETCHING AND
WRITING THEM OUT AT TOP
SPEED, AND THEN THE MEMORIES
WOULD FLOOD BACK FASTER
THAN I COULD COMMIT THEM
TO PAPER. EVEN STILL, THE
MEMORIES "AS KATINA," "AS
EMMA," OR "AS ED" WERE EACH
LOCKED IN SEPARATE PARTS
OF MY BRAIN, AND COULD ONLY
BE RECALLED SEPARATELY.

D. I. D.

DISSOCIATIVE IDENTITY DISORDER

DISSOCIATION IS BASICALLY A "TUNING OUT"—— A COPING MECHANISM IN WHICH YOUR CONSCIOUS MIND TEMPORARILY LEAVES YOUR BODY.

D.I.D., OR MULTIPLE PERSONALITY, IS CHARACTERIZED BY ONE OR MORE "ALTERS"— SEPARATE PERSONALITIES.

BOTH ARE BROUGHT ABOUT BY EXTREME, UNMANAGEABLE STRESS OR SEVERE TRAUMA.

D.I.D. SECTION

PAYMENT

THE TWO THERAPISTS I WAS SEEING (AFTER COLLEGE) BOTH DEMANDED PAYMENT IN FULL AT THE START OF EACH SESSION. (I PAID CASH.) IT WAS ACTUALLY A BAD WAY TO START EACH SESSION, BECAUSE IT IMPLIED AN IMMEDIATE LACK OF TRUST.

THE LAST THERAPIST I SAW INSISTED I COULD PAY AT THE END OF THE SESSION, BECAUSE SHE TRUSTED ME TO PAY HER. IT IMMEDIATELY MADE ME MORE TRUSTFUL OF HER.

THIS WAS JUST A DETAIL I
LEFT OUT BECAUSE IT WAS A
REPETITIVE ACTION, BUT I
SHOWED IT IF IT WAS RELEVANT
IN SOME WAY.

"TOBY" ALSO HAD A SMALL
TABLE NEXT TO HIS CHAIR, AND
AN OFFICE DESK IN THE CORNER,
WHICH WAS, I FELT, UNNECESSARY
DETAIL, DRAWN ONLY WHEN NEEDED.

BRACELET

IN THE FIRST TWO MONTHS
OF SESSIONS "AS KATINA," I
REGULARLY WORE A THICK,
METALLIC BRACELET. WHEN I
STARTED "SWITCHING" TO "ED,"
THE BRACELET WOULD BECOME
AN IRRITANT TO MY SKIN, AND
I WOULD HAVE TO TAKE IT OFF.

IT IS COMMON FOR DIFFERENT
"PARTS" TO HAVE DIFFERENT
ALLERGIES, SKIN SENSITIVITIES,
MODES OF SPEECH, ACCENTS, OR
SPEAK IN DIFFERENT LANGUAGES.

TAPE RECORDER

ONCE "TOBY" SUSPECTED
THAT HE WAS DEALING WITH A
POTENTIAL MULTIPLE PERSONALITY,
HE BEGAN TAPE-RECORDING
EVERY SESSION. HE SOON
REALIZED THIS WAS MAKING ME
SELF-CONSCIOUS, AND STOPPING
ME FROM OPENING UP TO HIM, SO
HE STOPPED AFTER ABOUT
HALF A DOZEN SESSIONS.

AT THE TIME, I HAD NO IDEA
WHY HE WAS DOING THIS.

JENNIFER BOYLAN

THE BOOK REFERRED TO IS <u>SHE'S NOT THERE</u>, AN AUTOBIOGRAPHY BY JENNY BOYLAN ABOUT HER MALE-TO-FEMALE TRANSITION.

THE GENDER THERAPIST SHE SAW, WHO APPROVED HER FOR THE TRANSITION, MENTIONED SHE WAS <u>NOT</u> SUFFERING FROM DISSOCIATIVE IDENTITY DISORDER.

D.I.D. IS GENERALLY MORE COMMON AMONG WOMEN THAN MEN.

T . M . J .

TEMPOROMANDIBULAR JOINT DYSFUNCTION

BASICALLY, A STIFFENING OF THE JAW MUSCLES AND THE JOINTS THAT CONNECT THE MANDIBLE TO THE SKULL. WITH ME, IT BECAME PSYCHO-SOMATIC, AND AN UNCONSCIOUS REFLEX.

IT IS, AGAIN, A CONDITION MORE COMMON IN WOMEN THAN IN MEN.